Information Security Policies Made Easy

A Comprehensive Set of Information Security Policies

Version 8

ISBN #1-881585-07-7

by
Charles Cresson Wood, CISA, CISSP
Independent Information Security Consultant & Author
InfoSecurity Infrastructure, Inc.
Post Office Box 2877
Sausalito, California 94966-2877 USA
Voice 415-289-0800; Fax 415-289-0808
ccwood@ix.netcom.com; www.infosecurityinfrastructure.com

Pentasafe Security Technologies, Inc
1233 West Loop South, Ste 1800
Houston, Texas 77027
Phone: 1-800-829-9955, 713-860-9390 (Outside USA & Canada); Fax 713-523-6393
www.pentasafe.com

Dedication

To Eva who's insight never ceases to amaze me.

Legal And Production Notices

Table of Contents

APPENDICES:

I. Introduction

Information security policies are a special type of documented business rule. Twenty years ago, there was no need for them. The explosion of information handling technologies, including cell phones, pagers, and portable computers has changed all of that. Those who work in the modern business environment must now have clear and definitive instructions which assist them in securing information in this complex new technological environment. Just as it is unthinkable that millions of automobile drivers would be on the road without laws about the right-of-way and when to stop, so it is unthinkable that millions of business people would operate modern information systems without information security policies.

The importance of business rules like information security policies is coming to be appreciated by management at many organizations. All around them are projects and endeavors which critically depend on clearly articulated business rules. For example, some of these managers may remember that when a legacy application was moved from the mainframe to the Internet, one of the important steps allowing this transition was the documentation of business rules. Without clear business rules, programmers and others creating a new system cannot be sure they are building something which will perform as management intends. Likewise, without information security policies, management cannot be sure that information systems are operated in a manner which is indeed secure.

The centrality of information security policies to virtually everything that happens in the information security field is increasingly evident. For example, systems administrators cannot securely install a new firewall unless they have first received a set of clear information security policies. Among other things, these policies will stipulate just what type of transmission services should be permitted, how to authenticate the identities of users, and how to log security-relevant events. Similarly, an effective information security training and awareness effort cannot be initiated without first writing information security policies. This is because policies provide the essential content which then can be utilized in training and awareness material.

As I see it, there are four fundamental building blocks that can be found in every organization that has a successful information security effort. Information security policies are of course of one of these essential building blocks. The others are information security risk assessment documents, information security roles and responsibilities documents, and an information security architecture document. These four building blocks will provide an information security effort with the direction and credibility needed to move ahead with significant velocity.

In days gone past those who worked in the information security field were often considered to be "sandbaggers" or people who slowed things down. Some people thought that information security was incompatible with the rapid pace of business that the new Internet-based economy required. This viewpoint quickly changed as people came to appreciate that Internet business was not possible unless an organization had done a good job in the information security area. To offer products or services via the Internet without adequately addressing information security is negligent and a reckless invitation to security incidents which could severely damage an organization's reputation. These days information security is instead coming to be appreciated as an expediter. To the extent that an organization can codify its business rules and internal processes, to that extent it can automate these same rules and processes, outsource these rules and processes, and enter into new business relationships (like extranets) based on these same rules and processes. For all of these projects and many others, information security policies provide clear-cut constraints defining a domain in which an acceptable solution can be found.

The more a manager knows about information security policies, the more he or she is likely to appreciate just how dependent an organization is on these special rules. For example, information security policies are important reference documents for internal audits and for the resolution of legal disputes about management's due diligence. Separately, new American case law indicates that policy documents can act as a clear statement of management's intent, and thereby help reduce management's potential liability. Policy statements can also serve as evidence of management's intention to safeguard organizational information, and this is an essential but often neglected step in the legal assertion of trade secret protection. Information security policies can furthermore serve as evidence of internal quality control processes. In this regard, not only can an information security policy statement give a business partner sufficient confidence to disclose confidential material, a policy statement can also assist with an ISO 9000 quality control certification process.

While recent information security technological developments like digital certificates are impressive and hold great promise, the state-of-the-art in information security is still relatively embryonic. There are many things that cannot be cost-effectively achieved with the existing technology. For example, a data classification label cannot be permanently attached to a piece of information so that the label follows the information no matter how the information has been summarized, edited, reformatted, retranscribed, or merged with other information. Recognizing the limitations of modern technology is an important step in the process of appreciating the importance of policies. Because so much cannot cost-effectively be done by technological tools, it must instead be <u>done by humans</u>. And policies provide the most important and most frequently referenced source of instructions detailing how workers should protect both information and information systems.

Some people say information security is a people problem, while others say it is a technology problem. They are both right. But before anything can be done about information security, management must get involved. Therefore, information security is <u>fundamentally a management problem</u>. Information security practitioners say that the number one key to information security success is the involvement of higher-level management. Without higher-level management support, there will be insufficient budgets for and insufficient attention paid to information security. Without sufficient budgets, necessary control changes will not be made. Similarly, without sufficient management attention, control decisions that need to be made will be ignored.

One of the most successful ways to garner <u>higher-level management support</u> for, awareness about, and involvement in information security is to prepare information security policies. Information security policies of course need to be reviewed and approved by higher-level managers. In fact, higher-level management's initial involvement in information security in many instances is occasioned by a policy development effort. The extensive list of pointers on the development and revision of information security policies found in the section entitled Instructions explains how to achieve these results.

Since policies for information security have such a profound and pervasive impact on all information security efforts, it's very important that the policies in effect be clear, sufficient, and responsive to the information systems at the organization in question. While this book can provide a starting point for most any organization, policies will need to be <u>customized</u> to suit the unique circumstances prevailing at the organization in question. Beyond this customization, information security specialists need to periodically reexamine information security policies to determine whether new circumstances dictate that the policies be modified or augmented. Accordingly, this book is intended to be used a reference to support both the practitioners who are writing policies for the first time and those who are rewriting/expanding existing policies.

Regardless of an organization's size, its industry, its geographical location, or the extent to which it uses computers, information security is an important matter that should be addressed by explicit policies. Harry DeMaio, former director of data security programs at IBM, says the lack of a well-defined corporate information security policy is the single biggest problem with most security efforts. This book provides the reader with concise already-written policies that can be quickly tailored to the needs of the reader's organization. The book can save weeks, even months, of effort since it provides a wide array of information that has heretofore never been provided in a single source.

Much as many of us would prefer it to be otherwise, effective information security policies cannot simply be taken "off the shelf," written-up, approved by a rubber-stamp process, and then issued. Instead policies must be uniquely tailored to the needs of each organization. This is because the factors which drive information security policies vary considerably from organization to organization. These factors include business objectives, legal requirements, organizational design, organizational culture, prevailing ethics and morals, the extent of worker education, and the information systems technology deployed.

Nonetheless, the ideas behind many information security policies are similar from organization to organization. Accordingly, this book provides the essential ideas that should go into all information security policy statements. But to have these ideas fit a particular organization, it will still be necessary for the reader to be familiar with the factors described in the prior paragraph. Perhaps the best way to acquaint oneself with these factors is to conduct a risk analysis (this topic is discussed at greater length in the section entitled Instructions).

This book includes most every policy now viewed as part of a non-military information security standard-of-due-care. (The book and CD-ROM is nonetheless still of considerable value to military organizations.) Many additional policies are included in the book and CD-ROM which could not properly be considered to be part of the standard-of-due-care. These additional policies are provided to give the reader a menu of options from which to choose appropriate policies.

A generally accepted standard-of-due-care for information security policies unfortunately does not currently exist. Because developments in the information systems area are coming at an increasingly rapid rate, there is some question whether such a generally accepted set of policies will ever exist. As the next best thing, this book and disk provide the most comprehensive collection of policies currently available anywhere. It is the responsibility of each reader to determine which of these policies are applicable to a specific organization.

II. Instructions

This section provides an orientation to the information security policy writing process. While it might be tempting to immediately start cutting-and-pasting policies together, it is very important that the policy writer read these instructions. (The term "policy writer" is used throughout this book to identify the person responsible for writing information security policies.) The instructions will provide background material that will make all subsequent policy writing tasks more efficient and more focused.

This section gives practical and down-to-earth guidance on the complex information security policy development process. This process includes writing policies, editing policies, obtaining management approval, communicating policies, and implementing controls to meet policy requirements. The last few subsections within this section contain hints and suggestions on how to best use this book and the accompanying computer readable material.

A. What Are Information Security Policies?

a. Distinct From Guidelines And Standards

"Policies" are management instructions indicating a course of action, a guiding principle, or an appropriate procedure which is expedient, prudent, or advantageous. Policies are high-level statements that provide guidance to workers who must make present and future decisions. It would also be correct to say that policies are generalized requirements that must be written down and communicated to certain groups of people inside, and in some cases outside, the organization. Policies can also be considered to be business rules. Although information security policies vary considerably by organization, they typically include general statements of goals, objectives, beliefs, ethics, controls, and worker responsibilities.

Policies are mandatory and can also be thought of as the equivalent of an organization-specific law. Special approval is required when a worker wishes to take a course of action that is not in compliance with policy. Because compliance is required, policies use definitive words like "do not ...," "you must ...," or "you are obliged to ...". The words used to indicate policies must convey both certainty and indispensability. For simplicity and consistency, throughout this book, the word "must" has been employed, but equivalent words are certainly acceptable.

Policies are distinct from, but similar to "guidelines," which are optional and recommended. In fact, the policies appearing in this book can be easily transformed into guidelines simply by replacing the word "must" with the word "should." As easy as this substitution may be, in general, transformation of the policies found in this book into guidelines is not recommended. This is because guidelines violate a basic principle of secure systems design called "universal application" (controls are significantly weakened if they are not consistently applied). Nonetheless, in some cases guidelines are desirable. For example, when work is to be done by a distributed group, then a centralized information security function may appropriately issue guidelines as opposed to policies. For example, this approach is common when a guideline for the preparation of departmental contingency plans is issued by a centralized information security group.

Policies are higher-level requirement statements than "standards," although both types of management instructions require compliance. Policies provide general instructions, while standards provide specific technical requirements. Standards cover details such as implementation steps, systems design concepts, software interface mechanisms, software algorithms, and other specifics. The phrase "information security architecture" is gaining increasing acceptance as a collection of integrated information security standards. Standards would for example define the number of secret key bits required in an encryption algorithm such as SSL (Secure Sockets Layer, a widespread Internet encryption protocol). Policies, on the other hand, would simply define the need to use an approved encryption process when sensitive information is sent over public networks such as the Internet.

Generally speaking, policies are intended to last for many years, while standards are intended to last for only a few years. Standards will need to be changed considerably more often than policies because the manual procedures, organizational structures, business processes, and information systems technologies mentioned in standards change so rapidly. For example, a network security standard might specify that all new or substantially modified systems must be in compliance with International Standards Organization (ISO) standard X.509 (which involves authentication of a secure communications channel via public key cryptography). This standard is likely to be revised, expanded, or replaced in the next few years.

Separately, policies are generally aimed at a wider audience than standards. For example, a policy requiring the use of computer virus packages would apply to all personal computer users, but a standard requiring the use of public key digital certificates could be directed only at staff who conduct organizational business over the Internet.

b. Distinct From Procedures And Controls

Policies are distinct from and considerably higher-level than "procedures" (sometimes called "standard operating procedures"). A policy statement describes only the general means for addressing a specific problem; it should not become detailed or lengthy -- otherwise it becomes a procedure or gets mixed up with procedures. Procedures are specific operational steps or manual methods that workers must employ to achieve a certain goal. For instance, in many information technology departments there are specific procedures for performing back-ups of server hard drives. In this example, a policy could describe the need for back-ups, for storage off-site, and for safeguarding the back-up media (using encryption, physical security, etc.). A standard could define the software to be used to perform back-ups and how to configure this software. A procedure could describe how to use the back-up software, the timing for making back-ups, and other ways that humans interact with the back-up system (how to restore a file, how to securely transport storage media to an off-site repository, etc.).

One of the problems that the author regularly observes in his policy writing consulting work involves the combination of policies, standards, and procedures in a single document. When it comes time to update the document, the process is needlessly time-consuming and confusing. This is because the three different types of document all have different levels of detail and focus on different things. Because these three document types are intended for different audiences, this combination approach also runs a high risk that the material will not be read. People are very pressed for time these days, and if a document contains a lot of material that's not relevant to them, they will be likely to stop reading. The combination of policies, standards, and procedures in a single document is also not recommended because it can make the location of relevant information much more difficult for the reader. This combination approach also is inefficient in terms of distribution because a lot of irrelevant information is sent to people who really don't need it. To simplify document maintenance, usage, and cross-referencing, be sure to use separate documents for policies, standards, and procedures.

Getting back to definitions, policies are also different from "controls" (also known as "countermeasures," "security measures," and "safeguards"). A control is a device or a mechanism used to regulate or guide the operation of a machine, apparatus, or system. An example of a control would be encryption of sensitive data stored on floppy disks. In many cases, policies provide broad objectives which are met with controls. For instance, a policy prohibiting actual or apparent conflicts of interest could be partially met via a control requiring employees to sign a statement indicating they have read the code of conduct and agree to comply. Likewise, in many instances, control measures are dictated directly by policy. For example, a requirement to sign a statement of compliance with a code of conduct might itself be a policy.

B. Why Are Policies Important?

With all of the attention that information security gets from the news media, the policy writer may at first believe that management understands what an information security policy is and why an information security policy is necessary. Unfortunately, this is often not the case. Before beginning to write a policy document, the policy writer should check with management to make sure that they are all talking about the same thing, and that they understand why a policy development effort is important.

To this end, the prior subsection, entitled "What Are Information Security Policies?," will give the policy writer specific words that can go into a memo to clarify the result of his or her work. A few of the sample policies at the end of this book can also be submitted to management as rough approximations of the finished products that the policy writer will produce. The section below provides specific ideas that can go into a memo detailing the reasons why an information security policy is important. A summary of justifications for the adoption of information security policies is provided in the table labeled Table 1. Some of the more important reasons to have information security policies are described in their own subsections.

a. Assuring The Proper Implementation Of Controls

With hopes of handling information security expediently, management in many organizations simply purchases one or more information security products. In these cases, management often thinks the new products -- be they hardware, software, information content, or services -- are all that's needed. Soon after the products are installed, however, management is often disappointed to learn that the hoped-for results have not materialized. In a large number of instances, this disappointment can be traced to the fact that management has failed to establish an adequate organizational infrastructure for information security. And one of the most critical components of an organizational infrastructure for information security is policies.

An example should help clarify this essential point. Suppose that a large organization has recently acquired an access control package for a multi-user computer system such as a super-server attached to an intranet. Simple installation of the package will do little to improve security. Management must first decide which users should be given access to which information resources, preferably defining the ways to make these decisions in a policy. Management must also establish procedures so that technical people can set-up access controls in a manner consistent with these decisions. Management should furthermore define the ways to review system logs and other records generated by the access control package. These and other efforts constitute part of the necessary organizational infrastructure to support security products. Most technology vendors do not provide policies, procedures, and the other things necessary for the turn-key usage of their products -- the purchasing organization must still come up with an organizational infrastructure. In part this is because organizational infrastructure is a function of, and must respond to each organization's unique requirements.

To establish a supporting organizational infrastructure, every organization needs a variety of documents. These include organizational responsibility statements, policies, standards, operational procedures, and enforcement mechanisms. Several management processes are also needed. These include a risks assessment (risk analysis) process, a process for coordinating an information security management oversight committee, as well as an information security budgeting and planning process. Once responsibility for information security has been defined (departmental mission statements, job descriptions, etc.), the next step is to perform a risk assessment. Once an initial risk assessment is completed, an initial information security policies document should be prepared. Other documentation such as standards and operational procedures then grow directly from the policy document and subsequent efforts. The timing issues surrounding the preparation of policies are discussed in greater detail below in the subsection entitled "When Should Policies Be Developed?"

b. Guiding The Product Selection And Development Process

Most organizations do not have the resources to design and implement controls from scratch. They often pick and choose from the set of controls provided by information security product vendors, and then they attempt to customize these controls with policies, procedures, standards, and other organization-specific integration efforts. This custom integration process is often performed without sufficient understanding of the security objectives and goals of the organization. As a result, the security products chosen and their implementation may not be responsive to the true needs of the organization. For example, the purchase of devices to bolt computers to desks may have been motivated by a rash of thefts; in the absence of guiding policies, management may have selected a product which does not easily allow for the secure storage of portable computers.

To avoid these problems, policies stating information security objectives and requirements can provide both the understanding and additional guidance that workers need in order to act as management intends they should. Such policies can be a way to make sure that in-house personnel are appropriately selecting, developing, and implementing information systems. For example, a policy can state that only virus screening software approved by the Information Security Department may be used on Company X systems. The actual vendor and product name can change from month to month without the need to change the policy (these details would instead be found in a standard).

c. Demonstrating Management Support

Some people (particularly users and Information Technology Department staff) often say, "When management tells me to, then I'll do something about information security." This attitude is not surprising when one appreciates that most people are unaware of the extent of the information security risks they face, just as they are not inclined to take the time to seriously analyze these risks. Beyond this, because they do not have the expertise, most people are unable to evaluate the need for certain control measures.

Policies are a clear and definitive way for management to demonstrate that (1) information security is important, and (2) workers should pay attention to information security. Policies can compensate for influences that may otherwise cause people to insufficiently protect information resources. One frequently-encountered example involves middle level managers who repeatedly refuse to allocate money for information security in their budgets. In this case, the other influence is often a bonus plan that rewards them for keeping costs down. But if policies dictating management support have been issued by top management, then middle level managers will not be able to continue to deny requests for information security funding.

According to a report issued by the National Research Council entitled "Computers at Risk," a California prosecutor recently observed that "We probably turn down more cases [involving computer break-ins] than we charge, because computer system proprietors haven't made clear what is allowed and what isn't." Don Ingram, a well-known district attorney in Alameda County, California, and an expert on computer crime, says it concisely when he notes that "If you can't define it [inappropriate behavior involving computers], how are you going to prosecute it?" Management at every organization needs to clarify its intentions with respect to the operation of computers and networks. If management takes the time to prepare an information security policy (and other documents such as a telecommuter policy), when the time comes for disciplinary action, prosecution, or litigation, the organization will not be subject to these same legal problems. Policies are thus a relatively inexpensive and straightforward way for management to define appropriate behavior.

d. Avoiding Liability

In addition to explicit statutes like the US Foreign Corrupt Practice Act (FCPA), an increasingly compelling body of case law is demonstrating that management and even technical staff may be held liable for inadequately addressing information security matters. The basis for this liability can be: negligence, breach of fiduciary duty, failing to use the security measures found in other organizations in the same industry, failing to exercise the due care expected from a computer professional (computer malpractice), or failure to act after an "actual notice" (such as a compromise of security) has taken place. Discussions about liability exposure and the need for policies are often successfully used to gain additional management attention and support for information security efforts. Be sure to speak with internal legal counsel prior to covering this topic with management.

Policies have been shown to be influential evidence in the eyes of the court that management has indeed been concerned about and done something about information security. If the policy writer's organization has not yet seriously addressed information security, it is important to promptly start work and to set the direction for future efforts. As intellectual property attorney George S. Cole (Menlo Park, California) recently put it, "The first line of defense is that you are doing something about [information] security, not necessarily that you have it solved. Ignoring the thing, hoping it will go away, will crucify you."

e. Protecting Trade Secrets

Although the laws related to trade secrets vary from jurisdiction to jurisdiction, in the United States and countries with similar legal systems, policies can provide extra protection for sensitive intellectual property. In a court of law, policies can serve as evidence indicating that an organization seriously took steps to protect its sensitive intellectual property, helping to convince the court that such intellectual property should be deemed a trade secret. If information is deemed a trade secret, an organization has additional legal remedies available which may help make a case for monetary damages, the issuance of an injunction, and the like.

Table 1. Reasons to Establish Policies

- Expand information security budget and add more personnel
- Establish top management communication path
- Show definitive progress with minor investment
- Establish information security effort credibility and visibility
- Shift worker attitudes and change perspectives
- Overcome ambiguity which leads to information overload
- Generate user support for information security
- Demonstrate clear top management support
- Avoid disputes and related internal politics
- Enable rapid development of new systems
- Coordinate activities of internal and external groups
- Achieve lower costs through control standardization
- Avoid problems because tasks are out of sequence
- Prevent decentralized groups from "reinventing the wheel"
- Establish benchmarks or reference points for future audits
- Guide security product selection and implementation

Table 1. Reasons to Establish Policies, cont.
- Assure consistent implementation of controls
- Arrange contractual obligations needed for prosecution
- Establish basis for disciplinary actions and termination
- Maintain trade secret legal protection for information assets
- Avoid liability for negligence and breach of fiduciary duty
- Document contract, law, and regulation compliance
- Demonstrate quality control processes (ISO 9000 compliance)

f. Adapting To A Dynamic Communications Environment

Workers in modern organizations are increasingly showing signs of burnout and information overload. The proliferation of new communications technologies such as computers, the Internet, fax machines, photocopying machines, and pagers has destabilized long-standing communications processes. For example, while it used to be polite behavior to return all telephone calls, this is no longer standard procedure if the one requesting a call-back is known to be a salesperson. The lack of clear rules dictating appropriate behavior in this dynamic new environment has made life more difficult for modern workers. To effectively manage worker expectations and to effectively guide behaviors, management must dispel this ambiguity by setting clear priorities and defining appropriate actions. The policy messages contained in this book are intended to do just that for the information security domain.

g. Achieving Consistent And Complete Security

One of the most serious problems in the information security field involves fragmented and inconsistent efforts. Too often one department will be supportive of information security efforts, while another department within the same organization will be resistant. To the extent that these departments share computing resources--such as an intranet--the resistant department will be likely to jeopardize information security in the supportive department. This could for example take place if a hacker were to gain access to an intranet via lax dial-up user authentication processes within a resistant department, and then use leverage this penetration to gain additional access that he would not otherwise have been able to obtain. Although it is neither feasible nor desirable to make all persons in an organization familiar with the complexities of information security, it is important that they all subscribe to some minimum level of protection. In high-level terms, policies can be used to define this minimum protection level (sometimes called a "baseline").

h. Coordinating Activities Of Internal And External Groups

Outsourcing and the use of contractors, consultants, and temporary personnel have become business necessities at many organizations. Likewise, today's organizations are also establishing close business partnerships with a variety of organizations, and in some cases these organizations are competitors. The large number of participants in modern business has made system access control, intellectual property protection, and related information security issues more difficult to manage. Because so many different parties are involved, there is a pressing need to consistently coordinate the activities of both internal and external groups. That's where information security policies can help. For example, a policy can address the circumstances where a confidentiality or non-disclosure agreement is necessary, and where it is not. Managers hiring contractors can then read this policy and manage these contractors so that internal information assets are properly protected.

In days gone past, sensitive information was often concentrated in the hands of middle and top management. These days, information is being pushed down the organizational hierarchy, out to lower-level employee desktops, and even further out to contractors, consultants, and temporaries. As a larger number of individuals get involved in the information management area, and as a larger number of people gain access to sensitive, valuable, or critical information, there is a resulting increase in the need for information security policies.

Direct supervision of all of these different people is impractical, and cost-effective technological tools to monitor every action they take are not yet available. Although organizations will rarely admit it, this means that all these people need to be largely self-managed, but they need instructions in the form of information security policies in order to do it right. In other words, the state-of-the-art in information security involves significant unsupervised reliance on people because sophisticated technological tools aren't yet available. The number one tool for managing the behavior of people in the information security area is a policies document.

C. How Should Policies Be Developed?

a. Gathering Key Reference Materials

Information security policies should be driven largely by the nature of the information handled by the organization in question. For example, information security policies at the Internal Revenue Service (IRS) are largely a function of the sensitive tax information that the agency handles. The policy writer should acquaint him- or herself with the nature of the information handled by the organization. One good source for this "information about information" (also known as metadata) is a data dictionary, also known as a data directory. Overviews of internal information systems prepared for top executives, board members, merger/acquisition candidates, and strategic partners, may also be useful background to the policy writing effort. Because information systems change so rapidly, available documentation is likely to be out-of-date; this means that the policy writer will most often need to interview knowledgeable workers to accurately identify the nature of the information currently being handled by the organization. When doing these interviews, the policy writer should be sure to ask what information is sensitive, what information is valuable, and what information is critical.

When developing a set of information security policies, the policy writer should reference a recent risk assessment (sometimes called a "risk analysis" or an "EDP audit") that clearly indicates the organization's current information security needs. A loss history, which documents the specifics of recent incidents, may also be helpful in terms of identifying areas in need of further attention. Lawsuits, formal written grievances, and other disputes may additionally be pointers to areas which need to be addressed in a policy document. To identify further problem areas, face-to-face meetings with interested parties such as the in-house legal counsel, the director of physical security, the chief information officer, the internal audit director, and the director of human resources are advisable.

To identify the policy areas needing further attention, the policy writer should additionally collect copies of all other relevant organizational policy documents now in effect. Relevant policies include application systems development policies, computer operations policies, computer equipment acquisition policies, human resources policies, information system quality control policies, and physical security policies. If obtainable, policies from other organizations in the same industry can also provide useful background information (unfortunately, these are generally not disclosed to the public). If the policy writer's organization is a subsidiary or affiliate of another organization, then the related organization's policies should also be obtained and used as reference material. If the organization is a participant in an electronic data interchange (EDI) value added network (VAN), a multi-organizational Internet commerce arrangement, or any other multi-organizational networks, the policies of these networks should be obtained and reviewed.

Some policy writers facing significant time or resource constraints will be tempted to skip the above-mentioned data gathering processes. Whenever data gathering is significantly abbreviated, the likelihood that the resulting document will be rejected by management increases dramatically. It is through this data gathering process that the policy writer can identify management's view of information security, the policies that already exist, the policies that need to be added or changed, how management enforces policies, the unique vulnerabilities that the organization faces, and other essential background information. If the policy writer has not given serious consideration to this background information, it is unlikely that a newly written information security policy will be responsive to the true needs of the organization in question.

Another major reason to do a good deal of background research in preparation for policy writing is to make sure that the requirements defined in the policy document are consistent with management's intentions. One of the fastest ways to lose credibility for an information security policy writing effort is to propose a policy which is clearly inconsistent with existing organizational norms. For example, at one well-known high-tech company, employees routinely downloaded games from the Internet and played these games on their powerful workstations during breaks and after-hours. Top management knew of and tacitly approved of these activities. At the same time, a published policy indicated that no personal use of the corporation's information systems would be tolerated. This glaring inconsistency caused a large majority of the workers at this company to dismiss the policy document as irrelevant window-dressing.

Still another important reason to spend considerable time on background research is to identify and define the organization's business-related strategic directions. A new or revised policy document needs to be consistent with these strategic directions if top management is going to approve and support the policy. For example, suppose an organization decides it wants to once again centralize its currently-decentralized information systems activities. A policy document that stresses many activities to be performed by a group of decentralized information security coordinators would then be out of step with management's intentions, and consequently would be unlikely to be approved.

Yet another reason to thoroughly research the current situation before beginning the policy writing process is to identify the internal information systems architecture. An information security policy document should be consistent with and fully support an existing information systems architecture. Note that we are NOT talking about an information security architecture here, we are talking about an information systems architecture. An information security policy document is typically developed after an information systems architecture is already in place. The development of an information security policy document will in turn allow an information security architecture to be developed. For example, a policy about permissible access through an Internet firewall will enable a security architecture to be specified (it will also enable an appropriate firewall product to be chosen and implemented).

b. Defining A Framework For Policies

After the above-mentioned reference materials have been collected, the policy writer should then compile a list of topics to be covered in a new and/or more comprehensive information security policy document. At least for the first draft, the list should include policies which are intended for immediate adoption as well as those which are intended for adoption some time in the future. This list should be prepared with a computer rather than by hand because it is likely to be revised several times. In most cases, the level of detail in this list will be inconsistent, and at this stage in the process, this shouldn't be cause for concern. For example, the list might include telecommuting, as well as password construction with a minimum of eight characters. When a high level outline is prepared (see the subsection below entitled "Preparing a Coverage Matrix"), the level of detail will be standardized.

Next the policy writer should attempt to define the ways in which the organization expresses information security policies. For example, policies may be placed in a standard operating procedures (SOP) manual. Alternatively, electronic mail memos summarizing policies may be periodically issued by the Director of the Information Security Department. Likewise, it is common these days for privacy policies to be posted on the Internet. Because modern-day workers are bombarded by communications from so many people through so many different communication channels, it is essential that information security policies be repeated and be sent through multiple communication channels. To assist with this effort, the appendix entitled "List of Suggested Awareness Raising Methods" provides a long list of ways to communicate policies. The channels used to express a policy will in turn determine how the policy should be written. For example, if a video tape will be used, then an abbreviated colloquial style should be employed; but if a policy document will reside on an intranet web server, a longer and more formal style is appropriate.

The policy writer should additionally examine the ways that the organization currently uses and/or intends to use information security policies. Policies may for instance be used to guide information system acquisition efforts, drive EDP audit plans, and simply assist users in securely operating their desktop computers. Additional ideas about potential uses were presented above in the table above labeled Figure 1. Defining the uses of policies will help identify the audiences to whom policies will be addressed (this topic is addressed in greater detail below in the section entitled "Preparing A Coverage Matrix"). Determining the uses for policies will also help focus the policy writer's attention on those areas which most need to be addressed. Certainly other uses will soon be apparent after the policy document has been distributed; this should not be considered poor planning on the part of the policy writer, but should instead be considered a successful initiative which has unforeseen contributions to the organization. In some instances, the uses of a policy document will be initially unknown, but these uses can be quickly identified through a series of meetings with interested parties.

The policy writer should also study the style in which existing policies are written, the use of certain words, the conventional format for documenting policies, the system for numbering and naming policies, as well as the linkages between policies and other management directives like procedures and standards. For example, existing policies may use the word "must" consistently; following suit, the information security policies should also use the word "must." Likewise, the existing policies may have a military-style numbering system like the one used in this book, or something entirely different. The issuance of an information security policy document will be controversial by its very nature; don't give critics additional ammunition by failing to be consistent with internal policy style guidelines (whether these guidelines are written or unwritten).

Part of the policy writer's study of the existing policies and how they are used should entail a review of the level of detail appropriate for the organization's policy statements. The organization may have defined existing policies in very specific terms, in which case many detailed information security policies may be appropriate. Alternatively, the organization may have defined policies in very high-level terms, in which case only a brief overall information security statement may be appropriate. Both of these alternatives may simultaneously exist in that separate policies are provided to different audiences. The level of detail is in part driven by the extent to which management trusts workers to use their judgement, the extent to which ISO 9000 and other documentation requirements are employed, and the extent to which the topics being addressed are new to the involved audiences.

Information about the expression, use, style, and level of detail found in internal policies is rarely written down, but it can be obtained by "reading between the lines" of existing policy statements. In very large organizations there may even be a document which provides directions on the policy writing process. In some large organizations, in-house staff in a Policy and Planning

Group can help with the policy writing effort. Whether or not explicit written guidance or in-house consulting assistance are available, to help ensure their prompt adoption, new and revised information security policies should be written in a manner that resembles and is at least in form indistinguishable from existing policies.

c. Preparing A Coverage Matrix

After preparing a rough list of the areas needing attention, and after becoming acquainted with the ways in which the organization expresses and uses policies, the policy writer is now ready to use the policies found in this book. At this point the policy writer is simply looking for additional topics which should be covered. The policy writer can skim one of the indexes in the back of the book looking only at title names. If the policy writer would like just a little more detail, he or she can look at the policies themselves, but skip the accompanying commentaries. This latter task is generally done most rapidly with the hardcopy book.

To get additional ideas for the areas to be covered, the policy writer can use the categories found in this book's Table Of Contents. While the Table Of Contents is useful and does provide good coverage of the major topics, policy writers are best advised to develop their own categories which uniquely respond to their organization's needs. Alternatively, categories reflecting the areas to be addressed may also be patterned after an internal audit report or an information security book that management values. Another way to segment the controls would be broad control objectives such as: avoid, prevent, deter, detect, mitigate, recover, and correct. Yet another way to organize a document is along technological lines such as: telecommuting, desktop computing, intranet, Internet, etc.

At this point a draft high-level outline reflecting the topics to be addressed should be developed. This outline is best if accompanied by a brief explanation with examples of topics to be covered in each section. The explanation can be only a sentence or two -- just enough to give a flavor of the topics included. At this point, distribution of the high-level outline to interested parties is recommended, and the meritorious feedback received should then be integrated with the high-level outline.

After revising a high-level outline in response to initial feedback, the policy writer is then advised to skim the "Index to Policies by Policy Number" found in the back of this book to find as many potential policies that respond to the organization's circumstances. Alternatively, the policy writer can read only the policies, again noting the number to each relevant policy. The numbers will be needed later in the policy development process. This step is also done expediently with the hardcopy book. Many people mark up the hardcopy book with a red pen or yellow highlighter.

Control Category / Audience	Computers	Data Communication	Management	Physical
End Users	12,35, 45, 46	12, 35, 46, 47 48, 49, 56, 58	435, 435, 504	12, 35, 36
Management	12, 36, 37, 345, 401	304, 305, 307 308, 309, 310	45, 47, 48, 49 54, 55, 57, 59	35, 36, 67, 38 44, 45, 134, 138 213, 214, 216
Info Sys Dept	34, 36, 59	189, 199, 200	501, 504, 523	12, 13, 14, 18 222, 223, 224 225, 226, 228 229, 332, 336
Customers	234, 235, 236	202, 203, 204	34, 36, 38, 39	34, 35, 36, 38
Business Partners	256, 257, 258	205, 206, 207	40, 41, 42, 43	34, 35, 36, 39

Figure 2. Coverage Matrix Example

At this point, the policy writer is still faced with the question: To which audiences should these messages be addressed? Often policies will be directed at several significantly different audiences because each audience has distinctly different needs. For example, end-users might receive a small booklet containing the most important information security policies that they need to keep in mind (the focus could be on desktop computer information security issues). At the same time, systems developers and other technical staff might receive a considerably longer document that provides much more detail, perhaps focusing on security as part of a standard systems development methodology. Management may get yet another document which deals primarily with the tasks of information owners.

While separate documents for separate audiences may at first sound like too much effort, the additional work is not great if the policy writer has first made a list of the essential messages to be communicated. This list can now be split by audience, and it is this splitting process which is discussed in the next few paragraphs. As an aside, the development and maintenance of separate documents for separate audiences is much easier these days if all of these so-called documents are placed on an intranet. Using browser links, those who read the policy can be quickly provided with only the information that is relevant to them. For example, at one large bank, an intranet is used to segment the information security policies by job title. Thus people need to read only those policies which directly apply to their own job. This intranet implementation also provides a key word search mechanism and an index, both of which help readers quickly find policies relevant to their current circumstances.

When more than two audiences will be addressed by separate policy documents, the author recommends that the policy writer prepare a "coverage matrix" before actually writing the first draft policy documents. (If the policy writer doesn't customarily think in terms of matrices, much the same result can be achieved if a separate detailed outline for each of the identified audiences is prepared.) A coverage matrix is simply an organizational tool to make sure that all the appropriate information security policy messages are presented to all the appropriate audiences. It is a way of looking at the work to be done and as such can bring order to what otherwise may be a complicated policy writing effort. Once the topics to be communicated have been identified, and organized in a coverage matrix, the preparation of policy documents will be relatively easy and straightforward.

A coverage matrix in its simplest form is a two-dimensional table. It can, for instance, use the primary audiences to which the policies are directed (for example, end-users, management, Information Technology Department staff, customers, and business partners) as row identifiers, and policy categories as column headings. These policy categories are the major sections appearing in the above-mentioned high-level outline. The cells in the center of the matrix should be filled with reference numbers separated by commas, each referring to a policy (as found in this book and perhaps elsewhere too).

Continuing with this discussion about a coverage matrix, Table 2 provides an example of a matrix that a policy writer might develop. Note that the policy numbers appearing in this matrix are place holders and are deliberately not the result of an analysis. Each organization will need to prepare its own coverage matrix, inserting policy numbers in the relevant cells to reflect its own unique business and information systems environment. If the policy writer considers the development of this type of a coverage matrix too time consuming, he or she can instead prepare a similar table using broad categories such as those found in the table of contents to this book (rather than using policy numbers).

Because there will probably be many columns, but only a few rows, the author suggests that the policy writer prepare a standard coverage matrix with the row headings filled in (for audiences), with blank column headings (for policy categories), and with blank cells in the middle (for specific policies). Such a template coverage matrix can then be photocopied many times to save the policy writer considerable time drawing coverage matrices. If the policy writer doesn't mind seeing only one portion of the coverage matrix at any one moment, is often more time-efficient if a spreadsheet program is used to construct and manipulate a coverage matrix. Use of a spreadsheet program also makes the generation of professional-looking hardcopy easier, just as it makes updates more straightforward.

Often only two or three audiences will be needed. Two possible audiences could be end-users and computer-literate technical staff. Using another approach, three possible audiences could be end-users, management, and computer support. In almost every instance, there will be a significant amount of overlap in the messages directed to each of these audiences. The policy writer should strive to minimize the number of audiences at the same time recognizing the needs of different groups to receive different information.

An alternative approach provides what could be considered a middle ground between a single policy and separate policies for different audiences. In this case, a broad umbrella policy document can apply to all staff, while separate specialized policy documents can be used to address audiences such as information owners, systems developers, telecommuters, etc. With this approach there is a basic set of rules which goes to everyone, but then there are also special policies which go only to selected audiences. At larger organizations with intranets, this approach is increasingly common.

In an effort to save time, policy writers often anticipate there will be only one audience. This one-size-fits-all approach may work for the first few policy statements that an organization issues, but the more sophisticated the information security effort, the less applicable this approach will become. It will often save the policy writer a significant amount of time if he or she deals with the different audiences from the beginning of a policy writing effort, rather than having to keep modifying a one-size-fits-all policy that was originally intended to meet the needs of multiple audiences. The use of separate documents will also be appreciated by the various audiences; if separate documents are employed, they will not need to be repeatedly notified about changes which in many cases will not apply to them. The use of separate documents will also allow differential treatment without confusion. For example, the rules for third party access to an organization's information systems can be quite different from the rules for permanent employee access.

Just because there are different audiences for policies doesn't necessarily imply that there should be different documents. It is possible to have different chapters or sections in an information security manual devoted to different audiences. This approach is attractive because all the policies are then found in one document rather than several. Having all information security policies in a single manual facilitates maintenance and revisions. It is also attractive because individuals often find themselves falling into two or more of the audiences (for example an individual may be both a general user and a systems developer).

Now that the policy writer is familiar with both the policies that are needed and the audiences to receive these policies, he/she should write the policy numbers directly into the body of the coverage matrix. The process of filling in the body of the coverage matrix often highlights the fact that certain audiences are not being adequately addressed, just as it often indicates that certain areas need additional policies to be truly responsive to the organization's needs. Note that if outlines for policy documents to different audiences were prepared, but no coverage matrix was used, these discrepancies may not have been revealed.

If an area is not adequately addressed, the policy writer can then go back to this book's indexes or Table Of Contents to get additional ideas. If the policy writer knows specifically what he or she is after, the computer-resident files provided with this book that have the word "policy" in the title can be searched based on key words. For example, if additional virus policies are needed, a search for the word "virus" would quickly yield results.

After the overall topics to be covered have been clarified through a coverage matrix, a detailed outline of the soon-to-be-prepared policy documents can be compiled. Depending on the management at the policy writer's organization, there may or may not be a need to get interested parties to review a detailed outline. If no such review is required, then a detailed outline may not be needed. In this case, using the coverage matrix, the policy writer can start preparing first draft policy documents.

Conservative policy writers who noticed a great deal of political uncertainty associated with the policy writing process may nonetheless wish to prepare a detailed outline and subject it to a review process. While this may slow the process down, it helps to ensure that the resulting document is on target and truly responsive to the organization's needs. Where only one audience is being addressed, the coverage matrix can be dispensed with, but policy writer does need a detailed outline. Either a coverage matrix or a detailed outline is important; without one or the other the policy writer risks weeks of wasted time writing policies on topics which are not needed or not wanted by management.

At this point, the policy writer must choose the categories to be employed in the policy document. The categories in the coverage matrix or the detailed outline will do, although they will often be modified during the subsequent review process. As an aside, the author recommends the use of a large number of subtitles. This will assist readers in their efforts to quickly locate topic(s) of interest. This will also allow readers to skip sections which don't pertain to them.

In those cases where a very large policy document is being developed, or if a significant amount of complexity must be addressed in the policy document, a "mind map" can be used. Mind maps are graphical representations of the relationships between ideas. They generally use circles to represent ideas and arrows to represent the relationship between ideas. A mind map can be readily converted into a complex outline, which in turn can be used to develop a draft policy document. One of the best books describing the mind mapping process is "Writing the Natural Way" by Gabriele Lusser Rico (published by J. P. Tarcher, Los Angeles, California, USA, 1983). Software programs are also available to assist the policy writer with the drawing and revision of mind maps. One of these is called Inspiration, and is available from Inspiration Software of Portland, Oregon, USA (http://www.inspiration.com).

After the policy writing process is complete (generally it takes several drafts), the policy writer is urged to save the coverage matrix, outlines, and related working papers. In a year or two a revised policy document will probably be needed. It will save a lot of time if the person writing revised policies can consult the original working papers. The coverage matrix and related working papers may also serve as important information in a court case, should there ever be any allegations that management did not seriously think about the risks and the policy messages which needed to be communicated. Similarly, the working papers should be retained for a year or two because internal and external auditors may wish to review them.

d. Making Critical Systems Design Decisions

Before a final version of a policy document can be published, management often needs to make a number of security-related systems design decisions. Examples of these decisions include: (1) which groups of users will be given Internet access, (2) how frequently will they need access (continuously, regularly, occasionally), (3) what type of access will they need (electronic mail, web surfing, file transfer, remote log-in, chat-rooms, etc.), (4) how will access be controlled (dynamic passwords, fixed passwords, smart cards, etc.), and (5) what types of user activity will be monitored (files transferred, web sites visited, hours per day of usage, etc.).

Identification of these systems design decisions is ordinarily indirect. Typically the policy writer will compile a draft policy document which incorporates a number of suggested options. Unfortunately, in an effort to expedite the policy writing process, the policy writer in many cases does not highlight alternative solutions. As a result, management may approve of a policy document incorporating decisions with far-reaching implications, many of which were unappreciated at the time of the approval. This may lead to excessive costs for information security as the initial approaches described in the policy document soon need to be replaced or revised. It may also mean that the policy document needs to be changed much sooner than it otherwise would be.

If the project schedule and resources permit, the policy writer should highlight the fundamental systems design decisions. If a paper draft of the policy is going to be circulated for comment, then this could be done by footnotes or endnotes which describe the options and the pros/cons of each. Wording reflecting the different design decisions can also be incorporated into the body of draft document; seeing the options in context will often help management make these decisions. If the draft policy is going to be placed on an intranet server with restricted access to selected interested parties, certain words can be highlighted and links can be used to illuminate options and supporting justifications.

In those organizations which have been attending to information security for some time, management will have already seriously considered all the necessary fundamental systems design options. In these cases, a policy writing effort will simply involve documenting the decisions already made, and choosing appropriate ways to express these decisions in the form of policies. In these cases, there will be no need for a separate review of the critical systems design issues as discussed above. Instead, the fortunate policy writer can focus on the extension of these existing design decisions to new information systems (such as extranets), as well as to new technologies (such as the programming language called Java).

e. Structuring Review, Approval, And Enforcement Processes

Once the first draft information security policy document(s) have been written, the policy writer should have a few friendly colleagues review them. After a few changes are made in response to feedback from these colleagues, the policy document(s) should then be sent to interested internal parties such as the Manager of the Internal Audit Department and the Intellectual Property Attorney. After changes have been made by a few critical allies, it is ready for review by the Information Security Management Committee. The next release of the draft can involve distribution to a much larger body of interested parties, for example all information owners and all people employed in the Information Systems Department. This multi-iteration review process is advisable because it builds on support from critical players, pre-selling the document to these critical players, and building grass-roots support from these same critical players.

Many review cycles, each with more changes to the policy document, are often necessary. This should be viewed as standard procedure, and should in no way be taken as a personal insult to the policy writer. Multiple reviews are in part a reflection of the fact that the information security policy development process is highly political, emotionally-charged, and highly unstructured (largely because it is so new). The policy writer should instead welcome input and appreciate that this iterative review process makes the policies more clear, concise, and responsive to prevailing conditions. Two appendices provide additional information; see the sections entitled "Overview Of Policy Development Process," and "Checklist Of Steps In Policy Development Process."

The final step in the review process is the signature of the General Manager, President, Chief Executive Officer, or Chairman of the Board. If there is simply no chance of getting this individual involved, the signature of the Chief Information Officer may suffice. The signature of the Information Security Department Manager is generally insufficient to show management adoption and support. While this effort may sound like unnecessary marketing, experience has shown that the signature (and ideally a brief message about expected compliance) is critical to widespread adoption. But before the policy writer submits the policy document to the final manager for approval and signature, the new document(s) should be reviewed by and approved by an Information Security Management Committee.

An Information Security Management Committee generally is composed of representatives from the major divisions in an organization and typically oversees the work of the Information Security Department. Typical participants include representatives from the following departments: Information Security, Internal Audit, Risk Management, Physical Security, Information Systems, Human Resources, Legal, Finance/Accounting, and various user departments. This Management Committee is used to get a reality check on proposed policies, procedures, organizational structures, and other information security initiatives. In some cases, a separate information security policy development committee is formed. If this latter approach is adopted, the committee should not actually write the policy (a single technically astute individual should instead do this). With this latter approach, the committee should be used to identify the topics which need to be addressed, to approve the high-level outline, to provide editing suggestions, etc.

Special early review cycles with the Internal Audit Department, the Human Resources Department, and the Legal Department are also highly recommended. Although there may be no representatives from these departments on the Information Security Management Committee, these groups are important allies of the Information Security Department. These departments also will be called upon to help enforce compliance with the policies.

One of the most important functions of an Information Security Management Committee is that it evaluates policies in light of their feasibility, costs/benefits, and implications in terms of internal politics. The Management Committee should ask itself: "Are these policies practical and readily implemented?" The Committee should also ask itself: "Are these policies clear and unambiguous?" After the policy reviewing process has been completed, at many organizations the Management Committee also provides guidance on policy implementation. For further information about such a Committee, see the policy in the middle of this book entitled "Information Security Management Committee."

Separately, while preparing new information security policies, the policy writer should make sure that an adequate enforcement process exists or will soon exist. If policies cannot be enforced, they will be little more than "window dressing," and they will in all probability not be effective. To have policies which are not enforced may in fact be worse than not having policies at all. This is because the policies may teach workers hypocrisy and tolerance for inappropriate behaviors. Having policies which are not enforced may also lull management into thinking that information security problems have been addressed when the reality is something else.

Management often believes that workers will naturally behave in a manner which is in the best interests of the organization. This is a dangerous and ill-advised assumption. Although policies are unlikely to affect the personal values of workers, through policies management can give workers the opportunity to conduct themselves in a manner consistent with organizational values. Policies tell workers what is expected of them, that is if they wish to continue to have a job. Assuming there will always be a variance between personal values and organizational values, policies will only be taken seriously if effective compliance mechanisms are in place.

In advance of the issuance of new policies, the policy writer should discuss the ways to achieve compliance with the Internal Audit or EDP Audit Department. These might include automated compliance checking tools such as software license management systems. The policy writer should also consider the difficulty and advisability of conducting periodic manual compliance check efforts. The manner and means for the accomplishment of these compliance checks should be envisioned. Human Resources Department policies, such as a disciplinary process and an employee performance evaluation process, will also be important, and will also need to be discussed in advance of writing policies.

Compliance in many instances can be assisted when computerized tools are used to assist the user. For example, at Sun Microsystems, it is reported that management-approved non-disclosure agreements (NDAs) can be found on an intranet server accessible to all employees. Whenever an NDA is needed, a user can simply print the relevant form found on this server. The ready availability of tools such as this will help users translate information security policies into action.

Policy enforcement need not be drudgery. William Hugh Murray, a security consultant, often tells a story about a security manager who walked the halls without a badge. When a worker finally asked him for his badge, he gave the worker a $100 bill. After news of that and a few similar events quickly spread through the organization, workers became more interested in who was wearing a badge. The policy writer may also wish to consider special procedures to make a point. For example, at IBM, if confidential information is left on top of a desk, the information is taken and a receipt is provided indicating how the worker can retrieve it. The second time confidential material is left out in the open, the worker and his manager must both retrieve the information. The third time requires the worker, his manager, and a vice president. IBM does not allow a fourth time.

Enforcement actions are very often more effective if workers have been made aware of exactly what activities would be information security policy violations, and exactly what penalties would be encountered if they were caught. Establishing clear expectations, via an information security awareness program, is a very important part of an effective and enforceable set of policies. Such awareness programs might, for instance, clearly state that business information is the property of

Company X, and that it is not to be copied, modified, deleted, or used for unintended purposes without prior management approval.

In general, the policy writer should attempt to guide workers and positively influence their behavior. It should not be the policy writer's intent to catch people and make them wrong and bad. While punishment should be used for offenders as necessary, it is not the intent of enforcement mechanisms to generate large numbers of out-of-compliance notices. Quite the contrary, if a large number of people are out-of-compliance, this is an indication that the policies and related awareness programs have been ineffective. In these situations, the motivations behind the policies may need to be communicated more effectively, or the policies may need to be modified to better reflect the organizational culture or operating circumstances.

f. Automating Policy Enforcement Via Policy Servers

At many organizations, the complexity of modern information systems is overwhelming the ability of staff to manage these systems. To deal with this complexity, new expert systems tools are being introduced. For example, some firewalls include an expert system which will tell the person doing the installation whether a configuration inadvertently has created a serious security vulnerability. To deal with this increased complexity, in the future, organizations will need to have more centralized network management systems which play an increasing array of information security roles. For example, network management systems can, and in some organizations do, act as a conduit for the relay of intrusion detection information to a network operator on duty.

An interesting new development along these lines is called a policy server. Policy servers take organization-specific policies and code them in a special machine-readable language which can then be accessed by a wide variety of operating systems, access control packages, network management systems, and the like. Examples of these policies or rules include the minimum number of characters in a password, the maximum number of log-in attempts permitted before a connection will be severed, and whether attachments to electronic mail files will be permitted to pass through firewalls. In many ways a policy server is expected to be like an active data dictionary because it will be called upon to provide definitive instructions from a centralized point. One example of a policy server is provided by Digital Equipment Corporation (the product is RMON Manager); many other policy servers are expected to appear over the next few years. For example, CheckPoint Software Technologies has announced details of a policy server to be integrated with their best-selling firewall. In the near future, suites of products from a single vendor, as well as suites from a combination of vendors, will start to perform some of the rationalizing and centralizing tasks of a policy server.

To prepare their organizations for these upcoming developments, policy writers should be thinking about how the policies they develop today will be put into the computer models of tomorrow (like policy servers). Policy writers should make an attempt to be as logical and straightforward as they possibly can. Not only will this help the readers understand how to behave when it comes to information security, but it will also help tomorrow's programmers in their efforts to create computer-enforced rules. Policy writers should also strive to achieve the most cross-organization, cross-network, cross-system, and cross-platform coordination of information security policies. This will also reduce complexity and allow the organization to more readily adopt new policy enforcement tools.

D. When Should Policies Be Developed?

Before one embarks on an effort to write and obtain management approval for information security policies, it is advisable to clarify who is responsible for issuing and enforcing policies. Only when a clear assignment of responsibility for information security policies exists, should a policy development effort be initiated. Often this means that a centralized information security group mission statement should be prepared and approved before a policy-writing effort gets underway. If responsibility has not yet been clearly assigned, this should be the first step in a policy development effort. If this important step is ignored, the policy writer should be prepared for a barrage of internal politics which is likely to significantly delay policy writing progress.

Another necessary prerequisite for successfully writing information security policies involves management's perspective. Only after management appreciates that information has become a critical factor of production will information security be recognized as a serious matter deserving their attention. This perspective is known by a number of phrases including "information resource management" and "recognizing information as an asset." Management first needs to realize that they are responsible for managing information itself; in days gone past, management thought information was used only to manage other resources such as people. Management must also appreciate that new tools and techniques are needed to manage information itself. In the midst of this discussion, it is appropriate to mention the significant contribution that policies can make. If management doesn't really understand how important information is to their organization, they will be unlikely to support information security policy writing efforts. This topic is discussed further in the subsection below entitled "How Should One Select the Objectives and Scope of Policies?"

Management should also acknowledge that there is an information security problem, and that policies are required to address this problem -- all this before a serious policy writing effort is initiated. While this may appear to be obvious, many good-intentioned policy writing efforts have gone nowhere because the necessary groundwork had not yet been laid. This groundwork often includes a brief awareness presentation. Topics at this presentation can include risks that the organization faces, the organization's loss history, incidents suffered by other firms in the same industry, and generally accepted approaches for dealing with these risks and incidents (like a policy document).
Ideally, a policies development effort should be initiated after the performance of a comprehensive information security risk assessment (also known as a risk analysis). The risk assessment should indicate – perhaps only in high-level terms – the value of the information in question, the risks to which this information is subjected, and the vulnerabilities associated with the current way of handling this information. A risk assessment will provide useful background information that the policy writer can use when selecting appropriate policies from this book. The general threat types faced by the organization, as well as other general background information from a risk assessment, may also be included in an information security policy document introduction or preface.

One of the best times to develop an information security policy is when an information security manual is being prepared. Because a manual is distributed widely throughout an organization, it is an excellent place to put information security policies. Specific written policies may also be prepared just before compiling the material for user training and awareness efforts. These efforts may include a videotape, lectures, posters, or articles in an in-house newspaper. See the appendix entitled "List of Suggested Awareness Raising Methods" for additional ideas along these same lines.

Another good time to prepare policies is right after a major information security breach, an unfavorable computer-related audit report, a security-related lawsuit, or some other type of loss which has received extensive top management attention. This is a good time to move ahead with policy development efforts because management--at these times--is especially supportive of and concerned about information security. At these times the policy writer should work fast because management's level of concern declines rapidly.

To provide direction for the preparation of system development guidelines, access control package implementation memos, computer technical standards, internal control procedural descriptions, and other more specific information security documents, policies should be prepared early in the life cycle of an information security effort. An initial set of policies is typically brief, and is followed by more detailed policy statements addressing specific areas of concern (examples include telecommuting policies, Internet policies, and user application development policies).

A good objective to keep in mind when writing policies is that they should be written so that they need not be modified for three years. In reality, because things change so often in the information systems field, policies will often be modified only a year or two after issuance. To prevent policies from quickly becoming out-of-date, the policy writer should write policies which are independent of specific commercial products, vendors, and organizational structures. Being independent of these areas does not preclude the policy writer from inserting general statements addressing these areas in a policy document. For example, the need for dynamic passwords is often articulated in policy documents, but the vendors and products used to provide dynamic passwords are not generally found in these documents.

Given the lightning-fast pace of changes in the information systems field, the policy writer should attempt to get management to agree in advance that time will be set aside to rewrite the policy document a year or two in the future. In recognition of the need to keep updating information security policies, this book is also periodically updated (generally every year or year-and-a-half). If you are using an older version of this book, you may wish to contact the publisher to inquire about more recent versions.

E. Length Of Policies Document

a. Determining An Appropriate Number Of Policies

To be effective, information security policies must be tailored to the unique needs of an organization. Some organizations have many policies, while others have only a few. For example, the information security policy manual at British Telecom (a telephone company) is over 150 pages, at Lockheed (an aerospace company) it is 75 pages, and at CSX (a railroad) it is 25 pages. While range in the number of pages across organizations is quite wide, the trend is clearly to have more detailed and therefore longer policy documents.

While industry is a critical determinant of the number of pages in a policy document, so too is management's view of centralization of the information security function. If local management discretion is valued and encouraged, the policy document will generally be less detailed and therefore shorter. If centralized control is valued and encouraged, then a policy document will generally be more detailed and therefore longer. Most organizations have a combination of these two, where certain information security activities are managed in a decentralized fashion, while others are managed in a centralized fashion. For example, local information security coordinators may handle user-ID issuance and password resets at a departmental level, but centralized information security staff may be used for network security matters such as firewall maintenance.

Some management teams will think it's appropriate to be perfectly clear about information security matters. In these cases, there may be a need for many policies. Some managers are reluctant to have many policies, preferring to stress reliance on the professional judgement of workers. Other managers want to keep a document brief because they fear that workers will get the impression that they're not trusted. But the policy writer should not be shy and overly concerned about minimizing the impact on corporate culture -- there are some basic information security requirements which must be communicated by policy, and those should be included in a policy document even if they will provoke thorny questions like the appropriate level of trust in workers.

The audiences to be addressed may be highly-literate, such as at a research institute, in which case more written material may be appropriate. Or the audiences may be marginally-literate, such as a manufacturing firm which employs immigrants from countries which speak a different language. Likewise, an organization may be accustomed to documenting internal business processes, in which case more policies will generally be appropriate. On the other hand, an organization may have deliberately chosen to keep documentation at a minimum, in which case fewer policies will generally be needed.

Although a concise set of policies is more likely to be completely read, there is much to be said for a comprehensive set of information security policies. For example, an employer will find it easier to defend itself in court against employee charges of privacy invasion if policies were very explicit. More importantly, a comprehensive set of policies provides definitive guidance for workers. The definitive guidance in a long policy statement can be quite useful in a court of law where there is need for evidence to show that management has been diligently addressing information security. Longer policy statements are also helpful with disciplinary actions because they explicitly define expected behavior patterns.

Another factor affecting the length of a policy document involves management's expectations for a high-level or a low-level policy document. A high-level document would typically briefly define worker responsibilities and a few major control measures such as dynamic password tokens. A low-level policy would typically get into much more detail, and may make reference to both tasks and procedures. If the policy writer has not already received guidance from management on this point, he or she should be sure to clarify this area before actually preparing a policy document outline.

Modern Internet and intranet technology is also altering the appropriate length of policy documents. In the past, policy documents were "pushed" at workers (typically via the delivery of paper). Now policy documents can instead passively reside on an intranet server, and can be "pulled" when workers need the information. This means that documents can be more detailed than they were before without imposing any additional burden on workers. Likewise, the "hot-links" that this technology provides facilitate the establishment of interconnections between documents, which in turn allows users to more quickly locate material of interest. So the policy writer should consider whether the policy document will be "pushed" at or "pulled" by workers, and this in turn will affect its length.

One overall strategy is to minimize the length of a policy document involves mentioning only prohibitions. With this strategy, readers of a policy document will hear primarily about what they should not do, not so much about what they should do. Of course there are exceptions to this overall rule. For example, workers should report security incidents to someone who is in a position to take appropriate action. This is certainly something that workers should do, not what they should not do. But in general there is merit to this strategy. With this strategy, document length can be minimized because the set of prohibitions is considerably smaller than the set of actions that workers are supposed to perform. Because it involves only minimal instructions, this strategy can also provide flexibility as business activities change; provided the supporting information systems don't significantly change, such a policy statement can still be relevant.

Looking at things in a slightly different way, as a general principle of policy writing, it is wise to issue only those policies which are absolutely needed. This is because people are inherently different, as are the groups that they form. To impose a single set of comprehensive rules for everyone is bound to lead to hardship and sub optimal results. To have only those policies which are absolutely needed, however, allows personal initiative, creativity, and expression to be manifested. Although humans have a tendency to generalize and standardize, this is often taken too far. An example would be an organization which has so many security policies and procedures that they interfere with getting the work done. With this in mind, the policy writer may select a minimum set of policies which will then be issued on an organization-wide basis, and then leave the rest up to departmental, divisional, and other local management.

Rather than starting out with a comprehensive effort, it is best to first focus only on the essentials, producing a slim and concise policy statement. Then only as circumstances warrant, the policy writer can add additional policies. This approach often takes the form of separate policy statements addressing problem areas such as the Internet and telecommuting. Because it asks for a smaller number of concessions at a particular point in time, this phased approach is also much more likely to get management approval as well as user compliance. Furthermore, both the visibility and the good reputation of an information security effort are more likely to be maintained at high levels with such a phased approach because it forces the policy writer to obtain frequent approval and feedback.

The truth is always situation-dependent. The truly best way to protect information and information systems will always depend on the circumstances. Factors like the type of users, the computer equipment configuration, and the sensitivity of the information will dictate what should be done when it comes to information security. Although some people would like it to be otherwise, policies can never define the true and optimal path for all situations at all times. An open mind and a willingness to deal with the circumstances will go a long way towards finding workable information security solutions. An exhaustive set of policies which denies the reality of each situation, and which denies personal responsibility, is bound to sub optimize information security -- if not generate rebellion and disdain. Accordingly, the policy writer should try to write policies which provide minimal guidance, yet allow situation-specific responses to the truth of the moment.

Still another way to look at the appropriate number of policies involves the intention to make information security as user-transparent as possible. The more information security is made user-transparent, the more likely it is to be accepted. Likewise, the more user-transparent it is, the less the need for written policies. Policies in large measure address areas where vendors don't yet have turn-key user-transparent automated solutions -- areas where we must still rely on users and other workers. When vendors provide sufficiently reliable user-transparent cross-platform security solutions, there will be a significantly reduced need for written policies. That ideal world seems many years away, so in the meanwhile a good number of policies will continue to be necessary.

The number of policies to prepare is also a function of the involved audiences. Many modern organizations prepare several information security policy documents. For example, separate documents might be respectively compiled for users, management, and technical staff. Many of the policies in each of these documents will be the same, although the degree of detail, the technical words used, and the number of examples will generally vary from one document to another. If the audience is composed of end-users, the number of policies ideally should be limited to several pages. For a management audience, there will be additional considerations--such as legal matters--and this is likely to expand the number of policies required. A set of policies for technical staff will most often be still longer and more detailed.

To assist the policy writer with this audience-related segmentation of policies, the commentary for each policy in this book is suffixed with an audience indicator. For example, the abbreviation "A: EMT" means that the audience in most cases will be end-users, management, and technical staff. As another example, "A: T" would indicate that the audience is generally technical staff only. There are other audience indicator combinations which are readily derived once the policy writer knows the meaning of these abbreviations.

Another factor affecting the number of policies needed is the degree of security required at the organization in question. As a broad and general indicator, the more information intensive the activities of an organization, the higher the need for security. For example, a bank (very information intensive) will have many policies, whereas a chain of coffee shops (not particularly information intensive) will have few policies. Of course, involvement in especially sensitive activities like human life support (such as medical organizations) or national defense (for instance military contractors) will also raise the need for security. Thus an organization with low level security needs, such as a car-wash company, will generally have fewer policies, just as it will have fewer implemented information security measures. An organization with significant security needs, such as an insurance company, will generally have more policies (no pun intended), just as it will have more implemented information security measures.

Although primarily commercial and civilian-government in their orientation, most the policies listed in this book are applicable to any organization. Nonetheless, there are some policies which are relevant only to organizations with certain levels of security. Accordingly, at the end of the commentary section for each policy there is an indication of the environment where this policy would best be used. For example, the abbreviation "E: LMH" means that this policy is applicable to environments where a low, medium, or high need for security is found. As another example, the abbreviation "E: H" indicates that generally this policy is only appropriate for those environments where there is a high need for security, such as a commercial bank.

b. Determining How Long Each Policy Should Be

Beyond the number of policies, the policy writer is invited to consider how long each policy should be. The policies appearing in this document are deliberately kept to a few sentences at most. This concise statement of policy helps to foster acceptance by workers since it is both easily read and easily understood. Keeping policy statements concise also helps to emphasize that policies provide overall guidance, not the details about handling every conceivable circumstance. Instead, the details typically appear in information security standard documents and standard operating procedure manuals.

Another policy length consideration to keep in mind when developing policies is that they need to be specific enough to be clearly understood and consistently interpreted. At the same time, policies should not be so specific that they eliminate an opportunity for local management to tailor them to local conditions. For example, management may issue a policy which specifies that all users must have passwords which are difficult for unauthorized persons to guess. This policy gives local management the latitude to determine whether they want to use system-generated passwords, or whether they want to allow users to choose their own passwords (perhaps accompanied by a mechanism to make sure users are doing a good job at this).

The length of each policy is also a reflection of how many options management wants to specify. For example, will it be sufficient to say that all connections to an internal network must have a firewall or another approved access control system (perhaps a modem pool accompanied by a dynamic password system)? Or will it be necessary to say what type of a firewall will be used, such as a packet-filtering firewall or an application-filtering firewall? Or will it be necessary to specify what services will be permitted through the firewall (ftp, telnet, etc.)? Generally, it is advisable to keep the policy statements relatively high-level, and to deal with the details, such as those described in the last two questions, in a standard or other supplementary document. Not only will this mean that the policy will be approved more quickly, it will also mean that the policy will not need to keep being modified as the circumstances change.

For those policy writers who feel they must produce a policy document with great specificity, the possible options should be identified and evaluated before the policy is written. Running all the options for every policy by management is generally a recipe for extending the project far into the future. Instead, an expedient way to proceed would be to have the technical decisions made by a small group of employees (perhaps an Information Systems Management Committee). For each controversial policy, the small group can then prepare a list of options, with an indication of the pros and cons. This list can then be taken to management for a brief discussion and pre-approval. This approach can significantly increase the likelihood that the final policy is approved because controversial points have been pre-sold with these supplementary lists and associated discussions.

Although it expands the length of each policy statement significantly, to help clarify policies, some organizations may wish to provide specific examples. As an illustration of this approach, a policy which prohibits the personal use of Company X information system resources could be followed by examples discussing Internet game playing, use of Internet Relay Chat (IRC) facilities, and use of the organization's telephones for socializing. Examples make a policy real and tangible rather than abstract. Examples also significantly reduce errors in the interpretation and application of a policy. At the same time, examples may appear to the reader to be demeaning, redundant, and unnecessary. In most cases, examples are not provided with policies except in those circumstances where confusion or disputes are expected.

Another important part of a policy document, which may also affect its length, involves explanations of the motivations for policies. If they are going to support information security policies, workers will need to understand why policies are important. The amount of material needed to convey the motivation for policies can vary considerably based on the audience involved. As information security is increasingly discussed in the news media, the general public is coming to appreciate what the risks are; this in turn means that the need for words explaining the motivation behind a policy document is markedly decreasing. Nonetheless, just in case the policy writer needs it, the overall motivation for each policy can be found in the commentary section after each policy. In most organizations, motivations are communicated by in-person training sessions, computer based training software, or some other means besides a written policy.

Other parts of an information security policy document, that are not mentioned above, but that may make a significant contribution to the size of a document include: a table of contents, an index, a glossary, an information-security-related organizational structure chart, a statement of information security responsibilities, a list of relevant internal documents, a risk assessment methodology description, a set of information systems security standards, a set of information security procedures, and a case study indicating how the material should be applied. The specific materials to include in a policy document must be determined by the needs of the organization in question, the organization's sophistication in the information security area, the documents which have already been released, and the responsibilities of the group preparing the policies. An information security policy document which includes all of the above-mentioned supplementary materials can be quite lengthy, for example 100 pages or more.

c. Iterative Development Process

If the policy writer decides to issue a more comprehensive set of policies, the author recommends a two-step process. The first step involves obtaining management approval for a generalized set of policies, and the second step involves approval for a more specific set of policies (perhaps addressing specific areas like the Internet). The generalized set of policies could include only 30-50 policies, and the specific set(s) could include another 50-150 policies. An example of a generalized policy would be the need to positively identify all users prior to giving them access to internal systems. An example of a specific policy would be the need to use identity tokens which generate dynamic passwords whenever a user connects to an internal network from an external location. In order to be able to accommodate both situations, the policy writer will find both general and specific policies in this book.

A two-step process is also advisable because it allows the information security group to initially focus on fundamental conceptual models (such as information ownership and data sensitivity classification). After these conceptual models have been emphasized with an initial policy document and communicated via a basic information security awareness program, more detailed requirements can be expressed in a larger policy document. Whether or not this two-step approach is employed, the policy writer should still identify the fundamental conceptual models on which the policies he or she is writing depends. These conceptual models should, of course, also be included in the policy document or other material previously-communicated to the relevant audiences.

The policy writer is well advised to take an audience-driven approach to policy development. Policies can generally be divided into two categories: (1) those for end-users and management, and (2) those for programmers, systems designers, and related technical people. In keeping with the two-step process discussed in the last two paragraphs, the first of these audiences may be addressed in an initial policy development effort, while a subsequent effort could address the second audience.

If the initial set of policies the policy writer sends to management is too long or too severe, management may reject it. As a result, the window to get policies approved may be closed for a certain period of time (often a year or more). Accordingly, the policy writer is advised to keep the first set of policies brief and relatively easy to comply with. Later, when the first set has been endorsed and absorbed throughout the organization, a more comprehensive and more stringent list of policies can be prepared. It is far better to proceed relatively slowly with a series of policy development efforts, in a manner that has credibility and lots of management communication, than it is to prepare a single giant policy document that is then rejected because it was perceived to be too much too fast too soon.

Expressed in a different way, the author suggests that policies be written with the classic trial-and-error strategy for dealing with complex problems. After a brief policy has been issued, the policy writer should observe the effects of this policy (including user reactions and problems with compliance). The policy writer should then correct the undesired effects by issuing new or modified policies. The policy writer should then observe the effects of these corrections, and then again correct for undesired side-effects, etc.

Policy writers should not be upset to receive many suggested changes to their draft policies. Information security is a highly-complex, highly-emotionally-charged, and rapidly-changing area. Not only will multiple iterations be required for the development of a first policy document, but this document will need to be revised every so often as the organization's circumstances change. This book is designed to be a reference that can be used for an initial set of policies as well as multiple upgraded sets of policies.

Policies should be reviewed periodically--preferably annually--to ensure that they are still relevant and effective. It is important to eliminate policies which have outlived their usefulness or that are no longer applicable. Efforts to streamline policies will be appreciated by both management and users. These efforts will also help improve the credibility of the information security function within the organization. Workers will appreciate that the information security staff is not out to establish a bureaucracy, but is instead focused on establishing the minimum controls needed to protect organizational information assets.

Delays associated with the information security policy approval process are understandably frustrating for many policy writers. Although policy writers may have done a respectable job developing policies, management often takes a long time to review and approve them. Policy writers must be patient. Even though information security is regularly discussed in daily newspapers and on TV, senior management at many organizations still doesn't really understand it. While waiting for their policies to be approved, policy writers can periodically submit newspaper clippings and other evidence of the need for policies to management. This will keep the topic alive in the minds of managers and also keep reinforcing the need for management attention to information security matters.

d. Table Of Contents For Typical Policy Document

The actual sections of a policy document will of course vary considerably from organization to organization. This should be a reflection of many organization-specific factors such as the sensitivity, value, and criticality of the information to be protected. The nature of the systems involved, the business activities performed, the local laws and customs, and other factors should also be considered. In many organizations, there will be several documents, each prepared for a different audience (see the subsection entitled "Preparing a Coverage Matrix" for further discussion).

There are many models around which information security policy documents can be written. The table of contents to this book uses an information attribute focus (confidentiality, integrity, and availability). Other possible models that can be used as a table of contents include: an information ownership and custodianship model (which deals with roles), reader employment status (employee, contractor, consultant, temporary, business partner, customer, etc.), job title (systems administrator, systems developer, user, manager, etc.), a data classification scheme (which deals with information sensitivity), a required time to restore scheme (which focuses on data criticality), an information valuation scheme (which focuses only on what's valuable), threat types (legal or business oriented), equipment types (mainframes, personal computers, etc.), geographical location (in the office, on the road, etc.), domains of trust on a network (which require different controls within different domains), and the decisions people face (how often to back-up, how to prevent virus problems, etc.). While duplication should be avoided whenever possible, no matter what model(s) the policy writer chooses to use as the backbone of a policy document, there will inevitably be some redundancy.

Typically, one would expect to find the following sections inside a policy document: a definition of information security, a statement of management's intention to support information security (a signed letter from the Chairman of the Board or the President is recommended), and a definition of general management and specific organizational responsibilities with respect to information security. Also included will be the specific policies themselves, perhaps with examples and/or explanations. Some policy documents may additionally include a discussion of the compliance review and disciplinary processes. Mention of the ways to report or otherwise handle out-of-compliance conditions may also appear. A list of related in-house documents is also helpful for those who want more information.

Although rare, of considerable assistance to readers of a policy document is a table showing the circumstances when certain policies apply. For example, when a document containing sensitive information is to be sent through traditional mail then policy A would apply, but when it is sent by a trusted third party courier, then policy B would apply. These tables can be formatted as decision tables. Rather than making reference to specific policies, a decision table could contain numbers which reference sections of the policy document. Two excellent books dealing with decision tables and related information displays are "Envisioning Information" and "The Visual Display of Graphic Information," both by Edward Tufte (published by Graphics Press, Cheshire, Connecticut, USA).

e. Which Topics To Address First

For an organization just beginning an information security effort, the complexity of the information security field can be overwhelming. As was mentioned above, to make it easier for users, managers, and other groups who may not be familiar with information security, the policy writer should issue only a few essential policies in the beginning. Later, as understanding and support build, additional policies can be issued. The section of this book entitled "Sample High-Level Information Security Policy" provides an example of this initial type of information security policy statement.

Rather than simply copying the policy appearing in the section entitled "Sample High-Level Information Security Policy," the policy writer should consider which topics most need to be addressed. Different for each organization, these are the topics that should be addressed in the initial policy statement. Typically these topics will include (as a minimum) the following areas: responsibility for information security, computer viruses, information backup, contingency planning, system interconnection, user identification, and system access control privileges. Taking the perspective of a farmer at harvest time, the policy writer could call these topics "low hanging fruit."

Another way of looking at an initial policy statement is that it should help lay the foundation for a successful information security effort. This foundation (or organizational infrastructure) includes policies, standards, and responsibility statements, and was discussed at length in the section of this reference book entitled "Assuring the Proper Implementation of Controls." An initial set of policies can be used to establish or clarify missing parts of an information security organizational infrastructure. For example, if enforcement mechanisms are missing, the initial set of policies can discuss responsibility for compliance checking, penalties for non-compliance, etc.

If an information security policy document already exists, the challenge will be to determine what new and changed policy ideas need to addressed in a new policy document. One of the fastest ways to make this decision is to use a coverage matrix as described in the section above entitled "Preparing a Coverage Matrix." In this case the existing policy document can be laid out in a coverage matrix, and the reference numbers of those policy ideas that need to change can be underlined or circled. Next the matrix can be populated with additional policies from this book. Then an outline for the new document can be prepared.

F. How Can These Policies Best Be Used?

a. Intended Target Audience

The policies provided in this book were written for the policy writer who is: (1) computer literate, and (2) working in a position related to information security. These assumptions allowed the author to ignore definitions for many common computer and communication system terms like "Internet service provider." To the extent possible, acronyms and technical computer and communication system terms have been deliberately avoided because policies must be approved by managers, who in most instances do not have extensive computer backgrounds. Likewise, general users are often unaware of technical terms.

In some instances, where the motivation for a policy in this book may not be readily appreciated, brackets ("[" and "]") are used to further explain why a policy is advisable. These bracketed comments are not intended to be part of a policy statement, although they may be rewritten to provide the motivation for a policy. Nonetheless, further explanation of the motivation for a policy may be in order, depending on the managers who will approve and the audience who will be expected to understand the policy.

b. Policy Customization Specifics

As discussed above, the author suggests the policy writer review the policies in this book and compare them with the policies (if any) at the policy writer's organization. Using any word processing package, the policies which appear relevant may be extracted (using "cut-and-paste" commands) and placed in a separate computer file. This new file can then be modified to reflect the unique circumstances prevailing at the policy writer's organization. To avoid damaging the original computer-readable files provided by Baseline Software, the policy writer should copy these files from the storage media provided (such as floppy disks) onto another storage media such as a hard drive.

Throughout the book, "Company X" is used to refer to a generic organization. This designator is just a placeholder for the policy writer's organization name. In spite of the apparent private sector bias, these policies are also relevant to, and have been successfully used by civilian government, military, and non-profit organizations. Likewise, use of this designation does not imply that the policies in this book must be used on an organization-wide basis; it may be appropriate for these policies to be applicable to a subsidiary, a division, a department, etc. Nonetheless, whenever possible, to keep long-run administrative, enforcement, and related costs down, policy writers should seek the widest-possible applicability of the policies they develop.

The policy writer should replace all occurrences of "Company X" with his or her own organization name, subsidiary name, division name, or the like. Additionally, the policy writer will need to change the job title names and department names appearing in this book. For instance, terms such as "Manager of Information Security" and "Information Security Department" will need to be modified to match those terms used by the policy writer's organization. Organizational unit terms such as "Information Systems Department" will likewise need to be modified to reflect the relevant terminology such as "Management Information Systems" or "Computer Services." Likewise, specific numbers (for example, "90") will appear in some of the policies. The policy writer should look to see whether these numbers are appropriate for his or her computing environment and make changes accordingly.

The policies in this book are deliberately written in generalized terms. For example, many policies are equally applicable to diskless workstations, microcomputers (PCs), super-servers, minicomputers, and mainframes. Rather than having a policy restricted to only one type of computer, a generalized policy is preferable since it fosters uniform protection of information no matter where it resides, no matter what technology is involved, and no matter what form the information takes. Accordingly, the policy writer is encouraged to use key word search terms that are general (such as "network") rather than narrow (such as "local area network"). As an aside, the policy writer is encouraged to simplify the work by taking a platform-independent perspective and thus create a set of policies which applies to all computing environments. Taking a hardware and software independent view will additionally prevent the policy writer from needing to update a policy document when a computing environment changes.

The policies set forth in this book generally take a most stringent position with respect to information security. For many environments these policies will be too severe. The policy writer should accordingly delete, dilute, and/or modify the policies to suit the needs of his or her organization. The strong form was stated throughout this material because it is much easier to water-down a strong policy than it is to bolster a weak policy.

c. Using Key Word Search Facilities

One of the most useful features of this book and its accompanying computer-readable form is the ability to employ word processor key word search commands to locate policies of interest. If the policy writer's organization is concerned about a certain topic such as viruses, then the policy writer should search the files on the provided floppy disks (or CD-ROM) with the character string "POLICY" in the file name. These files contain both the policies and the commentaries found in the hardcopy book. Of course, a separate already-written policy may also cover these same topics (for example, viruses are covered in the section entitled Sample Microcomputer Security Policy).

All of the other files on the CD-ROM besides the POLICY files are supporting in nature. For example, one index allows the policy writer to quickly identify the policy number associated with a certain policy title. Index files can be searched based on key words, but because they include titles rather than full text, the policy writer is less likely to find all the policies relevant to the topic of interest. So, for a quick reference, go to the index files. But for a comprehensive search, go the POLICY file(s) themselves. Note that the policy writer will need to refer back to the POLICY file(s) once relevant policy titles have been located via the indexes. The quickest way to do this is to search via policy numbers such as "120"; these numbers can be found in all indexes as well as in the POLICY file(s).

Key word searches can be performed using any word processing program or text editor -- there is no need for the policy writer to learn a new program. When the policy writer performs key word searches, he or she should be sure to use the most critical characters only. For example, if one is interested in networks, use the singular version of the word "network" rather than the plural. This will help the policy writer locate both the singular and the plural versions as well as related terms like "networking." Likewise, the policy writer should attempt to search with the most significant single words in a phrase rather than all of the words in a phrase. For example, the policy writer could search using "diligence" when looking for "due diligence."

Policy writers performing key word searches should also use synonyms. For example, if the policy writer is interested in information confidentiality matters, he or she can search for "confidentiality," "secret," "restricted," "internal use only," "private," "proprietary," "access control," and related terms. The policy writer is encouraged to search for all the synonyms he or she can think of which describe the area of interest. If the policy writer is not familiar with the area of interest, he or she would be well advised to ask someone who knows about it for some key words. In order to make it most likely that the policy writer will find relevant material, generally accepted terms used in both technical publications and general business publications are used throughout this book. To the extent possible, non-technical terms have been used if the essential ideas behind a policy could still be concisely communicated.

Another tip for searching the computer-readable version of this material involves the use of truncated rather than full words. For example, by searching for "copy" rather than "copyright," the policy writer will find more policies relevant to the topic of interest. If the policy writer is searching with a verb or a noun that has irregular plural forms, or that has letters at the end of the word that change, it may be appropriate to initiate several searches, each with a different form of the word. Continuing the same example, the policy writer might also search for "copies."

In an effort to be all-encompassing, to achieve consistent approaches to information security, and to simplify the already-too-complicated life of people in the information security field, the policies in this book have been prepared with general rather than specific terminology. For example, rather than using terms like "local area network," "gateway," and "router," more general terms like "network" have been employed. The policy writer should accordingly generalize his or her area of interest, pick a few words reflecting the general categories involved, and search for those using the key word features of his or her favorite word processing package.

Useful policies may be found in other sections of this book beyond the sections which seem most relevant based on a brief examination of the table of contents. Accordingly, the policy writer is encouraged to examine sections of the book beyond those that seem to directly address the area of interest. For example, if the policy writer reads only those policies appearing in the "Data Confidentiality" section, he or she may miss other important policies which are also relevant to data confidentiality which are located in other sections. As a specific example, policies dealing with the confidentiality of encryption keys will not be found in the "Data Confidentiality" section but in a separate section entitled "Encryption."

G. How Are These Policies Organized?

The policies in this book are hierarchically organized by generic category, such as "Logical Security -> Software Security -> Change Control." This hierarchy is intended to allow the policy writer an opportunity to easily access a large number of policies relevant to a topic of interest. This organizational approach also allows the policy writer to quickly identify related policies that may be germane to his or her topic of interest.

Within a section or subsection of the policies part of this book, policies of a similar nature are placed next to or close to each other. This means that the policy writer should, in many instances, read not only the entire section dealing with the topic of interest, but also those sections located nearby. The policy writer is urged to review the table of contents to identify other sections that may be relevant to the topic of interest.

Beyond this book's organization based on related topics, policies are loosely organized from the most general at the top of a section, to the most specific at the bottom of a section. If the policy writer needs only high-level policies, he or she could focus on the policies at the beginning of each section. Nonetheless, the author urges the policy writer to examine all the policies in each section of interest. The policy writer may also wish to consider how each of the policies can in turn be taken to a more specific level of detail.

H. How Should One Select The Objectives And Scope Of Policies?

a. Motivating Objectives

In most organizations, one of the primary assets at risk is information itself. Recent studies show that, in modern industrialized economies, from 10% to 95% of an organization's assets are now information-handling-related. It is this very important asset--information--that is addressed by the policies found in this book. Risks to people, equipment, buildings, land, and other assets are most often recognized in other policy documents, not an information security document. An introductory paragraph at the beginning of an information security policy should reinforce this basic idea.

Classical economic theory holds that the factors of production (also called assets or resources required to do business) are: land, labor, and capital (the latter is just a fancy term for money). More recent economic theory describes the factors of production as: people, money, plant (land, building, machines), and materials. As we move further into the information age, we must add a fifth factor of production: information. An introductory paragraph at the beginning of an information security policy should reinforce this fundamental idea.

Another motivating objective involves management's fiduciary duty to conserve and protect assets, and as noted above information is now considered an asset. This perspective can then serve as the foundation for explicit policies dealing with information security. This duty of management should also be acknowledged in the introductory paragraph to an information security policy. A "Sample High Level Information Security Statement" appearing at the end of this book includes these ideas.

Separately, many policy statements open with a brief overview of what might happen if information security was not adequately addressed. For example, many refer to a number of risks which the policies are intended to address. From a legal perspective, these include sabotage, terrorism, fraud and embezzlement, extortion, industrial espionage, errors and omissions, service interruption, equipment theft, and privacy violation. Another way to view risks is from a business perspective, with reference to business interruption, erroneous management decisions, competitive disadvantage, loss or destruction of assets, improper record keeping, statutory or regulatory sanctions, etc. The author recommends that all policy statements make reference to a set of motivating risks, however these risks may be characterized.

b. Operational Objectives

Policies should be tailored to suit the unique operating circumstances found within an organization. This tailoring process can start with policies that are linked to operational objectives. As an example, the policy writer may wish to use something like the following statement of objectives for a set of policies appearing in an information security manual:

This manual provides a definitive statement of information security policies to which all workers are expected to comply. It is intended to:

(a) Acquaint workers with information security risks and the expected ways to address these risks,

(b) Clarify worker responsibilities and duties with respect to the protection of information resources,

(c) Enable managers and other workers to make appropriate decisions about information security,

(d) Coordinate the efforts of different groups within Company X so that information resources are properly
and consistently protected, regardless of their location, form, or supporting technologies, and

(e) Provide guidance for the performance of information system security audits and risk assessments.

c. Scope

The scope of an information security policy document should be clarified early in the policies development project. Management should, for example, understand that so-called "netiquette" (manners) will not be addressed in this document. Likewise, a disciplinary process should be found in a Human Resources policy statement, not in an information security policy statement. Similarly, information quality control and information engineering topics should be outside the scope of an information security policy document. Physical security should be included within the scope of a policy document, but only to the extent that it directly relates to information security (theft of portable computers, access to the raised-floor computer room, protection of off-site back-up tapes, etc.). In an information security policy, generally insurance and legal issues are covered only in high-level terms, if at all.

Policy documents should furthermore include specific statements about their applicability. A policy statement could, for instance, state that the policies are: (a) applicable independent of the way information is represented (written, spoken, electronic, and other forms); (b) applicable independent of the technology used to handle the information (e.g., file cabinets, fax machines, computers, answering machines, cellular telephone systems, and local area networks); (c) applicable independent of the location of information (e.g., in an office, at a customer site, on an airplane); and (d) applicable to information throughout its life cycle (including origination, entry into a system, processing, dissemination, storage, and disposal).

As a further explanation of scope, policy statements should indicate who must observe the policies and when it may be acceptable for worker actions or activities to be inconsistent with policies. For example, a policy statement could say: (a) policies must be observed by employees, outsourcing firm staff, consultants, contractors, and temporaries, and (b) these workers must observe policies unless they have received specific permission to do otherwise from a Vice President or higher-level manager. This approach assumes that a centralized management group has the clout to dictate policy for an entire organization. Another way to look at the applicability of policies to specific individuals would be to require compliance for all system users. By continuing to use Company X systems, users implicitly (and in some cases explicitly through a window at sign-on time) agree to comply with security policies. In general terms, it is advisable to be very specific about the audiences for whom the policies have been written.

Writing an information security policy document that applies to an entire organization rather than sub-groups is the most efficient and frequently most effective way to proceed. This approach helps to achieve consistency and complete application of the rules defined in the policy document. Although this may be the ideal, in some cases this approach may be inconsistent with prevailing decentralized organizational structures. Having a centralized Information Security Department that issues policy for the rest of the organization is particularly difficult when subsidiaries and partially owned "sister companies" are involved. If a decentralized organizational structure prevails, an Information Security Department may instead issue suggested policies which it can then attempt to sell to the management of the other organizational units. In these cases, the scope of policy statements could: (a) make reference to the responsibility of the Information Security Department to provide advice on the protection of information assets, and (b) offer a set of policies as a recommended step in the direction of properly protecting information assets.

Many information policy statements have in the past applied only to the Information Technology Department. While this approach may have been sufficient ten years ago, modern distributed processing systems (local area networks, wide area networks, personal computers, departmental computers, voice mail systems, fax servers, the Internet, intranets, etc.) require that information security policies apply to all system users within the organization. Some organizations are expanding the scope of an information security policy effort still further, including suppliers, customers, and other strategic business partners. This very broad definition of the scope of information security policies is warranted by modern computer systems that include these outside parties as users. Examples of these more-broadly-scoped systems include electronic data interchange (EDI), electronic mail, electronic commerce on the Internet, and extranets.

As a matter of principle, each exception weakens security. For example, if an organization adopts a policy stating that all workers must wear photo-ID badges when in the computer center, and then allows top management to ignore the policy, security will be noticeably eroded. Not only will this cause other workers to question whether top management really supports the policy, but it will allow unauthorized visitors to wander about because authorized workers may assume they are part of the management team. While current organizational structures, organizational politics, and other matters will often prevent it, the policy writer should strive to have the scope of information security policies include as many organizational units, types of workers, and circumstances, as is feasible.

There should be consistency between the scope of responsibility of an information security group that is preparing policies and the scope of the policies themselves. If a group responsible for information security in a subsidiary company attempted to write policy for the parent company without prior management approval, problems will be likely. Often the documented scope of responsibility for those preparing information security policies is more narrowly defined than the scope of the soon-to-be-prepared policies. Given management support for broadly scoped policies has been obtained, this is an excellent opportunity for the information security group to expand both its influence and its formal responsibility.

Although it may at first appear obvious, it is important that the term "information security" be clearly defined. By its very nature, information security is multi-disciplinary, multi-departmental, and increasingly multi-organizational. Organizations are still having trouble determining where in the organization information security should report, just as they are having trouble determining the scope of an information security effort. One of the best operational definitions of information security that the author uses is "any activity which protects information and/or information systems." Note that, with this definition, confidential information might be owned by a third party, and be in the custody of the organization in question, yet it would still be within the scope of an information security effort. Likewise, this broad definition includes paper-based and voice-based information, not just computer- and network-resident information. It is advisable to augment this broad definition with specific mention of activities performed by certain internal groups such as contingency planning, systems administration, network management, and records management. Similarly, other activities should be specifically excluded, such as those performed by the EDP auditing, risk management, legal, and physical (industrial) security groups.

Another scope-related factor to keep in mind is the time when policies take effect. The policy document should clearly indicate when readers can expect the policies to take effect. Some situation-specific policies go still further, indicating when they will expire. For example, if certain security policies were adopted to facilitate business with a third party, those policies may expire at the same time that a contract with the third party expires. In some cases the issuance date for the policy document will precede the effective date by a month or two; this will give managers an opportunity to change their systems to be in compliance. Separately, some organizations recognize the fact that frequent changes in their policies are necessary and expected. To this end, organizations may append words to the end of their policy documents indicating that "Company X reserves the right to change these policies at any time without prior notice."

d. Handling Non-Compliance

According to a research report prepared by NetVital and World Research MIS Panel, compliance with information security policies is spotty at best. The 1998 survey indicated that only 23% of more than 500 respondents said user compliance is complete or near complete. At the other end of the spectrum, 22% said there was little or no compliance. Clearly non-compliance is a serious problem which undermines the usefulness of information security policies. Accordingly, the policy writer should spend some time thinking about how both compliance and non-compliance are going to be handled.

After policies have been written, workers must be notified that the policies exist and that they are expected to comply. Although outside the scope of this book, awareness and training efforts are essential to every successful information security policy endeavor. Awareness and training projects should help motivate workers to take information security seriously, help sell the benefits of controls, and help enlist worker participation in efforts to protect the organization's information assets. An appendix to this book entitled "List of Suggested Awareness Raising Methods" provides an overview of the various techniques to deliver these and related messages.

Inevitably, some people will think that a policy does not apply to them. If certain managers believe they may appropriately be out of compliance, it is prudent to require them to sign a "risk acceptance memo." Typically such memos indicate that a manager either believes other control measures compensate for the control indicated by a policy, or the manager is willing to assume the risk of being out of compliance. Because the provision of a signature on such a memo is a relatively intimidating and legally-meaningful prospect, many managers will prefer to comply rather than document the fact that they are out-of-compliance. The prospect of defending an out of compliance situation through the risk acceptance documentation process may also be daunting and a significant motivation for managers to comply. A copy of a risk acceptance memo is provided as an appendix to this book.

III. Specific Policies

Note on Abbreviations

At the end of each policy commentary, abbreviations are used to indicate both the audience for the policy as well as the type of organization for which the policy is intended. "A: EMT" indicates that the intended audience is end-users, management, and technical staff. As the material being discussed requires, only one or two of the three audience groups to the right of the first colon may be indicated. In a similar way, "E: LMH" means that the environment (the organization for which this policy is intended) is low-security, medium-security, or high-security. A typical low-security organization would be a restaurant, while a typical high-security organization would be a diplomatic governmental agency. As the policy being discussed requires, only one or two of these three organizational groups to the right of the second colon may be indicated.

1. Logical Security

1.1. Software Security

1.1.1. System Access Control

1.1.1.1. Password Management

1.1.1.1.1. Password And User-ID Construction

1. Minimum Password Length

Policy: The length of passwords must always be checked automatically at the time that users construct or select them. All passwords must have at least ten (10) characters.

Commentary: In many systems, fixed passwords are the first and only line of defense. Although it's a long-established hacker technique, guessing fixed passwords remains a popular and often successful attack method by which unauthorized persons gain system access. In the past hackers used manual methods, but these days password guessing is most often performed with automated tools like dictionary attack programs (so-called 'crack' programs). Passwords with only a few characters are much easier to guess than passwords with at least ten characters. Ten is generally considered by experts to be a good minimum password length for commercial systems. This policy may be expanded with additional requirements, such as a prohibition against repeating characters in a password. The policy is applicable to user-chosen passwords as well as system-generated passwords; this is why the words "construct or select" were used in the policy. If only user-chosen passwords are employed, then only "construct" is necessary; if only system-generated passwords are used, then only "select" is necessary. On most platforms, operating systems software or linked access control security software can be used to automatically enforce this policy. The policy can be restricted to system and network access control passwords, so as to allow database management systems, application programs, and voicemail systems to use fewer characters in a password. For related comments, see the policies entitled "Anonymous User-IDs," "Limit On Consecutive Unsuccessful Attempts To Enter A Password," "Maximum Permissible Password Attempts For Dial-Up Users," "Disclosure Of Information In System Log-in Banner," and "Requirement For Different Passwords On Different Systems." A: T; E: LMH.

2. Minimum Password Length Constrained By System Limitations

Policy: User-chosen fixed passwords must be at least ten (10) characters long, or the maximum length permitted by the system if that is less than ten characters.

Commentary: Perhaps the best known computer control mechanism, fixed passwords are widely-used even though they have been shown to be susceptible to interception when transmitted and guessing by parties who know something about the user. High security systems should consider other mechanisms to verify the identity of users, such as dynamic passwords which change every minute or every time that a user session is initiated. As much as fixed passwords have their problems, they will be around for a long time. Part of their continued use is dictated by systems which can only support fixed passwords, not the more sophisticated user authentication mechanisms like biometrics. These systems include mainframes and other legacy systems. The maximum number of characters in a password on these systems may be limited to six, seven, or eight, in which case a policy which specifies a minimum password length of ten will cause trouble. This policy recognizes the continued use of legacy systems, but says that every system that can support it must have a ten character minimum length. Separately, the long password requirement is a way to compensate for the deficiencies of fixed passwords. The longer a password is, the harder it is to guess, and the less likely it will succumb to a variety of automated attacks such as a dictionary attack (where entries in a dictionary are encrypted and then matched to the entries in an encrypted password file). For related considerations, see the policies entitled "Minimum Password Length" and "Extended User Authentication Required For In-Bound Internet Users." A: T; E: LMH.

3. Difficult-To-Guess Passwords Required

Policy: All user-chosen passwords for computers and networks must be difficult to guess. Words in a dictionary, derivatives of user-IDs, and common character sequences such as "123456" must not be employed. Likewise, personal details such as spouse's name, automobile license plate, social security number, and birthday must not be used unless accompanied by additional unrelated characters. User-chosen passwords must also not be any part of speech. For example, proper names, geographical locations, common acronyms, and slang must not be employed.

Commentary: The most frequently encountered problem with security systems is human error, and choosing an easily guessed fixed password is one of the most common security-related mistakes. This policy puts users on notice that they must choose passwords which are difficult for unauthorized parties to guess. Ideally, this policy should be enforced automatically by the system managing password changes, and the enforcement software should be invoked at the time users choose new passwords. Other specifics about what constitutes an easily-guessed password may be added to this policy. For example, technical and medical terms may be prohibited. This policy and the related control measures are particularly important if users are employing the same password on multiple systems (for instance on so-called "single sign-on systems"). If a single sign-on fixed password is guessed, an intruder then gains access to many systems, whereas access to only one system may be obtained if a single sign-on system were not employed. Separately, this policy may provide additional suggestions for constructing a difficult-to-guess yet easy-to-remember password. For instance, the policy may suggest that users employ methods such as: (a) string several words together (these passwords are also known as "passphrases"), (b) shift a word up, down, left or right one row on the keyboard, (c) bump characters in a word a certain number of letters up or down the alphabet, (d) transform a regular word according to a specific method, such as making every other letter a number reflecting its position in the word, (e) combine punctuation or numbers with a regular word, (f) create acronyms from words in a song, a poem, or another known sequence of words, (g) deliberately misspell a word--but don't use a common misspelling, or (h) combine a number of personal facts like birth dates and favorite colors. This policy is intended for distribution to users. Also see the policies entitled "Passwords Must Contain Both Alphabetic and Non-Alphabetic Characters," "Cyclical Passwords Prohibited," "In-Coming Dial-Up Calls Must Not Be Answered Until Fourth Ring," and "Suspected Disclosure Forces Password Changes." A: E; E: LMH.

4. Cyclical Passwords Prohibited

Policy: Users are prohibited from constructing fixed passwords by combining a set of characters that do not change, with a set of characters that predictably change. In these prohibited passwords, characters which change are typically based on the month, a department, a project, or some other easily-guessed factor. For example, users must not employ passwords like "X34JAN" in January, "X34FEB" in February, etc.

Commentary: Users are often annoyed by password systems which require them to change their passwords every so often. In an effort to defeat these systems, they will often employ passwords which change only partially. One technique they use is called "cyclical passwords," which allow users to continue to employ the same basic password, varying only a part of the password so as to satisfy an automated process which compares the old and new passwords to make sure that previous passwords are not reused. This security-eroding approach is particularly prevalent among users who must log-into many different machines. This policy prohibits users from using this approach. Separately, while single sign-on systems may make the log-in process easier for users, if these users employ cyclical passwords, the security of the network and connected systems will be reduced (perhaps becoming lower than before the deployment of the single sign-on system). Also see the policies entitled "Previous Password History File," "User-Chosen Passwords Must Not Be Reused," and "Difficult-To-Guess Passwords Required." A: EMT; E: LMH.

5. User-Chosen Passwords Must Not Be Reused

Policy: Users must not construct passwords that are identical or substantially similar to passwords that they had previously employed.

Commentary: The intention of this policy is to prevent users from recycling passwords that they had previously employed. For example, some operating systems like Novell's NetWare will prevent users from employing any of the last fifteen passwords. A user can then have a list of 16 passwords, generated by a rule of thumb, and repeatedly go through these same passwords. In other operating systems, only one previous password is recorded, so the user can then alternate between two passwords. Reuse of passwords increases the chances that a password will be divulged to unauthorized parties and that these unauthorized parties will then take advantage of this knowledge. Reuse also increases the chances that passwords will be guessed because they will be in use for considerably longer periods of time than other passwords (thus computer programs that crack passwords may be given more time to discover a password). A less stringent version of this policy would omit the words "or substantially similar." Instead of this policy, some organizations use a two policy system; for example, "Users with privileged user-IDs must never use the same password twice, while all other users must not employ the same password more than once in a twelve month period." Also see the policies entitled "Cyclical Passwords Prohibited" and "Previous Password History File." A: EMT; E: LMH.

6. Passwords Must Contain Both Alphabetic And Non-Alphabetic Characters

Policy: All user-chosen passwords must contain at least one alphabetic and one non-alphabetic character. Non-alphabetic characters include numbers (0-9) and punctuation. The use of control characters and other non-printing characters is discouraged because they may inadvertently cause network transmission problems or unintentionally invoke certain system utilities.

Commentary: The intention of this policy is to put users on notice that they must take specific steps to make their passwords difficult for unauthorized parties and system penetration software to guess. There are a number of specific steps that users can be told to perform (it is desirable that password change software enforces these rules). These include use of upper and lower case in the same password. Be sure to check systems documentation before writing this policy since some systems have rigid restrictions about the type of characters permitted (for instance DEC's VAX/VMS does not permit certain punctuation characters in a password). Note that so-called PINs (personal identification numbers), which are really just a type of password, are generally generated by a security system, and so would not fall within the purview of this policy. Such PINs may for example be used to activate smart cards or dynamic password tokens. If these PINs are user-chosen, however, the number of possible characters may be severely restricted (and combination of alphabetic with non-alphabetic characters may not be possible). The policy writer should consider all the possible systems on which user-chosen passwords are used, as well as the available keyboards, and then strive to have the policy embrace as many of these as possible. See the policies entitled "Difficult-To-Guess Passwords Required" and "Passwords Must Contain Both Upper And Lower Case Characters." A: EMT; E: LMH.

7. Passwords Must Contain Both Upper And Lower Case Characters

Policy: All user-chosen passwords must contain at least one lower case and one upper case alphabetic character. This will help make passwords difficult-to-guess by unauthorized parties such as hackers and industrial spies.

Commentary: The intention of this policy is to put users on notice that they must take specific steps to make their passwords are difficult to guess. There are a number of specific steps that users can be told to perform (it is desirable that password change software enforces these rules). These include use of the use of alphabetic and non-alphabetic characters in the same password. From a mathematical standpoint, the idea behind the use of both upper and lower case characters is to spread the actual passwords employed more evenly over the total possible values for passwords, thereby making password guessing more difficult and expensive. The mathematical expression of this idea is to spread passwords more consistently over the "password space." The policy writer should be sure to check systems documentation before adopting this policy since some systems have rigid restrictions about the type of characters permitted (for instance UNIX differentiates between upper and lower case characters in a password, while NetWare does not). See the policies entitled "Difficult-To-Guess Passwords Required" and "Passwords Must Contain Both Alphabetic And Non-Alphabetic Characters." A: EMT; E: LMH.

8. Seed For System-Generated Passwords

Policy: If system-generated passwords are used, they must be generated using the low order bits of system clock time or some other frequently changing unpredictable source.

Commentary: Because fixed passwords are often the only defense protecting a system, they must be constructed with care if they are to withstand various types of attack. System-generated passwords can be readily circumvented if an attacker gains access to the algorithm used to generate passwords and if the attacker has access to a predictable source for the inputs to this algorithm. Because the on-going secrecy of a password-generation algorithm is doubtful--especially when it is part of an operating system or some other widely-disseminated software--it is critical that the inputs to the algorithm be unpredictable. For instance, a number of system-generated password algorithms are readily obtained from hacker bulletin boards or in the public domain. Accordingly, the "seed" (starting point) for these computations should be very difficult to predict by unauthorized parties. Ideally, truly random seeds--like the number of particle emissions from radio-active decay processes--should be used. But in the real world, frequently-changing seed parameters, or better yet, a combination of frequently changing seed parameters, will suffice. For example, random noise on a communications line may be combined via an "exclusive-or" operation with the relevant user-ID to generate a seed parameter. Separately, the words "frequently-changing" in the policy are also important. If the current date or other predictable character strings that change infrequently are used to generate passwords, the resulting passwords may be easily-guessed. Separately, this same policy can be used for encryption key generation processes. Also see the policy entitled "Process For Generating Encryption Keys." A: T; E: MH.

9. Pronounceable System-Generated Passwords

Policy: So that users can more easily remember them, and so that users will not need to write them down, all system-generated passwords for end-users must be pronounceable.

Commentary: A system-generated password such as "X65Y98JJ8" begs to be written down because it's hard for a user to remember. On the other hand, a system-generated password such as "eatgreenhair" will be more easily remembered, and less likely to be written down. While system-generated passwords don't need to be constructed by stringing together actual words from the dictionary, it does help to construct them with pronounceable components (usually syllables). While the approach described in this policy makes system generated passwords more easily remembered, it also severely restricts the domain of total possible passwords, and therefore reduces the security that system-generated passwords provide. One way to compensate for this is to increase the minimum number of characters in system-generated passwords, perhaps to fifteen characters. Another approach is to allow users to pick from a list of ten or more possible system-generated passwords (the users should also have received instructions to choose the passwords which they find easiest to remember). This list of possible passwords would, of course, be generated differently for each user. Separately, some system-generated passwords are employed for end-user-transparent encryption key management, digital signatures, message authentication codes, and other security-related processes. There is no need for pronounce ability for these user-transparent passwords; that's why the phrase "for end-users" was added to the policy. Also see the policy entitled "Process For Generating Encryption Keys." A: T; E: MH.

10. Storage Of System-Generated Passwords

Policy: If passwords or Personal Identification Numbers (PINs) are generated by a computer system, they must always be issued immediately after they are generated. Regardless of the form they take, unissued passwords and PINs must never be stored on the involved computer systems.

Commentary: The basic idea behind this policy is to ensure that generated but unissued passwords do not fall into the wrong hands. To store system-generated passwords on a computer system--even in encrypted form--is ill-advised. The only time when passwords should be stored on a system is when they are encrypted with a one-way function. This prevents them from being decrypted ever, even by authorized parties. Thus, if passwords were to be stored using a one-way function, they could not be reconstructed into readable form. If they cannot be reconstructed into readable form, then they cannot be reissued. Thus passwords should be issued at the time they are generated. So the intent of this policy is to require that only when they are needed, will system-generated passwords be created. The policy also may be used as a justification for the restriction of both probes which test the workings of a password generation routine, as well as calls to a system-generated password routine by unauthorized programs (either of which may be performed with the intent to compromise system-generated passwords). Separately, this policy allows passwords and PINs to be generated at user request in real-time or on a batch basis. If done at user request, typically the user is presented with a few passwords and asked to choose one. The selected password is then stored, using a one-way function, in a password file. If done on a batch basis, the passwords would then be used to program smart cards, encode magnetic stripes for Automated Teller Machine (ATM) plastic cards, print secure mailers (sealed envelopes with embedded carbon paper that use an impact printer with no ribbon), or perform other security related activities. Separately, this same policy can also be used for the construction of encryption keys. See the policy entitled "Prevention Of Password Retrieval." A: T; E: MH.

11. Zeroization Of Password Generation Materials

Policy: If passwords or Personal Identification Numbers (PINs) are generated by a computer system, special care must be taken to erase all residual data used in the process. All computer storage media (magnetic tapes, floppy disks, etc.) used in the construction, assignment, distribution, or encryption of passwords or PINs must be "zeroized" immediately after use. Zeroization means that the media must be repeatedly overwritten with a series of ones and zeros. Additionally, computer memory areas used in the derivation of passwords or PINs must be zeroized immediately after use.

Commentary: Zeroization is necessary because magnetic computer media has "remanence." Remanence is a weaker signal reflecting prior values of the data rather than the current value. Accordingly, one-time overwriting of data in high security environments will be insufficient. Without multiple overwriting processes, persons knowledgeable about magnetic media can reconstruct the data several generations back. Zeroization of computer memory simply prevents utility programs and unauthorized applications from accessing memory areas that contain passwords, PINs, or the data used to construct these security parameters. In some very-high-security environments, such as within military units, magnetic media containing sensitive information must be destroyed by burning, shredding, or some related mechanism because zeroization does not provide sufficient security. In these cases, the security provided by the approach described in this policy is not sufficient. Separately, this same policy can be used for the construction of encryption keys. This policy goes hand-in-hand with the policy entitled "Protection Of Password Generation Algorithms." A: T; E: MH.

12. Protection Of Password Generation Algorithms

Policy: If passwords or Personal Identification Numbers (PINs) are generated by a computer system, all software and files containing formulas, algorithms, and other specifics of the process must be controlled with the most stringent security measures supported by the involved computer system.

Commentary: The essence of this policy is that information about the process by which system-generated passwords are constructed should be given the most stringent protection. If specifics about this critical security process are disclosed to unauthorized parties, then the entire system may soon be compromised. This is why the password generation mechanism is part of the "kernel" (most protected) portion of some operating systems. Some organizations may wish to include documentation, scratch paperwork, and other materials used to generate passwords within the scope of the policy. Separately, this policy also applies to processes by which encryption keys are generated. This policy goes hand-in-hand with the policy entitled "Zeroization Of Password Generation Materials." Also see the policies entitled "Encryption Of Passwords" and "Encryption Key Management Systems And Separation Of Duties." A: T; E: MH.

13. Previous Password History File

Policy: On all multi-user machines, system software or locally developed software must be used to maintain an encrypted history of previous fixed passwords. This history file must be employed to prevent users from reusing fixed passwords. The history file must minimally contain the last thirteen (13) passwords for each user-ID.

Commentary: The security provided by forced password changes is much less effective if users repeat the same passwords. A history file prevents users from flip-flopping between two passwords or following some other rotation scheme with a small number of passwords. Although some operating systems provide this security mechanism, other operating systems do not. It is important to establish a cross-platform policy for password management, especially if the organization currently uses or intends to move in the direction of single sign-on systems. One part of a cross-platform policy for password management is provided in this policy. Some organizations may want to additionally specify that the password encryption process must be one-way, so that stored passwords cannot be decrypted. Although historical passwords are no longer being used, it is desirable to keep them absolutely unavailable to unauthorized parties so that knowledge of them cannot be used to predict future passwords. For instance if one user employed dog breed names followed by a number as his previous passwords, an attacker could simply go through all dog breed names and concatenate numbers. This is why one-way encryption algorithms are desirable, even for outdated passwords. Separately, some organizations may want to increase the minimum number of passwords kept in the history file beyond 13. Because many firms force password changes on a monthly basis, many users employ a regular password combined with an indication of the month (JAN, FEB, etc.). Keeping a history of 13 or more previous passwords prevents them from using this approach from year to year. This is why 13 has become a rock-bottom parameter for a policy like this. See the policies entitled "Periodic Forced Password Changes" and "Cyclical Passwords Prohibited." A: T; E: LMH.

14. Anonymous User-IDs

Policy: User-IDs must be assigned in a sequential numeric fashion so that there is no obvious correlation between a user-ID and the actual name of the involved user.

Commentary: The intention of this policy is to prevent unauthorized persons from being able to employ user-IDs to break into systems, to masquerade as another user, to deduce confidential information, or to otherwise compromise system security. This might, for instance, take place if an industrial spy were going through the trash and was able to recover a phone book and also a system activity console log. If user-IDs were equivalent to last names, the spy would be able to determine what activities certain users performed on the system. He may then be able to gather personal information about them, using this information to guess their password. Alternatively, he may be able to use this information to decide who to bribe to perform certain actions on his behalf. This policy prevents unauthorized persons from guessing user-IDs (as would be easy to do if they were the same as last name), but unfortunately makes electronic mail and certain other system activities more difficult and less user-friendly. To alleviate this problem, the system may provide a conversion utility which allows users to address electronic mail to a specific name rather than a user-ID. The "sequential numeric" approach to assigning user-IDs reflected in this policy need not be used if some other way to conceal the actual identity of users is employed. For example, nicknames or some other more easily remembered character strings can be used. This unusual policy is designed for high security environments. Also see the policies entitled "Minimum Password Length" and "Naming Standard For A Single User-ID Used On All Platforms." A: T; E: H.

1.1.1.1.2. Design Of Password System User Interface

15. Displays And Printing Of Passwords

Policy: The display and printing of passwords must be masked, suppressed, or otherwise obscured so that unauthorized parties will not be able to observe or subsequently recover them.

Commentary: The intention behind this policy is to prevent passwords from falling into the hands of unauthorized parties. This policy supports two secure systems design principles: (1) each user should have a unique password and user-ID, and (2) each user should have a password known only to that user. Even the security administrator should not know user passwords (with the temporary exception of newly-issued or reissued passwords). This means that when a user password is employed -- provided certain other control measures are enforced -- the activity most likely is initiated by the involved user. Specifically, whenever a user types a password into a system, the password should not be displayed on a monitor or printed on a hardcopy terminal. If a password were to be displayed, persons nearby could "shoulder-surf" (look over the shoulder of the user) to obtain the password. Likewise, persons doing "dumpster-diving" (going through the trash) could recover passwords printed on a hardcopy terminal. For a display screen, the mechanism used most often is simple echo-off at the time a password is entered; for hardcopy terminals, over striking the password multiple times is sometimes used. On a related point, sometimes it is possible to recover passwords from temporary files or scratch memory locations. In high security environments, these temporary storage areas will need to be overwritten (see the policy entitled "Zeroization of Password Generation Materials"). Also see the policies entitled "Positioning Of Computer Display Screens With Respect To Windows" and "Assignment Of Expired Passwords." A: T; E: LMH.

16. User-Chosen Passwords Must Be Entered Twice If Masked When Entered

Policy: Whenever user-chosen passwords or encryption keys are first specified, they must be entered twice and masked so that onlookers cannot see what was typed. Both of these entries must match in order to be accepted by the system. This requirement will prevent typing mistakes from locking users out of the system or preventing access to important information.

Commentary: The intention of this policy is to prevent unknown typing errors from causing problems later on. Since masking (often done with large dots) prevents users from seeing what they enter, without entering parameters twice, users have no idea when they have made a typing mistake. Confirmation of a password or encryption key, also known as double entry of these parameters, will often but not always reveal this problem. For those rare situations where this approach does not detect a typing error because the same error was made twice, there are other control mechanisms (reset the password and use key escrow to recover encrypted data). Note that the policy only talks about the time when a user first specifies a password, for example when a password is being changed. Likewise, the policy deals with encryption keys that may be entered when a file is about to be encrypted. The policy need not apply to those times when the user later attempts to access a system using a previously-specified password, because the system will inform the user that a mistyped password is incorrect and will then invite the user to try again. Likewise, if an incorrect encryption key is provided at the time of file decryption, the program will either provide unintelligible results or provide an error notice. Either way, subsequent entry of passwords or encryption keys by users does not generally cause serious problems. For related ideas, see the policies entitled "Storage Of Passwords In Readable Form" and "Concealing Account Numbers On Customer Receipts." A: T; E: LMH.

17. Periodic Forced Password Changes

Policy: All users must be automatically forced to change their passwords at least once every ninety (90) days.

Commentary: The intention of this policy is to force users to change their passwords on a periodic basis. There is nothing special about once every ninety days--this is simply a common period for forced changes. The frequency could just have easily have been once every thirty or sixty days. The greater the need for security, the smaller the time frame here. In fact, some organizations have a tiered approach where different time intervals are used for different user populations, based on the nature of the privileges available to these users. For example, systems programmers may be forced to change their password every two weeks, while regular users may be forced to change their password once every month. Separately, if a password has fallen into the hands of an unauthorized party, then unauthorized system use could continue for some time in the absence of a forced password change process. This policy limits the time period in which this unauthorized use could continue. Likewise, if combined with a dormant user-ID privilege revocation process, this policy acts as a safety net if systems administrators forget to disable privileges when users change jobs or leave an organization. On a separate point, although it is against policy, people still often share passwords with co-workers; this policy limits the period of time that such a co-worker can masquerade as another user. On another note, two undesirable side-effects associated with frequent password changes are: (1) users write their passwords down, and/or (2) users develop simple-minded algorithms for generating passwords which can be guessed by unauthorized parties. Accordingly, unless a high security environment is involved, the policy writer should refrain from setting the frequency to a period of time less than sixty days. On still another note, this policy works well when combined with a policy requiring passwords to be changed if there has been a compromise or a suspected compromise of a password security system (see the policy entitled "Suspected Disclosure Forces Password Changes"). This policy also works well with another policy dealing with the construction of difficult-to-guess passwords (see the policy entitled "Difficult-to-Guess Passwords"). Also see the policies entitled "Password Change Interval Synchronization Across Platforms" and "Periodic Changes In Computer Communications Line Numbers." A: T; E: LMH.

18. Password Change Interval Synchronization Across Platforms

Policy: The fixed password change interval must be synchronized across all computer and network platforms at Company X.

Commentary: The intention of this policy is to lay the groundwork for single sign-on systems, whereby users can sign-in only once, but within a single on-line session they can use multiple systems. This policy is also helpful in terms of laying the groundwork for the use of security servers, through which administration of multiple platforms can take place. These administrative tools are increasingly popular and are expected to be more popular in the years ahead. The policy is also user-friendly because it allows users to simplify their password management activities, using a single fixed password across multiple systems. Some security experts complain that this is a risky approach, but in the real world users are overburdened with the complexity of information security systems, and they welcome any move in the direction of simplification. If fixed passwords are being used in a high security environment, and these fixed passwords are being transmitted without encryption, then indeed this approach is risky. But if a low security computing environment exists, or if fixed passwords are encrypted as they are send and stored, then the password synchronization mentioned in this policy makes sense and is advisable. This policy assumes that users are able to change their passwords whenever they wish; the existence of this ability will enable them to change all of their passwords on all systems on a certain date. For related ideas, see the policies entitled "Periodic Forced Password Changes" and "Password Changes After Compromise Of A Multi-User Computer System." A: T; E: LMH.

19. Assignment Of Expired Passwords

Policy: The initial passwords issued by a security administrator must be valid only for the involved user's first on-line session. At that time, the user must be forced to choose another password before any other work can be done.

Commentary: The intent of this policy is to make sure that only an involved end-user knows his or her own password. This will in turn allow system activity logged with a corresponding personal user-ID to be uniquely attributable to a certain user. The type of initial password in the policy is sometimes called an "expired password" or a "temporary password" in that it is valid for only one on-line session. Some vendors are now extending this idea to the default passwords that come with their computer or communications products. Thus both administrators and end-users are forced to change default or initial passwords before they do any work on the system. This policy assumes group user-IDs are not employed and also that users are permitted to choose their own passwords (no forced system-generated passwords). Also see the policies entitled "Difficult-To-Guess Passwords," "Changing Vendor Default Passwords," "Periodic Forced Password Changes," and "Computer Support Identification Codes." A: T; E: LMH.

20. Initial Passwords Transmitted To Remote Users By Authorized Means

Policy: The initial password for a new remote user must be sent via a communications channel other than the channel used to log-in to Company X systems. Authorized means of transmission include courier service requiring a signature, and in-person appearance at a trusted intermediary's office along with the provision of picture identification.

Commentary: The intention behind this policy is to distribute an initial fixed password, an identity token (often employing dynamic passwords), or any other user identity authentication mechanism in a secure fashion. The main focus in this case is preventing interception by an unauthorized party. Thus even if a courier service worker were to obtain a fixed password, he or she would still be missing a user-ID and other connection information (such as a URL), and would therefore be precluded from making unauthorized use of the service. The idea behind this policy is to split the information needed to log-in across multiple communications channels, thus making it considerably more difficult for an intruder to intercept them all. This approach is also called an "out-of-band" process. Separately, the reader should note that password resets can be handled remotely by phone, assuming that some other secret information that could be used to identify a remote user has been previously exchanged. This policy is particularly relevant to remote telecommuters or customers using the Internet from a foreign country. For related considerations, see the policies entitled "Separate Communication Channel For Data And Encryption Keys" and "Two Envelopes Required for Sensitive Information Sent by Mail." A: T; E: LMH.

21. Limits On Consecutive Unsuccessful Attempts To Enter A Password

Policy: To prevent password guessing attacks, the number of consecutive attempts to enter an incorrect password must be strictly limited. After three unsuccessful attempts to enter a password, the involved user-ID must be either: (a) suspended until reset by a system administrator, (b) temporarily disabled for no less than three minutes, or (c) if dial-up or other external network connections are involved, disconnected.

Commentary: One of the most frequently successful attack methods for gaining system access is simple password guessing. Besides simple context-sensitive guessing (knowing a bit about the user and the circumstances), attackers can use password cracker programs to exhaustively go through words in the dictionary. Whether it is a determined manual attack or an automated password guessing attack, this policy will help to ensure that the attack is unsuccessful. This is because the control mentioned in the policy will slow down any attempt at password guessing. Separately, some organizations may wish to put a time frame into the policy, so that the words "after three (3) unsuccessful attempts" become "after three (3) unsuccessful attempts within five minutes." Likewise a similar result may be achieved by qualifying this phrase with the words "during a single on-line session." It should be noted that, with this approach, some legitimate users will be locked out of their user-IDs if they are poor typists, if they are still learning how to use the system, or if they are having trouble remembering their password. These users will contact the security administrator for a new expired password. The contact with the security administrator also provides an opportunity for the security administrator to give the involved user the information needed to properly log-in the next time he/she uses the system. There is nothing sacred about the number three here, to support a more user-friendly (lower security) environment, this number could have just as easily been five or ten. This is one of a number of policies intended for systems administrators -- policies which instruct them on how they should set-up the systems they administer. Also see the policies entitled "Suspected Disclosure Forces Password Changes," "Assignment Of Expired Passwords," "Difficult-To-Guess Passwords," and "Maximum Permissible Password Attempts For Dial-Up Users." A: T; E: LMH.

22. Single Sign-On Process

Policy: Users must be asked for only one (1) user-ID and password combination at the time they reach the network and/or destination computer system. User identity related information must then be user-transparently passed to other computers, database management systems, and applications.

Commentary: As a systems design objective, some firms are attempting to minimize the number of times that users are required to enter user-IDs and passwords to identify themselves. In organizations with many computers this log-in process has become quite onerous, complex, and time consuming. In response to user demands for simpler interfaces, this policy states that users will identify themselves definitively only once. The process will then transparently convey the user's identity (user-ID) to the destination computer(s). This approach is for example manifested in DEC's proxy log-in system. An exception may need to be made to the single sign-on approach if an involved user has access to special privileges or multiple user-IDs (although an initial menu allowing the user to select the privileges or user-IDs is preferable). In this case, multiple passwords may be needed to control access privileges and log the activity. Increasingly this single sign-on approach is being incorporated into security front-ends that serve as gateways through which all users must pass (sometimes these are firewalls). This approach is also potentially much more economical because stringent user identification processes--such as those involving smart cards--need be applied only to one machine (the front-end). This policy is consistent with the increasingly-popular notion that users should sign-on to the network rather than specific destination computers. The policy could be expanded to include the notion that the suspension/revocation of a user-ID is immediately and automatically performed on multiple computers over the network. The policy may also be a part of an in-house systems security architecture. See the policies entitled "Consistent Protection Of Information Regardless Of Manifestation" and "Dial-Up Connections Must Always Utilize Firewalls." A: T; E: LMH.

23. All Workstations Must Have Password-Based Boot Protection

Policy: All workstations used for Company X business activity, no matter where they are located, must be using an access control system approved by the Information Security Department. In most cases this will involve screen-savers with fixed-password-based boot protection along with a time-out-after-no-activity feature.

Commentary: This policy is intended to prevent unauthorized persons from gaining access to workstations (PCs, portable computers, transportable computers, handhelds, palmtops, etc.) and the sensitive information that might be stored thereon. Because each of these computers generally include storage mechanisms such as a hard drive, they can also store sensitive information. By protecting every machine, the Information Security Department eliminates squabbles about who should or should not be using these workstation access control systems.

Note that some screen-saver based access control packages can be readily circumvented; the approval by the Information Security Department requirement in the policy means that only strong screen saver products will be employed (for example ACS from Harcom Security Systems, Baldwin, New York, USA). Separately, distributed information on the desktop means that distributed access control is also necessary. From another angle, it will be necessary to issue a standard about the number of minutes before a screen saver kicks-in; this can also be specified in a policy. On another note, it is desirable that a skeleton key is available, so that management may gain access to a workstation should an employee "forget" their password, or perhaps deliberately withhold this information. This skeleton key is similar to what is known as "key escrow" in the encryption area. For a related idea, see the policy entitled "General Purpose Encryption Systems Must Include Key Escrow." A: E; E: LMH.

1.1.1.1.3. Password System Internals Design

24. Passwords Never In Readable Form When Outside Workstations

Policy: Fixed passwords must never be in readable form outside a personal computer or workstation.

Commentary: The intention of this policy is to provide direction for the construction, integration, and management of password-based access control systems. Although dynamic passwords (typically different for each session) are the wave of the future, many organizations are still using fixed (reusable) passwords. This policy allows fixed passwords to continue to be employed so far as the end-user is concerned. For example, AT&T's product called S/Key transforms a fixed password provided by an end-user into a different parameter each time it is sent over a network (thus preventing reuse). The policy also allows, and in fact encourages, the use of dynamic passwords, such as the Secure-ID system from Security Dynamics (Bedford, Massachusetts). Because fixed passwords in the clear (readable form) can be easily captured as they travel over a network, it is critical that they be encrypted when on a network or other readily-accessible places. And simple encryption (such as the DES with electronic codebook mode of operation) is not enough; the encryption must be implemented such that passwords appear differently each time they travel over a network. If the passwords do not appear differently each time they are used, attackers could use replay methods to cause fraud, sabotage, and other abuses. This approach is used on the Internet with the encryption process known as SSL (Secure Socket Layer); after an encrypted connection is established, then a fixed password can safely be sent. Other approaches such as Kerberos allow fixed passwords to be used at the end-user level, but these same parameters will vary when they move over a network. This policy is thus consistent with Kerberos as well as network operating systems like Novell's NetWare, which encrypt passwords before they travel over a network. Likewise, with some of these systems, the encrypted password is never decrypted at the destination server (or some other place in a network like a telecom front-end, gateway, or firewall); instead, the encrypted password is matched directly with an encrypted password stored in a password file -- if there is a match, then this is the correct password, and access should be allowed. Separately, this policy is consistent with commercial products such as Netscape Navigator (the Internet browser) that allow passwords to be stored in log-on scripts (the actual password is not readable to unauthorized persons). In general, such password storage is a dangerous practice because unauthorized people can use these passwords, but in the real world, this is standard operating procedure for many users. This policy is particularly well suited for client/server systems, local area networks (LANs), and other small systems. Also see the policies entitled "Storage Of Passwords In Readable Form" and "User-ID & Password Required For Computer-Connected Network Access." A: T; E: LMH.

25. Customer Service Fixed Passwords Not Displayed By Company X Systems

Policy: The fixed passwords used to verify a customer's identity over the telephone must never be displayed by Company X information systems. Customer service representatives must instead type in passwords offered by customers and then receive system responses indicating whether these passwords are correct.

Commentary: The intention of this policy is to limit the number of internal Company X workers who have access to customer service passwords (which are often different from log-in passwords). If these customer service passwords were to be known by internal workers, the workers could masquerade as the involved customers, and then engage in fraud, privacy invasions, and other abuses. For example, the wire transfer departments at many banks utilize customer service passwords which authorize the disclosure of confidential customer information and which authorize the transfer of funds between accounts. This policy describes an easy-to-implement approach where the system only provides a "correct" or "not correct" response to a password typed in by a customer service representative. This approach prevents well-meaning customer service representatives from providing unauthorized hints, or from deciding that the provided passwords are close enough to system resident passwords, and then proceeding with sensitive transactions or disclosures (hints of course can be officially supported as part of the software, should management decide to do so). This policy is thus in keeping with the notion that only the customer (user) should know his or her password; the problem occurs when this confidential password must be disclosed to a customer service representative in order to complete a transaction or obtain restricted information. For related ideas, see the policies entitled "Concealing Account Numbers On Customer Receipts" and "Security Mechanisms Must Not Be Compromised for Customers." A: T; E: MH.

26. Fixed Password Changes Confirmed By Regular Mail To Detect Abuse

Policy: All fixed password resets or changes must be promptly confirmed by regular mail so that the authorized user can readily detect and report any abusive behavior.

Commentary: This policy is intended to utilize the user (who is often a customer) as a part of a security team to spot fraud and abuse. Many organizations supporting Internet commerce simply use fixed passwords and SSL encryption. The problem with this approach is that another person can, using the telephone, provide certain personal details and thereby masquerade as the authorized user and request a password reset or change. To reduce the damage that can be done by a masquerader, this policy notifies the authorized user that the password was changed. If the system is not a high-security system, then the mail notification can also include the new password (the usefulness of the password without the related user-ID is limited). Separately, this policy is also relevant to telephone bill payment and other telephone automatic response systems. In either case, if the user did not initiate the change of password process, he or she should contact the system provider and inform them of suspected foul play. The same policy can be used for the establishment of a new on-line service, such as wire transfer redemption of stock sale proceeds held with a mutual fund company. In this case, the mail notice would indicate that the new system capabilities were established, and ask the customer to contact the system provider if in fact this was not initiated by them. For new services, telephone companies in many jurisdictions use this mail confirmation approach without a password (mail notification only). Another reason for sending such notifications is to reduce the number of calls to customer service, calls which may be asking for the newly-issued password. For a related idea, see the policy entitled "Assignment Of Expired Passwords." A: T; E: LM.

27. Protection Of Passwords Sent Through The Mail

Policy: If sent by regular mail or similar physical distribution systems, passwords must be sent separately from user-IDs. These mailings must have no markings indicating the nature of the enclosure. Passwords must also be concealed inside an opaque envelope that will readily reveal tampering.

Commentary: The intention behind this policy is to make it more difficult for an unauthorized person to obtain both a user-ID and a password, that would in turn allow this person to gain system access. By sending these materials in separate envelopes, preferably at different times, the risk is reduced. If only one of the two is intercepted, then unauthorized system access cannot readily be achieved. Alternatively, multiple communications systems can be used; for example, a user-ID may be given over the phone, but the password may be sent by mail. Separately, the absence of markings on an envelope reduces the chance that unauthorized parties will notice these security-related materials. The last sentence in the policy reflects the fact that a password should be known only by the intended recipient (user), and that if it has been disclosed as it travels through the mails the user should report this to the security administrator (who will then issue another password). Such an opaque envelope is sometimes called a "secure mailer." An opaque envelope is also important so that people who handle the mail cannot hold the envelope up to the light to discover the password. High security environments may want to take this notion of segmenting user-ID from password one step further--they may break the password into "components" which are each sent separately. In this case, only when the full password is reconstructed by the user, and combined with a proper user-ID, will system access be possible. This approach involving components of secret parameters is also used in certain manual encryption key management activities. For a related idea, see the policy entitled "Encryption Key Management Systems And Separation Of Duties." A: T; E: LMH.

28. Re-registration Required For All Users Forgetting Fixed Passwords

Policy: Rather than resetting or changing existing passwords, all users who forgot or misplaced their passwords must once again register and receive both new user-IDs and new passwords.

Commentary: The intention of this policy is to prevent an unauthorized user from masquerading as an authorized user, using the telephone to request a password reset or change, and then using the privileges of the authorized user. For organizations that don't want to incur the costs associated with the issuance of a special password or secret code that the user may forget (separate from the log-in password, typically mother's maiden name), this policy provides a practical approach. Used extensively in the Internet commerce area, this policy might for example be appropriate for an information provider such as a subscription service that provided sports scores. Re-registration would involve once again providing a credit card number, name, address, and other important user details, perhaps including the creation of a customer profile. This policy thus eliminates one of the most troublesome areas for help desks, namely the resetting and changing of passwords (and the process of authenticating the identity of the requesting parties). The policy is also desirable because it can be completely automated; if a customer has never had any face-to-face (in person) interaction with the system provider, or even never had any voice-to-voice (telephone) interaction with the system provider, this policy can nonetheless allow the customer to continue to use the product or service all on their own. Separately, the policy works well when users get to choose their own user-IDs (as is the case with AOL), but requires the issuance of a new user-ID rather than re-use of a previously assigned user-ID. On a different note, this policy is best for customers, and less desirable for internal users such as employees who must have user-IDs which conform to a naming standard (the word "users" in the policy could be replaced with "customers"). Note also that with digital certificates there is no need for a policy like this because the identity of the user can be automatically validated without user-ID and password re-issuance. Separately, note that this policy increases security at the expense of user friendliness and ease-of-use. For similar ideas, see the policies entitled "Fixed Password Changes Confirmed By Regular Mail To Detect Abuse" and "Limit On Consecutive Unsuccessful Attempts To Enter A Password." A: T; E: LM.

29. Password Guessing Lockout Requires Help Desk Password Reset

Policy: Each user of the Company X computer systems which employ fixed passwords at log-on time will be given only three attempts to enter a correct password. If a user has incorrectly entered a password three consecutive times, the linked user-ID will be deactivated until Help Desk staff authenticates the user's identity and then resets the password.

Commentary: The intention of this policy is to prevent unauthorized system access occasioned by password guessing. The approach described in the policy helps to prevent a large number of passwords from being guessed, perhaps with the assistance of a computer program. Of course this policy cannot be of much help in those situations where the attacker has a copy of the encrypted password file. The latter unfortunate situation could occur, for example, if a UNIX system have been erroneously configured to allow outsiders to make a copy of the password file. Note that the policy makes it immediately clear to authorized users that somebody has been attempting to gain unauthorized access to their user-IDs (because the user-IDs will be deactivated). This important control goes hand-in-hand with another policy which requires that users choose difficult-to-guess passwords. Separately, the password reset manual work could be handled by people other than those in the Help Desk group; it could for example be performed by local systems administrators or by Information Security Department staff. On another note, the words "consecutive times" generally refer to attempts which take place within a certain time period such as an hour. Computer privileges generally are not revoked if the incorrect password entries took place over a longer time period. Although this opens up an opportunity for a coworker to occasionally attempt one or two undetected guesses of another user's password, this small risk is considered acceptable by most organizations. For other ideas, see the policies entitled "Initial Passwords Transmitted To Remote Users By Authorized Means" and "Fixed Password Changes Confirmed By Regular Mail To Detect Abuse." A: T; E: LMH.

30. Storage Of Passwords In Readable Form

Policy: Passwords must not be stored in readable form in batch files, automatic log-in scripts, software macros, terminal function keys, in computers without access control, or in other locations where unauthorized persons might discover or use them.

Commentary: The intention of this policy is to prevent readable passwords from falling into the hands of unauthorized persons. Thinking that it will save time, and/or help them remember their passwords, some users store their passwords in various computer-readable locations. While these practices may help achieve these user-oriented objectives, it unduly exposes the involved system(s) to unauthorized access. People breaking into systems using tiger-team (penetration attack) methods typically check terminal function keys, log-in scripts, and similar locations for passwords. This approach is very often effective. This policy is also applicable to other security parameters besides passwords, such as encryption keys, pseudo-random number generator seed parameters, personal identification numbers (PINs), initialization vectors, etc. Security parameters are the character strings which control a security process, such as those employed when logging-into a local area network server. Separately, because it covers an area where end-users can do considerable unintentional damage, this policy particularly applies to end-users employing microcomputers (PCs), workstations, and client/server systems. Note that this policy suggests a practice which is inconsistent with features found in several communications software packages (including some Internet browsers). These systems allow users to store passwords in log-in scripts; in order for this policy to be effective, users must be trained how to use such software packages without storing their passwords in log-in scripts. While the discovery of passwords is difficult with these packages (because a masking process is used), the use of these passwords is trivial. Also see the policies entitled "Writing Passwords Down" and "Passwords Never In Readable Form When Outside Workstations." A: EMT; E: LMH.

31. Encryption Of Passwords

Policy: Passwords must always be encrypted when held in storage for any significant period of time or when transmitted over networks. This will prevent them from being disclosed to wiretappers, technical staff who are reading systems logs, and other unauthorized parties.

Commentary: Encryption provides one of the few effective ways to safeguard passwords, encryption keys, pseudo-random number generator seeds, and other security parameters. Without encryption, these parameters may be inadvertently disclosed to persons who have access to telecommunication system buffers, temporary working memory inside a computer, etc. Special scavenger computer programs may also be able to record unencrypted security parameters for subsequent retrieval by unauthorized persons. The intention of this policy is to ensure that systems designers always use encryption to protect security parameters such as passwords. Ideally, the type of encryption would involve a randomizing factor such as an initialization vector (IV) that helps to ensure that the encrypted quantity differs over time, even though the unencrypted quantity does not. For example, the Data Encryption Standard (DES) has a cipher-feedback mode which provides such a randomizing process. The term "held in storage for any significant period of time" is used to exempt internal memory locations within a system which might temporarily contain an unencrypted password. This policy is particularly relevant to, and may be written so that it is restricted only to Internet communications; many password collection programs have been used to compromise Internet security. Two effective methods for protecting fixed passwords as they travel over a network are Kerberos (from Cybersafe, Redmond, WA) and S/Key (AT&T, Basking Ridge, NJ). Also see the policy entitled "Zeroization Of Password Generation Materials." A: T; E: MH.

32. Incorporation Of Passwords Into Software

Policy: To allow passwords to be changed when needed, passwords must never be hard-coded (incorporated) into software developed by or modified by Company X workers.

Commentary: To incorporate a password into software means that the password cannot readily be changed. This leads to inflexible security mechanisms which cannot be readily adapted to new circumstances. If passwords are not entered by users, it is better to use system tables or some other non-software location to store passwords (encryption of the passwords is of course needed too). The preferred approach, which is described in this policy, involves the notion of parameterization. Parameterization allows management to change security-related parameters from time to time, perhaps in response to break-ins or to the departure of a trusted employee who could cause damage using his or her technical knowledge. This policy is also applicable to other security parameters besides passwords, such as encryption keys, pseudo-random number generator seed parameters, personal identification numbers (PINs), initialization vectors, etc. Security parameters are the character strings that control a security process, such as those employed when logging-into a local area network server. Also see the policy entitled "Suspected Disclosure Forces Password Changes." A: T; E: LMH.

33. Prevention Of Password Retrieval

Policy: Computer and communication systems must be designed, tested, and controlled so as to prevent both the retrieval of, and unauthorized use of stored passwords, whether the passwords appear in encrypted or unencrypted form.

Commentary: The intention of this policy is to prevent unauthorized persons from obtaining access to passwords which might then be used to give them unauthorized system access. When a password is entered by a user, it should be encrypted using a one-way function (ideally at the workstation, but at the very least, at the destination computer), and this new encrypted string should then be compared to the relevant encrypted string in the destination machine's password file. Encrypted strings appearing in the password file should never be retrievable by users as this allows a dictionary attack to be mounted. A dictionary attack involves encryption of entries in a computer-readable dictionary, and then the comparison of these quantities to the entries in a password file; if a match occurs, then an unencrypted (cleartext) version of a password has been discovered. This cleartext password can then be used to compromise the security of the involved system. Even if one-way encryption functions are used, the dictionary attack can still be mounted (although there may be synonyms, i.e., several words which result in the same encrypted quantity). Accordingly, to avoid such attacks, the intention of this policy is to employ access controls such that all retrieval of passwords is prevented. The same concept can be extended to encryption keys, pseudo-random number generator seeds, and other security parameters. See the policy entitled "Storage Of System-Generated Passwords." A: T; E: LMH.

34. Reliance On Operating System User Authentication Process

Policy: Company X application systems developers must consistently rely on the password access controls provided by an operating system or an access control package that enhances the operating system. Developers must not construct separate mechanisms to collect passwords or user-IDs. Similarly, developers must not construct or install other mechanisms to identify or authenticate the identity of users without the advance permission of the corporate information security manager.

Commentary: This policy is useful to achieve consistent access controls across application systems. Generally speaking, operating systems and related access control packages (e.g., IBM's RACF) have the strongest access control mechanisms of any type of software. These two types of software also generally provide facilities which allow them to be called by applications, database management systems, and other types of software. Not only will this policy make application systems design easier and less expensive, but it will also make it more consistent across the organization and therefore easier to manage. The policy furthermore helps to eliminate duplicate security administration activities (for example, one at the operating system level and another at the application level). This policy becomes essential when an organization attempts to establish a consistent user interface and consistent application programming interfaces (APIs) across platforms within the organization. The policy is thus fully consistent with the notion of having a single sign-on process for a user, at which point the user authentication information is passed along to a destination machine or other software (DBMS, application, etc.). To keep application developers away from the development or maintenance of access control systems is a good idea because it limits Trojan horses and unauthorized access paths that they can establish. It also means that the access control system does not have to be reverified each time changes are made to application code. This policy is also particularly relevant to small systems environments (e.g., client/server systems) where end-users are designing their own application systems. See the policies entitled "Single Sign-On Process," "All Software Must Be Regulated By Access Control Systems Software," and "Prohibition Against Trap Doors To Circumvent Access Controls." A: T; E: LMH.

35. Special Privileges Associated With Secret User-IDs Or Passwords Prohibited

Policy: Developers are prohibited from building or deploying secret user-IDs or passwords which have special privileges and which are not clearly covered in the system documentation.

Commentary: This policy is intended to speak directly to an act that has been committed by many programmers. This act involves the definition of special user-IDs or passwords that nobody knows about (except the inside technical elite). Although relatively easy to code, and difficult for others to discover (unless these others do a line-by-line code review), these access mechanisms circumvent the developing organization's systems development life cycle controls. These access mechanisms also circumvent the end-user organization's standard request for privilege process and subsequent management authorization process. These mechanisms can give the programmers access to powerful functionality, even if these programmers no longer work for the employer who funded their efforts. Because they are fixed in the code, these access mechanisms cannot be readily removed or disabled when a developer leaves the employment of a software vendor, even if they do become generally known. Likewise, if hackers discover these same user-IDs or passwords, this could lead to bad publicity. This was the case when Microsoft engineers recently defined a secret password, a phrase deriding Netscape rivals as "weenies," that could be used to gain access to hundreds of thousands of Internet sites worldwide. Another reason to outlaw such user-IDs and passwords is that they give one or more individual developers control over the security of software when that control should have been transferred to the user organization when software was licensed, rented, or sold. Separately note that the reference to system documentation is intended to be a deterrent -- if developers would be embarrassed to have a special access mechanism described in the documentation, then it probably shouldn't be in the system at all. This policy can be seen as specific approach to the same topic covered in the policy entitled "Prohibition Against Trap Doors To Circumvent Access Controls." For related ideas, see the policies entitled "Removal Of All Unauthorized Access Paths In Production Software" and "Changing Physical Access Control Codes On Worker Termination."
A: T; E: LMH.

36. System Access Control With Individualized Passwords (Not Lockwords)

Policy: Computer and communication system access control must be achieved via passwords that are unique to each individual user. Access control to files, databases, computers, and other system resources via shared passwords (also called lockwords) is prohibited.

Commentary: The intention of this policy is to prevent systems administrators from establishing access control privileges with a scheme that leads to problems (specifically with lockwords rather than passwords). Lockwords, which are often used to control access to a file, can be easily passed along to another user. Thus the file owner who originally granted access can quickly lose control over who has access to, and who is changing the file. This defeats the principle of accountability, which attempts to attribute all system events to specific individuals. Use of an individualized password (and most often a user-ID too), along with specific access control privileges, will thus prevent this "secondary dissemination" of passwords because passwords must remain the exclusive knowledge of the involved users. This policy is consistent with the use of hand-held identity tokens (also called extended user authentication systems); nothing in this policy states that these systems cannot be used in addition to fixed password systems. The policy additionally prohibits the sharing of user-IDs, with so-called "group accounts;" at many organizations, the desirable security mechanisms incorporated into the operating system are not used properly -- group user-IDs are a common example. This policy is relevant to telephone systems, local area networks (including client/server systems), and other communication systems in addition to traditional mainframe-style access control packages like ACF2 (Computer Associates, Islandia,

New York). See the policies entitled "Password Sharing Prohibition," "Unique User-ID And Password Required," and "User-IDs Must Each Uniquely Identify A Single User." A: T; E: LMH.

37. Unique Passwords For Each Internal Network Device

Policy: All Company X internal network devices (routers, firewalls, access control servers, etc.) must have unique passwords or other access control mechanisms. A compromise in the security of one device will therefore not automatically lead to a compromise in other devices.

Commentary: In an effort to expedite administration, technical staff will often use the same fixed password for multiple devices of the same type (routers on a network for example), or even for a variety of different devices (firewalls, modem pools, etc.). This policy is intended to prevent the discovery or unauthorized disclosure of a network device fixed password from leading to extensive damage. If unique fixed passwords are used for each device, then the damage should be restricted to that device only, and what that device can do (perhaps capture other fixed passwords flowing through it). If the same fixed password is used in multiple places, it will also be more difficult to get rid of a hacker/cracker who keeps coming to visit. Likewise, the use of a single password for multiple network devices restricts management's ability to establish separation of duties and to restrict access based on job duties. This policy is consistent with the secure systems design principle called "least common mechanism." The principle encourages people to avoid situations where all of one's control "eggs are put in one basket." This policy is additionally essential if "defensive depth" is to be obtained in a network. Defensive depth refers to the establishment of multiple hurdles through which users must go if they are to reach a certain destination. These hurdles might be firewalls, routers, or other internal network machines. Defensive depth is used, for example, when firewalls are used to establish a demilitarized zone (DMZ) on an internal network. While lockwords, that is shared fixed passwords, are to be discouraged whenever the technology supports use of other methods (like dynamic passwords), the reality at many businesses is that shared fixed passwords must be employed. Separately, this policy addresses the age-old conflict between ease-of-use and security, coming down clearly on the side of the latter. For related ideas, see the policies entitled "Unique User-ID And Password Required" and "Assignment Of Expired Passwords." A: T; E: LMH.

38. Use Of Duress Passwords

Policy: Whenever system access to particularly valuable or sensitive data is given to a user, duress passwords must be employed to covertly signal the system that this user is being pressured to log-on. Duress passwords are special passwords used only in those circumstances where an alarm should be triggered, but where the user's safety may be jeopardized if people accompanying the user know the alarm has been triggered.

Commentary: Duress passwords may limit user privileges, limit the available balance in certain bank accounts, turn on supplementary logs, signal a remote alarm, or automatically initiate some other security-related action. Duress passwords are generally different from a regular password, both of which will let the individual onto the system in question. Because a duress password may be employed when an individual user's safety is endangered (such as when an industrial spy has a gun to a user's head), it is advisable to have system access provided. The duress password is a convenient way for the user to tip-off the system operators on duty or other people that something serious is happening. For normal business activities, duress passwords are not necessary. For related ideas, see the policies entitled "Immediate System Interruption If Human Beings Are Jeopardized" and "Special Sign-Off Required For Projects Involving Human Safety Issues." A: T; E: H.

39. Changing Vendor Default Passwords

Policy: All vendor-supplied default passwords must be changed before any computer or communications system is used for Company X business.

Commentary: One of the oldest, yet still most successful ways to break into systems is to employ default vendor passwords. These default passwords are typically strings such as "sysadm" or "sysmanager." Often the vendor-supplied default passwords are known by both the technical people with experience on this platform as well as the hacker/cracker community. Too many organizations forget to change these passwords before they press the involved systems into production mode. This policy specifically puts technical staff on notice that they must change all vendor default passwords in order to achieve the most basic level of security. To restrict the scope of this policy, the word "production" could be added to the policy (perhaps accompanied by a definition if the audience is not familiar with the notion of production systems). This policy is particularly important in Internet-connected, client/server, local area network, and small systems computing environments where system administrators may not be trained extensively in data processing. Separately note that some vulnerability identification packages can be used to monitor compliance with this policy (one such product is offered by Internet Security Systems, Atlanta, Georgia). Also see the policy entitled "Assignment Of Expired Passwords." A: T; E: LMH.

1.1.1.1.4. Password Related User Responsibilities

40. Requirement For Different Passwords On Different Systems

Policy: To prevent the compromise of multiple systems, computer users must employ different passwords on each of the systems to which they have been granted access.

Commentary: This policy prevents the users from putting "all of their eggs in one basket," and thereby allowing unauthorized persons to gain access to a variety of systems rather than a single system. If a hacker were to discover a fixed password through guessing, or perhaps recover a fixed password through a wiretap, then all the systems to which the individual with the same password had access would be compromised. As many users now have 5, 10, and as many as 25 different passwords, this policy encourages users to write their passwords down (undesirable because these passwords may then be recovered by other unauthorized parties). A policy like this may also cause significant user resistance, because users are trying to simplify their life by using the same password in multiple places; accordingly, this policy is appropriate only in high-security environments. A more friendly approach is to use a front-end -- such as an Internet firewall or a modem pool -- that requires people to log-in only once (a so-called "single sign-on system"). A preferred approach is described in the policy entitled "Single Sign-On Process." Also see the policies entitled "Writing Passwords Down And Leaving Where Others Could Discover" and "Permission To Use Same Password On Different Systems." A: EMT; E: H.

41. Permission To Use Same Password On Different Systems

Policy: Users must refrain from using the same password on multiple computer systems unless they have been informed by the Information Security Department that doing so will not unduly compromise security.

Commentary: This policy is intended to achieve much the same purpose as the policy entitled "Requirement for Different Passwords on Different Systems," yet it is a bit more lenient and user-friendly. Instead of an absolute prohibition against the use of the same password, it requires the user to first get permission. There are some users, who have relatively minor system privileges, for whom it would not be a serious security vulnerability if they were to use the same password on multiple systems. This stringent and user-unfriendly policy should be reserved for high security environments. See the policy entitled "Single Sign-On Process" for a preferred approach. A: EMT; E: H.

42. Suspected Disclosure Forces Password Changes

Policy: Each user must immediately change his or her password if the password is suspected of being disclosed, or known to have been disclosed to an unauthorized party.
Commentary: The basic secure systems design principle behind this policy is that ONLY the user should know his or her password (this policy assumes that all users have their own unique user-IDs). If the password in question has been disclosed to some other party, or if this is only suspected, then the password must be immediately changed. This policy implies that users are able to change their password whenever circumstances warrant. If this is not possible for technical or administrative reasons, as an alternative, a security administrator could reset the involved user's password immediately. If the latter option is used, to make sure the resulting password is known only by the user, a systems administrator can issue a new temporary password (also known as an "expired password"), which is then changed by the user the next time he or she logs onto the involved system. Also see the policies entitled "Assignment Of Expired Passwords," "Forced Change Of All Passwords After System Compromise," "Periodic Forced Password Changes," and "Password Change Interval Synchronization Across Platforms." A: EMT; E: LMH.

43. Password Changes After Compromise Of A Multi-User Computer System

Policy: If a multi-user computer system employs fixed passwords as its primary access control mechanism, all passwords on that system must be changed immediately after evidence of system compromise has been discovered. At this time, all users must be instructed to change their fixed passwords on other machines, if the passwords on the compromised machine are also used on these other machines.

Commentary: While this policy may at first appear to be obvious to those people who have been working in the information security field for a long time, it is not obvious to newly-appointed systems administrators, network managers, and other technical staff. While the changing of all fixed passwords may not eradicate the source of the compromise, it is a necessary step in the direction of reestablishing a trusted computing environment. Note that this policy also stresses that the passwords on other machines must be changed; far too few technical people appreciate that users often employ the same password across a variety of machines. Unless these other passwords are changed, the other machines are at significant risk of compromise as well. For a related idea, see the policy entitled "Required Actions Following Suspected System Intrusion." A: T; E: LMH.

44. Writing Passwords Down And Leaving Where Others Could Discover

Policy: Passwords must not be written down and left in a place where unauthorized persons might discover them.

Commentary: Discovering passwords written down and left in the top drawer, taped to a computer monitor, or in some other conspicuous spot is a surprisingly common way for penetration attackers (tiger team members) to break into computers. Surprising as it may seem, many users don't think about these risks unless management alerts them to the problems. Note that this policy does not say that users must not write their passwords down; only that they must not be left in a spot where others could recover them. This policy could be modified to become a stricter policy that absolutely prohibits users from writing their passwords down, but in many environments users will do it anyway. The policy thus recognizes the reality of common practices regarding writing down passwords. See the policies entitled "Pronounceable System-Generated Passwords," "Writing Passwords Down Using Secrecy Techniques," and "Requirement For Different Passwords On Different Systems." A: EMT; E: LMH.

45. Passwords Must Never Be Written Down Near Related Access Devices

Policy: Users must never write down or otherwise record a readable password and store it near the access device to which it pertains. For example, a personal identification number (PIN) must never be written down on an automated teller machine (ATM) card.

Commentary: The intention of this policy is to tip-off users that they should not store a password and the device to which it pertains. This happens often with portable computers, and users who record passwords and telephone access numbers inside their portable computers. To gain unauthorized access to remote computers, a thief only needs to examine these files. Likewise, PINs needed to initialize dynamic password tokens or smart cards should not be recorded on the devices themselves. This policy helps to support so-called "two factor authentication" (use of two techniques to authenticate a user's identity) -- if the password is combined with the device what was two factor authentication becomes only one factor authentication. For related ideas, see the policies entitled "Positive Identification Required For System Usage" and "Writing Passwords Down Using Secrecy Techniques." A: EMT; E: LMH.

46. No Fixed Passwords Stored In Dial-Up Programs Or Internet Browsers

Policy: Users must not store fixed passwords in dial-up communications programs or Internet browsers at any time.

Commentary: The objective of this policy is to prevent users from employing the nifty and user-friendly feature found in many communications programs that allows fixed passwords to be stored for future reference. Although these passwords are typically stored in encrypted form, and are masked when typed on the screen so that that unauthorized parties cannot view them, they can still be used by unauthorized persons who have access to the computer on which this communications software resides. In this manner, although the passwords are not revealed, they can nonetheless still be used to gain unauthorized system access. This policy is especially important for portable computers (laptops or handhelds) or any other computers which do not always have the benefit of physical access controls to protect them. Ideally communications software would be modified to prevent users from employing this "feature," but in most organizations this type of modification is not practical. The only alternative is to prohibit users from employing a feature that they would otherwise consider to be convenient and desirable (and hopefully to check-up on the users via internal audits). Looking at this from a secure systems design perspective, if users store their fixed passwords in a computer, then possession of that computer may be all that is needed to gain access to a remote machine, but if users keep these fixed passwords in their heads, then remote system access can be achieved only with such possession accompanied by the provision of a secret password. For related ideas, see the policies entitled "Storage Of Passwords In Readable Form" and "Prevention Of Password Retrieval." A: E; E: LMH.

47. User Controlled Machines Must Not Employ Cookies For Automatic Log-In

Policy: Company X computer users must refuse all offers by software to place a cookie on their computer so that they can automatically log-in the next time that they visit a particular Internet site.

Commentary: The motivation for this policy is to prevent users from accepting log-in cookies which could later be used by unauthorized parties to gain system access, order products, or obtain restricted information. A cookie is a small file which contains user-specific information that is placed on a user's hard drive, and can be used to uniquely identify that user. The use of log-in cookies thus simplifies and replaces the traditional log-in process. Many Internet merchants think they are doing users a great service when they offer to place this type of cookie on user machines. Nonetheless, the use of log-in cookies reduces security because it replaces information that the user knows (user-ID and password) with simple physical proximity to a remote machine. Many users only think of the time it would save them, how it reduces the need to remember a password, and the like. They don't think of how other people could masquerade as them, and perhaps commit computer crimes thereby. These users additionally don't generally think about the other things that such log-in cookies could do, for example create a detailed trail of their Internet activities. As an aside, if user machines have very strong access controls, such as encrypted hard drives and a boot password, then the restriction described in this policy may not be necessary. For related ideas, see the policies entitled "No Embedded Secret Personal Identifiers Or Serial Numbers" and "No Fixed Passwords Stored In Dial-Up Programs Or Internet Browsers." A: E; E: MH.

48. Dynamic Password Tokens Must Not Be Stored In Portable Cases

Policy: Dynamic password tokens must not be stored in the same briefcase or suitcase as portable computers used to remotely access Company X networks.

Commentary: The intention of this policy is to prevent convenience from winning-out over security. Without instructions to the contrary, users will keep dynamic password tokens (also called identity tokens) in the same carrying case as the computer to which it pertains. In some cases these tokens don't have enabling fixed passwords; this will mean that possession of both the token and the computer will be sufficient to gain unauthorized system access. Even if a fixed password is required to enable a token, the work factor (resources) required to compromise system security will be notably reduced when tokens are stored with portable computers to which they pertain. On another note, this policy advances the cause of "multi-factor" user authentication, which basically says that several different things will be required before system access is obtained (something the user knows, something the user has, something the user can do, something the user is (biometrics), etc.). This notion is not generally appreciated by users, but once they understand it, users will more readily comply with policies such as this. Unlike some policies, this one doesn't require users to think, it just tells them what not to do. Separately, with thefts of portable computers on the rise, this policy becomes more important. The dynamic password system mentioned in the policy could pertain to both the portable machine and to a remote computer, or just to the latter. For related ideas, see the policies entitled "Reporting Lost/Stolen Identification Badges And System Access Tokens" and "Positive Identification Required For System Usage." A: E; E: MH.

49. Personal Identification Numbers (PINs) Constructed Using Password Rules

Policy: All personal identification numbers (PINs) must be constructed with the same rules that apply to fixed passwords. Just because system access is assisted by a magnetic card, a dynamic password token, or some other user authentication technology, does not eliminate the need to employ PINs which are difficult to guess.

Commentary: The objective of this policy is to put both end-users and systems administrators on notice that they should not let their guard down when picking or constructing personal identification numbers, also known as PINs. Because PINs are often a part of a multi-factor user authentication scheme (where both a PIN and something else is required for system access), many people think that their PINs -- whether assigned by the system or user-generated -- don't need to be difficult to guess. This misconception about the role of a PIN, and the resulting choice of an easily guessed PIN, in turn makes it easier for an attacker to gain unauthorized system access. For example, if a PIN for a dynamic password token involved only the digits "1234," this string could be easily guessed, and this string typically would be one of the first PINs that an attacker would try. The need for difficult to guess PINs is underscored because PINs are often only four characters and this means that there aren't many possible combinations (in mathematical terms, the key space is small). This makes PINs subject to brute force attacks where all combinations are attempted, and makes it particularly important to have a lock-out mechanism after a certain number of incorrect log-in attempts. As an aside, because PINs include only numbers, certain password construction rules are irrelevant (such as don't use dictionary words or common names), but the same intention, to have them be difficult to guess, still applies to PINs. For related ideas, see the policies entitled "Extended User Authentication Systems Required For Dial-Up Lines" and "Maximum Permissible Password Attempts For Dial-Up Users." A: ET; E: LMH.

50. Writing Passwords Down Using Secrecy Techniques

Policy: Users must not write their passwords down unless (1) they have effectively concealed such passwords in a phone number or in other seemingly unrelated characters, or (2) they have used a coding system to conceal the password.

Commentary: This user-friendly policy gives specific guidance about the appropriate ways to write down passwords, with the expectation that users will write their passwords down. With the recent explosion in the number of passwords that users must remember, coupled with the need to periodically change some of these passwords, users often feel as though they have no choice but to write down their passwords. At the same time, writing down passwords can be an easy way for unauthorized persons to gain system access. This policy proposes a practical middle-of-the-road way to resolve these conflicting objectives. Separately, the coding practices that could be mentioned include what is called the "black night" method. With this method, passwords may be taped in a conspicuous spot because they have been altered using some standard approach, such as bump the first letter up the alphabet one letter, bump the second letter down one letter, etc. See the policies entitled "Writing Passwords Down And Leaving Where Others Could Discover" and "Passwords Never In Readable Form When Outside Workstations." A: EMT; E: LMH.

51. Password Sharing Prohibition

Policy: Regardless of the circumstances, passwords must never be shared or revealed to anyone else besides the authorized user. To do so exposes the authorized user to responsibility for actions that the other party takes with the password. If users need to share computer resident data, they should use electronic mail, public directories on local area network servers, and other mechanisms.

Commentary: In an effort to be polite, be more productive, or to save time, users often share their passwords. Sometimes system attackers masquerade as though they are information systems security staff, then asking users for their passwords. When requested to do so, a surprisingly large number of users will readily provide their password. Whenever users disclose their passwords, they inadvertently compromise system access controls and make logs of user activity less useful. It is important that users keep their passwords exclusively to themselves, and the intention of this policy is to remind them to do just that. The policy has a threat in it, specifically the part that talks about being responsible for the actions of another. This part of the policy could be expanded to mention that the way a user prevents him- or herself from being improperly held accountable for the actions of another is to keep his or her password secret. At many organizations, in the small systems environment (client/server, local area networks, etc.) a casual attitude toward security has traditionally prevailed; a policy like this seeks to counteract this attitude. See the policies entitled "In-Person Proof Of Identity To Obtain A Password," "Limitation On Number Of Daily Log-Ins Prevents Unauthorized Use," and "System Access Control With Individualized Passwords (Not Lockwords)." A: ET; E: LMH.

52. Users Responsible For All Activities Involving Personal User-IDs

Policy: Users are responsible for all activity performed with their personal user-IDs. User-IDs may not be utilized by anyone but the individuals to whom they have been issued. Users must not allow others to perform any activity with their user-IDs. Similarly, users are forbidden from performing any activity with IDs belonging to other users (excepting anonymous user-IDs like "guest").

Commentary: The intention of this policy is to make it clear that sharing user-IDs and associated passwords is prohibited. If users share user-IDs and passwords, logs will not reflect the true identity of the users, and will accordingly be less useful for disciplinary actions, prosecutions, and investigations. Likewise, user specific privilege controls mean little when users are sharing user-IDs and passwords. This policy has some positive side-effects that may not be readily apparent. For example, when an employee goes on vacation, to be in compliance with the policy, he/she may not give his user-ID and password to someone else so that other person can check the employee's electronic mail. The employee may instead use electronic mail forwarding mechanisms. Separately, in an indirect way, the fourth sentence in this policy forbids the hacking/cracking of external systems with the aid of Company X's systems. Separately, in some computing environments, individualized user-IDs are called "accounts" or sometimes "UIDs." On another note, this policy is not intended for those organizations (like some schools) which employ group user-IDs. Also see the policy entitled "Using An Electronic Mail Account Assigned To Another Individual." A: E; E: LMH.

1.1.1.1.5. Password Related Administrator Responsibilities

53. Forced Change Of All Passwords After System Compromise

Policy: Whenever a system has been compromised by an unauthorized party, system managers must immediately change every password on the involved system. Even suspicion of a compromise requires that all passwords be changed immediately. Under either of these circumstances, a trusted version of the operating system and all security-related software must also be reloaded. Similarly, under either of these circumstances, all recent changes to user and system privileges must be reviewed for unauthorized modifications.

Commentary: The purpose of this policy is to reestablish a "clean" (secure) operating system and associated password-based access controls following a break-in or some related compromise of the security measures. Immediate response is required because the longer the unauthorized parties are on the system the more the opportunity for them to establish unauthorized user-IDs, unauthorized privileges for existing user-IDs over which they have control, and trapdoors that would allow future system access. Reloading the operating system and scanning the logs for unauthorized changes that need to be undone will help to eliminate further unauthorized activity. Besides being relevant to Information Systems Department computer operators, this policy applies to LAN server administrators, departmental computer system managers, and similar persons who may be organizationally positioned outside the Information Systems Department. This policy is particularly important for those in charge of small systems such as client/server systems, local area networks, etc. Also see the policy entitled "Suspected Disclosure Forces Password Changes." A: T; E: LMH.

54. Forced Change Of All Passwords After Supervisor Account Compromise

Policy: If a privileged (supervisor) account has been compromised by an intruder or another type of unauthorized user, all passwords on that system must be immediately changed.

Commentary: The intention of this policy is to inform systems administrators and others who are managing information systems that all passwords are potentially compromised if a privileged account has been compromised. This is because privileged accounts (depending on the operating system) can be used to establish and modify privileges of any other account on the affected system. Accordingly, the passwords for all accounts must immediately be changed in order to prevent an unauthorized user from once again gaining system access. This policy is a quick fix, and it will not be able to keep an unauthorized user out of the affected system if operating system software has been modified. Separate control mechanisms can be used to detect changes in the operating system (such as cryptographic checksums). For related ideas, see the policies entitled "Forced Change of All Passwords After System Compromise" and "Password Changes After Compromise Of A Multi-User Computer System." A: T; E: LMH.

55. In-Person Proof Of Identity To Obtain A Password

Policy: Passwords must never be disclosed via voice telephone lines. To obtain a new or changed password, a user must show up in person and present suitable identification.

Commentary: The intention of this policy is to ensure that passwords are not disclosed to unauthorized parties. Many people have used "social engineering" to spoof others into disclosing passwords over the phone. To prevent improper disclosure of passwords, some organizations require proof of identity (such as an identification badge or a driver's license). As an alternative, users may be sent passwords in what are called "secure mailers." With this approach, passwords are automatically typed by impact printers using no ribbons into pre-sealed envelopes (this prevents unauthorized persons from viewing the passwords). This approach is discussed in the policy entitled "Protection of Passwords Sent Through the Mail." If a user must get a password in an emergency, some organizations require that the caller prove their identity by providing difficult-to-obtain information that an impostor would be unlikely to know, such as "What's the name of the school that you attended when you were in sixth grade?" Some organizations go one step further requiring a combination of personal information such as mother's maiden name, employee number, and automobile license plate number. See the policies entitled "Password Sharing Prohibition," "Assignment Of Expired Passwords," and "Computer Support Identification Codes." A: ET; E: LMH.

56. When And How Passwords May Be Disclosed By Security Administrators

Policy: Security administrators must only disclose passwords if a new user-ID is being assigned, if the involved user has forgotten or misplaced a password, or if the involved user is otherwise locked out of his or her user-ID. Security administrators must not reveal a password unless the involved user has first provided two pieces of definitive evidence substantiating his or her identity.

Commentary: This policy is intended to make it clear when and how security administrators (who are also often systems administrators) may disclose a password. There are many cases on record where "social engineering" (in this case masquerading as a legitimate user) is used to get security administrators to reveal a password over the phone. Note that this policy does allow a security administrator to reveal a password over the phone so long as adequate evidence of identity is provided (mother's maiden name, social security number, etc.). This over-the-phone process is expedient, although it is definitely less secure than requiring the user to show up in person. This policy assumes that fixed passwords are being used; if dynamic password systems are being used, then the policy may not be relevant (in some cases a fixed password or PIN may still be needed to activate a token which in turn generates dynamic passwords). To be truly effective, the policy needs to be accompanied by several related policies, such as one requiring that newly assigned passwords be changed during the first session when they are used (also known as "expired passwords"). The policy additionally assumes the term "security administrator" has been explicitly defined within an organization. For related ideas, see the policies entitled "Suspected Disclosure Forces Password Changes" and "Password Sharing Prohibition." A: T; E: LMH.

1.1.1.2. Log-In Process

57. Positive Identification Required For System Usage

Policy: All users must be positively identified prior to being able to use any multi-user computer or communications system resources.

Commentary: Positive identification ordinarily involves user-IDs and fixed passwords, but may also include biometrics, callback systems, dynamic password tokens, or digital certificates. The exact definition of positive identification can also vary based on platform or technology; for example accessing computers behind an Internet firewall may require dynamic passwords in addition to a fixed password, while using a telephone credit card may only require a fixed password. Some organizations may wish to alter this policy to require "two factor" user identity authentication (where two things are required for access, such as something a user knows--like a password, combined with something a user has--such as an identity token). The exact definition of positive identification may be deliberately omitted from the policy so that the technology may change over time, without the need to make corresponding changes to the policy. Some organizations may wish to add words to the policy making it clear that the Information Security Department will be the decision maker when it comes to a precise definition of "positive identification." In the version of the policy presented above, longevity of the policy is traded-off against making the policy clear and unambiguous. The intention of this policy is to ensure that no unauthorized persons access organizational computers or communication systems. Behind this approach is the notion of a moat, such as was used to protect medieval castles. A moat prevents unauthorized persons from getting inside of the castle (system) walls. As organizations adopt more interconnected systems, this policy becomes increasingly important. For example, a stand-alone departmental local area network poses a relatively limited vulnerability, but when such a LAN is connected to a wide area network, the need for all users to be positively identified is increased. As small systems (such as client/server systems) are increasingly used to run production applications, this policy likewise becomes commensurately more important. In the small systems environment, this policy may force certain network operating systems or workstation operating systems to be upgraded to support sufficiently strong access controls. Also see the policies entitled "Single Sign-On Process" and "Identification And Sign-In Process Required For All Visitors." A: EMT; E: LMH.

58. Access Controls For Remote Systems Connecting To Production Systems

Policy: All computers which have remote real-time dialogs with Company X production systems must run an access control package approved by the Information Security Department.

Commentary: This policy seeks to define the computers -- notably PCs and microcomputers -- that must have special access control packages (often fixed password boot-controlled, but increasingly using dynamic passwords). The policy acknowledges that the distributed processing associated with modern computer systems brings with it the need to secure all end-points that might be used to enter information into a production system. These end points might be a mobile computer, a personal digital assistant (PDA), or even a smart phone. To achieve an appropriate level of security for production systems, this policy says: "Don't connect a remote system with a production system unless you have an approved access mechanism." The exact definition of a "remote system" is deliberately not included in the policy so that it can cover a wide variety of systems. Note also that batch transmissions are in general more secure, and accordingly are not within the scope of this policy. To increase the coverage of this policy, batch systems could be included as well as real-time systems. On another note, this policy acknowledges the anarchy that often goes with PC or microcomputer usage, and insists that this must change if these same systems are going to connect to a production system. One additional advantage of this policy is that production system users' remote machines can be locked-down with a change control tool, which goes along with an access control system, and which prevents users from changing the configuration or internal software (and in the process reduces virus infections). In an indirect way, the policy also addresses down-loading of data; it helps establish access control packages on all the remote systems which might store production information. For related ideas, see the policies entitled "Where To Use Computer System Access Controls," and "Telecommuter Remote System Information Security Procedures." A: ET; E: LMH.

59. User-ID & Password Required For Computer-Connected Network Access

Policy: All users must have their identity verified with a user-ID and a secret password--or by other means which provide equal or greater security--prior to being permitted to use Company X computers connected to a network.

Commentary: The intent of this policy is to make sure that only authorized people can gain access to organizational networks. This policy implies that a password and user-ID could be shared by a group of people, although this practice is to be discouraged since it does not provide individual accountability. The policy also allows the organization to move to extended user authentication via biometrics, call-back systems, dynamic password identity tokens, digital certificates, etc. The policy could be written so that it applies to "multi-user systems" rather than "computers connected to a network." This would mean that it does not apply to microcomputers (PCs) and workstations. It may also be necessary to define what is meant by a "network" in this context; will, for instance, outgoing dial-up connections be considered "a network"? Also see the policies entitled "Computer Support Identification Codes" and "Granting User-IDs To Outsiders." A: T; E: LMH.

60. Unique User-ID And Password Required

Policy: Every user must have a single unique user-ID and a personal secret password. This user-ID and password will be required for access to Company X multi-user computers and computer networks.

Commentary: The primary intention of this policy is to facilitate security administration activities. With the ever-increasing number of computers and networks found in modern organizations, use of various user-IDs for the same person is getting to be too complex. This policy simplifies all that for both users and systems administrators. Another intention of the policy is to ensure that all multi-user systems and networks have access control software which can uniquely identify and restrict the privileges of each user. These access control facilities also allow special logging and monitoring software to be used. To further limit computer usage by unauthorized parties, some organizations may prohibit users from employing the same fixed password on every machine, although the same user-ID may still be (and ideally is) employed. The use of the same user-ID on all computers and networks across an organization is additionally desirable because it makes analysis of activity logs considerably easier. Before issuing a policy such as this, the reader may wish to investigate new security administration tools, such as Computer Associates' CA-Unicenter, which provide a consistent platform-independent administrative interface for access control systems. The use of the term "multi-user computer" in the policy effectively exempts workstations, microcomputers and other small systems. In many organizations, these small systems are increasingly taking on production and mission-critical functions; if this is true in the policy writer's organization, then there is merit to dropping the word "multi-user" from the policy. The policy described here also prohibits group user-IDs -- typically a significant problem in those organizations where the level of awareness about information security is low. On another point, some organizations may wish to replace the word "password" in the policy with a more general term such as "positive user authentication" -- this would allow for smart cards, dynamic password tokens, biometrics and other technologies. For similar ideas, see the policies entitled "Access To Secret Information Granted On Individual (Not Group) Basis," "Anonymous User-IDs," "User-IDs Must Each Uniquely Identify A Single User," "System Access Control With Individualized Passwords (Not Lockwords)," and "Requirement For Different Passwords On Different Systems." A: T; E: LMH.

61. Disclosure Of Incorrect Log-In Information

Policy: When logging into a Company X computer or data communications system, if any part of the log-in sequence is incorrect, the user must not be given specific feedback indicating the source of the problem. Instead, the user must simply be informed that the entire log-in process was incorrect.

Commentary: Persons attempting to break into systems can use specific feedback messages to determine what they are doing right, thereby narrowing the number of different combinations they need to try. This increases the likelihood that their system attacks will be successful. For example, if a message said "password incorrect," this may be helpful to an attacker because he or she would now know that the user-ID was acceptable. To prevent such attacks from being successful, this policy prohibits the provision of detailed feedback information to users. Note that this is slightly user-unfriendly, but the security advantage to be obtained more than compensates for the user-unfriendliness in most environments. To give specific feedback only after all the input has been entered by the user means that the timing of the feedback message cannot be used to deduce what part of the log-in was incorrect. For example, if an error message was given after the user-ID was entered, but before the password was entered, then this would be a good indication that the user-ID was erroneous (even if the message simply said "log-in incorrect"). See the policy entitled "Prohibition Against Any Feedback In Response To Incorrect Log-In." A: T; E: LMH.

62. Prohibition Against Any Feedback In Response To Incorrect Log-In

Policy: When logging-into a Company X computer or data communications system, if any part of the log-in sequence is incorrect, the user must not be given any feedback whatsoever indicating the source of the problem. Instead, the system must either terminate the session or wait for the correct log-in information to be entered.

Commentary: The objective of this policy is to provide absolutely no information which might be used by persons attempting to gain unauthorized system access. In some circumstances, the fact that a log-in sequence was expected may itself be a disclosure which would assist attackers. After reading the policy entitled "Disclosure of Incorrect Log-In Information," the reader can appreciate that the provision of any helpful information might be used to compromise the involved system. The approach in some cases is called the "black hole" response to log-in errors, making reference to the astronomy concept of a black hole into which all manner of things go, but nothing comes out. This is a relatively user-unfriendly policy, and is typically found only in high-security environments such as the military. This policy naturally accompanies a similar policy prohibiting any log-in banner information that might be used to identify a system, an organization, or otherwise provide information of use to a system attacker. See the policy entitled "Disclosure Of Information In System Log-in Banner." A: T; E: H.

63. Security Notice In System Log-in Banner

Policy: Every log-in screen for multi-user computers must include a special notice. This notice must state: (1) the system may only be accessed by authorized users, (2) users who log-in represent that they are authorized to do so, (3) unauthorized system usage or abuse is subject to criminal prosecution, and (4) system usage will be monitored and logged.

Commentary: For legal reasons, in many jurisdictions, it is wise to put all users on notice that the involved system may be used only for authorized purposes. In the event of a prosecution against those who entered a system unlawfully, one of the most successful defending claims is that there was no notice saying they could not enter. Hackers may cite log-in banners which include the word "welcome." Recent court cases have highlighted the need for organizations to put unauthorized users on notice that their systems are off-limits. As a result, a system log-in banner -- displayed on each user log-in screen -- should provide the electronic equivalent of a no-trespassing sign. Some organizations go further than the policy indicated above, indicating this is a private rather than a public system, and that they intend to prosecute unauthorized usage. A recent US Department of Justice opinion in fact requires that notice of activity logging be in the log-in banner if user keystroke monitoring is used (to do otherwise would be a violation of United States criminal code statute 15 USC 2510). The policy thus lets users know that management is serious about security and privacy. Separately, a policy such as this is desirable for all multi-user computers, especially those systems with external network connections (dial-up lines, Internet firewalls, etc.). The same type of banner can be used for selected data communication networks, not just computers. Also see the policy entitled "Disclosure Of Information In System Log-in Banner." A: T; E: LMH.

64. Disclosure Of Information In System Log-In Banner

Policy: All log-in banners on network-connected Company X computer systems must simply ask the user to log-in, providing terse prompts only where essential. Identifying information about the organization, operating system, system configuration, or other internal matters must not be provided until a user's identity has been successfully authenticated.

Commentary: The lack of specific information, such as the name of the organization, will keep unauthorized persons in the dark as to the system that they have reached. This may make the system less interesting to them, but it will certainly give them less information on which to base a password guessing attack. Lack of information about the computer operating system will also prevent the users from employing knowledge of specialized weaknesses in these operating systems. This banner disclosure policy is a more specific manifestation of the notion that information should be released based on the need-to-know. The last sentence of the policy is deliberately vague about the steps necessary to prove one's identity -- when an organization moves from user-IDs and fixed passwords to a more sophisticated technology, no change in the policy will be necessary. Some organizations may wish to replace this general user authentication statement with specific mention of a certain technology like smart cards. This policy may be restricted to network systems reachable from external networks, such as the Internet and dial-up lines. Also see the policies entitled "Difficult-to-Guess Passwords," "Inter-Processor Commands From Outside Locations Prohibited," and "Prohibition Against Any Feedback In Response To Incorrect Log-In." A: T; E: LMH.

65. Network Log-In Banner Wording Required

Policy: The following warning banner must be used when users connect to Company X's internal computer networks: "This system is for the use of authorized users only. Individuals using this computer system without authority, or in excess of their authority, are subject to having all of their activities on this system monitored and recorded by systems personnel. In the course of monitoring individuals improperly using this system, or in the course of system maintenance, the activities of authorized users may also be monitored. Anyone using this system expressly consents to such monitoring and is advised that if such monitoring reveals possible criminal activity, system personnel may provide the evidence of such monitoring to law enforcement officials."

Commentary: This policy is intended to put technical systems staff on notice that the words appearing in the quotes must be used in all computer network log-in banners. The words in quotes are supplied by the US Department of Justice and are intended to make sure that user activity monitoring is not inadvertently in violation of the Communications Privacy Act of 1986. For organizations outside the USA, the concept still applies: users should be put on notice that their activities may be logged. To encourage wider usage, the words supplied by the Department of Justice are deliberately not copyrighted. This policy is appropriate to dial-up connections, connections through value added networks (VANs) such as MCI Tymnet, as well as Internet connections. See the policies entitled "Security Notice In System Log-In Banner," "Disclosure Of Information In System Log-In Banner," "Notifying Subjects of Existing Monitoring Systems," and "Dial-Up Connections Must Always Utilize Firewalls." A: T; E: LMH.

66. Notice Of Last Log-In Time And Date

Policy: At log-in time, every user must be given information reflecting the last log-in's time and date. This will allow unauthorized system usage to be easily detected.

Commentary: The intention of this policy is to provide the end-user with the information needed to determine whether his or her user-ID has been used by an unauthorized party. Although this policy has been written for technical staff, the policy could be easily expanded to be applicable to end-users. If this were done, words would be added requiring the user to think back to the last time he or she used the system, and then requiring the user to determine whether there has been unauthorized activity. Certain operating systems, like DEC VAX/VMS, provide capabilities such as this; with other platforms, additional software may be needed to support this functionality. This policy works best if accompanied by a policy requiring reporting of suspected information security problems and violations. See the policies entitled "Required Reporting Of Information Security Incidents" and "Dormant User-IDs And Automatic Privilege Revocations." A: T; E: MH.

67. Limitation On Number Of Daily Log-Ins Prevents Unauthorized Use

Policy: Log-in passwords are personal and must never be shared with other individuals. To prevent unauthorized system usage, users are not permitted to log-in more than ten times a day. Any user-ID which reaches this threshold will be automatically blocked until the next day, and if this high usage level continues, the user-ID will be subject to immediate cancellation.

Commentary: The objective of this policy is to detect, and to some extent, prevent unauthorized system usage. Especially relevant to information providers in the Internet commerce area, this policy could for example be used by a provider of sports scores. If more than ten log-ins with a particular user-ID occur in a single day, this situation shows that there is unauthorized password sharing (and consequentially unnecessary revenue loss). Note that there is nothing special about the number ten referenced in the policy; this could just as easily be five or some other number high enough to prevent authorized users from encountering it. The intention is to limit the number of log-ins and to generate some sort of a report of excessive log-ins so that they can be investigated (and the user-IDs perhaps cancelled). This control is generally applicable to customers rather than in-house users such as employees. Separately, when the number of log-ins exceeds a certain threshold, then an entry in a log can be made. For related ideas, see the policies entitled "Password Sharing Prohibition," "Notice Of Last Log-In Time And Date," and "Prohibition Of Multiple Simultaneous On-Line Sessions." A: T; E: LM.

68. Prohibition Of Multiple Simultaneous On-Line Sessions

Policy: Unless special permission has been granted by the system manager, computer systems must not allow any user to conduct multiple simultaneous on-line sessions.

Commentary: Only a very small percentage of users (systems programmers and developers ordinarily) require multiple simultaneous on-line sessions. Multiple simultaneous sessions are often indicative of unauthorized usage (such as a bunch of hackers all using the same user-ID). System activity logging and access control software can alert computer operations or computer security staff to the existence of such sessions. If users are prohibited from having multiple simultaneous sessions, then this security software will be able to do its job without inappropriately notifying computer operators, security administrators, and users. In some instances, the "need" for multiple simultaneous sessions is a reflection of inappropriately assigned access privileges. This policy can therefore force a reevaluation of privileges where appropriate. See the policy entitled "Restriction Of Special System Privileges." A: T; E: LMH.

69. Automatic Log-Off Process

Policy: If there has been no activity on a computer terminal, workstation, or microcomputer (PC) for ten (10) minutes, the system must automatically blank the screen and suspend the session. Re-establishment of the session must take place only after the user has provided the proper password.

Commentary: The intention of this policy is to prevent unauthorized disclosure of information and unauthorized system usage resulting from authorized workers walking away from their desks without logging-out. Particularly in open offices where there are no walls, many people leave their computers on and available for anyone who happens to walk by. Although most effective when it applies to all workstations, this policy could be restricted to systems containing or accessing sensitive, critical, or valuable information. In many instances, because automatic log-out functionality is not a part of the operating system, for microcomputers and workstations a software security package will be needed to implement this policy. Larger multi-user computer systems often provide a feature such as this as part of the operating system. Note that nothing in this policy requires that a user lose his or her work in progress (such as a word processing file); after the correct password has been provided, the work can resume. The number of minutes (10) is reasonable, but by no means cast in concrete. Sometimes controls of this nature go by the name "reapers" (as in the "grim reaper" that kills idle jobs). Lastly, where no automatic log-out software is available, organizations can adopt a policy requiring users to log-out when they leave their workstations. See the policy entitled "Leaving Sensitive Systems Without Logging-Off." A: T; E: LMH.

70. Leaving Sensitive Systems Without Logging-Off

Policy: If the computer system to which they are connected or which they are currently using contains sensitive information, users must not leave their microcomputer (PC), workstation, or terminal unattended without first logging-out or invoking a password-protected screen saver.

Commentary: Like the policy entitled "Automatic Log-Off Process," this policy seeks to prevent unauthorized disclosure of information as well as unauthorized use. Instead of mandating a period of no activity beyond which jobs will be automatically terminated, this policy puts the onus of responsibility on the user. This approach is generally less effective than the policy entitled "Automatic Log-Off Process," but it does clearly emphasize that users are responsible for the security of information in their possession. Organizations ideally should not use both of these approaches. Note that, in this policy, there is no acceptable period during which systems with sensitive or valuable information may be unattended. A word or two indicating a time-frame, such as "15 minutes," could be provided in the policy, but this is not advised because it will make it harder to change the system settings. On another note, the reference to "logging-out" could be expanded to include password-based microcomputer access control packages. Also see the policy entitled "Logging-Off Personal Computers Connected To Networks." A: EMT; E: LMH.

71. Logging-Off Personal Computers Connected To Networks

Policy: If personal computers (PCs) are connected to a network, when unattended they must always be logged-off.

Commentary: The objective of this policy is to make sure that users log-off when they leave their PC, provided the PC is connected to a network. The single word "network" was used instead of local area network (LAN), wide area network (WAN), dial-up telephone network, or other more restrictive terms. This policy is particularly important in those cases where PCs have modems but no access control systems, in which case anyone dialing-up these systems can gain access to the PCs (and perhaps a connected LAN or another network as well). Note that ideally, the task mentioned in the policy would not be left exclusively up to the user; ideally, the system would automatically log-off after a certain period of inactivity. Even with automatic log-off facilities, users should still log-off when they leave their PCs. This policy assumes that some access control software is in use on the personal computers. See the policies entitled "Leaving Sensitive Systems Without Logging-Off," "Modems On Workstations Connected To Internal Networks," "Access Control Packages Required For Computers On The Network," and "Automatic Log-Off Process." A: EMT; E: LMH.

1.1.2. Privilege Control

1.1.2.1. Use Of Systems

72. Games May Not Be Stored Or Used On Company X Computer Systems

Policy: Games may not be stored or used on any Company X computer systems.

Commentary: The objective of this policy is to clearly state that games must not be used on Company X systems. Games are often down-loaded from bulletin boards, and may accordingly be infected with computer viruses or Trojan horses. Likewise, games may distract employees from their assigned duties. Games may additionally set an inappropriately playful and informal atmosphere that some organizations see as unbusinesslike. Because games are often duplicated and distributed illegally, games may also inadvertently subject an organization to liability for unauthorized software copying. Since most games reside on personal computers (PCs), workstations, and other small systems, this policy is particularly relevant to the small systems environment. Some conservative organizations will want to expand the scope of the policy to include public domain software (aka "freeware" or "shareware"); public domain software is similarly likely to contain viruses, Trojan horses, as well as other undesirable and unauthorized functionality. This policy may be enforced automatically via the new generation of software license managers, which prevent execution of software that has not first been approved by management. Some organizations claim that playing games helps people get over "computer phobia," but since computers are nearly everywhere in modern organizations, this is no longer as much of a concern as it used to be. For organizations such as these, words like "unless used for an authorized training effort" could be added to the policy. Separately, a new breed of products such as GameCop from Analytic Concepts of San Jose, California, can be used to set off an alarm when an employee plays a game during business hours. See the policies entitled "Personal Use Of Computer And Communications Systems" and "When Making Additional Copies Of Software Is Permissible." A: EMT; E: LMH.

73. Personal Use Of Computer And Communications Systems

Policy: Company X computer and communications systems must be used for business purposes only. Personal use is allowed only by special permission of a department manager.

Commentary: The intention of this policy is to provide clear guidance regarding personal use of computer and communication systems. Without such notice, an employee could, for instance, be covertly running his or her own computer service bureau using the employer's resources. Another may be using these system resources to run betting pools. Others may simply be amusing themselves with computer games, or making excessive long-distance personal phone calls. When confronted about such activity, they may say that they understood it was permissible, or that it was a fringe benefit. As a variation on the standard approach described in this policy, some organizations allow personal use if it's strictly personal (e.g., Christmas cards). With this variation, if the use is to support another business, such as selling insurance as a second job, then such use is prohibited. Other organizations permit personal usage during off-peak hours or during staff non-working hours. Whatever philosophy your organization adopts, it is wise to provide a precise definition of the term "personal use." This definition needs to address situations such as computer programming homework assignments for a course taken at a local university -- intended to augment the skills used on this employee's regular job (is this personal use or not?). Note that this policy applies to in-house staff rather than those who subscribe to a computer service bureau, run an outsourcing computer center, etc. Separately, in the policy, the person to provide approval is a department manager (perhaps a VP) instead of an information owner because this policy relates to an employee's use of systems rather than information. Unless special monitoring software is used, this policy may be difficult to police because mobile phones, portable computers, and related equipment is often used "in the field" away from management's eyes. That is not to say that the policy should be abandoned -- in fact the policy may become increasingly important as a way for an organization to prevent liability for unauthorized activity performed with its systems. Another good reason to adopt this strict policy is that it may prevent the use of electronic mail and other communication systems for union organizing. For a related idea, see the policy entitled "Use Of Company X Information For Non-Business Purposes." Also see the policies entitled "Use Of Telephones For Personal Purposes," "Personal Use Of Electronic Mail Systems," "Internet Use For Personal Purposes Prohibited," and "Games May Not Be Stored Or Used On Company X Computer Systems." A: EMT; E: LMH.

74. Incidental Personal Use Of Business Systems Permissible

Policy: Company X information systems are provided for, and must be used only for business purposes. Incidental personal use is permissible if the use: (a) does not consume more than a trivial amount of resources that could otherwise be used for business purposes, (b) does not interfere with worker productivity, and (c) does not preempt any business activity. Permissible incidental use of an electronic mail system would, for example, involve sending a message to schedule a luncheon.

Commentary: The intention of this policy is to be clear about personal use of business information systems such as telephone systems, electronic mail systems, Internet access dial-up systems, and the like. This policy is noteworthy because it describes prevailing practice at many organizations in a truthful way. This policy should be compared with many existing personal use policies which are excessively rigid. For example, the policy entitled "Personal Use of Computer and Communications Systems" would prohibit a worker from making a personal call to a baby-sitter to arrange a time to pick up a child; this could be counterproductive when the worker needs to make new arrangements so that he/she can stay overtime. The restrictions mentioned in this policy about incidental use allow personal usage so long as the stated conditions are met. This approach puts the onus of responsibility back on employees rather than on management. In reality, there is simply too much going on for management to be looking over every employee's shoulder (unless this process is automated, and then a several new problems like privacy invasion come up). For related ideas, also see the policies entitled "Use Of Telephones For Personal Purposes" and "Games May Not Be Stored Or Used On Company X Computer Systems." A: EMT; E: LMH.

75. Reasonable Personal Use Consistent With Conventional Ethical Standards

Policy: Company X allows computer users to make reasonable personal use of its electronic mail and other computer and communications systems. All such personal use must be consistent with conventional standards of ethical and polite conduct. For example, electronic mail must not be used to distribute or display messages or graphics which may be considered by some to be disruptive or offensive (such as sexual jokes or pornography).

Commentary: The intention of this policy is to clarify what constitutes acceptable personal use of Company X information systems, especially electronic mail (which has been widely abused in recent years). The policy is deliberately flexible in nature, and it need not be adjusted much, if at all, as "conventional standards of ethical and polite conduct" change. For example, flaming (the transmission of unrestrained and heated insults) is becoming less of a problem on the Internet and this change is a reflection of an evolving standard of conduct. Separately, the word "reasonable" was used to allow managers to have confidential talks with workers about their personal usage of system resources, which then hopefully will encourage these workers to spend more time on business matters and less time on personal matters. On another note, this policy works best if supplemented with controls which measure or block certain types of personal use. For example, a firewall can be used to block pornographic sites on the web. Likewise a content filter can be used to make a log of inbound graphics files which appear to be pornographic in nature. For related ideas, see the policies entitled "Personal Use Of Computer And Communications Systems" and "Incidental Personal Use Of Business Systems Permissible." A: EM; E: LMH.

76. Prohibition Against Non-Approved System Uses

Policy: Subscribers to Company X computing and communications services must not use these facilities for soliciting business, selling products, or otherwise engaging in commercial activities other than those expressly permitted by Company X management.

Commentary: The intention of this policy is to strictly limit the authorized uses of the computer and communications services provided by Company X. Unlike the policy entitled "Personal Use of Computer and Communications Systems," this policy applies to those who pay to use Company X's facilities. This policy is relevant to an electronic bulletin board (EBB), a computer service bureau, a value added network (VAN), an Internet service provider (ISP), an Internet information content provider, and similar firms. Many organizations are uneasy about the establishment of value-added products and services on top of their basic computer and communications services, and at the very least require that such value-added products and services be approved in advance. With recent abuses involving broadcast electronic mail solicitations on the Internet (alias "spamming"), a policy like this is becoming increasingly important. Some organizations may want to add a clause to this policy which prohibits charitable, political, religious, and other activities which are not directly business-related. Some organizations may find this policy especially helpful when denying future services to a user/subscriber. Also see the policy entitled "Personal Use Of Electronic Mail Systems." A: EMT; E: LMH.

77. Internet Use For Personal Purposes Prohibited

Policy: Use of Company X information systems to access the Internet for personal purposes will not be tolerated and may be considered cause for disciplinary action up to and including termination. All users of the Internet should be aware that firewalls can create a detailed audit log reflecting transmissions, both in-bound and out-bound.

Commentary: This strict policy about Internet access makes it clear that workers should not be using Company X facilities to access the Internet. Note that nothing in the policy prohibits workers from cruising the Internet on their own time, using their own systems. A policy such as this is often adopted by management out of frustration with the inordinate amount of time that workers spend on the Internet; it is thus primarily a productivity-enhancement policy. The policy also helps to reduce the incidence of unauthorized representations of Company X on the Internet; this is achieved by clearly separating work-related and personal uses of the Internet. This policy may be viewed as too strict for some organizations; they may wish to drop the second sentence which may seem a bit threatening. Other options include personal use of the Internet only after explicit management approval, or use only in response to an approved business purpose. Some firms may wish to give examples of prohibited personal use; these include operating an outside business, searching for jobs outside Company X, sending chain letters, and soliciting contributions for religious or political causes. See the policies entitled "Prohibition Against Non-Approved System Uses," "Personal Use Of Computer And Communications Systems," and "Use Of Telephones For Personal Purposes." A: E; E: LMH.

78. Personal Use Of Company X Internet Facilities Only On Personal Time

Policy: Company X management encourages workers to explore the Internet, but if this exploration is for personal purposes, it must be done on personal, not company time. Likewise, news feeds, discussion groups, games, and other activities which cannot definitively be linked to an individual's job duties must be performed on personal, not company time.
Commentary: The purpose of this policy is to make sure employees know that they should not be "surfing the 'net" during work hours. With good reason, some managers are concerned that the availability of Internet access will distract workers from their regular duties. This permissive policy allows users to take advantage of Company X facilities for personal purposes, but makes it clear when such use must take place. The policy writer should also consider deployment of a number of new monitoring products allow management to determine the nature of Internet usage, and then to determine whether this usage is consistent with in-house policy. Whether or not these products are used, a policy such as this puts a throttle on what could become a significant productivity issue. This policy recognizes that, at many organizations, personal Internet use is already recognized as a fringe benefit. The policy assumes that personal use will help workers become more proficient with Internet, and that this in turn will indirectly assist with business uses of the Internet. Separately, those organizations wanting to take a stricter approach may forbid all personal Internet use during business hours (the policy shown here implicitly allows personal use during breaks and lunch). For related ideas, see the policies entitled "Users

Responsible For All Activities Involving Personal User-IDs" and "Personal Use Of Computer And Communications Systems." A: E; E: LMH.

79. Personal Use Time Limit And Prohibited Activities

Policy: Incidental personal use of Company X computer and communication systems is permissible as long as this use is restricted to an hour or less per month. Such personal use must not include creation or distribution of chain letters, exchanging information which might be considered indecent, receipt or forwarding of jokes, moonlighting or searching for another job, participation in gambling activities, or engagement in political or charitable activities.

Commentary: This policy is intended to make it clear exactly what is expected in terms of personal use. A specific time limit on personal use is coupled with a list of prohibited activities to clarify expectations. Such a policy can be especially useful when disciplinary actions are taken in response to certain unauthorized usage. Some organizations may wish to extend the list in the second sentence to include issuance of solicitations or advertisements, as well as receiving messages from electronic mailing lists (listservs) that are not related to Company X business. The last item in the policy's second sentence ("charitable activities") may be too restrictive for those organizations which each year are directly supportive of certain charities such as the United Way. Separately, there is nothing sacrosanct about the one hour limit -- it could just as easily be thirty minutes. For related ideas, see the policy entitled "Internet Use For Personal Purposes Prohibited." A: E; E: LMH.

80. Permissible Uses Of Company X Information

Policy: Company X information must be used only for the business purposes expressly authorized by management.

Commentary: The intention of this policy is to state specifically that all non-approved uses of Company X information are prohibited. For example, an employee may want to use his employer's database of customers for a charitable mass mailing (direct mail campaign). The policy may apply across the board, or only be written on the label for storage media containing specific information likely to be abused (such as a customer mailing list). To prevent secondary dissemination problems, marking sensitive information is highly advised. Secondary dissemination problems typically involve passing information to a third party, who does not know about restrictions on the use of information, and who then goes on to do something inconsistent with these restrictions. The policy is relevant to all workers coming into contact with Company X information. Note that, in this policy, the focus is on use of the information rather than the systems which handle this information. Such a policy is appropriately augmented by a data classification policy such as the one entitled "Four Category Data Classification Scheme." Also see the policies entitled "Use Of Company X Information For Non-Business Purposes" and "Specific Handling Instructions For Recipients Of Sensitive Information." A: EMT; E: LMH.

81. Granting User-IDs To Outsiders

Policy: Individuals who are not employees, contractors, or consultants must not be granted a user-ID or otherwise be given privileges to use Company X computers or communications systems unless the written approval of a department head has first been obtained.

Commentary: The intention behind this policy is to make sure that unauthorized outsiders are not using Company X resources without specific management knowledge and permission. For example, although a disciplinary action is warranted as a result, it often happens that a technical computer staff member gives his or her friends user-IDs on an employer's system. This policy is also intended to make sure that outsiders like customers and utility service providers (e.g., telephone company employees) are kept off Company X systems unless specific management permission is obtained. Rather than approval of a department head, the approval could be granted by the Manager of Information Security or another manager with responsibility for organization-wide systems. Some organizations use a slight variation of this policy where a manager must "sponsor" (take responsibility for the actions of) an outsider prior to the issuance of any user-ID. Separately, note that the word "temporary" does not appear in the policy along with the words "employees, contractors, or consultants;" this is because temporaries are often hired with a neglible amount of background checking. Temporaries could be added to the policy, if the policy writer so desires. Also see the policies entitled "User-ID & Password Required For Computer-Connected Network Access," "Unique User-ID And Password Required," "Signed Forms Required For Issuance Of User-ID," and "Periodic Review And Reauthorization Of User Access Privileges." A: MT; E: LMH.

82. Third Party Access To Company X Systems Requires Signed Contract

Policy: Before any third party is given access to Company X systems, a contract defining the terms and conditions of such access must have been signed by a responsible manager at the third party organization. These terms and conditions must also be approved by both the Information Security Manager and the Law Department Vice President.

Commentary: In many organizations, outsourcing firms, consultants, contractors, and other third parties are given access to internal systems as if they were trusted insiders. This can lead to serious breaches of security, especially if the third party's systems are inadequately protected (an intruder may use the third party's systems as a conduit). This policy is intended put all internal staff on notice that third party access is a serious security issue, and that in all instances, it must be supported by a written and approved contract. After the internal managers who must approve such contracts have gone through this process several times, they will develop a checklist of criteria that must go along with each such contract. This checklist can be used to develop a pro-forma contract that can be used with all outsiders seeking access to internal information systems. The contract ordinarily would cover things such as: a non-disclosure agreement (NDA), a description of the specific control measures which must be used for Company X data, clarification of the responses that must be taken after a breach of security, and assignment of liability for any problems that occur. Also see the policies entitled "Unbecoming Conduct And The Revocation Of Access Privileges" and "Periodic Review And Reauthorization Of User Access Privileges." A: MT; E: LMH.

83. When Established, Outsider User-IDs Must Have Defined Expiration Date

Policy: Every user-ID established for a non-employee must have a specified expiration date. If the systems administrator setting-up such a user-ID is not provided with an expiration date, then thirty days will be used as a default.

Commentary: The intention of this policy is to make sure that user-IDs employed by outsiders do not continue to be activated long after these individuals have ceased to do any work for Company X. Without an expiration date, many of these user-IDs will remain enabled for a long period of time, especially at those organizations where the notification process about third party worker departures is informal or non-existent. By terminating these user-IDs promptly, the risk of unauthorized use, industrial espionage, sabotage, and other abuses is reduced. This policy will also help keep system response time high (because there will be fewer users) and disk space requirements low (because fewer files will be stored on the system). For related considerations, see the polices entitled "Dormant User-IDs And Automatic Privilege Revocations" and "Handling Involuntary Terminations Of Computer Workers." A: T; E: LMH.

84. Information Systems Access Privileges Terminate When Workers Leave

Policy: All Company X information systems privileges must be promptly terminated at the time that a worker ceases to provide services to Company X.

Commentary: The intention of this policy is to instruct systems administrators, network managers, and others in similar positions that they must promptly revoke the privileges of workers who are no longer employed by Company X. Often these boring administrative matters are ignored in favor of more pressing and interesting things. In some cases, system privileges are maintained as a courtesy to a worker who may not have access to electronic mail or Internet facilities. Whatever the reason, if privileges are not promptly terminated, former workers may be permitted to commit sabotage, industrial espionage, and other undesirable acts. Separately, some organizations may wish to qualify this policy, allowing the forwarding of electronic mail for a certain time after a worker stops work for Company X. On another note, this policy encourages the development of an in-house system to communicate changes in worker employment status to the systems administrators and others who must alter system privileges. For a related idea, see the policy entitled "Reporting Changes In User Duties To Systems Security Administration." A: T; E: LMH.

85. Time Limits For User-IDs And File Retention Period After Expiration

Policy: All user-IDs for multi-user systems at Company X have a time limit associated with them. To get user-IDs re-enabled, users must request authorization for an extension from their managers. For the month before their time limit expires, users will be sent weekly email notices reminding them about the need for re-authorization. If no re-enabling action is taken, these user-IDs will be disabled and the related files retained for a two week period thereafter.

Commentary: The intention of this policy is to define an organization's approach to authorizing and granting system privileges. This approach is particularly relevant to a university or any other organization with people coming in-and-out who have relatively uniform time periods for a relationship with the organization (students have semesters, faculty have academic years, etc.). Other organizations can certainly still use the policy even if they don't employ relationship time periods which are so concretely defined. The policy helps to automatically revoke privileges associated with dormant user-IDs, so that these user-IDs cannot be used by hackers or other unauthorized persons. The policy also forces managers to periodically examine the privileges that each user has, and to determine whether these same privileges should be renewed, or perhaps renewed but changed. Also note that the policy is written in such a way that systems administrators can define different time periods for different classes of users. Separately, the notice about a two week file retention period informs users that they need to make their own back-ups to preserve their data after their relationship with the organization has terminated. The two week clause additionally helps to conserve valuable disk space. For related ideas, see the policies entitled "Expiration Of User-IDs On Internet Accessible Computers" and "Periodic Review And Reauthorization Of User Access Privileges." A: E; E: LMH.

86. Disclaimer Of Responsibility For Damage To Data And Programs

Policy: Company X uses access controls and other security measures to protect the confidentiality, integrity, and availability of the information handled by computers and communications systems. In keeping with these objectives, management maintains the authority to: (1) restrict or revoke any user's privileges, (2) inspect, copy, remove, or otherwise alter any data, program, or other system resource that may undermine these objectives, and (3) take any other steps deemed necessary to manage and protect its information systems. This authority may be exercised with or without notice to the involved users. Company X disclaims any responsibility for loss or damage to data or software that results from its efforts to meet these security objectives.

Commentary: This policy is intended to define the privileges that systems administrators have as delegates of management. Rather legalistic in nature, it seeks to put users on notice that they cannot hold Company X liable for damages associated with management's attempts to secure its system. For example, if a systems administrator was performing a routine virus scan of all PCs on a LAN, he or she may detect what appears to be a virus. A virus eradication program may then be executed; this may alter the infected program rendering it useable. When the involved user determines that this program is inoperative, he cannot hold management responsible for damaging it. Thus, in an indirect way, this policy implies that users must make their own backups. Separately, this policy is best if Company X has facilities used by non-employees, as would for example be the case at a university that had student users. For related ideas, see the policies entitled "Restriction Of Special System Privileges" and "Disclaimer Of Responsibility Or Liability For Message Contents." A: E; E: LMH.

87. Gaining Unauthorized Access Via Company X Information Systems

Policy: Workers using Company X information systems are prohibited from gaining unauthorized access to any other information systems or in any way damaging, altering, or disrupting the operations of these systems. Likewise, workers are prohibited from capturing or otherwise obtaining passwords, encryption keys, or any other access control mechanism which could permit unauthorized access.

Commentary: The intention of this policy is to clearly establish management's position forbidding hacking (also called cracking) activities via Company X information systems. A policy of this nature is particularly desirable in those jurisdictions where hacking is not clearly illegal -- a situation which still prevails in a number of countries. The policy is also needed in academia, where hacking is often seen as justifiable in the name of discovering new information. The policy is written in such a way that it applies to both internal and also external information systems. The policy embraces a wide variety of hacker techniques, including social engineering (where a hacker masquerades as someone else), and password grabbers (which record passwords via wiretap like mechanisms). On a related note, the words "access control mechanism" are deliberately vague so as to include smart cards, dynamic password tokens, and the like. Separately, this policy can be used to discipline, and perhaps terminate, a worker who was hacking via Company X information systems; this is desirable if the organization wishes to keep the activity quiet (thus avoiding public relations problems, potential stockholder lawsuits, and the like). For related ideas, see the policies entitled "Prohibition Against Testing Information System Controls" and "Tools Used To Break Systems Security Prohibited." A: ET; E: LMH.

1.1.2.2. Information Driven Access Control

88. Where To Use Computer System Access Controls

Policy: All computer-resident information which is sensitive, critical, or valuable must have system access controls to ensure that it is not improperly disclosed, modified, deleted, or rendered unavailable.

Commentary: The intention of this policy is to require that the information which needs it will indeed be properly protected. Ideally, security measures are designed in a consistent manner, such that information is properly protected wherever it travels, whoever handles it, whatever technology is employed, and whatever form it takes. This policy mandates the use of access controls to support that notion. The policy assumes that a data classification system has been adopted (see the policy entitled "Four Category Data Classification Scheme"). Thus the words "sensitive," "critical," and "valuable" need to be specifically defined by management before this policy can be practically applied. It is also a good idea to define "system access controls" (perhaps secret passwords and user-IDs, perhaps smart cards, etc.). Although many personal computer operating systems (such as earlier versions of Microsoft's Windows) do not include access controls, most multi-user operating systems and network operating systems do include the type of access controls required by this policy. For those systems lacking native software to support access control, supplementary software packages may be required. This policy is also relevant to client/server systems, mobile computing systems, personal digital assistants (PDAs), and the like. Very small remote systems, such as alphanumeric pagers, may not be able to support the desired access control, in which case the organization in question must decide whether it will accept the risk, or prohibit the handling of such information on these systems. See the policy entitled "Four Category Data Classification Scheme." For related systems-design ideas, consider the policies entitled "Keeping Security Functionality Out of Business Applications" and "Systems Architecture For Logging Activities." A: T; E: LMH.

89. Personal Digital Assistant Use For Corporate Business Information

Policy: Personal Digital Assistants (PDAs), handheld computers, and smart phones must not be used for Company X business information unless they have first been configured with the necessary controls and approved for such use by the Information Systems Department. Exceptions will be made for calendars, address books, and stored connection information such as telephone numbers.

Commentary: This policy deals with a classic trade-off between ease-of-use and security. The new devices mentioned in this policy may be convenient and useful, but they may also unduly expose Company X information to unauthorized disclosure. Without guidance, users will most often opt for ease-of-use over security, and this policy seeks to prevent that decision. On another note, the policy acknowledges that these devices, as delivered by the vendor (with modification or enhancement) are often low budget models lacking security measures. For example, analog cellular phones still don't include encryption as a standard feature (this is available optionally). On yet another note, this policy acknowledges that Palm Pilots from Palm Computing (a 3Ccom company) are proliferating amongst the technological intelligentsia. To date, most of these and other small systems have been used simply as sophisticated calendars and address books. But the imminent introduction of wireless capabilities will radically change the way these small computers are used. It will soon be easy to send and receive electronic mail and to do limited web surfing. This time, encrypted communications for the wireless transmissions will be available, but still many users may not choose to use it. That's why approval by the Information Systems or Information Security Department is necessary. So this policy does not prohibit the use of these new systems, it only makes sure that they are adequately secured for use with business information. While an employer may not have jurisdiction over an individual's personal property such as a PDA, it does have the right to assert boundaries to its own information (and information entrusted to it by third parties). For a related idea, see the policy entitled "Use Of Cordless Or Cellular Telephones For Secret Discussions." A: E; E: MH.

90. No Sensitive Information On Personal Digital Assistants, Handhelds, Etc.

Policy: The security mechanisms available on Personal Digital Assistants (PDAs), handheld computers, smart phones, and similar small portable computers have not yet been shown to be effective and reliable. Accordingly, workers must refrain from using these computers with sensitive Company X information.

Commentary: The objective of this policy is to prohibit the use of small portable computers for sensitive Company X information in an effort to prevent this sensitive information from falling into the wrong hands (unauthorized disclosure). This might happen simply by the theft or loss of one of these devices. This might also happen because a user does not know how to properly operate security mechanisms on one of these small computers. This policy accordingly takes a conservative stance saying "don't use these small portable computers for sensitive information." The policy assumes that the term "sensitive information" has already been defined through a data classification scheme. If this is not the case, then the policy could be modified to prohibit these small computers from handling any Company X information (although that may adversely degrade worker productivity). For related ideas, see the policies entitled "All Workstations Must Have Password-Based Boot Protection," "Storing Secret Information On Transportable Computers," and "Never Lend Computers Containing Sensitive Information To Others." A: E; E: MH.

91. All Software Must Be Regulated By Access Control Systems Software

Policy: All software installed on Company X multi-user systems must be regulated by approved access control systems software. This means that a user's session must initially be controlled by approved access control systems software, and if defined permissions then allow it, control will then be passed to separate application software.

Commentary: This policy attempts to prevent the installation of software which cannot be regulated by an access control system (such as IBM's RACF in the MVS mainframe environment). Note that the "access control systems software" need not be an operating system; it could be an add-on access control package or even a front-end or firewall that performs access control. This policy is less necessary with new operating systems such as Microsoft's Windows NT because all requests for service are automatically mediated via the operating system's access control mechanisms. Older operating systems, however, such as IBM's VM and MVS, are in need of a policy such as this. The policy is not operating system specific -- it applies to all operating systems. Separately, this policy indirectly prohibits programmers from installing trap doors and other software that could circumvent an access control system. On another note, this policy would ordinarily be delivered only to systems programmers, systems administrators, and related technical support staff. Also see the policies entitled "Default To Denial Of Access Control Privileges" and "Reliance On Operating System User Authentication Process." A: T; E: LMH.

92. Systems Requiring Password-Based Access Control Package

Policy: If a small system (PC, LAN, etc.) handles either critical or confidential information, the system must also utilize a properly maintained version of an approved password-based access control system.

Commentary: The intention of this policy is to provide managers of small systems with a specific rule-of-thumb which can be used to determine whether they should employ a password-based access control system. Those systems which do not contain either critical or confidential information are, by default, not required to have access control systems. An example of such an access control system is the package called PC/DACs offered by Mergent International (Rocky Hill, Connecticut, USA). The words "properly maintained" were included in the policy to signify that the simple installation of a package is not sufficient. In some cases, the package may be installed, but it may not be used to protect either confidential or critical files. This policy assumes the words "confidential" and "critical" have already been defined; for further information about these distinctions, see the policy entitled "Four Category Data Classification Scheme." In some cases, the policy writer may also wish to use the word "valuable" in the policy. Also see the policies entitled "Access Control Packages Required For Computers On The Network" and "Physical Access Control For Areas Containing Sensitive Information." A: MT; E: LMH.

93. Privilege Restriction Based On The Need-To-Know

Policy: The computer and communications system privileges of all users, systems, and programs must be restricted based on the need-to-know.

Commentary: The intention of this policy is to prevent the granting of excessive privileges to users. Excessive privileges often allow users to perform abusive and unauthorized acts, such as viewing private information belonging to other users. Excessive privileges may also allow users to commit errors which have serious consequences, such as bringing a communications server down during business hours. Borrowed from the military, the need-to-know approach is a fundamental idea underlying nearly all commercial access control systems. The approach defined in this policy is significantly enhanced via a data classification scheme such as the one described in the policy entitled "Four Category Data Classification Scheme." Separately, this policy could be rewritten so that it focuses on information itself rather than systems; thus access to information would be granted only where a need-to-know exists. Likewise the term "need-to-know" could be replaced with similar but more general terminology such as "legitimate business need" or "demonstrable business need." See the policies entitled "Restriction of Special System Privileges" and "Process for Granting Access to Company X Information." For a different perspective on this topic involving information about information, see the policy entitled "Nature And Location Of Company X Information Is Confidential." Also see the policies entitled "Privilege Restriction Based On The Need-To-Withhold" and "Approval Required Before Access To Sensitive Or Valuable Information." A: MT; E: LMH.

94. Privilege Restriction Based On The Need-To-Withhold

Policy: Access to Company X computer and communications systems will be granted by default to all employees unless the manager controlling a specific system has specifically defined access control rules.

Commentary: This policy takes just the opposite approach from the policy entitled "Privilege Restriction Based On The Need-To-Know." The intention of this policy is to open up access to internal system resources to all employees, hopefully encouraging and motivating employees to better perform their jobs. While it may cause heartburn for information security specialists, this approach has received considerable attention from modern management experts. Rather than calling it a need-to-withhold approach to access control, these management experts often call it "open book management." This approach has been heralded as a way to facilitate faster and more efficient information flows within an organization, and has been adopted by some progressive companies such as Hewlett-Packard. Note that with the need-to-withhold approach, responsibility is shifted from users who must demonstrate a need for access (as is the case with the traditional need-to-know approach), to management who must demonstrate a need to restrict access. As a middle ground, some information security experts advocate use of the need-to-know for sensitive information, but need-to-withhold for non-sensitive information. The need-to-withhold approach is less expensive than the need-to-know approach because it can be implemented with fewer decisions about access permissions. As attractive as it may seem, the need-to-withhold approach suffers from a serious problem: if managers have not yet gotten around to defining necessary access control rules, then internal information systems could be left in a vulnerable and dangerously open state. Separately, notice that contractors, temporaries, and consultants are not mentioned in the policy -- these people do not receive default access. For related ideas, see the policies entitled "Nature And Location Of Company X Information Is

Confidential" and "Approval Required Before Access To Sensitive Or Valuable Information." A: MT; E: LMH.

95. Specific Information Access Policies Must Be Prepared

Policy: Designated information owners must establish specific written policies regarding the categories of people who will be granted permission to access information for which they are responsible. These policies must also specify limitations on the use of this information by those to whom access has been granted.

Commentary: This policy puts information owners on notice that they must take the time to specify who will, and who will not be able to gain access to information for which they have been designated the decision-maker. A specification of these access rights is a necessary precursor to implementing either a password-based access control package (like IBM's RACF) or the native access control facilities found in many operating systems (like Microsoft's NT). If an access control package implementation is attempted without first having decided what the rules will be, confusion inevitably results. The intention of this policy is thus to put management and technical staff on notice that such policies about information access must be not only specified, but also put in writing. If these policies are in writing, they will then also be auditable. This policy is effectively a high-level policy which sets the stage for more specific access control policies. Also see the policies entitled "Information Ownership Must Be Assigned" and "Granting System Privileges By Chain Of Authority Delegation." A: MT; E: LMH.

96. Information Ownership Must Be Assigned

Policy: The Chief Information Officer (CIO) must clearly specify in writing the assignment of information ownership responsibilities for databases, master files, and other shared collections of information. The CIO is also responsible for designating the individuals who will maintain access rights to these information collections on behalf of the owners.

Commentary: The intention of this policy is to establish a clear and documented delegation of information-access-control-related authority. A clear definition of delegated authorities is also very useful when determining access control permissions. Another intention of this policy is to clarify who is responsible for security and related matters for shared information resources such as a database. So often information security activities "fall between the cracks" (get forgotten) when several people are potentially responsible but no one has been explicitly assigned responsibility. This policy may also be helpful within organizations that rely on database management systems (DBMSs) and application programs to enforce access controls; often it is not clear that database administrators (DBAs) and technical systems support personnel are responsible for administering system access controls. The process of designating who is responsible for access control will also highlight those situations where nobody has been specifically designated as responsible, and hopefully this will then quickly be changed. See the policies dealing with owners, custodians, and users below, such as the policies entitled "Criteria For Assigning Information Ownership" and "Transfer Of Information Custodian Duties After Employee Terminations." A: M; E: LMH.

97. No Read Up Permissions To Access Sensitive Information

Policy: Workers who have been authorized to view information classified at a certain sensitivity level must be permitted to access only the information at this level and at less sensitive levels.

Commentary: The intention of this policy is explicitly instruct system administrators and others who set access control privileges, so as to prevent users from gaining unauthorized access to information. For example, if a person has been authorized to view secret information, he or she may also view confidential and public information because these are less sensitive than secret information. This person, however, may not view top secret information unless specific authorization has been granted. This approach is sometimes called "read down" or "no read up" because the user is only given permission to read at his or her classification level and those levels down (progressively getting less sensitive). This policy applies to all levels of data, no matter how many levels there are in a classification system. For example, if a user has only permission to read "unclassified" data (the least sensitive level), then he or she could not access any other levels. Conversely, if an individual had access to the highest level of data (perhaps this is termed "top secret" in the environment in question), then all other levels could be accessed by this individual. This idea is a part of the formal information security access control model called the "Bell-La Padula model." This policy is most often seen in military and diplomatic organizations, while commercial organizations often use less complex models. Unfortunately, a large number of commercial operating systems do not support this policy; additional software is required for policy implementation. Additional discussion of this policy can be found in the US Department of Defense's "Orange Book," also known as "Department Of Defense Trusted Computer System Evaluation Criteria." See the policies dealing with data classification such as the policy entitled "Four Category Data Classification Scheme." A: EMT; E: H.

98. No Write Down Permissions To Access Sensitive Information

Policy: Workers must not move information classified at a certain sensitivity level to a less sensitive level unless this action is a formal part of an approved declassification process.

Commentary: This policy is intended to prohibit users from moving data from one classification level to another so as to be able to gain unauthorized access to it. For instance, if an individual could copy "top secret" information and then write it to a "confidential" (less sensitive) file, he or she may be able to give access to another who is not otherwise authorized to view the information. The process of "writing [information] down" to a less sensitive classification level can also be considered to be effectively declassifying the information so that it may then be accessed by unauthorized parties. Some organizations may wish to add words to this policy describing the ways that users will know that a declassification process is approved (by who, when, etc.). Sometimes called the star property (*-property), this idea is a part of the formal information security access control model called the "Bell-La Padula model." This policy is most often seen in systems for military and diplomatic organizations rather than in commercial organizations. The policy can be enforced automatically, although most commercial operating systems do not support it -- additional software is required for implementation. Additional discussion of this policy can be found in the US Department of Defense's "Orange Book," also known as "Department Of Defense Trusted Computer System Evaluation Criteria." See the policies dealing with data classification such as the policy entitled "Four Category Data Classification Scheme." A: EMT; E: H.

99. Age Verification Required Prior To Adult Material Access

Policy: Prior to providing access to any material which the general public would consider inappropriate for children, all Company X systems must employ an age verification access control system approved by the Information Security Department.

Commentary: This policy is intended to put technical staff on notice about the circumstances where a special type of access control system is required. This access control system is not the usual type, which could for example involve dynamic or fixed passwords, but one which verifies a user's age. This could involve simply clicking on a button stating that a user affirms that they are at least a certain age (such as 18 years old). This could also involve collection of a legitimate credit card number, which could be confirmed on-line, as a surrogate for being an adult. The ability to provide a legitimate driver's license number can also be used as a mechanism to verify age. As these examples indicate, the technology behind the age verification process is crude; it is for this reason that the policy deliberately avoids reference to a specific technical solution. Separately, this policy is prompted by the exploding use of the Internet, and the access to "adult material" which children are gaining over the Internet. The policy is also motivated by the Child Online Protection Act (COPA), passed by the United States Congress in 1998. The existence of this policy can serve as evidence of management's intention to restrict access to certain materials to adults only, and to be in compliance with this and similar laws. Note that this policy is not limited to sexually explicit materials; it may also pertain to violent materials, ethically questionable materials, and the like. For this reason, the words "sexually explicit" were not used in the policy. For related ideas, see the policies entitled "Childrens' Personal Information Gathering Needs Parental Consent" and "Commingling Of Sensitive And Non-Sensitive Information." A: T; E: LMH.

1.1.2.3. User Separation

100. User-To-User Separation Of Activities And Data

Policy: Management must define user privileges such that ordinary users cannot gain access to, or otherwise interfere with, either the individual activities or the private data of other users.

Commentary: This policy prevents system managers from establishing the access controls on multi-user systems so that users can do damage to the files of other users, look at the work of other users, or otherwise exceed the privileges they need in order to do their own work. Much of this type of damage is often unintentional, as might be wrought by a program written by one user which alters the data belonging to another user. Implicitly this policy prohibits sharing of a single user-ID as well as the use of "lockwords" (passwords which are known and used by several people). The policy also assumes separate logical workspaces (rather than physical workspaces) for each user, an assumption which may not apply to groupware or certain virtual reality systems. Nothing in this policy prohibits the use of public directories for shared files, a restricted number of simultaneous execution software licenses that are shared, and other facilities to share resources as are commonly found on local area network servers. See the policy entitled "Privilege Restriction Based On The Need-to-Know." Also see the policy entitled "Separation Of Duties And Control Over Company X Assets." A: MT; E: LMH.

101. Default File Permissions For Networked Systems

Policy: File access control permissions for all Company X networked systems must be set to a default which blocks access by unauthorized users.

Commentary: This policy is intended to provide both users and systems administrators with guidance in the establishment appropriate access controls for networked systems. Systems which are not networked are not in such great need for logical access controls such as file permissions -- they can instead rely on physical security measures like a locked office door. All too often staff members decide on their own that logical access controls are too time consuming and resource intensive. This policy prohibits staff from making decisions like this which may not be in the organization's best long-run interests. The policy may also be helpful in those cases where local management does not want to spend the money to define access controls; the policy requires them to support technical staff who perform these tasks. For related ideas, see the policies entitled "Default User Privileges And Need For Explicit Written Approvals," "Default To Denial Of Access Control Privileges," and "Privilege Restriction Based On The Need-To-Know." A: ET; E: MH.

102. Existence Of User Access Capabilities Does Not Imply Usage Permission

Policy: Users must not read, modify, delete, or copy a file belonging to another user without first obtaining permission from the owner of the file. Unless general user access is clearly provided, the ability to read, modify, delete, or copy a file belonging to another user does not imply permission to actually perform these activities.

Commentary: The intention of this policy is to define appropriate boundaries around the files maintained by personal computer (PC) users, who often have no file access controls whatsoever. No mention of micros and PCs was made in the policy because the policy could conceivably also apply to larger systems. For larger systems, whenever access controls are deficient, or when a "hole" in the existing access controls has been discovered, this policy would apply. The policy essentially says "Just because you can do it, doesn't mean that you are allowed to do it." The policy makes reference to information owners, which ideally would make decisions about access to certain types of information. Nonetheless, for many types of information, the owner is by default the user on whose PC the information resides. Accordingly, some organizations may wish to change this policy so that it refers to the user of a system as a surrogate for the owner of a file. The word "file" could also be generalized to be an "information collection" (database, file, expert system software, etc.). For a related idea, see the policy entitled "Default To Denial Of Access Control Privileges." A: E; E: LMH.

103. User-IDs Must Each Uniquely Identify A Single User

Policy: Each computer and communication system user-ID must uniquely identify only one user. Shared or group user-IDs are not permitted.

Commentary: This policy establishes a definitive link between a user-ID and an individual (and in some cases a software process or a computer system). The converse is not necessary, i.e., individual users may have multiple user-IDs. Without unique user-IDs, logs cannot be used to definitively indicate the activities of a particular user. This problem in turn is likely to prevent an organization from taking disciplinary actions or entering into prosecutions for computer abuse; it may also prevent the provision of needed remedial training. Without unique user-IDs, privileges cannot be restricted on a user-by-user basis. If privileges cannot be restricted by user, then it will be very difficult to implement separation of duties, dual control, and other generally accepted security measures. This is a fundamental policy which underlies many access control policies, procedures, and the like. Some organizations will want to expand the words "uniquely identify only one user" to include software processes and computer systems. Nothing in this policy prevents the deployment of systems that make the specific computers involved user-transparent (e.g., client/server systems); for example, users may sign-into a network-based application and not a specific computer system. Note that this policy also implicitly forbids shared user-IDs (group user-IDs). See the policies entitled "Unique User-ID And Password Required" and "Accountability And Traceability For All Privileged System Commands." A: T; E: LMH.

104. Generic User-IDs Based On Job Function Prohibited

Policy: Generic user-IDs based on job function are prohibited. Instead, user-IDs must uniquely identify specific individuals.
Commentary: The intention of this policy is to prevent systems administrators and other technical staff from creating generic user-IDs based on job titles. This is a short-cut that many technical staff members employ to reduce the overhead associated with changes in worker employment status. With this short-cut, when someone leaves the organization, the password associated the user-ID can simply be changed. The new person who plays the role would employ the new password, while the person who departed would know only the old password. While

this approach may sound appealing in theory, there can be difficulties associated with system logs -- which individual's activity do the logs show? Of greater concern is the practice where generic user-IDs are assigned and shared passwords are employed; this may be necessitated by circumstances where several individuals have the same job title. Individual user accountability (via logs) is very difficult if not impossible to achieve in this environment. Another reason why the generic user-ID approach may be chosen has to do with database management systems, and the delegation of privileges. The same idea applies to privileges which may be incorporated into so-called "objects" (special programs). In either instance, the concept of privilege "inheritance" is used, which means that dropping a user may cause downstream problems with other users or processes. Accordingly, before this policy is adopted, the policy writer should investigate the implications with in-house programmers and other technical staff. Separately, the use of a generic user-IDs is furthermore ill-advised because it doesn't allow the files in a departed worker's directories to simply exist without modification until they are claimed by others, archived, or deleted. On another point, the policy is written such that group user-IDs cannot be assigned for contracting firms, outsourcing firms, or other third parties. For related ideas, see the policies entitled "Unique User-ID And Password Required" and "System Access Control With Individualized Passwords (Not Lockwords)." A: T; E: MH.

105. Re-Use Of Unique User-IDs Prohibited

Policy: Each Company X computer and communication system user-ID must be unique and forever connected solely with the user to whom it was assigned. After a worker or customer terminates their relationship with Company X, there must not be any re-use of the involved user-ID.

Commentary: This policy eliminates confusion caused by users who have the same legal name and therefore also the same user-ID (common in electronic mail networks). For example, if Sam Smith were to have an email address string of "s.smith@companyX.com" and he were to leave the company, and another Sam Smith were to be hired, without this policy the new Smith would get the same user-ID. Messages directed to the prior Sam Smith would come to the current Sam Smith. Separately, the policy also eliminates confusion about the true identify of a user in those cases where one or more users have received a user-ID that had been previously assigned to another. Thus, with this policy, system logs will be more authoritative and forensic investigations easier to conduct. If this policy sounds too difficult to implement in a certain organization, a helpful step in this direction would be the imposition of a long waiting period (say of one year) before previously used user-IDs can be reassigned to other users. As an aside, this policy is makes it easy to accommodate workers who leave and then later are rehired. On another note, user-IDs may be called other things such as "accounts," "user names," or "screen names," but the idea behind the policy is still the same. Also see the policies entitled "Dormant User-IDs And Automatic Privilege Revocations" and "Anonymous User-Ids." A: T; E: LMH.

106. Naming Standard For A Single User-ID Used On All Platforms

Policy: No matter how many systems they access, Company X workers must have only one computer system user-ID. Unless advance permission from the Director of Information Technology has been granted, all computer system administrators must consistently observe the user-ID naming standards specified by the Information Technology Department.

Commentary: The intention of this policy is to simplify both administrative and security work for networked computer systems. In medium- to large-sized organizations, a significant number of different user-IDs for a single individual can lead to great confusion. This confusion is particularly undesirable at the time that a worker leaves the organization, in which case staff may scramble to determine which user-IDs need to be deactivated. The policy simplifies these activities, as well as forensic activities like log analysis associated with computer crime investigation. A consistent approach to user-ID construction may, in some instances, be impossible if the technology does not allow it (for example some systems allow only a few characters in user-IDs); it is in recognition of these circumstances that exceptions are mentioned in the second sentence of the policy. Separately, the policy takes a strong stand in favor of centralized user-ID naming standards; in some computing environments this may be politically difficult to achieve. This policy may furthermore be costly to implement, especially if a significant number of computer systems are already in operation. Accordingly, the policy writer should perform a brief a cost/benefit analysis before adopting this policy. Note also that this policy will facilitate the establishment and administration of a single sign-on system. See the policies entitled "Single Sign-On Process," "Unique User-ID And Password Required," "Maintenance Of Master User-ID And Privilege Database," and "Anonymous User-IDs." A: T; E: LMH.

107. Separate User-IDs For Internet Connected & Internal Network Systems

Policy: All Company X workers must employ at least two different sets of user-IDs and passwords for two distinctly different classes of computers: those that are directly Internet-connected and those that are internal network-connected. The former includes Internet Service Provider (ISP) accounts and Internet commerce accounts with other businesses. The latter includes production servers on the Company X internal network and desktop machines.

Commentary: The intention of this policy is to prevent hackers and other intruders from exploiting a common time-saving practice that many users adopt. This practice involves choosing the same user-ID and password across a variety of computers. If users employ this time-saving approach, and if hackers break-into one of these user's accounts, then the hackers will find it easier to penetrate other machines to which these same users have been granted access. The policy makes life slightly more difficult for users, but the justification is easy to explain. Stated in another way, users must have different user-IDs and passwords for computers on the network periphery (Internet border) than they must have for computers on the internal network. Note that stand-alone machines, if there are any of these computers at the policy writer's organization, fall into the latter of these two categories (internal network-connected). For related ideas, see the policies entitled "Naming Standard For A Single User-ID Used On All Platforms" and "Unique User-ID And Password Required." A: E; E: LMH.

108. Exclusive Personal Use Of Access Codes Such As User-IDs & Credit Cards

Policy: In order to conduct business in an expedient manner, Company X issues computer accounts, user-IDs, network passwords, voicemail box personal identification numbers, credit card numbers, and other access codes. These access codes allow workers to utilize both the information systems of Company X and the systems of authorized third parties. These access codes are granted for the exclusive and individual use of the person to whom they were originally issued. Use of these codes by any other person is prohibited and constitutes a serious violation of Company X policies.

Commentary: The intention of this policy is to clearly and unequivocally state that the information system access codes must not be shared under any circumstances. This policy is different from related policies because talks about all access codes, not just user-IDs and passwords. It is therefore applicable to new technologies that an organization deploys in the future and need not be changed when these new technologies are introduced. This policy will help make system logs and other computerized records like telephone bills more reliable because the entries are more likely to be attributable to authorized persons. The policy also discourages unauthorized use, and this will help to keep operating expenses like telephone long-distance charges to a minimum. The policy furthermore helps to reinforce the concept of personal accountability. For related ideas, see the policies entitled "Users Responsible For All Activities Involving Personal User-Ids" and "Using An Electronic Mail Account Assigned To Another Individual." A: E; E: LMH.

109. Positive Identification Required For Initiation of Computer Transactions

Policy: The ability to execute business transactions on behalf of Company X must be restricted by both individual user-IDs and positive identification of the involved people using these user-IDs.

Commentary: The intention of this policy is to prevent unauthorized persons from being able to initiate binding business transactions on behalf of Company X. An example of such a transaction is a wire transfer sent using Company X systems. To achieve this end, it is customary to require that authorized users provide both their user-ID and a secret password. The policy is written in a general way such that passwords are not the only way to achieve positive identification. The same objective could for instance be achieved with smart cards, identity tokens, fingerprint readers, digital certificates, etc. It should also be kept in mind that positive identification of users is a must if separation of duties is to be enforced in a computerized environment. To be effective, it is likely that a definition of a "business transaction" will need to accompany this policy. The notion of "production business systems" may be a helpful idea when preparing this definition. See the policy entitled "Separation Of Duties And Control Over Company X Assets." A: EMT; E: LMH.

1.1.2.4. Special Privileges

110. Support For Special Privileged Type Of Users

Policy: All multi-user computer and network systems must support a special type of user-ID which has broadly-defined system privileges. This user-ID will in turn enable authorized individuals to change the security state of systems.

Commentary: The intention of this policy is to require that management set up a special type of user-ID which has greater privileges than the average user-ID. This more privileged user-ID would for instance be able to make backups of all data on a system disk, bring the system down, or terminate another user's session. Changing the security state of the system also takes place when new users are assigned a user-ID, when a new version of the operating system is installed, etc. By having a separate type of privileged user for these special tasks, management avoids giving all users "super-user" (also known as "God-like") privileges--an all too common situation. Note that it is not only possible, but desirable for staff backup reasons, that there be more than one privileged user for each system. Also see the policy entitled "Default User Privileges And Need For Explicit Written Approvals." A: MT; E: LMH.

111. Restriction Of Special System Privileges

Policy: Special system privileges, such as the ability to examine the files of other users, must be restricted to those directly responsible for system management and/or security. These privileges must be granted only to those who have attended an approved systems administrator training class.

Commentary: The intention of this policy is to restrict special system privileges, such as the ability to reboot a local area network (LAN) server, to those individuals who genuinely need these privileges to perform their jobs. The reader may wish to replace the words "system management and/or security" with the titles used by these individuals in his or her organization. Also see the policy entitled "Limited Number Of Privileged User-IDs" which focuses on the number of such user-IDs rather than privileges. Additionally see the policy entitled "Privilege Restriction Based On The Need-to-Know" (the latter policy deals with data access rather than system privileges). A: MT; E: LMH.

112. Restricted Remote Administration Of Internet-Connected Computers

Policy: Remote administration of Internet-connected computers is not allowed unless one-time passwords are employed over encrypted links.

Commentary: The purpose of this policy is to ensure that intruders (hackers, crackers, industrial spies, disgruntled ex-employees, what-have-you) do not take advantage of remote administration capabilities enabled on Company X Internet-connected machines. Because administration capabilities often have extensive privileges, these capabilities are an attractive target of intruders. The use of dynamic passwords (also known as one-time passwords) as well as encrypted links goes a long way to restricting this access to authorized persons. The policy could go still further by referencing things like restricted shells under UNIX version V (this is operating system specific so it was not mentioned in the policy). One well-known vendor of such one-time password systems is Security Dynamics, Bedford, Massachusetts, USA. For related ideas, consult the policies entitled "Real-Time External Network Connections Require Firewalls," "Reliance On Operating System User Authentication Process," and "Unique Passwords For Each Internal Network Device." A: T; E: LMH.

113. Limited Number Of Privileged User-IDs

Policy: The number of privileged user-IDs must be strictly limited to those individuals who absolutely must have such privileges for authorized business purposes.

Commentary: The intent of this policy is to provide systems administrators and security administrators with instructions on the assignment of privileged user-IDs to the general population of users. If a significant number of users have privileged user-IDs, it will be very difficult, if not impossible, to maintain adequate security. Separately, this policy implies an approval process for the granting of privileged user-IDs via the word "authorized." Some organizations may wish to make this management approval process more specific. Some organizations limit the number of privileged user-IDs to a specific number; this approach is not generally recommended because it may unduly interfere with the performance of normal business activities. The policy assumes that the words "privileged user-ID" (or privileged account) have been defined elsewhere. Generally these user-IDs allow users to examine the files of other users, change systems software, shut down the system, and otherwise run powerful system commands. See the policies entitled "Restriction Of Special System Privileges" and "End-User Access To Operating System Commands." A: T; E: LMH.

114. Two User-IDs Required For All Systems Administrators

Policy: Multi-user systems administrators must have at least two user-IDs. One of these user-IDs must provide privileged access and be logged; the other must be a normal user-ID for the day-to-day work of an ordinary user.

Commentary: This policy is intended to separate the work of systems administrators into two distinct categories, each of which has different access control privilege needs. By segmenting the work of systems administrators, this policy supports the notion of the need-to-know. In other words, no more privileges are used than is necessary to accomplish a specific business objective. Because systems administrators know their activities are logged and reviewed when they use privileged user-IDs, they will be encouraged to employ these user-IDs judiciously and with moderation. Without a policy like this, systems administrators may employ their privileged user-IDs to perform activities that they would otherwise be prevented from performing, had they been restricted to the privileges of a normal user. This distinction may not be noticed by systems administrators unless two or more user-IDs are actually employed. This policy also makes log analysis and review easier because a great deal of irrelevant information is not included in the detailed logs of privileged user-ID activities. This policy is particularly relevant to workers who are systems administrators on a part-time basis (they may for example be a programmer otherwise). As might be expected, this policy is not popular with systems administrators. See the policy entitled "Privilege Restriction Based On The Need-to-Know." A: T; E: LMH.

115. Logging And Reporting On Privileged User-ID Activity

Policy: All user-ID creation, deletion, and privilege change activity performed by systems administrators and others with privileged user-IDs must be securely logged and reflected in periodic management reports.

Commentary: The intention of this policy is to clearly specify which activities associated with privileged user-IDs need to be logged and reflected in periodic management reports. Too often management is unclear about this, and as a result, insufficient logs and management reports are generated. In the absence of specific instructions, systems administrators and others are likely to turn-off the logs and management reports to liberate scarce disk space. One variation of this policy would involve addition of another sentence requiring system owners, information owners, or others responsible for the involved systems to review these privileged user-ID activity management reports (designated delegates who perform these reviews would also be acceptable). The words "securely logged" imply that systems administrators and other privileged users cannot readily modify or delete a log. For related ideas, see the policies entitled "Accountability And Traceability For All Privileged System Commands" and "Generation And Review Of Logs Showing Use Of Override Facilities." A: T; E: LMH.

116. Default User Privileges And Need for Explicit Written Approvals

Policy: Without specific written approval from management, administrators must not grant system privileges -- beyond electronic mail and word processing -- to any user.

Commentary: This policy establishes a group of system privileges that all authorized users will be given so that they may communicate with other users and get their jobs done; beyond that, special permission is required. The basic set of privileges might for instance be given to all employees when they first join the organization. When their duties have been sufficiently defined, they will need to make specific requests for more privileges. These privilege requests are generally handled with special forms, which are increasingly handled by electronic mail. The idea behind this policy can be extended to include the establishment of default privileges by job title (such as those for all "consultants") as well as default privileges by department (such as those for the "accounting department"). Note that other privileges can be added to this default list of privileges; for example, Internet web surfing and spreadsheet programs could be added. See the policy entitled "Privilege Restriction Based On The Need-to-Know." A: MT; E: LMH.

117. Approvals Required For User-ID Creation And Privilege Assignment

Policy: User-IDs may be granted to specific users only when approved in advance by the user's immediate supervisor. Prior to being granted to users, business application system privileges must be approved by the involved information owner. System privileges beyond the capabilities routinely granted to general users must be approved in advance by the Manager of Technical Support.

Commentary: This policy is intended to clarify who must approve the issuance of a user-ID (account), and who must approve the granting of application and system privileges. The policy assumes that the user-ID and privilege granting process will be performed by a systems administrator or systems security specialist. As written, the policy does not mention permissible methods for communicating such approvals; these typically include electronic mail, internal paper mail, and telephone conversations. Some organizations will want to require communication methods that create a definitive audit trail (such as paper-based signatures); others will want communication methods that cannot easily be spoofed (such as digital signatures, perhaps accompanied by digital certificates). In some cases management authorization for system privileges must be "in writing," but just what that means in the information age will often require expert legal advice. Separately, the policy assumes the term "information owner" is defined elsewhere. For related ideas, see the policies entitled "Information Ownership And Management's Responsibilities" and "Default User Privileges And Need for Explicit Written Approvals." A: T; E: LMH.

118. Restriction Of Third Party Dial-Up Privileges

Policy: In-bound dial-up or in-bound Internet privileges must not be given to third party vendors unless the relevant system manager determines that these vendors have legitimate business need for such access. These privileges must be enabled for specific individuals and only for the time period required to accomplish approved tasks.

Commentary: Dial-up and in-bound Internet privileges (the latter through a firewall) have been used by a number of hackers, crackers, and other system attackers to gain unauthorized access to systems. It is ill-advised to leave these ports, such as those used by vendors for remote maintenance, open and available if they are not needed. The intention of this policy is to keep maintenance ports turned off, and keep third parties off the system unless they have first obtained approval from Company X management. Having a formal approval process will also discourage--if not prevent--others from attempting to masquerade as though they are a vendor representative as a way to get onto a system. To narrow the coverage of this policy, change "privileges" in the first sentence to "maintenance privileges." This policy could be expanded to apply to private branch exchanges (PBXs), network switching nodes, and other communication systems, as well as general purpose computer systems like minicomputers and mainframes. The use of the word "in-bound" in the policy provides an exemption for sophisticated maintenance systems, from vendors like Tandem, that automatically dial (via an out-bound connection) the vendor's system when they detect a problem. Also see the policies entitled "Conference Bridge Activated Only When Needed" and "Dial-Up Connections Must Always Utilize Firewalls." A: T; E: LMH.

1.1.2.5. Other Privilege Restrictions

119. Time Dependent Access Control

Policy: All multi-user computer systems must employ positive user identification systems to control access to both information and programs. Beyond this basic access control, user activities must be restricted by time of day and day of the week.

Commentary: The default access control found on many systems is based on files, i.e., on various types of access to information and/or application programs. Organizations wishing to bolster this control environment, can mandate additional restrictions based on time and day as mentioned in this policy. The policy's intent is to require more than simple access controls, normally based on user-IDs and passwords. Note that more than the ordinary user-IDs and passwords need not mean smart cards, biometrics, or some of the more expensive and esoteric technologies. Besides time dependent access controls, another example of a readily-available and low-cost way to augment user-IDs and passwords is via the terminal-ID codes (such as those available from IBM) built into the systems from various vendors. As another example, the Pentium III chip from Intel provides a unique identification number which could be used for this purpose. Note that each organization should base the specific positive user identification control measures it uses on a risk analysis (also known as a risk assessment). Recent studies of hacker activity show that they are most active at night, just the time that systems are sparsely staffed, if they are staffed at all. Separately, given so many people are working odd hours these days, this policy may be restricted to only those applications handling sensitive or valuable data (such as wire transfer systems). This policy is most relevant to organizations that have established hours of operation, such as a bank. The globalization that goes along with Internet commerce and organizational intranets may require that this policy be reworded to reflect local time zones. This policy is relevant to batch jobs as well as interactive sessions. Also see the policy entitled "Privilege Restriction Based On The Need-to-Know." A: MT; E: MH.

120. Dormant User-IDs And Automatic Privilege Revocations

Policy: All user-IDs must automatically have the associated privileges revoked after a thirty (30) day period of inactivity.

Commentary: Dormant user-IDs or accounts have been used by many to commit fraud and sabotage. Unauthorized users find dormant user-IDs attractive because the authorized users are unlikely to notice unauthorized activity. The intention of this policy is to eliminate the opportunity for unauthorized users to employ dormant user-IDs for various nefarious purposes (fraud, industrial espionage, etc.). There is nothing special about the 30 day period mentioned in the policy; this could just have easily been 45, 60, or 90 days. If an authorized user goes on vacation or leave-without-pay for an extended period, this policy will result in their user-ID being revoked. When the user returns, he or she can make a request that the security administrator reinstate privileges. The administrator would then check the individual's status with management, and follow-through with the request if it is consistent with management's intentions. Note that the involved user-ID can continue to be defined while the associated privileges have been revoked. Likewise, the files in a user's workspace can continue to reside on disk even though the user's privileges have been revoked. Separately, because systems administrators are often quite overworked, they may not get around to revoking privileges of users in a timely manner. Accordingly, an automated version of this policy acts as a safety net to reduce vulnerabilities brought on by the lack of timely attention on the part of an administrator. Another reason why user-IDs should be temporarily revoked but still defined is that it gives relevant managers an opportunity to review the files associated with the user-ID, and later to dispose of or transfer responsibility for these files as necessary. Separately, this policy applies to voice-mail and other systems besides multi-user general purpose computer systems. On still another note, some organizations revoke the privileges of outsiders (contractors, consultants, temporaries, customers, etc.) after a brief period of time without any activity, but provide a longer period of time for insiders (employees). See the policy entitled "Notice Of Last Log-In Time And Date." A: MT; E: LMH.

121. Default To Denial Of Access Control Privileges

Policy: If a computer or network access control system is not functioning properly, it must default to denial of privileges to end-users.

Commentary: Rather than allow open and uncontrolled access, the intention of this policy is to prevent access until the access control system can be fixed. For example, if a password-based access control system on a web server were to break-down, no end-user access to the system should be permitted. Of course, technical staff would need access in order to fix the problem. Restating the policy in other words, one could say that management would prefer not to do business if it would be done in an uncontrolled manner. Some organizations may wish to add specific exclusions to the policy in order to keep essential business processes going--such as continuing to clear checks at a bank. All such exclusions should be carefully considered before they are incorporated into the policy, lest they become the areas exploited by industrial spies, embezzlers, and others engaged in information system abuses. In general, if it accurately reflects the environment in question, it is desirable to keep a policy like this simple and straightforward, and to make exceptions on a case-by-case basis. For related ideas, see the policies entitled "Existence Of User Access Capabilities Does Not Imply Usage Permission" and "Privilege Restriction Based On The Need-to-Know." A: MT; E: LMH.

122. Trusted Host Relationships Must Not Be Established Without Permission

Policy: Unless the Information Security Department Manager has first approved in writing, Company X staff must not enable any trusted host relationships between computers connected to the Company X internal network. A trusted host relationship involves the sharing of data files or applications across computers, or the elimination of the need to log-into more than one computer.

Commentary: The intention of this policy is to put systems administrators and security administrators on notice that they must not enable NSF (Network File System for UNIX) or comparable software systems. These trusted host systems allow a user to log into one machine and then access the files remotely stored on another. If a hacker were to compromise one of two machines that had NSF enabled, the hacker would be able to sabotage or use both of those machines without any additional effort. Metaphorically speaking, use of trusted host relationships thus puts all of Company X's eggs in one basket. It is better security (although perhaps a greater inconvenience for technical staff) to have users log into each of these systems separately. For related ideas, see the policies entitled "Trusted Host Relationships Prohibited For Internet Connected Machines" and "Default To Denial Of Access Control Privileges." A: T; E: LMH.

123. Unbecoming Conduct And The Revocation Of Access Privileges

Policy: Company X management reserves the right to revoke the privileges of any user at any time. Conduct that interferes with the normal and proper operation of Company X information systems, which adversely affects the ability of others to use these information systems, or which is harmful or offensive to others will not be permitted.

Commentary: The intention of this policy is to put users on notice that they jeopardize their status as authorized users if they engage in the activities described. For example, crashing the system could reasonably be expected to be harmful to other users, and would accordingly subject the perpetrator to disciplinary action including privilege revocation. The policy attempts to broadly describe an ethic for computing, somewhat akin to the ecologist's ethic of minimum wilderness impact (for example "take only pictures, leave only footsteps"). Rather than specifying all the nasty things that people could do, such as crashing a system, this policy is discreet and high-level. The broadly-stated policy may also give management ample latitude when it comes to making a decision about privilege revocation. On a separate note, some organizations are a bit less discreet, adding words to this policy such as "Persons who abuse their privileges may also be subject to disciplinary action including civil or criminal legal action." Also see the policies entitled "Default User Privileges And Need For Explicit Written Approvals" and "Periodic Review And Reauthorization Of User Access Privileges." A: E; E: LMH.

124. End-User Access To Operating System Commands

Policy: After logging-in, all end-users of multi-user systems must be kept in menus which show the options that they have been authorized to select. End-users must not be allowed to invoke operating system level commands.

Commentary: The intention of this policy is to significantly restrict the damage that users can do and the trouble that they can cause. By preventing users from running operating system level commands, such as reformat a hard disk on a local area network server, the security of the system is improved. Besides, offering only menus is often more user-friendly than allowing the users to issue operating system commands. Note that the menus should only show the options that specific users have been authorized to run. Users should also be prevented from exiting from these menus (with the break character, escape, control-C, and related commands). When users wish to exit the menu system, they should be logged-off (there should be no other options). Software to implement this policy comes with some operating systems such as DEC's OpenVMS, while on other operating systems like Novell NetWare, a separate software package is required (such as the Saber menu system). See the policies entitled "Accountability And Traceability For All Privileged System Commands" and "Limited Number Of Privileged User-IDs." A: T; E: MH.

125. Limiting End-User Knowledge Of System Capabilities And Commands

Policy: End-users must be presented with only the system capabilities and commands that they have privileges to perform. For example, pull-down menus should show only the options which end-users can select.

Commentary: The intention of this policy is to limit the end-user choices to those options for which privileges have been granted. This makes system usage simpler and more direct, and also increases security. If users don't know that they can't do something they will be less likely to request those privileges, and thus the policy may trigger a marginal reduction in access control administration costs. This systems design related policy also prevents curious users from attempting to employ capabilities and commands for which they lack training and/or authorization. The policy makes it very clear which privileges are authorized and which are not, and may thus help administrators and systems designers make appropriate decisions about access control. On another note, this policy also helps with user problem diagnosis; if a certain option is not shown, this means that privileges have not yet been granted. Separately, note that this policy generally will be applicable only to software developed in-house; the software developed by third parties like Microsoft generally is not modifiable to make it comply with this policy. The policy is thus most applicable to a firm such as AOL, which writes its own user-interface and systems software. For related ideas, see the policies entitled "Restriction Of Special System Privileges," "Single Sign-On Process," and "Privilege Restriction Based On The Need-To-Know." A: T; E: LMH.

126. Termination Of User Processes Or Sessions And Removal Of User Files

Policy: Company X systems administration staff may alter the priority of, or terminate the execution of, any user process which it believes is consuming excessive system resources or is significantly degrading system response time. This staff may also terminate user sessions or connections if this usage is deemed to be in violation of security policies or consuming excessive system resources. This staff may furthermore remove or compress user disk files if it believes these files to consume excessive disk space. Any of these actions may be taken at any time without prior user notice and without user consent.

Commentary: The objective of this policy is to let users know what systems administrators may be doing and to prevent some complaints. The policy also lets all users know that the systems administration staff has great latitude to immediately deal with anything which they believe might jeopardize system availability, system integrity, or system security. The policy acts as a deterrent to abusive acts such as playing games with Company X systems (especially Internet based games, which may consume a great deal of network bandwidth). For a related consideration, see the policy entitled "Prohibition Against Programs Consuming Excessive System Resources." A: E; E: LMH.

127. Prohibition Against Testing Information System Controls

Policy: Workers must not test, or attempt to compromise internal controls unless specifically approved in advance and in writing by the Manager of the Information Security Department.

Commentary: When users attempt to break controls, this fosters an "attack ethic," i.e., an environment where it is acceptable for workers to attempt to break system controls. This policy eliminates an often invoked excuse for computer crimes, as the perpetrators may say that they were merely "testing the control system so as to be able to improve it." Of course, internal auditors already have this approval (in their departmental mission statement), and they should continue to test controls. While there is merit to regularly testing controls to illuminate weaknesses, this activity needs to be strictly controlled and performed in a confidential manner (lest the results be exploited by employees and others). The media discussion of the SATAN tool to detect vulnerabilities in Internet-connected UNIX systems points to the need to rigidly control who can probe systems to detect vulnerabilities. In general, this policy applies to the execution of public domain as well as commercial software packages used to break system controls (these go by names such as Crack and COPS). This policy will prevent users from running software like SATAN unless they have management approval. This policy also prohibits "tiger team attacks" (also known as "penetration attacks") unless approved in advance by management. See the policies entitled "Security Mechanisms Must Not Be Compromised For Customers," "Testing Physical Access Controls Forbidden," "Gaining Unauthorized Access Via Company X Information Systems," and "Tools Used To Break Systems Security Prohibited." A: ET; E: LMH.

128. Prohibition Against Exploiting Systems Security Vulnerabilities

Policy: Users must not exploit vulnerabilities or deficiencies in information systems security to damage systems or information, to obtain resources beyond those they have been authorized to obtain, to take resources away from other users, or to gain access to other systems for which proper authorization has not been granted. All such vulnerabilities and deficiencies should be promptly reported to the Manager of Information Security.

Commentary: The intention of this policy is to make it clear that users must not take advantage of information security vulnerabilities and deficiencies, even if they are aware of such problems. One example of such a problem involves having knowledge of a special password that allows a user to do things he or she would otherwise not be able to perform. In a broad sense, this policy is saying that users are given only the privileges explicitly granted to them--if they can do something else due to security problems, they are not authorized to take advantage of these problems. As written, the policy includes errors made by systems administrators, for example if a user was given too many privileges. While this example this may not involve a control vulnerability, it is decidedly a deficiency associated with the deployment of controls. For related ideas, see the policies entitled "Required Reporting Of Information Security Incidents" and "Restricted Use Of Diagnostic Test Hardware And Software." A: ET; E: LMH.

129. Recipient Screening For Distribution Of Powerful Security Tools

Policy: Before distributing vulnerability identification software or other tools that could be used to compromise the security of information systems, Company X staff must research and validate the recipient's need for such tools.

Commentary: This administrative policy is intended to restrict the distribution of tools (such as SATAN) that could be used to compromise the security of information systems. As is done by organizations like Bellcore (Basking Ridge, New Jersey, USA) for their product called Pingware, all would-be buyers should be screened to make sure that they are legitimate recipients. The idea behind the policy can be generalized beyond tools -- for example to information itself that could be used to compromise the security of systems; some organizations may wish to rewrite the policy to include sensitive security information. While intended primarily to be used by software developers and other organizations that issue or distribute such tools, the concept described in the policy is generally-applicable to all organizations. The policy is accordingly intended to prevent the distributing organization from being held responsible (liable) for some damage done with their tool. On a separate note, text accompanying this policy could specify how staff are supposed to validate the recipients' need for the tool. See the policies entitled "Prohibition Against Testing Information System Controls," "Tools For Determining Security Status Of System," "Limitation Of Functionality For Powerful Security Tools," "Tools Used To Break Systems Security Prohibited." A: T; E: MH.

130. Removal Of Vulnerability Identification Software When Not In Use

Policy: When vulnerability identification software is not being actively used, it must be removed from the system on which it has been run. Acceptable alternatives include special access control passwords or encryption of the software itself.

Commentary: The purpose of this policy is to ensure that unauthorized parties do not use vulnerability identification software to break into Company X systems. If this software is not removed or encrypted, it is possible that an intruder could use it to his or her advantage. The situation is akin to a locksmith leaving lock-picking tools near to a locked door; unauthorized people might use these tools to get through that locked door. While the use of vulnerability identification software from vendors like Internet Security Systems of Atlanta, Georgia, USA is quite the rage these days, few technical specialists think about how these tools are dangerous if in the wrong hands. Likewise, they don't think about how this software could be used to attack systems managed by other organizations, and how their employer might be held liable for those intrusions. Note that this policy, as written, applies to situations where the software runs on a centralized system that probes remote systems, as well as situations where the software runs on distributed systems and then reports back to a centralized system. Separately, note that the vendors of vulnerability identification systems are incorporating tools such as IP address limitations to restrict the way that these tools can be used; where available, these too should be used to achieve the same purpose as stated in the policy. For related ideas, see the policies entitled "Vulnerability Identification Software For Internet-Connected Systems" and "Tools Used To Break Systems Security Prohibited." A: T; E: LMH.

131. Limitation Of Functionality For Powerful Information Systems Tools

Policy: All powerful information systems tools, built or distributed by Company X, that could be used to cause significant damage must be automatically restricted such that they can only be used for their intended purpose(s).

Commentary: This systems design policy is intended to guide developers in the selection of appropriate functionality. The specific mechanisms to be used are deliberately not specified in the policy, lest this unduly constrain the developers. One example of this policy is provided by the product called Nebula Scanner from Milkyway Networks (Ottawa, Ontario, Canada). This vulnerability identification tool requires buyers to specify the IP addresses for their hosts so that the package cannot be used on unauthorized machines. Not only does this approach help make sure that buyers have up-to-date licenses, it also prevents their tool from being used on unintended hosts at other organizations. In overall terms, the policy instructs staff to help limit the liability of the developer or distributor. Separately, note that this policy is applicable to a wide variety of products such as floppy disk utilities (such as Symantec's Norton programs), not just information security tools. Also see the policies entitled "Prohibition Against Testing Information System Controls," "Tools For Determining Security Status Of System," "Limitation Of Functionality For Powerful Security Tools," "Tools Used To Break Systems Security Prohibited." A: T; E: MH.

132. Privileges For Modification Of Production Business Information

Policy: System privileges allowing the modification of "production" Company X business information must be restricted to "production" applications.

Commentary: Users must not be able to modify production data unless such modification is through well-defined and previously-approved production software. For example, employees should not be able to modify payroll amounts due unless this is done through a prescribed process including the access controls built into the payroll application system. Only when this process is followed can logging, data input validation, and other controls be consistently applied. Thus ordinary users should not be permitted to use text editors, programming debuggers, and other powerful system tools to modify production information directly. Of course there will always be an occasional need for certain staff, such as a select few systems programmers, to be able to modify production data directly--but even this should be severely restricted, supervised, logged, and periodically reviewed. Although found much less often in the real world than one would hope, this ideal approach is in keeping with the widely acclaimed Clark-Wilson information integrity model. Many microcomputer and local area network commercial operating systems make this policy hard to implement, although this is clearly an emerging trend. The policy might be implemented by the removal of certain utility programs like compilers and text editors (this is standard practice on Internet commerce servers). Also see the policy entitled "End-User Access to Operating System Commands." The policy entitled "Controlled Process For Modification Of Production Business Information" provides a less stringent approach which accomplishes some of the same objectives. A: T; E: MH.

133. Controlled Process For Modification Of Production Business Information

Policy: Privileges must be established such that system users are not able to modify production data in an unrestricted manner. Users may only modify production data in predefined ways that preserve or enhance its integrity. In other words, users must be permitted to modify production data ONLY when employing a controlled process approved by management.

Commentary: The objective of this policy is to make sure that unauthorized changes to production data are not being made. Similar to the policy entitled "Privileges For Modification Of Production Business Information," this policy is a derivative of the Clark-Wilson model's concept of a well-formed transaction. This policy is less stringent in that it does not require that the path be established via production software. It could instead be via manual procedures and separation of duties. This policy indicates there must be certain well-controlled paths by which production data is altered, and that the data should not be altered unless these paths are employed. For example, a database should only be modified if the associated database management system is employed. In this example, there are certain controls built into the DBMS, such as privilege restrictions, while there are less likely to be controls built into a general-purpose program that enables users to modify files of various formats. See the policy entitled "Separation Of Duties And Control Over Company X Assets." A: T; E: LMH.

134. Business Production Information Updates By Non-Production Staff

Policy: System privileges must be defined so that non-production staff (internal auditors, information security administrators, programmers, computer operators, etc.) are not permitted to update "production" business information.

Commentary: Updates should only be done via the normal channels, i.e., via production staff. For example, updates to the human resources database should only be allowed if initiated by authorized staff in the Human Resources Department. To allow other people to make updates invites abuses. The technical support staff should be able to examine the production business information, to detect errors and inconsistencies in this information, and to perform similar activities, but they should not be able to update the information itself. Particularly for small systems users, this policy may require an accompanying definition of the word "production." For a more general view, see the policy entitled "All Production Transactions Must Be Authorized by Management." Also see the policies entitled "Designated Security Administrator For All Multi-User Systems" and "Updating Company X Information Through The Internet." A: MT; E: LMH.

135. Database Updates Must Be Made Only Through Established Channels

Policy: Updates to production databases must only be made through established channels which have been approved by management. Unless permission of the Computer Operations Manager on duty has been obtained, the use of direct database access utilities in the production environment is not permitted because these programs will circumvent database synchronization and replication routines, input error checking routines, and other important control measures.

Commentary: The objective of this policy is to prevent well-meaning staff members from causing operational problems that could interrupt or otherwise interfere with production processing. In many instances computer operators on duty don't understand the delicate interconnectedness of distributed databases and other multi-location collections of information. This policy prohibits the use of utilities, which can circumvent database access controls, and which go directly to a database to modify the data contained therein. It thus provides the basis for disciplinary action should systems programming, systems administration, or computer operations staff commit such abusive acts (a log would of course be needed to record these activities). Some policy writers may wonder why such a policy is needed when access controls could prohibit the usage of such utilities; the answer is that this policy applies to privileged users who have the ability to defeat all such access control measures. For related ideas, consult the policies entitled "Controlled Process For Modification Of Production Business Information" and "Use Of Push Background Updates For Software Requires Approval." A: T; E: LMH.

136. Access Control Required For All Multi-User Production Applications

Policy: All production business applications supporting multiple users must be secured by an access control system approved by the Information Security Department.

Commentary: It is possible with some access control systems, such as Computer Associates' ACF2, to establish a list of applications to which access controls do not apply (sometimes called a "safe-list"). This is undesirable because it allows an exception which may not be consistent with other access controls, and may not be as well-secured or logged as other access controls. This policy, directed primarily to system administrators, states that all business applications must be controlled using standard and approved access control systems. One example of such an access control system involves fixed passwords and user-IDs, another involves dynamic passwords and hand-held identity tokens (such as those sold by Security Dynamics). Note that the policy applies to smaller systems too; it is on departmental servers and other small systems that applications without adequate access control often exist. This policy is a manifestation of the basic systems design principle called universal application, which holds that exceptions to a control will weaken it; in this case, any application which does not have a standard access control mechanism is unduly exposed. This policy also prompts the reader to ask what types of access control systems are approved by the Information Security Department, and the answer to this question is generally provided on a list of standard products and approved vendors (this list is in the domain of information security architectures and standards, rather than policies). See the policy entitled "Business Production Information Updates By Non-Production Staff." A: T; E: LMH.

137. Technical Staff Privileges And Production System Change Control

Policy: Beyond that which they need to do their jobs, computer operations staff must not be given access to--or permitted to modify--production data, production programs, or the operating system.

Commentary: This policy is a specific manifestation of separation of duties, as reflected by a typical mainframe shop. Because adequate separation of duties related access control mechanisms may not be available, the policy may not be practical for smaller systems such as microcomputers (PCs) or workstations. As the Internet continues to allow extranets and other automated business partnerships, the policy will become increasingly applicable to the small systems environment. The intention of the policy is to clearly indicate that computer operations staff should not be given "carte blanche" (universal) access to production data, production programs, and the operating system. Because this control is so often ignored in data processing shops, a specific policy may be required to clarify exactly what should be done. Also see the policies entitled "Privilege Restriction Based On The Need-To-Know" and "Separation Of Duties And Control Over Company X Assets." A: MT; E: LMH.

1.1.2.6. Administrative Activities

138. Signed Forms Required For Issuance Of User-ID

Policy: Users must sign both a confidentiality agreement and an information system security agreement prior to being given a user-ID allowing access to Company X systems.
Commentary: Users should be put on notice about security policies and their security-related responsibilities before they get access to any Company X system. The basic idea behind this policy is to withhold a user-ID until users have agreed in writing to respect the basic rules governing system usage. If users don't sign these agreements when they get their user-ID, it may be difficult to get them to sign them later. These signed agreements may also be important for prosecutions and disciplinary actions. The paperwork for the issuance of a user-ID can include the agreements mentioned in the policy and/or other agreements, depending on the needs of the organization. In broad terms, this policy is much like the process for driver's license tests; until people have been shown to know the rules and how to drive a car, they aren't given the right to drive. Also see the policy entitled "Annual Signature On Agreement To Comply with Security Policies." A: E; E: LMH.

139. Multi-Platform Systems Parameter Naming Conventions

Policy: To achieve consistent access control across different types of computer systems, standard user-ID codes, production program names, production file names, system names, and other naming conventions must be supported.

Commentary: This naming convention policy makes administration significantly easier for multi-platform user access control systems, logs, and audit trails. This policy is for example useful when establishing a single sign-on system. It is also helpful for systems designers putting together integrated application systems. Without such conventions, it is very difficult to perform certain security tasks. Examples of these tasks include tracing a user's activity on various systems, and revoking privileges for all user-IDs related to a specific individual after that individual has been terminated. Some organizations may wish to change the first few words in the policy to reflect additional motivations. For related ideas, see the policies entitled "Consistent Way Of Representing Employee Contact Information" and "Naming Convention For Production Files." A: MT; E: LMH.

140. Administrative Security Management For All Networked Computers

Policy: Configurations and set-up parameters on all hosts attached to the Company X network must comply with in-house security management policies and standards.

Commentary: The intention of this policy is to clearly state that all server (LAN) administrators, mainframe access control package administrators, and the like must consistently abide by internal security management policies and standards. Often these administrators are tempted to do things their own way, perhaps inadvertently opening an unauthorized access pathway to connected machines. This policy may at first seem unnecessary; some people may think that everyone else knows that the weakest link in a chain will be the first to break. But there is merit to stating this idea in writing, perhaps giving management something else to use when attempting to get administrators to abide by information security policies and standards. Perhaps in no other area is this policy so important as a network of UNIX machines; the many different options for establishing security on each machine, coupled with the do-it-yourself approach to many things in the UNIX community, can combine to create serious network vulnerabilities. Also see the policies entitled "Compliance With Organizational Systems Development Conventions" and "Required Compliance With Corporate Code Of Conduct." A: T; E: LMH.

141. Tools For Determining Security Status of System

Policy: Every multi-user system must include sufficient automated tools to assist the security administrator in verifying the security status of the computer. These tools must include mechanisms for the correction of security problems.

Commentary: This policy is intended to be used in the acquisition process for new and enhanced computer systems. It may also be helpful in the acquisition of tools assisting administrators in the maintenance of an adequate level of systems security. In general, it does little good to have security measures if one cannot determine whether or not they are working. Accordingly, this policy requires that each multi-user system have sufficient tools to determine whether the security is adequate and whether the security mechanisms are working as they should be. These tools could include a software package to check the logical consistency of assigned user privileges (for example, Braintree of Norwell, MA offers products like this). These tools include those which automatically review systems logs, and which automatically check whether security system set-up parameters match organizational policy. PCs (micros) were deliberately not included within the scope of this policy because such tools are rare on PCs; besides, most end-users don't yet have the technical sophistication to appreciate what these tools do, even if they were motivated to use them. Over time much of this functionality will be automated and incorporated into operating systems. For an important related idea, see policy entitled, "Tools Used To Break Systems Security Prohibited." A: MT; E: LMH.

142. Periodic Review And Reauthorization Of User Access Privileges

Policy: The system privileges granted to every user must be reevaluated by the user's immediate manager every three (3) months. This reevaluation involves a determination whether currently-enabled system privileges are still needed to perform the user's current job duties.

Commentary: As user job duties change, so should their associated system privileges. But in many cases, users change jobs, and the Information Security Department or others (like systems administrators) responsible for changing privileges are not notified about these changes. This policy seeks to keep privileges up-to-date and restricted to current job requirements. Because people are under pressure to produce results, there is a natural tendency for access controls to loosen over time; thus periodic reviews to restrict privileges are required. However, no periodic checking for the acquisition of privileges is necessary because users or their managers will complain until they get the privileges needed to do their current jobs. In order to implement this policy, many organizations issue a report of privileges by user. This electronic mail message or paper memo goes to the user's manager, and the manager has a certain period of time (two weeks for example) in which to respond. If no response is received, telephone calls are made, or other follow-up actions are performed to ensure that the manager actually did review the privilege list. In very high security environments, if the manager does not respond in a timely manner, user privileges may be revoked temporarily until the manager reauthorizes them. There is nothing special about three months; the period could be six months in a low security environment, but generally should not be any longer. Separately, in some cases, organizations will want to add these words to the end of the policy: "All privileges which are no longer needed will be revoked." Also see the policies entitled "Privilege Restriction Based On The Need-to-Know," "Time Limits For User-IDs And File Retention Period After Expiration," and "Periodic Identification Badge Reports Issued To Department Heads." A: MT; E: LMH.

143. Human Resources Sends Worker Status Changes To System Administrators

Policy: Every change in the employment status of Company X workers (including consultants, contractors, and temporaries) must be immediately reported by the Human Resources Department to the involved information systems administrators.

Commentary: The intention behind this policy is to foster an automated connection between the database maintained by the Human Resources Department and the access control database(s) maintained by information systems administrators. In far too many situations, systems administrators were not aware of promotions, transfers, retirements, leaves of absence, and related changes in the status of workers. Administrators accordingly do not make necessary changes in the access control privileges of these workers. Not making these changes in a timely manner can result in serious leaks of confidential information (if the worker is now employed by a competitor) or system sabotage (if the worker utilizes continued access to tamper with files). While the policy does not specifically talk about an automated connection, such a connection (often triggered by scripts in the Human Resources Department database system) is desirable in any organization with 100 or more workers. This policy is especially effective if an organization has an enterprise security management system which typically relies on a centralized database of user privileges across all operating systems and specific internal machines. The policy can be implemented on a manual basis, although delays and errors are more likely. Separately, this policy assumes that the Human Resources Department is kept informed of all changes in worker status; if managers in user departments can hire/fire/contract with individuals without the involvement of the Human Resources Department, then this policy is not going to be effective.

For similar considerations, see the policies entitled "Reporting Changes In User Duties To Systems Security Administration" and "Periodic Review And Reauthorization Of User Access Privileges." A: T; E: LMH.

144. Reporting Changes In User Duties To Systems Security Administration

Policy: Management must promptly report all significant changes in end-user duties and/or employment status to the system security administrators handling the user-IDs of the affected persons.

Commentary: The intention behind this policy is to support the notion of least privilege. End-user privileges must promptly be turned off if an individual has been terminated, transferred, promoted, put on leave without pay, or otherwise no longer in the same position. Systems security administrators don't generally know about these changes unless they receive notification from the involved managers (or alternately from the Human Resources Department). A separate but related policy requiring that all such status-change information be kept in strict confidence is advisable because a terminated employee may bring a defamation of character lawsuit. This policy may be particularly useful when it comes time to establish standard procedures for notifying administrators about worker status changes. In the most sophisticated of organizations, an automatic email notification of all changes in status goes from the HR database to security administrators. See the related policies entitled "Changing Physical Access Control Codes On Worker Termination" and "Transfer Of Information Custodian Duties After Employee Terminations." A: MT; E: LMH.

145. Users Must Inform Systems Administration About Status Changes

Policy: To enable Company X to accurately maintain information about each user, and if need be to immediately contact each user, every user is responsible for notifying the Systems Administration Unit about changes in their status with Company X.

Commentary: The objective of this policy is to inform users (workers) that they must inform Company X's systems administrators about changes in their status. For example, at a university, the students may be required to notify systems administrators if their expected graduation date has slipped a semester. If these users failed to notify systems administrators, the users would be likely to have their privileges terminated when these same system privileges were needed to complete their degrees. The policy is also suitable for Internet Service Providers (ISPs) and other system service providers who deal directly with individuals who may not work for Company X. This policy does not in any way prevent systems administrators from at the same time obtaining user status change notices from the Human Resources Department, and/or user managers. The more people reporting such changes, the more likely it will be that systems administrators will make suitable privileges changes in a timely manner. Some changes, such as involuntary terminations are not likely to be reported by the users themselves, and must instead come from other sources. Multiple information feeds coming into the systems administration unit are also desirable because often some of these sources fail to deliver information. For example, a worker who doesn't want to lose his or her system privileges associated with prior job duties may deliberately fail to notify systems administration. Multiple sources of status change information also allows systems administrators to corroborate unusual requests before acting upon them. Separately, the policy also provides systems administrators with the information needed to immediately contact users and ask them whether abusive activity was initiated by them or by an intruder using these same users' accounts. For related considerations, see the policies entitled "Human Resources Sends Worker Status Changes To System Administrators" and "Reporting Changes In User Duties To Systems Security Administration." A: E; E: LMH.

146. Maintenance Of Master User-ID And Privilege Database

Policy: So that their privileges may be expediently revoked on short notice, records reflecting all the computer systems on which users have user-IDs must be kept up-to-date.

Commentary: The intention behind this policy is to make sure that all user-IDs that an employee (or consultant, contractor, temporary, etc.) uses can be readily identified and the associated privileges quickly revoked. This will, for instance, be useful when an employee has been shown to be embezzling, in which case all user-IDs should be shut down immediately. Even when less dramatic changes in user status take place, such a database can be very helpful in determining which systems security administrators should be notified. Some organizations even keep a centralized database which is connected to the human resources database. In this case, changes in the human resources database automatically trigger the generation of electronic mail messages which are sent to those people maintaining the centralized database. Alternatively, the messages could be sent to systems security administrators or a script could be sent directly to the access control systems on which the involved employee had a user-ID. Also see the policies entitled "Transfer Of Information Custodian Duties After Employee Terminations" and "Naming Standard For A Single User-ID Used On All Platforms." A: MT; E: LMH.

147. Transfer Of Information Custodian Duties After Employee Terminations

Policy: When a worker leaves any position with Company X, both computer-resident files and paper files must be promptly reviewed by his or her immediate manager to determine who should become the custodian of such files, and/or the appropriate methods to be used for file disposal. The computer user's manager must then promptly reassign the computer user's duties as well as specifically delegate responsibility for the files formerly in the computer user's possession.

Commentary: The intention behind this policy is to clearly and expediently transfer custodian responsibilities, and thereby to ensure that security measures are maintained in minimally acceptable ways. The reassignment of duties process is especially important if the files contain sensitive, critical, or valuable information. This policy also implicitly puts employees on notice that their files will be examined by others after they leave the organization. Additionally, with this policy, managers are put on notice that they are responsible for the proper handling of a departed worker's information. The policy helps to avoid fraud, sabotage, and other abuses, which frequently take place when no specific person has responsibility for a certain area (perpetrators often take advantage of the confusion surrounding the departure of an employee). See the policies entitled "Changing Physical Access Control Codes On Worker Termination" and "Information Ownership And Management's Responsibilities." A: EMT; E: LMH.

148. Schedule For Deletion Of Files Following Worker Termination

Policy: Unless Computer Operations has received instructions to the contrary, four weeks after a worker has permanently left Company X; all files held in that user's directories will be purged.

Commentary: The intention of this policy is to establish a date for the automatic deletion of files held in user-specific directories (folders). A specific deadline will encourage managers responsible for departed workers to examine such files and reassign them to other workers. In those environments with significant user turnover, such as a large multi-user computer for university students, this policy can also be used to put users on notice about the need to backup their own data. Note that the words "permanently left" are used to prevent deletion of files when a worker is on a leave-of-absence, a sabbatical, a maternity leave, or some other extended but temporary absence. This policy will help conserve disk space. If accompanied by a script to automatically carry out its objectives, the policy can additionally be used to reduce the need for manual systems administration work. As a safety net, the files can of course be restored from backup tape, at least until such time as they are overwritten by new backup information. On another note, this policy assumes that a refined process for communicating worker departures to the people who manage systems already exists. The policy also assumes that the people who manage systems are able to readily identify the systems on which departed workers had user-IDs. It is advisable for Computer Operations to notify managers that departed worker files will be deleted as of a certain date to get them to take this policy seriously. Separately, the words "Computer Operations" could be "Systems Administration" or some other functional group designator. For related ideas, see the policies entitled "Maintenance Of Master User-ID And Privilege Database" and "Transfer Of Information Custodian Duties After Employee Terminations." A: M; E: LMH.

1.1.3. Logging

1.1.3.1. Information To Include In Logs

149. Logs Required On Application Systems Handling Sensitive Information

Policy: All production application systems which handle sensitive Company X information must generate logs that show every addition, modification, and deletion to such sensitive information.

Commentary: The intention behind this policy is to be able to account for all changes to sensitive information like personnel records, strategic plans, and product design specifications. For example, the payroll database in most organizations should have an associated log which shows who updated the payroll amounts and when. This type of information will be very helpful when attempting to investigate and correct problems like errors and defalcations. This policy essentially indicates which applications should have associated logs (also called "audit trails"). The log data elements (for example, whether a before-and-after image should be logged) will need to be determined on a case-by-case basis. The scope of the policy could be readily expanded to include "sensitive, critical, and valuable Company X information" rather than simply "sensitive Company X information." In some instances, the operating system, application system, or database management system will be able to capture sufficient log information. In other situations, supplementary logging software will be needed (either purchase of a commercial package or development of some code in-house). For a definition of words like "sensitive," see the policy entitled "Four Category Data Classification Scheme." A: MT; E: LMH.

150. Keystroke Logs Required For All Production System Privileged User-IDs

Policy: Activity with privileged user-IDs on Company X production systems must always be recorded with keystroke logs.

Commentary: The intention of this policy is to require that intensive logging be turned-on for privileged user-IDs on production systems. Every key pressed by these privileged users will go into a log so that all actions can be reconstructed precisely. Thus this policy is a deterrent against abuse of the capabilities which go along with privileged user-IDs (system administrators, auditors, installers, etc.). The policy also mandates extensive logging which could be most useful when investigating a computer crime, prosecuting a computer crime, or just trying to figure out what went wrong (a system crash for example). On another note, there is a still more intense type of log and that involves not only keystrokes but also mouse clicks -- sometimes called a "clickstream." In the very highest security environments, both types of information could be recorded for privileged user-IDs. As an aside, keystroke logging is applicable only to privileged user-IDs due to disk space limitations, but in very high security environments such as a bank's wire transfer room, it could be extended to all user-IDs on production machines. Separately, this policy assumes that the keystroke log cannot be readily disabled by privileged user-IDs. For related ideas, see the policies entitled "Security Notice In System Log-in Banner" and "Logs Required On Application Systems Handling Sensitive Information." A: T; E: MH.

151. Inclusion Of Security Relevant Events In System Logs

Policy: Computer systems handling sensitive, valuable, or critical information must securely log all significant security relevant events. Examples of security relevant events include: password guessing attempts, attempts to use privileges that have not been authorized, modifications to production application software, and modifications to system software.

Commentary: This policy is intended to specify which computer systems must have system logs reflecting security relevant events. It is particularly appropriate for microcomputers (PCs), workstations, local area network servers, client/server systems, and similar small systems that often lack adequate logs. It may be necessary to further specify what constitutes a "security relevant event" in the policy. Another way to handle this is to indicate that the Information Security Department will determine exactly what constitutes a security relevant event. Note that the policy only requires logs for systems handling sensitive, valuable, or critical information. Because it makes reference to "sensitive, valuable, or critical information," this policy implicitly relies on a data classification policy, such as the policy entitled "Four Category Data Classification Scheme." A: T; E: LMH.

152. Computer System Logs Must Support Audits

Policy: Logs of computer security relevant events must provide sufficient data to support comprehensive audits of the effectiveness of, and compliance with security measures.

Commentary: External auditors may not be able to rely on an organization's financial records if there is insufficient evidence that the controls are working as they should be. If this is the case, it means the external auditors will have to perform other tests of the records to verify their correctness, perhaps incurring significant additional auditing fees. Similarly, without sufficient logging information, internal auditors may not be able to do their jobs, which in turn should make management uneasy about systems security. Thus the intention of this policy is to make sure that logs provide sufficient information to allow both internal and external audits to proceed without excessive costs. Good logs can also be helpful with resolution of operational problems, such as determining the cause of a system crash. This policy is additionally helpful because it can prompt management to consider exactly what types of data should be recorded in logs. Some organizations may wish to expand this policy to include the data needed for legal actions and/or staff disciplinary actions. Also see the policy entitled "Internal Audit Review Of Information System Controls." A: MT; E: LMH.

153. Accountability And Traceability For All Privileged System Commands

Policy: All privileged commands issued by computer system operators must be traceable to specific individuals via the use of comprehensive logs.

Commentary: This policy is particularly relevant to servers, minicomputers, and mainframes, where more than one "operator" (trained user) could initiate certain commands. The intention of the policy is to maintain accountability and traceability for all privileged system commands that were issued (such as erase the contents of a magnetic tape). The policy is not intended for small systems such as microcomputers, for which specific operators are not usually designated. In those environments needing high security, the policy could be applied to small systems or systems containing particularly sensitive, valuable, or critical information. This policy instructs system management to keep records of all commands as well as an indication of who issued them. This policy and the controls used to implement it serve as a deterrent to abusive acts. Such logs also provide information that can be useful for disciplinary actions, legal proceedings, and the like. Most importantly, the logs of privileged system commands can be an important tool in both the resolution and understanding of system problems. Beyond computer system operators, the policy could also be expanded to include other types of people who typically have special privileges: information security administrators, internal auditors, systems programmers, local area network administrators, etc. Implicit in the policy is a definition of "privileged system commands" -- such a definition can be included in the policy or left for local system management to determine. Also see the policies entitled "End-User Access To Operating System Commands" and "Logging And Reporting On Privileged User-ID Activity." A: MT; E: LMH.

154. Contents of Logs For Systems Running Production Applications

Policy: All computer systems running Company X production application systems must include logs which record, at a minimum the following data: (1) user session activity including user-IDs, log-in date/time, log-out date/time, and applications invoked, (2) changes to critical application system files, (3) additions and changes to the privileges of users, and (4) system start-ups and shut-downs.

Commentary: The intention of this policy is to provide a minimum collection of log data that can be expected to be available on every internal system running a production application. Not only will this information assist with problem resolution efforts and system restore operations, it will also be invaluable to system penetration attack investigations, fraud investigations, and the like. By standardizing on a minimum logging requirement, an organization can assist system administrators with decisions about how to configure the internals of a system. A policy like this can also lay the foundation for an integrated multi-machine intrusion detection system. Separately, note that this policy applies to single user workstations as well as large machines such as mainframes. For related ideas, see the policies entitled "Inclusion Of Security Relevant Events In System Logs" and "Logs Required On Application Systems Handling Sensitive Information." A: T; E: LMH.

155. All Attempted System Log-Ins, Successful Or Not, Must Be Logged

Policy: Whether successful or not, all user initiated log-ins attempts to connect with Company X production information systems must be logged.

Commentary: The objective of this policy is to create a comprehensive set of operating system logs across all internal production information systems, that can then be used to investigate computer crimes (and perhaps used to support a computer resources charge-back system as well). Logs are also a very important input to computer intrusion detection systems, which can automatically alert technical staff that an attack is underway using pagers. A string of incorrect log-ins will be evidence of a password guessing attack or a user who needs additional training. Typically these system logs will show the user-ID, the time and date, the port that the user employed, and whether the login was successful or not. Separately, this policy is deliberately restricted to production information systems so that system logs will not be necessary on desktop machines and other computers which are not critical to the business. For related ideas, see the policies entitled "Contents Of Logs For Systems Running Production Applications" and "Clock Synchronization For Accurate Logging Of Events On Network." A: T; E: LMH.

156. Log-In Passwords Must Not Be Logged Unless In Encrypted Form

Policy: Log-in passwords must not be recorded in system logs unless these same system logs encrypt the passwords.

Commentary: The intention of this policy is to prevent passwords from being revealed to computer operators, systems administrators, and others who do not have authorization to view user passwords. If these technical people were to view user passwords it would be a violation of a fundamental approach to the design of fixed password systems. Specifically, in order to get accountability for a user-ID and a related password, only the involved user must know his or her own password. If logs record log-in passwords, then the technical staff who reviews the logs would discover the passwords of other users, and with this information could impersonate the other users. The policy writer will note that this policy prohibits even the logging of incorrect passwords. Often users will mistype a password and only one character will be off -- this may then allow anyone reviewing the log to use guessing techniques to determine the correct password. Recording of passwords with encryption is, however, permissible and may be warranted in high security environments. With this latter approach, encrypted passwords can be decrypted by a restricted group of security specialists in order to gain additional information which might help with the investigation of a computer crime. For related ideas, see the policies entitled "Disclosure Of Incorrect Log-In Information" and "Computer Operator Logs Must Be Periodically Reviewed." A: T; E: LMH.

157. Required Retention Period Of Logs

Policy: Computerized logs containing security relevant events must be retained for at least three (3) months. During this period, such logs must be secured such that they cannot be modified, and such that they can be read only by authorized persons. These logs are important for error correction, forensic auditing, security breach investigations, and related efforts.

Commentary: The intention of this policy is to clearly specify the retention period for logs as well as the need for secure storage of logs. The policy can be expanded to define explicitly what events are deemed as "security relevant." There is nothing special about three months; the figure will vary by industry and jurisdiction as well as the information involved. Be sure to check with internal legal counsel and records management staff about the appropriate time period to retain such records. The retention period for business transactions will generally be much longer than the retention period for logs of security relevant events and a log generally does not contain business transactions. Also see the policies entitled "Maintaining Building Access Control System Records" and "Retention Of Access Control Privilege Logs." A: MT; E: LMH.

158. Daily Removal Of Logs From Internet-Accessible Computers

Policy: If they are resident on Internet-accessible computers, system logs and application logs must be moved at least daily to other machines that are not directly Internet-accessible.

Commentary: The objective of this policy is to safeguard the integrity of logs. If logs are kept for a prolonged period on Internet-accessible machines, then the chances that hackers and other unauthorized parties have modified them is significantly increased. The need to protect logs is greatly magnified if the logs contain payment information such as credit card numbers, or if the logs contain private information such as customer telephone numbers. Daily transfer to a more secure machine could simply mean up-loading the logs to a machine behind another firewall. Alternatively, it may mean putting the logs on tape and storing them off-line (the latter is certainly preferred if the logs might need to be used as admissible evidence in a court of law). Rather than the process described in this policy, a more secure option is to refrain from keeping any logs on Internet-accessible machines (although this may introduce unacceptable network performance penalties). This might involve transfer of logging information on a real-time event-by-event basis to another machine which is behind another firewall (not in a DMZ). Getting back to this policy, another good reason to transfer logs to another machine on a daily basis is to free up disk space which may be needed for applications such as Internet commerce software. Yet another good reason to remove logs on a daily basis is to prevent overwriting previous log information (some logs have a fixed disk space allocation). For related ideas, see the policies entitled "Deletion Of Log Information About Customer Activities," "Resistance Of Logs Against Deactivation, Modification, Or Deletion," and "Retention Of Access Control Privilege Logs." A: T; E: LMH.

159. Logs Of User-Initiated Security Relevant Activities

Policy: To assure that users are held accountable for their actions on Company X production computer systems, one or more logs tracing security relevant activities to specific users must be securely maintained for a reasonable period of time.

Commentary: The intention of this policy is to clearly specify that all user-initiated security relevant activities must be logged and retained for a certain period (three months for instance). This information will be helpful to those people in security administration, computer operations, and internal auditing. The information also serves as a deterrent to abusive acts, as well as important information for the Help Desk to use when figuring out the nature of a problem. The policy makes reference to security relevant activities (alias security relevant events) like user changes to file access privileges, user changes to a secret password, and the like. If the policy was only distributed to management and technical people, the policy could include a specific definition of "security relevant activities." A specific definition may be contraindicated if the policy is to be distributed to users because the ambiguity of "security relevant activities" serves as a deterrent. It may also be appropriate to keep the term "security relevant activities" ambiguous so that local systems management can interpret it in light of their own situations. Thus local systems managers may determine that both applications and systems activities are "security relevant," or they may alternatively determine that only systems activities are "security relevant." For a related idea, consider the policy entitled "Informed Consent Required For Questionable System Actions." A: EMT; E: LMH.

160. Retention Of Access Control Privilege Logs

Policy: Computerized records reflecting the access privileges of each user of Company X multi-user systems and networks must be securely maintained for a reasonable period of time.

Commentary: As part of an investigation of a computer crime, management may wish to determine who could have performed certain actions on a system or network. Accordingly, the intention of this policy is to clearly specify that logs about user access control privileges be captured and maintained for a certain period of time. Some organizations will want to explicitly state a log retention period, such as three months, in the policy. Some other organizations will want to leave the retention period open so that it may be determined by local management. In this policy, reference was made to "multi-user systems" because the identity of the perpetrator of an abusive act is much less of an issue with a microcomputer (PC) or workstation. Likewise, these smaller systems are much less likely to have any sort of log reflecting user privileges (although add-on products such as PC/DACs from Mergent International can be purchased to do this). The policy could be expanded to include these smaller systems if desired; simple deletion of the phrase "multi-user" may be sufficient. The policy, as written, is relevant to both voice and data communication systems. Thus the policy will apply to PBX privileges, such as the use of the DISA feature (direct inward system access where users dial-in on an 800 number, and then dial-out to complete a long distance call and have it charged to Company X). Also consider the policy entitled "Granting System Privileges By Chain Of Authority Delegation." A: T; E: LMH.

161. Reconstructibility Of Changes To Production Information

Policy: To deter improper behavior, to foster user accountability, and to allow expedient systems management, all user activities affecting production information must be reconstructible from logs.

Commentary: The intention of this policy is to make sure that all errors, fraudulent changes, and other improper modifications to production information can be expediently detected and corrected. For example, in the event that a system crash damages a production database, such logs will be instrumental in reconstructing the database from a prior copy. In this case, database "snapshots" showing before-and-after images could be used. Unlike other policies found in this section, in this policy the emphasis is on being able to reconstruct data (preserve and/or enhance its integrity). As was discussed in the commentary to the policy entitled "Logs Of User-Initiated Security Relevant Activities," there is merit to keeping the term "activities affecting production data" ambiguous. Also see the policies entitled "Special Labelling For All Non-Production Business Transactions," "Orders To Change Internal Records Placed Via Phone," and "Management Notification Of Information Integrity Controls Failure." A: EMT; E: LMH.

162. Cryptographic Checksums To Detect Modifications Of System Logs

Policy: In order to immediately detect modification and/or deletion of system activity records, all Company X production information systems must employ cryptographic checksums to protect system logs.

Commentary: The intention of this policy is to ensure that unauthorized modification or deletion of system logs will be immediately evident. One of the first things that hackers and other intruders do when they gain system access is to shut off the system log. If intruders are concerned that turning off a system log may trigger an alarm and bring immediate attention by system operators, they may delete or modify the existing system log after they have done a nefarious deed in order to destroy any evidence that might be used against them. While the controls dictated by this policy will not detect that a log has been turned off, they will highlight the fact that a log has been tampered with, and hopefully this will be used as input to an intrusion detection system (IDS). Such cryptographic checksums are available in the form of commercial and shareware software, and one of best known is called Tripwire. These checksum methods involve a serial dependency of data such that modifying only one bit will cause an immediate alarm. Separately, because cryptography is involved, this policy introduces the need for a key management process. See the section entitled "Encryption Key Management" for ideas about that process. Just because a cryptographic checksum is used to detect modification and deletion doesn't mean that the entire log needs to be encrypted; using an encryption process only for a log checksum has less impact on system performance. For related ideas, see the policies entitled "Internet Connected Machines Must Have Intrusion Detection Systems" and "Resistance Of Logs Against Deactivation, Modification, Or Deletion." A: T; E: MH.

163. Information To Capture When Computer Crime Or Abuse Is Suspected

Policy: To provide evidence for investigation, prosecution, and disciplinary actions, certain information must be immediately captured whenever a computer crime or abuse is suspected. The relevant information must then be securely stored off-line until such time as the chief legal counsel determines that Company X will no longer need the information. The information to be immediately collected includes the current system configuration as well as backup copies of all potentially involved files.

Commentary: This policy is intended to put systems management staff on notice that certain information must be captured and securely stored until needed by internal auditors, corporate counsel, security administrators, and others. The policy allows evidence to be captured and properly secured, so that it will later be admissible in court. On the other hand, if the evidence remained on the involved computer for a certain period, there is a possibility that it could have been modified by unauthorized parties. If the evidence could have been modified, it will not be convincing in the eyes of the court. Note also that the process of capturing information should take place even if there is only a suspected problem. It is better to have this information and then dispose of it if it's not needed, than to not have the information and then be unable to take certain courses of action (such as prosecution). The policy thus makes sure that a snap-shot of the current situation is preserved for later use. Also consider the policy entitled "Accountability And Traceability For All Privileged System Commands." A: T; E: LMH.

164. Logs Required For Rapid Resumption Of Production System Activities

Policy: Because they are critical to Company X's business, certain production business applications require more extensive logging than others. All critical business applications must be supported by logs that allow system activities to be resumed within fifteen (15) minutes.

Commentary: The intention of this policy is to put both the Information Systems Department and user organizations which manage their own systems on notice that critical applications must be recovered within a certain time frame, and that extensive logs play an important part of the restoration process. Specification of a certain time frame for recovery makes it relatively easy for people to determine whether they are in compliance with the policy. The time frame will of course vary by organization, and ideally should be based on a business impact analysis (BIA). The time frame will also be a function of the criticality of the information handled by the involved application. The logs used to recover may take the form of replicated databases, database check-points, file snapshots, disk shadowing, and/or disk mirroring. Reference to these types of logs can appear in the explanatory remarks accompanying this policy, although in most instances it is best to keep such technical detail out of the policy itself. The specific time frame (here fifteen minutes) may also be stated elsewhere besides a policy since it is likely to change over time. For a good background policy, see "Four Category Data Classification Scheme." Also see the policy entitled "Annual Criticality Rating For Multi-User Applications." A: MT; E: MH.

165. Systems Architecture For Logging Activities

Policy: Application and/or database management system (DBMS) software must keep logs of user activities and statistics related to these activities which will allow them to spot and issue alarms reflecting suspicious business events.

Commentary: Consider a company which issues a credit card and which keeps a record of the number of transactions on each card per week. If this statistic far exceeds historical baseline statistics, it probably indicates that the card has been stolen and is being used to make fraudulent purchases. The intention of this policy is to specify where certain types of logs (aka audit trails) are to be maintained: in a computer operating system, in a network operating system, in access control software, in a database management system software, in an application software, etc. This policy says that business events, such as the amount of charges made to a credit card, should be captured in logs maintained by an application and/or DBMS. The organization can specify where other types of information, such as changes in user privileges, should be recorded as well. This policy is a technical systems design instruction, and is often part of an information security architecture. Many progressive organizations are now developing a plan (or architecture) specifying where critical controls such as logging will be supported. For a related architectural policy, consider "Where To Use Computer System Access Controls." A: T; E: LMH.

166. Clock Synchronization For Accurate Logging Of Events On Network

Policy: All multi-user computers connected to Company X's internal network must always have the current time accurately reflected in their internal clocks.

Commentary: Having synchronized clocks will assist system problem diagnosis and resolution, particularly for client/server and other systems involving interdependent hardware. This policy will also help with reliable event logging, automatic software updates, automatic encryption key changes, and other security-related activities. Beyond that, the intention of this policy is to allow investigators to reliably trace the actions of hackers or other unauthorized intruders on the network. If clocks are not synchronized and accurate, then investigations will be hampered. In addition, the evidence uncovered will most likely be unreliable, and therefore unusable as the reason for disciplinary action or prosecution. Accurate internal clocks are furthermore important because some access controls depend on this information, such as mechanisms which allow users to run privileged commands only during business hours. All clocks should be set to local standard time, and should be promptly changed to reflect daylight savings time (or whatever other periodic shifts are made with the seasons). Whenever there has been a system crash, a power outage, an operating system upgrade, or some other event that might affect the clock, the clock should be promptly reset. Also, computer clocks often drift with time, so they should be periodically resynchronized. A host of exciting new products, such as Tymeserve from Datum, San Jose, CA, use satellite synchronization to coordinate time across a network. The policy as stated here could be extended to all network-connected computer systems, although it is most important for multi-user systems. Also consider the policy entitled "Resistance Of Logs Against Deactivation, Modification, or Deletion." A: T; E: LMH.

167. Logs Of All Inbound And Outbound Faxes

Policy: Logs reflecting the involved phone numbers and the number of pages for all inbound and outbound fax transmissions must be kept. These logs must be retained for a period of one (1) year. Fax machines that do not automatically generate a log of faxes must be accompanied by a manual log.

Commentary: The purpose of this policy is to provide a legal record of the faxes that were sent and received. This is particularly important in those business environments where contracts, purchase orders, invoices, and other legally-binding promises are handled via fax. The maintenance and retention of a fax log can also assist day-to-day operational questions and problems (such as "Who received the fax from headquarters that was supposed to go to Mr. Y?"). The policy given here could be expanded to include other data fields to record such as the parties receiving the fax and/or the subject. Many new microcomputer-based software packages that support faxing come with their own logs, which according to this policy, should be turned on. Fax servers also support extensive logging. Also see the policy entitled "When Faxing Sensitive Information Is Permissible." A: EMT; E: MH.

1.1.3.2. Handling Of Logs

168. Resistance Of Logs Against Deactivation, Modification, Or Deletion

Policy: Mechanisms to detect and record significant computer security events must be resistant to attacks. These attacks include attempts to deactivate, modify, or delete the logging software and/or the logs themselves.

Commentary: The effectiveness of logs in large measure is dependent on the mechanisms used to protect the integrity of the logs as well as the mechanisms used to generate the logs. Thus, if a systems programmer was able to turn a log on and off, this would allow him or her to perform a nefarious act which did not appear in the log. The intention of this policy is to put technical staff on notice that proper access controls must be in place to protect both logs and the mechanisms used to generate logs. Some organizations may wish to add additional verbiage to this policy indicating that all changes to the logging system must themselves be logged; for example, if the log were turned off, this must result in an entry in the log. Readers may wish to consider a variety of mechanisms to protect logs including operating system based access controls, encryption, and file authentication codes. In some instances logs are also kept on separate machines which use a different operating system (this is advisable for Internet commerce). Also see the policy entitled "Encrypting Backup Media Stored Off-Site." A: T; E: LMH.

169. Writing Logs To WORM Storage Media Prevents Alteration

Policy: To prevent unauthorized alteration, production systems connected to the Internet must store all system logs on WORM storage media or similar technology approved by the Information Security Department.

Commentary: The intention of this policy is to prevent modification to system logs (the policy could be expanded to include application logs, but in some instances the volume of data generated by the applications may be too large). WORM storage media (write-once-read-many times) can be used to irreversibly record what happened on a production computer. An example of WORM storage media would be CD-ROMs. Note that the approach described in the policy doesn't record what happened if the logging facilities were deactivated, but the fact that the logging facilities were deactivated (and by whom) would still appear in a log. This policy is a recommended way to generate reliable logs which could then be admissible in a court of law. This policy is also recommended for Internet commerce. For related ideas, see the policies entitled "Controlled Process For Modification Of Production Business Information," "Make At Least One Copy Of Critical Backed-Up Files Prior To Use," and "Quarterly Archival Backups Required For All Critical Information." A: T; E: LMH.

170. Externally Accessible Systems Must Employ Remotely Mirrored Logs

Policy: All Company X production information systems which are accessible by any external network must employ remotely mirrored system logs.

Commentary: The objective of this policy is to require a certain design which is increasingly popular with Internet merchants. This secure systems design involves remote recording of system logs on another machine, ideally a machine with a different type of operating system. For example, an Internet commerce server may be running Microsoft Windows NT while a remote machine which is maintaining a real-time copy of the NT system log may be running Red Hat Linux. The use of a different operating system means that an intruder will have additional difficulty breaking into the remote logging system. This additional difficulty will impose a delay which should be enough for an intrusion detection system (IDS) to alert authorities to the intruder's presence on an internal network, and for these authorities to take some remedial action. Separately, the policy is based on the assumption that one of the first things that an intruder does when he or she compromises a machine is to turn-off, modify, or erase the systems log. These actions can conceal an intruder's logical footprints, but if the systems log is stored on another machine, then tampering with it will be much harder. For the very highest level of security, remote logs can be encrypted to prevent unauthorized disclosure and undetected modification, and also stored in a write-only fashion (perhaps on a CD-ROM) to prevent any modification whatsoever. For related ideas see the policies entitled "Logs Required For Rapid Resumption Of Production System Activities" and "Resistance Of Logs Against Deactivation, Modification, Or Deletion." A: T; E: MH.

171. Digital Signatures & Sequence Numbers Required For System Logs

Policy: To prevent undetected tampering, all Company X production computer system logs must be protected with digital signatures and log entry sequence numbers. These logs must also be automatically monitored to ensure that sudden decreases in size, failures of digital signatures, and/or gaps in log entry sequence numbers immediately trigger an alarm.

Commentary: The intention of this policy is to require that production systems be augmented with additional control measures which will most likely immediately detect tampering with system logs. One of the first things that intruders do when they gain unauthorized access to a system is to turn-off, delete, or modify the system log to cover their logical footprints. This policy ensures that production machine logging systems detect these activities and then promptly notify those who are in a position to remove the intruder from the involved system. Note that many operating systems do not include code to perform the functions defined in the policy, and that most often additional software will be required. The controls defined in this policy assume that an intrusion detection system (IDS) or a network management system (NMS) is in place for the machines in question. Separately, if an organization categorizes its machines by security needs, the words "production computer system" in the policy could be replaced with or augmented by the words "infrastructure servers and network periphery servers." For related ideas, see the policies entitled "Production Input Transactions Must Have Sequence Numbers" and "Externally Accessible Systems Must Employ Remotely Mirrored Logs." A: T; E: H.

172. System Log Rotation & Archive Process For High Security Systems

Policy: To prevent the overwriting of system logs or the expansion of these logs to the point where they consume all available disk space, a formal log rotation and archival process must be employed for all network periphery security systems (such as firewalls) and all multi-user production servers.

Commentary: The intention of this policy is to get systems administrators to establish and follow a formalized process for system log rotation and archive. In far too many organizations, system administrators don't really think about logs until they have gotten too big, at which point some essential logging data may be lost. Consider a relatively-full system disk on an important server. If an intruder were to gain system access to that server at midnight, he or she might quickly fill the disk because the system log recorded many unauthorized activities. At that time of night, the administrator may not be around to notice that the disk is full. If the attacker didn't delete or modify the system log, the log may still be considerably less useful than it would otherwise be, because available disk space constraints prevented important log data from being recorded. Separately, log files which are too large are difficult to handle, to move from machine to machine, and to search for specific events. Having reasonably sized log files which are rotated to separate storage media helps with these administrative activities. Archival storage of logs is advisable in case an intrusion is detected in the near future and then it is revealed that this intruder was on the involved system for quite some time. Only if archival logs are available can certain questions be answered such as: "When did the intruder first gain entry?" Having a rotation and archive process also gets logs off the involved machine, which reduces the chances that an intruder will be able to modify or erase them. For a related idea, see the policy entitled "Two Copies Of Critical Company X Records Stored Off-Site." A: T: E: LMH.

173. Persons Authorized To View Logs

Policy: All system and application logs must be maintained in a form that cannot readily be viewed by unauthorized persons. A person is unauthorized if he or she is not a member of the internal audit staff, systems security staff, systems management staff, or if he or she does not clearly have a need for such access to perform regular duties. Unauthorized users must obtain written permission from the Information Technology Manager prior to being granted such access.

Commentary: The intention of this policy is to limit access to logs--both application and system logs--to only those persons who have a bone fide need to have such access. Access by unauthorized persons can reveal user-IDs, transaction specifics, and other information that may be instrumental in fraud, sabotage, industrial espionage, and other abuses. In some instances passwords, particularly incorrectly typed passwords, may also appear in logs. The policy could make specific mention of encryption, although this is not necessary. If logs are encrypted, they will be exceedingly difficult for unauthorized people to view or modify. In terms of off-site storage, encryption is really the only truly effective way to prevent unauthorized access. Rather than encryption, in less secure environments, use of file access controls may be sufficient. In some circumstances, written permission for access to application logs may be granted by the information owner/sponsor, rather than the Information Technology Manager. A modification to the policy to reflect this expanded permission granting process may be appropriate for some organizations. This policy assumes that other types of access control will also be in place; see the policy entitled "Resistance Of Logs Against Deactivation, Modification, Or Deletion." A: T; E: LMH.

174. Regular And Prompt Review Of System Logs

Policy: To allow proper remedial action, computer operations or information security staff must review records reflecting security relevant events on multi-user machines in a periodic and timely manner.

Commentary: The intention of this policy is to require that computer operations or information security staff promptly review logs. This review process can be greatly facilitated if the logs produce exception reports indicating items of a suspicious nature in need of follow-up. To ask a person to go through a log reflecting all system events on a busy multi-user system is like asking them to find a "needle in a haystack." Prompt review of logs might, for example, be important if there was a hacker who was attempting to guess passwords via a dial-up line. If the logs were never reviewed, and if there were no other mechanism (like pager alerts) to notify the people who could do something about it, the organization may never have become aware of the attacks. If the attacks were not stopped--or at least discouraged by telling the hacker that he was being closely monitored--the hacker may be encouraged to continue. Likewise, the chronological window for taking remedial action (such as stopping an employee from making copies of proprietary product plans) closes quickly unless corrective steps are promptly initiated. In some environments, such as electronic funds transfer systems, the window in which adjustments must be made is very slim (a few days). In environments such as this, the time frame for log review may also be included in the policy. The policy could be expanded to include application logs, in which case user management or information owners/sponsors may be involved in the review process. Because they filter logs, modern tools such as intrusion detection systems (IDS) increasingly reduce the need for human review of logs, but people must still review the results from these systems, and of course then take prompt action. Also see the policies entitled "Computer Operator Logs Must Be Periodically Reviewed" and "Review Reasonableness And Accuracy Of Changes To Internal Records." A: T; E: LMH.

175. Notification Of Users About Logging Of Security Violations

Policy: Users must clearly informed which actions constitute security violations. Users must also be informed that such violations will be logged.

Commentary: The intention of this policy is to require that all users be clearly told about the actions which constitute security violations. To discourage users from engaging in these actions, they should be told that their activities will be logged. Disciplinary action will be very difficult if users have not been told about, and do not clearly understand what is expected of them. Along these same lines, if the policy is to be distributed to users, the policy may additionally include words indicating that "violations will subject users to disciplinary actions up to and including termination and prosecution." An advisable explanation that accompanies this policy--to be written by the reader because it is organization-specific--could give specific examples of security violations. Typically these violations would include attempts to compromise controls through password guessing, changing system access controls, masquerading as another user, as well as other actions such as crashing the system. Also see the policy entitled "Notifying Subjects Of Existing Monitoring Systems." A: T; E: LMH.

1.2. Software Development And Change Control

1.2.1. Computer Viruses And Worms

176. Users Must Not Attempt To Eradicate Computer Viruses

Policy: A computer virus is an unauthorized program which replicates itself and spreads onto various data storage media (floppy disks, magnetic tapes, etc.) and/or across a network. The symptoms of virus infection include considerably slower response time, inexplicable loss of files, changed modification dates for files, increased file sizes, and total failure of a computer system. Because viruses have become very complex, users must not attempt to eradicate them without expert assistance. If users suspect infection by a virus, they must immediately shut-down the involved computer, disconnect from all networks, and call the corporate help desk.

Commentary: The intention of this policy is to prevent users from attempting to eradicate computer viruses from their systems. These efforts often end up with the virus being spread still further in addition to the destruction of data or programs. For example, users may try to see whether a program resident on floppy disk works in a coworker's computer, and thus inadvertently spread a virus. Instead, the experts (either on staff in the Information Security Department, on the Help Desk, or at an external consulting firm) should be called in. Some organizations may wish to expand the last sentence in the policy to instruct the users to refrain from using diskettes or other data storage media which have been used on the infected computer. Separately, those organizations wishing a more abbreviated policy can skip the opening two sentences. Also see the policy entitled "Immediate Reporting Of Suspected Computer Virus Infestation." A: E; E: LMH.

177. Virus Eradication Requires Support Of Systems Administrator

Policy: Users are prohibited from attempting to eradicate a computer virus from their system unless they do so while in communication with a systems administrator. This communication will help minimize damage to data files and software, as well as ensure that information needed to detect a reinfection has been recorded.

Commentary: The intention of this policy is to prevent users from getting into trouble, for example by innocently spreading a computer virus in an effort to isolate and understand a problem. The policy assumes that a virus detection system is installed in all in-house small-scale systems susceptible to viruses (generally Unix systems are immune), and that users will be alerted to suspected virus infections. The policy instructs users to immediately get technical assistance rather than try to do this complex task themselves. This approach means that only systems administrators need to be trained in the use of eradication tools, not the general user population. This approach will also ensure that infections are centrally reported so that statistical tabulations can be prepared. Another important aspect of this approach is the enabling of log software associated with some virus detection packages (like Sweep from Sophos); the resulting logs indicate the actions taken to eradicate the virus. These logs are often essential references for restoring the computing environment which was in place prior to an infection. These logs can also capture the virus itself so that the virus detection software vendor can subsequently update its package to detect new viruses as well as mutated versions of old viruses. For related ideas, see the policy entitled "Users Must Not Attempt To Eradicate Computer Viruses." A: ET; E: LMH.

178. Prohibition Against Downloading Software From Third Party Systems

Policy: Workers must not down-load software from dial-up electronic bulletin board systems, the Internet, or any other systems outside Company X. This prohibition is necessary because such software may contain viruses, worms, Trojan horses, and other software which may damage Company X information and systems.

Commentary: The intention of this conservative policy is to significantly reduce the opportunities for infection from computer viruses, worms, Trojan horses and the like. Unauthorized externally-provided software may additionally cause software incompatibilities, disk space shortages, and worker productivity erosion (if the software is a game). Notice this policy does not prohibit down-loading data from third-party systems (only software) --some organizations may wish to add words to clarify this distinction. This is because viruses in most cases attach themselves to software, not data. A new breed of virus called a macrovirus does attach itself to data such as spreadsheet files; the only sure way to prevent these new viruses is to only download ASCII plain text data (permit no attachments to email messages). The policy as written here has a positive side effect: it encourages use of standard software packages rather than loosely allowing users to employ whatever software they choose. This in turn helps to create a more-easily-managed and controlled computing environment. Separately, organizations which are very concerned about viruses could adopt a strict policy such as this, although requiring all such third-party software to be scanned with a virus-screening software package prior to use may achieve much the same end. Another option is to require permission from a local information security coordinator prior to down-loading software. This policy describes a conservative approach that some organizations may prefer to implement via software rather than policies; consider tools such as LAN Protect from Intel, Santa Clara, CA, and InocuLAN from Cheyenne Software, Roslyn Heights, NY. Software license management software can also be used to prevent the execution of externally-supplied software that has not been approved by management. Note that some firewalls can enforce this policy. Because viruses and related malicious code historically have been a problem only on small systems, this policy applies primarily to workstations, PCs, local area networks, and client/server systems. This policy also becomes increasingly important as organizations connect to the Internet. See the policies "Testing For Viruses Prior To Use On Production Systems," "Telecommuting Data Entry Operators Must Employ Thin Clients," and "Process For Down-Loading Software From An Internet Mirror Site." A: EMT; E: MH.

179. Testing For Viruses Prior To Use On Company X Systems

Policy: To prevent infection by computer viruses, workers must not use any externally-provided software from a person or organization other than a known and trusted supplier. The only exception to this is when such software has first been tested and approved by the Information Security Department or a local information security coordinator.

Commentary: The intention of this policy is to keep all software used on Company X systems free from viruses, worms, Trojan horses, and other unauthorized programs. Note that the policy is not restricted to production systems; these unauthorized programs propagate rapidly and make no distinction between production and non-production systems. The policy requires only a negligible amount of extra work associated with the handling of externally-provided software. Normally, users would employ only that software which has been approved for internal use and which is in keeping with existing licenses with vendors. Thus this policy helps restrict the software routines that users may run. In a roundabout way, the policy also helps to discourage unauthorized copying of software for which Company X does not have a license. Although it does not need to be placed in the policy, the testing performed should always be done on a machine isolated from a network. Separately, some organizations may want to specify what constitutes a "known and trusted supplier" (ordinarily not an electronic bulletin board, an Internet-based users group, or some other non-commercial entity). Some other organizations may wish to expand the policy to require that all such testing of externally-supplied software be documented. On a different note, some organizations may wish to change the policy such that it requires all specific copies of software provided by non-trusted parties to be tested (rather than one copy, which is then alleged to be the same as other copies provided by the organization). On yet another note, this policy does not prohibit users from down-loading software from third party systems--it just prohibits them from executing it until it has been properly tested (this can be enforced by license management software or desktop change control software). See the policies entitled "Prohibition Against Down-Loading Software From Third Party Systems," "Loading External Programs Onto Network-Connected Computers," "Handling Software And Files Down-Loaded From Internet," and "Periodic Review Of Software Licensing Agreements." For a related idea, see the policy entitled "Immediate Reporting Of Suspected Computer Virus Infestation." A: ET; E: LMH.

180. Testing For Viruses On A Stand-Alone Non-Production Machine

Policy: Whenever software and/or files are received from any external entity, this material must be tested for unauthorized software on a stand-alone non-production machine before it is used on Company X information systems. If a virus, worm, or Trojan horse is present, the damage will be restricted to the involved machine.

Commentary: The intention of this policy is to maintain strict boundaries surrounding an organization's network and internal information systems. This policy states that software provided by vendors, files provided by associates at professional organizations, and all other externally-provided material must be tested prior to being used on Company X information systems. Note that viruses can now be embedded in data files like spreadsheet macros, not just in programs. This policy that may be too strict for many organizations. To maintain a separate machine for testing externally-provided material may be seen as excessively costly or inconvenient. Alternatively, screening of externally-provided material via programs like the SAM virus screening package from Symantec (Cupertino, California) -- which is invoked whenever a disk is inserted into a floppy drive -- may make the need for a separate non-production machine largely unnecessary. Likewise, some firewalls can scan both data files and email attachments, as well as executables. One benefit of this policy is that a log of all screening activity can be kept on the separate non-production machine. This log may provide essential information for the tracking and eradication a virus. The need to employ a stand-alone machine discourages users from bringing in non-standard software, thus helping to assure that standard software will be consistently used throughout the organization. In the long run, this policy will be superseded by personal computer license management software which will stop users from invoking unlicensed and unscreened software. On a separate note, Company X's definition of "production" is critical to this policy. If personal computers are, for the most part, not considered to be production machines, then the policy is easily implemented via products like SAM. If personal computers are, for the most part, connected to an intranet, then a separate machine or some intranet disconnection process will be needed. Also see the policy entitled "Handling Software And Files Down-Loaded From Internet." A: E; E: LMH.

181. All Outbound Software And Executable Files Must Be Virus Free

Policy: All files containing software or executable statements (including word processing and spreadsheet files) must be screened for viruses and shown to be virus free prior to being sent to any third party.

Commentary: This policy is motivated by an intention to avoid the bad press and public embarrassment which can come from being fingered as the source of a virus. The policy addresses the outbound transmission of files which is often unrestricted while the inbound transmission of files is often closely monitored. Note that this policy assumes that each user has the most recent virus screening utility on his or her computer, and has been trained in the ways to properly use this utility. Such screening is not necessary if an outbound file is in text format or rich text format (RTF) since no executable statements are included in such files. Note that the policy deliberately refrains from talking about a transmission path (Internet DSL connection, dial-up line, trusted courier, etc.) since the policy applies not matter what the transmission path. For related concepts, see the policies entitled "Prohibition Against Down-Loading Software From Third Party Systems" and "Required Process For Checking Software Down-Loaded From Internet." A: ET; E: LMH.

182. Virus Checking At Firewalls, Servers, And Desktop Machines

Policy: Virus screening software must be installed and enabled on all Company X firewalls, FTP servers, mail servers, intranet servers, and desktop machines.

Commentary: From a design standpoint, many people are confused about the best location for their virus screening software. For example, would it be sufficient to have this software run only on the mail server to catch incoming viruses from the Internet? This conservative policy clarifies the issue, requiring virus screening software to be resident and enabled on many distinct locations in an internal network (the policy does not, however, say how often scanning should take place). Because files may be encrypted or decrypted at any of these three spots, a virus screening package used at another location may miss a virus that has been part of transmission. The same could be said for data compression techniques, although many virus screening packages can adjust to data compression. Since a virus could be introduced at any of these three locations, and the sooner it is detected and eradicated the less it can spread, it is advisable to be checking for viruses at all of the specified locations. If an organization has a complex network involving other major types of computers, these too can be mentioned in the policy. For a related idea, see the policy entitled "At Least Two Virus Screening Software Packages Must Be Employed." A: T; E: LMH.

183. At Least Two Virus Screening Software Packages Must Be Employed

Policy: To assure that incoming viruses are immediately detected and eradicated, at least two virus screening software packages must be used at each point where electronic mail and other files enter Company X's network.

Commentary: The underlying motivation for this policy is diversification. With literally thousands of viruses now on the loose, it is increasingly difficult for virus screening software packages to detect all of them (even if the latest updates are faithfully applied). To reduce the level of risk, some organizations run several of these virus scanning systems on mail servers, firewalls, and other machines which accept incoming files including email. Note that this policy may have a performance impact which is unacceptable to the organization. For a related idea, see the policy entitled "Multiple Communication Channels For Electronic Offers & Acceptances." A: T; E: MH.

184. Virus Checking Decal Required For All Externally Supplied Floppy Disks

Policy: Externally supplied floppy disks may not be used on any Company X personal computer (PC) or local area network (LAN) server unless these disks have first been checked for viruses and received a decal indicating that no viruses were found.

Commentary: The objective of this policy is to provide a clear audit trail to make sure that all externally-supplied floppy disks are screened for viruses. The policy is also intended to discourage users from brining floppy disks into work for use on desktop systems. This policy removes reliance on end-users, assuming that they will not be qualified when it comes to checking for and responding to the presence of a virus. The policy assumes that one authorized person in each location or department will be the designated person to perform virus screening. This person, generally a local information security coordinator, would be the one to place decals on each externally-supplied floppy disk. The decals should include the person's initials and the date when the virus checking took place. Auditors can visually determine which floppy disks are externally-supplied based on the color of the plastic on the disks as well as the disk labels. They can then also visually determine whether these disks were checked for viruses and when. To make the identification of externally-supplied floppies still easier, an organization may want to purchase only one color of floppy disk. Beyond floppy disks, the scope of this policy could be expanded to include other small system storage media such as CD-ROMs, magneto-optical cartridges, and DAT tapes. Separately, some organizations take this one step further by putting bar codes on their floppy disks. Using the labels from vendors such as Avanti Associates (Valley Forge, Pennsylvania, USA), these organizations can then create a database indicating the origin, name, sensitivity classification, and contents of each floppy disk (or for that matter, any other user-controlled data storage media). For related ideas, see the policies entitled "Choosing Computer Storage Media Data Classifications" and "Limited Data Classification System Labelling Requirements." A: E; E: LMH.

185. Required Process For Checking Software Down-Loaded From Internet

Policy: Software down-loaded from non-Company X sources via the Internet may contain a virus (or similar programs such as worms or Trojan horses). Before such software is decompressed, users must log-out of all servers and terminate all other network connections. Then -- before it is executed -- the software must be screened with an approved virus detection package. If a virus is detected, the Information Security Department must immediately be notified, and no further work on this workstation may take place until the virus has been shown to be eradicated. If the software contains a virus, the damage will then be restricted to the involved workstation.

Commentary: The intention of this policy is to instruct users how to protect themselves against viruses contained in software down-loaded from the Internet. This policy takes a do-it-yourself approach to virus screening that eliminates the need for the Information Technology Department to get involved on a day-to-day basis. The policy assumes that users know when they are down-loading software from the Internet, and it assumes that users are somewhat knowledgeable about viruses and how they behave. Separately, new process on the Internet, called "server push" moves client software to an Internet-connected workstation without the involved user knowing that this transfer has taken place. While server-push mechanisms allow a new client/server functionality to be achieved, they also presents a significant threat of virus propagation. A new software package from McAfee Associates (Santa Clara, California, USA) scans such user-transparent software movements without user intervention. Accordingly, a policy such as this is expected to become obsolete in a few years as virus screening software automatically performs all the steps defined in the policy. Separately, the words following the second comma in the next-to-last sentence in the policy can be eliminated if this idea is believed to unduly interfere with productivity (it is, however, recommended that the words remain). See the policies entitled "Prohibition Against Down-Loading Software From Third Party Systems" and "Transferring Files Down-Loaded From Internet To Another Computer." A: E; E: LMH.

186. System Integrity Checking Programs Required For Personal Computers

Policy: To promptly detect and prevent the spread of computer viruses, all Company X personal computers (PCs) and servers must run integrity checking software. This software detects changes in configuration files, system software files, application software files, and other system resources. Integrity checking software must be continuously enabled or run daily.

Commentary: The mushrooming number of new computer viruses means that traditional virus scanners are no longer as effective as they used to be when it comes to detecting virus infections. There are now so many different viruses in circulation, and the number of new viruses is growing at such an alarming rate, that a lot of work (such as down-loading virus signatures from bulletin boards) is required to keep such scanners up to date. In addition, recent developments such as the "mutant engine" seriously jeopardize the effectiveness of virus scanning software that searches for bit sequences (signatures) to detect viruses. The mutant engine encrypts the body of a virus, thus changing its bit sequence, and therefore preventing many scanners from detecting it. More sophisticated virus detection tools are now required; these include algorithmic methods and heuristic scanning methods. Implementing these new tools, integrity checking software detects unexpected changes to software, configuration files, and the like, then prevents these changes or at least gives the user an opportunity to stop the virus infection process. Accordingly, this policy instructs local department management that they must use virus integrity checking software on a regular basis in order to protect Company X information and information systems. To make administration and eradication efforts easier, a particular vendor's virus integrity checking package can be made an in-house standard (but mention of the vendor's name generally does not appear in a policy). Some firms may wish to expand this policy to include mention of virus behavior detection and blocking facilities. This policy is also useful because it helps to detect intrusions where the attacker has modified files. Separately, to be effective, integrity checking software must also be accompanied by a policy that requires all problems to be promptly reported; see the policies entitled "Internal Reporting Of Information Security Violations & Problems" and ""Immediate Reporting Of Suspected Computer Virus Infestation." A: EMT; E: LMH.

187. Approved Virus Checking Programs Required On PCs And LAN Servers

Policy: Virus checking programs approved by the Information Security Department must be continuously enabled on all local area network (LAN) servers and networked personal computers (PCs).

Commentary: This policy doesn't make distinctions between integrity checkers, virus screening packages, virus behavior detection packages, and the like. Instead, it relies on the internal Information Security Department to identify one or more standard virus detection software packages. The emphasis is on networked machines because a virus or similar program can propagate much faster in a networked environment than it can in a stand-alone computing environment. Only intermittently networked machines, for example those which connect via dial-up, for purposes of this policy are still networked. The policy focuses on small systems because these are the computers which are most often hit by virus infections, not mainframes and other large-scale systems. Separately, the words "continuously enabled" were used to indicate that simply having the software on a hard disk drive is not sufficient -- it must be executing for protection to be provided. On another note, an increasing number of firewalls incorporate virus screening facilities. In those environments where the firewalls can support it, the policy should be expanded to include firewalls and mail servers. For related ideas, see the policies entitled "Testing For Viruses On A Stand-Alone Non-Production Machine" and "Immediate Reporting Of Suspected Computer Virus Infestation." A: E; E: LMH.

188. Current Virus Software Required For Certain Worker-Owned Computers

Policy: Every Company X worker who examines, processes, or stores Company X information using a computer that he or she owns must install and regularly run the most current version of an approved virus detection software package.

Commentary: The intention of this policy is to ensure that workers do not lose critical data due to malicious viruses, which among other things can erase the entire contents of a hard drive or insert spurious words into word processing documents. This requirement is not onerous for Company X workers because, if they were managing their systems well, they would have the most recent virus detection software package on their machines anyway. The policy becomes a service to the user community if Company X actually provides the software to these same workers. In order to maintain multi-location standardization and also to make remote technical support easier, this type of a software gift to workers is recommended. The cost of virus detection software is especially low when volume purchase agreements (VPAs) are arranged with vendors. For related considerations, see the policies entitled "At Least Two Virus Screening Software Packages Must Be Employed" and "Handling Software And Files Down-Loaded From Internet." A: E; E: LMH.

189. Material Must Be Decrypted Before Checking For Viruses

Policy: All externally-supplied computer-readable files (software programs, databases, word processing documents, spreadsheets, etc.) must be decrypted prior to being subjected to an approved virus checking process. Many virus checking programs cannot detect viruses in encrypted files.

Commentary: Many users do not understand that viruses may remain undetected in an encrypted file. This in turn can lead to serious problems where viruses are propagated when users believed they had been conscientious and had checked for viruses. The policy also makes reference to an "approved virus checking process" which undoubtedly will change over time as the sophistication of viruses accelerates. The last sentence in the policy could be deleted in those environments where only a bare-bones policy is needed; it is nonetheless desirable because it explains technical rationale for the policy. The policy could be expanded to include compressed files, which many virus checking programs cannot deal with either (although this has improved markedly over the last few years). Separately, note that viruses can now be found in data files and other computer-readable materials besides software; this is why the general term "files" is used in the policy. Also see the policy entitled "Users Must Not Attempt To Eradicate Computer Viruses." A: E; E: LMH.

190. Write Protection For Software On Micros And Workstations

Policy: All software running on micros and workstations must be write-protected such that an error will be generated if a computer virus tries to modify the software. An exception to this policy will be made in those cases where the software must modify itself in order to execute.

Commentary: The intention of this policy is to set microcomputer (PC) and workstation system parameters such that software cannot be modified unless specifically authorized by the user. For example, if a virus were to attempt to infect a word processing package, the user would get an error message saying that the requested write operation cannot be performed. This would be a tip-off to the user that a virus or some other unauthorized software had infected the system. Since many viruses do not inflict immediate damage, but lurk behind the scenes, this can be an important detective measure. The attractive aspect of this policy is that it is easy to implement and often effective in detecting viruses and related programs. Some modern operating systems, such as Apple's Macintosh OS, include a convenient button that users can employ to enable write protection of either system programs and/or application programs. Other mechanisms, such as write-protect tabs on floppy disks, can also be used to meet the requirements of this policy. Separately, note that some software packages will require that they be able to modify themselves at set-up time (for system parameters), but after that they will not need to modify themselves. Accordingly, after the initial system set-up, write-protection flags can be thrown. If the system parameters need to be changed later, the write-protection flags can be disabled, the system parameters changed, and then the write-protection flags once again enabled. For some software, using write protection will be problematic; it is the second sentence of the policy that allows an exception for these software packages. The policy given here could be expanded to include more discussion along these lines. It is generally accepted that this approach is not a sufficient defense against viruses; a separate virus detection system is needed (whether third-party software or part of the operating system as is the case with MS-Windows). See the policy "Immediate Reporting Of Suspected Computer Virus Infestation." A: ET; E: LMH.

191. Initial Backup Copies Of Microcomputer Software

Policy: All microcomputer software must be copied prior to its initial usage, and such copies must be stored in a safe and secure location. These master copies must not be used for ordinary business activities, but must be reserved for recovery from computer virus infections, hard disk crashes, and other computer problems.

Commentary: The intention of this policy is to make sure that all users have master backup copies of the software they employ. Of course, making backup copies of software should always be in keeping with the software vendor license agreements. Many licenses allow backup copies, so long as the backup copies are not used at the same time that another copy is being used. The reader should see the section of this book entitled Data Criticality for further policies dealing with backup and contingency planning. If a centralized technical support group distributes, updates, and manages microcomputer software, then there will be no need for a policy such as this to be distributed to end-users. This particular policy could be expanded to include other types of systems besides microcomputers (PCs), but the procedures on these larger systems are ordinarily more organized (so there is less of a need for an explicit policy like this). Some organizations may also want to specify that initial copies of all production software be stored both nearby and off-site (rather than simply in a "safe and secure location"). See the policy entitled "When Making Additional Copies Of Software Is Permissible." A: EMT; E: LMH.

192. Testing Of Software And Information Prior To Third Party Distribution

Policy: Prior to distributing any software or information in computerized form to third parties, Company X workers must first have subjected the software or information in question to appropriate testing, including comprehensive scanning to identify the presence of computer viruses. There are two notable exceptions to this need for testing: information contained within the body of an email message, and a file of information provided in text format.

Commentary: This policy helps avoid liability for bugs in software, for spreading a virus, etc. Although many organizations do not consider themselves to be publishers, this policy may still be relevant if they distribute software or information in any electronic form. For example, a large freight company in the USA provides its customers with a program on a floppy disk, allowing customers to determine the shipping charges, number of days to deliver a package to a certain location, etc. This freight company should subject this software to the tests described in this policy. The policy could be expanded to mention the title of the person, or the department, that determines what tests should be applied (the Information Security Department ideally determines this). The two exceptions are provided because they are unlikely to lead to the propagation of a virus or other nefarious code (unless the material is source or object code, but then questions will be asked and the material will not be executed). See the policy entitled "System Developers Must Not Perform Formal Testing." A: MT; E: LMH.

193. Prohibition Against Programs Consuming Excessive System Resources

Policy: Computer users must not run or write any computer program or process which is likely to consume significant system resources or otherwise interfere with Company X business activities.

Commentary: The intention of this policy is to prohibit game playing with recursive programs and other software that may damage Company X's ability to promptly process business transactions. Computer worms, like the one written by Robert Morris, Jr., would for instance be prohibited by this policy. Morris' worm caused 6,000+ computers on the Internet to be overloaded and crash. Likewise, Internet-based games can consume a great deal of bandwidth on internal networks, and are banned according to this policy. Often excessive system usage (computer cycles, disk space, etc.) is a good indicator of a virus or some other unauthorized program or process. Some computer operators will kill jobs which consume inordinate amounts of resources, and this policy will provide them with the management authorization to do so. Separately, the word "process" was included in the policy in addition to the word "program" so as to include things like macros, shell scripts, command files, and the like which may not, properly speaking, be computer programs. If users are prohibited from writing or running such programs or processes, then management can take disciplinary action, whereas management may be prevented from doing so if users were not placed on notice. Besides being a deterrent to playing around with viruses, worms, and similar software, this policy is a deterrent to playing around with production business systems just to find out what would happen. See the policies entitled "Limitation Of User Abilities To Delay Or Interrupt Service," "Termination Of User Processes Or Sessions And Removal Of User Files," and "Sending Large Quantities Of Unsolicited Email (Mail Bombing)." A: ET; E: LMH.

194. All User Involvement With Computer Viruses Prohibited

Policy: Users must not intentionally write, generate, compile, copy, collect, propagate, execute, or attempt to introduce any computer code designed to self-replicate, damage, or otherwise hinder the performance of or access to any Company X computer, network, or information. Such software is known as a virus, bacteria, worm, Trojan horse, and similar names.

Commentary: The intention of this policy is to clearly prohibit all involvement with viruses and the like. Most appropriate in the university environment where users consider these activities to be of academic interest, this policy makes it clear that all involvement with viruses is off-limits (on Company X systems or external systems reached via Company X systems). Because viruses are difficult to contain and isolate, the safest approach is to prohibit users from getting involved with them in any way. Separately, the policy also eliminates any possible claims that the organization encouraged a user to refine their computer skills and that these antics were really just efforts to learn computer programming. The word "generate" may at first seem superfluous, but it is actually different than "write." There are a number of programs freely-available in the computer underground which will allow users to construct their own viruses using already-written virus building software. If these tools are used, properly speaking, a user is not "writing" a virus. For a related idea, see the policy entitled "Immediate Reporting Of Suspected Computer Virus Infestation." A: ET; E: LMH.

1.2.2. Development Process

1.2.2.1. Development Tools And Techniques

195. Security Requirements Identification Prior To Development/Acquisition

Policy: Before a new system is developed or acquired, management of the user department(s) must have clearly specified the relevant security requirements. Alternatives must be reviewed with the developers and/or vendors so that an appropriate balance is struck between security and other objectives (ease-of-use, operational simplicity, ability to upgrade, acceptable cost, etc.).
Commentary: This policy is intended to require that user department management consider security requirements early in the systems development life cycle (SDLC). If a formal SDLC exists within an organization, then the policy could be expanded to make reference to specific milestones in the process where the consideration of security should occur. Separately, this policy makes it clear that, ultimately, it is the user department management (or perhaps the information owner) who is responsible for incorporating relevant controls into a new system. The scope of the policy could be expanded to include "significantly modified" systems, not just new systems. For related ideas, see the policies entitled "Incorporation Of Security Into Systems Development Life Cycle" and "Formal Specifications Required For Software Developed In-House." A: M; E: LMH.

196. Developers Embed Security In Systems If Commercial Solution Exists

Policy: In-house systems developers must embed security in the systems they build or enhance -- rather than requiring users to deal with security -- in every instance where a commercially-available and reasonably-priced solution exists.

Commentary: The intention of this policy is to save the organization a lot of money and also to make its systems easier to use. Studies show that organizations adding controls after a business application goes into production will pay ten times as much as those organizations who built-in security during the development process. This policy will require a higher expenditure up-front, but it will reduce the cost of information security over the long-run. Using packaged security solutions provided by third parties also reduces long-run costs, and this policy promotes a "purchase rather than build it in-house" philosophy. Likewise, whenever possible, information security should be automated and removed from the user's domain. For example, users should not be required to back-up their own data resident on a desktop machine; instead an automatic back-up process to a server at night can be employed over a local area network. Also see the policies entitled "Ease-Of-Use Required For Computer & Communications Security" and "Security Requirements Identification Prior To Development/Acquisition." A: T; E: LMH.

197. Compliance With Organizational Systems Development Conventions

Policy: Management must ensure that all software development and software maintenance activities performed by in-house staff subscribe to Company X policies, standards, procedures, and other systems development conventions.

Commentary: This policy instructs both local and centralized management to make sure that all software development activities performed by in-house staff are in compliance with standard systems development conventions. The growing popularity of end-user programming makes this policy increasingly important because end-users often construct and alter production application systems without proper testing, documentation, etc. This makes this policy particularly important for small system environments such as client/server systems, local area networks, PCs, etc. Even if end-user programming is prohibited (or simply not performed), there is still a need for a policy like this to ensure that local departmental management consistently observes Company X systems development related conventions. The policy assumes that such systems development conventions have already been specified. Hopefully these conventions are not so onerous that end-users would just dispense with them without serious consideration. The word "production" may be added to the policy to limit its applicability; if this is done, it would permit the unmanaged development of non-production software, but once that software was moved into production, it should be required to comply with these conventions. A definition of what "software development" entails may also be called for; this could, for instance, include development of new databases, new expert systems, and synchronized scripted updates between multiple files in a client/server network. See the policies entitled "Automatic Detection Of End-User Application Programs," "Incorporation Of Security Into Systems Development Life Cycle," and "Centralized Responsibility For Information Security." A: EMT; H: LMH.

198. Software Testing With Sanitized Rather Than Production Information

Policy: Unless written permission is first obtained from the Information Security Department manager, all software testing for systems designed to handle private information must be accomplished exclusively with "sanitized" production information. Sanitized information is production information which no longer contains specific details that might be valuable, critical, sensitive, or private.

Commentary: The "sanitization" process obscures certain information without significantly modifying the characteristics relevant to testing. For example, the actual first and last names of individuals in a human resources database might be mixed up such that they no longer reflect any specific persons. In this manner the actual field lengths required, the number of records in the database, and other statistics remain the same for testing purposes. The intention of the policy is to prevent unauthorized disclosure of testing information to persons such as in house programmers and contractors. This policy is appropriate for third party packages as well as software developed in-house. The policy is particularly relevant to those environments in which end-users are doing their own programming (client-server computing, local area networks, PCs, and the like) because these new programmers may not be familiar with traditional systems development approaches. Most organizations will want to specify how to sanitize data. On a separate note, rather than mentioning "valuable, critical, sensitive or private" information, the policy can make reference to certain data classifications used within Company X. For more information about classification approaches, see the policy entitled "Four Category Data Classification Scheme." Also see the policies entitled "Disclosure Of Private Information To Third Parties" and "Access To Production Business Information For System Testing." A: MT; E: MH.

199. Software Developed In-House--Notice Of Failure To Properly Operate

Policy: Whenever software developed in-house fails to produce the expected results, it must always provide either an error message or some other indication of failure, one or both of which must be presented to the user.

Commentary: It is dangerous for software to be producing erroneous results, particularly when users may be unwittingly relying on these results for their business activities. For example, if a program could not accept new input data, it might automatically use the last input data provided to it. This difference in input data might be undetectable to the user. Without specific notice of the problem, the user may go on to make erroneous decisions based on inaccurate information. Accordingly, the intention of this policy is to ensure that users are always made aware that in-house software is failing to operate as intended. This policy also partially compensates for the fact that so many users accept computer-generated reports without further thought, assuming reports to be correct. Externally-provided software generally includes failure notification features, although this policy could be extended to include external software. If this change to the policy were made, then the policy would be used for software acquisition decisions. This policy also implicitly requires that in-house developers incorporate reasonableness checks in the software they build--this is the only way they know whether the software produced the expected results. Also see the policies entitled "Software Developed In-House--Notice When No Action Taken" and "Preventive Maintenance On Computer And Communication Systems." A: T; E: LMH.

200. Software Developed In-House--Notice When No Action Taken

Policy: Whenever software developed in-house receives input from a user, some sort of feedback must be provided. If input from a user indicates a request, the user must always receive feedback indicating whether the request was performed.

Commentary: Great confusion can result when users think that they have instructed a system to perform a certain action, when in fact they have not. For example, when using an automated teller machine, a customer may think that he requested the system to transfer a certain sum from his money-market savings account to his checking account. Instead he may have hit the wrong button, thereby indicating that the money should be transferred from a regular savings account. If the customer does not have a regular savings account, then the automated teller machine may simply ignore his input. If the automated teller machine does not respond with an error message, the customer may assume the transfer has been made. Checks could then be bounced, and other problems may ensue. Accordingly, the intention of this policy is to require that systems designers always provide users with error messages indicating that the system did not perform their request if indeed this is the situation. On the other hand, the policy requires a confirmation when input is acceptable (a beep or other noise may be sufficient). The policy, as written, could apply to all software although having internal staff make modifications, patches, and the like to software packages written by third parties is often too much trouble. Also see the policy entitled "Software Developed In-House--Notice Of Failure To Properly Operate." A: T; E: LMH.

201. Formal Specifications Required For Software Developed In-House

Policy: All software developed by in-house staff, and intended to process sensitive, valuable, or critical information, must have a written formal specification. This specification must be part of an agreement between the involved information owner(s) and the system developer(s). A first draft of the agreement must be completed and approved prior to the time when programming efforts begin.

Commentary: Formal specifications define the functionality on which users, developers, auditors, and other parties can rely. Formal specifications should also clearly specify the control measures to be incorporated into software. Accordingly, this policy is intended to ensure that information owner(s) -- the surrogate for users -- know what they will be getting in advance of the time when development efforts get underway. An important part of knowing what they will be getting is the controls with which the information will be managed. This policy is deliberately aimed at countering an often-encountered problem where developers begin work before the nature of the intended system is clarified. Nothing in this policy prevents the use of prototyping as a mechanism for the refinement of requirements, for the testing of new ideas, and/or for the solicitation of user feedback. A specification can be modified as work proceeds, as users better understand what they need, and as business requirements change. This policy only requires an advance specification. Some organizations may wish to be more specific about what goes into the specification (business objectives served, system interfaces, platforms supported, controls to be incorporated, etc.). In most instances, what goes into an acceptable specification would be defined elsewhere, such as in systems development documentation. Because the specification deals with information of interest to the Information Security Department, some organizations may wish to add approval by the Information Security Department to the approval by the information owner(s). This policy is particularly relevant to those environments in which end-users are doing their own programming, such as client-server computing, intranets, local area networks (LANs), and PCs, because these new programmers may not be familiar with traditional systems development approaches. For a related idea, see the policy entitled "Information Security Impact Statements." A: MT; E: LMH.

202. Removal Of All Unauthorized Access Paths In Production Software

Policy: Prior to moving software which has been developed in-house to production status, programmers and other technical staff must remove all special access paths so that access may only be obtained via normal secured channels. This means that all trap doors and other short-cuts that could be used to compromise security must be removed. Likewise, all system privileges needed for development efforts -- but not required for normal production activities -- must be removed.

Commentary: The intention of this policy is to put programmers and other system developers on notice that they must eliminate all pathways which could be used to compromise security. An example justifying this policy involved the log-in program for what used to be called ARPANET (now Internet); the developers had a special password which allowed them to gain privileged access to any log-in program without having first been granted access by the system's management. This is exactly the type of access pathway that should be eliminated prior to placing systems in production status. Although programmers may only want to save themselves time at some point in the future, by leaving such unauthorized pathways in production systems, they also create pathways that can be exploited by unauthorized parties. The policy also implicitly requires all special access paths to be disclosed in documentation. This policy is particularly relevant to those environments in which end-users are doing their own programming (client-server computing, local area networks, intranets, PCs, and the like) because these new programmers may not be familiar with traditional systems development approaches. Also see the policies entitled "Security Mechanisms Must Not Be Compromised for Customers" and "Prohibition Against Trap Doors To Circumvent Access Controls." A: T; E: LMH.

203. Use Of Mature Development Tools And Techniques

Policy: In the absence of special management approval to the contrary, all in-house software development projects must use mature development tools and techniques.

Commentary: The use of new or untried tools and techniques, such as new compilers, increases the risks associated with development projects and the results produced. For example, developers may not be aware of security problems with new tools or techniques, and may inadvertently allow the results of these problems to be incorporated into production systems. Besides, mature tools and techniques often have the bugs and problems "ironed out," whereas new tools and techniques do not. Similarly, mature tools are often offered by vendors who have been in business for a good while and are therefore more likely to be financially stable. Accordingly, the intention of this policy is to eliminate the problems that new tools and techniques could bring. Of course, this policy also involves a tradeoff--for competitive or other reasons, management may want to use new tools and techniques. Since the definition of "mature" is not provided in the policy, there is some latitude for management to investigate new tools and techniques, and if they seem to do the job management wants, and if they have received good reviews in the media or from other customers, then they can be declared "mature." For related ideas, see the policies entitled "Use Of Most Current Computer Operating System Versions" and "External Network Interfaces Must Be Approved By Information Security." A: MT; E: LMH.

204. Use Of Software Tools & Languages With Unproven Security Attributes

Policy: Unless advance approval of the Information Security Department manager has first been obtained, Company X system designers and developers must refrain from utilizing software tools and languages which have unproven security attributes when they build web sites, extranets, or any other system having an interface to external parties.

Commentary: The intention of this policy is to get systems designers and developers thinking about which software tools and languages are proven to be secure. At this point Java has proven itself to be relatively secure, so it would be permissible under this policy. Likewise, CGI scripts (common gateway interface routines used for web pages), provided they are well-tested and avoid certain common mistakes, have been shown to be relatively secure. Other more recent software tools may not qualify, and thus should not be used yet. The delineation between proven to be secure and not proven to be secure is not quantitative or logically irrefutable, it must instead be the result of a conversation (hopefully with the Information Security Department manager). Note that the policy is restricted to external interfaces, where hackers or industrial spies could enter, and does not apply to internal systems. In this respect, the policy is a border protection policy. For related considerations, see the policies entitled "Use Of Mature Development Tools And Techniques" and "External Network Interfaces Must Be Approved By Information Security." A: T; E: LHM.

205. Use Of Higher Level Programming Languages

Policy: The use of higher level computer programming languages reduces the volume of code that must be developed, the difficulty of software maintenance, the time required to develop an application, and the number of bugs. Accordingly, unless Information Systems Department management permission is first obtained, all in-house system development projects involving over $100,000 of effort must be programmed in a higher-level language.

Commentary: The intention of this policy is to ensure that development staff consistently use higher level languages (the organization may wish to specify which languages in the policy). This is particularly important when end-users do their own PC-based programming outside the purview of the Information Systems Department. By limiting the nature and types of permissible languages, this policy seeks to ensure the maintainability and controllability of end-user programming efforts (particularly for client/server environments, local area networks, intranets, PCs, etc.). Ideally, modules for security procedures such as encryption would be pre-defined objects which could readily be incorporated into business applications via an object oriented programming environment (or CASE tool). Generally the Information Systems Department should set the standard for the higher level language to be employed, and should handle exceptions. For certain situations, it may be necessary to use a lower level language like assembler (for instance if a program is executed many times and the performance of an entire computer system would be adversely impacted if a higher level language were to be used for this task). Since many higher level languages provide some sort of self-documenting-code, this also helps with the frequently-encountered problem of inadequate and out-of-date documentation. For a related idea, see the policy entitled "Automatic Detection Of End-User Application Programs." A: EMT; E: LMH.

206. Re-Usability Of Software Developed In-House

Policy: All in-house development projects, with a budget over $100,000, must have as a secondary goal the development of reliable modular software which can be entered into a shared software repository.

Commentary: The development and use of standard shared modules not only reduces costs, but it also reduces risk of errors and the risk of inadvertent security exposures. The intention of this policy is to make sure that all major in-house software development effort produce code that can be reused in the future. Some organizations may want to add certain documentation requirements to this policy such that other developers will be able to understand what the original developers actually did. Other prerequisites for insertion into a software repository (such as extensive testing) may also be specified in this policy. The policy could also include some words urging developers to use modules stored in a repository whenever relevant. This type of policy is becoming increasingly important as computer-aided software engineering (CASE) tools and object oriented programming environments become more widely used. For a related idea, see the policy entitled "Control Over Movement Of Software From Development To Production." A: T; E: LMH.

207. Naming Convention For Production Files

Policy: A file naming convention must be employed to clearly distinguish between those files used for production purposes and those files used for testing and/or training purposes.

Commentary: Having a file naming convention which distinguishes production files from other files will assist with backups, log analysis, problem diagnosis, and system administration. Such a convention will also help with efforts to purge test and training files after testing and training have been completed. Another intention of the policy is to allow automated handling of files based on file name. For example, a local area network backup program may be instructed to only backup those files on each connected microcomputer (PC) with the suffix ".dat". Without such conventions, scripted processes -- such as searching backup tapes for a certain file -- will be very much more difficult. File naming conventions like this are especially important in those environments, such as client/server and Internet communications, where different operating systems are involved. Such file naming conventions are also very useful if data replication is being used across multiple machines. The convention itself may or may not be specified in the policy (generally not because these conventions would be expected to change more often than this policy). For a related idea, see the policy entitled "Multi-Platform Systems Parameter Naming Conventions." A: T; E: LMH.

208. Special Labeling For All Non-Production Business Transactions

Policy: Transactions used for auditing, testing, training or other non-production purposes must be labeled and/or otherwise separated from transactions used for production processing. This will help ensure that Company X records are not improperly updated by non-production transactions.

Commentary: The intention of this policy is to have a mechanism to clearly separate auditing, testing, training, and non-production transactions from legitimate business transactions. If this separation is achieved, it will avoid both confusion and improper updates of computerized records. Use of the EDP auditing technique know as a "test deck" for instance involves the submission of fictitious transactions to the system to determine whether they are handled correctly. Test deck analysis can show whether controls are working properly and whether transactions were posted to the proper accounts. One way to label these transactions is with a special transaction serial number (perhaps made up of letters rather than numbers). In other words, a special field devoted exclusively to a production designation need not be used; this information could be incorporated into other fields. For related ideas, see the policies entitled "Production Input Transactions Must Have Sequence Numbers" and "Reconstructibility Of Changes To Production Information." A: T; E: LMH.

209. Documentation Required For All Production Business Systems

Policy: Every user who develops or implements software and/or hardware to be used for Company X business activities must document the system in advance of its deployment. The documentation must be written so that the system may be run by persons unacquainted with it. Such documentation must be prepared even when standard software--such as a spreadsheet program--is employed.

Commentary: If the type of documentation described in this policy is not prepared and kept up-to-date, the sudden unavailability of a key person may mean that the production data processing they supervised comes to an abrupt halt. This policy is particularly relevant to small systems such as those with microcomputers (PCs), workstations, local area networks (LANs), client/server systems, and departmental systems. End-user programming of production business systems can lead to serious losses if proper documentation is not prepared; this might happen if the person who developed the system leaves the organization but nobody else knows how to run the system. Such documentation is also likely to be critical for contingency planning purposes. Words covering the need to update the documentation on a periodic basis, or whenever major changes are made, could also be included in the policy. For a related idea, see the policy entitled "Training & Operating Documentation Required For Production Systems." A: EMT; E: LMH.

210. Permissible Functionality Of Systems Developed In-House

Policy: With the exception of emergency fixes, only those functions described in an approved system design document may be included in a production computer or communications system that has been developed in-house.

Commentary: Undocumented functions, although they may be well-intentioned, may also pose grave security risks. For example, an undocumented mechanism to let the original programmer circumvent access controls, if left in the production version of an application, may be exploited by an unauthorized user. The intention of this policy is to make sure that all functionality gets documented and approved, and also that management knows about or can readily discover exactly what Company X systems do and don't do. In this context, "system" could be an entire computer or communications system, system programs, or application programs. This policy may also be used to discipline or terminate a programmer who built undocumented functionality into a system. This policy becomes more important as users develop their own client/server systems, local area network systems, departmental systems, intranets, and systems tying together PCs. Also see the policy entitled "Removal Of All Unauthorized Access Paths In Production Software." A: MT; E: LMH.

211. Immediate System Interruption If Human Beings Are Jeopardized

Policy: Robots and other computerized machinery must be programmed so that the current activity immediately stops if the activity is harming or is likely to harm a human being.

Commentary: This safety-related policy is a derivative of one of Isaac Isamov's rules of robot design. It is applicable to process control systems, computerized conveyor belts, manufacturing assembly lines, and similar computerized systems. The intention of the policy is that designers be forced to consider the circumstances when the system might jeopardize human safety. The policy could be expanded to include immediate notice to the operator of a dangerous condition. Such a policy may also be useful when demonstrating that the system was designed with human safety in mind; this might be useful when defending against a lawsuit alleging negligence. Such a policy may also help with management/employee relations (such as union negotiations) because it demonstrates a concern for worker safety. For a related idea involving danger to humans, see the policy entitled "Use of Duress Passwords." Also see the policy entitled "Human Intervention Required For Important Decisions." A: MT; E: LMH.

212. Restricted Use Of Diagnostic Test Hardware And Software

Policy: Diagnostic test hardware and software, such as communications line monitors, must be used only by authorized personnel for testing and development purposes. Access to such hardware and software must be strictly controlled.

Commentary: Diagnostic test hardware and software can be used to insert spurious messages on a communications line so that a fraud may be perpetrated. The tools may also allow people to read communications line traffic that they would otherwise not be able to examine. These wiretapping tools have, for instance, been used to capture readable passwords and user-IDs which are then later used to gain unauthorized system access. The intention of this policy is to restrict the use of such powerful tools to troubleshooting and other authorized business activities. The policy gives local management significant leeway in determining the ways in which they secure these hardware and software tools. For instance, some managers will require that line monitor devices be locked in a closet, while others will be satisfied with the use of a metal key to activate and deactivate the device. There is a greater need for this policy in those environments using fixed passwords (rather than dynamic passwords) for system access control. Likewise, this policy is not needed in those environments where all network traffic is encrypted. For a related idea, consider the policy entitled "Default To Denial Of Access Control Privileges." A: T; E: LMH.

213. Systems Utilities Resident On Production System Storage Media

Policy: Disks and other on-line storage facilities used on production computer systems must NOT contain compilers, assemblers, text editors, word processors, or other general purpose utilities which may be used to compromise the security of the system.

Commentary: In spite of the strong position taken in this policy, emergency use of these utilities will be required from time to time. As a practical matter, to meet these exceptional needs, the utilities may be kept on a tape or disk which is locked in a file cabinet in the computer machine room. After they are used, the utilities can be deleted from the system, and the tape can be once again locked in the file cabinet. This process might, for example, apply to the utilities from IBM for the MVS operating system called "Superzap" and "Diskanalyzer"--both of which could be used to circumvent controls. More specifically, Superzap allows a user to go directly to any file and modify it. Thus Superzap might be used to circumvent a password-based access control software package like Computer Associates' ACF2. This policy is equally important for smaller systems such as client/server systems, local area network servers, and PC systems, although it is more difficult to control; in these environments, software license management software may be used to spot these utilities. The intention of this policy is to prevent these utilities from being readily accessible to users, thereby reducing the chances that the utilities will be used to circumvent controls. Some of the utilities mentioned in the policy will be needed in certain environments, and so these may be deleted from the list of utilities found in this policy (most likely text editors and word processors). See the policy entitled "Restricted And Monitored Use Of Systems Software Utilities" and "Removal Of Unnecessary Systems Software At Installation Time." A: T; E: LMH.

214. Restricted And Monitored Use Of Systems Software Utilities

Policy: Access to systems software utilities must be restricted to a small number of trusted and authorized users. Whenever these utilities are executed, the resulting activity must be securely logged, and promptly thereafter reviewed by the computer operations manager.

Commentary: Most multi-user computer systems have one or more utilities that can be used to override either system access controls or application access controls. Examples include a database troubleshooting tool and a disk repair utility. These tools may allow a user to directly alter the payroll database, the accounts receivable check printing spool file, and other computer-resident collections of information--without going through the normal channels and the associated controls. The intention of this policy is to prevent dangerous utilities from being used by unauthorized persons. In those circumstances where these utilities must be used to get work done, the intention of this policy is to make sure that their usage is in keeping with management intentions. With the words "securely logged," the policy also seeks to have facilities to quickly identify unauthorized systems utility use. This policy assumes that the systems in question have access controls such as those based on passwords and profiles of user privileges (it is not applicable to unsecured microcomputers running only MS-DOS or Mac OS). If many people on a multi-user system are able to use such systems utilities, then the access controls are nearly worthless. Separately, the phrase "securely logged" means recorded in a manner that is not readily modifiable by users employing the involved system utility. Some organizations may wish to go further than the words shown in this policy--they may want to specifically authorize each and every use of a systems utility. Also see the policies entitled "Systems Utilities Resident On Production System Storage Media," "Approval Required For Changes To Production Operating Systems," and "Inclusion Of Security Relevant Events In System Logs." A: T; E: LMH.

215. External Network Interfaces Must Be Approved By Information Security

Policy: Company X systems designers and developers must restrict their usage of external network interfaces and protocols (FTP, TELNET, HTTP, etc.) to those which have been expressly approved by the Information Security Department manager.

Commentary: The intention of this policy is to prevent system designers and developers from writing software which employs new interfaces and protocols for which the security has not yet been proven to be robust, reliable, and operationally manageable. The policy also stops these people from using questionable interfaces and protocols which are employed by packaged software that the organization has purchased, rented, or leased. Use of new interfaces and/or protocols, or even old interfaces and/or protocols which are obscure and infrequently encountered, subjects the organization to a variety of unknown vulnerabilities. The more common interfaces and protocols have at least been closely examined, subjected to determined attacks, fixed and patched, as well as widely tested. This conservative policy thus minimizes the number of interfaces and protocols to the tried-and-true and generally-accepted alternatives (SHTTP, SSL, SNMP, etc.). A side effect of this policy is the promotion of internal network interface and protocol standardization, which in turn facilitates the establishment of centralized network management systems. Separately, note that the policy deliberately refrains from saying anything about the Internet, so it is equally applicable to other types of external networks such as the public switched dial network (PSDN). For related considerations, see the policies entitled "Latest Software Release On Systems Interfacing External Networks" and "Reliance On Operating System User Authentication Process." A: T; E: LMH.

1.2.2.2. Development Privileges And Relationships

216. Access To Production Business Information For System Testing

Policy: Where access to production business information is required so that new or modified business application systems may be developed or tested, only "read" and "copy" access may be granted on production machines. This access is permitted only for the duration of the testing and related development efforts, and must be promptly revoked upon the successful completion of these efforts.

Commentary: The intention of this access control policy is to clearly specify the times when access to production business data on production machines will be granted to testing personnel such as quality assurance experts. The policy also strictly limits the type of access they will have (no update or deletion privileges). Of course after they have read and/or copied production data over to a test system, then they can update and delete as much as they need to on the test machine. The policy thus enforces a clear distinction between production and development environments. The policy is also intended to make perfectly clear the type of access privileges that developers will be given. The policy attempts to consistently define access privileges for an area where excessive privileges are often commonplace. Without such a policy and associated control measures, it will be difficult to establish a clear separation between production and development computing environments. The policy also helps to prevent and discourage developer manipulation of production data (perhaps for sabotage, fraud, industrial espionage, or related reasons). For separation of duties reasons, the policy assumes that production users are different people than those doing the development and testing. Although not spoken to directly by this policy, the development personnel should also be different from the testing personnel. For related ideas, see the policies entitled "Privilege Restriction Based On The Need-to-Know," "Development Staff Access To Production Application Information," and "Software Testing With Sanitized Rather Than Production Information." A: T; E: LMH.

217. Separation Between Production And Development Environments

Policy: Business application software in development must be kept strictly separate from production application software. If existing facilities permit it, this separation must be achieved via physically separate computer systems. When computing facilities do not allow this, separate directories or libraries with strictly enforced access controls must to be employed.

Commentary: The separation between production (operations) and systems development is one of the most important aspects of a secure computing environment. If developers, users, and other can make changes to production software, then a wide variety of security exposures are introduced. These exposures include Trojan horse programs, logic bombs, and network worms which could be used to commit fraud, embezzlement, sabotage, and industrial espionage. This policy supports a variety of 'separation of duties' controls, such as the use of separate staff to run production applications from the staff used to develop and test applications. The policy also supports the restriction of production access privileges to a small number of people. Some organizations may wish to additionally specify separate storage media volumes (disks most likely) for production and development files. Although in some instances more difficult to achieve in the client/server, local area network, personal computer, and related small systems environments, this policy is not meant to be restricted to large scale systems. Note that the words in the policy "business application software in development" refer to both new software and also old software being modified. The policy could be further supported by having separate individuals work in development area and production area, just as it could be supported by having separate rooms for equipment for development and for production purposes. For related ideas, see the policies entitled "Privilege Restriction Based On The Need-to-Know," "Separation Between Programming And Testing Environments," and "Separation Of Duties And Control Over Company X Assets." A: T; E: LMH.

218. Separation Between Programming And Testing Environments

Policy: Production business application software in development must be kept strictly separate from this type of software in testing. If facilities permit it, this separation must be achieved via physically separate computer systems. When computing facilities do not allow this, separate directories or libraries with strictly enforced access controls must be employed.

Commentary: This policy is intended to take the policy entitled "Separation Between Production and Development Environments" one step further, adding additional security. This policy is intended to prevent unauthorized modification of software after tests have been performed, which could lead to a situation where the software is placed in a production environment and then used to commit fraud, embezzlement, sabotage, or industrial espionage. The policy could be further supported by having separate individuals work in the development area and the test area, just as it could be supported by having separate rooms for equipment for development and for test purposes. See the policies entitled "Privilege Restriction Based On The Need-to-Know" and "Separation Between Production And Development Environments." A: T; E: MH.

219. Development Staff Access To Production Application Information

Policy: Business application software development staff must not be permitted to access production information, with the exception of the production information relevant to the particular application software on which they are currently working.

Commentary: The intention of this policy is to limit each developer's access to production information such that access is granted only for that production information required to support his or her development work. For example, if a developer is working on a new accounts receivable system, he or she does not need access to accounts payable production information. The policy thus forces management to implement access controls at a level of detail that they may not have previously specified (they may have given all developers access to all production information). This policy supports the principle of separation of duties. Although perhaps more difficult to achieve in the client/server, local area network, personal computer, and related small systems environments, this policy is not restricted to large scale systems. For a more fundamental perspective, see the policies entitled "Privilege Restriction Based On The Need-to-Know" and

"Separation Of Duties And Control Over Company X Assets." Also see the policy entitled "Access To Production Business Information For System Testing." A: T; E: LMH.

220. System Developers Must Not Perform Formal Testing

Policy: Workers who have been involved in the development of specific business application software must not be involved in the formal testing or day-to-day production operation of such software.

Commentary: Granted, developers should test their programs as they build them. This policy does not address the informal testing that normally accompanies programming and development work. Using the words "formal testing," this policy refers to a process through which user management and/or systems management satisfies themselves that a system performs according to specifications. If a programmer or another developer were to do formal testing of his or her own work, there would be a great temptation to choose only those test cases which show that certain control measures work properly, to ignore certain potentially troubling test cases, etc. Even when there is no intention to be lazy, developers have a certain way of looking at an application that typically limits their appreciation of the real-world circumstances the application will be called on to handle. Thus another pair of eyes is needed to validate that the application works properly. Although more difficult to achieve in the client/server, local area network, personal computer, and related small systems environments, this policy is not restricted to large scale systems. This policy is a manifestation of the principle of separation of duties. See the policies entitled "Separation Of Duties And Control Over Company X Assets" and "Access To Production Business Information For System Testing." A: MT; E: LMH.

221. Special Sign-Off Required For Projects Involving Human Safety Issues

Policy: All in-house software projects that involve human safety risks must have a computer development project manager's signature on the testing approval papers prior to being used for production business purposes. These papers must state that this manager represents that--to the best of his/her professional ability and knowledge--all necessary controls have been integrated into the software in question, and such controls have been adequately tested.

Commentary: This policy reflects a regulation now found in England. In the regulation, development team project managers must personally sign-off on such projects, declaring that adequate controls have been incorporated into systems they developed. The intention of the policy is to make a specific individual accountable for the inclusion of appropriate safety-related control measures. If a specific individual can be sued or otherwise disciplined for insufficient security measures, the individual is more likely to take steps to ensure that adequate control measures are incorporated into systems developed in-house. Some organizations may wish to specify what is meant by the term "human safety risks," while others may deliberately wish to keep it vague to widen its applicability to potentially unforeseen future circumstances. If an organization chooses to get specific about this term, they may wish to make reference to repetitive motion and other ergonomic matters (carpal tunnel, eyestrain, etc.), not just severe personal injury that could be inflicted in a certain moment (robotic manufacturing systems, process control systems in a chemical plant, etc.). This policy attempts to counteract a tendency in the information security field where a number of people assume that security matters are someone else's responsibility; if everyone does this, then nobody has addressed the requisite security matters. For related ideas, see the policies entitled "Separate Approval Required For Production System Controls," "Immediate System Interruption If Human Beings Are Jeopardized," and "Use Of Duress Passwords." A: MT; E: MH.

222. Designers & Developers Must Notify Management Of Potential Problems

Policy: Systems designers and developers are individually responsible for notifying project management about any technical or social problems which might be caused by the applications they are building/modifying. Management must then decide what -- if any -- adjustments are appropriate.

Commentary: The intention of this policy is to make systems designers and developers personally responsible for notifying management about potential problems associated with the systems they are developing or enhancing. In many organizations, these more technical staff members don't say anything about serious issues such as fraud and privacy violation. Management may then put a system into production operation, and only later discover these previously-known problems. When asked why they didn't notify management, technical staff members often say "it's not my job" or "I wasn't asked to do that." This policy is consistent with an English law which makes developers personally liable for including adequate control measures in the software that they develop. Separately, new computer technology is often so far different from what people are used to, that they have trouble imagining how the new technology will operate once placed into production. Accordingly, the more people who think about potential problems before a system goes into production operation (not just information security specialists and internal auditors), the more likely these problems are to be discovered and corrected before serious losses are incurred. For related considerations, see the policies entitled "Inclusion Of Information Security Contact Information On Web Site" and "Users Must Not Distribute Information About System Vulnerabilities." A: T; E: LMH.

223. Complaints Regarding Errors & Security Problems Traced To Developers

Policy: All complaints about software errors, omissions, and security problems which are attributable to software developed in-house must be traced back to the designers, programmers, and other development staff involved. Such an inquiry must determine the cause(s) of the problems as well as the accountable individual(s).

Commentary: The intention of this policy is to encourage development staff to take security more seriously at the time that they put together a new or enhanced software system. All too often these technical staff are under great pressure to deliver something that works reasonably well according to unrealistic deadlines. In order to meet these deadlines, they often ignore security, and their choices in this matter are often supported by project management staff. This policy fosters a sense of accountability for the problems that may be encountered in the future. If development staff members know they will be held responsible for future problems, they will bring a new level of professionalism and concern to the security-related work that they perform. Separately, this policy will also help to illuminate those places where the systems development process breaks down, where it needs fixing. Notice that the words "development staff" do not refer to employees alone; these words include contractors, consultants, temporaries, etc. For related ideas, see the policies entitled "Special Sign-Off Required For Projects Involving Human Safety Issues" and "Originator Of Transactions Must Be Clearly Identified." A: T; E: LMH.

1.2.3. Change Control Process

224. Formal Change Control Procedure Required For All Production Systems

Policy: All computer and communications systems used for production processing at Company X must employ a formal change control procedure which is used to ensure that only authorized changes are made. This change control procedure must be used for all significant changes to software, hardware, communications networks, and related procedures.

Commentary: The intention of this policy is to stabilize the production processing environment by controlling all changes made to it. A formal change control process will help to ensure that only authorized changes are made, that they are made at the approved time, and that they are made in the approved manner. This will in turn, in most shops, increase the percentage of time the system is available for processing business transactions. Such change control processes are also a useful way to force the preparation of documentation, which will be important for problem resolution and contingency planning purposes. An explicit definition of "production processing" may be an important supplement to this policy. This policy is relevant to voice communications systems such as voice mail and PBXs, as well as data communications systems like intranets. Increasingly, software license management software and hardware inventory taking systems (such as NetCensus from Tally Systems, Hanover, New Hampshire) can be used to provide such change control for small systems like client/server, local area networks, and personal computers. For a higher level perspective, see the policy entitled "Authorization For Changes To Production Data And Programs." Also see the policy entitled "Incorporation Of Security Into Systems Development Life Cycle." A: T; E: LMH.

225. Production System Changes Must Be Consistent With Security Architecture

Policy: To prevent changes in hardware and software from contributing to or creating security vulnerabilities, prior to installation, every non-emergency change to production systems must be shown to be consistent with the information security architecture and approved by management as part of the formal change control process.
Commentary: The objective of this policy is to ensure that both computer operations staff and systems administration staff install only the hardware and software which is consistent with an information security architecture document. The policy thus states that production systems may only be changed in a manner which is compliant with an information security architecture. The policy accordingly establishes the importance of an information security architecture and specifies some of the circumstances when it must be referenced (system developers and designers should also reference it). Since the policy applies to the end of the systems development and testing process, it implies that systems developers and designers have already considered the architecture, that is if they are serious about getting their new systems into production. Note that a separate process is required if the changes are for an emergency situation (a contingency plan and a computer emergency response team should then be employed). Prior to adopting a policy like this, the organization in question should write and then obtain management approval for an architecture. This policy is partially motivated by the United States' Health Insurance Portability and Accountability Act (HIPPA). For related ideas, see the policies entitled "Loading External Programs Onto Network-Connected Computers" and "Establishing New Business Arrangements Via Internet." A: MT; E: MH.

226. User Installation Of Software On Personal Computers Is Prohibited

Policy: Users must not install software on their personal computers, network servers, or other machines without first receiving advance authorization to do so from a local information security coordinator.
Commentary: Internet access has made all sorts of new programs (including games) available to the general user population. With this comes the temptation to install and run these programs. If users do install such software, or at least acquiesce to an installation process performed by an automatic installation routine, viruses could be propagated, system crashes initiated, and other problems created. This policy seeks to prevent these problems by explicitly prohibiting users from installing any software unless previously approved by the information security coordinator. Note that new personal computer software packages, such as those offered by Gradient Technologies and Seven Locks Software, will prevent PC users from running any software besides the software specifically approved by management. Separately, by implication, this

policy prohibits the use of Java and ActiveX applets, but some users may not make the connection. Accordingly, a more explicit policy such as "Disabling Java Within Internet Web Browsers" may be also be necessary. A: E; E: LMH.

227. Users Prohibited From Upgrading Software For Personal Computers

Policy: Users are prohibited from installing new or upgraded programs on their workstations. This process will instead be done centrally by systems administrators via automatic network downloads.

Commentary: This policy seeks to establish a consistent set of applications running on all workstations within an organization. This can be achieved with automatic software distribution (ASD) software packages. Compliance with this policy can be checked by automatic license management software packages. A consistent set of applications is desirable because it is considerably easier to support (fewer exceptions), less expensive to acquire (thanks to volume purchase discounts), and likely to be more secure (management knows what's possible and what's not). Newer software such as Microsoft's Explorer is increasingly customizable and modular. This means that certain features can be turned off or removed before the software is distributed. For example, a radio comes with Explorer 5, and this may cause productivity and noise problems in open offices. A systems administrator can remove this module before using ASD to distribute this new browser over an internal network. Separately, those functions which support functionality considered to pose a significant risk (such as Java) can also be removed before centralized distribution takes place. On another note, this policy is deliberately silent about the method used for obtaining new or upgraded software because multiple methods might be employed (a CD-ROM distribution disk, Internet down-load, etc.). For a related idea, see the policy entitled "User Installation Of Software On Personal Computers Is Prohibited." A: E; E: LMH.

228. Access Controls Defined Prior To Cut-Over To Production Operation

Policy: All the user-level and administrative-level access controls required by Company X information security policies must be established and enabled before production information systems can be placed into operation.

Commentary: This policy is meant to prevent enthusiastic technical staff from placing a system into production operation without first having defined access controls at a reasonable level. To far to many situations, systems are placed in production but access controls have not been turned-on, or if they are turned on, they are not defined at a secure level of granularity. For example, in many cases, fixed password access controls are defined, but group user-IDs are employed. Unless individual user-IDs are employed, logs will not show which user took what actions, and separation of duties will be difficult to enforce. Thus, this policy adopts the following attitude: it is better to do it right the first time and be secure, than it is to do a sloppy job and later ask for forgiveness. The policy assumes that access control policies are previously or simultaneously established. For related ideas, see the policies entitled "Access Controls For Remote Systems Connecting To Production Systems" and "Where To Use Computer System Access Controls." A: T; E: MH.

229. Disabling Unnecessary Software Features At Installation Time

Policy: Software features which could be used to compromise security, and which are clearly unnecessary in the Company X computing environment, must be disabled at the time when software on multi-user systems is installed.

Commentary: The intention of this policy is to prevent unnecessary but enabled features from being used by hackers and others intent on compromising systems security. Modern software packages often have far more features than most organizations need; while this may attract buyers for the software, it also frequently provides additional vulnerabilities that can be exploited by unauthorized users. An example of this that's in the media these days is Java, the programming language from Sun Microsystems. There is great concern about Java applets being used as a mechanism to compromise the security of systems connected to the Internet. Separately, this policy could be expanded to apply to software on single-user systems, in which case the words "on multi-user systems" would be removed. Note that nothing in the policy – if it is used alone -- prevents disabled features from being enabled later, should circumstances require. Ideally users would be prevented from reenabling these features through access control mechanisms or other security measures. This policy is expected to meet with some resistance on the part of systems programmers, network managers, systems administrators, and others because it means extra work. On another note, this policy can be thought of as a specific application of the notion of least privilege (also called the need to know). For related ideas, see the policies entitled "Disabling Java Within Internet Web Browsers," "Removal Of All Unauthorized Access Paths In Production Software," and "Privilege Restriction Based On The Need-to-Know." A: T; E: LMH.

230. Disabling Privileged User-IDs Prior To Operating System Installation

Policy: Before any multi-user computer operating system is installed at Company X, technical staff must disable or rename all privileged user-IDs such as those named administrator, auditor, or installer.

Commentary: The intention of this policy is to make hackers work a good deal harder to break-into these systems. Privileged user-IDs are the target of many attacks such as password guessing attempts. By deleting or renaming them, Company X technical staff prevents them from being the targets of these hackers. While the policy as it stands will be effective against some automated attacks, to make the renaming process more effective, the policy can be changed to stipulate that new user-ID names must bear no resemblance to the prior names. Thus the auditor user-ID must not be renamed EDPauditor. In a broader sense, this policy uses the strategy of camouflage so that the enemy cannot properly target their weapons. Separately, for increased security, the words "multi-user" could be dropped from the policy, which would in turn make the policy apply to desktop PCs (this assumes that an access control package is found on each desktop PC). For a related idea, see the policy entitled "Where To Use Computer System Access Controls." A: T; E: LMH.

231. Removal Of Unnecessary Systems Software At Installation Time

Policy: All systems software which will definitively not be used at the present time, and which comes along with the operating system or other systems software, should be removed from production systems at the time when the operating system or other systems software is installed.

Commentary: The intention of this policy is to prevent hackers and others from utilizing systems software, which is not needed for business activity, in order to gain unauthorized entry to a system. The fewer the number of software packages found on a particular system, the fewer the avenues of attack for a hacker or other adversary. Reducing the number of systems software packages on a production system also potentially reduces the maintenance required (loading upgrades, investigating incompatibilities, etc.). This approach is used widely on firewalls and Internet commerce servers, both of which are known to use this "bare bones" approach to building systems software. Nothing in this policy prevents the removed software from being reinstalled if and when necessary. The policy does not state how to determine whether certain software packages will not be required (some investigation will be necessary), and who will make this decision; some organizations will wish to specify the latter of these two in the policy. For related ideas, see the policies entitled "Systems Utilities Resident On Production System Storage Media" and "Restricted And Monitored Use Of Systems Software Utilities." A: T; E: LMH.

232. When To Prepare Production Systems Change Documentation

Policy: Documentation reflecting all significant changes to production computer and communications systems at Company X must be prepared within a week from the time that a change took place. This documentation must reflect the proposed change, management approval, and the way in which the change was performed.

Commentary: The purpose of this policy is to force technical people--who are notorious about avoiding the preparation of documentation--to work to a deadline for the preparation of documentation. If there is no definitive deadline, many of these people will keep postponing the preparation of documentation for extended periods of time. If this happens, there is a high likelihood that the technical people involved will have left the organization, transferred to another position, or simply forgotten much about the change. Not having current documentation on hand is also a hindrance to resolving day-to-day problems, training new people, as well as contingency planning and disaster recovery efforts. Giving technical people a week to prepare documentation helps keep it current, and also allows them to make emergency changes without having to first document these changes. Some shops may find this policy a bit too lax; they may want to have full documentation prepared prior to a change (with the exception of emergency fixes). Others may want to state that documentation should be prepared in advance of a change, rather than afterwards. While some organizations may find it too rigid, it is also possible (and desirable) to prevent software from moving into a production processing environment unless documentation has first been prepared. See the policies entitled "Training & Operating Documentation Required For Production Systems" and "Approval Required For Changes To Production Operating Systems." A: T; E: LMH.

233. Training & Operating Documentation Required For Production Systems

Policy: Business application systems in development or undergoing significant modification must not be moved into a production processing environment without first having adequate training materials and operating documentation. The adequacy of these materials must be determined by user organization management.
Commentary: Undocumented systems and/or systems run by untrained people are very difficult to control. All too often significant losses ensue when operators don't know what they're doing (the Three Mile Island nuclear power plant accident is a famous example of this). Embezzlers and others intent on committing computer crimes frequently take advantage of the confusion surrounding a newly-introduced or improperly-documented system. The policy is thus intended to require that adequate training and operating documentation be prepared, and approved, before a system is formally moved to production status. Although generally more difficult to implement due to less sophisticated security tools, this policy is applicable to small systems such as those involving client/server systems, local area networks, and personal computers. Also see the policies entitled "Security Responsibilities of Information Users," "When To Prepare Production Systems Change Documentation," and "Documentation Required for All Production Business Systems." A: MT; E: LMH.

234. Loading External Programs Onto Network-Connected Computers

Policy: Users may not place any computer program developed outside of Company X on their own microcomputers (PCs), on their workstations, on network servers, or on computers connected to the network unless this program has first been approved by the Information Systems Department.

Commentary: The policy defines a software change control requirement for distributed networked systems. The policy's intention is to make sure that no software is placed on network-connected computers without having first been examined for viruses, worms, Trojan horses, and other unauthorized code. This policy can also be used to prohibit use of unauthorized software when organizational standard software has been adopted. For example, a user may wish to employ WordPerfect on his or her microcomputer (PC), while the organizational standard is MS-Word. Having consistent software throughout the network allows a help desk to provide better support and also allows the network to be more effectively managed. Some organizations may wish to enforce a policy like this using so-called "inventory" software; these packages automatically identify all software and hardware components in all micros or workstations connected to a local area network. Also see the policy entitled "Testing For Viruses Prior To Use On Company X Systems." A: ET; E: LMH.

235. Use Of Push Background Updates For Software Requires Approval

Policy: Automatic updating of software on Company X computers via background "push" technology is prohibited unless the involved software has first been tested by an authorized member of the Information Systems Department.

Commentary: A number of vendors, such as McAfee Associates, are distributing updates to their software products entirely without human intervention via the Internet. This "push" technology holds great promise, especially for the distribution of updates to virus screening software. Yet it also holds great risks, for instance an office where all the computers are unworkable because an incompatibility in newly-pushed software conflicts with existing software. While push software updating systems, such as those offered by BackWeb Technologies and PointCast, can save a lot of time for Information Systems Departments, the software testing processes performed by vendors may not be adequate substitutes for the software testing processes performed by user organizations. Accordingly, this policy seeks to maintain the stability of existing user systems by requiring that all software sent from vendors be tested before it is used within a user organization. In the future, when vendor testing processes are shown to be adequate, and when reliable vendor quality control measures exist, exceptions to this policy can be made on a vendor-by-vendor basis. Current exceptions to the policy may need to be made for virus software, since this type of software changes so rapidly. Exceptions may also be needed for intrusion detection software (IDS) which likewise requires frequent updates. For related ideas see the policy entitled "Formal Change Control Procedure Required For All Production Systems." A: T; E: LMH.

236. Testing Externally-Provided Software Prior To Use

Policy: Executable programs (software object code) provided by external entities must be tested before installation on any Company X production system. Program statement listings (software source code) provided by external entities must be visually reviewed prior to compilation, and then the resulting executable programs must be tested before installation on any Company X production system. Such testing and examination must be consistent with Company X standards and must also be properly documented.

Commentary: This policy is intended to prevent Trojan horses, worms, viruses, and other unauthorized code from doing damage to Company X systems, software, and data. It is common for hackers to modify games and other popular programs which are then placed on electronic bulletin boards, Internet web pages, and similar public places. One favorite antic is to append a virus to these programs. Note that this policy applies only to production systems, not the majority of PCs and LANs as they have been designated in most organizations. Thus the word "production" will need to have been defined before this policy makes sense. A testing process accompanied by a testing documentation preparation process will both need to be prepared for this policy to work as intended. Although public-domain software (such as shareware) is the most significant risk here, it is also good practice to test and examine code received from trusted vendors. Because it is technical in nature, this policy is intended for information systems department staff, rather than end-users. If end-users receive it, it will need to be simplified (for example removing the words in parentheses). Also see the policies entitled "System Developers Must Not Perform Formal Testing" and "Testing For Viruses Prior To Use On Company X Systems." A: T; E: LMH.

237. Free Software May Not Be Used For Production Applications

Policy: Software which supports production business applications (including operating systems, web browsers, and utility programs) must be either developed in-house, or obtained from a known and reliable third party vendor. Free software (also known as shareware) is not permitted unless specifically evaluated and approved by the Information Security Manager.

Commentary: This policy is intended to prevent workers from downloading free software over the Internet, some of which may contain viruses or Trojan horses. The policy is also intended to prevent computing environments from being built with technology which may not be regularly updated, which may not be robust, and which may not be supported by a business which is a going concern. While there are some good free software packages available over the Internet (such as web browsers), and while the Linux operating system is gaining increasing popularity, each of these packages should be evaluated before they are permitted to be used on production machines. The evaluation would typically determine that good documentation is available, decent training is available, on-demand technical support is available, updates are regularly provided, the vendor has a financially stable business, etc. This policy can be implemented with a change control software package on a personal computer, which can prevent end-users from making any changes to the software running on their personal computers unless initiated by approved administrators. Free software can also create incompatibilities and unexpected results in an otherwise stable computing environment; this is another reason to be staunch in a prohibition against free software. Also see the policy entitled "Testing Externally-Provided Software Prior To Use." A: ET; E: LMH.

238. Automatic Detection Of End-User Application Programs

Policy: All small systems (client/server systems, local area networks, personal computers, etc.) must use approved software license management software. Besides detecting unauthorized copies of third-party software, these license management systems must be configured to detect new and/or modified application programs developed by end-users.

Commentary: This policy supports a relatively laissez-faire (relaxed) computing environment in which end-users are permitted do their own application system programming so long as these systems are not used as production applications. The policy requires that license management software be used to police this activity. With license management software, all new applications will be flagged, and if later shown to be production applications, the involved users can be required to document the applications and to add supplemental controls. In some environments, a custom-developed screen can be shown to the developer in the end-user department, asking him or her to indicate whether the software is used for production purposes. If it is production software, then compliance with certain development and documentation standards will be required. Thus this policy supports prototyping and related evolutionary systems development approaches. Separately, the Information Systems Department does not lose control with this approach, since they can prevent the use of any software via the license management system. This step might be appropriate when such systems were missing proper testing and/or sufficient documentation. With license management software, the Information Systems Department can also monitor all new or changed software on networked systems. Also see the policies entitled "Compliance With Organizational Systems Development Conventions" and "Use Of Higher Level Programming Languages." A: T; E: LMH.

239. Critical Business Logic Must Not Reside On Desktop Computers

Policy: Production applications containing critical business logic must not run on desktop or portable computer systems. Instead, these applications must run on multi-user servers which have physical access controls, logical access controls, change controls, and contingency plans.

Commentary: The intention of this policy is to prevent critical business logic from falling into the hands of unauthorized persons if they were to steal a desktop or portable computer. From a different perspective, keeping critical business logic only on larger multi-user machines with physical access controls prevents copies of this logic from being dispersed, and in that respect helps control access to trade secrets, unique business practices, and other sensitive ideas. Desktop and portable systems are also notorious because they most often lack change controls, and are thus susceptible to viruses, worms, and other problems that multi-user systems with access controls do not generally encounter. Desktop and portable systems additionally often lack passwords, encryption, and other logical access controls to prevent the disclosure of data handled by these critical applications. Separately, this policy assumes that the word "critical" has been defined in contingency planning documentation. For additional ideas of this nature, see the policies entitled "Access Control Required For All Multi-User Production Applications" and "Automatic Detection Of End-User Application Programs." A: E; E: LMH.

240. Control Over Movement Of Software From Development To Production

Policy: Business application development staff must not have the ability to move any software into the production processing environment.

Commentary: This policy is another specific manifestation of the principle of separation of duties. Its intention is to prevent developers from prematurely moving their own application systems into production. They might, for example, do this to avoid comprehensive testing which would reveal inadequate control measures. They might also want to move their own systems into production quickly to avoid other scrutiny which might reveal a Trojan horse or other unauthorized code. The objective described in this policy may be difficult to achieve if there are very few people in an organization, or if microcomputers (PCs) and/or workstations are to run the production versions of these applications. Too few personnel will force certain compromises in terms of the separation of duties, while use of small systems like client/server systems or local area networks will often prevent the rigorous demarcation of a line between development and production (in some cases due to a restricted set of built-in control measures). See the policy entitled "Separation Of Duties And Control Over Company X Assets." A: T; E: LMH.

241. Vendor Provided Systems Software Must Go Through Change Control

Policy: Prior to being installed, new or different versions of the operating system and related systems software for multi-user production computers must go through the established change control process.

Commentary: It is not a foregone conclusion that vendor provided software will benefit all user organizations. In some cases, existing applications will fail when newer systems software is installed. In other cases, memory or disk space constraints will cause problems when systems software is updated. This policy accordingly attempts to prevent computer operations personnel from installing systems software unless the software has first been approved by management via the change control process. The policy also prevents systems programmers and others from testing new software on production systems, thus perhaps causing data corruption, system crashes, and related problems. This policy could easily be expanded to include applications provided by external vendors. The policy could also be expanded to include single-user production systems, but in most instances single-user systems do not have effective change control systems (although such products are now on the market). Software developed in-house would be handled by another change control policy, such as "Formal Change Control Process Required For Business Applications." Also see the policy entitled "Authorization For Changes To Production Data And Programs." A: T; E: LMH.

242. Review And Recompilation Required Before Movement To Production

Policy: Executable modules must never be moved directly from test libraries to production libraries. Fully-tested modules must be reviewed and then recompiled before being moved to production libraries. Review and recompilation activities must be performed by technical staff not associated with the testing process. This process will help to detect and eradicate errors as well as Trojan horses and other unauthorized code.

Commentary: Beyond the early detection and correction of errors and omissions, the intention of this process is to prevent the incorporation of unauthorized code--like Trojan horses--into production software. The policy also has an element of the separation of duties in that the reviewer(s) must not be the same person(s) as the tester(s). The policy could be further expanded to require that the tester(s) not be the same person(s) as the developer(s). Such separation of duties controls are generally possible only in large organizations which have the available staff to perform different jobs. This policy is relevant to client/server systems, local area networks, personal computers, and other small systems although it will generally be more difficult to implement (due to fewer access controls, lack of a separation between production and test environments, and lack of separation of duties). Another benefit of this policy is that it forces the preparation of adequate documentation for loading the new system -- without it another person cannot install the new software. The term "compilation" can be modified to suit the terminology used at the organization in question; alternative terms include "interpretation," "linking," "assembly," and "binding." See the policy entitled "Separation Of Duties And Control Over Company X Assets." A: T; E: LMH.

243. Formal Change Control Process Required For Business Applications

Policy: A formal written change control process must be used to ensure that all business application software which is in development moves into production only after receiving proper authorization from both Information Systems Department management and user organization management.

Commentary: The intention of this policy is to require a formal and written change control process for the development of production business applications. The benefits of a formal change control process include more up-to-date documentation, greater system stability (with consequent improvements in system availability), and a more structured systems environment which is more easily controlled and managed. Unlike the policy entitled "Control Over Movement Of Software From Development To Production," this policy addresses the requirement for a change control process (not the privileges used to support such a process). A definition of "business application software" considered to be "production" may also accompany this policy. The change control process described in this policy may be extended to packaged software and other parts of data processing operations. Additional words describing the change control process may be added to this policy; for example: "These change control procedures must include review of the need for all changes, proper testing of all changes, and preparation of supporting documentation." Any additional explanatory words for this policy should reflect only the essential components of a formal change control process; this is because there are many methodologies and because information systems departments often change methodologies. This policy may be used in those circumstances where the organization is not yet ready to extend change control to other information systems areas such as hardware and communications. Separately, the words "user organization management" can in some organizations be replaced with words "application owner." Also see the policy entitled "Approval For End-User Production System Development Efforts." A: T; E: LMH.

244. Separate Approval Required For Production System Controls

Policy: Before being used for production processing, new or substantially changed business application systems must have received written approval from the manager of the Information Security Department for the controls to be employed.

Commentary: This highly-recommended policy requires that the Information Security Department review major in-house software development efforts to ensure that adequate controls have been provided. The intention of the policy is thus to prevent applications from being moved into production if they do not have adequate controls built into them. Instead of the Information Security Department, the policy could make reference to the EDP Audit Department. In an indirect way, this policy will foster the use of systems development teams that include people knowledgeable about security. Some organizations may believe that this policy gives too much power to the Information Security Department. Distribution of this policy to end-users and management is recommended to let these audiences know that they are not permitted to modify production systems without going through the proper channels. Taking this one step further, some organizations are now requiring user department management to specifically sign-off on the controls found in productions application systems; this process helps get user department managers to take security more seriously (and to take personal responsibility). Also see the policies entitled "Formal Change Control Process Required For Business Applications," "Approval For End-User Production System Development Efforts," and "Special Sign-Off Required For Projects Involving Human Safety Issues." A: EMT; E: LMH.

245. Approvals Required For Production Multi-User Applications

Policy: Specific systems management, user department management, and EDP audit acceptance and sign-off procedures must be followed before a program will be granted production status on a multi-user machine.

Commentary: The intention of this policy is to make sure that multi-user machines run only those applications which have been appropriately approved by the right management representatives (information security management could be added to the policy). Local area network servers, mail servers, servers in client/server networks, and other small system machines are definitely within the scope of this policy. Unlike the policy entitled "Separate Approval Required for Production System Controls," this policy deals with approval by a number of different groups who have objectives above and beyond the inclusion of controls. The reference to "EDP audit" could be replaced with reference to Information Security, depending on the mission statements of the groups at the organization in question. The focus of this policy is multi-user systems, which typically have the greatest concentration of sensitive, valuable, and critical information. Multi-user machines are also networked in most instances, again indicating that such machines are deserving of special attention. The policy could be modified to include mention of substantial changes via the program maintenance process. Also see the policy entitled "Prior Approval Required For Set-Up of Multi-User Systems." A: T; E: LMH.

246. Approval For End-User Production System Development Efforts

Policy: All software that handles sensitive, critical, or valuable information, and that has been developed by end-users, must have its controls approved by the Information Security Department prior to being used for production processing.

Commentary: Development efforts by end-users are particularly of concern since users often set-up production processing environments in their own offices without the involvement of the Information Systems Department or the Information Security Department. This often leads to client/server systems, local area networks, and personal computers doing important work but without the requisite controls. This policy defines a process to ensure that needed controls are integrated into these systems. In many organizations, separate change control process policies will be needed for the end-user community and the technical community. Beyond what's described in this policy, additional approval by the Information Systems Department may be advisable to ensure that corporate networking standards, documentation standards, and other matters have been properly addressed. The words "Information Security Department" in this policy could be replaced with the words "EDP Auditing Department." For a related policy, see the one entitled "Separate Approval Required For Production System Controls." A: EM; E: MH.

247. Approval Required For Changes To Production Operating Systems

Policy: Extensions, modifications, or replacements to production operating system software must be made only if the written approval of the manager of the Information Security Department has been received in advance. To keep software maintenance costs down, and to prevent inadvertent security exposures from being created, such changes should be kept to a minimum.

Commentary: The intention of this policy is to discourage and rigidly control modifications to production computer operating systems. As a general rule, it is wise to keep a "standard vanilla" (standard vendor-provided) operating systems. This is because changes to operating systems software can and often do inadvertently introduce vulnerabilities. In addition, maintaining modified operating systems can be exceedingly time consuming and expensive. Customized or simply incompatible operating systems can also seriously interfere with attempts to connect computers to networks. Furthermore, if operating system changes have been extensive, then the organization may be prevented from rapidly moving to new releases of an operating system or application programs. This may also mean that new security fixes incorporated into a recent version of an operating system cannot be used by the organization. Likewise, special security fixes issued by Computer Emergency Response Teams (CERTs) or the operating system vendor may not work if operating systems have been modified in a custom way. In technically-sophisticated organizations, this policy may be appropriately distributed to end-users. See the policies entitled "Use Of Most Current Computer Operating System Versions" and "Restricted And Monitored Use Of Systems Software Utilities." A: ET; E: LMH.

248. Periodic Review Of Production Operating System Changes

Policy: Periodic reviews of production computer operating systems must be conducted to ensure that only authorized changes have been made.

Commentary: Since many access control functions are implemented at the operating system level, or at the access control package level (which extends the functions of the operating system), it is important to make sure that only authorized changes to the operating system have been made. Thus operating systems play an absolutely critical security role that should be periodically validated through a review (perhaps through a file compare program or perhaps through digital signatures). The intention of this policy is to mandate such a review. A policy specifying the need for such review is important because often organizations do not have in-house technical expertise to perform such a review. Increasingly these reviews are being done by software packages, such as the UNIX operating system security review service offered by AT&T. In microcomputer, client/server, and LAN environments, license management software containing check sums as well as periodic use of virus detection software could be used to implement this policy. The reader may wish to include "networked server operating systems" and "firewall operating systems" as a part of the policy. Also see the policy entitled "Approval Required For Changes To Production Operating Systems." A: T; E: LMH.

249. Prohibition Against Trap Doors To Circumvent Access Controls

Policy: Programmers and other technically-oriented staff must refrain from installing trap doors that circumvent the authorized access control mechanisms found in operating systems and/or access control packages.

Commentary: Trap doors are special code segments which secretly allow a systems programmer, technical support staff member, or someone else to get around standard access controls (like passwords and user-IDs). These hidden pieces of code are invoked with special undocumented commands known only to the person who wrote them. Ironically, most trap doors are installed with good intentions such as being able to install system maintenance code without rebooting the machine, being able to issue privileged systems programming commands from ordinary user workstations, or being able to bypass the access control system should the system freeze-up (crash). The intention of this policy is to force all accesses via standard access control mechanisms, thus achieving uniformity, auditability, and a more secure operating environment. If trap doors exist, they could be used by unauthorized parties to wreak havoc on the system. Likewise, if the person who installed a trap door leaves the organization under less than friendly terms, the former worker could do serious damage via the trap door. This policy could be modified to apply to application system access controls and/or database management system access controls, as well as the access controls found in operating systems and access control packages. See the policies entitled "Reliance On Operating System User Authentication Process" and "Removal Of All Unauthorized Access Paths In Production Software." A: T; E: LMH.

250. Prompt Implementation Of Security Problem Fix Software, Scripts, Etc.

Policy: All security problem fix software, command scripts, and the like provided by operating system vendors, official computer emergency response teams (CERTs), and other trusted third parties must be promptly installed.

Commentary: One of the major problems associated with the infamous "WANK worm" was that numerous systems managers on the Internet did not promptly install security fix command scripts to their operating systems. This allowed the worm to infiltrate their systems while it was not able to infiltrate those which had implemented the scripts. Accordingly, this policy is meant to instruct systems managers that they must promptly install security fixes. Often vendors wait until a problem can no longer be ignored before they issue a security fix. This means that user organizations need to promptly implement the fix if they are going to prevent losses. While the policy is meant to apply only to operating systems, it could be expanded to include applications, systems utilities, and other types of software. The policy could also be expanded to include mention of other trusted organizations such as user groups, in addition to trusted CERTs (Computer Emergency Response Teams -- such as the one at Carnegie-Mellon University, Pittsburgh, Pennsylvania, USA). This policy is particularly relevant to versions of the UNIX operating system, for which there have been many security fixes. Separately, in an indirect way, this policy also supports systems managers' attempts to keep up with the latest release of operating systems software. The implementation of this policy can be via automatic software distribution over a network, particularly for client/server systems, local area networks, and personal computers. There are a number of products like this on the market such as those offered by Frye Computer Systems, Boston, Massachusetts. See the policies entitled "Use Of Most Current Computer Operating System Versions" and "Incident Management Responsibilities." A: T; E: LMH.

251. Systems Software & Applications Software At Most Recent Stable Levels

Policy: All Company X production operating systems, database management systems, firewalls, and related systems software, as well as all production business applications software, must be kept at the most recent stable release level.

Commentary: The intention of this policy is to instruct computer operations staff about upgrading software resident on production systems. Operating systems, firewalls, database management systems, all have an important role to play in the security area. Likewise, application software often includes its own security mechanisms like passwords or privilege restrictions. The most recent software vendor release includes corrections for known security vulnerabilities (also known as holes), and thus provides the user organization with a higher level of security than can be achieved with older versions. As an aside, the word "stable" as included in the policy to prevent the user organization from being a beta test site when it did not intend to be acting in this capacity. Note that release levels are different than patches and fixes, which are discussed in the policy entitled "Prompt Implementation Of Security Problem Fix Software, Scripts, Etc." For related considerations, see the policies entitled "Latest Software Release On Systems Interfacing External Networks" and "Use Of Most Current Computer Operating System Versions." A: T; E: LMH.

252. Special Approval Required For Production Software Package Changes

Policy: Modifications to vendor-provided application software must be made only after first obtaining written permission from the director of the Information Systems Department. If modifications have been approved, prior to being placed into production, the altered software must be documented, tested, and otherwise follow change control procedures used for application software developed in-house.

Commentary: The intention of this policy is to force changes to third-party packaged software to follow the same change control process used for software developed in-house. Such modifications could jeopardize compatibility with subsequent versions of the software, cause the vendor to deny additional support for the software, or cause the vendor to justifiably renounce any responsibility for the software's behavior. Such changes may also cause the software to perform in an unauthorized, less secure, and/or undesired fashion. A version of this policy may be appropriate for users of microcomputers (PC), workstations, local area networks, client/server systems, etc., not just Information Systems Department development staff. Selection of certain parameters during either the installation process or the user-customization process does not constitute a modification of the software itself; some organizations may wish to clarify this in the policy. For related ideas, see the policies entitled "Formal Change Control Process Required For Business Applications" and "Customers Must Specifically Agree To Receive New/Enhanced Service." A: ET; E: LMH.

253. Software Maintenance With Source Rather Than Object Code

Policy: All permanent changes to production software must be made with source code rather than with object or other executable code.

Commentary: Maintenance of source code is considerably easier than maintenance of object code. Besides, changes to object code are considerably trickier, and more likely to lead to the introduction of new problems. It is also desirable to have a compiler or interpreter check the validity of new code prior to its execution; this cannot be done if changes are made directly in object code. Accordingly, the intention of this policy is to require that developers make changes in production software at the source rather than at the object level. Ideally, as many changes would be made with system tables, system generation parameters, and other mechanisms which do not require any modification to production software. This policy is also desirable because it forces certain rudimentary documentation to be prepared (for the source code). For a related idea, see the policy entitled "Escrow For Software Used In Critical Business Activities." A: T; E: LMH.

254. Timing of Changes To Company X Production Information Systems

Policy: Since the impact of changes to Company X's production information systems may be significant, all changes must be communicated to affected parties at least two weeks prior to the change, and all changes must be held until the first weekend of each month.

Commentary: This policy reflects standard practice at many telephone companies regarding phone switch software upgrades. The policy doesn't allow frequent and unannounced changes, both of which historically have caused many problems for users. For example, MCI put thousands of frame-relay network users out of commission for ten straight days in 1999. While frame-relay is a data network rather than a voice network, technicians are coming to appreciate that the scrupulous practices found in the voice network in many cases should be applied to data networks as well (and perhaps production information systems too). This policy is accordingly most relevant to those organizations which provide services to others such as common carriers, Internet service providers (ISPs), application service providers (ASPs), etc. On another note, organizations in this position should also have well-developed contingency plans to handle problems with new changes. Separately, the reason why changes are held until the first weekend is that accounting for the prior month (perhaps quarter or year too) will be done, and demand for services will be low; this stipulation will of course need to be modified depending on the issuing organization's industry. For example, this timing may be good for a traditional bank, but poor for an ISP. For related ideas, see the policies entitled "Formal Change Control Process Required For Business Applications" and "Prompt Implementation Of Security Problem Fix Software, Scripts, Etc." A: T; E: H.

255. Rapid Rollback To Prior Versions Of Production Software

Policy: Adequate "back off" procedures must be developed for all changes to production systems software and production application software. "Back off" procedures allow data processing activities to quickly and expediently revert to the prior version of such software, so that business activities can continue.

Commentary: It is wise not to burn your software "bridges" behind you. Given the complex interconnected nature of modern computer systems, to force a conversion to a new system without having clear back off procedures is to unduly tempt fate. In the interest of keeping production systems up and running as much of the time as possible, the intention of this policy is to ensure there will be at least one operational version of production software that can be used to get the business done. This policy is particularly important in the client/server and other complex computing environments where applications span multiple operating systems, multiple locations, and multiple sizes of computer. In these circumstances, it may not be sufficient to simply roll back to a prior version of an application, since many other things may have changed too. See the policy entitled "Production Software Conversion Contingency Plans." A: T; E: LMH.

256. Production Software Conversion Contingency Plans

Policy: Whenever cut-overs to new or significantly modified production software introduces potential problems which could cause a loss to Company X of over $1,000,000, special procedures are required. In these cases, management must prepare a conversion-related contingency plan which reflects ways to insure continued service to potentially-affected users.

Commentary: The intention of this policy is to ensure that management prepares specific procedures to deal with problems related to major conversions. There is nothing special about the figure used in the policy ("$1,000,000"); the actual number used should be a reflection of the needs of the organization in question. The use of a cut-off figure is useful from a security standpoint because it gets management to do a risk assessment (risk analysis) of sorts, in effect asking themselves whether they could lose $1,000,000 or more through a conversion effort. Some people may wish to specify what a loss of this nature involves (lost revenue, extra public relations efforts, extra consulting assistance, extra computer service bureau usage, etc.). Rather than just relating to the software aspects of a conversion, this policy implicitly addresses hardware, networking, customer relations and other factors. For related ideas, see the policies entitled "Procedures For Rapid Roll-Back To Prior Versions Of Production Software" and "Security Impact Statements For New Or Modified Business Applications." A: MT; E: LMH.

257. When Information Security Impact Statements Are Required

Policy: Whenever sensitive information is to be placed in computers--particularly computers connected to networks--an analysis of the potential security-related impacts must first be performed. Such an analysis must also be performed if sensitive information is to be used in new and/or substantially different ways. Besides addressing security risks such as industrial espionage, sabotage, fraud, and service interruption, the analysis must address business considerations such as product quality, customer confidence, and public image.

Commentary: Acknowledging that security can readily be defeated on many systems, some organizations prohibit the placement of their most sensitive data on any computers. For example, one large bank never stores staff performance evaluations on any computer or network (although they are prepared on PCs). The data is kept on floppy disks and is locked-up when not in use. Although this approach is overly cautious for most organizations, the underlying concern is valid. The policy shown above requires the equivalent of a computer-security-related environmental impact statement prior to the placement of certain information in computers or on networks. Some organizations may wish to restrict the policy only to network-connected computers (not all computers). The policy could be rewritten to refer to all major system changes involving sensitive information (rather than placing the information on a computer or a network). Similarly, to expand its scope, the policy could be rewritten to refer to "sensitive, valuable, and critical" information rather than just "sensitive" information (this change is recommended although the cost of implementing the policy increases substantially). The policy assumes the organization has already adopted a data classification policy defining the word "sensitive." For a similar idea, see the policy entitled "Formal Specifications Required For Software Developed In-House." Also see the policy entitled "Security Impact Statements For New Or Modified Business Applications." A: MT; E: LMH.

258. Security Impact Statements For New Or Modified Business Applications

Policy: Prior to being placed into production use, each new or significantly modified/enhanced business application system must include a brief security impact statement that has been prepared according to standard procedures.

Commentary: Much like an environmental impact statement, a security impact statement should discuss how security on the supporting system will change as a result of the new or modified application system. Unlike the policy entitled "When Information Security Impact Statements Are Required," this policy deals with changes to business applications (rather than changes to the way in which certain information is handled). One or the other of these two policies would be sufficient, generally not both. This policy may also be expanded to include an overview of the components of a security impact statement (ethical standards, risks to be considered, etc.). This policy may also be modified to state when in the systems development life cycle an impact statement must be prepared--the earlier the better, for instance, during the general systems design phase. The policy may additionally be expanded to require that the security impact statement be reviewed by the EDP Audit Department and/or the Information Security Department. See the policy entitled "When Information Security Impact Statements Are Required." A: MT; E: LMH.

1.2.4. Third Party Involvement

259. Vendor-Provided Written Integrity Statements

Policy: If procurement of third party software is being considered, management must obtain a written integrity statement from the involved vendor. This statement must provide assurances that the software in question does not contain undocumented features, does not contain hidden mechanisms that could be used to compromise the software's security, and will not require the modification or abandonment of controls found in the operating system under which it runs.

Commentary: The intention of this policy is to get written assurance from external providers of software that the software acts as represented, and that the software does not include other mechanisms which might be used to circumvent security. This written assurance can be later used in a court of law if it is shown that the vendor's software contained a Trojan horse, virus, worm, or other malicious code. The process of requesting and obtaining an integrity statement puts the vendor on notice that the purchasing organization is serious about security, and that it intends the vendor to bear some of the responsibility. This policy began many years ago with an IBM integrity statement provided to purchasers of the MVS operating system. More recently organizations have been requesting that other software vendors provide such statements. Some sites may wish to expand the policy to include a requirement that the vendor fix any major security problems that the purchasing organization discovers (perhaps within a certain period of time). Although the policy is written for application systems, the same policy can be readily applied to systems software (in this case the reference to "operating system under which it runs" would be changed). See the policy entitled "Security Mechanisms Must Not Be Compromised for Customers." A: T; E: MH.

260. Packaged Software And Unilateral Deactivation By Third Party Vendor

Policy: Every third party software package that Company X uses for production information systems purposes must be free of deactivation mechanisms that could be triggered by the vendor without Company X's consent.

Commentary: The objective of this policy is to prevent Company X from being in a position where it is dependent on a third party for critical software, but the third party then turns-off this software to compel Company X to perform a sought-after action (perhaps pay a disputed bill). This type of functionality has been incorporated into a number of software packages, but it has proven to be very disruptive to the user organization, and as a result it has been disparagingly discussed in information systems publications. The policy prevents Company X from entering into contracts where the organization might be at the mercy of a third party software vendor via a deactivation mechanism such as this. The mechanism can be implemented by a variety of techniques including a computerized timer, an execution counter, or remote access on/off switch. Whatever the mechanism, it's a bad idea for the user organization. Separately, the policy could be buttressed by adding these words: "Every written contract with a third party software vendor must include an assurance that no vendor-controlled deactivation functionality exists." While smaller firms will have trouble getting words such as this written into a contract, larger customers will have the power to make changes to a vendor's standard licensing contract. On another note, the United Kingdom (UK) now has a law which requires the user's prior consent before software is disabled by a vendor. For related ideas, see the policies entitled "Disabling Unnecessary Software Features At Installation Time" and "Rapid Roll-Back To Prior Versions Of Production Software." A: T; E: LMH.

261. Escrow For Software Used In Critical Business Activities

Policy: If third party software is being considered, and if this software will be used for a critical business activity, one of two conditions must be met prior to completing the transaction. The first condition is that the third party must license source code to Company X. The second condition is that the third party must periodically provide source code to a third party who will hold the source code in escrow. This policy allows Company X staff to continue to maintain the software even though the third party may have gone out of business, may have discontinued the product, or may be negligent in terms of fixing problems in the code.

Commentary: Under strict legally-defined conditions, software escrow allows the purchasing organization to gain access to previously restricted source code if the vendor does not live up to its contractual promises, goes bankrupt, etc. This policy is applicable to a wide variety of business relationships with a third party software vendor including software leasing, rental, and purchase. Separately, note that "software escrow" is distinctly different from encryption "key escrow." In this policy, the words "software" used for a "critical business activity" are deliberately ambiguous so that they will apply to systems software as well as application software. For a definition of the word "critical," this policy assumes the existence of an approved data classification policy such as the one entitled "Five Category Application Criticality Classification Scheme." Also see the policies entitled "Form Of Company X Software Distributed To Third Parties" and "Software Maintenance With Source Rather Than Object Code." A: T; E: MH.

262. Software In Escrow Must Be Verified By Independent Third Party

Policy: Each major release of software critical to Company X's business and held in third party escrow facilities must be verified by an independent third party. This verification process must involve the confirmation that all necessary software and documentation has been received by the escrow agent.

Commentary: The intention of this policy is to make sure that software escrow arrangements are going to provide the protection they were intended to provide. If an independent auditor or some other third party does not verify that all necessary materials are on deposit at the escrow agent's premises, then Company X may be in trouble should the software vendor go out of business, discontinue a product, refuse to fix a major bug, or otherwise be in violation of an agreement they worked out with Company X. The existence of this policy ideally is communicated to both the software vendor and the escrow agent prior to establishing a software escrow arrangement. The policy will then encourage both of them to strictly abide by the terms and conditions of the contract. Instead of this policy, some organizations may feel comfortable with reports from the escrow agent indicating what has been received (but these may not provide sufficient details). Other firms, such as the ones who adopt a policy like this, will want to have independent third party verify the materials that have been deposited at the escrow agent's premises. The escrow agent may not allow the user organization employees to gain access to the escrowed materials (unless one of the predefined circumstances exist); this rule may in turn require the use of a third party for auditing work. Also see the policy entitled "Escrow For Software Used In Critical Business Activities." E: T; E: LMH.

263. Form Of Company X Software Distributed To Third Parties

Policy: To prevent unauthorized copying and usage of Company X intellectual property, all software developed by Company X for use by prospects, customers, business partners, and others must be distributed in object code form only.

Commentary: Distribution in source code form would allow other parties to readily use the software in ways that are perhaps different from those originally intended by Company X. For example, purchasers may end up incorporating the code in a product that they sell. Likewise, purchasers may make unauthorized modifications which may cause the software to perform slowly or incorrectly. Of course, this policy does not rule out the possibility of a reverse compiler used to derive source code from object code, but use of these tools is relatively expensive and time-consuming. While not preventing reverse engineering, distribution in object form makes these types of unauthorized use much more difficult. The author additionally recommends the use of other anti-copying and anti-reverse-engineering control measures, such as encryption and dependence on certain software-readable parameters such as computer serial number. This policy may help in court if Company X is attempting to prove that they maintained sufficient controls to keep the software in question a "trade secret." Also see the policies entitled "Escrow For Software Used In Critical Business Activities" and "Third Party Agreements On Usage Of Company X Software." A: T; E: LMH.

264. Third Party Agreements On Usage Of Company X Software

Policy: To prevent unauthorized usage, all software developed by Company X for use by prospects, customers, business partners, and others, must be distributed only after the recipients have signed an agreement stating they will not disassemble, reverse engineer, modify, or otherwise use the programs except as agreed with Company X.

Commentary: The intention of this policy is to get written agreements about the approved usage of software developed by Company X prior to the distribution of the software. This will help prevent Company X intellectual property from being stolen or used in ways that Company X does not intend. The policy is intended for use by organizations that do not sell or develop software as their main business (those that do will have a much more formal and legalistic agreement). Some organizations may wish to add another sentence to this policy dealing with exceptions; such exceptions could involve an executive decision that the software in question does not incorporate proprietary Company X information. An example of such an exception would be a simple dial-up program sent to customers that allows these customers to call up a Company X computer and check on the status of an order (for example, Federal Express offers such a program). Disassembly is much the same as reverse compilation, the difference being the type of computer programming language used (Assembler or not). Reverse engineering is deducing the internal operation of a product based on its observable functionality. This policy is best used in conjunction with the policies entitled "Form Of Company X Software Distributed To

Third Parties" and "Clear Definition Of Third Party Information Security Responsibilities." A: T; E: LMH.

265. Release Of Systems Documentation To Third Parties

Policy: Prior to being released to third parties, all documentation that describes Company X systems or systems procedures must be reviewed by the manager of the Information Security Department to ensure that confidential information is not being inadvertently disclosed.

Commentary: It is important to communicate to workers that documentation, not just business records, may warrant restricted dissemination procedures. This policy puts staff on notice that they are not to release internal systems documentation without prior approval. The approval could also be provided by the Information Systems Department manager, the internal legal counsel, or some other manager. This policy is also called for because many system crackers/hackers use so-called "social engineering" (also known as "conning") to get information about internal systems, which in turn allows them to break into these systems. If employees are on notice that such information is not to be distributed to outsiders without prior permission, it is less likely that they will fall for such ploys. The prevalence of email systems connected to the Internet also makes the unauthorized transmission of internal documentation to outsiders considerably more likely than it was only ten years ago, and this development in turn increases the need for a policy such as this. See the policies entitled "Approval Required Prior To Release Of Company X Information" and "Internal Network Addresses Must Not Be Publicly Released." A: EMT; E: LMH.

266. Software Features & Functions Must Be Fully Revealed In Documentation

Policy: All features and functions of software released to the public must be fully revealed in the documentation provided to users. Covert software features or functions are incompatible with the honest and forthright manner in which Company X conducts its business.

Commentary: The intention of this policy is to prevent programmers and others involved in the systems development process from incorporating features or functions which are not fully revealed to users (or even fully revealed to internal management). For example, one well known Internet electronic mail package had a covert function which would contact a remote Internet server to get the most recent advertisement to display in a banner when the program was used. While the functionality was not nefarious or especially noteworthy, the way that the firm concealed this functionality's existence created considerable adverse publicity. To avoid erosion of customer confidence, to avoid allegations of bad intent (especially privacy violation), all features and functions should be revealed in the documentation. Users don't need to be able to change or disable these functions or features, just know that they exist. Separately, this policy is only relevant for software distributed to outsiders; if software is only for internal use, then this policy may not be necessary. For related ideas, see the policies entitled "Removal Of All Unauthorized Access Paths In Production Software" and "Prohibition Against Trap Doors To Circumvent Access Controls." A: T; E: LMH.

1.2.5. Computer Operations

267. Access To Company X Letterhead, Check Stock, And Other Forms

Policy: To reduce the risk of forgery and other unauthorized manipulations, access to Company X letterhead stationary, blank checks, and other forms must be made available only to those persons with a demonstrable need for such forms.

Commentary: The intention of this policy is to put staff on notice that Company X forms can be used to commit fraud and otherwise engage in unauthorized acts. For example, many cases of fraudulent letters of credit have been perpetrated via the unauthorized use of letterhead stationary. While access to most in-house forms, such as travel expense reports, poses little risk, others, like bank deposit slips, can be used to perpetrate high-loss abuses. Distinctions about the types of forms that will be restricted may also be incorporated into this policy; for example, those forms dealing with money-handling may be restricted while other forms may not be. In addition to a policy such as this, some forms--like printed check stock--should be locked up when not in use. Also see the policy entitled "Signed Forms Required For Issuance of User-ID." A: M; E: LMH.

268. Smoking, Eating And Drinking In The Computer Machine Room

Policy: Workers and visitors must not smoke, eat, or drink in the raised floor area in the computer machine room. To do so would risk electrical damage to equipment as well as risk particulate contamination to data storage devices.

Commentary: While it may seem to be an inconvenience to those people who do not want to leave the machine room when they work, this policy helps protect both equipment and information against damage. The policy may also be applied to workstations, microcomputers (PCs), local area network (LAN) servers, as well as other systems not resident in a computer machine room. Another example would be the Private Branch Exchange (PBX) phone system. Both the equipment and the data storage media on these systems is susceptible to damage from the above-mentioned substances. Volatile chemicals such as glue and solvents may additionally damage magnetic storage media, and can be mentioned in the policy. For fire prevention reasons, it is also wise to keep such chemicals out of a computer machine room. Also see the policies entitled "Physical Access Control For Areas Containing Sensitive Information" and "Computer Center Fire Resistance And Self-Closing Openings." A: EMT; E: LMH.

269. Production Computer Systems Must Be Physically Located In Data Center

Policy: All production computer systems including servers, firewalls, hubs, routers, voicemail systems, and the like must be physically located within the protected confines of the data center.

Commentary: The intention of this policy is to prevent departments and other distributed organizational units from placing production computer equipment in closets and in other unprotected places where it would be subject to sabotage, power outages, and fire. For example, one department located a production server in an unventilated closet along with toilet paper and cleaning supplies. Because the server was not managed by professional computer operators, no backups were made. One day the server had an electrical problem and the flammable cleaning liquids nearby caught fire, completely destroying all production records on the system as well as a portion of the organization's office building. If a computer system is important enough to be called a production system (used for regular and recurring business activities) then it should be protected by housing it in a machine room (data center) with fire suppression equipment, redundant power, physical access controls, etc. For related ideas, see the policies entitled "Critical Or Sensitive Activities Permitted Only In Physically Secure Areas" and "Location Of New Computer Or Communications Centers." A: E; E: LMH.

270. Computer Operator Logs Required For Multi-User Production Systems

Policy: All Company X multi-user production systems must have computer operator logs which show production application start/stop times, system boot/restart times, system configuration changes, system errors and corrective actions taken, and confirmation that files and output were handled correctly.

Commentary: This policy is intended to ensure that all multi-user production systems have a operator log which can be examined to assist with problem resolution efforts. Logs can also be instrumental with investigations should there be a fraud, embezzlement, sabotage, industrial espionage or related incident. Logs can additionally provide management with assurance that operators are following instructions correctly (perhaps indicating the need for more training). This assurance is important because operators often have the power to do significant damage. The specific details to include in an operations log could be dropped from the policy and replaced with the words "operational details specified by the Manager of Computer Operations." The latter approach allows these details to be changed without the need to modify the policy. This approach also allows different logging requirements for different operating systems (reflecting what's possible with different operating systems). As an aside, turning a log on or off could be considered to be a reconfiguration of the system, and so was not specifically mentioned in the policy. Note that this policy is not simply a mainframe requirement; it is relevant to LAN servers, Internet commerce servers, intranet servers, and other multi-user production systems. For related ideas, see the policy entitled "Business Production Information Updates By Non-Production Staff." A: T; E: MH.

271. Computer Operator Logs Must Be Periodically Reviewed

Policy: The logs from all Company X multi-user production systems must be regularly reviewed by the Computer Operations Manager or another technical specialist designated by the Information Systems Manager. These reviews are intended to ensure that operators are following established procedures and to identify problems in need of remedial action.

Commentary: This policy is intended to ensure that operators are following documented procedures, and that they are held accountable for their actions with production systems. If the logs are recorded, but never reviewed, they will be much less effective as a deterrent against abusive behavior by operators. Likewise, without regular reviews, some problems will come to management's attention only when they become so severe that they demand immediate responses. The person doing these reviews should not also act as a computer operator, in other words, this person should be independent. The need to designate someone to review the logs becomes apparent in the distributed computing environment (LAN servers for example). In this environment, there may be no Computer Operations Manager, and without a designated reviewer of the logs, this job may not get done. A policy is often needed because this task is frequently abandoned in favor of more pressing work. Note that this policy talks about logs of operator activity, whereas the policy entitled "Regular And Prompt Review Of System Logs" talks about user activity. This policy is more of a training and following procedures policy, whereas the policy just mentioned is more of an intrusion detection policy. For a related idea, see the policy entitled "Computer Operator Logs Required For Multi-User Production Systems." A: TM; E: MH.

1.3. Data Security

1.3.1. Intellectual Property Rights

1.3.1.1. Assignment Of Intellectual Property Rights

272. Information As An Important Company X Asset

Policy: Information is an important Company X asset. Accurate, timely, relevant, and properly protected information is absolutely essential to Company X's business. To ensure that information is properly handled, all accesses to, uses of, and processing of Company X information must be consistent with Company X information systems related policies and standards.

Commentary: This general policy helps to set the context for a number of other information security policies. Such a statement is frequently incorporated into the first set of policies as well as summary material oriented towards users and members of the top management team. It is necessary for these people to appreciate how information has become a critical factor of production in modern business--only then can they appreciate the pressing need for information security. The intention of this policy is thus to motivate the need for information security measures and to create a new understanding of the importance of information systems in modern organizations. This policy comes directly out of research in the Information Resource Management (IRM) area. For a related idea, see the policy entitled "Use Of Company X Information For Non-Business Purposes." A: EMT; E: LMH.

273. Assignment Of Patent, Copyright, And Other Intellectual Property Rights

Policy: While an employee of Company X, all staff members grant to Company X exclusive rights to patents, copyrights, inventions, or other intellectual property they originate and/or develop.

Commentary: This common policy assigns the rights to all intellectual property generated by employees to their employer. Some consulting and contracting agreements also contain provisions to this effect. Although generally not done, the policy could be restricted to material which in one way or another is related to Company X business. A more general approach is used instead to ensure that Company X retains the option to exploit such intellectual property. On another point, the policy could make reference to both working and non-working hours. Thus a research scientist might have a revelation about a new product while shaving in the morning; this would subsequently be assigned to Company X even though the scientist was not working at the moment he had the revelation. Separately, given the proliferation of outsourcing (formerly called facilities management) these days, it is especially important to clarify the rights to the work generated by outsiders. Without a policy like this, programmers in many instances will claim that code they developed is their own property. On a different note, to be sure there is no misunderstanding, many organizations get employees to sign agreements which include words similar to those found in the policy. Whether an agreement and/or a policy is used, readers should consult with internal legal counsel on this matter since there are jurisdiction-specific considerations. Furthermore, this policy may be an impediment to the hiring of certain creative people who wish to retain intellectual property rights to their work. The notion behind the policy may also be objectionable to some employees; they may believe that the policy reflects an attitude that Company X owns them and everything they create. This notion may be relevant to labor union negotiations and corporate culture redefinition efforts. For related ideas, see the policies entitled "Agreements Not To Compete Required for Employees," "Rights To Intellectual Property Developed Off-Site," and "Property Rights To Computer Programs And Documentation." Also see the policy entitled "Prior Review For Speeches, Presentations, Technical Papers, Etc." A: E; E: LMH.

274. Property Rights To Computer Programs And Documentation

Policy: Without specific written exceptions, all programs and documentation generated by, or provided by employees, consultants, or contractors for the benefit of Company X are the property of Company X. Management must ensure that all workers providing such programs or documentation sign a statement to this effect prior to the provision of these materials.

Commentary: Disputes about ownership of programs and documentation are frequently encountered. Programmers often claim that they have the right to take their creations to their next employer or to external consulting clients. Meanwhile, employers often claim that such materials are "works for hire" and as such are the property of the employer. This policy helps to clarify this nebulous area, and gives Company X additional influence in any related dispute, be the dispute an internal matter or a matter adjudicated in a court of law. The intention of this policy is to put programmers and related workers on notice about property rights; in this case the first sentence of the policy alone may be sufficient. Those organizations particularly concerned about this matter may wish to include the second sentence of this policy, which is intended to require that management get words to this effect incorporated in employment agreements, consulting agreements, and the like. This policy is not a formal agreement with a programmer, it only requires that one be involved whenever programming and documentation are prepared. The reader should speak with internal legal counsel about the development of both an agreement and a policy like this because there will be jurisdiction-specific considerations. For related ideas, see the policies entitled "Agreements Not To Compete Required For Employees," "Assignment Of Patent, Copyright, And Other Intellectual Property Rights," "Confidentiality Of Company X Computer Related Documentation," and "Recovery Of Computer-Related Property Belonging To Company X." A: T; E: LMH.

275. Legal Ownership Of Information Systems Files And Messages

Policy: Company X has legal ownership of the contents of all files stored on its computer and network systems as well as all messages transmitted via these systems. Company X reserves the right to access this information without prior notice whenever there is a genuine business need.

Commentary: This policy seeks to clarify the ownership of information resident on Company X systems. It can facilitate the examination of electronic mail files and personal computer (PC) file directories which users may otherwise consider to be confidential and private. The policy can also act as a deterrent, discouraging users from using Company X systems for personal purposes. In an indirect way, the policy may also help to resolve disputes about the ownership of software written by employees, contractors, or consultants. Separately, user organizations may wish to expand the scope of the policy to include telephone systems such as voicemail. This policy generally should accompany statements about the personal use of information systems. Separately, some organizations may wish to add a sentence acknowledging that Company X does not have legal ownership of information held in custody for a third party, or for software and other copyrighted, patented, or otherwise protected intellectual property obtained from third parties. See the policies entitled "Personal Use Of Computer And Communications Systems" and "Notifying Subjects Of Existing Monitoring Systems." A: E; E: LMH.

276. Recovery Of Computer-Related Property Belonging To Company X

Policy: Employees, temporaries, contractors, and consultants will not receive their final paycheck unless they have first returned all hardware, software, working materials, confidential information, and other property belonging to Company X.

Commentary: The intention of this policy is to make sure that confidential information, microcomputers, and other property of Company X get returned. This policy gives Company X some leverage to make sure these materials are returned. If a worker has already left, and if the worker has already been paid his or her last paycheck, there is very little incentive for the materials to be returned. The company should also keep accurate records of hardware, software, and other materials provided to workers so that these items can be recovered. Written acknowledgments of property ownership signed by the worker are also useful. Note that withholding a paycheck that has been earned may be illegal in some jurisdictions--check with internal legal counsel. As layoffs, reductions in force, terminations, and other separations become more common, there is an increasing need to specifically address the information issues associated with these changes in status. Also see the policies entitled "Property Rights To Computer Programs And Documentation," "Assignment Of Patent, Copyright, And Other Intellectual Property Rights," and "Removal Of Sensitive Information From Company X Premises." A: M; E: LMH.

277. Attribution Of Sources For Information

Policy: Company X workers must always give proper credit to the source of information used for Company X purposes.

Commentary: Not only does this policy foster what's technically called the right of paternity, but it also assists management in understanding the source of and reliability of information presented to it for review. The policy additionally helps to alert management to the existence of rights to the information which may have been ignored by a worker when preparing a report, developing a new product, etc. This behavior will in turn help reduce the frequency of allegations that Company X improperly appropriated certain information. This policy also helps foster an attitude respectful of intellectual property rights, which may be important when it comes to discouraging unauthorized software copying and other intellectual-property abuses. This policy additionally fosters responsible use of the Internet and electronic bulletin boards in that employees will be less likely to post information after eliminating reference to a source. See the policies entitled "Labelling For Paternity Rights To Intellectual Property" and "Misrepresentation Of Identity On Electronic Communication Systems." A: EMT; E: LMH.

278. Labeling For Paternity Rights To Intellectual Property

Policy: All users who submit information to the public area on Company X's web site or electronic bulletin board system (BBS) grant to Company X the right to edit, copy, republish, and distribute such information. If others besides the user who submits this information possess copyrights or additional rights to such information, the user who submits this material must indicate this fact at the time that the information is provided. The absence of such a notice implies that no other rights to the information are known by or claimed by the user.

Commentary: This policy clarifies the attribution of rights to information in what may otherwise be an ambiguous situation. It also clearly assigns responsibility for specifying paternity rights to the information submitted to a public area (this argues for a prohibition against anonymous submissions). The policy conveys the right of the web site operator or BBS operator to use posted information for marketing and other reasons without the need to get additional approval. Rather than being relevant just to web pages and BBSs, this policy is appropriate to any multi-organizational system such as the AOL/Compuserve on-line service. Also see the policies entitled "Attribution Of Sources For Information" and "Source And Date Labels Required For Major Decision Input." A: EMT; E: LMH.

1.3.1.2. Protection of Intellectual Property Rights

279. Copyright Notices On Computer Programs And Documentation

Policy: All computer programs and program documentation owned by Company X must include appropriate copyright notices.

Commentary: Although in the United States no such explicit notice is required for copyrights to be enforceable, the existence of a notice has a deterrent effect. Other jurisdictions may require explicit notices. The places where copyright notices should appear can also be specified in the policy. For example, notices could occur on screen displays, source code listings, object code listings, user manuals, etc. The policy may also be expanded to include the wording needed in the particular jurisdiction. In the United States, the characters "(c) 1999 Company X" are sufficient, although the words "All Rights Reserved" should be added for protection in South American countries. In the last sentence, of course the date "1999" would vary with the year involved. In some cases, the words "Electronic Archival Rights Reserved By Company X" may also be needed to restrict unauthorized inclusion of the material in on-line databases. Also see the policy entitled "Assignment Of Patent, Copyright, And Other Intellectual Property Rights." A: T; E: LMH.

280. Workers May Make Multiple Copies Only If Reasonable And Customary

Policy: Unless permission from the copyright owner(s) is first obtained, making multiple copies of material from magazines, journals, newsletters, and other publications is forbidden unless this is both reasonable and customary. This notion of "fair use" is in keeping with international copyright laws.

Commentary: Recent cases--such as American Geophysical Union et al vs. Texaco, Inc. (in the USA)--indicate that publishers are increasingly willing to prosecute copyright violators. Not only would a court action be costly but it would be embarrassing for the defendant. This policy seeks to prevent copyright problems before they get to the point of a court case or a formal complaint. It is intended to communicate the meaning of the legal term "fair use," which allows copies to be made without compensating the copyright owner(s). Some organizations may wish to expand the definition given here to include permissible single copies for personal use. The policy could also be expanded to instruct workers how to get permission before generating copies beyond the number that would generally be considered "fair use." The policy deliberately does not mention a particular technology, so the copies could just as easily be made with a personal computer (PC) as they could by a copy machine. Also see the policy entitled "Assignment Of Patent, Copyright, And Other Intellectual Property Rights." A: ET; E: LMH.

281. Periodic Review Of Software Licensing Agreements

Policy: The agreements for all computer programs licensed from third parties must be periodically reviewed for Company X compliance.

Commentary: Thanks to the Software Publishers Association (SPA), a number of surprise audits in large companies have revealed extensive unauthorized copying [the SPA has recently merged with the Information Industry Association]. More recently, the Business Publishers Alliance (BPA) has also initiated unauthorized copying audits, especially in Europe. The resulting lawsuits have most often been settled out of court, but substantial sums and press releases leading to public embarrassment are usually involved. New legislation in the United States makes willful copying of ten or more copies of software punishable by fines of $250,000 and larger amounts. It is best to avoid this type of problem by requiring periodic checking of compliance with the terms of license agreements. This policy may be helpful in showing that an organization is concerned about compliance with software license agreements, should Company X ever be taken to court for unauthorized copying. Checking compliance with license agreements is increasingly automated, for example on local area networks with so-called "inventory" taking programs. One example of such a program is NetCensus from Tally Systems, Hanover, New Hampshire, USA. These programs automatically survey the hardware and software in each microcomputer (PC) or workstation connected to a network. The existence of a policy like this may also serve as a deterrent to users who may be tempted to make unauthorized copies. Some organizations may wish to restrict this policy to microcomputers (PCs) and workstations, the small-scale systems environment in which most unauthorized copying takes place. See the policy entitled "Ordering Authorized Copies Of Software Needed For Business Activities." A: MT; E: LMH.

282. Systems Acquisition And Evidence Of Software Licenses

Policy: Whenever bundled systems are being procured, the source must provide written evidence of the software licenses conveyed.

Commentary: This policy is primarily intended for purchasing and procurement departments, although it is also relevant to any staff member who purchases computer and communications systems. Sources of bundled systems, like original equipment manufacturers (OEMs) and value added resellers (VARs), in some instances make unauthorized copies of software, in the process violating copyright licenses. There are an increasing number of cases on record where personal computer (PC) systems come with software on the hard drive but the software is not properly licensed. To prevent recipient organizations from being responsible for copyright license violations, recipients should obtain written evidence that the licenses are legitimate. Because there may be disputes about what was said at the time of purchase, verbal assurances from the vendor are not sufficient. A policy like this is strongly recommended by the British organization known as Federation Against Software Theft (FAST). For related ideas, see the policies entitled "Copyright Notices On Computer Programs And Documentation" and "Periodic Review Of Software Licensing Agreements." A: T; E: LMH.

283. Registration Of Information Systems Products With Vendors

Policy: To assure that support and discounted upgrades will be readily available, all hardware and software products must be registered with the appropriate vendors. This registration should take place when Company X staff takes delivery of new or upgraded information systems products, or soon after it has been determined that such products are not yet registered.

Commentary: The intention of this policy is to make sure that all hardware and software is properly registered with vendors. This will indirectly ensure that all these products are legitimately paid for, thus cutting down on unauthorized software copies and stolen equipment. Proper registration will also mean that users will receive notices of bugs, upgrades, and other relevant offers. Furthermore, proper registration will allow the user organization to get telephone and other types of technical support. Proper registration may additionally mean that the vendor will be helpful in the event of an emergency or disaster; under these circumstances, replacement copies might be obtained for free or at least at minimal cost if the product was previously registered. This policy may also be helpful in a court of law or during a SPA (Software Publishers Association) audit; it shows that management genuinely attempted to make sure that all in-use copies of software were authorized copies. Also see the policies entitled "Copying, Transferring, Or Disclosing Software Prohibited" and "When Making Additional Copies Of Software Is Permissible." A: ET; E: LMH.

284. Ordering Authorized Copies Of Software Needed For Business Activities

Policy: Company X provides a sufficient number of licensed copies of software such that workers can get their work done in an expedient and effective manner. Management must make appropriate arrangements with the involved vendors for additional licensed copies, if and when additional copies are needed for business activities.

Commentary: The intention of this policy is to make sure that management places orders for additional copies of needed software, rather than simply making unauthorized copies. Workers often claim they were forced to make additional unauthorized copies because management did not provide them with the needed number of authorized copies. This policy is intended to prevent that often-accurate claim from being the excuse for illegal software copying. This policy may be helpful in demonstrating that Company X intended to comply with its software licensing agreements, should there be a Software Publishers Association (SPA) audit. See the policy entitled "Periodic Review Of Software Licensing Agreements." A: EMT; E: LMH.

285. When Making Additional Copies Of Software Is Permissible

Policy: Third party software in the possession of Company X must not be copied unless such copying is consistent with relevant license agreements and either: (a) management has previously approved of such copying, or (b) copies are being made for contingency planning purposes.

Commentary: This policy is particularly relevant to microcomputers (PCs), workstations, local area network servers, client/server systems, and other small-scale systems. This is because the small-scale systems environment is where most unauthorized copying takes place. The intention of this policy is to put users on notice that all copying must be consistent with license agreements. The policy also lets users know that copying may not be allowed -- even if it is consistent with a license agreement -- unless management permission is obtained or unless the copying is for contingency planning (backup) purposes. See the policy entitled "Initial Backup Copies Of Microcomputer Software." A: ET; E: LMH.

286. Removal Of Unauthorized Copyrighted Information And Software

Policy: Third party copyrighted information or software, that Company X does not have specific approval to store and/or use, must not be stored on Company X systems or networks. Systems administrators will remove such information and software unless authorization from the rightful owner(s) can be provided by the involved users.

Commentary: Workers at many organizations are downloading copyrighted material from the Internet, electronic bulletin boards, on-line database services, and other public sources. In many instances, the copying is unauthorized and a violation of copyright laws. This policy is intended to put users on notice that they must not store these materials on Company X systems or networks. The policy is a good way to show management's intent to uphold the copyrights of others. The policy implies that systems administrators, internal auditors, and perhaps others have the right to browse through the file directories of users to identify unauthorized information and software. In some instances, the word "periodically" may be added to the second sentence of the policy, in which case there will be a regular user directory examination process. Note that the effectiveness of this examination process may be easily thwarted by users employing encryption utilities (and for this and other reasons, Company X may wish to ban the use of encryption). See the policies entitled "Removal Of Inappropriate Electronic Postings To Public Forums" and "Right To Remove Offensive Material Without Warning." A: E; E: LMH.

287. Default Copyright Protection For Information Posted To Internet

Policy: Much of the material on the Internet is copyrighted or otherwise protected by intellectual property law (for instance by license agreement). Workers must investigate intellectual property rights for all material they discover on the Internet before using it for any other purpose. One exception to this rule involves internal memos which cite this information.

Commentary: The intention of this policy is to prevent Company X workers from getting in trouble because they violated the intellectual property rights of other parties. One good example of this involves graphics; unauthorized copying and reuse of computer graphics found on the Internet is an epidemic. By reminding users about copyrights, Company X may also be able to at least partially protect itself against damages associated with the illegal acts of its workers. Note that this policy doesn't restrict itself to data, it is also relevant to software, and may therefore help make a case that the organization does not in any way encourage or support unauthorized software copying. For related ideas, see the policies entitled "Removal Of Unauthorized Copyrighted Information And Software" and "Responsibility For Making Unauthorized Software And Data Copies." A: E; E: LMH.

288. Copying, Transferring, Or Disclosing Software Prohibited

Policy: Users must not copy software provided by Company X to any storage media (floppy disk, magnetic tape, etc.), transfer such software to another computer, or disclose such software to outside parties without written permission from the Director of the Information Technology Department.

Commentary: The intention of this policy is make it clear that users are not to change the software configuration of their systems or make any copies, transfers, or disclosures that might violate software vendors' licenses. The policy may also be useful when it comes to preventing proprietary software developed in-house from going astray. The simplest way to achieve these objectives is to prohibit users from making any changes. New software such as that offered by Gradient Technologies (Hudson, Massachusetts, USA) will allow this policy to be enforced automatically, in which case there will be no need for a written policy. But until sophisticated software like this is generally used, a policy may be necessary. Separately, this policy does not interfere with normal business activities so long as adequate technical support is provided; when users must do their own technical support, this policy will be problematic. This policy works best when users have a pre-installed software configuration which meets their needs, and when they have been given a separate policy about only using software which has been adopted as an organizational standard. For related ideas, see the policies entitled "Copyright Notices On Computer Programs And Documentation" and "Make At Least One Copy Of Critical Backed-Up Files Prior To Use." A: E; E: LMH.

289. Responsibility For Making Unauthorized Software And Data Copies

Policy: Company X strongly supports strict adherence to software vendors' license agreements and copyright holders' notices. If Internet users or other system users make unauthorized copies of software, the users are doing so on their own behalf, since all such copying is strictly forbidden by Company X. Likewise, Company X allows reproduction of copyrighted material only to the extent legally considered "fair use" or with the permission of either the author or publisher.

Commentary: This policy is intended to clearly assign responsibility and legal culpability for unauthorized copying of both software and data. Since it is not feasible for management to supervise every act performed by workers, workers who make unauthorized copies are put on notice that they shoulder the risk of penalties. This policy is noteworthy in that it goes beyond the ordinary prohibition against making unauthorized copies of software, it specifically makes reference to making unauthorized copies of material taken from the Internet. A common example involves the graphics used on Internet home pages; many users steal such graphics and use them elsewhere without getting the owner's permission. On another note, it may not be possible for management to completely transfer blame for unauthorized copying; discussion with internal legal counsel is highly advised before issuance of a policy such as this. Also see the policies entitled "Initial Backup Copies Of Microcomputer Software" and "Periodic Review Of Software Licensing Agreements." A: E; E: LMH.

290. Tools Used To Break Systems Security Prohibited

Policy: Unless specifically authorized by the Information Security Department, Company X workers must not acquire, possess, trade, or use hardware or software tools that could be employed to evaluate or compromise information systems security. Examples of such tools include those which defeat software copy protection, discover secret passwords, identify security vulnerabilities, or decrypt encrypted files.

Commentary: Because these tools can be and often are used to circumvent controls, their possession and use should be severely restricted. Possession and use should be allowed only for those who have a need for such powerful tools, such as EDP auditors and tiger-team staff (penetration attack team members). While these tools are readily available on the open market, on the Internet, and on electronic bulletin boards, Company X users should not be in possession of these tools. Thus, ordinary users should not have a collection of vulnerability identification tools like SATAN and COPS stored on their hard drive. Likewise, users should not have a Sniffer(TM) in their possession because it can be used to perform a wiretap. For the same reason, users should not have a database which contains working serial numbers needed to operate stolen software. Separately, there is a potential problem with this policy -- it could prohibit use of powerful system utilities like Norton Utilities (from Symantec, Cupertino, California). In some cases these utilities can be used to circumvent control mechanisms, such as certain password-based access control systems for microcomputers (PCs). To make sure that users don't confuse these common utilities with the programs deliberately intended to break security, adjectives like "unauthorized" could precede each type of tools mentioned in the policy. Another way to handle this distinction is through the use of a list of organization approved hardware and software. Accompanying explanatory text added by the policy writer can clarify this distinction as the needs of the policy-reading audience require. Separately, some users may claim that they never intended to use such tools, that they only acquired them to learn about computers. This policy removes the whole question of the user's intent from the discussion; if users have the tools, they may be disciplined or terminated. Also see the policies "Prohibition Against Testing Information System Controls," "Disclosure Of Information About Information System Vulnerabilities," and "Tools For Determining Security Status Of System." A: ET; E: LMH.

291. Participation In Pirated Software Bulletin Boards & Related Internet Sites

Policy: Worker participation in any manner with pirated software bulletin boards or related Internet sites is strictly prohibited, even if this participation occurs during non-working hours. This prohibition extends to any other facility or system which exchanges illegal copies of music, books, or other copyrighted material over the Internet or through other communications channels.

Commentary: The intention of this policy is to let workers know that Company X does not tolerate any illegal activity involving unauthorized duplication of copyrighted material. The policy is partly motivated by the popularity of Napster, which was recently shut down by the courts in the United States because it illegally distributed copyrighted music. The policy is also motivated by the "warez" sites, which provide free but illegal copies of software, and which migrate rapidly across Internet sites in order to avoid prosecution and other trouble. The policy is furthermore motivated by the sites which distribute the serial numbers needed to activate software which is not copy-protected. Visiting, contributing to, or taking copies from any of these and other related sites are all prohibited by the policy. The organization adopting this policy seeks to clarify that it did not encourage a worker's involvement with these sites --hopefully this will help to show that the organization should not be held responsible for any damages sustained by third parties (even if the information systems of the policy-issuing organization were used by the involved worker). For related ideas, see the policies entitled "Copying, Transferring, Or Disclosing Software Prohibited" and "Publicly-Writable Directories On Company X Computers Cleared Nightly." A: E; E: LMH.

292. Handling Of Third Party Confidential And Proprietary Information

Policy: Unless specified otherwise by contract, all confidential or proprietary information that has been entrusted to Company X by a third party must be protected as though it was Company X confidential information.

Commentary: In many cases the people handling third party information do not have access to the contracts which define agreed-upon procedures for handling information entrusted to Company X. An expedient way to overcome this lack of information is to use the internal data classification scheme at the recipient organization to designate how the information should be protected. This policy by default assigns a classification of "confidential" to all such information. Alternatively, the policy could be modified to require that an internal Company X information owner/sponsor be assigned, who then is required to assign a data classification label consistent with an internal data classification scheme. As a general strategy, it is advisable for all such information sharing agreements to employ existing information security classifications, procedures, etc. One variation to this policy would require that third party information include a notice designating the information's true owner. For further information, see the policy entitled "Four Category Data Classification Scheme." A: MT; E: LMH.

293. Use Of Company X Information For Non-Business Purposes

Policy: Company X information (product specifications, databases, mailing lists, internal software, computer documentation, etc.) must only be used for the business purposes specifically allowed by management. Use of these information resources for any other reason will be permitted only after written permission has been granted by the designated owner of the information.

Commentary: The intention of this policy is to provide clear guidance regarding the use of Company X internal information resources for purposes other than ordinary business activities. Without such notice, an employee may mistakenly conclude that it's permissible to use the Company X's mailing list for a part-time business that he or she runs. It is advisable to attach an explanation to this policy providing examples of both acceptable and unacceptable business purposes. Many other similar scenarios will also be addressed by this policy. If an employee has a question whether a certain use of Company X information is in keeping with management's authorization, this policy implies that he or she should ask before using the information. The policy has another positive side-effect: staff will be more conscious about using internal information for a purpose other than the originally intended purpose. Requests to clarify certain uses of information will in turn force management to take a clear stand about appropriate use. Over time, the existence of the approval process may tend to discourage questionable practices that could get the organization into trouble. Separately, this policy eliminates those circumstances where an employee says that they didn't know that it was not acceptable to use internal information for non-business purposes; lack of employee notice has been effectively used as a defense in various legal proceedings. A similar policy focusing on the use of information systems rather than information itself is entitled "Personal Use Of Computer And Communications Systems." In some instances it may be appropriate to combine these two policies. Also see the policies entitled "Permissible Uses Of Company X Information" and "Personal Use Of Electronic Mail Systems." A: EMT; E: LMH.

294. Transfer Of Company X Information To Third Parties

Policy: Company X software, documentation, and all other types of internal information must not be sold or otherwise transferred to any non-Company X party for any purposes other than business purposes expressly authorized by management.

Commentary: Workers have been known to sell mailing lists and other in-house data. Similarly, at software firms, employees have been known to post pre-release copies of software on the Internet. This policy puts workers on notice that such information must remain in-house; the existence of such a notice can form the basis for disciplinary actions or prosecutions. In many instances transfer of information to a third party is in good faith, such as when an employee makes a copy of security documentation to show to colleagues at an information security professional association. In this case, disclosure of internal information may help outsiders to compromise the security of the organization involved. Some employees will be relieved to have a policy such as this because it permits them to decline to participate in research surveys, marketing research telephone interviews, and other interactions that they'd just as soon avoid. Also see the policy entitled "Software Or Data Exchanges With Third Parties Require Agreements." A: EMT; E: LMH.

295. Software Or Data Exchanges With Third Parties Require Agreements

Policy: Exchanges of in-house software or internal information between Company X and any third party may not proceed unless a written agreement has first been signed. Such an agreement must specify the terms of the exchange, as well as the ways in which the software or information is to be handled and protected. This policy does not cover release of information designated as public (marketing materials, help wanted postings, etc.).

Commentary: The intention of this policy is to prevent misunderstandings about the use of and protection of Company X proprietary or sensitive information. For example, if two companies exchange in-house mailing lists, it could be specified in writing that the lists are to be used one time only. Having a written contract also provides some assurance that controls will be used to prevent the information from being further disclosed to some unauthorized third parties (so called secondary dissemination) and from being used for purposes other than those originally intended. Because it encourages some restraint associated with the dissemination of information, this policy is relevant to electronic mail, electronic bulletin boards (EBBs), and the Internet. A special exception could be recognized in the policy: government requests for data (such as via a court order) need not have agreements; to some people this will be obvious and need not be specifically stated. Some readers will want to incorporate in the policy specific words about the topics that need to be addressed in an agreement. These could include: security responsibilities of each involved party, procedures for protecting the software or information, and assignment of copyrights and other intellectual property rights. This policy could be restricted such that it refers to confidential and proprietary information, not so-called "internal information." See the policies entitled "Formation Of Binding Contracts Via Electronic Systems" and "Exchanges Of Information Over The Internet." A: MT; E: LMH.

296. Designation Of Software And Systems As Competitive Information

Policy: The Information Security Department must annually prepare a list of software and systems which have been developed in-house and which provide Company X with a competitive advantage.

Commentary: The intention of this policy is to force the Information Security Department (or local information security coordinators) to periodically examine the importance of software and systems developed in-house. The existence of such a list should then be used as a mechanism to make sure that the software and systems information in question are properly classified according to an internal data classification scheme. Likewise, the list should be used to determine whether the associated controls are adequate. In this manner the policy helps organizations ensure that their most precious information resources are properly protected. This policy is most relevant for those organizations which have developed unique software, expert systems, knowledge management systems, and other materials that give them a distinct competitive advantage. The policy may also be used as a way to provide management with a report reflecting how information systems are (or are not) being used to achieve competitive advantage. In this respect, it may be appropriate for the Information Security Department to work with the Strategic Planning Department and/or the Systems Architecture Group within the Information Systems Department. In some organizations, the identification of materials which provide competitive advantage can be done by a data management or data warehousing group. Also see the policy entitled "Annual Information Security Planning Process Required." A: MT; E: LMH.

297. Monitoring Internet For Use Of Trademark And Copyrighted Materials

Policy: The Legal Department must monitor the Internet monthly to make sure that Company X trademarks, service marks, and brand names are not being used in an unauthorized fashion. Likewise, the Legal Department must also search for unauthorized postings of copyrighted materials owned by Company X.

Commentary: The intention of this policy is to assign a brand-new function which basically involves scanning the Internet on a regular basis to make sure that the organization's legal rights have not been infringed. Beyond trademark infringement and copyright infringement, this effort could include efforts to detect defamatory statements against the organization (libel and slander). The work could be done by other departments besides the Legal Department (perhaps the Information Security Department), but the Legal Department must follow-up with the other parties involved. Third party services who perform this function can use special software to perform much of this work automatically. Likewise, certain public domain software (so-called web spiders) can scan the world wide web looking for copyrighted materials including graphics. Of course, search engines like Alta Vista can be used to find occurrences of company names, trademarks, and service marks. On a different note, some firms may also wish to see who is linking to their site (via a search for URLs). Separately, keep in mind that organizations must take steps to protect their legal rights, or in some jurisdictions they may lose these legal rights. In all matters involving the law, be sure to consult an attorney. Also see the policies entitled "Monitoring Of Electronic Mail Messages" and "No Responsibility For Monitoring Content Of Information Systems." A: M; E: LMH.

298. Internet Use Of Other Organization's Trademarks And Service Marks

Policy: Company X web and commerce sites must not use any other organization's trademarks or service marks anywhere (text on pages, metatags, etc.) unless (a) the usage reflects the actual attributes of Company X products or services, and (b) advance permission has been obtained from Company X corporate legal counsel.

Commentary: The intention of this policy is to prevent legal problems, bad publicity, and soured relations with competitors. The use of another firm's trademark or service mark can be perceived to be a device to deceptively bring people into one's own web site through search engines such as Excite. This policy acknowledges the rights of third party firms to their own trademarks and service marks and takes a conservative position with respect to the use of these character strings. Beyond the avoidance of litigation, this policy may also help maintain good relations with prospective customers because complaints are minimized. For related concepts, see the policies entitled "Respecting The Intellectual Property Rights Of Others On The Internet" and "Unofficial Web Pages Permitted Only By Contract." A: T; E: LMH.

299. Prohibition Against Any Third Party Use Of Company X's Name

Policy: No third party organization may use Company X's name in its advertising or marketing materials unless the permission of corporate legal counsel has first been obtained.

Commentary: The purpose of this policy is to prevent third party activities from sullying the good name of a particular organization. For example, if a fly-by-night entrepreneur were to use the name of a large and prestigious company, saying that this company was endorsing his or her activities, this claim would bring great credibility. But if the claim were false, and he or she ended up defrauding customers, the good name of the large company might be degraded even though there was no conscious fault of the large company. In a worst case situation, some people may even hold the large company responsible for their fraud losses claiming an implied endorsement. To prevent such problems, this policy says that no usage is permissible unless it has first been approved by corporate legal counsel. Some companies are now enforcing this trademark protection policy by scanning the Internet via search engines, looking for all instances in which their company name appears. If any unauthorized appearance is found, the responsible parties are contacted and told to cease and desist. For related concepts, see the policies entitled "Respecting The Intellectual Property Rights Of Others On The Internet" and "Unofficial Web Pages Permitted Only By Contract." A: E; E: LMH.

300. Every Public Written Use Of Company X's Name Requires Approval

Policy: Every public written use of Company X's name in published material (web sites, marketing brochures, editorials, and the like) requires the advance approval of a vice president or the Public Relations Department. Use of the name on staff business cards or staff resumes does not require such approval.

Commentary: The intention of this policy is to prevent staff members from using the good name of Company X for unauthorized purposes. Workers may seek to use the organization's name as a way to obtain additional credibility for other endeavors. Unauthorized usage of the organization's name can lead to a variety of problems including liability for damages sustained by third parties who relied on an implied endorsement by the organization in question. Note that this policy also prohibits the use of broadcast email, contributions to Internet chat rooms, and other broadcast communications if the organization's name is mentioned (assuming that no management approval was first obtained). Staff members may of course participate in such forums if they don't mention that they work for Company X. This policy is thus a very conservative approach which reflects great concern about the preservation of the goodwill now held by Company X. For related ideas, see the policies entitled "Prohibition Against Any Third Party Use Of Company X's Name" and "Disclaimer Must Accompany All Internet Personal Messages." A: E; E: MH.

301. Loss Of Critical Knowledge And Employees Flying On Same Airplane

Policy: To protect Company X's pool of knowledge and skills, employees must not take the same airplane flight(s) if it would mean that three or more officers, five or more employees, or two or more engineers from the same department, would be on the same flight.

Commentary: This policy implicitly recognizes that one of the most important assets of an organization is the knowledge that its employees have in their heads. The policy's intention is to make sure that a plane crash will not severely damage the ability of the organization to achieve its goals. The policy could be expanded to include other modes of transport, but airplane crashes are one of the most sudden and catastrophic events where several employees could be lost. Although unusual, the policy could also be broadened to include life-endangering activities such as hang-gliding and motorcycle racing. There is nothing special about the numbers included in the policy; the number of engineers from the same department, for example, could have been three. One assumption behind the policy as written is that engineers are the organization's important type of employee. If this is not the case at the policy writer's organization, then appropriate substitutions of different words (like "information systems specialists") should be made. This policy assumes that Company X is a relatively large organization. For another approach to this same problem of putting "all of one's eggs in one basket," see the policy entitled "Cross Training For Staff In Critical Technical Jobs." Also see the policy entitled "Contact Numbers For Information Systems Department Staff." A: EMT; E: LMH.

1.3.2. Data Privacy

1.3.2.1. Restrictions Of Privacy Rights

302. Right Of Management To Examine Data Stored On Company X Systems

Policy: All messages sent over Company X computer and communications systems are the property of Company X. To properly maintain and manage this property, management reserves the right to examine all information stored in or transmitted by these systems. Since Company X's computer and communication systems must be used for business purposes only, workers should have no expectation of privacy associated with the information they store in or send through these systems.

Commentary: A number of court cases in the United States have focused on employee expectations of privacy while using an employer's computer and communications systems (particularly electronic mail). While management can choose to provide employees with the same privacy rights that they would enjoy when using a common carrier such as the telephone company, most employers are adopting a policy such as the one shown here. Whatever position management chooses to follow, it is important that the privacy status of employee-generated data on Company X systems be clearly specified. If employees know that such data may be examined by management, they will refrain from certain activities, such as sending love letters by electronic mail. Thus employee expectations must be clarified to avoid litigation, employee grievances, and morale problems. The reader may also wish to review the section of this book entitled "Assignment Of Intellectual Property Rights." For a similar but non-property oriented idea, see the policy entitled "Monitoring Of Electronic Mail Messages." For a decidedly more protective perspective, see the policy entitled "Privacy Of Personal Files Stored On Computers And In Desks." A: EMT; E: LMH.

303. Pretext Requests Used To Test Both Customer Service And Security Policies

Policy: As a general business rule, Company X believes that all business activities should be conducted in a forthright and honest manner. However, in certain circumstances authorized by the Director Of Physical Security, the organization may utilize investigators who pose as other persons in order to test customer service, test security policies, or investigate alleged wrongdoing.

Commentary: The intention of this policy is put employees on notice that there may be "moles" (spies) within the organization, who are posing as regular employees or other authorized personnel, but who are really investigators. These investigators may employ techniques like "pretext calling" where they use the telephone to masquerade as though they are someone else, in order to obtain certain information, or in order to determine a worker's response to certain questions. Having a policy like this shows management's attempt to be aboveboard and straight about a controversial topic, and a policy such as this may help prevent future allegations about being entrapped or mislead. Thus the policy may encourage employees to be on their best behavior. Separately, the policy is considered to be a restriction of privacy rights because the workers don't really know who they are dealing with over the phone, over the email system, or via some other communications channel. But taking that uncertainly seriously is the same attitude that many organizations seek to foster in order to prevent social engineering (spoofing) from leading to serious losses. For related ideas, see the policies entitled "Sender Contact Information Must Be Included In Electronic Mail" and "Validating The Identity Of External Parties On The Internet." A: E; E: MH.

304. Areas Where Electronic Monitoring Of Workers May Be Used

Policy: Workers may be subject to electronic monitoring while on Company X premises. This monitoring is used to measure workers performance as well as to protect worker personal property, worker safety, and Company X property. In areas where there is a reasonable expectation of privacy, such as bathrooms, dressing rooms, and locker rooms, no electronic monitoring will be performed.

Commentary: The intention of this policy is to put workers on notice that they are subject to electronic monitoring. This blunts any objection that they may later make stating that their privacy was invaded without their knowledge. The policy clearly states the areas where worker privacy will be honored. The policy is thus notable because it clearly establishes an understanding about the areas where electronic monitoring may be used. Also see the policies entitled "Electronic Mail Messages Are Company Records" and "Surreptitious Collection Of Customer Private Data Prohibited." A: E; E: LMH.

305. Disclosure Of Information On Company X Systems To Law Enforcement

Policy: By making use of Company X systems, users consent to allow all information they store on Company X systems to be divulged to law enforcement at the discretion of Company X management.

Commentary: This policy puts users on notice that they should not have an expectation of privacy with respect to Company X systems. It also puts users on notice that no search warrant will be necessary before law enforcement agents gain access to information that they store on Company X systems. Management may wish to reveal certain information (such as electronic mail logs) to law enforcement; this could be appropriate if management discovered the use of its computing facilities to conduct drug deals or some other illegal activity. Like the policy entitled "Right of Management To Examine Data Stored On Company X Systems," this policy helps to manage user expectations, making sure that users understand they do not have normal privacy protections applicable to public communications carriers (like the phone company). Also see the policy entitled "Disclosure Of Private Information To Third Parties" and "Electronic Mail Messages Are Company Records." A: EMT; E: LMH.

306. Privacy Rights Waived When Collecting Bills Or Enforcing Contracts

Policy: Company X retains the right to release private and confidential information to outside parties in order to collect outstanding bills or to otherwise compel performance with contractual terms and conditions.

Commentary: The intention of this policy is to make it clear to outside parties who may have provided Company X with personal information, and to internal workers, that there are some limitations to the privacy rights that the organization has published. For example, Company X may need to go to court to force a customer to pay their bill, but the process of finding the facts in court will necessitate the release of personal information. Company X doesn't want to restrict its own ability to collect bills, and so a policy like this may be necessary if other privacy assurances have been adopted. A policy like this may also be necessary in order to allow what the State of Connecticut (USA) has done with tax deadbeats. In 1999, the State has posted on the web the names of the 100 taxpayers with the largest tax debts to the State. This process of public shaming has reportedly been effective, and even the threat of posting names to the web (advance notice by letters) has caused people to promptly pay. Separately, those concerned about abuse of this "right" might consider inclusion of words in the policy that describe a process by which the legitimacy of a claim (back-due bill, broken contract, etc.) is verified prior to public release of personal information. For related ideas, see the policies entitled "Risk Acceptance Process And Permissible Exceptions To Policies" and "Minimum Information Retention Period." A: E; E: LMH.

307. Disclosures Of Private Information Without Data Subject Consent

Policy: Patient records must be disclosed only to those medical and insurance personnel who are actively engaged in a patient's treatment. Disclosures will be made to other parties only when a patient provides written authorization. An exception will be made in those cases involving a serious threat to public health.

Commentary: The intention of this policy is to clarify when disclosure of private information is permissible even though the data subject (the individual involved) has not expressly given consent. For example, if a patient in a hospital is in a coma, and is therefore unable to give consent, this policy will allow doctors not previously associated with the patient to view the patient's records and to assist with treatment. While this policy is found in the health care industry, it could be adapted to suit other industries as well. For example, a telephone company could use it to define who obtains access to customer calling patterns (pen registers). The policy is desirable because it minimizes the paperwork associated with the consent process, but at the same time establishes a minimum privacy protection level. The policy is also desirable because it allows the organization to disclose private data in order to safeguard the welfare of other parties. For example, if a doctor sees a married patient with a sexually transmitted disease, the patient may forbid the doctor from disclosing this information to his or her spouse. This would of course jeopardize the health of the spouse. The doctor, under this policy, would be free to contact the spouse even if the patient objects. The right to privacy thus must not be absolute; the general welfare of all concerned should be considered. See the policies entitled "Subjects Given Opportunity To Block Private Information Disclosures" and "Required Efforts To Ensure Personal Records Are Used Only As Intended." A: E; E: LMH.

308. Affected Individuals Notified About Material Changes In Privacy Policy

Policy: Company X staff members must take reasonable steps to promptly notify all affected individuals whenever there has been a material change in documented privacy policies.

Commentary: The motivation for this policy is to ensure that workers take steps to promptly notify affected individuals whenever there has been a significant change in a privacy policy. For example, a restriction of previously-promised privacy rights would warrant such a notice. Such a notification could, for example, be easily achieved by posting a few words on the home page at web site (although a button saying "I accept the new terms" is preferred). This policy is partially motivated by the United States law called the Health Insurance Portability and Accountability Act (HIPAA), and is additionally intended to provide evidence that management sought to notify all affected individuals when it changed its privacy policy. In the real world, of course, not all individuals will be reachable due to changes of address, unlisted phone numbers, bounced email addresses, and other problems. Reflecting difficulties associated with notifying the affected individuals, the policy uses the words "reasonable steps." The policy thus requires notice after the change has taken place and allows these affected individuals to change their relationship with the involved organization, should they wish to do so in response to the policy change. Thus the policy allows the notified individuals to then opt-in or opt-out of a new service, perhaps via an Internet URL with a form that can handle this process automatically. For related ideas, see the policies entitled "Personal Data Gathering Points And Corporate Privacy Policy Posting" and "Notifying Subjects Of Existing Monitoring Systems." A: M; E: LMH.

309. Privacy Policy Changes Require Posting Of Clear Differences Summary

Policy: If we change our privacy policy, we will clearly let you know that we have changed it, and when we have changed it. At each of these times, we will also provide you with a summary of the words that have changed and what these changes mean for you.

Commentary: The intention of this policy is to build user confidence about doing business with an on-line merchant. Customers and prospects want to know what their interaction with an organization is going to be like in the future. This policy helps to allay justified fears that about future abuse of private data collected by an Internet merchant. The policy says that the issuer of the policy will provide what is called a "difference file" which is generated when two files are compared and the changes are highlighted. This makes life much easier for users because they don't have to read the entire policy again, and then try to figure out what changed. This policy is in distinct opposition to the privacy unfriendly practices of some on-line merchants who expect the reader to look at their privacy policy periodically to determine, on their own, if the policy has been changed, and if it has, how it has changed. The latter approach puts an unreasonable burden on the user. For related ideas, see the policies entitled "Privacy Policy Pertains To All Types Of Interactions With Customers" and "Affected Individuals Notified About Material Changes In Privacy Policy." A: E; E: LMH.

310. Privacy Policy Pertains To All Types Of Interactions With Customers

Policy: Company X seeks to be straightforward and clear about its privacy policy. This statement contains our full policy and there are no exceptions to the policy which are not described here. This policy pertains to all interactions with customers, no matter what communications channel, no matter what involved department within Company X, and no matter what topic the interaction covers.

Commentary: This policy may at first appear to be unnecessary. But when the policy writer researches the latest privacy abuses by Internet merchants, he or she will appreciate the merits of the policy. Some health care web sites have posted a privacy policy for their web site which says that they will not share personal health information with third parties, but then they also have chat rooms or other facilities which have another policy saying that "anything a participant transmits or posts can be used for any purpose." Some visitors to the site may have read the web site policy but may not have carefully read the policy which pertains to the chat rooms or other facilities. Privacy policy is already a very complex area, and these Internet merchant maneuvers only confuse participants and give the industry a bad reputation. This policy lets policy readers know there is only one policy, that they do not have to locate and read separate policies for different types of interactions with Company X. This policy also lends itself to operational simplicity and information handling cost minimization. Arguing against a policy such as this are those same web merchants lambasted in this commentary who argue that they need to keep their options open lest they unduly "limit access and functionality" to their sites. For a related idea, see the policy entitled "Customer's Right-To-Know Nature Of Personal Information." A: E; E: LMH.

1.3.2.2. Collection Of Specific Types of Private Data

311. Permissible Information To Collect From Prospective Employees

Policy: Personal information about a prospective employee may not be gathered unless it is both necessary to make an employment decision and also relevant to the job in question. This policy addresses marital status, family planning objectives, off-hours activities, political affiliations, performance on previous jobs, previous employers, credit history, education, and other personal details.

Commentary: The intention of this policy is to maintain the privacy of prospective employees, as well as to keep personnel records orderly and clean (not overloaded with irrelevant facts). An additional objective of this policy is to prevent claims of illegal discrimination; if an organization did not collect certain information, then it is most unlikely that it could have used it to make employment decisions. Of course, this policy cannot be used to help defend against claims of discrimination based on race or sex, or other attributes which are readily observable and for which additional information gathering is not required. In an indirect way the policy also helps foster the identification of information relevant to an employment decision; this is desirable because it helps document the criteria used for making employment decisions, potentially assisting with a successful legal defense against charges of discrimination. Because this policy is heavily dependent on local laws and regulations, be sure to consult with an attorney before issuing such a policy. The policy could be expanded to more specifically state the types of information that must not be collected including sexual preference and the like. This policy permits the collection of current performance information (in those cases where a current employee is seeking a transfer) as well as other background information (vetting information). This policy also prevents certain employees from gaining unwarranted power because they have information which might be used to damage the reputation of the involved individual. Some organizations may wish to go further, prohibiting the retention of such information if the decision to which it applied has been made (although certain legal considerations should first be worked out with internal legal counsel). Policies such as this may bolster employee morale, indicating that an employer does indeed care about employee welfare. The policy may also help limit an employer's exposure to accusations that the privacy of certain individuals has been unreasonably invaded. Also see the policies entitled "Timing Of Notification About Electronic Performance Monitoring" and "Honesty And Emotional Stability Tests For Computer-Related Workers." A: M; E: LMH.

312. Collection Of Private Information Banned Except By Permission

Policy: Company X workers and information systems are banned from collecting private information (race, religion, political opinions, sexual orientation, etc.) unless the collection effort has been approved in advance by corporate legal counsel.

Commentary: The purpose of this policy is to keep the issuing organization out of trouble when it comes to collecting private information. Better to never have collected the information than to worry about protecting it, using it only for approved purposes, and releasing it only to authorized recipients. This approach is particularly well-suited to the new Internet commerce businesses which operate in many different countries; rather than having to keep track of all the relevant laws about private information handling, this policy makes it possible to ignore many of the issues. Many businesses don't require personal information for their activities, and for them the most economical and most expedient way to address privacy issues is to simply forbid the collection of such data. Note that the policy does not prohibit the collection of any private data forever; it is still possible to collect race data, for example, if a government agency required the compilation of an anti-discrimination report. This policy is patterned after the 1995 European

Union Directive On Data Protection, which bans the processing of certain private data except for a few enumerated cases. For related ideas, see the policies entitled "Permissible Information To Collect From Prospective Employees" and "Message Content Restrictions For Company X Information Systems." A: E; E: L.

313. Personal Information Necessary For Proper Functioning Of Business

Policy: Company X must collect, process, store, and disseminate only that information which is necessary for the proper functioning of its business.

Commentary: This policy can be expanded to prohibit the collection of information about employee religious, social, political, sexual, or other activities performed after hours that do not impinge on business matters. The intention of the policy is to preserve the privacy rights of employees, customers, and other people who may have some dealings with the organization in question. Another intention of the policy is to simplify the information systems by keeping the amount of information retained by Company X to a minimum. This may additionally counteract the tendency of some people to keep everything because it may be useful sometime in the future (also known as "packrats"). This policy discourages information hoarding by bringing the focus back to what's needed. In the latter respect, the scope of the policy is broader than just privacy matters, it pertains to all information. Separately, the policy does not provide detailed guidance about determining whether certain information is "necessary" -- this is a deliberate omission because both the decision process and the information to which it pertains will change dramatically over time. An organizational data dictionary (also known as a data directory) may also be an important adjunct to this policy. See the policies entitled "High-Level Inventory Of Information Assets" and "Regular Purging Of Information Which Is No Longer Needed." A: EMT; E: LMH.

314. Collecting Information About Expressions Of First Amendment Rights

Policy: Company X must not collect information about worker expressions of First Amendment rights (freedom of speech).

Commentary: In the United States, the First Amendment deals with the freedom of speech and the freedom of the press. In other countries, similar rights may be described in the constitution or other government rights documents; a suitable substitution may be appropriate. Separately, instead of referencing the "First Amendment," the policy can refer to "free speech and expression." Thus this policy is intended to prevent management or other people affiliated with Company X from collecting information such as the fact that an accountant in the Finance Department went to an environmental rally. This policy can be expanded to prohibit the collection of information about employee religious, social, political, sexual, or other activities performed after hours that do not impinge on business matters. If such free speech and expression information is collected by management, it may have chilling effect, i.e. workers may be afraid to express themselves lest it be judged adversely by management. This in turn can lead to a stagnant organization where people are afraid to do or say anything new or different lest they be punished for it. On another note, a policy such as this helps build employee trust for his or her employer because it shows the employer respects and wants to support employee rights like privacy. Separately, the term "worker" found in the policy could be substituted with appropriate distinctions such as "employee," "temporary," "contractor," and the like. For a related idea, see the policy entitled "Right To Free Speech Does Not Apply To Company X Systems." A: MT; E: LMH.

315. Need To Collect Private Information Must First Be Justified

Policy: Before Company X workers collect private information about workers, customers, or other people, the need for such information must first be documented and approved by the Director of Human Resources.

Commentary: This policy is intended to limit the collection of private information. This will, in turn, reduce the need for special controls to protect newly-collected private information. This policy also indirectly prevents Company X managers from keeping secret databases about employees, or from establishing covert performance monitoring systems. The policy is derived from legislation in the State of Florida (authored by the Florida Joint Committee On Information Technology Resources). While originally intended for government use, this policy is equally applicable to private sector organizations which want to keep the cost of information security down. Also see the policies entitled "Performance Monitoring Information And Relevance To The Job" and "Maintenance Of Index To Databases Containing Private Information." A: M; E: LMH.

316. Private Data Collection Only If Lawful And Necessary

Policy: The collection of private data by Company X workers will be permitted only if performed by lawful means, and only for a purpose related to the activities of Company X.

Commentary: The intention of this policy is to make it look like an organization is doing something about privacy, when really it is not. This policy is thus basically a public relations ploy rather than a substantial control that actually improves the privacy of data subjects. The policy holds the issuing organization to nothing substantive that it would not otherwise be required to live up to: that it operate lawfully, and that it engage in activities related to its business. As an aside, the policy does provide a means to terminate employees who deviate from these limits, but the employees in question probably could have been terminated for other reasons (such as insubordination or felony criminal conviction). This policy is included in this book because it is fairly common, and so that the policy writer can compare it with other policies that have some substance, and is not included because it is recommended. For related ideas, see the polices entitled "Need To Collect Private Information Must First Be Justified" and "Personal Information Necessary For Proper Functioning Of Business." A: E; E: LMH.

317. Surreptitious Collection Of Customer Private Data Prohibited

Policy: Company X computer and communications systems must never collect private data from customers or potential customers without having first obtained their clear and unambiguous consent.

Commentary: The intention of this policy is to improve the Company X public image as well as customer loyalty. By prohibiting clandestine private data gathering, customers and potential customers are given more confidence that they know about the private information they have entrusted to Company X. An example involves the debate about automatic number identification, also known as ANI (similar to caller-ID). ANI captures telephone callers' phone numbers without the potential customers' or existing customers' consent. Some organizations then use this information for follow-up telemarketing calls. Some organizations may also sell these numbers to other organizations without the consent of the callers. This policy prohibits the collection of ANI information in the absence of the callers' consent. Another example involves hidden programs which automatically send electronic mail back to the vendor of a software package; such a program was used by Performix to discover what, according to public reports, appears to be industrial espionage perpetrated by Mercury Interactive. Such programs can be used to indicate that a user is having trouble with software as well as inform the vendor where their software is installed. For more information on this intriguing case see "A '90s Espionage Tale Stars Software Rivals, E-Mail Spy," in The Wall Street Journal, 25 October 1995, p. B1. A good example of this policy implemented correctly can be found in Microsoft's Windows 95 operating system; the operating system sends e-mail back to Microsoft indicating what products are being used -- but only after the customer has first agreed to it. Separately, this policy is a manifestation of a more general idea that people should be the "owners" of the information describing their own lives. Also see the policies entitled "Notifying Subjects Of Existing Monitoring Systems," "Areas Where Electronic Monitoring Of Workers May Be Used," "Two-Party Consent For All Speaker Phone Use Or Tape Recording," and "Collection Of Personal Information Permissible But Distribution Prohibited." A: MT; E: LMH.

318. Personally-Identifiable Information Collection Requires Robust Notice

Policy: In every instance where personally-identifiable information is collected, robust (explicit and understandable) notice must be provided at the time and place the information is collected. Where information which is not personally-identifiable is collected, notice about this collection must nonetheless appear in the posted privacy policy.

Commentary: This policy is intended to clarify when and where notice about information collection should be provided. It is inspired by the Network Advertising Initiative (www.networkadvertising.org) and is a reflection of current United States industry proposals on Internet commerce privacy policy. The policy places the greatest emphasis on collection of personally-identifiable information (such as an email address) and seeks to mark all web locations where such collection is being performed irrespective of user knowledge or participation in the collection process. Thus if email addresses were harvested automatically from user web browsers when users visited a web site, this fact would need to be disclosed. Of lesser concern is information which is not personally-identifiable, such as click-stream data. Because this latter type of information is not associated with any particular person, the potential for abuse is considerably lessened, and this fact is reflected in the diminished need for notice. Some organizations may wish to mention an exception where private information may be collected secretly, and that involves the investigation of a suspected crime or an allegedly abusive activity. For related ideas, see the policies entitled "Monitoring And Recording Activity In An Anonymous Fashion" and "Customer Requests For Anonymity On Company X Systems." A: T; E: LMH.

319. Childrens' Personal Information Gathering Needs Parental Consent

Policy: Personal information about children may not be gathered by any Company X information system without first obtaining clear and unambiguous consent from the involved parents or guardians.

Commentary: The intention of this policy is to put technical staff on notice that they must not gather personal information from children unless parental or guardian consent is first obtained. Just how this consent is to be obtained is deliberately not stated in this policy because the mechanisms to do this have not yet been widely agreed-upon. Ideally, this consent would be through an electronic mail message signed by a parent with a digital signature that was verifiable through a digital certificate. This ideal can be rather time consuming, so something more expedient will in most instances be involved. For example, provision of a valid credit card number is often deemed sufficient evidence that one is indeed an adult. This policy is motivated by the increasing use of the Internet to gather personal information about people, notably children. Children, some people think, don't have the sophistication to protect their own privacy, and so their parents or guardians must step in to play this role. This policy attempts to prevent problems with the 1998 Internet Tax Freedom Act (United States legislation), which includes a provision that requires web sites to seek parental permission before they solicit information from children under 12. The policy is not specific to the Internet, because such information might be gathered by other means, for example via the telephone. The policy also attempts to establish that Company X is conscientious and socially-minded, thus hopefully improving its image. This policy could, in slightly modified form, be posted on a web site. Separately, the policy deliberately refrains from stating how the information is gathered; it might be explicitly solicited via user data entry and a web form, or it might be automatically gathered via user activity logging software. For related ideas, see the policies entitled "Age Verification Required Prior To Adult Material Access" and "Subjects Must Opt-In To Be Included In Systems Handling Private Data." A: T; E: LMH.

320. Personal Information Collection Permissible But Distribution Prohibited

Policy: The collection of personal information about potential customers and others with whom Company X does business is customary and expected. Access to this information must be strictly controlled on a need-to-know basis and the information must be used only for internal business purposes. Unless the clear and unambiguous consent of the party described by the information is first obtained, all third party sale, exchange, or other distribution is prohibited.

Commentary: The intention of this policy is to permit certain information to be gathered for business purposes, but to preserve the data subject's privacy by not permitting it to be distributed to third parties. Prohibition against unapproved distribution to third parties is a way to ensure that the information will not be used in a manner unintended by the data subject. Note that the policy permits the information to be used for internal purposes, including purposes other than those originally intended. This would, for example, permit "data mining" where new relationships are discovered between various types of customer data. Separately, the policy does not require the data subject to agree in advance about the collection of the information. The policy is exemplified by a recent New York State Public Service Commission ruling which permits businesses to collect phone numbers gathered via ANI (automatic number identification) systems, but it does not permit the businesses to market this information without the consumer's prior consent. This is a middle-of-the-road policy which may be an acceptable compromise for some businesses. Other businesses may consider this policy to grant the data subjects too many rights to data about them; these businesses will want to exchange mailing lists and other collections of personal information without first contacting the involved data subjects. Some organizations may wish to specify the need for consent when dealing with certain types of information (like telephone numbers), but no need for consent when dealing with other types of information (like mailing addresses). On a different note, the policy does not imply that personal information distribution required by law (such as release to the police in keeping with a search warrant) must go through the consent process; some organizations may wish to specify this in the policy. Also see the policy entitled "Surreptitious Collection Of Customer Private Data Prohibited." A: MT; E: LMH.

321. Permissible Information To Collect From Customers

Policy: Company X computer-supported procedures must never require the provision of customer personal information which is unnecessary for the completion of a transaction, or unnecessary for the provision of products or services.

Commentary: This restriction on the collection of unnecessary personal data is part of United States government privacy policies, as elaborated in the Privacy Act of 1974. This notion is applicable to commercial, non-profit, and other organizations as well. The policy is intended to simplify transactions and allow customers to decide not to provide certain personal information. Separately, a notice that the provision of certain personal information is optional may be added to certain paper forms, or be provided over the phone when collecting personal information. Some organizations may wish to mention the need for this notice in the policy. For example, a customer sending in a product warranty registration card can simply choose not to answer a question about his or her income; the registration process will proceed without this information. Note that this policy says nothing about requesting certain personal information, it only says that this information will never be required. Thus, market research and other efforts to understand customers will not be hindered. Of course, the policy does not interfere with the collection of necessary personal information, such as the collection of a social security number for the completion of certain income tax documents. Also see the policy entitled "Need To Collect Private Information Must First Be Justified." A: MT; E: LMH.

322. Least Intrusive Methods Available To Gather Private Information

Policy: Company X employs the least intrusive methods available to gather private information about its customers, prospects, employees, and others associated with its business. It does not ask for the same information more than once unless absolutely necessary for the accuracy and integrity of its records.

Commentary: This policy is intended to reassure customers, prospects, employees, and others that the issuing organization is deliberately trying to respect their privacy, and deliberately attempting to keep the burden of data gathering to a minimum (for both the issuing organization and data subjects). A statement such as this could be useful for marketing purposes, offering another reason to do business with the issuing organization. Separately, perhaps the reader remembers an occasion when they were asked to provide personal or private information, on multiple occasions within a brief time period, to the same organization -- it may have felt disrespectful and wasteful of time. Thus this policy assumes that the issuing organization has integrated customer records rather than isolated customer databases which serve various purposes. For related ideas, see the policies entitled "Surreptitious Collection Of Customer Private Data Prohibited" and "Permissible Information To Collect from Customers." A: E; E: LMH.

323. Involuntary Capture Of Personal Biometric Information Prohibited

Policy: Personal biometric information (voiceprints, fingerprints, eye blood vessel prints, DNA, etc.) may not be captured by any Company X information systems unless the individual described has been previously notified of and has consented to the capture.

Commentary: The objective of this policy is to prevent surreptitious collection of personal biometric information that could later be used to perpetrate a fraud or violate the privacy of the individual described by the information. A fraud could take place if the information was incorporated into a driver's license or some other counterfeit identification badge (this could involve identity fraud). Privacy violation could take place if biometric information were used to masquerade as the individual in question in order to obtain information that would otherwise be restricted. Covert collection of biometric information might also be a serious publicity problem if it later was revealed that such information were being collected without the knowledge or consent of data subjects. Separately, this policy assumes that strong mechanisms to protect such biometric information are in place (encryption is important here). On another note, this policy could be modified to specifically recognize an exception involving the investigation of alleged criminal activity (for example, fingerprints are captured at crime scenes). This exception was not written into the suggested policy because the data capturing process is most often performed by law enforcement staff, not Company X staff or information systems. For related considerations, see the policies entitled "Need To Collect Private Information Must First Be Justified" and "Positive Identification Required For System Usage." A: T; E: MH.

324. Prohibited Transfer Of Personal Biometric Data To Third Parties

Policy: Although Company X employs biometric identification systems such as fingerprint scanners, as a matter of policy, under no circumstances does it provide this data to third parties unless compelled to do so by law.

Commentary: The intention of this policy is to assure individuals who use biometric systems (customers, employees, contractors, volunteers, etc.) that their personal biometric data will not be released to third parties. This should be of particular concern to every person who is registered in a biometric system because such personal data could be used to commit identity theft. For example, fingerprint data could be incorporated into a magnetic strip which is on the back of a driver's license, and the existence of such a fraudulent driver's license could allow an individual to take out bank loans in the name of another person. Biometric personal data could also be used for purposes other than those to which the user agreed when he or she enrolled in the biometric system. For example, perhaps the facial recognition information gathered by certain English towns using closed circuit television (CCTV) could be used by a spurned spouse to prove adultery. Perhaps merchants could use such facial recognition information in shopping malls to see whether their direct mail campaign was working as anticipated. This policy helps to assure those who are considering enrolling in the system that there are no ulterior motives for a new biometric system. Admittedly, the organization gathering this special type of personal data could use it in new ways, but the risk of unauthorized uses is markedly reduced if the information is not shared with third parties. For a related idea, see the policy entitled "Involuntary Capture Of Personal Biometric Information Prohibited." A: E; E: MH.

325. Personal Data Gathering Points And Corporate Privacy Policy Posting

Policy: All points where personal data is gathered for use in Company X information systems must include a rendition of Company X's privacy policy approved by the manager of the Information Security Department.

Commentary: The purpose of this policy is to require that prospects and customers are consistently informed about Company X's privacy policy. The question is no longer "should your organization have a publicly posted privacy policy?" but "where should this policy appear?" This policy says that at every point where personal data is gathered (web page electronic forms, direct mail response postcards, applications for employment form, etc.), there must be a statement about privacy. Not all of these renditions of the privacy policy will need to be comprehensive; the information can instead be tailored to the nature of the information being collected. Separately, this policy helps prevent disputes occasioned by different departments saying different things about privacy (centralization achieves consistency). Likewise, if there are two different privacy policies used by a single organization, and if the information is later combined, how should the combined information (perhaps in a data warehouse) be handled? (The answer is according to the most stringent policy, but marketing people may not like the answer.) Note that this policy assumes that a corporate privacy policy has been developed and published. The policy also assumes that workers know what "personal data" is; a distinction between "secret" and "personal" may need to be made and some examples may be necessary. For related ideas, see the policies entitled "Notifying Subjects Of Existing Monitoring Systems" and "Prospective Employees Given Opportunity To Decline Credit Checks." A: T; E: LMH.

326. Name Of Organization Collecting Private Information Must Be Disclosed

Policy: Both the collecting organization's legal name and current contact information must be disclosed at each point where private information is collected. An exception will be made in those situations where this information can be easily determined from other information displayed on a user's screen.

Commentary: The intention of this policy is to prevent the collection of private information by third parties unbeknownst to a user (most often these users are Internet web surfers). Certain marketing firms now collect "click stream" (aka mouse movement) information from web surfers, but the entity collecting this information and the contact particulars for this entity are regularly not disclosed. To not disclose the third party's name, and to not provide contact information, to many people seems to be dishonest and reprehensible. Of course, the fact that the information is being collected should also be disclosed. This policy will help instruct web site and commerce site designers about the disclosures they must make. If some of these designers believe that the disclosures mandated by this policy will jeopardize their private information collection activities, then the propriety of the collection activities needs further examination. The word "private" may also need a definition at the organization adopting this policy. For example, if click stream data is anonymous, it generally would not be considered to be private, even though it describes activities of certain people. Separately, the second sentence allows links to be used to get contact information or other details, rather than requiring the information to be displayed at the time that the private information is gathered. For related ideas, see the policies entitled "Personally-Identifiable Information Collection Requires Robust Notice" and "Surreptitious Collection Of Customer Private Data Prohibited." A: T; E: LMH.

327. Full Explanation Why Private Information Is Required

Policy: Whenever private information is requested by Company X information systems or workers, the full and complete reasons for collecting this information must also be disclosed. Furthermore, the consequences of a data subject's refusal to provide private information must also be disclosed at this point in time.

Commentary: The intention of this policy is to give the individual disclosing private data sufficient information on which to base a disclosure decision. For example, someone applying for government welfare payments (also known as "the dole") may be required to provide information about their income, their financial resources, their personal property, etc. Without this information, the government may refuse to provide welfare, and this fact may be disclosed to the individual at the point of information collection. Note that this policy limits the things that the collecting organization can do with the private information since the purposes for collection were disclosed at the time that the information was provided. Some organizations may wish to delete the words "full and complete" from the policy, so as to give themselves an opportunity to use the information for other purposes in the future. The removal of these words is discouraged because subsequent use for undisclosed purposes is likely to place the organization in an awkward public relations and customer relations situation. For related ideas, see the policies entitled "Employee Right To Add Explanatory Statement To Personnel File" and "Notification Of Users About Logging Of Security Violations." A: T; E: LMH.

328. Performance Monitoring Information And Relevance To The Job

Policy: Management must not use computers to automatically collect information about the performance of workers unless the involved workers have first collectively agreed that such information realistically reflects their job-related performance. This restriction does not apply to information collected to manage and properly secure computer systems.

Commentary: Union contracts may dictate that a collective decision be made prior to the installation of such performance monitoring systems. Regardless of the presence of a union, from a personnel relations standpoint, it is advisable for employees to be a party to any decision to collect and use such data. The intention of this policy is thus to prevent management from installing and using performance monitoring technology unless it is first discussed with employees and acknowledged as relevant. The policy does not interfere with certain information systems security tools such as those that allow a computer operator to surreptitiously examine the information displayed on a remote user's screen. These tools are used by help desk personnel to resolve problems, as well as by information security staff to perform investigations. See the policies entitled "Need To Collect Private Information Must First Be Justified" and "Two-Party Consent For All Speaker Phone Use Or Tape Recording." A: EMT; E: LMH.

329. Privacy Expectations And Information Stored On Company X Systems

Policy: At any time and without prior notice, Company X management reserves the right to examine archived electronic mail, personal file directories, hard disk drive files, and other information stored on Company X information systems. This examination is performed to assure compliance with internal policies, to support the performance of internal investigations, to comply with legal requirements such as a subpoena or court order, and to assist with the management of Company X information systems.

Commentary: The intention of this policy is to put computer users on notice that the information they store, transmit, or otherwise process via Company X information systems is subject to management review. This will encourage them to use such information systems for business purposes only. It will also help to deter unethical or illegal activities such as down-loading child pornography from the Internet, and then storing such information on a Company X computer hard disk drive. The policy is particularly pro-monitoring rather than pro-privacy, but at least helps establish worker expectations. Separately, some organizations will want to use additional verbs besides "examine;" these verbs include access, retrieve, monitor, read, and disclose the involved information. See the policies entitled "Privacy Expectations And Electronic Mail," "Users Notified That All Data is Routinely Backed-Up," and "Privacy Of Personal Files Stored On Computers And In Desks." A: E; E: LMH.

330. Employee Permission Required Before Monitoring Is Used

Policy: Company X will not monitor the communications of an employee without first securing the employee's permission. An exception to this policy will be made in those instances where advance permission is likely to change the behavior in question (e.g., suspected criminal activity).

Commentary: The intention of this policy is to assure employees that they are not being monitored without their knowledge. Some organizations will want to augment this policy with further exceptions necessary to properly manage the involved information systems (to recover from a virus infestation, to gather evidence of unauthorized systems penetrations, etc.). Note that this policy covers only employees; it says nothing about temporaries, consultants, contractors, strategic business partners, and other third parties. If these other categories of individuals should be covered, then the word "workers" can be used. For a related idea, see the policy entitled "Monitoring Of Electronic Mail Messages." A: E; E: LMH.

331. No Blanket Monitoring Of Employee Communications

Policy: In general terms, Company X does not engage in blanket monitoring of employee communications. It does, however, reserve the right to monitor, access, retrieve, read, and/or disclose employee communications when: (a) a legitimate business need exists that cannot be satisfied by other means, (b) the involved employee is unavailable and timing is critical to a business activity, (c) there is reasonable cause to suspect criminal activity or policy violation, or (d) monitoring is required by law, regulation, or third-party agreement.

Commentary: The intention of this policy is to put employees on notice that their communications may be monitored under certain circumstances. The policy also seeks to assure employees that a "big brother" style blanket monitoring process does not exist, and the right to monitor will be used judiciously and only when a legitimate business need exists. Note that this policy covers only employees; it says nothing about temporaries, consultants, contractors, strategic business partners, and other third parties. Also note that the first part (section "a") in the second sentence of the policy covers a variety of technical problems such as recovery from a virus infestation. Separately, an example of the last part (section "d") in the second sentence of the policy would be execution of a search warrant. For a related idea, see the policy entitled "Privacy Expectations And Information Stored On Company X Systems." A: E; E: LMH.

332. Management Attention To Employee Off-the-Job Behavior

Policy: Management must not pry into the lives of employees or otherwise seek to manage off-the-job behavior unless it impairs the ability of the employee to perform regular job assignments (their own or others), or unless it affects the reputation of Company X in a significant way.

Commentary: This policy is a derivative of an internal IBM memo written in 1968 by Thomas Watson, Jr., then chairman of the board. For a long time, this statement has continued to be a guideline for internal IBM decisions about management's involvement in employee lives and the personal information management should seek. The intention of the policy is to restrict nosy managers from prying into the lives of employees. Certain events, such as an employee's stay in the hospital and the circumstances surrounding this stay should be discussed with the employee's manager. Romantic liaisons between coworkers is also fair game for management's attention since this could and most likely will affect what goes on in the office. The policy is written in such a general way that a wide latitude for interpretation is still provided. The policy can also be used to discourage behavior which may lead to sexual harassment and/or privacy invasion lawsuits. For additional ideas about worker off-hours behavior, see the policy entitled "Assignment Of Patent, Copyright, And Other Intellectual Property Rights." Also see the policy entitled "Permissible Information To Collect From Prospective Employees." A: M; E: LMH.

333. Notifying Subjects Of Existing Monitoring Systems

Policy: Tools for the monitoring or observation of computer user activities must not be used unless the involved users are first notified that their work may be monitored or observed. The only permissible exception to this policy involves investigations of suspected criminal activity.

Commentary: Remote monitoring programs may be useful for diagnosing problems that end-users may be experiencing, but can also be used to secretly watch their activities in real-time. There is great resistance to the notion of monitoring systems about which the subject knows nothing. This policy accordingly seeks to allay these fears and assure employees that they know of all monitoring systems. The policy does not require that subjects be told at the specific time they are monitored, it only says that they must be told that they may be monitored. Thus a manager may listen in on a telemarketer's conversation with a potential customer at any time, so long as the telemarketer has been notified that this might happen. The exception, involving criminal investigations, is appropriate because management in most instances will not want to tip-off the suspect that an investigation is in process; to do so would risk the suspect's escape or destruction of evidence. Some organizations may wish to replace the words "computer user" with "worker;" in this manner the policy is made more general and therefore applicable to voice communications and other systems. Also see the policies entitled "Surreptitious Collection Of Customer Private Data Prohibited," "Areas Where Electronic Monitoring Of Workers May Be Used," and "Notification Of Users About Logging Of Security Violations." A: EMT; E: LMH.

334. All User Monitoring Reported To User's Manager And Logged

Policy: Whenever a user's computer or network account is monitored for investigative or disciplinary purposes, the involved user's manager must be promptly informed of this activity. All user monitoring must itself be logged for subsequent management review and possible use in disciplinary or legal actions.

Commentary: Secret monitoring of user activity is a hot topic in the computer community. This policy attempts to allay some fears about the abuse of monitoring tools by requiring notification of the user's manager, and also by logging the activity. If the policy, as written, does not provide sufficient control over monitoring facilities, Company X may wish to require the user's manager to authorize the secret monitoring before it begins. Organizations looking to provide still more reassurance to users may wish to additionally require notification of a company ombudsman or corporate ethics officer. To tighten the policy still more, the policy may specify that only certain types of staff (such as information security personnel) are permitted to conduct the monitoring. See the policies entitled "Timing Of Notification About Electronic Performance Monitoring" and "Notifying Subjects Of Existing Monitoring Systems." A: T; E: LMH.

335. Managers Receive Logs And Determine Appropriate Internet Usage

Policy: Company X routinely logs web sites visited, files downloaded, and related information exchanges over the Internet. Department managers receive reports of such information and use it to determine what types of Internet usage are appropriate for their department's business activities.

Commentary: The intention of this policy is to put users on notice that their Internet activities are logged, and that a department manager then determines whether this usage is appropriate. The policy thus strongly encourages users to consistently follow existing policies, notably a policy regarding personal use. The policy is desirable because it places responsibility for disciplinary measures on the department manager's shoulders, not on the shoulders of a central information security group or the Information Services Department. Realistically, only departmental managers will know what type of activity is consistent with local business objectives. Note that this policy is a more flexible and potentially more economical alternative to blocking certain web sites, such as pornography sites. For related ideas, see the policies entitled "All User Monitoring Reported To User's Manager And Logged" and "Internet Use For Personal Purposes Prohibited." A: E; E: LMH.

336. No Internet Customer Usage Profiles Will Be Compiled

Policy: Company X will not capture key words, mouse clicks, or any other indications of customer system usage. Likewise, it will not compile system usage profiles beyond those needed to prepare accounting statements.

Commentary: The intention of this policy is to generate customer trust, which in turn should lead to additional traffic over the Internet (statistical studies support this assumption). This policy assures customers that there is no log being kept of their activities and that they can rest assured that this information will not in the future be used to compromise their privacy (for example through targeted advertisements). The policy is one of the new terms of service for AOL, which was recently investigated by the Federal Trade Commission (FTC) for privacy related matters. On another note, this policy assures users that no surreptitious gathering of user activity data is taking place -- a topic which remains a concern of many paranoid Internet users. Although it is most appropriate for service providers (such as Internet search engines), this policy can be adapted for use by any organization offering a product or service via the Internet. For related ideas, see the policies entitled "Routine Destruction Of Transaction Logs Prevents Profile Compilation," "User Control Over Information Gathered Via Internet Web Site," and "Disclosure Of Computer Logs Reflecting Customer Activities." A: E; E: LMH.

337. Monitoring Or Recording Telephone Conversations

Policy: Company X worker telephone conversations may not be monitored or recorded unless a clearly audible beeping tone accompanies the monitoring.

Commentary: A provision allowing unannounced monitoring to prevent or investigate illegal activities may be added to this policy as an exception. In keeping with certain USA state wiretapping statutes, this policy requires that the parties to a conversation be put on notice that a third party is listening or recording the conversation. In effect, the policy requires that non-private telephone conversations be clearly understood as such by both parties. The policy also requires that employees who are recording their own conversations with third parties put the third parties on notice about the recording activity. See the policy entitled "Group Monitoring Rather Than Individual Monitoring." A: EMT; E: LMH.

338. Group Monitoring Rather Than Individual Monitoring

Policy: The performance of Company X workers must not be monitored by computers unless the monitoring is performed on a group, rather than on an individual basis.

Commentary: Reflecting experience in Japan and Europe, computer monitoring of workers is much more likely to be both accepted and effective when done on a group basis, rather than on an individual basis. This approach also fosters teamwork. The policy does not interfere with management's personal observations about the performance of specific employees (such as attendance). The intention of this policy is thus to allow monitoring but in a manner that is most likely to foster both teamwork and worker acceptance. See the policy entitled "Monitoring Or Recording Telephone Conversations." A: MT; E: LMH.

339. Monitoring And Recording Activity In An Anonymous Fashion

Policy: Information about user activities may be anonymously collected to calculate system usage patterns, to identify problem areas, and to otherwise improve information systems. Except for authorized law enforcement purposes, no attempts to identify specific users or their system activities will be initiated.

Commentary: The intention of this policy is to permit a wide variety of system monitoring and logging but at the same time to ensure that the privacy of users is maintained. The policy is thus particularly applicable to web sites where users are concerned that their activities are being recorded. These sites might include those that post information about which many people have strong opinions, such as information about politics or sexual activity. The policy notably includes specific exemptions for law enforcement purposes, and thus may also prevent hackers from thinking that a privacy policy is in some way a shield against tracing their activities. Separately, note that the policy does not prevent the tracking of a specific user's clickstream (mouse movements) or typed material, only the attachment of an identity to that recorded information. For related ideas, see the policies entitled "Group Monitoring Rather Than Individual Monitoring" and "Personal Information Necessary For Proper Functioning Of Business." A: E; E: LMH.

340. Timing Of Notification About Electronic Performance Monitoring

Policy: If it applies to them, prospective employees, contractors, and consultants must be notified during their initial job interview that their work may be electronically monitored. This notification must be in writing and must include the type of information that will be gathered, how this information will be used, existing standards of production, and production expectations for the individual involved.

Commentary: This policy helps to prevent worker complaints about performance monitoring because the employees were put on notice when they first interviewed for their new positions. Without a notice about monitoring systems, workers may complain that they were mislead about the nature of the jobs they now hold. The intention of this policy is thus to force management to disclose the existence of performance monitoring systems before a prospective worker accepts a job offer. Special forms acknowledging the receipt of this information may also be used to create a paper trail showing that workers knew about and acquiesced to monitoring systems. See the policies entitled "Monitoring Or Recording Telephone Conversations" and "Permissible Information To Collect From Prospective Employees." A: M; E: LMH.

1.3.2.3. Disclosure Of Private Data

1.3.2.3.1. Disclosure Of Worker Private Data

341. Existence Of Secret Systems Containing Personnel Records

Policy: With the exception of criminal investigations, there must be no system of personnel records at Company X whose very existence is kept secret from the subjects or workers described therein.

Commentary: This policy prohibits "shadow databases" which may be kept by supervisors or others as a way to persecute, harass, intimidate, or otherwise control employees. In this case, the word "shadow" indicates behind-the-scenes or secret. The policy is inspired by law enforcement agencies in certain nations who kept (and in some case still do keep) detailed dossiers on so-called "enemies," and thereby obtained great power of these people. The policy helps build worker trust that they indeed know of all systems being used to judge their performance and promotion prospects. The intention of the policy is also to ensure that all systems containing personnel information are known by not only the subjects but also by the information security staff. If the information security staff knows about the existence of such systems, it will be better able to ensure that these systems incorporate appropriate control measures (such as access controls). The policy is additionally desirable because it forces the disclosure of all personal information, which could then be included in a data dictionary or data directory, thus assisting with efforts to standardize, categorize, and rationalize the different types of information across an organization. An exception for criminal investigations is called for because it would be counterproductive to inform a perpetrator that an investigation is in progress (this would invite suspect flight or evidence destruction). Also see the policies entitled "High-Level Inventory Of Information Assets" and "Notifying Subjects Of Existing Monitoring Systems." A: EMT; E: LMH.

342. Guaranteed Access To Personal Information Held In Company X Records

Policy: Upon written request, every individual must be granted access to the Company X records which contain personal information pertaining to the individual's life or condition.

Commentary: This policy follows the generally accepted practice used by consumer credit reporting bureaus in the United States. The credit bureaus in the US even provide a free copy of the record if an adverse decision has recently been made based on the information appearing in a credit record. Similarly, many businesses provide employees with the right to periodically view the information contained in their file. The intention of this policy is to give the subjects (workers, employees, etc.) the right to know the information that has been used in decisions about them. Knowledge of this information then allows the data subjects to object to (and hopefully get corrections to) inaccuracies or misleading statements appearing in the record. Separately, nothing in this policy requires the organization to disclose details which do not relate to the individual; these may be obscured (for paper records, through black magic markers and copying) before disclosure of the record to the data subject. Likewise, nothing in the policy prevents a thorough review of the record by management prior to release to ensure that only information directly applicable to the individual in question is released. On a different note, some organizations allow employees to insert a brief statement in their personal record if management has received a complaint about an inaccuracy or a misleading piece of information, but has decided not to change the information appearing in the individual's record. Thus this policy can indirectly be an information integrity policy. The integrity of personnel files can be further enhanced by the policies entitled "Employee Right To Add Explanatory Statement To Personnel File" and "Allegedly Incorrect Information To Be Corrected Or Labeled As Disputed." For related ideas, see the policies entitled "Conditions Under Which Employees May Examine Their Files," "Periodic Distribution Of Employee Personnel Records" and "Making Copies Of Information Appearing In One's Personnel File." A: EM; E: LMH.

343. Periodic Distribution Of Employee Personnel Records

Policy: To allow each employee an opportunity to acquaint himself or herself with the information, and to ensure that it contains no errors, every employee must be given a copy of his or her personnel file once a year.

Commentary: A large credit bureau has recently adopted a similar policy whereby free copies of one's record will be provided annually. This action was prompted because the United States Congress initiated an investigation of the many errors found in credit reports. The provision of a free copy of one's record is thus a way to reduce complaints about inaccurate reports, as well as a way to ensure that the information is current and accurate. The policy could be modified to state that "... each employee must be given an opportunity to receive a copy ...," thus considerably reducing the paperwork and expense associated with this information-integrity-related policy. For related ideas, see the policies entitled "Guaranteed Access To Personal Information Held In Company X Records" and "Prospective Employees Given Opportunity To Decline Credit Checks." A: EM; E: LMH.

344. Prospective Employees Given Opportunity To Decline Credit Checks

Policy: All prospective employees must be notified if their credit report will be examined or if a background check will be performed as part of the recruiting and selection process. These prospective employees must be given an opportunity to withdraw their application for employment if they choose not to disclose such personal information to Company X.

Commentary: The intention of this policy is to give prospective employees an opportunity to decide whether they want to disclose certain personal information to their future employer. By declining to disclose this information they effectively take themselves out of the competition for the job in question. Another objective is served by this policy: prospective employees know what information is used in reaching a decision about them. This allows the prospective employees to investigate if they believe that erroneous information led to an unfavorable decision. This policy is in keeping with the notion that data subjects should ultimately be the ones who control the flow of personal information about them. The policy is a derivative of laws currently on the books in both California and Minnesota, which deal with the requirement to disclose the use of a credit report in hiring situations. On a more general note, this policy could be broadened to include customers and other external third parties, in which case all personal data about these third parties that has been used in reaching a decision about them must be revealed to them. This wider approach might, for example, be used by a medical insurance company when deciding whether to issue a policy to an applicant. Banks increasingly use this disclosure-of-sources approach when deciding to make a loan such as a home mortgage. For related ideas, see the policies entitled "Periodic Distribution Of Employee Personnel Records" and "Fingerprinting For Employees With Access To Sensitive Information." A: MT; E: LMH.

345. Disclosure Of Private Information To Third Parties

Policy: Disclosure of private information about Company X workers to third parties must NOT take place unless required by law, or unless permitted by clear and explicit consent of the subject.

Commentary: This policy helps prevent invasion of privacy, defamation of character, libel, and slander lawsuits. The intention of the policy is to ensure that third parties are not given access to private information about employees (or more generally "workers"). The only exceptions are: (1) when specifically required by law--as would be the case if a subpoena was tendered, or (2) when the individual expressly authorized the transfer--as would be the case if the information was to be used by a prospective employer doing a background check. For this reason, without further authorization from the worker, many United States employers disclose only: (1) the fact that an individual worked/works at the organization, (2) the most recent place of work, (3) the dates of employment, and perhaps (4) an indication whether the employee would be rehired. Some organizations disclose just a subset of these types of information. Examples of the types of information to be withheld should accompany the explanation of this policy. For example, the reason for termination is not generally provided lest this lead to a defamation lawsuit. On another point, this policy implies that creditors, attorneys, private detective agencies, and others desiring non-job-related information do not receive it without the worker's consent (unless the law requires disclosure). Some organizations consider social security numbers to be private for purposes of this policy. For related ideas, see the policies entitled "Disclosure Of Reason For Termination Of An Employee" and "Disclosure Of Information On Company X Systems To Law Enforcement." A: EM; E: LMH.

346. Transfer Of Private Data Only To Organizations With Sufficient Controls

Policy: Company X will release private data only to third party organizations that commit in writing to maintain the information with an adequate level of protection, as determined by the Information Security Department. Exceptions will be made in those cases where the release is required by law or regulation.

Commentary: The intention of this policy is to prevent disclosure to those third party organizations which will not promise to adequately protect private information. The disclosures addressed by this policy are those chosen by the organization possessing the data, not to those chosen by the data subject (the one described by the data). This policy reflects common practice in the USA's mail order industry where lists are sold for "one time use," the exact use is specified in advance, and further usage is not permitted. While these contracts for list rental also help protect the disclosing organization's rights to the data, they do preserve the privacy of the involved individuals because each usage remains defined and limited. Separately, the policy is a derivative of Article 25 in the European Union's Data Protection Directive, which specifies that private data will not be released to countries which do not have privacy laws that are at least as good as those applicable to the country where the information is now stored. This policy is a sort of "transborder data flow" (TBDF) policy, although it applies to organizations rather than countries. Separately, note that the specific requirements will change over time and by jurisdiction, and that the policy sets the Information Security Department up to be the judge whether a particular release can proceed or not. For related ideas, see the policies entitled "Third Party Access To Company X Systems Requires Signed Contract" and "Default Restrictions On Dissemination Of Company X Information." A: E; E: LMH.

347. Keeping Records Of All Third Parties Receiving Private Information

Policy: Company X staff releasing private information to third parties must keep records of all such disclosures including specifically what information was disclosed, to whom it was disclosed, and the date of such disclosure.
Commentary: The intention of this policy is to protect the organization against unjustified accusations of privacy invasion. Certain individuals may accuse an organization of releasing personal information about them; without records such as those described in the policy, the organization would have harder time claiming that it did not release the information. In addition, the policy is intended to support individuals in their efforts to investigate and prosecute identity theft. With these disclosure records, a list of initial suspects can be developed. Likewise, these records can be used by individuals who are correcting errors which have been propagated across multiple databases or multiple organizations (so-called inherited errors). For related concepts, see the policies entitled "Use Of Personal Information For New Purposes," "Customer Right To Know Third Parties Receiving His Or Her Data," and "Customer Objection Opportunity For Subpoena Record Requests." A: E; E: LMH.

348. Transfer Of Private Information To Other Countries Requires Approval

Policy: Transfers of private information to another country, no matter what technology is employed, must not take place unless prior approval of the Information Security Manager has first been obtained. An exception is made in those cases where the data subject is, was, or will be located in the destination country, or when the data subject has specifically requested such a transfer.

Commentary: This policy is motivated by the European Union (EU) Data Protection Directive of 1998, which stipulates that private information may not be moved to another legal jurisdiction unless it can be shown that the receiving jurisdiction provides comparable security measures to protect the privacy of the involved data. This policy and the related law and regulations seek to prevent private data from slipping away from highly regulated jurisdictions into less regulated jurisdictions. Without impediments to this information flow, business would tend to make such a transfer to lower costs and perhaps to thwart the intention of the privacy laws and regulations. This policy thus helps prevent the development of data havens which are oases where business can do what they please, in relative terms of course, without the constrains of privacy laws and regulations. When an organization adopts this policy, especially an American organization, it shows that it is serious about privacy and wishes to prevent the movement of private data from defeating the protections provided by laws and regulations. When a European organization adopts a policy such as this it is simply formally acknowledging the laws and regulations to which it is already bound to comply. Note that the policy is deliberately technology neutral, and that it applies to the electronic mail transmission of a database, just as it applies to the movement of filing cabinets filled with paper records. Also see the policies entitled "Transfer Of Private Data Only To Organizations With Sufficient Controls" and "Chain Of Trust Agreements Required For Private & Sensitive Information." A: MT; E: LMH.

349. Subjects Given Opportunity To Block Private Information Disclosures

Policy: Data subjects must be given advance notice that their personal data held by Company X has been requested by a third party. Unless compelled to release the data by clear and authoritative law or regulation, a reasonable period of several weeks must be provided for a data subject to block this disclosure. No response from the data subject can, after that period, be considered to be acquiescence to the disclosure.

Commentary: The objective of this policy is to prevent future disputes where a data subject complains and says that Company X should have first obtained their permission before releasing certain personal data. This policy is a middle-of-the-road policy which is expedient (if no response, then release the information), but at the same time provides some privacy protection. The policy also provides considerable leeway for other uses of the information such as cross-marketing of other products and services (assuming these offerings are sold by the same organization). This policy helps to reestablish the data subject as the one in control of personal information (in the USA, there is a long way to go, but this a move in a socially-responsible direction). The policy applies to a wide variety of personal information including computer-resident address books and appointment calendars, as well as to information traditionally thought of as personal, such as medical records. For a related idea, see the policy entitled "Informed Consent Required For Questionable System Actions." A: T; E: LMH.

350. Disclosure Of Worker Names, Titles, And Other Contact Particulars

Policy: Company X does not disclose the names, titles, phone numbers, locations, or other contact particulars of its workers unless required for business purposes. Exceptions will be made when such a disclosure is required by law or when the involved persons have previously clearly consented to the disclosure.

Commentary: The intention of this policy is to protect the privacy of workers (employees, consultants, temporaries, etc.), especially from unwanted solicitations and marketing pitches. The invasiveness of modern telemarketing, for some organizations, warrants such a seemingly uncooperative policy. A potential side effect of this policy is that life will be made a bit more difficult for clients, customers, and others who have a legitimate need for this information. Many telemarketers call organizations asking for the name of the individual in a particular position, such as the Director of Marketing, and then ask to be put through to him or her. The Director of Marketing is then subjected to a sales pitch that he or she doesn't want to hear. This policy would prevent these calls. To make sure the organization doesn't lose important information (such as job applicants), receptionists and telephone operators can invite solicitors to send the material by mail addressed to "Director of Marketing" or whatever other position they are targeting (so-called "blind addressing"). Note that this policy does not address private information such as worker salary, only contact information. In general it is advisable that receptionists, telephone operators, security guards, and other people who have significant public contact be given specific instructions about the internal information they are permitted to release. For other ideas about private information, see the policy entitled "Disclosure Of Private Information To Third Parties." A: EM; E: LMH.

351. Disclosure Of Reason For Termination Of An Employee

Policy: To preserve the privacy of personnel information, the reason for termination of workers must not be disclosed to third parties. Two permissible exceptions are the prior approval of a Company X senior manager or if the disclosure is required by law.

Commentary: The intention behind this policy, beyond preserving the privacy of the involved employee, is to prevent libel, slander, defamation of character, and related lawsuits. Some organizations may wish to disclose this additional intention in the policy wording, while others may wish not to mention it explicitly. Note that, in some jurisdictions, the former employer may be held negligent if the reason for termination is criminal behavior and the former employee goes on to repeat this behavior at his/her next employer. This situation can be added to the policy as another permissible exception. As is the case with any new or changed policies, internal legal counsel review is recommended. The scope of this policy can be narrowed to relate to anyone who does not have a need-to-know; thus, other workers who did not ordinarily have any business interaction with a departed employee would not be given this information. This narrower scope further helps to lessen the risks of libel, slander, defamation of character, and related lawsuits. For a more general policy of this type, see the policy entitled "Disclosure Of Private Information To Third Parties." Also see the policy entitled "Disclosure Of Worker Change Of Status Information." A: EM; E: LMH.

352. Disclosure Of Worker Change Of Status Information

Policy: Detailed worker change of status information is strictly confidential, and must not be disclosed to anyone except those people who have a bona fide need-to-know. Detailed change of status information includes the reasons for terminations, retirements, resignations, leaves of absence, leaves of absence pending the results of an investigation, inter-departmental transfers, relocations, and changes to consultant/contractor status.

Commentary: The intention of this policy is to prevent people in the Human Resources Department and others who are privy to worker change of status information from disclosing it to people who do not need this information. Others may include receptionists, building guards, security department staff, and information security administrators. Ideally many of these so-called gatekeepers would be notified that there was a change of status for a certain worker, without the specific reasons. The type of information mentioned in the policy is typically a favorite topic of gossip if management has not yet made it clear that the information is strictly confidential. If the information is disclosed to people who do not have a need-to-know, then the individual involved may allege character defamation (libel or slander) or privacy invasion. This in turn could lead to a lawsuit or vengeful acts. Note that the policy entitled "Disclosure Of Reason For Termination Of An Employee" is a special case of this more general policy. Also note that this policy deals with internal as well as external disclosures whereas the policy entitled "Disclosure Of Reason For Termination Of An Employee" deals only with external disclosures. A: M; E: LMH.

353. Granting Workers Access To Disclosures Of Private Data Records

Policy: Workers must be given access to records reflecting the disclosure of their own private information to third parties. In addition, workers must be given sufficient information to allow them to contact such third parties to rectify errors or supply additional information.

Commentary: Workers should have an opportunity to provide their own interpretation of events, should that interpretation differ markedly from the interpretation found in Company X records. Accordingly, the intention of this policy is to allow workers to rectify what they may consider to be inaccurate or misleading information when Company X elects to take no action to correct their records. The policy could be modified to state that workers will be given this information only in those cases where Company X decides not to alter a private record in the manner requested by the subjects (i.e., the involved workers). This policy works as an adjunct to the policy entitled "Keeping Records Of Private Information Disclosed To Third Parties." A: MT; E: LMH.

354. Privacy Of Individual Worker Performance Information

Policy: Individual worker performance information must not be posted on bulletin boards or otherwise made available to others who do not have a legitimate business-related need-to-know.

Commentary: This policy is intended to prevent workers from feeling humiliated, harassed, and harried (which often leads to accidents) because their performance has been posted in a public place. Thus the policy seeks to prevent the use of peer pressure as a management control tactic. In many instances, coworkers will have a general idea of a worker's performance anyway, and the availability of this information will come as no surprise to them. In no way does this policy interfere with management's right to discipline or terminate the employee based on poor performance. The policy may help foster positive employee opinions about the motivations of management and the extent to which the organization cares about employee welfare. This policy may also help an organization stay out of trouble when it comes to privacy laws and regulations. This policy is a specific instance of the policy entitled "Privilege Restriction Based On The Need-to-Know." A: EM; E: LMH.

355. Confidentiality Of Internal Investigations Information

Policy: Until charges are pressed or disciplinary action taken, all investigations of alleged criminal or abusive conduct must be kept strictly confidential to preserve the reputation of the suspected party.

Commentary: Beyond the objective stated in the policy, this policy helps reduce the probability that Company X will be hit with a lawsuit alleging defamation of character. The intention of the policy is to clearly define the point in time when it becomes permissible to disclose information about employee investigations. One desirable aspect of this policy is that investigations which do not result in either prosecution (pressing charges) or disciplinary action will never be disclosed (declassified). If the employee and the employee's coworkers never knew about the investigation, then the employee can remain in good standing with a good reputation. On the other hand, if the employee heard about an investigation in process that later turned out to be inappropriate, he or she may become disgruntled or soon leave the organization. Likewise, if coworkers get wind of an investigation in progress and there turns out to be no justification for the related accusations, then the reputation of the accused as been degraded needlessly. The policy mentions the "reputation" of the individual rather than staying out of legal trouble because the dignity of the individual is a more noble goal, and because it is taken for granted that management wants to operate within the confines of the law. This policy assumes the existence of an internal data classification system; for additional information see the policy entitled "Four Category Data Classification Scheme." Also see the policies entitled "Required Investigation Following Computer Crimes" and "Transfer Of Certain Workers To Positions With Less Exposure." A: M; E: LMH.

356. Mandatory Disclosure Of Worker Health And Safety Information

Policy: Management must fully disclose to the involved workers the results of toxic substance tests and other information relating to the health and safety of workers.

Commentary: This policy is related to the so called "worker right to know" policy about dangers in the workplace. The policy helps avoid lawsuits. For instance, a lawsuit could allege that a worker would have quit or protected himself or herself differently if this information had been known. Perhaps the best known cases of this nature involve various American manufacturers of asbestos, many of which have gone bankrupt. The reader should also see the section of this book entitled Data Confidentiality - Right to Know. Beyond forcing management to disclose such information, this policy is also intended to build worker confidence that management genuinely cares about worker welfare. This policy is medical data related, while a more general policy is entitled "Workers Have Right To Know All Workplace Hazards." A: EM; E: LMH.

357. Use Of Tests To Determine Lifestyle, Political, & Religious Information

Policy: Candidates for a job with Company X must not be subjected to drug tests, AIDS tests, psychological tests, or other tests which may illuminate the candidates' lifestyle, political associations, or religious preferences. An exception may be made if this information is clearly needed to determine a candidate's suitability for a certain position.

Commentary: The intent of this policy is to prevent an organization from using tests to determine information about candidates for a job that the candidates did not willfully disclose. The policy is thus protecting the privacy of the individuals applying for a position with Company X (and perhaps also indirectly preventing Company X from being subjected to lawsuits or unfavorable publicity). The policy restricts the use of tests to those tests which are clearly job-related. AIDS tests may be required for health insurance purposes, and may thus be demonstrably needed (assuming eligibility for health insurance is a required qualification for the job). The words "AIDS tests" can be deleted from the policy without substantially altering its impact. Of particular concern to many employers are tests like the Reid Psychological Profile, which provides an indication of an employee's inclination to steal. These tests are consistent with the policy as written because honesty could be considered to be a requirement for certain jobs (such as cashiers). Also see the policy entitled "Use Of Convicted Felons In Computer-Related Positions Of Trust." A: M; E: LMH.

1.3.2.3.2. Disclosure Of Third Party Private Data

358. Privacy Of Personal Files Stored On Computers And In Desks

Policy: Personal files on Company X computers and in Company X worker desks must both be handled with the same privacy perspective given to personal mail and personal phone calls. This means that other workers, including managers and system administrators, must not read such personal files. Exceptions will be made if the action is part of: (a) a formal investigation initiated by the Security Department, or (b) an effort to dispose of or reassign files after a worker has left Company X.

Commentary: The intention of this policy is to clarify privacy expectations about the personal files of workers. Essentially this policy says that the files of workers, even though they may be work-related, are not to be read by other workers, including managers and system administrators. Thus the policy states that electronic mail messages should only be read by the sender and recipient(s). Another way to express this policy is the old phrase "Gentlemen don't read other people's mail." The policy can be modified to make specific mention of electronic mail, microcomputer (PC) and workstation files, and other examples. For a different and more invasive perspective, see the policy entitled "Right Of Management To Examine Data Stored On Company X Systems." Also see "Privacy Expectations And Electronic Mail." A: EMT; E: LM.

359. Keeping Records Of Private Information Disclosed To Third Parties

Policy: Every disclosure of private information to third parties must be recorded and these records must be maintained for at least five (5) years.

Commentary: The intention of this policy is to be able to definitively show exactly what information has been disclosed to which third parties, and that the disclosures have been in keeping with law, organizational policies, and general business practices. Keeping a log of disclosures will also be important when notifying information recipients of errors found in a private record. Thus, in the United States, credit bureaus keep a record of all third parties to whom they have disclosed details of an individual's debts and payment history; if an error in a record is detected, the credit bureaus are then in a position to immediately notify the recipients about the corrected information. This policy may be used in conjunction with the policy entitled "Disclosure Of Private Information To Third Parties," in which case the records about disclosures reflect only exceptions. Also see the policy entitled "Granting Workers Access To Disclosures Of Private Data Records." A: MT; E: LMH.

360. Protection Of The Privacy Of Customer Information

Policy: Information that can be directly linked to a specific customer (especially an individual) must ONLY be released to third parties if: (1) the customer has provided prior written consent, or (2) Company X is legally required to disclose the information.

Commentary: The intention of this policy is to restrict the unauthorized dissemination of information about an organization's customers--be they individuals or organizations. The policy is particularly relevant to those organizations which provide some personal product or service, such as medical insurance or psychological counseling. It may also be relevant to airlines, supermarkets, and other organizations which keep tabs on customer purchasing patterns. Frequent flier programs, customer supermarket discounts provided when customers allow personal data to be collected, and similar marketing initiatives may need a more-narrowly-defined version of this policy (in which case the policy would pertain only to the information used in these marketing efforts). The policy may interfere with certain database matching initiatives across organizations, but these are notoriously unpopular with the public and widely considered be a violation of privacy. Some organizations go farther than having an in-house policy of this nature--they include a different version of the policy in the materials distributed to customers. Several insurance companies, for example, explicitly inform customers about their policies regarding disclosures to third party organizations. Some people claim these types of customer communications improve the organization's public image and help bring in new business. Also see the policy entitled "Distribution Of Statistical Information About Customer Records." A: MT; E: LMH.

361. Disclosure Of Customer Information Including Customer Identity

Policy: Company X does not disclose information about its customers to external parties without explicit written permission. Even the identity of customers, or any other particulars which might be used to deduce the identity of customers, must not be disclosed without written permission.

Commentary: This very conservative policy helps give customers assurance that they can safely do business with Company X. A policy like this is especially useful for businesses such as psychologists, adult bookstores, and information security consulting firms, where even knowing that a customer does business with the Company X may be embarrassing. The policy is intended to be provided on a web site or in a brochure, not just distributed to in-house workers. Of course, if compelled to disclose customer information by force of law, this information will be disclosed. This is by some people considered to be obvious, and therefore not requiring reiteration in the policy itself. Separately, this policy also helps prevent trademark disputes where a customer says that a particular business is inappropriately using its name to lure people to its web site through search engines. For a related idea, see the policy entitled "Protection Of The Privacy Of Customer Information." A: E; E: MH.

362. Customer Right To Know Third Parties Receiving His Or Her Data

Policy: If requested in writing, Company X must promptly disclose the third parties receiving private information about any customer or data subject. This disclosure will include not only contact names, but also the telephone numbers and addresses of these third parties.

Commentary: The intention of this policy is to allow a customer or a data subject to readily determine who has received his or her private information. The policy parallels common practice in the American credit reporting industry, where data subjects can readily obtain a list of organizations that obtained information about the data subject. Note that the data subject does not have the "right" to object to this initial disclosure, just to determine after the fact who received the information. Rather than providing a high level of privacy protection and data subject control over private data, this policy at least provides accountability among those who are in possession of the information. The policy is also useful for those situations where identity fraud is being investigated. If identity fraud has taken place, in most cases the data subject must take on the task of informing all involved parties that someone else has been using his or her good name and credit without authorization. Without a policy such as this, it will be difficult for the data subject to stop continuing identity fraud. This policy thus has some public relations benefits, but really requires very little of the issuing organization. This policy assumes that records of disclosures to third parties are being kept (see the policy entitled "Keeping Records Of All Third Parties Receiving Private Information"). Also see the policy entitled "Identity Theft Prevention By Restricting Access To Personal Information." A: T; E: LMH.

363. Customer Objection Opportunity For Subpoena Record Requests

Policy: Company X does not release customer records to third parties unless a customer requests it, or unless compelled to do so by law or regulation. In the event that Company X receives a subpoena requesting access to customer records, so that that a legal challenge can be filed, the customer will be given two weeks advance notice prior to the release.

Commentary: This policy is intended to tighten the privacy policy observed by many organizations where they do not release personal customer records to third parties. The policy may prevent third parties from using a lawsuit as a mechanism to gain access to personal records that would otherwise be kept in confidence. The policy thus can be used to assist customers in their defense of their own privacy. The actual cost to the adopting organization is relatively minor -- only the administrative activity regarding notices sent in those instances where a subpoena is received; all legal costs associated with the challenge of a request for records are borne by the customer. This policy is modeled after California law which was originally intended to apply to telephone company billing records (so-called pen registers). The two week period is arbitrary, and could be lengthened so long as the organization holding the records isn't likely to be held in contempt of court for delaying the release of such records. Be sure to consult with legal counsel on all policies that involve the law. For related ideas, see the policies entitled "Approval Required Prior To Release Of Company X Information" and "Use And Disclosure Of Personal Information About Customers." A: T; E: LMH.

364. Privacy Policy Considered Contract Made At Time Information Provided

Policy: Company X takes its privacy policy very seriously. If we change our privacy policy, all customer information gathered after that date will be subject to the new policy. All information gathered under the a previous privacy policy will continue to be governed by that earlier privacy policy, unless we receive customer consent to act otherwise.

Commentary: The intention of this policy is to inform the policy reader that Company X considers its privacy policy to be akin to a legal contract. This contractual perspective relies on the fact that customers provide information under certain stated terms and conditions, and they expect the recipient organization to live up to its promises. Under this policy, Company X can not simply change its policy and then use customer information gathered under an older policy for purposes that are not allowed under the older policy (a number of Internet merchants have done this). This policy imposes additional overhead on the issuing organization because it must now use mechanisms to time-and-date stamp information from customers. Alternatively it could create special identifiers reflecting the privacy policy applicable to a certain customer record. Different mailing lists and different processing routines may also be required in order to handle two or more sets of customers in ways consistent with different privacy policies. Note that this policy reflects a trend in the Internet-posted privacy policy area; government regulators are increasingly holding organizations to the words appearing in their privacy policies, proceeding as though these same policies were legal contracts. For related ideas, see the policies entitled "Subjects Must Approve New Personal Data Uses After Merger/Acquisition" and "Subjects Must Opt-In To Be Included In Systems Handling Private Data." A: E; E: LMH.

365. Privacy Of Correspondent Email Addresses And Telephone Numbers

Policy: The electronic mail addresses and telephone numbers of correspondents with all users of Company X communication systems are considered confidential and will not be released to third parties unless Company X is compelled to do so by law or regulation.

Commentary: This policy is intended to clarify a privacy issue that remains nebulous in the United States, and perhaps in a few other countries as well. While members of the American public generally believe that both the phone numbers dialed and the email addresses of correspondents are confidential, this information can now legally be shared by a telephone company or another communication system provider without the consent of the involved users. The policy seeks to reassure users that information revealing correspondents will remain private. The policy assumes that the policy issuing organization already has a policy about the privacy of the content of these same communications (the words that go into an email message or the words spoken during a phone conversation). Students of history will remember that Adolf Hitler used information such as telephone numbers dialed (called a pen register) to determine who was Jewish and who was supporting Jewish people. The policy is thus an attempt to prevent communications system information from being used by abusive government authorities and other third parties (such as consumer marketing firms). This policy is intended to be adopted by a provider of information systems services, such as an Internet Service Provider (ISP) or a telephone company. For related considerations, see the policies entitled "Use And Disclosure Of Personal Information About Customers" and "Keeping Records Of Private Information Disclosed To Third Parties." A: T; E: MH.

366. Telephone Disclosures Require Positive Caller Identification

Policy: Requested customer information must not be disclosed by phone, unless the caller is able to positively identify themselves through a shared secret or through other caller identification measures approved by Company X management. Provision of additional information which is readily available to uninvolved third parties (such as a social security number) does not constitute positive identification.

Commentary: The intention of this policy is to prevent internal workers from improperly disclosing personal or private information, if a caller at the end of a telephone line has not adequately identified themselves. This policy would thus prevent an unauthorized relative from finding out how much their rich and old uncle had in his stock brokerage account. This policy would also prevent help desk staff from being duped by hackers using social engineering techniques; unless a shared secret such as a special password (in the USA, often mother's maiden name) can be provided, details about a certain customer's account will not be revealed by phone. While marketing specialists may consider this policy to be an impediment to speedy and efficient business, in today's business world it is a necessity if an organization is going to provide telephone disclosures. Besides this policy may give customers additional confidence that their money and information are properly protected. Separately, much the same approach could be used for telephone transactions. If the policy included transactions, a telephone company staff member would refuse to turn-on call forwarding for a business number based simply on a telephone request; they would instead call the customer back at a known number, or in some other way establish positive identification. At the present time, far too many businesses allow both disclosures and transactions based only on a telephone call. For a related idea, see the policy entitled "Orders To Change Internal Records Placed Via Phone." A: T; E: MH.

367. No Discussions Of Private Information In Public Places

Policy: Unless a customer's explicit permission is first obtained, all workers must refrain from discussing customer private information in public places such as in building lobbies or on public transportation. This policy applies even when the identity of the customer is kept confidential.

Commentary: Many organizations such as hospitals critically depend on customers to reveal private information. If customers withhold private information because they are concerned that unauthorized parties will obtain it, then the quality of the product or service that the organization provides will be severely compromised. For example, if a patient worries that a doctor will discuss his case in the lobby in front of other patients, he may not mention a certain type of medication that he is taking. This may lead to a dangerous situation where newly prescribed drugs interact with the secret medication to cause a serious reaction which could have been avoided. This policy attempts to emphasize the importance of maintaining private information in restricted places, such as inside a doctor's office. Note that the policy is very strict, it prohibits all discussion in public places, period. It doesn't matter if the identity of the customer is concealed. This strong position is called for because often workers are sloppy, and they reveal other information from which the customer's identity may be discovered. Nothing in this policy prevents workers from talking about research results in a general sense, perhaps including statistical conclusions, but avoiding mention of specific cases. If it is necessary to talk about specific cases, for example in a presentation given at a conference, advance permission of the individual(s) can be obtained. If this policy seems too strict for the policy writer's organization, the second sentence can be deleted. For additional ideas, see the policy entitled "Distribution Of Statistical Information About Customer Records." A: EMT; E: LMH.

368. Customer Requests For Anonymity On Company X Systems

Policy: To help preserve the privacy of customer information, Company X provides mechanisms for customers to remain anonymous when using Company X systems. Company X will not disclose the identity of the customers who elect to use these mechanisms unless compelled to do so by law.

Commentary: The intention of this policy is give customers a clear picture of what is meant by anonymous user-IDs, anonymous remailers (for electronic mail on the Internet), anonymous electronic cash (for financial transactions on the Internet), and similar anonymous mechanisms. Many people in the computer industry were shocked to hear that American On-Line (AOL) disclosed the sexual preference of an anonymous homosexual user to a military official without obtaining the user's advance permission (strange as it may appear, homosexuals are not allowed in the US military). In this case, the user expected that this sexual orientation would be kept secret, in fact his job depended on it. Here, as well as in many other places, there was confusion about the meaning of the word "anonymous." Separately, recent cases involving the Church of Scientology and an anonymous remailer in Finland met with some of the same dilemmas. For an interesting article about this issue, see "Anonymity On-Line? It Depends Who's Asking," appearing in The Wall Street Journal, 24 November 1995, p. B1. This policy is intended primarily for organizations offering computer and communications services to the public, although the same ideas apply to intranet discussion groups, automated internal suggestion boxes, etc. For related ideas, see the policies entitled "Anonymous User-IDs" and "Protection Of The Privacy Of Customer Information." A: EM; E: LMH.

369. Public Acknowledgement Of Or Reference To Famous Customers

Policy: Workers must not publicly acknowledge the identity of famous customers when in their presence unless the famous customers first openly state their names. Likewise, workers must refrain from talking about famous customers with anyone else other than Company X workers. An exception is made in those circumstance were workers need to reveal the identity of a famous customer in order to fill an order or to conduct other legitimate business activity. In these exceptional situations, workers must use a normal tone of voice and proceed in a normal businesslike manner.

Commentary: The intention of this policy is to preserve the privacy of famous customers, and to make them feel at home doing business with Company X. If a famous person is waiting in line at a check-out counter and the check-out clerk loudly exclaims "Its Mr. Z, the movie star!" this will bring attention to the famous person who may at that point wish to remain anonymous. Likewise, the second sentence in the policy prohibits gossip and unnecessary chatter which may lead to slander or defamation charges. This policy is also consistent with the security notion of maintaining a low profile. For other ideas dealing with anonymity, see the policies entitled "Monitoring And Recording Activity In An Anonymous Fashion" and "Anonymous User-Ids." A: E; E: LMH.

370. Distribution Of Statistical Information About Customer Records

Policy: Statistical information derived from customer records may be disclosed to parties outside Company X only if the customers involved cannot be identified by the information.

Commentary: The objective of this policy is to prevent workers from distributing reports to outsiders which might inadvertently reveal the identity of, or information about customers. This policy is thus relevant to the preparation of annual reports (financial statements), government forms, and the like. The word "statistical" could be replaced with "numerical." The idea behind this policy is that customer information be aggregated or summarized so much that its disclosure does not damage customers. If aggregated information cannot be changed to conceal the identity of customers (for example, if there is one large customer which skews the data), then the information should not be disclosed. Also see the policies entitled "Protection Of The Privacy Of Customer Information" and "Information Access Control Systems And the Mosaic Theory." A: MT; E: LMH.

371. Disclosure Of Computer Logs Reflecting Customer Activities

Policy: Logs reflecting the activities of computer users or those served by computers must not be disclosed to third parties unless Company X is: (1) compelled to do so by court order, law, or regulation, or (2) in receipt of written approval from the involved individuals.

Commentary: The intention of this policy is to protect the privacy of those individuals whose activities appear in logs. The policy covers library-provided literature searches, video tape rental histories, bank transaction records, supermarket frequent-buyer records, and the like. Common computer user activity logs are also covered (these typically contain information about when a user logged-on/off and what applications were executed). Some organizations may wish to restrict the scope of this policy by making reference to specific types of logs. This policy is a specific instance of the policy entitled "Privilege Restriction Based On The Need-to-Know." Also see the policy entitled "Deletion Of Log Information About Customer Activities." A: MT; E: LMH.

372. Deletion Of Log Information About Customer Activities

Policy: The individuals maintaining logs reflecting the activities of computer users or those served by computers, must expunge information which identifies users or persons served as soon as Company X's relationship with these individuals has been completed.

Commentary: The intention of this policy is to preserve the privacy of an individual user or person served with computers. If Company X no longer has a need for the information contained in the log, then this information must be promptly deleted. For example, a library would expunge the identity of the borrower of a book as soon as the book is returned and found to be in good condition. To do otherwise (to continue to maintain this log data) presents attractive opportunities for privacy violation. The words "as soon as" may be too immediate for some organizations; they may wish to substitute the words "within 30 days from the time when." Note that this policy does not restrict Company X from keeping statistics about business activity, it only restricts the keeping of information allowing this activity to be traced to individuals. Thus a library could keep statistics about which books are most frequently borrowed without the need for details about the specific customers who borrowed these books. The word "customer" in the title may need to be modified to suit the organizational vernacular; common alternatives include "client," "patient," and "user." Note also that this policy may need to be modified to reflect the fact that certain logs will need to be retained until such time as payments have been received, accounts have been balanced, or the security of a computer system has been shown to be acceptable. For example, computer user activity logs may need to be kept for three months. A time period like this may be necessary for management to be satisfied that there were no computer crimes, system crashes, or other incidents for which the logs might be of assistance. Also see the policy entitled "Disclosure Of Computer Logs Reflecting Customer Activities." E: MT; E: LMH.

373. Monitoring Of Electronic Mail Messages

Policy: Messages sent over Company X internal electronic mail systems are not subject to the privacy provisions of the Electronic and Communications Privacy Act of 1986 (which prohibits wiretapping), and therefore may be read by Company X management and system administrators.

Commentary: This policy makes it clear that management and technical staff may read worker electronic mail messages. Note that this is a "may" rather than a "must" policy. To avoid legal problems, an organization which monitors electronic mail should make every effort to inform its workers that it does such monitoring. If notified in advance, workers are then able to change their usage patterns to reflect the fact that they may be monitored (i.e., they will refrain from placing personal and private materials in electronic mail messages). This resulting behavior change is fully consistent with a policy indicating the organization's systems must be used for business purposes only (see the policy entitled "Use Of Company X Information For Non-Business Purposes"). Separately, in the policy wording, the legal reference to the "Electronic and Communications Privacy Act of 1986" is relevant to the USA only. Other jurisdictions should nonetheless be clear with the users of their electronic mail systems on this point, regardless of the legal reference (or absence of a reference). In order to manage the expectations of users, they could for example say that: "Messages sent over the Company X internal electronic mail system are not subject to law Z [where Z is a country specific law]." One of the most famous recent cases where notice to employees about e-mail monitoring has been a problem involved Epson of America. For a similar but property-oriented policy, see "Right Of Management To Examine Data Stored On Company X Systems." Also see the policies entitled "Electronic Mail Messages Are Company Records" and "Privacy Expectations And Electronic Mail." A: EMT; E: LMH.

374. Worker Rights To Read Third Party Electronic Mail Messages

Policy: Messages sent over Company X electronic mail systems that allow access by third parties (such as customers and suppliers) must be read by Company X workers ONLY if either the sender or the recipient has first given permission. Whenever electronic mail messages are forwarded to another party, by implication such permission has been granted. The internal Company X dissemination of electronic mail messages containing only general requests for products and/or services need not be so restricted.

Commentary: It is important to specify when electronic mail messages may be read. This becomes a special problem when an organization has third parties on its network, and thus comes closer to being a common carrier. This is an issue because common carriers have certain obligations not applicable to private networks. Likewise, users of common carrier systems have certain rights that do not apply if they are users of private networks. The intention of this policy is to clarify when it is permissible for Company X employees to examine electronic mail messages that may contain proprietary, confidential, or personal data relating to third parties. The policy seeks to address the secondary dissemination problem, whereby one recipient passes a message along to another person, and then this other person passes it to a third person who the original recipient never intended to have access. Separately, access rights may differ if a network provides public access versus if a network provides access only to third parties directly involved in business activities (customers, suppliers, consultants, etc.). For a related idea, see the policy entitled "Monitoring Of Electronic Mail Messages." In some instances, laws like the Electronic and Communications Privacy Act of 1986 (United States only) may dictate access rights. Consultation with internal legal counsel is advisable on all policies such as this. Also see the policies entitled "Privacy Expectations And Electronic Mail" and "Electronic Mail Messages Are Company Records." A: EMT; E: LMH.

375. Employee Observance Of Company X's Right To Privacy

Policy: Unless senior management permission is first obtained, workers must not consent to a violation of Company X's privacy or waive Company X's right to privacy. For example, workers must not allow police to have access to Company X information without a properly-executed search warrant.

Commentary: This policy partially defines a corporate (or organizational) right to privacy. The intention is thus to put employees on notice that such a right exists, that they are not to waive it without prior management permission, and that they are required to defend it. A policy such as this may be important when it comes to protecting confidential information potentially useful to an opposing party in a court battle. The notion of privacy for a legal person (an organization) rather than a physical person (an individual) is different and may at first appear odd to some people. To compensate for this unfamiliarity, some organizations may wish to further specify (in the policy) the ways in which Company X rights to privacy actually exist. For example, employees must not enter into legal contracts where they agree to disclose Company X confidential information unless management approval is first obtained. Similarly, the requirement for a search warrant can be overcome if the parties involved agree to a police search;

employees must not provide such agreement in the absence of top management approval. Consultation with internal legal counsel is advisable on all policies such as this. Also see the policies entitled "Signing Third Party Confidentiality Agreements Without Approval" and "Disclosure Of Information On Company X Systems To Law Enforcement." A: EM; E: LMH.

376. Informed Consent Required For Questionable System Actions

Policy: When in doubt about performing any particular computer-assisted action, Company X workers must inform those whom the action will affect. The communication must include a description of the action they propose to take, the intention behind the action, and the potential impacts that it may have on the recipients of the communication. Before the action is taken, those impacted must explicitly provide their clear and unambiguous consent, or at least be given an opportunity to object before the action is taken. In the absence of such consent, the permission of a vice president must be obtained before the action can be performed.

Commentary: This policy codifies a general ethical consideration proposed by Donn B. Parker at SRI International. The policy is meant to prevent workers from going ahead and performing some computer-related act which workers have reason to believe may harm other people. A good example involves a database product which Equifax (the credit bureau) was going to launch in conjunction with Lotus Development Corporation. The product would have facilitated direct mail advertising by a wide variety of organizations, at considerably lower prices, and would have included personal information about many individuals. Concerned about privacy violations, over 30,000 individuals objected to being included in the database, and the project was accordingly abandoned. Equifax and Lotus thus used this ethical consideration, although they probably did not have a written policy stating it. For some organizations, the policy may be too vague as stated here, and may need specific examples such as those dealing with privacy violation. Also see the policy entitled "Notification Of Suspected Loss Or Disclosure of Sensitive Information." A: MT; E: LMH.

377. Record Creators Decide Whether Record Subjects May View Records

Policy: Patients may not view their own medical records without the prior authorization of the health care provider who generated these records.

Commentary: This policy recognizes the privacy and professional courtesy rights of health care providers (medical doctors and others) as more important than a patient's right to know information about his/her own medical condition. As of 1999, a majority of American states have laws specifically regulating a patient's access to his/her health information. A conflict between the objectives of the patient and the health care provider can exist. For example, a patient may want to know what ails him, yet his doctor may not want him to know, thinking this will worsen his condition. A doctor may also want to restrict access to patient records for fear that these records will provide evidence for malpractice lawsuits. Separately, Federal US laws grant a right to access records about one's own medical condition, but this right does not apply to all types of patients. On another note, the policy title was deliberately generalized beyond the health care industry to show that the notion of record creator rights is applicable to other areas besides health care. For a related idea, see the policy entitled "Making Copies Of Information Appearing In One's Personnel File." A: E; E: LMH.

378. Disclosure Of Intended Uses Of Personal Information Prior To Collection

Policy: Before a customer places an order or otherwise discloses personal information, all Company X representatives must inform the customer of the ways that this personal information will be used.

Commentary: The intention of this policy is to make sure that all personal information gathered is obtained fairly, i.e., without misleading the consumers. A truthful and straightforward way to conduct business, this policy seeks to eliminate any ambiguity about the nature of the relationship between a consumer and an organization about to be established. Most consumers will have no objection, but those who do object can be placed in a special category (do not sell their names, do not call about other products, etc.). Because discussion about such a policy could jeopardize a sale, many organizations will deal with these matters after a sale has been completed. Others will take a more passive role, choosing to include a notice about uses of personal information in advertisements or brochures. Organizations which, as a matter of principle, do not resell mailing addresses or other personal information, may find that this policy provides them with a competitive advantage (this will be especially true if the organization sells products and services about which consumers might be self-conscious, such as pornography or psychological counseling services). This policy is based on a 1993 regulation by England's Data Protection Registrar Eric Howe. The regulation specifically deals with direct mail lists (mass mail), but it is relevant to telemarketing and other marketing activities with privacy implications. See a similar policy entitled "Subjects Given Opportunity To Opt-Out Of Private Data Systems." A: EM; E: LMH.

379. Customers Given Opportunity To Decide To Receive Direct Mail

Policy: Company X customers must be given an opportunity to inform Company X that they do not wish to be contacted via unsolicited direct mail promotions. Company X staff must faithfully observe and promptly act on these customer requests.

Commentary: The intention of this policy is to allow customers to tell Company X that they do not wish to receive promotional mass mail. Operationally the way this is often done is to let customers know that they should contact the company if they do not wish to receive solicitations (often called "interesting opportunities") by mail. A derivative of this notice could, for instance, be inserted into, or printed on monthly billing statements. By implication the policy prohibits Company X from selling these customer contact particulars to third parties who would then use it for mass mail. This policy is consistent with US mass mailer practices and post office regulations about "pandering matter." Note that if a customer asks for information by mail, even if this customer has previously expressed a desire not to receive direct mail, this policy would still allow the information to be sent. The words in the second sentence are most important in this regard. The words in the second sentence help to ensure that this policy is not just a mirage (window dressing), and that Company X does what it says it will do. The policy could be expanded to include fax solicitations, telemarketer phone solicitations, and electronic mail solicitations, particularly since these communication systems are also increasingly being used to send the equivalent of "junk mail." If its scope is expanded, this policy will help organizations prevent violations of laws and regulations. One example of a junk mail law (which is also applicable to fax transmissions) is provided by the Telephone Consumer Protection Act of 1992 (United States law). Also see the policy entitled "Maintaining Accurate Records To Prevent Unwanted Telemarketing" and "Subjects Given Opportunity To Opt-Out Of Private Data Systems." A: EM; E: LMH.

1.3.2.4. Handling Private Data

380. Placement Of Internet Advertising Only With Firms Valuing Privacy

Policy: Company X must not enter into any Internet advertising, referral, or lead generation relationship with other firms if these firms have failed to post on the Internet a privacy policy which is consistent with or more stringent than the policy adopted by Company X.

Commentary: The intention of this policy is to make it clear that people in the sales, marketing, and public relations departments must only place advertisements with, or otherwise enter into marketing arrangements with those firms which value privacy on the Internet. This policy is similar to a policy which has recently been adopted by Intel, and separately by IBM. The policy, which could itself be made public, sends a clear message that we don't do business with firms that don't value the privacy of personal information. This all makes good sense because these third party firms are often gathering personal information, and forwarding this information on to Company X. These third party firms are thus representatives or agents of Company X on the Internet, and if Company X has adopted a privacy policy (an assumption of this policy), then those firms which represent it on the Internet should also have a privacy policy. Note that ideally the privacy policies of both firms are substantially similar; if this is not the case, special care must be taken to assure that personal information gathered by the third party is not inadvertently merged with Company X's main sales and marketing database. The merging of personal information gathered under different privacy policies will make adherence to the relevant policy an administrative headache, or else raise costs unduly (because the most stringent privacy policy must apply to all information). For those firms which don't wish to make a decision about whether privacy policies are consistent, the last part of the policy could be altered to refer only to the existence of a posted privacy policy (this option is weak and is not recommended). Similarly, the scope of the policy could be restricted to include only advertising (not referrals or lead generation efforts). On another note, in an indirect way this policy prohibits spam (junk email) because those firms which broadcast spam often conceal their identities and don't post privacy policies. For similar ideas, see the policies entitled "Approval For Help Wanted Ads And Disclosure Of Sensitive Material," "Trading Partner Agreement Required Prior To Use Of EDI," and "Distribution Of Unsolicited Company X Marketing Materials." A: E; E: LMH.

381. Making Copies Of Information Appearing In One's Personnel File

Policy: Employees must be permitted to both examine and make one copy of the information appearing in their personnel file.

Commentary: To simply allow employees to look at their personnel files severely restricts their ability to rectify errors (as would be the case with the policy entitled "Guaranteed Access To Personal Information Held In Company X Records"). The intention of this policy is to allow employees to gather the information they need and then to be able to take it home, to an attorney, to a psychologist, or to some other third party. To allow employees to have a copy also allows them to better prepare letters and other requests for changes in their file. This policy thus provides a mechanism to increase the integrity of information. It is consistent with the ethic that data subjects should have control over information about them. A positive side effect of this policy is that it discourages the insertion of spurious and/or unsubstantiated information into personnel files. At the same time the existence of this policy may encourage shadow personnel files which do contain information that workers are not intended to see. Separately, the policy could be expanded so as to apply to all workers (including contractors, consultants, and temporaries). These shadow (or secret) personnel files can be prohibited with the policy entitled "Existence Of Secret Systems Containing Personnel Records." Also see the policy entitled "Periodic Distribution Of Employee Personnel Records." A: EM; E: LMH.

382. Conditions Under Which Employees May Examine Their Files

Policy: All employees wishing to examine their personnel file must first submit a written request to the Director of Human Resources. File reviews must only be conducted at appointed times, during business hours, and in the presence of a Human Resources representative.

Commentary: This policy is intended to prevent management from getting in "hot water" [trouble] inadvertently because materials are in personnel files that should not be there. The policy requires that a formal request first be filed; this gives management an opportunity to remove off-color references or inappropriate material. The removal of this material can help prevent discrimination or harassment lawsuits. The policy creates a controlled environment where questions about the record can be handled immediately by a Human Resources Department representative. This immediate problem resolution may help prevent grievances, unnecessary gossip, and unwarranted lawsuits. The presence of this representative also means that copying and removal of material in the file can be prevented. Limits on the number of times a record can be examined can also be established, although these limits in most cases are not required. For related ideas, see the policies entitled "Periodic Distribution Of Employee Personnel Records" and "Record Creators Decide Whether Record Subjects May View Records." A: E; E: LMH.

383. Employee Right To Add Explanatory Statement To Personnel File

Policy: If employees object to the accuracy, relevance, or completeness of information appearing in their personnel file, they must be given an opportunity to add a supplementary statement of up to two hundred (200) words.

Commentary: The intention of this policy is to allow employees to tell their side of a particular matter described in their personnel files. If the organization chooses not to make requested adjustments to a personnel file in response to an employee's complaint, then this right to insert a certain number of words may be applicable. Alternatively, the employee may not file a formal complaint about the information in the file, but they may wish nonetheless to add some explanation because the record may be misleading without the supplementary information although it may be correct. For example, the personnel file may state that a worker was late frequently and that she missed many days of work. The worker may wish to insert a statement that she was pregnant and that she had morning sickness which prevented her from showing up on time every day. Separately, the addition of a supplementary statement may be a one time privilege, or it may be used repeatedly for each contested piece of information. There is nothing special about the number of words referenced; this could just as easily have been 100 or some similar number. The policy may also be used for individuals other than employees (medical patients, tax accounting clients, etc.). Also note that there is deliberately no requirement that incorrect information be removed or changed under this policy. This policy works in conjunction with the policy entitled "Guaranteed Access To Personal Information Held In Company X Records." A: EMT; E: LMH.

384. Allegedly Incorrect Information To Be Corrected Or Labeled As Disputed

Policy: Whenever Company X receives notice that certain personal information held in its records is incorrect, it must promptly modify the information in question, or else append to the record an indication that this information is disputed and alleged to be incorrect.

Commentary: The objective of this policy is to make sure that records containing personal information are up-to-date and correct. If errors in personal records are not promptly corrected, the individuals described therein may suffer serious harm. For example, if a credit bureau did not correct (or label as incorrect) certain false bankruptcy information, then the person described in the record would be likely to suffer personal harm (home mortgage application denied, car purchase loan denied, etc.). Note that this policy does not require a change to a record if Company X personnel have misgivings about the accuracy of the corrected information (this is where a label indicating the existence of a dispute is appropriate). Separately, this policy assumes that a related policy has already granted the individuals described in personal records a right or opportunity to examine information appearing in Company X records. While this policy reflects good practice in the database management area, it is useful to put it in writing to give the people described in the records additional assurance that personal information about them will be treated with both respect and proper care. For related ideas, see the policies entitled "Guaranteed Access To Personal Information Held In Company X Records" and "Customer Right To Know Third Parties Receiving His Or Her Data." A: MT; E: LMH.

385. Required Efforts To Ensure Integrity Of All Personal Records

Policy: Management must make reasonable efforts to ensure that all personal information maintained by Company X is accurate, timely, relevant, and complete.

Commentary: The intention of this policy is to require management to diligently maintain records containing personal information. Thus, with this policy, management would be required to promptly make corrections if the organization has been informed about inaccuracies in a record by the person described therein. This is particularly important for those organizations which use personal information as part of their regular business (such as insurance companies and credit reporting bureaus), rather than organizations which use personal information in the course of their own internal human resources management activities. This is a good general policy on which other policies may rely. It is also appropriate for a brief policy statement. Some organizations may wish to add a description of the words "personal information" or simply provide examples (marital status, social security number, etc.). Note that personal information includes personnel information, but can be a more broadly defined category. Thus customer personal information would fall within the purview of this policy, while properly speaking it is not personnel (internal worker) information. In this policy, the word "private" might be used instead of "personal." Also see the policies entitled "Required Actions After Errors In Records Are Detected" and "Consistent Way Of Representing Employee Contact Information." A: MT; E: LMH.

386. Documented Procedures Required For Personal Record Handling Activities

Policy: To limit the inadvertent loss or disclosure of sensitive information, documented procedures for handling personal information must be established, consistently followed, and regularly updated.

Commentary: The objective of this policy is to inform those internal groups that handle personal information that they must get serious about handling personal (private) information. In part motivated by the United States' Health Insurance Portability and Accountability Act (HIPAA), this policy requires that operational groups which handle private data clearly conceptualize, document, and faithfully follow established procedures. The existence of these procedures will help ensure consistently secure handling of private data and also give internal auditors a reference point for their examinations. Should there be a publicly-revealed problem or a court case, these same procedures can also be used to show that management took prudent steps to protect this private data. Such procedures will typically deal with the routine and non-routine receipt of private data, the manipulation and processing of this data, the storage and retention of the data, the dissemination and transmission of this data, and the disposal and destruction of this data. For similar ideas, see the policies entitled "Computer Operator Logs Must Be Periodically Reviewed" and "Operations Staff Must Have Documented Intrusion Response Procedure." A: MT; E: LMH.

387. Required Efforts To Ensure Personal Records Are Used Only As Intended

Policy: Management must make reasonable efforts to ensure that all personal information is used only as intended, and that precautions preventing misuse are effective and appropriate.

Commentary: The intention of this policy is to force management to pay attention to secondary usage and secondary dissemination issues. Secondary usage refers to using certain information for purposes other than those originally intended (other than those purposes for which the person involved volunteered the information). Secondary dissemination refers to passing information along to third parties without the knowledge or consent of the person or originally created or provided it. This is a good overall policy on which other policies may rely. It is also appropriate for a brief policy statement. Note that personal information includes personnel information, but can be a more broadly defined category. Thus customer personal information would fall within the purview of this policy, while properly speaking it is not personnel (internal worker) information. In this policy, the word "private" might be used instead of "personal." Also see the policy entitled "Prohibition Against Non-Approved System Uses." A: MT; E: LMH.

388. Use Of Personal Information For New Purposes

Policy: Personal information about employees, consultants, or contractors, which has been gathered for one purpose, may not be used for another purpose without the clear and unambiguous consent of the parties to whom this information pertains.
Commentary: The intent of this policy is to stop the misuse of personal information for purposes other than those originally intended. Thus if a citizen of a national government disclosed certain information on his tax return so that the government could carry out tax laws, this policy would prohibit the information on his tax return from being used for child support payment disputes, student loan default collections, and other purposes. Note that this policy reduces the flexibility that management may otherwise enjoy to employ the information in whatever way it wishes (subject to laws, regulations, and ethical considerations). The existence of this policy may encourage data subjects to disclose information that they would not otherwise reveal. This is a widely-subscribed-to privacy policy, but in spite of general public support of the idea, many American organizations find the policy too restrictive. In this policy, the word "private" might be used instead of "personal." For related ideas, see the policies entitled "Use Of Telephones For Personal Purposes" and "Use Of Company X Information For Non-Business Purposes." A: EMT; E: LMH.

389. Linking Anonymous Information With Personally-Identifiable Information

Policy: Company X information systems and staff must not link anonymous information about user behavior or activities with personally-identifiable information unless the involved individuals have first given their consent.

Commentary: This policy addresses a serious problem associated primarily with Internet business activities. Certain personal information which is anonymous, such as click-stream data, is often gathered unbeknownst to the involved users. This information may then be surreptitiously linked with personally-identifiable information, such as a customer database, to form a still more revealing picture of individual behavior or activities. This policy prohibits this linkage in an effort to preserve the privacy of the individuals involved. By adopting this policy, an organization can show that it is genuinely concerned about privacy. This policy is suitable for posting on a web site. The words in the policy provided above are stringent; a watered-down version could replace the words about giving consent with words about robust notice (clear and evident warning). For related ideas, see the policies entitled "Use Of Personal Information For

New Purposes," "No Links Between Private Information And Other Information Types," and "Required Efforts To Ensure Personal Records Are Used Only As Intended." A: ET; E: LMH.

390. Use And Disclosure Of Personal Information About Customers

Policy: All customer records containing personal information that are in the possession of Company X will be used only for purposes directly related to Company X business. Social security numbers, products and services purchased, and account activity will be disclosed to outside parties only with the customer's permission or if Company X has received either a subpoena or court order.

Commentary: The intention of this policy is to clearly prohibit secondary uses of personal (private) information about customers. For example, a telephone company could prohibit the external disclosure of customer calling patterns (aka "pen registers" -- the numbers dialed). The policy is notable because it specifically identifies the types of information that will not be disclosed externally (the information that's not mentioned implicitly can be disclosed). This policy also prohibits the sale, rental, exchange, or any other method for conveying personal information to other organizations that might use it to solicit business from Company X's customers. Note that the term "in the possession of Company X" is used; Company X will have trouble exercising control over customer records that are not in Company X's possession (although this still may be possible if possession is held by outsourcing firms). The policy could be changed to incorporate an exception whenever the receiving party is an authorized government agency such as the Internal Revenue Service (IRS). Also see the policy entitled "Resale Or Subsequent Dissemination Of Customer Contact Information." A: EMT; E: LMH.

391. Customer's Right-To-Know Nature Of Personal Information

Policy: Customers have a right to obtain confirmation from Company X that personal information about them is kept on Company X systems. The nature of the information kept and the uses to which this information is put will generally be provided. If this cannot be done, the reasons why Company X has denied this request will nonetheless be promptly provided.

Commentary: The intention of this policy is to let both customers and internal workers know that customers are legitimately to receive certain types of internal Company X information. Note that the policy does not release the information itself, it only releases metadata (information about information). There will generally be far fewer disputes about metadata than there will be about the specific information. Regulations in some industries, such as the consumer credit reporting industry, will require that specific personal information be divulged, not just metadata. This policy has a pro-consumer sound to it, yet it requires very little of the organization adopting it. Separately, the word "right" is strictly a public-relations ploy since there is no legal grounding for this policy in generally-accepted American laws or regulations. For related ideas, see the policy entitled "Permissible Information To Collect From Customers" and "Personal Information Necessary For Proper Functioning of Business." A: E; E: LMH.

392. Resale Or Subsequent Dissemination Of Customer Contact Information

Policy: Information gathered about customers or potential customers, such as phone number and address, must only be used for internal Company X purposes.

Commentary: The intention of this narrowly defined policy is to guarantee that customer contact information will go no further than the organization that needs it in order to provide a product or service. This type of policy is particularly appropriate for those organizations providing a product or service about which the customer might be embarrassed or self-conscious. Thus psychological counseling organizations, debt problem counseling firms, AIDS victim relief services, political action committees, and similar organizations would need a policy such as this. The existence of a policy like this may also generate additional business for these organizations since some people may have refrained from becoming customers lest their name and contact particulars get on a list. In the USA, the most prevalent concern involves the sale or swap of customer phone and address data, leading to junk mail and unwanted telephone solicitations. This policy is intended to be distributed to customers and potential customers. Also see the policy entitled "Use And Disclosure Of Personal Information About Customers." A: MT; E: LMH.

393. Distribution Of Unsolicited Company X Marketing Materials

Policy: Workers must not use facsimile (fax) machines, electronic mail, auto-dialer robot voice systems, or any other electronic communications systems for the distribution of unsolicited advertising material.

Commentary: The intention of this policy is to prevent internal staff from using some of the new technologies for marketing purposes when the recipient has not indicated an interest in Company X's products and/or service. Such "cold call" solicitations are increasingly met with resistance and anger. In some jurisdictions such as California, these unrequested solicitations (privacy invasions) can be illegal. This policy preserves the privacy of the public and is a potential image enhancer (assuming the policy, or information about the existence of the policy, is made public). The policy could be extended to the telephone, in which case unrequested cold calls would be against internal policy. Likewise, no mention is made in the policy about use of the regular postal (mail) service. The mail system has been deliberately left out of the policy to allow mass mail (in large measure only because it is already common practice). For the same reason, some organizations may wish to deliberately exclude telephone systems from the scope of this policy. For another perspective on this topic, see the policy entitled "Subjects May Block Their Private Data From Being Used." A: MT; E: LMH.

394. Major Systems Changes And Privacy Impact Review Committee

Policy: Every major systems development or enhancement project, which could materially affect the privacy of individuals, must be reviewed in advance by an independent committee. This independent committee must: (a) determine whether individuals will be placed "at risk" or "at a disadvantage" as a result of the project, (b) as necessary, recommend remedial measures, and (c) if necessary, recommend the cancellation of the project.

Commentary: The intention of this policy is to force systems developers to consider the privacy implications of the new systems they build. A privacy committee could be made up of internal or both internal and external people. Some organizations may wish to include mention of how many people should be on the committee and what its composition should be. Such a committee is generally warranted only in those industries, such as banking and medicine, where privacy is a major concern. Nothing in the policy gives the committee any rights to cancel the project, delay it, or otherwise usurp management prerogatives. Nonetheless, the existence of a report by the committee may put management on notice that certain actions should take taken; if management does not take these actions they may be derelict in their fiduciary duty to protect organizational assets (and therefore unduly exposed to lawsuits). Also see the policy entitled "Information Security Management Committee." A: MT; E: LMH.

395. Source And Purpose Of Cookies And Web Bugs Must Be Revealed

Policy: All visitors to Company X Internet web sites and/or commerce sites must receive a clear notice indicating both the source of and purpose for all cookies and web bugs used by these sites.

Commentary: The intention of this policy is to force internal staff to inform remote users about existing data gathering mechanisms which employ cookies and/or web bugs. Cookies are small text files with unique user identifiers, while web bugs are tiny graphics embedded in html code that permit the exchange of user information. Many Internet users are suspicious about cookies (and many more don't know that web bugs exist). Both cookies and web bugs can be invisible to users, although more recent browsers can be configured to ask users whether they will accept a cookie from a particular site. Many sites place cookies on user machines or display web bugs on behalf of third party marketing firms, and these cookies or web bugs can be used to trace and later report on user activities. When users know what type of cookies are being employed, and who issues these cookies (hence the mention "source" in the policy), then they can decide whether they want to accept the cookies. Some sites provide an alternative way to interact with the site which does not require the acceptance of cookies, but users cannot intelligently opt for this type of interaction unless they first know the nature of and source of the cookies employed. Likewise, when users know the nature and source of web bugs employed, they can intelligently decide whether they want to interact with the site. This policy is thus an indication that the sponsor of a site is not in any wishing to conceal its use of cookies and/or web bugs, that it is helping users to make intelligent decisions about their relationships with the site, and that it wants to conduct Internet business in a forthright and honest manner. Certain law enforcement officials in the United States have threatened some Internet merchants with lawsuits if they don't notify visitors about existing cookies and web bugs; this policy would have prevented such threats or subsequent lawsuits. Separately, the policy could be further enhanced by requiring that all visitors be informed how they may delete cookies and web bugs. For related privacy ideas, see the policies entitled "User Controlled Machines Must Not Employ Cookies For Automatic Log-In" and "No Embedded Secret Personal Identifiers Or Serial Numbers." A: T; E: LMH.

396. Compelling Need Required Prior To Usage Of Cookies Or Web Bugs

Policy: Before cookies or web bugs are used on any Company X Internet web or commerce site, a compelling need to gather private data must be demonstrated and presented to the Information Security Management Committee. Only after this committee approves the use of either of these technologies can they be used on Company X web or commerce sites.

Commentary: The intention of this policy is to prevent privacy invasions which are not intended by management. In some organizations, technical staff establish web-based systems which perform functions that management doesn't really understand, and never expressly authorized. This policy helps to ensure that cookies and web bugs, both of which have a bad reputation in the privacy advocate community, will only be used if absolutely necessary. Of course, the organization in question should also disclose the use of these technologies if indeed it is going to use them. This policy is patterned after a new policy written by the Office of Management and Budget (OMB), which is a part of the United States government. The new OMB policy, much like the policy presented here, attempts to prevent privacy abuses rather than apologize for them later. Separately, both cookies and web bugs can be invisible to users, although more recent browsers can be configured to ask users whether they will accept a cookie from a particular site. Many sites place cookies on user machines or display web bugs on behalf of third party marketing firms, and these cookies or web bugs can be used to trace and later report on user activities. Also see the policies entitled "Source And Purpose Of Cookies And Web Bugs Must Be Revealed" and "User Controlled Machines Must Not Employ Cookies For Automatic Log-In." A: T; E: LMH.

397. No Embedded Secret Personal Identifiers Or Serial Numbers

Policy: Company X is serious about preserving customer privacy. Its information systems do not employ secret serial numbers, secret personal identification numbers, or any other secret mechanisms which might reveal the identity of, or activities of customers.

Commentary: This policy seeks to respond to the recent outcry surrounding the use of secret identifying numbers in Microsoft's Word and Excel documents. Using these numbers, it is possible to trace a file back to its originator. Users were not told about these numbers, and thus may have compromised their privacy unknowingly when they posted files to the Internet or some other public forum. This policy helps to gain additional business for an electronic commerce systems by reassuring customers that they will not be duped into conducting a transaction, only later to find out that there were some secret mechanisms used to compromise their privacy. In another highly publicized case, privacy groups are suing Intel about the use of a computer-identifying serial number in the new Pentium chip (this feature was well-publicized); this policy avoids these types of disputes. Note that this policy advances the cause of privacy, but at the expense of security. The policy is intended to be posted to a web site, an electronic bulletin board, or some other public place. For Internet commerce environments, specific mention can be made of "cookies," a mechanism to inconspicuously identify customers. Also see the policies entitled "Severing Link Between Identifying Information And Research Data" and "User Controlled Machines Must Not Employ Cookies For Automatic Log-In." A: E; E: LMH.

398. Personal Identifiers Must Not Appear On Publicly-Accessible Locations

Policy: Personal identifiers, such as social security numbers, must not appear on any publicly-accessible location managed by or controlled by Company X. This includes web pages, Internet commerce sites, product manuals, and magazine advertisements. An exception will be made for public encryption keys and digital certificates, both of which are intended to be widely available.

Commentary: The purpose of this policy is to preserve the privacy of both customers and employees (or anybody else who may be involved). If personal identifiers are not available, then the activities of these individuals cannot be traced back to them. For example, without social security numbers, the US government cannot do database matching, a widely-criticized practice which often uses information for purposes other than those for which it was originally disclosed. Another objective of this policy is to prevent identity theft. If social security numbers, telephone numbers, credit card numbers, electronic mail addresses, and other identifiers do not appear in publicly-accessible places, they cannot be stolen and used for identity theft. Separately, this policy is intended to be posted to a web site and other locations, hopefully thereby generating additional customer confidence and loyalty. Note that the policy does not prevent the organization from posting personal identifiers in restricted locations. This could for example be a list of soon-to-be-shipped orders posted to the Internet; a customer could see only his or her own order by providing a user-ID (thus the information is not public, but it is posted to a public network). In some cases, the word "real" could be added to the very beginning of the policy to distinguish between real and fictitious personal identifiers -- this in turn would, for example, allow usage of a dummy identifier in an advertisement ("John Doe" is the classic name). An example of how this policy gets violated in regular commerce involves the California Franchise Tax Board which recently sent six million tax forms via regular mail and social security numbers appeared on the address labels. For related ideas, see the policies entitled "No Embedded Secret Personal Identifiers Or Serial Numbers" and "Workers Must Not Conceal Their Identity When Using The Internet." A: ET; E: LMH.

399. Severing Link Between Identifying Information And Research Data

Policy: A link between an individual's name or other identifying information on one hand, and private data on the other, must be maintained no longer than is necessary to carry out the purpose(s) for which the data was originally gathered.

Commentary: The intention of this policy is to prevent archival medical records, customer activity databases, or some other information containing personal identifiers from inadvertently violating the privacy of the subjects. Used most often for research--such as research about alcoholics--this policy allows the background information for research to be gathered and analyzed, but then the link to personal identifiers is deleted. This can take the form of two files for each subject's record: a personal contact file and a research data file. The files are connected by serial numbers or pointers that cross-reference each other. When the data gathering is complete, the cross-reference information is deleted. At this point, the identification information is still on hand (perhaps for subsequent follow-up), and the research information is still on hand (for subsequent analysis), but the subject's privacy is assured. Beyond research, the policy may also be appropriate for certain commercial activities. For example a chain of bookstores that provides a frequent buyer program could create a contact file which it could use for solicitations and customer service, while it also maintained a separate anonymous market research file containing all the purchases made but no contact information. Also see the policies entitled "No Links Between Private Information And Other Information Types," "Anonymous User-IDs" and "Required Reporting Of Information Security Incidents." A: T; E: MH.

400. Retaining Personal Information Only As Long As Needed For Business

Policy: Personal information held in Company X information systems must be deleted at the point in time when the information is both no longer needed to conduct business, and when it is no longer needed to meet legal or regulatory requirements.

Commentary: The intention of this policy is to delete personal (private) information soon after it becomes unnecessary, thus preventing further use for unauthorized purposes. Such a policy about deletion also prevents additional disclosures which could violate the privacy of the individuals described in the records. Separately, the policy is deliberately vague about the meaning of the words "no longer needed." If Company X wanted to retain an individual's address and phone number for future notices about product upgrades or enhancements, that would be a business purpose, and therefore permissible under this policy. This policy also has a secondary intention and that is to keep business records to a minimum to thereby assist in their economical and orderly management. In this respect, this policy is an "information overload" reduction policy. As a tertiary intention, the policy also helps reduce historical records which might be the target of discovery legal proceedings which seek to find incriminating information that could be used by an opposing party in a lawsuit. For related ideas, see the policies entitled "Deletion Of Log Information About Customer Activities" and "Minimum Information Retention Period." A: E; E: LMH.

401. No Links Between Private Information And Other Information Types

Policy: Without written approval by the Information Security Manager, information systems must not support any links between private information and other types of information related to the same individual.

Commentary: To assure the privacy of individuals, this policy seeks to limit the number of people who have access to personal information (disciplinary history on a job, job performance evaluations, psychologist notes on a patient, etc.). In the health care industry, this policy prohibits the establishment of links between health care information and other types of information such as financial data and employment data. This would, for example, prevent staff in a hospital's billing department from seeing the specifics of the treatment given to a patient (there is no need-to-know). This policy may also help to avoid other types of abuses; for example, it may keep doctors from analyzing the services that generate the greatest fees for a particular patient, given the type of health insurance that the patient carries. Separately, there is a potentially adverse side-effect of this policy: it may discourage the establishment of a so-called customer information file (CIF) that describes all the different relationships maintained with a particular individual. CIFs and similar databases are common in the banking industry, and are also used elsewhere to allow customer service staff to respond to an individual in an intelligent and up-to-date manner. Note that the approval step at the beginning of the policy will allow an organization to have both a CIF or similar database and also a privacy policy such as this. On yet another note, the word "link" is deliberately vague so that it applies to a corporate data dictionary, an intranet, a database matching effort, etc. See the policies entitled "Severing Link Between Identifying Information And Research Data" and "Linking Anonymous Information With Personally-Identifiable Information." A: T; E: LMH.

402. Routine Destruction Of Transaction Logs Prevents Profile Compilation

Policy: Company X routinely destroys a transaction log entry after a transaction has been completed and after the period in which a refund might be provided has elapsed. Because it does not keep transaction logs, it cannot compile profiles showing customer activities.

Commentary: The intention of this policy is to routinely destroy the information which could be used to compromise the privacy of customers. This policy is thus suitable not only for internal consumption, but also for public release. The policy acknowledges that the archival storage of transaction logs introduces serious threats to individual privacy. Examples include histories of video tapes rented and books purchased. The policy writer should expect significant opposition from marketing people when it comes to the adoption of this policy. Marketing specialists will claim that they need transaction log information for a data warehouse, for data mining, and for the generation of customer profiles in order to provide better service. All this may be true, but unless the organization in question already has these tools, it doesn't need to be storing transaction logs right now. When it adopts these tools, it can amend its policy about log destruction. This policy is thus likely to be adopted only by conscientious organizations who truly believe in safeguarding the privacy of customers, and who understand how transaction dossiers can be serious privacy risks. On another note, it should be stated that nothing in this policy prevents an organization from gathering statistics about which products are selling well, when these products are bought, etc., since all such information could be provided on a general statistical basis rather than an individual basis. Separately, of course some accounting information needs to be maintained for tax and financial reporting purposes. This information can link to a particular credit card number or some other payment information rather than to customer name, social security number, or some other personal identifiers. For similar ideas, see the policies entitled "Periodic Destruction Of Archived Electronic Mail Messages" and "Severing Link Between Identifying Information And Research Data." A: E; E: LMH.

403. Subjects Given Opportunity To Opt-Out Of Private Data Systems

Policy: Prior to the implementation of any new or substantially modified information system that handles private data, the subjects involved must be given an opportunity to chose whether they wish to participate in the new system. This must be done in a straightforward, obvious, and low-cost way.

Commentary: The intention of this policy is to give the subjects--the people who are described by the private data involved--an opportunity to say "no-thanks, I don't want to participate in your new system." A hypothetical example involves people seeking welfare financial support ("the dole"). The bargain as it current exists in America requires that people agree to provide certain personal information in order to get financial assistance. If the government wanted to substantially increase the information required about each welfare recipient (asking how many job interviews have they gone to, for example), the participants could be given an opportunity to opt-out. By refusing to provide the additional information, they elect to no longer be a part of the welfare system, and necessarily their assistance would also stop. In many instances, however, new systems will be proposed. These will in turn require the system provider to be more proactive, contacting the data subjects, and explaining the new system. One example involves database matching (linking of two previously unconnected databases to illuminate new information). This is why the policy talks about getting permission prior to implementation; after implementation it may be too late (the privacy of the involved individuals may already be violated). Civil libertarians would say data subjects should be excluded by default and be given the right to "opt-in." This policy, which allows data subjects to "opt-out," is more in keeping with standard American pro-business practices. See the policies entitled "Subjects Must Opt-In To Be Included In Systems Handling Private Data," "Customers Given Opportunity To Decide To Receive Direct Mail," and "Disclosure Of Intended Uses Of Personal Information Prior To Collection." A: MT; E: LMH.

404. All Marketing Communications Must Provide An Opt-Out Opportunity

Policy: All written marketing communications with prospects or customers found in the Company X contact database must include words which clearly indicate how the recipients can prevent further communications from being sent.

Commentary: The objective of this policy is to make sure that direct mail, junk electronic mail, and all other unrequested written marketing communications include a mechanism to allow recipients to opt-out of further communications. In the electronic mail world, this is generally done at the end of the message, and recipients can simply reply to the sending address and indicate the word "remove" in the subject line. This policy helps to prevent complaints from people who do not want to be bothered with additional solicitations, who want to be left alone (this is considered to be an important aspect of privacy). Separately, this policy does not apply to rented mailing lists and other third party databases because Company X generally has little control over updates to those lists (although the policy could be modified to include these sources in which case requests to be removed would be forwarded to the involved third parties). For related ideas, see the policies entitled "Subjects Given Opportunity To Opt-Out Of Private Data Systems" and "Customers Must Specifically Agree To Receive New/Enhanced Service." A: T; E: LMH.

405. Subjects Must Opt-In To Be Included In Systems Handling Private Data

Policy: To be described in any Company X system which handles private data, the subjects involved must specifically elect to participate in the system. This must be done in a straightforward, obvious, and low-cost way.

Commentary: A common example of an opt-in database is the real estate broker Multiple Listing Service. This database contains information about houses that people have put up for sale. To get listed in this database, a seller must specifically request it and provide the necessary information. The intention of this policy is thus to prevent management from establishing systems where private data is stored against the wishes of the individuals described on the system. This approach eliminates many privacy issues, but may also eliminate some business opportunities. Some organizations may wish to set up a policy such as this only for certain types of data rather than all private data. Notice that no mention is made of system implementation since individuals would not be described in such a system if they had not specifically elected to be; thus, the system could be initially implemented with no personal data stored in it. This policy is a pro-consumer, rather than a pro-business policy. It would be to a business' advantage to adopt this policy if the contemplated system or business activity involved very private matters such as AIDS medical treatment data. See the policy entitled "Subjects Given Opportunity To Opt-Out Of Private Data Systems." A: MT; E: LMH.

406. Immediate Action For Individuals Requesting Database Removal

Policy: If an individual asks to be removed from a Company X internal customer and/or prospect database, workers must immediately remove the individual in question from the database.

Commentary: The objective of this policy is to make sure that Company X workers understand that they cannot dawdle when it comes to responding to requests to be removed from a regular slow mail mailing list, an email mailing list, a telephone calling list, or some other marketing-oriented list. If employees take their time with this task, the list is likely to be used for yet another mass mailing, email broadcast, or telephone campaign, and the individual in question will then be furious. Angry people like this cause great trouble for customer service representatives, and may take their complaints to top management or public forums such as Internet discussion groups. Separately, note that this policy makes reference to a Company X owned database -- not lists purchased or rented from third parties. Thus Company X has no obligation to notify third parties who provide lists for one-time use (although such notification would be desirable from a customer service standpoint). This policy prevents spam (unwanted junk email message), prevents junk snail mail, and prevents prohibited telephone solicitations. This policy will help Company X stay in compliance with privacy laws in countries such as the United States. From an operational standpoint, it is desirable to keep a record of the deleted individual, perhaps in an archival database, just in case there is a dispute, a mistake, or an unauthorized request for deletion. As an aside, the action described in the policy is sometimes referred to as "unsubscribing from a mailing list," but this term is not used in the suggested policy because most of the time individuals never subscribed in the first place. For related ideas, consider the policies entitled "Clearly Identified Source For Electronic Mail Marketing Material" and "Deletion Of Log Information About Customer Activities." A: E; E: LMH.

407. Subjects May Block Their Private Data From Being Used

Policy: Company X workers must diligently observe the unconditional right of data subjects to: block data about them from being included in mailing lists, block the sale of data about them to third parties, and to have data about them erased from direct marketing lists.

Commentary: The intention of this policy is to give data subjects (the ones described in a database or some other collection of data) the right to block the storage, usage, and distribution of data about them. The policy is specific to direct mail marketing activities, but could be expanded into other areas like telemarketing. The policy focuses on direct mail because that is the one of the major areas where consumers feel their privacy is most violated. This policy is a derivative of the Council of Europe's Recommendation on Direct Marketing (No. R85 20; 1985). Thus if a data subject requests any one of the three actions mentioned in the policy, Company X workers must follow through with their request in a conscientious manner. Problems with the follow-through may be encountered if this information has already been distributed to third parties. Some organizations may wish to include mention of procedures to be followed if this third party dissemination has taken place. Tracking of this information can be made possible via policies like the one entitled "Log Book Reflecting Movement Of Secret Documents." Underlying this policy is the idea that individuals should have control over the information about them, i.e., individuals should be the "owners" of their own private information. For a related idea, see the policy entitled "Distribution Of Unsolicited Company X Marketing Materials." A: EMT; E: LMH.

408. Subjects Must Approve New Personal Data Uses After Merger/Acquisition

Policy: If Company X or any of its personal information collections are sold, merged, acquired, or otherwise transferred to another organization, such personal information may not be used for new and unanticipated purposes unless the involved data subjects individually opt-in to these new uses.

Commentary: This policy is intended to provide customers and prospects with additional assurance that their personal information will not be used for new and different purposes that they did not approve simply because the custodian of their data happens to have been merged, been acquired, gone bankrupt, or in some other way changed the nature of its business. This topic has been of considerable concern to Internet commerce system users recently because one major Internet retailer has attempted to auction off its customer list to the highest bidder in the midst of bankruptcy proceedings. Note that this policy not only addresses changes in the ownership of the personal information custodian, but it also considers the outright sale of the personal information to another entity. The policy thus puts customers and prospects on notice that such a sale or transfer might take place, but it reassures them that new uses will not occur as a result of this change unless their explicit consent is obtained. This policy assumes that the uses of the personal or private data are explained elsewhere in the policy statement. Note that this policy deliberately restricts the activities of an internal Marketing Department that wishes to utilize the latest technology to learn about customers and prospects (data mining for example). Thus anticipated internal uses should be mentioned in the policy which could be posted to a web site or Internet commerce site. For related considerations, see the policies entitled "Privacy Policy Considered Contract Made At Time Information Provided" and "Subjects Must Opt-In To Be Included In Systems Handling Private Data." A: ET; E: LMH.

409. Business Structure Changes Do Not Permit Transfer Of Private Data

Policy: Company X is really serious about protecting the privacy of customer information. No matter what business changes our organization goes through (merger, acquisition, bankruptcy, etc.), we will not transfer customer private data to third parties.

Commentary: This policy seeks to respond to the concerns of Internet commerce customers who have been upset by developments surrounding the Toysmart.com bankruptcy. In this widely-watched legal case, the owners of Toysmart.com have attempted to sell private information to a third party in order to satisfy the still unpaid obligations of the now-defunct business. This has struck many people as a violation of the privacy policy posted on their site, but the privacy policy never specifically mentioned business changes such as bankruptcy. The information was originally provided to Toysmart.com under the assumption that it would not be shared with third parties, but the sale to another firm is a direct contradiction of that philosophy. Separately, while this issue has come to the public's attention through the bankruptcy of various dot-com firms, the practice of transferring customer private data as part of a merger or acquisition is common in the business world. The policy blocks such transfers, and helps to eliminate any gray areas that might later lead to a legal dispute. Some firms try to wriggle out of their prior commitments to privacy, stating that the name of the firm will be transferred along with the list, so technically they are not selling to a third party. But claims such as this give the Internet business community a bad name with privacy advocates. The policy described here will help to restore some of this lost confidence. See the policies entitled "Subjects Must Approve New Personal Data Uses After

Merger/Acquisition" and "Financial Condition Of Critical Vendors Reviewed Annually." A: E; E: LMH.

410. Maintenance Of Index To Databases Containing Private Information

Policy: Company X must annually update an index to all in-house databases containing private information. This index must be made available to workers and third parties described in the databases.

Commentary: The objective of this policy is to make sure that data subjects (the people who are described) are aware of all private computerized records about them. This knowledge will in turn allow subjects to check the records for accuracy, and to get involved with the proper distribution of this private information. If subjects don't know the information exists and where it is kept, they cannot object or otherwise exercise their rights regarding information about them. An index (or perhaps data dictionary) of all databases containing private information is also useful from an information security management standpoint, because it can be used to make sure that private information is receiving the protection it should get. It would, for instance, be helpful when determining whether information is protected in a manner commensurate with its sensitivity no matter where it resided, no matter what form it took, no matter what technology was used to handle it, and no matter what purpose(s) it served. Also see the policies entitled "Need To Collect Private Information Must First Be Justified" and "High-Level Inventory Of Information Assets." A: M; E: LMH.

411. Denial Of Benefits Due To Refusal To Provide Unnecessary Information

Policy: No benefit provided by Company X may be denied to any person if they refuse to provide unnecessary private information. Disputes about the definition of "necessary private information" will be resolved by Company X ombudsman.

Commentary: The intent of this policy is to prevent workers, customers, and others from suffering because they choose to withhold private information that is not required. In other words, people should not be penalized for safeguarding their own private information. For example, if a supermarket asked for information about marital status, then check cashing and other services of the supermarket should not be withheld because marital status information is not provided. Of course, products or services may be withheld if the information that has not been provided is indeed necessary. This policy is based on the Code of Fair Information Practices as placed into law in Quebec, Canada. This policy is applicable to both government and private sector organizations. If an organization doesn't have an ombudsman (impartial internal adjudicator), then corporate legal counsel may be used instead (although impartiality may suffer). The reader may wish to review the policies entitled "Default To Denial Of Access Control Privileges," "Adequate Grievance Resolution Procedures," and "Prospective Employees Given Opportunity To Decline Credit Checks." A: M; E: LMH.

1.3.3. Data Confidentiality

1.3.3.1. Overall Data Confidentiality Policies

412. Confidentiality Agreements Required For All Company X Workers

Policy: All employees and contractors (temporaries, consultants, outsourcing firms, etc.) must personally sign a Company X non-disclosure agreement. The provision of a signature must take place before work begins, or if a worker has been working without a non-disclosure agreement, a signature must be provided as a condition of continued employment.

Commentary: This policy is intended to prevent the disclosure of sensitive information to anybody unless they have previously signed a non-disclosure agreement (NDA). Organizations whose business depends on the continued protection of certain information, such as research labs, high-technology companies, and military organizations, will find this policy a necessity. Each organization's actual confidentiality agreement is often drafted by (or at least refined by) its legal department; to make things move faster for the policy writer, a draft NDA is included as an appendix to this book. Note that this policy requires that each individual sign the NDA -- blanket organizational NDAs are not allowed. This requirement prevents individuals from saying that they did not receive notice that the information was sensitive, and that they accordingly didn't take appropriate precautions. Personal modifications to the NDA made by workers should not be acceptable (if they want the job, they sign the form as it stands). To underscore the importance of confidentiality, in some organizations, workers are required to provide periodic signatures on NDAs (perhaps annually), although this is generally considered to be excessively strict. On a separate note, this policy assumes that NDAs are stand-alone contracts, but they could easily be integrated into employment contracts, consulting contracts, or related documents. Also see the policies entitled "Background Checks For Computer-Related Positions Of Trust," "Annual Signature On Agreement to Comply with Security Policies," "Confidentiality Agreements And Disclosures Of Sensitive Information," and "Third Party Non-Disclosure Agreements And Sensitive Information," A: EMT; E: LMH.

413. Chain Of Trust Agreements Required For Private & Sensitive Information

Policy: Private and/or sensitive information in the custody of Company X must not be disclosed to third parties unless these third parties have first signed an explicit chain of trust agreement approved by the Information Security Manager.

Commentary: The objective of this policy is to ensure that private and/or sensitive information is not disclosed to any third party unless this third party has first agreed to protect the information in a prescribed manner. Chain of trust agreements typically state that the recipient will return all the information when the project is completed, will destroy all copies of the information, and will refrain from using the information for purposes other than those expressly stated in the agreement. Other stipulations may also be included, for example the recipient may be required to keep the nature and existence of the information provided by the disclosing organization confidential. A chain of trust agreement may be incorporated in standardized contracts, such as a standard consulting services boilerplate contract, or it may be a standalone agreement. With chain of trust agreements, organizations can use outsourcing firms and other affiliated businesses with the assurance that the information security policies observed internally are also being observed at the recipient organization. Chain of trust agreements are thus a quick and dirty way to overcome the troublesome inconsistencies and incompatibilities in information security policies found at two or more organizations. For this reason they are popular with extranets and other Internet trading partner systems. Chain of trust agreements are also legally binding and they clearly identify who is responsible for what information security activities -- an important but often neglected area. For related ideas, see the policies entitled "Signed Forms Required For Issuance Of User-ID" and "Secondary Dissemination Of Secret Information." A: EMT; E: LMH.

414. Confidentiality Agreements Required For Office Machine Repair Staff

Policy: Prior to beginning their work, all external office equipment repair staff must have signed a Company X confidentiality agreement (non-disclosure agreement).

Commentary: The intention of this policy is to prevent industrial espionage (or perhaps military espionage). Recent models of ordinary office equipment such as copiers and fax machines now have up to five megabytes of recent information stored in them. If a repairperson were to swap the chip that contains this information, he or she could walk away with significant intellectual property but nobody would be the wiser. Likewise, if there is a paper jam, some sensitive information may have been printed on that paper but it may not have been removed from the machine. Note that the policy is written with a broad scope, and that general purpose computers (including palmtops and handhelds like the Palm Pilot) would be included within its purview. Some organizations call confidentiality agreements NDAs (non-disclosure agreements). For similar ideas, see the policies entitled "Confidentiality Agreements And Disclosures Of Sensitive Information," "Third Party Access To Company X Systems Requires Signed Contract," and "Sensitive Information Destruction/Concealment Before Servicing Done." A: E; E: MH.

415. Changes In Employment Require Review Of Confidentiality Agreements

Policy: Whenever there are changes in the terms of employment or contract, the terms and conditions of the confidentiality agreement must be reviewed with the individual's manager. At an absolute minimum, this review must take place when workers are scheduled to leave Company X or when their contract is coming to an end.

Commentary: This policy is intended to remind workers that they signed a confidentiality agreement, and that Company X intends to hold them to these terms and conditions. Customarily part of a so-called "exit interview" this review of the terms and conditions need not be a time-consuming process. It could instead simply be the manager saying: "You remember you signed a confidentiality agreement, right? Here's a copy, be sure to read it again ... the Company is serious about this stuff." The policy, as written, is deliberately vague about the exact words to be said by the manager, leaving it up to the circumstances and personal preference. In some cases, the reminder may come from a member of the Human Resources Department staff, rather than from the individual's manager (in either case, the job title of person to do the review should be stated in the policy). The existence and enforcement of this policy may help organizations in their legal efforts to demonstrate that they diligently attempted to protect trade secrets, and that they should therefore be eligible to receive some legal assistance against alleged wrongs of a worker. For a related policy, see "Confidentiality Agreements Required For All Company X Workers." A: EMT; E: LMH.

416. Default Restrictions On Dissemination Of Company X Information

Policy: All Company X internal information must be protected from disclosure to third parties by default. Third parties may be given access to Company X internal information only when a demonstrable need-to-know exists, and when such a disclosure has been expressly authorized by Company X management.

Commentary: The intention of this policy is to put workers on notice that, in the absence of further instructions, they should restrict the dissemination of internal Company X information. This is a good general policy on which more explicit subsequent policy statements can rely, or it can suffice for those organizations which don't have a great deal of confidential information. This policy is most applicable to those organizations which do not yet have a formal data classification system. Readers at those organizations which have already adopted a data classification system will note that no mention of data sensitivity labels is made in this policy. Labels can save time and money as well as standardize the handling of sensitive information. A somewhat crass way to summarize this policy is "if it's not public information, then don't give it to any outsider." For further information on sensitivity classification systems, see the policy entitled "Four Category Data Classification Scheme." Note that this policy is especially relevant to those organizations with connections to the Internet or other public computer networks. Recent cases have shown that employees often distribute internal information on electronic bulletin boards, in Internet chat sessions, and in other public forums unless specifically instructed not to do so. Restricting the flow of internal information onto external networks is also possible with certain firewall controls, such as those which examine the content of the data sent. Also note that the policy, as written, does not make use of formal non-disclosure agreements (NDAs). Also see the policy entitled "Default To Denial Of Access Control Privileges." A: EMT; E: LMH.

417. Notification Of Suspected Loss Or Disclosure Of Sensitive Information

Policy: If sensitive information is lost, is disclosed to unauthorized parties, or is suspected of being lost or disclosed to unauthorized parties, its owner and the Director of the Information Security Department must be notified immediately.
Commentary: Prompt notification of sensitive information loss or disclosure is a necessary precursor to performing effective damage control. For instance, if information about a new, but not yet released product has been mistakenly disclosed to a reporter by someone on Company X's staff, then the date for the official announcement of the product may need to be changed. The intention of the policy is therefore to require that all workers report all losses or disclosures of sensitive information. This policy works best when the word "sensitive" has been explicitly defined within the organization via a data classification system. For further information on this topic, see the policy entitled "Four Category Data Classification Scheme." Likewise, the term information "owner" (sometimes called information sponsor or information guardian) should be defined elsewhere. For more information on this latter topic, see the policy entitled "Information Ownership And Management's Responsibilities." Also see the policy entitled "Management Notification Of Information Integrity Controls Failure." A: EMT; E: LMH.

418. Revealing Information Systems Technical Details To Job Applicants

Policy: Information systems technical details (such as network addresses, network diagrams, and security software employed) must not be revealed to job applicants until they have signed a confidentiality agreement and also been hired/retained.

Commentary: The intention of this policy is to prevent a new type of attack which involves posing as an applicant for a technical information systems job (the relationship could be a contractor, a consultant, or a temporary). The attacker in this scenario would ask a variety of technical questions about the computing environment, ostensibly to determine whether the applicant had the right skills for a job. In the process, the attacker would obtain useful information that could be used for social engineering as well as mounting a narrowly focused attack (now that he or she knows what type of technology is being employed). This policy seeks to treat job applicants as untrusted outsiders, which is decidedly different from the traditional approach still used at most firms. At most organizations, there is a desire to welcome newcomers, to make them feel part of a family, or to otherwise encourage them to come aboard. In the absence of such a policy, to withhold information systems technical details from a job applicant would seem bizarre and uncalled-for. This policy is thus like the policy which specifies that people cannot piggy-back through a controlled door to a data center. In the latter case, politeness must give way to security. For related considerations, see the policies entitled "Release Of Systems Documentation To Third Parties" and "Software Or Data Exchanges With Third Parties Require Agreements." A: EMT; E: LMH.

419. Disclosure Of Information System Control Specifics To Third Parties

Policy: Workers must not disclose to any persons outside Company X either the information system controls that are in use or the way in which these controls are implemented. Exceptions will be made only if the permission of the Information Security Department manager is first obtained.

Commentary: If information about controls is disclosed, outsiders could use this information to reduce the work required to compromise information security systems. Efforts to obtain such information often involve so-called "social engineering" (spoofing ploys). In these cases, system attackers often pose as government officials, employees of the same organization, or other authorized persons so as to be credible. Social engineering may also be done by posing as a market researcher or official disseminator of information about system vulnerabilities. Without a policy such as this, users may attempt to be helpful, and thereby unwittingly compromise security. This policy could be expanded with examples of the types of information not to disclose (how to gain system access, what type of access control systems the organization uses, what third-party network connections are supported, etc.). Some organizations may wish to expand this policy to include physical security matters as well. The policy could additionally be enhanced by adding an exception for external auditors who have been authorized to receive this information by a vice president or another high-ranking manager. Separately, this policy is related to pre-publication review for technical papers; on this topic the reader can review the policy entitled "Prior Review For Speeches, Presentations, Technical Papers, Etc." This policy is also relevant to technical discussions on Internet chatrooms, on Internet listservs (discussion groups), on dial-up electronic bulletin boards, and in other public forums. These forums might, for instance, cover with the details of how to set up a network firewall. It is possible, and is in fact often desirable, for employees to engage in such technical discussions without providing detailed control information about their employer's systems. Department managers may need to instruct users who engage in these types of discussions so that detailed control information is not inadvertently disclosed. For a related topic, see the policy entitled "Disclosure Of Information About Information System Vulnerabilities." Also see the policy entitled "Insertion Of Computer-Related Contact Numbers In Directories." A: ET; E: LMH.

420. Material Financial Information Disclosures To Selected Parties

Policy: All workers must be careful about every disclosure of information about the financial condition of Company X, anticipated changes in financial position, and business developments which could reasonably be expected to materially alter the way investors view the company. All such disclosures must be cleared in advance with the Public Relations Department or a vice president, and made publicly available to all investors and interested parties at the same time.

Commentary: The intention of this policy is to prevent workers (especially top management) from making selected disclosures to certain securities analysts, who then use this information to formulate buy/sell/hold recommendations regarding the stock of Company X. This traditional approach allows the people with such restricted information to profit in the stock market while the general public (notably small investors) cannot trade on the information in question because they don't know about it. This policy is based on a new rule (called Regulation FD) proposed by the United States Government - Securities and Exchange Commission (SEC). The intention of the SEC is to establish a more equitable sharing of information regarding the prospects of and financial status of listed companies. The rule may, however, prevent any material disclosures unless they are delivered with Internet teleconferences, recorded in their entirety and posted to a web site, or otherwise made widely available. From an information security standpoint, it's desirable to be very careful about all disclosures to the public, especially in the litigious business environment now prevailing in the United States. This policy thus brings a greater awareness and concern about what is being said publicly as well as a modicum of fairness to the disclosure process. This policy is relevant only to companies listed on stock exchanges. For related considerations, see the policy entitled "Transfer Of Company X Information To Third Parties" and "Keeping Records Of All Third Parties Receiving Private Information." A: M; E: LMH.

421. Disclosure Of Information About Information System Vulnerabilities

Policy: Specific information about information system vulnerabilities, such as the details of a recent system break-in, must NOT be distributed to persons who do not have a demonstrable need-to-know.

Commentary: The intention of this policy is to let those few people, who have access to information about information system vulnerabilities, know that disclosure of this information should be strictly controlled. If vulnerability information were to fall into the hands of unauthorized parties, these people could use it to compromise the organization's systems. These unauthorized parties could also use it to blackmail (extort) or publicly embarrass the organization. Such information may also be of interest and useful for internal political battles. The vulnerability information may also erode the confidence that users and management have in the Information Systems Department, and for this reason should also be restricted. This policy is directly applicable to the SATAN vulnerability identification program, a publicly-available tool which tells Internet users what security problems exist in a network. This tool can and has been used to gain unauthorized entry into private networks. Newspapers report that the author of this tool was dismissed from his job for publicly-releasing vulnerability information in a manner inconsistent with this policy. Separately, some organizations may go further than this policy. For example, they may require that systems vulnerability information be labeled with special restricted access words. Similar to data classification labels such as "secret," these warning labels could get quite specific, forbidding distribution on electronic bulletin boards and similar publicly-accessible systems. Other organizations may keep logs of who this information was distributed to, when it was returned, and the like. All this will soon be electronically enforced via automatic program execution control, file authentication codes, and digital signatures, but for now, we must make do with policies. For related ideas, see the policies entitled "Disclosure Of System Penetration Software Source Code And Analysis" and "Presentation Of Low-Profile And Secure Image." A: MT; E: LMH.

422. Vulnerability Information Detail Level In Press Releases Must Be Low

Policy: Press releases or other public statements issued by Company X containing information systems vulnerability information must be free of explicit details.

Commentary: The objective of this policy is to prevent Company X representatives from causing trouble because they have released explicit details about information security vulnerabilities. If explicit details (the modus operandi or steps associated with compromising security) are provided, this may enable hackers and others to launch attacks against other sites, and Company X may be held responsible for the damage done thereby. Refraining from disclosing these details may be frustrating for the news media, but it will also help ensure that the attack method is not again used against Company X systems. Public disclosure of these explicit details may additionally inform the perpetrators that certain information about them is known, and this may cause them to destroy evidence that could otherwise be accessible to investigators, and could perhaps be useful in a prosecution. This policy will furthermore help to keep Company X representatives from speculating about exactly how attacks were carried out, and this may in turn help prevent charges of libel and slander. Note that disclosure to relevant vendors and to government agencies tracking computer break-ins are not covered by this policy and so are still permissible. For related ideas, see the policies entitled "Presentation Of Low-Profile And Secure Image" and "Disclosure Of System Penetration Software Source Code And Analysis." A: EMT; E: LMH.

423. Disclosure Of System Vulnerability Exploitation And Victim Data

Policy: Company X staff must not publicly disclose information about the individuals, organizations, or specific systems that have been damaged by computer crimes and computer abuses. Likewise, the specific methods used to exploit certain system vulnerabilities must not be disclosed publicly.

Commentary: This policy is akin to a policy used by the Computer Emergency Response Team (CERT) at Carnegie-Mellon University. This CERT monitors and reports on Internet vulnerabilities. The policy would be appropriate for vendors of information system products and services (in the future, most every organization of significant size will fall into this category). For instance, a workstation vendor may publicly release information about the existence of a security problem and how to install a patch to overcome the problem. Nonetheless, the customers who were victimized and the specific ways that the attacks were perpetrated should be kept confidential. This policy helps to ensure that unauthorized parties do not use the information to mount still further attacks against the victims (since they don't know who the victims are, which systems were involved, or the details of the attacks). It also makes it more difficult for unauthorized parties to exploit the vulnerability because they must still figure out the specific attack method. This policy does, nonetheless, allow the general information needed to improve the security of systems to be released publicly. For related ideas, see the policies entitled "Waiting Period Prior To External Disclosure Of Requested Information" and "Disclosure Of Information About Information System Vulnerabilities." A: ET; E: LMH.

424. Disclosure Of System Penetration Software Source Code And Analysis

Policy: Programming source code for computer viruses, worms, Trojan horses and other routines used to compromise security must be disclosed ONLY to those persons with a demonstrable need-to-know. Likewise, technical analyses of such software routines should also be disclosed only to those with a need-to-know.

Commentary: The intention of this policy is to prevent unauthorized persons from using this information to compromise systems security. There are many "copy-cat" computer criminals, who use previously written material to achieve new objectives. For example, many of the viruses currently infecting systems are simply derivatives of older viruses. Similarly, the WANK worm which successfully penetrated many systems on the Internet was a combination of previously written routines. Perhaps one of the worst things that could be done is to collect many attack programs and make them freely available on an electronic bulletin board; unfortunately the United States government is recently reported to have mistakenly done just this. Of course, such information is currently available via underground electronic bulletin boards and web sites, but those with such access are a small minority of the population. Separately, the analysis of such system penetration routines is also sensitive since it can be used by the system attackers to learn about what works and what does not. Such analysis can be considered to be a list of needed system enhancements for the next generation of system attack software. A minority of individuals see this policy as ill-advised; they claim that by making such information widely available the public will be able to improve the security of all systems. These people claim that by making such information available only to those who are masters in the "black art" of information security, access will be denied for systems administrators and others who need this information. Also of concern is an organization's liability for disclosing sensitive vulnerability information; will those who are damaged thereby come back and sue the disclosing organization? For a related idea, see the policy entitled "Disclosure Of Information About Information System Vulnerabilities." Also see the policies entitled "Security Mechanisms Must Not Be Compromised for Customers" and "Presentation Of Low-Profile And Secure Image." A: MT; E: LMH.

425. Security Mechanisms Must Not Be Compromised for Customers

Policy: Customer requests that Company X security mechanisms be compromised must NOT be satisfied unless: (a) an Executive Vice President first approves it in writing, or (b) Company X is compelled to comply by law.

Commentary: The intention of this policy is to clearly address the tradeoff between customer service and security. For example, a software company that makes word processing software with an encryption feature may receive a request from a customer. The customer may want the software company to break the encryption process so that the only copy of a file may be decrypted. This policy states that the software company must not do this unless one or both of the conditions in the policy are met. If the software company did break the encryption process, word might get out that the company can and will do this, and then the company would be requested to do it regularly. The company would also need to determine whether the requester indeed had the proper authority to request that the encryption process be reversed (a difficult and legalistic matter). Separately, the policy does not address the compromise of controls on systems external to Company X. Some organizations may wish to expand the scope of this policy to include external systems as well. This would, for example, prevent an information broker from compromising controls on an external system to obtain certain sought-after information. See the policies entitled "Disclosure Of System Penetration Software Source Code And Analysis," "Removal Of All Unauthorized Access Paths In Production Software," "Vendor-Provided Written Integrity Statements," and "Prohibition Against Testing Information System Controls." A: MT; E: LMH.

426. Presentation of Low-Profile And Secure Image

Policy: Company X must at all times present a low-profile and secure image to both the public and third parties. Information about the existence and nature of significant assets must be accessible only to those persons with a demonstrable need-to-know.

Commentary: The intention of this policy is to reduce potential losses as well as foster confidence on the part of the public and third parties (customers, suppliers, stockholders, etc.). For example, an organization should not have its mainframe data processing shop on the ground floor of a city block and keep large picture windows without curtains so that people passing by can look in. To do this would be to invite saboteurs and industrial spies. Although it may at first seem inconsistent with this policy, certain events, like a fire in an office building, should be made public knowledge because the public could be affected. In some jurisdictions and industries, reporting security incidents is required by laws or regulations. Although a security-relevant event can be acknowledged, the control measures used to prevent future problems should be kept confidential (at least the implementation details related to these control measures). This policy and accompanying explanations may be particularly useful background for a Public Relations Department when putting together press releases describing certain loss events. There is a trade-off decision implicit in this policy: it is assumed that a good secure image is a superior objective to deterring others from using the same techniques (that is, with this policy prosecution of computer criminals will be rare). For further ideas, see the policies entitled "Vulnerability Information Detail Level In Press Releases Must Be Low" and "Disclosure Of Information About Information System Vulnerabilities." A: MT; E: LMH.

427. Information Access Control Systems And The Mosaic Theory

Policy: If Company X sensitive information is resident on a computer system, and if users are permitted to request all or part of this information through on-line facilities, special access controls must be in force. These access controls must protect the information so that a series of permissible requests for information will not collectively reveal information that is otherwise restricted. Like a mosaic picture made of glass fragments, separate pieces of information must not be readily susceptible to assembly to create a larger picture. In many instances, to reduce the risk of unauthorized disclosure, access controls will prevent the segmentation of aggregate sets of information.

Commentary: The intention of this privacy-related technical policy is to give those responsible for security some guidance in the establishment of access control systems. For example, a network administrator in the process of setting-up an access control system could benefit from a policy such as this. Likewise, a programmer creating a database query facility to be placed on a server accessible via the Internet should keep this policy in mind. At its most fundamental level, this policy suggests that access control privileges should be defined in broad categories (such as job titles) rather than detailed categories (such as data about individuals). Accordingly, the last sentence in the policy may be moved from the policy into accompanying explanatory text. The accompanying explanation may also make reference to "dithering," a technique involving the introduction of minor inconsistencies and errors so as to conceal the true nature of the data. This policy addresses what is known as the "mosaic" theory. Looking at a single piece of glass in a mosaic mural will not reveal the big picture, but when a number of the pieces are collectively seen, new information is conveyed. Separately, the word "sensitive" may be replaced with a designation such as "secret" which is in keeping with an internal data classification policy. For further information about data classification systems, see the policy entitled "Four Category Data Classification Scheme." Also see the policies entitled "Distribution Of Statistical Information About Customer Records," "Responsibility For Assigning Data Classification System Labels," and "Labels For Collections Of Information With Various Sensitivities." A: T; E: MH.

428. Limitations On Third Party Collection Of Pricing Information

Policy: In an effort to prevent competitors from obtaining proprietary internal information, third parties are forbidden from gathering a significant number of prices for Company X products and services.

Commentary: The intention of this policy is to deliberately create an artificial barrier to free information flow. For example, software agents working in the background on the Internet may visit multiple vendor web sites selling audio CDs, and then determine which vendor has the lowest prices. This policy instructs systems designers to install mechanisms that will block agents from performing such price comparison tasks. While it may at first sound like a cut-throat competitive tactic, this practice is already well-established. The policy is similar to existing practices in the physical security world. For example, grocery stores will routinely bar employees from other stores from walking the isles collecting a significant amount of information about prices. In the future these types of obstructionist tactics will become more prevalent, blunting the true potential for "frictionless markets" supported by the Internet. In some instances it may be desirable to generalize this policy so that it limits any external information gathering activity which might then convey a competitive advantage to the third party. On another note, the word "significant" in the policy is deliberately vague, allowing information systems to evolve in response to changing conditions. Separately, this policy is most useful within an organization that offers many different products and/or services with different prices (a major airline for instance). For a related idea, see the policy entitled "Information Access Control Systems And The Mosaic Theory." A: T; E: LMH.

429. Identity Theft Prevention By Restricting Access To Personal Information

Policy: All identifying information about customers such as credit card numbers, credit references, and social security numbers, must be accessible only to those Company X personnel who need such access in order to perform their jobs.

Commentary: Identity theft has become a serious and increasingly common type of information crime. Among other things, it involves masquerading as someone else in order to make application for a loan or a credit card in the name of this other person. The policy intends to make it crystal clear that financial and personal information about customers must only be used by those people who have a genuine need for this information. This is desirable because it is the general availability of this information that often makes identity theft so easy to commit. This policy is deliberately silent about the mechanisms used to restrict access -- this gives local management significant leeway to choose the controls best suited to meet the objective defined in the policy (partially obscured database fields, encryption, passwords, etc.). The policy could be extended to employees and other groups of people for which the organization keeps records. The policy could additionally be useful for public relations (as an indication of the organization's proactive position). For a related idea, see the policy entitled "Shredding Of Credit Card Receipts And Other Payment Information." A: MT; LMH.

430. Data Warehouse Access Restricted To Top And Middle Management

Policy: Because the data warehouse contains sensitive information, access is restricted to Company X top and middle management.

Commentary: The idea of a data warehouse, able to produce all sorts of new reports that were never before possible, has many people excited about the new possibilities. In their enthusiasm, these people may ignore access control issues. As the policy entitled "Information Access Control Systems And The Mosaic Theory" implies, when a new collection of information is created, new patterns will be evident, and some of these patterns will be more sensitive than the underlying information. Access to a data warehouse should accordingly be restricted only to top and middle management (or some other select group of authorized workers). Although proponents of the "open book management" theory would argue for access by all employees, warehouse technology is still so new that information security professionals are still puzzled about the best ways to handle related access controls. Until a consistent and workable system that reflects the access control restrictions found on the systems supplying the underlying data can be applied to a data warehouse, it is conservative to allow only management to access the warehouse. An alternative approach would be to make it accessible only through an intermediary, such as a research assistant, who could also make an assessment of the requestor's genuine need for the requested information. While inefficient, this intermediary approach to implementing the policy has the advantage that it will be consistently applied. Separately, this policy should be distributed only to systems administrators and others who grant system privileges. On another note, this policy can be adapted for use in a variety of information collections including very large databases. For a related idea, see the policy entitled "Labels For Collections Of Information With Various Sensitivities." A: T; E: LMH.

431. Dithering To Conceal True Nature Of Signal

Policy: Information which is sensitive, which may be used by adversaries, and which is readily available in readable form over public channels must be slightly modified (dithered) to conceal its true high-integrity nature.

Commentary: The intention of this policy is to delineate the mechanism to provide information which is useful to the public and other constituencies, but not of such a high quality that it can be used by adversaries. Consider satellite clock information as an example. Military satellites may have so precisely defined these signals that a foreign power could use this information to guide nuclear missiles. So the encrypted version of these signals can be made available only to military systems (probably with padding and encryption so as to disguise the important information from extraneous information). Yet the public may need access to this information, for instance to guide boats and airplanes. The solution is a slightly modified or dithered version which can be made available in a readable form for these public constituencies. Although this policy is most relevant to military and government systems, the notion may also be applicable to commercial interests. Commercial organizations may consider this approach when trying to come to a workable solution for those apparently-paradoxical circumstances where information must be kept confidential, but must also be disclosed. Besides dithering, it may be appropriate in some instances to make available only summaries of such sensitive information. For this perspective, see the policy entitled "Information Access Control Systems And The Mosaic Theory." Also see the policy entitled "Reliability Of Information Down-Loaded From Internet." A: T; E: MH.

432. Right To Block, Conceal, Deny, Or Discontinue Service At Any Time

Policy: Company X reserves the right to block, conceal, deny, or discontinue its service at any time without advance notice. This right may be applied on an individual, organizational, regional, or national basis as business and security needs warrant.

Commentary: The intention of this policy is to prevent third parties from holding Company X responsible because it no longer provides an information service, or it no longer provides an information service with certain characteristics. The policy thus puts users on notice that the issuing organization may discontinue or change its service at any time without advance notice in order to advance or maintain its own business and security interests. The policy in effect says "don't hold us responsible for any dependent downstream uses of our service that we did not expressly agree to in writing." As an example, consider the Global Positioning System (GPS) which is maintained by the United States government. The GPS signal is used by civilian systems such as airplane autopilot systems and boat navigation systems. At the same time, this same signal could be used by an adversary to guide nuclear missiles. To handle this threat, the government has let the public know that it is able to "selectively deny the [GPS] signal on a regional basis when our national security is threatened." In days gone past, the government used a technique called "dithering" which degraded the GPS signal, but as of the year 2000, it no longer does this. Separately, this policy would generally be used by an organization offering a service (such as a time reference) to the public. On another note, this policy allows the issuing organization to discontinue its service without advance notice if the supporting systems have been compromised by a hacker; such a discontinuance would be warranted in order to reestablish a trusted computing environment. For related concepts, see the policies entitled "Payment Information Never Provided In Its Entirety To Customers" and "Dithering To Conceal True Nature Of Signal." A: E; E: H.

433. Information With Multiple Sensitivity Classifications On Single System

Policy: If a computer system contains information with varying sensitivity classifications, the controls used must reflect the most sensitive information on the system.

Commentary: The intention of this policy is to make sure that sensitive information is not improperly disclosed because it is on the same system as other less sensitive information. Although it is an expensive systems design objective, this policy states that information must be protected in accordance with the "highest" classification presently on the system. In the military, this is known as a "system high" policy. Security related costs can often be significantly lowered if the most sensitive information is moved to another system. Likewise, segmenting data by sensitivity onto different disk drives and other system components may help to lower security-related costs. Various segmented system components containing similarly classified data may be accessible only when processing on the system is at a certain level. For example, if confidential processing is being done on a system, then secret disks will be inaccessible. Separately, this policy would for example indicate that the operating system's access control mechanisms must be strong enough to protect the most sensitive information on the system; this means that all the other types of information must bear the overhead of this most sensitive type of information. This policy is most readily applied to a stand-alone system, and gets quite complex when networks are introduced. Taken to its logical conclusion, all systems connected to the network must have the same type of controls, consistent with the most sensitive data to be handled. A practical way to handle networks with this policy is through separate encrypted subnets or domains, which share certain keys. Reflecting the difficulties associated with implementation of this policy on networks, MILNET (the US military computer network) has these days become a separate network, while it was once part of the Internet. For more information about data classification systems, see the policy entitled "Four Category Data Classification Scheme." Also see the policy entitled "New Label After Storage Media Exposure To Secret Data Or Applications." A: T; E: MH.

434. Choosing Computer Storage Media Data Classifications

Policy: If information recorded on computer storage media with a higher sensitivity classification is moved to media with a lower sensitivity classification, then the media with the lower sensitivity classification must be upgraded so that its classification reflects the highest sensitivity classification.

Commentary: This policy provides specific guidance for end-users and others who handle data storage media (CD-ROMs, floppy disks, DAT tapes, nine track tapes, etc.). It tells them how they should proceed when files or other collections of data have different data classifications. For example, if a hard drive has secret information on it, and information from the hard drive is written to a floppy disk that has confidential information on it, then the floppy disk must be reclassified as secret. This policy is a more specific instance of the policy entitled "Information With Multiple Sensitivity Classifications On Single System." Rather than commingle information with different classifications, some organizations will chose to employ separate data storage media for each classification. For example, floppy disks can have colored labels indicating the classification of the information stored thereon. Other controls can also be used to more expediently deal with multiple data classifications stored on the same media; for example, secret data can be encrypted, while unclassified data can be left unencrypted. For a related idea, see the policy entitled "Commingling Of Sensitive And Non-Sensitive Information." A: EMT; E: LMH.

1.3.3.2. Data Classification Categories

435. Four Category Data Classification Scheme

Policy: Data must be broken into four sensitivity classifications with separate handling requirements: SECRET, CONFIDENTIAL, PRIVATE, and UNCLASSIFIED. This standard data sensitivity classification system must be used throughout Company X. These classifications are defined as follows:

SECRET: This classification applies to the most sensitive business information which is intended strictly for use within Company X. Its unauthorized disclosure could seriously and adversely impact Company X, its stockholders, its business partners, and/or its customers.

CONFIDENTIAL: This classification applies to less sensitive business information which is nonetheless intended for use within Company X. Its unauthorized disclosure could adversely impact Company X, its stockholders, its business partners, and/or its customers.

PRIVATE: This classification applies to personal information which is intended for use within Company X. Its unauthorized disclosure could seriously and adversely impact Company X and/or its employees.

UNCLASSIFIED: This classification applies to all other information which does not clearly fit into any of the above three classifications. While its unauthorized disclosure is against policy, it is not expected to seriously or adversely impact Company X, its employees, its stockholders, its business partners, and/or its customers.

Commentary: The intention of this policy is to provide all types of workers with information to guide their security-related handling of Company X sensitive information. This set of classification designations is appropriate for a medium to large organization which does not deal with especially sensitive information (such as national defense information). Organizations with many types of sensitive data will want to add additional categories to fine-tune sensitive information handling procedures. Beyond the four above-mentioned categories, a category for "public" information is often in order. This would apply to information which has been approved by management for public release. Disclosure of "public" information is consistent with policy, and will not adversely impact Company X, its employees, its stockholders, its business partners, and/or its customers. The default category to be used in the absence of further information, and the most prevalent category, is "unclassified." This policy may also be compressed so that only three or even two categories are involved. Note also that the policy as written here should not be used if the organization currently deals with, or will soon deal with military information; this is because the terms "confidential," "secret," and "unclassified" have special reserved meanings in the American national defense community. The organization can use the terms "restricted," "proprietary," and "for internal use only" instead. On a different note, most data classification policies include specific examples to help employees distinguish between the categories. Thus, salary data for employees would be considered "private." Some organizations may wish to add to the policy some words which indicate that draft versions of information should be classified and handled in the same matter as final versions. The policy given here could be made more explicit; this might, for example, involve replacement of the words about "adverse impact" with words about financial loss, gains to competitors, significant embarrassment to Company X, sizable loss of confidence in Company X, or notable reduction of Company X's standing in the community. Also see the policies entitled "Date For Declassification Must Be Specified If Known," "Annual Declassification Review For Sensitive Information," "Five Category Application Criticality Classification Scheme," and "Information With Multiple Sensitivity Classifications On Single System." A: EMT; E: MH.

436. Three Category Data Classification Scheme

Policy: All Company X information and information entrusted to Company X from third parties falls within one of three sensitivity classifications. If not designated, the default classification is Internal Use Only.

CONFIDENTIAL: Access to this information must be tightly restricted based on the concept of need-to-know. Disclosure requires the information's owner approval and, in the case of third parties, also a signed confidentiality agreement. Examples include employee performance reviews and new product development plans.

INTERNAL USE ONLY: This information must be disclosed only to third parties if a confidentiality agreement has been signed. Disclosure is not expected to cause serious harm to Company X, and access is provided freely to all internal workers via the organization's intranet. Examples include the organizational telephone book and staff automated calendars.

PUBLIC: This information has been explicit approved by the Marketing or Public Relations Department as suitable for public dissemination. Examples include marketing brochures and press releases.

Commentary: This policy is intended to establish a rudimentary data classification scheme suitable for a small or medium sized organization which does not deal with national defense information. The policy is deliberately simple and concise in an effort to minimize costs. The intention of the policy is to create some basic distinctions on which other policies and operational rules can be built. On another note, this policy combines two basic philosophies of access control: for the most sensitive information it uses the "need to know," and for less sensitive information it uses the "need to withhold." A key word search for these terms elsewhere in this book will provide further examples allowing the policy writer to further differentiate the two approaches. Separately, caution is in order because once a data classification system has been adopted, it is very expensive and difficult to change to another system. Accordingly, the policy writer should carefully examine the needs of the organization before adopting a policy like this or a policy such as "Four Category Data Classification Scheme." Classification systems are also used for data criticality, as described in the policy entitled "Five Category Application Criticality Classification Scheme." This policy assumes that the term "information owner" has been defined elsewhere; see the policy entitled "Information Ownership Must Be Assigned." A: EMT; E: LM.

437. Descriptive Prefixes For Data Classification Categories

Policy: Prefixes such as "medical" and "financial" must be used in front of approved data classification categories. These prefixes provide general indicators about the nature of the information and the persons who are authorized to access it.

Commentary: The intention of this policy is to provide greater granularity than standard data classifications provide. If specific information has to do with employee physical examinations, the information might be labeled "MEDICAL -PRIVATE." This will in turn designate that only persons dealing with employee medical matters should be given access to this information. In the absence of further access information, to simply label the information "PRIVATE" does not sufficiently restrict access. Note that these prefixes do not confer any additional protection than the data classification markings themselves provide. In other words, PRIVATE information should be handled a certain way, regardless of the prefix. Ideally specific prefixes are defined in this or a similar policy; alternatively, they may be chosen by the involved information owners. The second of these two options runs the risk of confusing people, especially when synonymous and overlapping terms are used. Also see the policies entitled "Limited Data Classification System Labelling Requirements" and "Choosing Computer Storage Media Data Classifications." A: MT; E: LMH.

438. Trade Secrets Specifically Identified Prior To Disclosure

Policy: As a condition of continued employment at Company X, workers must diligently protect from unauthorized disclosure all Company X information specifically identified as trade secrets. Trade secrets must be identified as such prior to being disclosed to any workers. For Company X internal purposes, trade secrets are classified as SECRET information.

Commentary: The intention of this policy is communicate to workers that Company X has certain types of information which it considers to be trade secrets, and that it expects all workers to diligently protect this information as a condition of continued employment. From a legal standpoint, the policy is also intended to make sure that workers who come in contact with certain highly-sensitive information know that such information is considered to be a trade secret. Because most organizations don't have a separate category in their data classification system for trade secrets, the policy defines where trade secrets fit in with respect to a data classification system ("secret" in the policy provided here). Separately, some organizations go one step further by requiring all new employees to sign a non-disclosure agreement (NDA) that specifies the types of information considered to be a trade secret. On another note, this policy only addresses workers (employees, consultants, contractors, etc.); different arrangements will be required for strategic business partners and other third party organizations. For a related idea, see the policy entitled "Internet Discussion Group Participation And Release Of Trade Secrets." A: E; E: MH.

439. Company X Trade Secrets Must Named & Described On Intranet Page

Policy: All Company X trade secrets are designated by the Chief Legal Counsel. Each of these trade secrets must be identified and very briefly described on the intranet so that workers are notified which types of information deserve special protection.

Commentary: The intention of this policy is to follow United States intellectual property law and to put workers on notice that certain types of information (deemed trade secrets) must get special protection. For example, the chemical formula for Coca-Cola is a trade secret and it is very closely-guarded. The employees of this soft drink bottler know that the information is a trade secret and they accordingly assist in protecting it. These employees know that its continued protection is intimately tied-up with the success of their employer. Before workers can be expected to treat certain information as worthy of special security precautions, they must know what information is in need of these precautions. One way to do this is with an intranet page that makes a list of trade secrets (note that the secrets are not divulged on the intranet, only named there). The preparation and the regular updating of a list of trade secrets can also be an indication that management takes the protection of these types of information seriously, and that a court of law should accordingly extend the special protections related to trade secrets to this information in the event of a dispute. Access to the intranet should be strictly controlled to prevent this list from being used by a corporate spy to identify interesting information to target. Separately, a data classification label should also be used for trade secrets (designations like "top secret" would be appropriate); posting a list to an intranet is probably not sufficient. Be sure to consult legal counsel before adopting a policy such as this. Also see the policies entitled "Internet Discussion Group Participation And Release Of Trade Secrets" and "Form Of Company X Software Distributed To Third Parties." A: M; E: MH.

440. Chief Legal Counsel Is Sole Person To Declare Information A Trade Secret

Policy: Company X's Chief Legal Counsel is the only person authorized to designate any Company X information to be a trade secret.

Commentary: The intention of this policy is to make it clear that a "trade secret" designation can be applied to certain information only after the Chief Legal Counsel has first done a proper analysis of the circumstances. Under United States law, trade secrets (sometimes called "proprietary" information) must be closely held, that is not generally known throughout the organization. Trade secrets must also have proven commercial value, specifically the organization must be able to show that it's exclusive knowledge of a trade secret allows it to make a profit. While in general terms these ideas can readily be understood by any lay person, they have a number of legal nuances associated with them that should really be left to the attorneys.

Note that the designation of certain information as a "trade secret" does not in any way interfere with the application of a data classification label such as "secret." This policy does not prevent an information owner from designating a data classification label, although trade secrets should generally get the highest classification (except in military and diplomatic environments). A data classification designation is separate and distinct from a trade secret designation. Each designation implies different actions to protect the applicable data. Separately, the policy prevents others within the organization from declaring information to be a trade secret when it in fact does not qualify. This policy will thus help keep the organization from spending money on information security that otherwise would be wasted. For related ideas, see the policies entitled "Trade Secrets Specifically Identified Prior To Disclosure" and "Critical Business Logic Must Not Reside On Desktop Computers." A: E; E: MH.

1.3.3.3. Data Classification Marking

441. Limited Data Classification System Labelling Requirements

Policy: All secret, confidential, and private information must be labeled (marked) according to standards issued by the Information Security Department. Information that does not fall into one or more of these categories need not be marked "unclassified." These markings must be maintained whatever technology is used to capture, store, or process the information.

Commentary: The intention of this policy is to clearly state what types of information require a sensitivity label. A label is simply one or a few words indicating the relative sensitivity of data. Thus "secret," "in confidence," and "for internal use only" are typical labels. Separate specifics about how to label information will also be required, although this information can be provided in procedure or standard documents. For example, where to put a label on a computer display, on a tape reel, on a floppy disk, on hardcopy, and other places could be specified in a related standard. The movement of information from one operating system to another can prove to be problematic since sensitivity label information may be stripped off along with file formatting and other operating-system-specific information. For this reason an organization may wish to additionally adopt standards for representing sensitivity labels inside files, for instance in the first line of text files. Separately, this policy presumes the existence of another policy which defines the terms "secret, confidential, and private." These terms may be readily replaced with the labels used within the organization in question. For an example of such a policy, see the policy entitled "Four Category Data Classification Scheme." For another approach to the labelling issue, see the policy entitled "Comprehensive Data Classification System Labelling Requirements." A: EMT; E: MH.

442. Information Treated As Secret Whenever Sensitivity Label Unknown

Policy: If information was obtained from Company X facilities that house secret information, and if no sensitivity label for this information can be determined, the information must be treated as though it is secret. This means that the information must be transported, stored, and destroyed according to policies for secret information.

Commentary: This policy clarifies how to handle information with an unknown or unspecified data classification label. The policy provides a high security approach for dealing with an ambiguous data classification label. Most data classification systems default to "internal use only" or a relatively low level of sensitivity. Unlike these data classification systems, to err on the safe side, this policy defaults to the highest category in a data classification scheme. Without this policy, if a worker were to remove or obfuscate a secret label, then the information would be automatically declassified to a "internal use only" status. This would be likely to result in disclosure to persons who should not have had access to the information. This policy will impose additional costs associated with handling information with an unknown classification, but it will also reduce the number of disclosure mistakes that workers make. The policy is accordingly appropriate for a research lab, a military unit, a diplomatic government agency, or some similarly highly-secure organization. See the policies entitled "Limited Data Classification System Labeling Requirements" and "Four Category Data Classification Scheme." A: E; E: H.

443. Department Specific Data Classification Labels Permissible

Policy: Department-specific data classification labels are permissible but must be consistent with and supplemental to the Company X data classification system.

Commentary: This policy attempts to clarify the circumstances under which it is permissible to employ departmental data classification labels. For example, at a hospital there may be an organization-wide label indicating that information is "private." But within the Archiving Department, additional labels like "private -- psychological" and "private -- financial" may be necessary. The use of the supplemental labels in this case would be consistent with the organization-wide labels, and would thus be acceptable. This policy attempts to prevent departments from coming-up with conflicting or confusing terms which will interfere with the proper handling of the information. In this case, if the Archiving Department were to designate private records as "confidential -- psychological" and "confidential -- financial," this would be a problem and a violation of the policy. Ideally, there would be no supplemental labels necessary, and all workers throughout the organization would use the same data classification labels. For a related idea, see the policy entitled "Department Managers Must Identify Vital Records." A: MT; E: MH.

444. Responsibility For Assigning Data Classification System Labels

Policy: For all existing production information types, the assigned business owner is responsible for choosing an appropriate data classification label. All workers who create, compile, alter, or procure a new type of production information must assign a classification which is consistent with prior designations made by the relevant information owners. If there is any question about the appropriate classification label for new information, the involved owners must be asked to determine an appropriate classification.

Commentary: The intention of this policy is to specify who must choose and apply a data classification label (also known as a marking). The responsibility assignment made in this policy is by no means the only option. Other parties who could be designated as decision-makers include an information originator's department manager and a third party who provided the information. The important objective here is to be clear about who makes the decision. Separately, this policy is appropriate for a research and development lab or other organizations where the staff have significant latitude to make their own decisions. Those organizations not wishing to give staff this much latitude may insist that data classification decisions be made by owners or managers. On another note, for cost-effectiveness reasons, the policy is deliberately limited to production information, but it could be broadened to include all types of information defined in a corporate data dictionary. Note that various types of relatively low sensitivity information may become more sensitive when combined; see the policy entitled "Information Access Control Systems And The Mosaic Theory" for more information. For a related idea, see the policy entitled "Use Of Labels Throughout Sensitive Information's Life Cycle." A: EMT; E: MH.

445. Responsibility For Labelling Externally Provided Information

Policy: With the exception of general business correspondence and copyrighted software, all externally-provided information which is not clearly in the public domain must receive a Company X data classification system label. The Company X worker who receives this information is responsible for assigning an appropriate classification on behalf of the external party. When assigning a Company X classification label, this staff member must preserve copyright notices, author credits, guidelines for interpretation, as well as information about restricted dissemination.

Commentary: The intention of this policy is to clearly specify who must label externally-supplied information which is not in the public domain. The policy goes further, specifying that the labels provided by the external party (such as copyright notices) must not be modified or deleted. The policy could also specify that the Company X recipient is the initial owner of the information, and that over time, the role of information owner may migrate to someone else -- probably the owner of related information. The policy attempts to clarify an area fraught with confusion and ambiguity; in far too many cases, sensitive externally-supplied information is not adequately protected by the recipient organization because responsibility for assigning a data classification system label has not been clearly assigned. This means that subsequent people who come in contact with the information will not handle it properly. Also see the policy entitled "Responsibility For Assigning Data Classification System Labels." A: ET; E: MH.

446. Creator Must Select Data Classification Label For New Files & Messages

Policy: The user who creates computer-files or messages must select one of the approved data classification labels at the time that these files and messages are first saved or sent.

Commentary: The intention of this policy is to get data classification labels on new files and messages from the time that they were created, and to keep these same labels attached to the associated information throughout the information's life cycle (unless of course the classification changes for some reason). If a label is attached at the time that information is created, and perhaps saved as part of the header or title to the file or message, it is much more likely to follow the information as it changes form and location. For example, if an electronic mail message was labeled as confidential when it was first prepared, when the recipient viewed this information he or she would be alerted to the fact that it was confidential. When this same recipient talks to someone else about the information over the phone, the label can and should be propagated with the information. This policy is thus consistent with the notion that information should be protected according to its sensitivity (and criticality and value as well) no matter what technology is used to process it, no matter what form it takes, no matter who comes in contact with it, and no matter where it goes. Note that this policy is inconsistent with other data classification policies which rely on information owners to assign the appropriate classification label. This policy takes the position that new information is being created by people throughout the organization on a continuous basis, and these creators don't have the time or inclination to repeatedly go back to the information owners to get the proper classification. See the policies entitled "Comprehensive Data Classification System Labeling Requirements" and "Information Treated As Secret Whenever Sensitivity Label Unknown." A: E; E: MH.

447. Comprehensive Data Classification System Labelling Requirements

Policy: All tape reels, floppy disks, and other computer storage media containing secret, confidential, or private information must be externally labeled (marked) with the appropriate sensitivity classification.

Commentary: The intention of this policy is to provide guidance for all workers on the need for sensitivity labels. Thus sensitivity labels will be required all of the time. This policy would typically be used by an organization very concerned about the handling of sensitive information. Other organizations will find it onerous and too expensive. Before using this policy, management should determine that the additional costs associated with comprehensive labelling are warranted given the risk of mistakes when information is not labeled. Separately, this policy presumes the existence of a policy which defines the terms "secret, confidential, and private." These terms may be readily replaced with the labels used within the organization in question. For an example of such a policy, see the policy entitled "Four Category Data Classification Scheme." For a less expensive and user-friendlier approach to the labelling issue, see the policy entitled "Limited Data Classification System Labelling Requirements." A: EMT; E: MH.

448. Location On The Page Of Hardcopy Sensitivity Labels

Policy: All printed, handwritten, or other human-readable manifestations of secret, confidential, or private information must have an appropriate sensitivity label (marking) on the upper right hand corner of each page.

Commentary: The intention of this policy is to give all workers guidance on the proper location of sensitivity labels. Some organizations may wish to add additional words about the placement of sensitivity labels (markings) on floppy disk labels and other computer storage media, in which case the scope (and title) of the policy would need to be changed. Note that the last two words in the policy require a label on each page; this helps prevent sensitive information from being mistakenly disclosed when it is copied or excerpted from a larger document. Some organizations will be less restrictive, requiring a classification label on every page only for the most sensitive types of information. Separately, this policy presumes the existence of a policy which defines the terms "secret, confidential, and private." These terms may be readily replaced with the labels used within the organization in question. For an example of such a policy, see the policy entitled "Four Category Data Classification Scheme." A: ET; E: MH.

449. Bound Hardcopy Material And Sensitivity Labels

Policy: When in hardcopy bound form, all printed, handwritten, or other tangible manifestations of secret, confidential, or private information must have an appropriate sensitivity label (marking) on the front cover, the title page, and the rear cover.

Commentary: The intention of this hardcopy-oriented policy is to provide specific guidance on the proper placement of sensitivity-related data classification labels (markings). A label on the title page is also called for, beyond labels on the front and rear covers, because the cover might be defaced, damaged, or missing. In addition, some organizations may wish to state that a label is needed on every page (generally done only for the most sensitive information). The policy could be modified to better reflect an organization's standard hardcopy policy for securely handling information, such as tractor-fed printed pages. Separately, this policy presumes the existence of a policy which defines the terms "secret, confidential, and private." These terms may be readily replaced with the labels used within the organization in question. For an example, see the policy entitled "Four Category Data Classification Scheme." Also see the policy entitled "Nature Of Labels On Hazardous Products And Services." A: ET; E: MH.

450. Labeling & Presentation Of Sensitive Information To Computer Users

Policy: If information is either secret, confidential, or private, all instances in which it is displayed on a screen or otherwise presented to a computer user must involve an indication of the information's sensitivity.

Commentary: The intention of this policy is to provide system developers with guidance about the display of data classification sensitivity labels (markings). This policy may be accompanied by diagrams and examples showing the specific wording to appear, exact screen location, etc. At some organizations, additional information such as instructions about down-loading or copying the sensitive data may also be provided in these examples. This policy presumes the existence of a policy which defines the terms "secret, confidential, and private." These terms may be readily replaced with the labels used within the organization in question. For an example of such a policy, see the policy entitled "Four Category Data Classification Scheme." For a more general but supporting policy, see the policy entitled "Comprehensive Data Classification System Labelling Requirements." Also see the policies entitled "Covering Sensitive Information When Interrupted At Work," "Display And Printing Of Passwords," and "Copyright Notices On Computer Programs And Documentation." A: T; E: MH.

451. Use Of Labels Throughout Sensitive Information's Life Cycle

Policy: From the time when information is created until it is destroyed or declassified, it must be labeled (marked) with a sensitivity designation if it is either secret, confidential, or private.

Commentary: The intention of this policy is to clearly indicate that labels must be attached to sensitive information wherever the information goes, whatever form it takes, and however it is processed. Thus if information previously resident on a departmental server was down-loaded to a microcomputer (PC), the sensitivity label should move with the information. Likewise, access controls should be consistent as the information's form, location, and presentation changes. The absence of proper labels will often prevent sensitive information from being handled appropriately. Thus if "secret" information is apparently "unclassified" (because it is not labeled), it will not be given the security-related handling it warrants. Removing a label can then be an effective way for an unauthorized person to declassify and gain access to sensitive information. Separately, this policy presumes the existence of a policy that defines the terms "secret, confidential, and private." These terms may be readily replaced with the labels used within the organization in question. For an example along these lines, see the policy entitled "Four Category Data Classification Scheme." For a more general but supporting policy, see the policy entitled "Comprehensive Data Classification System Labelling Requirements." A: EMT; E: MH.

452. Maintaining, Propagating, And Reestablishing Data Classification Labels

Policy: Workers in the possession of any information containing a Company X data classification sensitivity label must maintain, propagate, and if need be reestablish this same label whenever the information changes form, format, or handling technology.

Commentary: The intention of this policy is to tell users that they must be diligent when they change the form, format, or technology used to handle sensitive information. For example, assume that information labeled as "confidential" was sent by fax to a remote location. The recipient could then extract certain details from the fax and include these details in an email message. This policy would require that the "confidential" label be included in the email message. Because users are in control of many of the changes in form, format, and handling technology that occur, they must be the ones to make sure that a label continues to be attached to sensitive information (the technology can't do this reliably given the present state-of-the-art in information security). This policy could be expanded to include labels and restrictions provided by third parties such as copyright notices. For related ideas, see the policies entitled "Limited Data Classification System Labeling Requirements" and "Creator Must Select Data Classification Label For New Files & Messages." A: E; E: MH.

453. Labels For Collections Of Information With Various Sensitivities

Policy: When information of various sensitivity classifications is combined, the resulting collection of information must be classified at the most restricted level found anywhere in the sources.

Commentary: The intent of this policy is to guide users in the proper labelling of files, databases, floppy disks, magnetic tapes, CD-ROMs, and other collections of information. Often information with various sensitivities is combined, and users are confused about the label they should apply to the resulting product. This policy uses the military concept of "system high" which states that the resulting collection of information should adopt the highest (most stringent) requirements found amongst the source information. This is consistent with the notion of the mosaic theory, which says that new patterns may emerge when information from various sources are combined. If anything, the mosaic theory may imply that the resulting collection of information should, on occasion, be classified at a level higher than the most restrictive level found amongst the source information. This policy assumes that a classification system is already in place, and that the notion of sensitivity classifications has been communicated to the users. For related ideas, see the policies called "Information Access Control Systems And The Mosaic Theory" and "Information With Multiple Sensitivity Classifications On Single System." A: E; E: MH.

454. New Label After Storage Media Exposure To Secret Data Or Applications

Policy: Any writable computer storage media (floppy disk, magnetic tape, CR-RW, etc.) that has been exposed to secret data or applications must be reclassified at the secret level.

Commentary: This policy instructs users how to label computer storage media with an appropriate data classification after exposure to a secret application or secret data (rather than "secret," the policy writer can use another term for the most sensitive level of a classification system). The policy is necessary in high security environments because writable computer storage media can have temporary files, scratch files, and other work files stored on them, entirely without a user's knowledge. The system may not erase these files, or it may only delete the directory listing for the files (in which case the underlying data is still retrievable from the storage media). This policy makes reference to "exposure" to secret data or secret applications; in this context, "exposure" simply means use on a computer when either secret data or secret applications are active. A non-secret application may be working on secret data, in which case some of the secret data may be recorded on the computer storage media. Likewise, a secret application may store some temporary information on computer media. Separately, even when applications are well-designed (they erase all temporary files), this policy is still applicable because there could be a power outage, a user-initiated interrupt, an operating systems error, or some other problem which prevents the intended erasure from taking place as originally designed. Separately, note that reclassification at a secret level means that special disposal processes for storage media are required. For related ideas, see the policies entitled "Information With Multiple Sensitivity Classifications On Single System" and "Labels For Collections Of Information With Various Sensitivities." A: E; E: H.

455. User-Generated Classification Labels Do Not Bind Company X

Policy: Unless other written agreements have been reached, all information stored on or flowing through Company X information systems is the property of Company X. Sensitivity labels must not be assigned by individuals other than the designated information owner. If other individuals do assign labels, these labels do not in any way restrict Company X's right to access or otherwise use this information.

Commentary: The intention of this policy is to put users on notice that it doesn't matter if they put the word "private" (or some other label) on an email message, or in a file directory name. This material can still be accessed by Company X staff if, for any reason, they deem it necessary (but of course, encryption could be used to defeat the policy). This means that users have no computer-based private domain when they use Company X information systems. The policy thus encourages users to take care of personal matters on computers they have at home or at other locations (perhaps an Internet café). This policy accordingly discourages personal use of Company X information systems. The policy also makes it clear that only an owner can assign a sensitivity label, and that all other sensitivity labels can be ignored without penalty. For related ideas, see the policy entitled "Personal Use Of Computer And Communications Systems" and "Information Ownership And Management's Responsibilities." A: E; E: MH.

1.3.3.4. Classification System Implementation

1.3.3.4.1. Copying And Printing

456. Permission Required When Making Copies Of Sensitive Information

Policy: Making additional copies of, or printing of extra copies of secret, confidential, or private information must not take place without the advance permission of the information owner.

Commentary: The intention of this strict policy is to put on notice all those who come in contact with sensitive information that making unauthorized copies is against policy. Another way to do this would involve the owner (sponsor) as the only one who is permitted to make copies of sensitive materials; however, the owner can, and in most instances will, delegate this activity. An effective way to implement this policy is with paper copies of sensitive information that cannot be copied in an ordinary copy machine. These copies are usually blue or some other color besides white, and are described further in the policy entitled "Special Paper Preventing Copying of Sensitive Documents." The policy shown here is especially important in those cases where sensitive materials must be tracked in a log. For a policy relating to logs, see the policy entitled "Log Book Reflecting Movement Of Secret Documents." The policy shown here presumes the existence of a policy which defines the terms "secret, confidential, and private." These terms may be readily replaced with the labels used within the organization in question. For an example of such a policy, see the policy entitled "Four Category Data Classification Scheme." Also see the policy entitled "Tracking Copies Of Sensitive Information." A: EMT; E: LMH.

457. Tracking Copies Of Sensitive Information

Policy: Whenever additional copies of sensitive information are made, the number of copies and recipients of these copies must be recorded in a log. Each of the recipients must be informed that either further distribution or additional copying may take place only after the information owner's permission has been obtained.

Commentary: The intention of this strict policy is to make sure that all copies of sensitive information can be tracked. This will help with investigations of leaks or other unauthorized disclosures. Maintaining such records also helps foster responsible behavior when it comes to releasing the sensitive information to unauthorized parties, making further copies, destroying the information, etc. The log mentioned in the policy may be kept by the owner or an individual who the owner has designated as an authorized distribution point. The reference to a log in the policy is deliberately vague, since it could be implemented in various ways. For instance, the entire address of each recipient can be made a part of the document itself, or each of the copies can be numbered and a separate record of the recipients can be maintained. In many cases the words "sensitive information" should be replaced with the words "secret information" or some other indicator of the most sensitive type of information in use at the organization in question. See the closely-related policy entitled "Permission Required When Making Copies Of Sensitive Information." For a much more stringent approach, see the policy entitled "Log Book Reflecting Movement Of Secret Documents." A: EMT; E: LMH.

458. Destruction Of Intermediate Products Containing Sensitive Information

Policy: If a copy machine jams or malfunctions when workers are making copies of secret information, they must not leave the machine until all copies of the information are removed from the machine or destroyed beyond recognition.

Commentary: The intention of this policy is to ensure that bits and pieces of sensitive information are not inadvertently disclosed due to machine malfunction or related problems. This might happen when paper containing sensitive information is left in a jammed copy machine and later revealed to unauthorized persons. While the policy refers to copy machines, it can be broadened to include printing presses, fax machines, and other machines which might handle sensitive information. Separately, the scope of this policy may be restricted to the handling of very sensitive information related to internal controls, such as encryption keys. Separately, the policy shown here presumes the existence of a policy which defines the term "secret." This term may be readily replaced with the label(s) used within the organization in question. For an example of such a policy, see the policy entitled "Four Category Data Classification Scheme." A related policy requires that an authorized person be present whenever sensitive information is being transmitted over a fax machine, printed at a printer, etc. See the policies entitled "Prior Notice And Attended Operation For Sensitive Information Faxing" and "Attended Operation Required When Printing Sensitive Information." A: EMT; E: MH.

459. Destruction Of Waste Copies Of Sensitive Information

Policy: All waste copies of secret information that are generated in the course of copying, printing, or otherwise handling such information must be destroyed according to approved procedures.

Commentary: The intention of this policy is to put employees on notice that intermediate products of their work, in this case unacceptable copies, printouts, etc., should be destroyed according to approved procedures (shredding, burning, etc.). Unless otherwise put on notice, some workers may simply put these waste copies in a recycle bin (these copies can still be recycled after they have been shredded). This policy may be adopted only for the handling of sensitive information related to internal controls, such as the handling of encryption keys. Separately, the policy shown here presumes the existence of a policy which defines the term "secret." This term may be readily replaced with the label(s) used within the organization in question. For an example of such a policy, see the policy entitled "Four Category Data Classification Scheme." A related policy involves having an authorized person present whenever sensitive information is being transmitted over a fax machine, printed at a printer, etc. See the policies entitled "Prior Notice And Attended Operation For Sensitive Information Faxing" and "Attended Operation Required When Printing Sensitive Information." A: EMT; E: MH.

460. Attended Operation Required When Printing Sensitive Information

Policy: Printers must not be left unattended if sensitive information is being printed or will soon be printed. The persons attending the printer must be authorized to examine the information being printed. Unattended printing is permitted only if physically access controls are used to prevent unauthorized persons from both entering the area around the printer, and viewing the material being printed.

Commentary: The intention of this policy is to ensure that no unauthorized person examines sensitive printed materials. This is a particular concern when printers are shared among many people, or when the printer is physically located some distance away from the person who originated a printing request. While the policy is intended primarily for use with local area networks, it is also relevant to other computing environments including minicomputers, mainframes, as well as commercial print shops and manufacturing operations. Some organizations will want to augment the policy shown here with words requiring the person initiating the print commands to be responsible for the proper handling of the printed material. Separately, the policy shown here could be rewritten so that the word "sensitive" is replaced with the specific data classification labels used within the organization in question. For an example of such a policy, see the policy entitled "Four Category Data Classification Scheme." For a related policy see the policy entitled "Prior Notice And Attended Operation For Sensitive Information Faxing." A: EMT; E: LMH.

461. Page Numbering and Accountability for Sensitive Information

Policy: All sensitive Company X information manifested in paper form must indicate both the current and the last page (for example, "page X of Y").

Commentary: This policy helps to make sure that none of the sensitive information has gone astray. It also makes sure that readers of this information know they have read the whole document and not just the first part thereof. Likewise, this approach also helps those working in a copy shop or printing department properly account for all pages. The policy is not required for less sensitive types of information because accountability for hardcopy versions of less sensitive information is of less concern to management (and is likely to not be worth the trouble). The procedure described, however, is also extendable to less sensitive documents. On another note, this is an information integrity policy in that it helps to ensure completeness of the information. Separately, the policy shown here could be rewritten so the word "sensitive" is replaced with specific data classification labels used within the organization in question. For an example of such a policy, see the policy entitled "Four Category Data Classification Scheme." Also see the policy entitled "Tracking Copies Of Sensitive Information." A: EMT; E: LMH.

1.3.3.4.2. Shipping And Manual Handling

462. Third Party Non-Disclosure Agreements And Sensitive Information

Policy: Prior to sending any secret, confidential, or private information to a third party for copying, printing, formatting, or other handling, the third party must sign a Company X non-disclosure agreement.

Commentary: The intention of this policy is to define a clear boundary for the movement of sensitive information. Assuming that all Company X workers already have signed confidentiality agreements, the referenced types of information may be passed around inside the organization without further controls. But outsiders generally have not signed confidentiality agreements. Accordingly, these agreements will be required before sensitive internal information is provided to outsiders. The analogy of a moat around a castle is appropriate here. As an example, consider printers (people not machines) who are working on a public company's annual report (prepared for a stock exchange). These printers must sign confidentiality agreements to prevent them from using the information contained in the report to execute insider stock trades. Separately, this policy is relevant to computer data storage media, electronic mail, as well as old-fashioned hardcopy paper. As a result, the policy does not make specific mention of the technology that may be employed, although accompanying explanatory comments may do this. The policy shown here could be rewritten so that the words "secret, confidential, or private" are replaced with specific data classification labels used within the organization in question. For an example of such a policy, see the policy entitled "Four Category Data Classification Scheme." Also see the policy entitled "Confidentiality Agreements Required For All Company X Workers." A: EMT; E: LMH.

463. Disclosure Of Third Party Information In Possession Of Company X

Policy: Company X respects and safeguards the sensitive information which has been entrusted to it by third parties. Company X workers must not disclose this information to other third parties unless the originator of the information has provided advance approval of the disclosure, and unless the receiving party has signed an approved non-disclosure agreement (NDA).

Commentary: With the new business partnerships so prevalent in modern societies, there is often significant cross-organizational sharing of confidential information. Before this sharing of information can take place, originating organizations must feel confident that their information is not going to be disclosed to unknown third parties. To help generate this confidence, this policy makes it clear that Company X is going to require both an NDA and advance approval before any third party is going to get information which has been entrusted to Company X. To make this policy truly effective, it will be necessary to label information so that the originator is readily identifiable, or else provide other facilities (such as a corporate data dictionary) which will allow the originator to be readily identified. For related ideas, see the policies called "Disclosure Of Private Information To Third Parties," "Confidentiality Agreements And Disclosures Of Sensitive Information," and "Waiting Period Prior To External Disclosure Of Requested Information." A: ET; E: LMH.

464. Private And Confidential Information Sent By Internal Or External Mail

Policy: Private and confidential information must be shipped or sent through internal or external mails in a sealed opaque envelope marked "To Be Opened by Addressee Only."

Commentary: The intention of this policy is to give all types of Company X workers specific instructions on the proper way to mark "private and confidential" information sent by various types of mail (except electronic mail). The policy is intended to be used for sensitive information, but not the most sensitive type of information. Secret information may be handled by a separate policy, such as the policy entitled "Secret Information Sent By Internal Or External Mail." An opaque envelope prevents unauthorized people from holding the envelope up to a bright light to read the contents. Also note the use of the word "sealed" to indicate that reusable envelopes are not appropriate for this type of material. It is important that the recipient know if an unauthorized person has examined the involved material as it traveled en route. The policy shown here presumes the existence of a policy which defines the terms "private and confidential." These terms may be readily replaced with comparable label(s) used within the organization in question. For an example of such a policy, see the policy entitled "Four Category Data Classification Scheme." A: EMT; E: LMH.

465. Secret Information Sent By Internal Or External Mail

Policy: Secret information must be shipped or sent through internal or external mails in a sealed opaque envelope marked "To Be Opened By Addressee Only," which is in turn enclosed in a plain outer envelope which does not indicate the sensitivity of the contents.

Commentary: The intention of this policy is to give all types of Company X workers specific instructions on the proper way to mark "secret" information sent by various types of physical mail (except electronic mail). The policy is intended to be used for the most sensitive type of information, but does not apply to less sensitive types of information. "Private and confidential" information may be handled by a separate policy, such as the policy entitled "Private And Confidential Information Sent By Internal Or External Mail." An opaque envelope prevents unauthorized people from holding the envelope up to a bright light to read the contents. The plain outer envelope is intended to present a low-profile approach which is unlikely to draw the attention of those seeking such information. The innocuous words "To Be Opened By Addressee Only" are also a low-profile measure intended to subtly indicate that the contents might be sensitive. Note that there is no indication anywhere on either of the two envelopes of the sensitivity of the contents. For more about the low-profile approach, see the policy entitled "Presentation Of Low-Profile And Secure Image." Also note the use of the word "sealed" to indicate that reusable envelopes are not appropriate for this type of material. It is important that the recipient know if an unauthorized person has examined the involved material as it traveled en route. Separately, the policy shown here presumes the existence of a another policy which defines the term "secret." This term may be readily replaced with the label(s) used within the organization in question. For an example of such a policy, see the policy entitled "Four Category Data Classification Scheme." For a related idea where sensitivity labels are used rather than handling instructions, see the policy entitled "Two Envelopes Required For Sensitive Information Sent By Mail." A: EMT; E: LMH.

466. Two Envelopes Required For Sensitive Information Sent By Mail

Policy: If private, confidential, or secret information is to be sent through internal mail, external mail, or by courier, it must be enclosed in two envelopes or containers (double wrapped). The outside envelope or container must not provide any indication of the sensitivity of the information contained therein. The inside sealed and opaque envelope or container must be labeled "private," "confidential," or "secret," as circumstances warrant.

Commentary: The intention of this policy is to give all types of Company X workers specific instructions on the proper way to mark "private, confidential, or secret" information sent by various types of mail. The policy is intended to be used for all sensitive types of information (as opposed to having separate policies for different classifications of sensitive information). An opaque envelope prevents unauthorized people from holding the envelope up to a bright light to read the contents. The plain outer envelope is intended to present a low-profile approach which is unlikely to draw the attention of those seeking such information. For more about the low-profile approach, see the policy entitled "Presentation of Low-Profile and Secure Image." The policy shown here presumes the existence of a policy which defines the terms "private, confidential, or secret." These terms may be readily replaced with the label(s) used within the organization in question. For an example of such a policy, see the policy entitled "Four Category Data Classification Scheme." For a related idea where specific handling instructions are used rather than sensitivity labels, see the policy entitled "Secret Information Sent By Internal Or External Mail." A: EMT; E: LMH.

467. Permissible Methods For Transmitting Secret Hardcopy Information

Policy: Secret information in hardcopy form must be sent by trusted courier or registered mail. Because they don't allow the information to be tracked, other methods such as regular mail are prohibited.

Commentary: The intention of this policy is to put workers on notice that they must use the most secure transportation methods for "secret" hardcopy information. Special trusted transportation is warranted for the highest classification of sensitive information (whatever its label may be at the organization involved). This policy is intended to be used only for the most sensitive type of information. The policy does not address information held in computer data storage media (disks, tapes, etc.), since that could be encrypted and sent by any transportation method without worry of unauthorized disclosure. This policy does not cover the proper containers for hardcopy secret information since that topic is covered in the policies dealing with labelling; for example, see the policy entitled "Two Envelopes Required For Sensitive Information Sent By Mail." The policy shown here presumes the existence of a policy which defines the term "secret." For an example of such a policy, see the policy entitled "Four Category Data Classification Scheme." A: EMT; E: LMH.

468. Special Paper Preventing Copying Of Sensitive Documents

Policy: When private, confidential, or secret Company X information in hardcopy form must be released to third parties, it must always be distributed exclusively on special paper that cannot be copied using ordinary photocopy machines. All exceptions require the advance approval of the information owner.

Commentary: The intention of this policy is to prevent the receiving parties from making unauthorized copies, which in turn could lead to unauthorized secondary dissemination. Secondary dissemination involves the uncontrolled release of the information to still other unknown parties. For instance, in the early stages of a lawsuit, the opposing side may use discovery proceedings to gain access to certain sensitive internal information. The use of special paper, such as that provided by Nocopi Technologies (Wayne, Pennsylvania, USA), will help ensure that the receiving third party has one and only one copy of the information, which can later be returned to the information owner. The use of special paper also helps to ensure that the copy returned is indeed the copy originally distributed. Of course, there is nothing preventing the third party from reading the information and then re-entering it into a computer, or in some other way creating another version of the original material, which in turn can be copied. This policy does, however, prevent the use of optical character recognition (OCR) technology, not just photocopy technology. The policy is intended to make it considerably more difficult for unauthorized copies to be made. Given the choice of the representation for certain information (floppy disk, CD-ROM, hardcopy paper, etc.), some organizations may wish to distribute information only on paper like this since it is so easy for unauthorized copies to be made with other common data storage media. The policy could be expanded to apply to all hardcopy paper containing sensitive information, whether or not third parties are given copies. One drawback to this wider applicability is that such paper is often somewhat difficult to read (it may have a colored background). The reference to the "information owner" could be changed to refer to the Information Security Manager, the Industrial Security Manager, or the Chief Information Officer (CIO). This policy works best when accompanied by another policy requiring the tracking of all copies containing sensitive information. For example, see the policy entitled "Tracking Copies Of Sensitive Information." Also see the policy entitled "Acceptable Archival Storage Data Media." A: EMT; E: MH.

469. Secret Information May Only Be Printed On Paper Indicating Originals

Policy: Secret company X information may only be printed on paper which will clearly show whether it is an original or a copy. This can achieved with color borders, watermarks, or other technology approved for use by the Information Security Department.

Commentary: This policy is intended to keep all printed secret information exclusively on special paper that indicates it is an authorized original. The copying of secret information is often forbidden except when made with the permission of the owner, and then distribution should be tracked via logs and other mechanisms like acknowledgements of receipt. Because only the owner or his/her delegate should have a computerized version of the secret information, only these authorized parties should be able to generate a copy on special paper. All others, even if they have access to the paper original, will be able to only make paper copies (unless they go to considerable effort or expense). Although not foolproof, this control helps to limit unauthorized distribution of secret information to approved channels. Anyone who obtains a paper copy of secret information will know whether it is an unauthorized copy, and if it is, the recipient should report the situation to the owner (words to this effect can be placed in the document). Of course this owner reporting process is practical only if the document is still within the confines of the organization. Separately, note that the technology used to support this policy is basically the same technology used to prevent copying of currency, travelers checks, and regular checks (drafts). On a separate point, sufficient inventory of this special paper will need to be on hand if this policy is going to be practical (and this paper stock will need to be controlled with physical access controls). For related ideas, see the policies entitled "Log Book Reflecting Movement Of Secret Documents" and "Special Paper Preventing Copying Of Sensitive Documents." A: EMT; E: MH.

470. Delivery Of Sensitive Computer Output To Intended Recipients

Policy: Private, confidential, or secret computer system output must be personally delivered to the designated recipients. Such output should never be delivered to an unattended desk, or left out in the open in an unoccupied office. Alternatively, it may be made available to only the designated recipients via lockers or other physical security methods.

Commentary: The intention of this policy is to specifically instruct workers not to leave sensitive computer output (printouts) in places where unauthorized people could examine it (or steal it). This is especially relevant to environments where there are a lot of people who have access to computer output (for instance from the printers attached to a mainframe). Note that the policy does not prohibit computer operators, data control staff, and other people in a position of trust from handling the output in the normal course of their duties. Separately, the special handling for sensitive information required by this policy of course relies on the existence of appropriate labels printed on the computer output. For a germane idea, see the policy entitled "Use of Labels Throughout Sensitive Information's Life Cycle." The policy shown here presumes the existence of a policy which defines the terms "private, confidential, or secret." For an example of such a policy, see the policy entitled "Four Category Data Classification Scheme." A: T; E: LMH.

471. Delivery Via Courier Of Sensitive Hardcopy Information

Policy: Private, confidential, or secret information in hardcopy form which is sent via courier (United Parcel Service, Federal Express, etc.) must always be tracked with a weigh bill number and must always be marked recipient "signature required."

Commentary: This policy acknowledges the reality of modern business and the reliance on third party shippers such as Federal Express. Knowing how frequently these couriers are used, this policy specifies how sensitive material must be shipped. The weigh bill number allows the sender to find out where the package is and who received it, as well as if it has been received. The signature required designation means that delivery will not be made unless a signature of an authorized person is obtained (in other words it will not be left in a mailbox or on a doorstep where it could be stolen). Some organizations may wish to take this signature required step a little further insisting that only the designated addressee sign for the package (this is rare). Separately, this policy does not address storage media such as floppy disks sent via courier, since they can be encrypted, thereby significantly lowering the risk of transmission. On another note, this policy does not address how to label sensitive information inside a courier's envelope; for that information see a policy such as "Comprehensive Data Classification System Labelling Requirements." A: E; E: LMH.

472. Acknowledgement Required For Deliveries Of Secret Information

Policy: All deliveries of secret information must be conducted such that the recipient formally acknowledges the information has been received.

Commentary: The intention of this policy is to make sure that secret information goes where it is intended to go (to the designated recipient). This process is sometimes called "positive acknowledgement of receipt." The recipient could telephone the sender, could send electronic mail, sign a statement, etc. In really strict environments, the recipient must sign something before receiving it at all. A specific method for acknowledging receipt could be incorporated into the policy, although this diminishes its general applicability. Separately, the policy is also intended to prevent people from subsequently repudiating receipt of the information, thereby denying responsibility for the information's whereabouts. Specific time requirements for acknowledging receipt (such as within 24 hours) may also be mentioned in the policy. This policy complements the policy entitled "Log Book Reflecting Movement Of Secret Documents." The policy presumes the existence of a policy which defines the term "secret." This term may be readily replaced with the label(s) used within the organization in question. For suggested definitions of these labels, see the policy entitled "Four Category Data Classification Scheme." Also see the policies entitled "Immediate Written Acknowledgment Of Receipt For Secret Information" and "Conditions For Acceptance Of Third Party Sensitive Information." A: EMT; E: MH.

473. Immediate Written Acknowledgment Of Receipt For Secret Information

Policy: Recipients of secret Company X information must provide formal written acknowledgement of receipt at the time they take possession of the information. Delivery of such information to intermediaries is prohibited.

Commentary: The intention of this policy is to make sure that secret information goes only where it is intended to go (to the designated recipient) and the movement of the information is accurately tracked with up-to-date records. One common example of this policy in action is the delivery of a legal notice (so called "process serving"); delivery can take place only to the person named on the document. Separately, the written receipt is especially important as a mechanism to stop recipients from later repudiating receipt, perhaps disclaiming responsibility for the information involved. Sending sensitive information through intermediaries may be acceptable so long as it is encrypted or otherwise in some inaccessible form. Accordingly, this policy is most appropriate for, and may be limited to photographs, hardcopy paper, and other human-readable forms of information. This policy complements the policy entitled "Log Book Reflecting Movement Of Secret Documents." The policy presumes the existence of a policy which defines the term "secret." This term may be readily replaced with the label(s) used within the organization in question. For suggested definitions of these labels, see the policy entitled "Four Category Data Classification Scheme." Also see the policy entitled "Acknowledgement Required For Deliveries Of Secret Information." A: EMT; E: MH.

474. Log Book Reflecting Movement Of Secret Documents

Policy: When secret information is involved, a log must be kept reflecting the number of copies made, the location of copies, the names of recipients, the addresses of recipients, and any persons viewing the copies. This log must be maintained as long as such information retains a secret sensitivity classification. This log must also be classified as secret.

Commentary: The intention of this policy is to require that a log be kept for the most sensitive documents (be they labeled with the word "secret" or some other term like "in strict confidence"). The log can be instrumental in determining that all copies have been recovered and/or destroyed, just as it can be helpful when determining who is responsible for a so-called "leak" (unauthorized disclosure). The very existence of a log has a deterrent effect, reminding would-be policy violators that their actions are easily tracked. The policy could be expanded to require all copies to be sequentially numbered, but this was omitted since it is not absolutely necessary. This policy is intended for hardcopy documents, but could be expanded to be applicable to the more modern definition of "document," i.e., a computer file that can include audio, formatting, text, executables, and other types of information. For definitions of sensitivity labels, see the policy entitled "Four Category Data Classification Scheme." For related ideas, see the policies entitled "Permission Required When Making Copies Of Sensitive Information," "Immediate Written Acknowledgment Of Receipt For Secret Information," "Acknowledgement Required For Deliveries Of Secret Information," "Sequence Numbers For Secret Documents," and "Tracking Copies Of Sensitive Information." A: EMT; E: MH.

475. Sequence Numbers For Secret Documents

Policy: All copies of secret documents must be individually numbered with a sequence number to ensure that the persons responsible for the documents and the location of the documents can both be readily tracked.

Commentary: The intention of this policy is to ensure that all secret documents can be readily accounted for and that none will go astray ("fall between the cracks"). By requiring a sequence number, management may require that all secret documents be reflected in a log or described in a disposition report. If two copies with the same number show up, then this can be a tip-off that unauthorized copying has taken place. When this takes place, the person who should have prevented the copying can be readily identified. Likewise, the fabrication of and a subsequent fraud involving secret documents will be made more difficult if sequence numbers are carefully tracked. On another note, if secret information falls into the wrong hands, a sequence number will indicate who's copy it was that was not properly protected; this traceability is a motivator inducing recipients to carefully control access to their own copies. This policy works in conjunction with the policy entitled "Log Book Reflecting Movement Of Secret Documents." A: EMT; E: MH.

476. Those With Custody Of Sensitive Information Must Restrict Access

Policy: Workers in custody of Company X sensitive information must take appropriate steps to ensure that these materials are not available to unauthorized persons. Sensitive information is labeled "confidential" or "secret."

Commentary: The intention of this policy is to clearly state that those who have custody of sensitive materials have a duty to restrict access to these materials. Materials without a label are often by default defined as "for internal use only;" special access restrictions for internal staff are generally unnecessary for these materials. Thus the presence of a classification label can be used to indicate those cases where information is sensitive. On another point, the policy is deliberately vague about the ways to restrict access since these will vary by situation. Separately, it is important to note that being in custody of sensitive materials is different than being a "custodian" as defined in the policy entitled "Security Responsibilities Of Information Custodians." For a related idea see the policy entitled "Handling Hardcopy Sensitive Information Off Company X Premises." A: E; E: LMH.

1.3.3.4.3. Transmission By Fax And Phone

477. Prior Notice And Attended Operation For Sensitive Information Faxing

Policy: If secret information is to be sent by fax, the recipient must first have been notified of the time when it will be transmitted, and also have agreed that an authorized person will be present at the destination machine when the material is sent. An exception will be made if the area surrounding the fax machine is physically restricted such that persons who are not authorized to see the material being faxed may not enter.

Commentary: One often-encountered scenario for inadvertent disclosure involves sensitive materials that have been sent by fax but not yet picked up by the intended recipient. The objective of this policy is to ensure that no unauthorized person examines sensitive faxed materials. Separately, if the recipient knows the fax is coming, he or she will (hopefully) get concerned if it doesn't arrive when scheduled. The recipient in this case can initiate an investigation to determine where the information went (or if it went). Note that this policy is not especially strict; a stricter approach is provided by the policy entitled "Faxing Sensitive Information Requires Human Presence." On a different note, the policy shown here presumes the existence of a policy which defines the term "secret." This term may be readily replaced with the label(s) used within the organization in question. For an example of such a policy, see the policy entitled "Four Category Data Classification Scheme." Also see the policies entitled "Destination Physical Security For Sensitive Information Faxing," "When Faxing Sensitive Information Is Permissible," "Logs Of All Inbound And Outbound Faxes," and "Attended Operation Required When Printing Sensitive Information." A: E; E: LMH.

478. Faxing Sensitive Information Requires Human Presence

Policy: Sensitive materials must not be faxed unless at least one of the following conditions prevail at the receiving site: (1) an authorized staff member is on hand to properly handle the materials, or (2) a password protected fax mailbox is used to restrict unauthorized release of the materials.

Commentary: One often-encountered scenario for inadvertent disclosure involves sensitive materials that have been sent by fax, but not yet picked up by the intended recipient. This policy requires that human presence or a password protected fax mailbox be used to prevent such unauthorized disclosures. With respect to the first option, the policy could be modified to require the sending party to confirm the presence of an authorized staff member via telephone in advance of transmission. A still more strict approach would be to prohibit the faxing of sensitive information unless both the sending and receiving machine employ encryption (systems like this are available from Jones Futurex, Sacramento, California, USA). Also see the policy entitled "Prior Notice And Attended Operation For Sensitive Information Faxing." A: E; E: LMH.

479. Faxing Sensitive Information Via Untrusted Third Parties

Policy: Sensitive Company X information must not be faxed via untrusted intermediaries (hotel staff, rented mailbox store staff, etc.).

Commentary: While this policy may at first seem obvious to the cynical security-oriented individual, the idea behind it often escapes most workers. They may be travelling for business, pressed for time, and not really thinking about the people who may be exposed to sensitive information. The policy could be expanded to include preferred methods for sending the information (perhaps by courier). The use of encryption is irrelevant here because intermediaries can examine the information in hardcopy form. For related ideas, see the policies entitled "Prior

Notice And Attended Operation For Sensitive Information Faxing" and "Faxing Sensitive Information Requires Human Presence." A: E; E: LMH.

480. Cover Sheet Receipt Confirmation Before Faxing Sensitive Information

Policy: When sensitive information must be faxed, a cover sheet must first be sent and acknowledged by the recipient. After this is performed, the sensitive information may be sent via another call occurring immediately thereafter.

Commentary: The intention of this policy is to make sure that sensitive information is being faxed to the correct fax machine. The policy helps prevent unauthorized call forwarding from interfering with the intended fax communication path. Also, with so many fax machines in use these days, the chance that a wrong number would make connection with another fax machine is quite high. In past years, a wrong number would in most instances be readily identified because the fax would not go through (the receiving number would generally be a voice rather than a fax line). Another intention of this policy is to make sure that an authorized party is on-hand and actually watching the destination fax machine; this helps prevent unauthorized parties from viewing the sensitive faxed material. Confirming that an authorized recipient is on-hand is also desirable in case the fax goes astray during the second outbound call; in this case, the recipient will call and ask why the fax has not yet been sent. For especially conservative organizations, this policy could be augmented with another sentence requiring the recipient to confirm receipt of the second transmission. Likewise, conservative organizations can insist that the sender simply press a redial button on the fax machine rather than entering the numbers again (thus ensuring that no mistakes are made). Separately, the policy is quiet about how the destination party acknowledges receipt; this could occur on a separate line, on the fax line itself, or by other means such as a pager. See the policies entitled "When Faxing Sensitive Information Is Permissible" and "Faxing Sensitive Information Requires Human Presence." A: E; E: LMH.

481. When Faxing Sensitive Information Is Permissible

Policy: Sensitive information may be faxed over unencrypted lines only when both: (1) time is of the essence, and (2) no alternative and higher-security transmission methods are available. To assure that the sensitive information is not disclosed to unauthorized parties, in these instances, voice contact with the receiving party must be established immediately prior to transmission.

Commentary: The objective of this policy is to put staff on notice that sensitive information should not be faxed over unencrypted lines on a regular basis. If there is a need for regular transmission of sensitive information, then workers should request encrypting fax machines (note that some international export restrictions may apply to encryption technology). The policy shown here may also include words requiring confirmation of receipt of a fax that includes sensitive information. Transmission to an attended stand-alone fax machine may be preferable to transmission to a fax server, if that server does not have adequate access controls and if it may be readily-accessed by a number of people. This distinction may be stated explicitly in the policy. See the policy entitled "Prior Notice And Attended Operation For Sensitive Information Faxing." A: E; E: MH.

482. Destination Physical Security For Sensitive Information Faxing

Policy: Secret or confidential information must NOT be sent to an unattended fax machine unless the destination machine is in a locked room for which the keys are possessed only by people authorized to receive the information.

Commentary: The intention of this policy is to ensure that no unauthorized person examines sensitive faxed materials. By physically restricting access, unauthorized persons are prevented from seeing "secret or confidential" faxes. Notice that this policy says nothing about notification of the recipient, as is done in the policy entitled "Prior Notice And Attended Operation For Sensitive Information Faxing." The policy shown here presumes the existence of a policy which defines the terms "secret" and "confidential." For a policy showing definitions for such terms, see the policy entitled "Four Category Data Classification Scheme." Also see the policy entitled "Attended Operation Required When Printing Sensitive Information." A: E; E: LMH.

483. Encryption Required For Sending Secret Information By Fax

Policy: Secret information must NOT be sent by facsimile (fax) unless the transmission is encrypted using methods approved by Company X's Information Security Department.

Commentary: Encryption, also known as encoding or scrambling, prevents sensitive information from being revealed to wiretappers and others who may have access to it as it travels by common carriers. At the destination, the information can be decrypted, or recovered by reversing the encryption process. Thus, even though the transmission is encrypted, the information coming out of a destination fax machine will be readable to any person who happens to be present when the fax is received. To prevent this, other controls such as a password to print a fax will be required. Policies like "Destination Physical Security For Sensitive Information Faxing" may also be used. The intention of this policy is to thwart fax transmission wiretapping which is reportedly becoming more prevalent. It is relatively easy to place a wiretap, record a fax transmission, and later play it back into another fax machine to generate readable hardcopy. If this were done, neither the sender nor the recipient would be aware that a wiretap has taken place. This comment is equally true of the new faxing services that use the Internet rather than dial-up lines. Separately, the policy shown here presumes the existence of a policy which defines the term "secret." For a policy showing recommended definitions for terms like this, see the policy entitled "Four Category Data Classification Scheme." Also see "Secret Information Sent By Electronic Mail" and "Treat Electronic Mail As Public Communications." A: E; E: H.

484. Password Required For Sending Secret Information By Fax

Policy: Secret information must not be sent by facsimile (fax) unless a password is successfully provided by the receiving machine prior to the initiation of a transmission.

Commentary: The intention of this policy is to make sure that the correct fax machine has been reached. There have been quite a number of reported cases where sensitive faxes were sent to the wrong machine. In one case involving Cenith Partners and Ionics Inc., a "top-secret" merger and acquisition document was mistakenly sent to the Wall Street Journal, which subsequently printed an article about it (see the 20 December 1988 issue). Note that only the more expensive and more modern fax machines provide the ability to confirm connection to the right destination via passwords. Two compatible machines, each supporting passwords, are likely to be required. This in turn will reduce the number of machines to which secret faxes can be sent. Other passwords for printing faxes may also be required. Also see the policy entitled "Destination Physical Security For Sensitive Information Faxing." The policy shown here presumes the existence of a policy which defines the term "secret." For a policy showing recommended definitions for terms like this, see the policy entitled "Four Category Data Classification Scheme." Also see the policies entitled "Fax Cover Sheet Must Contain Restricted Dissemination Notice" and "Logs Of All Inbound And Outbound Faxes." A: E; E: MH.

485. Fax Cover Sheet Must Contain Restricted Dissemination Notice

Policy: All outgoing Company X faxes must include a cover sheet that has been approved by the manager of the Information Systems Department.

Commentary: This policy is intended to be responsive to the significant number of faxes which are mistakenly sent to the wrong number. Not only can this involve entering the wrong telephone number on the fax machine, it may also involve telephone system malfunctions, internal mail systems that misdeliver faxes, or monitoring by telephone company technicians. The reason for a standard cover sheet is to make sure that certain legal words precede all outbound faxes. Typically such a cover sheet includes a notice that the transmission is for use only by the intended individual or entity. This notice may also state that if the reader of the fax is not the intended recipient, then usage, dissemination, distribution, or copying of the information is strictly prohibited. The notice may go on to request that the sender be notified if the fax has been sent elsewhere besides the intended destination. The notice can be supplemented with words requesting the return of a misdirected fax at the sending party's expense. Separately, the words in the notice should be worked out with internal legal counsel. The policy shown above gives the greatest flexibility in that the words on the cover can be changed without the need to change the policy itself. Changes in the words on the cover will be necessary as the legal and business status of faxes evolves over time. For a related idea see the policy entitled "Password Required For Sending Secret Information By Fax." Also see the policy entitled "Warnings Required If Recipients Might Be Offended or Upset." A: E; E: MH.

486. Binding Signatures Must Be Sent By Traditional Paper Means

Policy: Because the law lags behind technology, many courts do not recognize faxed signatures as legally binding. Accordingly, all signatures on contracts, purchase orders and other important legally-binding documents provided by third parties must be in traditional paper form.

Commentary: The intention of this policy is to make sure that Company X is able to provide adequate evidence to demonstrate the existence of legally-binding agreements such as purchase orders. If agreements are only in fax form, some judges will claim this is insufficient evidence. Nothing in this policy prevents workers from obtaining a fax with signatures as a preliminary document, to be followed soon thereafter by signatures in traditional paper form. This two phase approach allows work to get underway immediately, with the paper documents being only a legal formality that is sent later. This policy is by implication also relevant to electronic mail and other forms of modern business communication, not just fax. Because the policy is more broadly applicable, some organizations may wish to replace the words "faxed signatures" in the first sentence with the words "signatures in non-paper form." Note that certain jurisdictions, such as the State of Utah, are increasingly recognizing digital signatures and digital certificates (both the result of cryptoprocesses) as legally binding. On a separate note, the policy focuses on signatures from third parties; to provide the maximum flexibility, it is deliberately silent about signatures from internal workers meeting these same criteria. For a related idea, see the policy entitled "Formation Of Binding Contracts Via Electronic Systems." A: E; E: LMH.

487. Discussion Of Secret Information And Use Of Speaker Phones

Policy: Secret information must not be discussed on speaker-phones unless all participating parties first acknowledge that no unauthorized persons are in close proximity such that they might overhear the conversation.

Commentary: The intention of this policy is to prevent the unauthorized disclosure of secret information when using speaker phones. All too often speaker phones are used in open offices (that use partitions rather than walls), lobbies, or in other locations where passers-by can overhear the conversation. This scope of this policy may be expanded to apply to teleconferences as well as speaker-phone conversations. Encryption of the phone lines is also advisable in many circumstances where secret information is being discussed. To be in compliance with this policy, at the beginning of a conversation, the parties to a conversation involving secret information can affirm that their location does not have unauthorized persons nearby. Alternatively, if a regular phone conversation is initiated, and later in this conversation it becomes necessary to discuss secret information, then the affirmation mentioned above can take place. Separately, the policy shown here presumes the existence of another policy that defines the term "secret." For a policy showing recommended definitions for terms like this, see the policy entitled "Four Category Data Classification Scheme." Also see the policy entitled "Leaving Sensitive Information On Answering Machines." A: E; E: MH.

488. Guarded Terms For Telephone Discussions Of Sensitive Information

Policy: Telephone lines may be tapped or otherwise intercepted by unauthorized parties. Accordingly, workers should take steps to avoid discussing sensitive information when on the telephone. If discussion of such information is absolutely required, workers must use guarded terms and refrain from mentioning sensitive details beyond those needed to get the job done.

Commentary: The objective of this policy is to put employees on notice that the phones may be tapped or otherwise intercepted, and to caution them not to discuss sensitive information if at all possible. Some organizations may wish to provide an example or two showing what is meant by "guarded terms." In this context, tricks like the use of codewords or nicknames can also be mentioned. The policy could be expanded to include mention of videoconferencing facilities, which are often unencrypted and likewise subject to interception. This policy assumes that an organization has already defined the term "sensitive" via a policy like "Four Category Data Classification Scheme." A: E; E: MH.

489. Use Of Cordless Or Cellular Telephones For Secret Discussions

Policy: Unless voice-line encryption gear approved by the Information Security Department is used, secret Company X information must NEVER be discussed on cordless or cellular telephones.

Commentary: The intention of this policy is to prevent the unauthorized disclosure of sensitive information. A number of highly publicized cases make it clear that it is easy and inexpensive to intercept such conversations broadcasted on the air waves. This is a particularly important policy to communicate to top management, who often have such phones, who often don't really understand the technology involved, and who often discuss secret matters. The scope of this policy can be expanded to incorporate other wireless networks such as personal communications services (PCS), personal digital assistants (PDAs) with wireless capabilities, alphanumeric pagers, wireless LANs, specialized mobile radio systems, ham radio networks, wireless packet networks, and satellite/VSAT (very small aperture terminal) networks. The term "secret" can be replaced with specific in-house data classification terms like "restricted" and "proprietary." For a policy showing recommended definitions for terms like these, see the policy entitled "Four Category Data Classification Scheme." Also see the policy entitled "Leaving Sensitive Information On Answering Machines." A: E; E: MH.

490. Secret Discussions On Wireless Microphones And Radio Networks

Policy: To prevent unauthorized interception, wireless microphones, walkie-talkies, radio local area networks (LANs), radio personal computer docking systems, and other unencrypted radio transmissions must never be used for the transmission of secret information.

Commentary: The motivation for this policy is obscure to a number of people, and for this reason the first four words of the policy have been added to help to create a motivation. Interception of radio transmissions is quite easy these days and all sorts of useful details (including telephone numbers, user-IDs, and passwords) can be obtained thereby. This policy puts users on notice that they must not use these types of technology, unless they know the transmissions are encrypted. Unfortunately, encryption is unavailable for a number of these systems (such as lavaliere microphones used by public speakers), so prohibition against the use of these systems for secret information is the only option. Note that the policy deliberately avoids a discussion about the transmission protocol (spread spectrum technology for example), and it avoids discussion of which frequency range the transmissions occur in (it is easier to intercept some ranges than others); all this information is considered too esoteric for users to understand and digest. This policy assumes the word "secret" has been clearly defined elsewhere. See the policies entitled "Electromagnetic Radiation (Emanation) Protection For Secret Systems" and "Use Of Cordless Or Cellular Telephones For Secret Discussions." A: ET; E: MH.

491. Internet Telephone Facilities May Not Be Used For Secret Discussions

Policy: Unless they are known to be encrypted, Internet telephone facilities must not be used for the transmission of secret Company X information.

Commentary: The intention of this policy is to get users who are employing Internet phone services to think about the nature of the information being transmitted, and if needed, to transmit secret information through other more secure channels. Internet phone services are becoming quite popular in large measure because they are inexpensive. At the same time, conversations that travel this way are sent through unknown machines managed by people who may or may not be monitoring transmissions. These transmissions could be recorded and later reviewed if the correspondent identities or other circumstances seem interesting. Separately, this policy assumes that the word "secret" has been clearly defined elsewhere, generally in a data classification policy. See the policies entitled "Guarded Terms For Telephone Discussions Of Sensitive Information" and "Monitoring Or Recording Telephone Conversations." A: ET; E: MH.

1.3.3.4.4. Movement Of Confidential Information

492. Secondary Dissemination Of Secret Information

Policy: Secret information must only be disclosed after the information owner's explicit authorization has been obtained. If an individual has been granted access to secret information, this does not imply the authority to disclose it to other persons.

Commentary: The intention of this policy is to prevent people who are in receipt of secret information from passing it to others when they don't have permission from the information owner. Thus, people in receipt of secret information do not inherit the right to disseminate it further. Since this notion is contrary to common practice (gossip for instance), there is often need for a specific policy. Another way to look at this policy is: the delegation of the authority to disclose secret information must be done explicitly, and in the absence of specific authorization to disclose the information, it has not been granted. This policy assumes the term "information owner" has been previously defined. For more about owners, see the policy entitled "Information Ownership And Management's Responsibilities." The word "secret" could be replaced by "sensitive" or a set of specific sensitive information classifications used by the organization in question. The policy assumes that the term "secret" has already been defined. For a policy showing recommended definitions for terms like this, see the policy entitled "Four Category Data Classification Scheme." Also see the policies entitled "Confidentiality Agreements And Disclosures Of Sensitive Information" and "Specific Handling Instructions For Recipients Of Sensitive Information." A: EMT; E: LMH.

493. Travelling On Public Transportation With Secret Information

Policy: Unless specific management approval has been granted, workers must avoid travelling on public transportation when in the possession of secret Company X information.

Commentary: The intention of this policy is to prevent secret information from falling into the wrong hands. A briefcase could be stolen, other passengers might look at the information when the involved worker is examining it, etc. This means that planes, trains, trolleys, busses, and the like must not be used when in possession of secret information. This also means that secret information will be less likely to be taken out of the office or places where it is stored; reducing the movement of such information lessens the probability that it will go astray. This very strict policy involves a tradeoff: the flexibility of working times and locations may be indirectly restricted as a result of this policy. Accordingly, telecommuters and employees who wish to work at home may have a problem with this policy. This does not mean that all work outside the office must be brought to a halt -- the solution can be to remove from the office only that information which is not secret. Separately, another option would be to encrypt all secret information when outside the office or other physically protected areas. On another note, the word "secret" could be replaced by "sensitive" or a set of data classification terms used by the organization in question. The policy assumes that the term "secret" has already been defined. For a policy showing recommended definitions for terms like this, see the policy entitled "Four Category Data Classification Scheme." For related ideas, see the policies entitled "Transportable Computers Must Be Hand Luggage On Airplanes," "Transportation Of Secret Data In Computer-Readable Storage Media," and "Removal Of Sensitive Information From Company X Premises." A: ET; E: MH.

494. Exposure Of Sensitive Information In Public Places

Policy: Secret, confidential, or private Company X information must not be read, discussed, or otherwise exposed on airplanes, restaurants, public transportation, or in other public places.

Commentary: The intention of this relatively-liberal policy is to help prevent the unauthorized disclosure of sensitive information. With the pressure to perform that so many employees face, it is not uncommon for them to work while sitting on a bus, an airplane, etc. Often they work with sensitive information. The policy seeks to prevent other travelers from looking over their shoulder on an airplane, read the material while using the same table at a restaurant, or in some other way being exposed the material. The policy does not address those circumstances where the information might be left behind in a hotel room, might be stored in a stolen briefcase, or otherwise goes astray. To address these circumstances, see the more strict policy entitled "Travelling On Public Transportation With Secret Information." In the policy given here, the adjective "sensitive" might be used instead of "secret, confidential, or private." The policy assumes that a data classification policy explaining these terms has been issued. For a policy showing recommended definitions for terms like this, see the policy entitled "Four Category Data Classification Scheme." Also see the policy entitled "Positioning Of Computer Display Screens With Respect To Windows." A: EMT; E: LMH.

495. Secret Information Discussions In Company X Administrative Areas

Policy: All company X offices have been divided into two separate areas referred to as administrative areas and secure areas. Administrative areas include corridors, cafeterias, visitor reception areas, and restrooms. Secure areas are those offices, data centers, and laboratories which are restricted by badge readers and/or other access control systems. Workers must not discuss secret information in administrative areas because these areas are likely to include persons who have not been expressly authorized to receive this information.

Commentary: The intention of this policy is to clarify where secret information may be discussed within the confines of Company X facilities. Far too many workers think that once they are on Company X premises, they can discuss anything they want, no matter how sensitive the information may be to the organization. The policy thus emphasize the distinction between those people who are authorized to receive secret information and those who are not. The policy should be used in conjunction with a data classification system, which can be employed to restrict worker access to information based on a label. This policy goes beyond the policy entitled "Exposure Of Sensitive Information In Public Places" in that it covers exposure of sensitive information within the confines Company X facilities. For related considerations, see the policies entitled "No Discussions Of Private Information In Public Places" and "Use Of Cordless Or Cellular Telephones For Secret Discussions." A: E; E: H.

496. Storing Secret Information On Transportable Computers

Policy: Workers in the possession of portable, laptop, notebook, palmtop, and other transportable computers containing secret Company X information must not leave these computers unattended at any time unless the secret information has been encrypted.

Commentary: The intention of this policy is to prevent secret information from falling into the hands of unauthorized persons. It has become a standard industrial espionage technique for spies to steal the transportable microcomputers (PCs) of executives. Encryption of the data held on the hard drive is the only definitive way to prevent this disclosure. Ideally, everything on the hard drive would be encrypted and the user would have to provide a password to gain access to the data (both at the time a session begins and after a certain period of inactivity). A number of low cost products on the market support this policy. The large number of very small computers available makes this policy increasingly appropriate. Nonetheless, for the very smallest systems (such as handhelds), there may be no commercially-available encryption systems; until such products are available, it may be necessary to keep secret information off these systems. The word "secret" in the policy could be replaced by "sensitive" or a set of data classification terms used by the organization in question. This policy assumes the term "secret" has already been defined. For a policy showing recommended definitions for terms like this, see the policy entitled "Four Category Data Classification Scheme." For a policy dealing with hardcopy sensitive information, see the policy entitled "Handling Hardcopy Sensitive Information Off Company X Premises." Also see the policies entitled "Transportable Computers Must Be Hand Luggage On Airplanes" and "Encrypting Backup Media Stored Off-Site." A: EMT; E: MH.

497. Controls For Transportable Computers With Sensitive Information

Policy: All portables, laptops, notebooks, and other transportable computers containing sensitive Company X information must consistently employ both hard disk encryption for all files as well as boot protection.

Commentary: The intention of this policy is to protect the sensitive information stored on transportable computers. These machines are often stolen, lost, or otherwise unaccounted for.

Unfortunately, when this happens, the information stored on the hard disk drives in these machines is also unaccounted for. While the cost of the hardware and software packages is often significant, this most often pales when compared to the cost of the information stored on these machines. The only truly reliable method to protect this information when the machines are unattended is to encrypt information on the hard disk drive. This policy requires that all files be encrypted when stored on the hard drive. Background encryption of all files makes the encrypt/decrypt process a system function rather than something that the user must get involved with. This means that user error (such as forgetting to encrypt a sensitive file) is not going to be a potential problem. Unfortunately, this approach also imposes a performance penalty. This policy goes further by requiring that a password be provided at the time the machine is turned on (so-called "boot protection"). In most instances the two controls mentioned in this policy will need to be acquired as separate hardware or software systems, and will not be native functions of the operating system. For a less strict but less effective approach, see the policy entitled "Storing Secret Information On Transportable Computers." A: EMT; E: MH.

498. Transportable Computers Must Be Hand Luggage on Airplanes

Policy: Workers in the possession of portable, laptop, notebook, palmtop, and other transportable computers containing sensitive Company X information must not check these computers in airline luggage systems. These computers must remain in the possession of the traveler as hand luggage.

Commentary: The objective of this policy is to prevent the theft/loss of transportable computers containing sensitive information. Numerous thefts from airline passenger luggage make it dangerous to check a computer with one's luggage (even if it is packed inside the luggage). Many bags are misdirected or lost when entrusted to the airlines. Keeping the machine in one's possession is a less risky approach. This policy is unnecessary if all user information on the computer's hard drive and accompanying storage media (CD-ROMs, floppy disks, etc.) is encrypted. But even with encryption the financial impact of replacing the hardware could be significant. Some organizations may want to augment the policy to allow an exception to this approach whenever such encryption processes are being used. Also see the policy entitled "Storing Secret Information On Transportable Computers." A: EMT; E: LMH.

499. Taking Secret Information Into A Foreign Country

Policy: Whenever secret information is carried by a Company X worker into a foreign country, the information must either be stored in some inaccessible form (such as an encrypted floppy disk) or must remain in the worker's possession at all times.

Commentary: The intention of this policy is to prevent foreign intelligence agents from obtaining secret information. According to the front page of The Wall Street Journal, 17 June 1991, many foreign governments routinely collect industrial secrets for the benefit of foreign companies. It is not advisable for such information to be left in hotel rooms unless it is in encrypted form. Practically speaking, to keep information in the worker's possession at all times is onerous; accordingly, encryption should be provided for all secret information stored on a computer. Storage of secret information on paper is less desirable because it can easily be photocopied, photographed, scanned with an optical character recognition wand, etc. The word "secret" could be replaced by "sensitive" or a set of sensitive data classifications used by the organization in question. The policy assumes that the term "secret" has already been defined. For a policy showing recommended definitions for terms like this, see the policy entitled "Four Category Data Classification Scheme." Also see the policy entitled "Instructions For Handling Sensitive Information Off Company X Premises." A: EM; E: MH.

500. Permission Required To Take Secret Information Into Foreign Country

Policy: Company X workers must not take secret Company X information into another country unless permission has first been obtained from the Industrial Security Manager.

Commentary: The purpose of this policy is to prohibit the unauthorized transportation of secret information into another country. A change of country brings a new set of laws under which industrial espionage may be legal or at least tolerated. As is mentioned in the policy entitled "Taking Secret Information Into A Foreign Country," many foreign country governments routinely engage in espionage on behalf of domestic companies. Organizations may also face troubles in their attempts to assert legal rights in another country. This policy attempts to prevent these types of problems. If secret information doesn't go into those countries, it will stand a much lower chance of going astray. A policy like this can be found in many military organizations, but is equally applicable to the private sector. The word "secret" is a placeholder, and can be replaced by the comparable words in use in the organization in question. The reference to the "Industrial Security Manager" could be changed to the Information Security Manager, or another manager who would know the relevant laws and risks. Separately, note that the policy is absolute -- it does not mention the form that the information takes (encrypted, protected by a password, etc.). A significant problem for many companies, particularly high-tech companies, has been the hiring of workers of foreign nationality who in turn take secret or proprietary Company X information back to their own countries. While this policy cannot prevent this activity, it can make it clear that such information is not to be removed from the country of origin. This policy may be difficult to implement for multinational companies which move secret information around the world in the normal course of their business. Also see the policies entitled "Handling Hardcopy Sensitive Information Off Company X Premises" and "Foreign Nationals Prohibited From Working On Information Systems." A: E; E: MH.

501. Floppy Disk Input/Output Encryption Drivers Prevent Disclosure

Policy: Company X has adopted a floppy disk management policy in which floppies are authorized, formatted, and issued only by the Information Technology Department. Information stored on these disks can be read only by Company X personal computers, and only Company X personal computers can write intelligible information to these disks without reformatting the disks. Each individual to whom one or more of these disks is issued is accountable for its safekeeping and return upon the termination of employment.

Commentary: The intention of this policy is to prevent workers from storing sensitive information on floppy disks and then walking out the door with these same floppies. In most offices, floppy disks remain the most portable and most easily removed data storage media. At most organizations, sensitive information stored on a floppy disk by a work computer will probably be readable on another computer at home (assuming the home computer is personally owned and managed). This policy makes use of custom encryption software which has been integrated with the floppy disk input and output drivers, such that each time a write-to or read-from floppy disk command is executed, the relevant encryption process is automatically invoked. These same disks are therefore unreadable by computers outside the organization (but they could be reformatted, in which case the sensitive data will be lost). Separately, if a user wanted to send information to an outside party via floppy disk, the intervention of the Information Technology Department would be required. Software could be entirely loaded from the Internet or from CD-ROM (the capacity of floppies is too small for major software packages these days). Other complimentary controls like outbound electronic mail content filters are recommended if this approach is adopted. For related ideas, see the policies entitled "Computer Storage Media Must Have A Pass When Leaving Premises" and "Special Paper Preventing Copying Of Sensitive Documents." A: E; E: H.

502. Removal Of Sensitive Information From Company X Premises

Policy: Sensitive Company X information may not be removed from Company X premises unless there has been prior approval from the information's owner. This policy includes portable computers with hard disks, floppy disks, hard-copy output, paper memos, and the like. An exception is made for authorized off-site backups.

Commentary: The intention of this policy is to prevent sensitive information from travelling around, and in the process being disclosed in unauthorized ways. The more information stays in one place, the easier it is to track and control. Note that this policy may restrict the activities of telecommuters and employees who wish to take work home with them. If such sensitive information routinely travels over computer networks, it may be difficult to identify its location at any particular point in time; in these cases, this policy will be difficult to implement and is most often inappropriate. On another note, this policy assumes the term "owner" has been previously defined. For more about owners, see the policy entitled "Information Ownership And Management's Responsibilities." Separately, this policy assumes that a data classification system has already been adopted. The word "sensitive" could be replaced by one or several data classification terms used by the organization in question. For a policy showing recommended definitions for terms like this, see the policy entitled "Four Category Data Classification Scheme." Also see the policies entitled "Log For Sensitive Information Removed From Company X Premises," "Provision Of Lockable Metal Furniture To Staff Working At Home," and "Recovery Of Computer-Related Property Belonging To Company X." A: EMT; E: MH.

503. Secret Information Must Not Leave Company X Offices In Any Form

Policy: Secret Company X information, no matter what form it happens to take, must not leave Company X offices unless the approval of the Information Security Manager has first been obtained.

Commentary: The objective of this policy is to ensure that workers do not take secret information home to work on it, do not carry it with them when they travel on business, or in any other way subject it to unauthorized disclosure because they took it away from Company X premises. This is a strict isolationist policy that requires the intervention of the Information Security Manager before such transportation takes place. Under this policy, this Manager could grant certain exceptions to the policy if the individual in question promises to use adequate security measures including floppy disk encryption software and password-based boot controls on portable computers. Note that these security measures are deliberately not specified in the policy so that they can change over time without the need to change the policy. This policy also provides an opportunity to respond to the risks of each type of secret information with a different set of controls. Separately, if the organization in question is participating in extranets or similar multi-organizational networks, then this policy is impractical and should be replaced with a policy specifying the ways to protect secret information when it is away from Company X premises. For ideas along these lines, see the policies entitled "Handling Hardcopy Sensitive Information Off Company X Premises," "Securing Sensitive Information In Unattended Rooms," and "Workers Must Show Contents Of Luggage When Leaving Premises." A: E; E: H.

504. Log for Sensitive Information Removed From Company X Premises

Policy: Whenever sensitive information must be removed from Company X premises, a record of the date, the information involved, and the persons possessing the information must be made.

Commentary: The intention of this policy is to keep track of all sensitive information that has been taken from Company X premises. Such records will assist with investigations following a "leak" or other unauthorized disclosures. The fact that such records are kept will also discourage theft or unnecessary removal of sensitive information by employees. The policy could be changed to specify who is to maintain these records and whether information owners are to be notified whenever sensitive information leaves Company X premises. The policy deliberately does not make a distinction between hardcopy and other ways to represent the information. To make the policy apply to a smaller proportion of the information at an organization, the word "sensitive" could be replaced with the word "secret." This policy, of course, assumes that the information involved has been properly labeled (marked) with a sensitivity designation. The policy also assumes that a another policy defining the word "sensitive" has been issued; see the policy entitled "Four Category Data Classification Scheme." Also see the policies entitled "Storing Secret Information On Transportable Computers" and "Removal Of Sensitive Information From Company X Premises." A: EM; E: LMH.

505. Handling Hardcopy Sensitive Information Off Company X Premises

Policy: Whenever a hardcopy version of sensitive information is removed from Company X premises, it must be carried in a locked briefcase or container when not in use. Such information must not be left in an unattended motor vehicle, hotel room, office, or some other location, even if the vehicle or room is locked.

Commentary: The intention of this policy is to put custodians of sensitive information on notice that they must handle the hardcopy versions of this information certain ways. The steps outlined in this policy help prevent the sensitive information from falling into the hands of hackers, industrial spies, competitors, and others who might have interests contrary to those of Company X. Many hotel rooms are easily accessed by housekeeping and other staff; there have also been reports of French government agents perpetrating industrial espionage against US Companies, including breaking into hotel rooms to obtain sensitive information. As another example, consider that during the Iraq/Iran war, a personal computer containing unencrypted battle plans was stolen out of a locked but unattended car. This policy can be expanded to include unencrypted floppy disks and other computer storage media. For a way to handle computer-resident sensitive information, see the policy entitled "Storing Secret Information On Transportable Computers." Also see the policies entitled "Log For Sensitive Information Removed From Company X Premises" and "Taking Secret Information Into A Foreign Country." A: EM; E: MH.

506. Transfer Of Sensitive Information To Third Parties On Computer Media

Policy: All computer storage media sent from Company X to a third party must never before have been used, or if used, must have been degaussed or zeroized prior to recording the information intended to be transferred.

Commentary: The intention of this policy is to ensure that residual information, which may have been "erased," is not left on the storage media, and therefore recoverable by a third party. This policy would for instance apply not only to sending demo disks out to potential customers, but also to those cases where old used computer hard drives are sent to a charity. Although not known by may people, information which has been "deleted" from a floppy disk is readily recoverable using various commercially available utility packages. Likewise, even though it has been overwritten, some information stored on magnetic storage media can be recovered using special equipment (the physics term for residual data is called remanence). Degaussing is one of the most secure mechanisms -- it subjects the media to very strong electro-magnetic fields and thus definitively erases information previously stored on the media. Zeroization involves successive writings of zeros and ones, thus obliterating the information previously stored on the media. Note that in very high security environments, zeroization may not provide enough protection. This policy may be restricted to those circumstances where sensitive information was previously recorded on the media. Also see the policies entitled "Certificate Of Destruction Rather Than Return Of Storage Media," "Sensitive Information Destruction/Concealment Before Servicing Done," and "Procedure For Release Of Used Equipment And Media To Third Parties." A: EMT; E: H.

507. Certificate Of Destruction Rather Than Return Of Storage Media

Policy: Whenever an external entity providing Company X with information on computer media (tapes, disks, CD-ROMs, etc.) requests that this media be returned, Company X staff must instead provide the external entity with written assurance that the information has been destroyed.

Commentary: The intention of this policy is to prevent Company X information from being unintentionally released to outside organizations. The computer media received might inadvertently have been used for temporary storage of sensitive information, and this sensitive information may not have been deleted before the media was returned. In a manner transparent to the user, the operating system might also have used the media to store scratch files containing sensitive information. The media might also contain a program which gathers information about Company X, in effect doing some automatic industrial espionage, perhaps under the guise of a demo disk. The only really reliable method to prevent these types of Company X sensitive information release is to keep the media. Software vendors or other information providers are most often willing to accept a written statement about the destruction of the material involved in lieu of return of the computer media. Separately, the policy could be toned-down by requiring such destruction rather than return only if data storage media can be written to (thus CD-ROMs could be returned, but floppy disks could not). On another note, the policy could be modified such that Company X staff are required to disclose the policy prior to receiving computer media from external entities. Since the non-return of submissions is relatively common in some industries such as the publishing industry (as is done with articles submitted for consideration), such prior notice is generally unnecessary. This policy is relevant only to those organizations with very stringent security needs such as research institutes, intelligence agencies, diplomatic units, criminal justice entities, and military groups. See the policy entitled "Transfer Of Sensitive Information To Third Parties On Computer Media." A: ET; E: H.

508. Confidentiality Of Company X Computer Related Documentation

Policy: All Company X computer related documentation is confidential, and must not be taken elsewhere when an employee, consultant, or contractor leaves the employ of Company X.

Commentary: The intention of this policy is to prevent programmers, editors, and others who have written Company X material from taking the documentation with them when they leave Company X. The policy is also intended to remind end-users, Information Systems Department staff, and others that computer related documentation is confidential and should not be disclosed to third parties without specific management permission. This policy once again gets back to who owns the information: is the it people who created it or is it the organization that employed them? Because this has been such a troublesome area, both in terms of communication between the people involved and also in terms of ambiguous laws, it is important to specify it in a policy (and ideally in contracts and other documents describing the relationships involved). If such documentation were to fall into the wrong hands, it could be used to break the controls found on the systems of the organization in question. The scope of this policy can be easily expanded to include communications systems, such as PBXs and local area networks. For a related idea, see the policy entitled "Property Rights To Computer Programs And Documentation." A: EMT; E: LMH.

509. Secret Information Sent By Electronic Mail

Policy: Unless each occurrence is specifically authorized by a vice president, readable secret information must not be sent by electronic mail. If encrypted with a Company X approved method, and if encrypted at the source and decrypted only at the destination, then secret information may be sent over an electronic mail system.

Commentary: This policy's objective is to communicate to users that electronic mail systems are not, as a general rule, to be trusted with secret information. Unencrypted electronic mail messages are easily intercepted by systems programmers, telephone system troubleshooters, wiretappers, and others. Note that the policy does not allow a blanket approval from a vice president (this is why the words "each occurrence" are used). If a user needs to send secret electronic mail messages on a regular basis, encryption facilities or other transmission media should be investigated. This policy is especially relevant to the Internet, external electronic mail services like Hotmail, as well as external value-added networks like BT Tymnet. For a more general approach, that does not require the establishment of a data classification system, see the policy entitled "Treat Electronic Mail As Public Communications." Also see the policies entitled "Acknowledgement Required For Deliveries Of Secret Information," "Encryption Required For Sending Secret Information by Fax," "Physical Security Or Encryption Required For All Sensitive Information," and "Government Standard Encryption Algorithm & Implementation." A: EMT; E: MH.

510. Diskless Workstations Must Be Used By R&D Department Workers

Policy: When working on new product development matters, all workers in the Research & Development Department must use diskless workstations tethered to an isolated departmental network.

Commentary: This policy helps prevent workers from walking away with new product designs and similar highly restricted material. It could be used in other high-security environments such as a strategic planning department, a mergers & acquisitions department, or a military battle strategy planning department. Since diskless workstations are used, workers cannot store information onto a floppy disk or other data media and then walk away with it. Since the network is isolated, workers cannot attach this information to an electronic mail message and thereby abscond with a copy. Separately, this policy achieves a degree of isolation not found in most modern offices, and as such it provides a markedly higher degree of security. On another note, when these workers are doing email or Internet web surfing, they will need to use other computers which are not connected to the diskless workstations. In the rare case where outside information needs to be posted to or removed from the isolated network server, a systems administrator can handle this task. For a related idea, see the policies entitled "Telecommuting Data Entry Operators Must Employ Thin Clients" and "Printers, Copiers, & Fax Machines Banned From Secret Information Areas." A: T; E: H.

1.3.3.4.5. Storage, Retention, And Declassification

511. Information Systems Unsuitable For Time-Sensitive Information

Policy: Lest it be disclosed to unauthorized parties, the most confidential time-sensitive information (details about mergers and acquisitions, layoff particulars, etc.) must not be handled by electronic mail, voice mail, telephone calls, or other computerized systems until the specifics have been publicly announced.

Commentary: This very conservative policy recognizes that information security for computer systems is embryonic and as a result is often unreliable. The policy informs management not to use computerized systems for such information until the information is publicly disclosed. While encryption programs and other automated controls have the potential to more securely protect information than was possible before the age of computers, these controls are often used inexpertly and ineptly, resulting in unintended disclosures. On another note, this policy may be best if adopted on a project-by-project basis, rather than being a standing policy appearing in a policies manual. The project assumes that the words "most confidential" have been previously defined; other words such as "top secret" may be used instead. Another benefit of this policy is that there is no electronic trail of events or other information which could be discovered in the course of legal proceedings. For related ideas, see the policies entitled "Regular Purging Of Information Which Is No Longer Needed" and "Existence Of Secret Systems Containing Personnel Records." A: M; E: MH.

512. Use Of Hard-Disk Drives For Storage Of Sensitive Information

Policy: Company X workers must not store private, confidential, or secret information on microcomputer (PC) or workstation hard-disk drives unless the Information Security Manager has determined that adequate information security measures will be employed.

Commentary: Since microcomputers (PCs) and workstations do not generally provide the same level of security as minicomputers or mainframes, some organizations prohibit sensitive information from being stored on micros and workstations unless adequate controls are first deployed. The intention of this policy is thus to require the use of adequate controls (such as a microcomputer password-based access control package). The intention is NOT to prohibit sensitive information from being stored on hard-disk drives. Special attention to hard-disk drives is warranted because they cannot easily be locked-up at the end of the day (as is the case for floppy disks). Special attention is also called for when a micro or workstation is connected to a local area network (LAN), in which case other users may be able to examine the contents of another's hard-disk drive (for instance if a cable modem is used). The policy deliberately is vague about what control measures are "adequate," since it is expected this will change over time. Also see the policy entitled "Data Stored On Hard Disk Drives Must Be Encrypted." A: EMT; E: LMH.

513. Commingling Of Sensitive And Non-Sensitive Information

Policy: Company X workers must not store confidential or secret information such that it is commingled with non-sensitive information on floppy diskettes or other removable data storage media.

Commentary: The purpose of this policy is to prevent confusion about the proper handling of removable data media such as floppy disks. Since handling procedures differ based on data classification, to commingle different classifications of data would force a disk or other storage media to be handled with the most stringent procedures, which in turn would be needlessly expensive and inconvenient. Thus another objective of this policy is to minimize costs associated with security. Alternatively, to not separate information by its classification runs the risk that workers will rebel claiming that the controls are onerous and inappropriate. This policy was designed for users of microcomputers (PCs) and workstations, although it is equally applicable to mainframe computer operators and others who handle data media. For more information about commingled data, see the policies entitled "Information With Multiple Sensitivity Classifications On Single System" and "Choosing Computer Storage Media Data Classifications." This policy assumes that the word "sensitive" has been defined in another policy; see the policy entitled "Four Category Data Classification Scheme." A: ET; E: LMH.

514. Clean Desks And Working Areas

Policy: Outside of regular working hours, all workers must clean their desks and working areas such that all sensitive or valuable data is properly secured.

Commentary: This policy is a modified "clean desk policy." This type of policy originated in the United States military. The traditional clean desk policy requires all information to be secured, lest an individual's judgement about the relative sensitivity of information be in error. The revised policy presented here is designed for microcomputer (PC) and workstation users--who often leave floppy disks and printouts out on their desk. The intention of the policy is to prevent people who happen to be in the building after hours from gaining access to sensitive information. The ways to properly secure information may be specified in another policy or in accompanying explanations provided by the reader of this reference book. This policy has a positive side effect: desks and work areas will be more neat and orderly. Another positive side effect: materials that are left out are more likely to be damaged or destroyed in a fire, explosion, or other disaster. In some cases the term "sensitive" could be replaced with specific mention of the sensitive data classifications found at the organization in question. The policy could be expanded to include mention of internal mail receptacles, unattended fax machines, black boards in conference rooms, and other places where sensitive information might be kept in the open. Although obvious to some, a few organizations specifically include mention in a clean desk policy that the policy is not meant to discourage workers from working outside normal working hours. For a policy showing recommended definitions for terms like "secret," see the policy entitled "Four Category Data Classification Scheme." The word "critical" might also be inserted between the words "sensitive" and "or valuable." Also see the policy entitled "Traditional Clean Desk Policy." A: EMT; E: LMH.

515. Traditional Clean Desk Policy

Policy: During non-working hours, employees in areas containing sensitive information must lock-up all information. Unless information is in active use by authorized personnel, desks must be absolutely clear and clean during non-working hours.

Commentary: This traditional clean desk policy intends to prevent inadvertent disclosure of sensitive information. The policy reflects a management attitude where workers are not trusted to decide what needs to be locked-up and what does not. The policy assumes that workers come in and do their job at regular times, for instance working from 9:00AM to 5:00PM. Many firms are moving to flexible schedules ("flextime"), so this policy may need to be modified so as to better define "non-working hours." Separately, a positive side-effect of this policy involves the requirement of a "ship-shape" environment where physical appearance (neatness) is valued. On another note, the policy assumes that the organization in question has the physical space and the financial resources to provide staff with the needed locking file cabinets, safes, and other containers. Also see the policy entitled "Clean Desks And Working Areas." A: EMT; E: MH.

516. Securing Sensitive Information In Unattended Rooms

Policy: When not in use, sensitive information must always be protected from unauthorized disclosure. When left in an unattended room, such information must be locked away in appropriate containers. If a custodian of such information believes he or she will be away for less than thirty minutes, the information may be left on a desk or in some other readily observed spot only if all doors and windows to the unattended room are closed and locked.

Commentary: The intention of this policy is to clarify when it is appropriate to leave sensitive information laying on a desk. The policy clearly states that this should only take place if the room is unattended and locked. Another possible exception may also be permissible: if the information is left in an area where all persons are authorized to view the sensitive information (as might be the case where cubicles rather than separate offices are used in a department). This additional exception could be added as a separate sentence at the end of the policy. The policy could also be expanded to indicate that the last person to leave an area that contains sensitive information must make sure that all sensitive information is properly secured. This policy assumes the word "sensitive" has been defined in other policy-related materials; see the policy entitled "Four Category Data Classification Scheme." Also see the policy entitled "Covering Sensitive Information When Interrupted At Work." A: EMT; E: LMH.

517. Storage Of Sensitive Information On Personal Computers

Policy: If sensitive information is to be stored on the hard disk drive or other internal components of a personal computer, it must be protected by either a password access control package or encryption. When sensitive information is written to a floppy disk, magnetic tape, smart card, or other storage media, the media must be suitably marked with the highest relevant sensitivity classification. Unless encrypted, when not in use, this media must be stored in locked furniture.

Commentary: This policy is intended to concisely delineate special procedures for handling sensitive information with personal computers (PCs). Because PCs are often not adequately physically secured, unauthorized persons may be able to gain physical access to them, and thereby to the sensitive information contained thereon. This policy assumes that the term "sensitive" has been previously defined in other policy-related documents. The term "sensitive" could be replaced with "confidential" or similar words. The words "or other internal components" were used to recognize that non-volatile flash memory and other internal PC memory subsystems may hold sensitive information, yet properly speaking, not be an internal hard drive. Separately, this policy is relevant to portables, handheld computers, laptops, and other transportable machines, not just desktop machines. Examples of personal computer encryption packages include offerings from RSA Data Security (Redwood City, California), while offerings of password access control packages include those from PC Guardian (San Rafael, California). Firms may also wish to investigate special disk and other storage media labels such as those which incorporate bar codes, as are offered by Avanti Associates (Valley Forge, Pennsylvania). On a different note, a separate policy detailing marking conventions will be needed to support the second sentence of this policy. For examples, see the policies entitled "Use Of Labels Throughout Sensitive Information's Life Cycle" and "Comprehensive Data Classification System Labelling Requirements." Also see the policy entitled "Storage Of Sensitive Information When Not In Use." A: EMT; E: MH.

518. Storage Of Sensitive Information When Not In Use

Policy: When not being used by authorized workers, or when not clearly visible in an area where authorized persons are working, all hardcopy sensitive information must be locked in file cabinets, desks, safes, or other furniture. Likewise, when not being used, or when not in a clearly visible and attended area, all computer media (floppy disks, CD-ROMs, etc.) containing sensitive information must be locked in similar enclosures.

Commentary: This policy is intended to provide specific guidance to end-users and others about the proper storage-related handling of sensitive information. It particularly applies to microcomputer (PC) and workstation users who often leave floppy disks and hardcopy printouts out on their desk. Periodic audits involving a night-time check of desks (also known as a "desk check") can be used to enforce a policy such as this. In the title, the word "sensitive" may be replaced with specific mention of the sensitive data classifications found at the organization in question. For a policy showing recommended definitions for terms like "secret," see the policy entitled "Four Category Data Classification Scheme." Also see the policy entitled "Storage Of Sensitive Information On Personal Computers." A: EMT; E: LMH.

519. Retention Period Required For All Sensitive Information

Policy: A retention period must be assigned to all secret information, regardless of the form that the information takes (paper documents, computer files, etc.).

Commentary: The intention of this policy is to encourage disposal of sensitive information when it is no longer needed; this reduces the chances of it falling into the hands of unauthorized persons. The information in question may still be classified as sensitive at the time it is destroyed (note simple disposal is generally not appropriate for sensitive information--a separate policy should specify destruction methods). See the policy entitled "Approved Methods For Hardcopy Sensitive Information Disposal." This policy facilitates disposal of the information at the proper time, thus reducing storage costs. The policy can be modified to include words which say that, in the absence of a specific date for disposal, a date when a decision about the date of disposal will be made may be used. If this option is provided, then a contact name and phone number may be needed. This policy assumes the existence of a policy which defines the term "secret." For this definition, see the policy entitled "Four Category Data Classification Scheme." Also see the policies entitled "Minimum Information Retention Period" and "Definition Of Archival Storage Data Retention Schedule." A: EMT; E: MH.

520. Date For Declassification Must Be Specified If Known

Policy: If known, the date that secret, confidential, or private information will no longer be sensitive must be indicated as part of the classification information. This policy also applies in those circumstances where sensitive information will be downgraded to a less sensitive classification.

Commentary: The intention of this policy is to ensure that information will be declassified or downgraded to a lower classification when the time to do so has arrived. For example, if certain information about a merger and acquisition is designated as secret, it should be noted that it will become public as of a certain date (the announcement date). Over time, there is a natural tendency for information to get progressively more classified (move up on a classification scale) or at least remain over-classified (not get declassified when it should). This policy fights these tendencies, and as a side-effect will help to keep security costs down because access controls costs will be reduced. The date for declassification or downgrading -- also known as an expiry date or expiration date -- may additionally help to identify the time for disposal of the information, thus reducing storage costs. In this regard, see the policy entitled "Retention Period Required For All Sensitive Information." The clear specification of a declassification or downgrading date also facilitates orderly handling of the information by different people who may not be in direct communication with the others involved. Separately, this policy assumes the existence of a policy which defines the terms "secret, confidential, or private." For definitions of terms like "secret," see the policy entitled "Four Category Data Classification Scheme." For a stricter alternative to this policy, see the policy entitled "Annual Review Of Sensitive Information Classification Assignments." A: EMT; E: LMH.

521. Accelerated Declassification And Downgrading Of Sensitive Information

Policy: The designated information owner may, at any time, declassify or downgrade the sensitivity classification applied to information. To achieve this, the owner must: (1) change the classification label appearing on the original document, (2) notify all known recipients, and (3) notify the Company X archives custodian.

Commentary: The intention of this policy is to make it clear exactly what has to happen to declassify or downgrade the classification for information. Declassification involves the removal of a sensitivity label, while downgrading involves only movement to a less sensitive level. The policy implicitly acknowledges that not all copies of the information will be located and either declassified or downgraded; the problems introduced by the incomplete location of recipients are acceptable because any resulting errors will provide more rather than less security. Separately, some organizations will want to change the words "original document" to make more specific reference to computerized versions of the original. This policy should be distributed only to information owners or those with the authority to declassify or downgrade information. In some cases, management will want owners to document the reason(s) for the declassification or downgrading; this too can be mentioned in the policy. Separately, instead of an "archives custodian" a data warehouse manager or similar job title could be used (someone who keeps track of "information about information," also known as metadata). For related ideas, see the policies entitled "Extension Of Declassification Or Downgrading Date" and "No Write Down Permissions To Access Sensitive Information." A: M; E: LMH.

522. Extension Of Declassification Or Downgrading Date

Policy: The designated information owner may, at any time prior to scheduled declassification or downgrading, extend the period that information is to remain at a certain classification level. To achieve this, the owner must: (1) change the declassification or downgrading date appearing on the original document, (2) notify all known recipients, (3) initiate a cost-effective search for additional recipients, and (4) notify the Company X archives custodian.

Commentary: The intention of this policy is to make it clear exactly what has to happen to extend the declassification or downgrading date for information (sometimes called an expiry date or an expiration date). The location of additional recipients of the information is essential if the information is to be protected adequately. Without a search, recipients who did not hear about the extension could in good conscience release the information to unauthorized parties. Such a search can be time-consuming and expensive unless detailed logs of recipients have been kept. To avoid the need to extend an expiration date, some organizations routinely add a month or a similar period of time to the expected declassification or downgrading date. Separately, some organizations will want to change the words "original document" to make more specific reference to computerized versions of the original. This policy should be distributed only to information owners or those with the authority to declassify or downgrade information. In some cases, management will want owners to document the reason(s) for the date extension; this too can be mentioned in the policy. For related ideas, see the policies entitled "Accelerated Declassification And Downgrading Of Sensitive Information" and "No Write Down Permissions To Access Sensitive Information." A: M; E: LMH.

523. Automatic Schedule For Downgrading Company X Information

Policy: The sensitivity classification of all Company X documents must be routinely downgraded according to the following table. An exception will be made in those instances where a document type is named on the attached special list. Another exception will be made in those cases where the information owner has provided other instructions for declassification or downgrading.

Existing Classification	New Classification	After Years
Secret	Confidential	10
Confidential	Internal Use Only	15
Internal Use Only	Public	20

Commentary: The intent of this policy is to force an automatic declassification or downgrading of sensitive information. Far too many documents are left at their original classification level for excessive periods of time. This in turn means that workers will have trouble locating and gaining access to information that would otherwise be available to them, and that information security costs will be higher than necessary. The automatic declassification of documents helps ensure that the information owner's declassification and downgrading job will be performed even when the owner hasn't gotten around to dealing with these matters (barring owner instructions to the contrary). An automatic declassification system also means that some of the subjectivity surrounding the declassification and downgrading process will be eliminated. Certainly the number of years before an automatic downgrading takes place will vary by organization; likewise, some organizations will prefer never to make information public. Separately, this policy assumes that only three levels of data classification (ignoring "public" information) are used at Company X. Since this automatic declassification process can get a bit complex, it is best applied with a document management system or similar computerized tools. On another point, the "special list" of documents not subject to automatic downgrading can include medical reports, personnel files, internal grievance and dispute resolution files, attorney-client files, and related types of information. Also, some organizations may wish to expand the policy (for privacy reasons) to specify that information involving an outside organization must not be downgraded to "public" without the outside organization's prior consent. This policy would generally be distributed only to information owners and others who make information classification decisions. For related ideas, see the policy entitled "Date For Declassification Must Be Specified If Known" and "Established Procedure For Review Of Information Released To Public." A: M; E: MH.

524. Annual Declassification Review For Sensitive Information

Policy: To determine whether sensitive information may be declassified or downgraded, at least once a year, information owners must review the sensitivity classifications assigned to information for which they are responsible.

Commentary: Sensitive information tends to get over classified over time (in part because of the system-high philosophy). Steps to declassify or downgrade it are therefore necessary if costs for information security are to be kept to a minimum. Declassification of information also helps keep government and corporations accountable to citizens and stockholders. The intention of this policy is to formalize a step to declassify and downgrade information and to require owners to participate in the process. Typically a status report showing the type of information and its classification will be prepared for review by information owners; the owners would then simply check off the items which should be declassified, downgraded, and/or remain classified as they are. The annual review period might be replaced with "periodically review" or another time period. For a more lenient alternative to this policy, see the policy entitled "Date For Declassification Must Be Specified If Known." This policy assumes that the term "owner" has been defined elsewhere such as in the policy entitled "Information Ownership And Management's Responsibilities." In most instances, this policy needs an accompanying policy that defines the term "sensitive." For such a definition, see the policy entitled "Four Category Data Classification Scheme." A: EMT; E: MH.

525. Declassification Of Sensitive Information Required As Soon As Practical

Policy: From the standpoint of sensitivity, information must be declassified or downgraded as soon as practical.

Commentary: To keep information at an excessive sensitivity classification also keeps costs for information security high. It additionally can be inappropriately used as a mechanism to prevent certain authorized people from viewing the information. When this comes to light, it often looks bad for management, implying that they had something to hide. The intention of this policy is thus to counter the tendency of information to become classified at excessive levels over time. This policy requires that the term "sensitivity" be defined in another policy. For example, see the policy entitled "Four Category Data Classification Scheme." Declassification may also be appropriate for information that was critical but is less critical now, and information that was valuable (had a pressing need for data integrity) but is no longer as valuable as it once was. Most organizations don't have classification schemes focusing on criticality or value, but the same approach could be adopted. Some organizations will prefer alternative wording for this policy such as: "information owners are responsible for ensuring that documents are classified at the lowest level consistent with Company X's business needs." Also see the policies entitled "Five Category Application Criticality Classification Scheme" and "Annual Declassification Review For Sensitive Information." A: EMT; E: MH.

1.3.3.4.6. Disposal And Destruction

526. Sensitive Information Destruction/Concealment Before Servicing Done

Policy: Before computer magnetic storage media is sent to a vendor for trade-in, servicing, or disposal, all Company X sensitive information must be destroyed or concealed according to methods approved by the Information Security Department.

Commentary: The intention of this policy is to ensure that sensitive information is not unwittingly disclosed to unauthorized persons working for vendors, charities, and other third parties. For example, if a hard disk drive were to crash, the drive might be sent to a computer repair service. The service company could examine the data on the drive, perhaps leading to unauthorized disclosure of sensitive information. To counter this risk, the drive could be degaussed prior to being sent to the service vendor. Of course, then the data held on the drive, that has not yet been backed-up, will be lost (this is a major disadvantage of the policy). Such sensitive information destruction makes sense only if the information has been properly backed-up or if the consequences of disclosure are very severe. Accordingly, this policy needs to be accompanied by definitive information backup policies; for example, see the policy entitled "What Data To Backup And Minimum Backup Frequency." A more practical alternative would be to require that all hard drives storing sensitive data employ encryption, in which case there is no problem about sending the drive to an outside vendor. This is why the word "concealed" is included in the policy in addition to the word "destroyed." Another approach is to require confidentiality agreements (NDAs) from all third parties. This policy assumes the term "sensitive" has been defined in another policy. For example, see the policy entitled "Four Category Data Classification Scheme." Also see the policies entitled "Transfer Of Sensitive Information To Third Parties On Computer Media" and "Information Destruction And Information Systems Equipment Disposal." A: EMT; E: MH.

527. Release Of Computer Storage Media Prior To Degaussing/Zeroizing

Policy: Computer storage media which has been used to record secret information must not leave controlled channels until it has been degaussed (demagnitized) or zeroized according to the standards published by the Information Security Department.

Commentary. This policy establishes the notion of a controlled channel for the custody of secret information (the policy writer can replace "secret" with another term indicating the most sensitive type of information). A "controlled channel" in this context is a conduit for the handling of information which preserves its security; this conduit may involve several people or only one person. Degaussing involves subjecting magnetic storage media such as floppy disks to a strong magnetic field which will then erase the information stored thereon. Zeroization involves overwriting the storage media with repeated sequences of zeros and ones, thereby obliterating the data (this would be appropriate for non-magnetic writable storage media such as CD-RW). The policy helps foster thinking on the part of users along the lines of "Just what is the controlled channel for the protection of the secret data in my possession?" It would for example foster thought about confidentiality agreements (NDAs) and encryption. For related ideas see the policies entitled "Transfer Of Sensitive Information To Third Parties On Computer Media" and "Destruction Of Sensitive Information On Computer Storage Media." A: E; MH.

528. Destruction Of Sensitive Information On Computer Storage Media

Policy: Destruction of sensitive information captured on computer storage media (such as CD-ROMs, tape reels, or floppy disks) must only be performed with approved destruction methods. These include the use of shredders or other equipment approved by the Information Security Department.

Commentary: The intention of this policy is to provide guidance on the approved methods for destroying sensitive information resident on computer storage media. The best destruction methods are burning, shredding, or some other approach which renders the media unusable. Next in order of preference is a degausser which uses electro-magnetic fields to definitively erase data (not relevant to CD-ROMs, magneto-optical cartridges, and other storage media which do not use traditional magnetic recording approaches). Next in order of preference are zeroization programs will write repeated sequences of ones and zeros over the information, thus reducing the chances that it can be recovered. The policy writer may need to seek technical assistance because zeroization may or may not be acceptable for certain storage media such as CD-RW (CD rewritable). In those organizations with less pressing security needs, one of the less definitive destruction methods mentioned above may be acceptable. On a separate note, this policy is written for military, diplomatic, and other organizations with very high security needs. The methods mentioned in this commentary which do not destroy the storage media will permit the media recycling, thus saving money and reducing environmental waste. Separately, this policy assumes the existence of another policy which defines the term "sensitive information." See the policy entitled "Four Category Data Classification Scheme." Also see the policies entitled "Zeroization Required For Erasure Of Sensitive Information," "Zeroization Of Password Generation Materials," "Protection For Encryption Key Generation Materials," and "Data Stored On Hard Disk Drives Must Be Encrypted." A: EMT; E: MH.

529. Zeroization Required For Erasure Of Sensitive Information

Policy: When sensitive Company X information is erased from a disk, tape, or other magnetic storage media, it must be followed by a repeated overwrite operation which prevents the data from later being scavenged.

Commentary: With most operating systems, standard disk file "delete" and "erase" commands simply delete the entry in a file allocation table (FAT) or directory; the information in the file is still resident on the computer media. A notable aspect of using this overwriting process (known as "zeroization") to obliterate sensitive information is that it can be programmed to happen automatically. A command file can be written to automatically scrub data storage media, using zeroization, each time that a sensitive file or other object (database, program, etc.) is erased. Some operating systems do this automatically; for example, IBM's RACF for MVS will "erase-on-scratch" those files which have been designated as in need of this protection. The user need not be aware of this process. Alternatively, in the absence of an automated approach, users can invoke an approved zeroization software utility to handle this "scrubbing" process whenever sensitive data is involved. The intention of this policy is thus to prevent unauthorized disclosure of sensitive information from computer media scavenging, whether the process is handled automatically or by the end-users. The automated approach is recommended since users cannot be counted on to conscientiously follow-through on this all of the time (not to mention the fact that it's more user-friendly to have the computer do it). Currently-available commercial packages now perform zeroization; for example, these are offered by Prime Factors (Eugene, Oregon). Note that this technology will not be relevant to WORM storage media (write once, read many times), which by its very nature is not reusable. This policy assumes that the term "sensitive" was defined in another policy; see the policy entitled "Four Category Data Classification Scheme." Also see the policies entitled "Deletion Of Log Information About Customer Activities," "Severing Link Between Identifying Information And Research Data," and "Transfer Of Sensitive Information To Third Parties On Computer Media." A: EMT; E: MI I.

530. Approved Methods For Hardcopy Sensitive Information Disposal

Policy: When disposed of, all secret, confidential, or private information in hardcopy form (paper, microfilm, microfiche, etc.) must be either shredded or incinerated.

Commentary: The intention of this policy is to prevent "dumpster diving" (the popular going-through-the-trash scavenging approach to recovering passwords, user-IDs, and other sensitive information). Scavenging information from the trash is a favorite tactic of hackers, private investigators, industrial spies, military spies, and the police. In many jurisdictions it is both legal and a successful method for gaining important information. In a related standard, many organizations specify the type of shredding required (for example, the pieces produced must be a certain size or smaller). This policy assumes the existence of a policy which defines the terms "secret, confidential, or private." For example, see the policy entitled "Four Category Data Classification Scheme." Also see the policies entitled "Sensitive Information Retention For Destruction Via Approved Method," "Destruction Of Encryption Key Generation Materials" and "Destruction Of Materials Used In Handling Sensitive Information." A: EMT; E: LMH.

531. Strip Shredders Must Not Be Used For Destruction Of Sensitive Information

Policy: Since the shredders which produce strips of paper allow the original documents to be easily reconstructed, strip shredders must not be used in any Company X facilities. Only shredders and other paper destruction equipment approved by the Information Security Department may be employed.

Commentary: The intention of this policy is to ensure that users are not shredding paper documents and establishing a sense of false security thereby. Although widespread, strip paper shredders can easily be overcome by a determined adversary who has the time to reconstruct original documents. This reconstruction was for example successfully done by Iranian students after they seized the US Embassy in Tehran. The widespread acknowledgement that their reconstruction effort was successful and had lead to the disclosure of US diplomatic secret information was not sufficient motivation for strip shredders to be widely shunned. Their widespread use continues in part because they are inexpensive. Instead of strip shredders, organizations should use shredders which produce confetti or some similarly small particles or shreds of paper. For ideas along these same lines, see the policies entitled "Destruction Of Sensitive Information On Computer Storage Media" and "Recording And Retention Of Electronic Mail." A: EMT; E: MH.

532. Areas Containing Sensitive Information Must Have Shredders

Policy: All Company X offices and other areas where sensitive information is handled must have operational shredders. The people working in these areas must also be informed which materials need to be shredded.

Commentary: The objective of this policy is to ensure that the right tools for information destruction are provided to the people who need to use them. All too often workers have been trained that they must destroy certain sensitive data using specified procedures, but then the tools (like shredders and zeroization software) are not provided. Not only does this policy state that shredders must be present, it states that they must be in good working order. The policy thus helps to counter the often massive disclosures which are occasioned via "dumpster diving" (searching the trash of organizations). Accordingly, this policy is intended to counter industrial espionage and the efforts of nosy reporters. For related concepts see the policies entitled "Destruction Of Waste Copies Of Sensitive Information," "Security Requirements For Work At Home Arrangements," and "Shredding Of Credit Card Receipts And Other Payment Information." A: E; E: MH.

533. Use Of Secure Containers For All But Secret Information Disposal

Policy: Sensitive information must not be discarded in trash bins, recycle bins or other publicly-accessible locations. Instead this information must be placed in a designated locked destruction container within Company X offices. An exception is made in the case of secret information, which must be immediately destroyed by approved methods (shredding, burning, etc.).

Commentary: This policy is intended to guide staff members in the proper disposal and destruction of sensitive materials. For confidential and other lower grade sensitive materials, depositing them in mailbox-like metal containers that are locked will be sufficient. Later, a member of the Security Department or a bonded contractor will remove these materials and destroy them according to a well-defined process (in some cases witnessed). Secret information, because it is so very sensitive must, however, be immediately destroyed. This will lessen the risk that someone could break into a locked destruction container, or even steal the whole container and later break into it. Separately, the policy assumes that the words "sensitive" and "secret" have been defined in other policies such as a data classification policy. The policy also assumes that approved methods for destruction of secret material have been published, or will soon be published. For related ideas, see the policies entitled "Shredding Of Credit Card Receipts And Other Payment Information," "Destruction Of Waste Copies Of Sensitive Information," and "Sensitive Information Retention For Destruction Via Approved Method." A: E; E: MH.

534. Security Staff Must Follow Information Destruction Instructions

Policy: Trash containing sensitive information that has been set aside for special destruction must not be sorted into destroy and do-not-destroy categories. All materials in the destruction container must be destroyed according to approved procedures regardless of recycling implications.

Commentary: The security staff members responsible for destroying information contained in destruction containers (sometimes called "burn bags") may rightfully be concerned about ecology. They may accordingly pick through the trash thinking that certain items need not be destroyed, and that these items can be recycled without harm to Company X. This policy prohibits them from making these decisions, and from doing any sorting whatsoever. The policy assumes that the worker who put the information in the destruction container intended it to be destroyed, and security staff member responsible for destruction cannot know the reasons why this worker thought the information should be destroyed. This policy helps ensure that all information that is intended for destruction is in fact destroyed. It also eliminates a reason why security staff members responsible for destruction might examine information they are not authorized to examine. Separately, as an aside, information destruction containers often resemble physical mail boxes; they are heavy metal containers locked with a key. For a related idea, see the policy entitled "Destruction Of Waste Copies Of Sensitive Information." This policy would generally only be distributed to security staff members. A: E; E: LMH.

535. Sensitive Information Destruction Must Follow Specified Procedures

Policy: After it becomes no longer needed, all sensitive or valuable Company X information must be securely destroyed using procedures approved by the Information Security Department.

Commentary: The intention of this policy is to require all persons who handle Company X sensitive information to dispose of it in a secure and authorized manner. The specific procedures to be used could be specified in a standard or a guideline rather than a policy. If the procedures were to be put into a policy, one could use policies like the one entitled "Approved Methods For Hardcopy Sensitive Information Disposal" as a model. The policy presented here is a higher level policy than the policy entitled "Approved Methods For Hardcopy Sensitive Information Disposal." This policy assumes the existence of a policy which defines the terms "sensitive or valuable." For example, see the policy entitled "Four Category Data Classification Scheme." Also see the policy entitled "Destruction Of Encryption Key Generation Materials." A: EMT; E: LMH.

536. Persons Authorized To Destroy Sensitive Company X Information

Policy: To ensure that it is in fact performed, the destruction of sensitive information must be carried out by Company X personnel or a bonded destruction service.

Commentary: The intention of this policy is to make sure that a trusted individual or organization is used for all sensitive information destruction efforts. There have been cases where destruction services did not shred sensitive data, instead simply dumping it in landfill. Others then discovered this sensitive information much to the dismay of the originating organization. To prevent such problems, this policy requires an employee or a destruction service that has gone through a background check and has received insurance (the bonding process). This policy would need to be used in conjunction with other policies stating how the destruction is to be performed; for example, see the policy entitled "Approved Methods For Hardcopy Sensitive Information Disposal." A: EMT; E: LMH.

537. Use Of Metal Boxes To Hold Sensitive Information To Be Destroyed

Policy: All secret, confidential, and private information no longer being used or no longer needed -- no matter what form it takes (disks, hardcopy, etc.) -- is to be placed in designated locked metal boxes until such time as authorized Company X personnel or a bonded destruction service picks it up.

Commentary: The intention of this policy is to ensure that sensitive information will not fall into unauthorized hands on the way to being properly destroyed. Collections of sensitive information waiting for destruction otherwise present an attractive target for industrial spies, nosy employees, and others. The boxes mentioned in the policy look much like public mail boxes, and are heavy enough and big enough so that the whole box cannot readily be stolen. To prevent theft of the whole box, in some cases boxes are chained, bolted, or otherwise secured to the floor or other furniture. Separately, this policy assumes that people responsible for disposal will sort the material based on recycling considerations (plastic, paper, etc.). In some cases it may be advisable to have separate containers for different sensitive materials to be recycled. On a different note, this policy would ordinarily be used with other policies specifying how information should be destroyed. For instance, see the policy entitled "Approved Methods For Hardcopy Sensitive Information Disposal." A: EMT; E: LMH.

538. Destruction Of Materials Used In Handling Sensitive Information

Policy: All materials used in the handling of sensitive information, which could be analyzed to deduce sensitive information, must be destroyed in a manner similar to that required for sensitive information. This policy covers typewriter ribbons, carbon papers, mimeograph stencil masters, photographic negatives, thermal fax transfer films, aborted computer hardcopy output, unacceptable photocopies, etc.

Commentary: The intention of this policy is to prevent unauthorized persons from gaining access to sensitive information by examining the discarded byproducts of sensitive information handling activities. Disposal of these materials in the trash may permit "dumpster diving" (scavenging) to be used to recover the sensitive information. Many people are not aware that sensitive information could be disclosed in these ways, so a specific notice to look after these byproducts is advisable. The list of byproducts found in the second sentence of this policy ideally should be expanded to include materials related to the technologies in use at Company X. For related ideas, see the policies entitled "Destruction Of Encryption Key Generation Materials" and "Approved Methods For Hardcopy Sensitive Information Disposal." This policy assumes that the word "sensitive" has been defined in another policy; see the policy entitled "Four Category Data Classification Scheme." A: EMT; E: MH.

1.3.3.5. Granting Access To Confidential Data

539. Approval Required Before Access To Sensitive Or Valuable Information

Policy: Access to Company X sensitive or valuable information must be provided only after express management authorization has been obtained.

Commentary: The intention of this policy is to restrict access to Company X sensitive and valuable data, not allowing people to gain access unless they have first obtained explicit (preferably written) management approval. Typically the management approval would involve answering the question: "Does this individual have a bone fide need-to-know?" The policy furthermore discourages workers from sharing such information with others workers (and with outsiders) in the absence of management approval. The policy is a general high-level policy under which various more-detailed policies related to access control could be added (perhaps at a later time). Rather than simply using the term "management authorization" the policy could refer to the "information owner." On another note, instead of "sensitive," the terms "secret," "confidential," and "private" could be used here. Although this policy can be used without an in-house data classification system, it is most effective when the words "sensitive" and "valuable" have been defined in another policy. See the policy entitled "Four Category Data Classification Scheme." Also see the policy entitled "Privilege Restriction Based On The Need-to-Know." A: EMT; E: LMH.

540. Access To Secret Information Granted On Individual (Not Group) Basis

Policy: Access to secret information must be granted only to specific individuals, not groups of individuals.

Commentary: The intention of this policy is to require that management make person-by-person decisions when granting access to the most sensitive types of information. If access is granted to groups of individuals, inevitably there will be greater access than is necessary to get the business done. Likewise, if access is granted to a group, it will be very much more difficult to trace leaks (unauthorized disclosures). When deciding to grant access to sensitive information, management should consider the individual's tenure with the organization, his or her current responsibilities, any disciplinary problems, potential conflicts of interest, and related matters. Separately, this policy supports the notion of having one user-ID for each individual (no group user-IDs). For ideas about group user-IDs, see the policy entitled "Unique User-ID And Password Required." A supplementary policy to the general policy entitled "Privilege Restriction Based On the Need-to-Know," this policy could be expanded to all types of sensitive information (not just "secret information"). The policy assumes that the word "secret" has been defined in another policy; see the policy entitled "Four Category Data Classification Scheme." Also see the policy entitled "Approval Required Before Access To Sensitive Or Valuable Information." A: EMT; E: LMH.

541. Granting System Privileges By Chain Of Authority Delegation

Policy: Computer and communication system privileges must be granted only by a clear chain of authority delegation.

Commentary: The intention of this policy is to clarify which managers can grant system privileges as well as the specific privileges they can grant. If a clear chain of delegation does not exist, a manager does not have the authority to grant access to other people. This notion is particularly important when departmental management and other end-user management is involved in system privilege granting activities. For example, in a mainframe database environment such as IBM's DB2, access privileges can be granted to another person. When a user's privileges are revoked, the ability to delegate privileges to others is also automatically revoked. The DB2 software automatically implements this policy. This policy also points to the notion of "inheritance" that will increasingly be important in object oriented programming (OOP). With OOP, programs have certain privileges that can be given to other programs, but these privileges must follow a clear line of access control delegation. For supporting ideas, see the policies entitled "Privilege Restriction Based On The Need-to-Know," "Approval Required Before Access To Sensitive Or Valuable Information," "Periodic Identification Badge Reports Issued To Department Heads," and "Maintenance Of List Showing Those Permitted To Grant Physical Access." A: MT; E: LMH.

542. Confidentiality Agreements And Disclosures Of Sensitive Information

Policy: All disclosures of secret, confidential, or private Company X information to third parties must be accomplished via a signed confidentiality agreement which includes restrictions on the subsequent dissemination and usage of the information.

Commentary: The intention of this policy is to prevent unauthorized uses of Company X information including what is called "secondary dissemination." When secondary dissemination takes place, the recipient of information passes it on to some other person, and this other person then has no agreements with the information's source about how the information should be handled. Specific directions about usage should prohibit additional distribution without the information owner's consent. This policy could be expanded to delineate the specific requirements that must be stated as part of a confidentiality agreement; these could include return of the information, how the information will be safeguarded, what the information will be used for, and who will be given access to the information. For related ideas, see the policies entitled "Secondary Dissemination Of Secret Information," "Specific Handling Instructions For Recipients Of Sensitive Information," and "Annual Signature On Agreement To Comply With Security Policies." A: EMT; E: LMH.

543. Specific Handling Instructions For Recipients Of Sensitive Information

Policy: All disclosures of secret, confidential, or private Company X information to third parties must be accompanied by an explicit statement describing exactly what information is restricted and how this information may and may not be used.

Commentary: This policy can be used to address "secondary dissemination" issues, unauthorized use, and related abuses of restricted information after it has left Company X. An "explicit statement" may be part of a non-disclosure agreement signed by a third party receiving the information, or simply given in narrative or verbal form at the time of disclosure. Some organizations will want to add the word "written" to the policy between the words "explicit statement." Simple verbal instructions may be sufficient if the recipient already has a signed confidentiality agreement with Company X or if the recipient has a trusted on-going business relationship with Company X. The intention of this policy is thus primarily to require those who disclose sensitive information to provide specific instructions on its proper handling. If this is done, the recipient will not be able to say: "But you didn't tell me I shouldn't do that." The policy assumes that the terms "secret, confidential, or private" have already been defined; see the policy entitled "Four Category Data Classification Scheme." Also see the policy entitled "Secondary Dissemination Of Secret Information." A: EMT; E: LMH.

544. Requests For Company X Information Referred To Public Relations

Policy: Unless authorized by top management, all requests for information about Company X and its business activities must be referred to the Public Relations Department. These requests include questionnaires, surveys, newspaper interviews, and the like. This policy does not apply to sales and marketing information about Company X products and services, nor does it pertain to customer support calls.

Commentary: The intention of this policy is to prevent workers, many of whom have only the best of intentions, from disclosing sensitive information to the press, market researchers, competitors, industrial spies, system crackers/hackers, and others. Effectively this policy says that only the Public Relations Department (or designated spokespersons who are often subject matter experts) are authorized to disclose information about Company X and its business activities. By funneling disclosures through Public Relations, an organization is also able to present a coordinated and orderly image to the public. By funneling calls through Public Relations, the organization also reduces the chances that industrial spies will use "social engineering" to get information from unwitting employees. Separately, this policy is important after a disaster or some other publicly-disclosed problem; under these circumstances, the press will seek out employees for interviews. When this happens, if disclosures are not carefully managed, an organization can appear poorly managed and confused. This policy may be a part of contingency planning efforts addressing what to do in the event of bomb blasts, earthquakes, and other disasters and emergencies. Separately, many employees will be relieved to have a quick-and-dirty approach to politely get rid of the people requesting information. On another note, in some firms, the Public Relations Department may have designated spokespersons who can speak about certain topics; for example, if an information security problem has taken place, the Director of Information Security may be authorized to speak with the public. Another example is Y2K surveys, where the Director of Y2K Remediation Efforts can represent the organization rather than routing these requests for information through the Public Relations Department. To be clear, some organizations may wish to add the words "and information systems" to the first sentence after "business activities." Separately, if no central funnel for information disclosure is to be used, see the policy entitled "Approval Required Prior To Release Of Company X Information." For related ideas, see the policies entitled "Centralized

Responsibility For Information Security" and "Presentation Of Low-Profile And Secure Image." A: EMT; E: LMH.

545. Prohibition Against Disclosing Customer Projects, Strategies, Etc.

Policy: Although the information may not be considered to be sensitive, Company X workers are prohibited from disclosing to anyone outside Company X the nature of customer projects, customer business strategies, or customer business relationships. This policy shows respect for customers and helps ensure customer loyalty and continued trust.

Commentary: The intention of this policy to err on the side of caution when it comes to disclosing information about customers (clients, patients, buyers, call them what you will). It would for example be relevant to a consulting firm which did fraud investigations. These customers would not appreciate it if such a consulting firm's personnel went to a conference and talked about the projects they did for various customers. Consulting firm personnel may want to do this to show competence and experience, and thereby generate additional work. Note that the policy is strict in that it doesn't permit any disclosure, even if the customer's identity is concealed (in some instances, the policy writer may want to add to the policy a sentence further emphasizing this). Separately, with the words "although the information may not be considered to be sensitive" the policy eliminates the need to reference the information's data classification label; these same words also eliminate any justification for a claim that "the information was known to other outsiders, so I didn't think it was a big deal to reveal it." On another note, the policy's scope could be expanded to include how it is to work with a particular customer; comments made to reporters like "they're very hard to work with" can damage ongoing relationships, even if they are not, strictly speaking, a disclosure of sensitive information. For related ideas, see the policies entitled "Marketing Information Must Never Be Shared With Competitors" and "Prior Review For Speeches, Presentations, Technical Papers, Etc." A: E; E: LMH.

546. Marketing Information Must Never Be Shared With Competitors

Policy: Although certain marketing information such as prices and sales policies are customarily disclosed to outsiders, they should never be disclosed to competitors. Likewise, marketing strategies, marketing plans, market share status, and other marketing information should never be shared with competitors.

Commentary: This policy is intended to clarify what is often a confusing point for people working in sales and marketing. On one hand, certain information such as prices and sales policies are discussed with just about any prospect or customer. On the other hand, this information is of great value to the competition. Granted, third parties working for the competition could gather this information on behalf of the competition, but this policy forces the competition to engage in a borderline unethical activity (changing or concealing their identity in order to get information to which they would not otherwise be entitled). Just because it's questionable, doesn't mean that the competition isn't going to use third parties to gather competitive intelligence (industrial espionage) information; this policy just makes it harder for them. Separately, the policy assumes that people working in sales and marketing know who the competition is; in some industries (like restaurants in a large city) there are so many competitors, it is not feasible to have an up-to-date list of them all (even in the yellow pages phone directory). On another note, each organization will need to clarify the precise types of information that it wishes to withhold from the competition (or implement a data classification system); the types mentioned here are merely placeholders. For related ideas, see the policies entitled "Refrain From Pressuring Employees Who Worked At Competitors" and "Notification And Handling Of Employees Leaving For A Competitor." A: E; E: LMH.

547. Information Released To The Public Must Have Single Official Source

Policy: Information generated by Company X and released to the public must be accompanied by the name of a designated staff member acting as the single recognized official source and point-of-contact. All updates and corrections to this information that are released to the public must flow through this official source.

Commentary: The intention of this policy is to bring some order to what has become, at some organizations, a relatively chaotic and disorganized process for the release of information to the public. Government agencies for example may conduct research, and then several different people may discuss that research with the media. This policy helps to ensure a consistent position with respect to the information in question, as well as a mechanism to control the different forms in which the information my be presented. It relies on designated sources rather than a public relations department to bring some order to this process. Separately, the policy could be changed to state that only the designated "owner" of the information can release it to the public. With computers on nearly everyone's desk these days, all workers are potential publishers. Separately, some organizations may want to specify a few exceptions to the policy, such as marketing brochures. For related ideas, see the policies entitled "All Public Representations Must Be Cleared Through Public Relations" and "Waiting Period Prior To External Disclosure Of Requested Information." A: E; E: LMH.

548. Approval Required Prior To Release Of Company X Information

Policy: Permission to disclose any internal Company X information to the news media or to other third parties must be obtained from Company X senior management prior to release.

Commentary: The intention of this policy is to prevent workers from disclosing sensitive information to the press, market researchers, competitors, industrial spies, system crackers/hackers, and others. Without explicit approval, disclosure is forbidden. Because the word "internal" is used, certain public information is not covered by the policy. Similarly, the word "internal" could be replaced by "sensitive" or "classified." This policy does not require that all information flow through a central clearing point, as is the case in the policy entitled "Requests For Company X Information Referred To Public Relations." Accordingly, this decentralized approach runs the risk of presenting a disorganized and poorly managed image to the public (as could be the case when various managers are involved). When compared to a centralized approach, this policy may be easier and less expensive to administer. One option that may be added to this policy would involve getting management's permission in writing prior to each release. For related ideas, see the policies entitled "Presentation Of Low-Profile And Secure Image" and "Release Of Systems Documentation To Third Parties." A: EMT; E: LMH.

549. Public Representations About Future Earnings Or New Product Prospects

Policy: To avoid shareholder class-action lawsuits, workers are forbidden from making any public representations about Company X future earnings or the prospects for new products.

Commentary: The rash of recent class-action lawsuits (many of which are frivolous) has made senior management at many American organizations worry about the repercussions of making any future projections. This policy accordingly prohibits any public statement along these lines. Not only will the policy help stop investor lawsuits, it will also stop gyrations in stock prices associated with actual financial results not meeting management's financial projections. This policy is relevant only to publicly traded companies; those companies without publicly-held stock need not have a policy such as this. This policy pertains to verbal representations made to reporters, as well as written representation made in stock offering prospectuses, annual reports, and related documents. Some organizations may consider this policy to be too stringent, and they may wish to add the words "with the exception of the CEO" after the word "workers." See the policies entitled "Requests For Company X Information Referred To Public Relations" and "Prior Review For Speeches, Presentations, Technical Papers, Etc." A: EM; T: LMH.

550. Waiting Period Prior To External Disclosure Of Requested Information

Policy: If Company X has received an outsider's request for internal information that is not of a sales, marketing, or public relations nature, then the following process must be followed. The information's owner and the corporate counsel must each be given five (5) business days to evaluate the merits of the request. If no objection is received from either the owner or the corporate counsel, then the information may be released. All requesters should be charged for the direct costs incurred in the process of fulfilling their requests.
Commentary: The intention of this policy is to define the ways to handle external requests for internal information that may be of a sensitive nature. This policy is used by the State of North Carolina, and the information involved is assumed to be public (under "freedom of information" laws or the equivalent thereof). Assuming that the information is public warrants a relatively lenient attitude about disclosure. The requested information might invade the privacy of a certain party, it might be national defense related information, it might be needed by law enforcement for an investigation in process, or for some other reason might not be appropriate to disclose. The possibility that it might be sensitive warrants the five day review period. The policy could be used by commercial organizations if it was restricted to certain information to which the public generally had a right to know. For example, at an electric utility monopoly, information about the systems used to generate electricity might be readily disclosed to the public in the absence of an objection from the parties named in the policy. When used in a governmental agency, the policy's reference to the parties able to veto the request could be changed to middle-level managers in charge of the systems and the related information. For a related idea, see the policy entitled "Requests For Company X Information Referred To Public Relations." A: MT; E: LMH.

551. Phased Public Release Of Controversial Sensitive Information

Policy: Controversial and sensitive Company X information must be released to the public in installments so that the impact of each disclosure can be measured and so that additional releases can be postponed if necessary.

Commentary: The intention of this policy is to assure that Company X's intended explanation accompanies each release of controversial information. In public relations jargon, the policy seeks to assure that the right "spin" is applied to controversial information released to the public. This will help to minimize damage to the reputation of Company X and will also help to assure that the information is used for intended purposes. A good example of this policy is provided by the United States Federal Bureau of Investigation (FBI) which has released information on the controversial email wiretapping tool called Carnivore in phases, each of which lasts 45 days. Of course, this policy's process for the release of controversial information may be in conflict with court orders, and then the court orders would prevail. But if Company X were voluntarily releasing information for the public benefit, or in order to assist a non-profit group (perhaps a privacy watchdog group), then this policy would be applicable. Note that this approach also provides time for the organization to fully research its internal records and to thereby determine all the information that will be released. This approach additionally allows Company X to release the least controversial parts of a sensitive information collection first, and to gradually provide progressively more controversial material. For related ideas, see the policies entitled "Presentation Of Low-Profile And Secure Image" and "Requests For Company X Information Referred To Public Relations." A: M; E: MH.

552. Approval For Help Wanted Ads And Disclosure Of Sensitive Material

Policy: All public help wanted advertising or announcements must be approved in advance by the Corporate Human Resources Department prior to being placed. The HR Department will ensure that labor law requirements are met, and that sensitive internal information is not inadvertently released.

Commentary: This policy is intended to prevent competitive intelligence analysts (that's a polite term for industrial spies) from using help wanted advertisements to determine what other firms are doing, what new products they will soon release, etc. Help wanted ads can additionally release management's priorities as well as internal problems. Examined over time, help wanted ads can also indicate a firm's strategic direction. All this is possible now that help wanted ads are on the Internet, and searchable by company name. For that reason, it is now advisable not to mention company name anywhere in an ad; some organizations may take it further, insisting on rotating the contact information such as telephone number of fax number. Separately, at the present time, head-hunters (recruiters) will withhold the name of their clients because this information might be used by others for unknown and unauthorized purposes. On another note, this policy is one of those ideas that most people would have never thought of, and so it is necessary if they are going to be prevented from inadvertently disclosing information useful to industrial spies. This policy is a move back to the centralization of information management. Only when all sensitive information goes through a funnel (such as a firewall) can certain pass/no-pass decisions be made. In the future, we will find many more gates such as this for information released to the public (review of articles to be published is one example). Many organizations are far too porous, allowing all sorts of sensitive information to seep out in unintended ways ("leakage" is the technical term). For related ideas, see the policies entitled "Prior Review For Speeches, Presentations, Technical Papers, Etc." and "Waiting Period Prior To External Disclosure Of Requested Information." A: E; E: MH.

553. Established Procedure For Review Of Information Released To Public

Policy: All information to be released to the public must have first have been reviewed by management according to an established and documented process.

Commentary: The intention of this policy is to require management to establish and observe a formal procedure for the review of information before it is released to the public. Beyond requiring such a procedure be used, this policy also requires the procedure to be documented. Separately, the policy could be expanded to require that documentation reflecting each request also be generated. Perhaps the most important part of the latter type of documentation is the specific approvals provided (signatures, dates, etc.). The existence of documentation is likely to have a sobering effect, such that conservative and well-reasoned decisions are more likely to be made. Although appropriate for those organizations with highly developed data classification schemes, this policy can also exist in the absence of a formal data classification scheme (it implies a two tiered approach in which information is either internal or public). For information about data classification, see the policy entitled "Four Category Data Classification Scheme." A less rigorous way to approach this issue may be found in the policy entitled "Approval Required Prior To Release Of Company X Information." A: EMT; E: LMH.

554. Prior Review For Speeches, Presentations, Technical Papers, Etc.

Policy: Every speech, presentation, technical paper, book, or other communication to be delivered to the public must first have been approved for release by the involved employee's immediate manager. This policy applies if the involved employee will represent Company X, if the employee will discuss Company X affairs (even if only in general), or if the communication is based on information obtained in the course of Company X duties. If new products, research results, corporate strategies, customer information, or marketing approaches are to be divulged, prior approval of the director of R&D and the director of the Legal Department must also be obtained.

Commentary: This policy requires that employees always obtain approval from their managers prior to delivering a speech, presentation, technical paper, or other communication. It thus helps prevent unauthorized (often inadvertent) disclosure of sensitive information. Additionally, the policy helps make sure that employees representing the organization will do a polished and professional job. The policy does not apply to personal matters, such as when an employee writes a paper on political matters or when he or she gives a speech at church. Nonetheless, if an employee discussed the general state of the industry in which Company X offered products or services, this too would need to be approved. This policy could be expanded to include the phrase "workers should disclose no more Company X-related information than is needed to achieve the desired purpose." Separately, the matters of particular concern to management are spelled out in the last sentence, and extra approvals are required if these matters will be communicated (this discourages employees from publicly discussing these matters). Of particular concern is the public disclosure of patentable material; if this information is published prior to the filing of a patent, then the patent can be invalidated (note that patent laws vary from country to country). See the policies entitled "Special Approval Required For Disclosure Of Patentable Ideas" and "All Public Representations Must Be Cleared Through Public Relations." For a more general policy, see the policy entitled "Approval Required Prior To Release Of Company X Information." A: EMT; E: LMH.

555. Conditions For Acceptance Of Third Party Sensitive Information

Policy: If an agent, employee, consultant, or contractor is to receive secret or confidential information from a third party on behalf of Company X, this disclosure must be preceded by the third party's signature of a release form approved by the Legal Department.

Commentary: This policy is intended to prevent Company X from being obliged to pay royalties or other compensation to third parties if, subsequent to this disclosure, Company X releases a product or service which is related to the ideas disclosed by the third party. A release form should make it clear that Company X is under no obligation to pay any such royalties or other compensation, and that receipt of the information does not imply any contractual arrangement whatsoever. This may be a particularly difficult issue if Company X has been secretly developing similar information (perhaps in the form a product). If this is the case, Company X may deliberately choose not to accept the information lest some dispute ensue. Some organizations--such as venture capital firms--are so concerned about this, without exception they refuse to sign other people's confidentiality agreements. Consultation with the Legal Department within Company X will be necessary prior to the release of a policy such as this. Also see the policy entitled "Acknowledgement Required For Deliveries Of Secret Information." A: EMT; E: LMH.

556. Signing Third Party Confidentiality Agreements Without Approval

Policy: Workers must not sign confidentiality agreements provided by third parties without the advance authorization of Company X legal counsel designated to handle intellectual property matters.

Commentary: In an effort to expedite discussions with suppliers, customers, and potential strategic partners, many workers will sign third party confidentiality agreements without thinking about it. They may thereby obligate their organization to pay royalties, should the organization later come out with a similar product or service. They may also thereby cause their employer to be accused of stealing ideas, when the same ideas were already known by their employer. Similarly, by signing a confidentiality agreement, they may legally prohibit their organization from introducing a similar product or service. To avoid these and other unfortunate and detrimental outcomes, this policy requires all confidentiality agreements to be routed through internal legal counsel (or designated external legal counsel). For a related idea, see the policy entitled "Third Party Non-Disclosure Agreements And Sensitive Information." A: E; E: LMH.

557. Sensitive Information Access For Temporaries And Consultants

Policy: Activities requiring access to sensitive Company X information must only be performed by full-time permanent employees unless one of the following conditions prevail: (1) the requisite knowledge or skills are not possessed by a full-time permanent employee, (2) an emergency or disaster requires the use of additional workers, or (3) permission of the Director of Human Resources has been obtained.

Commentary: The intention of this policy is to restrict access to sensitive information (information that requires a data classification designation besides "unclassified") to the most-trusted individuals. Full-time permanent employees (not newly-hired employees who may still be on probation) are generally more loyal than temporary employees or consultants, and are therefore more trustworthy. Once the employment relationship has ended, Company X has little control over the activities of temporary employees or consultants, but it maintains significant control over full-time employees. The risks of using people other than full-time permanent employees can be partially mitigated via confidentiality agreements. Entities which are virtual corporations, that use outsourcing extensively, or that have other modern decentralized/networked organization structures may have trouble with this policy because it's based on an assumption that a core group of employees runs the organization. See the policies entitled "Confidentiality Agreements Required For All Company X Workers" and "Four Category Data Classification Scheme." Also see the policy entitled "Privilege Restriction Based On The Need-to-Know." A: M; E: LMH.

1.3.3.6. Right To Know

558. Workers Have Right To Know All Workplace Hazards

Policy: Workers have a right to know the nature of all hazards that they may confront in the workplace. Management must inform workers about the existence of these hazards, provide safeguards to lessen the risk to workers, and train workers in the proper use of these safeguards.

Commentary: This policy is intended to be used to force management to disclose all hazards (robotic machinery that might cripple workers, quicksand on company property, ergonomic problems with certain computer equipment, etc.). The policy seeks to avoid lawsuits and other disputes, as well as foster worker confidence that management does indeed care about the workers' welfare. The policy discourages the use of workers as unknowing "guinea pigs" (test subjects). One of the classic cases of such unknown testing involves United States soldiers who witnessed an atomic bomb explosion at close proximity without knowing about related health risks; many of these soldiers subsequently succumbed to radiation poisoning. This policy is general in nature, while a policy that deals with medical matters is entitled "Mandatory Disclosure Of Worker Health And Safety Information." This policy is more proactive than the policy entitled "Mandatory Disclosure Of Worker Health And Safety Information" in that it requires management to take steps to properly protect workers (i.e., go beyond simple disclosure). For example, if a workplace is noisy, this policy requires that management inform workers of the danger to their hearing, provide ear protectors, and train workers in the proper use of these ear protectors. The other policy mentioned above would, for instance, require only disclosure of the danger to worker hearing. For a related idea, see the policy entitled "Waiting Period Prior To External Disclosure Of Requested Information." A: EMT; E: LMH.

559. Nature Of Labels On Hazardous Products And Services

Policy: All Company X products and services which may present a hazard to consumers, purchasers, workers, or other involved parties must have labels identifying the nature of the hazard, ways to avoid the hazard, and steps to take in the event that the hazard causes a loss.

Commentary: The intention of this policy is to prevent trouble (lawsuits, union grievances, worker accident related health insurance claims, etc.). It is better to put people on notice than to have to defend oneself against lawsuits alleging that people hurt themselves or others because they didn't know about hazards. This information security policy has recently been in the newspapers in the United States because some people allege that tobacco companies knew of the cancer causing nature of cigarettes but did not publicly disclose this information. Although organizations in the United States often go too far when it comes to hazard labelling, as the old adage goes: "Better safe than sorry." New US Federal Government laws in the United States are particularly stringent when it comes to labelling foodstuffs and medicines. This policy also applies to services. For example, a telephone sex service might have an initial outgoing message that warns callers about the nature of the service, and gives them an opportunity to hang up without being charged for the call. This policy requires extensive discussion with internal legal counsel. For a related idea about notices, see the policy entitled "Security Notice In System Log-in Banner." A: M; E: LMH.

560. Refrain From Pressuring Employees Who Worked At Competitors

Policy: Employees who formerly worked at competing organizations are encouraged to abide by the confidentiality agreements they signed with those organizations. Other employees must refrain from pressuring these employees to disclose information which might be beneficial to Company X.

Commentary: This policy is intended to make it clear that Company X has no intention of pressuring new recruits from competing organizations to disclose proprietary information from former employers. The policy also indicates that hiring staff from competing organizations is not part of a strategy for indirectly conducting industrial espionage. This policy is most relevant to organizations where turnover is high, such as high-tech firms in Silicon Valley, California, USA. As an aside, the significant amount of press given to a recent court case involving Borland and Symantec indicates this is an area where significant disputes exist. In that case, an executive was alleged to have stolen proprietary information from his former employer. Of course, some know-how will inadvertently be transferred from one organization to another whenever such a staff recruitment situation occurs. Although the specifics of the case involved will dominate any legal action that ensues, a policy like this may be helpful because it shows that management does not support indirect industrial espionage. For related ideas, see the policies entitled "Avoid Actual And Apparent Conflict of Interest" and "Requests For Company X Information Referred To Public Relations." A: E; E: LMH.

561. Disclosure Of Privacy Related Information Security Policies & Procedures

Policy: As a general rule, information security policies and procedures should be revealed only to Company X workers and selected outsiders (such as auditors) who have a legitimate business need for this information. A notable exception involves private data about individuals. In these cases, Company X has a duty to communicate the privacy related policies and procedures employed. In addition, Company X has a duty to disclose the existence of systems containing private information and the ways this information is used.

Commentary: This policy addresses a dichotomy that has many people confused. On one hand, information about security should be restricted to insiders only, but on the other hand, it should be revealed to outsiders. This policy explains why the dichotomy is necessary. Some organizations may wish to go one step further, adding a sentence at the end of the policy indicating that Company X recognizes that people have a vested interest in information about them. This policy is quite progressive and reflects the privacy policies in use at a number of telephone companies and government agencies. Commercial concerns in the United States, for the most part, have not yet adopted such a progressive stance. Commercial concerns in Europe, however, will find this common practice. The policy is deliberately vague about the specific information to be revealed, leaving that decision up to management (a data classification scheme should be used to designate information that is public). For related ideas, see the policies entitled "Customer Requests For Anonymity On Company X Systems" and "External Reporting Of Information Security Violations." A: MT; E: LMH.

1.3.3.7. Handling Confidential Data In Meetings

562. Uninvited Attendees At Meetings Covering Secret Information

Policy: Persons other than those specifically invited must not attend meetings where secret information will be discussed. Exceptions will be made only if advance management approval is obtained.

Commentary: The intention of this policy is to definitively instruct workers that no uninvited people may attend meetings where secret information is discussed. To allow this attendance would be to alter the set of people who have been authorized to access the information, and thus in effect usurp the authority of the secret information's owner. Note that this policy applies to in-person meetings, teleconferences, as well as virtual meetings where participants meet each other on-line (such as Internet Relay Chat or IRC). Separately, this policy could be modified such that approval is required from the secret information's owner rather than "management." The policy also helps overcome an inappropriate tendency where people are nice and polite, perhaps saying things like "of course you can stay." The term "secret" can be replaced with the most sensitive data classification label(s) used by Company X. This policy assumes the term "secret" has been defined; see the policy entitled "Four Category Data Classification Scheme." Also see the policy entitled "Oral Disclosure Of Confidential Information In Meetings." A: EM; E: MH.

563. Third Party Visitor Meetings In Enclosed Conference Rooms

Policy: If sensitive information is being handled by workers in the immediate vicinity of a conference room, all meetings with third party visitors (vendors, customers, regulators, etc.) who are not authorized to have access to such sensitive information must take place in fully-enclosed conference rooms.

Commentary: The intention of this policy is to prevent third parties from being inadvertently exposed to sensitive information. To reduce the chances of this happening, conference rooms must have walls on all sides, as well as a door that closes. Many modern offices are "open" and do not have complete walls or doors, and as a result sounds from the surrounding area can be overheard by visitors. This policy deals with acceptable places to have meetings more than it specifies the need for at least one fully-enclosed conference room. From a building construction standpoint, ideally visitors should not need to go through areas containing sensitive information in order to reach either a conference room or toilet facilities. This is one reason why conference rooms are often in a public area -- an area outside access control points such as doors that require an authorized badge before they open. By keeping them away from certain areas, the policy helps to prevent visitors from viewing sensitive information in written form as well. Also see the policy entitled "Clean Desks And Working Areas." A: EM; E: MH.

564. Oral Disclosure Of Confidential Information In Meetings

Policy: If confidential information is released orally in a meeting, seminar, lecture, or related presentation, the speaker must clearly communicate the sensitivity of the information. The speaker must also remind the audience to use discretion when disclosing it to others. Visual aids such as slides and overhead transparencies must include the appropriate confidentiality markings.

Commentary: The intention of this policy is to make sure that people who hear confidential information at a meeting treat it appropriately. Often the spoken word is handled more informally than the written word; unless specific steps to remind people about the proper handling of spoken information are taken, they may inadvertently disclose it to unauthorized parties. This policy furthermore implies that all workers who are giving presentations should clearly determine whether the information is confidential. The policy assumes that a data sensitivity classification scheme has already been adopted. See the policy entitled "Four Category Data Classification Scheme." Also see the policy entitled "Established Procedure For Review Of Information Released To Public." A: EM; E: MH.

565. Black Boards And White Boards Must Be Erased After Meetings

Policy: After each meeting is over, black boards and white boards in conference rooms must be erased.

Commentary: The intention of this policy is to make sure that any potentially sensitive information that is recorded on a black board or a white board is not inadvertently disclosed to unintended parties. Conference rooms are by their nature no-man's land, and anyone who happens to be in the building can enter them and perhaps write down what is recorded on the wall. Black boards and white boards in personal offices can, in some instances, be protected by locks on the door and the personal presence of an occupant. This policy is also courteous to the next users of the meeting room who may be people who wish to use the black board or white board. This policy makes no reference to the methods to erase the information, which most often are incomplete (someone who really tried to discern what was recorded can often obtain some information). For details about erasure methods, see the policy entitled "Erasure Of Sensitive Information On Black Boards And White Boards." Also see the policy entitled "Cameras Plus Audio Or Video Recording Equipment Prohibited." A: EMT; E: LMH.

566. Erasure Of Sensitive Information On Black Boards And White Boards

Policy: When sensitive information has been recorded on black boards or white boards, it must be definitively erased (with water or special cleaning fluids) before the authorized recipients of this information leave the area.

Commentary: The intention of this policy is to prevent the inadvertent disclosure of sensitive information to unauthorized parties. If sensitive information were to be left on a black board or a white board (in a conference room or in a private office), then the next people to enter the area could immediately obtain this information. Note that the policy is silent about the location of the black board or white board. In some military organizations, this policy is a standard operating procedure; it is nonetheless appropriate for commercial organizations as well. For related ideas, see the policies entitled "Uninvited Attendees At Meetings Covering Secret Information" and "Black Boards And White Boards Must Be Erased After Meetings." A: EMT; E: MH.

1.3.3.8. Miscellaneous Confidentiality Policies

567. Nature And Location Of Company X Information Is Confidential

Policy: Information about the nature and location of Company X information, such as that found in a data dictionary, is confidential and must only be disclosed to those who have a demonstrable need-to-know.

Commentary: The intention of this policy is to put workers on notice that information about information (also known as "metadata") is confidential. Note the distinction between restricting access to information based on the need-to-know, and restricting access to information about information based on the need-to-know. Metadata is of great use to system hackers/crackers, industrial spies, saboteurs, and others intent on doing harm to Company X. In many cases, metadata is more valuable than the information to which it refers. This is because metadata can include a data classification label (marking), a description of relevant control measures, the systems on which the information is resident, persons who have legitimate access rights to the information, etc. Looked at from a more commercial perspective, information about the existence of a soon-to-be-released product or service may be more important than the actual specifications for the product. Separately, while data dictionaries (also called "data directories" in government circles) can be important management tools, access to the information contained therein must be restricted based on the need-to-know. A new type of groupware software package called "document management systems" also contain metadata that should be restricted in accordance with this policy (one such vendor is Intellitactics based in Kitchener, Ontario, Canada). For more information about this notion, see the more general policy entitled "Privilege Restriction Based On The Need-to-Know." For more ideas about metadata, see the policy entitled "Management Must Be Notified Of Information Integrity Attributes" and "High-Level Inventory Of Information Assets." A: EMT; E: LMH.

568. Information Security Policies & Procedures Are For Internal Use Only

Policy: Unless the Information Security Manager has first approved their release in writing, all Company X information security policies and procedures are classified as Internal Use Only.

Commentary: The intention of this policy is to prevent workers from disclosing to outsiders the specifics of how Company X secures its information and information systems. These outsiders may in turn use the details of information security policies and procedures to compromise Company X information and information systems. For example, knowledge about an internal process may assist an industrial spy in perpetrating a credible social engineering fraud. Separately, because some information security policies are made public (for example a privacy policy posted on a web site), some workers may get the impression that other information security policies may also be publicly released without a problem. To the contrary, most information security policies should by default be declared to be Internal Use Only. This is not "security by obscurity" but a prudent approach where potential attackers are not given any more information about controls than is absolutely necessary. Thus, selected information security policies should be revealed to outsiders only when it is required for business reasons (for example when negotiating an extranet contract) or because it is the right thing to do (for example to give customers a sense for the ways that their personal data is handled). Note that not all of the information security policies need to be released in these instances. On another note, this policy can be included in a data classification subsection within a policy document. Each information security policy document should be marked with an appropriate classification in order to emphasize the fact that the policies are not public information. For related ideas, see the policies entitled "Work According To Information Security Policies & Procedures" and "Four Category Data Classification Scheme." A: EMT; E: LMH.

569. Location Of Data Processing Centers Considered Confidential

Policy: The computer center's physical address is confidential and must not be disclosed to those without a demonstrable need-to-know.

Commentary: The intention of this policy is to ensure that terrorists, saboteurs, industrial spies, hackers/crackers, competitors, and the like are not able to easily locate Company X data processing facilities. For correspondence, a post office box is recommended. Of course, vendors, consultants, and other third parties who are doing work for Company X will need to know the actual address. Phone company directories should similarly not list a physical location for these facilities. Likewise, there should be no sign at the street level indicating that the facility is the "Company X Data Processing Center." This policy could be expanded to include network control centers, record archive sites, and other major facilities for the handling or storage of information. Although reference is made to a "computer center," which often implies mainframes and larger systems, this policy is equally applicable to small systems such as those using personal computers, workstations, and client/server systems. Also see the policy entitled "Nature And Location Of Company X Information Is Confidential." A: EMT; E: LMH.

570. Browsing On Company X Systems And Networks Prohibited

Policy: Workers must not browse through Company X computer systems or networks. For example, curious searching for interesting files and/or programs in the directories of other users is prohibited. Steps taken to legitimately locate information needed to perform one's job is not considered browsing.

Commentary: The intention of this policy is to prohibit hacking, cracking, and related activities. In many instances, perpetrators of computer abuse are simply seeking thrills and are curious rather than deliberately malicious. Often these people go on to take advantage of the information they discover (such as credit card numbers). When caught, these people often claim that they were only looking around, and that they had no malicious, fraudulent, or other bad intentions. To counteract such claims, this policy makes it clear that browsing information systems is not acceptable. Separately, if workers do end-up browsing, this policy gives management a tool with which to discipline or terminate the worker. The policy is particularly relevant to microcomputers (PCs), workstations, client/server systems, and local area networks (LANs) because these small systems often have inadequate access controls. It should be noted that his policy is not an acceptable replacement for a real access control system. Separately, the policy could be expanded to mention intranet surfing, which is permissible and is not considered browsing. Also see the related policy entitled "Building Systems So That Errors And Manipulations Come To Light." A: EMT; E: LMH.

571. Authorized Systems Administrator Examination Of Private User Files

Policy: Systems administrators are authorized to examine private user files to handle emergencies such as virus infestations and system crashes. Whenever user files are examined in this manner, the involved user(s) must be notified. After the problem has been resolved, all copies of such files made by the administrator must be promptly destroyed.

Commentary: This policy is intended to put users on notice that their files may be examined and copied by a systems administrator in the course of normal business activities. The policy also informs administrators how they should go about accessing private user files (inform the user, and copy files into their own directory). Some organizations may also wish to require that administrators get management permission prior to examining private user files (although this will slow things down). An alternative and more expedient way to handle the management approval issue is to require administrators to notify management after the fact. Separately, some organizations may wish to limit the notification part of policy to internal users; notification to outsiders may cause problems such as allegations of snooping. On another note, the causes for an examination of user files could be expanded to include internal investigations, although user notification in these instances would jeopardize the investigation. The policy, as written, does not say that authorized personnel cannot review user files in the course of an investigation, and so the policy implicitly allows such a search. For related ideas, see the policies entitled "Approval Required Before Access To Sensitive Or Valuable Information," "Process For Granting Access To Company X Information," and "Privacy Expectations And Electronic Mail." A: ET; E: LMH.

572. Power Down Required For Systems Processing Sensitive Information

Policy: All computers that have been used for processing secret information must be powered-down at the end of the day, at a lunch break, or at the termination of a session. In most cases, this will erase residual information contained in the computer's memory (check the manufacturer's documentation to make sure), preventing it from being disclosed to unauthorized parties. An exception may be made for stand-alone computers located in areas with strict physical access controls which prevent unauthorized persons from gaining access to the system.

Commentary: This policy is intended to sensitize users the possibility that sensitive information may be scavenged from computer memory. Since most computers have volatile memory, this information will be erased when power is switched off. In some cases (depending on the type of chip employed), the memory is non-volatile. In these cases, the information will not be erased, and some other actions are called for (such as "zeroization" utilities which overwrite areas in memory). In recognition of the existence of non-volatile memory, the policy says "check the manufacturer's documentation." Separately, a turned-off computer is much more difficult to manipulate remotely (although special chips in the newest systems can be "woken-up" remotely); thus if equipment is off it is less likely to be used in a break-in. On another note, the policy is particularly relevant to stand-alone departmental servers, as well as microcomputers (PCs) and workstations located in an open office environment. The policy assumes that other policies instruct users not to store information on systems with inadequate access controls. For ideas along these lines, see the policy entitled "Use Of Hard-Disk Drives For Storage Of Sensitive Information." This policy assumes that the data storage media will also be physically removed, encrypted, locked in a piece of heavy furniture, or otherwise secured. For ideas about the security of secret information stored on computer data media, see the policy entitled "Choosing Computer Storage Media Data Classifications." This policy additionally assumes that the term "secret" has been defined in another policy; see the policy entitled "Four Category Data Classification Scheme." A: EMT; E: H.

573. Covering Sensitive Information When Interrupted At Work

Policy: Whenever a worker is handling Company X secret, confidential, or private information, if another person enters the area around the desk of the worker, steps to conceal the information must immediately be taken. If the information is in physical form, the information can be covered with other material. If the information is displayed on a computer screen, the worker may invoke a screen saver or log-off.

Commentary: The intention of this policy is to instruct users that they must conceal sensitive information when interrupted in their office or workplace. If they act as prescribed in this policy, workers will prevent the information from being disclosed to unauthorized persons (even though these interrupting parties are most often employees). One positive side-effect of this policy will be complaints from those people who find it difficult to work this way. For example, a receptionist will find it difficult to properly handle sensitive information and to handle visitors. Rather than indicating a deficiency in the policy, this complaint indicates that the individual's work on sensitive information is incompatible with her visitor reception duties. As a solution, the individual may do this work on a computer system located in a private office when not performing receptionist duties. This policy assumes that the terms "secret, confidential, or private" has been defined in another policy; for instance, see the policy entitled "Four Category Data Classification Scheme." In the policy itself, these three designations may entirely be replaced by the term "sensitive," or by some other terms used at Company X. Also the policies entitled "Securing Sensitive Information In Unattended Rooms," "Warnings Required If Recipients Might Be Offended or Upset," and "Leaving Sensitive Systems Without Logging-Off." A: EMT; E: H.

574. Never Lend Computers Containing Sensitive Information To Others

Policy: Never lend to others a personal computer, handheld computer, transportable computer, personal digital assistant (PDA), smart phone, or any other computer that you use for business activities if the machine contains sensitive information.

Commentary: The intention of this policy is to prohibit workers from lending their personal machine to others, often in an effort to be polite or accommodating. A wide variety of controls, such as personal computer fixed-password-based boot controls and encryption measures are set up for a specific individual, given that individual's present job duties and need-to-know. Allowing another person to access that machine (except perhaps a repair person), would permit the other person to circumvent these controls. To allow others to use a personal computer also jeopardizes the veracity of logs, and other mechanisms which monitor user behavior (firewalls examining web sites visited for example). Increasingly, personal computers need to be considered as unique and specifically assigned to a certain individual, just as is the case with user-IDs. Separately, this policy may be welcomed by many users who in the past felt uneasy about lending their computers to others, but up until the policy was issued, never really had a definitive basis for saying "no." On another note, the word "sensitive" will need to be defined elsewhere. For related ideas, see the policies entitled "Unique User-ID And Password Required" and "Password Sharing Prohibition." A: E; E: MH.

575. Locking File Cabinets Must Be Provided To And Used By All Workers

Policy: Since Company X handles sensitive information in the course of its regular business activities, all office workers must be provided with locking file cabinets. Workers must lock all sensitive material in these file cabinets when away from their desk, and must provide a backup copy of the key(s) to their department manager.

Commentary: The intention of this policy is to ensure that workers are given one of the basic tools for preserving data confidentiality -- a locking file cabinet. The policy also puts local management on notice that they must provide this type of furniture to all office workers (including temporaries, contractors, consultants, etc.). The policy additionally requires that employees use the locking file cabinets for sensitive material (the word "sensitive" will need to be defined elsewhere, perhaps in a data classification policy). Inevitably, the workers will lose or forget their keys, and that's why there is a backup with the department manager. In some cases backups will also need to be deposited with the physical security manager. For a related idea, see the policy entitled "All Workstations Must Have Metal Keys To Control Access." Also see the policies entitled "Traditional Clean Desk Policy," and "Security Requirements For Work At Home Arrangements." A: E; E: LMH.

576. Prohibited Trading Dates For Employee Stock Transactions

Policy: To prevent insider trading and also to preclude allegations of insider trading, employees must not buy or sell Company X stock or bonds between the end of the fiscal quarter and the time that financial results are publicly announced.

Commentary: The intention of this policy is to prevent employees who may have access to confidential information that is soon to be made public from exploiting their knowledge of this information in the stock market. The time frame given is the time period in which this manipulative exploitation could take place. After the public knows of the information, there is less of a special advantage for those who have insider knowledge. The policy is relevant only to companies which have stocks or bonds on public exchanges. It could be adapted to research institutes or government agencies that collect and analyze information (such as growth rate of the economy), the release of which alters the prices of stocks and bonds. Note that the policy applies to all employees, not just those who are working in the accounting department or who may otherwise know what the financial results were. The policy may be expanded to include instructing others (relatives, friends, attorneys, etc.) to buy or sell Company X stock on an employee's behalf or for their own benefit. A definition of insider trading may also be an appropriate adjunct to the policy (see local laws and regulations). Discussions with internal legal counsel will be needed on this policy. Also see the policy entitled "Avoid Actual And Apparent Conflict of Interest." A: EMT; E: LMH.

577. Dictation Machines And Tape Recorders For Sensitive Information

Policy: To reduce the chance of unauthorized disclosure, in general, workers should not record sensitive information with dictation machines, tape recorders, or similar devices. If the use of these devices is an operational necessity, the proper sensitivity classification must be specified at the beginning and end of each segment of sensitive information. In this case, the recording media must also be marked with the most stringent data classification found on the media. In addition, the media must be protected in accordance with the most stringent classification found on the media, and erased as soon as possible.

Commentary: The intention of this policy is to discourage the use of audio recording devices for sensitive information. If the use of these systems cannot be avoided, then the precautions specified in the policy should be taken. These precautions are not necessary if the media has been encrypted or scrambled (the technology for these processes is generally unavailable to non-military or non-diplomatic organizations). Tape spools, cassette tapes, and other recording media are easily stolen or copied, and accordingly expose sensitive information to unwarranted risks of unauthorized disclosure. For greater security, the requirement in the policy to "erase" the media as soon as possible can be replaced with words instructing the user to "destroy" the media according to approved methods. See the policy entitled "Leaving Sensitive Information On Answering Machines." A: EMT; E: MH.

578. Periodic Sweeps For Bugging, Interception, And Recording Equipment

Policy: The Telecommunications Department manger must initiate and supervise periodic sweeps for unauthorized bugging, interception, and recording equipment. These sweeps must cover all Company X offices and facilities where secret information is discussed, stored, or handled.

Commentary: The intention of this policy is to make it clear that sweeps for bugging and interception devices must be performed on a regular basis. The policy defines who must initiate and oversee this effort, so management can go directly to this person and ask them when the last sweep was done and what, if anything, was discovered. Long done in military establishments, these sweeps are now increasingly common in commercial firms because the industrial espionage business is booming and because it is now relatively easy to plant very small transmitting devices in telephones, under conference room tables, and in other inconspicuous places. Such sweeps also look for recording equipment in telephone closets, such as tape recorders that are turned on only when a conversation is underway. In most cases, an external consultant with specialized equipment will be needed, because most organizations do not have sufficiently trained personnel on staff. For related ideas, see the policies entitled "Guarded Terms For Telephone Discussions Of Sensitive Information" and "Encryption Of Passwords." A: T; E: MH.

1.3.4. Data Criticality

1.3.4.1. Systems Design

579. Specific Quantitative Goal For System Availability

Policy: While especially critical computer systems must be available more often, users must be able to access all shared computer systems at least 95% of normal working hours, as computed on a monthly basis.

Commentary: The intention of such a policy is to get top management to evaluate what type of system availability is needed at the organization in question. While the number ("95%" here) is bound to change over time (hopefully increase), there is considerable merit to defining it as a requirement. Specific contingency planning efforts and systems design decisions can be derived from such a policy. The exact number specified will be a function of an organization's unique needs. The number given here may be acceptable for a manufacturing company, but it is definitely not acceptable for a telephone company (99.98% would be more appropriate). A policy of this type may also be useful for outsourcing deals, requests for proposals, and other interactions with outside parties. Also see the policy entitled "Annual Information Security Planning Process Required." A: MT; E: LMH.

580. Limitation Of User Abilities To Delay Or Interrupt Service

Policy: The activities of users of shared computer systems must not cause these systems to unduly delay or interrupt the provision of service to other users. An exception is made for system security administrators, system managers, and computer operators, all of which need such privileges to do their jobs.

Commentary: While this policy has to do with proper settings for access controls, it also deals with the actions end-users are able to initiate. For example, a single mainframe user should not be able to consume all the system's resources such that all other users are prevented from obtaining processing services. This policy is therefore intended to direct the ways in which access controls are established, the ways system resources are allocated (performance tuning), as well as the ways in which application systems are designed. Computer worms, viruses, Trojan horses, and other unauthorized programs will often consume excessive system resources, leading to the denial of service for users. If the system has been configured to prevent this type of denial of service, then the system manager is more readily informed that a problem has been encountered. For a more general but related idea, see the policy entitled "Privilege Restriction Based On The Need-to-Know." Also see the policy entitled "Prohibition Against Programs Consuming Excessive System Resources." A: T; E: LMH.

581. Establishment And Use Of Control Override Facilities

Policy: Management must establish override facilities to be used in those exceptional circumstances where controls must be compromised to maintain on-going business operations. The ability to use override facilities must be severely restricted, and these facilities must be used only when absolutely necessary.

Commentary: The intention of this policy is to put systems designers, application programmers, and other technical staff on notice about the need for override facilities. The policy is also intended to describe management's intentions regarding the use of these override facilities, and thus indicate how access controls for these facilities should be defined. Separately, some organizations may also wish to add words to the policy requiring all override facility usage to be logged. On a different note, if override facilities are used on a regular basis, they effectively render the controls impotent. This is why the facilities must be used only when absolutely necessary. For a more general but related idea, see the policy entitled "Privilege Restriction Based On The Need-to-Know." For a more management-oriented perspective, see the policy entitled "Management Definition Of Circumstances For Use Of Control Overrides." Also see the policy entitled "Generation And Review Of Logs Showing Use Of Override Facilities." A: T; E: LMH.

582. Management Definition Of Circumstances For Use Of Control Overrides

Policy: Management must clearly define the specific circumstances when system controls may be overridden. Usage of override facilities for other circumstances requires the advance approval of the Manager of Computer Operations or the on-duty delegate for this Manager. Override mechanisms must only be used to remedy extraordinary conditions that are not otherwise resolvable.

Commentary: The intention of this policy is to specify the circumstances in which system control override facilities may be used. Referencing these instructions, staff can use override facilities without obtaining specific management approval. This is useful, for instance, if the system crashes at 3:00AM, the problem has been encountered before, and the solution is well-known and already scripted. In a case like this, it is unnecessary to get specific management approval for the use of override facilities. Separately, an example of a control override tool in the IBM MVS mainframe environment is the Superzap (IAMAZAP) program -- a utility that can modify any file at any time, regardless of existing access controls. Separately, this policy is also applicable to small systems such as local area networks, client/server systems, and multi-user workstations. On another note, some organizations may also wish to add words to this policy, stating that logging is required for all override facility usage. If override facilities are used on a regular basis, they effectively render the controls impotent. For a more general but related idea, see the policy entitled "Privilege Restriction Based On The Need-to-Know." For a systems-design-oriented perspective on this same topic, see the policy entitled "Establishment And Use Of Control Override Facilities ." Also see the policy entitled "Generation And Review Of Logs Showing Use Of Override Facilities." A: MT; E: LMH.

583. Generation And Review Of Logs Showing Use Of Override Facilities

Policy: Whenever system controls have been overridden, a log must be generated showing both the changes made and the privileged commands that were used. A technical manager or a delegate must promptly review these logs and related particulars to ensure that: (1) the use of override facilities was warranted, and (2) these facilities were used in a correct manner.

Commentary: The intention of this policy is to specify when control override logs must be generated, when they must be reviewed, and what management must determine when reviewing the logs. Reviewing logs is made considerably more palatable if exception reports are generated rather than requiring management to go through chronological activity logs. System logs on a busy computer can often be 100 pages per 24 hour period, so exception reports are a useful way of focusing management attention on suspicious or important matters. Use of exception reports will also reduce the time taken to perform the review. If there is no log reflecting usage of control override facilities, privileged users will be tempted to abuse these facilities (perhaps perpetrating fraud, embezzlement, sabotage, etc.). Note that modern intrusion detection systems (IDS) in some cases can perform this log review automatically; an example of such a system is provided by Intrusion Detection, New York, New York, USA. For related ideas, see the policies entitled "Establishment And Use Of Control Override Facilities " and "Management Definition Of Circumstances For Use Of Control Overrides." A: MT; E: LMH.

584. Computing Environment Supporting Equipment Required

Policy: Local management must provide and adequately maintain fire detection/suppression, power conditioning, air conditioning, humidity control, and other computing environment protection systems necessary to assure continued service for critical production computer systems.

Commentary: So often ignored, these environmental support systems can be essential to continuous computer and communications support. The intention of this policy is to require local management to provide the systems needed for computers handling critical production applications. This policy can be employed by end-users to compel departmental and other local managers to comply with the requirements defined by a centralized information technology management group. For instance, the users of microcomputers (PCs) running a critical application might need, but not have uninterruptible power supply (UPS) systems, and these users might be fighting with local management to buy such equipment. The policy could then be used to compel management to get a UPS system. As this example implies, the distribution or decentralization of information systems has meant that local management now makes decisions previously made by the Information Technology Department. To ensure that local management makes the right decisions, a policy such as this (accompanied by the standards which would be a separate document) is required. Note that smaller and more modern computer systems don't have the same environmental requirements as larger and older systems (air conditioning is a good example). This policy is deliberately vague about exactly which environmental systems will be required because these will be determined by geographical location, systems technology employed, business needs, etc. Separately, the policy assumes the word "critical" has been defined in another policy; see the policy entitled "Four Category Data Classification Scheme." For a related idea, see the policy entitled "Power Conditioning Equipment Required For All Microcomputers." A: MT; E: LMH.

585. Power Conditioning Equipment Required For All Microcomputers

Policy: All microcomputers (PCs) and workstations must be outfitted with either uninterruptible power supply (UPS) systems, electrical power filters, or surge suppressers which have been approved by the Information Systems Department.

Commentary: A high percentage of computer problems are attributable to dirty electrical power (surges, spikes, dips, brown-outs, etc.). Of course, this policy is also relevant to minicomputers, super-minicomputers, and other systems. In most cases, however, larger multi-user systems already have sufficient power protection measures. The intent of this policy is thus to require systems under local or departmental management (generally small scale systems) to be outfitted with appropriate electrical power conditioning equipment. The specific type of power protection equipment needed is a function of the criticality of the system in question, and is accordingly not specified in the policy. Also see the policy entitled "Static Electricity Protection Equipment And Local Conditions." A: EMT; E: LMH.

586. Static Electricity Protection Equipment And Local Conditions

Policy: If weather and building conditions pose a significant risk of static electricity discharge, all microcomputers (PCs) and workstations must be outfitted with static protection equipment which has been approved by the Information Systems Department. This will ensure that the discharge of static electricity does not damage computer equipment or information.

Commentary: The intention of this policy is to make sure that computer equipment is properly configured so as to prevent unwarranted loss of data, damage to systems, and related downtime. Most often found in colder climates with forced air heating, static electricity can be a significant problem. Specifically, microprocessor chips can burn out and information held in memory can be inadvertently erased. Specific control measures, such as static electricity floor mats, static electricity absorbing touch bars, and proper grounding for equipment, may also be mentioned in the policy. The specific control measures were not included in this policy since they are likely to change over time. This policy could easily be extended to include communications systems as well as computers. If the organization in question uses more traditional computing technology, it may wish to add the word "terminals" to the policy right next to reference to "workstations." This policy may be merged with a policy about electrical power protection, such as the one entitled "Power Conditioning Equipment Required For All Microcomputers." A: T; E: LMH.

587. Dispersion Of Computer And Communication Systems

Policy: The concentration of processing facilities in one or a few installations represents a greater threat than where facilities are dispersed. Accordingly, computer and communications systems must be geographically dispersed whenever possible, so long as this does not unduly hinder operational performance, unduly jeopardize security, or unduly increase costs.

Commentary: The intention of this policy is to highlight the contingency planning related benefits of distributed computing (also known as "decentralized computing"). For example, if a bomb were to go off at a large centralized data processing center, it would be likely to cause considerably more damage than if the same bomb were to go off at one of several data processing centers used by the same organization. This policy is derived from a policy used by Edgar's department store in South Africa where the threats of terrorism, riot, and sabotage are high. Although the policy is relevant to other jurisdictions, it is particularly important in those areas where such attacks might occur. The mention of ways to jeopardize security in a policy may at first seem counter-productive because it may give people ideas, but this policy remains at a general level and really gives no specific instructions on how to cause Company X specific harm. Instead it expresses a design intention which is fully consistent with modern systems evolution, particularly client/server systems. Note that many of the smaller modern systems, such as client/server systems, often have inadequate security measures, so a trade-off must be struck. In other words, the expanded contingency-planning security to be achieved by decentralization is in part traded-off against reduced access-control security. Also see the policies entitled "Consistent Protection Of Information Regardless Of Manifestation" and "Compliance With Standards Required For Emergency/Disaster Support." A: T; E: LMH.

588. Web And Commerce Servers Must Not Store Critical Information

Policy: Web and commerce servers must not be used to store any critical Company X business information.

Commentary: The intention of this policy is to prevent damage to critical information. Just as a general would not put the president of a country on the front line in a war, so too organizations should not put their critical information on the periphery of their networks where it could be damaged or modified by unauthorized parties. Critical information, such as a customer contact database, should instead be stored on internal machines which are behind additional firewalls or other security barriers. Critical information may still be processed by web and commerce servers, it's just shipped off to other machines after the processing is done. As an aside, this policy views web and commerce servers as "sacrificial lambs" which could be damaged by a hacker without major adverse impact to the organization. Increasingly web and commerce servers are being protected within a DMZ or demilitarized zone (a firewall-protected subnet which is less secure than an internal network), and in these environments these types of servers are not going to be sacrificial lambs. Either way one designs a network, it is wise to store critical collections of information on the most secure machines which are behind several layers of access controls. For related ideas, see the policies entitled "All Internet Web Servers Must Be Firewall Protected" and "Internet Commerce Servers Must Be In Demilitarized Zone (DMZ)." A: T; E: LMH.

589. Avoidance Of Communication Network Central Point Of Failure

Policy: Management must design Company X communications networks so that no single point of failure, such as a central switching center, could cause network services to be unavailable.

Commentary: The intention of this policy is to guide systems designers, network technicians, and others in the types of systems desired by management. High publicity failures of the phone system have recently highlighted the dependence of organizations on their networks (voice and data). This policy implies that the internal department dealing with telecommunications should look into the use of two long distance carriers, temporary microwave links to be employed if land lines are down, and the like. While not immediately realizable in many organizations, this policy serves as an objective to which the organization aspires. Note that the term "unavailable" was used rather than "disrupted" -- in most circumstances, if part of the network goes down one can expect some temporary problems. In these cases, after the system has been reconfigured, hopefully services will continue to be provided. For an example of more-narrowly-defined instructions, see the policy entitled "Diverse Long Distance Network Routing Required." A: T; E: LMH.

590. Diverse Long Distance Network Routing Required

Policy: Management must design Company X communications systems so that critical communications may immediately be sent via multiple long distance carriers over physically diverse routes.

Commentary: Several major failures of long distance carrier phone lines have recently demonstrated that, for many organizations, it is wise to have two long distance carriers. This policy thus provides definitive management guidance to those responsible for communication system management. Note that the policy covers both voice and data networks, and that it only applies to critical communications. The policy assumes the existence of another policy which defines the word "critical;" see the policy entitled "Four Category Data Classification Scheme." For a more general idea, see the policy entitled "Avoidance Of Communication Network Central Point Of Failure." A: T; E: LMH.

591. Compliance With Standards Required For Emergency/Disaster Support

Policy: If subsidiaries, divisions, departments, and other Company X organizational units wish to be supported by the Information Systems Department on a priority basis in the event of an emergency or a disaster, they must implement hardware, software, policies, and related procedures consistent with Company X standards.

Commentary: Supporting non-standard systems is a nightmare in the event of an emergency or a disaster. Non-standard systems also make the preparation of a contingency plan very much more difficult. This is because already-prepared contingency planning material cannot be used, and relevant in-house expertise is less likely to be available. Separately, this policy allows organizational units to go their own way, but puts them on notice that the Information Systems Department cannot support them as they do support organizational units which comply with in-house standards. The policy is considered by some to be an exceptionally effective tool for forcing organizational units to comply with information technology standards. The policy is helpful in the recentralization of information security (information security has become too distributed at many organizations, and as a result has often become ineffective). In some respects, this policy is like another policy (not really security related) that requires all microcomputers (PCs) or workstations to meet standards if they are to be connected to a local area network (LAN). In this case, local department managers can purchase non-standard equipment--they just can't network it, thus making the equipment very much less useful. Also see the policies entitled "Dispersion Of Computer And Communication Systems" and "Centralized Responsibility For Information Security." A: T; E: LMH.

1.3.4.2. Contingency Planning

592. Framework For Segmenting Information Resources By Recovery Priority

Policy: Computer Operations management must establish and use a logical framework for segmenting information resources by recovery priority. This will in turn allow the most critical information resources to be recovered first. All departments must use this same framework when preparing information systems contingency plans.

Commentary: One purpose of this policy is to specify which organizational unit is responsible for defining the categories and overall framework for prioritizing information resources. Another purpose is to require all departments to follow the same framework when developing their own contingency plans. This will in turn allow various contingency plans to be more readily coordinated, merged, and prioritized. The words "Computer Operations" could just as easily be changed to "Information Security" or some other organizational group. The framework could include categories like "mission critical" = must be recovered within one hour, "critical" = must be recovered within eight hours, and "all others" = must be recovered within 48 hours. See the policy entitled "Annual Criticality Rating For Multi-User Applications." A: T; E: LMH.

593. Annual Criticality Rating For Multi-User Applications

Policy: In conjunction with relevant information owners, the Information Systems Department must periodically prepare or revise an assessment of the degree of criticality of all production multi-user computer applications. This rating process will allow appropriate contingency plans to be prepared.

Commentary: The process whereby criticality ratings are assigned to applications is a necessary precursor to writing an effective contingency plan. With this dependency in mind, this policy requires Information Systems Department management (or alternatively Information Security Department management) to periodically prepare/revise a list of critical applications. As business systems change, so will the criticality of these systems. Likewise, some applications will be retired, others will be introduced, some will become more important, others will become less important. As a result of these and other changes, contingency plans should be periodically updated. Separately, this policy acknowledges the reality that user department management doing an evaluation often will say that their systems are critical when indeed they are not; to get a reasonable and consistent view across an organization it is often necessary to have a centralized authority perform this ranking. On another note, this policy makes it clear that both Information Systems Department management and information owners are responsible for an annual report showing application criticality. This policy assumes the word "production" has been defined clearly in other documents. The policy additionally assumes the existence of another policy which defines the word "critical;" for example, see the policy entitled "Five Category Application Criticality Classification Scheme." Also see the policy entitled "Annual Information Security Planning Process Required." See the policy entitled "Framework For Segmenting Information Resources By Recovery Priority." A: T; E: LMH.

594. Five Category Application Criticality Classification Scheme

Policy: All production computer applications must be placed into one of five criticality classifications, each with separate handling requirements: highly critical, critical, priority, required, and deferrable. This criticality classification system must be used throughout Company X, and must form an integral part of the system contingency planning process.

Commentary: The intention of this policy is to specify standard criticality categories to be used throughout an organization. Once standardization is achieved, then the applications can be ranked, and the most critical ones can receive special contingency planning attention. The number of criticality categories will vary from organization to organization, as will the meanings of the terms like "priority." Generally, each of these terms will have a time period during which the application must be recovered. For example, "highly critical" applications could be those which must be recovered within 15 minutes. This policy provides a classification scheme much like the more common sensitivity-related classification schemes; see the policy entitled "Four Category Data Classification Scheme." Information itself could be rated according to criticality, but because information is so often processed by many different applications, it is frequently easier just to focus on applications when preparing a contingency plan. Also see the policy entitled "Annual Criticality Rating For Multi-User Applications." A: T; E: LMH.

595. Preparation And Maintenance Of Computer Emergency Response Plans

Policy: For computer and communications systems, management must prepare, periodically update, and regularly test emergency response plans. These plans must provide for the continued operation of critical systems in the event of an interruption or degradation of service.

Commentary: A distinction between emergencies and disasters is helpful. Emergencies require immediate attention but may not have long-term implications or serious financial consequences. Disasters have long-term implications, have serious financial consequences, and may or may not require immediate attention. For example, if an automated teller machine (ATM) network were to go down at lunch hour on a Friday (when people want to deposit their paychecks and get cash for the weekend), this would be an emergency. It would, however, not be a disaster. An earthquake that decimated the data processing center of a large firm would be a disaster. Thus the intention of this policy is to require that management prepare, update, and test emergency response plans in addition to disaster response plans, which are assumed to be required by another policy. The reference to "degradation of service" may be omitted without serious damage to the policy; in some organizations (civilian government agencies and other non-competitive environments) degradation of service may not be particularly important. For this policy to be most effective, the term "critical" needs to have been previously defined; see the policy entitled "Five Category Application Criticality Classification Scheme." Also see the policy entitled "Annual Information Security Planning Process Required." A: MT; E: LMH.

596. Continuous Computer Center Staffing For Prompt Problem Resolution

Policy: To assist with speedy problem detection and resolution, the main computer center must be staffed by technically-competent staff twenty four hours a day, seven days a week, three hundred sixty five days a year (24X7X365).

Commentary: The intention of this policy is to ensure that downtime is minimized and customer service remains at a high level. The policy also ensures that someone is on duty to respond to an intruder's attack as it is happening. For international networks, such as telephone networks, such continuous staffing is an absolute necessity. Likewise, this policy is often found at Internet Service Providers (ISPs), Internet hosting firms, and large volume Internet merchants. The policy is applicable to large organizations which have the resources to support continuous coverage. Smaller organizations can change the policy to refer to continuously on-call staff, in which case communication would perhaps be facilitated by pager or cellular phone. The policy can also be changed to remove the central site reference; these days, some organizations have support staffs in different parts of the world who work when other people in close-by time zones are working. Separately, having staff on duty continuously enables them to notice things which could not be readily determined by electronic systems. For example, perhaps the water level for the river behind the computer center is rising because there has been extended heavy rain, and a flood is imminent. In some cases, having continuous staff on duty will lower insurance rates too. Also note that the policy is deliberately silent when it comes to defining "technically competent," leaving this decision up to information systems management staff. For a related idea, see the policy entitled "When To Seek Assistance With Unauthorized Access Problems." A: T; E: MH.

597. Organization/Maintenance Of Computer Emergency Response Team

Policy: Management must organize and maintain an in-house computer emergency response team (CERT) that will provide accelerated problem notification, damage control, and problem correction services in the event of computer related emergencies such as virus infestations, hacker break-ins, and the like.

Commentary: The classic CERT that has been the model for many in-house CERTs can be found at Carnegie Mellon University, in Pittsburgh, Pennsylvania, USA; their phone number is (412) 268-7090 and their Internet address is cert@cert.org. The Carnegie Mellon CERT assists users of the Internet network, while other CERTs coordinate investigations and problem eradication efforts on an international basis. Beyond these multi-organizational CERTs, in many organizations, there is a need for an in-house CERT to deal with in-house problems. By formally defining an in-house CERT, an organization becomes better prepared to deal with security-related contingencies. Use of an in-house CERT also reduces the probability that problems will become public knowledge; for more information about this idea, see the policy entitled "Presentation of Low-Profile and Secure Image." The intention of this policy is thus to require that Data Processing or related technical management set-up and support a CERT. Also see the policies entitled "Internal Reporting Of Information Security Violations & Problems," "Incident Management Responsibilities," "Expected Employee Assistance During Business Restoration," and "Information Security Alert System." A: MT; E: LMH.

598. Regular Simulated Incidents To Test Computer Emergency Response Team

Policy: At least once every three months, the Information Security Department must utilize simulated incidents to mobilize and test the adequacy of the Company X Computer Emergency Response Team (CERT).

Commentary: The intention of this policy is to dictate a certain frequency for exercises to test an internal Computer Emergency Response Team. If management specifies a certain minimum frequency for these tests, it helps to ensure that these tests will not be ignored in the interests of other pressing business activities (as is often the case with contingency planning matters). The policy helps to ensure that an internal CERT is operating efficiently and effectively. If the CERT is not operating in this manner, then this situation will be clearly illustrated by a failed simulation test. Separately, the policy could be augmented to include another sentence which requires the preparation of a one page report about the test results to be delivered to the Chief Information Officer (CIO) or some other middle-level executive. On another note, this policy assumes that a CERT already exists and has been adequately staffed. For similar ideas, see the policies entitled "Prompt Implementation Of Security Problem Fix Software, Scripts, Etc." and "Organization/Maintenance Of Computer Emergency Response Team." A: T; E: LMH.

599. Required Actions Following Suspected System Intrusion

Policy: Whenever a systems administrator has good reason to believe that a information security system has been compromised, the involved computer must be immediately removed from all networks. The systems administrator must then run a file comparison utility to identify all changes to systems software, and then restore the systems software environment from trusted backup copies. Before being reconnected to the network, the access control system must be reinitialized (for example all fixed passwords must be changed). The current system log must also be copied to separate data storage media which is then kept in a locked container.

Commentary: This policy seeks to establish the minimum actions that systems administrators must take in response to a system intrusion and related problems. All too often systems administrators get pressure from user management not to disconnect from an internal network, not to check to see which files have changed, and not to reestablish a reliable access control system. This policy overrides user management wishes, requiring these essential steps to be performed. In some cases, organizations may want the policy to simply state that the systems administrator must follow the approved list of recovery actions (rather than specifying them as is done here). The list can then go into these matters in greater detail, perhaps including examination of application files to see if they have been changed. An additional detail that might be added is the use of a hash total or digital signature applied to the system log which is stored in an off-line container; this could later be used in court to indicate the integrity of the evidence recorded in the log. Separately, this policy is also good for systems administrators because it ensures that the intruders are no longer logged-in; if a machine does not go off the network, the intruders may be watching and interfering with recovery actions. For related ideas, see the policies entitled "Password Changes After Compromise Of A Multi-User Computer System," "Power Down Required For Systems Processing Sensitive Information," and "Required Retention Period Of Logs." A: T; E: LMH.

600. Operations Staff Must Have Documented Intrusion Response Procedure

Policy: All computer operations staff must have an up-to-date documented procedure which clearly specifies how information security incidents will be handled. These staff members must also be regularly trained in the usage of these same procedures.

Commentary: This policy is motivated by the all-too-common situation where computer operations staff notice that an attack is underway, but they don't know what to do or who to contact. As a result, the hacker proceeds, and causes serious damage when he could have been stopped, logged, traced, discouraged, and otherwise dealt with in an expedient manner. While this policy is directed towards those who manage commerce servers, web servers, database servers, and other multi-user machines, it could also be applied to individuals who are not recognized as members of the Information Systems Department Computer Operations Group. Thus technical staff in user departments who look after production systems could be considered computer operations staff if the organization in question chose to define "computer operations staff" in a broad and inclusive manner. On another note, this documented procedure would typically specify the types of incidents that are covered by the document, who should be notified and when they should be notified, what should be done after an incident takes place, how to protect evidence such as logs, how to immediately limit the damage, how to prevent future problems of this nature, how to reestablish a trusted information systems environment, and how to document the actions that were taken in response to the incident. See the policies entitled "Regular And Prompt Review Of System Logs," "Internet Connected Machines Must Have Intrusion Detection Systems," and "System Integrity Checking Programs Required For Personal Computers." A: T; E: LMH.

601. Regular Monitoring Of Information Security Vulnerability Advisories

Policy: On a weekly or more frequent basis, systems administration staff must review all information security vulnerability advisories issued by trusted organizations such as the CERT at Carnegie-Mellon University.

Commentary: The intention of this policy is to ensure that systems administration staff (or another designated group such as information security staff) are regularly reading the advisories about information security. If these people know what's happening they can then request resources from management to upgrade or change their systems so that they will not be unduly vulnerable to attackers like hackers and industrial spies. Information systems technology, particularly Internet technology, changes so fast that it is imperative that staff be regularly monitoring these advisories. By the time that vendors notify customers of a fix, often significant periods of time have elapsed; this policy allows staff to close existing "holes" much more quickly. Separately, the policy deliberately did not say exactly which sources must be consulted, and it deliberately did not say what technology should be used to gather this information (email discussion groups, web site surfing, etc.). Both will change over time. Separately, note that some vendors are now filtering these advisories so that customers see only the information they need to see; one such organization is Netect of Boston, Massachusetts, USA. For related concepts, see the policies entitled "Preparation And Maintenance Of Computer Emergency Response Plans," "Prompt Implementation Of Security Problem Fix Software, Scripts, Etc.," and "Disclosure Of System Vulnerability Exploitation And Victim Data." A: T; E: LMH.

602. Information Security Alert System

Policy: Information Systems Department management must establish, maintain, and periodically test a communications system allowing workers to promptly notify appropriate staff about suspected information security problems. These problems include computer virus infestations, hacker break-ins, improper disclosure of internal information to outsiders, system service interruptions, and other events with serious information security implications.

Commentary: The intention of this policy is to make sure that management establishes and supports an appropriate communications system for the prompt notification of information security staff. This is different from an organizational structure for the prompt mobilization of information security staff, for example a Computer Emergency Response Team (CERT). Some organizations may wish to expand the scope of this policy to include efforts to notify in-house staff that this communications system exists and when it should be employed. Without such a communications system, all too often attacks are ignored, thus allowing attackers to continue to try other methods. Similarly, unless such problems are promptly communicated, there is a serious danger that total losses will be much greater than they need to be. This can be clearly seen with virus infestations on a computer network, where each minute of delay means further business interruptions and additional data destruction. In many organizations, the notification process will involve pagers, telephone number calling trees, and other methods. Separately, the second sentence in the policy may be dropped without loss of the policy's essential idea; the second sentence provides only a clarifying set of examples. The designated department responsible for the communications system could be the Information Security Department, the Institutional Security Department, or some other group; it is, however, important that responsibility be specifically assigned. Also see the policies entitled "Organization/Maintenance Of Computer Emergency Response Team," "Incident Management Responsibilities," and "Required Reporting Of Information Security Incidents." A: T; E: LMH.

603. Users Must Not Distribute Information About System Vulnerabilities

Policy: Users must promptly report all information security alerts, warnings, suspected vulnerabilities, and the like to the Information Systems Help Desk. Users are prohibited from utilizing Company X systems to forward such information to other users, whether the other users are internal or external to Company X.

Commentary: The intention of this policy is to prevent well-meaning users from needlessly causing concern and upset in the user community. This policy has recently become a necessity for many organizations because there have been so many hoaxes about viruses, time bombs, and the like. The policy indicates that the help desk will act as a filter for such information, screening out hoaxes, inaccurately reported problems, old problems that have already been resolved, etc. The help desk is also in a much better position to contact the parties who need to know than is an ordinary end-user. To make this policy work best, the help desk (often on duty 24 hours a day and seven days a week in multi-national companies) should be able to instantly mobilize a computer emergency response team (CERT). Help desks can additionally check digital signatures and valid electronic mail return addresses from official incident response teams to verify the validity of reported problems. On a related note, this policy prevents a well-meaning user from making false or potentially-libelous representations about systems security to outside parties. For a related concept, see the policy entitled "Organization/Maintenance Of Computer Emergency Response Team." A: E; E: LMH.

604. Users Must Notify Help Desk About All Production System Problems

Policy: All significant errors, incomplete processing and improper processing of production applications must be promptly reported to the help desk.

Commentary: This policy is intended to quickly alert technical staff that something is amiss on production applications. These problems may be more serious than a programming error. They may for example be an indication of a hacker attack in process, or of corrupted data, or of system unreliability. Requiring the reporting of all significant problems also prevents users from rationalizing that a problem is already known by the technical staff, or that it may already have been reported by others. This policy thus acts like a double-check on computer operations controls such as batch totals. This policy also provides a new and different set of criteria for determining whether applications ran successfully to completion -- the user has a business perspective that most people in the Information Technology Department do not. For related ideas, see the policies entitled "Notify Management Of Conditions That May Disrupt Work" and "Reporting Of Damage To Company X Off-Site Systems." A: E; E: LMH.

605. Notify Management Of Conditions That May Disrupt Work

Policy: Workers must promptly notify management of all conditions that could lead to a disruption of business activities.

Commentary: This policy requires that workers (employees, contractors, consultants, temporaries, etc.) be vigilant, promptly bringing any condition that could disrupt work to management's attention, so that remedial action may soon follow. Examples of topics that should be reported include: unexplained errors when writing to a hard disk drive, missing files on a personal computer (perhaps an indication of a virus), stolen computer equipment, fire extinguishers that are not charged, and other potential hazards. This policy requests that workers act responsibly--as though they were managers--at least when it comes to noticing problems; it is preferable to have many rather than a few sets of eyes to notice these things. See the policies entitled "Expected Employee Assistance During Business Restoration" and "Information Security Alert System." A: E; E: LMH.

606. Expected Employee Assistance During Business Restoration

Policy: Employees are expected to be present, and to assist to the best of their abilities, with the restoration of normal business activity after an emergency or a disaster disrupts Company X business activity. After an employee's family and personal assets are determined to be safe, employees are expected to put in overtime, work under stressful conditions, and otherwise do what it takes to maintain Company X as a going concern.

Commentary: This policy is intended to put employees on notice that they are expected to participate in the restoration of normal business operations, including the reestablishment of computer and communications services. Some organizations place a policy like this in their employee handbook to ensure that there is no misunderstanding about what is expected during these stressful times. In the event of a disaster, some employees may wish to volunteer with the Red Cross or other relief organizations; this policy informs them that the must first attend to the affairs of Company X. Other employees may claim that it's not their job to do such things; this policy eliminates disputes on that point. Separately, it is unreasonable to expect that employees will view their job as more important than their family or personal assets; this is the reason the second sentence acknowledges the need to first ascertain the safety of family and personal assets. Also note that this policy deals only with employees; contractors, temporaries, and consultants are not expected to assist in the same fashion because they do not have the same type of loyal relationship with Company X. Also see the policy entitled "Organization/Maintenance Of Computer Emergency Response Team." A: E; E: LMH.

607. Inventory Of Key Technical Jobs And Individuals Who Fill Them

Policy: Management must annually prepare an inventory of key Company X technical jobs and the names of the individuals who currently fill these jobs.

Commentary: This policy helps to highlight the reliance on certain people, encouraging cross training, job rotation, development of expert systems, and other ways of providing some redundancy for key people. In large corporations, a similar inventory reviewing key members of the top management team is often performed by a risk management department. Succession and new roles in the event that top managers are no longer able to fill their designated roles is a frequent topic of discussion in business circles. This same approach can and should be applied to critical technical personnel, such as the senior individuals who program telephone switches at a telephone company. See the policy entitled "Cross Training For Staff In Critical Technical Jobs." The process of identifying critical applications helps to focus attention on key human resources;

see the policy entitled "Five Category Application Criticality Classification Scheme." Also see the policy entitled "Annual Inventory Of Information Systems Hardware, Software, Etc." A: M; E: LMH.

608. Cross Training For Staff In Critical Technical Jobs

Policy: At all times, at least two staff members should be able to provide any given essential technical service for information systems critical to Company X business. If less than two staff members can provide these essential technical services, management must initiate cross training, additional hiring, outsourcing, or other remedial actions.

Commentary: The intention of this policy is to ensure that if a technical person who provides essential technical services (like systems programming) were to be unavailable, that critical business systems would not soon come to a halt. The list of methods management can use to remedy the problem was purposely kept incomplete, so that management can be creative when it comes to reducing the reliance on a single individual. This policy also applies to those situations where management wishes to alleviate the exposures it faces but no person on staff can provide essential technical services. For example, management may decide that it wishes to keep certain operational documentation up-to-date. The actions dictated by this policy can be avoided if management declares certain technical services as "non-essential." This is not a problem because management has made a decision, which is something that does not prevail in many organizations. Separately, this policy assumes that certain information systems have already been designated as "critical." For a policy which discusses the definition of this term, see the policy entitled "Four Category Data Classification Scheme." The policy presented here also assumes that Company X is an organization with a sufficient number of people where some staff redundancy can be achieved. Smaller organizations will need to get more creative, perhaps putting a technical consultant on-call for a small retainer. For a more fundamental idea, see the policy entitled "Inventory Of Key Technical Jobs And Individuals Who Fill Them." Also see the policy entitled "Reliance On A Single Person For Important Systems Expertise." For a related consideration, see the policy entitled "Loss Of Critical Knowledge And Employees Flying On Same Airplane." Attention should also be drawn to the policy entitled "Documentation Required For All Production Business Systems." A: MT; E: LMH.

609. Preparation And Maintenance Of Computer Disaster Recovery Plans

Policy: Management must prepare, periodically update, and regularly test a disaster recovery plan that will allow all critical computer and communication systems to be available in the event of a major loss such as a flood, earthquake, or tornado.

Commentary: The intention of this policy is to require management to financially support and diligently attend to disaster contingency planning efforts. Because disasters happen so rarely, technical management often ignores the disaster recovery planning process. These managers are increasingly changing their attitude about disaster recovery plans, in large measure because they are appreciating that having a good contingency plan is becoming a matter of competitive advantage (business partners may insist on one). These managers are also coming to appreciate that their job performance will increasingly be based on their having attended to these matters. Separately, the focus of this policy is on disasters, although it is also advisable to have a policy that deals with other types of interruptions. For example, see the policy entitled "Preparation And Maintenance Of Computer Emergency Response Plans." Note that a disaster recovery plan in most instances is going to fail unless the associated business facilities (phones, desks, etc.) are also available; see the policy entitled "Preparation And Maintenance Of Business Contingency Plans." This policy assumes that the term "critical" has been defined elsewhere. For a policy which discusses the definition of this term, see the policy entitled "Five Category Application

Criticality Classification Scheme." The specific natural disasters mentioned in this policy can be adapted to local conditions (such as tidal waves in Japan). Also see the policy entitled "Annual Information Security Planning Process Required." A: MT; E: LMH.

610. Preparation And Maintenance Of Business Contingency Plans

Policy: Management must prepare, periodically update, and regularly test a business recovery plan. This recovery plan must specify how alternative facilities such as offices, furniture, telephones, and copiers will be provided so workers can continue operations in the event of either an emergency or a disaster.

Commentary: Note that a business contingency plan deals with facilities and other business matters besides computers and communications systems. A computer and communications contingency plan is considerably narrower in scope. For further discussion on this point, see the policy entitled "Preparation And Maintenance Of Computer Disaster Recovery Plans." This policy is intended to supplement the policy dealing with disaster recovery plans because the business facilities will be necessary if the organization is going to remain operational. The people doing business contingency planning are often not the same as the people doing systems contingency planning. For example, physical security specialists may be doing business contingency planning, while information systems technicians may be doing system contingency planning. Nonetheless, a policy requiring business contingency planning is advisable, especially where subsidiaries and other decentralized management structures prevail. See the policy entitled "Preparation And Maintenance Of Computer Disaster Recovery Plans." A: MT; E: LMH.

611. Business And Computer Continuity Planning Process

Policy: A standard organization-wide process for developing and maintaining both business contingency plans and computer contingency plans must be documented and maintained by the Information Systems Department. In the absence of a vice president's approval, local managers responsible for these plans must comply with such organizational standards.

Commentary: This policy requires that a formal process exist for the preparation of both business contingency plans and computer contingency plans. To cover a wider variety of systems, the policy could be changed to reference "computer and communication system contingency plans" rather than simply "computer contingency plans." The planning process itself ordinarily would involve areas such as: identification and prioritization of critical business processes, identification of the risks facing the organization, assessment of the potential impacts of various types of emergencies and disasters, identifying and assigning responsibility for handling emergencies and disasters, documentation of procedures and processes, education of staff, and periodic testing of plans. The policy could be expanded to include mention of such specific activities. The standard process mentioned in the policy may be defined by an Information Security Group, although Information Technology, Risk Management, Insurance, Security, Operations Planning, or other departments may alternatively do this. Also see the policies entitled "Framework For Segmenting Information Resources By Recovery Priority" and "Risk Acceptance Process And Permissible Exceptions To Policies." A: MT; E: LMH.

612. Reversion To Manual Procedures Where Cost-Effectively Possible

Policy: If Company X critical business activities could reasonably be performed (even for a short while) with manual procedures rather than computers, a manual computer contingency plan must be developed, tested, and periodically updated. In most circumstances, this contingency plan should be integrated into computer and communication system contingency plans.

Commentary: The intention of this policy is to instruct management to look at the support of critical business activities via manual procedures. So often people get "locked" into a way of looking at things, in this case thinking about business activities as always computer-supported. This policy forces management to look at the manual performance of ordinary business activities. For example, a car rental desk at an airport may have trouble working without computer support, but they can probably still rent cars and handle many business activities on a manual basis (at least for a short while). In this case, clerks at the car rental desk could have manual procedures to follow if the computer were down (rather than simply sitting there waiting for the computer to come back up). These procedures might also require that price lists and other information be printed out every so often so that the hardcopy can be referenced when the computer system is down. Some organizations may wish to expand this policy to require the consideration of certain topics in a manual procedures contingency plan. Manual business procedures can additionally be the early steps in a business recovery plan. When this is the case, a contingency plan could cover the specific information that users must record manually, what business activities can be performed, and what restrictions apply. Also see the policy entitled "Preparation And Maintenance Of Computer Disaster Recovery Plans." A: T; E: LMH.

613. Annual Inventory Of Information Systems Hardware, Software, Etc.

Policy: So that the current computing environment may be quickly re-established following a disaster, Information Systems Department management must prepare an annual inventory of production information systems. This inventory must indicate all existing production hardware, software, and communications links.

Commentary: The intention of this policy is to compel management to prepare an annual inventory of production information systems hardware, software, and communications links. Only by knowing what system components exist can an organization properly plan for disasters. Examined from the standpoint of driving a car, when looking at a map, one must first know where he or she is to figure out how to get to a particular place. The information systems at many organizations change so rapidly that an up-to-date inventory will be a valuable management tool for other purposes, not just for contingency planning. For example, say the organization in question was going to adopt a new office automation software package which required all microcomputers (PCs) to run an Intel chip. Management could, by examining the equipment inventory, quickly determine which machines need to be upgraded before everybody in the office can use the new software. Likewise, the inventory will be helpful for other information security activities, like determining which microcomputers (PCs) are protected by virus screening software (such as after a virus infestation). Because LANs and other distributed computing systems are often insufficiently documented, this policy is particularly useful for LANs, client/server systems, office automation systems, and the like. Separately, new products allow the automatic taking of microcomputer hardware and software inventory when these machines are connected to a local area network. One such product is PC Census from Tally Systems, Hanover, New Hampshire, USA. If a comprehensive production system inventory is just too much to ask (and it's generally not that costly), then an inventory of equipment for critical applications would still be very helpful for contingency planning purposes. On another note, this policy involves what is known as a "periodic inventory" as opposed to a "perpetual inventory" (the latter is described in the policy entitled "Equipment Custodians Must Control Inventory With Serial Numbers"). Also see the policy entitled "Inventory Of Key Technical Jobs And Individuals Who Fill Them." A: MT; E: LMH.

614. Equipment Custodians Must Control Inventory With Serial Numbers

Policy: Company X equipment custodians must maintain perpetual inventory control and physical security over the equipment in their possession. Perpetual inventory involves the maintenance of current records indicating equipment manufacturer, model number and serial number. Equipment custodians must also maintain a record of the new location and new custodian of all equipment issued to others.

Commentary: As information systems equipment becomes increasingly distributed, there is a need to rely on rank-and-file staff to protect and account for this equipment. One common way to do this is through the use of designated equipment custodians, which are different from information custodians (the latter are described in the policy entitled "Security Responsibilities Of Information Custodians"). Equipment custodians keep track of equipment in their own office, at their home office, or in a computer lab. If an organization designates equipment custodians, and has written records to back up this designation, it will have less trouble with disputes about equipment ownership at the time of workers terminate their employment. Having custodians will also help in efforts to identify and control stolen and lost equipment. The existence of equipment inventories will also help with contingency planning efforts, equipment upgrade efforts, and missing equipment insurance reimbursement efforts. Separately, the words "perpetual inventory" can be contrasted with "periodic inventory," both of which are standard accounting terms that in some instances will need to be explicitly defined to equipment custodians. On another note, this policy could be modified to require equipment custodians to safeguard their inventory records (primarily against unauthorized alteration which may attempt to hide a theft). For related ideas, see the policies entitled "High-Level Inventory Of Information Assets" and "Annual Inventory Of Information Systems Hardware, Software, Etc." A: T; E: LMH.

615. Annual Determination Level Of Disaster/Emergency Support Levels

Policy: Each year user department management and Information Technology Department management must agree on the support levels that will be provided in the event of a disaster and/or emergency. These levels must appear in contingency planning documents or service agreements.

Commentary: The intention of this policy is to reach an understanding about the type of technical and administrative support that will be provided in the event of a disaster or emergency. For instance, if users understand that they will not be supported if they utilize non-standard systems, they may convert to standard systems. On this topic, see the policy entitled "Compliance With Standards Required For Emergency/Disaster Support." If users understand that their applications are not highly-critical, then they will not be upset when their application services are not restored at the same time as those of other departments. For some ideas about rating applications according to criticality, see the policy entitled "Five Category Application Criticality Classification Scheme." If users understand that Information Technology doesn't have the resources to bring their applications back up any sooner than a day from the time of a disaster, users may request additional funding from top management. This policy also helps to protect the Information Technology Department (or whoever is preparing a contingency plan) because it seeks to document the agreed-upon support levels. If these support requirements are in writing, users know they can't blame Information Technology for certain problems about which they had been given notice, and they will accordingly be encouraged to pay more attention to contingency planning. Early in the development of a contingency plan, a policy like this may also foster the performance of a risk assessment (risk analysis) to see exactly what would happen in the event of a disaster or an emergency. The policy could be expanded to include mention of the need for these support levels to be reviewed annually; this is appropriate given the many changes made to information systems within most organizations. Because end-users often make information systems decisions without the Information Technology Department's involvement, this policy is especially important for those organizations dependent on client/server systems, LANs, and other distributed computing systems. For a related idea, see the policy entitled "Preventive Maintenance On Computer And Communication Systems." A: MT; E: LMH.

616. Computer And Communications System Contingency Plan Testing

Policy: To the extent practical and feasible, computer and communication system contingency plans must be tested at regular intervals to assure that they are still relevant and effective. Each such test must be followed by a brief report to top management detailing the results of the test and any remedial actions that will be taken.

Commentary: The intention of this policy is to force the periodic testing of contingency plans. While many organizations ignore testing, a contingency plan that is never tested is of dubious value. Confidence in the ability to recover after a disaster or an emergency comes only from regular testing. Since the computer and contingency planning area at most organizations changes so rapidly, periodic testing is necessary just to make sure that previously-developed recovery strategies and procedures are still relevant. The requirement of a report to top management has several purposes: (1) it keeps top management in a conversation about contingency planning, (2) it forces the people doing the testing to document their work, and (3) it forces the people doing the testing to follow-through and actually make adjustments to the contingency plan. Of course, if an organization doesn't yet have a contingency plan, then the policy does not apply (because in this case it's not yet "feasible" to test). Some organizations may want the policy to be still more stringent, in which case a time frame for testing can be specified (such as once every six months for those systems supporting production applications). Testing at regular intervals rather than at surprise moments is recommended; although it's somewhat less realistic, a lot of ill-will can be generated if users are put through a test but they didn't know it was a test. Surprise tests that require staff to stay overtime or to come in during a weekend will garner especially negative responses. Surprise can be used for other EDP auditing matters (such as a surprise examination of a contingency plan). For a more fundamental idea, see the policy entitled "Preparation And Maintenance Of Computer Disaster Recovery Plans." A: MT; E: LMH.

617. Preventive Maintenance On Computer And Communication Systems

Policy: Preventive maintenance must be regularly performed on all computer and communications systems such that risk of failure is kept to a reasonably low probability.

Commentary: This policy begs the question: "Exactly what goes into preventive maintenance?" The policy is deliberately vague here. Middle management must determine what preventive maintenance is appropriate. Preventive maintenance can include replacing old magnetic tapes with new ones, cleaning and oiling disk drives, cleaning dust under raised floors, etc. An organization can run its information technology shop like a car. One approach involves driving until the car breaks down, at which point repairs are done. It is, however, better practice to change the oil, transmission fluid, tires, brake pads, and other parts every so often, to prevent the car from breaking down. Statistics show that preventive maintenance (PM) can reduce computer system down time. The policy is fully consistent with dial-out preventive maintenance systems that periodically notify the vendor of a system's internal status, automatically requesting certain remedial actions such as the replacement of a circuit board on which excessive faults have been detected. Such systems are offered by Tandem Computer of Cupertino, California, USA. If the scope of this policy seems too wide, the policy can be restricted to "production systems." PM is relevant to PCs, LANs, client/server systems, Internet commerce systems, and other small systems just as it is to mainframes and other large systems. Also note that the words "computer and communications systems" can refer to software and information collections (such as a database), as well as to hardware. For related ideas, see the policies entitled "Annual Determination Level Of Disaster/Emergency Support Levels" and "Information Systems Equipment Maintenance Requirements." A: T; E: LMH.

618. Information Systems Equipment Maintenance Requirements

Policy: All information systems equipment used for production processing must be maintained in accordance with the supplier's recommended service intervals and specifications. Repairs and servicing of equipment must be performed only by qualified and authorized maintenance personnel.

Commentary: The intention of this policy is to ensure that information systems equipment continues to operate as it should, thus supporting the organization in achieving its mission. Equipment downtime can be a serious problem bringing many information systems activities to a halt (especially if it is a mainframe, telephone switch or some other large multi-user system). Note that this policy doesn't state anything about the size of the system, and thus it applies to personal computers as well as the above-mentioned larger systems. This policy can be used to inform end-users that they must not try to repair their own personal computer (PC) equipment; instead, they must call the Help Desk (or some other authorized staff in the Information Systems Department). For a related policy, see "Preventive Maintenance On Computer And Communication Systems." A: ET; E: LMH.

619. Internet Domain Name Registration Payments Must Be Confirmed

Policy: Payments and paperwork for Internet domain name registrations for all of Company X official sites must be handled in a timely manner and promptly confirmed by the Telecommunications Manager to prevent interruptions in service.

Commentary: The intention of this policy is to prevent unnecessary interruptions in Internet web site and commerce site activity. A number of large and well-known organizations have recently had their sites go off the Internet for significant periods of time because they haven't paid their bills in a timely manner. While the future will probably bring insurance to prevent this type of outage, in the meanwhile, it is essential that all paperwork and payments be handled on time. Many companies don't believe that a registration authority (such as Network Solutions) will terminate the network router listings for their web and commerce sites just because payment is late, but this is now happening with an embarrassing frequency. For related ideas, see the policies entitled "Information Systems Equipment Maintenance Requirements" and "Preventive Maintenance On Computer And Communication Systems." A: T; E: LMH.

620. Contact Numbers For Information Systems Department Staff

Policy: All members of the Information Systems Department who travel out of town must wear a pager. These staff members must additionally provide both their manager and their group secretary with telephone numbers where they can be reached. These phone numbers must be provided in advance of the travel, and are required regardless of the reasons for travel.

Commentary: This policy acknowledges the significant reliance that is placed on information systems staff. The policy is intended to maintain the ability to quickly reach all technical people who might be needed for disaster or emergency recovery. The policy can be expanded to include members of user departments who are involved in technical computer and communications matters, contractors on which the organization relies, etc. The policy applies to those on vacation, attending conventions, etc. The policy also applies to holidays and other non-working hours. Some organizations may not need such an all-encompassing policy; for them, it may be sufficient to make sure that systems programmers, application programmers, and computer network specialists be on call via pagers (preferably national or international rather than local pagers). Unfortunately, sometimes technical staff travels to locations where pagers don't function (out of a metropolitan area for instance); it is this situation that makes it necessary to give other telephone numbers to a manager and a secretary. Organizations that must immediately be in contact with critical technical staff members will want to replace the word "pager" in the policy with the words "cellular phone." For related ideas, see the policies entitled "Organization/Maintenance Of Computer Emergency Response Team" and "Loss Of Critical Knowledge And Employees Flying On Same Airplane." A: T; E: LMH.

1.3.4.3. Backup And Archival Storage

621. Access Control For End-User File Restoration Processes

Policy: If end-users are given the ability to restore their own files, they must not be given privileges to restore other users' files or to see which files other users have backed-up.

Commentary: The motivation for this policy is to ensure that users don't employ a backup system as a way to circumvent an access control system. For example, on a local area network, one user might be able to restore personnel performance evaluation files saved by his or her supervisor, and thereby defeat the access controls normally applicable to these files. Only the local area network administrator (or security administrator for other environments) should have multiple-user access to file backups. One way to enforce this policy is to encrypt the backed-up files using one or more unique keys for each user. LAN or security administrators may also want to periodically check logs indicating which users restored which files to determine whether abusive activity has taken place. Some Internet firewall systems are now monitoring outbound traffic volume to determine whether excessive information flows are taking place (presumably an indication of suspicious activity such as industrial espionage). Other commercially-available firewalls are limiting the outbound volume of information that can be sent. These same data volume throttle approaches could be used to control backup information to which users have direct access. For related ideas, see the policies entitled "Default To Denial Of Access Control Privileges," "Encrypting Backup Media Stored Off-Site," and "Off-Site Storage Of Backup Media." A: T; E: LMH.

622. What Data To Backup And Minimum Backup Frequency

Policy: All critical business information and critical software resident on Company X computer systems must be periodically backed-up. These backup processes must be performed at least monthly, and with sufficient frequency to support documented contingency plans.

Commentary: The intention of this policy is to specify a minimum acceptable backup time frame and also to specify what type of data needs to be backed-up. Certain types of data will need to be backed up more frequently than monthly, but these decisions must be made on an organization-by-organization and data-type-by-data-type basis. These decisions will generally be covered in a contingency plan. Note that this policy is relevant to microcomputers (PCs), LANs, and client/server systems as well as larger machines; too often users on smaller systems forget or ignore backups. This propensity of end-users to forget about or ignore backups, in the long run, is best handled by automatic backup systems, such as those which operate in a user-transparent fashion at night. This policy assumes the word "critical" has been defined elsewhere; see the policies entitled "Four Category Data Classification Scheme" and "Five Category Application Criticality Classification Scheme." Also see the policy entitled "Specification Of Backup Process And Frequency." A: EMT; E: LMH.

623. Periodic And Supplementary Backups Required For Portable Computers

Policy: Because theft of portable computers is so common, workers using these computers must make backups of all critical information prior to taking out-of-town trips. These backups should be stored elsewhere than the portable computer's carrying case. This precaution supplements the periodic backups that must otherwise be made.

Commentary: The intention of this policy is to make sure that critical information stored on the hard disk drive of a portable machine is not lost forever when a portable computer is lost or stolen. This could happen if the even took place some time since the last periodic backup of a hard drive (if the backup was for example performed automatically over the Internet via a virtual private network or VPN). This policy also guards against police or customs agent confiscation of a portable computer, in which case the information stored thereon would be unavailable for business purposes. The policy uses out-of-town trips as a trigger for a supplementary backup process; this trigger may not be suitable for travelling sales staff or other workers who go out-of-town nearly every working day. For these people, an out-of-state or out-of-country trip may be the trigger. For a related idea, see the policy entitled "Transportable Computers Must Be Hand Luggage on Airplanes." A: EMT; E: LMH.

624. Do Not Use Hard Drives On Public Access Computers For Backup

Policy: The hard drives and other data storage devices attached to Company X desktop public access computers must not be used for backup purposes. These data storage locations should be used for temporary and scratch files only, should be considered volatile, and are subject to erasure at any time. Users are responsible for providing their own data storage media and making their own backup of important files.

Commentary: The intention of this policy is to let users know that they should not store their important files on public access machines (such as a computer lab at a university or a testing facility at a computer company). Since the involved computers don't have access controls, there is no practical way that Company X can prevent users from modifying or deleting files saved by other users on these machines. Establishing user expectations about the backup that is or is not performed is also highly desirable, and that intention motivated the last sentence in the policy. The policy also puts users on notice that systems administrators may at any time delete all user-provided files in order to free-up available disk space. For related considerations, see the policies entitled "Automatic Backup To Local Area Network Server" and "Access Control For End-User File Restoration Processes." A: E; E: LMH.

625. Encrypting Backup Media Stored Off-Site

Policy: To prevent it from being revealed to or used by unauthorized parties, all sensitive, valuable, or critical information recorded on backup computer media (magnetic tapes, floppy disks, optical disks, etc.) and stored outside Company X offices must be in encrypted form.

Commentary: Physical access controls at backup sites are often inferior to those at the organization's main site (such as a computer operations center). To make matters worse, backup sites are frequently unattended. The objective of this policy is thus to ensure that some access control remains over sensitive, valuable, or critical information stored off-site. For still more security, some organizations may want to require encryption for all backups, no matter where they are stored. This more stringent approach may be appropriate for telecommuters (people working at home), as well as those with portable computers and other systems removed from Company X premises. A tradeoff should be kept in mind: encryption of backup data will often slow if not prevent the recovery of the information involved. For example, keys for the decryption of backup media may be unavailable when there is an urgent need to recover data. This policy assumes the terms "sensitive, valuable, or critical" have been defined elsewhere; see the policies entitled "Four Category Data Classification Scheme" and "Five Category Application Criticality Classification Scheme." Also see the policies entitled "Storing Secret Information On

Transportable Computers" and "Secret Information Must Be Encrypted When Not In Active Use." A: EMT; E: MH.

626. Two Copies Of Sensitive, Critical, Or Valuable Information

Policy: Unless other backup arrangements are known to be operational, all end-users are responsible for making at least one current backup copy of critical files. These separate backup copies should be made each time that a significant number of changes are saved.

Commentary: The intention of this policy is to allow end-users to handle much of their own data reconstruction work because they have two or more copies of sensitive, critical, or valuable files. The policy is also intended to act as a safety-net for modifications to the important files which have not yet been backed up to a local server or backed-up to a tape drive located at the micro or workstation. To be effective, the policy will also require some user training about backups. The requirements specified in this policy are not onerous. For example, microcomputer (PC) or workstation users can store one copy on their hard drive and another on a LAN server, or they can store one copy on a floppy disk and one copy on their hard drive. With the cost of hard drives coming down in the last few years, it is now cost-effective for many end-users to employ two or more hard drives. This policy is relevant in those cases where automatic backup is performed over a LAN or WAN without user involvement. See the policy entitled "Make At Least One Copy of Backed-Up Files Prior to Use." This policy assumes the word "critical" has been defined elsewhere; see the policies entitled "Four Category Data Classification Scheme" and "Five Category Application Criticality Classification Scheme." A: EMT; E: LMH.

627. Two Copies Of Critical Company X Records Stored Off-Site

Policy: At least two recent and complete backups (not incremental backups) made on different dates containing critical Company X records must always be stored off-site.

Commentary: This policy is intended to ensure that a sufficient number of backup copies are always available for an important restore operation following an emergency or a disaster. If only one copy were used, that copy might be damaged during a restore operation. Likewise, one copy might be damaged in a backup tape delivery truck accident or another mishap associated with a major disaster. Another objective of this policy is to dictate a backup media rotation process (sometimes called "grandfather/father/son rotation") that involves at least two off-site copies. Separately, the word "recent" is deliberately vague, forcing management to interpret the word on a information type by information type basis. On another note, an incremental copy only provides the changes since the last backup, and would be of limited value unless the prior complete backup was also available. This policy is standard operating procedure for a number of third party data storage companies that run outsourced backup services. For a related idea, see the policy entitled "Two Copies Of Sensitive, Critical, Or Valuable Information." A: T; E: LMH.

628. Management Review Of End-User Backup Process

Policy: Department managers or their delegates must make sure that proper backups of sensitive, critical and valuable data are being made if such data is resident on microcomputers (PC), workstations, or other small systems.

Commentary: Unless end-users are reminded and in some instances forced to make regular backups, they may neglect to make backups, and this may have catastrophic consequences. All too often end-users don't really understand the notion of backing-up files until they have had a major data loss. This policy seeks to avoid major data losses and the consequences that result. The policy is appropriately accompanied by user training dealing with backups. Some systems can automatically backup changes that users make, storing the newest file copies on a server at the end of a business day. For example, on the Apple Macintosh, Applescript commands can be written to automatically backup the most recent copy of a database to a LAN server at the time that a workstation is shut-down. If the automatic approach is being employed, this policy still requires management to make sure that the process is effective. The policy assumes the word "critical" has been defined elsewhere; see the policy entitled "Five Category Application Criticality Classification Scheme." Also see the policies entitled "Automatic Backup To Local Area Network Server" and "What Data To Backup And Minimum Backup Frequency." A: MT; L: LMH.

629. Specification Of Backup Process And Frequency

Policy: Incremental backups for all end-user files must be performed by the on-duty administrator starting at 6:00PM each business day. An exception to this will be each Friday (or if this is a holiday, the first business day thereafter) when a full backup of all files must be performed.

Commentary: The intention of this policy is to clearly communicate when both incremental backups and full backups must take place. If a policy like this is put into writing, local area network administrators and others responsible for making backups cannot claim that they did not know what should be done. Although doing a backup at 6:00PM may be problematic for some backup software packages because certain files are still in-use, the more modern packages simply flag in-use files for subsequent retries. These modern packages will make multiple attempts to backup the in-use file, and if they fail with all attempts, will generate a command script that may be later run by a local area network administrator or the other person taking care of the backup process. If 6:00PM would still be problematic (due to high system usage, such as would be the case with automated teller machines in a bank), then the specified time can be 2:00AM or some other time. The important part is the regularity of the process, not the exact time of day. This policy could be changed to incorporate a courier who picks up backup disks and tapes at a certain time, then transporting them to an off-site storage location. See the policy entitled "Automatic Backup To Local Area Network Server" for a simpler and more user-friendly approach. A: T; E: LMH.

630. Automatic Backup To Local Area Network Server

Policy: All users with local area network (LAN) connections must leave their computers turned on at night so that an automatic backup can be performed.

Commentary: The intention of this policy is to make sure that end-users leave their machines (workstations, PCs, or other computers with local storage) turned on when they go home at night, so that an automatic backup process can proceed. Typically, such backups automatically copy all recently-changed files on client workstations to a server. Separately, there are ecological considerations associated with this policy. Leaving computers on all night tends to consume more electricity than turning them off when people go home. The best solution to this concern, if this backup-to-the-server approach is still employed, is to utilize the newest workstations that incorporate circuitry which reduces power consumption when the systems are not in use. If the backup software supports it, in some cases it will be possible to automatically and remotely power-down the workstations after a backup is completed. Separately, the words in the policy "so that an automatic backup can be performed" imply that workstation access controls should be set-up to allow a backup to proceed without human intervention. In other words, if a workstation is unattended, password-based workstation access control may not allow server-based backup software to read the contents of a hard disk drive unless some additional work is performed. Although automatic backup to a LAN server using timer-driven software is desirable, it may be necessary to have access control on workstations left connected to the network and unattended. If the LAN has external communication links (such as Internet firewalls or dial-up modem pools), such access control measures are absolutely essential. See the policy entitled "Access Control Packages Required For Computers On the Network." A: ET; E: LMH.

631. Users Notified That All Data Is Routinely Backed-Up

Policy: To prevent accidental loss, all files and messages stored on Company X systems are routinely copied to tape, disk, and other storage media. This means that information stored on Company X systems -- even if a user has specifically deleted it -- is recoverable and may be examined at a later date by systems administrators and others designated by management.

Commentary: This privacy-related policy seeks to put users on notice that their information may be examined by systems administrators, security investigators, and others authorized by management. To make this policy still more clear, the policy could be expanded to mention electronic mail messages, Internet FTP activities, dial-up Compuserve database searches, and other actions which could be logged and backed-up. In an indirect way, the policy also suggests that users consider not placing certain very sensitive information on Company X systems. While this policy may seem obvious to technically-sophisticated people, the idea behind the policy is not obvious to many users who are new to computers. Separately, as Oliver North, special assistant to US President Reagan discovered in the infamous Iran Contra scandal, backup systems may provide incriminating evidence that users thought they destroyed. Accordingly, this policy could be accompanied by a related policy indicating when data should be encrypted. For related ideas, see the policies entitled "Secret Data Sent Over Networks Must Be Encrypted," "Privacy Expectations And Information Stored On Company X Systems," and "Recording And Retention Of Electronic Mail." A: E; E: LMH.

632. Make At Least One Copy of Critical Backed-Up Files Prior To Use

Policy: Critical data which has been backed-up must not be used for data restoration purposes unless another backup copy of the same data exists on different computer storage media (tape, disk, smart card, CD-ROM, etc.). If a computer virus or other software problems are suspected, the additional backup copy should be made on a different computer. This policy will prevent the only current copy of critical backup data from being inadvertently damaged in the process of restoration.

Commentary: The intention of this policy is to make sure that the only current copy of critical data is not damaged or deleted in the process of being restored. In this policy, users (particularly end-users) are admonished to make another copy of such data prior to doing restoration work, provided an additional copy has not previously been made. If the set of policies the reader is preparing is at very high level of generality, the second sentence in this policy could be deleted. This multiple computer approach to making backup copies is advisable because the system to which data is to be restored may be infected by a virus, worm, Trojan horse or some other malicious software; in the process of restoring a file, the backup data storage media itself may be altered, scrambled, or otherwise changed in an unauthorized manner. Likewise, the act of making another copy of the data on different data storage media, if done on the machine to which the data is to be restored, may trigger such malicious software. As a preferred alternative to making an additional copy before restoration is performed, two copies can be generated when the original backup is made. Taking a different vantage point, the intention of this policy is to avoid having to put "all your eggs in one basket"--in this case the single backup copy of a critical file. See the policy entitled "Two Copies Of Sensitive, Critical, Or Valuable Information." The policy assumes that the word "critical" has been defined elsewhere; see the policy entitled "Five Category Application Criticality Classification Scheme." A: EMT; E: MH.

633. Production Batch Processing Only If Pre-Processing Backup Is Complete

Policy: Production batch processes must not begin unless a pre-processing backup of all involved master files and master databases has first been completed.

Commentary: The intention behind this policy is to prevent the involved organization from being in an awkward position when it comes time to open for business the following day. Without a control such as the one described in this policy, if a batch process failed during the night, and if there was no computer operator on duty to restart the process properly, when workers arrive at the office the next morning they may not be able to access customer records and other production data. This may be because the records have been partially modified and are not suitable for use until the batch process completes. In some organizations, it may be appropriate for these same workers to access a version of these same files and databases that has not been updated with batch transactions. The policy is also intended to ensure that the organization adopting it will have a useable backup copy of critical production files and databases, should the batch process damage these files or databases beyond repair. Because a batch process may run for several hours, and because it often consumes considerable processing resources, it is important to backup critical data before the process begins. This pre-processing backup should be in addition to a regular nightly backup, which could be performed after batch processes and all other production processes have been completed for the day. For related ideas, see the policies entitled "What Data To Backup And Minimum Backup Frequency" and "Input Data Validation And Rejected Item Handling." A: T; E: LMH.

634. Annual Audits To Determine Whether Production Backup Is Performed

Policy: The Internal Audit Department must perform an annual review of production computer system backup processes, including random tests, to determine whether critical data is indeed being adequately backed-up.

Commentary: The intention of this policy is to scare systems administrators and computer operators into paying attention to the very important -- but often neglected -- area of computerized information backup. The existence of this policy impresses them with the importance of diligently attending to backup every day of the year. These technical staff members know that every time a backup is performed they are creating extensive computer-readable records of their backup efforts (files backed-up have date/time stamps). While it's desirable to take the computer file backup process out of the hands of end-users in order to avoid errors and omissions, this policy also applies to end-users, should they be in charge of making backups for production systems. Generally, production systems do not run on desktop or portable machines over which end-users have control, and therefore this policy would not impact the end-user community. Separately, while it's common practice to let the Internal Audit Department determine the scope of the audits it performs, some things are so important that they are mandatory annual audits, and this area is one of those. For related ideas, see the policies entitled "Management Review Of End-User Backup Process" and "Archival Storage Of Every Version Of Internet Web & Commerce Sites." A: T; E: LMH.

635. Off-Site Storage Of Backup Media

Policy: Backups of essential business information and software must be stored in an environmentally-protected and access-controlled site which is a sufficient distance away from the originating facility to escape a local disaster.

Commentary: The intention of this policy is to ensure that backups of critical information are not destroyed by a local disaster such as a bomb blast or chemical spill. All too often, the backups are kept in the same room as the original copies of the information. Rather than specifying a certain distance from the originating facility, this policy leaves it up to local management to decide how far away the copies should be. In the real world, this remote location is generally five to one hundred miles away. Other organizations will find that it is sufficient to have current backup copies stored on-site at a primary location as well as off-site a few city blocks away. Local considerations, such as earthquake faults, may also affect the distance involved. Some organizations may wish to specify a certain minimum distance to increase the likelihood that the storage location will not be affected by the problem affecting the original site. Keep in mind is that the farther away the storage location, the more time and expense involved in retrieving the backups. This last tradeoff can be eliminated with the use of "electronic vaulting," where real-time backups are transmitted to a remote location via the Internet. For a related idea, see the policy entitled "Secret Information Must Be Encrypted When Not In Active Use." A: T; E: LMH.

636. Backup Media Stored In Separate Fire Zones From Originating Machine

Policy: Computer and network backup storage media must be stored in a separate fire zones from the machine producing the backup. Fire zones vary from building to building, and are defined by the Physical Security Department.

Commentary: This policy seeks to distance backup storage media from the machine which was used to produce the backup. Rather than requiring that the media be stored off-site, or even a certain number of miles away, this policy looks to isolated fire zones which are unlikely to be involved in the same blaze. Typically different buildings on the same corporate campus are different fire zones; similarly different parts of the same large building may be different fire zones. Because the specifics of a certain building will always differ, this policy mandates only the use of the notion of a fire zone, leaving the rest up to the Physical Security Department (which typically is responsible for fire suppression equipment, fire alarms, and the like). Separately, for greater protection, a backup media rotation system could move media through several fire zones. Also see the policies entitled "Off-Site Storage Of Backup Media" and "Encrypting Backup Media Stored Off-Site." A: ET; E: LMH.

637. Backup Media Storage Rooms, Vaults, & Cabinets Must Be Kept Locked

Policy: Unless they have an automatic closing mechanism which is triggered by a fire alarm, all fireproof computer backup storage rooms, vaults, cabinets, and the like must be kept fully closed when not in active use.

Commentary: The intention of this policy is to ensure that fireproof technology will do the job it is intended to do. If computer operations staff leaves a fireproof file cabinet containing the weekly backup open, and then a fire occurs, the file cabinet will not be able to provide any special protection for the backup tape, disk, or CD-ROM. Note that this policy doesn't really concern itself with access based on a legitimate business need; it is focused more on ensuring that fireproof systems are able to do their job. If there happens to be a lock on fireproof vaults, cabinets, etc., then there may be some access control benefits as well. For related considerations, see the policies entitled "Computer Center Fire Resistance And Self-Closing Openings" and "Securing Sensitive Information In Unattended Rooms." A: T; E: LMH.

638. Archival Storage Of Every Version Of Internet Web & Commerce Sites

Policy: Every version of Internet web site and commerce site files must be securely archived in two physically-separated locations.

Commentary: The intention of this policy is to create a redundant archive of every version of Internet web and commerce sites. Such an archive can be very important for legal purposes. For example, if there was a legal dispute about an offer posted to a web site, and if data integrity and access controls are part of the archiving process, then these records could be used to definitively prove what information was posted on the site. A bank, for instance, may use an archive like this to help resolve a dispute about the rate offered on a particular type of savings account of certificate of deposit. Such an archive can also be useful for contingency planning purposes, if for example a hosting firm destroys all copies of the site (or perhaps never made them). Because so many organizations use outsourced hosting firms these days, and because hosting firms may do a poor job of making backups, it is important that the organization paying the bills take care of its own archival backup process. In some jurisdictions there may also be legal reasons to keep copies of Internet sites (for example to show that the site had a privacy policy as of a certain date). For related considerations, see the policies entitled "What Data To Backup And Minimum Backup Frequency" and "Recording And Retention Of Electronic Mail." A: T; E: LMH.

639. Quarterly Archival Backups Required For All Critical Information

Policy: Critical business information and critical software must be backed-up onto archival storage media and kept for at least a year. These backups must be made every calendar quarter or more frequently if required by a relevant written contingency plan.

Commentary: This policy acknowledges that viruses or Trojan horses can alter files and that these alterations may not be detected for a long period of time. This means that several generations of backups may contain infected or altered files, and that the responsible parties may not be aware of the problem before all the backups have been corrupted or overwritten. When facing one of these unfortunate situations, the original installation storage media (disk or CD-ROM) may be the only hope for software, aside from going back to the vendor or software escrow agent. For critical business information, fraudulent modifications may have been made, and these modifications may be concealed for an extended period of time. Likewise, unless a policy like this is adopted, all the backups may contain fraudulent information. Recovery of the original and unmodified information may be very difficult if not impossible if the process described in this policy is not adopted. The cost of this policy is minor, especially when backup operations are automated, but the peace of mind that it provides is significant. On a separate note, the policy writer may wish to augment this policy with a policy specifying when and how these archival backups should be destroyed (consult your attorney about discovery and related legal issues). For related ideas, see "Two Copies Of Critical Company X Records Stored Off-Site" and "What Data To Backup And Minimum Backup Frequency." A: T; E: LMH.

640. Department Managers Must Identify Vital Records

Policy: Department managers must identify and maintain a current list of the vital records that their department needs to restore operations following a disaster.

Commentary: This policy is intended to clearly assign responsibility for the identification and maintenance of a list of vital records. The very fact that department managers must prepare and maintain the list forces them to think about the information that their department absolutely needs. This list can then be used for contingency planning as well as backup procedure purposes. Some organizations may want to define vital records more explicitly; they could for example mention the information needed to conduct ordinary business transactions, recreate Company X's financial and legal position, and preserve the rights of the company as well as its staff and customers. A definition of a disaster may also be appropriate. On another note, in some organizations, a worksheet is distributed by the contingency planning staff; this worksheet asks questions to help department managers identify vital records as well as the appropriate frequency of backups for this information. Separately, this policy would generally be distributed only to department managers. For related ideas, see the policies entitled "Two Copies of Sensitive, Critical, Or Valuable Information" and "Business Source Document Data Retention Requirements." A: M; E: LMH.

641. Directory Of Information Held In Archival Storage

Policy: All archival backup data stored off-site must be reflected in an up-to-date directory which shows the date when the information was most recently modified as well as the nature of the information.

Commentary: The intention of this policy is to facilitate the determination of whether certain information is held in archival storage, and if so, then discover its specific location. In some file storage management systems, such as those found in DEC's VAX/VMS, files are automatically moved between magnetic tapes, disk drives, and other media based on the last date they were accessed. A directory of the files and their locations is automatically generated as a by-product of the system's activity. These directories may also be maintained manually, although both the level of effort and the propensity to make errors is much higher than when they are done automatically. Such a directory may be useful when there is a business or legal dispute. Unfortunately, a directory like this can be used by the opposing side of a legal case to identify documents which might help the opponent's arguments. A directory like this can also be useful for contingency planning purposes as well as for insurance claim preparation purposes. This directory will be instrumental in carrying out a "purging" process mentioned in the policy entitled "Regular Purging Of Information Which Is No Longer Needed." A: T; E: LMH.

642. Acceptable Archival Storage Data Media

Policy: All media on which sensitive, valuable, or critical information is stored for periods longer than six (6) months must not be subject to rapid degradation. For example, thermal fax paper is not a suitable archival data storage media.

Commentary: The intention of this policy is to specify the storage media on which important records may be archived. Ideally, the same storage media is used widely throughout an organization (for example a certain size of magnetic tape cartridge for personal computer backups). If media of different sizes, formats, and types are used, recovery of the information stored thereon may be troublesome or even impossible. Examples of acceptable storage media, such as CD-ROM and non-acidic paper for books, may be provided as part of the policy. In the long run, this policy may be unnecessary when organizations use only the storage media which are suitable for archival purposes (machines using thermal fax paper may be replaced by those using ordinary copying paper). This policy assumes the words "sensitive, valuable, or critical" have already been defined in other documents; see the policies entitled "Four Category Data Classification Scheme" and "Five Category Application Criticality Scheme." Also see the policy entitled "Workers Must Show Contents Of Luggage When Leaving Premises" and "Special Paper Preventing Copying Of Sensitive Documents." A: EMT; E: LMH.

643. Regular Testing Of Archival Storage Data Media

Policy: Critical business information and critical software archived on computer storage media for a prolonged period of time must be tested at least annually to ensure that the information is still recoverable.

Commentary: The intention of this policy is to ensure that archival data will be readily recoverable if and when it is needed. If trouble is encountered, then efforts to move the data to more reliable data media should be promptly undertaken. An example of this problem involves information stored on magnetic tapes, which tend to "grow" errors over time. This policy may also be instrumental in discovering problems associated with an archival storage site, related procedures, and related software. For instance, there may be excessive dust in the storage area, and this may be interfering with the recovery of certain data stored on computer-readable magnetic tapes. If management has not yet noticed that problems such as this, the policy will force them to face reality. Also see the policy entitled "Regular Testing Of Used Data Media Employed for Archival Storage." A: T; E: LMH.

644. Regular Testing Of Used Data Media Employed For Archival Storage

Policy: The computer data media used for storing sensitive, critical, or valuable information must be high quality and must be periodically tested to ensure that it can properly record the information in question. Used data media that can no longer reliably retain information must not be used for archival storage.

Commentary: This policy requires that only reliable data storage media be used for backup purposes. Old and worn storage media cannot be relied upon to accurately preserve information. Many larger organizations have their own special-purpose machines which test the media on which information is stored. If these machines indicate that the media has an excessive number of errors, then the media should be removed from the backup cycle (sometimes called a "grand-father, father, son process." While end-users do not generally have the equipment to make thorough tests of data media, they are in a position to notice disk read and write errors as well as other indications that certain storage media is no longer reliable. This policy assumes the words "sensitive, critical, or valuable" have already been defined in other documents; see the policies entitled "Four Category Data Classification Scheme" and "Five Category Application Criticality Scheme." Also see the policy entitled "Regular Testing Of Archival Storage Data Media." A: EMT; E: LMH.

645. Preservation Of Data Held In Archival Storage

Policy: Computer media storage procedures must assure that sensitive, critical, or valuable information stored for prolonged periods of time is not lost due to deterioration. For instance, management must copy data to different storage media if the original backup media is showing signs of undue deterioration.

Commentary: This policy requires that management take steps to preserve important data held in archival storage. This policy dictates that actions be taken if there is reason to believe that data is deteriorating or will soon deteriorate. In this respect, the policy is the next step after the testing process described in the policy entitled "Regular Testing of Archival Storage Data Media." This policy may be expanded to include transferring data to more modern data media. For example, to increase the ease of accessing it, as well as to help preserve it, data kept on punched cards may be transferred to magnetic tapes. Likewise, data stored on paper that is deteriorating due to excessive acid content may be moved to more reliable storage media, such as CD-ROMs. This policy assumes the words "sensitive, critical, or valuable" have already been defined in other documents; see the policies entitled "Four Category Data Classification Scheme" and "Five Category Application Criticality Scheme." Also see the policy entitled "Acceptable Archival Storage Data Media." A: MT; E: LMH.

1.3.4.4. Retention Periods And Disposal Of Data

646. Minimum Information Retention Period

Policy: Unless the type of information is specifically listed on the Information Retention Schedule, information must be retained for as long as necessary but for no longer. Information listed on the Information Retention Schedule must be retained for the period specified. Other information must be destroyed when no longer needed--generally within two years.

Commentary: The intention of this policy is to clearly specify the retention periods for various types of information. Information is broadly broken into two categories: (1) those types listed on an Information Retention Schedule, and (2) those types not listed on the Schedule. For example, financial, tax, and medical information will generally be listed on a Schedule, while information about inventory on hand for certain products will generally not be on the Schedule. Often the Legal Department prepares a Schedule based on local laws and regulations. Separately, one attractive aspect of the approach embodied in this policy is that information types listed on the Schedule can change, whereas the words in the policy remain the same. This policy recognizes that the retention of information beyond the time when it is still needed slows down information retrieval processes, and may also subject Company X to legal problems (such as might be the case where the no-longer-needed information is used in a lawsuit against Company X). This policy could be modified so the reader is referred to the Records Management Department or departmental management in the event that there is doubt about the proper retention period. The policy could be expanded to allow extended retention of information in the event that legal proceedings may require it, if outside approval is needed for disposal/destruction (as might be specified in a contract), or if the information might help with the collection of a past-due account receivable. See the policies entitled "Definition Of Archival Storage Data Retention Schedule" and "Retention Period Required For All Sensitive Information." A: EMT; E: LMH.

647. Definition Of Archival Storage Data Retention Schedule

Policy: All financial accounting, tax accounting, and legal records must be retained for a period of at least seven (7) years. All other records must be retained for a period of at least five (5) years.

Commentary: The intention of this policy is to definitively specify the minimum time frames that certain types of records must be retained. After these time periods, the records can be discarded (perhaps destroyed according to approved procedures) without legal or other trouble. Some organizations may want to add a sentence to this policy requiring the destruction of such records after the retention period has run out. Destruction will prevent these records from being used by opponents in a legal discovery process. The policy may also specify time frames for information in certain forms, such as electronic mail messages, rather than just for information types. Check with the organization's legal counsel to find the suitable time periods for your jurisdiction, your industry, and your existing contracts. While the policy entitled "Minimum Information Retention Period" uses a separate Retention Schedule, this policy uses broad information categories in the policy itself to describe different retention requirements. The emphasis is on quick disposal of information in the policy entitled "Minimum Information Retention Period," while the emphasis in this policy is on making sure that information is retained at the very least for the specified period of time. See the policies entitled "Responsibility For Archival Storage Data Retention Schedule," "Approved Methods For Hardcopy Sensitive Information Disposal," and "Recording And Retention of Electronic Mail." A: EMT; E: LMH.

648. Responsibility For Archival Storage Data Retention Schedule

Policy: All Company X information must be securely retained according to a schedule published by the Legal Department.

Commentary: The intention of this policy is only to define who sets the retention periods for information. Generally it will be the Legal Department, but it may also be a Records Management Department or an Information Security Department. Some organizations may want to expand on the words "securely retained" so as to clarify where and how the information should be stored. These storage requirements could for example vary based on data sensitivity, criticality, and value. See the policies entitled "Definition Of Archival Storage Data Retention Schedule" and "Minimum Information Retention Period." A: MT; E: LMH.

649. Business Source Document Data Retention Requirements

Policy: Business source documents and original electronic input files must be retained until three events have taken place. Specifically, the related transactions must have been completed, a management review of the records incorporating these transactions must have been performed, and a period in which the transactions may be disputed must have passed.

Commentary: The intention behind this policy is to make sure that paper or electronic source documents are not destroyed prematurely. An example of a source document is the application form which people fill out when they are seeking a job at a company. Certain information from the application form frequently gets entered into a computer system, at which point the application form becomes a source document. Because many organizations do not put all information appearing on a source document into a computer, and because this process often involves errors, it is important to retain the source document until the transaction is complete. Continuing with the same example, management may not have enough information about a candidate to make an employment decision; they may then go back to the source document (application) to gather additional data. Separately, management review is necessary to ensure that the transaction was completed in accordance with management's intentions. This requirement allows the source documents to be used for audits, for example to reconcile the accounting records. Separately, the policy requires the time period for a dispute (in some cases, legally known as the "statute of limitations") to have elapsed, so that the source document can be discarded without problems. See the policies entitled "Minimum Information Retention Period," "Business Source Document Data Retention Period," and "Definition Of Archival Storage Data Retention Schedule." A: MT; E: LMH.

650. Business Source Document Data Retention Period

Policy: Business source documents containing input data must be retained for at least 90 days beyond the date when this information was entered into Company X computer system(s).

Commentary: The intention of this policy is to preserve original information that may be important should there be a computer problem (such as a virus) or data entry errors. The retained source documents may also be useful for quality control and/or auditing purposes. On a different point, there is nothing sacrosanct about the 90 day retention period; it could have been 120 days or a similar period. The retention period will vary based on industry practice, the nature of the information involved, local laws and regulations, as well as other considerations -- be sure to consult legal counsel on this point. This policy is a simplified version of the policy entitled "Business Source Document Data Retention Requirements." It seeks to give operations management a rule of thumb they can use to determine when source documents may be destroyed, preferably by shredding or some other secure means. Also see the policies entitled

"Business Source Document Data Retention Requirements" and "Definition Of Archival Storage Data Retention Schedule." E: MT; E: LMH.

651. Regular Purging Of Information Which Is No Longer Needed

Policy: All Company X information must be destroyed or disposed of when no longer needed. To support this policy, management must review the continued value and usefulness of information on a periodic and scheduled basis.

Commentary: The intention of this policy is to keep business records and files to a minimum and to thereby eliminate unneeded records. This process is sometimes referred to as "purging." The simplicity obtained thereby can help efforts to organize and properly secure the records. The process can also help eliminate information that could be used against the organization, and which might be disclosed during a legal discovery process. An important adjunct to this policy may be a data dictionary (in government circles, also known as a data directory); a data dictionary may be used to define what types of data exist within an organization, where this data exists (databases, files, file drawers, etc.), how old the data is, what controls apply to the data, and the like. For a related policy without mention of an accompanying process, see "Personal Information Necessary For Proper Functioning Of Business." Also see the policies entitled "Definition Of Archival Storage Data Retention Schedule," "Directory Of Information Held In Archival Storage," "Information Systems Unsuitable For Time-Sensitive Information," and "Approved Methods For Hardcopy Sensitive Information Disposal." A: MT; E: LMH.

652. Procedure For Release Of Used Equipment And Media To Third Parties

Policy: Before information systems equipment or storage media which has been used for Company X business is provided to any third party, the equipment or media must first be physically inspected by the Information Security Department to determine that all sensitive information has been removed. This policy does not apply when a non-disclosure agreement (NDA) has been signed by the third party.

Commentary: This policy is intended to prevent the inadvertent release of sensitive information to third parties. Thinking that they are recycling obsolete equipment, many local managers donate or sell old personal computers to charities, schools, or used equipment brokers. These managers may not have taken appropriate precautions to definitively remove all sensitive information from hard disk drives, non-volatile memory locations, and accompanying storage media. This policy transfers responsibility for removing data from local managers to the Information Security Department, but also establishes a strong perimeter to ensure that no donated or sold equipment or storage media is leaking sensitive information. This transfer of responsibility is appropriate because local managers don't often have the expertise to adequately determine that all sensitive information has been removed. The transfer is also advisable because it allows the Information Security Department staff to perform situation-specific risk assessments to determine whether equipment or media can be adequately desensitized, or whether destruction is necessary. This policy also prevents embarrassing publicity from leaks and assures that the Information Security Department knows which third parties are receiving equipment and media. Some policy writers will want to exclude from this policy certain equipment such as telephone handsets, fax machines, or copiers which have no data storage capabilities (these types of equipment are becoming increasingly rare). This policy goes well with policies which dictate centralized purchasing of information systems equipment such as the policy entitled "Hardware/Software Procurement Via Standard Purchasing Channels." Also see the policy entitled "Transfer Of Sensitive Information To Third Parties On Computer Media." A: MT; E: MH.

653. Information Destruction And Information Systems Equipment Disposal

Policy: Department managers are responsible for the prompt and proper disposal of surplus property no longer needed for business activities. Disposal of information systems equipment must proceed in accordance with procedures established by the Information Systems Security Department, including the irreversible removal of information and software.

Commentary: Some government agencies have been embarrassed to find that surplus computer equipment donated to charity contained considerable private or confidential information that should have been removed. Simple file deletion is generally not sufficient; the files must be expunged or overwritten (zeroized) by a separate systems utility to be truly irretrievable. This process can be complex, so separate procedures are often issued by the Information Security Department. Note that the way the policy is written, the procedures can be changed as the technology changes, without the need to change this policy. While the focus of this policy is on equipment, the real concern is the information which stored on the equipment (such as on the hard drive). This policy also helps prevent inadvertent violation of the license terms for copyrighted software. For related ideas, see the policies entitled "Transfer Of Sensitive Information To Third Parties On Computer Media" and "Sensitive Information Destruction Must Follow Specified Procedures." A: M; E: MH.

654. Destruction Of Records Or Information Requires Management Approval

Policy: Workers must not destroy or dispose of potentially important Company X records or information without specific advance management approval. Unauthorized destruction or disposal of Company X records or information will subject the perpetrator to disciplinary action including termination and prosecution. Records and information must be retained if: (1) they are likely to be needed in the future, (2) regulation or statute requires their retention, or (3) they are likely to be needed for the investigation or prosecution of unauthorized, illegal, or abusive acts.

Commentary: The intention of this policy is to put workers on notice that they must not destroy or dispose of potentially important information unless prior management approval has been received. This policy addresses destruction of records as a way to get revenge on another worker, concealing evidence needed for an investigation, etc. The policy also has another intention, and that is to clarify when information should be retained -- see the last sentence. This policy should be supported with other guidance (not necessarily policies) listing the time periods for which different types of information must be kept; this is often referred to as a "data retention schedule." On a different note, this policy indirectly holds management responsible for the destruction of records and information. This is desirable as a way to ensure management oversight of this important area. The policy is also a way to avoid problems where records are destroyed and then management disclaims any knowledge of the activities described in the records. Separately, restricting the persons authorized to do the destruction of records and information is another way to address the problem handled by this policy; see the policy entitled "Persons Authorized To Destroy Sensitive Company X Information." A: EMT; E: LMH.

655. Record Destruction Prohibited Unless Authorized By List Or Schedule

Policy: Workers must not destroy Company X records unless these records (1) appear on a list of records authorized for destruction, or (2) can be destroyed according to instructions appearing in the Company X Records Retention and Disposition Schedule. Destruction is defined as any action which prevents the recovery of information from the storage medium on which it is recorded (including encryption, erasure, and disposal of the hardware needed to recover the information).

Commentary: This policy is intended to inform workers that they may not destroy Company X records unless specifically authorized to do so by written documents. Without such specific instructions, workers may destroy records to cover-up their own misdeeds, or innocently destroy records that later prove to be useful. Separately, some organizations may wish to expand the exceptions mentioned in the policy to include verbal authorization by the organizational archivist or information owner. The authorized destruction list typically includes rough drafts that have not been circulated, copies made for short-term use, reference material, outdated publications, superseded backup copies, and blank forms. For related ideas, see the policy entitled "Sensitive Information Destruction Must Follow Specified Procedures." A: E; E: LMH.

656. Data Destruction Process Placed On Hold In Response To Discovery

Policy: Whenever an electronic discovery request is received by Company X, all organized and periodic electronic data destruction activities must immediately be placed on hold until the Legal Department determines whether these destruction activities jeopardize sought-after data.

Commentary: The intention of this policy is to notify systems administrators, data archivists, and computer operators that they must be ready to stop normal data destruction processes immediately if and when they receive notice from the Legal Department. In traditional English legal systems, the "discovery process" involves an opposing party in a lawsuit requesting certain internal records in the possession of the defendant. If the defendant negligently permits a data destruction process to proceed after a discovery notice has been received, the organization may suffer legal sanctions, and the defendant's position in the case may be damaged. The existence of a policy such as this is an indication that Company X intended to fully comply with legal requirements. Some organizations may wish to go beyond the requirements of this policy, including the establishment of a formal process for the immediate notification of all internal parties who engage in organized and periodic data destruction activities (paper shredding, back-up tape zeroization or erasure, etc.). Separately, note that an end-user deleting files from his or her hard drive to free up disk space is not intended to be an organized and periodic data destruction process, and therefore does not fall within the purview of this policy (the end-user should, however, be personally notified if their personal computer might contain sought-after information). For related considerations, see the policies entitled "Retaining Personal Information Only As Long As Needed For Business" and "Periodic Destruction Of Archived Electronic Mail Messages." A: T; E: LMH.

1.3.5. Data Integrity

1.3.5.1. Awareness Of Integrity Status

657. Management Must Be Notified Of Information Integrity Attributes

Policy: To the extent feasible, management must be periodically notified about the accuracy, timeliness, relevance, and other information integrity attributes that describe the information they use for decision-making.

Commentary: The intention of this policy is to achieve full disclosure about the nature of the information used for decision-making. Management needs to know the extent to which they can rely on the information they receive. This information about information (metadata) helps them make decisions about information reliability, and as a result, how likely it is that their decisions will be on-target. The reader can develop explanatory text to accompany a policy such as this; such text can give specific ways to measure information integrity. For example, the time period between data capture and processed information presentation can be provided (this is called "float"). Analysis of the integrity attributes of information is often done by database administrators, data modelers, systems architects, and others working to standardize data on a cross-application and cross-platform basis. Information security specialists should be involved, although this work is not the traditionally-appreciated mission of the information security specialist. For another metadata-related idea, see the policy entitled "Nature And Location Of Company X Information Is Confidential." For a different way to look at disclosing information integrity attributes, see the policy entitled "Suppression Or Labelling Of Incomplete Or Obsolete Information." A: MT; E: LMH.

658. Management Notification Of Information Integrity Controls Failure

Policy: If controls which assure the integrity of information fail, if such controls are suspected of failing, or if such controls are not available, management must be notified of these facts each time they are presented with the involved information.

Commentary: The intention of this policy, like the policy entitled "Management Must Be Notified Of Information Integrity Attributes," is to achieve full disclosure about the nature of information used for decision-making. If certain information is suspect or if it may be suspect, management must be notified. This policy requires that management be notified, rather than having the information be suppressed in the hopes that nobody will notice (after all, it might hurt some one's promotion potential to disclose such information). This policy thus requires that bad news be delivered, rather than tacitly permitting bad news to be suppressed. Particularly in large organizations, there is a tendency for bad news to be suppressed as information moves up the management hierarchy. This policy helps break that tendency. Also see the policy entitled "Notification Of Suspected Loss Or Disclosure Of Sensitive Information." A: MT; E: LMH.

659. Calculation Recipients Must Receive Information To Verify Correctness

Policy: All customers, employees, and other individual recipients of calculations performed on their account by Company X must be provided with sufficient information to independently verify that the calculations are correct.

Commentary: This policy attempts to overcome the obfuscation that tends to go along with computational complexity. It attempts to give individuals sufficient information so that they can verify that calculations were done correctly. This is desirable because it uses an outside party to help identify fraud and errors. For example, a bank customer should be able to calculate the interest due him, and if there is an error, he will bring it to management's attention. This policy is additionally desirable because it reduces the demands on customer service staff; if customers have the information they need to verify calculations, then they don't need to contact the customer service department. The policy is a reflection of existing labor laws in some jurisdictions, which require that paychecks show all deductions. This policy is additionally desirable because it will help foster customer goodwill and trust. On another note, as it is written, the policy doesn't apply to organizations, such as the Internal Revenue Service (IRS) or a business partner. This is because accounting standards define the preparation of financial statements and are thus the governing source of disclosures in the accounting domain. Nonetheless, it is desirable to apply this same concept to organizations to avoid disputes and to enable third party checking mechanisms. These third party checking mechanisms can be very useful when it comes to identifying fraud, errors, misunderstandings in contract terms, and other problems. For a related idea, see the policy entitled "Management Notification Of Information Integrity Controls Failure." A: T; E: LMH.

660. Nature Of Information Modifications Must Be Disclosed

Policy: If information issued by Company X has been modified in ANY way (photos retouched, numbers rounded up, etc.), the recipients must be notified about the nature of the modification. The notification must take place prior to recipient decisions based on such information.

Commentary: The intention of this policy is to make sure that the recipients of information do not make inappropriate decisions about modified information because they did not understand or know about modifications. The policy implicitly supports a perspective that "honesty is the best policy." Thus an organization with a policy like this would not knowingly run an advertisement that portrayed its products in misleading ways. This policy may also help to keep an organization out of trouble with the law. Likewise, the policy requires that the Information Systems Department notify users about changes made to information appearing in reports it generates; the policy can thus be interpreted to apply to both internal and external information consumers. Ultimately the information consumer is in the best position to determine whether certain modifications are material (important) in nature, and whether these modifications could affect a decision. This policy has a positive side-effect: scrupulous compliance with this policy will lead to loyal and supportive information consumers. An example of this policy in action involved the 1995 political discussions of California Senator Barbara Boxer with executives from the film industry. Boxer has been pushing for laws requiring that films altered for TV, videos, and the airlines be labeled with disclosure statements. Also see the policies entitled "Source And Date Labels Required For Major Decision Input" and "Altered Photographs Must Be So Labeled." A: MT; E: LMH.

661. Source And Date Labels Required For Major Decision Input

Policy: All data used for management decisions involving amounts over $100,000 must be marked ("labeled") with both its origin(s) and corresponding date(s). These marks must be retained whatever technology is used for the recording, storage, and processing of the information.

Commentary: The intention of this policy is to require special explanatory information -- information about information, also known as metadata -- whenever a substantial management decision is to be made. Having a cut-off (in this case it's $100,000, but it will vary by organization) helps to reduce the overall cost of collecting or generating special explanatory information. A similar policy may be appropriate for all data down-loaded from a multi-user machine to a smaller machine (microcomputer (PC), workstation, departmental processor, etc.). If management is not aware of the movement of data from machine to machine, decisions can be made assuming the information is current or correct when in fact is not. This policy thus seeks to address a widespread misconception that if information is from a computer, then it must be right. Also see the policy entitled "Labelling For Paternity Rights To Intellectual Property." A: MT; E: LMH.

662. Suppression Or Labelling Of Incomplete Or Obsolete Information

Policy: All incomplete or obsolete information must be suppressed and not distributed to users, unless it is accompanied by an explanation which describes the status of the information.

Commentary: The intention of this policy is to make sure that information consumers are aware of the nature of information they receive. If consumers are not aware that certain information is incomplete or obsolete, they may make erroneous decisions. This policy gives the information provider the option to either suppress the information or to explain its deficiencies. The policy-writer may wish to embellish on this policy, adding definitions for the terms "obsolete" or "incomplete." Another change could require that if there is a doubt as to the incompleteness or obsolescence of information, then the information provider must provide an explanation. In some respects, this policy is a different way of looking at the policy entitled "Management Must Be Notified of Information Integrity Attributes." For a different twist on this idea, see the policy entitled "Truthful Representations By Company X Employees." A: T; E: LMH.

663. Production Input Transactions Must Have Sequence Numbers

Policy: To facilitate tracking and problem resolution processes, each input transaction submitted to a production computer system must be assigned a unique sequence number or identifier.

Commentary: The intention of this policy is to properly account for all input transactions, and to facilitate the reconciliation of input transactions should there be a problem, or even suspicion of a problem. The existence of a serial number allows computer input data to be linked in a chronological way to source documents. It also helps to ensure that no transactions were duplicated and that no transactions were lost. For more information about source documents, see the policy entitled "Business Source Document Data Retention Requirements." To reduce its impact and cost, this policy may be limited to certain critical applications or other important activities. The policy assumes that the organization in question has already defined the terms "transaction" and "production" in a clear and unambiguous way. Also see the policies entitled "Changing Physical Access Control Codes On Worker Termination" and "Special Labelling For All Non-Production Business Transactions." A: T; E: LMH.

1.3.5.2. Integrity Of Information Sources

664. Authorization Required For All Production System Input Transactions

Policy: Methods must be in place to ensure that all input to production computer systems which has been submitted for processing has been properly authorized.

Commentary: The intention of this policy is to preserve the integrity of Company X books or records. If unauthorized transactions are posted to the books or records, all of the books or records become of questionable value. This policy also helps to prevent fraud, embezzlement, sabotage, and a number of other abusive acts that could be perpetrated by people who had information system access but who did not have proper authorization. Authorization could take the form of source document signature verification, digital signatures for electronic mail messages, message authentication codes (MACs) for wire transfers, etc. One of the most common way to indicate authorization is to use a secret password. While this policy deals with authorization methods, the policy entitled "All Production Transactions Must Be Authorized By Management" approaches the same idea with the notion of transaction acceptance. Also see the policies entitled "Authorization For Changes To Production Data And Programs" and "Originator Of Transactions Must Be Clearly Identified." A: T; E: LMH.

665. Changes To Sensitive, Critical, Or Valuable Information

Policy: Transactions affecting sensitive, critical, or valuable information must only be processed if the originating individual or system has been shown to be authorized to submit such transactions.

Commentary: The intention of this policy is to require that management establish and maintain an adequate access control system such that only authorized users can modify sensitive, critical, or valuable information. Another way to refer to this process is "user authentication." The most frequently encountered way to do this is with fixed passwords, although dynamic passwords are rapidly becoming the norm for dial-up and Internet-connected computers (the latter perhaps sent through a VPN). Authorization checking may also be performed by smart cards, digital signatures on electronic mail messages, message authentication code (MAC) comparisons for wire transfer instructions, etc. The policy assumes that the terms "sensitive, critical, or valuable" have already been defined elsewhere; see the policies entitled "Four Category Data Classification Scheme" and "Five Category Application Criticality Scheme." This policy employs an information-type orientation, whereas the policy entitled "Extended User Authentication Systems Required For Dial-Up Lines" takes a technological orientation. Also see the policy entitled "Reliance On Operating System User Authentication Process." A: T; E: LMH.

666. Input Data Validation And Rejected Item Handling

Policy: All transactions to be input to a multi-user production computer system must first be subjected to reasonableness checks, edit checks, and/or validation checks. Transactions which fail such checks must either be: (a) rejected with a notification of the rejection sent to the submitter, (b) corrected and resubmitted, or (c) suspended pending further investigation.

Commentary: The intention of this policy is to require that management properly validate all data submitted to multi-user computer systems. Validation in this case means subject the data to tests to clearly show that it has been properly formatted, defined, typed, etc. For example, an accounts payable program should reject an entry in the amount field which includes an alphabetic character. Input should be subjected to such tests before it ever gets an opportunity to update databases, master files, or other organizational books and records. If this validation is not performed, then eradicating what is called an "inherited error" (an error passed from system to system) becomes difficult and expensive. This policy thus attempts to detect and correct problems with data integrity at the earliest possible time (when information is first entered into a computer). Beyond errors and omissions, the policy provided here also indirectly protects against fraud, embezzlement, sabotage, and related intentional acts. One increasingly popular and potentially quite powerful way to implement this policy is via what is called an "active data dictionary." In this case, the data dictionary would be called upon for production processing by various application systems to figure out what input data validation routines to run. The attractive part about this approach is that data definitions and tests are defined only once even though they apply to a number of different applications. Separately, specific examples of problems that should fail data validation checks include: out-of-range values, invalid characters in data fields, missing or incomplete data, and unauthorized or inconsistent control data. This policy may be modified to require correction of the problem within a certain period of time (for example, three working days). For a more restrictive approach, see the policy entitled "Handling Of Rejected Input Transactions Via Suspense Files." Also see the policy entitled "Time For Problem Resolution Of Items In Suspense Files." A: T; E: LMH.

667. Email & Regular Mail Address Change Confirmed Via Previous Address

Policy: Customer requests to change a regular mail address and/or an email address will take effect one month after the change has been entered into the system. In the interim, an immediate change of address confirmation will be sent to the previous address in order to give the authorized customer an opportunity to correct any errors or irregularities.

Commentary: The intention of this policy is to ensure that unauthorized persons do not successfully request a change of address. Fictitious change of address requests often play a critical part in frauds, such as the fraudulent application for a credit card. This policy gives the authorized decision-maker on the account an opportunity to correct any errors or irregularities before the change goes into effect. To give customers a feeling that good customer service is provided, an acknowledgement of the change of address is sent immediately. A delay on a change of electronic mail or regular mail addresses will ordinarily not be problem because forwarding will be in effect (at least for a few months). There may be a few returned communications as a result of this policy, but these can be quickly taken care of because the relevant new address will be contained in a Company X customer database. For related ideas, see the policies entitled "Alternative Communications Channel Confirmation For Transactions" and "Validating The Identity Of External Parties On The Internet." A: T; E: LMH.

668. Double Keying Required For All Amounts Over $1,000

Policy: To reduce the probability of typographical errors, all keyboard-based production computer input processes involving amounts over $1,000 that will initiate a transaction must include entry of the amount twice.

Commentary: This policy seeks to prevent problems due to typing errors or other sloppiness. The policy would, for example, require a wire transfer data entry clerk to enter all amount fields over $1,000 twice. This policy would require that the whole process pertaining to that transaction be double-keyed. For example, the beneficiary bank account number would need to be entered twice. Separately, although it provides less effective data integrity checking, it may be sufficient in some environments for a computer to simply come back with a request for a confirmation (e.g., "You entered $1,500,000--is that correct? (Y or N)"). Because it's more effective, the actual entry of the amount twice is a preferred approach. On another note, the scope of this policy can be narrowed to only certain critical fields, such as the spelling of a beneficiary's name for a check over $1,000. Note that the entry of amounts over $1,000 into a spreadsheet or some other application that does not generate a transaction will not be within the scope of this policy. For added protection, the policy can be expanded to require that the second entry involve another individual (thus achieving separation of duties). This policy assumes that the word "production" has been defined elsewhere; the presence of this word exempts many single-user situations such as work on a personal computer where "back of the envelope" (informal) analysis not directly connected with a production application. Also see the policies entitled "Required Actions After Errors In Records Are Detected" and "Building Systems So That Errors And Manipulations Come To Light." A: T; E: LMH.

669. Line Numbering Required For Critical Free-Form Text Messages

Policy: In free-form text messages (such as electronic mail transmissions and faxes) that deal with critical or particularly important business matters, each line must be numbered. This process will highlight the omission or deliberate deletion of certain parts of the text.

Commentary: Line numbering for free-form (unformatted) text has long been used in legal documents to make sure that all changes are clearly evident. Some systems are using this approach as a part of the message itself. If line numbers are not automatically generated, users can add numbers to the left of each line using word processors, text editors, and similar programs. Some important multi-organizational networks, such as Electronic Data Interchange (EDI) systems, may wish to include line numbering for all free-form text messages. Some legal documents also use numbering such as this to clarify changes and make cross-referencing easier. Also see the policies entitled "Double Keying Required For All Amounts Over $1,000," "Required Actions After Errors In Records Are Detected," and "Building Systems So That Errors and Manipulations Come To Light." A: T; E: LMH.

670. Originator Of Transactions Must Be Clearly Identified

Policy: Transactions affecting sensitive, critical, or valuable information must be initiated only by source documents or computerized messages in which the originating individual or system is clearly identified.

Commentary: The ability to trace transactions back to the originating individual or system is critical for EDP auditing, forensic auditing (fraud auditing), problem resolution, and other efforts. In effect, the intention of this policy is to require that an audit trail exist for all transactions affecting sensitive, critical, or valuable information. Some organizations may wish to go beyond an indication of the source--they may want "proof" of the source. This can be achieved via digital signatures, message authentication codes (MACs), encryption, and hand-rendered signatures. The policy assumes that the terms "sensitive, critical, or valuable" have already been defined elsewhere; see the policies entitled "Four Category Data Classification Scheme" and "Five Category Application Criticality Scheme." While this policy specifies that a transaction originator must be identified, the policy entitled "Authorization Required For All Production System Input Transactions" helps to make sure that the proper person initiated the transactions. Also see the policy entitled "Prohibition Against Use Of Scanned Hand-Rendered Signatures." A: T; E: LMH.

671. Data Warehouse Input Requires Source, Classification, And Other Labels

Policy: All information included in the Company X data warehouse must be accompanied by information about its origin, its sensitivity classification, its reliability, and the date of its most recent revision.

Commentary: In general, the amalgamation or summarization of information should not imply that the underlying specifics are deleted (they may nonetheless be hidden from view). Along these same lines, this policy establishes a basic rule for populating a data warehouse (or any other large database). The input to the data warehouse should contain background information that will allow management to determine the underlying information's integrity, the extent to which the underlying information is reliable, and the underlying information's relevance for specific decision-making purposes. Without this background information, management may be only guessing about the integrity, reliability, and relevance of the information. This background information may also be important when doing a post-mortem for a failed decision making process; management may want to know what went wrong or what input data was erroneous. On a separate note, this background information can also assist with user access control decisions related to a data warehouse. For related ideas, see the policies entitled "Copyright Notices On Computer Programs And Documentation" and "Attribution Of Sources For Information." A: T; E: LMH.

672. Official Documents Prepared By Hand Must Exclusively Use Ink

Policy: All Company X official documents prepared by hand must use non-erasable ink. If an entry requires correction, the entry must be lined-out, initialed by the originator, and dated. Liquid paper correction fluid for these corrections is prohibited. Examples of official documents include travel expense reports, worker performance evaluations, and receiving dock logs.

Commentary: The intention of this policy is to prevent unauthorized and/or undetected modifications made to paper documents. The policy applies whether or not the paper documents are later used as computer input source documents. The first sentence could be expanded to say that the policy is relevant if the documents are prepared in any way by hand -- in whole or in part. Thus the policy covers the application of a signature to an otherwise typed or printed document. On a separate point, this policy also helps establish which document is an original and which is a copy; this is an important distinction from a legal standpoint. Much of this policy is common sense, if one knows the law. For related ideas, see the policies entitled "Special Paper Preventing Copying Of Sensitive Documents" and "Business Source Document Data Retention Requirements." A: E; E: LMH.

673. Review For Important Computer Analyses Done By Individuals

Policy: Company X business decisions which involve over $100,000, and which have been researched by one individual working alone with a spreadsheet or another computer application, must be reviewed in detail by at least one manager before any action is taken.

Commentary: This policy is particularly relevant to microcomputers (PCs), workstations, and other small computers like client/server systems. The notable aspect of this policy is that it requires another person to review the work of an individual working alone. This will hopefully bring to light errors in data entry, errors in logic, incomplete information, etc. The intention of this policy is to prevent an individual from arriving at a conclusion, upon which significant action is then taken, when this conclusion was incorrect or insufficiently researched. The policy imposes a sort of separation of duties in that major decisions must be made by at least two people. While the policy is primarily intended to catch errors, it also helps prevent fraud and other intentional acts which might be perpetrated if an individual were able to perform certain things alone. Most importantly, it helps prevent managers from unilaterally making incorrect decisions. Also see the policies entitled "Separation Of Duties And Control Over Company X Assets" and "Controls For Data Used To Arrive At Decisions Involving $100,000." For an external perspective on this internal review process, see the policy entitled "Need For Cross-Validation Of Important Information." A: EMT; E: LMH.

674. Controls For Data Used To Arrive At Decisions Involving $100,000

Policy: Prior to use in decisions involving over $100,000, all financial data critical to the decision at hand must be cross-checked via control totals, record counts, and/or similar controls.

Commentary: The intention of this policy is to make sure that data used for important decisions is reliable, complete, and adequately documented. The policy requires supporting data to be validated with standard control measures. This policy is particularly relevant to microcomputers (PCs), workstations, and other small computers such as client/server systems because such controls are so often missing in these informal computing environments. For example, a user may have mistyped when entering data into a spreadsheet, and this may not come to light unless controls such as those referenced in the policy are employed. There is nothing special about the cut-off for the amount involved ($100,000); this could just as easily have been $10,000, and should be based in part on the degree of risk that the organization is willing to accept (the accountants call this "materiality"). The notion of "criticality" may also need to be defined for this policy to be fully understood; see the policy entitled "Five Category Application Criticality Scheme." Also see the policies entitled "Need For Cross-Validation Of Important Information" and "Review For Important Computer Analyses Done By Individuals." A: EMT; E: LMH.

1.3.5.3. Modification Controls

675. Acceptable Risk Of Undetected Information Alteration

Policy: Management must establish and maintain sufficient preventive and detective security measures to ensure that Company X information is free from significant risk of undetected alteration.

Commentary: The intention of this policy is to guide systems designers, network specialists, and others to implement adequate control measures to prevent undetected information alteration. The exact nature of these controls will of course vary considerably from system to system. The policy communicates that it's important to be able to detect all unauthorized modifications, and also implies that unauthorized modifications should be prevented whenever possible. What's more, the policy also implies that it's important for all changes to information to have an audit trail, such that the reason for the changes and the person initiating the changes can be determined. Thus this policy is very much in support of the notion of EDP auditing. The controls used to achieve this policy could take many forms, such as digital signatures, message authentication codes (MACs), message encryption, and digital certificates. Information integrity and information availability are most important to private sector firms, while information confidentiality is most important to military organizations. Accordingly, this policy is most likely to be used by a private sector organization, although it is certainly still relevant to military organizations. A policy like this is especially important to organizations in the financial services industry because it sets the stage for controls that deal with fraud and embezzlement. Separately, some organizations may wish to modify the policy to restrict it to "sensitive, valuable, and critical" information. Such a modification to the policy may save some money because it will prevent controls from being used for certain end-user computing which does not deal with sensitive, valuable, and critical information. For a related idea, see the policy entitled "Security Requirements Identification Prior To Development/Acquisition." A: T; E: LMH.

676. Altered Photographs Must Be So Labeled

Policy: Photographs presented as a reflection of reality should not be altered. If photographs are altered, the viewer should be able to readily determine that changes have been made.

Commentary: The sophistication of computer-enhanced photographic processes makes it very difficult -- if not impossible -- to visually determine whether a photograph has been doctored (modified). This has lead to a number of abuses by the news media, some of which have resulted in lawsuits. New York University professor Fred Ritchin advocates an icon to designate digitally retouched photos, although this has not yet received public recognition or much support among the news media. An icon would be consistent with the second sentence of the policy which requires some sort of disclosure. The policy could be restated to say "Don't modify photos unless you make your modification obvious or put people on notice." Photos deserve special mention because it is so easy for laypersons (non-technicians) to make these modifications, and because photos have historically been used as a way to prove reality. The policy is relevant to all advertisements and other public representations, not just to those of the news media. For related ideas, see the policies entitled "Nature Of Information Modifications Must Be Disclosed" and "Reconstructibility Of Changes To Production Information." A: ET; E: LMH.

677. Handling Of Rejected Input Transactions Via Suspense Files

Policy: All rejected input transactions must be placed in a suspense file and listed in exception reports until such time as they are successfully resubmitted for processing or otherwise handled.

Commentary: The intention of this policy is to specify a standard method for handling rejected transactions so that all transactions will be promptly processed. A suspense file is a "holding tank" (weigh station) into which rejected items are placed. Suspense files should be cleaned out daily and items which are not cleaned out subjected to additional management scrutiny. Special management attention should be placed on the prompt resolution of the reasons why certain transactions were rejected. If this is not done, suspense files can be used to perpetrate fraud and other unauthorized acts. A recent case at a major commercial bank in California is exemplary in this regard; a loan officer put $10 million into a suspense account, and was able to defraud the bank for this amount because the suspense accounts were not promptly reconciled. As the case implies, it may be desirable for the reader's organization to expand the policy given here to require periodic purging of suspense files; alternatively the policy entitled "Time For Problem Resolution Of Items In Suspense Files" can be used. For an approach with a wider scope, see the policy entitled "Input Validation Procedures For Rejected Or Suspended Input." A: T; E: LMH.

678. Time For Problem Resolution Of Items In Suspense Files

Policy: All input transactions which are held in suspense status pending further investigation must either be resubmitted or otherwise handled within ten (10) business days of their original entry.

Commentary: The intention of this policy is to ensure that all rejected items are promptly resolved. As the commentary for the policy entitled "Handling Of Rejected Input Transactions Via Suspense Files" describes, if this is not done, fraud and other unauthorized acts may result. The time period would typically be much briefer for a bank, while it may be longer for a government agency. In some cases special permission may be required to keep an item in a suspense file longer than the specified number of days. Also see the policy entitled "Input Validation Procedures For Rejected Or Suspended Input." A: T; E: LMH.

679. Input Validation Procedures For Rejected Or Suspended Input

Policy: Input transactions which are corrected for resubmission, or which are suspended and later approved for resubmission, must be subjected to the same validation procedures that original input transactions receive. Examples of these validation procedures include reasonableness checks and format edit checks.

Commentary: The intention of this policy is to mandate the uniform application of controls to all input transactions. If the same validation procedures are not used for items which have been rejected or suspended, then a security vulnerability exists. This is because the people handling the items could reject or suspend an item, then modify it, and then resubmit it. If the same validation checks were not used, the modified item could effectively by-pass important control measures. Beyond fraud and embezzlement, this vulnerability could also lead to a degradation in information integrity. This policy is in keeping with standard testing procedures for software that require all tests to be performed again if there has been a change to the underlying code. Such testing procedures (and this policy as well) recognize the complexity of the modern computing environment, and the fact that humans fail to see the consequences associated with minor changes. For a related idea, see the policy entitled "System Developers Must Not Perform Formal Testing." Also see the policy entitled "Handling Of Rejected Input Transactions Via Suspense Files." A: T; E: LMH.

680. Personal Information Changed Only After Correct Prior Values Provided

Policy: Company X seeks to maintain accurate, up-to-date, and fully descriptive information in all of its computer systems. To reduce the probability of unauthorized modifications, before any personal information in production systems is altered based on a customer request, the correct prior information must be provided by the customer.

Commentary: The objective of this policy is to have customer service representatives confirm the prior version of personal information before these representatives make any changes to production information system databases. If a customer at the other end of an Internet connection or a phone line is not able to provide the correct prior version, chances are he or she is not the authorized person to make the change. For example, suppose a customer wants to change his billing address. In order to do this, he must provide the prior billing address before a new address will be posted to the production database. This is a weak control that needs to be used in conjunction with other security measures such as a customer specific password, or some other mechanism to verify the identity of the person submitting a change request. Some organizations allow customer service representatives to give hints which will prompt the customer to provide the correct prior information, even though this erodes the effectiveness of the control. For related ideas, see the policies entitled "Customer Service Fixed Passwords Not Displayed By Company X Systems" and "Computer Support Identification Codes." A: T; E: LMH.

681. Authorization For Changes To Production Data And Programs

Policy: Company X production data and production computer programs must be changed only by authorized people according to established procedures.

Commentary: The intention of this policy is to make sure special controls are used to protect the integrity of production computer data and programs. Since this data and these programs are used for critical business activities, special attention to security is warranted. Generally the number of authorized people will be small, and authorization will be granted only when such people have a bone fide need for these privileges. A formal change control system or a change management system may be used to automate and track the changes as well as associated authorizations. Authorization may be implemented via passwords, smart cards, digital signatures, digital certificates, encryption, manually-rendered signatures, and other methods. Computer programs can be considered a special type of computer data; for a computing environment to be secure, both need change controls. See the section of this reference book entitled Change Control Process for related policies, particularly the policy entitled "Formal Change Control Procedure Required For All Production Systems." Also see the policy entitled "Orders To Change Internal Records Placed Via Phone." A: EMT; E: LMH.

682. All Production Transactions Must Be Authorized By Management

Policy: Transactions that update business records must only be processed if they have first been authorized by Company X management.

Commentary: The intention of this policy is to make sure that only properly authorized transactions update production records (whether or not the records are computer-based). The policy can go on to specify what is meant by "authorization" -- generally a clear delegation of decision making power plus management approval to perform certain actions. Password-based computer access controls are the most frequently encountered means for checking that someone is, in fact, authorized to submit a transaction. Nonetheless, this policy is written in a general way such that the authorization process might also involve a manual signature on a paper document. While this policy deals with the notion of transaction acceptance, the policy entitled "Authorization Required For All Production System Input Transactions" addresses the same idea while emphasizing authorization methods. Also see the policy entitled "Business Production Information Updates By Non-Production Staff." A: T; E: LMH.

683. Review Reasonableness And Accuracy Of Changes To Internal Records

Policy: Management must review (or establish mechanisms for suitably-qualified and responsible people to review) the reasonableness and accuracy of all changes to internal records. These changes include posting sales transactions and recording accounts payable disbursements.

Commentary: The intention of this policy is to require that all updates to Company X records be reviewed by management or a properly authorized delegate of management (generally supervisors or internal auditors). Often this policy will be so much a part of the organizational culture at publicly-traded companies that it is superfluous. This is because securities laws have most stringent requirements for such review activities. For smaller companies, non-profit organizations, and government agencies the policy may still be warranted. Reasonableness checks are generally done via ratio analysis, reconciliation's, and similar procedures. Accuracy checks are done through physical inventories and similar review steps. Also see the policy entitled "Regular And Prompt Review Of System Logs." A: M; E: LMH.

684. Required Actions After Errors In Records Are Detected

Policy: If a customer brings error(s) in Company X records to the attention of Company X workers, an investigation of the error(s) must promptly be initiated. In the absence of a department manager's approval, resolution of the alleged error(s) must be completed within two weeks of receipt of the customer's communication. In addition, within two weeks of the time when the customer's communication was received a letter must be sent to the customer. The letter must specify either: (1) a change was made as requested, (2) no change was made and the reasons why no change was made, or (3) the date when a decision about the change will be made.

Commentary: The intention of this policy is primarily to build customer loyalty, but it is also to keep Company X records up-to-date. The policy specifically defines a response time for getting back to the customer, thus communicating to Company X workers that it is important that responses be generated promptly. Even if no definitive decision about a change is made, a response should still be sent to let the customer know that Company X is looking into it. This policy could be extended to include errors noticed by any third party (not just customers) or all errors (regardless of who noticed them). The emphasis on customers is warranted not only because accurate records containing personal data are a big concern of the public, but also because customer relations are critical to the success of any business. Separately, it should be noted that the term "resolution" does not necessarily imply a change to internal records. See the policies entitled "Employee Right To Add Explanatory Statement To Personnel File," "Building Systems So That Errors And Manipulations Come To Light," "Double Keying Required For All Amounts Over $1,000," and "Required Efforts To Ensure Integrity Of All Personal Records." A: EMT; E: LMH.

685. Standard Control Procedures For Correcting Business Records

Policy: If Company X business records are shown to be in error, they must be promptly corrected using standard control procedures.

Commentary: The intention of this policy is to require that standard control procedures be used to effect all error-correction-related changes to Company X business records. These control procedures might involve getting management approval before a change is made, or making changes via some sort of separation of duties with another worker. It is important to restrict who can make so-called "corrective" changes to business records, lest people abuse these powers to commit fraud, sabotage, and other unauthorized acts. It is not enough to know that records are in error; the records must be continuously corrected to maintain information integrity. Although not stated specifically, this policy also implies that a separate set of books--that does not describe the actual business circumstances--must not be maintained. For example, a deceptive sets of books could be kept for investor relations purposes, while a realistic set of books can be kept for insiders. Note that this policy does not prevent or discourage an organization from keeping different sets of books for different purposes if these books are still in keeping with standard procedures, such as generally accepted accounting principles (GAAP). This might, for example, involve one set of books for tax purposes and another for financial accounting purposes. Also see the policies entitled "Required Actions After Errors In Records Are Detected," "Control Implementations Consistent With Standard Of Due Care," and "Separation Of Duties And Control Over Company X Assets." A: MT; E: LMH.

686. Cellular Phones Must Not Be Used Anywhere In Data Center

Policy: To prevent possible interference with and/or disruption of computer and communications systems, cellular phones must not be used anywhere within the Company X computer machine room.

Commentary: The intention of this policy is to ensure that computer and communications systems resident in a data center are up-and-running as much as possible. There have been confirmed reports of cellular phones used near production servers and this usage causing crashes and hard disk corruption. Apparently the strong signals emitted by cellular phones interfere with the sensitive circuitry inside computers and communication systems. While this phenomenon may at first seem bizarre and unlikely, the policy writer only needs to remember that major airlines now forbid their passengers from using cellular phones during takeoff and landing. If cellular phones can affect the computers on airplanes, they can certainly can affect the computers inside a data center. This policy could be expanded to include two-way pagers, i.e., those pagers which can issue a reply of some sort to a page that has been received. For related ideas, see the policies entitled "Use Of Cordless Or Cellular Telephones For Secret Discussions" and "Property Pass For Removal Of All Computer And Communications Gear." A: E; E: LMH.

1.3.5.4. Consistent Representation Of Data

687. Truthful Representations By Company X Employees

Policy: All business related representations made by Company X employees, contractors, or consultants, must be truthful at all times. Such representations include those made in advertisements, in union negotiations, on product labels, and in government reports.

Commentary: The intention of this policy is to clearly put workers on notice that lying or "bending" the truth is prohibited. In general, the policy is intended to keep Company X workers (and Company X indirectly) out of trouble. This policy can be important if there are accusations that management systematically encouraged employees to misrepresent information (such as government environmental regulation compliance reports). Taking a different perspective with the same example, this policy is helpful in that it prevents "greenwashing" (disingenuous efforts to promote an organization as environmentally responsible when in fact it is not). The policy may also be helpful in any lawsuits involving fraud or misleading advertising. Recent US Federal Court decisions have underlined the importance of a written policy when it comes to assisting organizations in their efforts to avoid liability (for example, see "Sexual Harassment Ruling Limits Employers' Liability" in the Wall Street Journal, 15 August 1995, p. B3). This policy may also help prevent and/or defend from employee allegations that they were lied to during an employment interview process (so called "truth in hiring" cases). The policy may furthermore be useful in the prevention of practical jokes and clever humor which may ultimately cause problems. For a different twist on this idea, see the policy entitled "Suppression Or Labelling Of Incomplete Or Obsolete Information." A: EMT; E: LMH.

688. Misrepresentation Of Identity On Electronic Communication Systems

Policy: Misrepresenting, obscuring, suppressing, or replacing a user's identity on an electronic communications system is forbidden. The user name, electronic mail address, organizational affiliation, and related information included with messages or postings must reflect the actual originator of the messages or postings.

Commentary: The intention of this policy is to put users on notice that they may not misrepresent their identity on electronic communication systems, even for practical jokes or other humor. The scope of the policy is deliberately broad (specifically "electronic communication systems") so that it includes telephone systems as well as electronic mail systems. One example of an act which is prohibited by this policy is the extraction of certain text from an electronic mail message which is then incorporated into another electronic mail message without giving credit to the originator (thus violating the right of paternity). Note that this policy does not require all the routing information on an electronic mail message to be maintained, only the originator's identity. Separately, under this policy, the use of another person's user-ID is a policy violation (and technically electronic forgery). This policy assumes that no group user-IDs have been assigned; in other words, each user should have one or more personal user-IDs. For related ideas, see the policies entitled "Truthful Representations By Company X Employees," "Attribution Of Sources For Information," and "Internet Representations Including Company X Affiliation." A: E; E: LMH.

689. Consistent Way Of Representing Employee Contact Information

Policy: To assure the integrity of Company X records, all workers must choose a single way to represent their name, address, and other personal information, and must use this consistently for all Company X related matters.

Commentary: This policy prevents improper matching of files that belong to a single employee. For example, one database might have a "S. M. Smith" while another has a "Sam M. Smith," but the software may not be able to detect the fact that these names pertain to the same person. Improper matching could for instance lead to under reporting of taxable income, improper affirmative action (anti-discrimination) reports, etc. In some respects eliminating the need for this policy, some new software packages are able to detect possible duplicates in mailing lists and similar files. The explanation accompanying the policy should of course state that it is permissible for workers to change their name, move their residence, etc. Workers just need to consistently represent themselves with new contact information from the point in time when the change took place forward. This policy will also be appreciated by mail room workers, couriers, and receptionists. For a related idea, see the policy entitled "Multi-Platform Systems Parameter Naming Conventions." Also see the policies entitled "Required Efforts To Ensure Integrity Of All Personal Records" and "Management Must Be Notified Of Information Integrity Attributes." A: EMT; E: LMH.

690. Need For Cross-Validation Of Important Information

Policy: Important information on which management depends must be periodically compared with external sources or otherwise cross-validated to ensure that it conveys an accurate representation of reality.

Commentary: This policy seeks to periodically check important information to make sure that it is a reflection of reality. The notion of data integrity is meaningful only if one periodically compares the data to the outside world. An example involves inventory figures kept in a computer; if these figures are not periodically reconciled to the counts found in the real world, their integrity degrades. Likewise, as another example, technical staff should read professional publications to make sure that their current knowledge is still relevant. This policy begs the question: "How often is 'periodically'?" The answer will vary based on the type of information involved. If it is stock prices, then periodically may mean every business day. If it is the medical condition of staff in a position of significant trust, then periodically may mean annually. For internal rather than external validation of information, see the policy entitled "Review For Important Computer Analyses Done By Individuals." Also see the policy entitled "Controls For Data Used To Arrive At Decisions Involving $100,000." A: MT; E: LMH.

691. All Public Representations Must Be Cleared Through Public Relations

Policy: No media advertisement, Internet home page, electronic bulletin board posting, voice mail broadcast message, or any other public representation about Company X may be issued unless it has first been approved by the Corporate Public Relations Department.

Commentary: This policy seeks to prevent separate departments, although often meaning well, from independently initiating public representations about Company X. One of the major problems that organizations face is that different departments are so excited about advertising opportunities on the Internet, and so tired of waiting for assistance from centralized Information Technology Departments, that they have gone off and created their own Internet home pages (also called WWW pages or web pages). Unless a policy like this exists, there is a danger that such independent efforts will publicly embarrass the organization, confuse customers, or create unwanted news stories. This policy seeks to establish a single point-of-contact for interactions with the public. The leverage provided by modern communications technology (so many people can be reached so easily, inexpensively, and quickly) needs to be tempered by controls so that problems are not inadvertently created. Separately, in a conglomerate that owns autonomous companies (as well as in a large government entity), the Public Relations Department of each subsidiary would be involved rather than a centralized Public Relations Department. Also see the related policies entitled "Unofficial Web Pages Permitted Only By Contract," "Truthful Representations By Company X Employees," "Internet Discussion Group And Chat Room Participation Forbidden," and "Prior Review For Speeches, Presentations, Technical Papers, Etc." A: ET; E: LMH.

1.3.5.5. Censorship Of Data

692. Right To Free Speech Does Not Apply To Company X Systems

Policy: Company X computer and communications systems are not intended for, and must not be used for the exercise of the participants' right to free speech.

Commentary: The intention of this policy is to put system participants on notice that they should not expect management to support them in their rights to speak their minds when using Company X systems. This policy instead allows Company X to edit or censor electronic mail, electronic bulletin board entries, intranet sites, voice mail broadcasts, etc. The policy eliminates questions about legal problems associated with the infringement of free speech. The policy is American in its orientation, although it is equally applicable to other countries where the right to free speech is recognized. The on-line service called Prodigy recently got into trouble when subscribers complained in an open forum about certain of Prodigy's policies. Prodigy then censored the complaints and this lead to an even worse uproar because Prodigy had not notified the participants that their free speech rights did not apply. Another situation where this policy would be applicable involves so-called "flaming" (cursing out another person) on the Internet. The policy discourages users from speaking their mind if they are using Company X systems, which may be a prudent policy if Company X wishes to stay out of court (defamation, libel, etc.). Also see the policies entitled "Right To Censor Data On Organizational Systems" and "Collecting Information About Expressions Of First Amendment Rights." A: E; E: LMH.

693. Right To Censor Data On Organizational Systems

Policy: Management reserves the right to censor any data posted to Company X computers or networks. These facilities are private business systems, and not public forums, and as such do not provide First Amendment free speech guarantees.

Commentary: Although the "First Amendment" wording of this policy is relevant to the United States only, the general idea is more widely applicable. The intention behind the policy is that organizational systems not turn into mechanisms to damage the company. As mentioned in the commentary for the policy entitled "Right To Free Speech Does Not Apply To Company X Systems," something like this happened with Prodigy (the on-line service) a few years ago. It could happen elsewhere whenever members of a labor union, a group of dissatisfied customers, a minority stockholder faction, or another group of individuals disenchanted with the current management gets together on-line. Another intention is to be able to stop certain uses of the system if they are contrary to Company X policy or contrary to law. For example, if a system is being used to exchange stolen credit card numbers, management will want to censor messages dealing with this activity. Also see the policies entitled "Right To Free Speech Does Not Apply To Company X Systems," "Removal Of Inappropriate Electronic Postings To Public Forums," and "Disclaimer Of Responsibility Or Liability For Message Contents." A: E; E: LMH.

694. New Information Types Must Be Reflected In Corporate Data Dictionary

Policy: All new types of Company X information that are created and used for day-to-day business operations must be promptly reflected in the corporate data dictionary.

Commentary: This policy is intended to put all workers on notice that the corporate data dictionary must reflect all types of information used in day-to-day (so-called "production") operations. Through a corporate data dictionary, management can become aware of all the major types of operational information within an organization. They can thus promptly censor information where needed, as well as apply additional controls to those types of information that warrant these controls. Rather than an overt censorship approach, this policy takes a more information-management-oriented perspective, assuming that if management knows all the major types of information available within the organization, then it will be able to more readily control this information. Indeed, if management doesn't know what kind of information exists it will find it very difficult to properly manage this information (security in this context is a part of management). Separately, this policy could also insist that all new types of information be reflected in a data warehouse. For related ideas, see the policies entitled "Need To Collect Private Information Must First Be Justified" and "Existence Of Secret Systems Containing Personnel Records." A: EMT; E: LMH.

695. Right To Remove Offensive Material Without Warning

Policy: Company X retains the right to remove from its information systems any material it views as offensive or potentially illegal.

Commentary: This policy is intended to put users on notice that management has no obligation to retain information stored on its systems if it considers this information to be either offensive (harassing, pornographic, etc.) or otherwise questionable. It is notable that this policy does not say the system operator will exercise editorial control, that the operator will review material to determine whether it meets community standards, or whether the operator will subscribe to any particular standard of decency. It simply gives the organization the right to remove material as it sees fit -- in most instances in response to a complaint or a tip from another user. It is also notable that the policy deliberately says nothing about giving the involved user advance or concurrent notice of the removal process. This policy is particularly relevant to those organizations running electronic bulletin boards (EBBs), on-line chat rooms, Internet web pages with user feedback areas, and other systems that make information available to a wide audience. A policy like this is used by American On-Line (AOL) as part of its service agreement with users. For related ideas, see the policies entitled "Privacy Expectations And Information Stored On Company X Systems,"

"Removal Of Unauthorized Copyrighted Information And Software," and "Warnings Required If Recipients Might Be Offended or Upset." A: E; E: LMH.

696. No Responsibility For Monitoring Content Of Information Systems

Policy: Company X reserves the right to remove any message, file, database, graphic, or other material from its information systems. At the same time, Company X has no obligation to monitor the information content resident on or flowing through its information systems.

Commentary: This policy is intended to give management the maximum leeway in promptly removing material from its information systems (for whatever reason). At the same time, the statement of this right to remove material should not lead the reader to believe that all content will be monitored to meet certain standards (the standards are deliberately missing from this policy). This policy acknowledges that "community standards" (a legal notion associated with pornography and censorship) as well as business standards will evolve over time; nonetheless, this policy need not change as these standards change. The legal position that this policy attempts to establish is one of a common carrier like a telephone company in the United States; the telephone company is not responsible for illegal or unethical use of its facilities. In that respect, this policy is appropriate for an Internet Service Provider (ISP), a Value Added Network (VAN), an electronic bulletin board operator, or a similar organization. For related ideas, see the policies entitled "Standards Of Common Carriers Do Not Apply" and "Removal Of Inappropriate Electronic Postings To Public Forums." A: E; E: LMH.

697. Prohibited Uses Of Company X Computer & Communication Facilities

Policy: Company X internal computer and communication systems (voice mail systems, electronic bulletin boards, database management systems, and electronic mail facilities, intranet sites, etc.) must not be used as an open forum to discuss Company X organizational changes or business policy matters.

Commentary: The intention of this policy is to allow management to censor certain uses of internal computer and communication systems, and if need be to discipline the individuals using these systems for unauthorized activity. This would, for example, be important when layoffs (sackings) were being performed; for employee morale reasons, open discussion of such matters should not be found on these internal systems. Note that an announcement describing the appointment of a new manager or staff member would be permissible under the policy as it is written because this does not involve "discussion." It is free and open exchange about the referenced topics that many organizations find threatening and therefore wish to prohibit. The list of topics referenced may be expanded to include new products, strategic planning, product pricing, customer relations, and related considerations. This policy makes it clear that the named systems are not an appropriate place to address such matters. Note that this policy will take the policy-issuing organization in the opposite direction from collaborative computing, such as that available with the client/server system called Lotus Notes. See the policies entitled "Right To Free Speech Does Not Apply to Company X Systems" and "Internet Use For Personal Purposes Prohibited." A: E; E: LMH.

698. Disclaimer Of Responsibility Or Liability For Message Contents

Policy: Company X specifically disclaims any responsibility or liability for the contents of any message appearing on this web site. With respect to this site, Company X is acting like a common carrier, and as such does not control the content of messages on the system. Likewise, Company X does not verify the correctness, accuracy, or validity of the information appearing on this system.

Commentary: Historically, there have been many legal disputes dealing with bulletin board system (BBS) system operator responsibility for illegal activities taking place on their dial-up BBS. These same considerations apply to Internet web sites or any other electronic forum where third parties interact. This policy helps to put Company X in a position where it is not responsible for these activities (much like the way the telephone company is not responsible for the illegal acts that others perform using the telephone system). Note that with this policy, the system operator can still censor or delete messages. Although certain other legal doctrines will make an organization responsible for the acts of its employees, this policy helps to reduce Company X's exposure for messages posted on its systems. It is important to review this legalistic policy with in-house legal counsel. Separately, the words "this site" in the first sentence of the policy implies that this policy is presented to people when they log-into the site. The words "this site" in the second sentence could be changed or deleted to make the policy more generally applicable (perhaps to include Internet IRC systems, customer support discussion groups such as those on Compuserve, dial-up BBSs, etc.). The policy might also be used for an on-line service such as Prodigy. A recent New York State court ruling held Prodigy responsible for the libelous remarks of a user on its system. In this case the judge said that because Prodigy employs editors and has software screening systems that censor messages based on content, it will be deemed to be a publisher like a newspaper, and therefore is subject to liability (Stratton Oakmont Inc. v. Prodigy Services Co., New York Supreme Court, Mineola, Case No. 31063/94). This judicial opinion was in part rendered based on the fact that Prodigy advertised that it has a superior service because it exercised editorial control. Separately, the policy presented here expressly denies the use of such controls and therefore limits an on-line service provider's exposure. Also see the policies entitled "Comments On Systems Do Not Necessarily Reflect Company X Positions," "Disclaimer Must Accompany All Internet Personal Messages," "Disclaimer Of Responsibility For Damage To Data And Programs," and "Standards Of Common Carriers Do Not Apply." A: E; E: LMH.

699. Comments On Systems Do Not Necessarily Reflect Company X Positions

Policy: Comments that workers post to an electronic mail system, an electronic bulletin board system, or other electronic systems are not necessarily formal statements of or the official position of Company X.

Commentary: The intention of this policy is to put users on notice that they should not immediately assume what they read or otherwise observe on Company X systems is necessarily Company X policy. They should instead look for an indication that the material is a policy statement (soon organizations will require digital signatures to ensure that such policy statements are genuine and that they have not been tampered with). Another intention of this policy is to put users on notice that what they read or observe may soon be deleted. For example, messages could be sexually explicit or racially harassing. At any rate, the policy puts users on notice that the organization does not intend to be bound by these statements, nor does it make any guarantees that they are correct or authorized. Given the ease with which most electronic mail messages can now be spoofed, this conservative stance is warranted. Although the policy is intended for data-oriented systems like the Internet and electronic bulletin boards, voicemail and other communications systems could be added. Specific mention of the types of systems could be deleted from the policy, making reference instead to "electronic communications systems." Separately, this policy is the equivalent of the statement provided by many TV and radio stations which notes that "the opinions expressed are not necessarily those of the station or the station management." Also see the policy entitled "Disclaimer Of Responsibility Or Liability for Message Contents." A: E; E: LMH.

700. Warnings Required If Recipients Might Be Offended Or Upset

Policy: If the content of a phone message recording, voice mail message, letter, or some other Company X communication is likely to offend or upset certain segments of the expected recipient population, a clear warning must be provided on the cover, in the introduction, or in some other place such that the recipient may opt not to receive the information.

Commentary: This policy is intended to reduce the number of complaints about Company X advertising and communications. It is also intended to put recipients on notice about the nature of the information, giving them a chance not to proceed. For example, when calling a 900 area code recorded message in the USA, the service providers must provide callers with an introductory message about the nature of the service, how much it will cost, etc. The caller gets a grace period of perhaps 30 seconds before charges apply; this allows the caller to hang-up if they so choose. Likewise, firms sending pornographic direct mail (mass mail) material enclose their solicitations in an inner envelope which clearly indicates that the material may offend some people; the recipient then gets a chance to open it or discard it. Although the policy could apply to internal communications, it is primarily intended to be used for external communications. See the policies entitled "Fax Cover Sheet Must Contain Restricted Dissemination Notice" and "Covering Sensitive Information When Interrupted at Work." A: T; E: LMH.

701. All Information Posted To Internet Must Have Standard Content Labels

Policy: All information posted to Company X's commerce and web sites must be labeled so that content screening software can automatically determine the nature of the material.

Commentary: The intention of this policy is to keep the organization posting content to the Internet from getting into trouble with parents and employers (bad publicity, complaints, perhaps even legal problems). Parents can use content screening software to prevent their children from viewing material of a sexual, religious, or violent nature. Employers can use content filtering software such as that implemented in firewalls like Eagle from Raptor Systems (Waltham, Massachusetts). This software supports URL blocking so that employees will not be surfing the web and dealing with personal matters when at work. The content labels that can be employed will undoubtedly change but at the present time they are exemplified by the PICS standard (Platform for Internet Content Selection). While it is desirable for the organization posting material to do the labelling, these organizations should be aware that third parties also do their own independent categorization. For related concepts, see the policies entitled "Right To Censor Data On Organizational Systems" and "Warnings Required If Recipients Might Be Offended Or Upset." A: T; E: LMH.

702. Network Message Protection Services Not Provided

Policy: When providing computer networking services, Company X is acting as a common carrier. Company X is providing communications services, not message protection services. Accordingly, no responsibility is assumed for the disclosure of information placed on the network, and no assurances are made about the privacy of information placed on the network.

Commentary: This policy is intended to be communicated to subscribers who use Company X's network (say for electronic data interchange or EDI). It may also be sent to other external parties with which Company X communicates over its network (customers, employees, etc.). In some instances, this policy or a derivative thereof may be relevant to those firms supporting an Internet host which forwards mail or provides other services to the larger Internet community. The policy is intended to limit Company X's responsibility and liability for providing security measures. It clearly states that Company X does not do anything special to protect users' data (such as encrypt transmissions). While the implementation of appropriate security measures would be desirable, this policy is at least better than allowing users to hold onto their erroneous notions that some sort of security and/or privacy is provided. However, if encryption or other security facilities are provided on the network, the policy will need to be embellished to reflect that fact. The policy may be followed by a statement that it is the user's responsibility to provide encryption or other protection measures if the nature of the information involved so warrants. See the policies entitled "Consistent Protection Of Information Regardless Of Manifestation" and "Clear Definition Of Third Party Information Security Responsibilities." A: E; E: LMH.

703. Prohibition Against Sexual, Ethnic, And Racial Harassment

Policy: Sexual, ethnic, and racial harassment--including unwanted telephone calls, electronic mail, and internal mail--is strictly prohibited and is cause for disciplinary action including termination. Managers must make this policy clear to the workers in their group, as well as promptly investigate and rectify any alleged occurrences.

Commentary: The intention of this policy is to put workers on notice that harassing communications are not appropriate at work, and particularly not on Company X computer and communication systems. The reader's organization may already have a policy about harassment (from the Human Resources Department most likely), but that policy may say nothing about using Company X systems for harassment. Laws and morals about such behavior vary widely from jurisdiction to jurisdiction, so consultation with internal legal counsel is advisable. Also needed will be a definition of harassment (for example, repeated comments when the originator has been told that such comments are abusive and that he/she should stop). A recent American court case indicates that organizations can insulate themselves from liability if they have a strong anti-discrimination policy (see "Sexual-Harassment Ruling Limits Employer's Liability," in the Wall Street Journal, 15 August 1995, p. B3). Of course, it is not enough just to have a policy; there must be enforcement of the policy as well as communication of the policy to workers. Separately, the scope of this policy could be expanded to include harassment based on national origin, age, sexual orientation, disability, as well as religious or political beliefs. Also see the policies entitled "Management Attention To Employee Off-the-Job Behavior" and "Maintaining Accurate Records To Prevent Unwanted Telemarketing." A: E; E: LMH.

704. Restricted Behavior For Outbound Internet Communications

Policy: All outbound Internet communications (email, chat room remarks, discussion group postings, web form entries, etc.) must reflect well on Company X's reputation and public image. Inflammatory, defamatory, harassing, or disruptive communications are prohibited. Likewise, spamming or flaming is prohibited.

Commentary: This policy is intended to avoid legal complications and also to ensure that workers don't inadvertently embarrass an organization on the Internet. The policy dictates a certain standard of professionalism and a certain decorum that workers need to consistently follow. The policy thus provides the basis for disciplining or even terminating a worker who made the organization look bad in a public forum (the scope of the policy could be increased to include other public forums such as dial-up bulletin boards, but the Internet is by far the greatest risk). From a definitional standpoint, spamming is the transmission of junk email (unsolicited bulk advertisements); flaming is the use of cutting and nasty remarks sent electronically. For some related concepts, see the policies entitled "Right To Remove Offensive Material Without Warning" and "Removal Of Inappropriate Electronic Postings To Public Forums." A: E; E: LMH.

1.4. Communications Security

1.4.1. Establishment Of Access Paths And Systems

1.4.1.1. Flow Control Systems Including Firewalls

705. Internal Network Addresses Must Not Be Publicly Released

Policy: The internal system addresses, configurations, and related system design information for Company X networked computer systems must be restricted such that both systems and users outside Company X's internal network cannot access this information.

Commentary: This conservative policy seeks to prevent hackers and other unauthorized parties from obtaining information about Company X's internal network and connected systems. The idea behind this restriction is that attacks will be made significantly more difficult if this information is not readily obtainable. The more that an attacker knows about internal configurations the greater the chances that he or she will be able to obtain unauthorized entry (taken to the extreme, this statement means that insiders will be perpetrators of most computer abuse, a statement which is supported by various statistical studies). With many Internet firewalls, internal electronic mail address information is shared with machines outside the network, inadvertently revealing a target for future attacks. A number of firewalls provide address translation (aka address filtering or split DNS) as a way to increase security. When these translation services are used, the electronic mail address shared with outsiders is different than the address used on internal networks. This firewall feature thus supports the policy. Separately, this policy also requires that system administrators responsible for firewalls establish access control restrictions such that commands like PING cannot be used by external parties to gather information on machines connected to the internal network. This policy makes an assumption that Company X employs external network connections. If the policy is not clear as it stands, an example can be provided; for instance, "As an example involving the Internet, the Internet protocol (IP) addresses of internal computers must be translated and concealed at a firewall, router, gateway, or at other access points." Also see the policy entitled "Release Of Systems Documentation To Third Parties" and "Approval Required Prior To Release Of Company X Information." A: T; E: LMH.

706. Access Control Packages Required For Computers On The Network

Policy: If workers leave the power for their computers turned on during non-business hours, and if such computers are connected to a network, the computers must be protected by an access control system approved by the Information Security Department.

Commentary: The intention of this policy is to make sure that unauthorized persons don't gain access to Company X systems during off-hours when nobody is there to notice the intrusion. Many hackers, crackers, and others system attackers do their work, as the policy says, "during non-business hours." The scope of this policy could be narrowed to say that if computers are connected to a network with external connections (dial-up, value added networks, etc.), then there must be an access control package on each computer so connected. As written, this policy could also apply to all networks, such as an intranet, an extranet, and a dial-up telephone network. The reader may wish to provide examples of the different types of networks in the body of the policy itself. The policy, as written, may also discourage the connection to networks unless suitable controls have been arranged in advance. Separately, this policy is directly responsive to the frequently-occurring problem where end-users keep their computers on over the night, and at the same time have a connected modem that is left turned on. While this allows the end-users to connect with their office computers from home or some other location, it also allows unauthorized parties to access the same machine. The vulnerability that this practice presents is particularly serious when the computer is connected to an internal network (LAN, WAN, client/server system, etc.). For related ides, see the policies entitled "Modems On Workstations Connected To Internal Networks" and "Automatic Backup To Local Area Network Server." A: EMT; E: LMH.

707. Access Control Packages For Network-Connected Computers

Policy: All Company X computers that can be reached by third-party networks (dial-up lines, value added networks, the Internet, etc.) must be protected by a privilege access control system approved by the Information Security Department. This policy does not apply to computers which use modems to make outgoing dial-up calls, provided these systems do not receive unattended incoming dial-up calls.

Commentary: This policy is intended to clarify which systems must have a password-based access control system (such as PC/DACS offered by Mergent International in Rocky Hill, Connecticut, USA). The type of access control system is deliberately not included in the policy since this is expected to change over time -- for example, soon dynamic passwords will be widely used rather than fixed passwords. Likewise, different access control packages may be required for different computer platforms. Separately, to use a physical security analogy, the policy attempts to put the equivalent of a night-watchman at every entrance to the castle (in this case the network). The policy will also prevent well-meaning workers from establishing network connections that may jeopardize the security of internal networks and connected machines. For instance, this might take place if a user left work for the day and deliberately kept his modem turned-on with a communications package enabled inside his desktop office computer. While this may allow him to work from home, it may also allow others to readily gain access to the organization's systems. Separately, the exception provided in the last sentence could be deleted for organizations with very strict security requirements; in these environments, all dial-up activity may be prohibited. On another note, this policy is basically a statement about network security architecture, expressed in a manner to prevent users from saying "Hey, nobody told me about that..." Also see the policies entitled "Prior Approval Required For In-House System Interconnection" and "Access Control Packages Required For Computers On The Network." A: ET; E: LMH.

708. Large Networks Must Be Divided Into Separate Domains

Policy: All large networks crossing national or organizational boundaries must have separately-defined logical domains, each protected with suitable security perimeters and access control mechanisms.

Commentary: This policy requires network management staff to review access controls on large networks such as wide area networks (WANs). While each logical domain need not include a separate access control mechanism, management needs to justify this decision (hence the use of the word "suitable" in the policy). All too often large networks allow users to roam all over the network without encountering any barriers whatsoever. The no-restrictions approach is adopted by many network system designers because it is easier to establish and maintain a network such as this. The logical domains referred to in the policy might be organizational units (such as an accounts payable department), activities (such as order fulfillment), or locations (such as a headquarters building). The barriers may be implemented with communications front-ends, routers, gateways, firewalls, modem pools with dynamic passwords, and other network components that include access controls. The most common method used to restrict access to parts of a network is passwords, although other mechanisms like encryption can also be employed. Also see the policies entitled "Dial-Up Connections Must Always Utilize Firewalls,"

"Default Restrictions On Dissemination Of Company X Information," and "Positive Identification Required For System Usage." A: T; E: LMH.

709. Internet Connected Machines Must Have Intrusion Detection Systems

Policy: To allow Company X to promptly respond to attacks, all Internet-connected computers must be running an intrusion detection system approved by the Information Security Department.

Commentary: The intention of this policy is to ensure that those systems which are reachable via the Internet are protected with automated tools to immediately detect attacks, whether these attacks are successful or not. An IDS or intrusion detection system (offered by companies such as Internet Security Systems, Atlanta, Georgia, USA) looks at user activity and matches this activity against a database of known attack methods. If there is a match, an IDS will immediately notify systems administrators (for example by pager). This will allow immediate response, such as isolating a system from an internal network, disabling certain user-IDs, etc. Separately, there are less expensive alternatives that don't provide immediate notification, but that do show what has been modified by an attacker (the public domain package known as Tripwire is one example). It is up to the Information Security Department to determine which of these tools will be suitable for the organization adopting the policy. For related ideas, see the policies entitled "Regular And Prompt Review Of System Logs" and "Generation And Review Of Logs Showing Use Of Override Facilities." A: T; E: LMH.

710. Permissible Internet Access Without Firewalls

Policy: Until Company X establishes an approved firewall, only one method is permissible for connections to the Internet. This method involves use of dial-up outbound connections from a stand-alone computer. When an in-house computer is connected to a Company X internal network, this machine must not simultaneously be connected to the Internet unless a firewall is employed.

Commentary: This conservative policy is intended to control the ways that users connect to the Internet until such time as a proper firewall can be installed and cut-over to production operation. Although organizations are intrigued by the notion of doing business over the Internet, many still do not have firewalls. This policy allows users to nonetheless still exploit the Internet for research, electronic mail, and other purposes. The quick-and-easy way to do this is to establish accounts with Internet access providers (IAPs), which can provide such services as well as set-up a web site isolated from an organization's internal network. On another note, this policy puts emphasis on connectivity, a major concern in the age of software agents. For example, a new process on the Internet, called "server push" moves client software to an Internet-connected workstation without the involved user knowing that this transfer has taken place. While server-push mechanisms allow a new client/server functionality to be achieved, they also present a significant threat of virus propagation. For related ideas see the policies entitled "Real-Time External Network Connections Require Firewalls" and "Internet Connections Require Approved Firewalls." A: E; E: LMH.

711. All Internet Web Servers Must Be Firewall Protected

Policy: All web servers accessible via the Internet must be protected by a router or firewall approved by the Information Security Department.

Commentary: Putting a web server inside a firewall (or inside a router for less cost, but also less security) significantly increases the protection against hacker or cracker damage. One common scenario involves hackers posting pornography or other material that embarrasses the organization described on the site. Another scenario involves denial of service attacks that put the web server out of action for an extended period of time, or that are the precursor to a hacker or cracker gaining privileged system access. By putting a web server behind a firewall, organizations reduce the pathways that hackers or crackers could use to penetrate the system. For example, if TELNET is used to do remote web server maintenance, this same connection service could be used by a hacker if the web server is on the outside of a firewall. Putting a web server inside a firewall also makes maintenance easier. Of course, there should be other firewalls between the web server and any production machines on an internal network (if such a connection between an internal network and the Internet exists). This use of two or more firewalls is called a DMZ or demilitarized zone. For related ideas, see the policy entitled "Unique Passwords For Each Internal Network Device" and "Permissible Internet Access Without Firewalls." A: T; E: LMH.

712. Internet Commerce Servers Must Be In Demilitarized Zone (DMZ)

Policy: All Internet commerce servers including payment servers, database servers, and web servers must be protected by firewalls in a demilitarized zone.

Commentary: This policy seeks to protect Internet commerce servers from both users on the Internet and on an internal network. Firewalls are typically used for this task, and the architecture is generally called a DMZ. Firewalls can be used to limit the interactions with the commerce servers to only certain applications such as web surfing (http). This in turn will reduce the chances that hackers and other unauthorized persons are able to compromise these Internet commerce servers. Separately, the use of a DMZ does not preclude the transmission of information through the walls of a DMZ (either to/from a customer or to/from machines on an internal network). On another note, this policy uses the concept of isolation to help protect information systems. For a related idea, see the policy entitled "All Internet Web Servers Must Be Firewall Protected." A: T; E: LMH.

713. Public Servers On Internet Must Be Placed On Separate Subnets

Policy: Public Internet servers must be placed on subnets separate from internal Company X networks. Routers or firewalls must be employed to restrict traffic from the public servers to internal networks.

Commentary: The objective of this policy is to ensure that systems installers and administrators do not place public Internet servers (such as those hosting web pages) on the same network as intranets. If a separate subnet with flow controls is not employed, then the general public may be able to access internal computers, and the likelihood that unauthorized people may gain access to sensitive information is thereby significantly increased. Note that this policy is considerably more lenient than the policy entitled "Internet Commerce Servers Must Be In Demilitarized Zone (DMZ)" which requires the use of firewalls for this separation. This policy may be suitable for a conglomerate which has several web sites of varying sensitivities; some of these web sites may require firewalls and some may not. For a related idea, see the policy entitled "Web And Commerce Servers Must Not Store Critical Information." A: T; E: LMH.

714. Internet Commerce Servers Must Use Digital Certificates & Encryption

Policy: To prevent intruders from interfering with Internet commerce activities, all Internet commerce servers (web servers, database servers, payment servers, security servers, etc.) must employ unique digital certificates and must use encryption to transfer information in and out of these servers. An exception is made for web servers, FTP servers, and any other Company X servers supporting communications with customers, prospects, or other members of the public.

Commentary: The intention of this policy is to create a very high level of security for communications between Internet commerce servers and any other internal machines which might communicate with these servers (such as a mainframe). Digital certificates are used to uniquely identify each machine and communications encryption is used to protect information in transit. With this architecture (supported by a variety of products such as those from Open Market, Burlington, Massachusetts, USA), hackers and crackers will not be able to spoof Company X servers, nor will they be able to view the traffic sent between these servers, nor will they be able to modify the traffic sent between these servers. Separately, the exception in the second sentence is necessary because outside communications, such as ordinary web surfing (alias http), do not typically involve either digital certificates or communications encryption. For related ideas see the policies entitled "All Internet Web Servers Must Be Firewall Protected" and "Virus Checking At Firewalls, Servers, And Desktop Machines." A: T; E: MH.

715. Dial-Up Connections Must Always Utilize Firewalls

Policy: All inbound dial-up lines connected to Company X internal networks and/or computer systems must pass through an additional access control point (such as a firewall), which has been approved by the Information Security Department, before users reach a log-in banner.

Commentary: The intention of this policy is to restrict dial-in connections from parties such as customers, salespersons, travelling executives, and technicians working from home (telecommuters). It is highly undesirable for these dial-up users to directly connect with desktop systems in the office, perhaps thereby gaining access to internal networks. Such desktop systems often have no passwords or other access controls, or else only easily guessed fixed passwords. This policy instead channels all such calls through a central access point which the Information Security Department has determined is sufficiently secure. At this point, as an alternative to requiring two levels of passwords, some organizations may allow extended user authentication systems (smart cards with dynamic passwords, dial-back modems, etc.) to be used. The advantage to using extended user authentication technologies such as these is that users would not be required to log-in twice; the approach is therefore consistent with the notion of single sign-on. A sentence explaining this option could be added to the policy provided here. Used extensively on the Internet, firewalls (an access point) are a popular way to keep hackers and other intruders out of an organization's systems. In part this policy is an acknowledgement that traditional fixed password systems do not provide adequate security--at least when used the way that so many firms have implemented them. The scope of this policy could be restricted to multi-user machines thus excluding desktop systems (this change is not advised, but may be necessary in some environments). The policy can also be rewritten to require all directly connected dial-up systems to be isolated--no connections to internal networks or other multi-user machines will be permitted. Thus, this type of connection could be permitted for testing and other purposes, but only if other systems were not exposed thereby. While the scope of this policy includes all types of dial-up connections (both inbound and outbound), the wording could be changed to narrow the scope to dial-in connections only. While the major vulnerability (dial-in) would still be addressed, this narrower scope would be less of a burden on users. Also see the policies entitled "Approval Required For Systems Accepting In-Coming Dial-Up Calls," "Restriction Of Third Party Dial-Up Privileges," "Direct Dial Connections Prohibited Unless Modem Pool Is Used," "Modems On Workstations Connected To Internal Networks," and "Isolate Systems Containing Secret Information From Network." A: T; E: MH.

716. Real-Time External Network Connections Require Firewalls

Policy: All in-bound real-time external connections to Company X internal networks and/or multi-user computer systems must pass through an additional access control point (aka a firewall, gateway, or access server) before users can reach a log-in banner.
Commentary: This policy is intended to make sure that the periphery of an internal network always has strong access control mechanisms. If the boundaries to a network cannot be protected, then the controls inside the network may be superfluous. One of the reasons why Robert Morris' infamous worm program was able to overcome the defenses of 6,000+ computers on the Internet a number of years ago was that firewalls were not common at that time. A firewall is a dedicated-purpose machine that does not run business applications; its sole purpose is to act as a gatekeeper. This allows unnecessary systems software (like the UNIX routine called Sendmail) to be deleted from the system; the absence of these routines in turn means the system is less likely to be compromised. Separately, this policy requires all external real-time connections to have a firewall or comparable security system. Because they are not real-time, electronic mail, news feeds, and other store-and-forward network services do not need to have a firewall. On another note, use of separate machines as firewalls means that security-related systems administration staff can make errors in the access control systems for internal computers without allowing the world to get onto the organization's network. Separately, note that this policy has a broader scope than the Internet; for example, it also applies to value added networks (VANs) and dial-up lines. For related ideas, see the policies entitled "Positive Identification Required For System Usage" and "Access Control Packages Required For Computers On the Network." A: T; E: LMH.

717. Firewalls Must Be Configured So All Services Are Denied Unless Approved

Policy: All Company X firewalls connecting to the Internet must be configured so that every Internet service (telnet, ftp, http, etc.) is disabled by default. Only those services which have been specifically approved in writing by the Information Security Department manager may then be enabled.

Commentary: The intention of this policy is to prevent systems administrators from providing responsive customer service that compromises security. In an effort to be polite and responsive, administrators may open up a firewall to allow video, audio, and other services. Instead, these administrators (or whoever happens to be managing firewalls) need to get permission for the proposed new service(s). Certain services, such as inbound telnet, will generally be deemed too risky unless additional control measures are adopted (in this case extended user authentication like biometrics may allow secure inbound remote log-ins). If an organization were to allow all services through a firewall by default, this would be likely to create a chaotic computing environment which would in turn be difficult to secure. The policy writer will note that this policy does not apply to intranet firewalls. For related considerations, see the policies entitled "Default To Denial Of Access Control Privileges" and "Default Restrictions On Dissemination Of Company X Information." A: T; E: LMH.

718. Firewalls Must Run On Dedicated Computers

Policy: All firewalls used to protect Company X's internal network must run on separate dedicated computers. These computers may not serve other purposes such as act as web servers.

Commentary: The intention of this policy is to enhance the security of deployed firewalls by reducing the chances that they will be compromised by hackers. This policy uses the notion of simplicity to help ensure that firewalls will not be defeated via other applications which run on the same machine. If firewalls serve other purposes, other avenues of attack will exist which could be exploited by intruders. Thus if a firewall acted as a mail server, it may be compromised through a mail software bug. The use of a dedicated firewall is also desirable because firewalls have different and potentially conflicting design objectives than other machines. Having a dedicated purpose, such as security, ensures that unnecessary software (like compilers) can be removed without jeopardizing the functionality of the firewall. The relatively low cost of hardware makes this policy both feasible and a good practice. For a closely related idea, see the policy entitled "Removal Of Unnecessary Systems Software At Installation Time." A: T; E: LMH.

719. Firewall Configuration Change Requires Information Security Approval

Policy: Firewall configuration rules and permissible service rules have been reached after an extended evaluation of costs and benefits. These rules must not be changed unless the permission of the Information Security Department has first been obtained.

Commentary: This policy seeks to prevent on-the-fly modification of firewall rules that could jeopardize the security of an organization's internal network. For example, a system administrator may be responding to a user's complaint and may open up a new service through the firewall. In the process he or she may also open up the internal network to hacker intrusions. This policy seeks to establish firewall configuration rules and service rules as relatively fixed, not something that a single administrator can change at their own discretion. Since firewalls are the first point of entry to an internal network, it is imperative that their configuration and permissible services be strictly controlled. Separately, because the Information Security Department in many organizations doesn't directly administer firewalls, this policy keeps some control with the Information Security Department instead of turning it over wholesale to system administrators. For related ideas, see the policies entitled "Firewalls Must Run On Dedicated Computers" and "Internet Access With Company X Computers Must Go Through Firewall." A: T; E: LMH.

720. Internet Connections Require Approved Firewalls

Policy: All connections between Company X internal networks and the Internet (or any other publicly-accessible computer network) must include an approved firewall and related access controls.

Commentary: This policy is intended to prevent departments, divisions, and other organizational units from establishing their own connections to the Internet, or for that matter, any other external computer network. Many organizations lack a central authority to coordinate network security across the organization. As a result, it is common for separate organizational units to establish their own connections to the Internet. This policy mandates a standard way to make connections between internal networks and external networks. Consistency in network access controls is absolutely essential if effective security is going to be achieved. Without this policy, various parts of an organization are likely to establish their own external connections, and often these connections will lack adequate security; these connections may later be used by outsiders to gain unauthorized access to internal networks. This policy can be supplemented with a clarifying sentence indicating that dial-up connections from a stand-alone personal computer are permissible. For related ideas, see the policies entitled "Extended User Authentication Required For In-Bound Internet Users," "Restriction Of Third Party Dial-Up Privileges," "Large Networks Must Be Divided Into Separate Domains," "Single Sign-On Process," "Modems On Workstations Connected To Internal Networks," and "Isolate Systems Containing Secret Information From Network." A: T; E: LMH.

721. Trusted Host Relationships Prohibited For Internet Connected Machines

Policy: Unless the Information Security Department Manager has approved, all Company X computers that are Internet-connected or directly reachable through the Internet are prohibited from using shared directory systems, sometimes called shared file systems. These systems allow a user to obtain access to more than one computer's file system with only a single log-in process. Exceptions are made for Internet commerce and other systems where a multiple machine architecture involves automatically passing users with severely restricted privileges from one computer to another.

Commentary: The intention of this policy is to limit the damage that hackers and other intruders can do if they compromise the security of one computer which is reachable through the Internet. If a shared directory system is used (such as the ".rhosts" file on UNIX, or domain membership on NT), then the work of these intruders would be made significantly easier. Without a shared directory system, intruders must break-into each system individually. Separately, this policy assumes that fixed passwords or other access controls differ from one machine to another; if they are all the same, then this policy only makes work for systems administrators. On another note, the policy pertains to general purpose user-IDs, not to anonymous users and automatic forms that strictly limit what a user can do via the Internet (Internet commerce CGI scripts for example). On yet another note, this policy limits the places where single sign-on systems may be deployed, even though users like them because they save time and effort. For related ideas, see the policies entitled "Approval Required For Internet Connection Establishment" and "Trusted Host Relationships Must Not Be Established Without Permission." A: T; E: LMH.

722. Direct Network Connections With Outside Organizations (Tunnels)

Policy: The establishment of a direct connection between Company X systems and computers at external organizations, via the Internet or any other public network, is prohibited unless this connection has first been approved by the Manager of Information Security.

Commentary: Modern firewalls connected to the Internet have the ability to define a protected channel (called a tunnel or a Virtual Private Network) which allows individuals in one organization to go through the Internet and reach computers in another organization in a secure fashion. While this may be useful in certain circumstances, such as a joint-venture project, it also introduces additional security risks. This policy requires that users obtain approval of the information security manager or some other person responsible for information security before they establish such connections. Before approving such connections, a number of questions need to be answered, specifically: "Who will be able to access Company X systems?", "What information on Company X systems will be available to them?", "What logging systems will track the activity of these outsiders?", "What is the real business need underlying this type of a connection?", and "Is there another way that we can achieve the desired productivity without introducing additional information security vulnerabilities?" For related ideas, see the policies entitled "Restriction Of Third Party Dial-Up Privileges," "Large Networks Must Be Divided Into Separate Domains," "Single Sign-On Process," "Modems On Workstations Connected To Internal Networks," and "Isolate Systems Containing Secret Information from Network." A: ET; E: LMH.

723. Inter-Processor Commands From Outside Locations Prohibited

Policy: To stop unauthorized system access and related problems, all user-initiated commands received from external locations must not be fulfilled unless a user has first logged-in.

Commentary: One of the fastest ways to gain unauthorized system access to systems connected to the Internet network is to use the "finger" command. This command provides information about users which can then be used to guess user-IDs and passwords. Often no log-in is required to get this UNIX command to work. This policy expresses a systems design objective to be used when establishing system access controls and to be used when defining multi-processor security architectures. The idea is that outsiders should not be permitted to have any information about a system until they have properly identified themselves. In other words, don't disclose any information until you know who's requesting it and whether they are authorized to receive it. Note that the policy does not restrict the use of remote procedure calls (RPCs) initiated by a system (not a user) outside of Company X. Such RPCs might, for example, be used to exchange network pathing tables (as is done on the Internet). This policy is particularly relevant to client/server architectures. Also see the policies entitled "Disclosure Of Information In System Log-in Banner," "Extended User Authentication Systems Required For Dial-Up Lines," and "Reliance On Operating System User Authentication Process." A: T; E: LMH.

1.4.1.2. Making Network Connections

724. Isolate Systems Containing Secret Information From Network

Policy: Company X computer systems containing secret information must not be connected to any network or any other computer.

Commentary: The intention of this policy is to prevent the unauthorized disclosure of particularly sensitive information (call it "secret" or some other term). Knowing that network access controls are still somewhat unreliable, some organizations choose to prohibit network connections, lest the information somehow be improperly disclosed. This very conservative policy can often be replaced by a policy requiring strong encryption when the secret information not in use. Some organizations go one step further, by not allowing any other applications on the involved computer, effectively making it a dedicated computer. In the wake of the rush to interconnect virtually every system within organizations, some managers may wish to keep some high-security systems off the network, particularly the Internet. This need not cause major problems in terms of getting the work done; whenever there is a need to transfer data from a high security system to a lower security system, floppy disks or some other storage media can be used rather than a network. Also see the policies entitled "Prior Approval Required For In-House System Interconnection" and "Secret Information Must Not Be Placed On Internet or Intranet Systems." A: T; E: H.

725. Customers Must Specifically Agree To Receive New/Enhanced Service

Policy: Customers receiving computer or communications services from Company X must explicitly agree to receive new or enhanced services before these new or enhanced services are provided. In the absence of explicit acquiescence, Company X must continue to provide the services which were previously available.

Commentary: The intention of this policy is to maintain good customer relations as well as to ensure that customer computer and communication systems will continue to be compatible with Company X systems. Thus the policy in effect requires support of previously-available services (this does not preclude Company X from also offering new or enhanced services). An example was provided by New York Telephone Company in June 1993. New York Telephone turned on call-waiting for all customers in a certain area, without having first obtained their permission. As a result, consumers who had the service but were unaware of it found that it interrupted the transmission of computer data. Such consumers also found that, because the new service eliminated the busy signal, a calling party might mistakenly think that the person the party is trying to reach isn't there. After many complaints, the New York State Public Service Commission forced New York Telephone to discontinue call-waiting service. The policy as written is relevant to security because it helps ensure that previously effective controls will continue to be effective. Likewise, this policy prevents service providers from forcing a new service on customers before the customers are ready for it (being ready includes understanding the security implications of the new service). The policy also supports contingency planning efforts because it requires prior services to continue to be supported--if new or enhanced services introduce a major problem, Company X can always revert to the prior services. Note that this policy may be perceived by some Data Processing Managers as too restrictive (a good response to that is that the policy is intended for customers, suppliers, and other third parties, not necessarily internal systems users). The policy as written here can be expanded to include an exception clause in which previous services don't need to be offered if Company X top management agreement is first obtained; this will prevent Company X from having to offer obsolete and costly services. In some respects, this policy is similar to the opt-in/opt-out process used for systems handling private data; see the policy entitled "Subjects Given Opportunity To Opt-Out Of Private Data Systems." Also see the policy entitled "Special Approval Required For Production Software Package Changes." A: MT; E: LMH.

726. Prior Approval Required For All Communication Line Changes

Policy: Workers and vendors must not make arrangements for, or actually complete the installation of voice or data lines with any carrier, if they have not first obtained approval from the director of the Telecommunications Department.

Commentary: The intention of this policy is to ensure that only previously approved changes in communication lines are actually installed. Establishing unauthorized communication paths can significantly compromise the security of Company X systems. This is because unauthorized lines can provide hackers with avenues of attack that are not properly secured. The policy thus seeks to ensure that all lines are in compliance with existing access control requirements. This policy is relevant to microcomputers (PCs) and workstations, many of which have unauthorized modems attached to them. If there is no additional security for these systems (such as a password-based access control package), anyone may be able to dial-up into these systems using the public switched telephone network (PSTN). This may in turn allow an intruder to access a connected internal network. Some organizations may wish to expand the policy to make specific mention of such modems. Like some other aspects of computer and communication security, there are a number of things which should be done on a centralized basis. Establishing communication paths is one example, just as developing security policies is another. The words in this policy referencing approval by the Telecommunications Department could be replaced by approval by the Information Security Department. For a related perspective, see the policy entitled "Prior Approval Required For Set-Up Of Multi-User Systems." Also see the policies entitled "Prior Approval Required For In-House System Interconnection" and "Modems On Workstations Connected To Internal Networks." A: ET; E: LMH.

727. Prior Approval Required For Set-Up Of Multi-User Systems

Policy: Workers must not establish intranet servers, electronic bulletin boards, local area networks, modem connections to existing internal networks, or other multi-user systems for communicating information without the specific approval of the director of the Information Security Department. This policy helps ensure that all Company X networked systems have the controls needed to prevent unauthorized access.

Commentary: The intention of this policy is to make sure that users are not setting up communication systems which may inadvertently compromise an organization's systems and information. The policy is particularly important for the microcomputer (PC) and workstation environment (including client/server systems), where users so often do as they please regardless of in-house standards or Information Systems Department instructions. Unless there is a centralized approval process, supported by some sort of an audit and enforcement process, some users may create major information security vulnerabilities without the knowledge of the Information Security Department, the Telecommunications Department, or the Information Systems Department. The approving authority may easily be shifted to another relevant manager and away from the director of the Information Security Department. The emphasis on multi-user systems in this policy is a reflection of the fact that multi-user systems typically have more information than single-user systems, and as such generally pose greater risks. For similar perspectives, see the policies entitled "Prior Approval Required For All Communication Line Changes" and "Approvals Required For Production Multi-User Applications." A: ET; E: LMH.

728. Prior Approval Required For In-House System Interconnection

Policy: Real-time connections between two or more in-house computer systems must not be established unless the Information Security Department has first determined that such connections will not jeopardize information security.

Commentary: The intention of this policy is to keep certain information within certain areas in the organization, and to thereby be better able to control its dissemination. This basic design objective involves isolation to achieve security. For example, salary information about employees could be kept in Human Resources Department computers only. To establish a connection with the in-house LAN may open up a pathway for unauthorized dissemination of this private information. Note that this policy does not preclude the movement of tapes, disks, CD-ROMs, and other storage media between systems. Generally non-real-time movements of data (tapes, disks, etc.) are easier to control; a real-time connection often allows unauthorized persons to access information quickly with little or no audit trail. A recommended variation of this policy would broaden its scope such that any connection with an in-house system would need prior approval (not just in-house to in-house connections). Taking this policy one step further would have its scope expanded to include connections between internal and external systems. On another note, this is by no means the sole approach; for example, routers and firewalls can be used to create isolated subnets within an organization's internal network. Also see the policies entitled "Prior Approval Required For All Communication Line Changes," "Isolate Systems Containing Secret Information From Network," and "Intranet Server Establishment Requires Information Systems Approval." A: ET; E: MH.

729. Separate Subnet Required For Walk-Up Network Connections

Policy: In every instance where Company X provides walk-up network access for visitors to connect back to their home networks (for example to read electronic mail), a separate subnet that has no connection to the Company X internal network must be employed.

Commentary: The objective of this policy is to prevent unauthorized parties from gaining access to internal network-connected computers, and the information resources resident thereon. If an organization provides walk-up connections, which allow users to readily connect a portable computer to an organization's internal network, it significantly increases the risks of attacks such as packet sniffing and IP address spoofing. To isolate walk-up connections, but to still provide this useful connection service, a separate subnet can be used. On another note, although it is not mentioned in this policy, physical security over all these network access points (ports) should also be provided. For example, reception areas and conference rooms which have these access points should be locked when the involved organization is closed for business. For related ideas, see the policies entitled "Prior Approval Required For In-House System Interconnection" and "Public Servers On Internet Must Be Placed On Separate Subnets." A: T; E: MH.

730. Unattended Active Network Ports In Public Areas Prohibited

Policy: Unattended active network ports which connect to the Company X internal computer network are not allowed in public areas including building lobbies, company cafeterias, and conference rooms readily available to outsiders.

Commentary: The intention of this policy is to prevent network designers, network cable installers, and others from placing active data ports in places where unauthorized parties could employ these same ports to gain unauthorized entry to Company X internal information systems. The problem with active ports in public areas is that these ports are available to anybody and could be used to launch a password guessing brute-force attack, to place a computer virus on Company X systems, or to perpetrate some other abusive act. According to this policy, it is acceptable for these ports to be installed in public places; they must, however, not be turned-on (active). Separately, fixed passwords and/or other access control mechanisms should still be employed with a policy such as this. For related ideas, see the policies entitled "Separate Subnet Required For Walk-Up Network Connections" and "Configuration To Prevent/Detect Unauthorized Network Connections." A: T; E: MH.

731. Network Ports In Vacant Offices Must Be Promptly Disabled

Policy: All network ports in vacant offices and other areas which are not customarily in use must be promptly disconnected at the wiring closet or at another centralized location.

Commentary: The motivation for this policy comes from an understanding of a common attack method used by industrial spies and computer system intruders. This approach involves use of network ports found in vacant offices, conference rooms, or other unmonitored facilities. Intruders may use these ports to gain access to an internal network, and from there launch an attack against either internal Company X machines or perhaps external machines (perhaps using an assumed identity provided via Company X information systems). This policy informs network technicians and others who manage the physical infrastructure for an internal network that all unused network ports need to be disabled at a central location. It is not sufficient to disable the port at the remote location because an intruder could easily reestablish the connection with readily available tools like a screwdriver. Note that this policy assumes that telephone closets and other centralized wiring locations are physically protected or locked. For related ideas, see the policies entitled "Separate Subnet Required For Walk-Up Network Connections" and "Modems On Workstations Connected To Internal Networks." A: T; E: MH.

732. Configuration To Prevent/Detect Unauthorized Network Connections

Policy: All internal networks must be configured such that they can prevent and/or detect attempts to connect unauthorized computers.

Commentary: The intention of this policy is to prevent intruders from connecting unauthorized computers to an internal network. Even if an intruder is not immediately able to gain access to an authorized internal computer, the fact that an unauthorized machine is on the internal network may allow it to engage in various attacks. These attacks include masquerading via IP spoofing and cleartext password interception via packet sniffing. This policy dictates the use of secure hubs, encrypted intranet communications, or similar technologies which can be used to block all unauthorized machines from the network, or at least detect their presence. The detection of an unauthorized computer on an internal network can then be fed into an intrusion detection system, a network management system, or a problem management system, and hopefully technical staff (such as a computer emergency response team) will promptly respond. As an aside, the use of a policy like this also helps to ensure that a desktop computer standard is adhered to faithfully. Only after a new desktop computer has been shown to be consistent with in-house standards will network operations assign an internal address to that machine and allow it to access the internal network. For related ideas, see the policies entitled "Network Ports In Vacant Offices Must Be Promptly Disabled" and "Separate Subnet Required For Walk-Up Network Connections." A: T; E: MH.

733. Criteria For Connecting Company X Networks To Third Party Networks

Policy: Company X computers or networks may ONLY be connected to third party computers or networks after the Information Security Department has determined that the combined system will be in compliance with Company X security requirements.

Commentary: Many organizations are having trouble with systems interconnection issues related to decentralized systems management. For example, without examining the security implications, a marketing department manager may connect an internal Company X LAN to a consulting firm's internal network. To avoid the exposures that such actions introduce, a minimum amount of centralization is necessary (as reflected by this policy). The policy puts internal staff on notice that the Information Security Department does have requirements for connections with third party networks and systems, and that these requirements must be met before any connection will be permitted. The specific requirements are deliberately left out of the policy, but generally would include extended user authentication, user privilege access controls, and user activity logging. The specific requirements are expected to change over time, whereas the policy need not change with each change in the requirements. Note that the policy entitled "Security Requirements For Network-Connected Third Party Systems" is for third parties, not internal staff. For related ideas, see the policy entitled "Prior Approval Required For In-House System Interconnection." A: T; E: LMH.

734. Security Requirements For Network-Connected Third Party Systems

Policy: As a condition of gaining access to Company X's computer network, every third party must secure its own connected systems in a manner consistent with Company X requirements. Company X reserves the right to audit the security measures in effect on these connected systems without prior warning. Company X also reserves the right to immediately terminate network connections with all third party systems not meeting such requirements.

Commentary: The intention of this policy is to notify third parties who have access to Company X's network that they must maintain the security of their own systems in order to continue to do business over Company X's network. The ability to immediately terminate a connection which has been shown to be exploited by a hacker is increasingly important as hackers often use a number of different systems to hide their tracks (this is called "network weaving"). One case where this was a problem recently involved the US District Court in Seattle, Washington. The Court system was penetrated by hackers coming in through Boeing Computer Systems' computers. The aftermath included $75,000 of effort to scrub Boeing computers clean after the attack. Separately, this policy is an attempt to resolve what has become an increasingly difficult-to-manage problem, namely the reconciliation of differing security policies on separate networks. The policy actually gives third parties a relatively easy way to achieve consistent security: when connected to Company X's network, a stand-alone system observes Company X security requirements, but after this connection is terminated, the same machine can be connected to another organization's network and use a different set of controls. On another point, some organizations may wish to specify examples of the "third parties" (consulting firms, outsourcing firms, suppliers, customers, etc.). For related ideas, see the policies "Prior Approval Required For In-House System Interconnection," "Criteria For Connecting Company X Networks To Third

Party Networks," and "Direct Network Connections With Outside Organizations (Tunnels)." A: T; E: LMH.

735. Approval Required For Internet Connection Establishment

Policy: Unless prior approval of the Director of Information Systems has been obtained, workers may not establish Internet or any other external network connections which could allow non-Company X users to gain access to Company X systems and information. These connections include the establishment of multi-computer file systems (like Sun's NFS), Internet home pages, Internet FTP servers, and the like.

Commentary: Unlike the policy entitled "Prior Approval Required For In-House System Interconnection," this policy addresses connections via the Internet and other external networks. Some organizations may wish to merge the two policies, although connections between two or more internal systems present significantly less of a vulnerability than connections between inside and outside systems. This policy is meant to throttle the establishment of connections to the Internet. Without such a policy, users may establish their own world wide web site, or establish their own Internet file transfer protocol (FTP) site, and in either instance potentially embarrass the organization. There is a need to have all such connections conform to standard security measures, as well as a need to have them conform to content and format conventions dictated by the Marketing or Public Relations Department. This policy seeks to alert users that they open a Pandora's box of security problems when they make connections to outside machines. See the policies entitled "Security Responsibilities For Real-Time Connections With Third Parties," "Internet Connections Require Approved Firewalls," and "Direct Network Connections With Outside Organizations (Tunnels)." A: ET; E: LMH.

736. Security Criteria A Prerequisite For Intranet Connection

Policy: Before any computer system or network segment can be connected to Company X's intranet, it must first be deemed to have met the necessary security criteria established by the Information Security Department manager. These criteria include, but are not limited to, the following: no connection to the Internet which is not guarded by an acceptable firewall, an acceptable user-authentication system, an acceptable user privilege control system, an established change control process, a clearly written definition of system management responsibilities, and adequate operational documentation.

Commentary: The intention of this policy is to establish management's intention to prevent locally managed systems from connecting to an Intranet whenever the local system managers so desire. To allow unrestricted intranet server or network segment connections could jeopardize the security of other machines on the intranet. To be able to offer a department's information on the intranet is desirable for management of the involved department. A department's intranet pages can show how important the department is as well as how department members are making major contributions to the organization. Being connected to the intranet is thus desirable from a corporate politics perspective, and this policy leverages that desirability to bring remotely managed systems into compliance with some basic security measures. The policy specified a few of those basic security measures in the second sentence, but the policy writer should feel free to add others based on specific organizational needs (for example, a tested contingency plan could be appended to this list). Separately, the policy is a subtle way to help reestablish centralized organization-wide control over information security. For related ideas, consider the policies entitled "Criteria For Connecting Company X Networks To Third Party Networks" and "Approval Required For Internet Connection Establishment." A: T; E: LMH.

737. Inventory Of Connections To External Networks

Policy: The Information Security Department must maintain a current inventory of all connections to external networks including telephone networks, EDI networks, extranets, the Internet.

Commentary: The intention of this policy is to give the Information Security Department a clear picture of the access points to internal networks. Because hackers most often come in over networks, it is essential that the Information Security Department be aware of all of the external access points. The staff in the Information Security Department can then focus their attention on these access points, ensuring that controls such as firewalls and routers are properly established and operational. Special attention should be paid to business partner access to an organization's network (perhaps through an extranet), and this too would be within the scope of this policy. In a more general sense, this policy forces the Information Security Department to focus on a certain area. In the real world many organizations really don't know all the entry points into their networks and when they have intrusions it is not surprising that they have difficulties tracking down the pathways used by hackers, industrial spies, or other intruders. For related ideas, see the policies entitled "Annual Inventory Of Information Systems Hardware, Software, Etc." and "High-Level Inventory Of Information Assets." A: T; E: LMH.

1.4.1.3. Forming Contracts Over Networks

738. Standards Of Common Carriers Do Not Apply

Policy: The networking services provided by Company X are provided on a contractual carrier basis, not those of a common carrier. As the operator of a private network, this organization has a right to make policies regarding the use of its network systems without being held to the standards of common carriers.

Commentary: The intention of this policy is to avoid the need to provide equitable access to the network and other requirements of common carriers, some of which include security. Although Company X may have security superior to that found on common carrier systems, this policy gives Company X management more leeway to decide just how they want to set-up and maintain their network. Since this policy is legalistic in nature, it is especially important that it be approved by the organization's legal department. This policy is more general than most and is best used as an introductory comment appearing before more specific policies. Another intention of the policy is to establish realistic user expectations about the type of service and security that will be delivered. Also see the policies entitled "Network Message Protection Services Not Provided" and "Disclaimer Of Responsibility Or Liability For Message Contents." A: E; E: LMH.

739. Participation In Public Networks As Service Provider

Policy: Participation in public networks as a provider of services that others rely on is expressly prohibited unless two conditions are first fulfilled. Specifically, Company X legal counsel must first assess the extent and nature of the liabilities involved, and then top management must expressly accept these risks.

Commentary: Involvement as a message forwarding node on the Internet, as certificate authority, as an encryption key notarization center, as an encryption key distribution point, or some other provider of information services may open Company X up to liabilities that they had not previously considered. For example, if a fraud was perpetrated using Company X systems, to what extent is Company X responsible? If Company X systems are used by criminals to store stolen credit card data, is Company X responsible? The intention of this policy is to prevent

Company X personnel from volunteering Company X facilities until the liabilities and other responsibilities have been fully identified and accepted by top management. Although this policy has an American flavor (due to the emphasis on liability), the idea behind it is still relevant to other countries. Also see the policy entitled "Disclaimer Of Responsibility Or Liability For Message Contents." A: ET; E: LMH.

740. Formation Of Binding Contracts Via Electronic Systems

Policy: Although Company X seeks to aggressively implement Electronic Data Interchange (EDI) and other electronic business systems with third parties, all contracts must be formed by paper documents prior to purchasing or selling via electronic systems. EDI, electronic mail, and similar binding business messages must therefore be releases against blanket orders, such as a blanket purchase order.

Commentary: Contracts formed by electronic messages may not be enforceable from a legal standpoint. Some laws, like the United States statute of frauds, require a document, a writing, or a signature in order to be enforceable. The intention of this policy is to make sure that all contract-related EDI or electronic mail messages sent between organizations be legally binding. Be sure to get the organization's attorney to review this policy prior to promulgation. The policy could be expanded to include words which require all third party agreements to be approved by the Legal Department. Also see the policies entitled "Trading Partner Agreement Required Prior To Use Of EDI," "Software Or Data Exchanges With Third Parties Require Agreements," and "Binding Signatures Must Be Sent By Traditional Paper Means." A: MT; E: LMH.

741. Conducting Business Over The Internet With Foreign Companies

Policy: Unless advance approval of the Purchasing Department has been obtained, Company X workers are forbidden from purchasing any goods or services via the Internet if these goods or services are offered by a foreign firm.

Commentary: The intention of this policy is to prevent fraud, especially fraud with a remote probability of restitution, criminal prosecution, etc. Not all Internet fraud is local, and if the fraud is perpetrated by a foreign business, then it is likely to be prohibitively expensive and time consuming to try to set things right. On the other hand, if the firm is within the same country, legal dispute resolution remedies will be very much more available and cost effective. This is not to say that one should never do business with foreign firms over the Internet, just that these arrangements should be approached with skepticism. If one wishes to proceed, the assistance of the Purchasing Department can allow a background check to be performed, and if needed, special legal structures to be established (percentage of completion payment plans for example). On another note, foreign purchases are also to be approached cautiously because legal systems between countries can differ significantly; what is illegal in the purchaser's country may not be illegal in the seller's country. In addition, courts in some foreign countries may claim they have no jurisdiction over international transactions. Separately, this policy could be modified so that it applies only to transactions over a certain amount, such as $500. This policy is in keeping with recent warnings issued by the United Kingdom's Securities and Investment Board (a government agency). For related ideas, see the policies entitled "Hardware/Software Procurement Via Standard Purchasing Channels" and "Only Designated Employees May Form Contracts Via Email." A: E; E: LMH.

742. Trading Partner Agreement Required Prior To Use Of EDI

Policy: Prior to the use of Company X systems for Electronic Data Interchange (EDI) with any third party, a trading partner agreement, fixing the terms and conditions of EDI use, must be negotiated. This agreement must be approved by Company X legal counsel prior to using any EDI systems for business transactions.

Commentary: A trading agreement specifies who is liable if a message is lost, if the system goes down, or if other problems occur. The intention of this policy is to prevent user department management from employing an EDI system without first getting the terms and conditions properly worked out. This policy is intended to make sure that centralized control over EDI arrangements is maintained. This centralized control over EDI set-ups may also provide an opportunity to review the control measures on the system prior to use. See in-house legal counsel for the specifics of such agreements. A policy such as this is also useful when defining the meaning of digital signatures and message authentication codes (MACs) used for EDI messages and other transactions handled via multi-organizational systems. The formation of contracts to conduct business over the Internet should also be controlled lest users establish agreements without first getting management consent. To take this most recent development into consideration, some policy writers may wish to add a sentence to the policy recognizing the new "doing business over the Internet" transaction systems. Also see the policy entitled "Formation Of Binding Contracts Via Electronic Systems." A: EMT; E: LMH.

743. Only Designated Employees May Form Contracts Via Email

Policy: Correspondents with Company X workers may in some cases construe an email message as a legally-binding statement. Unless specifically authorized to enter into contracts on behalf of Company X, or otherwise authorized to legally represent Company X, all workers must include a notice at the end of each email message indicating that the message does not bind Company X to any contract, position, or course of action. The specific terms of this notice will be provided by the Legal Department and periodically updated.

Commentary: The intention of this policy is to strictly define who can and who cannot commit an organization to a certain course of action, contract, or position. Without a policy like this, correspondents may allege that a worker acted as though they were authorized to bind the organization, and that they had no reason not to believe that the worker was authorized. Correspondents may say that they relied on email, that they took action which put them at a "detriment," and that now Company X must follow-through on what it said it would do. This policy seeks to avoid such disputes and misunderstandings. Note that the policy doesn't restrict normal business activity, for example sales staff can negotiate price and delivery terms because they are authorized to do that. Likewise, the purchasing group can bind the organization for certain goods and services because they are authorized to do that. For related ideas, see the policies entitled "Formation Of Binding Contracts Via Electronic Systems" and "Establishing New Business Arrangements Via Internet." A: E; E: LMH.

744. Criteria For Accepting And Acting On Computerized Transactions

Policy: If transactions are sent and processed automatically (via Electronic Data Interchange for instance), then a message must not be accepted or acted on unless: (a) the message has been shown to match a trading profile for the initiating organization, or (b) the message has been shown to deviate from a trading profile but additional steps have been taken to verify the accuracy and authenticity of the message.

Commentary: The intention of this policy is to make sure that unusual messages are not automatically processed without further investigation. If an active wiretapper were to enter an EDI system and spoof one of the participants, then the other participants might blindly follow the instructions received. This type of problem is prevented with the general procedure defined in this policy. The implementation of part (b) in the second sentence might, for example, involve separate communication with the alleged sender via a method other than the EDI system that handled the original message (so a masquerader would be immediately detected). The words "trading profile" means the typical way that the other party interacts with Company X; this might for instance refer to the networks that the other party typically uses, the way the other party's messages are structured, the frequency of the other party's messages, etc. Note that the whole notion of a customer profile is increasingly incorporated into intrusion detection software (IDS); further ideas about this can be found in the policy entitled "Contents Of Logs For Systems Running Production Applications." Separately, note that this policy is written for inter-organizational networks, but it could also apply to intra-organizational systems. See the policies entitled "Multiple Communication Channels For Electronic Offers & Acceptances," "Orders To Change Internal Records Placed Via Phone," and "Authorization Required For All Production System Input Transactions." A: MT; E: LMH.

745. Multiple Communication Channels For Electronic Offers & Acceptances

Policy: All contracts formed through electronic offer and acceptance messages (fax, Electronic Data Interchange, electronic mail, etc.) must be formalized and confirmed via paper documents within two (2) weeks of acceptance.

Commentary: Confirmation by a different communication channel helps to catch fraud and also helps make agreements legally enforceable. The intention of this policy is to require that users always employ multiple communication channels for each contract. As digital signatures and message authentication codes become more pervasive, this policy is expected to become increasingly unnecessary. This is because controls built into computerized systems will provide an increased level of assurance that the contract is legitimate, comes from the party who is alleged to have sent it, and has not been modified in transit. Note that this policy is general business practice in the purchasing area, where an order may be initially placed over the phone (disclosing a purchase order number), and then a paper purchase order is sent by mail or fax. Also see the policies entitled "Criteria For Accepting And Acting On Computerized Transactions" and "Reliance On Operating System User Authentication Process." A: MT; E: LMH.

746. Internet Customers Must Specifically Agree To Terms & Conditions

Policy: All customers using the Internet to place orders must be presented with a summary of Company X's important terms & conditions, and in order to complete their orders, they must specifically indicate that they agree to be bound by these terms & conditions.

Commentary: The purpose of this policy to make it very clear exactly how an arrangement/sale between two parties is going to work over the Internet. The problem motivating this policy is fact that the Internet traverses many different jurisdictions with different laws about business contracts. The Uniform Commercial Code (UCC) handles this problem for transactions within the United States, but transactions on the Internet are often done from other countries. In these cases, the relevant jurisdiction, and the relevant set of laws is unclear. The policy requires either that a customer employ a mouse to click on a button which says "I agree," or that the customer type the words "I agree," or that some comparable mechanism be used to clearly show that the customer knew of and agreed to the merchant's terms & conditions. Such indications on the part of the customer can be considered to be the equivalent of a hand-rendered signature (in many jurisdictions, the legal basis of this electronic agreement is still largely undetermined). Separately, this policy assumes that the merchant has been diligent and posted important terms & conditions on the commerce site. For related ideas see the policies entitled "Formation Of Binding Contracts Via Electronic Systems" and "Trading Partner Agreement Required Prior To Use Of EDI." A: T; E: LMH.

1.4.2. Encryption

1.4.2.1. When To Use Encryption

747. Encryption Processes Must Not Be Used Unless Previously Approved

Policy: Encryption processes must not be used for Company X information unless the processes are first approved by the Information Security Department.
Commentary: The intention of this policy is to prevent users from damaging or destroying Company X information because they don't have the expertise or knowledge required to use encryption facilities properly. Only after the Information Security Department is satisfied that adequate "safety nets" exist to recover the involved information, should it approve the use of encryption. One of the best safety nets for encryption is to have management override keys, that allow management to decrypt information even if the key has been lost, misplaced, or intentionally withheld (these are also called "key escrow" or "key recovery" facilities). As the last sentence implies, one of the major risks that a firm faces when it allows its staff to use encryption is that important information will be ransomed by the staff (this happened in one British computer crime case). Separately, the policy is also intended to make sure that only approved algorithms, modes of operation, and other implementation aspects of cryptoprocesses (encryption processes) meet in-house standards. If all users were free to go their own directions, the resulting encryption "free-for-all" would interfere with the secure communication of confidential or private information. For example, if one group of users employed the RSA public key algorithm while another employed the DES symmetric algorithm, data would have to be decrypted and reencrypted before it could be moved between these two groups. In some jurisdictions, encryption is illegal (or the key may need to be disclosed to government agencies); to make sure that users are not inadvertently breaking the law, the Information Security Department should be involved in decisions to use encryption. See the policy entitled "Compliance With International Trade In Armaments Regulations." A: E; E: LMH.

748. Use Of Any Encryption Process Requires Prior Written Approval

Policy: Users are not permitted to employ encryption, digital signatures, or digital certificates for any Company X business activity or business information without the written authorization of their department manager. Before they utilize these complex technologies, users must also be properly trained and their systems must be configured by authorized personnel.

Commentary: This policy is intended to prevent staff members from getting into trouble (for example by encrypting a file, losing the key, and deleting the readable version). The policy forces all those who would use these increasingly important cryptoprocesses to first get management approval, then get trained, and lastly get their systems properly configured (note that the system configuration can at least in part be done remotely via automatic software distribution systems, aka ASD). This policy is conservative in that it seeks to prevent the use of these new tools until the need has been established and other prerequisites have been addressed. Without this approach, the chances are great that users will download encryption process software from the Internet and try to do it themselves, perhaps getting into trouble (representing the organization when they should not, inadvertently disclosing secrets, etc.). Note that this policy also allows the deletion from hard drives of cryptoprocess software that was discovered with "autodiscovery" software routines; this can all be performed automatically, and can help ensure that users are in fact not using these cryptoprocess tools. This in turn will help ensure that critical data is not maliciously encrypted and thus kept from those who need it for business reasons. For a related idea, see the policy entitled "Encryption Processes Must Not Be Used Unless Previously Approved." A: E; E: LMH.

749. Encryption Utilities With User-Provided Passwords Or Keys Prohibited

Policy: To prevent the loss of critical information, workers must never employ encryption utilities requiring a user to input a password or encryption key. If sensitive information needs protection, alternative information protection mechanisms approved by the Information Security Department must be used.

Commentary: This policy attempts to keep information perpetually available for business activities. The policy states that management does not want to run the risk that the password or key entered by a user is lost, forgotten, or deliberately withheld. A common scenario involves a disgruntled employee who is not happy with his or her employment severance arrangements; their memory of the password or key may be "faulty." Separately, this policy allows autodiscovery software to be used to detect the existence of encryption utilities. If a PC software change management system is used, an encryption utility can even be erased from a user's hard drive through remote commands. On a separate note, many word processing packages now include encryption features; some organizations may wish to disable these features. In general terms, it is desirable that users not be able to exclusively control organizational data (no separation of duties exists); this policy attempts to prevent such a dangerous situation. Note that the policy does not prevent the use of user-transparent encryption facilities that are embedded in networks, for instance via Cisco routers. Those businesses with particularly sensitive data will need user-controlled encryption utilities; for them, key escrow (key recovery) systems managed by an employer (not the government) will be a preferred option to this policy. For a related idea, see the policy entitled "Encryption Processes Must Not Be Used Unless Previously Approved." A: E; E: L.

750. Compliance With International Trade In Armaments Regulations

Policy: By proceeding further, users of this international network agree not to distribute, directly or indirectly, encryption software or any other munitions of war as defined in United States International Trade in Armaments Regulations (ITAR).

Commentary: One intention of this American policy is to reduce the liability risk faced by the provider of network services (or similar facilities). Another intention of this policy relates to training and awareness; the policy gives users an opportunity to acknowledge that they will not distribute encryption software or other items considered to be munitions of war by the United States government. Although these American regulations are widely considered to be antiquated and of questionable value, and although they are increasingly coming under attack as constraints to the expansion of both the US software business and Internet business, the regulations are still in effect. A recent court case involving Phil Zimmerman shows that the US government is still interested in enforcing these laws. Zimmerman is now famous for having written Pretty Good Privacy (PGP), a de-facto standard for performing encryption over the Internet. Because his encryption program was distributed via the Internet on an international basis, he became embroiled in court case dealing with the ITAR, but the government has now dropped the case. On another note, some organizations require users to acknowledge that they will comply with these regulations before they are given access to organizational facilities (sometimes this is done for physical entrance to offices too). This policy, as written, would be shown at the time that a new user is given an overview of available network services. If this policy is intended to be incorporated into a manual, a memo, or some other document, then the first three words in the policy can be dropped, and the sentence verb tense changed from "agree not to" to "must not." Another way to handle this type of acknowledgement is to have users sign a piece of paper stating that they will not knowingly export, directly or indirectly, any technical data, product, or software of United States origin to any restricted country, without first having obtained US government permission. Although this policy is decidedly American in its orientation, other countries such as England also restrict certain information security systems, tools, and data. If an illegal distribution of munitions of war does take place, this policy may be helpful in reducing fines or other penalties to the organization issuing the policy. Also see the policy entitled "When Faxing Sensitive Information Is Permissible." A: E; E: MH.

751. Secret Data Sent Over Networks Must Be Encrypted

Policy: If Company X secret data is to be transmitted over any communication network, it must be sent in encrypted form.

Commentary: The intention of this policy is to forbid the transmission of unencrypted secret data over a network where it could be wiretapped. Business can still get done, and secret data can still be sent over a network--it just needs to be encrypted. Encryption, also known as encoding or scrambling, conceals data such that it cannot be read by unauthorized parties. Encryption can also be used to provide an indication that a certain party sent a message and that the message was not modified in transit (most often via digital signatures, which are rendered via encryption). This policy may be supported with an application level encryption program and/or a network level encryption facility (in other words, the policy does not imply any particular type of implementation). The policy does not specify an encryption algorithm, although some organizations choose to put mention of an algorithm in such a policy. Separately, this policy is important for small systems such as PCs, LANs, client/server systems, intranets, and the like because users are often unaware of the protection that secret data requires; unless they are put on notice with a policy such as this, chances are that they will needlessly expose secret data. Note that this policy assumes that a data classification system has already been endorsed (implied by the use of the word "secret"). For further information, see the policy entitled "Four Category Data Classification Scheme." Also see the policies entitled "Government Approved Standard Encryption Algorithm & Implementation" and "When Faxing Sensitive Information Is Permissible." A: ET; E: MH.

752. Transportation Of Secret Data In Computer-Readable Storage Media

Policy: If secret data is to be transported in computer-readable storage media (such as magnetic tapes, floppy disks, or CD-ROMs), it must be in encrypted form.

Commentary: The intention of this policy is to prohibit workers from transporting secret data in computer-readable storage media when this secret data has not been encrypted. Transportation can still take place--the data just needs to be encrypted. Encryption of such media not only conceals the data, it can be used to detect system errors and tampering. When computer storage media goes through airport x-ray machines and is subjected to other magnetic fields en route, there is a chance that certain parts of the data will be erased or altered. If the data is encrypted (depending on the type of encryption used), such erasures and alterations can be made immediately evident, depending on the encryption algorithm employed (DES with the cipher-feedback mode would for instance detect this). Note that this policy assumes that a data classification system has already been endorsed (implied by the use of the word "secret"). For further information, see the policy entitled "Four Category Data Classification Scheme." Also see the policy entitled "Travelling On Public Transportation With Secret Information." A: ET; E: MH.

753. Secret Information Must Be Encrypted When Not In Active Use

Policy: All computerized secret information must be encrypted when not in active use (for example, when not manipulated by software or viewed by an authorized user).

Commentary: The intention of this policy is to prevent secret information from being inadvertently disclosed to unauthorized persons. If encrypted data was stored in unencrypted form, it may end up on backup tapes which then might be viewed by unauthorized persons. In this way, standard access controls could be circumvented. Although this policy may at first sound like a lot to ask, it is easily accomplished. For example, microcomputers (PCs) and workstations can employ commercially-available background encryption software packages that are user-transparent. With these packages, all the data on a hard drive is encrypted, but it is automatically decrypted when needed so that applications can use it. After the data is modified or otherwise used by an authorized application program, it is written back to the hard drive in encrypted form. The user's only involvement is the provision of an encryption key (password) at the time the system is booted. Note that this policy assumes that a data classification system has already been endorsed (implied by the use of the word "secret"). For further information, see the policy entitled "Four Category Data Classification Scheme." Also see the policy entitled "Encrypting Backup Media Stored Off-Site." A: ET; E: MH.

754. Data Stored On Hard Disk Drives Must Be Encrypted

Policy: To prevent unauthorized disclosure of data when computers are sent out for repair, when they are stolen, or when they are used by unauthorized parties, all data stored on hard disks must be encrypted via user-transparent processes.

Commentary: The intention of this policy is to prevent unauthorized persons from gaining access to Company X confidential or proprietary data. As was discussed in the commentary for the policy entitled "Secret Information Must Be Encrypted When Not In Active Use," various products now on the market make this process user-friendly and largely user-transparent. Unlike the policy entitled "Secret Information Must Be Encrypted When Not In Active Use," this policy does not require that users or others distinguish between secret and non-secret data. Removing users from the decision-making process can increase security because the chances of an inappropriate decision are decreased. At the same time, encrypting all data will tax computer system resources more than selectively encrypting data (reducing system response time). Because it defines the most effective (although often not the most efficient) way to protect data in a distributed computing environment, this policy is particularly relevant for microcomputers (PCs), workstations, LANs, intranets, and client/server systems. Separately, as an alternative to this policy, consider the use of a degausser to erase sensitive information stored on a computer hard disk before the computer is sent outside an organization for repair. Also see the policies entitled "Use Of Hard-Disk Drives For Storage Of Sensitive Information," "Transfer Of Sensitive Information To Third Parties On Computer Media," and "Destruction Of Sensitive Information On Computer Storage Media." A: ET; E: MH.

1.4.2.2. Encryption Key Management

755. Government Standard Encryption Algorithm & Implementation

Policy: If encryption is used, government-approved standard algorithms (such as the Data Encryption Standard or DES) and standard implementations (such as cipher-block chaining) must be employed.

Commentary: The intention of this policy is to require all systems within an organization (or on a multi-organizational network) employ the same encryption algorithm and the same encryption system implementation (sometimes called "mode of operation"). This policy will help ensure interoperability which in turn will lower costs and facilitate secure business communications. This policy will also help ensure compliance with local government laws and regulations, and thus may allow encryption to be used in situations where it would otherwise be illegal. For example, international network encrypted traffic may be illegal according to a certain country's laws, but these laws may be relaxed if government standard algorithms and implementations are used, and if certain bureaucratic approval processes are followed. Note that this policy has a major downside: government approved algorithms and implementations are more likely to have trap-doors, which may allow the government to monitor network traffic without the consent or knowledge of the participants. Suggested sources of information about encryption implementations include (US) Federal Information Processing Standard (FIPS) publication 1027, which provides specifications for crypto equipment; American National Standards Institute (ANSI) standard X9.9 provides information about message authentication codes (MACs), while ANSI standard X9.17 provides key management requirements. See the policy entitled "Hardware/Software Procurement Via Standard Purchasing Channels." A: T; E: MH.

756. Deployed Encryption Algorithms Must Be Publicly Evaluated (Open)

Policy: Every general purpose encryption algorithm used to protect Company X production information and information systems must be open (that is, the specific mechanisms are publicly disclosed) and must have been evaluated by cryptography experts.

Commentary: The intention of this policy is to prevent organizations from getting into trouble because they created their own insecure encryption systems or because they bought a "proprietary algorithm" from a certain vendor which turned out later to be weak. Cryptography is very complex and it's difficult to do it right. This policy helps to ensure that experts are involved in the intricate cryptographic design work, whereas a variety of others can be involved in the implementation of the systems these experts develop. In most instances this means that organizations will purchase modules which have been written by encryption vendors such as RSA Data Security and Baltimore. Examples of organizations which built their own encryption mechanisms, and which got into trouble thereby abound -- these organizations include Microsoft and Netscape. Likewise, a number of digital cellular phone encryption algorithms have recently received negative publicity for the same reason. Some people argue against this policy saying that confidentiality will make cracking the system more difficult, and there is some limited truth to that. But nothing prevents an organization from using open algorithms but not disclosing which algorithms are employed. This approach provides the assurance that the algorithm has been evaluated and shown to be strong, but at the same time because the implementation is kept confidential, increases the work factor (effort) required to break the system. Nonetheless, today many organizations cannot resist the public relations and marketing benefits that come from having experts evaluate their cryptography (especially if the cryptography is integrated into a product or service), and thus they wish to include the algorithms in publicly released information. Separately, the words "general purpose" were added to the policy to exempt encryption algorithms which are built into security systems; these include mechanisms to encrypt fixed passwords which are part of an access control program. Examples of open algorithms include PGP, SSL, S/MIME, IPSec, and SSH. For a related idea, see the policy entitled "Government Standard Encryption Algorithm & Implementation." A: T; E: LMH.

757. Disclosure Of Encryption Keys Requires Special Approval

Policy: Encryption keys are a most sensitive type of information, and access to such keys must be strictly limited to those who have a need-to-know. Unless the approval of a Senior Vice President is obtained, encryption keys must not be revealed to consultants, contractors, or other third parties.

Commentary: The intention of this policy is to clearly put workers on notice that encryption keys should be protected with the most stringent security measures. This is why most information technology shops will encrypt encryption keys if these encryption keys are kept in a file or in other locations (such as in computer system memory) that might otherwise be accessible by unauthorized persons. This means that encryption keys should not be stored in main memory on a multi-user machine unless they are in encrypted form (ideally a separate encryption peripheral device called a "security module" should be used). Ideally, key loading modules and other devices should be used to prevent any one individual from gaining access to a whole encryption key. See the policies entitled "Encryption Key Management Systems And Separation Of Duties" and "Suspected Disclosure Forces Password Changes." A: T; E: MH.

758. Encryption Key Management Systems And Separation Of Duties

Policy: Company X encryption systems must be designed such that no single person has full knowledge of any single encryption key. This must be achieved by separation of duties and dual control. Separation of duties refers to use of more than one individual to handle a certain important activity, while dual control means that two people must be simultaneously present for an important activity to be accomplished.

Commentary: The intention of this policy is to prevent any one individual from gaining access to a full encryption key. If a full encryption key was held by any one individual, then this individual could (depending on how the encryption system was set-up) decrypt other keys and/or decrypt sensitive information. This could lead to fraud, sabotage, privacy invasion and other problems. By breaking keys into components such activities are then not possible without collusion. Breaking keys into components usually involves creating two bit strings, which when combined via an exclusive-OR operation yield a production encryption key. This entire process is often automated via hardware called "key loaders." The notions described in this policy can be also applied to passwords, initialization vectors, pseudo-random number generator seeds, and other parameters used in security-related processes. See the policies entitled "Separation Of Duties And Control Over Company X Assets" and "Protection Of Password Generation Algorithms." A: T; E: MH.

759. Initialization Of Encryption Systems Requires Auditor Presence

Policy: Whenever an encryption system to be used for Company X production information systems is being initialized, installed, enabled, or reset, an EDP Auditor must be present to document and witness the process.

Commentary: While many things can be done to limit the damage that a particular insider can do to an organization's systems, management in large measure still trusts its technical staff to follow established procedures. This is especially important when loading encryption keys into Internet commerce servers and other production information systems on which the organization will place great reliance. The policy is thus intended to provide management with some additional assurance that the process has been done correctly, reliably, and securely. The presence of an auditor will have a sobering effect on all who are there, and may be important should there later be some allegations of negligence on management's part. Separately the focus here is on system set-up because that is the time of greatest vulnerability. After an encryption system has been established, keys can be automatically changed without much of a risk. Accordingly, this policy assumes that an automated key management process will be used; if this is not the case, then the presence of an auditor may be advisable for each key change process. The presence of an auditor may also be useful for marketing and public relations purposes, helping to establish a higher level of trust in the involved information system (if this is intended, an independent external auditor is recommended). For related ideas, see the policies entitled "Prior Approval Required For Set-Up Of Multi-User Systems" and "Internal Audit Review Of Information System Controls." A: T; E: MH.

760. Conditions For Delegation Of Key Management Responsibility

Policy: Key management responsibility may only be delegated to a party who has passed a background check, passed an operational security audit, and signed a confidentiality agreement.

Commentary: The intention of this policy is to keep middle management from delegating key management responsibility to outsourcing firms, service bureaus, business partners, and other external organizations which may not handle keys in as secure a manner as they should. A policy like this can also be used to define the internal staff who may take on key management duties. The policy describes a process for making sure that the receiving entity meets Company X's criteria for a trusted party. Separately, organizations must first precisely define with whom they will share sensitive key information. After this, they must decide how to screen people/organizations so that only trusted parties receive key information. It is the second step that is reflected in this policy. On a separate note, in this policy, the three criteria for determining trustworthiness could be modified to include other considerations, such as being registered with a governmental agency. As another option, they could also be well-known certificate authorities (CAs) which are increasingly being recognized as the keepers of the keys for Internet commerce activities. Two widely-known examples are Verisign and GTE. Getting back to the three criteria mentioned in the policy, they can be restated as: (1) personal character and historical records, (2) current operating practices, and (3) legal obligations. This policy could be generalized to include other security responsibilities on a shared network, such as user-ID issuance and password management. For related ideas, see the policies entitled "Granting System Privileges By Chain Of Authority Delegation" and "Restricted Delegation Of Information Owner Duties." A: MT; E: MH.

761. Protection Of Digital Certificate Root Keys At Certificate Authorities

Policy: Root keys for digital certificate hierarchies must be protected with rigorous physical security, dual control, split key components, and separation of duties.

Commentary: Many organizations are acting as their own certificate authority (CA) these days, issuing their own digital certificates either internally or externally. Because cryptoprocesses such as digital signatures and digital certificates critically depend on these root keys, it is imperative that the root keys (master keys) be kept with the utmost security. This policy is accordingly intended to specify four specific security mechanisms which in all cases must be employed. Rigorous physical security generally means storing sensitive information in safes, requiring badges for physical access to equipment, keeping logs of who had access to equipment, using closed circuit TV (CCTV), etc. Dual control refers to the use of no less than two people to perform critical acts such as generating root keys. Split key components are the result of mathematical transformations that conceal keys (generally using exclusive-OR operations). Separation of duties refers to the use of different people to perform different activities, such that each checks on the work of others. For related concepts, see the policies entitled "Conditions For Delegation Of Key Management Responsibility" and "Digital Certificate For All Company X Internet Web And Commerce Sites." A: T; E: LMH.

762. Separate Communication Channel For Data And Encryption Keys

Policy: If encryption is used, the information protected with encryption must be transmitted over a different communication channel than the keys used to govern the encryption process.

Commentary: The intention of this policy is to prevent a wiretapper from obtaining readable versions of both the keys and the sensitive data. If the wiretapper had broken the encryption process, then the wiretapper would have all the information needed for breaking new transmissions. Thus sending the keys over a separate communication channel raises the level of effort for a wiretapper (of course it also raises the cost to Company X). An example would be to send the keys by courier and not on a computer network linking the communicating parties. Note that this policy assumes the use of a traditional symmetric encryption algorithm such as DES (where the encryption key is the same as the decryption key). It is not needed if asymmetric algorithms are used (where the encryption key is different from the decryption key). The key management protocols on the Internet, such as SSL, are increasingly using the latter type of algorithm via a public key infrastructure (PKI). Thus this policy is not necessary if only standard Internet protocols are being employed for a network. On another note, this policy involves separation of duties applied to information, rather than people. See the policies entitled "Separation Of Duties And Control Over Company X Assets," "Storing Encryption Keys On Same Media As Protected Data Prohibited," and "Encryption Key Management Systems And Separation of Duties." A: T; E: H.

763. Automated Encryption Key Management Systems Preferred

Policy: Whenever such facilities are commercially available, Company X must employ automated rather than manual encryption key management processes.

Commentary: The intention of this policy is to save Company X money and time, as well as to obtain the most effective security system available. For some encryption systems (particularly those which are "home-grown"), there are no applicable commercially-available key management systems. But recent commercial offerings include a number of strong key management systems, such as those available from Information Resource Engineering of Baltimore, MD. Key management is very complex, and as such should be automated to reduce the probability of human error. Automation also reduces the probability of accidental key disclosure to unauthorized persons. Some organizations may wish to put the word "standard" into the policy to ensure interoperability with other key management systems. See the policies entitled "Explicit Assignment Of Encryption Key Management Functions" and "Encryption Key Management Systems And Separation Of Duties." A: T; E: MH.

764. Maximum Life Of Encryption Keys

Policy: Whenever encryption is used to protect Company X data, the keys must be changed at least every ninety (90) days.

Commentary: The intention of this policy is to force periodic changes in encryption keys. Changing the keys more rapidly will increase the security of an encryption system. If an adversary is able to derive a particular encryption key through cryptanalysis, he or she must start from the beginning whenever the key is changed (provided the adversary cannot determine a pattern in the generation of the keys). Because they are concerned about the strength of the Data Encryption Standard (DES) with its limited key length, some firms are now taking this policy to its logical extreme: requiring that keys be changed for every transmission (i.e., every transaction, on-line session, etc.). To further increase the "work factor" (level of required effort for adversaries), some organizations may also wish to change initialization vectors (IVs) on a periodic basis. See the policies entitled "Stated Life For All Encryption Keys" and "Periodic Forced Password Changes." A: T; E: MH.

765. Stated Life For All Encryption Keys

Policy: All encryption keys must have a stated life and must be changed on or before the stated expiration date.

Commentary: This policy is intended to make it clear that the people handling keys must assign a life span (expiration date) to all keys. Unless a Vernam cipher (one-time pad) or a similar cipher is being used, it is not acceptable to use keys that do not have an expiration date. A Vernam cipher -- inefficient, costly, and rarely used outside military or diplomatic circles -- never uses the same key twice. Because such keys are used only once, they don't need an expiration date or stated life. All other systems, like the Data Encryption Standard (DES), generally use the same key repeatedly. After a certain time period has elapsed, the security provided by these other encryption systems becomes degraded (an attacker has a greater amount of ciphertext with which to perform known-ciphertext cryptanalysis); accordingly, the key needs to be changed to bolster the security of the encryption process. With this line of reasoning, an encryption system where each session, or even each transaction, has its own key will provide higher security than if the same key is used for months. From a conceptual standpoint, a stated life for an encryption key is related to, and is somewhat similar to sensitivity classification labels for ordinary data. Note that this policy assumes a manual rather than an automated key management process. For related ideas, see the policies entitled "Maximum Life Of Encryption Keys" and "Use Of Labels Throughout Sensitive Information's Life Cycle." A: T; E: MH.

766. Process For Generating Encryption Keys

Policy: Whenever encryption is used, the keys employed must be generated by means which are not practically discernable by an adversary, and which will yield keys that are difficult-to-guess. An example of this key generation process is the use of a pseudo-random number generator which takes the low order bits of the computer clock as input.

Commentary: The intention of this process is to ensure that encryption systems provide all the security they are meant to provide. If encryption keys are easily guessed, then the security provided by encryption systems may be easily compromised. For example, if users choose their own encryption keys, a guessibility-related screening process is recommended. This policy is a derivative of a policy regarding so-called "weak keys" for the Data Encryption Standards (DES); certain weak keys make DES cryptanalysis quite easy and these keys must accordingly be avoided. Often the key generation process is part of an automated key management process, in which case this policy will not be necessary. See the policy entitled "Automated Encryption Key Management Systems Preferred." Also see the policies entitled "Minimum Length For User-Chosen Encryption Keys" and "Seed For System-Generated Passwords." A: T; E: MH.

767. Minimum Length For User-Chosen Encryption Keys

Policy: Whenever user-chosen encryption keys are employed, the encryption system must prevent users from employing keys made-up of less than ten (10) characters.

Commentary: Like the policy entitled "Process for Generating Encryption Keys," the intention of this policy is to make sure that an encryption system provides the security it was meant to provide. If encryption keys are easily guessed (because they are made up of too few characters), then an encryption system can be readily compromised. There is nothing special about ten characters; for very high-security environments the number will need to be higher, while for low- to medium-security environments the number may be slightly lower. Other screening mechanisms for user-chosen encryption keys may be warranted. For example, the DES algorithm has several "weak keys" which allow the encryption process to be easily defeated. These weak keys should not be permitted. For a related idea, see the policy entitled "Minimum Password Length." A: T; E: MH.

768. Protection For Encryption Key Generation Materials

Policy: Whenever encryption is used, materials to develop encryption keys as well as hardcopy versions of keys must be kept locked-up when not in use. Protective measures to prevent these keying materials from falling into the wrong hands must be observed throughout the life cycle of the information protected by the keys.

Commentary: The term "keying materials" is used to refer to data encryption keys, keys which encrypt other keys (master keys), initialization vectors (IVs), pseudo-random number generator seeds, and other parameters used to control or initialize encryption processes. The intention of this policy is to prevent the parameters used to construct encryption keys from falling into the wrong hands, and then being used to construct or intelligently-guess encryption keys. As soon as possible after their use, these keying materials should be destroyed according to approved procedures for most sensitive information (shredding, burning, etc.). For more on this, see the policy entitled "Destruction Of Encryption Key Generation Materials." The need for this policy may be partially overcome via the use of automated key management systems. See the policy entitled "Automated Encryption Key Management Systems Preferred." A: T; E: MH.

769. Protection For Plaintext Encryption Master Keys

Policy: Only two approaches for protecting plaintext (readable) master keys are acceptable to Company X. Master keys may be manually handled via dual control with split knowledge. Alternatively, they may be stored in tamper-proof modules. In all other places, they must appear only in encrypted form.

Commentary: This policy specifies the permissible ways to protect the keys at the top of a hierarchy of keys -- the most sensitive type of encryption keys. Master keys are used to encrypt all other keys, or at least encrypt keys that in turn encrypt other keys. If a master key is revealed, an entire encryption system can quickly be compromised. Accordingly, significant efforts are needed to prevent these keys from falling into the wrong hands. When in readable form, master keys must be chopped into segments (components), each of which does not reveal the original master key (also known as "split knowledge"). Alternatively, they may be stored in hardware modules that will automatically erase the keys if someone tampers with the module. These modules are sometimes called "security modules." They are sold by vendors such as ASC Systems, St. Clair Shores, Michigan, and USA. For related ideas, see the policies entitled "Protection For Encryption Key Generation Materials" and "Encryption Key Management Systems And Separation Of Duties." A: T; E: MH.

770. Destruction Of Encryption Key Generation Materials

Policy: All supplies used for the generation, distribution, and storage of keys (such as carbon copies, printer ribbons, and the like) must be protected from disclosure to unauthorized persons. When they are not longer needed, they must be destroyed by pulping, shredding, burning, or other approved methods.

Commentary: The intention of this policy is to prevent unauthorized parties from obtaining access to the information used to generate, distribute, or store encryption keys. This might allow these parties to obtain copies of the keys, which in turn would allow them to obtain the sensitive information protected with encryption. The policy also serves to make workers aware that these materials are sensitive and that they should be handled with care. See the policy entitled "Protection For Encryption Key Generation Materials." Also see the policies entitled "Approved Methods For Hardcopy Sensitive Information Disposal" and "Destruction Of Materials Used In Handling Sensitive Information." A: T; E: MH.

771. Time Frame For Destruction Of Key Exchange Material

Policy: Custodians of key exchange material must destroy this material according to approved procedures within a reasonable time -- not to exceed ten business days -- following the successful verification of a key exchange process.

Commentary: The intent of this policy is to clearly specify when custodians of keying materials (master keys, encryption key components, initialization vectors, random number generator seeds, etc.) must destroy the keying materials they have received. The smaller the amount of time that these materials exist outside the system, and the fewer the number of people that have them, the more secure the encryption process will be. For example, in a banking network involving shared automated teller machines (ATMs), the involved banks must all periodically change their own encryption systems to incorporate new keys. Multi-organizational networking environments are particularly in need of a policy like the one given here. While the key management process is increasingly being automated, there are still many encryption systems where manual key loaders and other technology requires human involvement. It is for those manual situations that this policy was intended. For related ideas, see "Destruction Of Intermediate Products Containing Sensitive Information" and "Destruction Of Materials Used In Handling Sensitive Information." A: T; E: MH.

772. Time Period For Protection Of Encryption Keys Used For Confidentiality

Policy: The secrecy of any encryption key used for confidentiality purposes (e.g., for data encryption or as a seed to an access control system) must be maintained until all of the protected information is no longer considered confidential.

Commentary: This policy provides systems designers and systems operators with a basic security principle for key management systems. The policy cautions them not to disclose encryption keys until all of the information protected with these keys is no longer considered confidential. From a practical standpoint, in many cases this time frame will be longer than an individual's lifetime. Separately, the secrecy of a key is assured if the key has been destroyed via authorized processes; for example, if confidential data was sent over the Internet some time ago, the key could be destroyed even though the information is still considered confidential. On another note, this policy communicates the great emphasis that must be placed on the continued secrecy of keys, a message which is often unknown to, or ignored by encryption system users. Note that the "life" a key is the time period in which it is employed, which for encrypted data in storage could be decades or longer. For related ideas, see the policy entitled "Maximum Life Of Encryption Keys" and "Stated Life For All Encryption Keys." A: ET; E: MH.

773. Time Period For Protection Of Private Digital Signature Keys

Policy: Private digital signature keys must be kept confidential and accessible for at least the number of years that they might be used in a legal challenge.

Commentary: The intention of this policy is to instruct users about how long to keep their private keys used for digital signatures. The exact number of years will vary by jurisdiction, and so was not stated in the policy. For a multi-national company, this policy could be accompanied by a table showing the requirements of different countries, or the maximum number of years could be placed into the policy itself. Separately, the policy could be expanded to include the need for a data integrity measure, such as a checksum to assure that the digital signature key has not been corrupted. On another note, some organizations may want to destroy private keys after they are no longer in use, thereafter relying on public keys to prove the authenticity of a message. This is possible with Internet-based public key systems (sometimes called PKI or public key infrastructure) where the private key differs from the public keys. On the other hand, those organizations who wish to retain the private keys for legal challenges would use this policy. It is to the latter type of organizations using PKI encryption systems, or to any type of organization using traditional symmetric key encryption systems (like the DES) that this policy applies. From a defini message was generated by a specific party and that this message has not been modified by unauthorized parties. Private digital signature keys must be kept secret, while public digital signature keys are widely available and are not generally kept secret. For related ideas, see the policies entitled "Digital Signature And User Authentication Keys Must Not Be Escrowed" and "Java Program Execution Prohibited Unless Digital Signature Validated." A: E; E: LMH.

774. Never Automatically Backup Private Key Used For Digital Certificates

Policy: Users must not allow automatic backup systems to make a copy of the readable version of their private key used for digital signatures and digital certificates. Automatic backups could allow unauthorized transactions to be generated in the involved users' names. These backups are prevented by keeping private keys in smart cards or otherwise in encrypted form.

Commentary: The intention of this policy is to preserve the confidentiality of private encryption keys used for both digital signatures and digital certificates. These private keys should be kept under the control of the specific user to whom they pertain. If users simply store the readable version of their private keys on personal computer hard disks, then automatic backup systems can transfer these private keys to backup storage media where unauthorized parties can find them. Note that this policy does not prevent a user from making a backup on a floppy disk and then locking this backup in a safe (an advisable step). Nonetheless, if a user loses control of his or her private key, he can always generate another one (correspondents may need to be notified). This policy is a reflection of an increasingly common phenomenon where one control (backup) can be used to circumvent another (digital signatures and certificates). For related concepts see the policies entitled "Digital Signature And User Authentication Keys Must Not Be Escrowed" and "Protection Of Digital Certificate Root Keys At Certificate Authorities." A: E; E: LMH.

775. Duplication Of Encryption Keys For Data That Has Been Backed-Up

Policy: Encryption keys used to conceal backup data must themselves be backed-up. These keys must also be stored with security measures comparable to or more stringent than measures applied to the involved backed-up data.

Commentary: The objective of this policy is to ensure that information systems staff has taken the necessary steps to securely back-up encryption keys used to protect backup data media. Encryption of backup media is often employed by financial institutions, credit bureaus, research labs, and other organizations handling sensitive, valuable, or critical data and storing its backups at an off-site location. The policy writer will note that this policy indicates that the keys should be protected in a manner at least as secure as the protected data. This is because physical security at an off-site location may be lax or easily compromised, in which case the encryption process is the only significant control preventing the disclosure of the backed-up data. For related considerations, see the policies entitled "Digital Signature And User Authentication Keys Must Not Be Escrowed" and "Storing Encryption Keys On Same Media As Protected Data Prohibited." A: T; E: MH.

776. Prevention Of Unauthorized Disclosure Of Encryption Keys

Policy: Encryption keys must be prevented from unauthorized disclosure via technical controls such as encryption under a separate key and use of tamper-resistant hardware.

Commentary: The intention of this policy is to specify that measures must always be taken to prevent the unauthorized disclosure of encryption keys. If encryption keys are disclosed, the security of encryption systems is in most instances defeated (assuming the algorithm and implementation are public knowledge, which they often are with the Data Encryption Standard (DES)). Tamper resistant hardware prevents people from opening encryption devices to recover the encryption keys stored inside. Also called "security modules," such hardware will automatically erase the keys contained inside if the module has been opened (it uses volatile memory). This hardware is also shielded so that electromagnetic emanations do not reveal the keys stored inside. In terms of encrypting encryption keys, rather than using only one master key to encrypt other keys, many organizations use a hierarchy of master keys. This can get quite complicated and this complexity presents another reason why it is desirable to automate key management processes; see the policy entitled "Automated Encryption Key Management Systems Preferred." Also see the policy entitled "Tamper Resistant Hardware Modules For Encryption Processes." A: T; E: MH.

777. Private Key For Digital Certificates Must Be Encrypted Or In Smart Card

Policy: The private key associated with each worker at Company X must be protected against unauthorized disclosure when not in use. This must be achieved by (a) an approved encryption process when stored on a hard drive or any other storage media such as a floppy disk, and/or (b) storage in a smart card. Use of physical security measures alone (such as locking an office door) in order to protect a private key is unacceptable.

Commentary: This policy seeks to put users on notice that they must protect their private keys against unauthorized disclosure and subsequent fraudulent usage. If an unprotected private key was discovered and later used by an unauthorized party, this party could bind the authorized user to contracts, buy products and services in the name of the authorized user, and otherwise wreak havoc with the life of the authorized user. The unauthorized party in this case would be engaged in a type of "identity theft." Separately, just as cardholders are told not to leave their credit cards on the dashboard of their cars (in order to prevent fraud), this policy says that private key holders must take certain precautions in order to maintain the security of the encryption processes which depend on their private keys (digital signatures, digital certificates, virtual private network -- or VPN -- connections, etc.). For a related idea, see the policy entitled "Time Period For Protection Of Private Digital Signature Keys." A: E; E: LMH.

778. Transmission Of Cleartext Private Encryption Keys Prohibited

Policy: If private encryption keys are transmitted over communication lines, they must be sent in encrypted form. The encryption of private keys should be performed with a stronger algorithm than is used to encrypt other sensitive data protected by encryption.

Commentary: The intention of this policy is to prevent users from inadvertently sending readable (cleartext) private encryption keys over communication systems. If this is done, then the encryption process (depending on the type of system involved) may be easily circumvented. Note that the second sentence is a guideline and not a policy (the word "should" is used rather than "must"). For example, if the organization in question were using a standard symmetric encryption algorithm, such as the Data Encryption Standard (DES), implementation of the guideline in the second sentence would be straightforward. In this case, encryption keys might be encrypted three times (using the "EDE" method), while data is encrypted only once. As it is written, this policy is applicable to both the new public key encryption systems (sometimes called PKI or Public Key Infrastructure) and the more traditional symmetric encryption systems (such as the DES). Whatever the underlying technology, private keys must never be sent in unencrypted form; with PKI, public keys can be sent without encryption. Separately, another way to implement this policy would be to use public key algorithms for key encryption (often easier from a key management standpoint), but the DES algorithm for encryption of text and other forms of data (the latter is often more efficient and faster). See the policy entitled "Separate Communication Channel For Data And Encryption Keys." A: T; E: MH.

779. Notifying Correspondents About Changes In Public Keys

Policy: If a public encryption key has been posted on a web server or in another publicly accessible location, all regular correspondents must be notified whenever there is a change in this public key.

Commentary: This policy is relevant only to those organizations that use public key encryption systems (alias PKI or public key infrastructure). Soon everyone will be using PKI systems because they are the systems of choice for Internet commerce. This policy recognizes that popular encryption systems such as PGP (Pretty Good Privacy) now allow a user to post their public key in a public spot. This allows electronic mail and other transmissions to be easily encrypted, and it also allows digital signatures to be easily checked (all without the use of digital certificates and without a third party called a Certificate Authority, or a CA). With this approach, there is a possibility that an imposter can pose as a legitimate user and post another public key in the legitimate user's public location. Until detected, this imposter may then be able to spoof correspondents into communicating with him or her rather than the legitimate user. This policy prevents such abuse, or at least significantly reduces the time period when this abuse could take place. The messages that notify correspondents of future changes in a public key can be signed with a current and not-yet-expired private key, thus assuring correspondents that they have received a message from the legitimate user and not an imposter. For related ideas, see the policy entitled "Transmission Of Cleartext Private Encryption Keys Prohibited." A: EMT; E: MH.

780. Compromised Keys Revoked Back To Last Time Known To Be Safe

Policy: Encryption keys which have been compromised, or revealed to third parties under a key escrow arrangement, must immediately be revoked retroactively to the last known time when the keys were safe.

Commentary: The intention of this policy is to support the resilience of key management systems (especially those which are a part of the PKI or public key infrastructure, which is fast becoming an integral part of Internet commerce). This policy supports the rapid notification of other participants in a key management system (perhaps through certificate revocation lists or CRLs), and then later the prompt issuance of new and trusted keys. If keys which had been revealed to third parties (i.e., compromised) were to be revoked only back to the point in time when this revelation is known to have occurred, there might have been earlier comprises which had not yet come to the attention of the key holder or the authority managing the keys. The continued support of transactions and messages executed and sent when there could have been still-undisclosed key compromises sets the stage for unrevealed fraud. To be on the safe side, a compromised key is instead revoked all the way back to the point when the key was known to be safe. This point often it coincides with a previous key change. For related considerations, see the policies entitled "General Purpose Encryption Systems Must Include Key Escrow" and "Encryption Utilities With User-Provided Passwords Or Keys Prohibited." A: T; E: MH.

781. Storing Encryption Keys On Same Media As Protected Data Prohibited

Policy: If encryption is used to protect sensitive data resident on computer storage media, the encryption keys and related encryption keying materials (initialization vectors, time-and-date stamps, salt parameters, etc.) used in the encryption process must not be stored anywhere on this storage media in unencrypted form.

Commentary: The intention of this policy is to prevent a cryptanalyst from taking advantage of the fact that the keying materials are stored on the same data storage media as encrypted data. If these materials are stored together, then the associated encryption process is easily circumvented. Surprising as it may seem, several commercial encryption packages use this approach. Use of hidden files or hidden directories for the unencrypted storage of these keying materials is not acceptable. To put both the keying materials and the encrypted data on the same media is like using tape to affix a front door key to one's locked front door. See the policy entitled "Separate Communication Channel For Data And Encryption Keys." A: T; E: MH.

782. Backup Encryption Keys Provided To Information Security Officer

Policy: If a Company X worker is going to employ encryption for production business information processing activities, the worker must first securely deposit backup copies of all keys with the Information Security Department manager. An exception will be made in those instances where the encryption software to be used includes key escrow functionality approved and tested by the Information Security Department.

Commentary: The intention of this policy is to make up for deficiencies in many encryption software packages. The policy allows an organization to enjoy the benefits of key escrow (the organization specific version, not the government sponsored version), even though the encryption package they are using includes no key escrow functionality. The objective of key escrow is to be able to read the protected data, even if the relevant encryption key is lost or stolen. Key escrow mechanisms can employ a separate skeleton key that allows encrypted data to be decrypted, even when the original encryption key is unavailable. This policy takes a more pedestrian approach whereby backup copies of keys are deposited with a trusted third party, in this case an in-house information security specialist. Note that this policy may be considered to be intrusive by some users because they may want to hide something from management. The policy, in its essence, is not really intrusive because it pertains only to production information, not to personal details. For related ideas, see the policies entitled "All Workstations Must Have Metal Keys To Control Access" and "Encryption Utilities With User-Provided Passwords Or Keys Prohibited." A: E; E: MH.

783. General Purpose Encryption Systems Must Include Key Escrow

Policy: All general purpose encryption processes running on Company X information systems must include key escrow functions. These special functions allow Company X management to recover encrypted information should there be system errors, human errors, or other problems.

Commentary: Although the US government's Clipper chip, key escrow, and key recovery proposals are unlikely to be widely adopted in the manner they were originally proposed over the last decade, the ideas behind them are still of use for information security management purposes. The intent of this policy is to require encryption systems used for regular business activities to employ a system with key escrow. Basically key escrow allows management (or some other trusted party) to circumvent the encryption process when and if needed. A secure process (known as escrow) is needed to protect the special "skeleton key" which allows the encryption process to be broken. This may be required in the event of emergencies, staff unavailability, personnel disputes, or criminal investigations. Without key escrow features, management runs a significant risk that staff will use the power that encryption provides for unintended purposes. For example, staff could use encryption facilities to conceal illegal activities like drug dealing; alternatively, staff could use such facilities to extort money, perhaps by encrypting important information, destroying backup copies, and then demanding payment for the release of the key. Note that the policy does not address encryption processes embedded in information systems, such as the password encryption facilities that go into Novell's NetWare network operating system. It only deals with "general purpose encryption systems," not special purpose encryption systems like those which handle message authentication codes, digital signatures, digital certificates, password encryption, and the like. Separately, the real issue is data held in storage in encrypted form; for that reason, the policy could be changed to exclude encryption for communications systems. Separately, key escrow is needed for stored data accessed via word processing packages and stand-alone encryption utilities. The policy is also consistent with new key escrow encryption system offerings from Bankers Trust (New York, New York, USA) and National Semiconductor (Santa Clara, California, USA). Also see the policies entitled "Automated Encryption Key Management Systems Preferred" and "Deletion Of Readable Data After Encrypted Version Has Been Made." A: T; E: LMH.

784. Digital Signature And User Authentication Keys Must Not Be Escrowed

Policy: Keys used for digital signatures, digital certificates, and user authentication must never be included in a key escrow arrangement. To make these keys available to third parties allows impersonation, which in turn facilitates fraud and deceit.

Commentary: This policy is intended to make sure that users cannot readily repudiate their encryption keys (also called non-repudiation). Repudiation would wreak havoc with legal proceedings which rely on digital signatures or other security mechanisms based on encryption keys. In general, digital signatures and a number of other control measures assume that only the involved user has control over a key (or password). But key escrow is an arrangement whereby encryption keys can be shared with certain parties. For a related idea, see the policy entitled "General Purpose Encryption Systems Must Include Key Escrow." A: T; E: LMH.

785. Explicit Assignment Of Encryption Key Management Functions

Policy: Whenever encryption is used to protect sensitive data, the relevant owner(s) of the data must explicitly assign responsibility for encryption key management.

Commentary: When encryption is employed, responsibility for protecting sensitive data has been changed to responsibility for protecting encryption keys. The protection activity is still needed, even though the quantity of information that needs to be protected shrinks dramatically. Thus, having the owners of the involved data explicitly assign key management responsibilities is important. The intention of this policy is to force owners to explicitly make such an assignment. For more information about owners, see the policy entitled "Information Ownership And Management's Responsibilities." Also see the policy entitled "Automated Encryption Key Management Systems Preferred." A: MT; E: MH.

1.4.2.3. Miscellaneous Encryption Matters

786. Deletion Of Readable Data After Encrypted Version Has Been Made

Policy: Whenever encryption is used, workers must not delete the sole readable version of data unless they have first demonstrated that the encryption process is able to reestablish a readable version of the data.

Commentary: The intention of this policy is to prevent all copies of sensitive data from being lost. Without first checking that an encryption process works, an encryption system malfunction could mean that the only copy of data is lost forever. On a different note, some organizations prefer the more technical term "cleartext" instead of "readable"--a substitution in the policy can easily be made. Separately, some organizations may wish to specify how to demonstrate that an encryption process works. Basically it involves encrypting the data, then decrypting it, and then comparing the result with the original readable version of the data. For this purpose, a file comparison program may be helpful, but is generally not required. See the policy entitled "General Purpose Encryption Systems Must Include Key Escrow." A: ET; E: MH.

787. Separate Keys For Encryption And Digital Signatures

Policy: If both encryption and digital signatures are used, separate keys must be used for each of these two control measures.

Commentary: Use of different keys is in keeping with the security principle of least common mechanism. The intention of this policy is to prevent an adversary who gains possession of one key from compromising both encryption and digital signature systems. If separate keys are used, the "work factor" (amount of effort required to defeat a system) is increased. Unfortunately, with separate keys, both the complexity and the cost of security systems is increased too. Digital signatures are short addendums added to messages (or in some instances files) to reflect the result of an encryption process applied to a message (or in some instances files). Digital signatures are used to show that messages (or files) come from an authorized source and that they have not been tampered with in transit (or during storage). Another name for digital signatures is message authentication codes. For related ideas, see the policies entitled "Storing Encryption Keys On Same Media As Protected Data Prohibited" and "Separate Communication Channel For Data And Encryption Keys." A: T; E: MH.

788. Compression And Encryption Of Sensitive Data To Be Held In Storage

Policy: If secret information is to be stored on a multi-user computer system, it must first be compressed and then encrypted using an approved encryption algorithm.

Commentary: By compressing the data, a good deal of the redundancy in natural languages such as English is eliminated. This makes the job of cryptanalysis considerably more difficult, which in turn helps protect the confidentiality of the data in question. Thus, by first compressing and then encrypting, the strength of the encryption process is enhanced. The intention of this policy is to require systems designers, programmers, and other technical people to implement data compression with encryption, as well as to specify the sequence in which these processes are to be applied to data. Separately, compression can be linked with encryption so that the two processes occur simultaneously, in a manner transparent to the end-user. On another note, "approved encryption algorithms" will be defined by each organization issuing a policy such as this; typically they include DES (the de-jure standard private key process) and RSA (the de-facto standard public key process). The need for external approval and endorsement, such as by government agencies, might also be added to this policy. See the policy entitled "Encryption Processes Must Not Be Used Unless Previously Approved." A: T; E: MH.

789. Tamper Resistant Hardware Modules For Encryption Processes

Policy: All encryption related processes must be performed in tamper-resistant hardware modules rather than in software. This approach minimizes the threat of software reverse engineering and unauthorized disclosure of key(s).

Commentary: Tamper-resistant modules will automatically erase sensitive data, such as encryption keys and initialization vectors, which are held in memory when the modules are opened or tampered with. Such modules are also shielded to prevent the keys and other security-relevant data from being revealed via electro-magnetic emanations. The intention of this policy is thus to require that all encryption processes be implemented using special gear that will increase the security of encryption processes. Such modules remove the keys from manual handling, thus reducing the chances that unauthorized persons will obtain them. Note that in some environments this policy will be difficult or prohibitively costly. For example, if the encryption process is expected to change frequently then each new change will require new hardware. In some cases, "tamper resistant modules" are called "security modules." Beyond encryption, tamper-resistant modules are also appropriate for a number of other security processes such as message authentication code (MAC) calculations, generation of encryption keys, generation of pseudo-random number passwords, etc. Also see the policies entitled "Prevention Of Unauthorized Disclosure Of Encryption Keys," "Electromagnetic Radiation (Emanation) Protection For Secret Systems," and "Disclosure Of Encryption Keys Requires Special Approval." A: T; E: MH.

1.4.3. Dial-Up Computer Communications

790. Insertion Of Computer-Related Contact Numbers In Directories

Policy: Information regarding access to Company X computer and communication systems, such as dial-up modem phone numbers, is considered confidential. This information must NOT be posted on the Internet, listed in telephone directories, placed on business cards, or otherwise made available to third parties without the advance written permission of the Information Systems Department director. Telephone numbers, fax numbers, and Internet electronic mail addresses are permissible exceptions to this policy.

Commentary: The intention of this policy is to prevent system access information from falling into the hands of unauthorized parties, who may then use it to break into Company X systems. Hackers/crackers can often discover such information using publicly-available sources; organizations are well advised to make the job of these people more difficult by withholding this information. Very security-conscious organizations may wish to extend this policy to include user-IDs and similar contact information, although this will make inter-organizational communications decidedly more difficult. For these organizations, in some cases it may be sufficient to prohibit the printing of this information on business cards and the like, at the same time permitting the involved persons to disclose it to specific outsiders on a case-by-case basis. For most organizations, however, the exceptions noted in the last sentence of the policy will be a necessary and customary way to do business. See the policies entitled "Telephone Book Contains Restricted Information," "Disclosure Of Information System Control Specifics To Third Parties," "Disclosure Of Bank Account Numbers," and "Disclosure Of Information In System Log-in Banner." A: ET; E: LMH.

791. Periodic Changes In Computer Communications Line Numbers

Policy: Company X dial-up computer communications telephone numbers must be changed at least once every twelve (12) months.

Commentary: This policy is intended to make it more difficult for hackers, crackers, and other unauthorized parties to locate Company X computer communication numbers. Hackers and crackers frequently trade such information, which means that over time an increasing number of individuals will know the particulars about access to an organization's systems. Changing dial-up numbers periodically can be considered much like changing passwords and encryption keys. At the very least, it will stop many types of unauthorized access that had up to that point in time gone unnoticed. Beyond hackers, crackers, and industrial spies, in many instances covert unnoticed usage is also be carried out by former employees. The time frame (12 months) mentioned in the policy can be changed without significantly altering the impact of the policy; the time frame might, for example, be twenty-four months instead. Many organizations will find this policy disruptive to normal operations, and therefore a clear assessment of the time and effort required to make adjustments to the new telephone numbers should be performed before the policy is adopted. Some organizations consider the impact of changed phone numbers to be too damaging to user and customer relations, and so this policy is unacceptable to them. There are other ways to compensate for not changing the dial-up number, for example, use of dynamic passwords. For related ideas, see the policies entitled "When To Prepare Production Systems Change Documentation" and "Periodic Forced Password Changes." A: T; E: H.

792. Extended User Authentication Systems Required For Dial-Up Lines

Policy: To positively identify the calling party, all inbound dial-up connections with Company X's internal computer data network must employ extended user authentication. These systems include call-back devices, dynamic password software, identity tokens (smart cards), biometrics (thumb-print readers, eye blood vessel readers, voice print readers, etc.), and other approved technologies which provide more security than traditional fixed password systems.

Commentary: The intention behind this policy is to require extra system access controls for every inbound connection with the public switched telephone network (PSTN). The author recommends that the scope of this policy be expanded to include all external network connections (including in-bound Internet connections). Since these interface points have historically been vulnerable spots, extra access controls are warranted. Extended user authentication systems are most often used in conjunction with user-IDs and passwords, although they may also replace user-IDs and/or passwords. Extended user authentication systems are often more expensive, less user-friendly, and more difficult to administer, so this policy can be modified so that it applies only to computer systems which contain particularly sensitive data. Organizations with extensively interconnected systems will find that a limitation of this policy to those machines with particularly sensitive data is relatively meaningless; depending on flow controls (mostly routers) in the internal network, once a user has gained access to a network, he or she may be able to establish connections with a wide variety of machines. Separately, the policy could be modified to make specific reference to certain products and vendors of extended user authentication systems that have been tested and approved by Company X. The inclusion of specific technologies, or even specific vendors, has much to recommend it from a standardization and ease-of-management perspective. Nonetheless, such specificity will mean that the policy has a more limited life. On a separate point, the word "modem" is deliberately not used in the policy because it implies analog communications; the policy should also apply to digital connections such as ISDN (Integrated Services Digital Network), cable modems, and DSL (Digital Subscriber Line). See the policy entitled "Modems On Workstations Connected To Internal Networks." While this policy uses a technological orientation, the policy entitled "Changes To Sensitive, Critical, Or Valuable Information" takes an information-type orientation. Also see the policies entitled "Validating The Identity Of External Parties On The Internet," "Extended User Authentication Required For In-Bound Internet Users," and "Reliance On Operating System User Authentication Process." A: T; E: LMH.

793. Dial-Out User Identity Must Be Authenticated Before Session Established

Policy: All dial-out connections from Company X offices must be established through a dedicated outbound modem pool. All users of these modem pools must have their identities definitively authenticated prior to establishing outbound calls.

Commentary: The intention of this policy is to prevent hackers and other unauthorized parties from engaging in what is called "network weaving." This maneuver involves the establishment of connections through multiple computers on different networks in an effort to thwart attempts to trace the call or log its activity. Hackers, industrial spies, and other unauthorized users are fond of network weaving (also called a "chain of logins") as a way to conceal their activities. This policy helps to ensure that hackers will not be able to dial-out if they have already broken into the systems at Company X. This policy furthermore allows the organization to define who it will authorize to establish outbound dial-up computer connections. Without an access control mechanism on a modem pool (and ideally removal of modems from desktop machines), any process to restrict such access is going to be ineffective. The policy additionally supports the use of a charge back system that allocates the costs of placing long-distance calls to specific departments, individuals, or projects. Note that the standard practice is to authenticate only inbound dial-up users, but that this policy goes beyond that to provide another layer of protection. An exception to this policy may be made for conference rooms or reception areas, where visiting people with portable computers can make outbound connections (or where analog public switched dial network ports may be provided). This exception will not in any way compromise the security provided by the policy since these portable computers are not connected to internal networks the way desktop units of employees typically are. Separately, this policy is deliberately vague about the ways to "definitively authenticate" user identities, which of course often forces the Information Security Department to define exactly what these words mean. The technology to support definitive authentication may in fact change over time without the need to rewrite this policy. For similar ideas, see the policies entitled "Restriction Of Third Party Dial-Up Privileges" and "Extended User Authentication Systems Required For Dial-Up Lines." A: T; E: LMH.

794. Use Of Cable Modems For Business Communications

Policy: Cable modems must not be used for any Company X business communications unless a firewall and a virtual private network (VPN) is employed on the involved computers.

Commentary: Cable modems provide a very fast alternative to dial-up lines, but unfortunately also have a major security deficiency (at least as they have been implemented to date). This security deficiency allows others in the local subnet to examine the activities of the involved user. This in turn could lead to the disclosure of data flowing over the cable modem connection. The speed advantages available with cable modems can, however, be achieved if a firewall and a virtual private network (encrypted channel) is used. No similar problems have been discovered for Digital Subscriber Line (DSL) or Integrated Services Digital Network (ISDN), although requiring a firewall and a VPN circuit is still advisable for these technologies as well. These technologies may be useful for telecommuters when they make connection to an employer's computer via the Internet. For a related policy, see "Extended User Authentication Systems Required For Dial-Up Lines." A: ET; E: LMH.

795. Modems On Workstations Connected To Internal Networks

Policy: Workers are prohibited from connecting dial-up modems to workstations which are simultaneously connected to a local area network (LAN) or another internal communication network.

Commentary: The purpose of this policy is to prohibit users from establishing a weak link in a system of network access controls. So that they may work at home, so that they may work while on a business trip, and so that others may work in real-time with them, users are fond of establishing dial-up modem connections to their workstations (PCs, personal computers, or LAN clients). Unfortunately, if a workstation is also connected to an internal network, such a modem connection can allow unauthorized parties onto the internal network (sometimes without a password or any other access controls). This in turn can allow the unauthorized parties to access intranet servers, connected mainframes, and other systems. While the policy may seem a bit strict, it does allow users to disconnect from an internal network whenever they are using a dial-up modem (the word "simultaneously" is critical here). This policy can be expanded to include Internet connections rather than just dial-up connections; in this case, users would not be allowed to be simultaneously connected to the Internet and also an internal network unless they go through an approved firewall system. Firewall software from vendors like Cypress Systems of McLean, Virginia, is now available to enforce a policy such as this. The policy may also be expanded to include both analog and digital dial-up communications, in which case the word "modem" should be avoided. Also see the policy entitled "Extended User Authentication Systems Required For Dial-Up Lines," "Dial-Up Connections Must Always Utilize Firewalls," "Prior Approval Required For All Communication Line Changes," and "Logging-Off Personal Computers Connected To Networks." A: ET; E: LMH.

796. Direct Dial Connections Prohibited Unless Modem Pool Is Used

Policy: With the exception of portable computers and telecommuting computers, the use of local modems to establish direct dial connections is prohibited. All dial-up connections with Company X systems and networks must be routed through a modem pool which includes an approved extended user authentication security system.

Commentary: The intention of this policy is to plug a security vulnerability which has been in existence at many organizations for a long time (dial-up connections which directly enter microcomputers, alias personal computers). To prevent these types of connections, some organizations will give users a standard computer hardware configuration which deliberately does not include a modem. In this policy, the words "extended user authentication" refer to smart card tokens and challenge/response dynamic password systems like Bellcore's S/Key. These authentication systems are necessary to definitively authenticate the identity of users prior to granting them inbound dial-up communications privileges. If the identity of users has not been reliably established, then privilege controls cannot effectively be enforced. Outbound restrictions in many cases are appropriate because proprietary or confidential information may easily communicated via dial-up lines. Less security-conscious organizations may wish to modify the policy so that it restricts only inbound connections. One of the best ways to enforce this policy is to physically remove modems from desktop hardware. This is because users may be able to enable previously-disabled inbound connections by simply changing the modem set-up parameters. For related ideas, see the policies entitled "Modems On Workstations Connected To Internal Networks" and "Dial-Up Connections Must Always Utilize Firewalls." A: ET; E: MH.

797. Registry Of All Modem Lines And Related Advance Approval Process

Policy: Workers are forbidden from installing or contracting for the installation of modem lines which connect to Company X computers or networks, unless these lines have first been approved by the Telecommunications Department Manager and entered into the organization-wide modem line registry.

Commentary: The intention of this policy is to prohibit users and others from simply calling the telephone company and installing modem lines which then connect to internal computers and networks. The policy puts these people on notice that they must first obtain approval and enter this line in a modem line registry. This registry can be used by information security staff when conducting penetration attacks or other types of risk analyses. Separately, the policy can be used as the basis for disciplinary actions, such as an instance where a worker set-up a modem connection but did not get proper authorization. On another note, the Telecommunications Department Manager should not approve all requests without determining whether internal information systems security would be jeopardized by the new modem line. This manager may require the use of extended user authentication systems (such as dynamic passwords) to further secure the dial-up connection. This manager should also check telephone bills and maintain the registry so that it is up-to-date. The registry may additionally be useful when investigating a computer crime because it shows possible avenues of network entry. In overall terms, this policy works best if an organization has a digital phone system, in which case regular analog modems will not work on the lines which go to each office. Also see the policies entitled "Direct Dial Connections Prohibited Unless Modem Pool Is Used" and "Approval Required For Systems Accepting In-Coming Dial-Up Calls." A: ET; E: LMH.

798. Approval Required For Systems Accepting In-Coming Dial-Up Calls

Policy: Company X workers must not establish any communications systems which accept in-coming dial-up calls unless these systems have first been approved by the Manager of the Information Security Department.

Commentary: The objective of this policy is to prevent inadvertent release of Company X information to outsiders, as well as to prevent workers from establishing unauthorized and insufficiently-secured pathways to access Company X networks. Because dial-up facilities are so widely available, it is relatively easy for even end-users to establish a server or desktop computer with some in-bound dial-up capabilities. To prevent these developments from later being a major embarrassment, there is a need to put users on notice that they must obtain approval for all such systems accessible over dial-up systems. Thus even temporary overnight dial-up access, for example established by plugging a modem into an analog voice line, is prohibited by this policy. Separately, a special and permissible exception may be added to the policy for stand-alone single-application systems such as interactive voice response (IVR) units. Other exceptions may be added, such as the testing of new systems which are not connected to any internal networks. Yet another permissible exception could involve the authorized use of vendor remote maintenance ports. While these exceptions could be mentioned in the policy, it is better to handle them through a risk acceptance process (a known and approved exception process). Many network managers don't really know all of the access points to their network; this policy helps keep the access points to a known and manageable number. Separately, the policy can be expanded to include Internet connections; this would mean that it would prohibit the establishment of any in-bound Internet connections unless management approval was first obtained. The approval process ideally would include a requirement that the connection use an approved access control system (such as a firewall for Internet connections). See the policies entitled "Dial-Up Connections Must Always Utilize Firewalls" and "Prior Approval Required For All Communication Line Changes." A: ET; E: LMH.

799. Prohibition Against Personal Computer Modems In Autoanswer Mode

Policy: Users must not leave modems connected to personal computers in autoanswer mode, such that they are able to receive in-coming dial-up calls.
Commentary: The purpose of this relatively permissive policy is to make sure that users don't go home or leave their desks when their modems are turned on. If users do this, they expose the organization to unauthorized visitors (especially because most of these modem connections have no access control system whatsoever). While the exposure might be serious if the PC in question was used for production purposes, this problem is particularly serious if the PC is connected to an internal network. Rather than prohibiting the use of modems, or even requiring the use of dynamic password systems, this low-security policy simply relies on users to turn their modems off, exit their communications software, or shut down their computers. For related ideas, see the policies entitled "Dial-Up Connections Must Always Utilize Firewalls" and "Extended User Authentication Systems Required For Dial-Up Lines." A: E; E: LM.

800. In-Coming Dial-Up Calls Must Not Be Answered Until Fourth Ring

Policy: All Company X dial-up modems must not answer in-coming calls until the fourth (4th) ring. This will thwart people who seek to gain unauthorized access to Company X computers with programs that identify computer-connected telephone lines. Because the modems don't pick up right away, these programs will erroneously conclude that these modem lines are voice lines.

Commentary: The intention of this policy is to prevent the disclosure of the modem telephone numbers to people who may wish to gain unauthorized access thereby. This policy imposes a slight delay on dial-in callers, yet also is likely to keep these lines off of modem line lists circulated in the underground computer hacker/cracker community. As used in the movie "War Games," automated "demon dialer" programs search for telephone numbers with connected computer modems; they often move on to the next number if no answer is provided after a few rings. In some cases, these programs are also called "war dialers." The last two explanatory sentences in this policy can be deleted for those organizations that prefer streamlined policies. Also see the policies entitled "Difficult-To-Guess Passwords Required" and "Maximum Permissible Password Attempts For Dial-Up Users." A: T; E: LMH.

801. Department Management Responsible For Dial-Up Compliance

Policy: Dial-up connections to internal systems and networks may be established by developers, system administrators, and others as long as they are fully consistent with published internal standards. Before dial-up connections are turned on, the manager of the department making the installation must make sure that these standards have been followed. All deviations from these standards must be approved in advance by the manager of the Information Security Department.

Commentary: Besides controlling unauthorized dial-up access, the intention of this policy is in part to reduce the work required by the Information Security group. This policy transfers responsibility for checking compliance with internal standards to local department management. Dial-up connections have become so common -- especially in the wake of telecommuting and mobile computing -- that they are often best managed on a local basis. In the era of decentralized and distributed computing, local management is often in the only position to exercise control over changes made to systems. This policy assumes that internal standards defining how to establish secure connections already exist (the very existence of such standards will also significantly reduce the amount of dial-up approval work required by the Information Security Department). Since dial-up lines are often used by hackers and other unauthorized parties to gain network access, this policy responds to one of the most pressing vulnerabilities in small systems (LANs, PCs, intranets, etc.) today. For related ideas, see the policies entitled "Dial-Up Connections Must Always Utilize Firewalls" and "Restriction Of Third Party Dial-Up Privileges." A: ET; E: LMH.

802. Maximum Permissible Password Attempts For Dial-Up Users

Policy: If a computer user attempting to gain access via a dial-up line has not provided a correct password after three (3) consecutive attempts, the connection must be immediately terminated.

Commentary: The intention of this policy is to prevent password guessing programs from cracking passwords used for dial-up access. Dial-up lines are frequently the avenue by which unauthorized users gain access to systems, so this policy addresses a major vulnerability found at many organizations. This approach, however, is not without its drawbacks. For example, attackers can immediately call back, but the password guessing process will take much longer and be much more expensive than it would be in the absence of this approach. Another good approach, used by organizations with custom-programmed access control systems, involves the progressive elongation of the time period between each attempt. In this case, the delay between the prompt for a user-ID and a password for the first log-in attempt employing a certain user-ID might be one second, between the second and third attempt might be two seconds, etc. This approach makes it infeasible to successfully use password guessing programs to try a large number of possibilities. On another note, this policy may be expanded to include Internet connections, in which case all in-bound Internet users would have the session dropped if they failed to provide a correct password after a certain number of attempts. A delay between log-in attempts using the same user-ID may then be imposed; this is the approach used by Novell's NetWare for supervisor user-IDs. This policy has historically been used for fixed password access control systems, but is also applicable to dynamic password systems. Also see the policies entitled "In-Coming Dial-Up Calls Must Not Be Answered Until Fourth Ring" and "Limit On Consecutive Unsuccessful Attempts To Enter A Password." A: T; E: LMH.

1.4.4. Down-Loaded Data

803. Process For Down-Loading Software From An Internet Mirror Site

Policy: Since software resident on Internet mirror sites may be corrupted with viruses or Trojan horses, Company X strongly discourages the use of mirror sites if the sought-after software can be downloaded directly from a known and trusted source. If a mirror site is used, it must be a well-known site and software verification tools like digital signatures must be employed to ensure that the software has not been corrupted.

Commentary: This policy is intended to direct technical staff on the safe way to down-load software over the Internet. Many popular information security tool sites like coast.cs.purdue.edu:/pub/tools are mirrored throughout the Internet. Because the integrity of the software resident on mirror sites is questionable, those people performing downloads should use only well-known sites as well as digital signature technology (like MD5 checksums) to ensure that the code has not been changed. While downloading software updates via the Internet is riskier than getting a CD-ROM directly from a vendor, it is much faster and often lower-cost. Separately, this policy assumes that no prohibition against down-loading software exists for technical staff, but such a prohibition could nonetheless still exist for other types of users. For related ideas, see the policies entitled "Prohibition Against Down-Loading Software From Third Party Systems" and "Free Software May Not Be Used For Production Applications." A: T; E: LMH.

804. Controls Needed For Down-Loading Sensitive Company X Information

Policy: Before any secret, confidential, or private information may be transferred from one computer to another, the person making the transfer must make sure that access controls on the destination computer are commensurate with access controls on the originating computer. If comparable security cannot be provided with the destination system's access controls, then the information must not be down-loaded.

Commentary: The intention of this policy is to force users to consider the security implications of down-loading (sometimes called "down-line-loading") sensitive information. Down-loading of information has been a significant security problem because controls on destination systems (particularly small-scale systems like PCs) are often more lax than those on the originating system. Down-loading can also be a problem because, in many instances, data sensitivity labels are not propagated from one operating system to another; for more about sensitivity labels, see the policy entitled "Four Category Data Classification Scheme." Another intention of the policy is to prohibit the down-loading of sensitive information that cannot be adequate protected. In this respect, the policy is a manifestation of the notion that information should be protected in a manner commensurate with its sensitivity, value, and criticality, no matter where the information resides and no matter what form it takes. Down-loading (sometimes without a hyphen -- "downloading") can take place over the Internet, via dial-up line, via on-line service bureau, and other methods. Separately, although it would imply significant changes in wording, this policy could be expanded to include controls over paper and other forms that the information may take after it is taken off a computer system with access controls. On a separate note, this policy is likely to generate calls to the Information Security Department because users will have questions about what the word "commensurate" means at Company X. These questions are justified and present a significant opportunity for information security staff to educate end-users and also to stay in touch with proposed changes in production systems. One way to reduce these inquiries is to employ control categories such as low-, medium-, and high-security systems with a definition of the controls that accompany each category. On another note, this policy assumes the words "secret, confidential, or private" have been defined elsewhere; see the policy entitled "Four Category Data Classification Scheme" for further details. Also see the policy entitled "Consistent Protection Of Information Regardless Of Manifestation." A: ET; E: LMH.

805. Down-Loading Sensitive Information Prohibited Without Permission

Policy: Sensitive Company X information may be down-loaded from a multi-user system to a microcomputer (PC) or a workstation ONLY after two conditions have been fulfilled. For this data transfer to take place, a clear business need must exist AND advance permission from the information owner must be obtained. This policy is not intended to cover electronic mail or memos, but does apply to databases, master files, and other information stored on mainframes, minicomputers, servers, and other multi-user machines.

Commentary: The down-loading (sometimes called "down-line-loading") of sensitive information continues to be insufficiently addressed in most organizations. Any information that a user of a mainframe, minicomputer, or departmental server can display at the same time can often be captured on a hard drive or floppy disk at a microcomputer (PC) or a workstation. In the absence of viable generally-available technical controls to take care of this problem, this policy defines acceptable behavior. The policy thus relies on people rather than technological controls. The intention of the policy is to clearly delineate the circumstances under which down-loading of data is prohibited; by implication, all other down-loading operations are permissible. This policy assumes that the important word "sensitive" has been defined; see the policy entitled "Four Category Data Classification Scheme." The notion of information ownership is covered in the policy entitled "Information Ownership And Management's Responsibilities." For additional information on similar topics, see the policy entitled "Controls Needed For Down-Loading Sensitive Company X Information" and "Prohibition Against Down-Loading Software From Third Party Systems." A: ET; E: LMH.

806. Automatic Device Synchronization Allowed Only With Permission

Policy: Systems which automatically exchange data between devices, such as a Personal Digital Assistant (PDA) and a personal computer, must not be enabled unless the systems have first been evaluated and approved by the Information Security Department.

Commentary: The intention of this policy is to prevent the inadvertent release of sensitive information to unauthorized parties, and to prevent operational problems which could have otherwise been avoided. The policy is prompted by the recent development of a wide variety of devices which automatically synchronize files such as directories between various devices including palmtop computers. While these systems employ useful and attractive technologies, they may also inadvertently release information to unauthorized persons. For example if a radio frequency (RF) broadcast is autonomously initiated between two devices, and if this transmission is not encrypted, the information sent might be intercepted by and used by third parties.

Likewise, unless certain device IDs are employed (as is the case with the Bluetooth standard developed by Ericsson, IBM, Intel and others), the information in question may be transferred to the wrong device, overwriting important files, thereby destroying important data, and otherwise causing operational problems. Evaluation by the Information Security Department ensures that these systems incorporate the necessary controls to be consistent with existing information security measures at the organization in question. Separately, because they work autonomously, sometimes these devices are called "silicon cockroaches." On another note, this policy does not prohibit the use of devices which have these features, it simply informs users not to utilize these features without advance permission. For related ideas, see the policies entitled "Clock Synchronization For Accurate Logging Of Events On Network" and "Secret Discussions On Wireless Microphones And Radio Networks." A: E; E: H.

1.4.5. Telephone Systems

807. Collect And Third-Party Bill-To Calls Prohibited On Voicemail Lines

Policy: Administrators in charge of Company X voicemail systems must make arrangements with the involved telephone company so that both collect and third party bill-to calls are prohibited on voicemail telephone lines. This will prevent hackers and other unauthorized parties from using the voicemail system at Company X's expense.

Commentary: When hackers get into a voicemail system, they often create their own mailboxes and then record outgoing messages that accept collect and third party bill-to calls. Beyond requiring long passwords for all regular user accounts and the system administrator's account, the system administrator should contact the relevant phone company and make arrangements to prohibit the calls mentioned in this policy. Many phone companies will do this at no extra charge; some will do it only if there have been some abuses in the past. Logically, it does not make sense to allow collect or third party bill-to calls coming into a voicemail system, so the limits imposed by this policy only close a back-door security vulnerability that could be exploited. In some cases this prohibition could be applied to regular telephone numbers. For example, using a personal phone line, an employee could make calls to phone-sex or other special service numbers, and then have these calls billed to Company X's telephone number. Also see the policy entitled "Leaving Sensitive Information On Answering Machines." A: T; E: LMH.

808. Disable Area Code 900 Calls On All Company X PBXs

Policy: Administrators in charge of Company X private branch exchange (PBX) systems must program PBX systems so that all area code 900 calls are prohibited. This will prevent unauthorized calls to information services--many of which are expensive--from being billed to Company X.

Commentary: The intention of this policy is to prevent Company X from being charged for unauthorized information service calls (such as sex talk party lines). In the process of prohibiting area code 900 calls (including 976, or whatever the local equivalents happen to be), Company X may inadvertently make it difficult for employees to obtain some information which they legitimately need to get their work done. This is, however, a rare occurrence, and these calls can be made using other phones such as a pay telephone along with a Company X telephone credit card. This policy could be broadened to include a prohibition on international calls originating from certain telephone stations (such as a retail store clerk's line). Likewise, cellular phones billed to Company X could have international calls blocked. Also see the policy entitled "Placement Of Telephone Credit Card Calls Through PBX Systems." A: T; E: LMH.

809. PBX Defined Calling Areas Must Be Restricted

Policy: To reduce the incidence of fraud, the numbers reachable via Company X PBXs must be restricted to only those needed for ordinary business purposes.
Commentary: The intention of this policy is to prevent telephone toll fraud (perpetrated by authorized users as well as external attackers, or so-called "phreaks"). A good deal of the fraud now encountered involves calls to certain less industrialized countries from businesses in more industrialized countries. So long as business activities would not be unduly hampered, organizations can prevent fraud if they block calls to these less industrialized countries. In some instances, such as for cellular phones, it is appropriate to block all international calls. In other instances, such as a shared factory floor phone, all long-distance domestic calls can be blocked. In certain business situations like as retail stores, only emergency out-bound calls (911 in the USA) and incoming calls will be allowed. Phone users can go through human attendants (operators) if they really need to reach an area that has been blocked. Certain area codes that assess additional charges, such as 900 in the USA, can also be blocked. Also see the policies entitled "Workers Must Not Return Area Code 900 Or Similar Calls" and "Privilege Restriction Based On the Need-to-Know." A: T; E: LMH.

810. Workers Must Not Return Area Code 900 or Similar Calls

Policy: Company X workers must not return regular phone calls or respond to pager phone calls where the return number has a 900 area code, where charges beyond those for normal telephone calls can be assessed, or where the charges will be reversed.

Commentary: One of the most lucrative scams going around these days involves the use of auto-dialers which seek pager numbers. These systems then leave a 900 area code number, and workers often dutifully return the call. For readers outside the USA, area code 900 numbers result in steep charges per minute (and are often used for telephone sex lines and the like). This policy accordingly seeks to sensitize workers to these frauds, instructing them not to return the call. The policy could be expanded to include mention of hanging up as soon as they hear that they will be assessed additional charges; in the USA, a brief introductory message is required so that the caller can determine whether he/she wishes to continue. Also see the policy entitled "Collect And Third-Party Bill-To Calls Prohibited On Voicemail Lines." A: ET; E: LMH.

811. Unusual Phone Operation Requests Must Be Denied And Reported

Policy: Unusual telephone operation requests, such as a caller asking for an outside line, must be consistently but politely denied. The circumstances and particulars of the request must then be immediately reported to the Telecommunications Department manager.

Commentary: The intention of this policy is to prevent outside parties from taking advantage of sophisticated phone system features in order to get a free outside line. The particular requests will vary by geographical location as well as PBX or other phone system in use. For example, in California there has been a wave of callers asking the person answering the phone to type "90#." If the person answering the phone does as requested (usually because they don't know why not, and they are trying to be helpful and polite), this will give the inbound caller a free line to call nationally or internationally. These connections are very useful for hackers who may want to conceal their tracks and have other people pay the bill for their calls. If the Telecommunications Department manager receives reports about a number of calls with a particular unusual request, he or she may choose to issue a memo to all staff (perhaps by email) reminding them about this policy. This policy will also help to prevent staff members from being victims of "social engineering" or "spoofing" ploys where the caller at the other end of a phone line makes believe that he or she is somebody authorized, when in fact that is not the case. The policy writer should note that this policy is intended for all users of a phone system, not just telephone operators. For a related idea, see the policy entitled "Reporting Unauthorized Data Changes & Questionable System Use." A: E; E: LMH.

812. Leaving Sensitive Information On Answering Machines

Policy: Workers must refrain from leaving messages containing sensitive information on answering machines or voicemail systems. This will help ensure that the information is communicated only to the intended party.

Commentary: The purpose of this policy is to put workers on notice that the person picking up messages on a message machine may not be authorized to receive sensitive information. Accordingly, workers should simply ask the intended recipient of the information to call them back. Not only can the person receiving the message be other than the intended recipient, but hackers can pick up messages off answering machines without ever having to physically access the answering machine (and sometimes without revealing the fact that they listened to the messages as well). This policy can be expanded to include prohibition on the use of remote access facilities that allow people to pick up messages from a different location--but this is likely to be burdensome and unpopular with the user community. The policy could also be expanded to include mention of leaving sensitive information on alphanumeric pagers. See the policies entitled "Discussion Of Secret Information And Use Of Speaker Phones," "Dictation Machines And Tape Recorders For Sensitive Information," "Collect And Third-Party Bill-To Calls Prohibited On Voicemail Lines," and "Use Of Cordless Or Cellular Telephones For Secret Discussions." A: ET; E: LMH.

813. Voicemail Passwords Not Subject To Password Construction Standards

Policy: Voicemail passwords need not be in compliance with Company X password construction standards because the information accessible via voicemail is quite limited in volume and short-term in nature. Users must, however, still pick a voicemail password which is different from their phone extension, their office number, their employee number, or any other number which could be easily guessed.

Commentary: The intention of this policy is to clarify why the minimum number of characters in voicemail passwords is typically fewer than the minimum for computer passwords. Some users have complained that their organization isn't living up to its own standards by not requiring the voicemail system to comply with a password construction standard. This policy explains why such compliance is not necessary, but at the same time reinforces the need to choose a strong (difficult-to-guess) password. Separately, this policy could be augmented by stating the minimum number of digits in a voicemail password. This type of password is really a personal identification number, or PIN, because only ten digits are available. Because the key space (a technical term for the number of possibilities) for a voicemail password with certain number of digits is quite limited, he author suggests that voicemail passwords be at least eight digits long. Separately, this policy is explicit about exceptions and in that respect is consistent with the ideas expressed in the policy entitled "Risk Acceptance Process And Permissible Exceptions To Policies." For other ideas, see the policies entitled "Difficult-To-Guess Passwords Required" and "Leaving Sensitive Information On Answering Machines." A: E; E: LMH.

814. Heard Voicemail Messages Deleted After One Month In Storage

Policy: Voicemail users are encouraged to check their voicemail at least once every business day and to promptly transfer information such as telephone numbers from voicemail to other storage media. All voicemail messages which have been heard and saved will be deleted after one month in the system.

Commentary: The objective of this policy is to get voicemail users to promptly remove their messages from the system, and to refrain from using the system as a database. This approach will help foster prompt response to requests from customers, prospects, vendors and others. This approach will also help minimize the sensitive information which is available via the voicemail system at any particular point in time, thus lowering the chances that unauthorized disclosures will take place via the voicemail system. This policy will furthermore lower the disk space requirements for a voicemail system, which these days often runs on an ordinary personal computer. For similar ideas, see the policies entitled "Daily Removal Of Logs From Internet-Accessible Computers," "Retaining Personal Information Only As Long As Needed For Business," and "Periodic Destruction Of Archived Electronic Mail Messages." A: E; E: LMH.

815. Placement Of Telephone Credit Card Calls Through PBX Systems

Policy: Workers must avoid the placement of direct dial telephone credit card calls though Private Branch Exchange (PBX) systems such as are used by many organizations and hotels. These PBX systems often record the credit card number and accompanying personal identification number. This information may later be used to place fraudulent calls. Where PBX systems are known to exist, workers should make their calls from a public telephone or another direct line.

Commentary: The intention of this policy is to prevent telephone credit card numbers and accompanying PINs from being recorded in call detail records. This will in turn prevent these records from being used as a source of credit card numbers that can facilitate fraudulent toll calls. When using a PBX system, workers could provide their credit card number and PIN to an operator verbally (not via a touch tone pad), but this runs the risk of someone overhearing the numbers. For this reason, verbal handling of numbers was not mentioned in the policy. Depending on the recipient audience for this policy, the term "PBX" may need to be defined more specifically. Also see the policy entitled "Disable Area Code 900 Calls On All Company X PBXs." A: EMT; E: LMH.

816. Use Of Credit Cards On Public Pay Phones

Policy: While using public pay phones, whenever circumstances permit, workers must swipe telephone or other credit cards rather than typing or speaking the numbers for bill-to information.

Commentary: This toll fraud related policy seeks to prevent bill-to numbers from falling into the hands of criminals, juveniles, and others who would use these numbers to place fraudulent calls. It is increasingly common for these people to listen-to, watch, or video tape other people entering their bill-to information into a keypad at a public phone. The video tape scam is perhaps the easiest because the tape can later be replayed in slow-motion repeatedly until the numbers can be ascertained. Likewise, if the bill-to information is spoken, other people can overhear it and later use it. The safest way to prevent these and related abuses is to swipe a credit card through the readers found in many pay phones. Some public phones will not have readers; this is one reason why the words "whenever circumstances permit" were used in the policy. Another reason is that Company X workers may not have a bill-to credit card with them. Separately, another reason to use bank credit cards (notably VISA and Mastercard) is that the liability of the user for fraudulent charges is limited to $50, and in many instances is waived entirely. Also see the policies entitled "Positioning Of Computer Display Screens With Respect To Windows" and "Reporting Lost/Stolen Identification Badges And System Access Tokens." A: E; E: LMH.

817. PBX - DISA Features Require Fraud Detection Facilities

Policy: Company X sites are prohibited from enabling the direct inward system access (DISA) features on private branch exchange (PBX) telephone systems unless they are accompanied by a fraud detection and limitation system approved by the Manager of Telecommunications.

Commentary: Reliable estimates now mark the cost to US business for toll fraud perpetrated via the DISA features of PBX systems at $3 billion per year. As a result, many telecommunications experts instruct phone system administrators to simply disable the DISA feature. DISA can actually save an organization a significant amount of money if implemented securely. With DISA systems, a caller places an 800 area code call to an organization's PBX, then using the PBX to place outgoing long distance calls, thus taking advantage of dedicated access virtual network or contract tariff plans. The intent of this policy is to prevent the use of DISA facilities unless they are accompanied by special fraud detection and caller privilege disabling systems. One example of such a system is provided by Northern Telecom (Washington, DC, USA). Separately, this policy is based on the assumption that user organizations will, at least for the near term, continue to be responsible for toll fraud losses. A pending rule proposed by the US Federal Communications Commission (FCC) that will shift liability for fraudulent telephone use to carriers and PBX manufacturers will alter the need for this policy because these carriers and manufacturers will be likely to build adequate security into their systems, rather than offer it as an option. In addition, recent toll fraud insurance coverage provided by some carriers like SPRINT will lessen the need for a policy like this. Also see the policies entitled "Use Of Credit Cards On Public Pay Phones" and "Required Investigation Following Computer Crimes." A: T; E: LMH.

818. Telephone Book Contains Restricted Information

Policy: Internal telephone books must not be distributed to third parties without specific authorization of a department manager. Contractors, consultants, temporaries and other third parties working for Company X may, of course, receive telephone books in order to perform their jobs.

Commentary: The intention of this policy is to change the way people have been thinking about the information contained in an internal telephone book. As a reflection of this, many organizations have now added the words "confidential" or "restricted" to each page in their telephone books, or at the very least on the cover. Telephone books may be used by recruiters (head-hunters) to locate people who they can hire away. In a similar manner, industrial spies could use a telephone book to identify workers they wanted to bribe, pressure, dupe, or otherwise exploit. Hackers could also use telephone books to identify modem numbers and other system-related numbers (like a help desk). Industrial spies could additionally use telephone books as a way to figure out which people they could best masquerade as when doing social engineering. Separately, this policy can be taken one step further by restricting the dissemination of information contained in the phone book. For example, if someone (usually a sales person) were to call Company X asking for the phone number and name of the director of the Information Systems Department, a telephone operator would be forbidden from releasing this information. This more restrictive policy was not written-up as a separate policy because the author considers it to be most unfriendly to prospective and existing customers (it may, however, be appropriate for military organizations). A consequence of designating an internal phone book as confidential is that it needs to be disposed of properly (shredded usually); some companies place words on the cover saying: "After New Book Is Issued, Return This Book To The Security Department For Secure Disposal." See the policy entitled "Insertion Of Computer-Related Contact Numbers In Directories." A: ET; E: LMH.

819. Two-Party Consent For All Speaker Phone Use Or Tape Recording

Policy: When using a telephone, workers must not use speaker phones, microphones, loud-speakers, tape recorders, or similar technologies unless they have first obtained the consent of both the originator(s) and recipient(s) of the call.

Commentary: The objective of this policy is to make sure that both parties know that other people are listening or could later be listening to the conversation. The originator(s) or the recipient(s) of the call are likely to speak differently when they know about the other people who might hear the conversation. If only one party to a conversation--perhaps the originator--knows about the use of such equipment, it is then a violation of wiretap statutes in ten states in the US. Although the US Federal Communications Commission requires the consent of the two (or more) parties to a conversation whenever such equipment is to be used, it no longer requires that a "beep tone" notify parties of the use of this equipment. Also see the policies entitled "Performance Monitoring Information And Relevance To The Job" and "Areas Where Electronic Monitoring Of Workers May Be Used." A: EM; E: LMH.

820. Special Permission Required To Record Video-Conferencing Sessions

Policy: Company X video-conferencing sessions must not be recorded unless this recording is (1) approved in advance by the manager of information security, and (2) communicated in advance to all video-conference participants.

Commentary: The intention of this policy is to prevent legal liability in the years ahead. If video-conferencing sessions are not recorded, they cannot be obtained during discovery proceedings or other legal maneuvers. In some ways similar to a policy at many organizations requiring the routine destruction of outdated electronic mail messages, this policy seeks to prevent sensitive internal information from being used in unintended and detrimental ways. This policy also helps to limit the amount of information that organizations must manage. For a related idea, see the policy entitled "Monitoring Or Recording Telephone Conversations." A: T; E: LMH.

821. Use Of Telephones For Personal Purposes

Policy: Company X telephones are provided to facilitate business activities. Telephones must not be used for personal purposes, unless the calls cannot be made during off-business hours. In these cases, the personal calls must be kept to a reasonable length.

Commentary: The intention of this policy is to clarify what is acceptable behavior regarding the use of the telephone system for personal purposes. This policy is a practical middle-of-the-road position reflecting a mix of the strict position that telephones must never be used for personal purposes, and the acknowledgement that workers will need to make personal calls to arrange baby-sitters, check to see if the mechanic has fixed their car, etc. A more stringent approach would involve prohibition of all personal use unless it relates to personal arrangements; thus friendly chats and personal visits would be prohibited. This more stringent policy is focused to a greater extent on reduced telephone expenses, while both versions help increase worker productivity. See the policies entitled "Personal Use Of Computer And Communications Systems," "Internet Use For Personal Purposes Prohibited," and "Personal Use Of Electronic Mail Systems." A: ET; E: LMH.

822. Reimbursement For Personal Telephone Calls

Policy: Company X telephones must not be used to place personal long-distance calls unless the calls are kept to a reasonable length, reported to management, and reimbursed to the Company.

Commentary: The intention of this policy is to clarify the use of Company X telephones for personal purposes, especially for long distance calls. Emphasis on long distance is appropriate because this is where the major expense for personal calls will be found. This policy implicitly permits local personal calls without the need to report or reimburse them. Some organizations may wish to add an additional sentence requiring that employees use a special accounting code to flag personal calls. In this case, a listing of personal calls can later be presented to employees for payment (or automatically deducted from their paycheck). Without such an accounting code entered at the time that a call is placed, it will be difficult in many situations to determine which calls were personal and which were business related. Separately, the words "reasonable length" were used in the policy to keep the productivity impact of such calls down. On another note, in the years ahead it will be increasingly difficult to determine which calls are long distance and which are not; the traditional way to do this was the provision of eleven digits rather than seven digits, but even local calls in some areas will soon be eleven digits (due to area code overlays). Are more precise definition of "long distance" will then be necessary (international calls may also be used instead). See the policy entitled "Use Of Telephones For Personal Purposes." A: E; E: LMH.

823. Maintaining Accurate Records To Prevent Unwanted Telemarketing

Policy: Company X must maintain records keeping track of prospects who have informed the company they do not wish receive sales-related telephone calls. These records must be employed by Company X sales representatives to prevent unwanted calls.

Commentary: This policy is intended to prevent certain potential customers from receiving telemarketing calls from Company X if the potential customers have previously indicated that they do not want to receive such calls. The policy will indirectly prevent public relations problems by preventing calls that could lead to embarrassing lawsuits, newspaper editorials, consumer boycotts, and the like. The policy is fully consistent with the US Telephone Consumer Protection Act, which forbids companies from making marketing calls to the homes of people who tell them not to. The 17 December 1993 issue of The Wall Street Journal describes a case where Citibank was sued for violation of this statute. The policy is also relevant to automated calling systems that handle calls via pre-recorded messages (sometimes called ADADS-- automatic dialing and announcing devices). See the policy entitled "Prohibition Against Sexual, Ethnic, And Racial Harassment" and "Warnings Required If Recipients Might Be Offended Or Upset." A: MT; E: LMH.

824. Orders To Change Internal Records Placed Via Phone

Policy: Orders to change any internal Company X records that are placed over the phone will not be honored unless the identity of the caller has first been verified by approved procedures.

Commentary: This policy is intended to define the circumstances under which telephone representations will be given credibility and be used as input for the update of internal records (be the records computer-resident or not). The process by which a caller's identity is verified can be as simple as providing a social security number or a telephone number, although neither of these are especially effective because this information is available publicly. It is better to call the involved party back at a predetermined number and then to verbally confirm that the transaction should proceed. (In the years ahead, caller ID -- also known as automatic number identification or ANI -- will meet this call back need without the need to place a separate confirming call.) The call back process is, for example, now used when money is being wired to another person using a credit card via Western Union. But even this can be defeated by call forwarding. To provide a higher level of security, a predetermined transfer code or special-use password is recommended; this process is generally employed for bank funds transfer orders placed by phone. The need for a policy like this was clearly shown by the 1995 incident where the alleged chief financial officer of Sybase (a database company located in Berkeley, California, USA) called the NASDAQ stock exchange and instructed the exchange to halt trading on Sybase's stock. NASDAQ officials relied on the instructions and suspended trading without confirming the individual's identity. Later it came to light that the whole affair was a prank intended to artificially inflate the price of Sybase stock (for details see The Wall Street Journal, 4 August 1995, pp. C1-C2). The scope of this policy could be expanded to include faxed orders, and in the near future should also include electronic mail orders. The notion of confirming the identity of callers can also be applied to those circumstances where callers request internal-use-only and more sensitive information. For related ideas, see the policies entitled "Reconstructibility Of Changes To Production Information" and "Authorization For Changes To Production Data And Programs." A: ET; E: MH.

825. Conference Bridge Activated Only When Needed

Policy: Conference bridges must be specifically activated only when needed. They must not be left in an activated state when authorized staff are not using them.

Commentary: The intention of this policy is to prevent unauthorized toll fraud. A favorite scam taking place these days involves a conference bridge left in an enabled state. Hackers/phreakers will sit on the bridge and accept third party collect calls for other hackers/phreakers. They may then place additional unauthorized outgoing calls through the bridge which in turn will be charged to the organization. Thus a conference bridge may be used to achieve "network weaving" where the work of a hacker/phreaker is concealed because he has traversed so many different systems and networks. These people may also take over a conference bridge and use it for their own purposes, such as exchanging stolen credit card numbers. To thwart these antics, conference bridges (effectively conference calling systems) can be controlled with passwords or other security mechanisms. For related ideas, see the policies entitled "Restriction Of Third Party Dial-Up Privileges" and "Leaving Sensitive Systems Without Logging-Off." A: T; E: LMH.

826. Computer Support Identification Codes

Policy: Unless the voice of a calling party is definitively recognized, the identity of persons placing telephone calls requesting computer support must be authenticated via a special identification code. This identification code is different from a computer password, must not be the same as a computer password, and is intended to be disclosed to authorized internal staff.

Commentary: The intent of this policy is to thwart what is called "social engineering." Social engineering involves masquerading as an authorized person, such as an executive. Industrial spies, systems hackers, and others frequently use social engineering in an effort to obtain employee numbers, telephone numbers, addresses, passwords, and other information that may be useful when it comes to accessing computers and networks. Because passwords should be known only by the person to whom they relate, computer passwords are not an appropriate way for staff to authenticate their identity to computer support staff (systems administrators, information security officers, help desk staff, telephone system operators, etc.). Likewise, employee numbers, social security numbers, or other readily-obtainable numbers specific to each worker are not definitive ways to authenticate the identity of internal staff. Computer support identification codes should only be available to those staff who have a bona fide need to know. In some organizations, use of these identification codes may be expanded to include release of sensitive information like salary and benefits information over the phone (or perhaps via a kiosk). Note that organizational culture may need to be slightly changed so that these codes are regularly used, lest the party who has been reached refrain from requesting a code in an effort to appear polite. Also see the policies entitled "System Access Control With Individualized Passwords (Not Lockwords)" and "Orders To Change Internal Records Placed Via Phone." A: T; E: MH.

1.4.6. Electronic Mail Systems

827. Using An Electronic Mail Account Assigned To Another Individual

Policy: Workers must not use an electronic mail account assigned to another individual to either send or receive messages. If there is need to read another's mail (while they are away on vacation for instance), message forwarding and other facilities must instead be used.

Commentary: This policy is intended to reinforce the notion that each user should have their own electronic mail user-ID, and that users should not share these user-IDs under any circumstances. The policy implicitly prohibits group accounts--a favorite way for some organizations to save system administration overhead costs. Although specific to electronic mail, the idea behind the policy is generalizable to other types of user-IDs (system log-in user-IDs, telephone credit cards, Internet user-IDs, on-line service provider use-IDs, etc.). The policy will help maintain the veracity and usefulness of electronic mail system logs, while at the same time reducing the confusion that might come about when someone uses another's account. The policy additionally supports the enforcement of privilege restrictions that may be associated with specific accounts. A written policy such as this also establishes electronic mail masquerading as a prohibited act, making termination and less severe forms of punishment justifiable responses. On a different note, this policy also prohibits a favorite tactic of those who send unsolicited bulk commercial email, also known as spam, in order to avoid tracing messages back to the true originator. For another perspective about sharing accounts, see the policy entitled "Unique User-ID And Password Required." Also see the policies entitled "Secret Information Sent By Electronic Mail," "Monitoring Of Electronic Mail Messages," "Worker Rights To Read Third Party Electronic Mail Messages," and "System Access Control With Individualized Passwords (Not Lockwords)." A: ET; E: LMH.

828. Using Electronic Mail Addresses Other Than Official Company X Addresses

Policy: Workers must not employ any electronic mail addresses other than official Company X electronic mail addresses for company business messages.

Commentary: The intention of this policy is to prevent workers from using Hotmail, and other free electronic mail services, as well as personal Internet service provider (ISP) accounts for company business. Some employees may be tempted to use these outside services because they can circumvent the controls that the organization has implemented for official company electronic mail. For example, by using a an unauthorized external address, message content screening systems may be circumvented. Likewise, by using an unauthorized external address, archival storage of all electronic mail will not be performed. Furthermore, use of an external address may allow virus-infected attachments to electronic mail messages to enter an internal network. This policy is additionally recommended because it helps to present a professional and organized image to customers and other third parties. When customers get electronic mail from a free services domain or some other external address besides the company in question, they may doubt the professionalism of the sending organization. An additional motivation for this policy involves prevention of confusion about personal use of company information systems; if workers are sending business messages on their personal accounts, and sending personal messages on their business accounts, it will be difficult to sort out whether the worker was using excessive amounts of business information system resources for personal purposes. Separately, at certain organizations, this policy may need to have a caveat added which would allow such outside addresses to be used in the event of an emergency or a disaster. For related ideas, see the policies entitled "Using An Electronic Mail Account Assigned To Another Individual" and "Forwarding Electronic Mail To An External Network Address." A: E; E: LMH.

829. Sender Contact Information Must Be Included In Electronic Mail

Policy: To facilitate communications and to properly identify the sending party, all electronic mail sent using Company X information systems must contain the sender's first and last name, job title, organizational unit, and telephone number.

Commentary: With the current state of Internet electronic mail technology, it's easy to spoof an electronic mail message (masquerade as another). This policy requires all who use Company X information systems to include a standard set of sender contact details in all electronic mail. This is an easy to meet requirement because many people simply have this information stored in a separate file (a so-called signature file, which is different from a digital signature) which can be quickly appended to each message (some electronic mail systems like Eurdora from Qualcom, San Diego, California, USA, will do this automatically). This policy also helps prevent confusion in those cases where messages have been forwarded or where excerpts are included in other messages. The policy additionally is useful because it requires all senders of electronic mail to identity themselves, even if the electronic mail passes through a remailer (a forwarding facility which strips off the sender's identity). Thus, in an indirect way, this policy encourages business use rather than personal use of electronic mail systems. Requiring identification also helps deter abuse and allows problem individuals to be more readily contacted so that inappropriate behavior can be changed. This policy also makes anonymous electronic mail, which might be harassing or derogatory in nature, against policy. On a related note, some organizations can expand this policy to include legal disclaimer notices (such as "messages don't necessarily reflect Company X policy") or notices of message monitoring and archival storage, either or both of which could be required at the end of each electronic mail message. For related ideas, see the policies entitled "Anonymous User-IDs" and "Using An Electronic Mail Account Assigned To Another Individual." A: E; E: LMH.

830. Clearly Identified Source For Electronic Mail Marketing Material

Policy: All marketing materials sent via electronic mail must include an accurate return address and must provide clear and explicit instructions allowing recipients to quickly be removed from the distribution list.

Commentary: The intention of this policy is to prohibit workers at Company X from deliberately sending marketing oriented electronic mail messages with inaccurate return addresses so they won't be bothered by recipients who object to receiving spam (junk email). To the contrary, this policy says that Company X is always going to be straightforward about the process associated with removal from a list. The policy also implies that Company X staff will delete names and related contact particulars from an electronic mail distribution list, even if this list is owned by third parties and rented or leased to Company X. Separately, this policy addresses one of the most troublesome areas in the Internet marketing area: spam recipients don't know how to get removed (unsubscribed) from a list. This policy will accordingly assist Company X in its efforts to be in compliance with privacy policies in certain countries such as the United States. For related considerations, see the policies entitled "Immediate Action For Individuals Requesting Database Removal" and "Attribution Of Sources For Information." A: T; E: LMH.

831. Forwarding Electronic Mail To An External Network Address

Policy: Unless the information owner/originator agrees in advance, or unless the information is clearly public in nature, workers must not forward electronic mail to any address outside Company X's network. Blanket forwarding of electronic mail messages to any outside address is prohibited unless written permission from the Information Security Manager has first been obtained.

Commentary: This policy is intended to make sure that confidential internal information does not inadvertently go astray. This could, for instance, take place when an internal memo is innocently forwarded to an associate at an outside firm. The perpetrator might not think about it at the time, but confidential information could be disclosed in the process. Taking a conservative position, this policy forbids all external forwarding of electronic mail messages. A less conservative position might allow it only after department head approval. On another note, of particular concern are blanket forwarding measures, such as those which might be established by an employee at the time that he left an organization. While these automated forwarding mechanisms may provide an expedient way for an employee to stay in touch with personal contacts and associates from a professional association, such arrangements risk the inadvertent disclosure of confidential information. For instance, a customer might send e-mail to the former employee -- thinking that the former employee still worked for his former organization -- and in the process unwittingly disclose information which might be strategically important to the employee's new organization. Separately, forwarded messages are virtually impossible to recall since they are now out of the sender's control. For related ideas, see the policies entitled "Handling Involuntary Terminations Of Computer Workers" and "Worker Rights To Read Third Party Electronic Mail Messages." A: ET; E: LMH.

832. Forwarding Externally Provided Electronic Mail Messages

Policy: Workers must not create their own, or forward externally provided electronic mail messages which may be considered to be harassment or which may contribute to a hostile work environment. Among other things, a hostile work environment is created when derogatory comments about a certain sex, race, religion, or sexual preference are circulated.

Commentary: This "politically correct" policy about forwarded electronic mail messages is intended to put workers on notice that they must not create or forward dirty jokes, pornography, and other material that could cause a hostile working environment. Although the policy will get resistance from users with comments like "that's no fun," it is an important step in the direction of avoiding liability for employment discrimination, sexual harassment, and other problems. For a related idea, see the policy entitled "Forwarding Copies Of Official Electronic Mail To Archival Records." A: E; E: LMH.

833. Recording And Retention Of Electronic Mail

Policy: Company X systems administrators must establish and maintain a systematic process for the recording, retention, and destruction of electronic mail messages and accompanying logs. The destruction of both logs and the referenced electronic mail messages must be postponed whenever a subpoena, discovery motion, or other legal notice is received. Such destruction should also be postponed if the material might be needed for an imminent legal action.

Commentary: Electronic mail provides a new and more effective way to chronicle the internal communications within an organization, and even between organizations. For this reason, electronic mail messages and logs are often sought as part of discovery proceedings accompanying a legal action. This policy accordingly requires that a standard process for handling messages and logs be established. The last two sentences are intended to put technical people on notice that in some instances, electronic mail messages and logs should be kept beyond their normal retention periods. For an historical perspective about the need for this policy, consider that the improper handling of electronic mail logs played an important part of the investigation of the Iran Contra Scandal perpetrated by Oliver North and others in the US National Security Council. Although rarely expanded in scope, the policy is equally applicable to voice mail. See the policies entitled "Definition Of Archival Storage Data Retention Schedule" and "Users Notified That All Data Is Routinely Backed-Up." A: T; E: MH.

834. User Retention Of Electronic Mail Messages For Future Reference

Policy: If an electronic mail message contains information relevant to the completion of a business transaction, contains potentially important reference information, or has value as evidence of a Company X management decision, it should be retained for future reference. Most electronic mail messages will not fall into these categories, and so can be erased after receipt.

Commentary: This policy is intended to reduce information overload as well as prevent the improper destruction of valuable information. Many users are uncertain which electronic mail messages should be retained and which should be erased after receipt. This policy provides explicit instructions about the types of information that should be retained (stored in electronic form and/or printed on paper). Many organizations will want to tinker with the description of the types of messages that should be kept. An explicit definition of a "business transaction" may also assist readers of this policy. For a related idea, see the policy entitled "Recording And Retention Of Electronic Mail." A: E; E: LMH.

835. Users Must Not Employ Electronic Mail Systems As A Database

Policy: Users must regularly move important information from electronic mail message files to word processing documents, databases, and other files. Electronic mail systems are not intended for the archival storage of important information. Stored electronic mail messages may be periodically expunged by systems administrators, mistakenly erased by users, and otherwise lost when system problems occur.

Commentary: This policy addresses what has become a bad habit for many users. Overwhelmed by the volume of communications they receive, users simply elect to save certain electronic mail messages. Unfortunately they assume that a saved message will be there when they go back for it later. Many electronic mail systems were not designed as databases, and accordingly they do not have adequate mechanisms to protect important information. This policy thus attempts to preserve important information (an integrity issue). Similar to the whole concept of backing-up personal data, so often users take this matter seriously only after they have lost important material. If a policy like this is used, hopefully, the pain of learning through the "school of hard knocks" can be avoided. For a related idea, see the policy entitled "Recording And Retention Of Electronic Mail." A: E; E: LMH.

836. Periodic Destruction Of Archived Electronic Mail Messages

Policy: While management encourages periodic backups of computer-resident data, internal correspondence must be disposed of when no longer needed. To this end, all multi-user electronic mail logs must be destroyed one year after being archived. Electronic mail messages relevant to current activities, or that are expected to become relevant to current activities, should be saved as separate files and retained as long as needed.

Commentary: This policy is intended to keep the volume of archived electronic mail messages down, thus conserving scarce disk space and simplifying information management activities. From a legal standpoint, the policy is additionally intended to prevent an organization from being caught in a difficult place where management thought it had deleted all records pertaining to a certain matter, when in fact archived e-mail was still available. A number of lawyers are using e-mail as a favorite new source of information coming to light during discovery motions. When a policy like this exists, there will be no legitimate charges that the involved organization deliberately deleted incriminating evidence because such deletion has been made into an ordinary business procedure. An accompanying explanation, telling end-users what information types to retain and for what periods of time is also advisable. Separately, although this policy applies to file servers and other multi-user systems, not to individual worker personal computers (PCs), it could be extended to PCs. On another note, the time period could be shortened from one year to three months (discuss this with legal advisers). Also see the policies entitled "Destruction Of Sensitive Information On Computer Storage Media" and "Data Destruction Process Placed On Hold In Response To Discovery." A: ET; E: LMH.

837. Privacy Expectations And Electronic Mail

Policy: Workers must treat electronic mail messages and files as private information. Electronic mail must be handled as a private and direct communication between a sender and a recipient.

Commentary: The intention of this policy is to clearly specify what type of privacy workers should expect when it comes to electronic mail. A clear understanding of the privacy they can expect will enable users to make appropriate decisions about the types of information to send via electronic mail. This policy is purposely vague about matters such as looking at messages in order to support the administration of an electronic mail system. Such message examination would be fully in keeping with this policy so long as the intention was to maintain/administer the system, and not to violate another's privacy. This policy is decidedly pro-privacy, and may be too pro-privacy for some managers who wish to use electronic mail systems to spy on workers, monitor worker performance, discover misconduct, ensure proper use of the system, etc. If these uses are to be off-limits, the policy can be expanded to include words such as: "Electronic mail must not be routinely monitored to discover misconduct." This policy can also be expanded to include specific prohibited actions like: "Electronic mail must not be monitored, viewed, reproduced, or otherwise used by anyone other than the sender and the recipient." The words "messages and files" in the policy make it apply to messages in transit, messages that have not yet been read that are stored in a holding file, and messages that have been read and archived. This policy may also be expanded to apply to voice mail messages. Also see the policies entitled "Privacy Of Personal Files Stored On Computers And In Desks," "Monitoring of Electronic Mail Messages," and "Worker Rights To Read Third Party Electronic Mail Messages." A: EMT; E: LMH.

838. Treat Electronic Mail As Public Communications

Policy: Consider electronic mail to be the electronic equivalent of a postcard. Unless the material is encrypted, users must refrain from sending credit card numbers, passwords, research and development information, and other sensitive data via electronic mail.

Commentary: The intention of this policy is to impress users with the fact that their electronic mail communications are not protected the way an ordinary letter going through the postal service is. The postcard analogy seems apt because users are familiar with the fact that anyone in the delivery chain can read a postcard. The policy puts Internet users on notice that sensitive information should not be sent over the Internet unless it's in encrypted form. This policy thus attempts to alter the popular perception that the Internet has adequate built-in security, which it generally does not. Separately, some organizations may wish to expand this policy to define a standard encryption process for Internet electronic mail (often PGP, alias Pretty Good Privacy from Network Associates, Santa Clara, California). It is common these days for Sniffers (from Network General, Menlo Park, California) and other network analyzers to be used to capture and store information travelling over Internet links. Of particular concern are fixed passwords and credit card numbers, both of which can be used for subsequent unauthorized purposes. Separately, this policy could be modified to make reference to "Internet and other external electronic mail systems" rather than simply "electronic mail;" this would allow internal electronic mail systems to handle sensitive information, whereas the use of external electronic mail systems for sensitive information would be prohibited. The policy assumes that those reading the policy already know what the word "sensitive" means when applied to information; if this is not the case, a policy such as "Four Category Data Classification Scheme" may be appropriate. Unlike the policy entitled "Secret Information Sent By Electronic Mail," this policy does not require an established data classification scheme. Also see the policies entitled "Encryption Of Passwords" and "Encryption Required For Sending Secret Information by Fax." A: E; E: LMH.

839. Authorization To Read Electronic Mail Messages Of Other Workers

Policy: When the Director of Information Services and the Director of Human Resources collectively agree to it, electronic mail messages flowing through Company X systems may be monitored for internal policy compliance, suspected criminal activity, and other systems management reasons. Unless electronic mail monitoring tasks have been specifically delegated by the above-mentioned managers, all workers must refrain from this activity.

Commentary: This policy seeks to clarify who can read electronic mail messages, as well as the approved circumstances when messages can be examined. The policy implicitly puts workers on notice that their electronic mail may be monitored -- an important step in establishing user expectations. It is advisable to check local laws about the monitoring of electronic mail messages to get additional input when writing a policy such as this. In the United States, the Electronic Communications Privacy Act (ECPA) prohibits interception of messages unless prior consent is established (and a policy like this can help to establish prior consent, especially when signed by workers). Some organizations may wish to replace the words in the policy "other systems management reasons" with words more directly reflecting the ECPA; these words might read "supervision, control, and efficient operation of the workplace." For a related idea, see the policy entitled "Electronic Mail Messages Are Company Records." A: EMT; E: LMH.

840. Modifying Electronic Mail Message Contents Or Header Prohibited

Policy: Modifying personal email or news sent via email is strictly prohibited. Such modification includes forging and removing information appearing anywhere in an email message including the body of the message or the header.

Commentary: The intention of this policy is to let users know that they must not play games with the electronic mail system, that it is to be used for business activities only, and always with a businesslike manner. The policy additionally prohibits modifications to electronic mail messages which might cause office politics to be problematic (for example, forging the sender's name on a bogus love letter). The policy is necessary because it is actually quite easy to modify an electronic mail message without the modification being detected by the recipient (unless the sender uses encryption or a digital signature). For related ideas, see the policies entitled "Digital Certificate For All Company X Internet Web And Commerce Sites" and "Using An Electronic Mail Account Assigned To Another Individual." A: ET; E: LMH.

841. Profane, Obscene Or Derogatory Remarks In Electronic Mail Messages

Policy: Workers must not use profanity, obscenities, or derogatory remarks in electronic mail messages discussing employees, customers, or competitors. Such remarks -- even when made in jest -- may create legal problems such as trade libel and defamation of character. Special caution is warranted because backup and archival copies of electronic mail may actually be more permanent and more readily accessed than traditional paper communications.

Commentary: Many users consider electronic mail to be more informal than traditional paper letters. This can lead to the inclusion of obscenities or derogatory comments that would not have been included in a paper letter. This policy is intended to put workers on notice that their electronic mail may come back to haunt them, and be a legal problem for their employer. The policy also indirectly discourages "flaming," the practice of venting negative emotions via electronic mail (as well as other ways to communicate such as Internet chat rooms). Some organizations may wish to expand the policy and making mention of "harassing, embarrassing, indecent, intimidating or other unethical, immoral or unlawful material." For a related idea, see the policy entitled "Disclaimer Must Accompany All Internet Personal Messages." A: E; E: LMH.

842. Message Content Restrictions For Company X Information Systems

Policy: Workers are prohibited from sending or forwarding any messages via Company X information systems that a reasonable person would consider to be defamatory, harassing, or explicitly sexual. Workers are also prohibited from sending or forwarding messages or images via Company X systems that would be likely to offend on the basis of race, gender, national origin, sexual orientation, religion, political beliefs, or disability.

Commentary: The intention of this policy is to protect Company X against a variety of legal problems including defamation of character, libel, sexual harassment, and the creation of a hostile work environment. The policy seeks to let workers know that Company X information systems are not to be used for the exercise of rights to free speech (in the United States, the First Amendment). A policy like this should be accompanied by another policy restricting the use of Company X information systems to business activities. For related ideas, see the policies entitled "Disclaimer Of Responsibility Or Liability For Message Contents" and "Personal Use Of Computer And Communications Systems." A: E; E: LMH.

843. Notification Of Content Monitoring For Electronic Mail Transmissions

Policy: Company X routinely employs automatic electronic mail content scanning tools to identify selected keywords, file types, and other information. Users should restrict their communications to business matters in recognition of this electronic monitoring.

Commentary: The purpose of this policy is to put users on notice that their electronic mail messages will be automatically scanned for certain keywords (which might indicate the presence of sensitive data), and file types (which might indicate unauthorized graphics such as pornography). The policy is deliberately vague about the exact nature of the scanning that will be done, thus allowing these facilities to be upgraded without further notice to the user community. The vague nature of the policy is also desirable because it creates some doubt in the mind of users, thus potentially acting as a deterrent against electronic mail transmissions which are illegal or against policy. Be sure to consult legal counsel about all matters dealing with employee monitoring. The monitoring mentioned here is often implemented at the firewall level, or at the mail server level, so that it can detect (and in some cases block) the outbound flow of sensitive information. For related ideas, see the policies entitled "No Responsibility For Monitoring Content Of Information Systems" and "Disclaimer Of Responsibility Or Liability For Message Contents." A: E; E: LMH.

844. Reporting Offensive Electronic Mail Messages To Originator And HR

Policy: Workers are encouraged to respond directly to the originator of offensive electronic mail messages, telephone calls, and/or other communications. If the originator does not promptly stop sending offensive messages, workers must report the communications to their manager and the Human Resources Department.

Commentary: This policy is meant to encourage workers to initially deal directly with the originator of material that they consider to be offensive (sexist, racist, bigoted, etc.). Only when the originator fails to take action based on the feedback, should workers escalate the matter to their manager and the Human Resources Department. In many instances, the originator does not appreciate that certain material is offensive, and a simple complaint sent to the originator will be sufficient to stop the communications. Note that an "originator" might be an individual who simply forwards material obtained from another source (sexist jokes for example). Separately, the existence of this policy is an indication that an organization takes legal issues such as sexual harassment and a hostile work environment seriously. The policy shows that management is so serious about these matters that they established a process for their resolution. For related ideas, see the policies entitled "Right To Remove Offensive Material Without Warning" and "Prohibition Against Sexual, Ethnic, And Racial Harassment." A: E; E: LMH.

845. Sending Unsolicited Personal Email Messages After Request To Stop

Policy: Users of Company X information systems must immediately stop sending unsolicited personal electronic mail messages to any recipient if the recipient requests that such messages stop.

Commentary: The primary intention of this policy is to prevent legal problems such as allegations of sexual harassment or a hostile working environment. The secondary intention of this policy is to prevent workers from bothering prospects or customers who have requested that they no longer be contacted. An overly aggressive salesperson may, for example, badger a prospect into buying a product. While such messages are not "spam" (unsolicited bulk email), they are unwelcome and a nuisance. In a serious case of such email harassment, the recipient may also be able to claim that his or her privacy (right to be left alone) has been violated. As a general business matter, it is wise to promptly respond to the requests of external parties for no further contact, and this policy makes it clear that workers should do exactly that. See the policies entitled "Prohibition Against Sexual, Ethnic, And Racial Harassment" and "Profane, Obscene Or Derogatory Remarks In Electronic Mail Messages." A: E; E: LMH.

846. Prohibition Against Unsolicited Bulk Email Advertisements (SPAM)

Policy: Users are prohibited from using Company X computer systems for the transmission of unsolicited bulk email advertisements or commercial messages which are likely to trigger complaints from the recipients. Colloquially known as "spam," these prohibited messages include a wide variety of unsolicited promotions and solicitations such as chain letters, pyramid schemes, and direct marketing pitches.

Commentary: The intention of this policy is to prevent users from abusing the network connectivity that electronic mail systems provide to reach a very large number of people at a very low cost. The policy helps to reduce customer complaints, and the costs that would otherwise be incurred dealing with these complaints. The policy makes it clear that Company X does not permit or employ spam, and that if spam was sent, then it was strictly an individual's decision to do so. The policy also allows an organization to terminate a worker who sent spam messages with its computer facilities. Separately, spam is increasingly being regulated, and this policy helps to ensure that the policy issuing organization stays on the right side of the law. Note that the policy could be buttressed by including a provision which forbade the collection of responses from unsolicited bulk email transmissions. For related ideas, see the policies entitled "Immediate Action For Individuals Requesting Database Removal" and "Clearly Identified Source For Electronic Mail Marketing Material." A: E; E: LMH.

847. Forwarding Is Appropriate Response To Junk Email (SPAM)

Policy: When workers receive unwanted and unsolicited email (also known as SPAM), they must refrain from responding directly to the sender. Instead, they should forward the message to the email administrator who will take steps to prevent further transmissions.

Commentary: The intention of this policy is to help ensure that internal electronic mail systems are used exclusively for business purposes, and only by authorized workers. SPAM (junk email) creates an erosion of worker productivity as well as a degradation in system availability (by clogging networks and incoming electronic mail boxes). This policy tells workers not to respond; this is because a response means that there is someone actively monitoring the user-ID's inbound email box. This is just further invitation for a spammer to send additional material, and maybe sell the email address to other spammers. Instead, forwarding to an administrator allows the administrator to establish filters at the firewall level or at the email server level to prevent these messages from reaching inbound mail boxes. Administrators can also report this activity to various black-lists on the Internet that are then used to block email messages. If an administrator is feeling particularly upset, he or she can even contact the ISP from which the message originated and complain that the account should be revoked. Note that the forwarding process is a recommendation, but the instruction regarding responding is mandatory (note the use of "should" and "must"). Separately, "spam" is a registered trademark for a meat product from Hormel Foods, but has become a slang word for unsolicited commercial email. For related ideas, see the policies entitled "Authorization To Issue Broadcasts On Electronic Mail And Voice Mail" and "Forwarding Externally Provided Electronic Mail Messages." A: E; E: LMH.

848. Sending Large Quantities Of Unsolicited Email (Mail Bombing)

Policy: Users are forbidden from sending large quantities of unsolicited email to specific addresses or Usenet groups (this practice is colloquially known as "mail bombing").

Commentary: The objective of this policy is to let users know that it's unacceptable to get even with somebody by sending large quantities of email. Not only does this practice consume computer and network resources unnecessarily, a great deal of time on the recipient's part is required to sort through all the unwanted messages, trying to find those which are indeed desired. As a result of a mail bomb attack, the mail server at the recipient's end may also have a disk full condition which requires operator intervention. While some electronic mail programs are able to filter and drop messages from selected addresses, this policy tries to stop the practice at its originating point. Note that a mail bomb is different from a spam message in that a mail bomb is intended to disrupt and sabotage, while a spam message is intended to sell a product or service. Separately, the transmission of a large number of messages with no substantive content to a Usenet group is called "flooding" and this type of abuse is prohibited by the policy. For related ideas, see the policies entitled "Prohibition Against Programs Consuming Excessive System Resources" and "User Retention Of Electronic Mail Messages For Future Reference." A: ET; E: LMH.

849. Electronic Mail Messages Are Company Records

Policy: The Company X electronic mail system is to be used only for business purposes. All messages sent by electronic mail are Company X records. The Company reserves the right to access and disclose all messages sent over its electronic mail system, for any purpose. Supervisors may review the electronic mail communications of workers they supervise to determine whether they have breached security, violated Company policy, or taken other unauthorized actions. The Company may also disclose electronic mail messages to law enforcement officials without prior notice to the workers who may have sent or received such messages.

Commentary: This policy is very employer-rights-oriented, placing more importance on the ability to monitor electronic mail than on the rights of workers to communicate privately. The policy seeks to put workers on notice that their communications can be monitored without prior consent. This notice is intended to eliminate disputes about the propriety of management actions to monitor e-mail traffic. Wherever an organization draws the line in terms of employer rights vs. worker communications privacy, it is important to manage the expectations of the people who use the system. Note that the procedures which go along with this policy could be defeated via encryption; to be truly effective a policy prohibiting encryption will be necessary -- see the policy entitled "Encryption Processes Must Not Be Used Unless Previously Approved." Also see the policies entitled "Areas Where Electronic Monitoring Of Workers May Be Used," "Notifying Subjects Of Existing Monitoring Systems," "Monitoring Of Electronic Mail Messages," and "Worker Rights To Read Third Party Electronic Mail Messages." A: E; E: LMH.

850. All Electronic Mail Archived And Subject To Supervisory Review

Policy: All electronic mail sent through the Company X mail server is archived and subject to review by people other than the recipient and sender.

Commentary: The intention of this policy is to make it clear that all email sent through a particular organization is being archived. The senders and recipients are placed on notice that their communications are not private. This policy is also required by some government agencies that are concerned about misrepresentations made to customers. For example, in the USA, the Securities and Exchange Commission (SEC) imposes rules including the mandatory archive and review of all customer communications. Among other things, the SEC is concerned about stockbrokers saying things like "if you buy this stock, you can't lose." Separately, this policy is often appended to electronic mail so that all external correspondents know that their messages will be archived and reviewed. For related ideas, see the policies entitled "Periodic Destruction Of Archived Electronic Mail Messages" and "Recording And Retention Of Electronic Mail." A: E; E: LMH.

851. Forwarding Copies Of Official Electronic Mail To Archival Records

Policy: All official Company X electronic mail messages, including those containing a formal management approval, authorization, delegation, or handing over of responsibility, or similar transaction, must be copied to the Archival Records Department.

Commentary: This policy acknowledges the changing nature of the archival records function in modern organizations. Rather than being a paper-handling group, it is increasingly an electronic records management group. The copying of such electronic mail messages provides evidence and accountability, should there be disputes, disciplinary actions, or legal proceedings. The process of storing an official copy of correspondence is in fact an announced Internet electronic mail service to be provided by the United States Postal Service. But organizations need not use the public postal service; other firms provide this service on the Internet, and it can be done within an organization as well. Separately, the policy says nothing about encryption; if the message contents are sensitive, then the message should be encrypted. This, of course, introduces another factor that will need to be considered: how to manage the encryption keys. On another point, in some cases it may be sufficient for a message hash, digital signature, or extract to be stored rather than the actual message; for example, on a stock exchange, the archival trade records may be only a hash, digital signature, or extract. This would allow the verification of a specific trade, by certain parties, for certain amounts, at a certain time/date; but would not allow the original message to be reconstructed. For a related idea, see the policy entitled "Recording And Retention Of Electronic Mail." A: EMT; E: LMH.

852. Personal Use Of Electronic Mail Systems

Policy: Electronic mail systems are intended to be used primarily for business purposes. Any personal use must not interfere with normal business activities, must not involve solicitation, must not be associated with any for-profit outside business activity, and must not potentially embarrass Company X.

Commentary: The intention of this policy is to clearly specify what type of personal use of an electronic mail system is permissible. In many organizations, workers are using electronic mail systems for personal purposes already. This policy will make sure that the personal use is kept within certain limits. At some organizations, the term "outside business activity" will need to be defined; it can simply be defined as personal business affairs unrelated to Company X business. An example might be teaching a night class at a local university. See the policies entitled "Personal Use Of Computer And Communications Systems," "Prohibition Against Non-Approved System Uses," "Use Of Telephones For Personal Purposes," and "Use Of Company X Information For Non-Business Purposes." A: EMT; E: LMH.

853. Authorization To Issue Broadcasts On Electronic Mail And Voice Mail

Policy: Broadcast facilities found in electronic mail systems and voice mail systems may only be used by top management or with top management approval.

Commentary: This policy is intended to reduce junk mail. The productivity of many workers is adversely impacted by messages about kittens for sale, the wind surfing club meeting, and all sorts of low priority announcements. For some organizations, this policy may too severely restrict the use of broadcast facilities; they may wish to add words permitting use of the facilities in the event of an emergency or disaster (although this is obvious to many people). Other organizations may wish to establish a formal review and approval procedure for the issuance of broadcast messages. Still others may wish to grant to both systems administrators and members of the security department some blanket permission to issue broadcasts without advance top management approval. Separately, in some cases, organizations may wish to restrict end-user system privileges allowing them to issue such broadcasts. On another note, the scope of this policy could be extended to include public address (PA) facilities (audio speakers throughout a building). A policy similar to this is alleged to be in effect at Microsoft. For related ideas, see the policies entitled "Right To Free Speech Does Not Apply To Company X Systems" and "Prohibition Against Non-Approved System Uses." A: E; E: LMH.

854. Authorization To Issue Electronic Mail Or Voice Mail To Groups

Policy: Electronic mail or voice mail messages that will be sent to groups with more than ten recipients must first be approved by a department manager.

Commentary: The objective of this policy is to prevent workers from sending inaccurate, embarrassing, or inappropriate material to a large number of people via electronic mail or voice mail systems (such incidents often make interesting news stories). The policy thus prohibits workers from distributing notices about the "availability of free kittens" or "an old car for sale" via electronic mail or voice mail systems. With this policy, department managers are put in the position of interpreting and applying electronic mail and voice mail policies for workers who may not understand them. This policy also imposes a certain formality to these communications which causes workers to think hard before they prepare a message and seek department manager approval. If the message really isn't important, then workers probably will not go to the trouble of seeking manager approval, and the potential recipients will then not be bothered by yet another piece of irrelevant material. Note that this policy indirectly prevents the use of broadcast facilities, but the policy is broader in scope and includes things like private email lists. Separately, note that the policy applies to both internal and external recipients of the messages in question. For related ideas, consider the policies entitled "Internet Discussion Group And Chat Room Participation Forbidden" and "All Public Representations Must Be Cleared Through Public Relations." A: E; E: LMH.

855. Placement On Electronic Mail Distribution List Requires Opt-In

Policy: Nobody outside Company X will be placed on an electronic mail distribution list without first indicating their intention to be included on the list through an opt-in process.

Commentary: This policy seeks to prevent complaints and bad publicity associated with spam or unwanted electronic mail (junk email). In a small number of jurisdictions, it may also prevent legal troubles. With this policy, organizations would first ask potential customers and others whether they wish to receive a certain type of information, and then only if the recipients respond affirmatively, would they be placed on an a specific electronic mail distribution list. Note that many marketers will object to this policy saying that it unduly constrains their sales activities, but those with a strong ethical stand will appreciate how it preserves the privacy of individuals (and if publicized, may even generate positive comments about the organization). For related concepts, see the policies entitled "Customers Must Specifically Agree To Receive New/Enhanced Service" and "Subjects Must Opt-In To Be Included In Systems Handling Private Data." A: E; E: LMH.

856. Prohibition Against Use Of Scanned Hand-Rendered Signatures

Policy: Workers must not employ scanned versions of hand-rendered signatures to give the impression that an electronic mail message or other electronic communications were signed by the sender.

Commentary: This policy seeks to restrict the dissemination of hand-rendered signatures in digitized form. If these scanned signatures fall into the wrong hands, they could be used to forge checks, fraudulently authorize credit card transactions, and improperly obtain identification cards. Often attempts to replicate manual controls (like signatures) in an automated environment are at the very least suboptimal, and sometimes disastrous. There are other much more reliable controls to authenticate the identity of electronic mail message originators; these include digital signatures, digital certificates, encryption, and dynamic password systems. Financial institutions that use scanned versions of hand-rendered signatures for their internal operations may wish to change the policy so that it is restricted to public networks like the Internet. For related ideas, see the policies entitled "Originator Of Transactions Must Be Clearly Identified" and "Validating The Identity Of External Parties On The Internet." A: E; E: LMH.

857. Prohibition Against Opening Attachments Unless They Were Expected

Policy: Workers must not open electronic mail attachments unless they were expected from a known and trusted sender.

Commentary: This policy seeks to prevent virus infections on desktop computers. Perhaps the best known recent virus which automatically replicated itself via electronic mail is the I LOVE YOU virus. Executable attachments are a favorite way for viruses to enter an internal network, and the resulting disruption can be significant and costly. Many of these viruses will look at the address book found in the electronic mail application and then automatically send the virus out to all recipients in the address book. These transmissions will be from a known sender, but the attachment will not be expected, so hopefully the recipient will not open the attachment. Of course, certain attachments, such as those in rich text format (RTF) will be innocuous because they will not contain any executable statements. The policy could be modified to permit the opening of text and RTF attachments, but users cannot be relied upon to definitively know the format of the attached files they receive (regardless of the file extensions). Without question, this rule of thumb policy is not going to keep viruses out of internal networks, but it will definitely help. Separately, these words could be added to the policy: "Opening an attachment is permissible if the explanation accompanying the attachment makes sense given your current business activities, and if the attachment was sent by a known and trusted party." For related ideas, see the policies entitled "Prohibition Against Down-Loading Software From Third Party Systems" and "Using Electronic Mail Addresses Other Than Official Company X Addresses." A: E; E: LMH.

858. Inbound Attachments To Internet Electronic Mail Prohibited

Policy: Attachments to inbound Internet electronic mail messages sent to Company X users will be automatically deleted. If a formatted file, an executable program, or some other non-text message must be sent, other methods such as FTP must instead be employed.
Commentary: This strict policy seeks to prevent the new macroviruses from inadvertently being transmitted to Company X machines via Internet electronic mail attachments. It also partially protects an organization against dynamic content (Java, ActiveX, etc.), which is an increasingly dangerous risk that all Internet users face. The policy forces users to put word processing documents, spreadsheets, and other files in simple text (ASCII) format, and embedded in the body of an email message. This conservative policy acknowledges that, aside from diskettes, electronic mail attachments have become the primary mechanism used to spread macroviruses such as Word.Concept and Wazzu. Macroviruses attach themselves to data rather than executable programs. This policy also reduces the transmission of executables, which in turn is likely to reduce infections from ordinary viruses (which attach themselves to executables). Assuming that it is better to automatically enforce a policy, rather than rely on users, this policy assumes that special code has been written for email handling programs. Many firewalls now have the capabilities to do this type of filtering, but the filtering may be incomplete or unreliable. On another note, this policy has a positive productivity side-effect: users do not need to waste time finding the right program to view attachments because the senders restrict their material to text. Note that entire messages will not be lost; Company X users will still know that someone attempted to send them an attachment. This policy is very restrictive and will be too heavy-duty for many organizations. For a related idea, see the policy entitled "Right To Censor Data On Organizational Systems." A: ET; E: H.

859. Browser Electronic Mail Features Must Not Be Used For Business Activities

Policy: The electronic mail features found in Internet browsers are not compatible with the Company X electronic mail system and must not be used for any business communications.

Communications: The motivation for this policy is to prevent users from employing browser electronic mail facilities, and in the process circumventing the controls embedded in an internal electronic mail system. If users employ a browser for electronic mail, especially if they connect with their personal Internet Service Provider (ISP) via a dial-up line, they could download an attachment which contains a virus. If this email attachment instead went through the organization's standard electronic mail server, it could have been filtered and deleted, preventing any damage. Likewise, use of a browser for electronic mail could circumvent electronic mail header logging systems and content filtering systems. This policy also stops workers from giving customers and prospects personal electronic mail addresses because they consider an internal electronic mail system to be too slow or burdensome. For related ideas, consider the policies entitled "Monitoring Of Electronic Mail Messages" and "User Retention Of Electronic Mail Messages For Future Reference." A: E; E: LMH.

1.4.7. Telecommuting Arrangements

860. Telecommuting Data Entry Operators Must Employ Thin Clients

Policy: All Company X data entry operators must employ thin clients as configured by the Information Systems Department. At the beginning of each business day, these operators must down-load the software for their work.

Commentary: This policy reflects a relatively high-security environment where data entry operators (claims adjusters for an insurance company, billing clerks for a hospital, etc.) can use their machines for no other activity than Company X business. Because the machines are "thin clients," they do not have a hard drive and cannot permanently store the software they execute. With this approach, each completed transaction must be submitted to Company X's server, which is where business data is stored. If peripheral devices like a floppy drive are locked out, this approach prevents telecommuters from taking business information that is the property of Company X (unless they write it down by hand, which is laborious and inconvenient). Separately, the configuration must have a fast modem or other type of connection because the software can be quite large, and may otherwise take a long time to down-load. Also, this configuration assumes that a relatively reliable network connection is available (perhaps through the Internet and VPNs); otherwise, telecommuter work may be seriously impeded when communications interruptions occur. This approach is very restrictive, and is not appropriate for general office telecommuters, only those with narrowly-defined jobs. On another note, this approach allows Company X to change the software daily, and to ensure that all client machines were updated at the same time. A change control mechanism on the thin client can be used to prevent any changes in the operating system or other software. In some instances, thin clients are also known as "network computers" (although the latter term is archaic). For related ideas, see the policies entitled "Diskless Workstations Must Be Used By R&D Department Workers," "Prohibition Against Down-Loading Software From Third Party Systems," and "Controls Needed For Down-Loading Sensitive Company X Information." A: T; E: MH.

861. Permissible Equipment For Telecommuting

Policy: Employees working on Company X business at alternative work sites must use Company X-provided computer and network equipment. An exception will be made only if other equipment has been approved as compatible with Company X information systems and controls.
Commentary: The intention of this policy is to make sure that telecommuting workers do not use information systems which could: (a) cause malfunctions or damage to Company X systems or information, or (b) insufficiently protect Company X information. The latter might, for instance, occur if telecommuting equipment was not able to encrypt sensitive information stored on a computer at an employee's home. A burglary could then lead to unauthorized disclosure of this sensitive information. Separately, many organizations have a checklist of standard information systems equipment issued to telecommuters. This list can include a modem, a special high-speed phone line (such as an ISDN line), a pager, an answering machine, a fax machine, a copier, a printer, and a personal computer. The list could include software and documentation such as standard application programs and standard utilities (such as a disk scrubber or zeroization program, a file and communications encryption program, and a password-based access control program). On a related note, organizations may wish to issue a separate policy stating that Company X is not responsible for loss, damage, or wear-and-tear of employee-owned equipment

used for Company X business. It may also be desirable to state that such employee-owned equipment may continue to be used for personal activities provided Company X information is not jeopardized. On another note, these policies should be supplemented by words defining terms like "alternative work site" and "telecommuter." Beyond computers at home, these policies are additionally applicable to mobile computers like laptops, palmtops, and portables. For related ideas, see the policies entitled "Security Requirements For Work At Home Arrangements," "Controls For Transportable Computers With Sensitive Information," and "Provision Of Lockable Metal Furniture To Staff Working at Home." A: ET; E: LMH.

862. Alteration/Expansion Of Computers Provided By Company X

Policy: Computer equipment provided by Company X must not be altered or added to in any way (e.g., upgraded processor, expanded memory, or extra circuit boards) without departmental management knowledge and authorization.

Commentary: The intention of this policy is to ensure that users know that they must not tamper with Company X provided equipment. Such tampering could inadvertently cause any of various security measures to malfunction; for example, a boot protection system (which requires a password when the system is turned on) could lock a user out of a computer altogether. Tampering could also be used to deliberately circumvent security measures. In addition, in an indirect way, the policy prohibits theft of internal components like memory chips. Furthermore, the policy helps to ensure the equipment issued to a user is the equipment that will be delivered when the user leaves the employ of Company X. Although this policy is unnecessary if users only employ desktop machines in the office, when the computers are taken off-site (portables, laptops, etc.) the need for this policy increases dramatically. Separately, although generally less of a concern, stand-alone communications equipment (such as external modems) could also be included within the scope of this policy. For related ideas, see the policies entitled "Permissible Equipment For Telecommuting" and "Controls For Transportable Computers With Sensitive Information." A: E; E: LMH.

863. Reporting Of Damage To Company X Off-Site Systems

Policy: Workers must promptly report to their manager any damage to or loss of Company X computer hardware, software, or information which has been entrusted to their care.

Commentary: The intention of this policy is to make sure that telecommuting workers, as well as those workers with mobile computers, report all damages or losses promptly. This will in turn allow remedial measures, such as the replacement of a portable computer, to take place expediently so as to minimize the impact on business activity. This will also allow prompt notification of the information owner if the loss of sensitive information was involved (and by extension, this will additionally allow prompt remedial action when necessary). The policy could be augmented with another sentence requiring department managers to report these damages or losses to the Physical Security Department, which generally keeps loss history records. Alternately, users could be told to report all such damage or loss to the help desk, which in turn would report it to the appropriate internal groups (perhaps including an insurance department, which may then collect insurance for stolen portable computers and the like). In many cases, the user reporting a loss will need to fill out a loss report, but this is a procedure, so would not typically be detailed (but it may be mentioned) in a policy. Separately, note that this policy requires the reporting of information loss or damage; this may be a particularly important issue for organizations concerned about industrial espionage and portable computer theft. On another note, this policy is deliberately written so that it could apply to all locations, not just off-site systems (the policy title may need to change if the policy writer wishes to make this wider applicability more clear). For a similar ideas, see the policies entitled "Required Reporting Of

Information Security Incidents" and "Internal Reporting Of Information Security Violations & Problems." A: E; E: LMH.

864. Protection Of Company X Property At Alternative Work Sites

Policy: The security of Company X property at an alternative work site is just as important as it is at the central office. At alternative work sites, reasonable precautions must be taken to protect Company X hardware, software, and information from theft, damage, and misuse.

Commentary: The intention of this policy is to impress telecommuters (and others working with Company X information systems at locations other than a central office) that the same security measures apply no matter where they are located. In some respects, this policy is another way of saying that information should be protected in a manner consistent with its value, sensitivity, and criticality. Protective measures should apply no matter where the information is located, no matter what form it takes, and no matter what technology is used to handle it. For example, if sensitive information is being handled, it should be encrypted when in storage, no matter if a computer is in the main (traditional or central) office or at an alternative work site. This policy allows an organization to avoid having to specify a new set of control requirements for off-site information handling; it basically says that the same controls should be used at alternative work sites as are used at central work sites. Separately, this policy applies to mobile computing users just as it does for users who work at home. For related ideas, see the policies entitled "Consistent Protection Of Information Regardless Of Manifestation," "Removal Of Sensitive Information From Company X Premises," and "Controls Needed For Down-Loading Sensitive Company X Information." A: ET; E: LMH.

865. Rights To Intellectual Property Developed Off-Site

Policy: Intellectual property developed or conceived of while an employee is working at alternative work sites is the exclusive property of Company X. This policy includes patent, copyright, trademark, and all other intellectual property rights as manifested in memos, plans, strategies, products, computer programs, documentation, and other materials.

Commentary: This policy seeks to notify telecommuters and others working off-site that their intellectual property work is still Company X property, even though it was developed at another location. Some organizations may wish to restrict this policy such that it only makes reference to materials developed during working hours; others may want to restrict it so that it only makes reference to intellectual property related to Company X's business. As written now, the policy has the broadest possible applicability, and so will tend to protect Company X more than the employee. Detailed discussions with internal legal counsel about this topic are highly advisable. This policy is equally applicable to mobile computer users and others who might not be at an officially-designated alternative work site (satellite offices, neighborhood work centers, and virtual offices). For related ideas, see the policies entitled "Assignment Of Patent, Copyright, And Other Intellectual Property Rights" and "Property Rights To Computer Programs And Documentation." A: ET; E: LMH.

866. Information Stored In Portable Computers Owned By Company X

Policy: Company X provides selected members of its workforce with portable computer equipment so that they can perform their jobs at remote locations including hotel rooms and personal residences. The information stored in these computers is Company X property, and like the equipment, it must be returned to Company X at the time workers are no longer employed by Company X. Likewise, since the information belongs to Company X, it can be inspected or used in any manner, and at any time, by Company X.

Commentary: The intention of this policy is to prevent confusion about ownership regarding the information stored in portable computers such as handhelds or personal digital assistants (PDAs). Because these computers stay with an workers, they are considered by some people to be personal property. This policy overcomes that perspective by stating that these devices are provided to perform specific duties with the implication that the devices should be used primarily for business purposes. At the very least, after reading this policy users of these devices will know that they shouldn't store anything on the devices that they would be ashamed about, should an auditor from Company X examine its contents. In a broader sense, this policy seeks to extend the boundary between organizational property and personal worker property because the technology has allowed new types of distributed computing. On another note, according to this policy, if a worker employs his or her own equipment, then an employer has no stated rights to the information contained therein. For related ideas, see the policies entitled "Storage Of Sensitive Information On Personal Computers" and "Removal Of Information Upon Termination Of Employment." A: E; E: LMH.

867. Telecommuters And Structured Working Environments

Policy: To retain the privilege of doing off-site work, all telecommuters must structure their remote working environment so that it is in compliance with Company X policies and standards. Commentary: This policy is intended to put telecommuters on notice that being a telecommuter is a privilege, not a right, and as such this privilege may be revoked if the workers do not abide by Company X policies and standards. The policy specifically avoids dictating the specifics of remote working environments, since these are expected to change often. When it comes to security, these specifics typically include keeping equipment and other materials in a locked room, as well as regular use of a surge protector, a hard disk drive password-based access control system, a paper shredder, and a virus screening program. There will be other specifics not related to security (typically dealing with human resource issues, like accounting for time worked). For related ideas, see the policies entitled "Periodic Review And Reauthorization Of User Access Privileges" and "Storing Secret Information On Transportable Computers." A: E; E: LMH.

868. Use Of Computer Systems Belonging To Workers On Company Property

Policy: Workers must not bring their own computers, computer peripherals, or computer software into Company X facilities without prior authorization from their department head.

Commentary: This policy prevents: (1) propagation of viruses, (2) disputes about ownership of hardware and software, and (3) improper removal of hardware, software, or data at the time when a worker's employment is terminated. The policy is also desirable because it helps make sure that everyone uses the same type of software (this makes it easier to provide access control, contingency planning services, and technical support services). This policy is particularly relevant to microcomputers (PCs) and workstations, as well as client/server systems, for which the ownership status is often unclear. This policy can be supported by another policy requiring all computer and communications equipment to have a pass before it can be removed from Company X premises. For more about this, see the policy entitled "Property Pass For Removal Of All Computer And Communications Gear." Also see the policy entitled "Hardware/Software Procurement Via Standard Purchasing Channels." A: ET; E: LMH.

869. Security Requirements For Work At Home Arrangements

Policy: Work at home (telecommuting) arrangements are a management option, not a universal employee benefit. Permission to telecommute is the decision of the involved employee's manager. Before a telecommuting arrangement can begin, this manager must be satisfied that an alternative work site (such as a home office) is appropriate for the Company X work performed by the involved employee. Considerations include physical and information security for Company X property, a distraction-free work environment, ways to measure worker performance, and methods to stay in touch with other workers.

Commentary: Discussions about "alternative work sites" (notably home offices) have become more prevalent in the last few years. In some instances, at least in the USA, air pollution regulations are forcing organizations to support these arrangements. Whenever these arrangements are being considered it is important to consider what happens to Company X physical assets (such as computers) as well as information assets (such as customer lists). This policy is intended to give management broad latitude to decide who will be allowed to telecommute, and under what circumstances. Many organizations have adopted a checklist which, among other things, lists the security requirements for telecommuting. These generally include tools such as hard disk encryption packages, locking file cabinets, and paper shredders. Some organizations take it one step further, requiring telecommuters to sign a statement where they promise to abide by specific rules for securing off-site information. Separately, the policy could be augmented with definitions clarifying terms such as "alternative work site," "telecommuter," and "central work location" (generally the traditional centralized office). See the policies entitled "Property Pass For Removal Of All Computer And Communications Gear," "Current Virus Software Required For Certain Worker-Owned Computers," and "Provision Of Lockable Metal Furniture To Staff Working at Home." A: EMT; E: LMH.

870. Sensitive Information Retention For Destruction Via Approved Method

Policy: Workers must not discard sensitive information in hotel waste baskets or other publicly-accessible trash containers. Instead, sensitive information must be retained until it can be shredded, or destroyed with other approved methods.

Commentary: Overwhelmed by the great volume of paper that so many of us receive (information overload), workers may simply throw away sensitive information. Without thinking about it much, they may discard sensitive documents which can be scavenged by industrial spies, hackers, and other interested parties (this practice is called "dumpster diving"). This policy seeks to have workers retain sensitive information until they can dispose of it properly. Note that nowhere in the policy is hardcopy paper mentioned, so the policy is applicable to floppy disks and other ways to capture sensitive information. To make the policy more readily understood by readers, some policy writers will want to specifically mention different ways that sensitive information can be recorded (tapes, disks, etc.). This policy recognizes that many workers are on the road, away from the office where shredders, degaussers, and related information destruction equipment (or software) may be located. The policy is equally applicable to mobile workers as it is to telecommuters. See the policies entitled "Security Requirements For Work At Home Arrangements" and "Approved Methods For Hardcopy Sensitive Information Disposal." A: E; E: LMH.

871. Telecommuter Remote System Information Security Procedures

Policy: As a condition of continued employment, telecommuters agree to abide by all remote system security policies and procedures. These include, but are not limited to, compliance with software license agreements, performance of regular backups, and use of shredders to dispose of sensitive information.

Commentary: The intention of this policy to make telecommuters aware of the procedures they must perform on a day-to-day basis. Some organizations may need a more detailed procedural description of the security requirements associated with telecommuting, in which case the second sentence in the policy could be replaced with a separate memo. In most cases, organizations will want to augment this precaution list with other considerations, such as returning the organization's equipment at the time that the working relationship ends. If an organization is going to permit its sensitive information to be used in remote locations that cannot be easily supervised, it is reasonable for it to insist that certain security precautions be observed. Because telecommuting introduces new risks, a more stringent and specially-documented policy dealing with telecommuters may be appropriate in those instances where no similar policy exists for workers who come into the office every day. This policy may also be appropriate for workers which are not -- properly speaking -- telecommuters, but who nonetheless take organizational information to their home or on business trips. For related ideas, see the policies entitled "Agreements With Third Parties Which Handle Company X Information" and "Annual Signature On Agreement To Comply With Security Policies." A: E; E: LMH.

872. Right To Conduct Inspections Of Telecommuter Environments

Policy: Company X maintains the right to conduct inspections of telecommuter offices with one or more days advance notice.

Commentary: The intention of this policy is to put telecommuters on notice that Company X representatives may conduct inspections of their home offices. This will help ensure that telecommuters observe both safety and security policies and procedures. In return for permitting employees to telecommute, Company X can receive the right to conduct inspections of its property kept in the houses of telecommuters. Thus, by conducting inspections, Company X management is carrying out its duty to protect Company X assets. A separate policy is generally not needed to put computer users on notice that EDP auditors will examine the controls in the organization's office -- this is expected. It is only because the home is generally the domain of the employee that such a right to inspect must be clearly communicated and/or negotiated. Separately, a first inspection is often conducted as soon as workers have set up their offices; thereafter, annual or on-demand inspections may be sufficient. The policy allows multiple follow-up inspections to correct deficiencies that were detected during prior visits. On another note, some organizations may not wish to give any advance warning, in which case the last seven words in the policy can be deleted. Besides safety factors like fire dangers, these inspections can be motivated by ergonomic factors, such as preventing carpal tunnel syndrome. Also see the policy entitled "Internal Audit Review Of Information System Controls." A: E; E: LMH.

873. Training Course Required Prior To Use Of Remote Access Systems

Policy: Company X workers must complete an approved remote systems access training course prior to being granted privileges to use dial-up, Internet telnet, or any other remote access data communications system.

Commentary: Recognizing the potentially serious security problems associated with telecommuting and other types of remote system access, this policy insists that all users of Company X remote access facilities be adequately trained. The training course mentioned in this policy would typically include security issues such as protecting remotely-located equipment from theft, encryption of sensitive files stored on a remote machine hard disk, shredding of sensitive hardcopy prior to disposal, locking sensitive hardcopy in cabinets or similarly secure containers, and security-related steps required to establish a data communications system connection. For related ideas, see the policies entitled "Security Requirements For Work At Home Arrangements" and "Telecommuter Remote System Information Security Procedures." A: E; E: LMH.

874. Workers Must Keep Portable Computers In Their Possession Or Locked

Policy: Workers must keep Company X portable computers in their possession at all times unless they have been deposited in a secure location such as a locked closet or a hotel safe.

Commentary: The theft of portable computers (handhelds, transportable PCs, etc.) has become an epidemic. This policy seeks to limit the loss of these computers due to theft, and also to limit the loss of the information which may be stored on such computers. So long as a computer is in an employee's possession it's unlikely to be stolen, but if it is left in an unattended office or in some other relatively public place, it's likely to be gone when the user returns. Note that this policy says nothing about encryption or access control systems, both of which are important for portables, but are addressed in other policies found in this book. This policy could be modified to include anti-theft devices such as locking cables as another option besides a locked closet. For related ideas, see the policies entitled "Controls For Transportable Computers With Sensitive Information," "Storing Secret Information On Transportable Computers," and "Dynamic Password Tokens Must Not Be Stored In Portable Cases." A: E; E: LMH.

875. Mobile Computer Alternatives For Protecting Company X Information

Policy: When away from Company X offices, mobile computer users must utilize at least one of the following approaches to protect sensitive Company X information from unauthorized access: encryption software to protect the information when in storage, storage of the information only on disks or other removable storage media which are then kept with the worker at all times, or storage of this information only on a hard drive which is then removed and securely vaulted when unattended by the worker.

Commentary: The objective of this policy is to clearly specify how mobile computer users should protect Company X sensitive information when they are away from the office. The policy specifies three basic alternatives which involve either concealment of the information without removing it from the machine, removal of the information and keeping it with the worker, or removal of the information and keeping it in a secure location. Special attention is necessary for mobile computers as opposed to telecommuting computers because mobile computers are more likely to be stolen. With this policy, theft of the computer itself while the worker was away from it would not result in the unauthorized disclosure of sensitive information. Separately, this policy assumes that the worker knows what is and what is not "sensitive information;" if this distinction has not been made, the organization in question could require at least one of these three approaches for all Company X information resident on a mobile computer. The policy could be further enhanced, for secret (the most sensitive) information, by requiring both encryption and one of the two other alternatives mentioned in the policy. The policy writer should note that this policy addresses only sensitive information in storage, and additional controls will be needed for sensitive information in transmission (to prevent interception). For related ideas, see the policies entitled "Permissible Equipment For Telecommuting," "Travelling On Public Transportation With Secret Information," and "Exposure Of Sensitive Information In Public Places." A: E; E: MH.

1.4.8. Internet Connections

1.4.8.1. Access Control For Internet Connections

876. Access To Internet Requires Completion Of Training Course

Policy: Only those workers who have received department management approval may access the Internet via Company X facilities. Approval will be granted after these workers have completed an Internet policies and practices training course.

Commentary: The intention of this policy is to prevent unrestricted usage of the Internet by Company X workers. Because Internet usage presents a number of new and serious potential security problems, a separate training course is appropriate (generally only an hour or two). Ideally the training course would be delivered by computer based training (CBT), thus allowing users to complete it when their schedules permit. Separately, note that the policy does not inhibit departmental management from establishing additional requirements for granting permission to access the Internet. These requirements might include a business need for such access. For related ideas, see the policies entitled "Information Security Training Required For All Information Workers" and "Information Security Training Time Required." A: ET; E: MH.

877. Internet Privileges Reserved For Those With A Business Need

Policy: While electronic mail is provided to all workers, all other types of Internet access are reserved for those who have a demonstrable business need for such access. With the exception of electronic mail, all access to the Internet with Company X information systems must be approved in advance in writing by the relevant department manager.

Commentary: Many organizations are providing full access to the Internet to all office employees without really thinking about it (ftp, http, etc.). In the process, they are unwittingly creating various problems including productivity erosion (as people are distracted), and release of confidential and proprietary information (as people for example mistakenly post messages to discussion groups). This strict policy applies the concept of "need-to-know" to Internet access -- an approach that should have been adopted at many organizations long ago. Note that this policy is distinctly in opposition to the prevailing attitudes held by many employees, that Internet access is a fringe benefit. This policy will probably not be acceptable in a high-technology firm, where access to the latest technological toys is considered a perk. Operationally, this policy could be implemented by providing all office workers with a standard suite of applications including a word processing package, a spread sheet package, and an electronic mail program (but not an Internet browser). Generally-available Internet access can still be provided in a corporate library or in other common areas, thus making it much more difficult for users to waste time "surfing" the Internet. Separately, the policy could be further buttressed if workers requesting Internet access besides email were required to describe how their productivity will be enhanced by the additional access privileges. For a related idea, see the policy entitled "Privilege Restriction Based On The Need-to-Know." A: T; E: MH.

878. Workers Who Do Not Perform Research Denied Internet Web Access

Policy: Only those Company X workers who perform regular research as a part of their job will be granted Internet web access. All other workers will be given access to Internet web-resident data through news groups, electronic mail discussion groups, and push data feeds from the Internet to the Company X intranet.

Commentary: The intention of this policy is to limit access to the Internet web, and in the process to limit a variety of security problems. Such a limitation will, for example, reduce the risk of virus infestation due to dynamic content (Java, ActiveX, etc.). Similarly, this limitation will prevent workers from wasting time surfing the net while they are at work. This policy thus reduces the need for content screening software at a firewall (although it will still be desirable to screen electronic mail messages and attachments). This policy can be effectively implemented with products like Castanet from Marimba, which is a push content management software suite. This software can collect information, such as the latest interest rates, from Internet locations and then push that information to selected intranet sites. Users who need the information then go to the intranet sites, and do not have Internet web surfing access. For related ideas, see the policies entitled "Internet Privileges Reserved For Those With A Business Need" and "News Feeds From Internet For Company X Related Topics." A: ET; E: MH.

879. Expiration Of User-IDs On Internet Accessible Computers

Policy: User-IDs on Internet accessible computers must be set to expire six months from the time they are established. Renewals of these user-IDs are permissible, but must be restricted to six month intervals.

Commentary: The intention of this policy is to discourage and limit the use of user-IDs on Internet accessible computers. These user-IDs can be exploited by intruders, so it is best to keep them to an absolute minimum. The periodic renewal of such user-IDs is a minor inconvenience to the users involved. Most importantly, if a user-ID is no longer active, the requirement described in this policy eliminates a possible pathway to compromise the involved system. Most user activity (FTP, telnet, web surfing, etc.) can be performed from machines behind a firewall, and thus don't need to be done with user-IDs on Internet accessible machines. Likewise, in some instances, users will need to be informed that they don't need a user-ID on an Internet accessible machine in order to do Internet electronic mail; typically any mail server on an internal network will also be able to send and receive Internet electronic mail. Taking this policy one step further, some organizations give users a hard time, challenging their need for an user-ID on an Internet accessible machine; users may request these user-IDs because they provide an easier way to perform a variety of tasks that are also achievable with better-protected internal systems. Separately, there is nothing sacrosanct about the six month interval; it could just as easily be three months. For related ideas, see the policies entitled "Assignment Of Expired Passwords" and "Time Limits For User-IDs And File Retention Period After Expiration." A: T; E: LMH.

880. Company X Blocks Certain Non-Business Internet Web Sites

Policy: Company X information systems routinely prevent users from connecting with certain non-business web sites. Workers using Company X information systems who discover they have connected with a web site that contains sexually explicit, racist, or other potentially offensive material must immediately disconnect from that site. The ability to connect with a specific web site does not in itself imply that workers are permitted to visit that site.

Commentary: This policy is intended to prevent various problems, such as those resulting from the down-loading of pornographic pictures. These activities might be construed as creating a "hostile working environment," which in turn might expose an organization to lawsuits. The policy also recognizes a new breed of products which screen web activity, keeping it within certain limits. One example of a product like this is the Eagle firewall from Raptor Systems (Waltham, Massachusetts). Because so many sites are being added to the Internet so rapidly, it is not currently possible for these programs to prevent users from visiting all sites which are off limits according to existing policy. In response to this reality, this policy tells users to move on, and not to continue to pursue things at a particular off-limits site. For a complementary policy forbidding personal use, see the policy entitled "Personal Use of Computer And Communications Systems." Also see the policies entitled "Message Content Restrictions For Company X Information Systems" and "News Feeds From Internet For Company X Related Topics." A: E; E: LMH.

881. News Feeds From Internet For Company X Related Topics

Policy: News feeds, email mailing lists, push data updates, and other mechanisms for receiving information over the Internet must be restricted to material which is clearly related to Company X business as well as the duties of the receiving workers.

Commentary: The purpose of this policy is to put systems administrators on notice that they should screen news feeds from the Internet such that only business-oriented material gets through. This policy also implicitly gives management the right to examine email and push data updates to determine that the material is not only business related but germane to the duties of the receiving worker. In some cases, the policy can also be issued to users, in effect acting as a response to their requests for certain news feeds and other information services. Distribution of this policy to users is increasingly necessary as the new "push" information distribution technologies gain momentum on the Internet. The policy will prevent news feed discussions about sexual fetishes, bizarre hobbies, and other irrelevant things from distracting internal staff (thus the policy helps with productivity). The policy will also help conserve disk space and other system resources such as network bandwidth. The policy assumes users are not dialing-out to reach the Internet, but that they go through an internal firewall and related systems. If users are dialing-out, then decisions about news feeds will be made by an Internet access provider (IAP) and the involved users. For related ideas, see the policies entitled "Real-Time External Network Connections Require Firewalls" and "Personal Use Of Company X Internet Facilities Only On Personal Time." A: ET; E: LMH.

882. Extended User Authentication Required For In-Bound Internet Users

Policy: All users wishing to establish a connection with Company X computers via the Internet must authenticate themselves at a firewall before gaining access to Company X's internal network. This must be done via an extended user authentication process approved by the Director of Information Systems. Use of extended user authentication systems will prevent intruders from guessing fixed passwords or from replaying a fixed password captured via a wiretap. Designated "public" systems, such as Internet web sites, do not need these authentication processes because anonymous interactions are expected.

Commentary: Firewalls have been widely acclaimed to be the cure-all for Internet security problems. Although they have an important role to play, there is much more to Internet security than firewalls. This policy describes one of the major functions that should be performed by an effective Internet firewall. In most instances, firewalls allow unimpeded out-bound connections, but will stop or provide significant hurdles to those who wish to establish an in-bound connection through the firewall. This policy deliberately avoids discussing the technology that will be employed, in large measure because it is expected to change rapidly in the years ahead. Most often dynamic password systems (such as the Secure-ID system offered by Security Dynamics of Boston, Massachusetts, USA) are used at the firewall to authenticate the identity of in-bound users. Besides these smart-card based systems, other dynamic password technology like user-transparent challenge/response systems can be used (Softkey from Enigma Logic in Concord, California, USA is one example). Full session encryption can also be used as an alternative to dynamic passwords. Also see the policies entitled "Internet Connections Require Approved Firewalls," "Passwords Never In Readable Form When Outside Workstations" and "Extended User Authentication Systems Required For Dial-Up Lines." A: T; E: LMH.

883. Telnet Connections With Fixed Passwords Over Internet Prohibited

Policy: Telnet connections (also known as remote log-in connections on UNIX systems) using traditional fixed passwords over the Internet for Company X computers are prohibited unless these connections are established using dynamic passwords or some other approved extended user authentication technology.

Commentary: The intention of this policy is to prevent fixed passwords from being intercepted over the Internet and replayed later to gain unauthorized access to Company X systems. With Sniffers (from Network General, Menlo Park, California, USA) and other wiretapping devices readily available, it is straightforward for intruders to automatically capture passwords moving over the Internet. These attacks can be thwarted with dynamic password systems such as those offered by Security Dynamics (Boston, Massachusetts, USA), as well as other extended user authentication technologies like voiceprints and user typing patterns. This policy is also intended to put technical staff on notice about the privileges that should be allowed via a firewall or other Internet connection devices (routers, gateways, etc.). As a side comment, the words "remote log-in" are often abbreviated "rlogin" in a manner consistent with a UNIX command of the same name. See the policies entitled "Extended User Authentication Required For In-Bound Internet Users" and "Extended User Authentication Systems Required For Dial-Up Lines." A: ET; E: LMH.

884. Updating Company X Information Through The Internet

Policy: Users connecting to Company X systems via the Internet are not permitted to directly modify any Company X information.

Commentary: This policy reflects the evolving security facilities for the Internet and the concerns that many managers still have about inadequate security. The policy seeks to maintain the integrity of internal records through a filtering process. Internet-connected users (whether customers, suppliers, employees, or some other group) can, according to this policy, submit requests for internal record updates, but these requests must be reviewed by either a person or an automated process before being posted to Company X's production information stores such as databases, data dictionaries, master files, web pages, etc. This policy is intended to reassure management that current systems will not allow a dangerous activity -- but from a technological standpoint, the policy really is unnecessary. With strong user authentication mechanisms (like dynamic password tokens) and strong encryption systems, the modification of internal records via the Internet can be secure. This policy, if adopted, may need to be modified in a few years as Internet-based electronic commerce facilities are installed. For example, a definition of "direct modification" may be a "real-time update based on user-provided information without reasonableness checks." For related ideas, see the policies entitled "Business Production Information Updates By Non-Production Staff" and "All Production Transactions Must Be Authorized By Management." A: T; E: LMH.

885. Disabling Java Within Internet Web Browsers

Policy: All Internet users must disable Java programs by changing the default configuration of their Internet browser software. This setting can be changed only when users visit the web sites of known and trusted organizations, or when they use the Company X intranet. If this setting is changed, it must be promptly changed back as soon as users go onto the Internet.

Commentary: Although many of the threats from unauthorized Java applets have been generated in research labs rather than experienced in the real world, there exists a significant risk that Java programming language could be used to circumvent existing access control mechanisms. The resulting damage would be very much like a computer virus (file erasure, file modifications, system crash, etc.). While some firewalls can screen out Java applets, in many organizations such firewalls have not yet been installed. Until reliable security mechanisms for Java applets become more widely available, users may need to be told to disable Sun Microsystems' Java at the browser level (Java derivatives, such as the one offered by Hewlett-Packard may also need to be turned off). This policy is likely to generate significant resistance from users since the capabilities that the Java language provides are powerful and for many users quite exciting. Separately, the policy could be modified to make reference to Microsoft's ActiveX, Microsoft Visual Basic scripts, and Macromedia Shockwave files, all of which from a security standpoint present some of the same risks as Java (and all of which are considered "active content"). Note that Netscape's Java Script also presents some serious security problems, and it too can be turned off at the browser level. For a related policy see "Prohibition Against Down-Loading Software From Third Party Systems." A: ET; E: LMH.

886. Java Program Execution Prohibited Unless Digital Signature Validated

Policy: Workers are prohibited from executing Java applets downloaded from the Internet unless (1) the applet is from a known and trusted source, and (2) the digital signature has been checked and no problem has been discovered.

Commentary: This permissive approach to running Java applications (or "applets") on desktop machines is intended to prevent viruses, Trojan horses, and other malicious code from being executed on Company X computers. The policy assumes users can distinguish between those circumstances where a digital signature has been checked and no error message is presented to the user, and those circumstances where the digital signature checking mechanism has been turned off. The policy thus assumes a technically aware audience. For a less technically sophisticated audience, many organizations will want to simply block the inbound passage of applets at a firewall. On a different note, the scope of this policy could be expanded to include Microsoft's ActiveX, Microsoft Visual Basic scripts, and Macromedia Shockwave files, all of which from a security standpoint present some of the same risks as Java (all are considered "active content"). For a more stringent approach that does not assume such firewall blocking, see the policy entitled "Disabling Java Within Internet Web Browsers." A: E; E: LMH.

887. Firewalls Screen Out All Active Content (Java, Active X, Etc.)

Policy: Because the security surrounding active content (Sun's Java, Microsoft's Active X, Microsoft's Visual Basic scripts, Macromedia Shockwave files, etc.) does not meet Company X standards, all inbound applets containing this type of code will be automatically removed by a firewall.

Commentary: The intention of this policy is to prevent damage to users' computers and information. The types of damage include hard disk erasure and other malicious events that one would customarily see when a malicious virus delivered its "payload." Active content programs on the Internet are increasingly being used to circumvent existing access controls and to cause serious damage. For example, Netscape's Java Script was used by one hacker to get Hotmail users to reenter their passwords and user-IDs; meanwhile these were being stored for subsequent use by the hacker. To prevent such problems, some firms are simply prohibiting all inbound active content (it still may be used on an intranet). This approach, involving screening things out at the firewall level, eliminates user choices, and thus achieves an overall higher level of security than any approach which depends on user actions (like disabling certain types of programs in a browser). For related ideas, see the policy entitled "Java Program Execution Prohibited Unless Digital Signature Validated" and "Disabling Java Within Internet Web Browsers." A: T; E: LMH.

888. Internet Access With Company X Computers Must Go Through Firewall

Policy: Internet access using computers in Company X offices is permissible only when users go through a Company X firewall. Other ways to access the Internet, such as dial-up connections with an Internet Service Provider (ISP), are prohibited if Company X computers are employed.
Commentary: This policy prevents users from deliberately or unwittingly circumventing the controls supported by a firewall. These controls include the ability to: screen inbound (down-loaded) files for viruses, scan outbound files for keywords indicating sensitivity, bar the connection with certain web sites, log the user's activity, and block the down-loading of Java applets and other active content. If users wish to access the Internet via an ISP, they can do so on their own time with their own equipment (unless they are on the road or telecommuting). The

policy is restricted to computers in Company X offices because telecommuters and mobile computer users cannot practically abide by the requirements of this policy. Separately, while firewalls were originally conceived of as stripped-down computers dedicated to network access control tasks, their functionality is rapidly expanding, further underscoring their role as funnels through which certain types of external communications must flow. For a related idea, see the policy entitled "Permissible Internet Access Without Firewalls." A: ET; E: LMH.

1.4.8.2. Internet Representations And Identity Validation

889. Disclaimer Must Accompany All Internet Personal Messages

Policy: Whenever a worker posts a message to an Internet discussion group, an electronic bulletin board, or another public information system, this message must be accompanied by words clearly indicating that the comments do not necessarily represent the position of Company X. Such statements are required even when Company X's name does not appear in the text of the message and/or when an affiliation with Company X has not been explicitly stated. Exceptions will of course be made in those instances where the message has been approved for release by the Public Relations Department.

Commentary: The intention of this policy is to shield Company X against libel claims, copyright infringement claims, unauthorized release of trade secrets, or other problems that may be created when one of its workers makes a posting to a public information system. Such disclaimers are needed even when the name of the organization does not appear in the message text. A number of different pieces of information could reveal the involved organization; these include the nature of the comments made, the electronic mail address involved, or the individual's name alone (when combined with knowledge that this person works at a certain organization). Also see the policies entitled "Disclaimer Of Responsibility Or Liability For Message Contents," "All Public Representations Must Be Cleared Through Public Relations," and "Comments On Systems Do Not Necessarily Reflect Company X Positions." A: E; E: LMH.

890. Internet Representations Including Company X Affiliation

Policy: When engaged in discussion groups, chat rooms, and other Internet offerings, only those individuals authorized by management to provide official support for Company X products and services may indicate their affiliation with Company X. This may be accomplished explicitly by adding certain words to their messages. Alternatively, it can be accomplished implicitly via the use of an electronic mail address. In either case, unless they have received instructions to the contrary, whenever workers disclose an affiliation with Company X, they must clearly indicate that "the opinions expressed are my own, and not necessarily those of my employer."

Commentary: The intention of this policy is to strictly limit the number of official representations on the Internet coming from Company X. This will help reduce the chances of libel, defamation, misrepresentation, and similar legal problems. Organizations adopting this policy may additionally wish to put those authorized to represent them on the Internet through a public relations training class. Separately, an area that may need additional clarification involves official pronouncements such as press releases. In most cases, however, the policy words "unless they have received instructions to the contrary" will cover these cases. For related ideas, see the policies entitled "Disclaimer Must Accompany All Internet Personal Messages" and "Comments On Systems Do Not Necessarily Reflect Company X Positions." A: E; E: LMH.

891. Internet Discussion Group And Chat Room Participation Forbidden

Policy: Unless expressly authorized by the Public relations department, when using Company X information systems, all Company X workers are forbidden from participating in Internet discussion groups, chat rooms, or other public electronic forums.

Commentary: The intention of this policy is to prevent embarrassment to Company X, and perhaps legal trouble as well. All too often one person within a certain organization says one thing while another person says something quite different. This can be the genesis of an investigation, lawsuit, or simply bad press. This policy seeks to strictly limit who is representing the organization on the Internet. The policy is necessary because so many people take an informal attitude towards posting material on the Internet; in effect, the policy says "watch what you say in public." Separately, the words "public electronic forums" could include on-line teleconferences and other arrangements. The words were deliberately vague in order to be able to embrace new technologies without having to change the policy. For related ideas, see the policies entitled "All Public Representations Must Be Cleared Through Public Relations," "Internet Discussion Group Participation And Release Of Trade Secrets," and "Right To Free Speech Does Not Apply To Company X Systems." A: E; E: LMH.

892. Internet Representations About Company X Products & Services

Policy: Workers must not advertise, promote, present, or otherwise make statements about Company X products and services in Internet forums such as mailing lists, news groups, or chat sessions without the prior approval of the Public Relations or Marketing Departments.

Commentary: The intention of this policy is to control what workers say about Company X products and services. This policy helps ensure that public representations are consistent and a reflection of management's intentions. The communications facilities provided by the Internet open up a vast new array of ways for workers to communicate, but if legal problems such as libel and defamation of character are to be avoided, these communications need to be carefully controlled. In many instances, workers are well-meaning, hoping to help their employer; but the net effect (pun intended) may be quite different. Separately, this policy allows the organization to train designated people who then regularly monitor these forums, and respond as the discussion thread warrants. For related ideas, see the policies entitled "Prior Review For Speeches, Presentations, Technical Papers, Etc." and "Approval Required Prior To Release Of Company X Information." A: E; E: LMH.

893. Disclosure Of Personal Contact Information In Public Internet Forums

Policy: Children (as well as adults concerned about stalking, harassment, or other invasions of their privacy) should not disclose their real names, addresses, or telephone numbers on electronic bulletin boards, chat rooms, or other public forums reached by the Internet.

Commentary: A version of this policy is suggested by the Interactive Services Association and is intended to prevent children (or adults who are concerned about stalking, harassment, or other invasions of their privacy) from being needlessly bothered. The policy is a reaction to attempts by pedophiles to lure children into meetings, by crazy people who stalk others they have met on-line, and to a California case where a movie star was murdered by someone who located her address through computerized motor vehicle department public records. Intended for personal use of the Internet, the policy is impractical for most Internet business activities because the parties will need to exchange money or physical items, in which case contact information must be correct. The policy puts people on notice that they can conceal their identity and that they need not disclose such information when on-line (many are not aware of this). The policy is most relevant to off-hours use of the Internet. Organizations giving this policy to their users may also want to include instructions to the following effect: (1) children need not respond to messages they consider suggestive, belligerent, or that in some other way makes them feel uncomfortable, and (2) children must not arrange face-to-face meetings with another computer user without prior parental consent. Parents may also be advised to look into software that can monitor the content of Internet sessions as well as other software that can block access to certain Internet sites which contain what the parents consider to be "inappropriate material" (generally this means pornography). Organizations taking a proactive approach to these potential problems with the children of employees will help reduce personal problems that may in turn interfere with employee work performance. For related ideas, see the policies entitled "Privacy Expectations And Electronic Mail" and "Validating The Identity Of External Parties On The Internet." A: E; E: LMH.

894. Political Advocacy Statements And Product/Service Endorsements

Policy: Whenever an Internet user provides an affiliation with Company X --whether implicitly or explicitly -- care must be taken not to make any political advocacy statements or product/service endorsements unless the permission of the Public Relations Department has first been obtained.

Commentary: Chat rooms, newsgroups (listservs), and electronic mail give Internet users a tremendous and unprecedented opportunity to reach others. This policy is intended to blunt that opportunity, making sure that it is used in a manner which furthers an organization's interests, and which does not create legal or public relations trouble. The reference to "implicit or explicit" could be explained in greater detail if the audience is not familiar with these distinctions (an electronic mail address alone may implicitly convey an affiliation, whereas the provision of contact information at the end of a posting may explicitly convey that affiliation). Separately, this policy in no way prevents Internet users from making the prohibited statements as an individual (without any affiliation to Company X), using a personal electronic mail address and other non-Company X facilities. On another note, some organizations will want the legal department to approve rather than the public relations department. For a related idea, see the policy entitled "Internet Representations Including Company X Affiliation." A: E; E: LMH.

895. Internet Discussion Group Participation And Release Of Trade Secrets

Policy: Participation in discussion groups, chat rooms, and other public Internet forums related to Company X business is restricted to designated workers who have been briefed about the release of trade secrets. Simply reading the postings of others is acceptable for those who have not been so designated.

Commentary: The intention of this policy is to prevent inadvertent release of trade secrets in public forums such as Internet discussion groups (listservs). Often well-meaning employees will be participating in discussions and only later realize that they have said something which could be considered to be confidential or proprietary. Note that this policy deliberately says nothing about participation in public forums on topics that are not related to Company X business. The policy's scope could also be expanded to include chat rooms on the Internet. For related ideas, see the policy entitled "Internet Representations Including Company X Affiliation," "Disclaimer Of Responsibility Or Liability For Message Contents," and "Trade Secrets Specifically Identified Prior To Disclosure." A: E; E: LMH.

896. Validating The Identity Of External Parties On The Internet

Policy: It is relatively easy to spoof the identity of another user on public networks such as the Internet. Before workers release any internal Company X information, enter into any contracts, or order any products via public networks, the identity of the individuals and organizations contacted must be confirmed. Identity confirmation is ideally performed via digital certificates, but in cases where these are not yet available, other means such as letters of credit, third party references, and telephone conversations may be used.

Commentary: There have been a number of cases where individuals have represented that they were somebody else, such as the president of the United States. In overall terms, this policy is therefore intended to put workers on notice that they need to perform a due diligence process before they rely on the alleged identity of those they correspond with over public networks. Identity confirmation is not built into the Internet, and must be achieved via controls added by user organizations (such as this policy). Over the next ten years the most prevalent and most expedient way to confirm the identity of other users will be via digital certificates (offered by firms such as Verisign, Redwood City, California, USA). Digital certificates are the equivalent of an Internet passport, providing a third party's vouching for a certain individual's identity or organization's identity. Digital certificates in turn allow digital signatures to be performed; digital signatures indicate that a message was not modified in transit, and that it definitively came from the designated originating individual or organization. One increasingly popular digital signature system is provided by a subsidiary of RSA Data Security (Redwood City, California, USA). Use of encryption systems which incorporate source authentication features, as is the case with Privacy Enhanced Mail (PEM), provides another way to confirm the identity of a correspondent over the Internet. Also see the policy entitled "In-Person Proof Of Identity To Obtain A Password," "Disclosure Of Personal Contact Information In Public Internet Forums," and "Extended User Authentication Systems Required For Dial-Up Lines." A: E; E: LMH.

897. Digital Certificate For All Company X Internet Web And Commerce Sites

Policy: A current digital certificate is required for every Internet server handling Company X business to which customers, prospects, and others may connect.

Commentary: The intention of this policy is to prevent third parties from establishing Internet systems that masquerade as though they are Company X systems (or at least prevent these third parties from doing business without being detected). Digital certificates are like passports because they definitively authenticate the identity of either individuals or organizations, in this case the latter. Digital certificates include certain encryption related information that allows a remote third party to check that they have reached a genuine Company X system (preventing so-called "node spoofing"). This usage of digital certificates does not require that remote third parties have digital certificates, or that they even check the digital certificate that is posted by Company X on its Internet systems (although recent browsers can perform this task). This usage is relatively inexpensive and provides one of the basic control mechanisms necessary for Internet commerce activities. On another note, the word "current" in the policy is necessary because third party certificate authorities (such as Verisign, Redwood City, California, USA) issue digital certificates for brief periods of time, which means that they need to be periodically renewed. For related ideas, see the policies entitled "Use Of Any Encryption Process Requires Prior Written Approval," "Positive Identification Required For System Usage," and "Personal Identifiers Must Not Appear On Publicly-Accessible Locations." A: E; E: LMH.

898. Workers Must Not Conceal Their Identity When Using The Internet

Policy: When using Company X information systems, or when conducting Company X business, workers must not deliberately conceal or misrepresent their identity. This policy includes participating in discussion groups and chat rooms, as well as establishing accounts on other computers. Use of anonymous FTP log-ins, anonymous UUCP log-ins, HTTP (web) browsing, and other access methods established with the expectation that users would be anonymous are permissible.

Commentary: This policy is intended to prevent workers from employing Company X systems for questionable activities such as purchasing pornography via the Internet. Without valid user identity information, logs will be considerably less useful. Likewise, the absence of an identifier may encourage people to do things which they would not otherwise do (perhaps engage in illegal acts like threatening violence). One of the fundamental principles of secure systems design is that positive user identification must be obtained before access controls can be applied; if the identity of a user has not been established, then the effectiveness of access controls is considerably diminished. If workers wish to conceal their identity, perhaps for a special interest discussion group, they can always do so with a personal user-ID obtained from an Internet Service Provider (ISP). On another note, this policy forbids the use of electronic mail remailers, which have allegedly been used to commit crimes and conduct questionable activities. For a related idea, see "Extended User Authentication Required For In-Bound Internet Users." A: ET; E: LMH.

1.4.8.3. Internet Content Management

899. Respecting The Intellectual Property Rights Of Others On The Internet

Policy: Although the Internet is an informal communications environment, the laws for copyrights, patents, trademarks, and the like still apply. To this end, workers using Company X systems must for example (1) repost or reproduce material only after obtaining permission from the source, (2) quote material from other sources only if these other sources are identified, and (3) reveal internal Company X information on the Internet only if the information has been officially approved for public release.

Commentary: While this policy may appear at first to fall in the domain of on-line manners ("netiquette"), it is intended to remind users that the informal environment found on the Internet does not mean that they can ignore intellectual property laws. The informality surrounding the Internet has already sparked a number of libel cases, which conceivably could have been avoided if this policy were stressed. While the policy may at first seem obvious, there is a great deal of confusion about these matters in the user community. Accordingly, it is necessary to be crystal clear in order to set user expectations, and if necessary, be able to discipline the offending user. Separately, some organizations will want to expand the policy to make reference to libel, slander, defamation of character, and related legal issues. For related ideas, see the policies entitled "User Checking Of Information Before Posting To The Intranet" and "Assignment Of Patent, Copyright, And Other Intellectual Property Rights." A: E; E: LMH.

900. Sending Software And Other Sensitive Information Over The Internet

Policy: Company X secret, proprietary, or private information must never be sent over the Internet unless it has first been encrypted by approved methods. Unless specifically known to be in the public domain, source code must always be encrypted before being sent over the Internet.

Commentary: The intent of this policy is to put users on notice that the Internet does not, by default, provide information protection. This policy is a general version of the policy entitled

"Treat Electronic Mail As Public Communications" with a different emphasis. It seeks to ensure that encryption is being used for all sensitive information sent over the Internet. Organizations should consider the adoption of Internet encryption standards such as PEM (Privacy Enhanced Mail) and PGP (Pretty Good Privacy). Ultimately, encryption facilities will be incorporated by default into many networks, but until these facilities are provided, it will be necessary to get users involved in the encryption process. Separately, note that source code is especially proprietary and needs to be acknowledged as such by many organizations. This policy takes special steps to recognize source code as a type of information in need of special protection. This policy is accordingly most suitable for organizations like telephone companies and software houses, which generate their own source code. See the policies entitled "Physical Security Or Encryption Required For All Sensitive Information," "Automated Encryption Key Management Systems Preferred," and "Encryption Required For Sending Secret Information by Fax." A: E; E: LMH.

901. Removal Of Inappropriate Electronic Postings To Public Forums

Policy: Electronic mail sent by Company X workers to Internet discussion groups, electronic bulletin boards, or other public forums may be removed if determined to be inconsistent with Company X's business interests or existing Company policy. Messages in this category include: (a) political statements, (b) religious statements, (c) cursing or other foul language, and (d) statements viewed as harassing others based on race, creed, color, age, sex, physical handicap, or sexual inclination. The decision to remove electronic mail must be made by the Information Security Manager or the Human Resources Manager. When practical and feasible, individuals responsible for the message will be informed of the decision and given the opportunity to remove the message(s) themselves.

Commentary: The motivation for this policy is to put employees on notice that their public postings may be censored if these postings are later determined to be inconsistent with Company X business interests or policies. This policy is intended to make employees more thoughtful about their postings (hopefully avoiding "flames" and related angry outbursts). The policy is also intended to give Company X the unequivocal right to quickly delete inappropriate postings without a formal decision process and without the need to consider objections. Some organizations may wish to change the policy slightly to make it clear that if individuals in no way state or imply their affiliation with Company X (including implied affiliations via an electronic mail address), then Company X will have no right to censor their messages. One advisable exception to the restriction mentioned in the last sentence involves messages which deal with Company X business activities. For example, if a Company X customer service representative made a personal statement on a Compuserve forum which painted Company X in a bad light, and if the individual's affiliation was in no way linked to the Company, then the Company could still delete that message. On another note, the ability to delete messages sent by others will become increasingly difficult in the years ahead as digital signatures, encryption routines, and access controls will be used to prevent others from deleting a message they did not send. In many of these instances, all an employer will be able to do is request deletion from the system manager or service provider. In light of this trend, the existence of a policy like this can facilitate message deletion arrangements between Company X management and the involved system operator. Separately, the legal rights of Company X suppressing an individual's right to free speech is an issue here, and should be discussed with internal legal counsel. Also see the policies entitled "Right To Censor Data On Organizational Systems," "Disclaimer Of Responsibility Or Liability For Message Contents," and "Standards Of Common Carriers Do Not Apply." A: ET; E: LMH.

902. Search Engines To Detect Misleading Web Sites With Similar Names

Policy: Company X Legal Department staff must periodically employ web search engines to determine whether any web sites with similar names are masquerading as Company X authorized or sponsored sites.

Commentary: The intention of this policy is to make sure that an internal staff member (typically in the Legal Department) is using search engines to ferret out potentially confusing sites which may be using a similar name. For example, a short while back, if a user typed "wwwbankofamerica.com," then the user would be connected to "www.wwwbankofamerica.com" rather than the intended site which was "www.bankofamerica.com." Simply missing a period in this case would take a user to a fraudulent site which gathered passwords and user-IDs, and could conceivably use these parameters to break into legitimate bank accounts. This policy informs internal staff that they must search for such spoof sites, and once they detect one, hopefully they would bring it to the attention of somebody who could do something about it (typically the general counsel). In the case noted above, the bank did sue the site to force it to change its name or take the site down. Banks aren't the only ones being targeted by these types of fraud; Paypal.com was recently spoofed by paypai.com. This policy would generally only be used by Internet commerce sites that were concerned about fraud, or other sites that were concerned about their good name being tarnished by an authorized web site. For related considerations, see the policies entitled "Monitoring Internet For Use Of Trademark And Copyrighted Materials" and "Unofficial Web Pages Permitted Only By Contract." A: E; E: H.

903. Posting Company X Material On The Internet

Policy: Users must not place Company X material (software, internal memos, press releases, etc.) on any publicly-accessible Internet computer system unless the posting has first been approved by the Director of Public Relations.

Commentary: The intention of this policy is to put workers on notice that they are not allowed to release information to outsiders via the Internet unless it has first been approved by the Public Relations Director. A policy like this would, for example, provide a software development firm with sufficient justification for terminating an employee who posted copies of new software to the Internet a few days before the software was officially released. Many users of the Internet have the belief that information should be shared and spread-around; this policy explicitly notifies them not to act using that philosophy. In some other cases, individuals may think they are being helpful, for example by posting a list of known bugs to a commercial software package to the Internet. Misguided helpfulness can therefore also be prevented by this policy. Separately, this policy could be expanded to include other examples, such as business prospects, product performance information, union negotiation information, and the like. To motivate compliance, an accompanying explanation could make reference to possible libel and defamation problems, as well as fluctuations in Company X's stock price. See the policies entitled "Removal Of Inappropriate Electronic Postings To Public Forums," "All Public Representations Must Be Cleared Through Public Relations," "Unofficial Web Pages Permitted Only By Contract," "Truthful Representations By Company X Employees," and "Prior Review For Speeches, Presentations, Technical Papers, Etc." A: E; E: LMH.

1.4.8.4. Electronic Commerce And The Internet

904. Establishing New Business Arrangements Via Internet

Policy: Unless the Director of Information Technology and the Chief Legal Counsel have both approved in advance, users are prohibited from using Internet connections to establish new or different business channels. These channels include electronic data interchange (EDI) arrangements, electronic malls with on-line shopping, on-line database services, etc.

Commentary: The intention of this policy is to stop in-house initiatives to conduct business via the Internet (also known as "electronic commerce" in some circles) until security can be assured. Because standard security measures for such arrangements are largely undefined, it is critical that in-house staff examine the security of such arrangements before Company X goes live with production systems. Although certain specialty trade associations for doing business on the Internet have recently cropped up (Commercenet of Santa Clara, California, USA is one example), most organizations have not yet defined the essential controls that must accompany Internet business transactions. (A document containing these essential control ideas is generally known as a "security architecture.") Advance approval by the managers identified in the policy is accordingly required. Advance approval of electronic commerce systems by the procurement department may also be required in some instances. See the policies entitled "Formation Of Binding Contracts Via Electronic Systems" and "Trading Partner Agreement Required Prior To Use Of EDI." A: ET; E: LMH.

905. Production In-House Systems May Not Be Directly Internet Connected

Policy: In-house production information systems, such as a mainframe, must not be directly connected to the Internet. Instead these systems must connect with a commerce server, a database server, or some other intermediate computer that is dedicated to Internet business activity.

Commentary: The objective of this policy is to limit the damage that a hacker or cracker can do if he or she breaks into the first Company X computer accessible via the Internet. Some organizations these days are directly connecting their production systems to the Internet. This practices is not recommended because if that machine were compromised, all the production data on that machine would be at risk (including the materials that are not Internet related). Likewise, if that production machine were damaged by a hacker, then all production activity done by that system would be stopped, not just Internet activity. This policy reflects good practice for Internet commerce, and given the low cost of computers today, it does not impose a heavy financial penalty on the organization adopting it. On another note, to be still more effective, the policy could state that the intermediate computer must have another operating system or another access control mechanism than the attached production computer (this provides "defensive depth" against intrusions). For related ideas, see the policies entitled "Direct Network Connections With Outside Organizations (Tunnels)" and "Establishing New Business Arrangements Via Internet." A: T; E: MH.

1.4.8.5. Sending & Receiving Internet Information

906. Publicly-Writable Directories On Company X Computers Cleared Nightly

Policy: All publicly writable directories on Company X Internet-connected computers will be reviewed and cleared each evening. This process is necessary because pirated software, purloined passwords, stolen credit card numbers, erotica, and other information inconsistent with Company X's business may otherwise be anonymously exchanged in such areas.

Commentary: This policy intends to prevent Company X computers from being used as a free staging-point for the exchange of illegal, immoral, abusive, or simply personal information. There are a number of publicly-disclosed cases where hackers have used publicly-writable directories on web servers, ftp servers, and similar Internet-connected machines to store the types of information mentioned in this policy. This policy is also desirable because it helps prevent Company X from unwittingly being named as an accomplice to a crime, or the provider of a controversial and high-visibility computer system. On another note, the procedures to support this policy can be automated via command scripts, so the policy's implementation need not be expensive. The policy and the procedures used to implement it are a direct outgrowth of the fundamental policy entitled "Use Of Company X Information For Non-Business Purposes." A: T; E: LMH.

907. Encryption For Files Left On Anonymous FTP Servers

Policy: All user-provided files which have not been explicitly approved for public release by the Marketing Department, and which are resident on Company X's anonymous FTP server, must be encrypted using Company X standard software.

Commentary: The intention of this policy is to let the user community know that they must not leave readable files on an anonymous file transfer protocol (FTP) server unless these files have been approved for public release. A few organizations have employees who have developed a dangerous (although convenient) habit of leaving readable files on an anonymous FTP server so that the files can be picked up by business partners, customers, and others external to the organization. Of course, this exposes these same files to unauthorized access by other people who happen to visit that same server (although having an unpublished address for the web server will decrease this risk). It is relatively easy to write a script to periodically erase all files on the anonymous FTP web server which are not encrypted with an in-house standard encryption package (such as Viacrypt's Pretty Good Privacy, alias PGP). This is accordingly an automatic enforcement process for the policy shown here. This policy also allows an organization to abandon the ill-advised but still often-encountered security practice where user-IDs and fixed passwords were shared by both inside and outside parties, thereby allowing the outside parties to gain access to files placed on a web server. Another desirable aspect of encrypting these files is that unauthorized modifications will be immediately evident; without encryption for this purpose, digital signatures may be required to quickly spot unauthorized changes. For related ideas, see the policy entitled "Secret Data Sent Over Networks Must Be Encrypted." A: ET; E: LMH.

908. Encryption Of All Payment Information On Internet-Accessible Machines

Policy: To prevent unauthorized disclosure, all payment information, such as checking account numbers and credit card numbers, must be encrypted when stored on any Company X Internet-accessible computer.

Commentary: The motivation for this policy is to ensure that payment information will not be disclosed to hackers, industrial spies, disgruntled ex-employees and other unauthorized parties if these same parties were able to defeat the access control systems of Internet-accessible computers. Disclosure is an issue with respect to these payment parameters because they are equivalent to a fixed password (access to the parameters allows unauthorized persons to obtain money). This policy provides a second level of security, which would be effective even if firewalls and password-based access controls had been compromised. The policy deliberately avoids making reference to the type of file in which the payment information resides (database files, word processing files, etc.) in order to apply across-the-board to all such files. This policy is a standard recommendation coming from the major credit card companies, but still many Internet merchants don't follow this basic and important rule. Note that this policy deals only with the storage of the information; the information still needs to be protected in transit (via SSL or Secure Sockets Layer encryption for example). The policy writer should also note that this policy makes reference to "Internet-accessible computers" not just "Internet-connected computers;" this means that the policy applies to all machines that an intruder might reach via the Internet, not just the computers on the periphery directly interfacing with the Internet. For similar ideas, see the policies entitled "Identity Theft Prevention By Restricting Access To Personal Information," "Daily Removal Of Logs From Internet-Accessible Computers," and "Shredding Of Credit Card Receipts And Other Payment Information." A: T; E: LMH.

909. Avoid Tipping-Off Competition Through Public Network Postings

Policy: Care must be taken to properly structure comments and questions posted to electronic bulletin boards, electronic mailing lists, on-line news groups, and related forums on public networks like the Internet. If workers aren't careful they may tip-off the competition that certain Company X projects are underway. If a user is working on an unannounced software product, a research & development project, or related confidential Company X matters, all related postings must be cleared with one's manager prior to being posted to any public network.
Commentary: This policy is intended to sensitize Company X workers about postings on public electronic systems. While at first the policy may seem to be a restatement of common sense, by explicitly putting workers on notice Company X gains several advantages: (a) the ability to discipline or terminate workers who do not abide by it, and (b) the ability to successfully defend against wrongful termination lawsuits brought by those who have been terminated for offenses of this nature. The Internet and other public forums are new to many users, and often users don't draw a clear line between internal and external networks; this policy is intended to remind them about the importance of drawing such a distinction. For related ideas, see the policies entitled "Confidentiality Agreements And Disclosures Of Sensitive Information" and "Notification Of Suspected Loss Or Disclosure Of Sensitive Information." A: E; E: LMH.

910. Handling Software And Files Down-Loaded From Internet

Policy: All software and files down-loaded from non-Company X sources via the Internet (or any other public network) must be screened with virus detection software. This screening must take place prior to being run or examined via another program such as a word processing package.

Commentary: The intention of this policy is to clearly define the process that users must go through before they execute software or open data files that have been down loaded from public networks. While viruses, Trojan horses, and worms used to be threats only with software, they are now increasingly being included with data files (such as macros that come along with spreadsheet programs). Accordingly, screening of both programs and data files is necessary. And to contain the spread of these unauthorized programs, the screening must take place before any other program is used (with the possible exception of decompression and/or decryption programs). Separately, the most cost-effective place to deal with viruses or similar unauthorized programs is at the point where they enter an organization, as addressed in this policy. Dealing with these unauthorized programs after they have started to spread throughout an organization is considerably more expensive. This policy helps to reduce the negative side-effects occasioned by viruses and related programs; these include system down-time, unauthorized erasure of data files, and subtle unnoticeable modification of data files. On another note, this policy will be considerably easier to implement if each user has a current virus-detection program on his or her workstation. Also see the policies entitled "Prohibition Against Down-Loading Software From Third Party Systems," "Controls Needed For Down-Loading Sensitive Company X Information," and "Testing for Viruses Prior To Use On Company X Systems." A: EMT; E: LMH.

911. Transferring Files Down-Loaded From Internet To Another Computer

Policy: Internet access is only permitted from stand-alone personal computers. All files down-loaded from the Internet must be checked with an authorized virus detection package prior to being moved to any other computer.

Commentary: This very conservative policy is intended to prevent viruses, Trojan horses, worms, and other malicious code from being propagated across internal computer networks. It allows Internet access, but only from personal computers which are isolated from other internal machines (in some instances specific instructions about how to isolate a personal computer will be necessary). This policy then goes on to insist that all down-loaded files be checked for viruses prior to being transferred to any other machine. Note that the policy is not limited to software -- it includes data files as well; this approach acknowledges the reality of modern "macroviruses." The policy also emphasizes the role that networks and interconnectivity plays in the propagation of viruses, a topic that many end-users do not yet appreciate. Note that this policy differs from the policy entitled "Required Process For Checking Software Down-Loaded From Internet" because it requires personal computer isolation prior to the establishment of an Internet connection. A: E; E: H.

912. Reliability Of Information Down-Loaded from Internet

Policy: All information taken off the Internet should be considered suspect until confirmed by another source. There is no quality control process on the Internet, and a considerable amount of Internet information is outdated, inaccurate, or deliberately misleading.

Commentary: The intention of this policy is to make workers aware that much of the information on the Internet is not reliable. Workers often naively believe that what they read on the Internet is trustworthy. The Internet is, for the most part, unregulated and unsupervised. As a result, con games and other scams are now being perpetrated via the Internet. One of the most prevalent Internet misrepresentations involves provision of information allegedly for the public's benefit, when it is in fact a disguised advertisement. This policy defines proper expectations regarding the quality of Internet-provided information (in some respects this is information engineering). A positive side-effect of this policy is that it causes staff to think more deeply about the quality of the information they use for decision-making. Separately, the policy could be expanded to include a prohibition against updating or modifying Company X records until the Internet information has been confirmed by another source. See the policy entitled "Dithering To Conceal True Nature Of Signal" and "Regular Testing Of Used Data Media Employed For Archival Storage." A: E; E: LMH.

913. Exchanges Of Information Over The Internet

Policy: Company X software, documentation, and all other types of internal information must not be sold or otherwise transferred to any non-Company X party for any purposes other than the business purposes expressly authorized by management. Exchanges of software and/or data between Company X and any third party may not proceed unless a written agreement has first been signed by a vice president. Such an agreement must specify the terms of the exchange, as well as the ways in which the software and/or data is to be handled and protected. Regular business practices--such as shipment of technical information in response to a customer purchase order--need not involve such a specific agreement since the terms of the exchange are already defined.

Commentary: There is a large and growing underground market in information flourishing on the Internet. Often individuals will swap credit card numbers, trade secrets, and other information via the Internet. This policy is expressly intended to prohibit the unauthorized exchange of inside information via the Internet. Often organizations are surprised to find that their workers have been releasing information that management considered to be confidential. Consider the case of Hydro Quebec, a Canadian utility company (for details, read the 29 February 1988 issue of Computerworld). Only after the issuance of a policy about the release of customer information did management discover that customer information had been routinely sold to outsiders by certain employees. The lesson of this story is that assuming that workers understand these ideas may lead to dysfunctional results. Also see the policies entitled "Software Or Data Exchanges With Third Parties Require Agreements," "Posting Company X Material On The Internet" and "Notification Of Suspected Loss Or Disclosure Of Sensitive Information." A: E; E: LMH.

914. Up-Loading Software To Other Machines Via The Internet

Policy: Users must not up-load software which has been licensed from a third party, or software which has been developed by Company X, to any computer via the Internet unless authorization from the user's department manager has first been obtained.

Commentary: Unauthorized distribution of copyrighted software via the Internet continues to be a serious problem. Companies that don't take a strong stand against this activity can be accused of contributing to the problem or being negligent in the protection of intellectual property belonging to other organizations. This policy seeks to put users on notice that up-loading any software is forbidden unless a manager first approves. Because this is really a user-related information management issue rather than a technical issue, the approving manager is a departmental manager rather than the information security manager. For good measure, the policy goes beyond licensed software, including software which has been developed in-house; the policy could go one step further, including mention of software that had been entrusted to Company X and perhaps not licensed. The policy thus helps to prevent unauthorized distribution of software which may be a trade secret or simply critical to Company X. Because the Internet makes it so easy for users to transfer files, including software, explicit policies preventing up-loading activities are necessary. An extension to this policy prohibits the transfer of software from one computer to another, no matter what communications system is involved. Separately, in the future, the need for a policy like this is expected to dwindle as sophisticated firewalls, which can block the in-bound or out-bound transfer of software, are increasingly deployed (one such firewall is offered by Secure Computing Corporation of Roseville, Minnesota, USA). Also see the policies entitled "Prohibition Against Down-Loading Software From Third Party Systems" and "Handling Software And Files Down-Loaded from Internet." A: E; E: LMH.

915. User Control Over Information Gathered Via Internet Web Site

Policy: Whenever Company X gathers information about people who visit its web site(s), the users must be notified of this monitoring process. These users must be given an opportunity to specify how this information will be used and to whom it will be disclosed.

Commentary: Web sites now have the ability to gather all sorts of information about individuals who visited their site (sometimes this is called a "click stream"). The information now available includes the screens an individuals examined, how long they examined these screens, where they clicked the cursor, etc. Internet electronic mail addresses may also be gathered without a user's knowledge. On another note, new products such as I/Pro from Internet Profiles Corporation (San Francisco, California, USA) allow users to provide demographic information about themselves in return for certain benefits. Other new tools such as a search engine from Deja News (Austin, Texas, USA) allow private investigators and anyone else to see what messages an individual has posted to Usenet. With marketers eager to get a definitive picture of Internet web site activity, and traditional tools limited to "hits" or some other relatively unhelpful activity metrics, there is considerable pressure to utilize these new tools and newly-available data. This policy thus seeks to avoid a privacy backlash, which might lead to bad press for the organization which established or owns the web site. For related ideas, see the policies entitled "Protection Of The Privacy Of Customer Information" and "Subjects Given Opportunity To Opt-Out Of Private Data Systems." A: T; E: LMH.

1.4.8.6. Using Information From The Internet

916. Acceptance Of Unsolicited Ideas Through The Internet

Policy: If a mechanism to receive comments or suggestions is provided on Company X Internet web sites, it must be accompanied by the following words: "The receipt of unsolicited ideas by Company X does not obligate the company to keep these ideas confidential, nor does it obligate the company to pay the person who submits them."

Commentary: This strict (and somewhat unfriendly) policy is intended to clearly establish the expectations of external parties when they send unsolicited ideas to Company X. The typical mechanism to receive such ideas is through electronic mail, but the ideas could also be received through other mechanisms. While the policy's scope could be expanded to include other communications mechanisms besides Internet web pages, generally only web pages allow a notice to be posted in a conspicuous spot. For instance, it would be onerous to ask staff to say these words to when people use the telephone to contact the organization. Some organizations may wish to go one step further, specifying that externally supplied ideas be funneled through a designated internal person who is not in the operational side of the business. If the designated person was in the operational side of the business, he or she might be tempted to use the idea to improve operations. This designated person may then follow-up with the submitter of the idea, asking them to sign a release form. If the submitter refuses to sign, then the designated person can destroy all copies except for one copy placed in a sealed and dated envelope (which could be used for evidence). This process allows the designated person to say that he or she was the only one (aside perhaps from the initial recipient) within Company X who saw the submission. Separately, the notice in this policy could be expanded to include words indicating that all material received becomes the property of Company X. For a related idea, see the policy entitled "Signing Third Party Confidentiality Agreements Without Approval." A: T; E: LMH.

917. Production Systems Must Not Rely On Free Internet Information

Policy: Aside from information provided by prospects, customers, suppliers, business partners, or government agencies, Company X information systems must not depend on free information obtained through the Internet. This is because the timeliness, accuracy, author bias, and continued availability of such information is not reliable.

Commentary: The intention of this policy is to ensure that production information systems are resilient, reliable, and dependable. If a production system would fail whenever a remote web site changes its format, or fails to update its information in a timely matter, then the production system cannot be described as resilient, reliable, or dependable. Reliance on free information provided by a third party is ill-advised because the third party can change or withdraw such information at will, and the dependent organization then has no say whatsoever about these changes or withdraws. Note that the policy does not prohibit usage of information obtained over the Internet if there is payment. Thus it would be acceptable for a company to rely on Internet-supplied information from a market research firm such as Gartner Group, or even a subscription newspaper such as The Wall Street Journal. Some organizations may wish to delete the words "government agencies" from the policy because they don't consider this information reliable or timely (these words were included primarily for the financial industry, which obtains information about interest rates and other macroeconomic data via the Internet). Other organizations may wish to modify the policy so that they do not place reliance on free Internet information alone; reliance in this case would acceptable if the information was independently corroborated. For related concepts, see the policies entitled "Reliability Of Information Down-Loaded from Internet" and "Required Process For Checking Software Down-Loaded From Internet." A: T; E: LMH.

1.4.8.7. Internet Web Page Management

918. Unofficial Web Pages Permitted Only By Contract

Policy: Unofficial web pages dealing with Company X products or services are prohibited, unless the sponsor of these home pages has a contract signed by the Director of Public Relations. Workers who notice a new Internet reference to Company X products and/or services are requested to promptly notify the Director of Public Relations.

Commentary: The motivation for this policy is the existence of so-called unofficial (unauthorized) web pages on the Internet. Organizations which don't closely monitor and police these unofficial web pages could find themselves in legal trouble including misrepresentation, trademark infringement, and copyright violation. This policy is intended to take a strong stand against such unofficial web pages unless the operator has agreed to be bound by terms that the Director of Public Relations finds acceptable. One of these terms should be that Company X can, at any time and for any reason, force the operator to remove any or all references to Company X products and/or services. Another advisable term would be that the word "unofficial" must appear in these web pages, along with other words clearly showing that Company X is not sponsoring or taking any responsibility for the home page. Separately, some organizations may be flattered and consider such unofficial web pages to be good advertising (see the Lego(TM) enthusiast web pages for an example). Nonetheless, if such unofficial home pages are permitted at all, the affected organization should keep a tight reign on them via a legally-binding contract. Discussions with an in-house attorney are appropriate because certain legal rights may be lost if they are not asserted; for example, if an organization allows others to use its trademark without authorization, it risks the loss of its rights. On a different note, this policy additionally informs workers that they should let Public Relations know whenever they see something new about Company X on the Internet; this helps track what is being said about the organization in user discussion groups, FAQ (frequently asked question) lists, media-sponsored vendor evaluations, etc. Also note that this policy prohibits insiders from constructing web pages without the prior written consent of the Director of Public Relations. See the policies entitled "Disclaimer Must Accompany All Internet Personal Messages" and "Search Engines To Detect Misleading Web Sites With Similar Names." A: ET; E: LMH.

919. Responsibility For Content Posted To Personal Web Pages

Policy: Company X provides the computer and communications facilities for its workers to create and publish their own complimentary personal web pages. Every worker who seeks to use these systems must first sign a statement acknowledging that they are responsible for all content posted on that site before their site will be enabled. If a problem with design or content is reported or discovered, the personal page owner will be contacted with a request to correct the problem. If the problem is not promptly corrected, the page will be rendered inaccessible until the matter is resolved to Company X's satisfaction.

Commentary: The intention behind this policy is to provide workers with a free mechanism to create and publish their own personal web pages. An increasing number of organizations now offer this fringe benefit and it is actually a good way to get to know people that one has been corresponding with over the phone or email. Typically users post pictures or a summary of their background and current responsibilities at Company X. This policy clarifies responsibility for the page, even though Company X provides the computers and other facilities to support it (which could be accessible via the Internet, or simply via an intranet). One danger of Internet-accessible personal web pages is that recruiters (headhunters) are more easily able to find and lure away top technical talent because personal information is readily accessible. Separately, one desirable aspect of adopting the approach described in this policy is that Company X can easily determine what its workers are posting on the Internet, and has some control over the content (it can revoke the connection if it doesn't like what it sees). For related ideas, consider the policies entitled "Disclaimer Must Accompany All Internet Personal Messages" and "Unofficial Web Pages Permitted Only By Contract." A: E; E: LMH.

920. Company X Internet Web Page Management Committee

Policy: Prior to being posted, all changes to the Company X corporate Internet web page must be approved by a special committee established by the Public Relations Department. This committee will make sure that all posted material has a consistent and polished appearance, is aligned with business goals, and is protected by adequate security measures.

Commentary: At a number of businesses, it has become clear that the Public Relations Department doesn't really know much about the Internet and the technical aspects of web page maintenance. Accordingly, this policy reflects a practical solution whereby decisions about material posted to a web site are delegated to the committee (which in many instances will also need higher management approval). The committee typically includes a few web systems administrators, an information security specialist, an intellectual property attorney, a marketing expert, and a public relations expert. This policy would ordinarily only be distributed to information systems technical staff because only they typically have the access privileges to make changes. For related ideas, see the policies entitled "All Public Representations Must Be Cleared Through Public Relations" and "Right To Remove Offensive Material Without Warning." A: T; E: LMH.

921. Internet Web Page Design Requirements

Policy: All Company X Internet web pages must conform to layout standards, navigation standards, legal wording standards, and similar requirements specified by the Internet Web Page Management Committee.

Commentary: This policy makes it clear that all Internet web pages must conform to a standard set of requirements. Rather than explicitly describing these requirements in the policy, the policy only states that they exist and that all web pages must conform. This is because the requirements will often change over the next few years. Typical items to include on the requirements list are: (1) always make transfers of a user's session from Company X's web site to another organization's web page very clear, (2) always make a transfer from the Internet to an intranet very clear, (3) put Company X's name on all pages to prevent other sites from representing that the material is their own, and (4) on all hot-link pages include a disclaimer saying that Company X is not responsible for the material found on the referenced sites. For a related idea, see the policy entitled "All Public Representations Must Be Cleared Through Public Relations." A: T; E: LMH.

922. Management Approval Required For Internet Hot-Link Establishment

Policy: Hot-links which transfer a user's Internet session from a Company X web site to the web site of any outside entity are not permitted unless the approval of the Internet Web Page Management Committee has first been obtained.

Commentary: The intention of this policy is to prevent web site designers, web site administrators, and others managing internal web sites from establishing hot-links to other sites that could embarrass Company X. Along with each hot-link goes an implied endorsement. Accordingly, all hot-link proposals should be screened by a committee, or approved in advance by a designated executive. In some cases specific criteria will be established, and outside entities must meet these criteria before any hot-link can be set-up. The criteria might include: a stellar business reputation, not in competition with Company X, likely to be of interest to those who visit Company X's web site, and the willingness to establish a reciprocal hot-link. This policy is especially important when one appreciates the real-world actions of a disgruntled employee at a major retail chain. This systems administrator established a hot-link to his own web site, where he made nasty remarks about his employer. Likewise, hackers are fond of establishing unauthorized hot-links to pornographic web sites. For related ideas, see the policies entitled "Intranet Site Developers Must Use Company X Style Guide" and "Internet Hot-Links Must Be Accompanied By Legal Disclaimer." A: T; E: LMH.

923. Internet Hot-Links Must Be Accompanied By Legal Disclaimer

Policy: Hot-links that transfer a user's Internet connection from a Company X web site to a web site associated with a third party are not permitted unless an approved disclaimer from the Legal Department is clearly displayed.

Commentary: The intention of this policy is to prevent customers, prospects, and others from claiming that Company X is legally responsible for third party staff behavior, products, or services. This accusation is quite possible, especially in the United States, where the legal notion of "joint and several liability" is favored by many lawyers. The notion here is that a party who believes that he or she is wronged will sue all other associated parties in an attempt to get money or some other benefit. A wronged party may claim that the existence of a link was Company X's implied endorsement of a third party's site, their products, their services, etc. This policy requires a disclaimer that should expressly disavow all such implied endorsements (the disclaimer wording will change over time as Internet law changes, and for this reason, the disclaimer wording is not included in the policy itself). For related ideas, the policy writer is directed to the policies entitled "Company X Internet Web Page Management Committee" and "Management Approval Required For Internet Hot-Link Establishment." A: T; E: LMH.

924. Daily Review Of Contents And Hot-Links For Company X Web Page

Policy: A staff member from the Marketing Department must check the Company X web page daily to confirm that the page is up-and-running, that no unauthorized changes have been made, and that no unauthorized links have been established. Upon detecting any of these conditions, the staff member must immediately contact the Information Security Department manager.

Commentary: The intention of this policy is to promptly detect the fact that Company X's web page has been defaced by a hacker, a disgruntled ex-employee, a dissatisfied customer, or a malicious competitor. Hackers often change web pages to promote a cause or to embarrass the organization which posted the material. They may also add links to pornographic sites, hate groups, and other sites which are likely to embarrass the organization in question. This policy ensures that modified web pages and/or links will not last long, and that they will be promptly changed (thus reducing the damage to the organization's reputation). In the real world, these types of attacks are often brought to the organization's attention by customers. But just in case customers haven't reported such changes yet, this policy requires a staff member to check-up on the web page. The policy is a frugal approach for organizations that don't want to spend money on an intrusion detection system (IDS). For those organizations which have available funds, a better alternative would be to employ a software package (like Tripwire) which automatically detects modifications to a web page, and which then pages technical staff or feeds directly into a network management system (NMS). For related considerations, see the policies entitled "Controlled Process For Modification Of Production Business Information" and "Resistance Of Logs Against Deactivation, Modification, Or Deletion." A: E; E: LMH.

1.4.9. Intranet Connections

925. Owner/Department Manager Permission Required For Intranet Postings

Policy: Before any information is posted to the Company X intranet, two approvals must be obtained. First, the department manager in charge of the relevant intranet page must approve. Second, the owner of the involved information (or creator of the information if the owner has not yet been designated) must approve.
Commentary: The intention of this policy is to prevent employees from posting all sorts of information to an intranet that should not be available over an intranet. The approval processes described in the policy gives management an opportunity to review whether the information belongs on the proposed intranet page, whether the information should be disclosed on an intranet, and what if any supplementary access controls will be necessary. Besides preventing inappropriate disclosure of sensitive information (perhaps to outsiders who use the intranet in question), this policy will help keep intranet postings organized and consistent with business purposes. A separate set of guidelines for selecting information to post to an intranet is recommended; this set of guidelines can be distributed to the department managers with intranet web pages so that they can better perform their duties as described in this policy. For related ideas see the policies entitled "Removal Of Inappropriate Electronic Postings To Public Forums" and "Posting Company X Material On The Internet." A: EMT; E: LMH.

926. All Content Posted To Intranet Is Owned By Company X

Policy: Unless approved in advance by the director of the Information Services Department, and explicitly noted on the intranet web page in question, all content posted to the Company X intranet is the property of Company X.

Commentary: The policy is intended to eliminate disputes about who owns content posted to intranet web pages. For example, at many universities, a dispute currently rages between students and the administration. Students claim that content on their intranet pages is their personal property, while the administration claims that the university owns the network, and by implication the page contents as well. It is advisable for an organization to maintain ownership of the content so that it can censor this content when need be. While little argument will be found with copyright infringement or libel issues, there may be a significant dispute about content which is in poor taste, in poor judgement, or may reflect badly on Company X. Note that if Company X owns intranet web pages, then it may also be liable for the content. This implies that there should be a review process prior to posting material to the intranet. This policy is a natural extension of other business-use-only policies, such as the one entitled "Personal Use Of Computer And Communications Systems." A: E; E: LMH.

927. User Checking Of Information Before Posting To The Intranet

Policy: Before posting material to the intranet, workers must thoroughly check all information and programs to make sure they do not include viruses, Trojan horses, and other malicious code. Workers must also confirm the information's accuracy, timeliness, and relevance to Company X business before posting it. Likewise, all legal issues such as disclosure of confidential information and copyright infringement must be resolved prior to posting.

Commentary: This policy defines the quality control steps that users must take before they post something to an intranet. The policy assumes that users may post things to an intranet without going through a review committee or some other approval process. While the author does not recommend that all users be given permission to post whatever they want to an intranet; this policy can be used in computing environments where that "lay-back" management approach prevails. Standard tools that can be used to check for viruses, malicious Java applets, and the like could also be provided, and perhaps mentioned in the policy. The policy assumes that personal information is kept off the intranet; if this is not the case, the words "relevance to Company X business" could be deleted. For related ideas, see the policies entitled "Respecting The Intellectual Property Rights Of Others On The Internet" and "Owner/Department Manager Permission Required For Intranet Postings." A: E; E: LMH.

928. Staging Area For New/Changed Intranet Content Review And Testing

Policy: All new and/or changed content to be posted to the Company X intranet must pass through a staging area where approved personnel will review the content and test its operation. An exception will be made in those instances where content is automatically downloaded from the Internet, verified, and posted to the intranet. These exceptions are established only through the written approval of the Information Security Department manager.

Commentary: The intention of this policy is to impress upon internal workers that the intranet is a production system which deserves formal change control procedures. This policy seeks to restrict intranet content, so that only high-quality material is ever posted. The policy helps support the posting of only that content which has been screened and shown to be accurate, relevant, current, and in violation of no internal security policies. Although not stated in the policy, access to the staging area should be restricted with mechanisms like password-controlled file directories (the words in the policy "where approved personnel will review" imply this but do not require it). The last two sentences recognize the reality of automatically updated intranet content. For related considerations, see the policies entitled "Authorization For Changes To Production Data And Programs" and "Intermediate Holding Area Required To Restrict Computer Room Access." A: E; E: LMH.

929. Cleansing Process For Downloaded Internet Content Moved To Intranet

Policy: All content downloaded from the Internet must go through a structured and documented cleansing process before being posted to the Company X intranet.

Commentary: The intention of this policy is to ensure that content downloaded from the Internet doesn't include viruses, worms, and other malicious software which could be propagated across desktop systems within Company X. While the cleansing process should include use of virus screening software packages, it should also involve stripping-off (or at least testing) of dynamic content such applets written with Java, ActiveX, and CGI scripts. These dynamic content applets could conceal Trojan horses like logic bombs which would do damage to Company X systems. The cleansing process additionally should include visual examination of the downloaded content to make sure that it can be reposted internally without restriction (examination of copyright notices and related restrictions). For similar ideas, consider the policies entitled "Testing For Viruses On A Stand-Alone Non-Production Machine" and "Software Testing With Sanitized Rather Than Production Information." A: T; E: LMH.

930. Intranet Sites Must Not Use Unapproved Active Content

Policy: Only those active content applets (Java, ActiveX, CGI scripts, etc.) which have been tested and approved by the Information Systems Department may be used on sites connected to the Company X intranet.

Commentary: The intention of this policy is to ensure that developers working for a certain department or some other decentralized organizational unit don't incorporate active content applets into an intranet site and in the process propagate a virus, worm, or some other nefarious software program. The policy assumes that intranet content is provided by a variety of decentralized units, and that there is no central screening process for this same content. If a central screening process is employed, then this policy is unnecessary. Separately, the policy supports a repository of tested, approved, and documented programs which can be reused repeatedly. This repository need not be limited to active content, but ideally includes a wide variety of programs including encryption routines as well as access control system extensions to support extended user authentication. Separately, this policy helps to promote standardization of software across the organization so that incompatibilities are only infrequently encountered (for example some version of Java do not work with browsers on Apple Macintosh computers). For related ideas, see the policies entitled "Disabling Java Within Internet Web Browsers" and "Java Program Execution Prohibited Unless Digital Signature Validated." A: T; E: LMH.

931. Webmaster Review Of Intranet Web Pages Prior To Posting

Policy: Prior to being posted to the Company X intranet, all user-developed web pages must be tested for security and operational problems according to an approved process issued by the Information Security Department.

Commentary: This policy is intended to prevent vulnerabilities with user-developed intranet web pages such as Common Gateway Interface (CGI) scripts which can introduce security problems. Other vulnerabilities which can be detected by a webmaster review include the presence of viruses, non-compliance with organizational format conventions, use of unauthorized software (such as Java), and broken hyper-links. The policy deliberately avoids mentioning these tests since they are rapidly evolving over time. The approved testing process can be changed regularly to reflect these new developments, while the policy remains the same. For related ideas, see the policy entitled "Intranet Site Developers Must Use Company X Style Guide." A: ET; E: LMH.

932. All Information Posted On Intranet Pages Must Have Designated Owner

Policy: All information posted to the Company X intranet must have a designated owner. Contact information for this owner must be clearly indicated on the page where the information appears.

Commentary: The intention of this policy is to insist that all information posted to an intranet (or for that matter any company LAN-based electronic bulletin board, organization-wide shared disk space, etc.) have a designated owner. Sometimes this type of an owner is called a "pagemaster." If such an owner is indicated, then errors can be reported back to this same person, and this same person also can approve corrective action. Likewise, this owner typically makes decisions about dissemination to users other than those who can currently access the information. Decisions about the use of this information in other contexts (for example the establishment of hot-links to it) an also be made by this type of owner. This type of owner furthermore often makes final decisions about the design of the intranet page itself. This policy additionally fosters efforts to designate owners for all types of important internal information. This policy ordinarily would be distributed only to those responsible for maintaining intranet web pages (so-called "webmeisters" or "webmasters"). Also see the policy entitled "Criteria For Assigning Information Ownership." A: T; E: LMH.

933. All Intranet Pages Must Include Information Owner Digital Signatures

Policy: All information owners who post the information for which they are responsible on the Company X intranet must generate digital signatures indicating their approval of the final versions of the applicable pages. These same digital signatures must be posted along with the pages.

Commentary: The intention of this policy is to be able to readily detect unauthorized modification to intranet pages. If digital signatures are posted along with the related pages, an intrusion detection system (IDS) or some other software such as Tripwire can be used to automatically determine whether any unauthorized changes have taken place. The use of digital signatures for intranet pages also prevents workers from posting certain pages to an intranet, and then later saying "Oh, sorry, I thought you approved of that." Either the approval was obtained or it was not. If approval was obtained, a digital signature will be there, and it can be easily checked by other workers. The existence of a valid digital signature can thus be part of the screening process that all pages must go through before they are posted to an intranet. Note that this policy assumes that a public key infrastructure (PKI) encryption system is implemented at the organization adopting the policy. PKI allows some interesting twists to this control, including having the signature of more than one owner on a single page, if indeed more than one owner is involved with the information appearing on a single page. Separately, nothing in this policy prevents the automated update to an intranet page; because an owner can sign sections of a page rather than the whole page, the automatically updated part of a page could be left unsigned. To recognize this dynamically changing content, an additional sentence describing the owner's approval of an update process could be added to this policy. For related considerations, see the policies entitled "Java Program Execution Prohibited Unless Digital Signature Validated" and "Digital Signatures & Sequence Numbers Required For System Logs." A: T; E: MH.

934. Secret Information Must Not Be Placed On Internet Or Intranet Systems

Policy: Because Internet and intranet security technology is still relatively new and untested, Company X secret information must not be resident on either Internet or intranet servers.

Commentary: This policy acknowledges that when one uses Internet or intranet technology, one takes on additional risk. To prevent unauthorized disclosure of the most sensitive type of information, it should be handled by more traditional means including face to face meetings, personal telephone calls, and the like. The most sensitive type of information in this policy is designated as "secret," but the label could change based on the internal data classification system in use. For a related idea, see the policy "Isolate Systems Containing Secret Information From Network." A: T; E: LMH.

935. Intranet Reviewed Quarterly To Confirm Sensitive Data Not Posted

Policy: The Information Security Department must review all postings to the Company X intranet quarterly to confirm that none of these postings contain confidential or secret information.
Commentary: The intention of this policy is to establish a mechanism to make sure that intranet users are not posting information with a more sensitive classification than "for internal use only" ("secret" and "confidential" are only two possible data classification system categories which are more sensitive). This policy assumes that there exists no central approval authority for placing information on the intranet, that users can place material on the intranet as they see fit (or

perhaps only get their manager to approve). If there is a central approval authority, this policy is unnecessary since screening will have already been performed. On another note, a trained eye from an information security professional is recommended because such a person can imagine future problems associated with the posting of certain information that the original person did not think about (even if all relevant policies have been followed exactly by the original person). Separately, this policy assumes that the organization has already adopted a data classification system. Also see the policies entitled "Three Category Data Classification Scheme" and "Company X Trade Secrets Must Named & Described On Intranet Page." A: M; E: MH.

936. Intranet Server Establishment Requires Information Systems Approval

Policy: Before they are connected to the internal network, all Company X intranet servers must be preauthorized by the network services manager in the Information Systems Department.

Commentary: This policy seeks to control what is often an unpredictable and uncontrolled process whereby various departments will establish their own intranet servers. Some network management systems (NMS) can generate alarms indicating the presence of unauthorized machines on a network; these capabilities can be used to enforce this policy. Approval of the network services manager is advisable because it provides an opportunity to ensure that only standard software and hardware are used, that a proper network address for the server has been assigned, and that other similar set-up tasks have been performed. For a related idea, see the policy entitled "Prior Approval Required For In-House System Interconnection." A: M; E: LMH.

937. Real-Time Connections To Company X Production Systems Via Intranet

Policy: The intranet must not be used to provide real-time connections to any Company X production information system which has extended user authentication access controls (anything beyond a fixed password and a user-ID), unless the approval of the Information Security Department manager has first been obtained.

Commentary: This policy is intended to prevent users and other from employing the intranet as a new and less burdensome pathway to access internal Company X information systems. For example, one production accounting system might have a dynamic password access control system (perhaps smart cards with passwords that change each minute). If the intranet were used to access this system, the dynamic password access control system may be circumvented, thus lowering the hurdles that users must clear in order to gain access. The rapid speed with which intranet systems are deployed can mean that management is not able to keep up with all new connections; this policy seeks to prevent these connections from circumventing an important type of access control. To make this policy still more rigorous, the reference to extended user authentication systems could be dropped; instead, reference could be simply made to any access control system. For related ideas, see the policies entitled "Real-Time External Network Connections Require Firewalls" and "Prior Approval Required For In-House System Interconnection." A: ET; E: LMH.

938. Approval Required For Access To Internal Systems By Third Parties

Policy: All third party access to Company X internal computer systems which are not clearly public (such as a web server containing company brochures) must be approved in advance by a designated information security coordinator.

Commentary: The objective of this policy is to prevent systems administrators and others from readily granting third parties access to internal machines, be these machines on an intranet or some other type of an internal network. So-called "extranets" (intranets with access by external third parties) are becoming popular and in the rush to exploit these new systems, many managers are granting access to third parties without first going through established access control approval processes. The involvement of an information security coordinator is indicated because these distributed representatives of a centralized information security infrastructure know the established rules for approving access control privileges. In the policy, the "information security coordinator" could be replaced by an "information security manager" or others who, in one way or another, are already tied-into the existing centralized information security infrastructure. As information systems become increasingly distributed and decentralized, end-users are taking on many of the traditional roles of systems administrators, and are thus often in a position where they can and often do grant access to third parties. On another note, this policy covers a wide variety of access types (electronic mail accounts, Internet access user-IDs, inventory checking applications, etc.). For related ideas, see the policy entitled "Privilege Restriction Based On The Need-to-Know." A: E; E: LMH.

939. Forwarding Information On Company X Intranet To Third Parties

Policy: The Company X intranet is for the exclusive use of authorized persons. Unlike the Internet, information on the intranet may be disseminated only to authorized persons. Workers must not forward information appearing on the intranet to third parties without going through the appropriate internal channels (such as Human Resources, Marketing, or Public Relations). Commentary: Although Internet tools such as browsers are used to access an intranet, the open and free exchange of information found on the Internet does not apply to an intranet. Accordingly, this policy puts workers on notice that they must not allow unauthorized third parties to gain access to the intranet, and that they must not forward intranet information to third parties without the proper authorization. A policy such as this seeks to prevent the release of sensitive information, incomplete information, and information that may be taken out of context. Separately, note that nothing in this policy prevents an organization from turning an intranet into an extranet (where authorized third parties gain access to an intranet). For a related idea, see the policy entitled "Secondary Dissemination Of Secret Information." A: E; E: LMH.

940. Direct Transfer To Internet Sites Not Permitted From Intranet

Policy: Company X intranet users must not be transferred directly to an Internet site without first seeing a clear notice. This notice must indicate that the users are about to be transferred to the Internet. Before connecting to the Internet, all such users must click a button that says "OK," or in some other manner provide feedback indicating they have read the notice.

Commentary: The intention of this policy is to make it very clear when users are on an intranet and when they are on an Internet. It is easy for users to get confused because both intranets and the Internet are accessed via web browsers. Confusion is made still more likely by hot-links which conceal the destination web site address from users. If there is confusion, users may release confidential Company X information on the Internet, and then later find out that they were not, as they thought, on the intranet. The notice referred to in this policy would generally include words that remind users about the dangers of communications on the Internet (for example, the need to encrypt all fixed passwords, credit card numbers, and other sensitive information before it is sent over the Internet). The intention behind the clicking process is to force users to pay attention to the notice, not to have the notice displayed for a certain period of time, perhaps ten seconds, and then disappear. For related ideas, consider the policies entitled "Management Approval Required For Internet Hot-Link Establishment" and "Production In-House Systems May Not Be Directly Internet Connected." A: T; E: LMH.

941. Intranet Site Developers Must Use Company X Style Guide

Policy: All workers developing intranet sites must consistently observe the intranet style guide and use the resources found the intranet implementation repository.

Commentary: The intention of this policy is to require that all intranet web page developers (alias "webmeisters," or in some cases "webmistresses") subscribe to the intranet style guide. Such a guide typically defines legal disclaimers, ways to handle hot-links to other pages, page layout templates, standard graphics, and the like. The policy also requires these people to use the approved utilities found in the intranet implementation repository. These resources typically include Java applets, various scripts, tools for establishing interfaces to in-house applications, tools for creating custom graphics, and tools for editing pages. Without the consistent use of these tools and requirements, an intranet may become disorderly, difficult to navigate and inadequately secured. This policy also prevents the use of unapproved externally-supplied software, which may include serious undocumented bugs, Trojan horses, or viruses. For a related idea, see the policy entitled "New Information Types Must Be Reflected In Corporate Data Dictionary." A: T; E: LMH.

1.4.10. Electronic Payment Systems

942. Concealing Account Numbers On Customer Receipts

Policy: The account numbers appearing on computer-generated receipts provided to customers must be partially-concealed or truncated. This will help prevent unauthorized parties from committing fraud or masquerading as an authorized customer.

Commentary: The primary intention of this policy is to prevent unauthorized parties from using the information printed on discarded or lost receipts to commit a fraud. At the same time, if account information is partially provided, customers will be able to determine which of their accounts was involved in the transaction. This policy thus meets the objectives of both fraud prevention and good customer service. One of the most prevalent examples of this involves receipts for automated teller machine (ATM) transactions; on these receipts, a credit card cash advance number may have certain (usually the "bin number" or rightmost digits) account digits obscured. For credit card receipts, the expiration date may deliberately not be provided. Note that this policy is not relevant to transactions where the receipt is a source document for subsequent computer input. For example, the policy is not suitable for credit card sales drafts done manually because the entire number will later be needed to complete the transaction. But it is suitable for transactions that have been recorded inside an information system, or that have already been completed (such as a credit card transaction for which an authorization number has been received). Separately, the partial-concealment mentioned here can be achieved by "masking" part of the account number with other characters such as an "X." Also see the policies entitled "Disclosure Of Computer Logs Reflecting Customer Activities," "Secondary Dissemination Of Secret Information," and "Acknowledgement Required For Deliveries Of Secret Information." A: T; E: LMH.

943. Receipt Must Be Provided For Every Purchase Or The Purchase Is Free

Policy: Cashiers must offer every customer a receipt. Failure to offer every customer a receipt will be cause for disciplinary action up to and including termination. A sign indicating "customers who are not offered a receipt will be given their purchase for free" must be prominently displayed on every cash register.

Commentary: The objective of this policy is to prevent cashiers from secretly taking money from cash registers (a form of computer). This control requires that every transaction be entered into a cash register (closed circuit TV or CCTV is also advisable). If cashiers are allowed to accept cash for transactions, but not ring them up on the register, they can easily pocket the cash without being caught. This policy thus requires that the cash collected by a cashier on their shift must match the amount tallied by the cash register (allowing for exceptions such as "overrings," which are handled differently). The provision of free food in a restaurant or some other free goods makes the customer motivated to become a part of the internal control system. The prominent display of a sign describing this arrangement is necessary if the customer is going to be notified of their role in the internal control system. Separately, a similar division of responsibilities can be applied to other situations where there is a risk of theft of cash, checks, bonds, or other forms of money. For related ideas, see the policies entitled "Separation Of Duties And Control Over Company X Assets" and "Concealing Account Numbers On Customer Receipts." A: E; E: LMH.

944. Payment Information Never Provided In Its Entirety To Customers

Policy: When customers are confirming the use of a particular credit card number, checking account number, or other payment information on file with Company X, only the last few digits of this information can be shared.

Commentary: The objective of this policy is to prevent fraud. If somebody calls a customer support telephone number and wants to confirm a credit card number stored in the information systems managed by the organization, the telephone customer support representatives should only provide the last four digits. Similarly, in an Internet commerce application, if the customer needs to confirm the use of a particular credit card, only the last four digits will be displayed as part of their profile. Because the full set of numbers is not revealed, impersonators cannot obtain this payment information and use it for unauthorized purposes, but the authorized user will still have enough information in order to confirm that he or she wants to use that particular payment method. The least significant digits (last few digits) of the payment information are used because they are the most likely to change from customer to customer and from account to account. For example, if the same credit card issuer has provided several cards to a certain individual, the first four numbers (also called bin numbers) will be the same for all these cards. Likewise, if an impersonator were to determine that an individual had a relationship with a certain credit card company, the first four numbers would be predetermined because they apply to all customers, and they would thus be inadequate when it comes to uniquely identifying a credit card number. Also note that this policy applies to those situations where payment information is changing (such as when a credit card expiration date has come and gone). These same concepts are applicable to checking account numbers, electronic cash account numbers, and other payment methods. The provision of partial information is also addressed in the policy entitled "Dithering To Conceal True Nature Of Signal." For additional ideas of this nature, consult the policies entitled "Orders To Change Internal Records Placed Via Phone" and "Exchanges Of Information Over The Internet." A: T; E: LMH.

945. Disclosure Of Bank Account Numbers

Policy: Company X disbursement (debit) bank account numbers are confidential and must not be disclosed to third parties on forms, stationery, brochures, and the like.

Commentary: This is a new policy being adopted by a number of European companies in response to a new type of computer crime involving unauthorized debits to bank accounts. Frauds have been easily committed by unauthorized individuals who have entered publicly-available bank account numbers on automatic debit request forms. The amounts involved are often relatively small, and many organizations don't bother to reconcile their accounts for a significant period of time. Accordingly, these transactions don't come to light soon, and in the interim the perpetrators may have closed the receiving bank accounts and left town. This policy assumes that the organization adopting the policy has both receiving bank accounts or credit accounts (which can be placed on forms, such as wire transfer instructions to customers), and separately, disbursement (or debit) bank accounts. When a policy like this is adopted, organizations should make arrangements with their bank to reject all debits to accounts reserved for incoming funds (credit accounts). Note the way the policy is worded--it is permissible for employees to disclose disbursement bank account numbers to authorized third parties on a case-by-case basis. This policy is well-suited for electronic commerce on the Internet, as it is for Electronic Data Interchange (EDI). For a discussion of the frauds motivating this policy, see Computer Fraud & Security Bulletin, September 1995. Also see the policy entitled "Insertion Of Computer-Related Contact Numbers In Directories." A: T; E: LMH.

946. Shredding Of Credit Card Receipts And Other Payment Information

Policy: The disposal of all paper documents which contain payment information (bank account numbers, credit card numbers, etc.) must involve shredding or other approved destruction methods.

Commentary: The intention of this policy is to prevent payment information from falling into the wrong hands, and then being used to commit a fraud. Perhaps the most pervasive example of this involves credit card charge receipts, which are often retrieved from trash bins, and then used to place telephone orders (which do not require a signature, and which cannot entail matching the purchaser's face to an ID picture on the card). Far too many businesses discard such payment information without shredding it. If shredding is not used, the information unearthed from a fraud investigation could be embarrassing to explain to customers; it might also become a public relations or legal problem. The vulnerability addressed by the policy is so widely understood, and is so frequently discussed in the news media, that taking no action borders on irresponsibility. Separately, this policy could complement existing policies requiring shredding of sensitive information. On another note, this policy also helps prevent identity fraud, where an unauthorized person poses as another person in order to obtain credit cards, loans, or other benefits using the good reputation of that other person. For related ideas, see the policies entitled "Destruction Of Waste Copies Of Sensitive Information," "Business Source Document Data Retention Period," "Identity Theft Prevention By Restricting Access To Personal Information." A: E; E: LMH.

947. Encrypt Credit Card Numbers & Other Payment Data When Not Used

Policy: Payment information, such as credit card numbers or bank checking account numbers, must be encrypted when not in active use for authorized business purposes. These numbers must be encrypted when transmitted over a public network as well as encrypted when held in storage on computer disk or tape.

Commentary: This policy seeks to prevent credit card numbers and bank checking account numbers from falling into the wrong hands. For both types of numbers, simple possession of the number may be enough to initiate a fraudulent funds transfer. This is because the numbers are basically fixed passwords authorizing funds transfers. Encryption will prevent the readable versions of these parameters from being accessible to unauthorized individuals. For example, if these parameters are encrypted when stored on a backup tape, they will be unavailable for fraud, even though the tape is stored at a remote location without strong physical access controls. This policy is consistent with the regulations of major credit card issuing and processing firms, and is especially important for those organizations who have Internet commerce operations. For related ideas, see the policies entitled "Treat Electronic Mail As Public Communications" and "Personal Identifiers Must Not Appear On Publicly-Accessible Locations." A: T; E: LMH.

948. Credit Card Numbers Must Be Used Only For Payment Processing

Policy: Credit card numbers must not be used for customer identification or any other purpose other than processing payments for goods and/or services.

Commentary: The more that credit card numbers are used for other purposes besides payment processing, the more likely they are to appear in readable form in places where they will not be adequately protected. This in turn may lead to fraud, identity theft, and other abuses. In far too many retail establishments, credit cards are used as some sort of identification, for example to cash a check. Clerks at these retail establishments may even write down a credit card number on a check, which then exposes it to every person who handles the clearing of and customer account preparation associated with that check. This policy also helps to set the tone for fraud and identity theft prevention, and may be useful when showing that the organization took diligent steps to protect credit card numbers from unauthorized use. For related ideas, see the policies entitled "Encrypt Credit Card Numbers & Other Payment Data When Not Used" and "Disclosure Of Bank Account Numbers." A: E; E: LMH.

949. New Account Opening Requires Robust Identity Authentication

Policy: Whenever Company X opens a new account with a customer, it must first authenticate the identity of this customer in a definitive way (by checking a driver's license, receiving a voided check, or viewing information or documents such as a passport that only the customer would be expected to possess).

Commentary: The intention of this policy is to prevent perpetrators of fraud or identity theft from using the anonymity of the Internet, the telephone, and other remote communications systems as a excuse preventing them from providing definitive identification. Consider the case of an Internet bank called X.com, which allowed new customers to transfer money into their X.com bank account from any other bank account in the United States banking system. New customers did not need to definitively validate both their identity and the fact that they were the signers on the account from which the funds were taken. Thus fraudulent wire transfers were initiated and the proceeds were placed into new X.com accounts. Thus X.com's efforts to make business over the Internet as easy as possible led to fraud. Obtaining robust identification is not so hard, and it could have been accomplished via the provision of a voided check (this approach is widely used in the banking industry to authorize automated clearing house payments). Separately, the policy writer will note that this policy is deliberately vague when it comes to opening accounts remotely or in-person (both require robust identity validation). For related ideas, see the policies entitled "Identity Theft Prevention By Restricting Access To Personal Information" and "Validating The Identity Of External Parties On The Internet." A: E; E: MH.

950. Any Demonstrated Fraud Forces Immediate Financial Account Closure

Policy: Any demonstrated fraud on a financial account with Company X (checking account, savings account, certificate of deposit, credit card account, etc.) requires that the account be immediately closed.

Commentary: The intention of this policy is to prevent additional fraud if some fraud has already been shown to exist. The policy is suitable for adoption by any organization that maintains financial accounts with various organizations including banks, loan companies, credit card companies, etc. The policy is also appropriately adopted by organizations which offer financial accounts, such as an Internet-only bank. If there has already been fraud on an account, then the perpetrator is familiar with the account number and all other details necessary to complete the fraud. If the perpetrator did it once, he or she is likely to do it again, especially if it appears as though the fraud was not detected. By closing an account, the organization adopting this policy prevents the same type of fraud using the same account (hopefully remedial measures to prevent similar frauds with other accounts will also be initiated, but that is another matter). An example of the application of this policy involves checking account fraud. Here a perpetrator could steal a check and use a computer with a high-quality printer to generate a credible version of that same check stock, with the same account number but with a check number several numbers in advance of the check that was stolen. The perpetrator could then write a fictitious name into the payee line of the check, and cash it at a bank teller window with fraudulent identification such as a bogus driver's license. If the account were not immediately closed, the perpetrator would be encouraged to repeat this crime. For related ideas, see the policies entitled "Payment Information Never Provided In Its Entirety To Customers" and "Disclosure Of Bank Account Numbers." A: E; E: LMH.

951. Alternative Communications Channel Confirmation For Transactions

Policy: To help deter and detect fraud, all transactions initiated via the Internet, the telephone, or any other electronic system must be promptly confirmed by an alternative communications channel such as regular mail.

Commentary: Identity theft is a growing problem on the Internet and elsewhere in modern industrial countries. It involves the theft of details about an individual, and then the subsequent masquerading as that person. Because orders can be placed using stolen credit card numbers, stolen checking account numbers, stolen user-IDs, and the like, it is advisable for merchants and other service providers to always confirm each transaction. In this context, a transaction could include a change of address as well as more traditional transactions such as a purchase of goods. For an address change, many banks will send a confirmation to the old address; thus, if the address change was part of a fraud, it will then be detected by the customer, and the customer will notify the involved bank (hopefully). Likewise, when orders are sent via Internet commerce, email is used to confirm that an order was placed (Amazon does this). The confirmation should be sent through a channel other than the channel used to place the order (transaction) because if it is sent via the same channel it will simply go back to the potential perpetrator of fraud. For related concepts, see the policies entitled "Multiple Communication Channels For Electronic Offers & Acceptances" and "Validating The Identity Of External Parties On The Internet." A: T; E: LMH.

952. Daily Balancing And Reconciliation Of Accounting Records

Policy: To detect errors and fraud, accounting records reflecting activity on Internet commerce payment systems must be balanced and reconciled daily.

Commentary: The intention of this policy is to require accounting records to be up-to-date and accurate, and thus useful for the prompt detection of errors and frauds. Because everything moves so fast in the Internet commerce area, it is essential to perform these activities daily, if not more often. Balancing involves the preparation of a balance sheet and related accounting statements which are based on a dual-entry accounting system (many if not all of these activities can be automated). A dual-entry accounting system will allow assets to equal liabilities plus equity. If the records don't balance, an error exists somewhere. Likewise, reconciliation involves comparison of external records (such as a credit card clearing house's daily activity report) with internal records, so that all differences are explained and understood. These activities will allow management to perform other tests of the accounting records such as balance analysis and ratio analysis. Balance analysis involves comparison of a balance (such as monthly sales) in a certain accounting period to the same balance in other periods, thereby highlighting problems and trends. Ratio analysis involves the construction of ratios using certain account balances (such as current assets divided by current debt), which then show financial strength and other management success/failure indicators. For a related idea, see the policy entitled "Accountability And Traceability For All Privileged System Commands." A: M; E: LMH.

953. Receipt Must Be Confirmed Before Payment Token Will Be Activated

Policy: Payment tokens (such as credit cards) must be activated only after the intended recipient has indicated receipt through the provision of some information that only that recipient could provide.

Commentary: The purpose of this policy is to prevent fraud with a payment mechanism such as a smart card, a debit card, or a credit card. Since these payment mechanisms are often sent via regular mail, there often needs to be a mechanism by which the authorized recipient communicates to the issuing organization that he or she has received the payment mechanism. With credit cards this is often done with a toll-free telephone call, where the authorized recipient provides the last four digits of their social security number or some other information generally known only to that individual. The same approach can be used for information systems identity tokens such the as the dynamic password systems sold by Security Dynamics, Bedford, Massachusetts. The user-ID to which the token provides access can then be activated only after proper receipt has been indicated. After a certain period of time has elapsed, if the intended recipient has not provided confirmation of receipt, it can be assumed that the token was lost or stolen, at which point a new token can be issued. For related ideas, see the policies entitled "Dynamic Password Tokens Must Not Be Stored In Portable Cases" and "Alternative Communications Channel Confirmation For Transactions." A: T; E: MH.

2. Managerial Security

2.1. Administrative Security

2.1.1. Training And Awareness

954. All New Workers Must Receive Information Security Policy Pamphlet

Policy: All new Company X workers -- be they employees, contractors, consultants, or temporaries -- must promptly receive a copy of the information security policy pamphlet. These workers must also be informed that their continued employment or contractual relationship depends on their compliance with the requirements described in that pamphlet.

Commentary: The objective of this policy is to ensure that all new workers know the information security rules, have read these rules, and understand that they must abide by these rules. Many organizations don't distribute a full information security manual these days, preferring instead to provide a brief pamphlet which contains the most important points. These pamphlets typically contain a URL which can then be used on an intranet to locate all information security policies, standards, procedures, and responsibilities. This approach allows the information security requirements to be updated quickly and automatically without the need to distribute new hardcopy manuals to all workers. Instead, an electronic mail notice can be sent to all people who must abide by these requirements. Giving new workers a pamphlet with their new hire package of material emphasizes management's commitment to information security and brings information security to their attention at the very beginning of the employment relationship. For related ideas, see the policies entitled "Signed Acknowledgement For Understanding The Code

Of Conduct" and "Information Security Training Required For All Information Workers." A: M; E: LMH.

955. Information Security Training Required For All Information Workers

Policy: All workers (employees, consultants, contractors, temporaries, etc.) must be provided with sufficient training and supporting reference materials to allow them to properly protect Company X information resources.

Commentary: The intention of this policy is to require that sufficient information security training and documentation be delivered to those workers who handle Company X information. The specific material to be delivered to workers will vary based on the nature of the jobs that these workers perform. For example, telephone order-takers should generally receive different training than computer programmers. In most modern organizations, nearly every worker accesses Company X information in order to do their job. Nonetheless, many workers need only rudimentary training. The word "information" may accordingly be deleted from the end of the title without major changes to the meaning. The policy thus communicates from top management to lower level management requirements for training and documentation (which could be on-line rather than in hardcopy form). This policy relies on the local manager to decide what constitutes sufficient information security training; some organizations may prefer to say that the Information Security Department will determine what constitutes sufficient training. See the policies entitled "Information Security Training Time Required," "Current Information Security Manual Required," "Security Responsibilities Of Information Users," and "Technical Information Systems Staff Training & Continuing Education." A: M; E: LMH.

956. Information Security Training Only After Workers Pass Other Training

Policy: Workers must have successfully completed all other basic training needed in order to perform their new jobs before they receive information security training.

Commentary: The intention of this policy is to prevent people from going through information security training if they are not going to pass other training courses. The delay in training mentioned by this policy will also give many organizations additional time for new hire background checks to be completed, if they have not already been completed. Thus the policy will prevent unsuitable people from gaining access to information which might be used to compromise information security at Company X. Consider standard practice at many banks. Tellers are not given security training until they have passed other training and until they have shown that they can handle whatever the job requires. In a sense, this policy restricts information about security to those who have a need for it, and in that respect it is a manifestation of the "need to know." Separately, nothing in this policy is meant to imply that new workers should be placed on the job before they receive information security training. For related ideas, see the policies entitled "Training Course Required Prior To Use Of Remote Access Systems" and "Limiting End-User Knowledge Of System Capabilities And Commands." A: EM; E: MH.

957. Information Security Policy Change Notices Distributed To All Workers

Policy: All Company X workers must receive prompt notice of changes in the Company X information security policy, including how these changes may affect them, and how to obtain additional information.

Commentary: The objective of this policy is to ensure that all workers know about the latest version of the information security policy. Without a policy such as this, there may be legal problems associated with discipline and termination actions which were based on an information security policy that had not been communicated to the involved workers. These workers may say that they cannot reasonably be held to a standard of behavior (defined in a policy) about which they have not been informed. This policy clearly states management's intention to inform all affected workers, although it does not specify how to inform them -- this will vary by recipient group and available information systems. Electronic mail is one of the most economical approaches, and email can contain a URL which provides all the details via an intranet. Also effective is a notice inserted into paycheck envelopes if checks rather than automatic deposit are being used at the organization in question. See the appendix entitled "List Of Suggested Awareness Raising Methods" for further suggestions. Also see the policies entitled "Affected Individuals Notified About Material Changes In Privacy Policy" and "Signed Acknowledgement For Understanding The Code Of Conduct." A: M; E: LMH.

958. Information Security Department Responsible For Related Training

Policy: The Information Security Department must provide refresher courses and such other materials to regularly remind employees, temporaries, consultants, and contractors about their obligations with respect to information security.

Commentary: The intention of this policy is to clarify responsibility for the provision of information security training, documentation, and related materials. All too often this responsibility is not adequately assigned, and important information security work does not get done. Instead of (or in addition to) an Information Security Department, some other departments might have been referred to in the policy. These include Human Resources, Industrial Security (Physical Security), Information Technology, and Training. Another objective of the policy is to underline the fact that training and awareness is not a one-time effort; such work needs to be done periodically. Written between the lines of this policy is an acknowledgement that departmental and other lower level management must give their workers sufficient time to attend refresher courses, run computer-based instruction (CBI) software, read documentation, etc. Separately, the policy mentions "employees, consultants, and contractors" with the intent to cover all persons who may be in a position where they would need to know the proper protection of Company X information resources. Some organizations may prefer to simply use the word "workers," and then use some discretion when it comes to deciding who should receive training, documentation, etc. Also see the policy "Information Security Training Time Required" and "Specific Tasks Performed By The Information Security Department." A: MT; E: LMH.

959. Information Security Training Time Required

Policy: Management must allocate sufficient on-the-job time for employees to acquaint themselves with Company X security policies, procedures, and related ways of doing business.

Commentary: It is not realistic to expect employees to read information security materials during their own time. The intention of this policy is to clearly let management know, not only that such training is required, but also that they must give their employees enough time to acquaint themselves with information security materials. Some managers do not consider information security to be a worthwhile use of an employee's time because it does not directly contribute to the bottom line. For related ideas, see the policies entitled "Required User Training For Production Systems" and "Information Security Department Responsible For Related Training." A: M; E: LMH.

960. Work According To Information Security Policies & Procedures

Policy: Every worker must understand Company X's policies and procedures about information security, and must agree in writing to perform his or her work according to such policies and procedures.

Commentary: The intention of this policy is to require every worker not only to familiarize themselves with information security policies and procedures, but also to sign a statement acknowledging the fact that he or she understands and agrees to be bound by these policies and procedures. From a legal standpoint, it is desirable to have employees acknowledge in writing that they understand information security is a part of their job. If they are subsequently terminated (sacked, fired, etc.) due to an information security violation or related problems, there is no doubt that the employee understood what was required of him or her. This policy therefore reduces the probability of a wrongful termination lawsuit. Obtaining something in writing also lends a new credibility that many people may not have previously brought to matters involving information security. Also see the policy entitled "Attendance At Information Security Class Mandatory." A: M; E: LMH.

961. Attendance At Information Security Class Mandatory

Policy: Every worker must attend an information security awareness class within three months of the date when they began employment with Company X. To provide evidence that every employee has attended such a class, each employee must sign a statement that they have attended a class, understood the material presented, and had an opportunity to ask questions.

Commentary: The intention of this policy is to require every new worker to attend a class discussing information security. For existing employees, a modification of this policy could state they must attend within six months of the date when such courses become available. To make sure that people actually attend a class, they are asked to sign a statement acknowledging the fact that they understood the material presented. From a legal standpoint, it is desirable to have employees acknowledge in writing that they understand information security is a required part of their job. If they are subsequently terminated (sacked, fired, etc.) due to an information security violation or related problems, there is no doubt that the employee understood what was required of him or her. This policy therefore reduces the probability of a wrongful termination lawsuit. If the classes are scheduled for working hours, then another intention of this policy is to put lower level management on notice that they must provide working hours time for their employees to attend information security training events. There is nothing special about the time periods mentioned in the policy (e.g., three months); these can be changed to suit organizational needs and resources. On a different note, ideally information security material is included in new employee orientation, in which case, the three month period will be met. Also see the policy entitled "Work According To Information Security Policies & Procedures." A: EM; E: LMH.

962. Information Security Training Course Prior To Gaining System Access

Policy: All Company X workers -- no matter what their status (full-time employee, part-time employee, consultant, contractor, temporary, intern, volunteer, etc.) -- must complete an approved information security training class before they are granted access to any Company X computer systems.

Commentary: The intention of this policy is to inform all parties involved that new workers must not be given any information system access privileges until they have completed an information security training class. The training class is not just any old training class, it must be "approved" (and generally written) by the Information Security Department. This policy ensures that every worker knows the rules for information security, so they are then able to sign a form in good conscience which says that they agree to abide by these rules whenever they use Company X information systems. In some organizations, workers are expected to sign such a form but they haven't yet gone through a training class, so they don't really know what they are agreeing to (but workers do it anyway because they need a job). This policy is easily implemented via computer based training (CBT) systems which are set up in a library, a conference room, or some other unrestricted area. New recruits can be sent to this location and at their convenience take a pre-recorded course. An attractive aspect of a CBT system is that it can also be used to give users tests to gauge their understanding of the material (systems like this are available from vendors like PentaSafe, in Houston, Texas). For related considerations, see the policies entitled "Sensitive Information Access For Temporaries And Consultants" and "Information Security Training Required For All Information Workers." A: EM; E: LMH.

963. Required Compliance With Corporate Code Of Conduct

Policy: As a condition of a continued working relationship with Company X, all workers must read, understand, and behave in accordance with the corporate code of conduct.

Commentary: The intention of this policy is to put all workers on notice that compliance with the corporate code of conduct is a mandatory part of their job. A code of conduct (for corporations or other types of organizations) ordinarily includes mention of matters like accepting gifts from suppliers, having conflicts of interest, and the like. In many cases it also involves information security matters such as disclosure of sensitive information. Rather than being a good place for information security policies, a corporate code of conduct is intended to be a brief and handy guide to doing business the Company X way. Honesty and other higher-level considerations are typically addressed in a code of conduct, while information security policies (as they might appear in an information security manual or some other document) generally are more detailed. On another note, the words "continued working relationship" are more general than the words "continued employment relationship," in acknowledgement of the so-called contingent workforce which includes consultants, temporaries, and contractors. For additional information, see the policy entitled "Signed Acknowledgement For Understanding The Code Of Conduct." A: E; E: LMH.

964. Signed Acknowledgement For Understanding The Code Of Conduct

Policy: All workers must indicate their understanding of the code of conduct by annually signing a form acknowledging that they agree to subscribe to the code.

Commentary: The intention of this policy is to annually remind employees that they must abide by the organization's code of conduct. From a legal standpoint, it is desirable to have employees acknowledge in writing that they understand that a code of conduct is a required part of their job. If they are subsequently terminated (sacked, fired, etc.) due to code of conduct related problems, there is no doubt that the employee understood what was required of him or her. This policy therefore reduces the probability of a wrongful termination lawsuit. For more discussion about a code of conduct, see the policy entitled "Required Compliance With Corporate Code Of Conduct." A: E; E: LMH.

965. Required User Training For Production Systems

Policy: Company X workers must not use any software for production business processes unless they have first completed approved training for such software.

Commentary: The intention of this policy is to require that workers complete an approved training effort prior to running software that affects production business operations. The policy is additionally aimed at assuring that users have sufficient training before a cut-over to a new or significantly enhanced software system takes place. Nothing in the policy prevents workers from running the software in a test environment so that they may familiarize themselves with the software. The policy prevents workers from being in a position where they could adversely affect business records (by errors, omissions, frauds, etc.) unless they have first completed approved training. Beyond the system interruptions and delays, other risks of inadequately trained users involves poor customer service and adverse public relations. This policy helps avoid embarrassment for users who may be too proud to admit that they don't know how to use the software, and/or too afraid to ask. Training should, of course, also include familiarization with controls and related security matters. On a separate note, the word "approved" in the policy is deliberately vague, allowing management considerable leeway when it comes to choosing the type of training that each system requires. Hardware or networks were not mentioned explicitly in this policy since, by implication, new hardware and networks have accompanying new or different software; some organizations may wish to add the words "hardware and networks" to the policy. See the policy entitled "Information Security Training Time Required." A: M; E: LMH.

2.1.2. Reporting Of Security Problems

966. Required Reporting of Information Security Incidents

Policy: All suspected information security incidents must be reported as quickly as possible through the correct Company X internal channels.

Commentary: This policy is intended to require that all problems and violations are promptly brought to the attention of those who can actually do something about them. If problems and violations go unreported, they may lead to much greater losses for the organization than would have been incurred, had the problems been reported right away. A good example of this involves computer viruses, which if unreported and uncontained, will continue to spread. On a different note, some organizations go further by requiring that reporting take place within a certain time frame, for instance 24 hours. Other organizations add specific penalties for not reporting problems. The implementation of this policy could involve an area code 800 telephone number to prevent the caller from having to pay toll charges. To encourage reporting, anonymity can partially be achieved by turning off any automatic caller-ID (also known as ANI) features available with the receiving telephone. Likewise, the Information Security Department may wish to publicize the fact that reports can be made anonymously. It may also encourage people to call if they know they will always get an answering machine, never a person on the receiving end of the line. Separately, reference is made to the "correct channels" to encourage people to go to the Information Security Department or other people who are recognized as responsible for investigations. The words "correct ... channels" also encourage the establishment of such channels for information flow if they are not already clearly defined. Also see the policies entitled "Reporting Of Damage To Company X Off-Site Systems ," "Internal Reporting Of Information Security Violations & Problems," "Information Security Alert System," "Leave Without Pay Required During Extended Investigations," and "When To Prosecute Or Seek Restitution." A: E; L: LMH.

967. Computer Crime Investigation Information Is Legally Privileged

Policy: All evidence, ideas, and hypotheses about computer crimes experienced by Company X, including possible attack methods and perpetrator motivations, must be communicated to internal legal counsel and treated as restricted and "legally privileged" information.

Commentary: The purpose of this policy is to severely restrict who has access to information about computer crimes suffered by Company X. This in turn can help prevent Company X from suffering negative publicity, declining stock prices, and other adverse events that may result from inappropriate disclosures. When information is legally privileged, it is also protected from certain types of legal information gathering, such as discovery. Thus the policy may help keep computer crime information in the hands of a restricted few managers and technical staff at the organization even though a lawsuit is underway. This policy additionally helps to emphasize that computer crime information is very sensitive and should only be distributed to those who have a bona fide need for the information. The policy furthermore helps reduce the chances that spokespersons for Company X will offer unsubstantiated theories about perpetrator motivations, attack methods, and the like to the media, and then get Company X into legal trouble due to slander or libel. The word "internal" could be deleted from the policy if the organization uses only external legal counsel. For related ideas, see the policies entitled "Public And Governmental Disclosure Of Computer System Attacks" and "Centralized Reporting Of Information Security Problems." A: TM; E: LMH.

968. Issuance Of Cease And Desist Messages To Attackers

Policy: A stern cease and desist message must be sent to the source of all attacks mounted against Company X computers whenever the source or intermediate relay points can be identified.

Commentary: The intention of this policy is to send a message to attackers that their activities have been noticed and that they should stop immediately. Such a message may, in some instances, be enough to discourage an attacker (hacker, industrial spy, disgruntled ex-employee, etc.) from further efforts. If an attacker is using a shield such as a relay site, then the message can still be sent to the relay site's administrator. Even if the attacker doesn't get the cease and desist message, someone who manages that site can still take action such as revoke the privileges of the offending user-ID or otherwise tighten-up security. Separately, this policy assumes that an organization has an intrusion detection system (IDS) already installed and operational. This policy could also be supported by new software that is just starting to hit the market that will trace the source of attacks. Also note that this policy applies to a wide variety of networks, not just the Internet; for example, it could apply to an intranet too. For additional ideas, see the policies entitled "Notification Of Suspected Loss Or Disclosure Of Sensitive Information" and "Users Must Notify Help Desk About All Production System Problems." A: T; E: LMH.

969. Inclusion Of Information Security Contact Information On Web Site

Policy: The opening pages of all Company X web sites must include contact information (email address, phone number, etc.) for the Information Security Department.

Commentary: The intention of this policy is to make sure that outsiders who notice there is a problem can promptly report their observations to the correct person. This would for example be useful if a web page were to be modified by hackers, and then noticed by a potential customer. The policy thus in an indirect way solicits outsiders to assist with information security. Often customers and prospects are the first to notice there is a problem (although intrusion detection systems should immediately notify relevant personnel). The inclusion of such contact information on web pages also allows outsiders to report problems that are not of a security nature (slow response time, erroneous results to a calculation, etc.). Some words that go along with the contact information could be "Please report any suspected security violations or problems to ..." Separately, the scope of the policy could be broadened to include all intranet sites. For related concepts, see the policies entitled "External Reporting Of Information Security Violations" and "Required Reporting Of Information Security Incidents." A: E; E: LMH.

970. Internal Reporting Of Information Security Violations & Problems

Policy: Company X workers have a duty to report all information security violations and problems to the Information Security Department on a timely basis so that prompt remedial action may be taken.

Commentary: The intention of this policy is to require workers to promptly report information security violations and problems. For example, immediate reporting is absolutely essential to limit losses from hacker system penetrations and other potentially serious security problems. Delays in reporting can mean massive additional losses for the organization. This policy acknowledges that the people who use systems are often the ones to spot problems; lest this information go to waste, this policy requires that it be reported to someone who can do something about it. The reporting process here is to a central group as opposed to line management or a service provider (it could be either or both). The reporting process could also go through line management, although this takes longer and is likely to unduly delay corrective actions. The policy could be expanded to state that workers must not, under any circumstances, attempt to prove the existence of these weaknesses unless they have been specifically charged with this work by top management. This caveat could be added to discourage hacking and other system intrusions that might be interpreted as system misuse. Separately, the policy here could be expanded to require a written report following the initial oral report. On a different note, the scope of this policy could be expanded to include "suspected problems," not just "problems and violations." The word "weaknesses" may also be used instead of "problems." While internal reporting is to be encouraged and required, external reporting is fraught with significant dangers, as is discussed in the policy entitled "External Reporting Of Information Security Violations." Also see the policies entitled "Organization/Maintenance Of Computer Emergency Response Team" and "Immediate Reporting Of Suspected Computer Virus Infestation." A: E; E: LMH.

971. Centralized Reporting Of Information Security Problems

Policy: All known vulnerabilities -- in addition to all suspected or known violations -- must be communicated in an expeditious and confidential manner to the Information Security Department. Unauthorized disclosures of Company X information must additionally be reported to the involved information owners. Reporting security violations, problems, or vulnerabilities to any party outside Company X (except external auditors) without the prior written approval of the Legal Department is strictly prohibited.

Commentary: This policy is intended to establish a centralized Information Security Department as the focal point for all reports of vulnerabilities and violations. In many organizations, these reports go only to lower level managers (such as department managers), and never find their way back to a centralized group. Unless there is centralized reporting, no loss history can be compiled, no loss analysis can be conducted, and no related decision-making can be performed. Centralized reporting is also useful for the mobilization of a computer emergency response team (CERT), an organization-wide contingency plan, and other important defensive resources. The policy is also helpful because it alleviates the reporting party's concerns about short-circuiting the chain of command; without a policy like this, local managers may get upset because problem reports make them look bad and they didn't get a chance to stop the reporting process from reaching top management. The policy is also helpful because it indicates what needs to be communicated and to whom. Separately, this policy assumes that a separate policy defining information owners is already in place. For related ideas, see the policies entitled "Reporting Of Damage To Company X Off-Site Systems" and "Legal Framework For Information Security Policies." A: E; E: LMH.

972. Interference With Reporting Of Information Security Problems

Policy: Any attempt to interfere with, prevent, obstruct, or dissuade a staff member in their efforts to report a suspected information security problem or violation is strictly prohibited and cause for disciplinary action. Any form of retaliation against an individual reporting or investigating information security problems or violations is also prohibited and cause for disciplinary action.

Commentary: This policy attempts to encourage workers who wish to report an information security problem or violation, yet are concerned that they may find it difficult, problematic, or otherwise ill-advised. These "whistle blowers" often are concerned that their own immediate management will penalize them for reporting problems or violations. This policy attempts to foster a perspective that is in the best interest of the organization, rather than the internal political interests of certain managers who may look bad. For a related idea, see the policy entitled "Problem Reporting And Management Process." A: EMT; E: LMH.

973. Protection Of Workers Who Report Information Security Problems

Policy: Company X will protect workers who report in good faith what they believe to be a violation of laws or regulations, or conditions that could jeopardize the health or safety of other workers. This means that such workers will not be terminated, threatened, or discriminated against because they report what they perceive to be a wrongdoing or dangerous situation. Before taking any other action, these workers must report the problem to their manager or the Internal Auditing Department, and then give the organization time to remedy the situation.

Commentary: The intention of this policy is to assure workers who are considering reporting problems that the organization will protect them. This should encourage workers to make reports when they may otherwise have been deterred by the potential adverse consequences. Beyond that, the policy is also intended to instruct workers to report problems internally rather than externally (thereby reducing adverse publicity and loss of customer confidence). This policy does not prohibit external reporting -- it only states that the problem should first be internally reported and the worker should give Company X some time to remedy the situation. These words are very important because they allow the termination of a worker who goes public with the information immediately after reporting the problem internally. Likewise nothing in this policy prevents Company X from firing the worker for other reasons, such as poor performance in other areas. Separately, the policy defines the specific person(s) or departments to whom a report should be directed (this should be tailored to the policy writer's organization). The policy is deliberately defined in a broad manner so that it includes information security problems; it also includes physical security problems as well as worker safety problems. For a related idea, see the policy entitled "External Reporting Of Information Security Violations." A: EM; E: LMH.

974. External Reporting Of Information Security Violations

Policy: If required by law or regulation, management must promptly report information security violations to external authorities. If no such requirement exists, in conjunction with representatives from the Law Department, the Security Department, and the Internal Audit Department, management must weigh the pros and cons of external disclosure before reporting these violations.

Commentary: Many organizations still refrain from reporting computer crimes because the public embarrassment, cost, and diversion of staff resources appear to outweigh the benefits. Benefits include setting an example to discourage other violations, giving employees the impression that management believes in the criminal justice system, and obtaining restitution. It is often desirable that management be given the ability to choose to report violations on case-by-case basis. Accordingly, the intention of this policy is to require management to look at the pros and cons of each case before actually making an external report (provided local law gives management such leeway). Although it is rare, some organizations may wish to establish a committee that will evaluate the merits of external reporting on a case-by-case basis. Of course, law enforcement and criminological researchers rally for public reporting because they need statistics to better understand the nature of crime. As it stands, a significant number of computer crimes go unreported, and a significant number go undetected. Note that required external reporting is restricted to violations of laws and regulations, while required internal reporting could include violations of policies and other non-legal requirements. The policy provided here is narrowly-scoped in that it deals with information security violations; the policy could be broadened to focus on all security-related violations. Also see the policies entitled "Retention Of Information Security Violation & Problem Information," "Internal Reporting Of Information Security Violations & Problems," and "Problem Reporting And Management Process." A: M; E: LMH.

975. Reporting Problems To Investors & Government Regulatory Authorities

Policy: Since Company X is publicly-listed on a stock exchange, investors must be informed of significant negative events at Company X which may affect their decisions. In some cases, information security problems including downtime, intrusions, and fraud, may qualify as significant negative events. The information security manager must inform both the vice president of the Law Department and the vice president of the Finance Department of any event which in his or her estimation could qualify as a "material event." These two senior executives must then decide whether public disclosure is necessary and appropriate.

Commentary: Under the securities laws of the United States, and some other countries as well, significant negative events must be promptly disclosed. The Securities and Exchange Commission (SEC) has termed these events "any important information" which may affect an investor's decision process. The test here is whether the investor would consider the information to affect their decision-making; if no, then no disclosure is necessary, and if yes, then disclosure is required. Most organizations are quiet about bad news for fear that it may impact their image, customer confidence, supplier confidence, employee morale, and other factors. But a number of companies have been recently hit with lawsuits from shareholders which allege delayed or insufficient reporting of adverse events. The intention of this policy is to require management to consider disclosures, to pay attention to the relevant disclosure laws, and to establish a formal process for handling these disclosures. By acting promptly and properly, management may curb or avoid shareholder class action lawsuits. By using this policy, management may also avoid a severe drop in the stock price caused by a loss of investor confidence prompted by the revelation of more details about the problem in the midst of a scandal (brought on because the information was initially suppressed). Note that other organizational structures will be required for reporting other types of "material events," such as a staff layoff. This policy applies primarily to publicly-listed companies, but it could also be reformulated for other organizations to take into consideration things that a local community should know. For related ideas, see the policy entitled "External Reporting Of Information Security Violations." A: M; E: LMH.

976. Public And Governmental Disclosure Of Computer System Attacks

Policy: Unless compelled by law to disclose attacks against its computer systems or networks, Company X does not publicly report these incidents, nor does it disclose the incidents to government agencies.

Commentary: The intention of this policy is to keep organizations out of the newspapers if they are to be shown in an uncomplimentary light. This helps keep customer confidence high as well as keep stock prices high. For firms in regulated industries, such as utilities and transportation, this policy is also intended to keep the organization and out of trouble with regulators (if lawmakers and regulation-makers knew a firm was having a trouble, they might step-in and create new rules). The policy furthermore acknowledges that most governments (and the US government is no exception here) do not have a trusted and secure mechanism to protect information about attacks. Thus sharing attack information with a government agency would actually be irresponsible because it could lead to the unauthorized exploitation of this information. So what many organizations are doing is just keeping a low profile, and not disclosing attack information. This policy is often unwritten, but in many situations it may be advisable to put it in writing to keep workers from publicly disclosing such information. Another good reason to put this policy in writing is to show that it's a legitimate and justified approach, not a decision rule that must be concealed. On a separate note, the policy deliberately does not distinguish between a successful attack and an unsuccessful attack -- both of which may include sensitive information. For related ideas, see the policy entitled "External Reporting Of Information Security Violations." A: E; E: LMH.

977. Immediate Reporting Of Suspected Computer Virus Infestation

Policy: Computer viruses can spread quickly and need to be eradicated as soon as possible to limit serious damage to computers and data. Accordingly, if workers report a computer virus infestation to the Information Security Department immediately after it is noticed, even if their negligence was a contributing factor, no disciplinary action will be taken. The only exception to this early reporting amnesty will be those circumstances where a worker knowingly caused a computer virus to be introduced into Company X systems. However, if a report of a known infestation is not promptly made, and if an investigation reveals that certain workers were aware of the infestation, these workers will be subject to disciplinary action including termination.

Commentary: This policy is intended to encourage quick reporting of viruses, which is essential if their growth is to be limited and consequential losses are to be contained. A notable aspect of the policy is that disciplinary action will be taken if there is a delay in reporting a problem. Because even minutes can make a great difference when it comes to the propagation of computer viruses, the word "immediately" was used in the policy. Of course, if a worker has written a virus and let it loose on Company X computers, then this should still be cause for disciplinary action, even if the employee did call the Information Security Department promptly after it got out of hand. The policy, as written, does not stop such a disciplinary action because it refers to "negligence" rather than a deliberate malicious act. On a different note, the policy could be expanded to include worms, Trojan horses, and other unauthorized programs that pose a risk to Company X systems. For a related idea, see the policy "Testing For Viruses Prior To Use On Company X Systems." For a more general approach, see the policy entitled "Internal Reporting Of Information Security Violations & Problems." Also see the policy entitled "Users Must Not Attempt To Eradicate Computer Viruses." A: E; E: LMH.

978. Required Reporting Of Software Malfunctions

Policy: All apparent software malfunctions must be immediately reported to line management or the information system service provider.

Commentary: The intention of this policy is to require users to note and report any software which appears to be functioning incorrectly (i.e., in a manner that differs from documentation). This will help to uncover Trojan horses, viruses, out-of-balance accounting problems, frauds, and other problems. The policy will also indirectly encourage the maintenance of up-to-date documentation. This policy could be expanded to instruct users to stop using the computer and to disconnect it from any attached networks; these actions help isolate the problem to minimize further damage. Likewise, in a policy like this, users could be instructed not to attempt a recovery; in these instances, the actual recovery effort should be performed by experts. This policy could be changed to require reporting to the Information Security Department. As organizations expand the connectivity of their networks (such as hook-ups with the Internet), this policy is increasingly important because such interconnectivity can provide new pathways for the transmission of viruses, worms, Trojan horses, and other unauthorized software. See the policy entitled "Immediate Reporting of Suspected Computer Virus Infestation." A: E; E: LMH.

979. Reporting Unauthorized Data Changes & Questionable System Use

Policy: Users of Company X information systems must immediately report to the Information Security Manager any unauthorized loss of, or changes to computerized production data. Any questionable usage of files, databases, or communications networks must likewise be immediately reported to the same manager.

Commentary: The intention of this policy is to provide users with specific examples of the types of events that should be reported to the Information Security Manager. The policy seeks to enlist the participation of users on an information security team, and use their eyes and minds to detect unusual events which may be indicative of sabotage, fraud, system malfunction, and other information-security-relevant events. The policy may need some explanation when delivered to the end-user community, lest they think that they are being turned into unwilling shills who are now required to "rat on" their fellow employees. This policy fits nicely with the policy entitled "Required Reporting Of Software Malfunctions." Also see the policies entitled "Internal Reporting Of Information Security Violations & Problems" and "Centralized Reporting Of Information Security Problems." A: E; E: LMH.

980. Required Investigation Following Computer Crimes

Policy: Whenever evidence clearly shows that Company X has been victimized by a computer or communications crime, a thorough investigation must be performed. This investigation must provide sufficient information so that management can take steps to ensure that: (1) such incidents will not be likely to take place again, and (2) effective security measures have been reestablished.

Commentary: This policy is intended to make sure that management takes appropriate action in response to computer or communications system crimes. Too often management is inclined to "sweep" the whole affair "under the rug." To prevent management from trying to suppress information about vulnerabilities (often because it would make them look bad), this policy requires that they initiate an investigation. In most instances, department and other local management will not have the expertise to carry out such a sophisticated investigation. Thus, the policy indirectly requires these managers to contact the Information Security Department, the Internal Audit Department, or some other group with the requisite expertise. The policy also helps guard against lawsuits alleging that management did not take care of problems even though they were "on notice" that security problems existed. Examples of computer and communications crimes (which may be suitably included in an accompanying explanation) include theft of computer-resident trade secrets and PBX toll fraud. Some organizations may wish to take this policy one step further: instead of requiring investigations after an organization has been shown to have been victimized, investigations can be required if such acts are only suspected. Another variation on the policy is to require that an investigation be performed after an abuse has been noted, even if this abuse is not legally a crime; this approach of course requires that the term "abuse" be defined. An example of a computer abuse that is not a computer crime in many jurisdictions is privacy violation. Separately, reporting of such incidents to the Audit Committee on the Board of Directors may additionally be required in the policy. Also see the policy entitled "Confidentiality Of Internal Investigations Information." A: MT; E: LMH.

981. When To Seek Assistance With Unauthorized Access Problems

Policy: Whenever unauthorized system access is suspected or known to be occurring, Company X personnel must take immediate action to terminate the access. If these actions do not completely suppress the unauthorized activity, assistance from the Corporate Information Systems Help Desk must immediately be sought.

Commentary: This policy informs both technical staff (and perhaps users) that they must take immediate action to suppress unauthorized system access. The policy also informs workers that they must immediately seek expert technical assistance via the help desk if they are not able to completely stop the unauthorized access. In many organizations, the help desk would then contact information security technical specialists (typically by pager). The policy is necessary because many systems administrators, network managers, and other technical staff are embarrassed to admit that they have not been able to rid a system of a hacker or some other unauthorized user. As a result they may spend considerable time trying to outsmart the intruder, and in the process unduly jeopardize both information assets and systems availability. On another note, rather than having the policy get overly complicated with various responses to a variety of problems, it simply directs all such problems to the help desk (which is hopefully on duty 24 X 7 X 365). Procedures to deal with a variety of contingencies can then be developed by the help desk staff in conjunction with in-house attorneys, physical security specialists (for investigation expertise), and information security specialists. For a related idea, see the policy entitled "Required Reporting Of Information Security Incidents." A: T; E: LMH.

982. Retention Of Information Security Violation & Problem Information

Policy: Information describing all reported information security problems and violations must be retained for a period of three (3) years.

Commentary: The intention of this policy is to put management on notice that certain important information security related information must not be destroyed. The information referred to in the policy is helpful when doing risk assessments, when planning information security projects, and when developing budgets. It may also be useful for prosecution or disciplinary actions. The policy applies to computer logs and internal correspondence, as well as notes from secret investigations. Management may want to quickly destroy certain information for fear that it will be used to discredit them or otherwise paint the organization in a bad light. Some organizations may want to forgo this policy because they may want the leeway to destroy certain information for fear that parties opposing the organization in a lawsuit could gain access to the information, and thereby achieve an advantage in court. This concern can be dealt with by adding words such as "unless approved in advance by corporate counsel." In support of the notion that information describing information security problems is valuable, certain government regulations (such as those pertaining to commercial banks in the United States) now require the reporting of information security problems to government regulators. The scope of the policy could be changed to deal with all security problems and violations, not just those related to information security. Also see the policies entitled "Annual Analysis Of Information Security Violations & Problems" and "External Reporting Of Information Security Violations." A: MT; E: LMH.

983. Annual Analysis Of Information Security Violations & Problems

Policy: An annual analysis of reported information security problems and violations must be prepared by the Information Security Department.

Commentary: The intention of this policy is to require the Information Security Department to prepare a status report of actual losses and problems encountered. Such a loss history analysis is helpful when performing risk assessments, when preparing job performance evaluations, and also when preparing budgets and project plans for the coming year. Although it may sound like more work for often-overworked information security staff, this policy can help establish and maintain a regular communication path with top management. Notice that the methodology for performing such analyses is not mentioned so as to give the Information Security Department the leeway to change its approach as it becomes more sophisticated. The policy could be expanded to include mention of submitting a written report to the Chief Information Officer (CIO), the Chief Executive Officer (CEO), or the Audit Committee on the Board of Directors. Also see the policies entitled "Required Investigation Following Computer Crimes" and "Retention of Information Security Violation & Problem Information." A: MT; E: LMH.

984. Problem Reporting And Management Process

Policy: Information reflecting the effects of system faults, breakdowns, and computer related problems must be made available to users on a regular basis. A formal problem management process must be in place to record the problems, reduce their incidence, and to prevent their recurrence.

Commentary: The intention of this policy is to require that users be able to determine the effects that certain system problems have on their data and the quality of service they receive. Only with a good understanding of these problems can users properly appreciate the value of the service they receive as well as the integrity of the data they use for decision-making. Another intention of this policy is to require that a problem management system be established and operational. Problem management systems can be important tools in the reporting and resolution of information security problems such as virus infestations and unauthorized system use (e.g., occasioned by "hackers"). The policy deliberately omits mention of reports about computer crimes and other sensitive matters which may be restricted to a few people. This policy looks at internal reporting; for ideas about external reporting see the policy entitled "External Reporting Of Information Security Violations." Also see the policy entitled "Internal Reporting Of Information Security Violations & Problems." For more of a hardware maintenance perspective on this matter, see the policy entitled "Preventive Maintenance On Computer And Communication Systems." A: MT; E: LMH.

985. Systems Designers & Developers Must Inform Management Of Problems

Policy: All potentially serious problems associated with information systems being designed or developed, that are not being adequately addressed by planned or existing projects, must be promptly reported to the Information Security Manager.

Commentary: The intention of this policy is to give workers a reporting channel other than the standard management hierarchy with which they normally operate. As the Y2K problem has made painfully clear, standard reporting channels are often not sufficient for the reporting of major problems because management doesn't like bad news, doesn't want to look bad, doesn't want to spend money now when they can spend it later, doesn't have the technical expertise to understand the problem, etc. This policy makes it officially required for technical staff members to bring problems to the attention of the Information Security Manager (as an alternative, the

Internal Audit Manager could be used). Separately, note that the nature of the problems was not defined; by leaving this word ambiguous, a very broad scope of possible problems is covered by the policy. In a broader sense, this policy seeks to establish that all people throughout an organization are responsible for information security, not just the members of the Information Security Department. Also note that this reporting process could proceed anonymously, for example through a hot line that is never answered by a person but that connects to an answering machine without caller-ID. For related ideas, see the policies entitled "Designing Controls With Large Margins Of Error" and "Risk Acceptance Process And Permissible Exceptions To Policies." A: E; E: LMH.

2.1.3. Control Selection

2.1.3.1. Controls And Systems Design

986. Reliance On New Information Systems Security Products

Policy: Information systems security products on the market less than a year must not be used as an integral component of any critical Company X production information system.
Commentary: The intention of this policy is to prevent systems designers and others from using very new information security products for production systems. Nothing in the policy prevents Company X from acting as a beta site, or from testing these new products. It does, however, prevent Company X from "betting the business" on these products. The major concern here is discovery of security deficiencies which then later embarrass the organization, cause it to discontinue the production systems involved, or allow other crimes like fraud to be perpetrated. By waiting a year (or a comparable period like six months), Company X relies on the marketplace to identify major security problems. Some of these problems were encountered in 1995 with the Netscape Communications browser Internet software and the public key encryption mechanisms found therein. Separately, although rare, this policy or a derivative policy with a smaller time frame could also apply to major releases of existing information systems security products. For the most conservative organizations, the policy could apply to all information systems products, not just information systems security products. Separately, if this policy seems too restrictive as written, a special approval process can be provided to deal with exceptions. Note that this policy need not be in conflict with another policy entitled "Use Of Most Current Computer Operating System Versions," since operating systems are already in use and are therefore not new. Also see the policies entitled "Use Of Mature Development Tools And Techniques" and "Prompt Implementation Of Security Problem Fix Software, Scripts, Etc." A: T; E: MH.

987. Ease-Of-Use Required For Computer & Communications Security

Policy: All computer and communications security measures must be simple and easy to use, simple and easy to administer, and simple and easy to audit.

Commentary: The intention of this policy is to require that all computer and communications controls be practical and sustainable. If security measures are too complex they are likely to be misunderstood, misinterpreted, or misapplied. Additionally, whenever controls are awkward, cumbersome, or otherwise poorly designed, users will bypass and/or resist them. This policy acknowledges reality in that, to be successful, controls must have a balance between security objectives and practical concerns (cost, ease of use, etc.). On another note, the term "user-friendly" may be used in this policy, but it has been used so much that it has lost much of its meaning. To make the policy cleaner, some readers may wish to eliminate two of the three instances of the words "simple and easy." The policy is intended for systems designers, systems integrators, and others who set-up information systems. Nothing in this policy prevents systems designers from building complex systems; this policy only requires that the complexity be hidden from the users and others who must interact with the system. See the policies entitled "Minimum Information System Controls Dictated By Standard Practice" and "Required User Acceptance Of Information Security Measures." A: T; E: LMH.

988. Required User Acceptance Of Information Security Measures

Policy: All information security controls must be both accepted and supported by the people who are monitored by and work with the controls.

Commentary: Often overlooked until it becomes a problem, acceptance by the subjects (or users) is essential to the success of all controls. These individuals should be involved in the control-related decision-making process. For example, employee union representatives could be involved in discussions about using computer systems to monitor the work of employees. An example where this acceptance and support was not obtained reportedly involved an IBM facility in Italy. After an employee movement monitoring system was installed, the employees went on strike because they considered use of the system to be a privacy invasion. Shortly thereafter, the system was deactivated. In keeping with the example, this policy implicitly forces management to explain and justify controls to employees. Such communications go long way toward motivating employees to comply with security measures. If employees understand the reasons why security measures are called for, they will be able to achieve the same objectives even when these security measures fail. The policy could be changed to incorporate some indication of when acceptance and support must be obtained (for instance before a new system goes into production mode). See the policies entitled "Minimum Information System Controls Dictated By Standard Practice" and "Where To Use Computer System Access Controls." A: T; E: LMH.

989. Incorporation Of Security Into Systems Development Life Cycle

Policy: For all business application systems, security must be considered by systems designers and developers from the beginning of the systems design process through conversion to a production system.

Commentary: While consideration early in the development process is desirable because it is considerably more efficient and effective, this should not be the end of the control selection process. Typically the systems development life cycle will involve several points where security is formally included in the process. Hand-rendered signatures (or perhaps digital signatures) indicating the adequacy of security work may be required at these points. The intention of this policy is to require the technical staff to consider security as a formal part of the systems development life cycle. This policy assumes that an enforced systems development life cycle (SDLC) exists -- this may not be the case in the PC, workstation, client/server, intranet, and LAN computing environments. See the policies entitled "Formal Specifications Required For Software Developed In-House," "Formal Change Control Process Required for Business Applications," and "Compliance With Organizational Systems Development Conventions." A: T; E: LMH.

990. Hardware/Software Procurement Via Standard Purchasing Channels

Policy: To assure compliance with in-house information security standards, all hardware and software must be procured through the Purchasing Department.

Commentary: Users often thwart standard purchasing channels to: (1) get their software or hardware more quickly, or (2) to avoid having to comply with internal technical standards. This practice may also allow them to purchase hardware and software that inadvertently compromises network or computer system security. For example, they may purchase desktop computers which have a floppy disk drive when diskless workstations are standard equipment. Allowing users to go their own way also creates chaotic computing environments where systems are not readily supportable, interoperable, or interconnectable. The intention of this policy is to require that all such purchases go through a single organizational unit, which can then monitor the requests for compliance with in-house technical standards. Whenever there is a question about compliance, the Purchasing Department can forward requests for information security related hardware and software to the Information Security Department for approval. Separately, the policy could be written in a more general sense in which case the words "information security" would be dropped. The policy could also be rewritten such that all purchases go through the Information Technology Department. Also see the policies entitled "Purchase Rather Than Build Information Security Solutions," "Centralized Responsibility For Information Security," "Use Of Computer Systems Belonging To Workers On Company Property," as well as "Procedure For Release Of Used Equipment And Media To Third Parties." A: ET; E: LMH.

991. Consistent Protection Of Information Regardless Of Manifestation

Policy: Information must be protected in a manner commensurate with its sensitivity, value, and criticality. This policy applies regardless of the media on which information is stored, the locations where the information is stored, the systems used to process the information, or the processes by which information is handled.

Commentary: The intention of this policy is to require that systems designers consistently handle information no matter what manifestation it takes. So often part of a system will have good controls while another has poor controls. In keeping with the "weakest link in a chain" adage, if there is to be a security problem, it's likely to be where controls are poor. This policy encourages a more holistic view of information, including examination of the ways information flows through an organization. The policy also implicitly points to the scope of an Information Security Department's work: throughout and often even outside an organization (wherever the information goes). The policy additionally encourages internal audit departments to use integrated techniques such as data flow analysis. The idea behind this policy is important for those preparing a systems security architecture; integrated access control systems using this idea can include single sign-on to a network of computers, single-point for user registration, centralized access control administration, and centralized access control system auditing. Separately, in some cases, the policy writer will want to provide examples to clarify this policy. Examples of media for information storage include paper, overhead transparencies, and computer floppy disks. Examples of locations where information is stored include in a headquarters building or a remote sales office. Examples of systems used for information processing include voice mail systems, fax machines, and laptop personal computers. Examples of processes used to handle information include the in-house systems development methodology, annual budget preparation procedure, and employee background checking procedure. See the policy entitled "Single Sign-On Process." For related ideas, see the policies entitled "Control Implementations Consistent With Standard Of Due Care," "Information Security Management Committee," and "Dispersion Of Computer And Communication Systems." A: T; E: LMH.

992. Every Information System Privilege Not Specifically Allowed Is Forbidden

Policy: Every information system privilege which has not been specifically allowed by the Information Security Manager is forbidden. Such privileges may not be employed for any Company X business purpose until they have been approved in writing.

Commentary: This policy is an expression of what is called restrictive design. It is intended to prevent privileges that have been enabled but not sufficiently examined from being used by intruders and other unauthorized individuals. For example, according to the configuration of a firewall, certain Internet services will be allowed and certain services will be forbidden. Vendors often ship products with many, if not all, services allowed to enable customers to get the systems up and running quickly. Likewise, the Internet is designed with a permissive design approach that says everything which is not specifically forbidden is allowed (e.g., all communications protocols will be supported unless a firewall is installed to block them). This policy imposes a certain degree of inflexibility because privilege changes must be approved in advance, but it helps to assure that services which have not been adequately investigated aren't going to be used against the organization in question. Separately, this policy suggests that the Information Security Manager is the one to make decisions about new types of privileges; some organizations may wish to employ information owners instead. As this policy implies, the author suggests that owners be used only to implement the decision-making systems and guidelines established by an Information Security Manager; this is because owners often do not understand the technological implications associated with the approval of a new type of privilege. As an aside, in an indirect way, this policy also informs users that they should not attempt to discover privileges which they have not been expressly authorized to utilize. For related ideas, see the policies entitled "Privilege Restriction Based On The Need-To-Know" and "Minimization Of Reliance On Common Mechanism For Controls." A: T; E: LMH.

993. Minimization Of Reliance On Common Mechanism For Controls

Policy: Within the confines of cost-justification, information security controls must be selected and designed such that reliance on a common mechanism is minimized.

Commentary: If a common mechanism, such as a PBX telephone switch, is used by many controls, its failure or unavailability will have a serious effect on overall security. For example, if a single node on a network was the sole provider of gateway-style access control services, then the unavailability of this one node might mean that the whole network is unavailable. This policy instructs systems designers and other technical staff to avoid such vulnerable designs. At the very least, the policy requires that systems designers raise the question of reliance on a common mechanism. Some readers may wish to include in the policy a definition of "common mechanism." One definition could be "a systems component that provides security services to a variety of other systems." This policy is often in opposition to other systems design objectives like simplicity and cost--part of the information security specialist's job is to achieve a workable balance between such competing objectives. The scope of the policy could readily be expanded to include all systems components (not just controls). See the policies entitled "Independent Security Systems For Each Computer System," "Control Implementations Consistent With Standard Of Due Care," and "Human Intervention Required For Important Decisions." A: T; E: LMH.

994. Independent Security Systems For Each Computer System

Policy: The security of a computer system must never be entirely dependent on the security of another computer system.

Commentary: In a well-secured network of systems, ideally each system can maintain its own security in a decentralized manner. This design approach provides greater resilience to a variety of attacks. For example, if a small system was entirely dependent on another system on a network, then a successful compromise of the security on the other system would leave both systems vulnerable. This might be the case if so-called "single-sign-on" systems were employed because the same password could allow access to a variety of systems. The intention of this policy is to force designers and other technical staff to consider whether a system is in fact dependent on another system. The policy indirectly encourages control measures which compensate for deficiencies or failures of other controls. An example of such a control would be an active logging system which might shut-down a certain user-ID because activity on the user-ID was very different from the authorized user's profile. This active logging system could step-in if the access control system, perhaps a single-sign-on system, were to be defeated. This policy is increasingly important the more systems are interconnected (for example via client/server technology), especially when an Internet connection is employed. See the policies entitled "Reliance On A Single Person For Important Systems Expertise," "Reliance On Operating System User Authentication Process," and "Minimization Of Reliance On Common Mechanism for Controls." A: T; E: LMH.

995. Dedicated Computers & Networks For High-Security/High-Reliability

Policy: Unless approved in advance by the Information Security Department manager, every high-security and high-reliability system managed by or owned by Company X must have its own dedicated computers and networks.

Commentary: The purpose of this policy is to clearly delineate an essential requirement for every high-security and high-reliability system that Company X owns or manages. If dedicated computers and networks are used, there is considerably less complexity associated with a system. This simplicity will make it much easier to make the system secure and reliable. Dedicated systems also reduce the number of people and organizations who have something to do with the system, and this in turn reduces the chances for errors and omissions, and will also allow Company X to make modifications more quickly. Examples of modern systems which are dedicated include automated teller machine (ATM) networks. If ATM networks were to sell theater tickets, allow people to vote, and allow a myriad of other functions to be performed with the same computers and networks, a host of security and reliability issues would be introduced. Note that this policy has implications for systems outsourcing arrangements as well as systems managed in-house. For related ideas, see the policies entitled "Internet Commerce & Financial Systems Must Be Physically Isolated" and "Isolate Systems Containing Secret Information From Network." A: T; E: MH.

996. Designing Controls With Large Margins Of Error

Policy: When designing information security measures, workers must use large margins of error and large time horizons. For example, encryption key lengths must be sufficiently large so that encryption systems will not be likely to be defeated within the next decade.

Commentary: The intention of this policy is to underscore that information security systems design must incorporate significant margins of error and long time horizons. The Y2K (millennium bug) crisis is a good example of a problem encountered because programmers and their project managers took a short-term perspective. This policy thus acknowledges that systems built today are likely to be used a decade from now. The policy also provides for unexpected developments, such as new mathematical techniques which make cryptanalysis easier and faster. Such an unexpected development could mean that existing encryption systems are now readily compromised even though they could not be readily compromised in the recent past. This policy is not just relevant to encryption key length; it also applies to fixed password length, random number generator seed length, and other security parameters. Separately, this policy directly addresses the tendency to minimize costs, which if used as the primary decision factor, in many instances will lead to information security systems that are obsolete or weak within a short period of time. For related ideas, see the policies entitled "Building Systems So That Errors And Manipulations Come To Light" and "Minimization Of Reliance On Common Mechanism For Controls." A: T; E: LMH.

997. Use Of Most Current Computer Operating System Versions

Policy: To take advantage of recent security improvements, after a delay of several months, Company X must use the most recent version of all multi-user computer operating systems.

Commentary: When it comes to installing the latest release of an operating system, a delay is often called for unless the organization is willing to discover and deal with bugs found in new versions (depending on the vendor's history with testing and bugs). The intention of this policy is to make sure that the organization in question has implemented the most recent versions of operating systems because these most recent versions include various security fixes. Thus, by using the most current versions of operating systems, the best operating system security is achieved. The policy could be expanded to include network operating systems (like Novell's NetWare), not just computer operating systems (like Microsoft's Windows 98). For further discussion of this point, see the policy entitled "Approval Required For Changes To Production Operating Systems." For related ideas, see the policies entitled "Reliance On New Information Systems Security Products," "Use Of Mature Development Tools And Techniques" and "Prompt Implementation Of Security Problem Fix Software, Scripts, Etc." A: T; E: LMH.

998. Latest Software Release On Systems Interfacing External Networks

Policy: To help ensure that attackers don't utilize the newest penetration methods against Company X systems, all systems interfacing external networks (Internet firewalls, Internet commerce servers, dial-up modem banks, etc.) must be running the latest version of the vendor-supplied operating software.

Commentary: The intention of this policy is to reduce the success that hackers, crackers, and other third party attackers will have when attempting to use the latest penetration attack method. Many systems administrators are overwhelmed and preoccupied with pressing issues, and they postpone upgrading the software on firewalls and other systems which have external interfaces. This is a dangerous approach to security, and will be prevented with this policy. Of course, the vendors involved don't always release patches and fixes in sufficient time to prevent major problems, but if an attack method is serious enough the vendors ordinary release patches shortly after vulnerabilities are discovered in order to limit their own liability. The presence of vulnerability identification software on the Internet (such as SATAN) makes this policy especially important. Such software allows attackers to automatically see what version of software a particular system is running and then to readily determine the vulnerabilities which go along with that version of software. The more recent the operating software, generally, the fewer the vulnerabilities. This policy is also useful when it comes to Y2K compliance because recent software is more likely to be compliant. Separately, some organizations may not wish to use the word "release" -- instead they may prefer to use the term "security patches or fixes." This rewording makes it clear that bug fixes which are not of a security nature need not be immediately posted. For a related idea, see the policy entitled "Use Of Most Current Computer Operating System Versions." A: T; E: LMH.

999. Network Security Measures Must Not Be Backwards Compatible

Policy: Network security measures used on Company X production systems must not be backwards compatible.

Commentary: The objective of this policy is to prevent what is called a version rollback attack, which can lead to the compromise of the involved control. While backwards compatibility is user-friendly and desirable from an interconnectivity and interoperability standpoint, it is definitely dangerous from a network security standpoint. If an attacker can get a new version of a control to roll back to a prior version's protocol, then the attacker may be able to take advantage of a prior version's vulnerabilities, even though these same vulnerabilities may have been fixed in the new version. This is why users who had 40 bit SSL (secure sockets layer) plug-ins for their Internet browsers now need to load a new version of the software in order to support 128 bit SSL encryption. It is exceedingly hard to design a control which is backwards compatible just enough to be functional, but at the same time prevent attackers from exploiting vulnerabilities in the prior version. This policy recognizes that difficulty and opts for the more secure approach prohibiting backwards compatibility. For related considerations, see the policies entitled "Use Of Most Current Computer Operating System Versions" and "Latest Software Release On Systems Interfacing External Networks." A: T; E: H.

1000. Keeping Security Functionality Out Of Business Applications

Policy: Whenever feasible and cost-effective, system developers must rely on system services for security functionality rather than incorporating such functionality into applications. Examples of system services include operating systems, network operating systems, database management systems, access control packages, front-end processors, firewalls, gateways, and routers.

Commentary: The purpose of this policy is to make sure internal system developers employ standard security functionality, such as the log-in process associated with operating systems like DEC's VMS. If developers write their own versions of such routines, these routines are likely to be inadequately tested, inadequately documented, and inadequately supported in the years ahead. By insisting that all developers use system services, a consistent level of security can be maintained on a cross-application basis. Improvements to the security of the system services, as are naturally provided by new releases of operating systems, will thus be easy to integrate with applications. On the other hand, numerous proprietary security routines built into applications may prevent an organization from moving to the latest release of an operating system, or at the very least prove administratively unmanageable. Of course, there will be certain functions that cannot be achieved with system services, and these are best done at the application level. For example, a routine which performs input error checking is generally done at the application level (although in the future these tasks will increasingly be performed via centralized systems services, such as active data dictionaries). Separately, this policy works best if there is a formal review and approval process associated with software development efforts, in which case deviations from this policy can be readily identified. The policy also works better if the organization has a set of approved security software routines which have been tested, documented, and made generally-available to developers; this in many respects is similar to IBM's concept of a repository for software. For related ideas, see the policies entitled "Where To Use Computer System Access Controls" and "Formal Change Control Process Required For Business Applications." A: T; E: LMH.

1001. Systems Must Be Configured & Customized According To Templates

Policy: Every general purpose computer at Company X is considered to be a desktop system, an infrastructure server, or a border server. To assure these computers are adequately secured, they all must be configured and customized according to one of three security templates issued by the Information Security Department.

Commentary: This policy is intended to: (1) establish the existence of a three tier computer template scheme, and (2) require all general purpose computers to be customized and configured according to the template requirements. A three tier scheme such as this recognizes that each of the three types of computers have different security requirements. For example, a desktop system will typically have minimal or non-existent logging, while an infrastructure server (like a mail server) will have heavy-duty logging, and border server (like a firewall) will have the maximum logging available. Requiring extensive logging on a desktop system would unduly interfere with productivity and would be too expensive. The templates thus require security only where needed, and thus reduce the overall cost of security. The existence of a three tier scheme like this additionally helps to reestablish centralized control over the configuration and customization of computers. In many organizations, end-users have taken over local computer operations, and a wide variety of configuration and customization approaches are accordingly used within the same organization. By standardizing these templates, an organization can help restore operational order and security across all departments. Use of such templates also makes the addition of centralized information security services like a network management system or a centralized intrusion detection system (IDS) easier to implement. Separately, a configuration decision example involves specification of the minimum number of characters in a password. A customization decision example involves specification of the virus detection software package that must be installed and enabled on all machines within a template class. For related considerations, see the policies entitled "Intranet Site Developers Must Use Company X Style Guide" and "Where To Use Computer System Access Controls." A: ET; E: LMH.

2.1.3.2. Controls And Business Considerations

1002. Risk Assessments Required For Production Information Systems

Policy: All "production" computer information systems must be periodically evaluated by the Information Security Department to determine the minimum set of controls required to reduce risk to an acceptable level.

Commentary: The process described in the policy is often called a "risk analysis" or "risk assessment." The intention of this policy is to require a risk assessment for all production information systems, thus ensuring that critical business systems have received at least a rudimentary level of security attention. Some readers may wish to put a time period into the policy, although simply using the term "periodic" is recommended. The way the policy is written now, production systems can be prioritized by risk, and those which present a greater risk can be examined more frequently and in greater detail. Instead of the Information Security Department, these evaluations could be performed by an Internal Audit Department or an EDP Audit Department. It is advisable to specify which group is responsible for performing risk assessments, either via this policy or via a separate policy dealing with overall responsibilities. A risk assessment is required because Certified Public Accountants (called Chartered Accountants in some countries) do not look closely at information security measures as part of their regular financial statement related audits. A risk assessment provides background information on which information security management decisions such as budgets, staffing plans, and project plans can be based. For related ideas, see the policies entitled "Response Required For Every Significant Information Security Risk," "Specific Tasks Performed By The Information Security Department," "Annual Information Security Planning Process Required," and "Minimum Information System Controls Dictated By Standard Practice." A: M; E: LMH.

1003. When To Perform An Information Systems Security Risk Assessment

Policy: Information systems security risk assessments for critical information systems and critical production applications must be performed at least once every two years. All major enhancements, upgrades, conversions, and related changes associated with these systems or applications must be preceded by a risk assessment as defined in the Information Security Manual.

Commentary: The intention of this policy is to require staff to perform risk assessments before major changes are made to critical information systems (such as an in-house electronic mail system) or critical production applications (such as sales lead tracking). This policy assumes that the organization has already ranked its information systems along a criticality continuum (see the policy entitled "Five Category Application Criticality Classification Scheme"). The policy also assumes that a methodology for performing risk assessments has been defined in another internal document such as an Information Security Manual. The exact methodology for the risk assessment is deliberately not specified in the policy; this allows the methodology to evolve over time without the need to change this policy. The type of risk assessment (alias risk analysis) will in many cases also vary based on circumstances. For example, if a risk assessment was performed on the application in question six months ago, then only an abbreviated update to the prior assessment may be required. But if no risk assessment has ever been performed, then a full-scale risk assessment may be needed. For a related idea see the policy entitled, "Annual Information Security Planning Process Required." A: T; E: LMH.

1004. Vulnerability Identification Software For Internet-Connected Systems

Policy: To ensure that Company X technical staff has taken appropriate preventive measures, all systems directly-connected to the Internet must be subjected to an automated risk analysis performed via vulnerability identification software at least once a month.

Commentary: The purpose of this policy is to ensure that Company X knows what vulnerabilities a hacker or cracker could use to break into its systems. Armed with this information, Company X staff can make appropriate adjustments, such as install the latest version of certain systems software. If staff doesn't know what the vulnerabilities are, then taking the appropriate next steps will be impossible. This policy is in support of the conclusion reached by various statistical studies: it is much cheaper to prevent problems than it is to correct things in response to them and to otherwise recover from them. Vulnerability identification software is especially important for Internet-connected systems because these systems are exposed to much more severe attacks than any other systems (even dial-up systems). One vendor offering vulnerability identification software is Internet Security Systems, Atlanta, Georgia, USA. For related ideas, see the policies entitled "Internet Connected Machines Must Have Intrusion Detection Systems," "Changing Vendor Default Passwords," and "Tools Used To Break Systems Security Prohibited." A: T; E: LMH.

1005. Purchase Rather Than Build Information Security Solutions

Policy: To keep costs down and to facilitate systems development, Company X must purchase commercially-available information security solutions rather than build the solutions in-house. Exceptions to this policy must only be made when the cost-effectiveness of an in-house solution has been clearly analyzed, documented, and approved by Information Security Department management.

Commentary: The intention of this policy is to save the organization money as well as free-up its personnel to address business problems rather than information security system development problems. Commercially available solutions are generally much cheaper than in-house solutions, although they may not be as much fun to put together (for some technical people anyway). Commercial solutions are also generally more extensively tested than in-house systems, as well as more extensively documented than in-house solutions, and so are likely to be more secure. However, in certain instances, no commercial products meet organizational needs, and in these cases it is necessary to develop in-house solutions. Even in these cases, it is often possible to put together an in-house solution which incorporates several commercial products. Some readers may wish to extend this policy to apply to all information systems (not just "information security solutions"), but that is outside the normal scope of an information security manager's responsibility, so it's not addressed here. Given commercial products are often in compliance with standards, for a related idea, see the policy entitled "Compliance With Industry Specific Information Security Standards." Also see the policies entitled "Hardware/Software Procurement Via Standard Purchasing Channels" and "Compliance With Standards Required For Emergency/Disaster Support." A: MT; E: LMH.

1006. Best-Of-Breed Solutions For Critical Information Security Functions

Policy: Unless they will be handled with in-house resources, all critical information security functions must be supported with best-of-breed commercially available products and services.

Commentary: This policy expresses a secure systems design philosophy and specifies how it should be implemented from a business standpoint. The policy is intended to ensure that all critical information security products (smart card systems, single sign-on systems, digital certificate systems, encryption systems, etc.) as well as related services (network intrusion detection monitoring, network privilege assignment administration, etc.) are supported with the best currently available commercial solutions. The policy explicitly specifies commercial solutions because non-commercial solutions may not be supported or may not be kept up-to-date (in this context, the Linux operating system would be considered a commercial solution, because a variety of businesses support it, even though the code itself may be free). Separately, the Information Security Department would ordinarily determine which functions are critical, and which should be supported by best-of-breed solutions. Note that this policy requires that internal staff perform additional research to understand what the market now has to offer -- that they do not simply opt for what they know or what a salesperson is suggesting that they buy. For related ideas, see the policies entitled "Reliance On New Information Systems Security Products" and "Purchase Rather Than Build Information Security Solutions." A: T; E: H.

1007. Compliance With Industry Specific Information Security Standards

Policy: Company X information systems must employ industry-specific information security standards. No exceptions are permitted unless it can be demonstrated that the costs of using a standard exceed the benefits, or that use of a standard will clearly impede Company X's business activities.

Commentary: The intention of this policy is to require that systems designers and other technical people employ industry standard controls. For example, in the banking industry, encryption systems should use industry specific systems for key management. Various other industry specific controls are also relevant to the medical services industry, the aerospace/defense community, and other industry groups. Additional specifics may also be obtained from industry associations. Separately, given commercial products are often in compliance with standards, for a related idea, see the policy entitled "Purchase Rather Than Build Information Security Solutions." Also see the policies entitled "Control Implementations Consistent With Standard Of Due Care" and "Minimum Information System Controls Dictated By Standard Practice."
A: T; E: LMH.

1008. Legal Framework For Information Security Policies

Policy: Company X acknowledges the complexity of legal requirements found in the global networking environment created by the Internet. Company X's information security policies were drafted to meet, and in some instances exceed the protections found in existing laws and regulations. If any Company X information security policy is believed to be in conflict with existing laws or regulations, this observation must be promptly reported to the Information Security Department Manager.

Commentary: The intention of this policy is to create a context for the requirements specified in an information security policy document. Policies go beyond laws and regulations, or at least ensure that an organization will meet the requirements specified by laws and regulations. This policy seeks to acknowledge in writing support for laws and regulations, as well as express an intention to stay in compliance with existing laws and regulations. The policy goes further by acknowledging the incredible complexity of the current legal and regulatory environment and, in an indirect way, apologizes for any oversight that might have occurred. The policy is suitable for both internal information security policies and those made available to the public (perhaps posted on a web page). For related ideas, see the policies entitled "Required Reporting Of Information Security Incidents" and "Legal Ownership Of Information Systems Files And Messages." A: E; E: LMH.

1009. Risk Acceptance Process And Permissible Exceptions To Policies

Policy: Exceptions to information security policies will be permitted in rare instances where a risk analysis examining the implications of being out of compliance has been performed, where a standard risk acceptance form has been prepared by the responsible manager, and where this form has been approved by both the Information Security Manager and the Internal Audit Manager.

Commentary: Inevitably, management will be called upon to approve certain exceptions to policies. This policy makes it clear that exceptions will be granted only after a risk acceptance form has been filled-out, signed, and approved. These forms typically ask a number of questions such as "What compensating controls exist?" Other questions typically found on these forms include "What would the cost of compliance be?" and "What readily-available technology exists to comply?" An example of such a form is provided in the appendix to this reference book. The policy writer should note that the form includes a statement where the responsible manager takes personal responsibility for any losses occasioned by the out-of-compliance situation. Because this prospect is a bit intimidating, the actual use of the forms is rare. Nonetheless, the existence of such a form provides an "escape value" that can be used to address those unavoidable situations where users insist on being out-of-compliance with policies. Separately, it is desirable to make all out-of-compliance situations both known and documented. This means that if ever there were to be a loss that occurred as a result of the situation, management could demonstrate to a judge or jury that it was aware of the situation, it examined the risks, and it decided to waive the relevant policy or standard. On another note, the scope of the policy could be expanded to embrace standards, procedures, and related requirements beyond policies. For related ideas, see the policies entitled "Disciplinary Measures For Information Security Non-Compliance," "Privacy Rights Waived When Collecting Bills Or Enforcing Contracts," and "Security Measures Must Be Enforceable Prior To Installation." A: M; E: LMH.

1010. Non-Enforcement Of Any Policy Does Not Constitute Consent

Policy: Management's non-enforcement of any policy requirement does not constitute its consent. Management may, at its discretion, choose to enforce the provisions of policy requirements at any time without prior notice.

Commentary: The intention of this policy is to put readers of a policy statement on notice that they should not expect out-of-compliance conditions to be continued just because management hasn't yet gotten around to forcing them to change things. This policy furthermore eliminates any claim to "grandfathering" in which a local manager may claim that an out-of-compliance condition should be permitted to remain as it is because the condition has been in existence for a considerable period of time. For related ideas, see the policies entitled "Internal Audit Review Of Information System Controls" and "Network Log-In Banner Wording Required." A: E; E: LMH.

1011. Minimum Information System Controls Dictated By Standard Practice

Policy: At the very least, all Company X information systems must include standard controls found in other organizations facing similar circumstances. Beyond this, the unique risks faced by Company X must be addressed with custom solutions.

Commentary: This policy refers to the legal notion of the "standard of due care." The standard of due care defines the minimum acceptable set of controls that an organization would be expected to have, given its industry, its location, the nature of its business, and other aspects of its situation. This policy is intended to keep the organization out of trouble because not having standard of due care controls subjects the organization's management to accusations of negligence, breach of fiduciary duty, computer professional malpractice, etc. The policy goes on to require that management must address the unique risks faced by the organization, thus implicitly requiring a risk assessment (risk analysis). It may be appropriate for some readers to drop the second sentence in the policy (although it is recommended that the sentence be retained). See the policies entitled "Risk Assessments Required For Production Information Systems," "Control Implementations Consistent With Standard Of Due Care," and "Periodic Independent Review Of Information System Controls." A: MT; E: LMH.

1012. Response Required For Every Significant Information Security Risk

Policy: For every significant information systems security risk, management must make a specific decision about the degree to which Company X will (a) be self-insured, (b) seek external insurance, or (c) adjust controls to reduce expected losses.

Commentary: The intention of this policy is to force management, particularly user department managers acting as "information owners," to respond to auditor or other findings that significant security vulnerabilities exist. Too often management ignores the whole situation, implicitly becoming self-insured. This policy forces them to make explicit choices. To make sure such choices are explicitly made, some organizations may wish to put the words "in writing" into this policy. The policy can be changed to communicate to managers that insurance is available to address some of these problems, although the primary decision is to invest in controls or just accept the risk. The explanatory text accompanying this policy can include reference to different types of insurance coverage including: professional errors & omissions (liability), property (hardware theft), employee bond (fidelity), computer crime, records reconstruction, and business interruption. This policy addresses with the "What now?" questions that a risk assessment (risk analysis) generates. Also see the policies entitled "Control Implementations Consistent With Standard Of Due Care" and "Risk Assessments Required For Production Information Systems." A: MT; E: LMH.

1013. Approval Before Disabling Critical Components Of Security Infrastructure

Policy: Critical components of Company X's information security infrastructure may not be disabled, bypassed, turned-off, or disconnected without prior approval from the Information Security Manager. Doing any of these without proper approval subjects the involved worker to severe discipline including termination.

Commentary: This policy is motivated by the natural tendency of systems administrators to respond quickly to complaints from users. The policy informs administrators and other workers that they must not remove a critical control without first obtaining the proper approval. Imagine that a firm suffers repeated denial of service (DoS) attacks which shut down its firewall. Users then complain that they can't utilize the Internet, and they ask the administrator to disable the firewall. Unless the administrator appreciates what the firewall does, he or she may inadvertently make the internal network vulnerable when he or she disconnects the firewall. Just as this policy would prohibit an administrator from removing a firewall, in an indirect way, it would prohibit an end-user from disabling a virus detection software package on a desktop machine. This policy helps to strike the proper balance between information security and other business objectives -- in this instance the competing objective is getting the work done. The policy is deliberately avoids a definition for a "critical component," thereby encouraging the policy reader with a question to seek management interpretation and guidance. For related considerations, see the policies entitled "Disabling Unnecessary Software Features At Installation Time" and "Limit On Consecutive Unsuccessful Attempts To Enter A Password." A: T; E: LMH.

1014. Adequate Information Security Insurance Coverage Must Be Maintained

Policy: Adequate insurance coverage must be obtained and kept in force for every major threat facing the confidentiality, integrity, and availability of information handled by Company X computer and communication systems.

Commentary: The intention of this policy is to require that management look at the insurance needs of the organization in question, particularly as they relate to the confidentiality, integrity, and availability of information. The policy requires that insurance coverage be maintained (but management must determine how much is adequate -- sometimes no insurance is adequate). For many types of coverage, this also means that the insurance company's requirements must be observed by the insured company (these can include certain controls such as fire suppression systems). Separately, the policy implicitly communicates that such insurance does exist--this may be news to certain members of the management team. Of course, the financial implications of different types of insurance will also need to be reviewed; use of the word "adequate" implicitly covers this consideration, although explicit words may be added to the policy. Note that this policy does not require any action with respect to trivial threats (threats are called "perils" in the insurance business). This policy is especially important to the financial services industry, the high-tech industry, and to other industries where information is becoming the essence of their business. See the policies entitled "Risk Assessments Required For Production Information Systems," "Directory Of Information Held In Archival Storage," and "Bonding Of Persons In Computer-Related Position Of Trust." A: MT; E: LMH.

1015. Allocation Of Sufficient Resources To Address Information Security

Policy: Management must allocate sufficient resources and staff attention to adequately address information systems security.

Commentary: The intention of this policy is to communicate to lower level managers that information security is important and is not to be ignored. The policy is particularly appropriate for decentralized organizations, such as a holding company with subsidiaries. This policy should also help garner the budget money necessary to properly protect Company X information and systems. Separately, this policy may be especially helpful to those organizations which employ charge-back systems for computer and telecommunications services; all too often such charge-back systems discourage users from using these services to address information security. On another point, the meaning of the word "sufficient" is deliberately vague; the policy thus implies that a risk assessment (risk analysis) needs to be performed. See the policy entitled "Risk Assessments Required For Production Information Systems." Another view of the word "sufficient" may be found in the policy entitled "Minimum Information System Controls Dictated By Standard Practice." A: MT; E: LMH.

1016. Information Security Is Overhead, Not A Charge-Back Item

Policy: Information security products and services are provided through corporate overhead budgets, and must not be charged-back to each subsidiary company.

Commentary: This policy is intended to encourage the allocation of sufficient funds for information security within large organizations that have divisions, subsidiaries, or other types of organizational units. When charge-back systems are used to transfer the costs for information security, all too often unit managers will decide to reduce or eliminate information security. This is not a serious problem if each unit has independent and unconnected information systems, but if they are connected via a network (as they increasingly are), consistency is absolutely required if adequate security is to be achieved. Thus, by providing a central overhead budget, the compliance with internal information security standards is significantly enhanced. Separate organizational units can still go their own way with special approval -- if they wish to pay for custom systems. This policy helps ensure that all units have sufficient controls, no matter what their budget or recent financial performance may be. This policy addresses one of the organizational design issues that often conspires to render information security ineffective, impotent, and/or irrelevant. See the policies entitled "Allocation Of Sufficient Resources To Address Information Security" and "Prompt Review Of Invoices For Computer & Communications Services." A: M; E: LMH.

1017. Security Measures Must Be Enforceable Prior To Installation

Policy: All information systems security controls must be enforceable prior to being adopted as a part of standard operating procedure.

Commentary: Controls which are not enforced have a tendency to become useless, or worse, a mockery of management's attempts to control operations. For example, if management has a policy about clean desks (locking all sensitive materials up after work), and if it is not enforced, then employees quickly learn to ignore the policy. This policy is intended to force management to look at what it means to enforce a control, a question that they may not otherwise ask themselves before adopting a control. For instance, management may adopt a policy about reviewing the access control logs for unauthorized activity, but then after adopting the policy, management may find that the policy takes too much staff time. A definition of the word "enforceable" may be advisable in some instances; the author suggests that for a control to be enforceable, it must be possible for management to clearly determine: (a) whether staff is in compliance with the control, and (b) whether the control is effectively doing its intended job. Note that the policy is purposefully vague about what constitutes "standard operating procedure" (SOP). This allows the policy to apply to a wide variety of circumstances, whether or not the control is documented, specific to a certain department, or used in an experimental way. In some instances, this policy may force the control designers to add "instrumentation" to the control; this is a monitoring mechanism which reports on the status of the control. For example, encryption boxes from some vendors have lights which indicate that they are working as they should. For related ideas, see the policies entitled "Internal Audit Review Of Information System Controls" and "Agreements With Third Parties Which Handle Company X Information." A: MT; E: LMH.

1018. Whenever They Are Available, Use Of Evaluated Products Required

Policy: If all essential functional requirements can otherwise be met, an information systems security product which has been evaluated by the US Government's Computer Security Center is preferred and must be used rather than a product which has not been evaluated.

Commentary: The intention of this policy is to put systems designers on notice that management prefers products which have been evaluated by the Computer Security Center (physically located at Ft. George G. Meade, Maryland, USA). Evaluated products have been extensively documented and tested according to a predefined set of security objectives. In addition, a grade indicating the level of security provided by the product has been issued to these products by the evaluating governmental agency. In general, evaluated products will be more secure than those which have not been evaluated. It is likely that certain of these evaluation tasks will soon be performed by private-sector organizations rather than defense related governmental agencies (European countries already delegate certain of the work to private consulting firms). Separately, to tailor this policy to the needs of other countries, the government references can modified to reflect the equivalents in those countries where similar efforts are underway (England, Australia, France, Germany, etc.). If the country from which this policy is issued does not have a governmental unit that evaluates products according to a criteria such as the "Orange Book," then reference to the US Government's evaluation process may still be appropriate. Political factors (socialism/ capitalism, geographical location, etc.) are also likely to affect the reference country. Note that the policy is written in a manner that allows management to deal with security as a secondary consideration -- all other functional requirements must be met before security will affect the decision. If management does not wish to downplay security to this extent, then it may wish to change the first seven words in the policy. Also note that the policy assumes military or governmental security objectives will closely match the organization's security objectives; if this not so, then this policy may not be appropriate. For a related idea, see the policy entitled "Compliance With Industry Specific Information Security Standards." A: T; E: MH.

2.1.4. Outsourcing And Third Party Contracts

1019. Agreements With Third Parties Which Handle Company X Information

Policy: All agreements dealing with the handling of Company X information by third parties must include a special clause. This clause must allow Company X to audit the controls used for these information-handling activities, and to specify the ways in which Company X information will be protected.

Commentary: The intent of this policy is to prevent Company X employees from inadvertently giving away responsibility for the security of Company X information. This might, for instance, happen when an outsourcing firm takes over data processing operations. While Company X may elect to have contractors or other organizations handle information security activities, it should always retain the right to specify information protection requirements as well as the right to make sure that the third party in question is living up to these requirements. One major computer manufacturer makes a big deal of this process, particularly when it denies contracts to organizations which don't pass its proprietary information audits. This makes sense since proprietary information is the essence of success in the computer industry, and control over the dissemination of this information is very important. On a separate point, note that the policy is worded such that the auditing could be done by humans or via automated auditing tools, such as Netcensus from Tally Systems, of Hanover, New Hampshire (a software inventory tool). Also see the policies entitled "Clear Definition Of Third Party Information Security Responsibilities," "Termination Of Outsourcing Contracts For Security Violations," and "Third Party Access To Company X Systems Requires Signed Contract." A: MT; E: LMH.

1020. Outsourced Hosting Arrangements Require Backup Plan And Testing

Policy: All contracts with web site hosting firms, application service providers (ASPs), and other information systems outsourcing firms must include both a documented backup plan and a periodic third-party testing schedule.

Commentary: This policy is motivated by a number of horror stories recently experienced by firms who retained the services of application service providers. These Internet commerce sites have suffered severely and in some cases gone out of business because their hosting firms were not keeping backups of their data. This policy is intended to establish a minimum control measure (backup plans), that all to often doesn't get written into contracts. If this requirement is incorporated into a contract and if the hosting firm doesn't deliver, then there is legal recourse and a subscribing firm may be able to recover damages. Whatever the words in a contract, due diligence dictates that backup plans must be periodically tested to show that they are working correctly. A subscriber to a hosting firm's service can retain a consultant to perform these tests. Note that small firms may not have the leverage to change the contractual terms with a hosting firm (it may be a "take it or leave it" boilerplate contract). Also note that just because a hosting firm is big doesn't mean that it's going to do a good job when it comes to backup. In more general terms, every subscriber should also establish and periodically update a contingency plan which uses these backups to set-up an Internet business using another hosting firm (but a backup plan should be in place at the very least). For related ideas, consider the policies entitled "Chain Of Trust Agreements Required For Private & Sensitive Information" and "Agreements With Third Parties Which Handle Company X Information." A: M; E: LMH.

1021. External Firms Gathering Company X Information Must Make It Available

Policy: Every contract with an outsourcing firm, a contract programmer, or any other external firm which handles Company X information systems and/or communication systems must stipulate that all information gathered about Company X will be provided on demand to Company X at no additional charge.

Commentary: The motivation for this policy is a variety of recent attempts by third party vendors to lock-in paying customers. For example, a firm which maintains information systems equipment for a company may keep detailed records, but later refuse to provide these same records to the company. This refusal will make it much more difficult for the company to bring this activity back in-house, just as it will make it more difficult for the company to switch outsourcing firms. The third party seeks to make switching providers prohibitively expensive and/or time-consuming. This policy follows the general practice of telephone companies, where they provide a list of numbers called, calling patterns to different parts of the world, and similar information to the company who pays the bill. In many ways this policy is a way to protect the company against exploitation by third parties based on denied access to certain information. This policy could be enhanced by requiring that the information in question be delivered in computer-readable form using widely-accepted file conventions. This enhancement will prevent a third party from providing the information in a form which is unusable, for example providing a 5GB database via paper reports. For related ideas, see the policies entitled "Customer's Right-To-Know Nature Of Personal Information" and "Guaranteed Access To Personal Information Held In Company X Records." A: MT; E: LMH.

1022. Security Responsibilities For Real-Time Connections With Third Parties

Policy: Before any third party users are permitted to reach Company X systems via real-time computer connections, specific written approval of the Information Security Department manager is required. Requests for approvals must specify the security related responsibilities of Company X, the security related responsibilities of the common carrier (if used), and the security related responsibilities of all other involved third parties. These responsibility statements must also address the liability exposures of the involved parties.

Commentary: The purpose of this policy is to prevent real-time (as opposed to store-and-forward) connections of Company X systems with third parties unless these have been shown to be adequately secure. This policy would for instance prevent salespeople from opening up the order entry system to customers unless security issues had previously been examined, and approved controls had been properly implemented. Only after clearly specifying security responsibilities can Company X determine whether they want to accept the risks that the connection presents. The policy would allow internal users to employ out-bound dial-up systems to access third party electronic mail services and on-line database retrieval services without the need for a security evaluation and approval process. This policy would also allow Internet electronic mail connections because these are store-and-forward (not real-time) connections. This policy would, however, prevent a department from establishing their own Internet firewall. Also see the policies entitled "Prior Approval Required For In-House System Interconnection," "Prior Approval Required For All Communication Line Changes," and "Internet Connections Require Approved Firewalls." A: MT; E: LMH.

1023. Clear Definition Of Third Party Information Security Responsibilities

Policy: Company X's business partners, suppliers, customers, and other business associates must be made aware of their information security responsibilities via specific language appearing in contracts which define their relationship with Company X.

Commentary: The intention of this policy is to clearly state that management must consider the assignment of information security responsibility when they strike deals with third parties. Not only must these topics be considered, but specific details about the way these things are going to get handled must be included in contracts. A good example of this is outsourcing facilities management deals, where a third party takes over the information technology operations of an organization. Too often companies forget (or deliberately ignore) information security when it comes to these negotiations. As a result, information security suffers. When the organization which outsourced its operations complains, the outsourcing outfit will point to the contract saying that they are not required to provide security, and that the organization must pay extra if it wants extra service. This example assumes that some major problem (such as a public relations 'faux pas' has not already taken place). The policy equally applies to other environments such as the use of a third party value-added network service. Be sure to talk with internal legal counsel on this important topic. See the policies entitled "Agreements With Third Parties Which Handle Company X Information," "Third Party Agreements On Usage Of Company X Software," "Who Must Comply With Information Security Requirements," "Network Message Protection Services Not Provided," "Security Requirements For Network-Connected Third Party Systems," and "Cross Training For Staff In Critical Technical Jobs." A: MT; E: LMH.

1024. Termination Of Outsourcing Contracts For Security Violations

Policy: All information-systems-related outsourcing contracts must be reviewed and approved by the Information Security Manager. It is this manager's responsibility to make sure that these contracts sufficiently define information security responsibilities, as well as how to respond to a variety of potential security problems. It is also this manager's responsibility to make sure that all such contracts allow Company X to terminate the contract for cause if it can be shown that the outsourcing firm does not abide by the information security terms of the contract.

Commentary: The intention of this policy is to clearly assign responsibility for examining outsourcing contracts to make sure that contracts are sufficiently explicit and clear in the area of information security. In many cases, the organization which hired an outsourcing firm has been lax about defining security responsibilities and how to handle problems. As a result, when a security problem occurs, the outsourcing firm many then act lackadaisical because it is not rewarded or punished based on information security. This policy seeks to change that, to give the organization explicit legal mechanisms (such as contract termination) which can be used to get the outsourcing firm to take security seriously. This problem was classically shown by the 1999 episode involving the US Department Of Energy's retention of the University of California as an outsourcing firm to run Los Alamos nuclear weapons lab. DOE told UC to restrict the access to classified bomb material available to Chinese-linked spy Wen Ho Lee, but according to The Wall Street Journal (9 August 1999), UC officials did not appropriately respond. This allowed Mr. Lee to continue to remove classified material. The head of DOE was powerless to discipline these officials, he could only recommend reprimands. This indicates that the contract with UC apparently did not give DOE sufficient power to properly manage information security. Separately, the policy is intended to prevent situations where the information security department never sees outsourcing agreements until there is a problem. On another note, the last sentence in the policy could be dropped (it could be handled by the legal department). For related ideas see the policies entitled "Restricted Delegation Of Information Owner Duties," "Agreements With Third Parties Which Handle Company X Information," and "Involvement Of In-House Information Security Department." A: M; E: MH.

1025. Financial Condition Of Critical Vendors Reviewed Annually

Policy: The financial condition of vendors providing or supporting critical Company X production information systems must be reviewed annually by the Chief Information Officer (CIO) or an individual designated by the CIO. The objective of this review is to determine whether these vendors are going concerns and whether remedial measures must promptly be taken.

Commentary: The intention of this policy is to force those responsible for information systems management to periodically consider the financial condition of essential vendors. With mergers, acquisitions, bankruptcies, initial public offerings, and other major events are taking place with increasing frequency in the information systems industry, relationships with the vendors on which a business depends may accordingly change quite rapidly. An increasing number of information systems products and services are delivered by outside vendors, and purchasing organizations are as a result that much more dependent on these vendors. If management knows that there is some question about a vendor being a "going concern" (being a financially viable business), it can take remedial measures such as arrange software escrow, establish back-up contracts with other vendors, and investigate the ways that production data can be converted in order to run with other vendors' software. As an aside, note that this policy is written in a general way so that it includes both services as well as products. Separately, in their contracts, many organizations require privately-held vendors to disclose annual financial statements in order to perform the task described in this policy. For related ideas, see the policies entitled "Vendor Provided Systems Software Must Go Through Change Control" and "Vendor-Provided Written Integrity Statements." A: M; E: LMH.

2.2. Human Resources Matters

2.2.1. Discipline And Termination

1026. Avoid Actual And Apparent Conflict of Interest

Policy: All workers must avoid the actual or apparent conflict of interest in their business-related dealings with Company X. Should there be any doubt as to the existence of a potential conflict of interest, the worker must consult his or her manager.

Commentary: The intent of this policy is to put workers on notice that it is not enough to have no conflict of interest--there must be no appearance of a conflict of interest. For example, a manager may own a significant block of stock in a competing company through a trust. Although the manager may not be able to exercise any influence over the competing company, and although he may not have any special relationship with or access to information at the competing company, the manager's ownership implies a conflict of interest. If this ownership information were to get into the newspapers, or if major customers were to become aware of it, it may damage the company's reputation, not just the manager. Many organizations will want to supplement this policy with examples, such as having a close relative who works for a competitor. More than any other policy in this book, this policy is likely to be integrated into an organizational Code of Conduct. For a related idea, see the policy entitled "Prohibited Trading Dates For Employee Stock Transactions." A: E; E: LMH.

1027. Researchers Must Disclose Sponsors And All Potential Conflicts

Policy: Whenever Company X performs polls, analytical studies, or other research that is intended for public consumption, the participants in the research must mention in their report both the sponsor(s) and all potential conflicts of interest.

Commentary: The intention behind this policy is to restore integrity to the news gathering, drug research, market research, and related fields which have been stung by recent allegations of conflicts of interest. If a researcher, perhaps a university professor, also happens to be doing consulting on the side for a pharmaceutical company that has retained him or her to evaluate a new drug, this fact should be disclosed. Likewise, the fact that the pharmaceutical company is paying such a professor to do the drug evaluation should also be revealed in the published findings. Readers can then choose to discount the findings or not, as the case may be. To not reveal such information is considered by many people to be deceptive. Separately, a similar problem is taking place at a few major newspapers in the United States. Editors at these newspapers focus on positive news associated with advertisers, ignoring negative news that deals with these same advertisers. The traditional separation between the advertising department and the news department in these publishing firms is often being torn down with new articles/documentaries dubbed "infomercials." Infomercials are a mix of supposedly objective reporting combined with an advertisement. These new information delivery mechanisms bring the implied credibility of objective news reporting to commercials, and thereby help an advertiser (but the harm coming to the advertiser if the truth is later revealed may more than erase any positive benefit originally enjoyed). Separately, while use of this policy in various organizations may require rewording and/or adjustment, the idea is still fundamentally useful in order to promote a business climate characterized by integrity and fair play. Possible adjustments in wording including requiring the disclosure of any restrictions on the research results specified before the project got underway. Note that this policy is only relevant if Company X publicly publishes newsletters, research reports, or similar material. For related considerations, see the policies entitled "Second Job Impact On Objectivity And Competition With Employer" and "Refrain From Pressuring Employees Who Worked At Competitors." A: E; E: LMH.

1028. Workers May Not Have Romantic Relationships With Competitor Staff

Policy: Company X workers must not have any romantic partners or immediate family working at competing firms.

Commentary: The intention of this policy is to prevent the unintentional disclosure of confidential information (also known as leakage). Even an informal comment might convey information which would be of use to a competitor. Of course the policy is also a safeguard against industrial espionage (or military espionage) where a romantic partner also happens to be a spy. This strict policy allegedly reflects a policy previously in place at IBM (the firm has since loosened-up some and now simply transfers people to less sensitive positions). For related ideas, see the policies entitled "Marketing Information Must Never Be Shared With Competitors" and "Refrain From Pressuring Employees Who Worked At Competitors." A: E; E: MH.

1029. Disciplinary Measures For Information Security Non-Compliance

Policy: Non-compliance with information security policies, standards, or procedures is grounds for disciplinary actions up to and including termination.

Commentary: The intention of this policy is to emphasize that information security is important, and that significant disciplinary action may result if a worker is not in compliance. The policy is also intended to provide justification for management actions if a worker were to complain that a disciplinary measure is unwarranted or unfair. Some organizations may wish to specify some of the possible disciplinary actions (suspension without pay, demotion, etc.). In this case, the last two words in this policy could be changed to "up to and including termination." Nonetheless, in the majority of cases, this will be unnecessary because other personnel policies will address the specifics of disciplinary measures. Also see the policy entitled "Disciplinary Measures For Various Information Security Violations." A: E; E: LMH.

1030. Disciplinary Measures For Various Information Security Violations

Policy: Assuming the action is inadvertent or accidental, first violations of information security policies or procedures must result in a warning. Second violations involving the same matter must result in a letter being placed in the involved worker's personnel file. Third violations involving the same matter must result in a five-day suspension without pay. Fourth violations involving the same must result in dismissal. Willful or intentional violations, regardless of the number of violations, may result in disciplinary action up to and including immediate dismissal.

Commentary: Many jurisdictions require that a worker be put on notice before receiving severe disciplinary action or termination. This policy is intended to provide an increasingly severe set of disciplinary actions reflecting information security violations. In many organizations it will be unnecessary to specify such steps because a more general personnel policy will already have covered these matters. The specifics are provided in this book for those organizations that do not have a documented progression of increasingly severe disciplinary measures. Of course, the specific disciplinary measures mentioned here could be replaced with others that may be more common in the reader's organization or in the reader's country. See the policy entitled "Disciplinary Measures For Information Security Non-Compliance." A: EM; E: LMH.

1031. Unauthorized Information Disclosure and Loss of Stock Options

Policy: If the recipient of stock options discloses internal Company X information to unauthorized parties, these options will be revoked.

Commentary: The objective of this policy is to send a very clear and emphatic message about the need to keep confidential information under wraps. All too often management ignores information security thinking that all is fine and that it's "business as usual" (until a serious security problem occurs, but even those are quickly forgotten). This policy is especially relevant to companies that are about to, or have recently gone public (had an initial public offering or IPO). It hits workers at private sector companies where it counts -- in the wallet. The policy is more potent the greater the percentage of an employee's income that comes from stock options. Thus top management would generally pay a great deal of attention to this policy because they often derive a large percentage of their income from stock options (the president of Chrysler motor company had 100% of his income in stock options during the turn-around about 10 years ago). Separately, the policy could be modified to include other information security violations, not just unauthorized disclosures. But since unauthorized disclosure is frequently the greatest issue for a new high-tech company, that's the way the author wrote the policy (which is now in use at least one major Fortune 500 company). This policy provides an action-forcing mechanism that has so far often been missing, and because it has been missing, little has been done to improve information security at many organizations. For related ideas, see the policies entitled "Disciplinary Measures For Information Security Non-Compliance" and "Security Violations Requiring Instant Terminations." A: EM; E: MH.

1032. Security Violations Requiring Instant Terminations

Policy: Unless the special permission of a Senior Vice President is obtained, all workers who have stolen Company X property, acted with insubordination, or been convicted of a felony, must be terminated immediately. Such instant terminations must involve both escort of the individual off Company X premises, as well as assistance in collecting and removing the individual's personal effects.

Commentary: The intention of this policy is to force managers to terminate workers who have shown themselves to be an unwarranted threat to the security of the organization and/or the safety of its workers. For example, if an employee has been convicted of murder while employed by Company X, his or her continued presence in the office may constitute an unwarranted risk. Note that this policy gives management significant leeway in terms of determining options besides termination (like suspension without pay if there was an intention to bring the employee back). Lesser responses to these serious problems can always be decided on and approved by a Senior Vice President. Because keeping these individuals around (particularly if they are in a computer-related position of trust) poses special risks, top management consideration is required before their continued presence is permitted. The specific circumstances leading to instant terminations (like "stealing Company X property") can be changed to suit Company X management preferences. Instant removal is a way to quickly remove the individual and eliminate the continued risk that they pose. Also see the policy entitled "Disciplinary Measures For Various Information Security Violations." A: M; E: LMH.

1033. Notifications And Handling Of Employees Leaving For A Competitor

Policy: All workers intending to work for a competitor must immediately notify Company X management at the time they accept an offer to work for a competitor. Accompanied by an escort, every worker in this position must immediately gather their personal belonging and be shown to the door. All Company X rights, privileges, and accesses which have been extended to such workers must be immediately revoked.

Commentary: This policy is intended to make it clear that every employee who will soon go to work for a competitor should not remain on the premises, and should not remain an authorized user of information systems. This is true no matter what the type of separation (firing, resignation, retirement, etc.). This policy deals with problems encountered in the infamous court case between Borland and Symantec, in which an executive is alleged to have sent some of his former employer's proprietary information to his new employer. In this case electronic mail was used, but access to any system provides a tempting opportunity for departing employees to take customer mailing lists and other information which might be of use. One of the most effective things an organization can do to handle these situations is to establish a policy expelling all workers who announce they will be going to work for a competitor. This also sends a message to all remaining staff that the former employee is no longer a member of the trusted group. The existence of a policy like this makes it diplomatically and socially acceptable to deal decisively with this type of departing employee. This policy is a special manifestation of the notion of a conflict of interest. Separately, the policy is most suitable for those firms with a high staff turnover, such as high-tech organizations. Also see the policies entitled "Transfer Of Information Custodian Duties After Employee Terminations" and "Schedule For Deletion Of Files Following Worker Termination." A: EM; E: LMH.

1034. Immediate Notification Of Employees Regarding Worker Terminations

Policy: All employees must be immediately notified as soon as a worker has been terminated. With each such notice, the Human Resources Department must regularly remind employees that departed workers are no longer permitted to: be on Company X property (unless escorted by an employee), use Company X resources, or in any other way be affiliated with Company X. Commentary: The intention of this policy is to enlist the support and participation of all remaining employees to tighten the fence separating insiders from outsiders. Remaining employees cannot act as an early-warning system (alerting security guards perhaps) if they are not informed that certain terminated workers are no longer permitted inside Company X buildings, no longer permitted on Company X computers, and no longer permitted to be in any other way connected to Company X. This policy goes well with a challenge policy that requires remaining employees to challenge all people currently inside restricted areas who are not conspicuously wearing a valid identity badge. This policy is a broader scope notification than the notification performed by many organizations, where only systems administrators and others who are responsible for updating computer access controls receive such a notice. Separately, this policy deliberately makes no distinction between involuntary and voluntary terminations, although the scope of the policy could be narrowed to include only involuntary terminations. On another note, such notification can easily be performed with email, and if there are worker head-shot pictures on an intranet, this policy is made more effective (because the individual can be more readily recognized). For related considerations, see the policies entitled "Security Guard Escort For Workers Who Are Involuntarily Terminated" and "Reporting Changes In User Duties To Systems Security Administration." A: E; E: MH.

1035. Informing Relevant Contractors And Vendors Of Worker Terminations

Policy: If a terminated worker had authority to direct contractors, consultants, or temporaries, or if this same worker had the authority to bind Company X in a purchase or another transaction, then the Human Resources Department must promptly notify all relevant third parties that the terminated worker is no longer employed by Company X.

Commentary: The objective of this policy is to prevent a terminated worker from directing third parties in any way. A terminated worker may be in a vengeful spirit and may obligate Company X to purchase certain goods, or may bind Company X to another transaction (such as an expensive on-line directory listing). A departed worker can also embarrass his or her past employer by acting in an unprofessional manner, perhaps offering to sell certain confidential information. If third parties think that the departed worker is still employed at Company X he or she will have more credibility (this is one reason to collect business cards, credit cards, and other evidence of affiliation at the time of termination). A former worker may also use the implied trust that goes along with employment to engage in social engineering (spoofing) to get passwords and other system access codes, which in turn could be used to break-into a former employer's computers. This policy helps to make a clean and clear-cut distinction between current workers (still trusted) and former workers (not trusted any longer). Separately, the act of notifying third parties can also bring to light certain irregularities that may not have been noticed before. For example, if a special and unauthorized discount was being given to a distributor, this distributor may ask whether the discount will still be available. On another note, some firms accomplish the same result when a replacement worker contacts each relevant contractor, consultant, temporary, or vendor, to inform them that the former worker is no longer responsible for certain activities. For related ideas, see the policies entitled "Changing Physical Access

Control Codes On Worker Termination" and "Responsibility For Taking Action In Response To Worker Terminations." A: M; E: LMH.

1036. Handling Involuntary Terminations Of Computer Workers

Policy: In all cases where information technology support workers are involuntarily terminated, they must be immediately relieved of all of their duties, required to return all Company X equipment and information, and escorted while they pack their belongings and walk out of Company X facilities.

Commentary: Since information technology workers can do considerable damage, it is wise to immediately eliminate the possibility that they might strike back at their former employer in revenge. The intention of this policy is to single out information technology support workers for special handling (since they are most often in a significant position of trust). Some firms may wish to add words to the policy mentioning security workers and others who are likewise in a position of significant trust. Notice that the policy does not mention end-users per se, only those who have special privileges to affect what end-users do; in this respect, a distinction is made between information technology support workers and information technology workers (the latter are expected to be almost every worker sometime in the near future). Additional words dealing with the immediate revocation of system privileges are also a possible expansion of the policy. See the policy entitled "Security Violations Requiring Instant Terminations." A: MT; E: LMH.

1037. Security Guard Escort For Workers Who Are Involuntarily Terminated

Policy: In every case where workers are involuntarily terminated by Company X, the termination must take place in the presence of a security guard. These workers must immediately pack their personal belongings in the presence of the guard and be shown to the door. These workers must also be informed that they must not reenter the building unless invited to do so by management.

Commentary: The intention of this policy is to prevent vengeful acts, especially damage to computerized information. After workers are involuntarily terminated (perhaps due to a lay-off), they must not be permitted to log-in and to once again gain access to Company X computerized records. If workers have personal information resident on Company X information systems, and if there is a policy against personal use, then the information can be abandoned because it is evidence of a policy violation. If no personal use policy exists, a supervisor can retrieve the personal information and send it to the employee on a floppy disk or similar data storage media (or perhaps by email). On another note, to further reduce the chances of vengeful acts, the involved worker's system access privileges should be revoked prior to formal notification that he or she has been terminated (doing this without tipping-off the worker about the impending termination can be tricky, but nonetheless quite feasible). Separately, this policy assumes that there is another process for collecting phone cards, credit cards, cell phones, office building keys, identity badges, and the like. The policy also assumes that the organization has security guards. For related considerations, see the policies entitled "Security Violations Requiring Instant Terminations" and "Responsibility For Taking Action In Response To Worker Terminations." A: M; E: LMH.

1038. Removal Of Information Upon Termination Of Employment

Policy: Upon termination of employment, workers may not retain, give away or remove from Company X premises any Company X information other than personal copies of information disseminated to the public and personal copies of correspondence directly related to the terms and conditions of their employment. All other Company X information in the custody of the departing worker must be provided to the worker's immediate supervisor at the time of departure.

Commentary: This policy makes it clear that internal Company X information must not be removed when a worker departs from Company X. Often workers walk away with all sorts of information thinking it may help them with their subsequent jobs. The policy's second sentence is particularly of note because it implies that workers must not try to negotiate about the provision of information to their supervisor when they depart (perhaps in an effort to get a better severance package). The words "in readable form" could be added to the second sentence to make it very clear that all information turned over to the worker's immediate supervisor must be accessible (not encrypted). Ideally this policy is used in conjunction with a policy stating that Company X owns all information created by workers during the course of their employment, except where written agreements provide for alternative arrangements. Separately, some organizations may wish to generalize the policy to include contractors, consultants, temporaries, and other types of workers besides formal employees. For related ideas, see the policy entitled "Transfer Of Information Custodian Duties After Employee Terminations." A: EMT; E: LMH.

1039. Return Of Information By Contractors, Consultants, And Temporaries

Policy: Upon the termination or expiration of their contract, all contractors, consultants, and temporaries must hand over to their project manager all copies of Company X information received or created during the performance of the contract.

Commentary: A complement to the policy entitled "Removal Of Information Upon Termination Of Employment," this policy also intends to make it crystal clear that contractors, consultants, and temporaries must return over all information they received in order to complete a contract. Ownership of the information created during the performance of the contract may be an issue unless this topic was specified in the contract. In the absence of a formal written agreement, legal issues, such as whether the work generated was a "work for hire," may control actual ownership. Note that "ownership," as used here, refers to legal ownership, not to the role of information security owners. For related ideas, see the policy entitled "Property Rights To Computer Programs And Documentation." A: EMT; E: LMH.

1040. Return Of Company X Property At Time Of Separation From Company X

Policy: At the time that every employee, consultant, and contractor terminates his or her relationship with Company X, all Company X property must be returned. This includes portable computers, library books, documentation, building keys, magnetic access cards, credit cards, outstanding loans, and the like. These terminating individuals must inform management about all Company X property they possess, as well as all computer system privileges, building access privileges, and other privileges that they have been granted.

Commentary: The intention of this policy is to collect all Company X property before the individual leaves Company X (and ideally before they are paid their last paycheck). If Company X property is not collected at that time, it may be quite difficult to collect it later. Special problems are encountered when Company X property is located at the worker's home, in the worker's car, or in other places not under the direct control of Company X. In these cases, on the worker's last day, Company X should obtain from the worker a written acknowledgement of possession of the property accompanied by a promise to return it. This is the reason for the third sentence in the policy, requiring the employee to identify the property belonging to Company X. Another reason for this sentence is that the worker's representations about property in his/her possession can be matched against Company X inventory records, perhaps revealing property that had not previously been identified. Separately, if a computer is to be kept by a former employee, then representatives from Company X should examine its hard disk to make sure it contains no Company X sensitive information. The second sentence in this policy provides only a suggested list of property to be returned; each organization would ordinarily come up with their own list depending on the nature of the business and the tools of the trade employed. This list is ordinarily not specified in the policy but on a separate terminations checklist for managers. See the policies entitled "Responsibility For Taking Action In Response To Worker Terminations" and "Changing Physical Access Control Codes On Worker Termination." A: M; E: LMH.

1041. Responsibility For Taking Action In Response To Worker Terminations

Policy: In the event that an employee, consultant, or contractor is terminating his or her relationship with Company X, the worker's immediate manager is responsible for: (1) ensuring all property in the custody of the worker is returned before the worker leaves Company X, (2) notifying all administrators handling the computer and communications accounts used by the worker as soon as the termination is known, and (3) terminating all other work-related privileges of the worker at the time that the termination takes place.

Commentary: The purpose of this policy is to put specific managers on notice that they must take certain systems-related actions at the time that a worker leaves an organization. These actions should be taken even if a consultant's or a contractor's project has ended. Many cases on record show that disgruntled employees who have been fired (sacked) can do significant information-systems-related damage. Of particular concern are those employees who have computer or communication system access and who are in a significant position of trust. For these trusted employees, some organizations may wish to develop a separate policy with more stringent requirements (such as immediate escort out the building at the time of termination). Early preparation for terminations is a wise idea, including consultations with internal legal counsel and the director of the Human Resources Department. An organization's empathy and consideration for departing employees will go a long way to limit revenge and related losses. Outplacement (new job search) consulting, judicious and low-profile handling of the reason for the employee's departure, and generous severance pay allowances are examples of the compassionate things that organizations can do. See the policy entitled "Return Of Company X Property At Time Of Separation From Company X." A: M; T: LMH.

1042. Those Involuntarily Terminated Not To Be Re-Hired Or Retained

Policy: Former employees, consultants, and contractors who were involuntarily terminated must not be re-hired or retained without the written permission of a Senior Vice President.

Commentary: Among other things, this policy prevents terminated employees from becoming consultants or contractors to Company X. Because these individuals may harbor ill feelings toward the organization, it is wise to avoid placing them in a position of trust where they could do serious damage (such as a privileged computer-related spot). Another motivation for this policy is strictly economic; technical computer specialists who know they are indispensable have been known to quit, thus requiring their former employer to retain them as consultants or contractors at a considerably higher rate of pay. This policy discourages these manipulative ploys. On another note, some organizations take this policy one step further, indicating that all people who are terminated (involuntarily or voluntarily) are prohibited from being re-hired or retained. In small towns and other areas with a severely limited number of technical persons, this more stringent version of the policy may unduly prevent Company X from utilizing local talent. Separately, in some industries, such as academia, it is customary for staff to leave for a few years and later come back; this policy is not appropriate for these industries. Also see the policy entitled "Probationary Period For New, Re-Hired, Or Retained Again Workers." A: M; E: LMH.

1043. Probationary Period For New, Re-Hired, Or Retained Again Workers

Policy: All new workers, as well as those workers who have been re-hired or retained again after a poor performance evaluation, must be placed on a six (6) month probationary period. During this period, management to whom they report must actively monitor the performance and attitude of these workers. These workers may be dismissed without cause during the probationary period.
Commentary: The intention of this policy is to give management a significant period of time to evaluate the performance of employees, and to allow them to terminate the employees if the employees are performing poorly, refuse to follow internal controls, or in any other way are deemed unsuitable. The policy also puts management on notice that they are to closely scrutinize the work of these workers to make sure that they are suitable members of the organization. Often managers do not really get to know the people who directly report to them; this can often lead to security problems. For example, if an employee has a gambling problem and they must get money quickly in order to pay a past due debt, they may commit a computer fraud. If management knew about the problem, it could refer the employee to confidential psychological counseling or suggest other remedial measures. A policy like this also gives management additional leeway when it terminates an employee (so long as it is within the six month period); this may discourage litigation or complaints. There is nothing special about the six month period; it could just as easily have been three months. See the policy entitled "Those Involuntarily Terminated Not To Be Re-Hired Or Retained." A: M; E: LMH.

1044. Leave Without Pay Required During Extended Investigations

Policy: Extended investigations of security breaches must be performed while the suspected worker is given leave without pay. The reason for a suspect's leave without pay must not be disclosed to co-workers without the express permission of the Director of Security.

Commentary: The intention of this policy is to provide management with time to gather the information it needs to determine if an employee was the perpetrator of an alleged crime or abuse. Because brief investigations need not involve time off with pay, the word "extended" was used in the policy (since the policy is deliberately vague, management may decide which investigations will be 'extended' on a case-by-case basis). To have the suspected employee off-site prevents important evidence from being concealed, modified, or destroyed. The policy also prevents early judgements about the guilt or innocence of the involved employee; to be off-site and paid for time off says nothing. Avoiding preliminary judgements about guilt are also desirable because it prevents defamation of character lawsuits (slander or libel). The confidentiality requirement found in the second sentence further prevents defamation of character lawsuits. As a more compassionate and recommended alternative, many organizations give leave with pay rather than leave without pay. See the policies entitled "Incident Management Responsibilities" and "Required Reporting Of Information Security Incidents." A: M; E: LMH.

1045. Annual Signature On Agreement To Comply With Security Policies

Policy: As a condition of continued employment, employees, consultants, and contractors must annually sign an information security compliance agreement.

Commentary: The intention of this agreement is to require all employees to sign a compliance statement each year, thereby forcing them to acknowledge without a doubt that compliance with security policies and procedures is part of their job. These agreements typically say the individual agrees to comply with information security policies and procedures, has read the security manual, understands the manual, and furthermore understands that violations are cause for disciplinary action up to and including termination. The act of signing something not only provides employers with legally-admissible evidence that workers were on notice about information security, but also changes the way that workers view information security (they, for instance, might think, "I guess this is really important after all ..."). For related ideas dealing with signing agreements when a worker first joins an organization, see the policies entitled "Confidentiality Agreements Required For All Company X Workers" and "Confidentiality Agreements And Disclosures Of Sensitive Information." A: M; E: LMH.

1046. When To Prosecute Or Seek Restitution

Policy: To communicate that abusive and criminal behavior will not be tolerated, Company X management must seriously consider prosecution for all known violations of the law.

Commentary: The intention of this policy is to encourage the prosecution of abusive and criminal acts. While a decision to prosecute will be contingent on the specifics of the case (does sufficient evidence exist, will prosecution adversely affect customer relations, will confidential information be disclosed in court, etc.), management should not simply dismiss prosecution without further thought. While lawyers would applaud this policy, it may also be important in terms of communicating to those would-be perpetrators of abusive or criminal acts. Many computer crimes are not prosecuted and perpetrators often know this, expecting victim organizations to simply terminate them and "hush-up" the entire affair. A policy like this is, for example, used by a number of telephone companies for those individuals who fraudulently obtain telephone service. Rather than being stated in general terms, this policy could require prosecution for certain events which normally happen in the course of the involved business (such as credit card fraud victimizing a bank issuing the credit card). For several related policies, see the section of this book entitled "Administrative Security - Reporting Of Security Problems." A: M; E: LMH.

2.2.2. Reliance On People

1047. Human Intervention Required For Important Decisions

Policy: All computer-assisted processes must involve human intervention prior to initiating any action which could result in human life-threatening or human safety-threatening events.

Commentary: The intention of this policy is to prevent systems designers from entirely turning over important decisions to computers. For example, triggers for nuclear missiles in the USA require two authorized people to simultaneously initiate them--they cannot be initiated by a computer acting without human intervention. The reference to "life-threatening" and "safety-threatening" situations could be expanded to include significant financial decisions, as well as decisions that could significantly impact other areas (such as customer relations). Notice that no mention is made of expert systems, neural networks, artificial intelligence, or other specific technology; this helps to ensure that the policy will be relevant five to ten years in the future as well as in the present. Also see the related policy entitled "Minimization Of Reliance On Common Mechanism For Controls" and "Immediate System Interruption If Human Beings Are Jeopardized." A: T; E: LMH.

1048. Reliance On A Single Person For Important Systems Expertise

Policy: Expertise in important computer- or communications-related areas must be possessed by at least two available persons. Having such backup expertise prevents undue interruptions in systems service, and also increases the likelihood that unauthorized and abusive acts will be noticed.

Commentary: The intention of this policy is to prevent an organization from finding itself in an awkward spot where there are no available persons to assist with technical matters. For example, this might happen when an earthquake damaged a data processing center and killed a critical client/server systems programmer. Because nobody else knows what he or she knew, the recovery of production systems at an off-site location could then be significantly delayed. Note that the policy does not indicate that the people with the important expertise must be employees; they could be contractors or consultants. The important word in the policy in this regard is "available." The policy supports the development and maintenance of a skills bank--a database containing information about the skills possessed by employees and others working at an organization. The policy indirectly requires management to consider which areas are important; this fosters an awareness of risks (particularly those related to contingency planning). Some organizations may wish to use the word "critical" rather than "important." Likewise, either of the terms "mission-critical" or "strategic" could be used instead of "important." See the policies entitled "Cross Training For Staff In Critical Technical Jobs" and "Independent Security Systems For Each Computer System." A: MT; E: LMH.

1049. Five Consecutive Days Of Vacation Required Each Year

Policy: To give others an opportunity to cross-train, and to increase the likelihood that improprieties will be revealed, all workers must take a vacation of at least five (5) consecutive days once a year. Managers who fail to enforce this policy with workers who report to them will be held personally accountable.

Commentary: The primary intention of this policy is to prevent workers from concealing a fraud or other illegal or abusive acts. If workers come to work every business day, they are much more likely to be able to conceal these activities (such as a pyramid scheme where the money from new customers is used to pay interest on the investments of existing customers). A vacation of five business days is long enough that some other worker must get involved with the activities done by the person on vacation. When someone else gets involved, some cross-training takes place (but often it is superficial and haphazard). This policy can serve as a significant deterrent to on-going internal fraud and related abuses. Another benefit of the policy is that it forces employees to take vacation time; this in turn may help prevent significant build-ups of vacation time which would then be a major liability on the organization's balance sheet. The policy may also help stressed-out employees take a significant vacation when they would not be inclined to otherwise do so. This policy may be an appropriate adjunct to a policy which requires employees to take their vacation time or lose it. Separately, the last sentence in the policy discourages managers from half-heartedly supporting the policy, all the while secretly wanting the involved employee to continue working in order to complete a time-sensitive project. Also see the policy entitled "Cross Training For Staff In Critical Technical Jobs." A: M; E: LMH.

1050. Second Job Impact On Objectivity And Competition With Employer

Policy: Workers are permitted to have second jobs only under certain circumstances. A second job is not permissible if it may in any way jeopardize or compromise a worker's objectivity when performing duties on behalf of Company X. Likewise, a second job is not permissible if the other employer is in any way in competition with Company X.

Commentary: Many people feel the economic pressure to take on a second job. This policy is intended to ensure that these second jobs do not lead to information security problems with the first employer (Company X). For example, if a purchasing agent took a second job with a vendor to Company X, this would compromise his or her ability to objectively perform purchasing duties, and would therefore be grounds for termination. This type of second job may also involve off-the-books payments to the Company X employee for steering business towards the vendor.

These payments may be undetectable without a policy such as this and some monitoring of employee second jobs. Likewise, if a worker took a job with a competitor, there may be some pressure to steal proprietary information from the first employer. Separately, the policy could be augmented with words that say that "if there is any question about the interpretation of these words, consult your manager or the Human Resources department." On another point, the policy should apply to consulting engagements, contractor assignments, temporary positions, etc., not just to traditional full-time permanent "jobs." For related ideas, see the policies entitled "Second Jobs Must Be Disclosed At Initial Interview Or When Taken," "Avoid Actual And Apparent Conflict of Interest," and "Five Consecutive Days Of Vacation Required Each Year." A: E; E: LMH.

1051. Second Jobs Must Be Disclosed At Initial Interview Or When Taken

Policy: Workers must inform their immediate manager that they have second or third jobs at the time when they are interviewed for a position with Company X. After they are retained by Company X, workers must inform their manager at the time when they take on these other jobs.

Commentary: The objective of this policy is to make sure that management is informed about second and third jobs that Company X staff currently perform. This will help managers understand variances in worker performance, perhaps because they aren't getting enough sleep. It will more importantly help management determine whether a conflict of interest exists, or whether the other job may in some way compromise a worker's objectivity when performing duties on behalf of Company X. The policy can additionally help to spot potential public relations or legal problems such as interlocking directors of large and influential companies. The information provided via this policy can furthermore be useful when investigating potential frauds or other problems which involve multiple organizations. The policy is thus a mechanism to ensure that management has a good idea of the motivations driving worker behavior. For related ideas, see the policies entitled "Second Job Impact On Objectivity And Competition With Employer," "Notification And Handling Of Employees Leaving For A Competitor," and "Five Consecutive Days Of Vacation Required Each Year." A: E; E: LMH.

1052. Periodic Job Rotation For Computer-Related Workers

Policy: All computer-related workers in significant positions of trust must be rotated to another position every eighteen (18) months.
Commentary: The intention of this policy is to bring to light any improprieties or other abuses that a worker in a computer-related position of trust may be perpetrating. A secondary intention is to cross-train staff so that several people are able to perform in critical positions. This policy might, for example, be useful for wire transfer system operators. After a certain period of time in that position, they are moved to some other position. In some cases, by keeping staff in certain positions for a limited period of time, the chance that they will notice and exploit weaknesses in the system of internal controls is diminished. There is nothing special about the eighteen month period; it could just as easily be twenty-four months or some similar time period. Rotation is also consistent with efforts to expand the skill-sets of workers, also known as "professional development." Such rotation is additionally consistent with management training programs that attempt to acquaint workers with a variety of jobs within the organization. Also see the policy entitled "Reliance On A Single Person For Important Systems Expertise." A: MT; E: LMH.

1053. Bonding Of Persons In Computer-Related Position Of Trust

Policy: All workers in particularly sensitive computer related positions of trust must be surety bonded for a minimum of $1,000,000.

Commentary: Bonding is a type of insurance policy against various acts of disloyalty such as fraud, embezzlement, and industrial espionage. Bonds are sometimes called "fidelity bonds" or "fidelity insurance." The process of getting a bond for persons in a significant position of trust ordinarily involves a background check (vetting). This can be an illuminating process through which management gets an idea of the person's history. Using information from the background check, management will be much better able to make decisions about the degree of trust that should be placed in the individual. Even if a background check reveals nothing indicating there might be a problem, getting a bond (insurance policy) against loss helps to defray the costs of problems encountered. Such a background check also impresses management with the extent to which certain people hold the keys to the organization's future. Knowing that a background check will be performed is likely to discourage certain inappropriate people from even applying for those jobs which involve significant trust. Separately, some insurance coverage underwriting processes (like financial institution computer crime insurance) require a company to obtain bonds for certain types of employees. See the policies entitled "Who Must Comply With Information Security Requirements," "Use Of Tests To Determine Lifestyle, Political, & Religious Information," "Background Checks For Computer-Related Positions Of Trust," and "Use Of Convicted Felons In Computer-Related Positions Of Trust." A: M; E: LMH.

1054. Staff Qualifications For Working On Most Sensitive Company X Projects

Policy: Only financially stable employees with good to excellent performance reviews and a tenure at Company X of at least two years may work on new product development and other highly sensitive Company X projects.

Commentary: The objective of this policy is to limit the people who work with the most sensitive information to those who are least likely to succumb to bribes, to be manipulated by an industrial spy who offers sex in return for information, or to exploit their position to obtain information and then sell it outside Company X. The two year waiting period makes it more difficult for industrial spies to take a job at Company X simply to gain access to information (perhaps on behalf of a competitor). The policy is also intended to prevent people who are under duress, perhaps financial pressure, from working on projects where they would have access to the most sensitive information. The policy also justifies another background check before an employee is assigned to a project which involves handling the most sensitive information. Separately, the policy makes it an honor to work on these projects, and this may encourage further loyalty and additionally insulate Company X against social engineering attacks such as those mentioned above. On another note, there will of course be occasions when specialized external expertise is needed in order to complete a project -- in those instances an approved departure from this policy may be obtained. Note that this policy is only appropriate for well-established and relatively large organizations; start-up organizations typically lack sufficient qualified staff who meet the criteria mentioned in the policy. For additional ideas, see the policies entitled "Granting User-Ids To Outsiders" and "Prospective Employees Given Opportunity To Decline Credit Checks." A: M; E: MH.

1055. Workers In Positions Of Trust Must Not Also Be Company X Customers

Policy: Workers currently in a computer-related position of trust at Company X must not also be customers of Company X.

Commentary: The intention of this policy is to avoid temptation and prevent a variety of abuses which might be encouraged because workers have privileged access to Company X information systems. For example, if a wire transfer clerk at a commercial bank were to have an account at the same bank, this might facilitate fraudulent wire transfers. This policy thus helps to reduce suspicion of workers in computer-related positions of trust. The policy is intended primarily for those organizations which are dealing with valuable types of information, especially those dealing with computerized money. For example, a chain of grocery stores probably would not adopt a policy such as this. The policy may also be useful in those circumstances where separation of duties is inadequate. On another note, the criteria for determining whether a position is indeed a computer-related position of trust will need to be defined if this policy is adopted. This criteria could include: (a) the ability to readily cause computer-related damage to Company X of over $100,000, (b) the ability to modify production system files so that computer-based fraudulent activity could be readily concealed, or (c) the ability to alter customer records anonymously. For related considerations, see the policies entitled "Bonding Of Persons In Computer-Related Position Of Trust" and "Staff Qualifications For Working On Most Sensitive Company X Projects." A: M; E: H.

1056. Duty To Report Status Changes Affecting Eligibility For Certain Position

Policy: Employees have a duty to promptly report to their immediate manager all changes in their personal status that might affect their eligibility to maintain their current position. If employees fail to disclose material information about their changed status, they subject themselves to disciplinary action up to and including termination. Examples of such status changes include convictions for job-related crimes and outside business activities.

Commentary: The intention of this policy is to extend the time when employees must disclose information about their personal status beyond the point in time when an employment decision is made. In most organizations, there is usually no mandatory post-employment disclosure policy. Changes in employee status affect the degree to which management can trust them with access to sensitive information and access to other assets (such as cash). Computer workers are in a powerful position of trust that can be exploited to an employer's detriment; this policy seeks to prevent such troublesome situations. Separately, most conservative organizations may wish to change the words "job-related crimes" to "all felony crimes." For a related idea, see the policy entitled "Background Checks For Computer-Related Positions Of Trust." A: E; E: MH.

1057. Transfer Of Certain Workers To Positions With Less Exposure

Policy: Workers who have given notice of their intention to leave the employment of Company X, as well as those who are aware of an impending involuntary employment termination, must be transferred to positions where they can do minimal damage to Company X assets. This policy also applies to those workers who are known to be disgruntled. At the worker's supervisor's option, these individuals may alternatively be placed on a paid leave of absence.

Commentary: The intention of this policy is to prevent disgruntled or upset employees from being kept in positions where they could cause serious damage to organizational property (including the information handled by computer and communications systems). For example, to keep a systems programmer on the job after he or she had received notice of being laid off would invite problems. Notice that the policy does not make specific reference to computers and communications related workers, since this policy should apply to all types of workers. For example, a building entrance security guard who has given notice could be, according to this policy, removed from his or her job. The policy has deliberately been written in a manner that forces management to use its discretion. In some firms a security guard may be in a position to do serious harm to organizational assets (or to allow others to do serious harm), while in others a security guard would not be able to do much of consequence. See the policies entitled "Changing Physical Access Control Codes On Worker Termination" and "Confidentiality Of Internal Investigations Information." A: M; E: LMH.

1058. Use Of Convicted Felons And A Safe Work Place

Policy: Job offers must not be extended to individuals who have been convicted of crimes involving violence which, if repeated, would pose a physical danger to Company X employees or property.

Commentary: The objective of this policy is to help ensure that the work force is made up of law-abiding and safe employees. Seen a bit differently, the policy seeks to make sure that workers are not unduly exposed to workplace violence. If management knowingly hires such a person, and then the person hurts other employees, management may be held liable (at least in the USA). Safe employees are also less likely to damage computer and communications systems in a fit of rage (as has happened in a number of reported cases). For example, one user shot a display screen with a gun, another took a sledge hammer to his workstation. This policy can be extended to include contractors, consultants, temporaries, and others besides ordinary employees. Also see the policy entitled "Use Of Convicted Felons In Computer-Related Positions of Trust." A: M; E: LMH.

1059. Use Of Convicted Felons In Computer-Related Positions Of Trust

Policy: Persons who have been convicted of a felony must not be hired into, retained for, promoted into, or maintained in computer-related positions of trust.

Commentary: The intention of this policy is to ensure that the people who Company X depends on are indeed worthy of the trust that has been extended. While some people may object, saying that this policy does not give convicted felons a chance to become reintegrated with the rest of society, the policy takes a strong stand in terms of not hiring those who have shown themselves to be untrustworthy. If written too broadly as it stands, this policy can be restricted to felonies which have a bearing on the job that the person will do. For example, banks would not hire a teller who had been convicted of a felony such as fraud or embezzlement. Alternatively, the policy can be restricted by making reference to convictions which show "dishonesty or breach of trust." For example, one large computer company hired an individual who had been convicted of white-collar fraud to be their information security manager. This would clearly be a violation of the policy (whether or not it was restricted as indicated above). Another variation on this policy involves restricting it to workers who will have "access to sensitive, critical, or valuable information." The policy shown here implies that a background check (so-called vetting in Europe) will be performed to determine whether the individual has a criminal record. The policy is relevant to employees as well as contractors, consultants, temporaries, and outsourcing firms. See the policies entitled "Use Of Convicted Felons And A Safe Work Place," "Background Checks For Computer-Related Positions Of Trust," "Bonding Of Persons In Computer-Related Position Of Trust," and "Use Of Tests To Determine Lifestyle, Political, & Religious Information." A: M; E: LMH.

2.2.3. Background Checks

1060. Background Checks For Computer-Related Positions Of Trust

Policy: All workers to be placed in computer-related positions of trust must first pass a background check. This process shall include examination of criminal conviction records, lawsuit records, credit bureau records, driver's license records, as well as verification of previous employment. This policy applies to new employees, re-hired employees, transferred employees, as well as third parties like temporaries, contractors, and consultants.

Commentary: The intention of this policy is for management to know who it is they are hiring or retaining. For instance, if a background check reveals that an individual has a history of bank robbery, management may want to reconsider a "proceed with an offer" hiring decision. Separately, too often computer criminals are not prosecuted and they go on to perpetrate much the same abuse with a new employer. While privacy laws often restrict what a previous employer can say about a former employee, those doing background checks can often pick-up significant reservations about the individual. Often the question "Would you re-hire this individual?" is sufficient to give a clear overall picture of the former worker's status. Even without the details behind the reservations, this is often enough to disqualify a candidate or cause for further research. This process is often called obtaining a character reference, and this too could be added to the policy as it is now written. Other things which could be added to the list of tasks that must be performed are: verification of the completeness and accuracy of the worker's resume, confirmation of academic and professional qualifications, verification that the applicant is a citizen or legal alien, and verification of the applicant's identity (via passport or driver's license). On another note, some organizations may want to eliminate mention of the types of background checks to be performed (the second sentence in the policy), instead saying only that "a background check must be performed according to standard in-house procedures." In this case, a separate memo from the Human Resources Department can then delineate the types of background checks required for different job titles. This approach gives management additional flexibility in its determination of the background checks which will be performed for each open position. Also see the policies entitled "Use Of Convicted Felons In Computer-Related Positions Of Trust," "Duty To Report Status Changes Affecting Eligibility For Certain Position," and "Bonding Of Persons In Computer-Related Position Of Trust." A: M; E: LMH.

1061. Staff Must Pass Background Check Before Accessing Private Information

Policy: To prevent unnecessary and inappropriate disclosures, only those staff members who pass a background check will be permitted to access private information.

Commentary: The objective of this policy is to require a background check, above and beyond a pre-employment background check, for each and every worker who will have access to private (i.e., personal) information. In part motivated by the United States' Health Insurance Portability and Accountability Act (HIPAA), this policy states that only a restricted group of staff members should be able to access private information. Thus a temporary employee or a volunteer who helps with seasonal increases in the workload should not be given access to private data unless he or she has first passed this additional background check. The policy assumes that the organization in question has already defined what data is private and what data is not private (a data classification system will help in this regard). The policy is deliberately silent about the components of the background check, or vetting process as the British would call it, but these components should be documented in a separate procedure. This policy is appropriate for a hospital, a medical doctor's clinic, a medical insurance company, or any other organization which acts as a custodian of private data above and beyond employment records. For related ideas, see the policy entitled "Background Checks For Computer-Related Positions Of Trust" and "Required Efforts To Ensure Integrity Of All Personal Records." A: M; E: LMH.

1062. Sensitive Product Information Access Requires Background Check

Policy: All workers who will have access to sensitive product information (marketing plans, engineering specifications, manufacturing procedures, etc.) must first pass a standardized background check performed by the Human Resources Department.

Commentary: The intention of this policy is to segregate trade secrets or other information of a proprietary nature, and to give only those workers who have passed a background check access to this sensitive information. While a background check is not a panacea, it can help to eliminate certain individuals from consideration who are clearly not good risks. For example, a background check could unearth the fact that an applicant for a job recently worked for a competitor. This may be sufficiently disturbing to management to prevent the individual from gaining access to sensitive product information. This policy is intended for use at private sector firms which offer a product. The policy could be expanded to include all information which has a designated sensitivity, perhaps "secret." If it were so altered, it would mimic a standard policy found in many military organizations. If the policy were expanded to be linked to a data classification label, then another policy describing the data classification system will also be necessary. Separately, the policy writer should notice that the policy applies equally to contractors, consultants, temporaries, interns, and volunteers, just as it applies to employees (hence the use of the word "workers"). Also note that "product information," as used here, refers to not just new and unreleased products, it also applies to information about existing products. For related considerations, see the policies entitled "Confidentiality Agreements Required For All Company X Workers" and "Granting User-Ids To Outsiders." A: M; E: MH.

1063. Fingerprinting For Employees With Access To Sensitive Information

Policy: Prospective employees who will have access to sensitive information must be fingerprinted before they begin work. Such fingerprints must be promptly sent to the Federal Bureau of Investigation to determine whether the prospective employees have a criminal record.

Commentary: The intention of this policy is to obtain specific identification data about individuals that can then be run against government databases of known criminals. This policy requires a nationwide background check, while local criminal record background checks may be restricted to state/provincial databases. In some cases, an international background check via Interpol may be possible. Although the future promises that other technologies like DNA prints will be used, at the present time fingerprints are the most sophisticated, definitive, and generally-used identification technology. This policy could be broadened to include consultants, contractors, temporaries, and others who are not regular employees. Those organizations outside the USA can replace their own governmental agency name where the words "Federal Bureau of Investigation" appears. The words "sensitive information" may also be expanded to "sensitive, critical, and/or valuable information." Likewise, the policy can be expanded to include those who are being promoted or transferred into such a position rather than only new-hires. Significant explanation may be required to make sure this policy does not cause problems with workers; some may get the impression that management thinks they are a bunch of criminals. See the policies entitled "Bonding Of Persons In Computer-Related Position Of Trust," "Prospective Employees Given Opportunity To Decline Credit Checks," and "Positive Identification Required For Initiation Of Computer Transactions." A: M; E: MH.

1064. Honesty And Emotional Stability Tests For Computer-Related Workers

Policy: All workers to be placed in computer-related positions of trust must first pass honesty and emotional stability tests which have been approved by the Human Resources Department.

Commentary: The objective of this policy is to make sure that lower-level management administers tests to make sure that workers who are placed in computer-related positions of trust are indeed worthy of that trust. These tests can be written tests, question and answer interviews, situation case studies, or other types of tests. Statistical studies have shown such tests to be an effective and fair way of determining views on honesty and other morals. The tests are increasingly being used as a means to make sure that a prospective worker will perform as intended, particularly when working under pressure or adverse circumstances. One of the most-widely-used of these tests is provided by Reid Psychological Systems (Chicago, Illinois, USA).

Such tests are sometimes euphemistically called "attitude tests." See the policies entitled "Permissible Information To Collect From Prospective Employees" and "Fingerprinting For Employees With Access To Sensitive Information." A: M; E: LMH.

1065. Foreign Nationals Prohibited From Working On Information Systems

Policy: Company X does not permit foreign nationals to work on its information systems. This policy applies no matter what the relationship between Company X and the worker (part-time employee, contractor, consultant, temporary, outsourcing staff, etc.).

Commentary: The intention of this policy is to ensure that the people who are working on internal information systems are trustworthy. A number of high profile real-life cases have shown that some foreign nationals take on information systems jobs so that they can engage in industrial espionage and/or information warfare (sabotage). While there are undoubtedly many trustworthy foreign nationals, and this policy should not be construed as a condemnation of all foreign nationals, citizens or those who are in the process of becoming a citizen have at least shown some intention to stay in a particular country. If workers permanently reside in the country where they work, they will at least be subject to the laws of that country; but if the workers will soon leave, they may feel less inclined to follow the rules of their temporary country. Separately, this policy acknowledges that information systems have become critical to modern organizations and that not just anybody should work on these information systems. Fears about foreign nationals working on Y2K remediation projects, and embedding Trojan horses and other unauthorized code in their "fixed" software, have prompted some organizations to once again look at adopting a policy such as this. On another note, this policy is consistent with military security clearance process criteria, but it is also applicable to the private sector. Care should also be taken to ensure that this policy is not illegal under anti-discrimination laws in the jurisdiction in question. For additional ideas, see the policies entitled "Taking Secret Information Into A Foreign Country" and "Background Checks For Computer-Related Positions Of Trust." A: M; E: MH.

1066. Significant Unexplained Increases In Wealth Must Be Investigated

Policy: If any Company X worker shows unexplained significant increases in wealth (big new house, fancy new car, massive stock portfolio, etc.), management has a duty to discreetly investigate the source of this new wealth.

Commentary: The intention of this policy is to tip-off local management that significant unexplained increases in wealth may be an indication of internal fraud. If such a change in wealth is noted, management should interview the involved employee and also investigate the individual's computer privileges and access to organizational funds. While there should of course be respect for the involved individual's privacy, this change in wealth is often a valid indicator that something is seriously amiss. Many computer criminals are identified because they foolishly spend their ill-begotten gains ostentatiously. For related considerations, see the policies entitled "Workers In Positions Of Trust Must Not Also Be Company X Customers" and "Required Investigation Following Computer Crimes." A: M; E: LMH.

2.2.4. Miscellaneous Personnel Matters

1067. Adequate Grievance Resolution Procedures

Policy: In an effort to quickly resolve employee relations problems, management must establish and provide adequate staff for procedures which promptly address each and every written worker grievance.

Commentary: The objective of this policy is to communicate to lower-level management a requirement for the prompt "resolution" of all worker grievances. Notice the policy does not require that the grievances be resolved in a manner that is satisfactory to the workers, only that each and every one be promptly addressed. Having an effective grievance resolution process also helps to build employee morale, communicating that management does care what employees have to say. This policy is also consistent with a commitment to having quality be a part of all business processes (potentially helpful with ISO 9000 certification). Some grievances may relate to control deficiencies, and so the complaints may provide valuable information for improving internal control (not to mention other areas within the organization). The prompt resolution of grievances also lessens the risk of a computer crime or other abuse because a worker felt the need to seek revenge or get attention. In some organizations, an internal ombudsman is established as an impartial judge to which unresolved grievances can be taken. See the policy entitled "Denial Of Benefits Due To Refusal To Provide Unnecessary Information." A: M; E: LMH.

1068. Free Confidential Counseling Services For Workers

Policy: All workers with personal problems such as drug addition, alcoholism, or divorce must be given free and confidential counseling services.

Commentary: The intention of this policy is to assist workers with the resolution of personal problems so that these problems do not unduly interference with the workers' ability to perform their jobs. For example, if a worker were a drug addict, this would could affect his or her reasoning ability, which may lead to a problem for the employer. Similarly, if a worker were under severe financial pressures, he or she might be tempted to sell confidential information to competitors. Many organizations provide some counseling services as a part of a medical insurance plan or a health maintenance organization (HMO) arrangement. Research performed for the US Department of Justice shows that many computer criminals had personal problems that they considered unshareable. These individuals went on to commit computer crimes with the belief that the crimes would resolve their problems. If counseling were offered, many of these computer crimes might never have been committed. Separately, the duration of the counseling (10 one-hour sessions for instance) and the nature of the specific services (like drug addiction counseling) in some cases may best be left out of the policy. This gives management the ability to change the services offered as health insurance and related fringe benefits are modified. Although rare, the policy may also set a limit on the number of visits to a counselor, the total cost, or the time-period when free services will be provided (this information is generally provided elsewhere). Co-payment arrangements, where the worker pays part of the cost, are also common. For similar reasons, organizations would be well advised to consider interest-free loans (for instance of up to $1,000) for those employees who find themselves in desperate need of extra money. Also see the policies entitled "Drug-Free And Alcohol-Free Work Place" and "Adequate Grievance Resolution Procedures." A: M; E: LMH.

1069. Drug-Free And Alcohol-Free Work Place

Policy: With the exception of prescriptions ordered by licensed health care professionals, workers must not use or be under the influence of either drugs or alcohol when in the workplace.

Commentary: The intention of this policy is to encourage workers to be sober when working for their employer. Sober employees, in turn, are more likely to make rational decisions in keeping with the organization's objectives. For example, at an insurance company one computer operator overwrote the only copy of critical backup tapes because he was high on marijuana. Separately, some organizations may wish to have a written policy giving them a rule that may be pointed to in the event that they discipline or terminate a worker for the use of drugs or alcohol when at work. With telecommuting (including salespeople working out of their cars), the location of "the workplace" is no longer as clear as it used to be. In the so-called "virtual organization" the workplace is wherever people do their work; the policy reflects this intention (i.e., when people do work, they should be sober). This policy may cause a problem with some employees who drink during lunch periods, particularly if entertaining prospective customers. Exercising good judgement on these rare occasions would in all likelihood be sufficient--thus eliminating the need for specific mention of these occasions in the policy. A policy like this may also encourage employees to take time off from work if they are under the influence rather than go to work (as would be appropriate for people who operate trolley-cars). To enforce a policy like this, a small but increasing number of organizations are using computer-based sobriety tests, which are video games that test worker reflexes to make sure that workers are sober before they begin work. See the policy entitled "Free Confidential Counseling Services For Workers." A: EMT; E: LMH.

1070. Agreements Not To Compete Required For Employees

Policy: At the time they join Company X, all employees must sign an agreement not to compete for six (6) months after their separation from Company X.

Commentary: Agreements not to compete essentially prevent former employees from going into business in direct competition with their former employer. They are often constrained by time (as is this policy) as well as constrained by geography (for example, setting up shop across town is unacceptable but in another state may be). Former employees may be a significant competitive challenge to their former employer if they steal proprietary information (like customer lists). Agreements not to compete may be quite useful in court if ever there is a dispute about the actions of former employees. Although theft of information may not be something that a former employer can prove in court, going into business in competition with this employer is relatively easy to prove. This policy requires the signing of an agreement not to compete--it is not the actual agreement with the employee. Readers should consult internal legal counsel about the agreement and its use in conjunction with a policy like this. The intention of this policy is to require managers to get employees to sign such an agreement. For a related idea, see the policy entitled "Assignment Of Patent, Copyright, And Other Intellectual Property Rights." A: M; E: LMH.

1071. Technical Information Systems Staff Training & Continuing Education

Policy: All technical information systems staff must have sufficient initial training as well as continuing education in all critical aspects of their jobs including security, quality assurance, and customer relations.

Commentary: The intention of this policy is to ensure that technical information systems staff get the training and education they need in order to do their jobs properly, including doing their jobs with adequate security. A wide variety of problems occur because staff don't know what they are doing, then they try something, and this turns out to create a serious problem. The resolution of security problems should not be left to inadequately trained staff who are guessing what to do. This policy will also foster worker loyalty which in turn should encourage workers to stay with their employer instead of taking the first job offer they get which pays more money. Separately, this policy runs counter to current business practice in the United States but is consistent with business practice in both Germany and Japan. In the United States, employers want experienced and well-trained workers, but they often refuse to pay the bill for this training. This policy insists that employers pay for training, at least for information systems staff. Note that this policy addresses different subject matter than the subject matter which would ordinarily be delivered by an information security awareness effort. For related ideas, see the policies entitled "Regular Monitoring Of Information Security Vulnerability Advisories" and "Information Security Training Required For All Information Workers." A: MT; E: LMH.

2.3. Organizational Structure

2.3.1. Responsibility For Information Security

2.3.1.1. Management Role

1072. Information Security Management Committee

Policy: Until further notice, an information security management committee must be composed of senior managers or their delegates from each of Company X's major divisions. This committee will meet quarterly to: (a) review the current status of Company X's information security, (b) review and monitor security incidents within the Company, (c) approve and later review information security projects, (d) approve new or modified information security policies, and (e) perform other necessary high-level information security management activities.

Commentary: The objective of this policy is to provide a mission statement for a middle-level management committee that addresses information security issues. This policy effectively describes what the committee is expected to do. Some organizations have a perpetual (or "standing") committee, while others choose to have only a temporary committee. Temporary committees are most often used until an information security effort builds sufficient momentum to get along without the committee's influence. The specific objectives of the committee can be modified to suit organizational needs. Other objectives which could be included in the policy include: (a) defining specific roles and responsibilities as they relate to information security, (b) approving the use of specific methodologies and processes for information security (such as for risk assessment), (c) ensuring that information security is integrated with other Company X planning processes, (d) coordinating the implementation of specific information security measures, and (e) promoting the visibility of information security within the Company. The objectives should not make reference to detailed activities because the work of the management committee should be restricted to oversight, policy, and related higher-level matters. Likewise, detailed activities are likely to change substantially over time, and this policy should be written such that it will be relevant for several years. Committees like this have been shown to be an excellent way to increase management awareness about information security, and also to achieve consistent information security across large organizations with different departmental/divisional organizational cultures and work processes. Also see the policies entitled "Centralized Responsibility For Information Security" and "Major Systems Changes And Privacy Impact Review Committee." A: M; E: LMH.

1073. Information Ownership And Management's Responsibilities

Policy: All production information possessed by or used by a particular organizational unit must have a designated owner. Owners must determine appropriate sensitivity classifications as well as criticality ratings. Owners must also make decisions about who will be permitted to access the information, and the uses to which this information will be put. Owners must additionally take steps to ensure that appropriate controls are utilized in the storage, handling, distribution, and regular usage of information.

Commentary: The intention of this policy is to make sure that all production information (such as accounts receivable records) has a designated owner, and that the owner knows what he or she must do when it comes to information security. While the owner does not specify how to protect information with a certain sensitivity classification, he or she will designate the classification and the appropriate controls will follow directly. Likewise, the owner does not specify how to backup or otherwise provide for the continued availability of critical information; the degree of criticality the owner assigns will in turn (in well run organizations) imply the availability-related controls which are needed. The access control decisions to be made by the owner include rights to create, modify, delete, view, and use information; again, the mechanisms for implementing these privileges ordinarily will be determined by a standard process (not by the owner). The owner does, however, specify which people, or which groups of people, will be given which access privileges. Practically speaking, owners are too busy--and generally not technically-inclined--so it would not be appropriate for them to get involved with technical security implementation issues. However, they are a critical connection between business management and information systems management, and as such their view should dictate what type of security will be applied. Separately, owners are typically user department middle-level managers; some organizations may wish to mention this in the policy itself. On a different point, it is difficult to designate owners if there has not previously been some sort of an information inventory taking effort (this may involve the compilation of an organization-wide data dictionary or a data directory). Also see the policies in the section entitled "Owner, Custodian And User Responsibilities." This policy assumes that both sensitivity classifications and also criticality ratings have been adopted by the organization; see the policies entitled "Four Category Data Classification Scheme" and "Five Category Application Criticality Classification Scheme." Also see the policies entitled "Restricted Delegation Of Information Owner Duties" and "High-Level Inventory Of Information Assets." A: MT; E: LMH.

1074. Divisional Plans For Information Security Compliance

Policy: Management within each Company X division must prepare an annual plan for bringing its computer and communications systems into compliance with published policies and standards.

Commentary: The intention of this policy is to require middle management to prepare specific written plans reflecting the ways that they will improve information security. Middle management is often the most reluctant management layer when it comes to getting into action with information security. For organizations which are just beginning to get serious about information security, a policy such as this may help to communicate to middle management that they must pay attention to information security. By requiring middle management to prepare plans and periodic reports reflecting progress on these plans, this policy can be an important way to get people into action. Separately, this policy helps to ensure that distributed systems management will adequately address information security; it is therefore of particular use in those organizations heavily dependent on LANs, departmental systems, PCs, client/server systems, and similar equipment. The reference to "division" could, of course, be replaced with "department," "unit," "subsidiary," or some other organizational grouping. See the policy entitled "Annual Information Security Planning Process Required." A: M; E: LMH.

1075. Assignment Of Responsibility For Information Asset Controls

Policy: Management must specifically assign responsibility for the control measures protecting every major information asset.

Commentary: The intention of this policy is to make sure that responsibility for the controls protecting major information assets (such as a customer contact information database) has been assigned. Some people differentiate between responsibility and accountability, but this policy does not make that distinction (nor does the author think that distinction is particularly helpful). The policy assumes the major information assets have been identified, for instance in a corporation-wide data dictionary. Identification of the major information assets of an organization can also take place when risk assessments are performed and when contingency plans are prepared. Note that, unlike policies dealing with information ownership, this policy refers to assignment of responsibility for the controls (not the information itself). Such responsibility is, in many instances, assigned to those with job titles like business analyst (which may or may not be physically located in a user department), data center computer operator, security administrator, and LAN administrator. Whoever is responsible, it is important that the responsibility for controls be clear. When such responsibility is not definitively assigned, there are often control lapses followed by puzzled exclamations like: "I thought you were going to handle that!" Separately, the words "information assets" may also be referred to as "information resources" (particularly in government agencies). See the policies entitled "High-Level Inventory Of Information Assets," "Annual Inventory Of Information Systems Hardware, Software, Etc.," "Maintenance Of Index To Databases Containing Private Information," "Nature And Location Of Company X Information Is Confidential," and "Designated Custodian Required For All Major Information Types." A: MT; E: LMH.

1076. Control Implementations Consistent With Standard Of Due Care

Policy: Managers are responsible for implementing information system controls in a manner that is consistent with generally-accepted business practice. In addition, managers are responsible for implementing these controls in a fashion which is consistent with the criticality, value, and sensitivity of the information being handled.

Commentary: The intention of this policy is to alert management that they must implement controls that are consistent with what a court of law would consider to be "due diligence." In other words, generally-accepted business practices (also called "standard of due care" controls) should be followed at the organization in question. This policy will help to reduce management liability for inadequate controls because it specifically acknowledges the need for such controls, although the controls themselves may not yet have been put into place. As attorney George S. Cole of Menlo Park, California, USA stated, "The first line of defense is that you are doing something about [information] security, not necessarily that you have it solved... ignoring the thing, hoping it will go away, will crucify you." If an organization does not get into action, it runs the risk of being accused of negligence, breach of fiduciary duty, failing to use the security measures found in other organizations in the same business, failing to exercise the due care expected from a computer professional (computer malpractice), or failure to act after an "actual notice" (such as a compromise of security). The existence of a published policy has been an important factor in a number of recent American court cases. Separately, reflecting the fact that each organization has its own unique needs, the second sentence in the policy indicates that the controls should be customized to the business environment found at the organization. Also see the policies entitled "Standard Control Procedures For Correcting Business Records," "Consistent Protection Of Information Regardless Of Manifestation," "Noting And Correcting Variances From Generally Accepted Control Practices," "Periodic Independent Review Of Information System Controls," and "Compliance With Industry Specific Information Security Standards." A: MT; E: LMH.

1077. Handling Variances From Generally Accepted Control Practices

Policy: Managers are responsible for noting variances from generally accepted information system control practices, and also for promptly initiating corrective action.

Commentary: The intention of this policy is to put managers explicitly on notice that they should note "variances" from the standard of due care, as well as take steps to correct these variances. In this sense, the word variances refers not only to those situations where standard of due care controls are absent, but also to those circumstances where the organization is not in compliance with previously-specified or previously-implemented controls. In most organizations, internal auditors are delegated the job of looking into these matters (sometimes the job goes to external auditors or to specialist consultants). Management, however, is ultimately responsible for being aware of and implementing appropriate internal controls. This is why some people say that security is a "line" rather than a "staff" responsibility. Also see the policies entitled "Control Implementations Consistent With Standard Of Due Care" and "Compliance With Industry Specific Information Security Standards." A: M; E: LMH.

2.3.1.2. Information Security Department Role

1078. Information Security Is Every Worker's Duty

Policy: Responsibility for information security on a day-to-day basis is every worker's duty. Specific responsibility for information security is NOT solely vested in the Information Security Department.

Commentary: The purpose of this policy is to clarify the fact that information security is multi-departmental, multi-disciplinary, and multi-organizational in nature. This means that information security cannot possibly be adequately addressed by a single department within Company X. Thus every worker must do their part in order to achieve appropriate levels of information security. After all, information can be found nearly everywhere in the organization and nearly every worker utilizes information in order to do their job. It is only natural that every worker should be specifically charged with responsibility for information security. Some organizations go one step further than this policy, incorporating a question into performance review forms. The question could read something like this: "Does the employee observe information security policies in the course of his/her work?" To be truly effective, this policy must be supplemented with additional instructions, telling workers exactly what is expected of them. On another note, some organizations may wish to drop the second sentence in the policy given here (they may consider it implied). This policy is typically followed by specific user-oriented instructions dealing with choosing strong passwords, not disclosing passwords to other people, and the like. Separately, because the reliance on users is increased, this policy is increasingly important as distributed systems (LANs, PCs, client/server systems, etc.) are used for production information processing activities. Also see the policies entitled "Information Security Considered In Employee Performance Evaluations" and "Specific Tasks Performed By Information Security Department." A: EMT; E: LMH.

1079. Centralized Responsibility For Information Security

Policy: Guidance, direction, and authority for information security activities is centralized for the entire organization in the Information Security Department.

Commentary: The intention of this policy is to clearly communicate to all workers that the Information Security Department calls the shots when it comes to information security matters. Since information security is still a relatively new field, many organizations have internal arguments about who is ultimately responsible for information security. This area is particularly problematic with LANs, personal computers (PCs), client/server systems, and other small systems that have been largely managed by user departments rather than a centralized Information Systems Department. Of course, this policy does not imply that all the information security work will be done by the Information Security Department; there still should be departmental coordinators, local security administrators, and others specifically charged with information security work. Nonetheless, to be effective in the age of integrated networks, information security policies, standards, architectures, and related infrastructure matters must be dictated centrally by an organization-wide information security group. Also see the policies entitled "Information Security Management Committee," "Compliance with Organizational Systems Development Conventions," "Requests For Company X Information Referred To Public Relations," "Prior Approval Required For All Communication Line Changes," and

"Hardware/Software Procurement Via Standard Purchasing Channels." For a contrarian view, see the policy entitled "Avoidance Of Communication Network Central Point Of Failure." A: MT; E: LMH.

1080. Overview Of Tasks Performed By Information Security Department

Policy: The Information Security Department is responsible for establishing and maintaining organization-wide information security policies, standards, guidelines, and procedures. The focus of these activities is on information, no matter what form it takes, no matter what technology is used to handle it, no matter where it resides, and no matter which people possess it.

Commentary: One intention of this policy is to make it clear that the Information Security Department has organization-wide responsibility. Another intention is to clearly emphasize that the Information Security Department focuses on information per se, not on computers (it should no longer be called the "Computer Security Department"). Although it may organizationally report to the Chief Information Officer (CIO) of a large subsidiary or the Director of the Information Technology Department, the Information Security Department needs to be clearly seen as an authority throughout the organization. Another purpose of this policy is to clearly communicate to workers what the Information Security Department actually does. Many workers have an erroneous view that the Information Security Department will do everything related to information security, and that they need not be involved. The tasks outlined in the policy should be modified to reflect the organizational structure and design at Company X. For example, the policy could be expanded to include investigations, compliance review, and other activities. Some organizations would prefer to put the material found in this policy in a mission statement (or charter) rather than a policy. Also see the policies entitled "Centralized Responsibility For Information Security," "Information Security Is Every Worker's Duty," "Information Security Department Mission Supports Company X Goals," and "Specific Tasks Performed By The Information Security Department." A: E; E: LMH.

1081. Specific Tasks Performed By The Information Security Department

Policy: The Information Security Department must provide the direction and technical expertise to ensure that Company X's information is properly protected. This includes consideration of the confidentiality, integrity, and availability of both information and the systems that handle it. The Department will act as a liaison on information security matters between all Company X departments and divisions, and must be the focal point for all information security activities throughout Company X. The Department must perform risk assessments, prepare action plans, evaluate vendor products, participate on in-house system development projects, assist with control implementations, investigate information security breaches, and perform other activities which are necessary to assure a secure information handling environment.

Commentary: The intention of this policy is to provide specific information about the responsibilities of the Information Security Department. Because information security is a new field, many workers will be unclear about the duties of and the contribution to be made by an Information Security Department. This policy (or if you prefer material for a mission statement or charter) can help to eliminate arguments about and focus the work of the Department. Note that the policy defines information security in a broad sense so that it includes paper-based, voice-oriented, hand-rendered graphic, product-embodied, and other manifestations of information (not just computer and communication systems manifestations). Also see the policy labeled "Overview Of Tasks Performed By Information Security Department." A: MT; E: LMH.

1082. Information Security Department Mission Supports Company X Goals

Policy: The Information Security Department is charged with the prevention of serious loss or compromise of Company X's critical, valuable, and sensitive information resources. It must coordinate and direct specific actions that will help provide a secure and stable information systems environment consistent with Company X goals and objectives.

Commentary: The intention of this Information Security Department mission statement is to make it clear that the Department supports Company X goals and objectives. Too often the Information Security Department is perceived as a hindrance to, or an obstacle to the attainment of Company X goals and objectives. This mission statement (or charter) tries to minimize statements about negative events (for example, prevent and recover from: fraud, embezzlement, service interruption, data integrity corruption, industrial espionage, sabotage, terrorism, extortion, errors and omissions, public embarrassment, and privacy violation). This positive characterization of the Department helps to foster a view that the Department is a contributor to, rather than an inhibitor of growth and expansion. The mission statement is also intended to be clearly in support of Company X goals and objectives; in a policy like this, some organizations may wish to be still more specific about the ways that the Department can support the organization's goals and objectives. Also see the policy entitled "Overview Of Tasks Performed By Information Security Department." A: MT; E: LMH.

1083. Authority To Create Information Security Standards And Procedures

Policy: The Information Security Department has the authority to create, and periodically modify, both technical standards and standard operating procedures (SOP) which support this information security policy document. These standards and procedures, when approved by appropriate Company X management, have the same scope and authority as if they were included in this policy document. When a standard or procedure is intended to become an extension of this policy document, the document will include these words: "This standard or procedure has been created by the authority described in the Company X Information Security Policy, and must be complied with as though it was part of the Policy document."

Commentary: The intention of this policy is to prevent users and others from contesting the Information Security Department's authority to create and modify technical standards and standard operating procedures. The policy is intended to lay the groundwork for the development of and adoption of more detailed documents (standards and procedures). The policy allows the Information Security Department to focus on what needs to come next, not on "reinventing the wheel" in terms of information security related organizational structure, responsibilities, and management approvals. Also see the policies entitled "Centralized Responsibility For Information Security" and "Assignment Of Responsibility For Information Asset Controls." A: EMT; E: LMH.

1084. Annual Information Security Planning Process Required

Policy: Working in conjunction with the responsible management, the Information Security Department must annually prepare plans for the improvement of information security on all major Company X information systems.

Commentary: The intention of this policy is to require staff from the Information Security Department and managers from other departments to annually prepare a formal plan for improving information security. So much of the work in the information security field is "putting out fires" (handling urgent problems) that information security people need to periodically step back and take another look at what is now being done and what should be done. In other words, this policy requires that staff focus on what's important, not just what's urgent. Separately, this policy communicates that not only should information security people do this but management from relevant departments should also participate. The policy also indirectly supports the periodic performance of a risk assessment (risk analysis); without specific knowledge of the current risks and vulnerabilities, an organization cannot prepare information security plans that truly respond to its unique business needs. Use of the term "plans" may be changed to "plan" if needed; the plural was used in the policy because the work to be done will probably show up in several places such as user department budgets, a central Information Security Department budget, the Human Resources department budget, etc. Also see the policies entitled "Designation Of Software And Systems As Competitive Information," "Preparation And Maintenance Of Computer Disaster Recovery Plans," "Preparation And Maintenance Of Computer Emergency Response Plans," "Divisional Plans For Information Security Compliance," "Annual Analysis Of Information Security Violations & Problems," and "Centralized Responsibility For Information Security." A: M; E: LMH.

1085. Annual Organization-Wide Information Security Risk Assessment

Policy: Each year the Information Security Department must conduct (or manage an independent party who conducts) an organization-wide risk assessment. The report resulting from this project must include a detailed description of the information security risks currently facing the organization, as well as specific recommendations for preventing or mitigating these risks.

Commentary: The intention of this policy is to require the Information Security Department to annually get the big picture about important threats, important recent developments, and important next steps. Information security is an incredibly complex field, and it is important for those working in the field to step-back once in a while and reprioritize what they are doing. Without a policy such as this, information security resources are likely to be spent on effort which don't have much impact. Far too many information security efforts are narrowly focused on contingency planning and system access control, while there is a great deal more to information security that desperately needs attention. An annual risk analysis (alias risk assessment) will help point out these additional tasks. Separately, no two organizations are alike, and the steps that will need to be taken need to be customized for each organization. In order to perform this customization process, or even plan for it, a risk analysis must be performed. A risk analysis is also a very important reference document when preparing policies, standards, procedures, architectures and other organizational infrastructure material. Note that the policy deliberately avoids specifying the method for a risk analysis -- this is because it should change over time to give a better understanding of the true situation. For related ideas, see the policies entitled "Annual Analysis Of Information Security Violations & Problems" and "Risk Assessments Required For Production Information Systems." A: M; E: LMH.

1086. Risk Assessments Performed By Organizational Units Managing Systems

Policy: Each organizational unit within Company X that manages its own computers or networks must annually perform a security-related risk analysis of these same systems, and then certify that adequate security measures have been implemented.

Commentary: The objective of this policy is to delegate responsibility for performing regular risk assessments to the distributed organizational units (departments, divisions, platoons, subsidiaries, etc.) which manage local information systems. This policy states that information security is also a line management responsibility, not just the responsibility of a centralized information security group. While annual risk assessments are called for by each unit managing information systems, a centralized information security group, an EDP audit group, or an independent consulting firm should periodically do their own independent risk assessments of these same information systems (as a double check to make sure that all important matters are addressed). A centralized information security group should also perform risk assessments of centrally-managed resources like a wide area network. While some readers may point out that this policy has distributed organizational units evaluating their own security, and may therefore introduce a conflict of interest, the policy writer will note that distributed units are not the only groups evaluating the security of distributed systems. To the contrary, having distributed groups evaluate their own security is the first step in responsibly managing security. Distributed groups cannot effectively or efficiently manage information security if they do not understand what the risks are. On a related note, this policy can be supported by a guideline for performing risk assessments which could be issued by a centralized information security unit. For similar ideas, see the policies entitled "Risk Acceptance Process And Permissible Exceptions To Policies" and "Annual Organization-Wide Information Security Risk Assessment." A: MT; E: MH.

1087. Current Information Security Manual Required

Policy: The Information Security Department must prepare, maintain, and distribute one or more information security manuals which concisely describe Company X information security policies and procedures.

Commentary: The objective of this policy is to require the Information Security Department to prepare and maintain a document which describes how things will be done at the organization in question. Without specific instructions on information security, the organization may have a hard time justifying disciplinary actions against employees. Likewise, without specific written instructions, the authority to conduct awareness and training efforts may be problematic. Typically a manual would include how to handle internal mail of various sensitivities, how to handle passwords and user-IDs, and other end-user oriented topics. Separately, the specific content of the manual should not be mentioned in the policy since that will change from year to year. The policy could be modified to require subsidiaries, divisions, or other large organizational units to prepare their own manuals. Alternatively, a centralized training department could be responsible. Without a clear indication of which organization is responsible, there will often be considerable finger-pointing accompanied by words like "That's your department's responsibility." The need for this policy comes from the fact that information security is, by its very nature, multi-disciplinary, multi-departmental, and increasingly multi-organizational. On another note, the word "pamphlets" or simply "instructions" could be used instead of the word "manuals." The use of the word "manuals" need not imply a paper document; it could be resident on an intranet, a local area network (LAN) server, an electronic bulletin board (EBB), or made available via other electronic means. See the policy entitled "Training & Operating Documentation Required For Production Systems," "Information Security Training Required For All Information Workers," and "Information Security Training Time Required." A: M; E: LMH.

1088. Involvement Of In-House Information Security Department

Policy: All information security problems must be handled with the involvement and cooperation of in-house information security staff. The use of external consultants, computer security response teams, or other outsiders is specifically prohibited unless these have been approved by the Company X Information Security Department.

Commentary: This policy helps keep security problems inside the organization, lessening the probability that they will become known to unauthorized parties like the press. The policy also fosters the use of the in-house information security group rather than alternative suppliers of information security services. It thus keeps costs down and also assures that in-house policies, standards, methods, and the like will be consistently applied. Just as end-user departments have gone off on their own when it comes to personal computers (PCs), local area networks (LANs), and client/server systems, they are increasingly also going off on their own in the information security area. Although this policy does not require that all work be done by a central in-house information security group, it does require the group's approval. Outsourcing is therefore still an option, particularly when there are not enough in-house staff members to handle a certain project. Some people may think that the threat of user departments going outside will help make an in-house group competitive (just like outsourcing of data processing supposedly has), but this approach often leads to confusion, wasted resources, and internal political problems. See the policies entitled "Termination Of Outsourcing Contracts For Security Violations," "Clear Definition Of Third Party Information Security Responsibilities," and "Restricted Delegation Of Information Owner Duties." A: EMT; E: LMH.

2.3.1.3. Other Information Security Roles

1089. Prompt Review Of Invoices For Computer & Communications Services

Policy: Computer users must promptly review the details of their computer and communications bills (including internal charge-back statements) to ensure that the charges are appropriate, that no significant mistakes have been made, and that no significant unauthorized usage has occurred.

Commentary: The intention of this policy is to require user department managers to review their statements to promptly determine unauthorized usage and other errors which may be information-security-related. The statements referred to in the policy may be computer service bureau invoices, phone system long distance call detail accounting reports, or internal accounting charge-back reports. The policy does not differentiate between in-house or external computing or communications service providers, and so, as written, it is relevant to both. The policy is particularly important for private branch exchange (PBX) telephone switches, where a $100,000 bill for unauthorized toll calls can be run-up in a single weekend. Separately, some organizations may wish to extend the policy's scope to credit card statements as well. See the policies entitled "Information Security Is Overhead, Not A Charge-Back Item" and "PBX - DISA Features Require Fraud Detection Facilities." A: M; E: LMH.

1090. Who Must Comply With Information Security Requirements

Policy: Outside consultants, contractors, and temporaries must be subject to the same information security requirements, and have the same information security responsibilities, as Company X employees.

Commentary: The intention of this policy is to clearly state who must comply with information security requirements (policies, standards, procedures, etc.). This policy informs lower-level managers that they need to provide consultants, contractors, and temporaries at least some information about how things are done at the organization. The policy also puts management on notice that they should not use consultants, contractors, and temporaries as a way to get around security requirements that apply to employees. This policy is another way to express the notion of "universal application" which holds that controls should apply to all people across all computing environments. For example, every person should be wearing a badge when inside a secured building. On a separate point, many people consider it wise to reserve certain privileged or highly-trusted activities, such as systems security administration, for employees only. The idea behind this is that employees are generally more loyal than outsiders. See the policies entitled "Bonding Of Persons In Computer-Related Position Of Trust" and "Clear Definition Of Third Party Information Security Responsibilities." A: M; E: LMH.

1091. Designated Security Administrator For All Multi-User Systems

Policy: Every Company X multi-user computer system must have a designated security administrator to define user privileges, monitor access control logs, and perform similar activities. For purposes of this policy, local area network (LAN) servers and private branch exchange (PBX) switches are considered to be multi-user systems.

Commentary: The intention of this policy is to make sure that a specific person is designated as the one responsible for security. When it is not clear who is responsible for security, often security tasks get neglected, and as a result the organization is unduly exposed to various problems. All multi-user systems (even workstations used by more than one person) that handle sensitive, critical, or valuable information should have some sort of access control system. Most often this will involve fixed passwords, but other technologies such as smart cards, identity tokens, fingerprint recognition, and the like may also be used. For purposes of this policy, all computer networks are multi-user systems, and as such should have one or more designated security administrators. There is no requirement that security administrators do their job full-time; part-time administrators are often used in smaller organizations or for those systems which are managed by departments or other decentralized organizational units. On a different point, this policy is increasingly important as information systems are distributed, as is the case with LANs, PCs, and client/server systems. For other security administrator responsibility ideas, see the policy entitled "Business Production Information Updates By Non-Production Staff." Also see the policy entitled "Each Department Must Have Information Security Liaison." A: MT; E: LMH.

1092. Backup Security Administrator Must Be Designated And Trained

Policy: Every multi-user Company X system with an access control system must have a designated employee who is responsible for user-ID assignment and user access privilege control. This systems administrator must also have a designated and trained backup employee who can fill-in when necessary.

Commentary: This policy is intended to prevent awkward situations where a security administrator does not have a designated and/or trained backup person, in which case business activity may be impaired or interrupted. Separately, if a backup administrator is ready to fill-in for a regular administrator, then it is unlikely that security systems will need to be compromised in order to continue necessary business activity. Note that both the regular and the backup persons should be employees; this is because employees are generally more loyal and most often have a longer tenure with Company X than contractors, consultants, temporaries, and the like. Furthermore, this policy can be used to obtain both necessary staffing and training resources. On another note, this policy assumes that the words "access control system" have been defined elsewhere; generally these words mean a fixed password user identification system with associated user access privilege controls, but many other options such as dynamic password tokens are also available. Also see the policy entitled "Designated Security Administrator For All Multi-User Systems." A: T; E: LMH.

1093. Each Department Must Have An Information Security Liaison

Policy: Every department manager must designate an information security liaison, and give this liaison sufficient training, supporting materials, and other resources to properly perform his or her job.

Commentary: The intention of this policy is to clearly communicate to departmental and other lower-level managers that information security liaisons are important and that they must be adequately supported. Since information security does not directly contribute to the "bottom line," many departmental managers erroneously assume that it's not important. This policy seeks to overcome this old-fashioned attitude. The policy is particularly suitable for those organizations which have part-time liaisons. Liaisons often act as both a local contact for information security matters, and a knowledgeable person regarding information security. Liaisons are frequently LAN administrators or security administrators (who take care of access control on systems). Separately, this policy is particularly important for departments using microcomputers (PCs) and workstations, LANs, client/server systems, etc., because the security of these smaller systems is often neglected. Also see the policy entitled "Designated Security Administrator For All Multi-User Systems." A: MT; E: LMH.

1094. Annual Review Of Trade Secrets, Copyrights, Etc. By Legal Department

Policy: Each year the Legal Department, working in conjunction with the Information Security Department, must perform an intellectual property and information protection law review. This project involves: (1) development of an inventory of the legal issues surrounding Company X information, (2) assessment of the efficiency and effectiveness of the controls which address these issues, and (3) compilation a list of recommended changes for subsequent review and discussion by the Information Security Management Committee.

Commentary: The intention of this policy is to compel the Legal Department and the Information Security Department to pay attention to the legal issues associated with information security. These issues include trademark and service mark infringement, patent infringement, copyright violation, and privacy violation. Legal and regulatory requirements in many instances will dictate information systems requirements. But in many organizations the legal and regulatory issues have not yet been adequately explored, and these organizations are then at a great disadvantage because they are operating in the dark, hoping that they are doing the right things. This policy shifts the ordinary way of dealing with these legal matters from a reactionary approach to a proactive approach. On another note, the policy writer should make a clear distinction between this type of a legal and regulatory analysis and an information security risk analysis (or a risk assessment). Although some of the same topics may be addressed in each type of project, the two projects involve different methodologies, different specialists, and separate topics. Separately, nothing in this policy is meant to imply that an outside consultant or some other third party assistance cannot be used for this specialized work. For related ideas, see the policies entitled "Annual Organization-Wide Information Security Risk Assessment" and "Chief Legal Counsel Is Sole Person To Declare Information A Trade Secret." A: M; E: MH.

1095. Internal Audit Review Of Information System Controls

Policy: The Internal Audit Department must periodically review the adequacy of information system controls as well as compliance with such controls.

Commentary: The intention of this policy is to clearly state in a policy (or a mission statement or a charter) the information-security-related responsibilities of the Internal Audit Department. In many organizations, Internal Audit doesn't have the requisite expertise to do this job, so they ignore information security. This policy puts Internal Audit on notice that they should get trained so that they can perform this job, hire an EDP auditor, or else retain an outsider to assist with this work. The policy is also intended to clarify a question which is often a point of confusion between the Information Security Department and the Internal Audit Department: who should do information systems security reviews (also known as risk assessments or risk analyses)? Instead of the Internal Audit Department, the Information Security Department could do these security reviews. The important objective here is the clear assignment of responsibility. Separately, the policy provided above could be modified to reflect the fact that often Internal Audit checks-up on the adequacy of information security rather than performing detailed technical work. See the policies entitled "Computer System Logs Must Support Audits," "Risk Assessments Required For Production Information Systems," and "Security Measures Must Be Enforceable Prior To Installation." A: M; E: LMH.

1096. Internal Audit Performs Information Security Compliance Checking

Policy: The Internal Audit Department must periodically perform compliance checking related to information security policies, standards, and procedures.

Commentary: The intention of this policy is clearly state that the Internal Audit Department, NOT the Information Security Department, must perform compliance checking. If the Information Security Department were to do this, it would be a conflict of interest. It's not desirable for people who designed, installed, and administered a system to also check up after themselves. This policy will thus keep the Information Security Department on their toes. Far too often management has the erroneous idea that compliance checking will be done by the Information Security Department. While the Information Security Department may install and run tools which can help enforce policies, standards, and procedures, the job of compliance checking should go to the Internal Audit Department. Examples of tools which the Information Security Department can use to enforce these rules include change control software, software license management, and network management software. But an independent report to management indicating whether these tools are doing the job they are intended to do, that should come from the Internal Audit Department. For a related idea, see the policy entitled "Internal Audit Review Of Information System Controls." A: MT; E: LMH.

1097. Periodic Independent Review Of Information System Controls

Policy: An independent and externally-provided review of information system controls must be periodically obtained. These reviews must include efforts to determine both the adequacy of, and compliance with controls. The reviews must not be performed by persons responsible for implementing and maintaining controls.

Commentary: The purpose of this policy is to require management to periodically seek outside feedback about information system controls. Far too many organizations assume they are adequately secure, when in fact they are not aware of the significant vulnerabilities they face. This problem is particularly severe in organizations where Information Systems Department management has been employed by the same organization for many years. In these cases, staff often becomes complacent and does not keep up with either the technology or the new risks that this technology introduces. An outsider's review may also be a useful way to overcome internal loyalties and conflicts-of-interest that have conspired to keep vulnerabilities hidden. It is also useful for an independent outsider to come in and provide a reality check, particularly to assure that "standard of due care" controls are being employed. Increasingly, Certified Public Accountants (CPAs)--or Chartered Accountants (CAs) in Canada and England--are required to look at computer-based internal controls during financial audits. CPAs examine controls to determine the degree to which they can rely on the results of the systems employing these controls. Nonetheless, at this point in time, as part of a financial audit, CPAs generally do not investigate information system controls in sufficient depth to notice other vulnerabilities besides those directly associated with financial information systems. This is why additional external review, perhaps provided by an outside technical consultant or a specialist at the CPA firm, may be appropriate. A new and more specific designation called Certified Information Systems Auditor (CISA) is now being used to identify those competent to do this work. Also see the policy entitled "Minimum Information System Controls Dictated By Standard Practice." A: M; E: LMH.

1098. Information Security Responsibilities In Job Descriptions

Policy: Specific information security responsibilities must be incorporated into all worker job descriptions if such workers have access to sensitive, valuable, or critical information. Commentary: The intention of this policy is to require management to formally acknowledge the information security responsibilities (in job descriptions) for those positions which handle sensitive, valuable, or critical information. If job descriptions contain these statements, workers are more likely to take information security responsibilities seriously. When workers see that their promotions and salary increases are related to information security, they will take it all more seriously. For a wider scope, the words "access to sensitive, valuable, or critical information" can be changed to "manage or use Company X information systems." This change would for example be appropriate when the organization does not have a data classification system. As currently written, this policy assumes the existence of a data classification system (and perhaps related policies for ranking information based on value and/or criticality). In some organizations, it may be appropriate to delete the words "valuable, or critical" because only a sensitivity ranking scheme (such as a data classification policy) is available. As a service to the managers who write job descriptions, the centralized Information Security Department is urged to prepare a standard set of words for job descriptions. See the policy entitled "Four Category Data Classification Scheme." Also see the policy entitled "Information Security Considered In Employee Performance Evaluations." A: M; E: LMH.

1099. Information Security Considered In Employee Performance Evaluations

Policy: Compliance with information security policies and procedures must be considered in all employee performance evaluations.

Commentary: The intention of this policy is to require managers--at the time they write performance evaluations--to first of all decide whether the employee should be concerned about information security, and if the answer is yes, then to determine whether the employee has acted in compliance with policies and procedures. The policy provided here makes direct reference to a management activity (evaluating employees), and only indirectly to a rank-and-file employee activity (complying with policies and procedures). Nonetheless, it implies that both are expected by management. The words "information security policies and procedures" could be changed to "information security requirements" or other generic terms used at the organization in question. For a more limited approach, see the policy entitled "Incorporation Of Information Security Responsibilities Into Job Descriptions." Also see the policy entitled "Information Security Is Every Worker's Duty." A: M; E: LMH.

1100. Separation Of Duties And Control Over Company X Assets

Policy: Whenever a Company X computer-based process involves sensitive, valuable, or critical information, the system must include controls involving a separation of duties or other compensating control measures. These control measures must ensure that no one individual has exclusive control over these types of Company X information assets.

Commentary: The intention of this policy is to prevent fraud, embezzlement, and other abuses which take advantage of an individual's unrestricted access to Company X information or the systems which handle such information. For example, a bank teller who checked her own work, prepared her own reports, and who handled everything else herself may be able to abscond with bank money without causing suspicion. Getting another person involved in a process helps to make sure that the entire process was performed in accordance with management intentions. Because only a data classification scheme may be in place, at some organizations, it may be advisable to drop the words "valuable, or critical" from the policy provided here. This policy is especially important in those organizations where small systems (LANs, PCs, client/server systems, and the like) are used for production processing. This is because the flexibility and power of these small systems allows downsizing (reengineering), and often a single person is left doing the jobs that formerly took several people. Separately, an example of a "compensating control measure" would be increased automatic user activity monitoring. Also see the policies entitled "User-To-User Separation Of Activities And Data," "Building Systems So That Errors And Manipulations Come To Light," "Specific Instructions Regarding Separation Of Duties," "Computer Center Is A Closed Shop," "Working Alone In Restricted Areas Forbidden," and "Positive Identification Required For Initiation Of Computer Transactions." A: MT; E: LMH.

1101. Building Systems So That Errors And Manipulations Come To Light

Policy: Company X computer systems must be built so that no single person can make an error or manipulate the records without such events being detected by some other person during the routine execution of that other person's duties.

Commentary: This policy is a detection-oriented expression of the principle of separation of duties. Rather than focusing on preventing problems, it takes a less stringent approach requiring only that errors and manipulations readily be discovered. This approach may involve fewer controls or less costly controls than the more stringent preventative approach, and therefore may be attractive to small businesses. Nonetheless, in the long run, total costs (controls plus losses) will generally be higher than they would be with a preventative approach. See the policies entitled "Separation Of Duties And Control Over Company X Assets," "Double Keying Required For All Amounts Over $1,000," and "Required Actions After Errors In Records Are Detected." A: MT; E: LMH.

1102. Specific Instructions Regarding Separation Of Duties

Policy: Whenever practical, no person should be responsible for completing a task involving sensitive, valuable, or critical information from beginning to end. Likewise, a single person must not be responsible for approving their own work. To the extent possible, for every task involving sensitive, valuable, or critical information, at least two people must be required to coordinate their information-handling activities.

Commentary: This policy specifically delineates what the separation of duties means within a certain organization. It is intended to accordingly provide specific guidance for business process reengineering specialists, computer systems designers, new application programmers, maintenance programmers, and related personnel. The nature of the business performed by each organization will in turn dictate the specifics to be covered in a policy such as this. Industry-specific laws and regulations may likewise point to the specifics to be mentioned here. In some organizations, it may be appropriate to delete the words "valuable, or critical" (particularly if no policies relating to these considerations exist). See the policy entitled "Separation Of Duties And Control Over Company X Assets." A: MT; E: LMH.

1103. Incident Management Responsibilities

Policy: To ensure a quick, effective, and orderly response to incidents, the individuals responsible for handling information systems security incidents must be clearly defined. These people are in turn responsible for defining procedures for handling incidents.

Commentary: All too often management is surprised when a security incident (like a hacker break-in) takes place. Typically, people will not know who to turn to, nor will they know what should be done next. The purpose of this policy is to require that specific individuals be defined as responsible for handling such incidents and that these people know that they are responsible for developing and maintaining procedures for handling incidents. The word "incidents" as used here could be construed in its widest sense--in its contingency planning sense--to include emergencies as well as disasters. In addition to normal contingency plans, the procedures that these individuals develop can include ways to document an investigation, ways to determine how to prevent the problem's recurrence, ways to report the incident to management and third parties, and ways to protect logs and audit trails should they be needed for disciplinary or prosecution purposes. The most famous organization performing these duties is the Computer Emergency Response Team (CERT) at Carnegie-Mellon University, Pittsburgh, Pennsylvania. While the Carnegie-Mellon CERT deals with Internet problems, this policy talks about the creation of an internal CERT. See the policy entitled "Leave Without Pay Required During Extended Investigations," "Organization/Maintenance Of Computer Emergency Response Team," "Information Security Alert System," and "Prompt Implementation Of Security Problem Fix Software, Scripts, Etc." A: M; E: LMH.

2.3.1.4. Owner, Custodian And User Responsibilities

1104. High-Level Inventory Of Information Assets

Policy: The Information Systems Department must compile and annually update a corporation-wide data dictionary and other high-level descriptions of the major Company X information assets.

Commentary: The intention of this policy is to force the Information Systems Department to organize and document information about information (sometimes called 'metadata'). Most often in the form of a data dictionary (data directory), this information is invaluable when it comes to planning future application development projects, migrating applications from mainframes to client/server systems, and designing an executive information system (EIS). It is also helpful when conducting risk assessments (risk analyses) and when preparing contingency plans. A data dictionary can additionally be used by EDP auditors to determine whether controls have been applied to information consistently across applications and across systems. A data dictionary is furthermore essential if the notion of owners, custodians, and users is to be successfully applied within a particular organization. These distinctions rely on the ability to clearly define, locate, control, and otherwise manage information, as can only be done via a data dictionary or similar tool. This policy is really a complexity management policy, helping organizations come to terms with the incredible complexity of their modern information systems. The policy is therefore most relevant to large organizations, although many middle-sized organizations will also find the policy appropriate. On another point, it should not be forgotten that access controls for a data dictionary are essential; not everyone will need-to-know everything contained in the data dictionary. See the policies entitled "Assignment Of Responsibility For Information Asset Controls," "Designated Custodian Required For All Major Information Types," "Personal Information Necessary For Proper Functioning Of Business," "Existence Of Secret Systems Containing Personnel Records," "Maintenance Of Index To Databases Containing Private Information," and "Nature And Location Of Company X Information is Confidential." A: MT; E: LMH.

1105. Criteria For Assigning Information Ownership

Policy: If there are several potential information owners, higher-level management must assign ownership responsibility to the single individual who makes the greatest use of the information.

Commentary: The intention of this policy is to make it clear how information owners should be assigned. If the criteria is not specific, all too often an owner will not be assigned, and as a consequence security for the involved information will be lax. With intranets, integrated distributed databases, client/server systems, and other multi-departmental applications, these days the assignment of ownership can be a non-trivial question. The term "greatest use" is deliberately kept vague since there will be different factors in each decision (most linked with strategically-important businesses activities, most critical to continuing operations, most frequently accessed, etc.). Separately, another way to determine ownership is identify who pays the bill for the storage and other information services associated with the information in question (assuming an internal charge-back or external service bureau billing system is in place). Yet another way to assign ownership would be identify the department manager responsible for maintenance of the information and/or related information system. For further guidance, see the policy entitled "Information Ownership And Management's Responsibilities." A: M; E: LMH.

1106. Information Systems Department Must Not Be Owner Of Information

Policy: With the exception of operational computer and network information, the Information Systems Department must not be the owner of any information.

Commentary: The intention of this policy is to make it clear that the Information Systems Department, which often serves as a custodian, should not at the same time be an owner of information. This would create a conflict of interest where security is likely to be inadequately addressed. For example, the Information Systems Department might decide that minimal controls were appropriate for sensitive information because this would speed access and keep costs down. It is this same conflict of interest that has many people working in the information security field saying that the Information Security Group should not report to the Information Systems Department. Of course, the term "Data Processing" can be replaced with "Information Technology" or other vernacular used at the organization in question. See the policy entitled "Information Ownership And Management's Responsibilities." A: MT; E: LMH.

1107. Designated Custodian Required For All Major Information Types

Policy: Each major type of information must have a designated custodian. Each custodian must properly protect Company X information in keeping with the designated owner's access control, data sensitivity, and data criticality instructions.

Commentary: The objective of this policy is to require that a custodian be assigned for all significant information types. To determine whether information is "important" or significant, one may look to see if the information is included in an organization-wide data dictionary. Another objective of the policy is to clearly specify the responsibilities of information custodians. This policy also implies that owners should pay custodians so that they may properly protect the involved information. This idea may be manifested via an internal charge-back system, inter-organizational transfer prices, or other accounting mechanisms. If the owner does not provide sufficient resources to protect the involved information, the custodian must then notify the owner that the information is not being protected in a manner consistent with instructions. Although custodians may be either individuals or organizational entities, it is best if they are restricted to individuals; this helps to foster accountability which in turn is more likely to lead to desired results. Separately, organizations may wish to augment the stated responsibilities of custodians to include the provision of, and maintenance of, a general security system for information systems. See the policies entitled "Assignment Of Responsibility For Information Asset Controls," "Information Security Is Overhead, Not A Charge-Back Item," and "High-Level Inventory Of Information Assets." A: MT; E: LMH.

1108. Security Responsibilities Of Information Custodians

Policy: Information custodians are responsible for defining specific control procedures, administering information access controls, implementing and maintaining cost-effective information control measures, and providing recovery capabilities consistent with the instructions of information owners.
Commentary: The intention of this policy is to explicitly define what it means to be an information custodian. For example, the policy makes it clear that custodians do not call the shots when it comes to security (the owners do). Custodians instead provide a service in a manner consistent with instructions from owners. This policy is written with the assumption that the Information Security Group organizationally reports to the Information Systems Department (the most common arrangement, even though it presents some conflicts of interest). If this is not the case, mention of administering access controls, may need to be removed from this policy. Ideally, responsibilities should be assigned such that the Information Security Group is not be a custodian for any production information (just security-related information). See the policy entitled "Designated Custodian Required For All Major Information Types." A: MT; E: LMH.

1109. Security Responsibilities Of Information Users

Policy: All users of Company X information must comply with the control requirements specified by the information's owner and/or custodian. Users may be employees, temporaries, contractors, consultants, or third parties with whom special arrangements have been made.

Commentary: The intention of this policy is to put users on notice that they are permitted to use information with the understanding that they must properly protect it. Some organizations make this policy more specific by requiring users to sign a statement that they agree to abide by information security policies and procedures. A signature on a form with this statement, and perhaps a summary of the policies and procedures, can be required before a user is given a user-ID and a password. It should be emphasized that the users do not own or control the information to which they have been granted access, and that they should not be making security-related decisions about this information. Without a specific written statement to this effect, users may decide that they can share the information with their friends, their acquaintance at a competing firm who asked for a copy, etc. As more and more information is distributed to intranets, LANs, PCs, client/server systems, and the like, there is a pressing need for policies like this to clarify user security responsibilities. For more relevant policies, see the section of this book entitled "Password Related User Responsibilities." A: EMT; E: LMH.

1110. Process For Granting Access To Company X Information

Policy: Access to Company X information must always be authorized by a designated owner of such information, and must be limited on a need-to-know basis to a reasonably restricted number of people.

Commentary: The intention of this policy is to clearly state who makes decisions about access to certain information (the owner). Note that the policy allows owners to create categories of users, such as accounts payable clerks, to which a predetermined set of privileges may then be granted. This allows custodians to grant basic privileges to an individual based on their job title, eliminating the need for the owner to consider the circumstances of each individual. This policy is just as applicable to external requests for information as it is to internal requests. Separately, the policy also reminds all who read it that access to information is not granted simply because access was requested (the need-to-know must also be present). A small minority of organizations are replacing the traditional notion of need-to-know with the notion of need-to-withhold (at least for information that has not been designated as sensitive). For further information about this emerging change in practice, see the policy entitled "Privilege Restriction Based On The Need-to-Know." Also see the policies entitled "Access Control Packages Required For Computers On The Network" and "Default To Denial Of Access Control Privileges." A: MT; E: LMH.

1111. Restricted Delegation Of Information Owner Duties

Policy: An information owner's responsibility for the specification of appropriate information controls may not be delegated to service providers outside Company X.

Commentary: The objective of this policy is to make sure that insiders (who generally have a better understanding of the business and its needs than outsiders do) make decisions about the security of information. Outsiders may be committed to maximizing profit and minimizing their own staff's time involvement with this customer, and as a result security may very well be significantly eroded. In other words, this policy is saying that certain fundamental security decisions must be made by the management of an organization, not by outsiders. An analogy might help here: management should not delegate decisions about business strategy to consultants, since this would be akin to abrogating their responsibility to manage the business. Similarly, to delegate responsibility for security decisions is to annul management's fiduciary responsibility to protect and conserve assets (information systems related and otherwise). Note that the actual implementation of the security decisions can still be done by outsiders. This policy may be incorporated into outsourcing agreements, facilities management agreements, consulting requests for proposals (RFPs), and the like. See the policies entitled "Information Ownership And Management's Responsibilities" and "Involvement Of In-House Information Security Department." A: MT; E: LMH.

3. Physical Security

3.1. Physical Access Security

3.1.1. Building Access Control

3.1.1.1. Locks And Barriers

1112. Physical Access Control For Areas Containing Sensitive Information

Policy: Access to every office, computer room, and work area containing sensitive information must be physically restricted. Management responsible for the staff working in these areas must consult the Security Department to determine the appropriate access control method (receptionists, metal key locks, magnetic card door locks, etc.).

Commentary: The intention of this policy is to first of all require that local management restrict who has access to areas where sensitive information may be found. Note that the specific technology required to handle this information is deliberately not stated. Accordingly, the information could be on hardcopy computer output, could be discussed over the phone, could be on building construction blueprints, and the like. A second intention of this policy is to require that local management consult internal security specialists to determine what type of access control technology should be used. Circumstances often vary so much from work area to work area that it may not be expedient to require all offices to use a certain access control technology (particularly in multinational companies which face widely differing local customs and requirements). On the other hand, from a cost-containment standpoint, there is a lot to recommend standardization of certain physical access control technology like magnetic cards. This policy is particularly relevant to computing environments containing microcomputers (PCs), LANs, workstations, client/server systems and the like because the logical access controls on such systems are often lax or missing. Separately, this policy could be expanded to include mention of granting physical access based on the need-to-know, although it is implied as the policy is now written. The scope of the policy could also be expanded to include "valuable, or critical" information (not just "sensitive information"). For further guidance on this matter, see the policies entitled "Four Category Data Classification Scheme" and "Five Category Application Criticality Classification Scheme." Also see the policy entitled "Changing Physical Access Control Codes On Worker Termination." A: M; E: LMH.

1113. When Personal Offices Are Not In Use, The Doors Must Be Locked

Policy: All workers with separate personal offices must lock the doors when these offices are not in use. Although other measures will also be necessary, this practice will help to restrict unauthorized access to sensitive information.
Commentary: The intention of this policy is to get workers to employ the office door locks which in many instances are standard equipment in office buildings. Often this basic control measure is ignored, and unauthorized disclosure of sensitive information takes place after hours or when an area is unattended. This policy seeks to establish a practice which may make life more difficult for managers, who may want a memo sitting on a desk which is inside a locked office. If adopted, the policy should be accompanied by a strong physical key management system which allows managers and secretaries to gain access to locked offices when circumstances require. This policy assumes that separate offices are fully enclosed; this policy is not appropriate if all workers have cubicles or other only partially enclosed offices. While this policy may seem basic, obvious, and perhaps not even worth mentioning in an information security policy document, it is important to clarify these instructions in writing if consistent compliance is going to be achieved. For a related idea, see the policy entitled "Physical Access Control For Areas Containing Sensitive Information." A: EMT; E: LMH.

1114. Multi-User Computer Or Communications Systems In Locked Rooms

Policy: All multi-user computer and communications equipment must be located in locked rooms to prevent tampering and unauthorized usage.

Commentary: No matter how sophisticated software access controls may be, if physical access to servers and similar equipment can be obtained, then software access controls can be overcome. For example, on many LAN servers, a simple reboot process will allow an unauthorized person to completely control the machine. The policy seeks to alert technical management at remote sites that all multi-user systems must be located behind locked doors. Typical recipients of the policy include systems administrators, network managers, and others responsible for remotely-located equipment. Note also that the policy requires that switches, PBXs, hubs, routers, firewalls, and other network equipment must be located in a locked room. Separately, this policy indirectly encourages the location of servers and similar equipment in raised floor computer rooms (at many organizations, this will be a move towards recentralization). Also see the policies entitled "Provision Of Lockable Metal Furniture To Staff Working At Home" and "Equipment Isolation Between Company X And Third Party Systems." A: T; E: LMH.

1115. Guards Or Receptionists For Areas Containing Sensitive Information

Policy: Visitor or other third party access to Company X offices, computer facilities, and other work areas containing sensitive information must be controlled by guards, receptionists, or other staff. Visitors and other third parties must not be permitted to use employee entrances or other uncontrolled pathways leading to areas containing sensitive information.

Commentary: The objective of this policy is to require that an authorized staff person get involved in the process of determining whether visitors or other third parties should be allowed to come into areas containing sensitive information. Unchecked access to such areas may otherwise lead to industrial espionage, fraud, equipment theft, and other problems. This policy defines a way to implement the strategy known as "control the perimeter," a classic approach used since the days of medieval castles. To implement this policy, employee entrances can have man-traps, turnstiles, and other mechanisms to make sure that only authorized workers using a badge or some other access control mechanism are let through that door. Separately, the scope of the policy can be expanded to include "valuable, or critical" information (not just "sensitive information"). For further guidance on this matter, see the policies entitled "Four Category Data Classification Scheme" and "Five Category Application Criticality Classification Scheme." Also see the policy entitled "Physical Access Control For Areas Containing Sensitive Information." A: M; E: LMH.

1116. Badges Must Be Worn In Visible Places When In Company X Premises

Policy: Whenever in Company X buildings or facilities, all persons must wear an identification badge on their outer garments so that both the picture and information on the badge are clearly visible.

Commentary: The purpose of this policy is to put all workers on notice that they must wear their badges in a conspicuous place. This will allow guards and other workers to determine whether a worker is permitted in a certain area. The policy will thus allow workers to readily notice if someone is using a stolen (or "borrowed") badge. This policy assumes picture badges are used by at least some of the workers, but reference to pictures can be deleted if this is not the case. This policy or a derivative of it can apply to several different types of premises: (a) where authorized workers have picture badges but visitors do not, (b) where every person in a restricted area has a picture badge, or (c) where none of the badges have pictures on them. This policy works well with a policy dealing with challenges of unauthorized persons in restricted areas. If only certain areas are restricted via badges, the policy can refer to "restricted areas," rather than stating that it deals with all Company X "buildings or facilities." Some workers don't like the picture on their badges (they may for example think it's not flattering). These people may seek to conceal their badges; this behavior is not acceptable according to this policy. Those individuals should be invited to sit for another picture and to then get a new badge that they will feel more comfortable wearing. See the policy entitled "Individuals Without Identification Badges Must Be Challenged." A: E; E: LMH.

1117. Temporary Badges For Workers Who Have Forgotten Their Badges

Policy: Workers who have forgotten their identification badge must obtain a temporary badge by providing a driver's license or another piece of picture identification. Such a temporary badge is valid for a single day only.

Commentary: The purpose of this policy is to emphasize that everyone must have an identification badge, even if they forgot their regular badge. The process of issuing a temporary badge takes a few moments and therefore discourages people from forgetting their badges. If workers habitually forget their badges, this will be readily noted by the Security Department records showing temporary badges issued. If the number of temporary badges for a specific individual is excessive, this may be cause for a notice to the individual's manager. Temporary badges should expire at the end of the day in case visitors forget to bring them back and also as an inducement to regular workers to bring in their regular badge the next day. To make expiration readily apparent, some types of temporary badges will discolor after a certain period from the time of issuance has elapsed. The time consumed by the temporary badge issuance process will encourage employees to remember their badge the next time. Separately, identification should be required to prove that a worker is who they say they are; this will help prevent third parties from gaining access to restricted areas by alleging they are authorized workers who forgot their badges. A temporary badge system implies that worker access privileges (and ideally photos) are resident in a computer database, and that these privileges can be readily recorded on a new badge. If this is not the case, this policy and the procedures it implies may be impractical. Note that the policy applies to all types of "workers" (consultants, contractors, temporaries, etc.). See the policies entitled "Positive Identification Required For Initiation Of Computer Transactions" and "Periodic Identification Badge Reports Issued To Department Heads." A: E; E: LMH.

1118. Reporting Lost/Stolen Identification Badges And System Access Tokens

Policy: Identification badges and physical access cards that have been lost or stolen--or are suspected of being lost or stolen--must be reported to the Security Department immediately. Likewise, all computer or communication system access tokens (smart cards with dynamic passwords, telephone credit cards, etc.) that have been lost or stolen--or are suspected of being lost or stolen--must be reported to the Security Department immediately.

Commentary: The intention of this policy is to require all workers to notify the Security Department of all badges or tokens that may have been lost or stolen. The Security Department can then take steps to immediately block the privileges associated with these badges or tokens. In this way, losses occasioned by lost or stolen badges or tokens can be minimized. Ideally there are other mechanisms which prevent badges or tokens from allowing either work area or system access. For badges, the picture is the most common mechanism. For a smart card, a separate fixed password known only by the user might be the mechanism. See the policy entitled "Use Of Credit Cards On Public Pay Phones." A: E; E: LMH.

1119. Each Individual Must Have Their Badge Read At Every Controlled Door

Policy: Each person must present his or her badge to the badge reader before entering every controlled door within Company X premises. Before proceeding through every controlled door, each person must wait until the badge reader indicates that they have permission to enter the area.

Commentary: This policy is intended to ensure that the physical access control log (supported via badges) reflects the individuals who were actually in an area at a specific time. All too often a group enters a controlled door, and only the first person is actually logged as having entered. This policy accordingly seeks to change what many people would consider to be polite behavior. People want to help others, and holding doors open for them has long been a matter of courtesy. But this practice can be, and often is, exploited by industrial spies, competing firm staff, and others seeking to gain access to areas containing sensitive information. The specifics of how this policy is implemented will vary based on the physical access control technology involved. For example, if a green light on the card reader indicates access is permitted, then this fact might be mentioned in the policy. Adding such specifics to the policy is, however, not recommended because the policy will need to change when the access control system is replaced. Ideally turnstyles are used, in which case piggy-backing or tail-gating is very difficult if not impossible. Note that the policy refers to "persons" rather than "workers" because some persons in the area will be visitors, vendors, etc. Separately, note that this policy may cause a backlog just before work is scheduled to begin as many people all converge on controlled doors at much the same time (more controlled doors or turnstyles may be needed). For a related idea, see the policy entitled " No 'Piggybacking' Through Controlled Doors Permitted." A EMT; A: LMH.

1120. No 'Piggybacking' Through Controlled Doors Permitted

Policy: Workers must not permit unknown or unauthorized persons to pass through doors, gates, and other entrances to restricted areas at the same time when authorized persons go through these entrances. While this may at first seem rude, it is essential if the security of Company X premises and Company X workers is to be maintained.

Commentary: This policy is known as a "no piggybacking" or "no tailgating" policy. It is intended to prevent unauthorized persons from following authorized persons into restricted areas (for instance, by using the authorized person's key or card to open the door). If turnstiles or mantraps are used, then this policy is less important, because piggybacking is physically prevented. The policy could be expanded to require authorized workers to refer all unknown or unauthorized persons to a receptionist or guard station. In the policy statement, the term "restricted areas" can be replaced by specific areas such as "the computer center." See the policies entitled "Individuals Without Identification Badges Must Be Challenged" and "Each Individual Must Have Their Badge Read At Every Controlled Door." A: E; E: LMH.

1121. Propped-Open Doors To Computer Center Requires Presence Of A Guard

Policy: Whenever doors to the computer center are propped-open (perhaps for moving computer equipment, furniture, supplies, or similar items), the entrance must be continuously monitored by an employee or a contract guard from the Physical Security Department.

Commentary: The intention of this policy is to make sure that equipment and information are not improperly removed because doors to the computer center are not sufficiently controlled. The policy can also be used to make sure that the movers do not make off with materials that they didn't come for, whether intentionally or accidentally. This policy is necessary because many shops are loose about physical access controls, but the computer center is perhaps the most central repository of important organizational information (and therefore a prime target for an industrial spy). The operational implementation of the policy need not be onerous; the computer operator on duty need only call the Physical Security Department and ask them to send a guard over. Note that the policy, in an indirect way, also forbids propping-open of the doors because the air conditioning isn't working well enough (unless of course, someone monitors the entrance). For several related ideas, see the policies entitled "Property Pass For Removal Of All Computer And Communications Gear" and "Computer Center Is A Closed Shop." A: T; E: LMH.

1122. Testing Physical Access Controls Forbidden

Policy: Workers must not attempt to enter restricted areas in Company X buildings for which they have not received access authorization.

Commentary: The intention of this policy is to put workers on notice that they are not to attempt to defeat physical access controls. If workers need access to a certain area, they must go through the proper authorization channels rather than taking matters into their own hands. Granted, there will always be emergencies and disasters where this policy does not apply; in these circumstances, workers will do what they need to do, and explain the situation later (there is no need to discuss it in a policy). Modern access control systems will log repeated attempts to gain access to areas that an individual does not have permission to enter. This policy establishes the basis for disciplinary action whenever there have been repeated attempts to gain access to an off-limits area. See the policy entitled "Prohibition Against Testing Information System Controls." A: E; E: LMH.

1123. Working Alone In Restricted Areas Forbidden

Policy: Workers must never be permitted to work alone in restricted areas containing sensitive information.

Commentary: The intention of this policy is to prevent workers from taking advantage of the fact that they are the only person in an area containing sensitive information. For example, one worker might look at the private personnel file of another worker, something they would not do if other people were around. Depending on the other policies in force, this policy can be expanded to include mention of "valuable, or critical" information (not just "sensitive" information). Separately, to make the policy more restrictive, the word "sensitive" could be changed to "secret." This policy helps to make sure that a separation of duty policy is effective. See the policies entitled "Separation Of Duties And Control Over Company X Assets" and "Working In Restricted Areas Only During Official Business Hours." A: E; E: MH.

1124. Working In Restricted Areas Only During Official Business Hours

Policy: If access to a particular Company X facility has been restricted because sensitive, critical, or valuable information is handled therein, workers must be allowed to access these facilities ONLY during official business hours.

Commentary: If employees stay late or come in early, they may be unsupervised, and may therefore be able to engage in computer abuse (such as using another employee's computer to view confidential data). If workers are restricted to normal hours, they may not engage in abusive acts because they would not risk being caught or because they would be prevented from performing these acts by other people. This policy is thus a background policy that helps to ensure that separation of duties policies are effective. Separately, in the policy, the word "official" may be replaced by "authorized" to give management additional leeway in setting working hours. Also see the policies entitled "Separation Of Duties And Control Over Company X Assets" and "Working Alone In Restricted Areas Forbidden." A: E; E: H.

1125. Physical Security Or Encryption Required For All Sensitive Information

Policy: All information storage media (such as hard disk drives, floppy disks, magnetic tapes, and CD-ROMs) containing sensitive information must be physically secured when not in use. An exception will be made if this information is protected via an encryption system approved by the Information Security Department.

Commentary: The intention of this policy is to require all local managers to implement either physical security measures or encryption (or both) for sensitive information. This policy is particularly relevant to portable, laptop, palmtop and other small microcomputers (PCs). Since physical security cannot be assured when these systems are moved from building to building, encryption will be required (perhaps for just the sensitive information, or perhaps for the entire hard drive). This policy also helps prevent theft of microcomputers containing sensitive information. Based on the other policies in force, the policy given here may be expanded to include "valuable, or critical" information (not just "sensitive" information). See the policies entitled "Physical Security Measures For Computers & Communications Systems," "Data Stored On Hard Disk Drives Must Be Encrypted," and "Secret Information Sent By Electronic Mail." A: ET; E: MH.

1126. Property Pass For Removal Of All Computer And Communications Gear

Policy: Typewriters, cellular telephones, portable computers, modems, and related information systems equipment must not leave Company X premises unless accompanied by an approved property pass.

Commentary: The intention of this policy is to make sure that workers are not stealing equipment (and perhaps the information stored inside such equipment). Guards at controlled exit points can check property passes to make sure they are properly approved by management, still up-to-date, and apply to the equipment in question. This policy is particularly relevant to microcomputers (PCs) and workstations, many of which are stolen. Often people use excuses like "I'm using it to do some work at home," or "I'm taking it to be fixed," when they are really stealing the equipment. For the benefit of guards, a property pass will confirm or deny these claims. Note that a property pass is required for both personally-owned and Company X-owned property. Separately, new technology will set off alarms at controlled building entrance/exit points if tagged equipment is being removed. The property pass process can be a method to prevent these alarms from being triggered (because the equipment is passed outside the monitored area). On another note, this policy could be expanded by prohibiting visitors, temporary staff, and employee family members from removing any equipment from Company X premises. For related ideas, see the policies entitled "Guards Or Receptionists For Areas Containing Sensitive Information" and "Moving Microcomputer Equipment Without Approval Prohibited." A: E; E: LMH.

1127. Computer Storage Media Must Have A Pass When Leaving Premises

Policy: All computer storage media (CD-ROMs, floppy disks, etc.) leaving Company X offices must be accompanied by a properly authorized pass. All such removals of storage media must be logged at the building's front desk.

Commentary: The intention of this policy is to ensure that workers are not walking off with sensitive or valuable information (such as a customer list). The primary risks that this policy attempts to counteract are industrial espionage, privacy violation, intellectual property theft (perhaps software copyright infringement), and sabotage (perhaps removal of the only copy of critical information or software). The policy may be difficult for organizations which have a large contingent of telecommuting staff, many of whom may customarily carry storage media into and out of an office building. This difficulty is expected to be diminished in the years ahead as a large number of authorized data transfers will be done through the Internet rather than through physical transport of computer storage media. Of course, portable computer hard disks are also computer storage media, and they too should have passes. This policy is appropriate for high security environments, such as a diplomatic embassy, a bank data processing center, or a military command post. This policy goes well with the policy entitled "Property Pass For Removal Of All Computer And Communications Gear." Also see the policy entitled "Workers Must Show Contents Of Luggage When Leaving Premises." A: E; E: H.

1128. Workers Must Show Contents Of Luggage When Leaving Premises

Policy: All briefcases, suitcases, handbags, and other luggage must be opened for Company X building guards to check when people leave the premises. This will ensure that sensitive or valuable information is not being removed from the premises without authorization.

Commentary: The objective of this conservative policy is to discourage people from walking out with sensitive or valuable information (in whatever form). Without question the policy is a gesture and a deterrent, not a foolproof method to prevent the theft of sensitive or valuable information. This policy suffers from a serious flaw: guards are unlikely to spot sensitive or valuable information even if it was right under their noses. For example, generally a security guard is not going to take the time to check the information resident on a floppy disk contained in a briefcase. While sensitive or valuable information can be printed on special colored paper that stands out, or can be tagged with magnetic markers which set off alarms when removed from a building, these and related approaches are relatively ineffective against a determined thief. Likewise, Internet connections can quietly permit the rapid transmission of gigabytes of sensitive or valuable information. This policy is more effective in its intent to discourage and occasionally apprehend theft of computer equipment and supplies. See the policies entitled "Property Pass For Removal Of All Computer And Communications Gear" and "Secret Information Must Not Leave Company X Offices In Any Form." A: E; E: H.

1129. Provision Of Lockable Metal Furniture To Staff Working At Home

Policy: All workers who must keep sensitive Company X information at their homes in order to do their work must receive lockable furniture for the proper storage of this information. At the time of separation from Company X, both the furniture and sensitive information stored therein must be immediately returned to Company X.

Commentary: The purpose of this policy is to make sure that telecommuters and other staff who work in their homes have the proper furniture to securely store sensitive Company X information. If a worker already has suitable furniture, then it need not be provided by Company X (although a key should be provided). If furniture was provided, ownership of the furniture remains with Company X (labels on the furniture should probably note this, and a memo to the employee clarifying ownership is also appropriate). To make this policy more selective, the word "sensitive" could be replaced with "secret." This policy assumes the word "sensitive" has been defined elsewhere. If this is not the case, see the policy entitled "Four Category Data Classification Scheme." Separately, with an increasing number of people working in their cars or trucks, this policy could be expanded to include transportation vehicles (in which case some sort of a safe or lockable container could be used). The policy could also be expanded to include other security tools needed to work at home, such as encryption programs for a personal computer (PC) or workstation. Also see the policies entitled "Permissible Equipment For Telecommuting," "Physical Security Or Encryption Required For All Sensitive Information," "Security Requirements For Work At Home Arrangements," and "Removal Of Sensitive Information From Company X Premises." A: M; E: MH.

3.1.1.2. Building Access Records

1130. Maintaining Building Access Control System Records

Policy: To facilitate emergency evacuation and to support investigations, the Security Department must maintain records of the persons currently and previously inside Company X buildings. This information must be securely retained for at least three (3) months.

Commentary: The purpose of this policy is to force the recording of information about who comes and goes through a building containing sensitive, valuable, or critical information. This information may be especially important when physical access control systems are combined with computer access control systems. For example, if a user-ID was used to commit a fraud, but the individual who is authorized to use the user-ID was not in the building at the time, this might show that an unauthorized person was using the user-ID. Knowing who is in a building is very important if there is a fire, a bomb threat, or some other emergency or disaster. If records are kept of entrances and exits, this may also serve as a deterrent to various unauthorized acts such as stealing computers. Such records may also be important for showing that certain time cards are fraudulent. Maintenance of such records may also help with the enforcement of policies about permitting only those with a need-to-know to have access to certain areas. See the policies entitled "Required Retention Period Of Logs" and "Periodic Identification Badge Reports Issued To Department Heads." A: MT; E: LMH.

1131. Changing Physical Access Control Codes On Worker Termination

Policy: When a worker terminates his or her working relationship with Company X, all physical security access codes known by the worker must be deactivated or changed. For example, the password entered on a cipherlock to get into the building must be changed.

Commentary: This policy is intended to limit further access by terminated workers (employees, contractors, temporaries, etc.). The policy is written in a general way so that it includes shared codes like combination lock numbers for the front door, as well as individual codes such as the identification numbers recorded on a magnetic stripe on a badge. This policy helps prevent confusion about the identity of the person who is using an access code. The policy may also prevent a terminated worker from using a copy of the access mechanism (like a magnetic card) to gain unauthorized entry to Company X work areas. This last objective is particularly important if the worker is disgruntled and potentially vengeful. The policy makes mention of "access codes known by the worker," but could be changed to "access codes known by or available to the worker." This change would be called for if the codes were embedded in a smart card, but strictly speaking, unknown to the worker. Separately, the Human Resources Department may need to define what constitutes a termination; for example, if an employee becomes a contractor, is that a termination of the working relationship? Distribution of this policy ordinarily would be restricted to Information Security and Physical Security Department staff. See the policies entitled "User-To-User Separation Of Activities And Data," "Return Of Company X Property At Time Of Separation From Company X," "Transfer Of Certain Workers To Positions With Less Exposure," and "Reporting Changes In User Duties To Systems Security Administration." A: T; E: LMH.

1132. Access Rights To Restricted Areas Must Be Revoked On Termination

Policy: Whenever a worker terminates his or her working relationship with Company X, all access rights to Company X restricted areas must be immediately revoked.

Commentary: The purpose of this policy is to make sure that workers who have terminated their working relationship with an organization are no longer permitted into the offices (or into other controlled areas such as a manufacturing plant's floor). Just when the access rights should be revoked is a tough question. For example, if someone resigns with two weeks notice, should the person be shown to the door immediately, or should the person be allowed to continue and keep their access rights for the two week period. Human Resource Department policies should address these questions. This policy supports information security because if an organization can't control who is inside restricted areas, it is going to have a great deal of trouble restricting who can gain access to restricted information. This policy is written for managers, who often must handle the termination process. For related ideas, see the policies entitled "Changing Physical Access Control Codes On Worker Termination" and "Privilege Restriction Based On The Need-to-Know." A: M; E: LMH.

1133. Maintenance Of List Showing Those Permitted To Grant Physical Access

Policy: A list of managers who are authorized to grant access to Company X premises must be kept up-to-date. This list must also be periodically reviewed by the higher-level managers who delegated authority to these managers.

Commentary: The objective of this policy is to establish a clear hierarchy showing the delegation of authority regarding granting of physical access. The managers mentioned in the first sentence are the ones who, on a day-to-day basis, actually authorize certain workers to gain access to restricted areas. The "higher-level managers" mentioned in the second sentence are the ones who decided which managers would make the day-to-day decisions. The existence of a clear and up-to-date delegation of authority will prevent demoted, transferred, terminated, or otherwise no-longer-authorized managers from misusing their authority. Likewise, the existence of this hierarchy will focus attention on the appropriate rights to grant various managers, thereby helping to ensure that the rights actually granted are commensurate with business needs. A foundation of basic physical security (including the policies found in this section) is necessary for many information security controls to work properly. See the policies entitled "Granting System Privileges By Chain Of Authority Delegation," "All Production Transactions Must Be Authorized By Management," and "Periodic Identification Badge Reports Issued To Department Heads." A: M; E: LMH.

1134. Periodic Identification Badge Reports Issued To Department Heads

Policy: Every department head must receive a monthly listing of all persons in their area who currently have authorized identification badges. Department heads must promptly report to the Security Department all enabled badges which are no longer needed.

Commentary: The intention of this policy is to force the issuance and review of a report reflecting currently authorized badges. This will in turn help to identify and eliminate expired badges which have not yet had the associated privileges revoked. If unauthorized persons are permitted to gain access to Company X premises, then the security of the information found in these premises will be unduly at risk. The process of generating and reviewing a report can also be effectively used with computer user-IDs, telephone credit cards, and other access mechanisms. The report mentioned pertains to all types of workers (employees, consultants, contractors, temporaries, etc.), and this is why the term "in their area" is used. Also see the policies entitled "Maintenance Of List Showing Those Permitted To Grant Physical Access," "Periodic Review And Reauthorization Of User Access Privileges," and "Access To Secret Information Granted On Individual (Not Group) Basis." A: M; E: LMH.

3.1.1.3. Handling Visitors

1135. Identification And Sign-In Process Required For All Visitors

Policy: All visitors must show picture identification and sign-in prior to gaining access to restricted areas controlled by Company X. Visitors must be admitted to Company X premises only for specific authorized purposes.

Commentary: The objective of this policy is to require that all visitors (even employees from different locations) show definitive identification proving who they are before they are permitted to enter restricted areas. This will discourage unauthorized persons from masquerading as though they are authorized. It will also help ensure that a log showing who entered/left the restricted area (the so-called "sign-in" process) is accurate and reflects the actual identity of the individuals involved. If the organization considers the display of picture identification to be too intrusive, it may scale the policy back, requiring only the sign-in process. If only the sign-in process is used for most people, then access can be restricted to those who had appointments; all others may be required to show identification. Separately, the policy could be modified to require both sign-in and sign-out with a time/date for both. The advantage of requiring a sign-out is that if there is an emergency like a fire or an incident such as a theft, management will be able to readily determine who was, or who still is in the building. Another objective of this policy is that it discourages employees from bringing their family and friends into the office (thus avoiding unauthorized information disclosure and possible damage to property). On another note, this policy is intended to be used with an escort policy such as "Escorts Required For All Visitors." Also see the policies entitled "No 'Piggybacking' Through Controlled Doors Permitted" and "Positive Identification Required For System Usage." A: E; E: LMH.

1136. Escorts Required For All Visitors

Policy: Visitors to Company X offices must be escorted at all times by an authorized employee, consultant, or contractor. This means that an escort is required as soon as a visitor enters a controlled area, and until this same visitor goes outside the controlled area. Visitors requiring an escort include customers, former employees, worker family members, equipment repair contractors, package delivery company staff, and police officers.

Commentary: The intention of this policy is to prevent unauthorized persons from gaining access to confidential, proprietary, or private information while inside a controlled area such as an office. They may, for example, simply read a memo that happens to be sitting on a worker's desk. If visitors are escorted, their actions can be supervised and such unauthorized disclosures prevented. This policy also helps to prevent theft of office property like modems and personal property like handbags. This policy works best if toilets are located right off of the reception area; if visitors must go through controlled doors to reach toilets, then they may be able to thwart the escort policy because a receptionist will not be allowed to leave his/her post. See the policies entitled "No 'Piggybacking' Through Controlled Doors Permitted," "Third Party Supervision In Areas Containing Sensitive Information," and "Identification And Sign-In Process Required For All Visitors." A: EM; E: MH.

1137. Escorts Required For All Visitors Outside Normal Business Hours

Policy: Visitors must be escorted by an employee authorized by a department manager whenever they are in Company X offices or facilities outside of normal business hours.

Commentary: The objective of this policy is to prevent visitors from roaming around offices and facilities outside of normal business hours, and perhaps obtaining confidential information, stealing valuable items, placing wiretaps, or otherwise engaging in unauthorized activities. Outside normal business hours there will be many fewer people to notice that a visitor is doing something unauthorized. This policy also only allows an authorized employee to be an escort, thus preventing contractors, consultants, and temporaries from being an escort (the latter three categories are generally less trusted). Note that this policy does not prevent deliveries at a shipping dock, building remodeling or reconstruction, and similar activities -- it only dictates that these activities be performed in the presence of an authorized employee. Separately, the policy does permit visitors to move unimpeded within certain areas during normal business hours, and thus keeps worker productivity high since no escort is required during those hours. In high-security organizations, automatic electronic tracking of visitor movements (generally with proximity badges) could be used in place of an escort, and if this approach was followed, then the policy would need to be modified to reflect this modern approach. For similar ideas, see the policy entitled "Security Violations Requiring Instant Terminations" and "Unescorted Visitors In Restricted Areas Must Be Challenged." A: EM; E: LMH.

1138. Third Party Supervision In Areas Containing Sensitive Information

Policy: Individuals who are neither Company X employees, nor authorized contractors, nor authorized consultants, must be supervised whenever they are in restricted areas containing sensitive information.
Commentary: The intention of this policy is to ensure that third parties, whose motivations are largely unknown, are not permitted to roam unescorted in areas containing sensitive information. If these people are permitted unsupervised access, industrial espionage, privacy violation, equipment theft, and other problems may occur. For example, a technician installing a DSL (Digital Subscriber Line) connection should, under this policy, be escorted at all times when in restricted areas. Separately, this policy could be expanded to include "valuable, or critical" information, not just "sensitive" information. This policy is a "watered-down" (less stringent) version of the policy entitled "Escorts Required For All Visitors." Also see the policy entitled "Individuals Without Identification Badges Must Be Challenged." A: EM; E: MH.

1139. Individuals Without Identification Badges Must Be Challenged

Policy: Individuals without a proper Company X identification badge in a clearly visible place must be immediately questioned about their badge. If they cannot promptly produce a valid badge, they must be escorted to the receptionist desk.

Commentary: The purpose of this policy is to ensure that everyone wears their badge at all times when inside a restricted area. All authorized people must wear badges when inside restricted areas; if they don't there is no way to readily determine who is authorized and who is not. Physical security is a necessary prerequisite to information security; if an organization cannot control who is inside restricted areas, then controlling information security is going to be very difficult, if not impossible. On another note, this policy can be made into a game if certain employees occasionally go without a badge, and then those people who challenge them receive a $100 bill on the spot. On another note, some organizations will want to add another sentence to the policy which says that if someone is concerned about their physical safety after a challenge, an acceptable alternative is to immediately call the Physical Security Department. Also see the policies entitled "Unescorted Visitors In Restricted Areas Must Be Challenged" and "Temporary Badges For Workers Who Have Forgotten Their Badges." A: E; E: MH.

1140. Removal Of Badges After Leaving Company X Facilities

Policy: Immediately after workers leave Company X facilities, they must remove their identification badges and store them in a safe and convenient place away from public view.

Commentary: The intention of this policy is to prevent workers from walking around town with their badges on, in the process indirectly notifying everybody that they work for Company X. Keeping a badge on in public may attract corporate spies or hackers, who are intent on obtaining information from the involved worker. Thus wearing a badge in public needlessly makes workers a target. This policy is especially important for those organizations who wish to have their personnel remain anonymous (the Central Intelligence Agency, the National Security Agency, etc.). Wearing a badge in public is also gauche and it implies that the worker involved is unconscious about his or her circumstances. This policy additionally foster awareness about the correct placement of a badge and how its placement corresponds to the physical location of a worker (wearing it visibly when on the premises, safely putting it away when away from the premises). For related ideas, see the policies entitled "Guards Or Receptionists For Areas Containing Sensitive Information" and "Security Guard Escort For Workers Who Are Involuntarily Terminated." A: E; E: H.

1141. Handling Badges When Workers Are Away From Company X Facilities

Policy: When off Company X premises, workers must protect their identification badges with the same level of protection as their wallets and credit cards.

Commentary: The intention of this policy is to emphasize that Company X identification badges are valuable, that badges need protection comparable to a wallet, and that workers are expected to protect their badges from theft and/or unauthorized use. In too many situations, workers leave their badges in unlocked cars (for example on the dashboard) or in other locations where the badges are visible and could easily be stolen. Separately, an intruder intent on gaining access to Company X facilities seeks to get a badge and analyze its components in order to determine how to make a counterfeit. If the intruder cannot put his or her hands on an existing badge, this counterfeit making process will be that much harder. Likewise, if the badge technology being used is not sophisticated, an intruder may be able to remove the existing picture and insert his or her own image into the card. On another note, the policy writer should notice that this policy is deliberately technology-neutral. The policy doesn't even require that a photo-ID badge system be used at the organization in question. For related considerations, see the policies entitled "Individuals Without Identification Badges Must Be Challenged" and "Guards Or Receptionists For Areas Containing Sensitive Information." A: E; E: MH.

1142. Unescorted Visitors In Restricted Areas Must Be Challenged

Policy: Whenever a worker notices an unescorted visitor inside Company X restricted areas, the visitor must be immediately questioned about the purpose for being in restricted areas. The visitor must then be directly accompanied to either a reception desk, a guard station, or the person they came to see.

Commentary: This "challenge" policy is intended to prevent unauthorized people from roaming around controlled areas where sensitive, proprietary, or private information is handled. It helps to make sure that only authorized persons wearing proper identification badges are in restricted areas. The policy is applicable to those environments where badges are required, as well as smaller office environments without badges where everybody knows everyone else. If this policy is too harsh, it can instead require workers to ask third parties "Can I help you?" If workers are in potential physical danger, they can alternatively call the Physical Security Department rather than directly confronting a strange or menacing person in the area. Also see the policies entitled "No 'Piggybacking' Through Controlled Doors Permitted," "Escorts Required For All Visitors," and "Badges Must Be Worn In Visible Places When In Company X Premises." A: EM; E: MH.

1143. No Visitors Allowed In Data Center Or Information Systems Department

Policy: Visitors who don't need to perform maintenance on Company X equipment, or who otherwise don't absolutely need to be inside the Data Center or the Information Systems Department, are prohibited from entering these same areas. Customers, investors, auditors, and all other visitors can instead view worker activities through the picture windows provided.

Commentary: The intention of this policy is to prevent visitors from learning trade secrets, from stealing system manuals which could be used to break into information systems, from sabotaging equipment, from placing bombs, and from otherwise engaging in activities which would be harmful to Company X. In order to perform these acts, physical access is often required. Separately, the policy acknowledges that certain visitors (computer vendor maintenance personnel for example) must have physical access, and for these people a perpetual escort can be employed. All other visitors can use a picture window which opens to an internal hallway to get a rough idea of what is going on. This policy can be very impressive to visitors because it shows that management is more concerned about security than public relations and marketing. For related ideas, see the policies entitled "Unescorted Visitors In Restricted Areas Must Be Challenged" and "Escorts Required For All Visitors Outside Normal Business Hours." A: EMT; E: H.

3.1.2. Restricted Access To Computer Facilities

1144. All Workstations Must Use Metal Keys To Control Access

Policy: All Company X desktop workstations must employ a metal key lock to control access to authorized persons. A copy of this key must be provided to the department manager.

Commentary: This relatively old-fashioned policy may nonetheless still be used as an adjunct to software-based access controls such as a boot protection mechanism which employs fixed passwords. The intention of this policy is to prevent unauthorized parties from gaining access to workstations, which may have sensitive information stored thereon. The trouble with this approach is that users will lose or forget their metal keys, in which case they may be prevented from using their workstations. This is why a backup key is provided to the department manager (as well as for investigations, duress terminations, and related situations). On a separate note, the word "desktop" was used in the policy to exempt portable computers such as handhelds and palmtops. Because they didn't come with a key from the manufacturer, in order to implement this policy, some computers may need separate security products which use a metal key and which cover the keyboard, floppy drive slot, or other components. Depending on the configuration of the locking mechanism, some keys can also be used to prevent unauthorized people from opening the computer's case, thereby preventing theft of components such as modems and memory. For related ideas, see the policies entitled "Locking File Cabinets Must Be Provided To And Used By All Workers" and "All Workstations Must Have Password-Based Boot Protection." A: E; E: LMH.

1145. Computer & Communications Equipment Rack Doors Must Be Locked

Policy: All doors on computer and communications equipment racks located in the computer center must be kept locked unless an authorized technician is actively engaged in repair, maintenance, or reconfiguration activities.

Commentary: The intention of this policy is to establish another layer of physical access control over computer equipment located within the protected confines of a computer data center. In many organizations, a large number of people are permitted inside a data center. These include programmers picking up their output, computer operators hanging tapes, computer performance analysts measuring system characteristics, etc. While it's desirable to keep the number of people in a computer room to a minimum to reduce opportunities for sabotage and other types of abuse, sometimes that is not practical or it is not politically expedient. Two alternatives then open up: add additional walls or locking metal cages to segment the computer room into different zones each with their own security level, or lock the cabinets which house production equipment. This policy speaks to the latter option. A policy about locking metal cage doors or regular wall doors inside the data center could be written in much the same format as this policy. For related ideas, consult the policies entitled "Locking File Cabinets Must Be Provided To And Used By All Workers" and "Security Requirements For Work At Home Arrangements." A: T; E: MH.

1146. Internet Commerce & Financial Systems Must Be Physically Isolated

Policy: All Internet commerce servers and equipment (such as firewalls), as well as those systems that handle wire transfers and other financial activities, must be physically isolated and secured in a manner that is separate from other computers occupying the same computer center.

Commentary: The intention of this policy is to segregate and separately protect the computers which handle digitized money, in an effort to reduce the possibility of fraud. If computer operators are able to reboot a server, they are likely to be able to change the access controls, change the operating system parameters, or in some other way compromise the security of the system. Permitting physical access to these systems may also allow unauthorized parties to steal backup tapes which may contain credit card numbers, checking account numbers, or other information which could be used to commit fraud. This policy thus acknowledges that some level of physical security is necessary before real information security can be achieved. This policy assumes that a computer center is locked and that only a restricted number of people are given access to that area. This policy provides a further level of physical access control beyond the door to the computer center. The policy is fully consistent with Internet hosting service standard computer center design specifications, which for example employ locked metal cages to separate the machines of various subscribers. But even if a firm does its own hosting, the Internet commerce and related financial servers should still be placed in a separate secured room, or in some other way physically isolated from the rest of the machines in the computer center. For related idea, see the policies entitled "Equipment Isolation Between Company X And Third Party Systems" and "Critical Or Sensitive Activities Permitted Only In Physically Secure Areas." A: T; E: MH.

1147. Equipment Isolation Between Company X And Third Party Systems

Policy: Computer and communications equipment managed by Company X staff must be physically isolated from equipment managed by third parties.

Commentary: The objective of this policy is to prevent third parties from gaining unnecessary access to Company X computer and communications equipment. Physical access can allow unauthorized persons to reboot the operating system (which could then allow them to take over the access control system), steal magnetic media such as backup tapes, and to sabotage equipment. If equipment is commingled in a data center, then third parties must be in the same room where Company X managed equipment is located. But if separate rooms are used, then physical access controls (usually employing magnetic stripe card readers) can be used to prevent where third parties can go. Separate rooms need not be employed; a metal locking cage can be used, or glass partitions to an existing room can be added. This policy is relevant, for example, where Company X has equipment resident in an Internet commerce hosting firm's data center. Note that physical access controls for Company X managed equipment may be a prerequisite to using remote network management tools as well as to establishing lights-out operations. For related ideas, see the policies entitled "Physical Security Measures For Computers & Communications Systems," "Backup Media Stored In Separate Fire Zones From Originating Machine," and " Multi-User Computer Or Communications Systems In Locked Rooms." A: T; E: LMH.

1148. Physical Security Measures For Computers & Communications Systems

Policy: Buildings which house Company X computers or communications systems must be protected with physical security measures that prevent unauthorized persons from gaining access.

Commentary: The intention of this policy is to ensure that rudimentary physical security measures are used to protect both computers and communications systems. This will in turn prevent equipment theft, unauthorized system use, and other information security related problems. Because they are so often inadequately protected, the policy is particularly relevant to microcomputers (PCs), workstations, LANs, and client/server systems, although it applies to all types of information systems. The policy is particularly important because smaller computers and office equipment are often protected only by physical security measures. The policy could be restricted to those computer systems handling critical and/or sensitive information, but is ideally left as it stands with a wider scope. Also see the policies entitled "Guards Or Receptionists For Areas Containing Sensitive Information" and "Physical Security Or Encryption Required For All Sensitive Information." A: MT; E: LMH.

1149. Critical Or Sensitive Activities Permitted Only In Physically Secure Areas

Policy: All critical or sensitive Company X information handling activities must take place in areas that are physically secured and protected against unauthorized access, interference, and damage.

Commentary: The intention of this policy is to ensure that local management has suitable physical access controls for computer centers, telephone call centers, archival file vaults, and other places where critical or sensitive information is handled. The actual technologies to be used are deliberately not stated in the policy because local management should decide (and internal auditors should concur). The actual physical security technologies should be a function of the criticality, value, and/or sensitivity of the information, as well as the location of the site. The emphasis in this policy is on information rather than equipment, and for that reason, this policy has a broader scope than the policy entitled "Physical Security Measures For Computers & Communications Systems." Also see the policy entitled "Secret Information Must Not Leave Company X Offices In Any Form." A: MT; E: LMH.

1150. Computer Center Is A Closed Shop

Policy: Company X computer centers are closed shops. Programmers, users, and others without a business need for such access are not permitted inside computer machine rooms.

Commentary: The term "closed shop" means that the doors are locked and that programmers, users, and others who do not have a need to be inside the machine room do not get access. The objective of this policy is to physically enforce separation of duties between computer operators on one hand and programmers and users on the other. The policy also helps to reduce congestion and confusion in the machine room. The policy also indirectly prohibits visitors taking tours, which in turn increases security. On another note, the policy could be rewritten so the words "computer centers" are replaced by "computer centers containing minicomputers, mainframes, and/or network control systems." Separately, this policy is not generally applied to departmental systems, client/server systems, or local area network (LAN) servers, although it could be. Note that this policy is a physical interpretation of the policy entitled "Privilege Restriction Based On The Need-To-Know." Also see the policies entitled "Separation Of Duties And Control Over Company X Assets," "Authorization For Changes To Production Data And Programs," and "Restricted Access To Magnetic Tape, Disk, And Documentation Libraries." A: MT; E: LMH.

1151. Computer Center Authorized Staff Access List Reviewed Quarterly

Policy: The list of authorized staff members who are permitted inside the computer center must be reviewed and updated by the Computer Operations Manager quarterly. Only those staff members who have a legitimate business need to be in the computer center may be granted access.

Commentary: The intention of this policy is to establish a mechanism whereby management will periodically review the list of authorized people who may enter the computer center. In all too many computer shops, management doesn't even know who is permitted in the computer center and who is not. Having a quarterly review will help to get people who no longer work there deleted from the access list, just as it will help to get people who have transferred to another department removed from this same list. While many organizations pay a lot of attention to who gets into the building (badges, guards, etc.), many fewer organizations really scrutinize who can get into the data center and the reasons why data center access should be granted. See the policies entitled "Computer Center Is A Closed Shop" and "Physical Security Measures For Computers & Communications Systems." A: T; E: MH.

1152. Centralization Of All Critical Voice And Data Networking Devices

Policy: All business critical devices supporting the Company X telephone system, intranet, local area networks, and the wide area network must be centralized in dedicated rooms with physical access controls, closed circuit TV, environmental monitoring systems, and other security measures indicated by the Information Security Manager.

Commentary: The intention of this policy is to deny unauthorized people physical access to voice and data networking devices such as PBXs, hubs, and routers. This will in turn make it significantly more difficult for them to place wiretapping devices, and it will make it more difficult for them to sabotage these systems. Because networking systems are used by so many people, they are a favorite target for saboteurs (who may also be on the payroll). The policy also counters the tendency to place these devices throughout an office, subjecting them to a variety of unnecessary dangers such as spilled coffee and jostling by people passing by. Note that this policy will increase cabling costs. Separately, the policy's scope could be expanded to include all servers or multi-user computers. On another note, the policy assumes the word "critical" has been formally defined through a contingency planning effort. For related ideas, see the policies entitled "Multi-User Computer Or Communications Systems In Locked Rooms" and "Physical Access Control For Areas Containing Sensitive Information." A: T; E: LMH.

1153. Restricted Access To Magnetic Tape, Disk, And Documentation Libraries

Policy: The magnetic tape, disk, and documentation libraries are controlled areas within the computer center. Access must be restricted to workers whose job responsibilities require their presence in these libraries.

Commentary: The intention of this policy is to physically restrict access to areas containing sensitive, valuable, or critical information (the libraries). This will in turn reduce the chance that such information will be disclosed, manipulated, deleted or otherwise handled in a manner which is not in keeping with management intentions. This policy is a specific manifestation of the separation of duties principle. Reference to the "computer center" could be changed to "computer centers containing minicomputers, mainframes, and/or network control systems" or some other organization-specific system descriptions. The storage media could also be changed to reflect whatever Company X happens to be using (magneto-optical disks, CD-ROMs, etc.). See the policies entitled "Separation Of Duties And Control Over Company X Assets" and "Computer Center Is A Closed Shop." A: MT; E: MH.

1154. Vacated Equipment Areas Must Be Locked And Periodically Checked

Policy: All information systems equipment areas that are vacated must be locked and periodically checked by either remote monitoring systems and/or a security guard.

Commentary: This policy is in part motivated by insurance requirements, which in this case are a reflection of good information systems management. Locking the premises will prevent industrial spies, disgruntled ex-employees, and curious neighbors from gaining entrance. Checking the premises ordinarily involves confirming that all doors are locked and that everything seems to be secured (red lights indicate fire alarms are working, intrusion detection systems panels indicate normal status, etc.). This policy doesn't apply only to data centers, it is equally applicable to offices which have desktop personal computers (PCs). Adoption of and implementation of this policy may allow an organization to lower its insurance premiums (so-called premium rating). Also see the policy entitled "Computer Center Is A Closed Shop." A: MT; E: MH.

1155. Locked Communications Equipment Areas And Escorted Access

Policy: Telephone closets, network router and hub rooms, voicemail system rooms, and similar areas containing communications equipment must be kept locked at all times. Visitor access to these areas must be provided only with an authorized technical staff escort who monitors all work being performed.

Commentary: The objective of this policy is primarily to prevent third parties from placing wiretaps in Company X communications areas. The policy is also intended to prevent unauthorized persons from damaging or interfering with critical equipment needed to perform business activities. Thus, disgruntled employees will find it more difficult to damage or interfere with these highly complicated systems if the areas are off-limits. The use of an escort will further deter unauthorized activity because every action will be watched. While the use of an escort may at first seem to be a waste of valuable technical staff time, it is important that internal staff knows what was done, why it was done, and how to reverse any changes that were made. While accompanying a visitor, the escort can thus fill out change control paperwork at the same time that a visiting technician is doing the work. For related considerations, see the policies entitled "Network Ports In Vacant Offices Must Be Promptly Disabled" and "Intermediate Holding Area Required To Restrict Computer Room Access." A: T; E: H.

1156. Public Tours Of Computer Facilities Prohibited

Policy: Public tours of major computer and communications facilities are prohibited.

Commentary: The intention of this policy is to eliminate public tours, which can be a covert means for industrial spies, hackers, disgruntled employees, and others intent on doing harm to gain access to restricted areas. Individuals such as these have been known to pick up information while on a tour, which was then instrumental in subsequent compromises of system access controls. Other individuals have used their proximity to computer and communications equipment while on a tour to sabotage systems. The policy does not prevent private tours, such as those for employees, consultants, and/or contractors who have a business need-to-know about the facilities. Likewise, this policy does not prevent tours for top management, investors, stockholders, important customers, and the like. However, educational tours and tours for tourists are prohibited. In years gone past, part of the unauthorized access via tours problem was generated by management's pride in their "glass house" containing expensive equipment. Now that computers are no longer special and unusual devices, and now that management appreciates the merits of a "low profile" approach, they are much less likely to permit public tours. Also see the policies entitled "Privilege Restriction Based On The Need-to-Know," "No Signs Indicating Location Of Computer Or Communications Center," and "Badges Must Be Worn In Visible Places When In Company X Premises." A: EMT; E: LMH.

1157. Cameras Plus Audio Or Video Recording Equipment Prohibited

Policy: Within the controlled perimeters of Company X offices, personally owned cameras and audio or video recording equipment is not allowed.

Commentary: This policy is intended to prevent cameras, plus audio or video recording equipment, from being used to capture confidential information. Confidential information may include the physical shape of a new product, or even the building lay-out for a data processing facility. Prohibiting such equipment reduces the chances that it will be used to capture confidential information on black boards or white boards, exchanged in a conversation, or expressed in a memo laying on a staff member's desk. Some organizations will wish to post a sign at the guard's desk to this effect. If a camera, or audio or video recording equipment has been used in violation of this policy, the physical security department could remove the film (destroying the information) or else confiscate the film and have it developed, and later return the materials which are not specific to Company X. On another note, the words "personally owned" appear in a comparable policy used by the US National Security Agency (NSA), but the author prefers the words "not authorized by the Information Security Department." This policy was publicly discussed due to fears about bringing a smart toy called a Furby into NSA offices. Furby dolls have a microphone built into them but it turns out that the dolls only use the microphone to initiate predefined activity, not to turn on or otherwise work with an audio recording device. Nonetheless, to be on the safe side, the NSA bans Furbys from secure areas. For related policies, see the policy entitled "Special Paper Preventing Copying Of Sensitive Documents" and "Positioning Of Computer Display Screens With Respect To Windows." A: EMT; E: H.

1158. Printers, Copiers, & Fax Machines Banned From Secret Information Areas

Policy: To prevent unauthorized removal of secret information, all printers, copiers, and fax machines are banned from the physically isolated zones within Company X offices that contain secret information.

Commentary: The intention of this policy is to prevent people from making paper copies, from printing computer resident information, and from otherwise removing hardcopy versions of secret information. If the devices to perform this process are not provided within a secured area (which may have only diskless workstations), then those people who seek to make unauthorized copies will be thwarted in their efforts. All other avenues through which secret information could flow must also be blocked -- for example an isolated local area network could be used to prevent users from sending the secret information out over the Internet as part of an email message. The very high security approach reflected in this policy works best if the movement of paper-resident secret information is strictly controlled, perhaps with sensors which detect that it has been removed from an isolated area. This policy also helps to create a paperless office, which when deployed in high security areas has the potential to be more secure than any paper-based office could ever be. For related ideas, see the policies entitled "Diskless Workstations Must Be Used By R&D Department Workers" and "Telecommuting Data Entry Operators Must Employ Thin Clients." A: MT; E: H.

3.2. Computer Location And Facility Construction

1159. Location Of New Computer Or Communications Centers

Policy: All new Company X computer or communications centers must be located in an area unlikely to experience natural disasters, serious man-made accidents (chemical spills, dangerous release of nuclear materials, etc.), riots, and related problems.

Commentary: The intention of this policy is to force management to consider the consequences in advance of locating a computer or communications center in a dangerous area. All too often a decision is made to locate a facility and only later are the serious risks appreciated. In effect, this policy requires management to prepare a security impact statement (not far different from what Americans call an "environmental impact statement"). Although it could be clarified, the phrase "computer or communications centers" is deliberately kept vague, thus giving the policy a general applicability which may extend to departmental systems, local area network (LAN) servers, client/server systems, and other smaller systems. Also see the policies entitled "Redundant Supplies For Public Utility Resources" and "Computer And Communications Facility Location Within A Building." A: MT; E: LMH.

1160. Redundant Supplies For Public Utility Resources

Policy: All new Company X computer or communications centers must be located such that they have ready access to two electrical power substations and two telephone central offices.

Commentary: This policy is intended to establish a minimum design objective for the individuals who are designing new computer or communications centers. The policy specifies that redundant sources of supply for public utilities must be employed. Water could be included in this policy, but it is rarely required to support computer and communications systems anymore (except for so-called "legacy" or mainframe systems which use it for cooling). Besides, water can be stockpiled much more easily and inexpensively than electrical power (a company swimming pool is a possibility). The policy could be enhanced to incorporate an additional provision which states that the lines for electricity and telephone services must run on separate poles and/or through separate conduits. Without this separate routing requirement, a backhoe or a crane could cut both supply lines. See the policy entitled "Location Of New Computer Or Communications Centers." A: MT; E: LMH.

1161. Adequate Construction For Computer Or Communications Centers

Policy: New and remodeled Company X computer or communications centers must be constructed so that they are protected against fire, water damage, vandalism, and other threats known to occur, or that are likely to occur at the involved locations.

Commentary: The purpose of this policy is to force those responsible for building new and remodeled computer or communications centers to consider local security risks in advance of construction. For example, several computer centers located near the Mississippi river in the United States were not built to withstand a major flood such as those experienced in 1994. The policy is a specific construction-oriented version of the standard of due care; see the policy entitled "Control Implementations Consistent With Standard Of Due Care." Also see the policy entitled "Location Of New Computer Or Communications Centers." A: MT; E: LMH.

1162. Computer And Communications Facility Location Within A Building

Policy: To minimize theft and water damage, multi-user computers and communications facilities must be located above the first floor in buildings. To minimize potential damage from smoke and fire, kitchen facilities should be located away from (including not directly above or below) multi-user systems. Likewise, to minimize potential water damage, rest room facilities should not be located directly above these systems. To minimize potential damage from bombs, and to minimize unauthorized electromagnetic eavesdropping and interference, these systems must be separated from the building's exterior wall by an additional internal wall. Likewise, to prevent authorized entry as well as remote information observation, there must be no windows to these facilities.

Commentary: The intention of this policy is to provide guidance for those responsible for the location of a multi-user computer facility within a building. Many of the managers responsible for locating computer centers do not consider these matters, and problems are encountered after the installation is complete. At least the awareness of these problems will help management install other controls which would reduce or eliminate losses, even if the location of a computer center did not change. This policy may be changed to be a series of construction guidelines rather than a policy per se. See the policies entitled "Positioning Of Computer Display Screens With Respect To Windows" and "Location Of New Computer Or Communications Centers." A: MT; E: LMH.

1163. Computer Equipment Locations Must Have Water Damage Precautions

Policy: All Company X locations which house computer and communications equipment must meet minimum water damage prevention requirements as well as minimum water damage alarm precautions which have been established by the Information Security Department. These include being above ground level, being above flood levels of nearby rivers and sewers, having adequate drainage, and not being situated immediately below water tanks or water pipes.

Commentary: The objective of this policy is to establish some minimum standards for computer and communications equipment protection against water damage. Because this type of equipment is powered by electricity, there is a danger of staff member electrocution in addition to severe damage to equipment if it gets wet while power is still applied. Likewise, even if the power is off, many types of computer equipment (like disk drives) are so finely calibrated that any significant amount of dirt, dust, or rust that gets into the equipment via water would cause it to malfunction, even if the equipment has been dried out completely. These are some of the reasons why many installations use chemical fire suppression systems like Halon and/or carbon dioxide rather than water sprinklers. The policy was deliberately silent about sprinklers, allowing an Information Security Department to make a decision as it deems appropriate. For related ideas, see the policies entitled "Continuous Computer Center Staffing For Prompt Problem Resolution" and "Fire, Water, And Physical Intrusion Alarms Trigger Immediate Action." A: T; E: LMH.

1164. Intermediate Holding Area Required To Restrict Computer Room Access

Policy: A secured intermediate holding area must be used for computer supplies, equipment, and other deliveries. Delivery personnel must not be able to directly access rooms containing multi-user computer facilities.

Commentary: The intention of this policy is to protect computer rooms from unauthorized access, such as from delivery service personnel. For example, loading dock doors should not open directly to the computer room. By restricting the movement of materials, this policy also helps bolster access controls to a computer room. The policy furthermore helps keep the risk of fire down by requiring that paper and other supplies be stored elsewhere than in the computer room (there have been many reported cases of printing paper spontaneously catching fire). Keeping these materials out of the computer room also helps reduce the exposure of systems to paper dust, cleaning fluids, and other potentially dangerous substances. This policy is also in support of a separate Receiving Department, that will inspect and account for shipments received. The Receiving Department will then help transport the goods to the locations in need of these goods. Separately, this policy helps stop the all-too-common practice where high-value goods are stored in a computer machine room because that is one of the few physically-secured places available. See the policy entitled "Default To Denial Of Access Control Privileges." A: MT; E: LMH.

1165. No Signs Indicating Location Of Computer Or Communications Center

Policy: There must be no signs indicating the location of computer or communications centers.

Commentary: This policy means that organization name signs, communications center signs, computer room signs, Information Systems Department signs, technical support group signs, and the like should not be visible from public areas. The policy is intended to prevent terrorist attack or sabotage. Besides preventing physical attack, the absence of signs may also help prevent attacks on data (such as wiretapping). A problem with this approach is that employees and others will often be confused and will need to ask for directions or be escorted. Accordingly, receptionists and others must not be so polite that the intent of the policy is entirely undone. For a related idea, see the policy entitled "Public Tours Of Computer Facilities Prohibited." A: M; E: LMH.

1166. Computer Center Fire Resistance And Self-Closing Openings

Policy: Fire walls surrounding computer facilities must be non-combustible and resistant to fire for at least one hour. All openings to these walls (doors, ventilation ducts, etc.) should be self-closing and likewise rated at least one hour.

Commentary: The intention of this policy is to clearly specify a minimum acceptable fire resistance construction for computer centers. The same could apply to communications facilities, such as a network control center. Openings such as ventilation ducts can be self-closing, and doors can have automatic release latches that close them if a fire alarm is initiated. Fire is the most common cause of a major disaster at computer centers, and often a fire starts in adjacent areas, then spreading to the computer center. If adequate fire resistance is built into the premises, the likelihood that a fire is put out before major damage is caused will be increased. Note that "fire walls" (two words), as used here, deal with physical facility construction matters, whereas Internet "firewalls" (one word) deal with logical access control matters. See the policy entitled "Smoking, Eating and Drinking In The Computer Machine Room." A: MT; E: LMH.

1167. Computer Facilities And Doors Resistant To Forcible Entry

Policy: Computer facility rooms must be equipped with riot doors, fire doors, and other doors resistant to forcible entry.

Commentary: A number of terrorists have rammed computer room doors down before setting the place on fire, taking hostages, or doing some other nefarious acts. The intent of this policy is to make sure that the doors to a computer room provide adequate protection for the expensive equipment contained therein. In many offices, there is no locked door to computer facilities (particularly where small systems like local area network (LAN) servers are located). The policy can be expanded to include the requirement that such doors automatically unlock whenever there is a fire alarm, and/or whenever there is an emergency need for someone on the inside to get out. The policy could be expanded to include communications facilities, such as network management centers. Also see the policies entitled "Computer Center Fire Resistance And Self-Closing Openings" and "Computer Facilities And Automatically Closing Doors." A: M; E: LMH.

1168. Computer Facilities And Automatically Closing Doors

Policy: Computer facility rooms must be equipped with doors that automatically close immediately after they have been opened, and which set off an audible alarm when they have been kept open beyond a certain period of time.

Commentary: The requirements embodied in this policy prevent people from propping doors open with chairs, books, etc., so that others can enter. Such doors help to ensure that the physical access control that management intended is actually being used (and that worker entrances and exits are being recorded in a log). These doors have been shown to be very effective when it comes to forcing people to use a physical access control system. The policy could be expanded to include communications facilities, such as network management centers. Also see the policies entitled "Computer Center Fire Resistance And Self-Closing Openings" and "Computer Facilities And Doors Resistant To Forcible Entry." A: M; E: LMH.

1169. Secondary Computer Center Doors Must Have Alarmed Crash Bars

Policy: All secondary computer center doors must be equipped with crash bars which allow the occupants to quickly exit in the event of an emergency, but also set-off a loud battery-powered alarm when they are opened.

Commentary: This policy specifies construction standards for computer centers including network operations centers. It states that all secondary doors, i.e., doors besides a main entrance, must have crash bars. Now a standard part of data center hardware, these crash bars will signal an audible alarm even if the power to the computer center is out. In this way the crash bars can alert staff on duty that a door has been opened and that an unauthorized person may be gaining access to restricted areas, or that expensive equipment or sensitive data storage media may be going out that door. For related considerations, see the policies entitled "Physical Access Control For Areas Containing Sensitive Information" and "Securing Sensitive Information In Unattended Rooms." A: T; E: MH.

1170. Computer-Assisted Equipment Tracking

Policy: All Company X computer and communications equipment must have a unique computer-readable identifier attached to it such that physical inventories can be efficiently and regularly conducted.

Commentary: Many information systems departments don't know exactly what equipment they own, lease, rent, or otherwise have control over. Having an up-to-date inventory of equipment is an important management tool for making various decisions like: (a) determining whether equipment has been stolen, (b) determining what equipment needs to be upgraded, and (c) planning network reconfigurations. Such inventories are especially useful when an employee is terminated (fired or sacked). In this case, there is often a dispute about what equipment the employee had in his/her possession and which of these pieces of equipment belong to the employer. The "unique identifier" mentioned in the policy can be a bar code, an optical character recognition mark, or some other computer-sensed marking. Ideally the mark is invisible to the naked eye, thus making its removal difficult. This policy is particularly relevant to inventories of microcomputers (PCs), workstations, fax machines, and other small office equipment. For related information, see the policies entitled "Formal Change Control Procedure Required For All Production Systems" and "Periodic Review Of Software Licensing Agreements." A: T; E: LMH.

1171. Marking Information Systems Equipment With Identification Codes

Policy: All Company X computer and communications equipment must have an identification number permanently etched onto the equipment. This code will assist police in their attempts to return the property to its rightful owner.

Commentary: The theft and illegal resale ("fencing") of computer and communications equipment has become a very large problem. Much of the lost and stolen equipment that has been recovered is never returned because law enforcement officials don't know to whom it belongs. New technologies for the marking of equipment with a social security number (SSN), a tax-related employer identification number (EIN), a telephone number, or some other unique number are now available. Many of these markings are invisible to the naked eye, so thieves are unlikely to make attempts to obscure the markings. Separately, these markings can also be used in the future as input data for databases describing stolen equipment. This policy is especially important for portables, laptops, and other mobile personal computers (PCs). On another note, the policy may be useful at the time of employee terminations, when it comes to determining the rightful owner of a piece of equipment. For a related idea, see the policy entitled "Computer-Assisted Equipment Tracking." A: T; E: LMH.

1172. Moving Microcomputer Equipment Without Approval Prohibited

Policy: Office computer equipment (desktop computers, fax machines, LAN servers, network hubs, etc.) must not be moved or relocated without the prior approval of the involved department manager. An exception will be provided for equipment for which a move approval form has been obtained (mobile computing equipment, telecommuter equipment, etc.).

Commentary: This policy seeks to prevent employees from stealing computer equipment, claiming they are using the equipment to perform business activities, when in fact they are not. It also helps maintain some semblance of change control in the small systems environment. It gives local management rather than a centralized Information Technology Department the ultimate say-so regarding the location and uses of small systems equipment. Separately, unauthorized movement of equipment may cause unanticipated problems such as network addressing problems, electrical wiring problems, fire hazards, ventilation problems, etc. For related ideas, see the policies entitled "Marking Information Systems Equipment With Identification Codes" and "Property Pass For Removal Of All Computer And Communications Gear." A: E; E: LMH.

1173. Fire, Water, And Physical Intrusion Alarms Trigger Immediate Action

Policy: All Company X computer centers must be equipped with fire, water, and physical intrusion alarm systems that automatically alert those who can take immediate action.

Commentary: The intention of this policy is to ensure that adequate alarm systems are included in all computer centers (the scope could be changed to include network operations centers as well). With the price of computers declining rapidly, production hardware is increasingly being stuck in closets or in regular offices which are not adequately protected by alarms. As the technology becomes more "rugged," the protective enclosures and related environmental systems that surround mainframes are not being used for smaller machines. Separately, in terms of "those who can take immediate action," the fire department could be called by a fire alarm. Likewise, a private guard service could be called if water was detected, and the police could be called if there were a physical intrusion. The building code specifications of these alarms is deliberately missing from the policy; the policy only says that these things must be in place. If the policy seems a bit expensive, it can be restricted so that it instead requires these alarms only for computer centers containing equipment which supports critical business activities, such as Internet commerce. Note also that fire, water, and physical intrusion alarms can be tied into a network management system (NMS). For related ideas, see the policies entitled "Property Pass For Removal Of All Computer And Communications Gear" and "Internet Connected Machines Must Have Intrusion Detection Systems." A: T; E: LMH.

1174. Positioning Of Computer Display Screens With Respect To Windows

Policy: The display screens for all microcomputers (PCs), workstations, and dumb terminals used to handle sensitive or valuable data must be positioned such that they cannot be readily viewed through a window, by persons walking in a hallway, or by persons waiting in reception and related public areas.

Commentary: The intention of this policy is to reduce the chance that unauthorized people will be able to view sensitive information displayed on a computer screen. A number of industrial espionage cases involved use of high-power telescopes to read material displayed on a screen through a window. On a more mundane level, many people gain access to sensitive or valuable information simply by being in the vicinity of a computer displaying this information (often by so called "shoulder surfing"). Some organizations may wish to extend this policy to include keyboards and keypads. If unauthorized persons can view typing at a keyboard or keypad they can recover the information that has been entered. Recently, organized criminals have been using binoculars and video cameras at airports to steal telephone credit card numbers. To prevent these abuses, workers can be instructed to cover the keypad with one hand while the other hand types in the numbers. The idea is nonetheless the same. A positive side effect of this policy is likely to be increased concern about unauthorized viewing on the part of those people who work on transportable computers (portables, notebooks, laptops, palmtops, etc.). This policy assumes the terms "sensitive and valuable" have been defined; see the policy entitled "Four Category Data Classification Scheme." For a related idea, see the policy entitled "Travelling On Public Transportation With Secret Information." A: EMT; E: LMH.

1175. Electromagnetic Radiation (Emanation) Protection For Secret Systems

Policy: Company X systems containing secret information must employ hardware which meets military standards for electromagnetic radiation (emanation) control. These systems must also be protected inside locked rooms encased with wire mesh or other electromagnetic radiation blocking materials as specified by military standards.

Commentary: This policy addresses a problem largely unknown in the non-military and non-diplomatic world: electromagnetic radiation generated by computer and network equipment. This type of radiation can be detected at significant distances and then converted into readable signals. For instance, the information appearing on a computer monitor can be picked up at 1,000 feet using relatively inexpensive equipment, even though there exists no line of sight connection with the involved monitor. The commercial world has ignored this problem, but will soon need to pay greater attention to it. Separately, the relevant military standards are country-specific, so they are not included in the policy provided here. On another note, this policy should apply only to the most sensitive types of information. To this end, rather than referring to "systems containing secret information," the policy could be rewritten to refer to "systems containing collections of security parameters (encryption keys, passwords, random number generator seeds, etc.)." For example, a credit card transaction processing company might apply this policy to the computers which store Personal Identification Numbers (PINs) for credit cards and debit cards.

IV. Sample High-Level Information Security Policy

Role Of Information And Information Systems: Company X is now critically dependent on both information and information systems. If important Company X information were disclosed to inappropriate persons, unavailable, or unreliable, the company could suffer serious losses or even go out of business. The good reputation that Company X enjoys is also directly linked with the way in which it manages both information and information systems. For example, if private customer information were to be publicly disclosed, the organization's reputation would be harmed. For these and other important business reasons, executive management working in conjunction with the Board of Directors has initiated and continues to support an information security effort. One part of that effort is definition of these information security policies.

Team Effort: To be effective, information security must be a team effort involving the participation and support of every Company X worker who deals with information and/or information systems. In recognition of the need for teamwork, this policy statement clarifies the responsibilities of users as well as the steps they must take to help protect Company X information and information systems. This document describes ways to prevent and respond to a variety of threats to information and information systems including unauthorized access, disclosure, duplication, modification, appropriation, destruction, loss, misuse, and denial of use.

Involved Persons: Every worker at Company X -- no matter what their status (employee, contractor, consultant, temporary, volunteer, intern, etc.) -- must comply with the information security policies found in this and related information security documents. Workers who deliberately violate this and other information security policy statements will be subject to disciplinary action up to and including termination.

Involved Systems: This policy applies to all computer and network systems owned by and/or administered by Company X. Similarly, this policy applies to all platforms (operating systems), all computer sizes (personal digital assistants through mainframes), and all application systems (whether developed in-house or purchased from third parties). The policy covers only information handled via computers and/or networks. Although this document includes mention of other manifestations of information such as voice and paper, it does not directly address the security of information in these forms. For information about the protection of information in paper form, see the Information Classification Policy [link to intranet page for that document goes here].

Primary Departments Working On Information Security: Guidance, direction, and authority for information security activities is centralized for all Company X organizational units in the Information Security Department [intranet link to Information Security Department mission statement]. The Information Security Department is responsible for establishing and maintaining organization-wide information security policies, standards, guidelines, and procedures. Compliance checking to ensure that organizational units are operating in a manner consistent with these requirements is the responsibility of the EDP Audit Unit within the Internal Audit Department [link to Internal Audit Department mission statement]. Investigations of system intrusions and other information security incidents is the responsibility of the Physical Security Department [link to Industrial Security Department mission statement]. Disciplinary matters resulting from violations of information security requirements are handled by local managers working in conjunction with the Human Resources Department [link to Human Resources Department mission statement].

Three Categories Of Responsibilities: To coordinate the team effort referred to above, Company X has established three categories, at least one of which applies to each worker. These categories are: Owner, Custodian, and User. These categories define general responsibilities with respect to information security. More detailed information about these responsibilities can be found in the Information Ownership Policy [link].

Owner Responsibilities: Information Owners are the Department Managers, Top Management, or their delegates within Company X who bear responsibility for the acquisition, development, and maintenance of production applications which process Company X information. Production applications are computer programs which regularly provide reports in support of decision making and other business activities. All production application system information must have a designated Owner. For each type of information, Owners designate the relevant sensitivity classification (described below), designate the appropriate level of criticality, define which users will be granted access, as well as approve requests for various ways in which the information will be utilized.

Custodian Responsibilities: Custodians are in physical or logical possession of either Company X information or information that has been entrusted to Company X. While Information Technology Department staff members clearly are Custodians, local system administrators are also Custodians. Whenever information is maintained only on a personal computer, the User is necessarily also a Custodian. Each type of production application system information must have one or more designated Custodians. Custodians are responsible for safeguarding the information, including implementing access control systems to prevent inappropriate disclosure, and making back-ups so that critical information will not be lost. Custodians are also required to implement, operate, and maintain the security measures defined by information Owners.

User Responsibilities: Users are responsible for familiarizing themselves with and complying with all Company X policies, procedures, and standards dealing with information security. Questions about the appropriate handling of a specific type of information should be directed to either the Custodian or the Owner of the involved information. As information systems become increasingly distributed (through mobile computing, desktop computing, etc.), Users are increasingly placed in a position where they must handle information security matters that they did not handle in days gone past. These new distributed systems force users to play security roles that they had not previous had to play.

Consistent Information Handling: Company X information, and information which has been entrusted to Company X, must be protected in a manner commensurate with its sensitivity and criticality. Security measures must be employed regardless of the media on which information is stored (paper, overhead transparency, computer bits, etc.), the systems which process it (personal computers, firewalls, voice mail systems, etc.), or the methods by which it is moved (electronic mail, face-to-face conversation, etc.). Information must also be protected in a manner that is consistent with it classification (defined below), no matter what its stage in the life cycle from origination to destruction.

Information Classification Designations: Company X has adopted an information classification system which categorizes information into four groupings. All information under Company X's control, whether generated internally or externally, falls into one of these categories: Secret, Confidential, Internal Use Only, and Public. All workers are expected to familiarize themselves with the definitions for these categories and the steps that must be taken to protect the information falling into each of these categories. Details can be found in the Information Classification Policy [link]. For purposes of this policy, "sensitive information" is information which falls into either the Secret or Confidential categories.

Information Classification Labelling: If information is sensitive, from the time it is created until the time it is destroyed or declassified, it must be labeled (marked) with an appropriate information classification designation. Such markings must appear on all manifestations of the information (hardcopies, floppy disks, CD-ROMs, etc.). The vast majority of Company X information falls into the Internal Use Only category. For this reason, it is not necessary to apply a label to Internal Use Only information. Information without a label is therefore by default classified as Internal Use Only. Further instructions about labelling sensitive information can be found in the Information Classification Policy [link].

Need-To-Know: Access to information in the possession of, or under the control of Company X must be provided based on the need-to-know. In other words, information must be disclosed only to people who have a legitimate business need for the information. At the same time, workers must not withhold access to information when the Owner of the information in question instructs that it be shared. To implement the need-to-know concept, Company X has adopted an access request and Owner approval process. Workers must not attempt to access sensitive information unless they have been granted access rights by the relevant Owner. When a worker changes job duties (including termination, transfer, promotion and leave of absence), his or her supervisor must immediately notify the Information Security Department [link with another screen showing details on this notification process]. The privileges granted to all workers will be periodically reviewed by information Owners and Custodians to ensure that only those with a current need-to-know presently have access.

User-IDs And Passwords: To implement the need-to-know process, Company X requires that each worker accessing multi-user information systems have a unique user-ID and a private password. These user-IDs must then be employed to restrict system privileges based on job duties, project responsibilities, and other business activities. Each worker is personally responsible for the usage of his or her user-ID and password.

Anonymous User-IDs: With the exception of electronic bulletin boards, Internet web sites, intranet web sites, and other systems where all regular users are intended to be anonymous, users are prohibited from logging into any Company X system or network anonymously. Anonymous access might, for example, involve use of "guest" user-IDs. When users employ system commands that allow them to change active user-IDs to gain certain privileges, they must have initially logged-in employing user-IDs that clearly indicated their identities. This might, for example, take place on UNIX systems with the SU command.

Difficult-To-Guess Passwords: To ensure that password systems do the job they were intended to do, users must choose passwords which are difficult-to-guess. This means that passwords must NOT be related to one's job or personal life. For example, a car license plate number, a spouse's name, or fragments of an address must not be used. This also means passwords must not be a word found in the dictionary or some other part of speech. For example, proper names, places, technical terms, and slang must not be used.

Easily Remembered Passwords: Users can choose easily-remembered passwords that are at the same time difficult for unauthorized parties to guess if they:

(a) string several words together (the resulting passwords are also known as "passphrases"),
(b) shift a word up, down, left or right one row on the keyboard,
(c) bump characters in a word a certain number of letters up or down the alphabet,
(d) transform a regular word according to a specific method, such as making every other letter a number reflecting its position in the word,
(e) combine punctuation or numbers with a regular word,
(f) create acronyms from words in a song, a poem, or another known sequence of words,
(g) deliberately misspell a word (but not a common misspelling), or
(h) combine several preferences like hours of sleep desired and favorite colors.

Repeated Password Patterns: Users must not construct passwords with a basic sequence of characters that is then partially changed based on the date or some other predictable factor. For example, users must NOT employ passwords like "JIM01JAN" in January, "JIM01FEB" in February, etc. Additionally, users must not construct passwords that are identical or substantially similar to passwords they have previously employed.

Password Constraints: To make guessing more difficult, passwords must also be at least eight characters long. To ensure that a compromised password is not misused on a long-term basis, passwords must also be changed every 90 days or at more frequent intervals. Whenever a worker suspects that a password has become known to another person, that password must immediately be changed.

Password Storage: Passwords must not be stored in readable form in batch files, automatic log-in scripts, software macros, terminal function keys, in computers without access control systems, or in other locations where unauthorized persons might discover them. Similarly, passwords must not be written down in some readily-decipherable form and left in a place where unauthorized persons might discover them.

Sharing Passwords: If workers need to share computer-resident data, they should use electronic mail, groupware databases, public directories on local area network servers, manual floppy disk exchange, and other mechanisms. Although user-IDs are shared for electronic mail and other purposes, passwords must never be shared with or revealed to others. Systems Administrators and other technical information systems staff have all the system privileges they need to do their work -- they will never need a worker to reveal their personal password. The only time when a password should be known by another is when it is first issued; these temporary passwords must be changed the first time that the authorized user accesses the system. To share a password (or for that matter any other access mechanism such as a dynamic password token) exposes the authorized user to responsibility for actions that the other party takes with the disclosed password. If a user believes that his or her user-ID and password are being used by someone else, the user must immediately notify the Systems Administrator for the information system in question.

Compliance Statement: All workers wishing to use Company X multi-user computer systems must sign a compliance statement prior to being issued a user-ID [link to the statement itself]. Where users already have user-IDs, such signatures must be obtained prior to receiving annually-renewed user-IDs. A signature on this compliance statement indicates the involved user understands and agrees to abide by Company X policies and procedures related to computers and networks (including the instructions contained in this policy).

Release Of Information To Third Parties: Unless it has specifically been designated as public, all Company X internal information must be protected from disclosure to third parties. Third parties may be given access to Company X internal information only when a demonstrable need-to-know exists, when a Company X non-disclosure agreement [link to a copy of the agreement] has been signed, and when such a disclosure has been expressly authorized by the relevant Company X information Owner [link to a corporate data dictionary with a list of Owners and the types of information they manage]. If sensitive information is lost, is disclosed to unauthorized parties, or is suspected of being lost or disclosed to unauthorized parties, the information Owner and the Information Security Department must both be notified immediately [link to a separate screen with telephone numbers and additional instructions for this notification process].

Third Party Requests For Company X Information: Unless a worker has been authorized by the information Owner to make public disclosures, all requests for information about Company X and its business must be referred to the Public Relations Department. Such requests include questionnaires, surveys, newspaper interviews, and the like. This policy does not apply to sales and marketing information about Company X products and services, nor does it pertain to customer technical support calls. If a worker is to receive sensitive information from third parties on behalf of Company X, this receipt must be preceded by the third party's signature on a Company X release form [link to form]. For further details on this topic, consult the External Party Information Disclosure Policy [link]. Additional relevant information may also be found in the External Communications Security Policy [link].

Physical Security To Control Information Access: Access to every office, computer machine room, and other Company X work area containing sensitive information must be physically restricted to those people with a need-to-know. When not in use, sensitive information must always be protected from unauthorized disclosure. When left in an unattended room, sensitive information in paper form must be locked away in appropriate containers (safes, file cabinets, etc.). If a

Custodian of such information believes he or she will be away for less than thirty minutes, information in paper form may be left on a desk or in some other readily observed spot only if all doors and windows to the unattended room are closed and locked. During non-working hours, workers in areas containing sensitive information must lock-up all information. Unless information is in active use by authorized people, desks must be clear and clean during non-working hours to prevent unauthorized access to information. Similarly, workers must position their computer screens such that unauthorized people cannot look over their shoulder and see the sensitive information displayed.

Internal Network Connections: All Company X computers that store sensitive information, and that are permanently or intermittently connected to internal computer networks must have a password-based access control system approved by the Information Security Department. Regardless of the network connections, all stand-alone computers handling sensitive information must also employ an approved password-based access control system [link to approved information security products list and procurement details on how to order them]. Users working with all other types of computers are advised to employ the screen saver passwords which are provided with operating systems, so that after a period of no activity the screen will go blank until the correct password is again entered. Similarly, multi-user systems throughout Company X must employ automatic log-out systems which automatically terminate a user's session after a defined period of inactivity.

External Network Connections: All in-bound session connections to Company X computers from external networks (Internet, public dial-up lines, etc.) must be protected with an approved dynamic password access control system [link to approved information security products list again]. Dynamic passwords are different each time they are used, and therefore cannot be replayed to gain unauthorized access. Users with personal computers connected to external networks are prohibited from leaving unattended modems turned-on while data communications software is enabled, unless an authorized dynamic password system has been previously installed. In general terms, Company X workers must not establish connections with external networks (including Internet Service Providers) unless these connections have been approved by the Information Security Department; for further information on this process, see the External Communications Security Policy [link].

Network Changes: Changes to Company X internal networks include loading new communications software, changing network addresses, reconfiguring routers, adding dial-up lines, and the like. With the exception of emergency situations, all changes to Company X computer networks must be: (a) documented in a work order request, and (b) approved in advance by the Information Technology Department. All emergency changes to Company X networks must only be made by persons who are authorized by the Information Technology Department. This process prevents unexpected changes from inadvertently leading to denial of service, unauthorized disclosure of information, and other problems. This process applies not only to "workers" as defined in the Scope section of this policy, but also to vendor personnel.

Telecommuting: At management's discretion, certain qualified workers can do some of their work at home. Permission to telecommute is granted by each worker's immediate supervisor based on a checklist of relevant factors [link to the checklist, which may be a subsidiary intranet page under the Human Resources Department's main intranet web page]. Continued permission to telecommute is partially dependent on continued compliance with a number of information security policies and standards; for further information on these requirements, see the Telecommuting Policy [link]. Periodic checking of electronic mail while on the road or from home is not considered telecommuting, but does require that workers follow many of the same security precautions.

Internet Access: Workers are generally provided with Internet web access to perform their job duties, but this access may be terminated at any time at the discretion of a worker's supervisor. Internet web access is monitored to ensure that workers are not visiting sites unrelated to their jobs, and also to ensure that they continue to be in compliance with security policies. Workers must take special care to ensure that they do not represent Company X on Internet discussion groups and in other public forums, unless they have previously received top management authorization to act in this capacity. All information received from the Internet should be considered to be suspect until confirmed by reliable sources; there is a great deal of inaccurate and deliberately misleading information available on the Internet. Separately, workers must not place Company X material (software, internal memos, press releases, databases, etc.) on any publicly-accessible computer system such as the Internet unless the posting has first been approved by both the information Owner and the Director of the Information Technology Department. The establishment of Internet web pages is separately handled by an approval process involving the External Communications Committee [link to Public Relations Department]. Likewise, users are prohibited from establishing any electronic commerce arrangements over the Internet unless the Information Technology Department and the Information Security Department have first evaluated and approved of such arrangements. On a related note, sensitive information, including passwords and credit card numbers, must not be sent across the Internet unless this information is in encrypted form. These and related considerations are discussed in greater detail in the Internet Communications Policy [link].

Electronic Mail: Every Company X worker who uses computers in the course of their regular job duties will be granted an Internet electronic mail address and related privileges. All Company X business communications sent via email must be sent and received using this company email address. Use of a personal Internet Service Provider (ISP) email account or any other electronic mail address for Company X business is forbidden. When transmitting messages to groups of people outside Company X, workers must always use either the blind carbon copy (bcc) facility or the distribution list facility; this will prevent recipients from learning the electronic mail addresses of other recipients. Unsolicited email transmissions to prospects and customers (so-called spam) are prohibited. Flaming (emotional outbursts sent via email) and mail bombing (overloading the email account of someone through a deluge of messages) are likewise forbidden. All business email communications must be proofread before they are sent, as well as professional and businesslike in both tone and appearance. Electronic mail is a public communication much like a postcard; all Company X workers must accordingly refrain from sending credit card numbers, passwords, or other sensitive information which might be intercepted. All Company X staff must additionally employ a standard email "signature" (not necessarily a digital certificate) which includes their full name, their job title, their business address, and their business phone number. Users should not store important messages in their email inbox because, as a matter of policy, Company X deletes from its servers all messages which have already been read and which are 90 days old or older. Additional details can be found in the Electronic Mail Security Policy [link].

Computer Virus Screening: Viruses can now spread by data files, not just by program files. The symptoms of virus infection include much slower computer response time, inexplicable loss of files, changed modification dates for files, increased file sizes, and total failure of personal computers and servers. To assure continued uninterrupted service for both computers and networks, all personal computer users must keep the current versions of approved virus screening software enabled on their computers [link to list of approved information security products]. This screening software must be used to scan all software and data files coming from either third parties or other Company X groups. This scanning must take place before new data files are opened and before new software is executed. Workers must not bypass or turn-off the scanning processes which could arrest the transmission of computer viruses.

Computer Virus Eradication: If workers suspect infection by a computer virus, they must immediately stop using the involved computer and call the Help Desk [link to Help Desk page]. Floppy disks and other magnetic storage media used with the infected computer must not be used with any other computer until the virus has been successfully eradicated. The infected computer must also be immediately isolated from internal networks. Users must not attempt to eradicate viruses themselves; qualified Company X staff or consultants will be called in to complete this complex task in a manner that minimizes both data destruction and system downtime.

Clean Back-Ups: To assist with the post-virus-infection restoration of normal personal computer activities, all personal computer software must be copied prior to its initial usage, and such copies must be stored in a secure location such as a locked file cabinet. These master copies must not be used for ordinary business activities, but must be reserved for recovery from computer virus infections, hard disk crashes, and other computer problems.

Software Sources: Larger computer systems do not generally suffer from viruses, but they do suffer from worms and Trojan horses. Worms are much like viruses, but do not attach themselves to other programs. Trojan horses are unauthorized programs hidden within authorized programs. To prevent problems with viruses, worms, and Trojan horses, Company X computers and networks must not run software that comes from sources other than: (a) other Company X departments, (b) knowledgeable and trusted user groups, (c) well-known systems security authorities such as Carnegie-Mellon University's Computer Emergency Response Team (aka CERT), (d) established computer or network vendors, or (e) established commercial software vendors. Software down-loaded from electronic bulletin boards, shareware, public domain software, and other software from untrusted sources must not be used unless it has first been subjected to a rigorous testing regimen approved by the Information Security Department [link to a page describing this process, who to contact, etc.].

Written Specifications For Owners: All software developed by in-house staff, and intended to process critical or sensitive Company X information, must have a formal written specification. This specification must include discussion of both security risks and controls (including access control systems and contingency plans). The specification must be part of an agreement between the involved information Owner and the system developer(s). Macros in spreadsheets, word processing documents, and the like are not considered software for purposes of this paragraph.

Security Sign-Off Required: Before being used for production processing, new or substantially changed application systems must have received written approval from the Information Security Department for the controls to be employed. This requirement applies to personal computers just as it does to larger systems [link to form requesting Information Security Department review and sign-off].

Formal Change Control: All computer and communications systems used for production processing at Company X must employ a documented change control process which is used to ensure that only authorized changes are made. This change control procedure must be used for all significant changes to production system software, hardware, communications links, and procedures. Again, this policy applies to personal computers running production systems, just as it applies to larger multi-user systems. For further information on this topic, see the Software Development and Change Control Policy [link].

Systems Development Conventions: All production software development and software maintenance activities performed by in-house staff must subscribe to Information Technology Department policies, standards, procedures, and other systems development conventions. Among other things, these conventions include the proper testing, training, and documentation. For further information on this topic, see the Software Development and Change Control Policy [link].

Adequate Licenses: Company X provides a sufficient number of licensed copies of software such that workers can get their work done in an expedient and effective manner. Company X management must make appropriate arrangements with the involved vendors for additional licensed copies, if and when additional copies are needed for business activities. To ensure compatibility with Company X networks and computers, and to allow licenses to be centrally managed, all software must be purchased through the Procurement Department [link to list of approved software products for the desktop; perhaps a link to the Procurement Department's purchase request form].

Unauthorized Copying: Users must not copy software provided by Company X to any storage media (floppy disk, magnetic tape, etc.), transfer such software to another computer, or disclose such software to outside parties without advance permission from their supervisor. Ordinary back-up copies are an authorized exception to this policy.

Back-Up Responsibility: To protect Company X's information resources from loss or damage, personal computer users are responsible for regularly backing-up the information on their personal computers, or else making sure that someone else is doing this for them. For multi-user computer and communication systems, a Systems Administrator is responsible for making periodic back-ups. If requested, the Information Technology Department will install, or provide technical assistance for the installation of back-up hardware and/or software [link to list of approved security products]. All back-ups containing critical and/or sensitive information must be stored an approved off-site location with either physical access controls or encryption. A contingency plan must be prepared for all applications that handle critical production information; it is the responsibility of the information Owner to make sure that this plan is adequately developed, regularly updated, and periodically tested.

Theft Protection: All Company X computer and network equipment must be physically secured with anti-theft devices if located in an open office environment. Local area network servers and other multi-user systems must be placed in locked cabinets, locked closets, or locked computer rooms. Portable computers must likewise be secured with locking cables, placed in locking cabinets, or secured via other locking systems when in the office but not in use. Computer and network gear may not be removed from Company X offices unless the involved person has first obtained a property pass from the building manager. Pagers and cellular phones are not subject to these requirements.

External Disclosure Of Security Information: Information about security measures for Company X computer and network systems is confidential and must not be released to people who are not authorized users of the involved systems unless the permission of the Director of Information Security has first been obtained. For example, publishing modem phone numbers or other system access information in directories is prohibited. Nonetheless, public disclosure of electronic mail addresses is permissible.

Rights To Material Developed: While performing services for Company X, workers grant to Company X exclusive rights to patents, copyrights, inventions, or other intellectual property they originate and/or develop. All programs and documentation generated by, or provided by workers for the benefit of Company X are the property of Company X. Company X asserts the legal ownership of the contents of all information systems under its control (subject to prior claims such as copyrighted software licensed from third parties). Company X accordingly reserves the right to access and use this information at its discretion.

Right To Search And Monitor: To ensure compliance with Company X internal policies as well as applicable laws and regulations, and to ensure employee safety, Company X management reserves the right to monitor, inspect, and/or search at any time all Company X information systems. This examination may take place with or without the consent, presence, or knowledge the involved workers. The information systems subject to such examination include, but are not limited to, electronic mail system files, personal computer hard drive files, voicemail files, printer spool files, fax machine output, desk drawers, and storage areas. All searches of this nature will be conducted after the approval of the Legal and Security Departments has been obtained. Since Company X's computers and networks are provided for business purposes only, workers should have no expectation of privacy associated with the information they store in or send through these information systems. Company X management additionally retains the right to remove from its information systems any material it views as offensive or potentially illegal. For further information on this topic, see the Information Privacy Policy [link].

Personal Use: Company X information systems are intended to be used for business purposes only. Incidental personal use is permissible if the use: (a) does not consume more than a trivial amount of resources that could otherwise be used for business purposes, (b) does not interfere with worker productivity, and (c) does not preempt any business activity. Permissible incidental use of an electronic mail system would, for example, involve sending a message to schedule a luncheon. Other types of personal use require the permission of a department manager. Games which are shipped with computer operating systems (like Microsoft Windows) can be played during scheduled breaks or lunch so long as this activity doesn't interfere with either worker productivity or motivation. Games which take the form of separate software packages are prohibited. Use of Company X information systems for chain letters, charitable solicitations, political campaign material, religious work, and any other non-business use is prohibited.

Unbecoming Conduct: Company X management reserves the right to revoke the system privileges of any user at any time. Conduct that interferes with the normal and proper operation of Company X information systems, which adversely affects the ability of others to use these information systems, or which is harmful or offensive to others will not be permitted.

Security Compromise Tools: Unless specifically authorized by the Information Security Department, Company X workers must not acquire, possess, trade, or use hardware or software tools that could be employed to evaluate or compromise information systems security. Examples of such tools include those which defeat software copy-protection, discover secret passwords, identify security vulnerabilities, or decrypt encrypted files. Similarly, without this type of approval, workers are prohibited from using "sniffers" or any other hardware or software which monitors the traffic on a network or the activity on a computer.

Prohibited Activities: Users must not test, or attempt to compromise computer or communication system security measures unless specifically approved in advance and in writing by the Director of the Internal Audit Department. Incidents involving unapproved system cracking (hacking), password cracking (guessing), file decryption, bootleg software copying, or similar unauthorized attempts to compromise security measures may be unlawful, and will be considered serious violations of Company X internal policy. Likewise, short-cuts bypassing systems security measures, as well as pranks and practical jokes involving the compromise of systems security measures are absolutely prohibited.

Mandatory Reporting: All suspected policy violations, system intrusions, virus infestations, and other conditions which might jeopardize Company X information or Company X information systems must be immediately reported to the Information Security Department (voice mail with pager alert XXX-XXX-XXXX) [link with computer emergency response team intranet web page]. Messages may be left anonymously in this voice mail box.

Effective Date: DD/MM/YY
Date Of Last Revision: DD/MM/YY

V. Sample Detailed Information Security Policy

Executive Summary

Everyone recognizes that the highway system and motor vehicles are essential to modern commerce. But people are only recently coming to appreciate how information systems made up of computers and networks are another infrastructure essential to modern commerce. In recognition of the critical role that information systems play in Company X business activities, this policy defines the rules of the road and other requirements necessary for the secure and reliable operation of the Company X information systems infrastructure.

Just as every driver has a role to play in the orderly and safe operation of the transportation infrastructure, so too there are information security roles and duties for every worker at Company X. For example, just as it is a driver's duty to report accidents, so too it is an worker's duty to report information security problems. Similarly, just as car manufacturers are required to provide safety belts with their vehicles, system designers at Company X are required to include necessary security measures such as user access restrictions based on the need-to-know.

This policy also defines "baseline" control measures that everyone at Company X is expected to be familiar with and to consistently follow. Sometimes called "standard of due care" controls, these security measures are the minimum required to prevent a variety of different problems including: fraud and embezzlement, industrial espionage, sabotage, errors and omissions, as well as system unavailability. On another level, these policies also define the minimum controls necessary to prevent legal problems such as allegations of negligence, breach of fiduciary duty, or privacy violation. When preparing these policies, the Information Systems Security Department has considered these and other threats; the result of their efforts is this policy document detailing reasonable and practical ways for all of us at Company X to prevent unnecessary losses.

Company X critically depends on continued customer confidence. This confidence has been built up gradually and is the result of many years of dedicated effort on the part of Company X workers. While it is slow to grow, this confidence can be rapidly lost due to problems such as hacker intrusions causing system outages. The trust that customers have in Company X is a competitive advantage that must be nurtured and grown with efforts such as this information security initiative.

Introduction

Critical Business Function: Information and information systems are necessary for the performance of just about every essential activity at Company X. If there were to be a serious security problem with this information or these information systems, Company X could suffer serious consequences including lost customers, reduced revenues, and/or degraded reputation. As a result, information security must now be a critical part of the Company X business environment.

Supporting Business Objectives: This information security requirements document has been prepared to ensure that Company X is able to support further growth of the business, as well as ensure a consistently high level of customer, supplier, employee, and business-partner service. This document is also intended to support the firm's reputation for high-integrity and high-quality business dealings. Because prevention of security problems is considerably less expensive than correction and recovery, this document will also help reduce costs in the long run.

Consistent Compliance Essential: A single unauthorized exception to security measures can jeopardize other users, the entire firm, and even outside organizations such as business partners. The interconnected nature of modern information systems requires that a minimum level of security be observed by all workers. This document defines that minimum level of due care. In some cases, these requirements will conflict with other objectives such as improved efficiency and minimized costs. Top management has examined these tradeoffs and has decided that the minimum requirements defined in this document are appropriate for all workers at Company X. As a result, as a condition of continued employment, all workers (employees, contractors, consultants, temporaries, etc.) must consistently observe the requirements set forth in this document.

Team Effort Required: The tools now available in the information security field are still relatively unsophisticated. Many of the tasks that need to be done cannot be achieved with products now on the market. This means that Users at Company X must step-in and play an important role in the information security area. Now that information and information systems are distributed to the office desktop, and are used in remote locations, the worker's role has become an essential part of information security. No longer is information security the exclusive domain of the Information Systems Department -- information security is now a team effort requiring the participation of every worker who comes into contact with Company X information and/or information systems.

Information Security Responsibilities

Information Owners: Middle level managers in user departments must be designated as the Owners of all types of information used for regular business activities. In other words, each type of "production system information" (as defined in the section below entitled Systems Development) needs an Owner. When information Owners are not clearly implied by organizational design, the Chief Information Officer will make the designation. Information Owners do not legally own the information in question; they are instead members of the Company X management team who make decisions on behalf of the firm. Information Owners or their delegates are required to make the following decisions and perform the following activities:

(a) Approve information-oriented access control privileges for specific job profiles,
(b) Approve information-oriented access control requests which do not fall within the purview of existing job profiles,
(c) Select a data retention period for their information, relying on advice from the Legal Department,
(d) Designate a system-of-record (original source) for information from which all management reports will be derived,
(e) Select special controls needed to protect information (such as additional input validation checks or more frequent back-up procedures),
(f) Define acceptable limits on the quality of their information (accuracy, timeliness, time from capture to usage, etc.),
(g) Approve all new and different uses of their information,
(h) Approve all new or substantially enhanced application systems that use their information before these systems are moved into production operational status,
(i) Review reports about system intrusions and other events which are relevant to their information,
(j) Review and correct reports which indicate the current production uses of their information,
(k) Review and correct reports which indicate the job profiles which currently have access to their information,
(l) Select a sensitivity classification category relevant to their information and review this classification every five years for possible downgrading, and

(m) Select a criticality category relevant to their information so that appropriate contingency planning can be performed.

Information Owners must designate a back-up person to act if they are absent or unavailable. Owners may not delegate ownership responsibilities to third party organizations (such as outsourcing firms) or to any individual who is not a full-time Company X employee. When both the Owner and the back-up Owner are unavailable, pressing Owner decisions may be made by the Department Manager who ordinarily handles the information.

Worker's Manager: Ordinary access control requests are not approved by Owners. Instead, a worker's immediate manager approves a request for system access based on existing job profiles. If a job profile doesn't exist, it is the manager's responsibility to create the profile, obtain the approval of relevant Owners, and inform the Information Security Department. Similarly, when a worker leaves Company X, it is the worker's immediate manager's responsibility to promptly inform the Information Security Department that the privileges associated with the worker's user-ID must be revoked. User-IDs are specific to individuals, and must not be reassigned to, or used by others. Shortly after separation from Company X, a worker's manager is additionally responsible for reassigning the involved duties and files to other workers.

Information Custodians: Custodians are in physical or logical possession of information and/or information systems. Like Owners, custodians are specifically designated for different types of information. In many cases, a manager in the Information Systems Department will act as the Custodian. If a Custodian is not clear based on existing information systems operational arrangements, then the Chief Information Officer will designate a Custodian. Custodians follow the instructions of Owners, operate systems on behalf of Owners, but also serve Users authorized by Owners. Custodians must define the technical options, such as information criticality categories, and then allow Owners to select the appropriate option(s) for their information. Custodians also define information systems architectures and provide technical consulting assistance to Owners so that information systems can be built and run to best meet business objectives. If requested, Custodians additionally provide reports to Owners about information system operations, information security problems, and the like. Custodians are furthermore responsible for safeguarding the information in their possession, including implementing access control systems to prevent inappropriate disclosure, as well as developing, documenting, and testing information systems contingency plans.

Information Users: Users are not specifically designated, but are broadly defined as any worker with access to internal information or internal information systems. Users are required to abide by all security requirements defined by Owners, implemented by Custodians, and/or established by the Information Security Department. Users are required to familiarize themselves with, and act in accordance with all Company X information security requirements. Users are also required to participate in information security training and awareness efforts. Users must request access from their immediate manager, and report all suspicious activity and security problems (see the section below entitled Reporting Problems).

Information Security Department: The Information Security Department is the central point of contact for all information security matters at Company X. Acting as internal technical consultants, it is this Department's responsibility to create workable information security compromises which take into consideration the needs of Users, Custodians, Owners, and selected third parties. Reflecting these compromises, this Department defines information security standards, procedures, policies, and other requirements applicable to the entire organization. The Information Security Department is responsible for handling all access control administration activities, monitoring the security of Company X information systems, and providing information security training and awareness programs to Company X workers. The department is additionally responsible for periodically providing management with reports about the current state of information security at Company X. While information systems contingency planning is the responsibility of information Custodians, the Information Security Department must nonetheless provide technical consulting assistance related to emergency response procedures and disaster recovery. The Information Security Departments is also responsible for organizing a computer emergency response team (CERT) to promptly respond to virus infections, hacker break-ins, system outages, and similar information security problems.

Internal Audit Department: The Company X Internal Audit Department periodically performs compliance checks to make sure that the above-mentioned parties are performing their assigned duties, and to make sure that other information security requirements are being consistently observed. Internal Audit acts as the eyes and ears of top management at Company X, making sure that internal controls (including those related to information security) are consistent with both top management expectations and organizational goals.

Information Sensitivity Classification

Reasons for Classification: To assist in the appropriate handling of information, a sensitivity classification hierarchy must be used throughout Company X. This hierarchy provides a shorthand way of referring to sensitivity, and can be used to simplify information security decisions and minimize information security costs. One important intention of a sensitivity classification system is to provide consistent handling of the information, no matter what form it takes, no matter where it goes, and no matter who possesses it. For this reason, it is important to maintain the labels reflecting sensitivity classification categories. Company X uses four sensitivity classification categories:

Public -- This information has been specifically approved for public release by Public Relations Department or Marketing Department managers. Unauthorized disclosure of this information will not cause problems for Company X, its customers, or its business partners. Examples: marketing brochures and material posted to the Company X Internet web page. Disclosure of Company X information to the public requires the existence of this label, the specific permission of the information owner, or long-standing practice of publicly distributing this information.

Internal Use Only -- This information is intended for use within Company X, and in some cases within affiliated organizations, such as Company X business partners. Unauthorized disclosure of this information to outsiders may be against laws and regulations, or may cause problems for Company X, its customers, or its business partners. This type of information is already widely-distributed within Company X, or it could be so distributed within the firm without advance permission from the information Owner. Examples: the Company X telephone book and most internal electronic mail messages.

Confidential -- This information is private or otherwise sensitive in nature and must be restricted to those with a legitimate business need for access. Unauthorized disclosure of this information to people without a business need for access may be against laws and regulations, or may cause significant problems for Company X, its customers, or its business partners. Decisions about the provision of access to this information must always be cleared through the information Owner. Examples: customer transaction account information and worker performance evaluation records.

Highly Restricted -- This information is the most private or otherwise sensitive, and must be strictly monitored and controlled at all times. Unauthorized disclosure of this information to people without a business need for access may be against laws and regulations, and/or may cause severe problems for Company X, its customers, or its business partners. Decisions about the provision of access to this information must always be cleared through the information Owner. Examples: merger/acquisition plans and legal information protected by client/attorney privilege.

Default Category: If information is not marked with one of these four categories, it will by default fall into the Internal Use Only category. If information falls into the Internal Use Only category, it is not necessary to apply a sensitivity label. Information which falls into either the Confidential or Highly Restricted categories is designated "sensitive information."

Labeling: Computer system vendors have not adopted a consistent approach to sensitivity labeling. It is up to the Owner or creator of information to designate an appropriate label, and up to the User or recipient of this information to consistently maintain an assigned label. Labels for sensitive information should be used in the subject field of electronic mail messages or paper memos. Labels for sensitive information should appear on floppy diskettes, magnetic tape reels, CD-ROMs, audio cassettes, and other storage media. If a storage volume (such as a floppy diskette) contains information with multiple classifications, the most sensitive category should appear on the outside or overall label. Likewise, when creating a collection of information from sources with various classifications, the collection must be classified at the highest sensitivity level of the source information.

Handling Instructions: All Users must observe the requirements for handling information based on its sensitivity which are defined in the accompanying table [see the section of this book entitled Data Classification Quick Reference Matrix]. Owners may designate additional controls to further restrict access to, or to further protect their information.

Access Control

Access Philosophy: To keep costs down, access to Public and Internal Use Only information is not restricted with access controls that discriminate by specific User. For example, Public information is available at the Company X web site, and Internal Use Only information is available on the Company X intranet. On the other hand, access to Confidential and Highly Restricted information will be granted only when a bona fide business need has been demonstrated and access has been approved in advance by the information Owner. Likewise, access to special hardware and/or software (such as diagnostic test equipment called "sniffers") must be restricted based on business need.

Access Approval Process: The access control approval process must be initiated by a worker's manager, and the privileges granted remain in effect until the worker's job changes or the worker leaves Company X. If either of these two events take place, the manager must immediately notify the Information Security Department. All non-employees (contractors, consultants, temporaries, outsourcing firms, etc.) must also go through a similar access control request and authorization process initiated by the project manager. The privileges of these non-employees must be immediately revoked through the Information Security Department when the project is complete, or when the non-employees stop working with Company X. The need for the continuing privileges of non-employees must be reviewed every three months by the relevant project manager.

Default Facilities: All Users will by default be granted basic information systems services such as electronic mail and word processing facilities. These basic facilities will vary by job title and be determined jointly by the Information Security and the Information Systems Department. All other system capabilities will be provided via job profiles or by special request directed to the Owner of the involved information. The existence of certain access privileges does not, in and of itself, mean that an individual is authorized to use these privileges. If Users have any questions about access control privileges, they should direct these questions to the Information Security Department.

Departures From Company X: When a User leaves Company X, all system privileges immediately cease, and access to Company X information must likewise immediately cease. For example, departed Users are not permitted to continue to maintain an electronic mail account with Company X. At this point in time, all Company X information disclosed to Users must be returned or destroyed. For example, customer contact lists must remain with Company X. All work done by Users for Company X is Company X property, and it too must remain with Company X when Users depart. For instance, a computer program written by a member of the Information Systems Department while employed by Company X is Company X property and must remain with Company X.

Unique User-IDs: Each User will be assigned their own unique user-ID. This user-ID follows an individual as they move through the firm. It will be permanently decommissioned when a User leaves Company X; re-use of user-IDs is not allowed. Every Company X user-ID and related password is intended for the exclusive use of a specific individual. While user-IDs can be shared in electronic mail messages and in other places, passwords must never be shared with anyone (information systems technicians have all the privileges they need to do their job, and will never need to obtain a user's password). User-IDs are linked to specific people, and are not associated with computer terminals, departments, or job titles. With the exception of Internet web pages, intranet pages, and other places where anonymous interaction is both generally understood and expected, anonymous user-IDs (such as "guest") are not allowed unless approved in advance by the Information Security Department.

Privilege Deactivation: After a period of no activity defined in minutes by the Information Security Department, on-line sessions with multi-user machines will be terminated automatically. To prevent unauthorized people from using the privileges associated with a user-ID, Users must be sure to log-off from multi-user computers when they leave their desks for any more than a few minutes. Dormant user-IDs on multi-user computers which have not seen any activity for a period defined in weeks will have their privileges automatically revoked (the related files will be archived). Users who come back from an extended vacation or a leave of absence must have their manager contact the Information Security Department to reestablish their privileges.

User Authentication: All production information system user-IDs must have a linked password or a stronger mechanism (such as a dynamic password token) to ensure that only the authorized user is able to utilize the user-ID. Users are responsible for all activity that takes place with their user-ID and password (or other authentication mechanism). Users must immediately change their password if they suspect that it has been discovered or used by another person. Likewise, Users must notify the Information Security Department if other access control mechanisms are broken or if they suspect that these mechanisms have been compromised.

Fixed Password Management

Choosing Passwords: Users must choose difficult-to-guess passwords. This means that fixed passwords must not be in the dictionary and must not be a reflection of the User's personal life. For example, license plate number and spouse's name are both unacceptable passwords. All fixed passwords must be at least eight characters, and where systems support it, this minimum length must be enforced automatically. Users must also choose fixed passwords that include both alphabetic and numeric characters (for example "POWER711"). Strong passwords are easier to remember when memory techniques are employed; for example, several familiar words can be strung together or an acronym can be derived from words in a favorite song.

Changing Passwords: User-chosen fixed passwords must not be reused or recycled. Switching between two or a similar small number of passwords is therefore prohibited. Where systems support it, fixed passwords must be forced to change every sixty days. Likewise, where systems support it, expired passwords must be employed. Expired passwords are passwords which must be changed the first time they are used. If Users suspect that somebody else may know their password, the password must be immediately changed. The Information Systems Department's Help Desk will not reset User passwords unless a User first definitively identifies him- or herself.

Protecting Passwords: Fixed passwords are a very important way to authenticate the identity of users. Users must not share a fixed password with anyone, including their manager or co-workers. Instead, Users must employ authorized mechanisms to share information such as local server shared directories, electronic mail, intranet pages, or floppy disks. Users must not store their fixed passwords in any computer files (such as log-in scripts or computer programs) unless the passwords have been encrypted with authorized encryption software. Likewise, passwords must not be written down unless they have been concealed by a transformation process, or they are physically secured (such as placed in a locked file cabinet). All fixed passwords set by default by the hardware or software vendor must be changed before the involved system can be used for Company X business activities.

Privacy

Expectations of Privacy: Users should have no expectation of privacy when using information systems at Company X. To manage systems and enforce security, Company X may log, review, and otherwise utilize any information stored on or passing through its systems. For these same purposes, Company X may also capture User activity such as telephone numbers dialed and web sites visited.

Collecting Information: As a general rule, Company X does not collect information which is not necessary for business purposes (such as information about employee off-hour activities). Likewise, Company X does not collect information from third parties such as customers unless these parties are first notified about the data collection activities.

Third Party Information Privacy: A wide variety of third parties have entrusted their information to Company X for business purposes, and all workers at Company X must do their best to safeguard the privacy and security of this information. The most important of these third parties is the individual customer; customer account data is accordingly Confidential and access will be strictly limited based on business need for such access. Similarly, customer account information must not be distributed to third parties without advance authorization by the customer (exceptions will be made in the case of customer incapacitation or death).

Third Party Disclosures

Preauthorization For Public Statements: To maintain customer confidence, all workers who will be delivering speeches, writing papers, or otherwise disclosing information about Company X and/or its business must obtain preauthorization from the Public Relations Department. Only designated individuals are authorized to be spokespersons for Company X. Unless a worker is one of these designated spokespersons, all inquires from the media must be directed to the Public Relations Department.

Company X Non-Disclosure Agreements: Whenever communications with third parties necessitate the release of sensitive Company X information, a standard non-disclosure agreement (NDA) must be signed by the third party. Information released to these third parties must be limited to the topics directly related to the involved project or business relationship.

Third Party Non-Disclosure Agreements: In some instances, before discussions can be commenced, third parties will ask that workers at Company X sign their NDAs. Recipients of third party NDAs should forward these agreements to the Legal Department. To be effective, third party NDAs can only be signed by members of the Company X Legal Department. Without this double check on NDAs, Company X may later find that it has inadvertently agreed to unnecessarily restrict its business activities.

Acceptable Use Of The Internet

Not A Fringe Benefit: Internet access (beyond electronic mail) will be provided only if necessary to perform a worker's job. If a User needs additional access to Internet facilities, a request should be directed to the User's manager, who in turn will contact the Information Security Department.

Information Reliability: All information taken off the Internet should be considered suspect until confirmed by separate information from another source. There is no standard quality control process on the Internet, and a considerable amount of information on the Internet is outdated, inaccurate, and in some cases deliberately misleading. Similarly, it is relatively easy to spoof the identity of another user on the Internet. As a result, Users must not rely on the alleged identity of a corespondent via the Internet unless the identity of this person is confirmed through methods approved by the Information Security Department (digital certificates, digital signatures, etc.).

Posting Information To Discussing Groups: Users must not post to public discussion groups ("listservs"), chat rooms, or other public forums on the Internet unless they have been preauthorized by the Public Relations Department to make this type of representation on behalf of Company X. Management reserves the right to remove any Internet posting by a worker at Company X that it deems inappropriate and potentially damaging to the firm's reputation.

Downloading Software: Users must not download software from the Internet unless specifically authorized to do so by the Information Systems or Information Security Department. Users may download data files from the Internet, but must check these files for viruses before executing them (decompression and decryption, when they are used, must be performed first).

Sending Security Parameters: Users must not send any sensitive parameters such as credit card numbers, telephone calling card numbers, fixed passwords, or customer account numbers through the Internet unless the connection is encrypted (SSL in an on-line session is acceptable). Users must not include sensitive parameters in electronic mail messages sent through the Internet unless these messages are encrypted with software approved by the Information Security Department.

International Transfer Of Data: The movement of private information (such as human resources records) across international borders in some countries is illegal. Before transferring any private information across a border, Users must first check with the Information Security Department to ensure that these Trans-Border Data Flow laws are not violated.

Setting Up Extra Services: Subscription to real-time automatic information distribution services on the Internet (so-called "push services") is prohibited unless approved by the Information Systems Department. Subscription to electronic mail distribution lists (also known as "news groups") is permissible without this approval. The establishment of any network connection with a third party (such as an "extranet") is forbidden unless the Information Security Department has approved the controls associated with this connection. Users must not establish any web pages, electronic bulletin boards, or other mechanism which provides public access to information about Company X, without the advance approval of both the Information Security and the Public Relations Department. Likewise, the establishment of Electronic Data Interchange (EDI) and other electronic business system arrangements is prohibited unless approved by both the Information Security and the Information Systems Department.

User Anonymity: Users must not misrepresent, obscure, suppress or replace their own or another user's identity on the Internet or on any other Company X information system. In all instances, the user name, electronic mail address, organizational affiliation, and related contact information must reflect the actual originator of a message or posting. The use of anonymous remailers or other identity hiding mechanisms is forbidden and is not in keeping with the Company X culture of straight and honest communication. The use of web browsers, anonymous FTP log-ins, and other methods established with the expectation that users do not need to identify themselves is permissible.

False Security Reports: The Internet has been plagued with hoaxes alleging various security problems like viruses which will erase hard drives. Many of these hoaxes take the form of chain letters which request that the receiving party send the message to other people. All Users in receipt of information about system vulnerabilities should forward this information to the Information Security Department, which will them determine what if any action is appropriate. Users must not redistribute system vulnerability information.

Establishing Network Connections
Company X computers or networks may only be connected to third party computers or networks after the Information Security Department has determined that the combined systems will be in compliance with Company X security requirements. Similarly, real-time connections between two or more in-house Company X computer systems must not be established unless the Information Security Department has first determined that such connections will not jeopardize information security. Connections of internal Company X computers to the Company X internal network (aka intranet) do not require such permissions, unless the involved systems store Confidential or Highly Restricted Information. Likewise, connections to the Internet through Company X firewalls do not require such permissions.

Workers must not connect their own computers with Company X computers or networks without prior authorization from their department head. Likewise, personally owned systems may not be used to process any Company X information unless the systems have first been approved for use by the Information Security Department.

Workers and vendors working for Company X must not make arrangements for, or actually complete the installation of voice or data lines with any carrier, unless they have first obtained written approval from the director of the Telecommunications Department.

All connections between Company X internal networks and the Internet (or any other publicly-accessible computer network) must include an approved firewall or related access control system. The privileges that will be permitted via this firewall or related access control system will be based on business needs, and will be defined in an access control standard issued by the Information Systems Security Department [link to that document could go here].

Dial-Up Access
With the exception of portable computers and telecommuting computers, the use of modems directly attached to, or integrated into, personal computers to establish communications sessions with Company X computers or networks is prohibited. Instead, all dial-up connections with Company X computers and networks must be routed through a modem pool which includes an extended user authentication security system approved by the Information Security Department.

Third Party Access
Before third party users are permitted to reach Company X internal systems via real-time computer connections (dial-up lines, the Internet, value added networks, etc.), specific written approval of the Information Security Department manager must be obtained. These third parties include information providers such as mutual fund companies, business partners such as payment clearing agents, as well as contractors and consultants working on special projects.

Third party information system vendors must only be given in-bound connection privileges (dial-up, Internet TELNET, etc.) when the applicable system manager determines that they have a legitimate business need. These privileges must be enabled only for the time period required to accomplish previously-defined and approved tasks. Third party vendor access which will last longer than one day must be approved by the Information Security Department.

Unless the relevant information Owner has approved in advance, workers must not place anything other than Company X public information in a directory, on a server, or in any other location where unknown parties could readily access it. One example of this prohibited placement involves posting files to an Internet connected server such that unknown third parties could access these files via FTP services.

As a condition of gaining access to Company X's computer network, every third party must secure its own connected systems in a manner consistent with Company X requirements. Company X reserves the right to audit the security measures in effect on third party connected systems without prior warning. Company X also reserves the right to immediately terminate network connections with all third party systems not meeting such requirements.

Encryption

Default Protection Not Provided: Company X networks as well as the Internet and other public networks are not protected from wiretapping by default. In all but a few rare instances, if information is to be protected, then the User must take specific action to enable encryption facilities. Thus Users who employ cellular or mobile phones must not discuss sensitive (Confidential or Highly Restricted) information unless they have taken steps to encrypt the call. Likewise, videoconferences should not involve discussion of sensitive information unless encryption facilities are known to be enabled.

When To Use Encryption: Whenever sensitive (Confidential or Highly Restricted) information is sent over a public computer network like the Internet, encryption methods authorized by the Information Security Department must be used to protect it. Whenever Highly Restricted information is stored in a computer, this storage must be achieved with similar authorized encryption methods. The accompanying table defines these circumstances in greater detail [link to a table like Sample Data Classification Quick Reference Matrix].

Key Selection: Many encryption routines require that the User provide a seed or a key as input. Users must protect these security parameters from unauthorized disclosure, just as they would protect passwords from unauthorized disclosure. Rules for choosing strong seeds or keys should likewise follow the rules for choosing strong passwords (described in the section entitled Choosing Passwords).

Electronic Mail

Sharing and Forwarding: Electronic mail accounts, like user-IDs, are for specific individuals and must not be shared. If a User goes on vacation or is otherwise unable to check their mail for extended periods, mail can be forwarded to another Company X worker. Likewise, notices can be established which will automatically notify correspondents that the recipient will not be responding for a certain period of time. Upon departure from Company X, a User's electronic mail account must be terminated. To restrict the dissemination of sensitive information, no forwarding of electronic mail to addresses outside Company X is permitted. If an electronic mail message contains sensitive information, Users must not forward it to another recipient unless (1) the other recipient is authorized to view the information, or (2) the originator approves the forwarding. The covert use of the blind carbon copy feature in electronic mail systems is discouraged because it is inconsistent with the open and honest communication at Company X.

Broadcast electronic mail message facilities should not be employed unless department manager approval is first obtained, but the use of selected distribution lists is both advisable and permissible without such approval.

Default Protection: Electronic mail is not protected from prying eyes by default. Electronic mail has comparable privacy to that of a post card. Accordingly, Users must be careful about the inclusion of sensitive information in electronic mail messages which are not protected by encryption. To protect information from unauthorized disclosure, Users must employ encryption facilities approved by the Information Security Department.

Message Recording: By default all electronic mail messages are recorded in logs and back-ups. This means that even though an electronic mail message may have been deleted from a User's in-box, it may still be retrievable with other methods. Nonetheless, because electronic mail messages that have been read will be purged from these systems every six months, Users are responsible for saving important messages which might be needed at a future date. Electronic mail systems are not intended to be used as databases; Users must move important messages from electronic mail systems into other storage places such as word processing documents.

Contents of Messages: Users must not use profanity, obscenities, or derogatory remarks in any electronic mail messages discussing employees, customers, competitors, or others involved with Company X business. Such remarks, even when made in jest, may create legal problems such as trade libel and defamation of character. Special caution is warranted because back-up and archival copies of electronic mail made by third parties may actually be more permanent and more readily accessible than traditional paper communications.

Harassing or Offensive Messages: Company X information systems must not be used for the exercise of a User's right to free speech. Sexual, ethnic, and racial harassment -- including unwanted telephone calls, electronic mail, and internal mail -- is strictly prohibited and is cause for disciplinary action. Users are encouraged to respond directly to the originator of offensive electronic mail messages, telephone calls, and/or other communications. If the originator does not promptly stop sending offensive messages, workers must report the communications to their manager and the Human Resources Department.

Printing, Copying and Fax Transmission

Destruction Of Waste Copies: If a printer, copier, or fax machine jams or malfunctions when printing sensitive (Confidential or Highly Restricted) information, the involved Users must not leave the machine until all copies of the sensitive information are removed or are no longer legible. All paper copies of sensitive information must be disposed of by shredding or other methods approved by the Information Security Department.

Faxing Precautions: Sensitive materials must not be faxed unless: (1) an authorized staff member is on-hand at the time of transmission to properly handle the materials at the receiving site, (2) the fax is sent to a locked room to which only authorized workers have access, or (3) a password-protected fax mailbox is used to restrict release to an authorized recipient. Sensitive information must not be faxed via untrusted intermediaries (hotel staff, rented mailbox store staff, etc.). As the table accompanying this document indicates, Highly Restricted information may only be faxed if the connection is protected with encryption systems approved by the Information Security Department. The receipt of sensitive information via fax must be confirmed promptly. All faxes must employ a standard cover page which includes language approved by the Company X Legal Department. To ensure their enforceability in court, third party signatures on contracts, purchase orders, and similar legal documents sent by fax must always be followed-up with an exchange of paper originals.

Printer Precautions: When printing sensitive information, the User must: (1) be present at the printer at the time of printing to prevent the information from being revealed to unauthorized parties, or (2) direct the output to a printer inside an area where only authorized workers are permitted to go.

Copy Machine Precautions: Unless permission from the copyright owner(s) is first obtained, making multiple copies of material from magazines, journals, newsletters, and other publications is forbidden unless this is both reasonable and customary. This notion of "fair use" is in keeping with international copyright laws. Additional information about copying software and other materials can be found below in the section entitled Intellectual Property Rights.

Repair Services: Because modern fax machines, printers, and copy machines may have storage areas and internal logs which could contain sensitive Company X information, the repair of these machines must only be performed by third party vendors who have signed a Company X non-disclosure agreement (NDA).

Mobile Computing and Work at Home

Approval For Remote Access: Remote access to Company X computers will be granted only to those Users who have a demonstrable business need for such access. Permission to access Company X computers remotely is granted by and annually reviewed by a User's manager. All remote Users must attend a special class before their remote access privileges are granted or annually renewed. To ensure that the requirements for remote access are consistently observed, Company X reserves the right to conduct surprise audits of Users with remote access privileges. These surprise audits could include visits to remote sites as well as a review of the contents of a computer used to access Company X systems.

Location Independence: The security of Company X information and physical property at remote locations is just as important as it is in the office. All the same security requirements apply at remote locations, although they may be implemented in different ways. For example, paper-based Confidential and Highly Restricted information needs to be locked up when not in active use. In Company X offices, a file cabinet might be used, but on the road, a locking briefcase might be employed.

Access Control Packages: All portable and remote computers which are under the control of Company X workers, and which are used to process Company X business information must be protected with an access control package approved by the Information Security Department. These access control packages will prevent unauthorized use of the machines and unauthorized access to Company X information. These access control packages will also help prevent virus infections and other types of damage from malicious software.

Handling Of Sensitive Information: In general, sensitive (Confidential and Highly Restricted) information should not leave Company X offices. If it is necessary to remove computer-readable sensitive information from Company X offices, this information must be protected with encryption facilities approved by the Information Security Department. Likewise, if sensitive information is transmitted over public computer networks such as the Internet, this transmission must take place with encryption facilities approved by the Information Security Department. All portable and remote systems storing sensitive Company X information must also employ hard disk encryption systems.

Authentication Of Remote Users: Remote access to Company X computers and networks requires that all Users be definitively authenticated with dynamic passwords or other identification systems approved by the Information Security Department. All remote users must connect to Company X computers and internal networks via authorized communications systems such as firewalls and modem pools. Inbound connection to Company X computers or networks through an office desktop modem is prohibited unless specific approval has been obtained from the Information Security Department. Outbound connection to third party networks including the Internet is permissible through office desktop modems or other types of modems. Leaving personal- computer-linked modems in auto-answer mode is prohibited unless a remote User identification system approved by the Information Security Department has been installed.

Theft Of Equipment: If information systems equipment used to handle Company X information is not stored in a locked area, Users should employ anti-theft equipment approved by the Information Security Department. Because theft of these systems is so common, Users must not store passwords, user-IDs, or any other access information in portable or remote systems. Likewise, dynamic password tokens or other access control mechanisms employed for remote access must not be stored in the same case as portable computers.

Remote Office Security: Before approval for working at home or telecommuting is granted, a User's manager must review the security environment of the proposed working environment. If the User works with sensitive information, a shredder must be employed or issued by Company X. Similarly, if sensitive information will be stored in paper form, locking furniture or a safe must be available or provided by Company X. Users must also make sure that their files will be remotely backed-up over the network, or that they will have appropriate remote systems to perform their own back-ups.

Travel Considerations: Users must be careful not to discuss sensitive information when in public places like hotel lobbies, restaurants, and elevators. Viewing sensitive information on a computer screen or hardcopy report is prohibited when a User is in a public place such as seated on an airplane. Similarly, Users must be careful not to provide sensitive information in voicemail messages or alphanumeric pager messages.

Viruses, Malicious Software, and Change Control

Virus Checking Required: Virus checking systems approved by the Information Security Department must be in place on all personal computers with operating systems susceptible to viruses, as well as on all firewalls with external network connections, and on all electronic mail servers. All files coming from external sources must be checked before execution or usage (if encryption or data compression has been used, these processes must be reversed before the virus checking process takes place). Users are not authorized to turn off or disable virus checking systems.

If A Virus Is Detected: If Users obtain virus alerts, they must immediately disconnect from all networks and cease further use of the affected computer, and then call the Information Systems Help Desk and get technical assistance. To prevent possible damage to Company X information and information systems, Users are not permitted to remove viruses on their own. If Users believe they may have been the victim of other malicious software such as a Java applet, they must immediately call the Help Desk to minimize the damage. User possession or development of viruses or other malicious software is prohibited.

Change Control: Users are not permitted to install new or upgraded operating systems or application software on personal computers or other machines used to process Company X information. Systems used to process Company X information may or may not be owned by Company X, but have been specifically recognized as systems used for regular business activities (reimbursement by Company X for the cost of the machine would be a clear indication of this status). This approach allows Company X to perform automatic software distribution, automatic software license management, automated remote back up, and related functions on a centralized and coordinated basis. While change control will be maintained through the above-mentioned access control packages, Users can, however, change the preferences on software packages, such as the fonts for a word processing package.

Personal Use of Information Systems

Personal Use: All User activity is subject to logging and subsequent analysis. Users must not perform any activity on Company X information systems that could damage the reputation of Company X. Unbecoming conduct could lead to disciplinary action including revocation of access control privileges. Incidental personal use of Company X information systems (including the telephone) is permissible so long as the usage does not interfere with job performance, does not deny other Users access to the system resources, and does not incur significant costs. Personal use of Company X information, such as a mailing list, requires the advance approval of the relevant information Owner. Use of software licensed to Company X on a personal computer owned by a User is not authorized unless the system has been designated a "system which is used to process Company X information" (as defined in the prior paragraph).

Testing Prohibition: Users must not test, or attempt to compromise any information security mechanism unless specifically authorized to do so by the Information Security Department. For example, Users must not attempt to compromise anti-copying mechanisms built into commercial software. Users are prohibited from possessing software or other tools that are designed to compromise information security (for example, password cracking software).

Intellectual Property Rights

Legal Ownership: With the exception of material clearly owned by third parties, Company X is the legal owner of all business information stored on or passing through in its systems. Unless a specific written agreement has been signed by the Chief Information Officer, all business-related information (including patents, copyrights, and inventions) developed while a User is employed by Company X is Company X property.

Making Copies Of Software: Users must not make copies of or use software unless they know that the copies are in keeping with the vendor's license to Company X. If a "system which is used to process Company X information" has been set-up by the Information Systems Department, Users can rely on the fact that all software on this system is licensed and authorized. Questions about licensing should be directed to the Information Systems Department, which maintains documentation reflecting software licenses throughout Company X. Making regular back-ups of software for contingency planning purposes is permissible. The Information Systems Department will remove all software which is not authorized on "systems which are used to process Company X information."

Labeling: In addition to maintaining the labels mentioned above in the section entitled Information Sensitivity Classification, for all information provided by third parties, Users must maintain information about source, date, and usage restrictions. These labels will be important for management decision making purposes, and will also help demonstrate that Company X observed appropriate copyright and other intellectual property laws. Users should assume that all materials on the Internet are copyrighted unless specific notice states otherwise.

Systems Development

Production System Definition: Information systems which have been designated "production systems" have special security requirements. A production system is a system which is regularly used to process information critical to Company X's business. Although a production system may be physically situated anywhere, the production system designation is assigned by the Information Systems Department computer operations manager.

Special Production System Requirements: All software developed in-house which runs on production systems must be developed according to the Information Systems Department's systems development methodology (SDM). Among other things, this methodology ensures that the software will be adequately documented and tested before it is used for critical Company X information. The SDM will also ensure that production systems include adequate control measures. Production systems must also have designated Owners and Custodians for the critical information they process. The Information Security Department must perform periodic risk assessments of production systems to determine whether the controls employed are adequate. All production systems must have an access control system to restrict who can access the system as well as restrict the privileges available to these Users. A designated access control administrator (who is not a regular User on the system in question) must be assigned for all production systems.

Separation Between Production, Development, and Test Systems: Where resources permit, there should be a separation between the production, development, and test environments. This will ensure that security is maintained in a much more rigorous way for the production system, while the other two environments can maximize productivity with fewer security restrictions. Where these distinctions have been established, development and test staff must not be permitted to have access to production systems. Likewise, all production software testing must proceed with sanitized information (where Confidential or Highly Restricted information is replaced with dummy data). All security fixes provided by software vendors must also go through the SDM testing process, and must be promptly installed. On a related note, application programmers must not be given access to production information. A formal and documented change control process must also be used to restrict and approve changes to production systems. All application-program-based access paths other than the formal User access paths must be deleted or disabled before software is moved into production.

User Programming: Users are not permitted to write production computer programs unless specifically authorized by the Chief Information Officer. The construction of spreadsheet formulas, automatic execution scripts which are run when a system is booted, or databases is not considered programming for purposes of this document. Both Users and Programmers must be careful never to embed user-IDs or readable passwords in any file.

Reporting Problems

What To Report: All workers must promptly report to the Information Security Department any loss of, or severe damage to their hardware or software. For example, if a portable computer were stolen, this must be reported. Workers must also report all suspected compromises to Company X information systems. For instance, if a hacker is believed to have broken-into Company X systems, then this too must be reported. Likewise, if a serious information security vulnerability is known to exist, this too must be reported. All instances of suspected disclosure of sensitive (Confidential or Highly Restricted) information must additionally be reported.

How To Report: An unattended voicemail hotline (phone number XXX-XXX-XXXX) with a pager alert has been established to handle information security problem reports. Callers to the hotline can leave messages on this line anonymously if they wish. Reports must not be sent by electronic mail unless the message is encrypted with software authorized by the Information Security Department. All reports will be investigated before any action is taken. This hotline may also be used by workers with a question about information security, for example a worker wondering whether a certain proposed action would jeopardize security.

Non-Compliance Situations

Risk Acceptance: Non-compliance with these and other information security requirements can result in disciplinary action up to and including termination. In rare cases, a business case for non-compliance can be established; in all such cases the non-compliance situation must be approved in advance through a risk acceptance process. This process requires a risk acceptance memo signed by a department manager and approved by the following departments: Information Security, Information Systems, and Internal Audit. Further details on the risk acceptance process can be obtained through the Internal Audit Department.

Further Information: Questions about this document should be directed to Information Security Department manager at XXX-XXX-XXXX. Further policy information can be found in the Human Resources Manual.

VI. Sample Telecommuting & Mobile Computer Security Policy

MANAGEMENT ISSUES

Telecommuting Privileges: Working at home or alternative site work arrangements (both known as telecommuting) are a management option, not a universal employee fringe benefit. Permission to telecommute is granted by the involved employee's manager. Before a telecommuting arrangement can begin, this manager must be satisfied that the job can be effectively performed off-site, that the worker has the personality and work habits suitable for telecommuting, and that an alternative worksite (such as a home office) is appropriate for the Company X tasks performed by the involved worker. Worksite considerations include physical and information security for Company X property as well as a low-distraction work environment. Managers must also be satisfied that the ways to measure worker performance are both clearly specified and realistic, and that the methods to stay in touch with other workers are adequate. A worksheet/checklist for making these approval decisions is available from the Help Desk [intranet link to this checklist goes here].

Periodic Privilege Reevaluation: The system privileges granted to all users, including the privilege to telecommute and to make remote access to Company X systems, must be reevaluated by management every six months. Consistent compliance with the policies described in this document as well as related policies is an important factor in management's decision regarding the continuation of a telecommuting arrangement. Related policies include, but are not limited to, compliance with software license agreements and reporting suspected computer virus infections. Many related policies are not reiterated here because they appear in other Company X documents [link to table of contents for the information security policies intranet site]. This document is restricted to security matters relevant to telecommuters and mobile computer users.

Work Site Inspections: Company X maintains the right to conduct inspections of telecommuter offices without advance notice. Company X also maintains the right to examine the contents of any computer which contains or is thought to contain Company X internal information, including computers which have been purchased by employees, contractors, consultants, temporaries, and others.

Consistent Security: Company X information must be protected in a manner commensurate with its sensitivity, value, and criticality. The precautions described in this policy apply regardless of the storage media on which information is recorded, the locations where the information is stored, the systems used to process the information, or the processes by which the information is handled. This means that workers must protect information in a similar manner no matter whether they are in a Company X office, a hotel room, or at a home office.

Required Training: Company X workers must complete an approved remote systems access training course prior to being granted privileges to use dial-up, in-bound Internet telnet, or any other Company X remote access data communications system [link to the intranet site which allows them to sign-up for and download this computer based training (CBT) course].

Intellectual Property Rights: As is the case when workers are in the office, intellectual property developed or conceived of while a worker is attending to Company X business at an alternative worksite is the exclusive property of Company X. Such intellectual property includes patent, copyright, trademark, and all other intellectual property rights as manifested in memos, plans, strategies, products, computer programs, documentation, and other Company X materials.

Reporting Loss Or Damage: Workers at remote working locations must promptly report to their manager any damage to or loss of Company X computer hardware, software, or sensitive information which has been entrusted to their care [link to Help Desk intranet trouble ticket system].

ACCESS CONTROL

Encryption And Boot Protection: All computers used for telecommuting, as well as portables, laptops, notebooks, and other transportable computers containing sensitive Company X information must consistently employ both hard disk encryption for all files as well as boot protection via a password. These two essential controls must be provided via software and/or hardware systems approved by the Information Security Department [link to list of approved information security products]. Personal Digital Assistants (PDAs), handheld computers, and smart phones must not be used for Company X business information unless they have first been configured with the necessary controls, such as encryption and boot protection, and approved for such use by the Information Systems Department. Exceptions will be made for calendars, address books, and stored connection information such as telephone numbers.

Sharing Access Devices And Systems: Telecommuters must not share dynamic password token cards, smart cards, fixed passwords, or any other access devices or access parameters with any other person without prior approval from the Information Security Department. This means that a remote computer used for Company X business must be used exclusively by the involved telecommuter -- family members, friends, and others must not be permitted to use this machine. Likewise, telecommuters must never lend to others a handheld computer, a personal digital assistant (PDA), a smart phone, or any other computer that stores information about Company X business activities.

BACKUP AND MEDIA STORAGE

Back-Up: Telecommuters are responsible for seeing to it that their remote systems are backed-up on a periodic basis, either automatically through the network or remotely with tape drives or similar equipment. If network backup is not available or feasible, Company X will provide telecommuters with local backup equipment. If backups are made locally, telecommuting workers must store copies of these same backups at a secure location away from the remote working site at least every two weeks.

Sensitive Media Marking And Storage: When sensitive information is written to a floppy disk, magnetic tape, CD-ROM or other storage media, the media must be suitably marked with the highest relevant sensitivity classification. Unless encrypted, when not in use, this media must be stored in heavy locked furniture (safes, credenzas, etc.). Smart cards and tamper-resistant security modules are an exception to this rule because they have their own protective enclosures as well as encryption measures.

Automatic Device Synchronization: Systems which automatically exchange data between devices, such as a Personal Digital Assistant (PDA) and a personal computer, must not be enabled unless the systems have first been evaluated and approved by the Information Security Department. These synchronization systems can crash computers and overwrite critical data if not properly configured and used.

Setting Date & Time: To facilitate backup file restoration processes, and to assist with the recording of system logs, telecommuting workers must diligently keep their remote computers' internal clocks synchronized to the actual date and time.

COMMUNICATIONS LINKS

Establishing Dial-Up Facilities: Workers must not leave their personal computers unattended with a modem turned-on and communications software enabled unless they have installed an access control system approved by the Information Security Department [intranet link to approved information security products list]. Unless an approved access control system is enabled, leaving a work computer or home computer turned-on in this fashion could allow unauthorized persons to gain access to both this system and a connected network. Workers must not establish any communications systems which ordinarily accepts in-coming dial-up calls unless these systems have first been approved by the Information Security Department manager [link to the External Communications Security Policy].

Inbound Dial-Up To Company X Networks: All inbound dial-up lines connected to Company X internal networks and/or multi-user computer systems must pass through an additional access control point (a firewall, modem pool, telecommunications front-end or similar system) before users are permitted to reach an operating system-based computer log-in screen asking for a user-ID and fixed password.

Establishing Internet Connections: Workers must not establish firewalls, routers, communications servers, or any other facilities on their remote computer systems that handle Company X business if these facilities permit telnet or any other type of real-time in-bound remote access via the Internet. Out-bound connections from a remote system through the Internet are permissible so long as these connections are secured in a manner consistent with the requirements specified in the External Communications Security Policy [link].

Other Connections: Other than dial-up and Internet connections, workers must not establish any other interface between a remote computer used for Company X business activities and another network (such as Value Added Networks), unless prior approval of the Information Security Department has been obtained in writing. This means that workers are prohibited from establishing their own personal accounts with Internet Service Providers (ISPs) and using these accounts for Company X business; instead, all Company X business Internet electronic mail and Internet web surfing must be accomplished through a Company X-managed firewall [link to that part of the External Communications Security Policy].

DSL Lines And Cable Modem Lines: Digital Subscriber Line (DSL) lines, cable modem lines, and other high-speed lines must not be used for any Company X business communications unless a firewall and an approved virtual private network (VPN) is employed. Telecommuters must contact the Help Desk for assistance in the establishment of these facilities before making any arrangements with third party vendors.

Radio Networks: Workers transmitting sensitive Company X information must not employ radio networks, such as cellular modems, unless these network channels are encrypted. The use of digital communications protocols rather than traditional analog communications protocols does not qualify as encryption.

Telephone Discussions: To prevent interception (taps), workers should take steps to avoid discussing sensitive information when on the telephone. If discussion of such information is absolutely required, workers must use guarded terms and refrain from mentioning sensitive details beyond those needed to get the job done. On a related note, secret information must not be discussed on speaker-phones unless all participating parties first acknowledge that no unauthorized persons are in close proximity such that they might overhear the conversation. Because the risk of interception is considerably higher than for other technologies, unless an encryption or scrambling system approved by the Information Security Department is used, secret Company X information must never be discussed on cordless or cellular telephones.

Message Machines: Unless the receiving message machine or voicemail system is known to be password protected, workers must refrain from leaving messages containing sensitive information on these recording systems. This will help ensure that sensitive information is released only to the intended party. In addition, unless their message machine or voicemail system is password protected, telecommuting workers must record an outgoing message informing callers that their incoming message recording system is not secure and is not suitable for sensitive information.

SYSTEM MANAGEMENT

Telecommuting Systems: Workers attending to Company X business at alternative worksites must only use Company X-provided computer software, hardware, and network equipment. An exception will be made only if other systems have been approved by the Information Systems Department as compatible with Company X information systems and controls. Similarly, workers should not bring their own computers into Company X offices to process or otherwise handle Company X information without prior approval from the Information Systems Department.

Changes To Configurations And Software: On Company X-supplied computer hardware, workers must not change the operating system configuration or install new software. If such changes are required, they will be performed by Help Desk personnel with remote system maintenance software.

Changes to Hardware: Computer equipment supplied by Company X must not be altered or added to in any way (e.g., upgraded processor, expanded memory, or extra circuit boards) without prior knowledge and authorization from the Information Systems Department.

Down-Loading Software: Without prior authorization, workers must not down-load software from dial-up electronic bulletin board systems, the Internet, or other systems outside Company X onto computers used to handle Company X data. This prohibition is necessary because such software may contain viruses, worms, Trojan horses, and other routines which may damage Company X information and systems. Such software may also introduce software incompatibilities and related technical problems.

Ownership Vs. Possession: If Company X supplied a telecommuter with software, hardware, furniture, information and/or other materials to perform Company X business remotely, the title to, and all rights and interests to these items will remain with Company X. In such instances, telecommuter possession does not convey ownership or any implication of ownership. Accordingly, all such items must be promptly returned to Company X when a telecommuter separates from Company X, or when so requested by the telecommuter's manager.

Liability For Company X Property: If Company X supplied a telecommuter with software, hardware, furniture, information or other materials to perform Company X business remotely, Company X assumes all risks of loss or damage to these items unless such loss or damage occurs due to the telecommuter's negligence. Because these items are not under the direct control of other Company X personnel, Company X expressly disclaims any responsibility for loss or damage to persons or property caused by, or arising out of the usage of such items.

Electromagnetic Interference: In some cases, use of computers or other electronic devices will generate electromagnetic interference (EMI) which will affect televisions, radios, and/or other machines. If a telecommuting system set-up to perform Company X business generates such interference, it's use must be terminated immediately until such time as the specific nature of and a solution for the problem has been identified. The Company X help desk will assist telecommuters with this process [link to Help Desk intranet page].

TRAVEL CONSIDERATIONS

Removal Of Information: Sensitive (confidential or secret) information may not be removed from Company X premises unless the information's Owner has approved in advance. This policy includes sensitive information stored on portable computer hard disks, floppy disks, CD-ROMs, magnetic tape cartridges, and paper memos. An exception is made for authorized off-site backups which are in encrypted form [link to Information Classification Policy].

Travelling With Secret Information: Unless specific approval from a local Department Manager has been granted, workers must avoid travelling on public transportation when in the possession of secret Company X information.

Foreign Transport: Whenever secret information is carried by a Company X worker into a foreign country, the information must either be stored in some inaccessible form (such as an encrypted floppy disk) or must remain in the worker's possession at all times. Company X workers must not take secret Company X information into another country unless the permission has first been obtained from the Physical Security Department manager.

Public Exposure: Sensitive (confidential or secret) Company X information must not be read, discussed, or otherwise exposed in restaurants, on airplanes, on trains, or in other public places where unauthorized people might discover it.

Checked Luggage: Workers in the possession of portable, laptop, notebook, palmtop, handheld, smart phones, personal digital assistants, and other transportable computers containing sensitive Company X information must not check these computers in airline luggage systems. To avoid damage and theft, these computers must remain in the possession of the traveler as hand luggage.

Securing Hardcopy Sensitive Information: Whenever a hardcopy version of secret information is removed from Company X premises, it must either be stored in a safe, locking furniture, or some other heavy container with a lock, or carried in a locked briefcase when not in use. Such information must not be left in an unattended motor vehicle, hotel room, or external office, even if this vehicle or room is locked.

Faxing Sensitive Information: If secret information is to be sent by fax, the recipient must first have been notified of the time when it will be transmitted, and also have agreed that an authorized person will be present at the destination machine when the material is sent. An exception will be made if the area surrounding the fax machine is physically restricted such that persons who are not authorized to see the material being faxed may not enter. This means that sensitive Company X information must not be faxed through a hotel desk or other untrusted third parties. Another exception will be made in those instances in which the destination fax machine is password protected and authorized parties are the only ones who have access to the involved password.

PHYSICAL SECURITY

Provision Of Secure Containers: Workers who must keep secret or confidential Company X information at their homes in order to do their work must have safes or lockable heavy furniture for the proper storage of this information. If these workers do not have such furniture or safes, Company X will loan these items to the telecommuting worker.

Shredders: Telecommuters must also have or be provided with a shredder to appropriately dispose of printed versions of sensitive information. Shredders which make strips of paper are not acceptable for the disposal of Company X sensitive material; acceptable shredders make confetti or other small particles. All sensitive Company X paper-resident information plus any information containing financial account numbers (like credit card numbers) must be shredded. Intermediate work products related to sensitive information, such as carbon copies, photocopies, or memo drafts, must also be shredded. Telecommuting workers must not throw away Company X sensitive information in hotel waste baskets or other publicly-accessible trash containers. Instead, sensitive information must be retained until it can be shredded, or destroyed with other approved methods.

Property Passes: Portable computers, cellular phones, PDAs, modems, and related information systems equipment belonging to Company X must not leave Company X offices unless accompanied by an approved property pass. Property passes should be obtained when bringing personally-owned equipment into Company X offices, lest the removal of this equipment be delayed.

Screen Positioning: The display screens for all systems used to handle Company X sensitive information must be positioned such that they cannot be readily viewed by unauthorized persons through a window, over a shoulder, or by similar means.

Call-Forwarding: Workers handling Company X internal information on a remote computer must never employ call forwarding on remote modem lines to gain access to Company X systems which employ call-back user-authentication.

Logging-Out: After a worker has completed a remote session with Company X computers, the worker must log-out and then hang-up, rather than simply hanging-up. Because some modems take a while to drop a line after a call has been terminated, simply hanging up may leave the modem port open. This means that, if the worker did not log-out, the next caller could resume the session where the worker left off. Workers using remote communications facilities must wait until they receive a confirmation of their log-out command from the remotely connected Company X machine before they leave the computer they are using.

Moving Residence Location: If a telecommuting worker moves his or her residence or off-site work location to another site, the worker must notify his or her manager prior to the move. The worker must also follow Information Security Department instructions associated with telecommuter residence moves. The new location must meet all the current telecommuter site requirements [link to telecommuter checklist goes here].

VII. Sample External Communications Security Policy

Policy Objectives and Scope: This policy describes the security requirements for remote information systems connections to Company X internal computers and networks. It covers a wide variety of technologies including cellular phone connections, dial-up modem links, value-added networks, and Internet encrypted tunnels (also known as value added networks or VPNs). Every individual worker or organization making these and other types of automated connections to Company X internal computers and networks must abide by the rules described here.

External Connections Require Approval: Access to Company X internal networks from remote locations including worker homes, hotel rooms, and customer offices, must in all instances be approved in advance by the involved worker's immediate manager. Such remote access is not a universal fringe benefit, and may be revoked at any time for cause including unsatisfactory performance and non-compliance with security policies. Further details about this approval process can be found within the Telecommuting Security Policy [link to intranet site document by that name].

Third Party Access to Company X Internal Networks: In strictly controlled situations, Company X does allow third parties to access Company X internal networks and connected computer systems. Both the Owner of the information to which the third party will be given access and the project manager in charge of the third party's work must agree in writing to such access before it will be established. The decision-making process for granting such access includes consideration of the controls on the systems to be connected, the third party's security policies, and the results of a background check. Privileges for such third parties must be strictly limited to the system facilities and information clearly needed to achieve predefined business objectives. These access privileges must be reviewed every six months by the relevant project manager to determine whether they need to be continued.

Third Party Vendor Access: Third party vendors which have sold Company X hardware, software, or communication services are not automatically granted repeated access to Company X internal computers and/or networks. They must either go through the approval process described in the last paragraph, or go through a separate remote access for systems maintenance process administered by the Information Security Department [intranet link to contact information for the department]. Temporary remote access privileges for vendors may, however, be enabled by a systems administrator without going through either of these approval processes. This temporary access must be granted only for the time period required to accomplish approved tasks (one day or less). This temporary access must be provided by positive identification of the vendor personnel before the connection is established, as well as logging of all activity while the connection exists.

Third Party Compliance Statement: All third parties wishing to remotely access Company X internal computers or networks must sign a compliance statement prior to being issued a user-ID. If a certain third party already has a user-ID, a signature must be obtained prior to receiving a renewed user-ID (as indicated above, this renewal process takes place every six months). A signature on this compliance statement indicates the involved user(s) understand and agree to abide by Company X policies and procedures related to computers and networks. Company X retains the right to periodically audit third parties who have access to Company X computers and networks to ensure compliance with this and other policies and requirements.

Responsibility for User-IDs: All workers (including third parties) are responsible for the activity performed with their personal user-IDs, whether or not these user-IDs are connecting via external network facilities. User-IDs must never be shared with associates, friends, family members, or others. User-IDs may not be utilized by anyone but the individuals to whom they have been issued. Similarly, workers are forbidden from performing any activity with user-IDs belonging to other individuals (excepting authorized anonymous user-IDs like "guest").

Default to Denial: If a Company X computer or network access control system is not functioning properly, it must default to denial of privileges to users. If access control systems are malfunctioning, the systems they support must remain unavailable until such time as the problem has been rectified.

Dynamic Passwords: All computer network connections (for example by dial-up line or the Internet) initiated from a location outside an official Company X office, and connecting to a Company X internal network, must employ dynamic password systems approved by the Information Security Department. Dynamic passwords are passwords which change each time a new session is established. Dynamic passwords are necessary because traditional fixed passwords can be intercepted and later replayed by third parties to gain unauthorized access to Company X computers and networks. Store-and-forward network connections, such as those used for electronic mail and Internet news services, need not employ dynamic passwords. These dynamic passwords can be provided as part of a virtual private network (VPN) system.

Outbound Connections: Computer network connections initiated from inside an official Company X office, and connecting to an external network or computer, do not need to employ dynamic passwords. These connections must however be routed through dial-up modem pools, Internet firewalls, and other systems expressly established to provide secure network access.

Modems on Desktop Systems: Modems inside or connected to office desktop microcomputers (PCs) are not permitted. Home based, mobile and/or telecommuting microcomputers are an exception to this rule. As indicated above, connections to remote computers and networks must instead be routed via modem pools or the Company X Internet firewall. Unless a dynamic password system is installed, workers with home based, mobile, or telecommuting PCs must not leave modems in auto-answer mode, with communications software enabled, such that in-coming dial-up calls could be received.

Encrypted Links: Whenever a computer network connection is established between a Company X computer and another computer at a location outside an official Company X office, and whenever this connection transmits or is likely to transmit either Confidential or Secret information, the link must be encrypted. Such encryption must be accomplished only with systems approved by the Information Security Department [intranet link to approved products list issued by the Information Security Department]. These systems include virtual private networks (VPNs) which incorporate not only encryption but also user authentication mechanisms.

Using Radio Technology for Data: Portable phones using radio technology as well as cellular phones must not be used for data transmissions containing Company X Secret or Confidential information unless the connection is encrypted. Likewise, other broadcast networking technologies--such radio-based local area networks--must not be used for these types of Company X information unless the link is encrypted. Such links may be used for electronic mail as long as involved users understand that the transmissions must not contain readable Secret or Confidential information. Similarly, workers must not discuss Confidential or Secret matters on cordless or cellular phones employing a regular voice connection, unless this connection has been encrypted with technology approved by the Information Security Department [another intranet link to approved products list]. Phones using digital transmission rather than traditional analog transmission protocols (such as PCS) are not considered to be encrypted for purposes of this policy.

Privilege Access Controls: All computers permanently or intermittently connected to either external networks or Company X networks must operate with privilege access controls approved by the Information Security Department [another intranet link to approved products list]. Multi-user systems must employ user-IDs unique to each user, as well as user privilege restriction mechanisms including directory and file access permissions. Network-connected single-user systems must employ approved hardware or software mechanisms that control system booting and that includes a time-out-after-no-activity screen blanker.

Changing Initial Passwords: All vendor-supplied default passwords (or other alternative access mechanisms) must be changed before any computer or communications system is used for any Company X business activity. This policy applies to passwords associated with end-user user-IDs, as well as passwords associated with systems administrators and other privileged user-IDs.

Shared File Systems: The establishment of a connection between any external computer or network and a Company X internal computer or network must not involve the use of shared file systems such as UNIX's NFS (Network File System). This will help to ensure that sensitive information is not inadvertently disclosed to unauthorized persons. An exception will be made if the Information Security Department approves the configuration prior to usage.

Required Virus Checking Programs: Up-to-date virus checking programs approved by the Information Security Department [intranet link to approved products list] must be continuously enabled on all web servers, LAN servers, mail servers, firewalls, and networked PCs. An exception will be made in those cases where the operating system, such as UNIX, is not generally subject to viruses.

Eradicating Viruses: Because viruses are often complex and sophisticated, workers must not attempt to eradicate them without expert assistance. If workers suspect infection by a virus, they must immediately stop using the involved computer, disconnect from all networks, and call the corporate help desk [insert telephone number or link to their intranet page]. If the suspected virus appears to be damaging information or software, workers must turn the microcomputer off immediately.

Decompress Before Running Virus Software: All externally-supplied computer-readable files (software programs, databases, word processing documents, spreadsheets, etc.) must be decompressed prior to being subjected to an approved virus checking process. Many virus checking programs cannot detect viruses in compressed files. The same applies to files which have been encrypted.

Downloading Software: Workers must not down-load software from dial-up electronic bulletin board systems, the Internet, or other systems outside Company X. This prohibition is necessary because such software may contain viruses, worms, Trojan horses, and other software which may damage Company X information and systems. An exception is made for systems administrators and other authorized technical personnel downloading patches and the latest releases of software packages. An exception is also provided for external network automated software distribution systems (such as those which distribute the latest virus checking software), which have been approved by the Information Security Department [intranet link to approved products list issued by the Information Security Department].

Downloading Content and Assigning Sensitivity Labels: With the exception of general business correspondence and copyrighted software, all externally-provided information which is not clearly in the public domain must receive a Company X information classification system label. The Company X worker who receives this information is responsible for assigning an appropriate classification on behalf of the external party. When assigning a classification label, this worker must preserve copyright notices, author credits, guidelines for interpretation, as well as information about restricted dissemination. Further details can be found in the Information Classification System Policy [intranet link to that document].

Reliance on Downloaded Content: All information taken off the Internet and other external networks should be considered suspect until confirmed by separate information from another source. There is no standardized quality control process on the Internet, and a considerable amount of its information is outdated and inaccurate, and in some instances even deliberately misleading.

Time-Out After No Activity: All information systems accepting remote connections from public networks such as the dial-up phone network or the Internet must include a time-out mechanism. This time-out mechanism must terminate all sessions without activity for a period of 30 minutes or less (a smaller time period is recommended). In addition, all user-IDs registered to networks or computers with external access facilities must be automatically suspended after a period of 30 days of inactivity.

Failure to Establish a Connection: All Company X computers with interfaces to external networks must temporarily terminate the connection or time-out the user-ID for at least ten minutes following a sequence of several unsuccessful attempts to log-in. For example, if an incorrect dynamic password is provided three consecutive times, dial-up systems should drop the connection. Repeated unsuccessful attempts to remotely establish a connection using a privileged user-ID must not result in the revocation (suspension as opposed to time-out) of the user-ID because this could interfere with the ability of authorized parties to respond to security incidents.

No Trespassing Banners: Where systems software permits, log-in banners must be used on all Company X networks and computers which are directly accessible through external networks. These banners must employ standard no trespassing warning notices adopted by the Information Security Department. These banners must also refrain from disclosing the fact that Company X systems have been reached, the nature of the information available on these systems, as well as the specific systems software running on these computers. Web servers, telephone voice response units (VRUs), and other systems which are designed to respond to anonymous users do not need to have such banners.

Anonymous Interaction: With the exception of web servers, electronic bulletin boards, or other systems where all regular users are anonymous, users are prohibited from logging into any Company X system or network anonymously (for example, by using "guest" user-IDs). If users employ systems facilities which allow them to change their active user-ID to gain certain privileges, they must have initially logged-in employing a user-ID that clearly indicates their identity.

Logs for Externally Connected Systems: All Company X computers and networks which interface to external networks must maintain system logs which indicate the identity and activity performed by each user who gains access to these systems. These logs must indicate the time of day, the date, the user-ID employed, any special privileges utilized, and other details associated with all connections (whether permitted or denied). Systems administrators must regularly review these logs or use automated intrusion detection systems to immediately inform them of suspicious activity.

Flow Control for Externally Connected Systems: All Company X networks which are connected to external networks must employ flow control mechanisms to restrict the machines to which users can connect based on the need for such access. Flow control can be implemented via internal firewalls, routers, gateways, and other network systems. The intention of this flow control is to contain intrusions by unauthorized parties.

Browsing: With the exception of the Company X intranet, workers must not browse through Company X computer systems or networks. For example, curious searching for interesting files and/or programs in the directories of other users is prohibited. Steps taken to legitimately locate information needed to perform one's job is not considered browsing. This statement on browsing does not apply to external networks such as the Internet.

Gaining Unauthorized Access: Workers using Company X computer networks are prohibited from gaining unauthorized access to any information system or network to which they have not been expressly granted access. Workers using Company X computer networks are also prohibited from in any way damaging, disrupting, or interfering with the operations of multi-user information systems to which they are connected. Likewise, workers are prohibited from capturing or otherwise being in possession of passwords, encryption keys, or any other access control mechanisms which has not been expressly assigned to them. Workers are furthermore prohibited from possessing or using software tools which could provide unauthorized access to system resources (these include password dictionary attack programs, encryption key brute-force discovery programs, and software for defeating copy-protection mechanisms).

Changes to Company X Networks: Changes to Company X internal networks include loading new software, changing network addresses, reconfiguring routers, adding dial-up lines, and the like. With the exception of emergency situations, all changes to Company X computer networks must be documented in a work order request [intranet link to that form here], and must be approved in advance by the Information Technology Department. Emergency changes to Company X networks must only be made by persons who are authorized by the Information Technology Department. This process prevents unexpected changes from inadvertently leading to denial of service, unauthorized disclosure of information, and other problems.

Establishing System Connections: Workers must NOT establish or make arrangements for the establishment of electronic bulletin boards, local area networks, modem connections to existing local area networks, or other multi-user systems for communicating information without the specific approval of the Director of the Information Technology Department. Likewise, new types of real-time connections between two or more in-house computer systems must not be established unless such approval has first been obtained. This policy helps to ensure that all Company X systems have the controls needed to protect other network-connected systems. Security requirements for a network-connected system are not just a function of the connected system, they are also a function of all other Company X connected systems.

Installation of Communications Lines: Workers and vendors must not make arrangements for, or actually complete the installation of voice or data lines with any carrier, if they have not first obtained approval from the director of the Information Systems Department [intranet link to a form for this].

Subscription to External Networks: Workers must not establish connections with Internet Service Providers (ISPs) or other external networks for the transmission of Company X data unless this arrangement has first been approved by the Director of the Information Security Department. For further information about ISPs, see the Internet Security Policy [intranet link].

Establishing New Business Networks: Unless the Director of the Information Technology Department and the Chief Legal Counsel have both approved in advance, workers are prohibited from using the Internet or any other external network to establish new or different business channels. These channels include electronic data interchange (EDI) arrangements, electronic malls with on-line shopping, on-line database services, acceptance of credit cards through the Internet, etc.

Participation in External Networks: Participation in external networks as a provider of services that external parties rely on is expressly prohibited unless two conditions are first fulfilled. Specifically, Company X's chief legal counsel must identify the legal risks involved, and then the Director of the Information Technology Department must expressly accept these and other risks associated with the proposal. Acting as an Internet node is an example of such participation.

Disclosure of Systems Information: The internal addresses, configurations, and related system design information for Company X computers and networks is confidential and must not be released to third parties who do not have a demonstrable need-to-know such information. Likewise, the security measures employed to protect Company X computers and networks is confidential and should be similarly protected.

Related Information: For additional information on a related topic, see the policies entitled Telecommuting Security Policy [intranet link], and External Party Information Disclosure Policy [intranet link].

Approved by: [insert approving executive's name].
Approved on: DD/MM/YY.
Effective date: DD/MM/YY.
Version number: XX.

VIII. Sample Microcomputer Security Policy

DOCUMENT OVERVIEW

Objectives And Scope: A large portion of Company X's business is conducted with microcomputers (PCs, Macintoshes, UNIX workstations, portable computers, handheld computers, personal digital assistants, and similar computers dedicated to a single user's activity). Protection of these microcomputers and the information handled by these systems is an essential part of doing business at Company X. To this end, this policy provides information security instructions applicable to all workers (employees, contractors, consultants, temporaries, etc.) who use Company X microcomputers. All microcomputer users are expected to comply with this policy as a condition of continued employment. This policy applies whether microcomputers are stand-alone or connected to a network such as a LAN or the intranet. [This policy can be supplemented by several other policies found in this book entitled "Telecommuting & Mobile Computer Security Policy," "Sample Internet Security Policy," and "Sample Intranet Security Policy."]

BUSINESS USE ONLY

Business Use Only: Company X computer and communication systems must be used only for business purposes. Incidental personal use is permissible if the use: (a) does not consume more than a trivial amount of resources that could otherwise be used for business purposes, (b) does not interfere with worker productivity, and (c) does not preempt any business activity. Permissible incidental use of a microcomputer would, for example, involve responding to an electronic mail message about a luncheon. Separately, examples of personal use include game playing, writing a resume, and surfing the Internet for entertainment purposes.

CONFIGURATION CONTROL

Changes To Application Software: Company X has a standard list of permissible software packages that users can run on their microcomputers [a link to an intranet-posted microcomputer configuration standard could be provided here]. Workers must not install other software packages on microcomputers without obtaining advance permission from the Microcomputer Group in the Information Systems Department. Likewise, workers must not permit automatic software installation routines to be run on Company X microcomputers unless these routines have first been approved by the Microcomputer Group. Unless separate arrangements are made with the Microcomputer Group, upgrades to authorized software will be downloaded to microcomputers automatically. Auto-discovery license management software is used to remotely determine which software packages are resident on worker microcomputer hard disks. Unapproved software may be removed without advance notice to the involved worker.

Changes To Operating System Configurations: On Company X-supplied computer hardware, workers must not change operating system configurations, upgrade existing operating systems, or install new operating systems. If such changes are required, they will be performed by corporate help desk personnel (in person or with remote system maintenance software).

Changes To Hardware: Computer equipment supplied by Company X must not be altered or added to in any way (e.g., upgraded processor, expanded memory, or extra circuit boards) without the prior knowledge of and authorization from the Microcomputer Group within the Information Systems Department. Auto-discovery software is used to determine what equipment is installed in each microcomputer, so unauthorized hardware reconfigurations are detected automatically.

ACCESS CONTROL

Access Control Package: All Company X microcomputers must run an access control package approved by the Information Security Department. Typically these packages require a fixed password at the time a microcomputer is booted and again after a certain period of no activity. Users must set the time frame for this period of no activity -- at which point the contents of the screen are obscured -- to 15 minutes or less. If sensitive information resides on a microcomputer, the screen must immediately be protected with this access control package, or the machine turned off, whenever a worker leaves the location where the microcomputer is in use (for example, when leaving one's desk to go to the coffee machine).

Choice Of Passwords: The user-chosen passwords employed by access control software packages, as well as the keys employed by encryption packages, must be at least eight characters in length. These passwords and keys must be difficult-to-guess. Words in a dictionary, derivatives of user-IDs, and common character sequences such as "123456" must not be employed. Likewise, personal details such as spouse's name, license plate, social security number, and birthday must not be used unless accompanied by additional unrelated characters. User-chosen passwords and keys must also not be any part of speech. For example, proper names, geographical locations, common acronyms, and slang must not be employed.

Storage Of Passwords: Workers must maintain exclusive control of their personal passwords; they must not share them with others at any time. Passwords must not be stored in readable form in batch files, automatic log-in scripts, software macros, terminal function keys, in computers without access controls, or in any other locations where unauthorized persons might discover them.

Encryption Of Secret Information: All computerized secret information must be encrypted when not in active use (for example, when not manipulated by software or viewed by an authorized user). The use of physical security measures such as safes, locking furniture, and locking office doors is also recommended as a supplementary measure to protect secret information.

Logging Of Events Related To Secret Information: Microcomputers handling secret information must securely log all significant computer security relevant events. Examples of computer security relevant events include: password guessing attempts, attempts to use privileges that have not been authorized, modifications to production application software, and modifications to system software.

VIRUSES

Virus Program Installed: All microcomputers must continuously run the current version of virus detection package approved by the Information Security Department. The current version of this virus package will be automatically downloaded to each microcomputer when the machine is connected to Company X's internal network. Workers must not abort this download process. At a minimum, this package must execute whenever external storage media is supplied (for example when a floppy disk is inserted).

Decompression Before Checking: Externally supplied floppy disks, CD-ROMs, and other removable storage media must not be used unless they have first been checked for viruses. Externally supplied computer-readable files (software programs, databases, word processing documents, spreadsheets, etc.) must be decompressed prior to being subjected to an approved virus checking process. If the files have been encrypted, they must be decrypted before running a virus checking program. Many virus checking programs cannot detect viruses in compressed or encrypted files.

Eradicating Viruses: Because viruses can be complex and sophisticated, workers must not attempt to eradicate them without expert assistance. If workers suspect infection by a virus, they must immediately stop using the involved computer, disconnect from all networks, and call the Information Systems Department Help Desk. If the suspected virus appears to be damaging information or software, workers must immediately turn-off the microcomputer.

Playing With Viruses: Users must not intentionally write, compile, copy, propagate, execute, or attempt to introduce any computer code designed to self-replicate, damage, or otherwise hinder the performance of any Company X computer system. Such software may be called a virus, bacteria, worm, or a Trojan horse.

BACK UP

Archival Copies: All microcomputer software must be copied prior to its initial usage, and such copies must be stored in a safe and secure location. These master copies must not be used for ordinary business activities, but must be reserved for recovery from virus infections, hard disk crashes, and other computer problems. Documentation about the licenses for such software must be retained to get technical support, qualify for upgrade discounts, and verify the legal validity of the licenses.

Periodic Back-Up: All sensitive, valuable, or critical information resident on Company X computer systems must be periodically backed-up. Such back-up processes must be performed at least weekly. Unless automatic back-up systems are known to be operational, all end-users are responsible for making at least one current back-up copy of sensitive, critical, or valuable files. These separate back-up copies should be made each time that a significant number of changes are saved. User-generated back-ups must be periodically stored off-site in a physically secure location. Selected files from back-ups must be periodically restored to demonstrate the effectiveness of every back-up process. Department managers must verify that proper back-ups are being made on all microcomputers used for production business activities. Help Desk technical support is available for those workers that are having difficulty specifying, configuring, or otherwise establishing backup systems.

Reporting Software Purchases: All purchases of microcomputer software which have not been handled through the Purchasing Department must promptly be reported to the Information Systems Department Help Desk (this will allow Company X to keep a master database of licensed software, to support efforts to obtain favorable licensing terms, and to support related contingency planning initiatives).

Copyright Protection: Company X strongly supports strict adherence to software vendors' license agreements and copyright holders' notices. Making unauthorized copies of licensed and copyrighted software, even if only for "evaluation" purposes, is strictly forbidden. Likewise, Company X allows reproduction of copyrighted materials only to the extent legally considered "fair use" or with the permission of the author/owner. If workers have any questions about the relevance of copyright laws, they should contact corporate legal counsel. Unless they receive information to the contrary, workers should assume that software and other materials are copyrighted.

DESTRUCTION

Deletion of Old Information: Workers are required to delete information from their microcomputers if it is clearly no longer needed or potentially useful. Prior to deleting any Company X information, workers should consult the Document Retention Schedule prepared by corporate legal counsel [intranet link could go here]. Use of an "erase" feature (e.g., putting a document in a trash can icon) is not sufficient for sensitive information because the information may still be recoverable. Sensitive information should be deleted via an overwrite (zeroization) program approved by the Information Security Department.

Destruction Of Information: Prior to disposal, defective or damaged floppy disks containing sensitive information must be destroyed using scissors or other methods approved by the Information Security Department. Other storage media containing sensitive information must be disposed of in the locked destruction bins found in Company X offices. All hardcopy containing sensitive information must be disposed of in these bins or via a shredder.

DOCUMENTATION

Documentation For Production Systems: Every user who develops or implements software and/or hardware to be used for Company X production business activities must document the system in advance of its deployment. The documentation must be written so that the system may be run by persons unacquainted with it. Such documentation must be prepared even when standard software--such as a spreadsheet program--is employed. Production business activities are periodic repeated activities, such as payroll calculations.

Production System Development Conventions: To facilitate the movement of production applications from microcomputers to larger multi-user systems, all workers who are creating or upgrading production Company X applications that run on a microcomputer must abide by the Information Systems Department abbreviated systems development requirements. These abbreviated requirements have been specifically prepared for microcomputers and require much less effort that the requirements for multi-user systems. These requirements include a brief risk assessment, a quick check to make sure that the involved production system is in compliance with existing technical standards, and the use of standardized file names.

Contingency Plans: When a microcomputer is used as a critical part of any production business application it must have a documented and tested contingency plan. Contingency plans should be prepared in accordance with the guidelines issued by the Information Security Department [intranet link could go here].

Consistent Classification Marking: If information is sensitive, from the time when it is created until it is destroyed or declassified, it must be labeled (marked) with an appropriate data classification designation. Such markings must appear on hardcopy versions of the information, as well as the labels for storage media containing this information (floppy disks, CD-ROMs, etc.). Further information about data classification and marking can be found in the Data Classification Policy [intranet link could go here].

NETWORKING

Modems: Modems in office desktop microcomputers are not permitted. Mobile and telecommuting microcomputers are an exception to this rule. Communications software must always employ a password with at least eight characters which has been constructed according to the rules found elsewhere in this document. When in Company X offices, users needing to make outbound connections with remote computers must route their connections through modem pools or the Internet firewall.

Internet: As a matter of policy, inbound Internet connections to Company X microcomputers (or any other computer other than an Internet web or commerce server) is forbidden unless these connections employ an approved virtual private network (VPN) software package. These VPN systems must employ both user authentication features (most often simply fixed passwords) as well as data interception prevention features (encryption).

Downloading Sensitive Information: Sensitive Company X information may be down-loaded from a multi-user system to a microcomputer only after two conditions have been fulfilled. For this data transfer to take place, a clear business need must exist and advance permission from the information Owner must be obtained. This policy is not intended to cover electronic mail or memos, but does apply to databases, master files, and other information stored on mainframes, minicomputers, servers, and other multi-user machines.

Installation Of Communications Lines: Workers and vendors must not make arrangements for, or actually complete the installation of voice or data lines with any carrier, if they have not first obtained approval from the director of the Information Systems Department.

Establishing Networks: Workers must not establish electronic bulletin boards, local area networks, modem connections to existing internal networks, Internet commerce systems, or other multi-user systems for communicating information without the specific approval of the Information Security Department. This policy helps ensure that all Company X networked systems have the controls needed to prevent unauthorized access.

PHYSICAL SECURITY

Equipment Theft: To prevent theft, all office desktop microcomputers (with the exception of portables) must be physically secured to desks with approved devices such as locking wires or plates that bolt the equipment to furniture. All microcomputer equipment is marked with an invisible identification information which clearly indicates it is Company X property. Periodic physical inventories are used to track the movement of microcomputers and related computer equipment.

Custodians For Equipment: The primary user of a microcomputer is considered a custodian for the equipment. If the equipment has been damaged, lost, stolen, borrowed, or is otherwise unavailable for normal business activities, a custodian must promptly inform the involved department manager. With the exception of portable machines, microcomputer equipment must not be moved or relocated without the knowledge and approval of the involved department manager.

Use Of Personal Equipment: Workers must not bring their own computers, computer peripherals, or computer software into Company X facilities without prior authorization from their department head. Likewise, workers must not use their own microcomputers for production Company X business unless these systems have been previously evaluated and approved by the Information Security Department. Writing memos or reports is not considered production Company X business for purposes of this policy.

Property Pass: Microcomputers, portable computers, typewriters, and related information systems equipment must not leave Company X offices unless accompanied by a property pass signed by a department manager. Equipment owned by workers and brought into Company X offices must also have a property pass; workers neglecting this requirement may discover that they are not able to remove their own equipment. Guards in the lobby of all Company X buildings will check the contents of briefcases, suitcases, handbags, and other luggage to ensure that all equipment leaving Company X offices has an approved property pass. Remote sensing devices have also been installed at selected locations to trigger an alarm if certain Company X computer related devices are removed from Company X offices.

Positioning Display Screens: The display screens for all microcomputers used to handle sensitive or valuable data must be positioned such that the information cannot be readily viewed through a window, by persons walking in a hallway, or by persons waiting in reception and related areas. Care should also be taken to position keyboards so that unauthorized persons cannot readily see workers enter passwords, encryption keys, and other security related parameters.

Locking Sensitive Information: When not being used by authorized workers, or when not clearly visible in an area where authorized persons are working, all hardcopy sensitive information must be locked in file cabinets, desks, safes, or other furniture. Likewise, when not being used, or when not in a clearly visible and attended area, all computer storage media (floppy disks, tapes, CD-ROMs, etc.) containing sensitive information must be locked in similar enclosures.

Environmental Considerations: To reduce the damage done by electrical power problems, all microcomputers in Company X offices must use surge suppressers. Those microcomputers running production applications must also have uninterruptible power systems (UPSs) approved by the Information Security Department.

Static Discharges And Electromagnetic Fields: If weather and/or building conditions pose a significant risk of static electricity discharge, microcomputers must be outfitted with static protection equipment which has been approved by the Information Systems Department. This will help prevent damage to equipment and the resident information. On a related note, magnetic storage media such as floppy disks and magnetic tapes must be kept at least several inches away from electric fields, such as those generated by magnets and a telephone when it rings.

Smoking, Eating & Drinking: Workers are strongly advised not to smoke, eat, or drink when using microcomputers. Storage media such as floppy disks are susceptible to the particles in tobacco smoke; food and drink can also cause damage to electronic equipment such as keyboards.

MANAGEMENT

Rights To Programs Developed: Without a specific written exception, all computer programs and documentation generated by, or provided by workers for the benefit of Company X are the property of Company X. All other material developed by Company X workers using microcomputers is considered a "work for hire," and is accordingly the property of Company X. This material includes patents, copyrights, and trademarks.

Browsing: Workers must not browse through Company X computer systems or networks. For example, curious searching for interesting files and/or programs in the directories of other users is prohibited. Steps taken to legitimately locate information needed to perform one's job is not considered browsing. Use of the Company X intranet is not considered browsing.

Tools To Compromise Systems Security: Unless specifically authorized by the Information Security Department, Company X workers must not acquire, possess, trade, or use hardware or software tools that could be employed to evaluate or compromise information systems security. Examples of such tools include those which defeat software copy-protection, discover secret passwords, identify security vulnerabilities, or decrypt encrypted files. Unless specific permission has been obtained from the Information Security or Internal Auditing Departments, workers are prohibited from using such tools.

Reporting Problems: Users must promptly report all information security alerts, warnings, suspected vulnerabilities, and the like to the Information Systems Help Desk. Users are prohibited from utilizing Company X systems to forward such information to other users, whether the other users are internal or external to Company X.

Additional Information: Every department has a designated information security liaison, which should be the reader's first stop in a search for more information. If this liaison cannot answer a question or provide a satisfactory resolution to a problem, the next step is to call the corporate Information Security Department at XXX-XXX-XXXX.

Effective Date: DD/MM/YY
Approval Date: DD/MM/YY
Version Number: XX
Approving Executive Name: YY

IX. Sample Electronic Mail Security Policy

Company Property: As a productivity enhancement tool, Company X encourages the business use of electronic communications systems (notably the Internet, voice mail, electronic mail, and fax). Unless third parties have clearly noted copyrights or some other rights on the messages handled by these electronic communications systems, all messages generated on or handled by these systems are considered to be the property of Company X.

Authorized Usage: Company X electronic communications systems generally must be used only for business activities. Incidental personal use is permissible so long as: (a) it does not consume more than a trivial amount of system resources, (b) does not interfere with worker productivity, and (c) does not preempt any business activity. This means that Company X electronic communication systems must not be used for charitable fundraising campaigns, political advocacy efforts, private business activities, or personal amusement and entertainment. On a related note, news feeds, email mailing lists, push data updates, and other mechanisms for receiving information over the Internet must be restricted to material which is clearly related to both Company X business and the duties of the receiving workers. Workers are reminded that the use of corporate information system resources should never create either the appearance or the reality of inappropriate use.

Default Privileges: Electronic communication systems must be established and maintained such that only the privileges necessary to perform a job are granted to a worker. This approach is widely known as the concept of "least privilege." For example, when a worker's relationship with Company X comes to an end, all that worker's privileges on Company X electronic communications systems will also come to an immediate end (electronic mail will not be forwarded, voicemail will not be stored pending pick-up, etc.). Likewise, with the exception of emergencies and regular system maintenance notices, broadcast facilities must be used only after the permission of a department manager has been obtained.

User Separation: Where electronic communications systems provide the ability to separate the activities of different users, these facilities must be implemented. For example, electronic mail systems must employ personal user-IDs and associated passwords to isolate the communications of different users. Unless a computerized fax mailbox system is employed, fax machines that do not generally have separate mailboxes for different recipients, so such user separation is required. If user separation has been established by Company X, workers must not employ the user-ID or other identifier of any other user.

User Accountability: Regardless of the circumstances, individual passwords must never be shared or revealed to anyone else besides the authorized user. Information Technology Department staff have all the privileges they need in order to do their jobs; they will never ask users to reveal their passwords. To give a password to somebody else exposes the authorized user to responsibility for actions the other party takes with this password. If users need to share computer resident data, they should utilize message forwarding facilities, public directories on local area network servers, groupware databases, and other authorized information-sharing mechanisms. To prevent unauthorized parties from obtaining access to electronic communications, users must choose passwords that are difficult-to-guess (for example, not a dictionary word, not a personal detail, not a name, and not a reflection of work activities).

User Identity: Misrepresenting, obscuring, suppressing, or replacing another user's identity on an electronic communications system is forbidden. The user name, electronic mail address, organizational affiliation, and related information included with electronic messages or postings must reflect the actual originator of the messages or postings. With the exception of hot-lines which are intended to be anonymous (such as the Information Security Department's voicemail problem reporting system), workers must not send anonymous electronic communications. At a minimum, all workers must provide their name and phone number in all electronic communications. Electronic mail "signatures" indicating job title, company affiliation, address, and other particulars are strongly recommended for all electronic mail messages. Digital certificates are also recommended for electronic mail, and will be more widely used by Company X communications systems in the years ahead.

Use Only Company X Electronic Mail Systems: Unless permission from the Information Security Manager has first been obtained, workers must not use their personal electronic mail accounts with an Internet Service Provider (ISP) or any other third party for any Company X business messages. To do so would circumvent logging and backup controls that Company X has established. Likewise, workers must not use the electronic mail features found in web browsers for any Company X business communications; they must instead employ authorized Company X electronic mail software.

Use Of Encryption Programs: Workers are reminded that Company X electronic communications systems are not encrypted by default. If sensitive information must be sent by electronic communication systems, encryption or similar technologies to protect the information must be employed. PGP (Pretty Good Privacy) is recommended as a relatively simply way to send sensitive information in encrypted form over the Internet. Workers must not use encryption for any production electronic communications system unless a backup key or a key escrow system has been established with the cooperation of the Information Security Department.

Respecting Intellectual Property Rights: Although the Internet is an informal communications environment, the laws for copyrights, patents, trademarks, and the like still apply. To this end, workers using Company X electronic mail systems must for example (1) repost or reproduce material only after obtaining permission from the source, (2) quote material from other sources only if these other sources are properly identified, and (3) reveal internal Company X information on the Internet only if the information has been officially approved for public release. As an aside, all information taken off the Internet should be considered suspect until confirmed by another source. There is no quality control process on the Internet, and a considerable amount of Internet information is outdated, inaccurate, and/or deliberately misleading.

Respecting Privacy Rights: Except as otherwise specifically approved by management, workers may not intercept or disclose, or assist in intercepting or disclosing, electronic communications. Company X is committed to respecting the rights of its workers, including their reasonable expectation of privacy. Company X also is responsible for operating, maintaining, and protecting its electronic communications networks. To accomplish these objectives, it is occasionally necessary to intercept or disclose, or assist in intercepting or disclosing, electronic communications. To meet these objectives Company X may employ content monitoring systems (which scan for certain key words) as well as other electronic system management tools.

No Guaranteed Message Privacy: Company X cannot guarantee that electronic communications will be private. Workers should be aware that electronic communications can, depending on the technology, be forwarded, intercepted, printed, and stored by others. Furthermore, electronic communications can be accessed by people other than the intended recipients in accordance with this policy. Because messages can be stored in backups, electronic communications may actually be retrievable when a traditional paper letter would long since have been discarded or destroyed. Workers should accordingly be careful about the topics covered in Company X electronic communications, and should not send a message discussing anything that they would not be comfortable reading about on the front page of their local newspaper.

Contents Of Messages: Workers must not use profanity, obscenities, or derogatory remarks in electronic mail messages discussing employees, customers, competitors, or others. Such remarks -- even when made in jest -- may create legal problems such as trade libel and defamation of character. It is possible that such remarks would later be taken out of context and used against Company X. International communications are also problematic when humor is attempted but misunderstood; this is an increasingly serious problem with Internet electronic mail (avoid smiley faces, etc.). To prevent these and other problems, stick to business matters in Company X electronic communications. As a matter of standard business practice, all Company X electronic communications must be consistent with conventional standards of ethical and polite conduct (no "flaming" is allowed).

Statistical Data: Consistent with generally accepted business practice, Company X collects statistical data about its electronic communication systems. As an example, call detail reporting information collected by telephone switching systems indicates the numbers dialed, the duration of calls, the time of day when calls are placed, etc. Using such information, technical support personnel monitor the use of electronic communications to ensure the ongoing availability and reliability of these systems. Company X employs computer systems which analyze these types of statistical information to detect unauthorized usage, toll fraud, and other problems.

Incidental Disclosure: It may be necessary for technical support personnel to review the content of an individual worker's communications during the course of problem resolution. Technical support personnel may not, however, review the content of an individual worker's communications out of personal curiosity or at the behest of individuals who have not gone through proper approval channels (advance approval by the Physical Security Manager is required for all such monitoring).

Handling Attachments: Attachments to electronic mail messages, if they have any executable code embedded in them, may contain a virus or may in some other way damage a worker's computer. Accordingly, when sending an attachment to a third party, workers should attempt to use RTF (rich text format) or simple text files whenever possible. Often information can be embedded in the body of a message rather than appended in an attachment. Workers should encourage third parties to send them files in these same formats whenever reasonable and practical. All other attachment files should be scanned with an authorized virus detection software package before opening and/or execution. Unexpected attachments received from third parties should be viewed with suspicion. Even if the third party is known and trusted, viruses may still cause an infected attachment to be sent unbeknownst to the trusted third party.

Message Forwarding: Recognizing that some information is intended for specific individuals and may not be appropriate for general distribution, electronic communications users should exercise caution when forwarding messages. Company X sensitive information must not be forwarded to any party outside Company X without the prior approval of a local department manager. Blanket forwarding of messages to parties outside Company X is prohibited unless the prior permission of the Information Security Department Manager has been obtained. Messages sent by outside parties outside should also not be forwarded to other third parties unless the sender clearly intended this and unless such forwarding is necessary to accomplish an ordinary business objective. In all other cases, forwarding of messages sent by outsiders to other third parties can only be done if the sender expressly agrees to this forwarding.

Handling Alerts About Security: Users must promptly report all information security alerts, warnings, reported vulnerabilities, and the like to the Information Security Department. Many of these notices are hoaxes and cause workers to be unnecessarily distracted from their work. The Information Security Department is the only organizational unit authorized to determine appropriate action in response to such notices. Users are prohibited from utilizing Company X systems to forward these notices to other users, whether the other users are internal or external to

Company X. Similarly, users must promptly report all suspected security vulnerabilities or problems that they notice to the Information Security Department [intranet link to a form for reporting problems could be provided here].

Public Representations: No media advertisement, Internet home page, electronic bulletin board posting, electronic mail message, voice mail message, or any other public representation about Company X may be issued unless it has first been approved by the Marketing or Public Relations Departments. Likewise, Company X, as a matter of policy, does not send unsolicited electronic mail (so-called "spam"), nor does it issue unsolicited fax advertising. If workers are bothered by an excessive amount of spam from a particular organization or electronic mail address, they must not respond directly to the sender. Instead, they must forward samples of the messages to the Systems Administrator in charge of the electronic mail system in question, and that Administrator will then take the matter up with the sender's Internet Service Provider (ISP). Workers are also prohibited from "mail bombing" other users in retaliation for any perceived wrong (this involves sending a large number of message in order to overload a server or user's electronic mailbox).

User Back-Up: If an electronic mail message contains information relevant to the completion of a business transaction, contains potentially important reference information, or has value as evidence of a Company X management decision, it should be retained for future reference. Most electronic mail messages will not fall into these categories, and accordingly can be erased after viewing. Users must regularly move important information from electronic mail message files to word processing documents, databases, and other files. Electronic mail systems are not intended for the archival storage of important information. Important but old electronic mail messages can be periodically expunged by systems administrators, mistakenly erased by users, and otherwise lost when system problems occur.

Archival Storage: All official Company X electronic mail messages, including those containing a formal management approval, authorization, delegation, or handing over of responsibility, or similar transactions, must be copied to the Archival Records Department.

Purging Electronic Messages: Messages no longer needed for business purposes must be periodically purged by users from their personal electronic message storage areas. After a certain period -- generally six months -- electronic mail messages stored on Company X mail servers will be automatically deleted by systems administration staff. Not only will this increase scarce storage space, it will also simplify records management and related activities.

Harassing Or Offensive Materials: Company X computer and communications systems are not intended to be used for, and must not be used for the exercise of the workers' right to free speech. These systems must not be used as an open forum to discuss Company X organizational changes or business policy matters.

Likewise, as a further restriction of free speech, sexual, ethnic, and racial harassment -- including unwanted telephone calls, electronic mail, and internal mail -- is strictly prohibited and is cause for disciplinary action up to and including termination. Workers who receive offensive unsolicited material from outside sources must not forward/redistribute it to either internal or external parties (unless this forwarding/redistribution is to the Company X Human Resources Department in order to assist with the investigation of a complaint).

Responding Directly To The Sender: Workers are encouraged to respond directly to the originator of offensive electronic mail messages, telephone calls, and/or other electronic communications. If the originator does not promptly stop sending offensive messages, workers must report the communications to their manager and the Human Resources Department. Company X retains the right to remove from its information systems any material it views as offensive or potentially illegal.

Establishing Electronic Business Systems: Although Company X seeks to aggressively implement Electronic Data Interchange (EDI), Internet commerce, and other electronic business systems with third parties, all contracts must be formed by paper documents prior to purchasing or selling via electronic systems. EDI, electronic mail, and similar binding business messages must therefore be releases against blanket orders, such as a blanket purchase order. All electronic commerce systems must be approved by the Information Systems Department director and in-house legal counsel prior to usage.

Paper Confirmation For Contracts: All contracts formed through electronic offer and acceptance messages (fax, EDI, electronic mail, etc.) must be formalized and confirmed via paper documents within two weeks of acceptance. Separately, because it could facilitate identity theft and other types of fraud, workers must not employ scanned versions of hand-rendered signatures to give the impression that an electronic mail message or other electronic communications were signed by the sender.

X. Sample Computer Network Security Policy

PURPOSE

The purpose of this policy is to establish management direction, procedures, and requirements to ensure the appropriate protection of Company X information handled by computer networks.

SCOPE

This policy applies to all employees, contractors, consultants, temporaries, and other workers at Company X, including those workers affiliated with third parties who access Company X computer networks. Throughout this policy, the word "worker" will be used to collectively refer to all such individuals. The policy also applies to all computer and data communication systems owned by and/or administered by Company X.

GENERAL POLICY

All information travelling over Company X computer networks that has not been specifically identified as the property of other parties will be treated as though it is a Company X corporate asset. It is the policy of Company X to prohibit unauthorized access, disclosure, duplication, modification, diversion, destruction, loss, misuse, or theft of this information. In addition, it is the policy of Company X to protect information belonging to third parties--that has been entrusted to Company X--in a manner consistent with its sensitivity as well as in accordance with all applicable agreements.

RESPONSIBILITIES

An Information Systems Security Committee will be composed of management or their delegates from each of Company X's major divisions and subsidiaries, as well as the Director of Information Technology, the Director of Security, and the chief Company X attorney responsible for intellectual property. At quarterly and ad hoc meetings, this committee will: (a) periodically review the status of Company X's computer and network security, (b) as needed, review and monitor remedial work related to computer and network security incidents, (c) authorize and later judge the results of major projects dealing with computer and network security, (d) approve new or modified information security policies, standards, guidelines, and procedures, and (e) perform other high-level information security management activities.

The Information Security Manager is responsible for establishing, maintaining, implementing, administering, and interpreting organization-wide information systems security policies, standards, guidelines, and procedures. This manager is therefore also responsible for activities related to this policy. While responsibility for information systems security on a day-to-day basis is every worker's duty, specific guidance, direction, and authority for information systems security is centralized for all of Company X and its subsidiaries in the Information Security Department. Accordingly, this Department will perform information systems risk assessments, prepare information systems security action plans, evaluate information security products, and perform other activities necessary to assure a secure information systems environment.

The Physical Security Manager is additionally responsible for conducting investigations into any alleged computer or network security compromises, incidents, or problems. All security compromises or potential security compromises must be reported to the Physical Security Manager.

System Administrators are responsible for acting as local information systems security coordinators. These individuals are responsible for establishing appropriate user privileges, monitoring access control logs, and performing similar security actions for the systems they administer. They are also responsible for reporting all suspicious computer and network-security-related activities to the Physical Security Manager. System Administrators also help implement the requirements of this and other information systems security policies, standards, guidelines, and procedures. If information security is not handled by another department or group, each Company X department must designate an individual to serve as a System Administrator.

Departmental Managers are responsible for ensuring that appropriate computer and communication system security measures are observed in their areas. Besides allocating sufficient resources and staff time to meet the requirements of these policies, Departmental Managers are also responsible for making sure that all users are aware of Company X policies related to computer and communication system security.

Users are responsible for complying with this and all other Company X policies defining computer and network security measures. Users are also responsible for bringing all known information security vulnerabilities and violations that they notice to the attention of the Physical Security Manager.

SYSTEM ACCESS CONTROL

End-User Passwords

Users must always choose fixed passwords that are difficult-to-guess. This means that passwords must NOT be related to a user's job or personal life. For example, a car license plate number, a spouse's name, or fragments of an address must not be used. This also means passwords must not be a word found in the dictionary or some other part of speech. For example, proper names, places, technical terms, and slang must not be used. Where such systems software facilities are available, users must be prevented from selecting easily-guessed passwords.

Users can choose easily-remembered passwords that are at the same time difficult for unauthorized parties to guess if they:

(a) string several words together (the resulting passwords are also known as "pass phrases"),
(b) shift a word up, down, left or right one row on the keyboard,
(c) bump characters in a word a certain number of letters up or down the alphabet,
(d) transform a regular word according to a specific method, such as making every other letter a number reflecting its position in the word,
(e) combine punctuation or numbers with a regular word,
(f) create acronyms from words in a song, a poem, or another known sequence of words,
(g) deliberately misspell a word (but not a common misspelling), or
(h) combine a number of personal facts like birth dates and favorite colors.

Users must not construct passwords that are identical or substantially similar to passwords they have previously employed. Where systems software facilities are available, users must be prevented from reusing previous passwords.

Users must not construct passwords using a basic sequence of characters that is then partially changed based on the date or some other predictable factor. For example, users must NOT employ passwords like "X34JAN" in January, "X34FEB" in February, etc.

Passwords must not be stored in readable form in batch files, automatic log-in scripts, software macros, terminal function keys, in computers without access control, or in other locations where unauthorized persons might discover them.

Passwords must not be written down and left in a place where unauthorized persons might discover them. Aside from initial password assignment and password reset situations, if there is reason to believe that a password has been disclosed to someone other than the authorized user, the password must be immediately changed.

Regardless of the circumstances, passwords must never be shared or revealed to anyone else besides the authorized user. To do so exposes the authorized user to responsibility for actions that the other party takes with the disclosed password. If users need to share computer resident data, they should use electronic mail, public directories on local area network servers, and other mechanisms. This policy does not prevent the use of default passwords--typically used for new user-ID assignment or password reset situations--which are then immediately changed when the user next logs-onto the involved system.

All passwords must be immediately changed if they are suspected of being disclosed, or known to have been disclosed to anyone besides the authorized user.

Password System Set-Up

All computers permanently or intermittently connected to Company X networks must have password access controls. Multi-user systems must employ user-IDs and passwords unique to each user, as well as user privilege restriction mechanisms. Network-connected single-user systems must employ hardware or software controls approved by the Information Security Department that prevent unauthorized access including a screen blanker triggered by a certain period of no keyboard activity.

Computer and communication system access control must be achieved via passwords which are unique to each individual user. Access control to files, applications, databases, computers, networks, and other system resources via shared passwords (also called "group passwords") is prohibited.

Wherever systems software permits, the display and printing of passwords must be masked, suppressed, or otherwise obscured such that unauthorized parties will not be able to observe or subsequently recover them.

Wherever systems software permits, the initial passwords issued to a new user by a Security Administrator must be valid only for the new user's first on-line session. At that time, the user must be forced to choose another password. This same process applies to the resetting of passwords in the event that a user forgets a password.

All vendor-supplied default passwords must be changed before any computer or communications system is used for Company X business. This policy applies to passwords associated with end-user user-IDs, as well as passwords associated with System Administrator and other privileged user-IDs.

To prevent password guessing attacks, where systems software permits, the number of consecutive attempts to enter an incorrect password must be strictly limited. After three (3) unsuccessful attempts to enter a password, the involved user-ID must be either suspended until reset by a System Administrator, or temporarily disabled for no less than three (3) minutes. If dial-up or other external network connections are involved, the session must be disconnected.

Whenever system security has been compromised, or even if there is a convincing reason to believe that it has been compromised, the involved System Administrator must immediately: (a) reassign all relevant passwords, and (b) force every password on the involved system to be changed at the time of the next log-in. If systems software does not provide the latter capability, a broadcast message must be sent to all users telling them to change their passwords.

Whenever system security has been compromised, or even if there is a convincing reason to believe that it has been compromised, a trusted version of the operating system and all security-related software must be reloaded from trusted storage media such as CD-ROMs, magnetic tapes, or original source code floppy disks. The involved system(s) must then be rebooted. Similarly, all changes to user privileges taking effect since the time of suspected system compromise must be immediately reviewed by the System Administrator for unauthorized modifications.

Log-In/Log-Off Process

All users must be positively identified prior to being able to use any multi-user computer or communications system resources. Positive identification for internal Company X networks involves both a user-ID and a fixed password, both of which are unique to an individual user.

Positive identification for dial-up lines involves the use of hand-held tokens, cryptographic challenge/response protocols, or other approved extended user authentication techniques. The combination of a user-ID and a fixed password does not provide sufficient security for dial-up connections to Company X systems or networks. Modems attached to network-connected workstations situated in Company X offices are forbidden because they do not provide adequate positive user identification. Modems connected to isolated computers (such as portable computers and home computers) are permissible.

Positive identification for users originating external real-time connections to Company X systems or networks via value added networks, private business networks (like the Company X extranet), public networks (like the Internet), or any other external communications system must also involve extended user authentication techniques.

Where systems software permits, every log-in banner on multi-user computers must include a special notice. This notice must state: (1) the system is for the use of authorized users only, (2) by continuing to use the system, the user represents that he/she is an authorized user, (3) the user acknowledges that all system usage is logged, and (4) the user understands that violations of Company X information security policies and other requirements may trigger disciplinary action up to and including termination, as well as civil or criminal prosecution.

The log-in process for network-connected Company X computer systems must simply ask the user to log-in, providing prompts as needed. Specific information about the organization managing the computer, the computer operating system, the network configuration, or other internal matters must not be provided until a user has successfully provided both a valid user-ID and a valid password.

If there has been no activity on a computer terminal, workstation, or microcomputer for a certain period of time, the system must automatically blank the screen and suspend the session. Re-establishment of the session must take place only after the user has provided a valid password. The recommended period of time is fifteen (15 minutes). An exception to this policy will be made in those cases where the immediate area surrounding a system is physically secured via locked doors, secured-room badge readers, or similar technology.

With the exception of electronic bulletin boards or other systems where all regular users are anonymous, users are prohibited from logging into any Company X system or network anonymously (for example, by using "guest" user-IDs). If users employ systems facilities which allow them to change the active user-ID to gain certain privileges, they must have initially logged-in employing a user-ID that clearly indicates their identity. On UNIX systems, this means that users must be prevented from initially logging-in as "root," but must instead first log-in employing their own user-ID. If such users have been granted the ability to achieve superuser privileges, they may then "set userid" ("su") to gain "root" access. Whatever the operating system, logs must record all such changes of current user-IDs.

System Privileges

Limiting System Access

The computer and communications system privileges of all users, systems, and independently-operating programs (such as "agents") must be restricted based on the need-to-know. This means that privileges must not be extended unless a legitimate business-oriented need for such privileges exists.

Default user file permissions must not automatically allow anyone on the system (on UNIX systems, the "world") to read, write, or execute a file. Although users may reset permissions on a file-by-file basis, such permissive default file permissions are prohibited. Nonetheless, default file permissions granted to limited groups of people who have a genuine need-to-know are allowed.

Users with microcomputers (Macintoshes and IBM-PCs) are responsible for administering a screen saver program securing access to their machine's hard disk drive, and setting passwords for all applications and systems software that provide the capability.

Company X computer and communications systems must restrict access to the computers that users can reach over Company X networks. These restrictions can be implemented via routers, gateways, firewalls, and other network components. These restrictions must be used to, for example, control the ability of a user to log-into a certain computer then move from that computer to another.

Process For Granting System Privileges

Requests for new user-IDs and changed privileges must be in writing and approved by the user's manager before a System Administrator fulfills these requests. To help establish accountability for events on the related systems, documents (perhaps in electronic form) reflecting these requests must be retained for a period of at least a year.

Individuals who are not Company X employees must not be granted a user-ID or otherwise be given privileges to use Company X computers or networks unless the advance written approval of a department head has first been obtained.

Privileges granted to users who are not Company X employees must be granted for periods of 90-days or less. As needed, users who are not Company X employees must have their privileges reauthorized by the sponsoring department head every 90 days.

Special system privileges--such as the default ability to write to the files of other users--must be restricted to those directly responsible for systems administration and/or systems security. An exception to this policy can be made only if a department head has approved the exception in writing. For example, end-users must not be granted "root" privileges (or comparable access rights on non-UNIX platforms), unless they have first received specific written authorization from their department managers. Similarly, configuration changes, operating system changes, and related activities that require "root" privileges must be performed by System Administrators, NOT end-users.

Third party vendors must NOT be given dial-up privileges to Company X computers and/or networks unless the involved System Administrator determines that they have a legitimate business need. These privileges must be enabled only for the time period required to accomplish the approved tasks (such as remote maintenance). If a perpetual or long-term connection is required, then the connection must be established by approved extended user authentication methods (hand-held tokens, software-based challenge/response protocols, etc.), as discussed above.

All users wishing to use Company X internal networks, or multi-user systems that are connected to Company X internal networks, must sign a compliance statement prior to being issued a user-ID. If a certain user already has a user-ID, a signature must be obtained prior to receiving a renewed user-ID. The latter process must be performed periodically. A signature on this compliance statement indicates the involved user understands and agrees to abide by Company X policies and procedures related to computers and networks (including the instructions contained in this document).

Process For Revoking System Access

All user-IDs must automatically have the associated privileges revoked after a certain period of inactivity. The recommended period is thirty (30) days.

If a computer or communication system access control subsystem is not functioning properly, it must default to denial of privileges to users. If access control subsystems are malfunctioning, the systems they support must remain unavailable until such time as the problem has been rectified.

Users must not test, or attempt to compromise computer or communication system security measures unless specifically approved in advance and in writing by the Information Security Manager. Incidents involving unapproved system cracking (hacking), password cracking (guessing), file decryption, bootleg software copying, or similar unauthorized attempts to compromise security measures may be unlawful, and will be considered serious violations of Company X policy. Customer requests that Company X security mechanisms be compromised must NOT be satisfied unless: (a) the Information Security Manager approves in advance, or (b) Company X is compelled to comply by law. Likewise, short-cuts bypassing systems security measures, as well as pranks and practical jokes involving the compromise of systems security measures are absolutely prohibited.

The system privileges granted to users must be reevaluated by management every six (6) months. In response to feedback from management, System Administrators must promptly revoke all privileges no longer needed by users.

Management must promptly report all significant changes in worker duties or employment status to the System Administrators responsible for user-IDs associated with the involved persons. For all terminations, Human Resources must also issue a notice of status change to all System Administrators who might be responsible for a system on which the involved worker might have a user-ID.

Establishment Of Access Paths

Changes to Company X internal networks include loading new software, changing network addresses, reconfiguring routers, adding dial-up lines, and the like. With the exception of emergency situations, all changes to Company X computer networks must be: (a) documented in a work order request, and (b) approved in advance by the Information Technology Department except as explicitly delegated by the Information Technology Department. Emergency changes to Company X networks must only be made by persons who are authorized by the Information Technology Department. This process prevents unexpected changes from inadvertently leading to denial of service, unauthorized disclosure of information, and other problems. This process applies not only to "workers" as defined in the Scope section of this policy, but also to vendor personnel.

Workers must NOT establish electronic bulletin boards, local area networks, FTP servers, web servers, modem connections to existing local area networks, or other multi-user systems for communicating information without the specific approval of the Information Security Manager. Likewise, new types of real-time connections between two or more in-house computer systems must not be established unless such approval has first been obtained. This policy helps to ensure that all Company X systems have the controls needed to protect other network-connected systems. Security requirements for a network-connected system are not just a function of the connected system, they are also a function of all other Company X connected systems.

Participation in external networks as a provider of services that external parties rely on is expressly prohibited unless two conditions are first fulfilled. Specifically, Company X legal counsel must identify the legal risks involved, and then the Director of Information Technology must expressly accept these and other risks associated with the proposal. Acting as an Internet node is an example of such participation.

All Company X computers that intermittently or continuously connect to an internal or external network must employ password-based access controls. Multi-user computers must employ software which restricts access to the files of each user, which logs the activities of each user, and which has special privileges granted to a System Administrator. Single-user systems must employ access control software approved by the Information Security Department that includes boot control and an automatic screen blanker which is invoked after a certain period of no keyboard (or other input device) activity. Portable computers and home computers that contain Company X information are also covered by this policy, as are network devices such as firewalls, gateways, routers, and bridges.

To stop unauthorized system access and related problems, all inter-processor commands from non-Company X locations are prohibited unless a user or process has first properly logged-in. Examples of such commands include remotely-initiated requests for a list of users currently logged-in as well as a remote procedure call.

Users initiating sessions via dial-up lines connected to Company X internal networks and/or multi-user computer systems must pass through an additional access control point (firewall) before users employing these lines can reach a log-in banner. Although other forms of firewalls are possible, Company X now provides such access via dynamic passwords (specifically a hand-held token system). Unless approved in advance by the Director of Information Security, dial-up connections that do not go through approved firewalls in order to reach Company X internal-network connected systems are prohibited. This policy applies to Internet inbound calls as well as Electronic Data Interchange (EDI).

Remote maintenance ports for Company X computer and communication systems must be disabled until the specific time they are needed by the vendor. These ports must then be again disabled immediately after use. Alternatively, dial-up connections can be established with vendors via outbound calls initiated by Company X workers. No firewall access control is needed for either type of connection.

Portable phones using radio technology as well as cellular phones must not be used for data transmissions containing Company X "confidential" or "secret" information unless the connection is encrypted. Likewise, other broadcast networking technologies--such radio-based local area networks--must not be used for these types of Company X information unless the link is encrypted. Such links may be used for electronic mail as long as users understand that it "confidential" or "secret" information must not be transmitted using this technology.

COMPUTER VIRUSES, WORMS, AND TROJAN HORSES

A computer virus is an unauthorized program that replicates itself, attaches itself to other programs, and spreads onto various data storage media (floppy disks, magnetic tapes, random access memory, etc.) and/or across a network. The symptoms of virus infection include much slower computer response time, inexplicable loss of files, changed modification dates for files, increased file sizes, and total failure of computers.

To assure continued uninterrupted service for both computers and networks, all microcomputer (Macintosh and IBM-PC) users must keep approved virus screening software enabled on their computers. This screening software must be used to scan all software coming from either third parties or other Company X departments. This scanning must take place before the new software is executed. Users may not bypass scanning processes that could stop the transmission of computer viruses.
Users are responsible for eradicating viruses from all microcomputer systems under their control whenever viruses have been detected using software installed by Company X staff. As soon as a virus is detected, the involved user(s) must immediately call the Information Security Department's "hot-line" to assure that no further infection takes place and that any experts needed to eradicate the virus are promptly engaged [hot line number could be provided here].

To assist with the post-virus-infection restoration of microcomputer computing environments, all microcomputer software must be copied prior to its initial usage, and such copies must be stored in a safe place. These master copies must not be used for ordinary business activities, but must be reserved for recovery from computer virus infections, hard disk crashes, and other computer problems. These master copies must also be stored in a secure location.

Larger systems do not generally suffer from viruses, but they do suffer from worms and Trojan horses. Worms are much like viruses, but do not attach themselves to other programs. Trojan horses are unauthorized programs hidden within authorized programs. To prevent problems with viruses, worms, and Trojan horses, Company X computers and networks must not run software that comes from sources other than: (a) business partners, (b) knowledgeable and trusted user groups, (c) well-known systems security authorities such as Carnegie-Mellon University's Computer Emergency Response Team (aka CERT), (d) computer or network vendors, or (e) commercial software vendors. Software down-loaded from electronic bulletin boards, shareware, public domain software, and other software from untrusted sources must not be used unless it has first been subjected to a rigorous testing regimen approved by the Information Security Manager.

DATA AND PROGRAM BACK-UP

To protect Company X's information resources from loss or damage, microcomputer users are responsible for backing-up the information on their machines. For multi-user computer and communication systems, a System Administrator is responsible for making periodic back-ups. If requested, the Information Technology Department will install, or provide technical assistance for the installation of back-up hardware and/or software.

All sensitive ("secret" or "confidential"), valuable, or critical information resident on Company X computer systems and networks must be periodically backed-up. User department managers must define which information and which machines are to be backed-up, the frequency of back-up, and the method of back-up based on the following guidelines:

1. If the system supports more than one individual and contains data that is critical to day-to-day operations within Company X, then back-up is required daily.

2. If the system is used to support job related functions and contains key data critical to the day-to-day operations of that job, then back-up is required weekly.

3. If the system is primarily used as a personal productivity tool and contains no data that would be classified as job or departmental in nature, then back-up is at the discretion of the individual user.

Nothing in the timeframes for periodic back-up mentioned immediately above restricts the generation of more frequent back-ups, as will occasionally be required for operational and business reasons.

Company X requires the use of at least three (3) sets of back-up storage media (tapes, CD-ROMs, etc.) to be used in rotation. For multi-user machines, whenever systems software permits, back-ups should be performed without end-user involvement, over an internal network and during the night.
Storage of back-up media is the responsibility of the microcomputer user or multi-user machine System Administrator involved in the back-up process. Media should be stored in fireproof safes, at a separate location at least several city blocks away from the system being backed-up.

Unless the type of information is specifically listed on Company X's Information Retention Schedule (available from the Legal Department), information must be retained for as long as necessary but for no longer. Information listed on the Information Retention Schedule must be retained for the period specified. Other information must be destroyed when no longer needed--generally within two (2) years.

To prevent it from being revealed to or used by unauthorized parties, all Company X "secret" or "confidential" information stored on back-up computer media (magnetic tapes, floppy disks, optical disks, etc.) must be encrypted using approved encrypting methods.

ENCRYPTION

When Company X "confidential" or "secret" information is transmitted over any communication network, it must be sent in encrypted form. Likewise, whenever Company X source code, or source code that has been entrusted to Company X by a business partner, is to be sent over a network, it too must be in encrypted form. Specific definitions of the words "confidential" and "secret" can be found in the Data Classification Policy [intranet link to that policy goes here].

Similarly, whenever "confidential" or "secret" information is not being actively used, it must be stored in encrypted form. This means that when "confidential" or "secret" information is stored or transported in computer-readable storage media (such as magnetic tapes or floppy disks), it must be in encrypted form.

Encryption of information at rest (in storage) or in transit (on a network) must be achieved via commercially-available products approved by the Information Security Department. The algorithm called the Advanced Encryption Standard (AES) is recommended, but because only certain of its implementations are exportable, secured international communications will often need to use other algorithms.

Whenever encryption is used, workers must not delete the sole readable version of the information unless they have first demonstrated that the decryption process is able to reestablish a readable version of the information.

Encryption keys used for Company X information are always classified as "confidential" or "secret" information. Access to such keys must be strictly limited to those who have a need-to-know. Unless the approval of the Information Security Manager is first obtained, encryption keys must not be revealed to consultants, contractors, temporaries, or third parties. Likewise, encryption keys must always be encrypted when sent over a network.

Whenever such facilities are commercially available, Company X must employ automated rather than manual encryption key management processes for the protection of information on Company X networks.

PORTABLE COMPUTERS

Workers in the possession of portable, laptop, notebook, palmtop, and other transportable computers containing "secret" or "confidential" Company X information must not leave these computers unattended at any time unless the information is stored in encrypted form.

To prevent unauthorized disclosure, workers in the possession of transportable computers containing unencrypted "secret" or "confidential" Company X information must not check these computers in airline luggage systems, with hotel porters, etc. These computers must remain in the possession of the traveler as hand luggage.

Whenever "secret" or "confidential" information is written to a floppy disk, magnetic tape, smart card, or other storage media, the storage media must be suitably marked with the highest relevant sensitivity classification. When not in use, this media must be stored in a locked safe, locked furniture, or a similarly secured location. Further information can be found in the Telecommuting Information Security Policy [intranet link goes here].

REMOTE PRINTING

Printers must not be left unattended if "secret" or "confidential" information is being printed or will soon be printed. The persons attending the printer must be authorized to examine the information being printed. Unattended printing is permitted if the area surrounding the printer is physically protected such that persons who are not authorized to see the material being printed may not enter.

PRIVACY

Unless contractual agreements dictate otherwise, messages sent over Company X computer and communications systems are the property of Company X. To properly protect and manage this property, management reserves the right to examine all data stored in or transmitted by these systems. Since Company X's computer and communication systems must be used for business purposes only, workers should have no expectation of privacy associated with the information they store in or send through these systems.

When providing computer networking services, Company X does not provide default message protection services such as encryption. Accordingly, no responsibility is assumed for the disclosure of information sent over Company X's networks, and no assurances are made about the privacy of information handled by Company X internal networks. In those instances where session encryption or other special controls are required, it is the user's responsibility to make sure that adequate security precautions have been taken. Nothing in this paragraph should be construed to imply that Company X policy does not support the controls dictated by agreements with third parties (such as organizations which have entrusted Company X with confidential information).

LOGS AND OTHER SYSTEMS SECURITY TOOLS

Every multi-user computer or communications system must include sufficient automated tools to assist the System Administrator in verifying a system's security status. These tools must include mechanisms for the recording, detection, and correction of commonly-encountered security problems.

Whenever cost-justifiable, automated tools for handling common security problems must be used on Company X computers and networks. For example, auto-discovery software (which automatically checks microcomputer software licenses via a local area network) must be used on a regular basis.

To the extent that systems software permits, computer and communications systems handling sensitive, valuable, or critical Company X information must securely log all significant security relevant events. Examples of security relevant events include: users switching user-IDs during an on-line session, attempts to guess passwords, attempts to use privileges that have not been authorized, modifications to production application software, modifications to system software, changes to user privileges, and changes to logging subsystems.

Logs containing computer or communications system security relevant events must be retained for at least three (3) months. During this period, logs must be secured such that they cannot be modified, and such that they can be read only by authorized persons. These logs are important for error correction, security breach recovery, intrusion investigations, and related efforts.
To provide evidence for investigation, prosecution, and disciplinary actions, certain information must be captured whenever it is suspected that computer or network related crime or abuse has taken place. The relevant information must be securely stored off-line until such time as it is determined that Company X will not pursue legal action or otherwise use the information. The information to be immediately collected includes the system logs, application audit trails, other indications of the current system states, as well as copies of all potentially involved files.

To allow proper remedial action to be taken in a timely manner, records reflecting security relevant events must be periodically reviewed in a timely manner by computer operations staff, information security staff, or systems administration staff.

Users must be put on notice about the specific acts that constitute computer and network security violations. Users must also be informed that such violations will be logged.

Although System Administrators are not required to promptly load the most recent version of operating systems, they are required to promptly apply all security patches to the operating system that have been released by either: (a) knowledgeable and trusted user groups, (b) well-known systems security authorities such as Carnegie Mellon University's Computer Emergency Response Team (aka CERT), and (c) the operating system vendor. Only those systems security tools supplied by these sources or by commercial software firms may be used on Company X computers and networks.

HANDLING NETWORK SECURITY INFORMATION

From time to time, the Director of Security will designate individuals to audit compliance with this and other computer and network security policies. At the same time, every worker must promptly report any suspected network security problem--including intrusions and out-of-compliance situations--to the Physical Security Manager.

Computer viruses can spread quickly and need to be eradicated as soon as possible to limit serious damage to computers, networks, and Company X information. Accordingly, provided no intention to damage Company X systems existed, if workers report a computer virus infestation immediately after it is noticed, even if their negligence was a contributing factor, no disciplinary action will be taken.

All network or systems software malfunctions must be immediately reported to the Information Technology Department and/or the involved external information system service provider. Ignoring these malfunctions could lead to serious problems such as lost or damaged information as well as unavailable network services.

Information about security measures for Company X computer and communication systems is confidential and should not be released to people who are not authorized users of the involved systems unless the permission of the Information Security Manager has first been obtained. For example, publishing modem phone numbers or other system access information in directories is prohibited. Nonetheless, release of Internet electronic mail addresses is permissible.

PHYSICAL SECURITY OF COMPUTER AND COMMUNICATIONS GEAR

All Company X network equipment must be physically secured with anti-theft devices if located in an open office environment. Additional physical access control may also be used for these devices. For example, local area network servers must be placed in locked cabinets, locked closets, or locked computer rooms. Computer equipment located in sales service offices must additionally be secured with anti-theft devices.

Access to systems development staff offices, telephone wiring closets, computer machine rooms, network switching rooms, and other work areas containing "secret" or "confidential" information must be physically restricted. Management responsible for the staff working in these areas must consult the Information Security Department to determine the appropriate access control method (receptionists, metal key locks, magnetic card door locks, etc.).

All workers who must keep "secret" or "confidential" Company X information at their homes in order to do their work must receive lockable furniture for the proper storage of this information. At the time of separation from Company X, both the furniture and the information stored therein must be immediately returned.

"Secret" or "confidential" information must not be down-loaded to remote locations--such as sales offices--unless proper physical security and encryption facilities are installed and faithfully observed.

EXCEPTIONS

The Information Security Manager acknowledges that under rare circumstances, certain workers will need to employ systems that are not compliant with these policies. All such instances must be approved in writing and in advance by the Information Security Manager.

VIOLATIONS

Company X workers who willingly and deliberately violate this policy will be subject to disciplinary action up to and including termination.

GLOSSARY

Access control: A system to restrict the activities of users and processes based on the need-to-know.

Agents: A new type of software that performs special tasks on behalf of a user, such as searching multiple databases for designated information.

Algorithm: A mathematical process for performing a certain calculation; in the information security field, it is generally used to refer to the process for performing encryption.
Badge reader: A device which reads worker identity badges and interconnects with a physical access control system, which in turn may control locked doors.

Booting: The process of initializing a computer system from a turned-off or powered-down state.

Bridge: A device which interconnects networks or that otherwise allows networking circuits to be connected.

Compliance statement: A document used to obtain a promise from a computer user that such user will abide by system policies and procedures.

Confidential information: A sensitivity designation for information, the disclosure of which is expected to damage Company X or its business affiliates (also see Secret information).

Critical information: Any information essential to Company X's business activities, the destruction, modification, or unavailability of which would cause serious disruption to Company X's business.

Cryptographic challenge/response: A process for identifying computer users involving the issuance of a random challenge to a remote workstation, which is then transformed using an encryption process and a response is returned to the connected computer system.

Default file permission: Access control file privileges (read, write, execute, etc.) granted to computer users without further involvement of either a security administrator or users.
Default password: An initial password issued when a new user-ID is issued, or an initial password provided by a computer vendor when hardware/software is first delivered.

Dynamic password: A password which changes each time a user logs-into a computer system.

Encryption key: A secret password or bit string used to control the algorithm governing an encryption process.

Encryption: A process involving data coding to achieve confidentiality, anonymity, time-stamping, and other security objectives.

End-user: A user who employs computers to support Company X business activities, who is acting as the source or destination of information flowing through a computer system.

Extended user authentication technique: Any of various processes used to bolster the user identification process typically achieved by user-IDs and fixed passwords (such as hand-held tokens and dynamic passwords).

Firewall: A logical barrier stopping computer users or processes from going beyond a certain point in a network unless these users or processes have first passed some security check (such as providing a password).

Front-end processor (FEP): A small computer used to handle communications interfacing (polling, multiplexing, error detection, etc.) for another computer.

Gateway: A computer system used to link networks which can restrict the flow of information and which employs some access control method.

Hand-held token: A commercial dynamic password system which employs a smart card to generate one-time passwords that are different for each session.

Information retention schedule: A formal listing of the types of information that must be retained for archival purposes and the timeframes that these types of information must be kept.

Isolated computer: A computer which is not connected to a network or any other computer; a stand-alone personal computer is an example.

Log-in banner: The initial message presented to a user when he or she first makes connection with a computer.

Log-in script: A set of stored commands which can log a user into a computer automatically.

Master copies of software: Copies of software which are retained in an archive and which are not used for normal business activities.

Multi-user computer system: Any computer which can support more than one user simultaneously.

Password guessing attack: A computerized or manual process whereby various possible passwords are provided to a computer in an effort to gain unauthorized access.

Password reset: The assignment of another (temporary) password when a user forgets or loses his/her password.

Password-based access control: Software which relies on passwords as the primary mechanism to control system privileges.

Password: Any secret string of characters used to positively identify a computer user or process.

Positive identification: The process of definitively establishing the identity of a computer user.

Privilege: An authorized ability to perform a certain action on a computer, such as read a specific computer file.

Privileged user-ID: A user-ID which has been granted the ability to perform special activities, such as shut down a multi-user system.

Router: A device that interconnects networks using different layers of the Open Systems Interconnection (OSI) Reference Model.

Screen blanker: See screen saver.

Screen saver: A computer program that automatically blanks the screen of a computer monitor or screen after a certain period of no activity.

Secret information: Particularly sensitive information, the disclosure of which is expected to severely damage Company X or its business affiliates (also see Confidential information).

Security patch: A software program used to remedy a security or other problem (commonly applied to operating systems, database management systems, and other systems software).

Sensitive information: Any information, the disclosure of which could damage Company X or its business associates.

Shared password: A password known by and/or used by more than one individual.

Software macro: A computer program containing a set of procedural commands to achieve a certain result.

Special system privilege: Access system privileges allowing the involved user or process to perform activities which are not normally granted to other users.

Suspending a user-ID: The process of revoking the privileges associated with a user-ID.

Systems Administrator: A designated individual who has special privileges on a multi-user computer system, and who looks after security and other administrative matters.

Terminal function keys: Special keys on a keyboard that can be defined to perform certain activities such as save a file.

User-IDs: Also known as accounts, these are character strings that uniquely identify computer users or computer processes.

Valuable information: Information of significant financial value to Company X or another party.

Verify security status: The process by which controls are shown to be both properly installed and properly operating.

Virus screening software: Commercially-available software that searches for certain bit patterns or other evidence of computer virus infection.

XI. Sample Internet Security Policy

INTRODUCTION

Opportunities & Risks: The wide array of new resources, new services, and interconnectivity available via the Internet all introduce new business opportunities as well as new security and privacy risks. In response to the risks, this policy describes Company X's official policy regarding Internet security.

Applicability: This policy applies to all workers (employees, contractors, consultants, temporaries, volunteers, etc.) who use the Internet with Company X computing or networking resources, as well as those who represent themselves as being connected--in one way or another--with Company X. All Internet users are expected to be familiar with and fully comply with this policy. Questions about the policy should be directed to the reader's Departmental Information Security Coordinator or the Corporate Manager of Information Security. Violations of this policy can lead to revocation of system privileges and/or disciplinary action up to and including termination.

Prior Management Approval: Access to the Internet (aside from electronic mail) will be provided to only those employees who have a legitimate business need for such access. The ability to surf the web and engage in other Internet activities is not a fringe benefit to which all workers are entitled. If a worker does not have sufficient Internet access, but needs such access for a particular project, he or she can use the special shared systems found in the Corporate Library. In order to receive Internet access privileges, all workers must first attend the Company X information security training and awareness course.

INFORMATION INTEGRITY

Information Reliability: All information taken off the Internet should be considered suspect until confirmed by separate information from another source. There is no quality control process on the Internet, and a considerable amount of its information is outdated and inaccurate, and in some instances even deliberately misleading. Accordingly, before using free Internet-supplied information for business decision-making purposes, workers must corroborate the information by consulting other sources.

Virus Checking: All non-text files (databases, software object code, spreadsheets, formatted word processing package files, etc.) downloaded from non-Company X sources via the Internet must be screened with virus detection software prior to being used. Whenever an external provider of the software is not trusted, down-loaded software should be tested on a stand-alone non-production machine that has been recently backed-up. If this software contains a virus, worm, or Trojan horse, then the damage will be restricted to the involved machine. Downloaded files must be decrypted and decompressed before being screened for viruses. Separately, the use of digital signatures to verify that a file has not been altered by unauthorized parties is recommended, but this does not assure freedom from viruses.

Push Technology: Automatic updating of software or information on Company X computers via background "push" Internet technology is prohibited unless the involved vendor's system has first been tested and approved by the Internet Group within the Information Systems Department. While powerful and useful, this new technology could be used to spread viruses, and cause other operational problems such as system unavailability.

Spoofing Users: Unless tools like digital signatures and digital certificates are employed, it is relatively easy to spoof the identity of another user on the Internet. Before workers release any internal Company X information, enter into any contracts, or order any products via public networks, the identity of the individuals and organizations contacted must be confirmed. Identity confirmation is ideally performed via digital signatures or digital certificates, but in cases where these are not available, other means such as letters of credit, third party references, and telephone conversations may be used.

User Anonymity: Misrepresenting, obscuring, suppressing, or replacing a user's identity on the Internet or any Company X electronic communications system is forbidden. The user name, electronic mail address, organizational affiliation, and related information included with messages or postings must reflect the actual originator of the messages or postings. If users have a need to employ remailers or other anonymous facilities, they must do so on their own time, with their own information systems, and with their own Internet Service Provider (ISP) accounts. Use of anonymous FTP log-ins, anonymous UUCP log-ins, HTTP (web) browsing, and other access methods established with the expectation that users would be anonymous are permissible.

Java: All Internet users must disable Java by changing the default configuration of their Internet browser software. Reliable mechanisms to prevent damage to Company X systems, software, and data from Java (as well as ActiveX and related programs) are not yet generally available. In the interim, running Java (and similar programs) on a Company X system is prohibited unless specifically authorized in advance by the Internet Group within the Information Systems Department.

Attachments: Workers must not open electronic mail attachments unless they were expected from a known and trusted sender. Such attachments may include viruses or other malicious software.

Web Page Changes: Workers may not establish new Internet web pages dealing with Company X business, or make modifications to existing web pages dealing with Company X business, unless they have first obtained the approval of the Internet Management Committee. Modifications include the addition of links to other sites, updating the information displayed, and altering the graphic layout of a page. This committee will make sure that all posted material has a consistent and polished appearance, is aligned with business goals, and is protected with adequate security measures.

Web Page Archives: Every version of the Company X Internet web site and commerce site files must be securely archived in two physically-separated locations. The Internet Management Committee will designate a web master who will keep this archive and provide copies of historical pages on demand.

INFORMATION CONFIDENTIALITY

Information Exchange: In keeping with the confidentiality agreements signed by all workers, Company X software, documentation, and all other types of internal information must not be sold or otherwise transferred to any non-Company X party for any purposes other than business purposes expressly authorized by management. Exchanges of software and/or data between Company X and any third party may not proceed unless a written agreement has first been signed. Such an agreement must specify the terms of the exchange, as well as the ways in which the software and/or data is to be handled and protected. Regular business practices--such as shipment of a product in response to a customer purchase order--need not involve such a specific agreement since the terms and conditions are implied.

Posting Materials: Workers must not post unencrypted Company X material (software, internal memos, policies, etc.) on any publicly-accessible Internet computer which supports anonymous FTP or similar publicly-accessible services, unless the posting of these materials has first been approved by the Director of Public Relations. In more general terms, Company X internal information must not be placed in any computer unless the persons who have access to that computer have a legitimate business need-to-know the involved information.

Message Interception: Wiretapping and other types of message interception are straightforward and frequently encountered on the Internet. Accordingly, Company X secret, proprietary, or private information must not be sent over the Internet unless it has first been encrypted by approved methods. Unless specifically known to be in the public domain, source code must always be encrypted before being sent over the Internet. For the same reasons, Internet telephone services must not be used for Company X business unless the connection is known to be encrypted.

Security Parameters: Unless a connection is known to be encrypted, credit card numbers, telephone calling card numbers, fixed log-in passwords, and other security parameters that can be used to gain access to goods or services, must not be sent over the Internet in readable form. The SSL or AES encryption processes are both acceptable Internet encryption standards for the protection of security parameters. Other encryption processes, such as PGP, are permissible if they are approved by the Corporate Manager of Information Security.

PUBLIC REPRESENTATIONS

External Representations: Workers may indicate their affiliation with Company X in mailing lists (listservs), chat sessions, and other offerings on the Internet. This may be done by explicitly adding certain words, or it may be implied, for instance via an electronic mail address. In either case, whenever workers provide an affiliation, unless they have been expressly designated as a spokesperson of Company X, they must also clearly indicate the opinions expressed are their own, and not necessarily those of Company X. Likewise, if an affiliation with Company X is provided, political advocacy statements and product/service endorsements are also prohibited unless they have been previously cleared by the Director of Public Relations. With the exception of ordinary marketing and customer service activities, all representations on behalf of Company X must first be cleared by the Director of Public Relations.

Appropriate Behavior: To avoid libel, defamation of character, and other legal problems, whenever any affiliation with Company X is included with an Internet message or posting, "flaming" or similar written attacks are strictly prohibited. Likewise, workers must not make threats against another user or organization over the Internet. All Internet messages intended to harass, annoy, or alarm another person are similarly prohibited.

Removal Of Postings: Those messages sent to Internet discussion groups, electronic bulletin boards, or other public forums, which include an implied or explicit affiliation with Company X, may be removed if management deems them to be inconsistent with Company X's business interests or existing Company policy. Messages in this category include: (a) political statements, (b) religious statements, (c) cursing or other foul language, and (d) statements viewed as harassing others based on race, creed, color, age, sex, physical handicap, or sexual orientation. The decision to remove electronic mail must be made by the Corporate Manager of Information Security or the Director of Human Resources. When practical and feasible, individuals responsible for the message will be informed of the decision and given the opportunity to remove the message(s) themselves.

Disclosing Internal Information: Workers must not publicly disclose internal Company X information via the Internet that may adversely affect Company X's stock price, customer relations, or public image unless the approval of the Director of Public Relations or a member of the top management team has first been obtained. Such information includes business prospects, products now in research and development, product performance analyses, product release dates, internal information systems problems, and the like. Responses to specific customer electronic mail messages are exempted from this policy.

Inadvertent Disclosure: Care must be taken to properly structure comments and questions posted to mailing lists (listservs), public news groups, Usenet, and related public postings on the Internet. Before posting any material, workers must consider whether the posting could put Company X at a significant competitive disadvantage or whether the material could cause public relations problems. Workers should keep in mind that several separate pieces of information can be pieced-together by a competitor to form a picture revealing confidential information which could then be used against Company X. Although it may seem to be different than the prevailing Internet culture of openness, to avoid this mosaic picture problem, workers should be reserved rather than forthcoming with internal Company X information.

INTELLECTUAL PROPERTY RIGHTS

Copyrights: Company X strongly supports strict adherence to software vendors' license agreements. When at work, or when Company X computing or networking resources are employed, copying of software in a manner that is not consistent with the vendor's license is strictly forbidden. Likewise, off-hours participation in pirate software bulletin boards and similar activities represent a conflict of interest with Company X work, and are therefore prohibited. Similarly, the reproduction, forwarding, or in any other way republishing or redistribution of words, graphics, or other copyrighted materials must be done only with the permission of the author/owner. Workers should assume that all materials on the Internet are copyrighted unless specific notice states otherwise. When information from the Internet is integrated into internal reports or used for other purposes, all material must include labels such as "copyright, all rights reserved" as well as specifics about the source of the information (author names, URLs, dates, etc.).

Publicly-Writable Directories: All publicly-writable directories on Company X Internet-connected computers will be reviewed and cleared each evening. This process is necessary to prevent the anonymous exchange of information inconsistent with Company X's business. Examples include pirated software, purloined passwords, stolen credit card numbers, and inappropriate written or graphic material (for instance, pornography). Workers using Company X computers must not be involved in any way with the exchange of the material described in the last sentence.

ACCESS CONTROL

Inbound User Authentication: All users wishing to establish a real-time connection with Company X internal computers via the Internet must authenticate themselves at a firewall before gaining access to Company X's internal network. This authentication process must be achieved via a dynamic password system approved by the Corporate Manager of Information Security. Examples of approved technology include hand-held smart cards with dynamic passwords and user-transparent challenge/response systems. These systems will prevent intruders from guessing fixed passwords or from replaying a fixed password captured via a "sniffer attack" (wiretap). Designated "public" systems (anonymous ftp, web surfing, etc.) do not need user authentication processes because anonymous interactions are expected.

Browser User Authentication: Users must not save fixed passwords in their web browsers or electronic mail clients because this may allow anybody who has physical access to their workstations to both access the Internet with their identities, as well as read and send their electronic mail. Instead, these fixed passwords must be provided each time that a browser or electronic mail client is invoked. Browser passwords may be saved if and only if a boot password must be provided each time the computer is powered-up, and if a screen saver password must be provided each time the system is inactive for a specified period of time. Similarly, Company X computer users must refuse all offers by software to place a cookie on their computer so that they can automatically log-in the next time that they visit a particular Internet site.

Internet Service Providers: With the exception of telecommuters and mobile computer users, workers must not employ Internet Service Provider (ISP) accounts and dial-up lines to access the Internet with Company X computers. Instead, all Internet activity must pass through Company X firewalls so that access controls and related security mechanisms can be applied. Likewise, users must always employ their Company X electronic mail address for Internet electronic mail; use of a personal electronic mail address for this purpose is prohibited.

Establishing Network Connections: Unless the prior approval of the Manager of Telecommunications Services has been obtained, workers may not establish Internet or other external network connections that could allow non-Company X users to gain access to Company X systems and information. These connections include the establishment of multi-computer file systems (like Sun's NIS), Internet web pages, Internet commerce systems, ftp servers, and the like.

Establishing New Business Channels: Unless the VP of Information Systems, the VP of Marketing, and the Chief Legal Counsel have all approved in advance, workers are prohibited from using new or existing Internet connections to establish new business channels. These channels include electronic data interchange (EDI) arrangements, electronic malls with on-line shopping, on-line database services, etc.

PERSONAL USE

Personal Use: Company X management encourages workers who have been granted Internet access to explore the Internet, but if this exploration is for personal purposes, it must be done on personal, not company time. Likewise, games, news groups, and other non-business activities must be performed on personal, not company time. Use of Company X computing resources for these personal purposes is permissible so long as the incremental cost of the usage is negligible, and so long as no Company X business activity is preempted by the personal use. Workers must not employ the Internet or other internal information systems in such a way that the productivity of other workers is eroded; examples include chain letters and broadcast charitable solicitations.

Blocking Sites: Company X firewalls routinely prevent users from connecting with certain non-business web sites. Workers using Company X computers who discover they have connected with a web site that contains sexually explicit, racist, violent, or other potentially offensive material must immediately disconnect from that site. The ability to connect with a specific web site does not in itself imply that users of Company X systems are permitted to visit that site.

PRIVACY EXPECTATIONS

No Default Protection: Workers using Company X information systems and/or the Internet should realize that their communications are not automatically protected from viewing by third parties. Unless encryption is used, workers should not send information over the Internet if they consider it to be confidential or private.

Management Review: At any time and without prior notice, Company X management reserves the right to examine electronic mail messages, files on personal computers, web browser cache files, web browser bookmarks, logs of web sites visited, and other information stored on or passing through Company X computers. Such management access assures compliance with internal policies, assists with internal investigations, and assists with the management of Company X information systems.

Logging: Company X routinely logs web sites visited, files downloaded, time spent on the Internet, and related information. Department managers receive reports of such information and use it to determine what types of Internet usage are appropriate for their department's business activities.

Junk Email: Users are prohibited from using Company X computer systems for the transmission of unsolicited bulk email advertisements or commercial messages which are likely to trigger complaints from the recipients. Colloquially known as "spam," these prohibited messages include a wide variety of unsolicited promotions and solicitations such as chain letters, pyramid schemes, and direct marketing pitches. When workers receive unwanted and unsolicited email (also known as spam), they must refrain from responding directly to the sender. Instead, they should forward the message to the email administrator at Company X who can then take steps to prevent further transmissions. To respond to the sender would be indicate that the user-ID is monitored regularly, and this would then invite further junk email.

REPORTING SECURITY PROBLEMS

Notification Process: If sensitive Company X information is lost, disclosed to unauthorized parties, or suspected of being lost or disclosed to unauthorized parties, the Corporate Manager of Information Security must be notified immediately. If any unauthorized use of Company X's information systems has taken place, or is suspected of taking place, the Corporate Manager of Information Security must likewise be notified immediately. Similarly, whenever passwords or other system access control mechanisms are lost, stolen, or disclosed, or are suspected of being lost, stolen, or disclosed, the Corporate Manager of Information Security must be notified immediately. Because it may indicate a computer virus infection or similar security problem, all unusual systems behavior, such as missing files, frequent system crashes, misrouted messages, and the like must also be immediately reported to the Help Desk. The specifics of security problems should not be discussed widely but should instead be shared on a need-to-know basis.

False Security Reports: The Internet has been plagued with hoaxes alleging various security problems. Many of these hoaxes take the form of chain letters which request that the receiving party send the message to other people. Workers in receipt of such information about system vulnerabilities must forward it to the Corporate Manager of Information Security, who will then determine what if any action is appropriate. Workers must not personally redistribute system vulnerability information.

Testing Controls: Workers must not "test the doors" (probe) security mechanisms at either Company X or other Internet sites unless they have first obtained permission from the Corporate Manager of Information Security. If workers probe security mechanisms, alarms will be triggered and resources will needlessly be spent tracking the activity. Likewise, both the possession and the usage of tools for cracking information security (such as SATAN) is prohibited without the advance permission of the Corporate Manager of Information Security.

XII. Sample Intranet Security Policy

Business Use Only: The Company X intranet is intended to facilitate more efficient and more effective ways for Company X staff to communicate and conduct business. Like other Company X information systems, because it is intended for business purposes, personal use is permitted only if the approval of a department manager has first been obtained.

Respecting Intellectual Property Rights: Although the intranet is an informal internal communications environment, the laws for copyrights, patents, trademarks, and the like still apply. To uphold these rights, and also to ensure the quality and security of the intranet, workers may post material to the intranet only after they follow these steps:

(1) If material to be posted originates outside Company X, written permission from the source must first be obtained, and the source must be given adequate credit,

(2) If copyright infringement, confidential information disclosure, libel, defamation of character, and/or other possible legal issues could be involved, Company X legal counsel must approve the posting,

(3) Workers must independently confirm the material's accuracy, timeliness, and relevance to Company X business, and

(4) All user-developed web pages must be tested for security and operational problems by a webmaster according to an approved process issued by the Information Security Department.

Prohibited Content: Because Internet and intranet security technology is still relatively new and untested, Company X secret information must not reside on either Internet or intranet servers.

Approvals For Postings: Before any information is posted to the Company X intranet, two approvals must be obtained. First, the department manager in charge of the relevant intranet page must approve. Second, the owner of the involved information (or creator of the information if the owner has not yet been designated) must approve. In some cases, these two approvals may come from the same person. A formal change control procedure must be used for all changes to the content posted to the Company X intranet, and this procedure must include documentation reflecting management approvals as well as archival storage of all prior versions of posted material.

Classification For Postings: The content posted to the Company X intranet must be classified as either Public or Internal Use Only. Confidential or Secret information must never be posted to the intranet. Staff in the Information Security Department must review all postings to the Company X intranet quarterly to confirm that none of these postings contain Confidential or Secret information.

Legal Ownership Of Material Posted: Unless approved in advance by the director of the Information Technology Department, and explicitly noted on the intranet web page in question, all content posted to the Company X intranet is the property of Company X.

Designated Information Owner: All content posted to the Company X intranet must have a designated "owner" (responsible manager). Contact information for this owner must be clearly indicated on the page where the content appears.

Third Party Access: All third party access to Company X internal computer systems which are not clearly public (such as the intranet) must be approved in advance by the Information Security Department.

Restricted Dissemination: The Company X intranet is for the exclusive use of authorized persons. Unlike the Internet, information on the intranet may be disseminated only to authorized persons. Workers must not forward information appearing on the intranet to third parties without going through the appropriate internal channels (such as Marketing, Human Resources, or Public Relations).

Relevant Standards And Resources: All Company X intranet pages must conform to layout standards, navigation standards, legal wording standards, and similar requirements specified by the Intranet Management Committee. All personnel developing intranet sites must consistently observe the intranet style guide and use the resources found in the intranet implementation repository.

Connections To Production Systems: The intranet must not be used to provide real-time connections to any Company X production information system which has extended user authentication access controls (anything beyond a fixed password and a user-ID), unless the approval of the Information Security Department manager has first been obtained.

Connecting Systems To The Intranet: Before any computer system or network segment can be connected to Company X's intranet, it must first be deemed to have met the necessary security criteria established by the Information Security Manager. These criteria include, but are not limited to, the following: no connection to the Internet which is not guarded by an acceptable firewall, an acceptable user-authentication system, an acceptable user privilege control system, an established change control process, a clearly written definition of system management responsibilities, and adequate operational documentation.

Server Approval: Before they are connected to the internal network, all Company X intranet servers must be preauthorized by the network services manager in the Information Technology Department.

Establishing Internet Links: Links which transfer a user's session from a Company X intranet web site to the web site of any outside entity are not permitted unless the approval of the Information Security Department manager has first been obtained. Whenever these links are established, they must clearly notify the user that they are leaving the intranet and entering the Internet.

XIII. Sample Privacy Policy (Stringent)

OVERVIEW AND APPLICABILITY

Company X supports the right to privacy, including the rights of Data Subjects to control the dissemination and use of personal data that describes them, their personal choices, and/or their life experiences. Company X additionally supports domestic and international laws and regulations which seek to protect the privacy rights of such Data Subjects.

This policy applies to all Company X employees, contractors, temporaries, and consultants, and other workers. All of these people are expected to be familiar with and fully in compliance with these policies. Workers who are not in compliance are subject to disciplinary action up to and including termination.

This policy also applies to outsourcing firms which perform information processing services on behalf of Company X. Use of outsourcing firms to process personal data must always include a contractual commitment to consistently observe these policies and related Company X procedures and standards as specified by the Information Security Department. All outsourcing firms handling personal data provided by Company X must periodically issue certificates of compliance with this policy, as well as allow Company X to initiate independent audits to determine compliance with this policy.

DEFINITIONS

Personal data means any information relating to an individually identifiable natural person (also known as a Data Subject). Such data includes name, address, telephone number, address, social security number, driver's license number, and personal business transaction details. For example, such a natural person could be a purchaser of Company X products. The following policies do not apply to statistical reports or other collections of information in which specific natural persons are not identifiable.

Processing of personal data (simply "processing" below) means any operation or set of operations performed on personal data, whether or not by automatic means, such as collection, recording, organization, storage, adaptation or alteration, retrieval, consultation, use, disclosure by transmission, dissemination or otherwise making available, combination, blocking, erasure or destruction.

Owner means the Company X manager or executive, which jointly or alone determines the purposes for processing personal data, and which makes decisions about the security mechanisms to be used to protect such personal data.

Custodian means the Company X manager (or third party organization manager if processing is outsourced) which processes personal data according to the instructions provided by the Owner.

Third party means any natural or legal person, partnership, corporation, public authority, government agency or any other entity other than the Data Subject, the Owner, the Custodian, and the persons who, under the direct authority of the Owner or the Custodian, are authorized to process the data.

Recipient means the natural or legal person, public authority, government agency or any other entity to whom personal data are disclosed, whether a third party or not.

The Data Subject's consent means any freely-given informed indication of his or her wishes by which the Data Subject signifies his or her agreement to have his or her personal data processed (this may include disclosure).

No distinction between data, information, knowledge, or wisdom is made in this policy.

SPECIFIC REQUIREMENTS

1. All personal data must be processed fairly and lawfully (according to the laws and regulations of all jurisdictions where Company X does business).

2. Personal data must be collected for purposes communicated to the Data Subject and not further processed in a way incompatible with those purposes. Further processing of such data for historical, statistical or other business purposes is not incompatible with the original purpose provided the further processing includes adequate additional controls protecting the rights of the Data Subject.

3. The amount of personal data collected must be adequate, relevant and not excessive in relation to the purposes for which they are collected and/or for which they are further processed.

4. Personal data must be accurate and complete, and where necessary, kept up to date. Every reasonable step must be taken to ensure that personal data which are inaccurate or incomplete -- keeping in mind the purposes for which they were collected or for which they are further processed -- are definitively erased or corrected.

5. Data Subjects must be given an opportunity to examine, and thereafter issue complaints about, inaccuracies and incompletions in records containing their personal data. Investigations of Data Subject complaints must be performed promptly, and must be answered with a letter informing the involved Data Subjects about the courses of action that Company X will take. Any resulting erasures or corrections must likewise be performed promptly and at no cost to the Data Subjects. Reasonable steps to prevent reoccurrence of the same inaccuracies or incompletions must also be taken, for instance by adding an explanatory paragraph in the subject's file. An exception to the requirements stated in this paragraph is allowed for personal data in management sucession planning records, criminal activity investigation records, and other legitimate business activities where disclosure to the Data Subject would be highly likely to jeopardize the project then underway.

6. Personal data must not be kept in a form which permits identification of Data Subjects for any longer than is necessary for the purposes for which the data were collected or for which they are further processed. This can for instance be implemented with linked separate files respectively containing Data Subject identification information and related sensitive information.

Owners of personal data are responsible for ensuring that items in the preceding five points are complied with.

7. Personal data may be processed only if:
   - (a) the Data Subject has given his/her consent unambiguously, or
   - (b) processing is necessary for the performance of a contract to which the Data Subject is party (such as completing an order for goods), or
   - (c) processing is required to respond to a request made by the Data Subject, or
   - (d) processing is necessary for compliance with a legal obligation to which the Owner is subject, or
   - (e) processing is necessary in order to protect the vital interests of the Data Subject, or

(f) processing is necessary to explore or provide new business products and/or services which may be of use to the Owner, so long as these new products and/or services do not override the fundamental rights or freedoms of the Data Subject.

8. The processing of personal data revealing racial or ethnic origin, political opinions, religious or philosophical beliefs, trade-union membership, criminal offenses, health, or sex life is prohibited unless:

(a) the Data Subject has provided explicit consent to such processing, or
(b) processing is necessary for the purposes of carrying out the obligations and specific rights of the Owner in the field of employment law, or
(c) processing is necessary to protect the vital interests of the Data Subject or of another person where the Data Subject is physically or legally incapable of giving his consent.

Custodians of personal data are responsible for ensuring that items in the preceding two points are complied with.

INFORMATION TO BE GIVEN TO THE DATA SUBJECT

The Owner or his or her representative must provide Data Subjects with the following information:

(a) the identity of the Custodian and of his or her representative, if any,
(b) the purposes of the processing for which the data are intended,
(c) the policies related to handling personal data, including material changes to these policies that have gone into effect since the personal data was collected,
(d) any further information such as
- the Recipients or categories of Recipients of the data,
- whether replies to the questions are obligatory or voluntary, as well as the possible consequences of the failure to reply, and
- the existence of the right of access to and the right to correct the data concerning the Data Subject.

Where personal data has not been obtained directly from the Data Subject, the Owner or his or her representative must notify the Data Subject at the time when personal data will be processed. Alternatively, if a disclosure to a third party is envisaged, the Data Subject must be notified no later than the time when the data are first disclosed. The Owner must provide the Data Subject with at least the following information, except where the Data Subject already knows it:

(a) the identity of the Custodian and the Custodian's representative, if any,
(b) the purposes of the processing,
(c) any further information such as,
- the categories of data concerned,
- the Recipients or categories of Recipients, and
- the existence of the right of access to and the right to correct information concerning the Data Subject.

Upon request, the Owner or his or her representative must provide all Data Subjects with a brief written summary of the subject's rights to learn about, get copies of, lodge objections to, and correct personal data. Trained personnel who can explain a Data Subject's rights must also be available to subjects by telephone.

THE DATA SUBJECT'S RIGHT OF ACCESS TO DATA

1. Every Data Subject has the right to obtain from the Custodian:Without undue constraint at reasonable intervals and without excessive delay or expense:

- confirmation as to whether or not data relating to him or her are processed and information at least as to the purposes of the processing, the categories of data concerned, and the Recipients or categories of Recipients to whom the data are disclosed;
- details as to the source(s) of information about the Data Subject, if such information is recorded;
- communication of the personal data to the subject in an intelligible form; and
- knowledge of the logic involved in any automatic processing of data concerning him at least in the case of the automated decisions affecting the Data Subject's welfare (creditworthiness, performance at work, etc.).

2. When appropriate, an indication that his or her personal data has been corrected, erased, or blocked because it was incomplete or inaccurate.

3. Notification to third parties to whom the data have been disclosed of any correction, erasure or blocking carried out in compliance with the prior paragraph, unless this proves impossible or involves a unreasonable effort or expense.

THE DATA SUBJECT'S RIGHT TO OBJECT

Data Subjects may object, free of charge, to the processing of personal data which the Owner anticipates will be processed for the purposes of direct marketing. Owners must provide prompt processing mechanisms that allow Data Subjects who objected to be removed from direct marketing lists.

Data Subjects must be informed before personal data are disclosed for the first time to third parties or used on their behalf for the purposes of direct marketing. Data Subjects must be expressly offered the right to object free of charge to such disclosures or uses. Owners must provide processing mechanisms that allow Data Subjects who objected to block such a disclosure.

DISCLOSURE OF PERSONAL DATA TO THIRD PARTIES

Company X may provide third parties with personal data processed on its systems for generally accepted business purposes such as court orders, subpoenas, employment verification, governmental licensing, underwriting, and other reasons. All Recipients of such information must definitively identify themselves, certify in writing the legal and customary purposes for which the information is sought and also certify that the personal data will be used for no other purposes.

All disclosures to government agencies and other third parties must be preceded by written or other notice sent to the Data Subject; a blanket one-time Data Subject approval of such disclosures is sufficient. Sufficient time must be provided between the receipt of such notice to the Data Subject and the actual disclosure to the third party to allow the Data Subject to object, should he or she so elect.

PROCESSING CONFIDENTIALITY AND SECURITY

The Owner must implement appropriate technical and organizational measures to protect personal data against accidental or unlawful destruction, accidental loss, unauthorized alteration, and unauthorized disclosure or access. These measures must be consistent with the standards and procedures issued by the Information Security Department.

Transfers of private information to another country, no matter what technology is employed, must not take place unless prior approval of the Information Security Manager has first been obtained. An exception is made in those cases where the Data Subject is, was, or will be located in the destination country, or when the Data Subject has specifically requested such a transfer.

Company X information systems and/or staff must not link anonymous information about Data Subject behavior or activities with personally-identifiable information unless the involved Data Subjects have first given their consent. Such a linkage could for example tie Internet shopping purchase information with web browsing logs.

The Owner or his or her designated representative must prepare a documented risk analysis to determine the privacy implications of all significantly new or different uses of personal data. Such a risk analysis must be completed before these uses take place, and must include all steps in the proposed processing, including access, storage, transmission, destruction. Such a risk analysis must include not only consideration of the risks, but also the security measures to be employed, such as access controls, encryption, logs, data retention schedules, and data destruction procedures.

When building, testing, enhancing, and maintaining processing systems, developers must not use "live" personal data. Instead, they must use "fictional" (sanitized) personal data which preserves the essential characteristics of the data, but which does not relate to identifiable Data Subjects. In emergency situations, where processing with "live" personal data is required, use of such information is permitted under strict security procedures defined by the Information Security Department.

All user access to processing systems and networks containing personal data must be logged so that every recent access to personal data can be traced to a specific user. Custodians of these systems and networks are responsible for the routine monitoring of such logs as well as the follow-up on potential security-relevant events.

When not in use, personal data must be stored in encrypted form if held inside a computer or network, or in a locked or similarly secured containers if held in paper, microfiche, or other non-computerized form. Similarly, when sent over public computer networks such as the Internet, personal data must be protected by encryption. Procedures and standards issued by the Information Security Department provide additional details on these topics.

When they are no longer needed, all copies of personal data, including those on back-up tapes, must be irreversibly destroyed according to standards and procedures defined by the Information Security Department. A document describing the personal data destroyed and the reasons for such destruction must be prepared for each destruction process, and promptly submitted to the relevant Owner. Permission to destroy personal data may only be granted by the Owner, and only then if all legal retention requirements and related business purposes have been met.

MONITORING OF INTERNAL ACTIVITIES

In general terms, Company X does not engage in blanket monitoring of internal communications. It does, however, reserve the right at any time to monitor, access, retrieve, read, and/or disclose internal communications when: (a) a legitimate business need exists that cannot be satisfied by other means, (b) the involved individual is unavailable and timing is critical to a business activity,

(c) there is reasonable cause to suspect criminal activity or policy violation, or (d) monitoring is required by law, regulation, or third-party agreement.

Company X may at any time log web sites visited, files downloaded, and related information exchanges over the Internet. Similarly, Company X may record the numbers dialed for telephone calls placed through its telephone systems. Department managers may receive reports detailing the usage of these and other internal information systems, and are responsible for determining that such usage is both reasonable and business-related.

To prevent accidental loss, all files and messages stored on Company X processing systems are routinely backed-up to tape, disk, and other storage media. This means that information stored on Company X information processing systems -- even if a worker has specifically deleted it -- is often recoverable and may be examined at a later date by systems administrators and others designated by management.

At any time and without prior notice, Company X management reserves the right to examine archived electronic mail, personal computer file directories, hard disk drive files, and other information stored on Company X information processing systems. This information may include personal data. Such examinations are typically performed to assure compliance with internal policies, support the performance of internal investigations, and assist with the management of Company X information processing systems.

XIV. Sample Privacy Policy (Lenient)

Company Intentions And Management Responsibilities

Intentions And Objectives: In the course if its business, it is necessary for Company X to record, store, process, transmit, and otherwise handle private information about individuals. The Company takes these activities seriously and seeks to provide fair, secure and fully legal systems for the appropriate handling of this private information. All such activities at Company X are additionally intended to be consistent with both generally accepted privacy ethics and standard business practices.

Management Responsibilities: To this end, management must take reasonable efforts to ensure that all private information maintained by Company X is reasonably accurate, timely, relevant, and complete. Management must also make reasonable efforts to ensure that all private information is used only as intended, and that precautions preventing misuse are both effective and appropriate. Management is additionally responsible for establishing appropriate controls to ensure that private information is disclosed only to those who have a legitimate business need. Management must furthermore establish and maintain sufficient controls to ensure that all Company X information is free from a significant risk of undetected alteration.

Data Classification Labels: To identify the information in need of special handling, management (specifically information Owners) must consistently apply a standard data classification label indicating that information is private. For example, this label must appear on computer screens when private information is displayed, and it must also be stamped on hardcopy versions of private information. This label must follow private information no matter what form it takes, no matter what technology is used to handle it, and no matter where the information resides.

Disclosure Of Private Information

Revealing Information About Policies And Procedures: As a general rule, information security policies and procedures should be revealed only to Company X workers and selected outsiders (such as auditors) who have a legitimate business need for this information. A notable exception involves the policies which deal with private information about individuals. All involved individuals have a right to receive an officially-approved statement of Company X's policies and procedures regarding the handling of information about them. In addition, Company X has a duty to disclose the existence of systems containing private information and the ways that this information is used. With the exception of criminal and policy-violation investigations, there must be no system of personnel records within Company X whose very existence is kept secret from the people described therein.

Handling Private Information Requests: All requests for private information coming from a person or organization outside Company X must be forwarded to the Company X intellectual property counsel. Similarly, all requests for private information that fall outside normal business procedures and that come from a Company X insider must be forwarded to the director of the Human Resources Department. These managers will then decide whether the requests will be granted.

Appropriate Handling Of Private Information

Collect Only Necessary Information: In general, Company X may collect, process, store, transmit, and disseminate only that private information which is necessary for the proper functioning of its business. For example, Company X management must not collect information about worker activities during non-work hours unless these activities are highly likely to influence the involved worker's performance, or unless they could adversely affect the reputation of Company X.

Destruction Of Private Information: When private information is no longer needed, it must be destroyed by shredding or other approved destruction methods. Destruction of private information resident on computer disks and other magnetic media must be accomplished with an overwriting process (a simple "erase" process is not sufficient). To assure the proper destruction of private and/or confidential information, disposal of computers with embedded hard disk drives or other data storage systems must proceed according to procedures issued by the Information Security Department.

Removal Of Private Information: In general, private and/or confidential information should not be removed from Company X offices. Permission to take such information off-site may be granted by a departmental manager provided the involved worker has completed the information security segment of telecommuter training. Signed third party non-disclosure agreements may additionally be required when private information is removed from Company X offices. Private information must not be moved to another country unless the permission of the manager of the Information Security Department is first obtained.

Preventing Inadvertent Disclosure on Screens: The display screens for all microcomputers (PCs), workstations, and dumb terminals used to process sensitive or valuable data -- including private information -- must be positioned such that they cannot be readily viewed through a window, by persons walking by a hallway, or by persons waiting in reception and related areas.

Preventing Inadvertent Disclosure Via Hardcopy: Whenever a worker is handling private information, if a person who is not authorized to view that information enters the immediate area, steps to conceal the information must promptly be taken. If the information is in physical form, the information can be covered with other material. If the information is displayed on a computer screen, the worker can invoke a screen saver or log-off.

Private Information On Computer And Communication Systems

Expectation Of Privacy: All messages sent over Company X internal computer and communications systems are the property of Company X. To properly maintain and manage this property, management reserves the right to examine all information transmitted through these systems. Examination of such information may take place without prior warning to the parties sending or receiving such information. Since Company X's computer and communications systems must be used for business purposes only, workers should have no expectation of privacy associated with the information they store in or send through these systems.

No Blanket Monitoring: In general terms, Company X does not engage in blanket monitoring of employee communications. It does, however, reserve the right at any time to monitor, access, retrieve, read, and/or disclose worker communications when: (a) a legitimate business need exists that cannot be satisfied by other means, (b) the involved employee is unavailable and timing is critical to a business activity, (c) there is reasonable cause to suspect criminal activity or policy violation, or (d) monitoring is required by law, regulation, or third-party agreement.

Examination Of Stored Information: At any time and without prior notice, Company X management reserves the right to examine archived electronic mail, private file directories, hard disk drive files, and other information stored on Company X information systems. Such examinations are typically performed to assure compliance with internal policies, support the

performance of internal investigations, and assist with the management of Company X information systems.

Manager Involvement In Monitoring: Whenever a worker's computer or communications user-ID (account) is monitored for investigative or disciplinary purposes, the involved worker's manager must be promptly informed of this activity. All worker monitoring must itself be logged for subsequent management review and possible use in disciplinary or legal actions.

Department Manager Activity Review: Company X routinely logs web sites visited, files downloaded, and related information exchanges over the Internet. Similarly, Company X records the numbers dialed for telephone calls placed by each worker. Department managers routinely receive reports detailing the usage of these and other internal information systems, and are responsible for determining that such usage is both reasonable and business-related.

Changing Information Resident On Systems: Management reserves the right to delete, summarize, or edit any information posted to Company X computers and/or communication systems. These facilities are privately-owned business systems, and not public forums, and as such do not provide First Amendment free-speech guarantees.

Routine Usage Of Back-Up Systems: To prevent accidental loss, all files and messages stored on Company X systems are routinely copied to tape, disk, and other storage media. This means that information stored on Company X information systems -- even if a worker has specifically deleted it -- is often recoverable and may be examined at a later date by systems administrators and others designated by management.

Encryption Of Electronic Mail: Workers should consider electronic mail to be the computerized equivalent of a postcard. Unless material sent by electronic mail is encrypted, workers must refrain from sending credit card numbers, passwords, research and development information, medical histories, computer programming source code, and other private and/or confidential information via electronic mail.

Links Between Separate Types Of Private Data: Without advance consent from the manager of the Information Security Department, Company X information systems must not be configured to support new links between private information and other types of information related to the same individual. This review process is intended to verify that new links do not inadvertently create an invasion of privacy or a security problem. One widely used approach for establishing such links is called 'database matching.'

Testing With Sanitized Data: Unless written permission is first obtained from the Information Security Department manager, all software testing for systems designed to handle private data must be accomplished exclusively with "sanitized" production information. Sanitized information is production information which no longer contains specific details that might be valuable, critical, sensitive.

Activity Monitoring

Physical Security Systems: Workers may be subject to electronic monitoring (closed circuit TV, intercoms, etc.) of their activities while on Company X premises. This monitoring is used to measure workers performance as well as to protect worker private property, worker safety, and Company X property. In areas where there is a reasonable expectation of privacy, such as bathrooms, dressing rooms, and locker rooms, no electronic monitoring will be performed.

Handling Personnel Information

Access To Own Personnel File: Upon written request, every worker must be given access to his or her own personnel file. Employees must be permitted to both examine and make one copy of the information appearing in their personnel file. If employees object to the accuracy, relevance, or completeness of information appearing in their personnel file, each year they may add a supplementary statement of up to two hundred (200) words.

Disclosure To Third Parties: Disclosure of private information about Company X workers to third parties must not take place unless required by law or permitted by explicit consent of the worker. Company X does not disclose the names, titles, phone numbers, locations, or other contact particulars of its workers unless required for business purposes. Exceptions will be made when such a disclosure is required by law or when the involved persons have previously consented to the disclosure. To preserve the privacy of personnel information, the reason for termination of workers must not be disclosed to third parties. Two permissible exceptions are the prior approval of a Company X senior manager or if the disclosure is required by law. Separately, every disclosure of private information to third parties must be recorded by the Human Resources Department and these records must be maintained for at least five (5) years.

Summary Of Disclosures: If they request it, workers must be provided with a summary of all disclosures of their private information to third parties. In addition, workers must be given sufficient information to allow them to contact such third parties to rectify errors or supply additional explanatory information.

Change Of Status Information: Detailed worker change of status information is strictly confidential, and must not be disclosed to anyone except those people who have a bona fide need-to-know. Detailed change of status information includes the reasons for terminations, retirements, resignations, leaves of absence, leaves of absence pending the results of an investigation, inter-departmental transfers, relocations, and changes to consultant/contractor status.

Private Information From Job Seekers

Gathering Unnecessary Information: Private information about a prospective employee may not be gathered unless it is both necessary to make an employment decision and also relevant to the job in question. This policy addresses marital status, family planning objectives, off-hours activities, political affiliations, performance on previous jobs, previous employers, credit history, education, and other personal details.

Permissible Tests: Candidates for a job with Company X must not be subjected to drug tests, AIDS tests, psychological tests, or other tests which may illuminate the candidates' lifestyle, political associations, or religious preferences. An exception may be made if this information is clearly needed to determine a candidate's suitability for a certain position.

Credit And Background Checks: Whenever a credit report will be examined or a background check will be performed, prospective workers must first provide a written release indicating their approval of the process. These prospective workers must be given an opportunity to withdraw their application for employment or contract work if they choose not to disclose such private information to Company X.

Private Information About Customers

Consent For Collection Required: The collection of private information about potential customers and others with whom Company X does business is customary and expected. However, Company X workers must not collect private information from customers or potential customers without having first obtained their knowledge and consent.

Consent For Uses Required: Before a customer places an order or otherwise discloses private information, all Company X representatives must inform the customer about the ways that this private information will be used.

Collection Of Unnecessary Information: Company X workers or information systems must never require the provision of customer private information which is unnecessary for the completion of a transaction, or for the provision of products or services. No product or service provided by Company X may be denied to any person if they refuse to provide unnecessary private information. All disputes about necessary private information will be resolved by the Company X intellectual property counsel.

Anonymity Mechanisms: To help preserve the privacy of customer information, Company X provides mechanisms for customers to remain anonymous when using Company X systems. Company X will not disclose the identity of the customers who elect to use these mechanisms unless compelled to do so by law.

Opting Out From Unsolicited Contacts: Company X customers must be given an opportunity to inform Company X that they do not wish to be contacted via unsolicited direct mail, telemarketing, and related promotions. Company X staff must faithfully observe and act on these customer requests. Company X workers must diligently observe the unconditional right of data subjects to: block data about them from being included in mailing lists or calling lists, block the sale of data about them to third parties, and to have data about them erased from direct marketing lists.

XV. Sample Web Privacy Policy

Company X has created this security & privacy statement in order to document and communicate its commitment to doing business with the highest ethical standards and appropriate internal controls.

Our site's request-for-more-information form requires users to give us contact information (like name, email address, and telephone number). This information is used to provide information to those who inquire about our products and services, to ship orders, to bill orders, and to handle related business matters. This information is also used to get in touch with customers when necessary. From time to time, the information gathered via this site will be used to notify you about products and services which we think will be of interest to you. Information gathered via this site is not shared with third parties unless the involved individual requests such sharing or unless disclosure is required by law.

Our site does not capture information regarding the specific activities of any particular user. It does, however, produce reports which allow us to view activity in anonymous aggregated form. We do not use JavaScript, cookies, web bugs, or any other active content mechanism to capture or maintain information about users without their prior consent. The only personal information we capture has been specifically submitted to us through the request-for-more-information form.

This site contains links to other sites. Company X is not responsible for the security or privacy practices of these sites, the products or services offered by these sites, or the content appearing at these sites. Likewise, Company X does not endorse any of the products or services marketed at these other sites.

Our site is protected with a variety of security measures such as change control procedures, passwords, and physical access controls. We also employ a variety of other mechanisms to ensure that data you provide is not lost, misused, or altered inappropriately. These controls include data confidentiality policies and regular database backups.

With respect to this web site, there are two options regarding your personal information: (1) if you wish to contact us about our products or services, then you need to disclose your contact information so that we can service your request(s), or (2) if you do not wish to contact us about our products or services, then we will have gathered no information about you, and you do not need to take further action. If you have elected to pursue the first of these options, after you have obtained the information you sought, you may at any time tell us to remove your name and other contact particulars from our database.

If you wish to remove your name and related information from our database, we will promptly take action to comply with your request. Likewise, we are pleased to process address error correction notices and address change requests through any of the following communication channels:

1. Sending email to [insert email address]
2. Sending regular slow mail to [insert physical address]
3. Calling [insert telephone number] during regular business hours [time zone]
4. Faxing [insert fax number] any time of day or night

If you have any questions about this security & privacy statement, the practices of this site, or your dealings with our company, you can contact us using any of the above communications channels.

XVI. Sample Data Classification Policy

INTRODUCTION AND OVERVIEW

Worker Responsibility: All workers who have any type of access to either Company X information or Company X information systems have an important information security role to play. They are, for instance, personally responsible for the protection of information which has been entrusted to their care. To simplify the protection of information, to minimize information protection costs, and to clarify information protection requirements, management has compiled, approved, and issued this policy. This document defines a conceptual model for viewing the sensitivity of information as well as required methods for protecting information based on its sensitivity classification. All workers who come into contact with "sensitive" Company X internal information are expected to familiarize themselves with this data classification system policy and to consistently use it in their Company X business activities. "Sensitive" information is either "Confidential" or "Secret" information (the latter two quoted words are defined below). Although this policy provides overall guidance, to achieve consistent information protection, workers will be expected to apply and extend these concepts to fit the needs of day-to-day operations.

Addresses Major Risks: Company X's data classification system, as defined in this document, is based on the well-known concept called "need to know." This term means that information is not disclosed to any person who does not have a legitimate and demonstrable business to receive the information. This fundamental concept, when combined with the policies defined in this document, will help to protect Company X information from unauthorized disclosure, use, modification, and deletion.

Consistent Approach Required: A single lapse in information security can have significant long-term consequences. Consistent use of this data classification system is absolutely essential if sensitive information is to be adequately protected. Without the consistent use of this data classification system, Company X unduly risks loss of customer relationships, loss of public confidence, internal operational disruption, excessive costs, and competitive disadvantage. The intention of this policy is thus to consistently protect sensitive information no matter what form it takes, no matter what technology is used to process it, no matter who handles it, no matter where the information may be located, and no matter what stage in its lifecycle (creation, production usage, archival storage, destruction, etc.) the information may be.

Applicable Information: This data classification policy is applicable to all information in Company X's possession or under Company X's control. For example, Confidential information entrusted to Company X by customers, business partners, suppliers, and other third parties must be protected with this data classification policy. Workers are expected to protect third party information with the same care that they protect Company X information. Separately, no distinctions between the words "data," "information," "knowledge," and "wisdom" are made for purposes of this policy.

Trade Secrets: One special type of sensitive information is called a Trade Secret. Trade Secrets are proprietary information which give Company X competitive advantage in one form or another. This document covers Trade Secrets, all of which need to be separately designated as a Trade Secret. Trade Secrets must also be identified as such prior to being disclosed to any worker. By default, all Trade Secrets are classified as Secret information (see definitions below). Company X's Chief Legal Counsel is the only person authorized to designate any Company X information to be a Trade Secret.

ACCESS CONTROL

Need to Know: Every one of the policy requirements set forth in this document are based on the concept called "need to know." If a worker is unclear how the requirements set forth in this policy should be applied to any particular circumstance, he or she must conservatively apply the need to know concept. That is to say that information must be disclosed only to those people who have a legitimate business need for the information. This principle applies to private employee information such as medical histories, just as it applies to proprietary corporate information such as plans for a new product.

System Access Controls: All sensitive computer-resident information must be protected via access controls to ensure that it is not improperly disclosed, modified, deleted, or rendered unavailable. Traditional access control systems employ fixed passwords, but these are giving way to more secure technologies including dynamic passwords and biometrics. These access control packages must not only control access based on the need to know, they must also log which users accessed what sensitive data, and the time and date of such access.

Access Granting Decisions: Access to Company X sensitive information must be provided only after the written authorization of the information Owner has been obtained. Custodians of the involved information must refer all requests for access to the relevant Owners or their delegates. Standard templates of system privileges are defined for all job titles, and these privileges are approved in advance by Owners. Special needs for other access privileges will be dealt with on a request-by-request basis.

No Read Up Permissions: Workers who have been authorized to view information classified at a certain sensitivity level must be permitted to access only the information at this level and at less sensitive levels.

CLASSIFICATION LABELS

Owners & Production Information: All production information possessed by or used by a particular organizational unit within Company X must have a designated Owner. Production information is information routinely used to accomplish business objectives. Examples include payroll summaries, shipping schedules, and managerial cost accounting reports. Information Owners are responsible for assigning appropriate sensitivity classifications as defined immediately below. Owners do not legally own the information entrusted to their care. They are instead designated members of the Company X management team who act as stewards who supervise the ways in which certain types of information are used and protected [hot-link to Data Ownership Policy could go here].

SECRET: This classification label applies to the most sensitive business information which is intended strictly for use within Company X. Its unauthorized disclosure could seriously and adversely impact Company X, its customers, its business partners, and/or its suppliers. Examples include merger and acquisition documents, corporate level strategic plans, litigation strategy memos, reports on breakthrough new product research, and Trade Secrets such as certain computer programs.

CONFIDENTIAL: This classification label applies to less sensitive business information which is intended for use within Company X. Its unauthorized disclosure could adversely impact Company X, its customers, its suppliers, its business partners, and/or its employees. Information that some people would consider to be private is included in this classification. Examples include employee performance evaluations, customer transaction data, strategic alliance agreements,

unpublished internally-generated market research, computer passwords, identity token personal identification numbers (PINs), and internal audit reports.

FOR INTERNAL USE ONLY: This classification label applies to all other information which does not clearly fit into the above two classifications. While its unauthorized disclosure is against policy, it is not expected to seriously or adversely impact Company X, its employees, its suppliers, its business partners, and/or its customers. Examples include the telephone directory, dial-up computer access numbers, new employee training materials, and internal policy manuals.

PUBLIC: This classification applies to information which has been explicitly approved by Company X management for release to the public. By definition, there is no such thing as unauthorized disclosure of this information and it may be freely disseminated without potential harm. Examples include product and service brochures, advertisements, job opening announcements, and press releases.
Other Labels: Company X department- or division-specific data classification labels are permissible but must be consistent with and supplemental to the Company X data classification system. These supplementary labels might for example include the use of words like "Private" or "Financial."

Owners & Access Decisions: Owners must make decisions about who will be permitted to gain access to information, and the uses to which this information will be put. Owners must additionally take steps to ensure that appropriate controls are utilized in the storage, handling, distribution, and regular usage of information. Readers of this policy can quickly determine the appropriate Owner by consulting the Information Security Department's page on the Company X intranet.

LABELING

Consistent Classification Labeling: If information is sensitive (Confidential or Secret), from the time it is created until the time it is destroyed or declassified, it must be labeled (marked) with an appropriate data classification designation. Such markings must appear on all manifestations of the information (hardcopies, floppy disks, CD-ROMs, etc.). Workers are forbidden from removing data classification system labels from sensitive information unless the permission of the Owner has first been obtained.

What Gets Labeled: The vast majority of Company X information falls into the Internal Use Only category. For this reason, it is not necessary to apply a label to Internal Use Only information. Information without a label is therefore by default classified as Internal Use Only.

Information Collections: Workers who create or update a collection of information are responsible for choosing an appropriate data classification label for the new collection. This label must be consistent with the decisions made by the relevant Owners and generally should be the most restricted classification level found in the collection. For example, if a new database is being created, and if it contains Internal Use Only as well as Confidential information, then the entire database must be classified as Confidential. Other examples of such collections include internally-generated competitive intelligence report, management decision background reports, and access-controlled intranet web pages. At the time that it is being compiled, every worker creating a new collection of this nature must notify the involved information Owner(s) about the creation of their new collection.

Storage Media: If information recorded on computer storage media with a higher sensitivity classification is moved to media with a lower sensitivity classification, then the media with the lower sensitivity classification must be upgraded so that its classification reflects the highest sensitivity classification. For example, if information labeled Secret were to be placed on a floppy disk containing information with no label (which is by default Internal Use Only), then the floppy disk must immediately be reclassified as Secret. Likewise, if information with several different data classification levels is resident on a single computer, then the system controls must reflect the requirements associated with most restrictive data classification level (this approach is sometimes called "system high"). In general, because it increases handling costs as well as operational complexity, commingling of information with different sensitivity classifications is discouraged.

Labels For Externally-Supplied Information: With the exception of general business correspondence and copyrighted software, all externally-provided information which is not clearly in the public domain must receive a Company X data classification system label. The Company X worker who receives this information is responsible for assigning an appropriate classification on behalf of the external party. When assigning a Company X classification label, this staff member must preserve copyright notices, author credits, guidelines for interpretation, as well as information about restricted dissemination.

Labeling Hardcopy: All printed, handwritten, or other paper manifestations of sensitive information must have a clearly-evident sensitivity label on the upper right hand corner of each page. If bound, all paper manifestations of sensitive information must have an appropriate sensitivity label on the front cover, the title page, and the rear cover. The cover sheet for faxes containing sensitive information must also contain the appropriate classification label. Microfiche and microfilm must also contain labels if they contain sensitive information.

Labeling Computer Storage Media: All tape reels, floppy disks, and other computer storage media containing sensitive information must be externally labeled with the appropriate sensitivity classification. Unless it would adversely affect the operation of an application, computer files containing sensitive information must also clearly indicate the relevant classification label in the first two data lines.

Other Displays: If information is sensitive, all instances in which it is displayed on a screen or otherwise presented to a computer user must involve an indication of the information's sensitivity classification. Teleconferences and telephone conference calls where sensitive information will be discussed must additionally be preceded by a statement about the sensitivity of the information involved. Teleconferences and telephone calls where sensitive information is discussed must be preceded by a determination that all parties on the line are indeed authorized to receive the sensitive information.

Additional Public Information Labels: Unless it is unquestionably already public information (such as a printed marketing brochure), all Company X information with a Public label must also be labeled "Approved For Public Release" along with the date when the Owner declared the information Public.

Dictation Machines And Tape Recorders: To reduce the chance of unauthorized disclosure, in general, workers should not record sensitive information with dictation machines, tape recorders, or similar devices. If the use of these devices is an operational necessity, the proper sensitivity classification must be specified at the beginning and end of each segment of sensitive information. In this case, the recording media must also be marked with the most stringent data classification found on the media. In addition, the media must be protected in accordance with the most stringent classification found on the media, and erased as soon as possible.

THIRD PARTY INTERACTIONS

Third Parties And The Need To Know: Unless it has specifically been designated as Public, all Company X internal information must be protected from disclosure to third parties. Third parties may be given access to Company X internal information only when a demonstrable need-to-know exists, and when such a disclosure has been expressly authorized by the relevant Company X information Owner.

Disclosures To Third Parties And Non-Disclosure Agreements: The disclosure of sensitive information to consultants, contractors, temporaries, or any other third parties must always be preceded by the receipt of a signed Company X non-disclosure agreement (NDA). Disclosures of Company X sensitive information to these third parties must be accompanied by a running log indicating exactly what type of information was provided. This log will be important when the time arrives to recover these materials (or obtain a letter certifying the destruction of the materials) at the end of a contract.

Disclosures From Third Parties And Non-Disclosure Agreements: Workers must not sign non-disclosure agreements provided by third parties without the advance authorization of Company X legal counsel designated to handle intellectual property matters. These forms may contain terms and conditions which unduly restrict Company X's future business directions.

Third Party Requests For Company X Information: Unless a worker has been authorized by the relevant information Owner to make public disclosures, all requests for information about Company X and its business must be referred to the Public Relations Department. Such requests include questionnaires, surveys, newspaper interviews, and the like. This policy does not apply to sales and marketing information about Company X products and services, nor does it pertain to customer support calls.

Prior Review: Every speech, presentation, technical paper, book, or other communication to be delivered to the public must first have been approved for release by the involved employee's immediate manager. This policy applies if the employee will represent Company X, if the employee will discuss Company X affairs (even if only generally), or if the communication is based on information obtained in the course of performing Company X job duties. If new products, research results, corporate strategies, customer information, or marketing approaches are to be divulged, prior approval of the director of R&D and the director of the Legal Department must also be obtained.

Owner Notification: If sensitive information is lost, is disclosed to unauthorized parties, or is suspected of being lost or disclosed to unauthorized parties, the information Owner and the manager of the Information Security Department must both be notified immediately.

SHIPPING AND HANDLING

Making Copies: Making additional photocopies of, or printing of extra copies of sensitive information must not take place without the advance permission of the information Owner. Workers should be aware that selected photocopy machines keep logs of the information copied along with the associated audit card number.

Unattended Printing: Printers must not be left unattended if sensitive information is being printed or will soon be printed. The persons attending the printer must be authorized to examine the information being printed. Unattended printing of sensitive information is permitted only if physical access controls are used to prevent unauthorized persons from both entering the area around the printer and viewing the material being printed.

Use Of Outside Services: Prior to sending any sensitive information to a third party for copying, printing, formatting, or other handling, the third party must sign a Company X non-disclosure agreement.

Page Numbering: To help recipients determine that no pages have gone astray, and that all pages have been provided, all sensitive Company X information manifested in paper form must indicate both the current and the last page ("Page X of Y").

Back-Up Storage Media: To prevent it from being revealed to or used by unauthorized parties, all sensitive information recorded on back-up computer media (magnetic tapes, floppy disks, optical disks, etc.) and stored outside Company X offices must be in encrypted form. If an encryption system with key escrow is not used for this purposes, all keys used to make these backup copies must be promptly provided to the Information Security Department shortly after their initial use.

Envelopes: If sensitive information is to be sent through internal mail, external mail, or by courier, it must be enclosed in two envelopes or containers (double wrapped). The outside envelope or container must not indicate the classification of the nature of the information contained therein. The inside sealed and opaque envelope or container must be labeled with the appropriate classification label. Envelopes containing sensitive information must always be addressed to a specific person, and must also contain sufficient return address information. To assist with information tracking and related investigations, all sensitive Company X information sent through these delivery systems must require a signature by an authorized party at the destination.

Delivery Of Computer Output: Sensitive computer system output must be personally delivered to the designated recipients. Such output must not be delivered to an unattended desk, or left out in the open in an unoccupied office. Alternatively, it may be made available to only the designated recipients via password-protected fax mailboxes, departmental/personal computer output lockers, or other physical security methods.

Removal From Offices: Sensitive Company X information may not be removed from Company X premises unless there has been prior approval from the information's Owner. This policy includes portable computers with hard disks, floppy disks, hard-copy output, paper memos, and the like. An exception is made for authorized off-site back-ups.
Locked Containers In The Office: Sensitive information in hardcopy form must be locked-up when not actively in use, even if it is within a building to which access is controlled. In keeping with the clean desk policy, if not encrypted, all sensitive information must be locked in safes, heavy furniture, or other containers approved by the Information Security Department.

Locked Containers Off-Site: Whenever a hardcopy version of sensitive information is removed from Company X premises, it must be carried in a locked briefcase or container when not in use. Such information must not be left in an unattended motor vehicle, hotel room, office, or some other location, even if the vehicle or room is locked.

Oral Warnings: If Confidential information is released orally in a meeting, seminar, lecture, or related presentation, the speaker must clearly communicate the sensitivity of the information. The speaker must also remind the audience to use discretion when disclosing it to others. Visual aids such as projector slides and overhead transparencies must also include the appropriate data classification labels.

Cellular Phones: Because the risk of interception is high, unless an encrypted link has been established, workers must never discuss sensitive matters over cellular or portable phones. Likewise, computer links established over cellular phone or other broadcast systems must not include the transfer of sensitive information unless the link is encrypted.

DECLASSIFICATION/DOWNGRADING

Dates For Reclassification: If known, the date that Secret or Confidential information will no longer be sensitive (that is, the date when it will be "declassified") must be indicated on all Company X sensitive information. This will assist those in possession of the information with its proper handling, even if these people have not been in recent communication with the information's Owner.

Classification Extensions: The designated information Owner may, at any time prior to scheduled declassification or downgrading, extend the period that information is to remain at its current classification level. To achieve this, the Owner must: (1) change the declassification or downgrading date appearing on the original document, (2) notify all known recipients and Custodians, (3) initiate a cost-effective search for additional recipients, and (4) notify the Company X archives Custodian. Because such an extension can be expensive and time consuming, Owners are urged not to specify a date for declassification or downgrading unless they are relatively sure that the date will not be changed.

Notifications: The designated information Owner may, at any time, declassify or downgrade the classification of information entrusted to his or her care. To achieve this, the Owner must: (1) change the classification label appearing on the original document, (2) notify all known recipients and Custodians, and (3) notify the Company X archives Custodian.

Schedule For Review: To determine whether sensitive information may be declassified or downgraded, at least once a year, information Owners must review the sensitivity classifications assigned to information for which they are responsible. From the standpoint of sensitivity, information must be declassified or downgraded as soon as practical. Owners must follow the guidelines for declassification and downgrading as specified in the Information Ownership Policy [link to that policy could be placed here].

No Unauthorized Downgrading: Workers must not move information classified at a certain sensitivity level to a less sensitive level unless this action is a formal part of a declassification or downgrading process approved by the Owner.

DESTRUCTION AND DISPOSAL

Destruction And Disposal: All Company X information must be destroyed or disposed of when no longer needed for business purposes. To support this policy, information Owners must review the continued value and usefulness of information on a periodic basis. Owners must also review the data retention schedule issued by the Legal Department to determine the minimum legal periods that information must be retained [intranet link to the data retention schedule could be placed here].

Destruction And Locked Boxes: All sensitive information no longer being used or no longer needed -- no matter what form it takes (floppy disks, hardcopy, etc.) -- is to be placed in designated locked metal boxes until such time as authorized Company X personnel or a bonded destruction service picks it up. If no locked disposal boxes are in the immediate vicinity, sensitive information in hardcopy form (paper, microfilm, microfiche, etc.) must be either shredded or incinerated, while sensitive information in all other forms must be delivered to the Industrial Security Department for secure destruction. The shredders used for this purpose must create confetti or other similar small particles; strip cut shredders may not be used for this purpose because they allow unauthorized parties to readily reconstruct shredded hardcopy documents. Erasing or reformatting magnetic media such as floppy disks is not an acceptable data destruction method because the data previously stored thereon can still be recovered.

Destruction Approval: Workers must not destroy or dispose of potentially important Company X records or information without specific advance management approval. Unauthorized destruction or disposal of Company X records or information will subject the worker to disciplinary action including termination and prosecution. Records and information must be retained if: (1) they are likely to be needed in the future, (2) regulation or statute requires their retention, or (3) they are likely to be needed for the investigation or prosecution of unauthorized, illegal, or abusive acts. Any questions about data destruction should be referred to the information Owner or his or her delegate.

Permissible Destruction: Workers may, however, destroy Company X records when approval has been granted by (1) verbal instructions from the Owner or his or her delegate, (2) an Information Security Department or Archive Department memo detailing the type of records that may be destroyed and when, or (3) the records retention and disposition schedule issued by the Legal Department. Destruction is defined as any action which prevents the recovery of information from the storage medium on which it is recorded (including encryption with unknown keys, erasure, reformatting, or disposal of the hardware needed to recover the information).

Intermediate Products: All materials used in the handling of sensitive information, which could be analyzed to deduce sensitive information, must be destroyed in a manner similar to that required for sensitive information. This policy covers typewriter ribbons, carbon paper sheets, mimeograph stencil masters, photographic negatives, aborted computer hardcopy output, unacceptable photocopies, etc.

Photocopies: All waste copies of Secret information that are generated in the course of copying, printing, or other sensitive information handling must be destroyed according to the instructions found in this policy. If a copy machine jams or malfunctions when workers are making copies of Secret information, the involved workers should not leave the machine until all copies of the information are removed from the machine or destroyed beyond recognition.

Equipment Disposal Or Servicing: Before computer or communications equipment is sent to a vendor for trade-in, servicing, or disposal, all Company X sensitive information must be destroyed or concealed according to methods approved by the Information Security Department. Removable computer storage media such as floppy diskettes and magnetic tapes may not be donated to charity or otherwise recycled unless they have first been subjected to zeroization (wipe/obliteration) processes approved by the Information Security Department.

PHYSICAL SECURITY

Office Access: Access to every office, computer room, and work area containing sensitive information must be physically restricted. Management responsible for the staff working in these areas must consult the Physical Security Department to determine the appropriate access control method (receptionists, metal key locks, magnetic card door locks, etc.).

Locked When Not In Use: When not in use, sensitive information must always be protected from unauthorized disclosure. When left in an unattended room, such information must be locked away in appropriate containers. If a Custodian of such information believes he or she will be away for less than thirty minutes, the information may be left on a desk or in some other readily observed spot only if all doors and windows to the unattended room are closed and locked.

Unauthorized Screen Viewing: The screens on computers used to handle sensitive information must be positioned such that unauthorized persons cannot readily look over the shoulder of the person using the workstation. Screens should also be positioned such that sensitive information cannot be seen through windows using binoculars or telescopes.

SPECIAL CONSIDERATIONS FOR SECRET INFORMATION

Numbering Document Copies: All copies of Secret documents must be individually numbered with a sequence number to ensure that the persons responsible for the documents and the location of the documents can both be readily tracked. To help control its dissemination, hardcopy manifestations of Secret information should also include the words "Do Not Copy Without Explicit Permission From The Information Owner."

Secret Information Logs: When Secret information is involved, the Owner or delegate of the Owner must keep a log reflecting the number of copies made, the location of copies, the names of recipients, the addresses of recipients, and any persons viewing the copies. This log must be maintained as long as such information retains a Secret sensitivity classification. This log must also be classified as Secret. Separately, all production application systems which handle Secret Company X information must generate logs that show every addition, modification, and deletion to such Secret information.

Removal From Offices: Secret Company X information, no matter what form it happens to take, must not leave Company X offices unless the approval of the Information Security Manager has first been obtained. This requirement will help to ensure that appropriate information security measures safeguard the Secret information when it is located elsewhere besides Company X offices.

Couriers: Secret information in hardcopy form must be sent by trusted courier or registered mail. Because they don't allow the information to be tracked, other methods such as regular mail are prohibited. All deliveries of Secret information must be conducted such that the intended recipient personally acknowledges that the information has been received. Delivery of Secret information to intermediaries such as receptionists is prohibited.

Transportation With Computers: Workers in the possession of portable, laptop, notebook, palmtop, personal digital assistant, and other transportable computers containing Secret Company X information must not leave these computers unattended at any time unless the Secret information has been encrypted. Likewise, if Secret data is to be transported in computer-readable storage media (such as magnetic tapes, floppy disks, or CD-ROMs), it must also be in encrypted form.

Viewing In Public: In general, workers should avoid travelling on public transportation when in the possession of Secret information. Secret information must not be read, discussed, or otherwise exposed on airplanes, or in restaurants, elevators, restrooms, or other public places. Company X workers must not take Secret Company X information into another country unless permission has first been obtained from the Industrial Security Manager.

Storage: As noted above, computerized Secret information must be encrypted when not in active use (for example, when not manipulated by software or viewed by an authorized user). Separately, to avoid unauthorized access to temporary computer memory and scratch files, all systems used for the processing of Secret information must either be: (a) powered down immediately after processing is completed, or (b) have these temporary storage locations overwritten with zeroization (wipe/obliteration) programs approved by the Information Security Department.

Internet/Intranet Servers: Because Internet and intranet security technology is still relatively new and untested, Company X Secret information must not be resident on either Internet or intranet servers unless the advance permission of the Information Security Department has first been obtained.

Transmission Over Networks: If Company X Secret data is to be transmitted over any communication network, it must be sent only in encrypted form. Such networks include internal electronic mail systems, the Internet, and dial-up lines. A secure process for exchanging the keys used in an encryption process must also be employed, as approved by the Information Security Department.

Transfer To Another Computer: Before any Secret information may be transferred from one computer to another, the person making the transfer must make sure that access controls on the destination computer are commensurate with access controls on the originating computer. If comparable security cannot be provided with the destination system's access controls, then the information must not be down-loaded.

Fax Transmission: Secret information must not be sent to an unattended fax machine unless the destination machine is in a locked room for which the keys are possessed only by people authorized to receive the information. Transmission to a fax server that uses passwords to control access to received faxes is a permissible exception to this policy. All fax transmissions containing Secret data must also employ an encrypted link.

Speaker Phones: Secret information must not be discussed on speaker-phones unless all participating parties first acknowledge that no unauthorized persons are in close proximity such that they might overhear the conversation. Workers must also refrain from leaving messages containing Secret information on answering machines or voicemail systems. This will help ensure that the information is communicated only to the intended party.

Telephone Conversations: Telephone lines may be tapped or otherwise intercepted by unauthorized parties. Accordingly, workers should take steps to avoid discussing sensitive information when on the telephone. If discussion of such information is absolutely required, workers must use guarded terms and refrain from mentioning sensitive details beyond those needed to get the job done.

Meeting Attendance: Persons other than those specifically invited must not attend meetings where Secret information will be discussed.

Approved By: [executive manager's name]
Approval Date: [date signature obtained]
Date When Policy Takes Effect: [date implementation expected]
Policy Number: XXX [adjust number to suit numbering system]
Responsible Department For Updates: Information Security

Label Name	Storage on Fixed Media (e.g. hard drive)	Storage on Exchangeable Media (e.g. floppy disk)	Copying	Faxing	Sending by Public Network (e.g. Internet)	Disposal
HIGHLY RESTRICTED	Encrypted	Encrypted	Permission of Owner Required	Encrypted Link plus Password Protected Recipient Mailbox or Attended Receipt	Encrypted	Shredding or Secure Disposal Boxes
CONFIDENTIAL	Encrypted or Physical Access Control	Encrypted	Permission of Owner Advised	Password Protected Recipient Mailbox or Attended Receipt	Encrypted	Shredding or Secure Disposal Boxes
INTERNAL USE ONLY	Encryption Optional	Encryption Optional	No Restrictions	No Restrictions	Encryption Optional	Ordinary Trash Can
PUBLIC	Encryption Not Advised	Encryption Not Advised	No Restrictions	No Restrictions	Encryption Not Advised	Ordinary Trash Can

XVII. Sample Data Classification Quick Reference Matrix -- Page 632 -- Copyrighted & Licensed Material

Label Name	Release to Third Parties	Electronic Media Labelling Required	Hardcopy Labelling Required	Internal and External Mail Packaging	Granting Access Rights	Tracking Process By Log
HIGHLY RESTRICTED	Owner Approval and Non-Disclosure Agreement	External and Internal Labels	Each Page if Loose Sheets; Front and Back Covers and Title Page if Bound	Address to Specific Person But Label Only On Inside Envelope	Owner Only	Recipients, Copies Made, Locations, Addresses, Those Who Viewed, and Destruction
CONFIDENTIAL	Owner Approval and Non-Disclosure Agreement	External and Internal Labels	Each Page if Loose Sheets; Front and Back Covers and Title Page if Bound	Address to Specific Person But Label Only On Inside Envelope	Owner Only	Not Required
INTERNAL USE ONLY	Non-Disclosure Agreement	No Label Required	No Label Required	Only One Envelope With No Markings	Local Manager	Not Advised
PUBLIC	No Restrictions	Release Date Plus Classification	Release Date Plus Classification	Only One Envelope With No Markings	No Restrictions	Not Advised

XVIII. Sample External Party Information Disclosure Policy

DETERMINING IF DISCLOSURE IS APPROPRIATE

Duty To Take Special Care: To the extent required to perform their job duties, workers are given access to Company X sensitive internal information. Proper protection of this information is essential if the interests of not only Company X, but also customers and business partners, are to be preserved. These interests include maintenance of competitive advantage, trade secret protection, and preservation of personal privacy. Accordingly, as indicated in the non-disclosure agreement signed by all workers, special care should be taken to prevent disclosure of sensitive internal information to unauthorized third parties.

Sources Of Additional Information: While this policy describes the considerations that workers should bear in mind before, during, and after disclosure to third parties, it cannot specifically address every possible situation. Questions about the disclosure of specific information should be directed to the relevant information Owner [link to the corporate data dictionary, which then indicates who is the Owner for various types of information]. Workers are additionally expected to extend these policies to fit the specific circumstances they face, to use their professional judgement, and ask the Information Security Department for guidance in those instances where the appropriate handling of sensitive information is not clear.

Two Types Of Information: For purposes of this policy, there are basically two types of information. The first type of information has been approved for release to a specific group (such as customers), an organization (such as a regulatory agency), or an individual (such as a contractor). Information which has been specifically designated as "Public" also falls into this first category. If the party requesting information falls within the limits of the approved group of recipients, or if the Public label has been applied, then no Owner approval is required. The second type of information has not yet been approved for release to a specific group, organization, or individual. This policy discusses the specific requirements for dealing with the second category. Additional guidance may be found in the Information Classification Policy [intranet link to that policy].

Third Parties And The Need To Know: Unless it has specifically been designated as Public, all Company X internal information must be protected from unauthorized disclosure to third parties. Third parties may be given access to Company X internal information only when a demonstrable need-to-know exists, and when such a disclosure has been expressly authorized by the relevant Company X information Owner.

Non-Disclosure Agreements: The disclosure of sensitive information to consultants, contractors, and temporaries must always be preceded by the receipt of a signed non-disclosure agreement (NDA). When a NDA pertains to an organization, to be valid, an officer of the recipient organization must sign the NDA. Workers must not sign NDAs provided by third parties without the advance authorization of Company X legal counsel designated to handle intellectual property matters.

Disclosing Information Belonging To Third Parties: Company X respects and safeguards the sensitive information which has been entrusted to it by third parties. Company X workers must not disclose this information to other third parties unless the third party providing the information or the legal owner of the information has provided advance approval of the disclosure, and unless the receiving party has signed an approved non-disclosure agreement (NDA).

Third Party Requests For Company X Information: Unless a worker has been authorized by the information Owner to make disclosures, all requests for information about Company X and its business must be referred to the Public Relations Department [intranet link to that department's page]. Such requests include questionnaires, surveys, newspaper interviews, and the like. This policy does not apply to sales and marketing information about Company X products and services, nor does it pertain to customer requests for information that has been approved for release to customers.

Prior Review: Every speech, presentation, technical paper, book, or other communication to be delivered to the public must first have been approved for release by the involved employee's immediate manager. This policy applies if the employee will represent Company X, if the employee will discuss Company X affairs (even if only generally), or if the communication is based on information obtained in the course of performing Company X duties. If new products, research results, corporate strategies, customer information, or marketing approaches are to be divulged, prior approval of the director of R&D and the director of the Legal Department must also be obtained.

Releasing Information About Internal Events: Specific information about Company X internal events, including new products and services, staff promotions, reorganizations, and information system problems, must not be released to third parties, including members of the news media, without specific authorization from a Vice President.

Discussions In Public Forums: Care must be taken to properly structure comments and questions posted to electronic bulletin boards, electronic mailing lists, on-line news groups, and related forums on public networks like the Internet. If workers aren't careful they may tip-off the competition that certain Company X projects are underway. If a user is working on an unannounced new financial service, a research & development project, or related confidential Company X matters, all related postings must be cleared with one's manager prior to being posted to any public network. Likewise, workers should be careful not to reveal specifics about Company X's internal systems (such as configurations or products used) via public postings.

Mosaic Theory: Both the worker performing the disclosure and the Owner need consider the mosaic theory. A mosaic is made up of many little pieces, which when combined paint a picture that could not otherwise have been seen. The plethora of information available from the Internet and other sources like on-line databases means that one additional piece of information could lead to card holder privacy violation, identity theft, publicity problems, or other undesirable repercussions. Both the workers handling the disclosure and the Owner should consider how the release of the information in question could be just enough to allow these and other abuses.

RESOLVING PROBLEMS WITH DISCLOSURE PROCESSES

Unassigned Owner: If the Company X internal information being considered for disclosure to a third party does not have a designated Owner, then the disclosure decision must be made by the Company X Legal Department. Before referring such decisions to the Legal Department, those workers handling a request for disclosure must consult the corporate data dictionary to determine whether an Owner has been assigned [insert link to the corporate data dictionary here, which in turn indicates the Owners for certain types of information]. Workers can also ask the designated information Custodian to identify the Owner.

Unmarked Information: If the information being considered for disclosure to third parties is not marked with an appropriate information classification, then workers must assume that the information is Company X Internal Use Only information, and not approved for public release. Information marked Public does not require Owner approval prior to release to third parties.

Marking Preservation: The worker disclosing Company X internal information to third parties must preserve markings indicating author, date, version number, usage restrictions, and other details which might be useful in determining the approved usage, currency, accuracy, and relevance of the information in question. An exception may be made, with Owner approval, in those cases where such markings would reveal Company X information which should not be disclosed to the third party (for example the identity of a confidential source).

Disclaimers: It is the information Owner's responsibility to make sure that when controversial, frequently changing, highly uncertain, or potentially-damaging information is released to third parties that it contain the appropriate legal disclaimers. Such disclaimers, generally provided by the Company X Legal Department, include words which limit Company X's liability, define the information's intended uses, and place recipients on notice of potential problems associated with the information.

Naming: The terminology used to refer to information released to the third parties must be consistent with the terminology employed in Company X's corporate data dictionary. Exceptions are permissible in those cases where specialized technical terms would not be readily understandable to a third party, or where use of such terms would reveal information that Company X does not wish to disclose. If there is any difference between the terminology used within Company X and the terminology used within the information disclosed to a third party, then this difference must be approved in advance by the designated Owner. Consistent information naming terminology will reduce errors and confusion, and also allow a third party receiving the information to better adapt its information systems to interface with Company X's information systems.

REQUIRED DISCLOSURE RECORDS

Disclosure Records: Records reflecting the sensitive Company X internal information (not information designated Public) that has been distributed to third parties must be maintained by the worker releasing the information to the third party. Such records must indicate the types of information disclosed, the receiving third party's name and contact particulars (generally address, telephone number, and email address), as well as the date of release. Maintenance of such records will allow errors to be quickly corrected, allow updates to be quickly provided, allow recovery of the information, and also allow Company X to take legal action (should the third party use the information in unintended and unauthorized ways). It should be noted that even though a confidentiality agreement may have been signed, and even though management has approved third party access to certain information, it is still the responsibility of the worker releasing the information to keep records reflecting the information disclosed.

Recovery Or Destruction: All copies of Secret information provided to third parties must be returned to the worker within Company X who provided it. Alternatively all such copies must be destroyed and a certificate of destruction sent to the worker within Company X who provided it. Such recovery or destruction should generally take place within a month of the time when the information ceases to be useful for the intended purposes. The Company X worker who provided the information is responsible for recovering the information or obtaining a certificate of destruction. This Company X worker must also note the recovery or destruction of the information in his or her records reflecting disclosures.

Reporting Improper Disclosures: If sensitive information has been inappropriately disclosed, or is believed to have been inappropriately disclosed, the circumstances must immediately be reported to the relevant information Owner. If a Owner has not been assigned for the information in question, then the Legal Department must immediately be informed. It is the Owner's responsibility to determine whether the disclosure or suspected disclosure needs to be reported to third parties such as government banking regulators, criminal justice system personnel, customers, and others. If no Owner has been assigned, this decision is the Legal Department's responsibility.

PREPARING INFORMATION FOR DISCLOSURE

Using The Best Information: Authorized disclosures of Company X internal information must be done with the best (most current, accurate, timely, and relevant) information available. In other words, the worker disclosing the information must be aware of and extract the information from the "system of record," or the definitive master copy of such information within Company X. If the worker involved is not aware of the system of record, the corporate date dictionary can provide this information.

Updates To Previously Disclosed Information: Owners have a duty to correct information that has been made public, or that has been disclosed to certain third parties, if subsequent events have made this information misleading or materially incorrect. Timely and prompt correction of the previously disclosed information is especially important in those instances where the public or a third party is likely to rely on the information in its decision making processes. This requirement does not apply if the disclosure took place a year or more in the past, and the information is unlikely to be still in use.

Designated Source For Public Disclosures: Information generated by Company X and released to the public must be accompanied by the name of a designated staff member acting as the single recognized official source and point-of-contact. All updates and corrections to this information that are released to the public must flow through this official source.

Phased Disclosure Of Controversial Information: Controversial and sensitive Company X information must be released to the public in installments so that the impact of each disclosure can be measured and so that additional releases can be postponed if necessary.

XIX. Sample Information Ownership Policy

New Centrality Of Information: Information is no longer simply something which supports the provision of a product or service. Information itself has become a product which Company X now offers. Information has additionally become a critical and integral part of other products and services that Company X provides. The new centrality of information necessitates the establishment of new roles and responsibilities to properly manage and protect it. To this end, this policy defines the information security roles and responsibilities of Owners, Custodians, and Users. Information security can no longer be a concern of technical specialists alone -- it must instead be addressed by a large team of individuals. This team is made up of every Company X worker who comes into contact with Company X information and/or information systems.

Policy Scope And Applicability: This policy applies to the handling of all Company X production information, regardless of the origin of this information (customer transactions, third party market research, etc.). "Production information" is information routinely used to perform important business activities or routinely used to support management decision making. This policy applies no matter what information handling technology is used, no matter where the information resides, no matter how the information is employed to meet business needs, and no matter which Users have access to the information. This policy applies to all Company X units, all geographical regions, and all subsidiaries.

Roles And Responsibilities Of Owners: Information Owners are senior business unit managers (full-time Company X employees) with the authority for acquiring, creating, and maintaining information and information systems within their assigned area of control. Owners are responsible for categorizing the information for which they have been designated an Owner using the classifications defined in the Data Classification Policy [link to that document via the intranet]. To assist with contingency planning efforts, Owners are also responsible for categorizing information (or specific application systems) according to a criticality scale defined by the Information Security Department [link to a separate intranet page dealing with contingency planning matters goes here]. Owners are additionally responsible for authorizing User access to information based on the need-to-know. To this end, Owners must establish written policies regarding the categories of people who will be granted access to the information for which they are the designated Owner; these policies must also specify the type of access that each such category of person will be granted. Owners must also make decisions about the permissible uses of information including relevant business rules. Owners are furthermore responsible for choosing relevant controls for information consistent with policies and standards issued by the Information Security Department [intranet link to these policies]. For example, Owners must define the validation rules used to verify the correctness and acceptability of input data. These validation rules and other controls for protecting information must be formally approved in writing by the relevant Owner before major modifications can be made to production application systems. Separately, Owners must understand the uses and risks associated with the information for which they are accountable. This means that they are responsible for the consequences associated with improper disclosure, insufficient maintenance, inaccurate classification labeling, and other security related control deficiencies pertaining to the information for which they are the designated Owner.

Roles And Responsibilities Of Custodians: Information Custodians are individuals (often staff within the Information Systems Department or local department systems administrators) in physical or logical possession of information from Owners. Custodians are charged with the provision of information systems services consistent with the instructions of Owners, including information security measures such as encryption. Using physical and logical access control systems, Custodians must protect the information in their possession from unauthorized access, alteration, destruction, or usage. Custodians are also responsible for providing and administering general controls such as back-up and recovery systems consistent with the policies and standards issued by the Information Security Department. Custodians are likewise responsible for establishing, monitoring, and operating information systems in a manner consistent with policies and standards issued by the Information Security Department. Furthermore, Custodians must provide Owners with regular reports about the resources consumed on their behalf (often via a charge-back system), as well as reports indicating User activities. Custodians are forbidden from changing the production information in their possession unless they have received explicit and temporary permission from either the Owner or an authorized User.

Roles And Responsibilities Of Users: Information Users are individuals who have been granted explicit authorization to access, modify, delete, and/or utilize information by the relevant Owner. Users must use the information only for the purposes specifically approved by the Owner. Users must also comply with all security measures defined by the Owner, implemented by the Custodian, and/or defined by the Information Security Department. Users must additionally refrain from disclosing information in their possession (unless it has been designated as Public) without first obtaining permission from the Owner. Users must additionally report to the Information Security Department all situations where they believe an information security vulnerability or violation may exist. Local management must also provide Users with sufficient time to receive periodic information security training, and Users are required to attend such training on a periodic basis. Users of personal computers have special responsibilities (for example relating to back-up and virus screening) which are defined in the Personal Computer Security Policy [link to that document via intranet].

Multiple Roles And Responsibilities: It is likely that certain individuals will act in multiple capacities with respect to certain types of information. For example, an employee may be the creator of a new type of production information which is stored in a desktop personal computer. In this case, the worker must, at least temporarily, act in the capacity of Owner, Custodian, and User. To achieve a more secure operating environment, in general the roles of Owner, Custodian, and User should be performed by separate individuals wherever production information has more than one User. Creators of new types of production information must promptly inform the Information Architecture Department so that appropriate roles and responsibilities may be established and maintained.

Designating Owners: If there are several potential information Owners, higher-level management must assign Ownership responsibility to the senior manager of the business unit which makes the greatest use of the information. When acting in his or her capacity of Owner, this individual must take into consideration the needs and interests of other stakeholders which rely upon or have an interest in the information. With the exception of operational computer and network information, managers in the Information Systems Department must not be Owners for any information. An Owner's roles and responsibilities may be delegated to any full-time manager in the Owner's business unit. An Owner's roles and responsibilities may not be assigned or delegated to contractors, consultants, or individuals at outsourcing firms or external service bureaus.

Designating Custodians: Management must specifically assign responsibility for the control measures protecting every major production type of information. Owners are responsible for identifying all those individuals who are in possession of the information for which they are the designated Owner. These individuals by default become Custodians. Although special care must be taken to clearly specify security-related roles and responsibilities when outsiders are involved, it is permissible for Custodians to be contractors, consultants, or individuals at outsourcing firms or external service bureaus.

Designating Users: Users may be employees, temporaries, contractors, consultants, or third parties with whom special arrangements (such as non-disclosure agreements) have been made. All Users must be known to and authorized by Owners. The security-relevant activities of all Users must be tracked and logged by Custodians. To allow proper privilege assignment and activity logging, Users must always be specific individuals; Users must not be defined as departments, project teams, or other groups.

Changes In Status: Due to promotions, transfers, retirements, etc., the individuals who play the roles of information Owners, Custodians, and Users will change on a regular basis. It is the responsibility of the local manager of all individuals to promptly report status changes to the Corporate Human Resources Department. As soon as they are known, status changes must be immediately reflected in the Corporate Human Resources database [these changes in worker status will be automatically communicated to the Information Security Department and local systems administrators]. Custodians must maintain access control systems so that previously provided User privileges are no longer provided whenever there has been a User status change. When a Custodian has a change in status, it is the responsibility of the Owner to promptly assign a new Custodian, and to assist the new Custodian with the assumption of tasks previously performed by the former Custodian (including necessary training). When an Owner has a change in status, it is the Chief Information Officer's responsibility to promptly designate a new Owner [Owners should be listed via the corporate data dictionary page which is accessible via the intranet].

Handling Of Information Following Status Changes: Users who change their status must leave all production information with their immediate manager. Soon after a User has a change of status, both computer-resident files and paper files must be reviewed by the User's immediate manager to determine who should be given possession of the files, and/or the appropriate methods to be used for file disposal or destruction. The manager must then promptly reassign the User's duties as well as specifically delegate responsibility for information formerly in the User's possession. It is this manager's responsibility to train the new User so that the new User is able to fully perform the tasks previously performed by the former User.

Externally-Supplied Information: In the course of normal business activities, Company X often takes possession of third party sensitive information. Whenever a non-disclosure agreement (NDA) has been signed, an internal Company X Owner must be assigned for information so received. The manager of the business unit utilizing the information is ordinarily designated as the Owner. The Owner must promptly report the existence of this third party information to the Information Architecture Department for inclusion in the corporate data dictionary [a link for a form to report such information could be provided here]. This third party information must also be labelled with the appropriate data classification category and treated as though it was Company X internal information with the same classification. The roles and responsibilities for Custodians and Users are also relevant to externally-supplied information.

Corporate Data Dictionary: To assist with the management of information, the Information Systems Department must compile and annually update a corporation-wide data dictionary and other high-level descriptions of the major Company X information assets found in production systems. It is the responsibility of the Chief Information Officer to ensure that this data dictionary includes an up-to-date indication of the Owners for all major Company X production information assets.

Supporting Role Of Information Architecture Department: Although not directly involved with Owners, Custodians, and Users in day-to-day information handling activities, the Information Architecture Department is responsible for developing and maintaining an enterprise information architecture. The Information Architecture Department is also responsible for the creation and maintenance of a corporate data dictionary, including appropriate definitions for various types of production information. The Information Architecture Department is furthermore responsible for building a database which tracks the people playing the roles of Owner and Custodian. Working in conjunction with the Information Security Department, the Information Architecture Department is additionally responsible for fostering the efficient and appropriately secured sharing of Company X production information.

System-Of-Record: Each Owner must designate a "system-of-record" which will serve as the most authoritative copy of the information under his or her care. Updates to this information must be made to the system-of-record before or at the same time that updates are made to other systems containing this information. It is the Owner's responsibility to ensure that all production copies of the information for which he or she is the designated Owner are maintained with appropriate controls to ensure a reasonable degree of information accuracy, timeliness, and integrity.

Risk Acceptance Process: In rare circumstances, exceptions to information security policies and standards will be permitted if the information Owner, the Director of the Information Security Department, and the Chief Information Officer have all signed a properly completed risk acceptance form. In the absence of such management approval reflected on a risk acceptance form, all Owners, Custodians, and Users must consistently observe relevant Company X information security policies and standards.

Approved by: (executive name)
Approved on: DD/MM/YY
Version number: XX
Document reference number: XXX
Effective date: DD/MM/YY

XX. Sample Firewall Policy

Policy Objective And Scope: Firewalls are an essential component of Company X's information systems security infrastructure. Firewalls are defined as security systems that control and restrict both Internet connectivity and Internet services. Firewalls establish a perimeter where access controls are enforced. Connectivity, as the word is used here, defines which computer systems can exchange information. A service, as the word is used here, is sometimes called an application, and it refers to the way for information to flow through a firewall. Examples of services include FTP (file transfer protocol) and HTTP (web browsing). This policy defines the essential rules regarding the management and maintenance of firewalls at Company X and it applies to all firewalls owned, rented, leased, or otherwise controlled by Company X workers.

Playing The Role Of Firewalls: In some instances, systems such as routers, air gaps, or gateways may be functioning as though they are firewalls when in fact they are not formally known as firewalls. All Company X systems playing the role of firewalls, whether or not they are formally called firewalls, must be managed according to the rules defined in this policy. In some instances this will require that these systems be upgraded so that they support the minimum functionality defined in this policy.

Policy Applicability: All firewalls at Company X must follow this policy. Departures from this policy will be permitted only if approved in advance and in writing by the Information Security Department Manager.

Defined Decision Maker: Before being enabled, all new firewall services and new connectivity paths must be evaluated in terms of business advantages and security risks. The Information Security Department Manager is the only recognized decision maker who can either approve or deny these requests.

Default To Denial: Every Internet connectivity path and Internet service not specifically permitted by this policy (and supporting documents issued by the Information Security Department) must be blocked by Company X firewalls. The list of currently approved services must be documented and distributed to all systems administrators with a need-to-know by the Information Security Department. Likewise, every network connectivity path not specifically permitted by the Information Security Department must be denied by firewalls. Prior to the deployment of every Company X firewall, a diagram of permissible paths with a justification for each must be submitted to the Information Security Department. Permission to enable any paths will be granted by the Information Security Department Manager only when (1) the paths are necessary for important business reasons, and (2) sufficient security measures will be consistently employed.

Regular Auditing: Because firewalls provide such an important barrier to unauthorized access to Company X networks, they must be audited on a regular basis. At a minimum, this audit process must include consideration of defined configuration parameters, enabled services, permitted connectivity, current administrative practices, and adequacy of the deployed security measures. These audits must also include the regular execution of vulnerability identification software. These audits must be performed by technically proficient persons other than those responsible for the administration of the involved firewalls.

Logs: All changes to firewall configuration parameters, enabled services, and permitted connectivity must be logged. In addition, all suspicious activity which might be an indication of unauthorized usage or an attempt to compromise security measures must also be logged. The integrity of these logs must also be protected with checksums, digital signatures, encryption, or similar measures. These logs must be promptly removed from the recording systems and stored in a physically protected container for at least six months after the time they were recorded. These logs must be reviewed periodically to ensure that the firewalls are operating in a secure manner.

Intrusion Detection: All Company X firewalls must include intrusion detection systems approved by the Information Security Department. These intrusion detection systems must each be configured according to the specifications defined by the Information Security Department. Among other potential problems, these intrusion detection systems must detect unauthorized modifications to firewall system files. Such intrusion detection systems must also immediately notify technical staff who are in a position to take corrective action. All technical staff working on firewalls must be provided with remote access systems and privileges so that they can immediately respond to these incidents even when they are physically removed from the firewall in question.

Contingency Planning: Technical staff working on firewalls must prepare and obtain Information Security Department approval for contingency plans which address the actions to be taken in the event of various problems including system compromise, system malfunction, system crash, and Internet Service provider (ISP) unavailability. These contingency plans must be kept up-to-date to reflect changes in the Company X information systems environment. These plans must also be periodically tested to ensure that they will be effective in restoring a secure and reliable information systems environment.

External Connections: All in-bound real-time Internet connections to Company X internal networks and/or multi-user computer systems must pass through a firewall before users can reach a log-in banner. Aside from personal computers which access the Internet on a single-user session-by-session dial-up basis, no Company X computer system may be attached to the Internet unless it is protected by a firewall. Such computer systems include web servers, electronic commerce servers, and mail servers. This means that all personal computers with digital subscriber line (DSL) or cable modem connectivity must employ a firewall approved by the Information Security Department. Wherever a firewall supports it, log-in screens must have a notice indicating that: (1) the system may only be accessed by authorized users, (2) users who log-in represent that they are authorized to do so, (3) unauthorized system usage or abuse is subject to disciplinary action including criminal prosecution, and (4) system usage will be monitored and logged.

Extended User Authentication: Inbound traffic (with the exception of Internet electronic mail, regular news distributions, and push broadcasts previously approved by the Information Security Department) making access to Company X networks through a firewall must in all instances involve extended user authentication measures approved by the Information Security Department. Extended user authentication involves a technology more secure than fixed passwords and user-IDs. Examples of approved extended user authentication systems include dynamic passwords and digital certificates.

Virtual Private Networks: To prevent unauthorized disclosure of sensitive and valuable information, all inbound traffic (with the exception of Internet mail and push broadcasts) making access to Company X networks must be encrypted with the products approved by the Information Security Department. These connections are often called virtual private networks or VPNs. Many VPNs combine extended user authentication functionality with encryption functionality.

Firewall Access Mechanisms: All Company X firewalls must have unique passwords or other access control mechanisms. In other words, the same password or access control code must not be used on more than one firewall. This will prevent an intruder from using the same mechanism to compromise multiple firewalls. Whenever supported by the involved firewall vendor, those who administer Company X firewalls must have their identity validated via extended user authentication mechanisms (as defined above). In certain high security environments, such as the Company X Internet commerce site, remote access for firewall administrators is prohibited; to prevent intruders from altering firewall configurations and causing other trouble, for these environments, all firewall administration activities must take place in person.

Firewall Access Privileges: Privileges to modify the functionality, connectivity, and services supported by firewalls must be restricted to a few technically-trained individuals with a business need for these same privileges. Unless permission from the Information Security Department Manager has been obtained, these privileges must be granted only to individuals who are full-time permanent employees of Company X (no temporaries, contractors, consultants, or outsourcing personnel). All firewalls must have at least two staff members who are adequately trained to make changes as circumstances require. Care must be taken to schedule out-of-town vacations so that at least one of these firewall administration staff members is readily available at all times.

Secured Subnets: Portions of Company X's internal network that contain sensitive or valuable information, such as the computers used by the Human Resources Department, must employ a secured subnet. Access to this and other subnets must be restricted with firewalls and other control measures. Based on periodic risk assessments, the Information Security Department will define the secured subnets required.

Demilitarized Zones: All Internet commerce servers including payment servers, database servers, and web servers must be protected by firewalls in a demilitarized zone (DMZ). Demilitarized zones are subnets which are protected by a firewall from the Internet, but themselves have another firewall preventing users of the systems in the DMZ from gaining access to other network-connected Company X computers outside the DMZ.

Network Management Systems: Firewalls must be configured so that they are visible to internal network management systems. Firewalls must also be configured so that they permit the use of remote automatic auditing tools to be used by authorized Company X staff members. Unless deliberately intended as a test, such automatic auditing tools must not trigger a response sequence through firewall-connected intrusion detection systems.

Disclosure Of Internal Network Information: The internal system addresses, configurations, and related system design information for Company X networked computer systems must be restricted such that both systems and users outside Company X's internal network cannot access this information. One example of this involves split DNS (Domain Name Service).

Secure Back-Up: Current off-line back-up copies of firewall configuration files, connectivity permission files, firewall systems administration procedural documentation files, and related files must be kept close to the firewall at all times. A permissible alternative to off-line copies involves on-line encrypted versions of these files. Either of these options will help to keep a trusted copies away from intruders, but at the same time immediately available to reestablish a secure and reliable computing environment.

Virus Screening & Content Screening: Virus screening software approved by the Information Security Department must be installed and enabled on all Company X firewalls. Both content screening software and software which blocks users from accessing certain non-business web sites must also be enabled on all Company X firewalls.

Firewall Dedicated Functionality: Firewalls must run on dedicated machines which perform no other services (such as acting as a mail server). To reduce the chances of security compromise, firewalls must have only the bare minimum of operating systems software resident and enabled on them.

Firewall Change Control: Because they support critical Company X information systems activities, firewalls are considered to be production systems. This means that all changes to the software provided by vendors (excluding vendor-provided upgrades and patches) must be approved in advance by the Information Security Department Manager, and then tested and approved by the Quality Assurance Department before being used in a production environment.

Posting Updates: Because hackers and other intruders use the latest attack techniques, Company X firewalls must be running the latest software to repel these attacks. Where available from the involved vendor, all Company X firewalls must subscribe to software maintenance and software update services. Unless approved in advance by the Information Security Department Manager, staff members responsible for managing firewalls must install and run these updates within two business days of receipt.

Monitoring Vulnerabilities: Company X staff members responsible for managing firewalls must subscribe the CERT (Computer Emergency Response Team) advisories and other relevant sources providing current information about firewall vulnerabilities. Any vulnerability which appears to affect Company X networks and systems must promptly be brought to the attention of the Information Security Department.

Standard Products: Unless advance written approval is obtained from the Information Security Department Manager, only those firewalls appearing on the list of approved vendors and products may be deployed with Company X networks. This list is issued and periodically updated by the Information Security Department.

Firewall Physical Security: All Company X firewalls must be located in locked rooms accessible only to those who must have physical access to such firewalls to perform the tasks assigned by management. The placement of firewalls in the open area within a general purpose data processing center is prohibited, although placement within separately locked rooms or areas which themselves are within a general data processing center is acceptable. These rooms must have burglar alarms as well as an automated log of all who gain entry to the room.

Approving Executive: [manager's name]
Approval Date: [date sign-off provided]
Date When This Policy Goes Into Effect: [date when compliance is required]
Policy Reference Number: XXXX

XXI. External Network Interface Security Policy Harmonization

Many information systems specialists are confused when they have been instructed by management to connect their own organization's internal network with the internal network of another organization. The other organization could be a supplier, a major customer, a subcontractor, a government agency, or an outsourcing firm. These connections could for example be established via an extranet, a third party Electronic Data Interchange (EDI) network, or a third party business-to-business (B2B) web intermediary.

Whoever the third party or parties, and whatever the nature of the business arrangement, it is critical that the participants in this new network agree on certain fundamental security policies. If the security policies are incompatible, then there is a possibility that lax security at one organization could lead to security compromises at the other. For example, suppose one organization employed group user-IDs and had a serious argument with a particular worker, who then became disgruntled. This worker could then go on to disrupt the network, but the system logs and could not pinpoint exactly who was causing the trouble. Because a connection has been enabled to an outside organization, that organization's network-connected systems could be damaged by this same disgruntled worker.

To assist with the harmonization of security policies for organizations seeking to establish a network connection, this chapter provides a list of essential policy points. Ideally these points will be used by management when negotiating the arrangement, but if that did not happen, they can at least be used by technical staff when implementing the arrangement which has already been renegotiated. In some cases, a review of this list will indicate that the arrangement needs to be renegotiated before systems reflecting this arrangement are implemented.

The intention of harmonizing security policies is to establish a "baseline" or a "standard of due care" to which all parties to the arrangement must abide. This baseline must define the minimum information security requirements that must be maintained in order to participate in the networking arrangement. Not being willing or able to meet these requirements should be sufficient justification for exclusion from (or expulsion from) the multi-organizational networking arrangement.

To the right of each of the information security topic areas found below, the reader will find a section number in ISPME. Reference to the Table Of Contents at the beginning of the book will provide further details about the topic in question as well as related topics. The following list assumes that the connection to an outside organization is done through the Internet; if the connection is via dial-up lines the reader should see section 1.4.3.

Access Control Considerations

User-IDs reflecting individual users rather than groups of people (1.1.1.1.1)
Length of fixed passwords employed and construction rules (1.1.1.1.1)
Forced password changes after a certain time period has elapsed (1.1.2)
Forced password changes for all newly-assigned or reset passwords (1.1.1.1.2)
Extended user authentication systems like one-time passwords (1.1.1.2)
Cookies to authenticate the usage of a specific computer used to log-in (1.1.1.1.6)
Encrypted or digital-signature-protected cookies to prevent spoofing (1.1.1.1.6)
Anonymity of users prevented through log-in processes (1.1.1.2)
Assigned privileges of users based on the need-to-know (1.1.2)

Removal of access privileges as soon as an authorized worker departs (1.1.2)
Dormant user-IDs automatically have privileges revoked (1.1.2)
Session time-out after no activity for a designated period (1.1.2)
Use of single sign-on systems or other gateways for users (1.1.2)
Types of firewalls, routers, and other flow control systems (1.4.1.1)
Use of demilitarized zones (DMZs) as a buffer against attackers (1.4.1.1)

Encryption And Public Key Infrastructure (PKI) Considerations

Encryption process employed for sensitive transmitted data (1.4.2)
Encryption key management process used to automatically handle keys (1.4.2.2)
Use of hardware and/or software for provision of encryption (1.4.2)
Digital certificates as a mechanism to identify users (1.4.2)
Digital certificates as a mechanism to identity servers (1.4.2)
Digital certificates to restrict privileges of specific users (1.1.1.1.6)
Background checking for issuance of digital certificates (1.1.1.1.6)
Cross-certification of certificate authorities to support digital certificates (1.1.1.1.6)
Certificate revocation lists and other procedures for disabling users (1.1.1.1.6)
Electronic wallets to protect digital certificates and other information (1.1.1.1.6)
Digital signatures to assure absence of changes to certain data (1.3.5)
Digital signatures to assure that data originated with certain parties (1.4.2)

Change Control And Contingency Planning Considerations

Virus detection and eradication software and procedures (1.2.1)
Change control approval process for all modifications to the network (1.2.3)
Rapid installation of patches from firewall & operating system vendors (1.2.3)
Testing of new software prior to use in production network environment (1.2.2)
Computer emergency response team (CERT) to mobilize against attacks (1.3.4.2)
Intrusion detection systems to notify technicians about break-ins (1.3.4.2)
Physical security measures for all data centers connected to network (3.1.1)
Uninterruptible power systems prevent downtime when power fails (1.3.4.2)

Network Management Considerations

Management observation of information sent over the network - privacy (1.3.2)
Timestamps and date-stamps to validate that certain activity occurred (1.3.5)
Network time synchronization sources and procedures (1.1.3.2)
Logs and audit trails recorded on servers and client machines (1.1.3)
Network management systems and visibility of specific machines (1.4.8)

Appendix 1.
Abbreviated List Of Information Security Policy References

Earlier editions of this reference book contained a very long list of references that the author has consulted. The Internet's key word search engines along with key word search facilities found in Bowker's "Books In Print" makes such a long list of marginal additional value to the reader. Instead, the author has chosen to provide a short list of recommended supplementary references which the policy writer may wish to consult when writing original or updated policies.

American Health Information Management Association, Guidelines on Safeguards for On-line Medical Records, (includes a statement on patients' rights), 1996, write them at 919 N. Michigan Ave., Suite 1400, Chicago, IL 60611-1683 USA, or phone: 312-787-2672, 1995

Anonymous, A Checklist of Responsible Information-Handling Practices, Privacy Rights Clearing House, University of San Diego -- Center for Public Interest Law, Fact Sheet #12, January 1995

Anonymous, Access to and Use and Disclosure of Electronic Mail on Company Computer Systems: A Tool Kit for Formulating Your Company's Policy, Electronic Messaging Association (Arlington, Virginia), 1996

Anonymous, Draft United Nations Manual on Computer Related Crime, September 1992, published by the Canadian Department of Justice, Ottawa, Canada

Anonymous, Fair Information Practices Checklist, Direct Marketing Association (New York, New York), 1992

Anonymous, Fair Information Practices Manual, Direct Marketing Association (New York, New York), 1994

British Standards Institution, A Code of Practice for Information Security Management, Department of Trade and Industry, British Government, London, 1995 (second edition); also known as BS 7799

Cobb, Steven, NCSA Firewall Policy Guide, National Computer Security Association, Carlisle, Pennsylvania, 1996 (www.ncsa.com)

Corby, Michael, and Robert E. Johnston, "Intranet Security Guidelines: How To Protect The Enterprise As Your Intranet Grows," Computer Security Journal, Vol. XIV, Number 4, 1998

Computer-based Patient Record Institute Inc., Guidelines for Establishing Information Security Policies at Organizations Using Computer-based Patient Record Systems, (write them at 1000 E. Woodfield Road, Suite 102, Schaumburg, IL 60173 USA; or phone: 708-706-6746), February 1995

Computer-based Patient Record Institute Inc., Guidelines for Information Security Education Programs at Organizations Using Computer-Based Patient Record Systems, (write them at 1000 E. Woodfield Road, Suite 102, Schaumburg, IL 60173 USA; or phone: 708-706-6746), June 1995

Gilbert, Gregory A., "How to Develop a Computer Security Policy," Datapro Reports on Information Security, McGraw-Hill, January 1989

Gritzalis, Dimitris, "A Baseline Security Policy For Distributed Healthcare Information Systems," Computers & Security, Vol. 16, No. 8, pp. 709-719, 1997

Lindup, Kenneth, "A New Model for Information Security Policies," Computers & Security, Vol. 14, pp. 691-695, 1995

Nordic Council of Ministers (Kobenhavn, Denmark), Datapolicy: Information Security in Nordic Countries, 1993

On Technology Corporation (Cambridge, Massachusettes, USA; www.on.com), Internet Usage and Security Template, 1997

Overbeek, Paul, Wim Sipman, and Leon Strous, Handbook of Information Security Standards, Kluver Academic Publishers, Dordrect, The Netherlands (fax 078-334911), 1994

Ozier, Will (committee chair), Generally-Accepted System Security Principles (GSSP), Exposure Draft 2.0, November 1995, published by the Information Systems Security Association, Chicago, IL (posted on www.ibm.com/security/ wpconsul.htm)

Ruthberg, Zella G., and Harold F. Tipton, Handbook of Information Security Management, Auerbach Publishers, Boston, Massachusetts, USA, 2000

Schweitzer, James, "Classifying Information for Security," DataPro Reports On Information Security, IS15-250-101, January 1989

Wood, Charles Cresson, "Establishing Internal Technical Systems Security Standards," Computers & Security (UK), pp. 193-200, Elsevier, Oxford, England, August 1986

Wood, Charles Cresson, Best Practices In Internet Commerce Security: A Standard Of Due Care Requirements List For Merchants; Publisher: PentaSafe, Houston, Texas, 1998

Wood, Charles Cresson, Information Security Roles & Responsibilities Made Easy; Publisher: PentaSafe, Houston, Texas, 2001

Wood, Charles Cresson, "Principles of Secure Information Systems Design," Computers & Security (UK), vol. 9, no. 1, pp. 13-24, Elsevier, Oxford, England, February 1990

Wright, Benjamin, The Law of Electronic Commerce: EDI, Fax, and E-Mail --Technology, Proof, and Liability, Little Brown and Company, Boston, Massachusetts, USA, 1991

Appendix 2.
List Of Information Security Periodicals

Note: Several publications have "The" preceding other words in the title. For purposes of this alphabetical listing, the inconsequential word "The" has been dropped.

2600 -- The Hacker Quarterly; P.O. Box 752, Middle Island, NY 11953-0752 USA; phone (631) 751-2600; fax (631) 474-2677; www.2600.com and E-mail: 2600@well.sf.ca.us [an underground hacker how-to newsletter]

Cipher--Newsletter of the Technical Committee on Security & Privacy; Institute of Electrical and Electronics Engineers (IEEE), Code 5540, Naval Research Laboratory, Washington, DC 20375-5337 USA; phone (202) 404-7931; fax (202) 404-7942; www.ieee-security.org/cipher.html [engineering research oriented articles]

Computer Fraud & Security; Elsevier Advanced Technology; P.O. Box 7247-7682, Philadelphia, PA 19170 - 7682, USA; phone (212) 633-3730; fax (212) 633-3680; www.elsevier.com [newsletter dealing with the latest computer crime cases and practical management tips]

Computer Law and Security Report; Elsevier Advanced Technology; P.O. Box 7247-7682, Philadelphia, PA 19170-7682, USA; phone (212) 633-3730; fax (212) 633-3680; www.elsevier.com [legalistic analysis of recent high-tech problems such as telephone toll fraud and what to do about them intended for lawyers and information security specialists]

Computer Professionals For Social Responsibility Newsletter; Computer Professionals For Social Responsibility; PO Box 717, Palo Alto, CA 94302-0717 USA; phone (650) 322-3778; fax (650) 322-3798; djlin@quark.cpsr.org; www.cpsr.org [an ethics-oriented review of recent developments related to information security, particularly privacy and freedom issues]

Computers & Security; Elsevier Advanced Technology; P.O. Box 7247-7682, Philadelphia, PA 19170-7682, USA; phone (212) 633-3730; fax (212) 633-3680; www.elsevier.com [the best-known international information security research journal; deals with innovative developments in the information security field and focuses on recent research]

Computer Security Alert; Computer Security Institute (Division of CMP), 600 Harrison St., San Francisco, CA 94107 USA; phone (415) 947-6320, fax (415) 947-6023; www.gocsi.com; csi@cmp.com [a monthly newsletter providing practical hands-on advice and experience from other information security practitioners working in the trenches]

Computers Security Journal; Computer Security Institute (Division of CMP), 600 Harrison St., San Francisco, CA 94107 USA; phone (415) 947-6320; fax (415) 947-6023; www.gocsi.com; csi@cmp.com [a semi-annual journal providing case studies and articles by experienced practitioners]

Contingency Planning & Management; Witter Publishing Company, 84 Park Ave., Flemington, NJ 08822; phone (908) 788-0343; fax (908) 788-3782; www.contingencyplanning.com [periodical dealing with management issues associated with information systems and other types of contingency planning]

CyberSecurity Advisor; Bureau of Business Practice (division of Aspen Publishers), 7201 McKinney Circle, Frederick, MD 21704 USA; richard.dann@ aspenpubl.com;

www.aspenpubl.com [newsletter dealing with the highlights of new developments in the information security field]

Cybertek; Cybertek Magazine, PO Box 64, Brewster, NY 10509 USA; www3.l0pht.com/~oblivion//cybertek/cybertek.html [archival material, no longer published; survival and technological magazine combined with computer anti-security]

Disaster Recovery Journal - The Journal Dedicated to Corporate Disaster Recovery Planning; Systems Support, Inc., PO Box 510110, St. Louis, MO 63151 USA; phone (314) 894-0276; fax (314) 894-7474; www.drj.com [for those responsible for managing, preparing, or supervising contingency planning (information systems related and otherwise)]

E-Business Advisor; Advisor Media, 5675 Ruffin Road, Suite 200, San Diego, CA 92123 USA; phone (858) 278-5600; fax (858) 279-4702; www.advisor.com; order@advisor.com [periodical dealing with strategies and tools for Internet commerce which deals with many security issues in a high-level manner]

EDPACS -- The EDP Audit, Control, and Security Newsletter; CRC Press LLC (Auerbach Division); 2000 NW Corporate Blvd., Boca Raton, FL 33431 USA; phone (800) 272-7737 or (561) 994-0555; fax (800) 374-3401; www.crcpress.com [general newsletter covering a wide variety of computer-security-related topics]

Emergency Preparedness Digest; Emergency Preparedness Canada - Communications Directorate, 122 Bank Street, 2nd Floor, Ottawa, Ontario K1A 0W6 CANADA; phone (613) 991-7077; fax (613) 998-9589; Communications@epc-pcc.x400.gc.ca; www.epc-pcc.gc.ca [deals with many contingency planning issues, many computer related]

Emergency Preparedness News; Business Publishers, 8737 Colesville Rd., Ste. 1100, Silver Spring, MD 20910-9973 USA; phone (800) 274-0122 or (301)589-5103; fax (301) 585-9075; www.bpinews.com; bpinews@bpinews.com [newsletter devoted to various contingency planning matters including crisis management; in operation for 20+ years]

Frontline Solutions (incorporating Automatic I.D. News for Automated Data Capture Systems Management); Advanstar Communications, Inc., 7500 Old Oak Blvd., Cleveland, OH 44130 USA; phone (440) 891-2766; www.advanstar.com [deals with bar codes, fingerprint recognition, eye blood vessel recognition, and related technologies -- product oriented]

HackTic – www.hacktic.nl [a paper-only Dutch-only magazine dealing with computer hacking; has ceased publication and there is no available contact information but archives can be accessed through website]

ID World; Faulkner and Gray, Eleven Penn Plaza, New York, NY 10001 USA; phone 800-535-8403 USA; www.faulknergray.com [provides detailed information about smart cards, biometrics and other ways to identify people]

Information Executive; Association of Information Technology Professionals (AITP), 315 South Northwest Highway, Suite 200, Park Ridge, IL 60068-4278 USA; phone (800) 224-9371 x226 or (847) 825-8124; fax (847) 825-1693; www.aitp.org/publications/contents.html [monthly newsletter dealing with a variety of technology topics including information security]

Information Management and Computer Security; MCB University Press Ltd., 60/62 Toller Lane, Bradford BD8 9BY, West Yorkshire, ENGLAND; phone +44 (0) 1274 777700; fax +44 (0) 1274 785200; www.mcb.co.uk [a five-times-a-year journal, established in 1993, dealing with current developments in management and control]

Information Security Bulletin; Chi Publishing Ltd.; Technology House, Lissadel Street, Salford M6 6AP ENGLAND; phone +44 161 278 2778; fax +44 161 278 2777; subs@chi-publishing.com; www.chi-publishing.com; isb@chi-publishing.com [monthly magazine covering a wide variety of current technical and management topics]
Information Security Magazine; published by TruSecure, formerly ICSA (International Computer Security Association), and before that NCSA (National Computer Security Association); 1200 Walnut Bottom Road, Carlisle, PA 17013 USA; phone (717) 258-1816 or (781) 255-0200; fax (781) 255-0215; www.trusecure.com or isca.net [widely read publication dealing with all areas of information security management]

Information Systems Auditor; International Newsletters, PO Box 133, Witney, Oxon OX8 6ZH ENGLAND; phone +44 (0) 1993 824130, fax +44 (0) 1993 824150; www.intnews.com; sales@intnews.com [an international publication which deals with all aspects of information systems auditing in a concise manner]

Information Systems Security; Auerbach Publications; CRC Press; 2000 Corporate Blvd. NW, Boca Raton, FL 33431 USA; phone (800) 272-7737; www.crcpress.com [practical management-oriented advice about information security matters]

Inside Fraud Bulletin; Maxima Partnering Limited, Hillend House, Nutley, East Sussex TN22 3HB, ENGLAND; phone +44 (0) 1825 712868 or +44 (0) 1825 712069; fax +44 (0) 1825 712026; www.insidefraud.com; ifbulletin@maxima-group.com [high-tech and low-tech investigator oriented news and articles]

Intelligence Newsletter; Indigo Publications Group, 142 rue Montmarte, F-75002 Paris, FRANCE; phone +33 1 44 88 26 10; fax +33 1 44 88 26 15; www.indigo-net.com; indigo@indigo-net.com [spying-related information security newsletter]

Information Systems Control Journal (formerly IS Audit and Control Journal); Information Systems Audit and Control Association (ISACA), 3701 Algonquin Road, Suite 1010, Rolling Meadows, IL 60008 USA; phone (847) 253-1545; fax (847) 253-1443; www.isaca.org/ jrnlhome.htm [very well-known professional association's primary journal dealing with EDP auditing, also known as computer auditing]

Journal of Computer Security; IOS Press, Nieuwe Hemweg 6B, 1013 BG Amsterdam THE NETHERLANDS; phone +31 20 688 3355; fax +31 20 620 3419; market@iospress.nl; www.iospress.nl [a quarterly academic journal dealing with research topics]

Law Enforcement Product News (LEPN), General Communications, 100 Garfield St., #300, Denver, CO 80206-5550 USA; phone (303) 322-6400; fax (303) 322-0627; www.law-enforcement.com [new products and services for the law enforcement, security, and corrections industries; includes some information security products]

Legal Information Alert; Alert Publications; 401 West Fullerton Parkway, Suite 1403E, Chicago, IL 60614; phone (773) 525-7594, fax (773) 525-7015; www.alertpub.com; info@alertpub.com or alertpub@compuserve.com [a brief newsletter containing abstracts of recent events including privacy, trans-border data flows, and other information security related legal matters; based on over thirty other publications]

Managerial Auditing Journal, Customer Service Executive, MCB University Press, Limited, 60/62 Toller Lane, West Yorkshire BD8 9BY ENGLAND; phone +44 (0) 1274 777700; fax +44 (0) 1274 785200; www.mcb.co.uk/maj.htm; customerservices@mcb.co.uk [provides guidance on how the new expanded role of the internal auditor is being accomplished, including ways to help rather than criticize management; covers some information systems issues]

Manufacturing and Logistics IT Magazine; IBC Ltd., Latimer House, 189 High Street, Potters Bar, Herts EN6 5DA ENGLAND; phone +44 (0) 1707 664200; fax +44 (0) 1707 664800 ; www.ibcpub.com/logit/contact-log.htm [independent newsletter devoted to reporting the latest developments in IT security on a world-wide basis, giving special emphasis to Internet commerce supply chain security]

News and Views; Federal Information Systems Security Educators' Association, c/o US Department of Commerce, National Institute of Standards & Technology, Gathersburg, MD 20899-0001 USA; www.csrc.nist.gov/organizations/fissea.html [newsletter dealing with awareness and training issues]

Operations Management; Institutional Investor Inc., 488 Madison Ave., New York, NY 10022 USA; phone (212) 224-3800; fax (212) 224-3689; www.operationsmanagement.com; customerservice@iinews.com [a financial services newsletter dealing with the legal and security issues associated with an Internet presence]

Password; Information Systems Security Association (ISSA), 7044 S. 13th Street, Oak Creek, WI 53154 USA; phone (414) 768-8000, fax (414) 768-8001; www.issa-intl.org [periodic newsletter for information security specialists dealing with certification of professionals, standards, policies and related issues]

Privacy and Security 2001; Ross Engineering, 8785 Commerce Court, Manassas, VA 20110 USA; phone (703) 365-2200 or (800) US-DEBUG; fax (703)365-0363; www.rosseng.com; dchq@rosseng.com or info@rosseng.com [10 issues/year newsletter dealing with counter espionage techniques and technology, as well as telecom toll fraud]

RCMP Technical Security Branch Bulletin; Technical Security Branch, Technical Operations Directorate, Royal Canadian Mounted Police, 1426 St. Joseph Blvd., Gloucester, Ontario, K1A OR2 CANADA; phone (613) 993-7977; fax (613) 993-7060; www.rcmp-grc.gc.ca/tsb/pubs/index_e.htm; brian.feagan@rcmp-grc.gc.ca [free high-level newsletter dealing with information security management issues; written in both English and French]

Risk Management; Risk Management Society Publishing, Inc., 655 Third Ave., New York, NY 10017 USA; phone (212) 286-9292; fax (212) 922-0716; www.rims.org [monthly management-oriented publication from professional society called the Risk and Insurance Management Society, also known as RIMS]

SC Magazine (incorporating InfoSecurity News); Westcoast Publishing; 161 Worchester Road, Suite 201, Framingham, MA 01701 USA; phone (508) 879-9792; fax (508) 879-2755; www.scmagazine.com [widely read magazine covering the latest product developments and reviews of these same products]

Security; Cahners Publishing, PO Box 7592, Highlands Ranch, CO 80163-9392 USA; phone (800) 637-6072; fax (800) 334-2812; www.securitymagazine.com [a physical security magazine that runs a monthly column on information security and often additional information security articles]

Security Industry Buyers Guide; Phillips International, Inc., 7811 Montrose Road, Potomac, MD 20854 USA; phone (800) 777-5006 or (301) 424-3338; www.phillips.com/sibguide.htm [annual directory of vendors and products, including information security products]

Security Insider Report; phone (727) 556-0833; fax (727) 556-0834; www.infowar.com/chezwinn/sir/sir_home.html-ssi [a dramatic down-to-earth monthly review of information security developments; in 1995 ceased to be published but will soon be archived in its entirety at the previously mentioned website]

Security Law Newsletter; Crime Control Research Corp., 3507 Baring St., Philadelphia, PA 19104; phone (301) 390-9577; fax (301) 390-1749 [informal newsletter dealing with court cases, some of which are information-security-related]

Security Management; American Society for Industrial Security, 1625 Prince St., Alexandria, VA 22314-2818 USA; phone (703) 519-6200, fax (703) 519-6299; www.asisonline.org; asis@asisonline.com [monthly publication covering a wide variety of security topics including occasional coverage of information security]

Security Watch (formerly Security Management Bulletin); Bureau of Business Practice (division of Simon & Schuster), 125 Eugene O'Neill Drive, Suite 103, New London, CT 06320 USA; phone (800) 876-9105 toll-free or (860) 442-4365 international; fax (800)437-3150 toll-free; www.bbpnews.com; customer.service@ aspenpubl.com [a semimonthly tips-oriented newsletter that focuses on physical security issues, but that includes information security articles]

Telecom & Data Network Security; Telecommunications Reports International, 1333 H St., NW, Suite 100 East, Washington, DC 20005-4707 USA; phone (800) 822-6338 or (202) 312-6116; fax (202) 842-3023; www.tr.com/newsletters/tns/ index.htm; customerservice@tr.com [practical tips about protecting PBXs from toll fraud and "telabuse"]

White Paper: Topical Issues on White Collar Crime; Association of Certified Fraud Examiners, The Gregor Building, 716 West Ave., Austin, Texas 78701 USA; phone (800) 245-3321 or (512) 478-9070, fax (512) 478-9297; www.cfenet.com; info@cfenet.com [deals with forensic/investigative nature of computer crime]

Appendix 3.
List Of Information Security Professional Associations And Related Organizations

(a) Generic

American National Standards Institute (ANSI), 11 West 42nd Street, 13th Floor, New York, NY 10036 USA; phone (212) 642-4900 or (212) 764-3274; fax (212) 398-0023; URL: http://www.ansi.org [wrote standards on various information security issues such as encryption]

American Society for Industrial Security (ASIS), 1625 Prince St., Alexandria, VA 22314 USA; phone (703) 519-6200; fax (703) 519-6299; URL: http://www.asisonline.org [physical security oriented professional society; from time to time addresses selected computer security issues in conferences and publications; very large membership]

Association for Computing Machinery (ACM) -- Special Interest Group on Security, Auditability and Control (SIGSAC), One Astor Plaza, 1515 Broadway, 17th floor, New York, NY 10036 USA; phone (212) 869-7440; fax (212) 944-1318; URL: http://www.acm.org [most prestigious professional association; SIG is relatively quiet, although some technically astute publications have been generated; irregularly issues a newsletter on information security]

Association of Information Technology Professionals, (AITP) (formerly known as DPMA), 315 South Northwest Highway, Suite 200, Park Ridge, IL 60068-4278; phone (847) 825-8124; fax (847) 825-1693; URL: http://www.aitp.org; e-mail: Nan_Tammone@aitp.org [management oriented computer professional association; hosts conferences dealing with security; has special interest group addressing security issues]

Association For Information Management Professionals, formerly Association of Records Managers & Administrators (ARMA International), 4200 Somerset Dr., Suite 215, Prairie Village, KS 66208 USA; phone (913) 341-3808; fax (913) 341-3742; URL: http://www.arma.org; email hq@arma.org [deals with paper-resident information primarily]

Canadian Institute of Chartered Accountants, 277 Wellington Street West, Toronto ON M5V 3H2, CANADA; (416) 977-3222; fax (416) 977-8585; URL: http://www.cica.ca [has developed and published several information security related standards; believed to have a special interest group dealing with security]

Computer Emergency Response Team (CERT), Software Engineering Institute, Carnegie Mellon University, Pittsburgh, PA 15213-3890 USA; phone (412) 268-7090; fax (412) 268-6989; URL: http://www.cert.org; e-mail cert@cert.org [monitors loss experience on the Internet, preparing special reports about vulnerabilities]

Computer Professional for Social Responsibility (CPSR), P.O. Box 717, Palo Alto, CA 94302 USA; (650) 322-3778; fax (650) 322-4748; URL: http://www.cpsr.org [the conscience of the computer community; focuses on privacy violation, ethics, and related information security issues; members often give testimony before Congress; a relatively new but influential player in the association area]

Computer Security Institute (CSI), 600 Harrison St., San Francisco, CA 94107 USA; (415) 905-2626; fax (415) 905-2218; URL: http://www.gocsi.com [historically the first organization involved with information security training matters; puts on several excellent information security conferences including the largest information security conference in the world; also markets an information security technical journal, related books, and a monthly newsletter; has an interesting website]

Data Interchange Standards Association, Inc. (DISA), 333 John Carlyle St., Suite 600, Alexandria, VA 22314 USA; phone (703) 548-7005; fax (703) 548-5738; URL: http://www.disa.org [handles data formatting and communications standardization issues which include security matters]

Electronic Funds Transfer Association, 950 Herndon Parkway, Suite 390, Herndon, VA 20121 USA; phone (703) 435-9800; fax (703) 435-7157; URL: http://www.efta.org [handles financial services issues including security of electronic payments]

Electronic Industries Alliance, 2500 Wilson Blvd., Arlington, VA 22201-3834 USA; phone (703) 907-7500; fax (703) 907-7501; URL http://www.eia.org [involved with lobbying]

Electronic Messaging Association, 1655 North Fort Myer Drive, Suite 500, Arlington, VA 22209 USA; phone (703) 524-5550; fax (703) 524-5558; URL: http://www.ema.org [worked on electronic mail security issues]

Federal Information Systems Security Educator's Association (FISSEA), US Department of Commerce, National Institute of Standards and Technology, Bldg. 820, Rm. 426, Gaithersburg, MD 20899 USA; Kathie Everhart (301) 975-3868; fax (301) 948-6213; URL: http://csrc.nist.gov/organizations/fissea.html [sponsors annual conference and coordinates activities of educators]

Information Technology Industry Council (ITIC), 1250 Eye St., NW, Suite 200, Washington, DC 20005 USA; phone (202) 737-8888; fax (202) 638-4922; URL: http://www.itic.org [gets involved in lobbying and standards activities associated with information security]

Information Systems Audit & Control Association (ISACA), 3701 Algonquin Road, Suite 1010, Rolling Meadows, IL 60008 USA; phone (847) 253-1545; fax (847) 253-1443; URL: http://www.isaca.org [largest and oldest professional society directly related to information security; formerly called EDP Auditors Association (EDPAA); international constituency; several publications on standards; monthly magazine; more than 15,000 members in 92 countries]

Information Systems Security Association (ISSA), 7044 S. 13th Street, Oak Creek, WI 53154 USA; phone (414) 768-8000; fax (414) 768-8001; URL: http://www.issa.org [information security practitioner-oriented professional society; hosts annual conferences with MIS Training; provides quarterly newsletter called The Password; local chapters in approximately 15 cities; rapidly growing group with an international membership]

Institute of Electrical and Electronics Engineers (IEEE), 3 Park Avenue, 17th Floor, New York, NY 10016-5997 USA; phone (212) 419-7900; Fax (212) 752-4929; URL: http://www.ieee.org [annual conferences on information security, participates in standards activities, issues quarterly crypto newsletter, publishes books related to information security]

Institute of Internal Auditors (IIA), 249 Maitland Ave., Altamonte Springs, FL 32701-4201 USA; phone (407) 830-7600; fax (407) 831-5171; URL: http://www.theiia.org; email: iia@theiia.org [financial internal auditor viewpoint; has new special interest group dealing with information security; well established with approximately 50 chapters around the world; funds some information security research]

International Federation for Information Processing (IFIP), Hofstraße 3, A-2361 Laxenburg, Austria; phone +43 2236 73616; fax +43 2236 736169; URL: http://wwwifip.or.at; email: ifip@ifip.or.at

International Information System Security Certification Consortium (ISC2), services office – PO Box 1117, Dunedin, FL 34697; phone (727) 738-8657; fax: (727) 738-8522; operations office – 860 Worcester Rd., Suite 101, Framingham, MA 01701; phone: (508) 875-8400; fax: (508) 875-8450; URL: http://www.isc2.org [administers tests for the Certified Information Systems Security Professional (CISSP) examination]

International Standards Organization (ISO), Brussels, Belgium; c/o American National Standards Institute (ANSI), 11 West 42nd Street, 13th Floor, New York, NY 10036 USA; phone (212) 642-4900; fax (212) 398-0023; URL: http://www.ansi.org; email: ansionline@ansi.org [develops international standards on information security]

MIS Training Institute, 498 Concord St., Framingham, MA 01702 USA; phone (508) 879-7999; (508) 872-1153; URL: http://www.misti.com [provides a variety of audit-related information security conferences and training seminars; one of the largest providers of information security training; publishes the most widely-distributed information security magazine, Infosecurity News]

National Computer Security Center (NCSC), 9800 Savage Road, Fort Meade, MD 20755-6765 USA; phone (410) 854-4371; fax (410) 854-4375; URL: http://www.nsa.gov or http://radium.ansc.mil [government agency associated with the US Department of Defense; provides evaluations of information security products and hosts an annual conference in Washington, DC]

Security Industry Association, 635 Slaters Lane, Suite 110, Alexandria, VA 22314-9990 USA; phone (703) 683-2075; URL: http://www.siaonline.org [primarily an association of equipment manufacturers and other vendors in the physical security industry, this group deals with some information security issues, develops technical standards, and engages in lobbying to obtain certain legislative results]

Society of Competitive Intelligence Professionals, 1700 Diagonal Rd., Suite 600, Alexandria, VA 22314, USA; phone (703) 739-0696; fax: (703) 739-2524; email info@scip.org; URL http://www.scip.org [deals with ethical competitive intelligence gathering and industrial espionage prevention]

Software Information Industry Association, 1730 M Street NW, Suite 700, Washington, DC 20036 USA; phone (202) 452-1600; fax (202) 223-8756; URL: http://www.siia.net [addresses privacy and related information security issues in its studies and Congressional testimony; does not spend considerable resources on information security matters]

The World Institute for Security Enhancement (WISE), PO Box 770727, Miami, FL 33177 USA; phone (305) 773-0048; URL: http://www.worldinstitute.org [provides education and interdisciplinary research on safety and security issues, including information security]

(b) By Industry

American Bankers Association, 1120 Connecticut Ave. NW, Washington, DC 20036 USA; phone (202) 663-5000; fax (202) 663-7543; URL: http://www.aba.com [prepares and promulgates standards specific to the commercial banking industry]

American Institute of Certified Public Accountants, 1211 Avenue of the Americas, New York, NY 10036 USA; phone (212) 596-6200; fax (212) 596-6213; URL: http://www.aicpa.org [prepares guidelines for auditors working on information security matters; monthly magazine deals with information security issues]

Bank Administration Institute, One North Franklin, Suite 1000, Chicago, IL 60606-3421 USA; phone (312) 683-2464; fax (312) 683-2373; URL: http://www.bai.org [publishes a newsletter which deals with information security issues; involved in relevant standards activities]

Information Technology Industry Council, 1250 Eye St. NW, Suite 200, Washington, DC 20005 USA; phone (202) 737-8888; fax (202) 638-4922; URL: http://www.itic.org [involved in computer crime legislation hearings; funds computer security research and conferences]

International Association for Healthcare Security & Safety, P.O. Box 637, Lombard, IL 60148 USA; phone: (630)953-0990; fax: (630)953-1786; email only: nancy@iahss.org [professional organization which deals with security and safety issues such as patient privacy and provides educational material]

International Association of Financial Crimes Investigators, 385 Bel Marin Keys, Suite H, Novato, CA 94949 USA; phone (415) 884-6600; fax (415) 884-6605; URL: http://www.iafci.org [association of specialists in credit card fraud, which is a computer-related crime]

(c) By Market Segment

Computer Associates, World Headquarters, One Computer Associates Plaza, Islandia, NY 11749 USA; phone (516) 342-5224; fax (516) 342-8179; URL: http://www.cai.com [users groups for the top IBM mainframe access control packages]

Association of Contingency Planners (ACP), 7044 S. 13th Street, Oak Creek, WI 53154 USA; phone (414) 768-8000 x 116; URL: http://www.acp-international.com [a specialty niche within information security area; a new player in the association area; largest contingency planning organization]

International Biometric Association, 1444 I Street NW, Suite 700, Washington, DC 20005 USA; phone (202) 712-9049; fax (202) 216-9646; URL: http://www.tibs.org; e-mail ibs@bostromdc.com [association of vendors of biometric equipment and systems; few users involved]

SHARE (IBM users group), 401 N. Michigan Ave. Suite 2400, Chicago, IL 60611 USA; phone (312) 321-5160; fax (312) 644-6363; URL: http://www.share.org [with GUIDE, most influential IBM users group; has prepared security requirements for IBM; published papers on information security]

(d) Others

Electronic Bulletin Agency: Dockmaster, National Computer Security Center, National Security Agency, 9800 Savage Rd., Fort Meade, MD 20755-6000 USA; phone (301) 688-6311 or (800) 688-6115; fax (301) 688-6198; URL: http://www.nsa.gov [electronic bulletin board discussing information security issues; only those demonstrating qualifications to get on the bulletin board are allowed to gain access]

Subscription service with periodic meetings: I4 (International Information Integrity Institute), SRI International, 333 Ravenswood Ave., Menlo Park, CA 94025 USA; phone (650) 859-2000; fax (650) 326-5512; URL: http://www.sri.com [exclusive subscription service for very large organizations; focuses on practical administration aspects of information security]

Electronic Privacy Information Center (EPIC), 1718 Connecticut Ave., NW, Suite 200, Washington, DC 20009 USA; phone (202) 483-1140; fax (202) 483-1248; URL: http://www.epic.org [publishes a number of influential reports about privacy and testifies before Congress on privacy and related issues]

Appendix 4.
List Of Suggested Awareness Raising Methods

The following topics are not organized in priority order; they are instead clustered by the type of communication involved. Consider this list to be a menu from which appropriate activities may be selected. The policy writer should not select just one or two of the following methods, but ten or twenty of them. Repetition of information security policy ideas is essential; repetition impresses users and other audiences with the importance that management places on information security.

In-Person

Provide special classroom-style training courses at convenient locations every year or so (for users, systems administrators, remote site information security coordinators, new hires, and other audiences identified in a needs analysis).

Deliver policy ideas and other material at new employee orientation meetings.

Send influential information systems staff to off-site information security conferences.

Hold video conferences where people from various sites discuss information security.

Stage vulnerability demonstrations (aka tiger-team attacks or penetration attacks).

Conduct information security risk assessments, especially when interviewing and other methods are used to engage staff in the process.

Have the Legal Department conduct an intellectual property inventory and an associated risk assessment.

Give small prizes like free lunches to exemplary staff who observe policies & procedures.

Give traffic ticket warnings (little pieces of paper) reflecting policy violations.

Conduct internal EDP audits, actually checking the extent to which compliance exists.

Bring in an outside consultant to conduct an external EDP audit looking at compliance.

Initiate an unauthorized software duplication inventory project where personal computers are checked for illegal software.

Install a software license management system that checks that all software in use is legitimately licensed, and then have discussions with people who have unauthorized software.

Integrate information security training content with other face-to-face computer training materials, such as a course for telecommuters (required before they telecommute).

Establish and promote the existence of a Information Security Management Committee.

Establish a committee of systems administrators and other first-line staff who must deal with Information security.

Host quarterly luncheons for systems administrators from various sites to discuss security.

Start disciplining staff for violations of information security policies, and let the reasons why Disciplinary actions were used be known to others (and used as an example).

Initiate strategic planning, new product development, and other initiatives which see information and information systems as a key to future competitive advantage.

Prevent the use of certain new and desired system services (such as Internet access) until certain Security projects (like a firewall) have been completed.

Prevent new business application software from being moved into production until adequate controls have been installed (and talk to management about the issues).

Institute a new or more serious change control approval process, such as the prohibition against the establishment of new phone lines without first getting the information security manager's approval (and talk to management about the issues).

Declare an amnesty day for information security violators who wish to obtain technical or other assistance so that they may now be in compliance.

Test the backups being made by departmental systems administrators and have discussions with department managers about the adequacy of these backups.

Adopt an annual information security day on which special educational materials are presented and special events take place (coordinate with national computer security day if possible).

Initiate a high-profile investigation into an information security breach and engage a significant number of staff members in the investigation.

Schedule special top management briefings where the strategic issues regarding changes in corporate culture to support information security are addressed.

Conduct an internal survey of mid- and lower-level managers asking them what they think should be done to improve information security (thereby getting them to think about something that they probably don't think about much).

Conduct a survey of customers, suppliers, and other third parties asking them what they think should be done to improve the security of computerized business activities.

Conduct a "gap analysis" whereby existing information security training and awareness materials are compared to an ideal set of messages that management wants to communicate, and then prepare a management proposal to upgrade the materials.

In Writing

Add information security questions to written performance reviews (a simple yes/no may be sufficient in many organizations).

Require a signature on personal responsibility statement (indicates that employees consider compliance with policies to be a condition of continued employment).

Require a signature on a form verifying that a worker has received a copy of, read, and understood the information security manual.

Require all employees to annually sign a statement saying they have read and understood the Information security policy manual.

Require users to sign a security compliance statement before they get user-Ids.

Write security articles for in-house newspapers, newsletters, and magazines.

Periodically issue written policy statements, procedures, and technical standards.

Issue pamphlets or brochures to end users describing a code of conduct.

Ghostwrite memos from top management reminding staff about security.

Distribute relevant clippings from newspapers and technical magazines.

Hang posters and signs to remind people (some also use stickers and decals).

Make up special labels for disks, tape reels, etc. indicating sensitivity, handling instructions, ownership, and the like.

Post notices on both paper and electronic bulletin boards.

Insert security notices in pay-check envelopes, air flight ticket envelopes, etc.

Integrate security ideas with systems development process documentation.

Issue information security responsibility organizational design memos that clarify areas of confusing responsibility.

Write expanded job descriptions for systems administrators and others such that information security is explicitly included.

Write expanded mission statements for various departments so that information security is Explicitly recognized as a part of their charter..

Prepare an information security architecture document or otherwise integrate security into the organization's technology plans.

Issue an information security manual containing policies, contact persons, and a list of approved in-house products.

Write detailed back-up instructions and insist that staff comply.

Develop and test a contingency plan to deal with information system emergencies and disasters.

Require that information security risk acceptance forms be signed by all managers who are in charge of units which are not in compliance and which don't intend in the near future to come into compliance.

Prepare non-disclosure agreements and educate staff when they should be used.

Prepare non-complete agreements and educate staff when they should be used.

Prepare notices to be given to all people who come into contact with trade secrets notifying them that certain information is a trade secret and that it must be handled according to special security rules (policies).

On Systems

Add security instructions to application program and system utility help-screens.

Purchase computer based training (CBT) software that runs on personal computers and require staff to go through it; this should ideally automatically reporting back to an information security officer's PC just how many workers have completed the training (ideally with time/date stamps and digital signatures to create evidence that could be admissible in court demonstrating that the worker read the policy).

Establish on-line quizzes/questionnaires which determine just how well staff understand Information security policy material (perhaps providing prizes, or at least entries into a drawing for prizes, for those who get perfect scores).

Before users gain access to certain applications or systems facilities, force them to first go through a brief on-line training program.

Prepare a personal computer security utility software disk including encryption routines, a password access control utility, a disk scrub (zeroization) utility, and a self-assessment questionnaire.

Employ written or automated questionnaires to gauge the (self-assessed) level of compliance.

Use special vulnerability identification software to check security parameters, alerting security staff that problems exist (O/S installed incorrectly, passwords easily guessed, etc.).

Install intrusion detection software to monitor attempts to break-into internal systems and use these reports as evidence of the need for greater funding.

Set-up an in-house intranet server and post all information security documentation to that server (including forms).

Establish web site blocking software at the firewall to control the sites that staff visit and then issue a memo explaining the new system and why it has been adopted.

Install content monitoring software which looks at the material flowing through the firewall, and let staff know their communications are being monitored.

Require that all portable personal computers used for Company X business employ an access control software package including a boot password and screen blanker.

Adopt a commercial encryption product as an in-house standard and internally publicize the ways that this will assist the organization with a move towards implementing PKI (public key infrastructure).

Establish logging systems that detect security violations as well as a formal process for (as needed) notifying users and their managers.

Change the log-on banner to prohibit electronic trespassing, state that the system facilities are for business use only, and that all user activity is subject to monitoring.

Place a notice on log-in screens (perhaps at a firewall or dial-up modem pool) that says users should proceed no further unless they have reviewed and understand Company X's information security policy.

Require users to click on a button indicating their agreement to comply with all information security polices at the time they log-in to Company X information systems or networks.

Change the initial invocation banners for specific applications (including e-mail) to provide application specific security policies and/or other security instructions.

Install regularly changing on-screen reminders, such as those which display at log-in time.

Use software agents that remind staff to perform certain security activities such as regularly back up their systems.

Give all systems administrators the email address of the Computer Emergency Response Team (CERT) at Carnegie-Mellon University and get them to sign-up for free notices about vulnerabilities.

On Other Things

Write information security messages on coffee mugs, mouse pads, glass coasters, and other trinkets that are given to staff.

Write information security messages on T-shirts and sweat shirts and give these to staff who have been supportive of information security efforts.

Prepare video tapes that can be distributed to all remote locations (most often splicing material from previously-prepared videos).

Establish a hot-line with a message machine where information security problems can be reported (perhaps anonymously).

Cycle awareness materials on kiosks with built-in personal computers, or on closed-circuit TVs in staff-only areas like a lunch-room.

Provide messages on the organization's in-house TV station (some large firms have their own).

Write security messages on air fresheners that staff hangs from their car rear view mirror.

Appendix 5.
Checklist of Steps In Policy Development Process

This checklist is intended to provide a quick overview of the major steps associated with the development, refinement, and approval of an internal information security policy document. A more detailed description of the necessary development, refinement, and approval steps can be found in the chapter of this book entitled "Instructions." Similarly, a list of steps to take after a policy document has been produced is found in an appendix entitled "Suggested Next Steps Now That Policies Are Written." Note that many of the following steps can be pursued simultaneously or in an order different than the order shown below.

1. Perform a risk assessment or EDP audit to determine your organization's unique information security needs; these needs must be addressed in a policy document.
2. Clarify what the word "policy" means within your organization so that you are not preparing a "standard," a "procedure," or some other related material.
3. Make sure that roles and responsibilities related to information security are clarified (including responsibility for issuing and maintaining policies).
4. Convince management that it's advisable to have documented information security policies
5. Identify the top management staff who will be approving the final information security document as well as all influential reviewers.
6. Collect and read all existing internal information security awareness material and make a list of the bottom-line messages contained therein.
7. Conduct a brief internal survey to gather ideas that stakeholders believe should be included in a new or updated information security policy.
8. Examine other policies issued by your organization, such as those from the Human Resources Department, to identify prevailing format, style, tone, length, and cross-references, so what you produce fits with what came before.
9. Identify the audience(s) to receive information security policy materials and determine whether they will each get their own document.
10. Determine the extent to which the audience is literate, computer knowledgeable, and receptive to security messages (this includes understanding the corporate culture surrounding information security).
11. Decide whether some other awareness efforts must take place before information security policies are issued (for example, one effort might show that information itself has become a critical factor of production).
12. Using ideas from the risk assessment, prepare a list of absolutely essential bottom-line policy messages that must be communicated (consult the files on the CD-ROM with the names POLICY1, POLICY2, and POLICY3, as well the as already-written policies at the end of this book called "sample policies").
13. If there is more than one audience, match-up the audiences with the bottom-line messages to be communicated via a coverage matrix (this process is described at length in the chapter called "Instructions").
14. Determine how the policy material will be disseminated (an intranet site is recommended, but the appendix dealing with awareness methods provides many other alternatives), noting the constraints and implications of each medium of communication.
15. Review the compliance checking process, disciplinary process, and enforcement process to make sure that they all can work smoothly with the new policy document.
16. Determine whether the number of messages is just too large to be handled all at one time, and if so, identify different categories of material that will be issued at different times.

17. Run the outline of topics to be included in the first document by several stakeholders (an Information Security Management Committee is the ideal review board, if your organization has one).
18. Based on comments from the stakeholders, revise the initial outline and prepare a first draft, extracting policies as needed from this book's CD-ROM.
19. Run the first draft document by the stakeholders for initial reactions, presentation suggestions, and implementation ideas.
20. Make changes to the draft in response to comments from stakeholders (expect that this step will repeat several times).
21. Get top management to approve and sign-off on the policy (changes may be necessary here, in which case this step can repeat several times too).
22. Prepare extracts of the policy document for selected purposes, for example for a form signed by users receiving brand new or renewed user-IDs and passwords.
23. Develop an awareness plan which uses the policy document as a source of ideas and requirements.
24. Create a working papers memo indicating the disposition of all comments received from reviewers (even if no changes were made).

Write a memo about the project, what you learned, and what needs to be fixed so that the next version of the policy document can be: prepared more efficiently, better received by the readers, and more responsive to the unique circumstances facing your organization

Basic Steps Related To Information Secturity Roles & Responsibilities

For Organizations Just Starting To Get Organized In the Information Security Area

For Organizations That Have Already Done Considerable Information Security Work

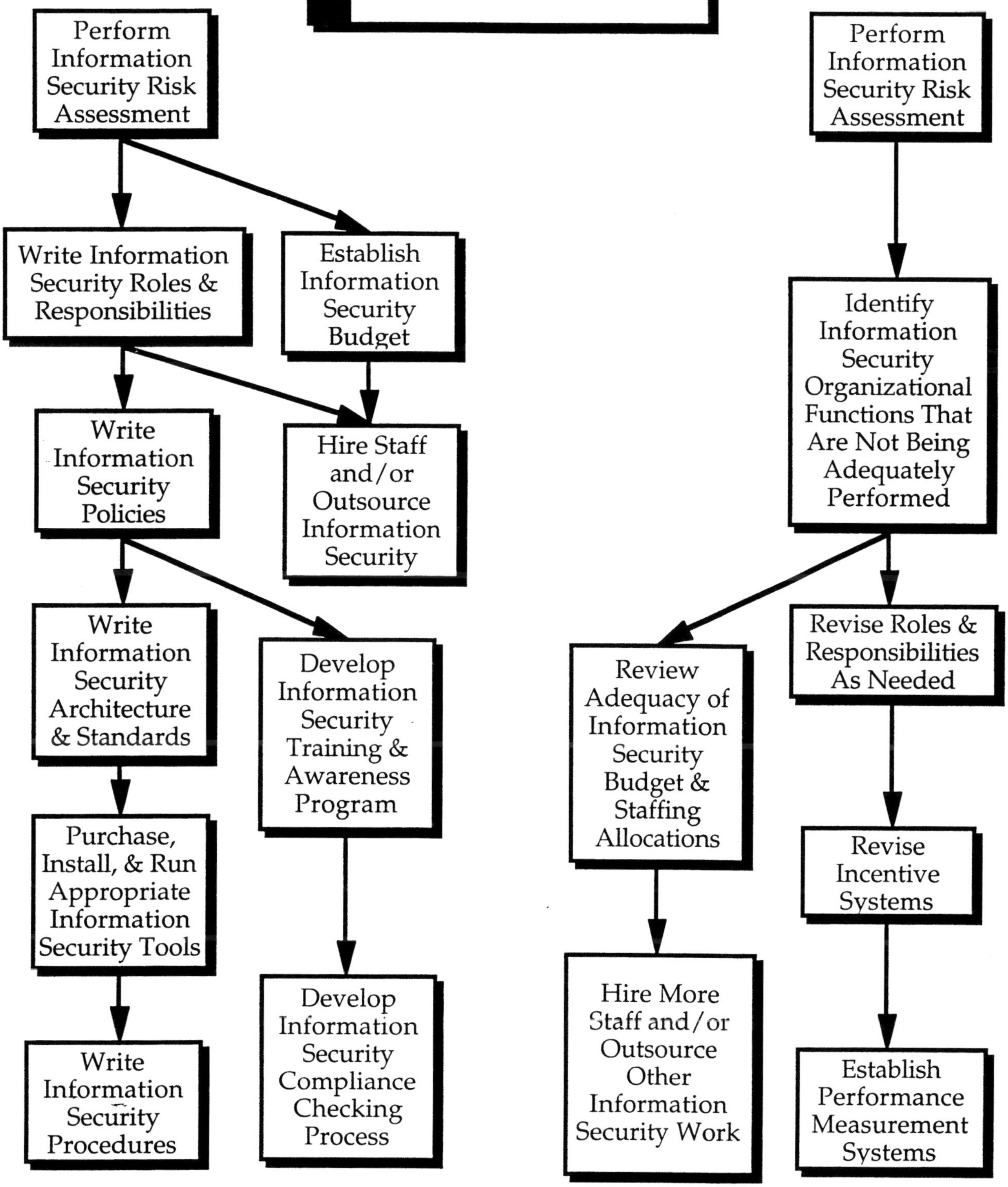

Appendix 7.
Suggested Next Steps Now That Policies Are Written

After an information security policy has been approved by top management at the policy writer's organization, what should be done next? The following list of suggested next steps provides some answers, but it is not intended to provide a comprehensive list of all possible next steps. Each of these suggested next steps are commonly encountered, although not all the items will apply to all organizations. Rather than following the list in a rote fashion, the policy writer is urged to use it as a starting point when drawing-up an information security policy implementation project plan. The suggestions listed below are organized in a rough chronological order, and may be addressed one-by-one. A better alternative would be to pursue several of these steps at the same time in order to make significant progress.

The policy writer should note that there will typically be many other projects that are initiated as a result of preparing an information security policy document. For example, a policy preparation effort may have illuminated the fact that an existing information security requirement is obsolete. A specific example might involve callback technology for dial-in access to an organization's networks. If this requirement is widely subscribed to within the organization, an effort to adopt a more modern alternative may be yet another project to add to a project plan. Continuing with this specific example, dynamic password tokens could be used instead of callback systems.

1. Post Polices To Intranet Or Equivalent: The new policies document should be placed on Company X's intranet and then links to related documents should also be added. Multiple indexes should also be prepared so that users can quickly locate material of interest. A key word search facility should also be added. Other electronic bulletin board equivalents, such as a Human Resources kiosk, could also include the information security policy document. Further ideas about the places to post policies can be found in the appendix to this book entitled "List Of Suggested Awareness Raising Methods."

2. Develop A Self-Assessment Questionnaire: The essential requirements found in the new information security policy document should be extracted and reformatted in the form of a questionnaire. The Internal Audit Department should then issue the questionnaire to department managers. Responses to the questionnaire will highlight those areas where departments are out of compliance and where additional control enhancements are needed. Based on the results of the survey, remedial projects can then be proposed. Later the questionnaire can be used as part of a regular compliance-checking internal audit process. Other ideas about obtaining compliance can be found in the subsection entitled "Handling Non-Compliance" found in the chapter entitled "Instructions."

3. Develop Revised User-ID Issuance Form: A form is used at many organizations as a way to document management approval prior to the issuance of a user-ID. This control is described in greater depth in the policy entitled "Signed Forms Required for Issuance of User-ID." A summary of the critical ideas in the new information security policy document should be included as part of this form along with words such as "the user mentioned below has read and agrees to abide by Company X information security policies as a condition of his/her continued use of Company X information systems." All new or reissued user-IDs should then be enabled only after the form is signed.

4. Develop Agreement To Comply With Information Security Policies Form: A legal document reflecting an agreement by employees to comply with information security policies should be drawn-up, edited, and later approved by management. This form should be signed by all

workers, or at the very least by all newly hired/retained workers. An example of a such an agreement is provided in the appendix to this book entitled "Annual Signature On Agreement To Comply With Information Security Policies." Then the policy writer should initiate an awareness program to publicize the existence of the new policy document and to get signed forms. For further information, the policy writer is directed to the appendix entitled "Agreement To Comply With Information Security Policies."

5. Assign Information Security Coordinators: Many centralized information security departments are understaffed. Clearly these centralized staff members cannot handle all the information security jobs that need to be done. To assist in the implementation of the controls described in the new policy document, decentralized information security coordinators should be assigned. Systems administrators, systems mangers, network managers, and other technical staff often serve in this part-time capacity. Coordinators serve as a local liaison with the central information security group, interpreting policies for a department or division. The role of an information security coordinator is taken up in greater detail in the policy entitled "Each Department Must Have an Information Security Liaison."

6. Train Information Security Coordinators: Before the above-mentioned information security coordinators can be expected to do substantive work, they should receive a training course. A half-day course should be developed to acquaint them with the requirements defined in the new information security policy document, existing organizational resources, and the best ways to deal with a variety of problems such as power failures, hacker intrusions, and computer virus infections. A handbook for local information security coordinators is also recommended. The policy writer is directed to the appendix entitled "List Of Information Security Periodicals" for sources of information that could be included in these trainings.

7. Prepare And Deliver A Basic Information Security Training Course: A brief training course should be prepared and presented to the rank-and-file at Company X. The policy document can be the primary source of ideas for a training and awareness course. A variety of other material -- such as the corporate code of conduct -- should also be drawn upon when preparing this course. After this course has been presented several times, it can be revamped and then recorded via video tape or computer based training (CBT) software. In some instances, separate audiences may need different training courses. Possible audiences include: (1) new hires going through orientation, (2) current employees in need of additional training, (3) systems administrators, LAN administrators, office technology coordinators, and others likely to be designated as information security coordinators, and (4) systems analysts, application programmers, systems related project managers, systems quality assurance staff, and other technical staff who will not be serving in an information security coordinator capacity. See the section entitled "Intended Target Audience" appearing in the chapter called "Instructions" for further discussion of this point.

8. Develop Application Specific Information Security Policies: Certain highly sensitive applications (such as those used by Company X's Cash Management Department) will need additional application-specific policies and procedures. Now that the new information security policy document has been prepared, more detailed policies and related requirements for high-risk application systems should be developed. Certain computing environments (not just applications), such as Internet electronic commerce, may likewise warrant more detailed policies and procedures. The conceptual hierarchy described immediately below can be used to describe the linkage between these application specific documents and the new information security policy. For additional ideas about more detailed and specific policies, the policy writer is directed to the subsection entitled "How Should One Select The Objectives And Scope of Policies?" found in the chapter called "Instructions."

9. Develop A Conceptual Hierarchy Of Information Security Requirements: The information security area is unfortunately very complex, and this complexity shows up in various and sundry documents which define information security requirements. In many organizations, these include standards, guidelines, policies, procedures, architectures, and the like. A general information security policy document should be at the top of a conceptual hierarchy, with application related information security policy documents falling underneath. Likewise, standards, guidelines, procedures, and other documents should be controlled by the general organization-wide information security policy statement. A conceptual hierarchy should also indicates when certain documents apply, which documents take precedence when a conflict exists, and which documents are current or outdated. This conceptual hierarchy will be useful for training and awareness purposes, and can be posted to the Company X information security intranet page. Further discussion on this point can be found in the subsection entitled "What Are Information Systems Security Policies?" found in the chapter called "Instructions."

10. Assign Information Ownership And Custodianship: Management ownership of specific types of information should be assigned according to the requirements set forth in the new information security document. After ownership roles have been assigned, custodianship roles can should come next. In many instances, these efforts will be a natural adjunct to the compilation of a corporate data dictionary, an electronic document management system, or a similar project. This topic is taken up in greater detail in the policies entitled "Designated Custodian Required for All Major Information Types" and "Information Ownership Must Be Assigned."

11. Establish An Information Security Management Committee: To supervise the various information security initiatives now underway, a committee should be formed with middle-level managers from each of the major divisions at Company X. This committee will ensure that current and proposed information security activities are consistent with business objectives. The committee will also serve as a sounding board for proposals, prior to presenting these same proposals to top management. The committee ordinarily would meet once a quarter, and would not provide any technical assistance to the Information Security Department. A committee is discussed in the policy entitled "Information Security Management Committee." A mission statement and related details about such a committee can also be found in the author's book entitled "Information Security Roles & Responsibilities Made Easy."

12. Develop An Information Security Architecture Document: Even though the basic rules for information security are specified in a policy document, in most cases there is still a need to put together a grand vision for designing secure systems. The larger an organization, the more the need for a document such as this (complexity is much more of a problem there). An architecture should specify the controls that will be used now and in the near future, as well as provide a plan for the migration to controls to be adopted in the near future. Some organizations also use an architecture document as a place to specify certain approved information security products and vendors. An architecture deals with system interfaces, technical standards, and other more technical considerations than a policy document. Further ideas about an information security architecture can be found in the policy entitled "Systems Architecture For Logging Activities."

Appendix 8.
Top Ten Impediments To Implementing Policies

You worked hard to write an information security policy that uniquely reflects your organization's ways of doing business, its organizational culture, and its information technology. After many discussions and a few presentations, you were able to strike compromises that allowed the document to be endorsed by the chief executive officer. Perhaps the document even made it onto your organization's intranet or into the employee handbook. But that's about as far as things went.

You were frustrated when you discovered that the internal audit department doesn't use the policies when they conduct audits. With dismay, you noticed that new hire orientation still doesn't indoctrinate newly recruited men and women in the ways of information security. Likewise, you observed that systems administrators have not yet made changes in the computer access control systems which would bring these systems into compliance with the policy. You furthermore observed that the Information Technology Department didn't seem to pay any attention to the policy when they bought many new systems and upgraded pieces of equipment. In other words, your policy isn't being implemented.

Before you quit your job, consider that there may be several impediments which prevent the implementation of your policy document. Clarification of these blockages is the first step to clearing them out of the way. While there are certainly other impediments to progress, over the last twenty one years of information security consulting I've noticed ten of these which keep coming up again and again. You'll find these impediments described below in non-prioritized order with a few suggestions for moving things ahead.

Of course, in an ideal world, all of these impediments would be addressed and handled before the information security policy document is developed, or at least at the time when it was created or updated. Implementation can then be part of a formal project plan approved by management, and can follow in a logical and straightforward way.

1. Other Priorities Take Precedence, Sorry, There's Insufficient Budget

Perhaps the most common objection to implementing an information security policies document is "we don't have the money right now." This can be a code word for a wide variety of situations -- situations that management may or may not wish to share with you. It's a bit awkward to ask "why not?" But that retort actually makes a lot of sense. Many information security specialists are left to wonder why they wrote a policies document if management isn't going to follow through with implementation.

On a more fundamental level, budgetary objections are a reflection of failure to sell management on the importance of both information and information systems to the business. The reader may at first wonder why this is necessary when our designated focus is information security. The answer is that management must understand how the organization has become inextricably dependent on both information and information systems. When they really get this, then information security becomes a significant priority. When management truly understands, the money and other forms of support will be there.

Far too many information security efforts postpone awareness and training efforts, thinking these can be deferred. Instead they focus on the technical aspects of information security like access control systems. If this approach is taken, the nature of the information security effort at an organization can be unduly technical for a prolonged time. Information security is not just a technical problem, it is a people problem, and it is a management problem. There are many ways to do management awareness raising, but one of my favorites is a penetration attack. This is a great way to wake management up, to show them that systems are not as secure as they thought.

2. Why Do You Keep Talking About Policy Implementation?

Another reason why policies may not be implemented at your organization may have to do with management's understanding about the benefits of policies. Management may not, for example, appreciate how policies establish benchmarks or reference points for audits, how they lower costs through control standardization, and how they help demonstrate that management acted with due diligence (thus, we hope, avoiding liability). There are at least twenty good reasons to have policies and to actively use them in the management of information security [these are listed in the chapter called Instructions].

Management needs to understand that policies are a way to efficiently ensure that their intentions are being consistently applied throughout the organization. Management needs to appreciate that if policies are widely adopted, then their job will be made considerably easier (having fewer exceptions to agonize over is but one example). Management also needs to understand that information security is incredibly complex field and that policies (not to mention standards and procedures) are needed to establish and maintain a secure computing environment.

Just as a policy writing effort may have been defined as a specific project, so too should policy implementation be defined as a specific project (or better yet, several projects). Putting implementation into the framework of a project will give the person preparing a proposal an opportunity to tout the benefits of policies. Often an investigation of the merits of policies has broader top management implications, for example pointing to a change in the way that business is conducted. To the extent that an information security specialist can establish an alliance with an internal auditor or a management consultant who can tout the merits of policies in general, to that extent an information security policy will be seen as that much more worthy of management attention.

3. Wasn't This Supposed To Be Only A Policies Development Effort?

Management may not really understand that it's not sufficient to just have an approved and published policies document. Management may not appreciate how leaving it at that can foster cynicism and the belief that management doesn't really mean what they say. Management may not appreciate that by leaving it at that they are sowing the seeds of future non-compliance -- workers will surely notice that management doesn't show any further interest in a policies document, and in their minds, that may mean that management doesn't care.

Often management has signed-off, but they did not understand exactly what implementation required. This can frequently be attributed to inadequate disclosure at the beginning of the policies development effort; management may not have appreciated the so-called "total cost of ownership." In this case, some information security people advise others to conceal these total costs, to write the policies, and to "do it anyway, and then later ask for forgiveness." I don't believe that this approach fosters goodwill or open communications between the information security staff and top management. I also think that this approach cannot help but make it look like the information security staff doesn't know what they are doing.

Instead, information security practitioners are urged to disclose all the changes that will need to take place as a result of implementing a policies document. Practitioners are urged to additionally say that there will be other things, that we don't yet appreciate, but that we will understand when the time comes to implement the policies. The list of implementation tasks that will need to be funded and supported by management include replacing certain technology that is out of compliance, establishing additional procedures to support the policies, hiring information security training staff, and many other things.

4. Are We Really Required To Do All Of These Things?

Top management at some firms may keep it to themselves, but they secretly only wanted an information security policies document as window-dressing, that is, to keep the auditors happy. Management in these cases may never have been behind the development of a document for its own sake, it was only supportive because they thought it was a necessity. An increasing majority of people in business now have the impression that a policies document is a part of the standard of due care. Even external auditors are talking about policies these days, and the threat of a qualified opinion on financial statements can be a significant motivator for managers.

While some would say that it's good that policies got written, whatever the motivation, in the real world there is a big price to pay for such shallow management support. If management thought of a policies development effort as a chore, they probably didn't put much if any time into developing customized policies that really fit their organization. Whatever policies they have are likely to be broad and sweeping; these policies are likely to omit the details that are absolutely essential if a policies effort is going to be successful.

What we have here are basic resistant managers, managers who don't do things until they are forced by circumstances. It is these managers who often face a serious crisis when a hacker breaks in or an employee is caught engaging in computer fraud. They may be so-called 'crisis managers,' who believe in changing things only when they are broken. It is especially with these managers that the information security practitioner needs to demonstrate how a proactive approach to information security is the least costly alternative. The practitioner needs to talk about the impact of a security problem on customer confidence and on public opinion. The practitioner also needs to talk about statistics that show that information security is much less expensive if you deal with it largely from a 'prevent, deter and detect' perspective, rather than simply from a 'correct and recover' perspective.

5. What Do You Mean When You Say There Are Some Dependencies?

Many information security policies implementation efforts are going nowhere because the people tasked with these efforts are missing important information. In many instances, this information could have been provided through a risk assessment or an information security architecture development project. What we have here is a failure to adequately identify and manage project dependencies.

An example should clarify this point. Suppose a policies document requires an extended user authentication technology (biometrics, dynamic passwords, etc.) for all remote access. Nonetheless, no information security architecture has been prepared, and no in-house standard products have been selected. Meanwhile, staff members are complaining because they aren't allowed to work from home. Management then steadfastly insists that working from home isn't possible because they don't have the technology to accomplish this securely.

Information security policies are an important seminal document on which many information security efforts depend, but they are not the only such document. In cases like this, management doesn't appreciate the basic documents that need to be prepared before serious project planning can proceed. Because information security efforts can often take years to achieve a major result (such as implement a secure data warehouse system), a lot of long-term planning is absolutely essential. To get around this impediment to progress, information security needs to be a line item on an organizational budget, and a manager of the information security group needs to be very specific about project plans, staffing, deliverables, and dependencies.

6. What Do You Mean That Nobody Knows What You Should Do Next?

It must be a good time to be a recruiter of information security specialists. Salaries are going through the roof and competent experienced people are very difficult to find. In many organizations this means that information security has been assigned to someone who really knows very little about the field. While a fresh perspective may sometimes be helpful, especially if the individual truly knows the underlying business, it is most often a serious drawback unless some source of competent outside assistance is readily available.

Far too many information security policies languish on the shelf because information security staff really didn't understand the big picture. Too many policies languish because staff didn't understand how they needed to follow through and implement the rules and instructions defined in a policy document. Every organization needs a technical leader, someone who has a vision for where information security is going over the next few years. If this person isn't an employee, then perhaps he or she can be a contractor or consultant. Courses, conferences, videos, and books are especially helpful in this regard.

7. This Is Dauntingly Complex; I've Never Dealt With Anything Like It

The Internet is the most complex system ever created by man. Working with the Internet we have operating systems, application programs, firewall software packages, manual procedures, and many other components to a total information system. Like many technical people, managers often don't understand just how complex these systems are, nor do they understand the many points where problems might take place. But without an appreciation for this complexity, managers are not going to allocate sufficient resources to adequately deal with information security.

Even those specializing in information security are overwhelmed by the complexity of it all. But just because something is complex doesn't mean we should ignore it. We should instead be using automated tools to help us come to terms with this complexity, for example, contingency planning software is now a standard of due care for anybody who seriously wants to prepare a contingency plan for anything but the smallest of organizations.

The complexity found in information systems should also be the reason why management allocates funds for network management systems, intrusion detection systems, automatic software distribution systems, automatic software license checking systems, and other automated mechanisms that can handle a task that no single human can hope to do all himself. The practitioner should speak with management about the existence of these new tools, and why they are so popular. This in turn should start management thinking about the extent to which their current computing environment is, or is not still manageable given the complexity it entails. This should lead to an understanding about how these tools can be used to implement information security policies.

8. My Power As A Manager Is Going To Be Eroded By These Policies!

In many organizations the lack of a centralized policy on certain topics, like disciplinary actions, is a tacit statement that local management can do as they see fit. While this may work in some areas like flextime, it doesn't work when it comes to information security policy enforcement and discipline. Every exception weakens a control, and universal compliance is a must if the security of a network of connected systems is to be preserved. Consider how just one careless person could cause misery for many other network users when it comes to a computer virus. With this in mind, there is no practical alternative -- information security policies will need to be dictated centrally and every manager will need to support these rules and instructions.

But local managers may have grown accustomed to doing things their own way, and they may consider local autonomy to be a perk of working at the organization involved. They may resist the development and implementation of a policies document, thinking that it will be a direct threat to their power and prestige. While the document may be these things, the emphasis in discussions with these people should instead be on how a coordinated and centralized effort is essential, and how local management support is likewise a necessity.

In a broader sense, many organizations are tolerating a wide variety of exceptions on a regular basis, and these exceptions are running the people who work there absolutely ragged. Access control administration is a good example. If there is a standardized procedure for requesting system access, and if this has been put into a policies and procedures document, then things are going to go a lot more smoothly. But if each department does things their own way, expecting the information security group to adapt, then chaos, upsets, and delays will be the norm. Often a campaign needs to be waged to sell the merits of standardized processes, and of course standardization should include an information security policies document.

9. Why Should I Be Worried About Policy Implementation? It's Not My Job!

For far too long, management hasn't wanted to deal with the technical details of information security, instead considering this to be the domain of information technology staff. While IT staff will no doubt need to be involved, middle and top-level management must also be engaged in the process. This point, however, is rarely made clearly, and even more rarely accepted among the ranks of management.

Managers need to understand that information security policies will go nowhere unless they are clearly supported by management. Managers also need to know that their active participation in the development and implementation of policies is essential for success. Many of the decisions associated with the writing and implementation of policies are business decisions that should not be made by technical staff. For example, assume that management has adopted a change control policy that prevents workers from changing the software on their desktop office computers. At the same time, management may be encouraging the use of portable computers when workers are on the road, but workers are using their own systems for this purpose. Imposing change control on a computer owned by a worker would be unreasonable and impractical. So management is faced with a business decision: do they pay extra money to purchase portables for workers who need them, or do they allow computers owned by workers to be used with sensitive data, perhaps leading to a security problem?

The way to overcome this impediment is through a clear definition of roles and responsibilities in the information security field. This is often hard because the field is new, and because there are so many different ways to do things. For example, should the information security group be doing policy compliance checking? While I suggest that the answer to that question should be no (for conflict of interest reasons), the major point here is to be clear about roles and responsibilities. Practitioners also need to stress that information security is multi-disciplinary, and that help from many different people is required.

10. We Can't Make A Big Deal About This -- There's No Disciplinary Process!

In far too many organizations, often organizations with stellar reputations and very public personas, the centralized disciplinary process is crude and dysfunctional when it comes to information security. Consider the case of a telephone company that fired a bunch of workers for downloading pornography from the Internet. The workers were not given any warnings; they were simply fired to set a very visible example for the rest of the staff. Unfortunately, one side effect of this disciplinary action was to discourage Internet usage; people from that point forward were afraid that they were going to mistype a URL and in the process mistakenly end up at a porn site.

Organizations should use a phased disciplinary process, where people are given a chance to come into compliance with policies. A large computer company uses a four step process: (1) initially only a personal note is left on the employee's desk, (2) if the condition persists, another memo is issued and copied to the employee's manager, (3) if things still don't change, then the worker is suspended from work for two weeks, and (4) if that doesn't create the desired result, the worker is terminated. People respond much better to a phased process, and they consider it to be both fair and equitable.

Before an internal audit reveals serious out-of-compliance situations, a set of penalties for being out-of-compliance needs to be established. Responsibility for these and related activities needs to be defined. For example, should the human resources group or should the information security group do this disciplinary work? Information security specialists should try to draw on a centralized human resources disciplinary process as much as possible, rather than "reinventing the wheel." Only when an adequate disciplinary process that is actually used by management has been established, will people take policies seriously.

Conclusion: An On-Going Organizational Function

Far too many organizations still look at information security as a project to be completed once in a while. Instead, organizations these days need to see information security as an on-going organizational function like accounting and marketing. When management adopts this more progressive view, they will bring the tools and techniques used for other functional areas to the information security area. Then management will see that writing a policies document is just one of many important steps in an on-going process to create and maintain a secure information systems environment.

This appendix originally appeared as the cover story in Information Security magazine's August 1999 issue. For further information about the magazine, direct your web browser to www.infosecuritymag.com.

Appendix 9.
Real World Problem Cases Caused By Missing Policies

At A Government Agency...
A clerk spent a great deal of time surfing the Internet while on the job. Because there was no policy specifying what constituted excessive personal use, management could not discipline this employee. Then management discovered that the clerk had downloaded a significant amount of pornography. Using this as justification, management fired him. The clerk appealed the termination with the Civil Service Board, claiming that he couldn't be fired because he had never been told that he couldn't download pornography. After a Civil Service hearing, the Board ordered him to be reinstated with back pay. This situation could have been avoided if the employer had a clear and up-to-date policy dealing with personal use of information systems.

At A Law Firm ...
The manager of data processing took a job with a competing law firm. Because his former employer had nobody who could do the job that he did, they kept him on as a part-time contractor. For months, this sophisticated technician performed a wide variety of systems management tasks for his former employer. In order to do these tasks he needed full privileges on the former employer's network. One day a partner at the former employer learned that the manager's new employer was opposing them in a high-visibility lawsuit. The partners at the manager's former employer started asking some questions, such as could the former data processing manager gain access to any file on the network and perhaps the legal strategies for this case? The answer was yes, but nobody knew whether the manager had exploited these capabilities because no data access logs were being kept. This situation could have been avoided if the former employer had policies about conflicts of interest, system access privileges, and keeping logs.

At An Oil Company ...
An oil company computer technician compiled a list of jokes about sex. Proud of his list, he broadcasted this list on the Internet, appending his electronic mail address to the end, just in case the recipients happened to have heard any new ones. Management was able to have the posting deleted from several discussion groups, but was not able to control copies that had already been made. Around the same time this technician had printed a copy of his list, and when distracted by something else, had left it in the hopper of a departmental printer. Women in the department objected that they had been subjected to sex jokes via email that they didn't want to hear. They pointed to the Internet postings and the printer output as examples. The pending sexual harassment lawsuit was settled for an undisclosed sum. A policy about permissible use of the Internet, as well as a policy about representations made with the company name over the Internet were noticeably lacking.

At A Local Newspaper ...
A local newspaper had no policy requiring the termination of user-ID and password privileges after an employee had left. A senior reporter left the newspaper, and shortly thereafter, the newspaper had trouble because a competing local newspaper consistently picked-up on their exclusive investigative reporting stories (scoops). A review of the system logs revealed that the departed reporter had been consistently dialing-up his former employer's computer to get ideas for stories to use at his new employer.

At A Midwest Manufacturing Company ...
A virus hoax sent by email through the Internet indicated that if people receive a message with the heading "Join the Crew" they should not read it. The hoax went on to state that this email

would erase a hard drive if ever it should be displayed. Thinking that they were doing others a favor, 10% of the staff at a large manufacturing company broadcasted the hoax to all the people they knew. Because no policy defined how they should handle these warnings, they flooded the company's internal networks with email and caused a great deal of unnecessary technical staff time to be wasted. A policy requiring all reported information security vulnerabilities to be forwarded to the Information Security Department could have avoided this loss of worker productivity.

At a West Coast Manufacturing Company ...
Because it had no policy requiring employee private data to be encrypted when held in storage, a large manufacturing company found itself facing a public relations problem. A thief made off with a computer disk containing detailed personal details and bank account information on more than 20,000 current and former employees. The press speculated that this could be used to facilitate identity theft, including application for credit cards in the names of other people. The event precipitated a massive notification process including recommendations on changes to bank account numbers.

At a Major On-Line Service Company ...
A Navy enlisted man registered with an Internet on-line service company and filled out a profile form which indicated that he was gay. An employee at the service company, after an inquiry from the Navy, shared this profile information with the Navy's "top brass." Based on this information, the enlisted man was given a dishonorable discharge. The enlisted man sued the Navy for violating its own "don't ask, don't tell" policy, and won an honorable discharge with retirement benefits as a result. The on-line service company publicly stated that its employee had violated "the privacy policy," but this policy had been violated on multiple occasions before including top management's publicly stated intention to sell customer home telephone numbers to telephone marketers. At least the service firm now admits that it has a policy. Training associated with policies is absolutely essential if these policies are going to be faithfully observed.

Appendix 10.
Index To New Policies Since The Last Edition

The following policies have been added to Information Security Policies Made Easy (ISPME) since the last version. This list is intended for those licensees who have a copy of version 7 and who wish to update their existing policy statements focusing only on new policies. There are 171 new policies in this new version of ISPME and one policy was deleted from the prior version.

2. Minimum Password Length Constrained By System Limitations
16. User-Chosen Passwords Must Be Entered Twice If Masked When Entered
20. Initial Passwords Transmitted To Remote Users By Authorized Means
25. Customer Service Fixed Passwords Not Displayed By Company X Systems
29. Password Guessing Lockout Requires Help Desk Password Reset
35. Special Privileges Associated With Secret User-IDs Or Passwords Prohibited
46. No Fixed Passwords Stored In Dial-Up Programs Or Internet Browsers
47. User Controlled Machines Must Not Employ Cookies For Automatic Log-In
49. Personal Identification Numbers (PINs) Constructed Using Password Rules
54. Forced Change Of All Passwords After Supervisor Account Compromise
75. Reasonable Personal Use Consistent With Conventional Ethical Standards
83. When Established, Outsider User-IDs Must Have Defined Expiration Date
85. Time Limits For User-IDs And File Retention Period After Expiration
90. No Sensitive Information On Personal Digital Assistants, Handhelds, Etc.
107. Separate User-IDs For Internet Connected & Internal Network Systems
108. Exclusive Personal Use Of Access Codes Such As User-IDs & Credit Cards
122. Trusted Host Relationships Must Not Be Established Without Permission
126. Termination Of User Processes Or Sessions And Removal Of User Files
143. Human Resources Sends Worker Status Changes To System Administrators
145. Users Must Inform Systems Administration About Status Changes
155. All Attempted System Log-Ins, Successful Or Not, Must Be Logged
156. Log-In Passwords Must Not Be Logged Unless In Encrypted Form
162. Cryptographic Checksums To Detect Modifications Of System Logs
170. Externally Accessible Systems Must Employ Remotely Mirrored Logs
171. Digital Signatures & Sequence Numbers Required For System Logs
172. System Log Rotation & Archive Process For High Security Systems
181. All Outbound Software And Executable Files Must Be Virus Free
188. Current Virus Software Required For Certain Worker-Owned Computers
196. Developers Embed Security In Systems If Commercial Solution Exists
204. Use Of Software Tools & Languages With Unproven Security Attributes
215. External Network Interfaces Must Be Approved By Information Security
222. Designers & Developers Must Notify Management Of Potential Problems
223. Complaints Regarding Errors & Security Problems Traced To Developers
225. Production System Changes Must Be Consistent With Security Architecture
228. Access Controls Defined Prior To Cut-Over To Production Operation
251. Systems Software & Applications Software At Most Recent Stable Levels
260. Packaged Software And Unilateral Deactivation By Third Party Vendor
266. Software Features & Functions Must Be Fully Revealed In Documentation
269. Production Computer Systems Must Be Physically Located In Data Center
291. Participation In Pirated Software Bulletin Boards & Related Internet Sites
300. Every Public Written Use Of Company X's Name Requires Approval
303. Pretext Requests Used To Test Both Customer Service And Security Policies

308. Affected Individuals Notified About Material Changes In Privacy Policy
309. Privacy Policy Changes Require Posting Of Clear Differences Summary
310. Privacy Policy Pertains To All Types Of Interactions With Customers
318. Personally-Identifiable Information Collection Requires Robust Notice
323. Involuntary Capture Of Personal Biometric Information Prohibited
324. Prohibited Transfer Of Personal Biometric Data To Third Parties
326. Name Of Organization Collecting Private Information Must Be Disclosed
348. Transfer Of Private Information To Other Countries Requires Approval
364. Privacy Policy Considered Contract Made At Time Information Provided
365. Privacy Of Correspondent Email Addresses And Telephone Numbers
369. Public Acknowledgement Of Or Reference To Famous Customers
384. Allegedly Incorrect Information To Be Corrected Or Labeled As Disputed
386. Documented Procedures Required For Personal Record Handling Activities
389. Linking Anonymous Information With Personally-Identifiable Information
395. Source And Purpose Of Cookies And Web Bugs Must Be Revealed
396. Compelling Need Required Prior To Usage Of Cookies Or Web Bugs
400. Retaining Personal Information Only As Long As Needed For Business
404. All Marketing Communications Must Provide An Opt-Out Opportunity
406. Immediate Action For Individuals Requesting Database Removal
408. Subjects Must Approve New Personal Data Uses After Merger/Acquisition
409. Business Structure Changes Do Not Permit Transfer Of Private Data
413. Chain Of Trust Agreements Required For Private And Sensitive Information
418. Revealing Information Systems Technical Details To Job Applicants
420. Material Financial Information Disclosures To Selected Parties
422. Vulnerability Information Detail Level In Press Releases Must Be Low
432. Right To Block, Conceal, Deny, Or Discontinue Service At Any Time
439. Company X Trade Secrets Must Named & Described On Intranet Page
440. Chief Legal Counsel Is Sole Person To Declare Information A Trade Secret
442. Information Treated As Secret Whenever Sensitivity Label Unknown
446. Creator Must Select Data Classification Label For New Files & Messages
452. Maintaining, Propagating, And Reestablishing Data Classification Labels
495. Secret Information Discussions In Company X Administrative Areas
501. Floppy Disk Input/Output Encryption Drivers Prevent Disclosure
503. Secret Information Must Not Leave Company X Offices In Any Form
531. Strip Shredders Must Not Be Used For Destruction Of Sensitive Information
551. Phased Public Release Of Controversial Sensitive Information
568. Information Security Policies & Procedures Are For Internal Use Only
578. Periodic Sweeps For Bugging, Interception, And Recording Equipment
598. Regular Simulated Incidents To Test Computer Emergency Response Team
600. Operations Staff Must Have Documented Intrusion Response Procedure
619. Internet Domain Name Registration Payments Must Be Confirmed
624. Do Not Use Hard Drives On Public Access Computers For Backup
633. Production Batch Processing Only If Pre-Processing Backup Is Complete
634. Annual Audits To Determine Whether Production Backup Is Performed
637. Backup Media Storage Rooms, Vaults, & Cabinets Must Be Kept Locked
638. Archival Storage Of Every Version Of Internet Web & Commerce Sites
656. Data Destruction Process Placed On Hold In Response To Discovery
667. Email & Regular Mail Address Change Confirmed Via Previous Address
680. Personal Information Changed Only After Correct Prior Values Provided
686. Cellular Phones Must Not Be Used Anywhere In Data Center
717. Firewalls Must Be Configured So All Services Are Denied Unless Approved
729. Separate Subnet Required For Walk-Up Network Connections
730. Unattended Active Network Ports In Public Areas Prohibited
731. Network Ports In Vacant Offices Must Be Promptly Disabled

732. Configuration To Prevent/Detect Unauthorized Network Connections
736. Security Criteria A Prerequisite For Intranet Connection
775. Duplication Of Encryption Keys For Data That Has Been Backed-Up
780. Compromised Keys Revoked Back To Last Time Known To Be Safe
782. Backup Encryption Keys Provided To Information Security Officer
793. Dial-Out User Identity Must Be Authenticated Before Session Established
797. Registry Of All Modem Lines And Related Advance Approval Process
803. Process For Down-Loading Software From An Internet Mirror Site
811. Unusual Phone Operation Requests Must Be Denied And Reported
813. Voicemail Passwords Not Subject To Password Construction Standards
814. Heard Voicemail Messages Deleted After One Month In Storage
828. Using Electronic Mail Addresses Other Than Official Company X Addresses
830. Clearly Identified Source For Electronic Mail Marketing Material
840. Modifying Electronic Mail Message Contents Or Header Prohibited
845. Sending Unsolicited Personal Email Messages After Request To Stop
846. Prohibition Against Unsolicited Bulk Email Advertisements (SPAM)
848. Sending Large Quantities Of Unsolicited Email (Mail Bombing)
854. Authorization To Issue Electronic Mail Or Voice Mail To Groups
857. Prohibition Against Opening Attachments Unless They Were Expected
859. Browser Electronic Mail Features Must Not Be Used For Business Activities
875. Mobile Computer Alternatives For Protecting Company X Information
878. Workers Who Do Not Perform Research Denied Internet Web Access
902. Search Engines To Detect Misleading Web Sites With Similar Names
908. Encryption Of All Payment Information On Internet-Accessible Machines
919. Responsibility For Content Posted To Personal Web Pages
923. Internet Hot-Links Must Be Accompanied By Legal Disclaimer
924. Daily Review Of Contents And Hot-Links For Company X Web Page
928. Staging Area For New/Changed Intranet Content Review And Testing
929. Cleansing Process For Downloaded Internet Content Moved To Intranet
930. Intranet Sites Must Not Use Unapproved Active Content
933. All Intranet Pages Must Include Information Owner Digital Signatures
935. Intranet Reviewed Quarterly To Confirm Sensitive Data Not Posted
940. Direct Transfer To Internet Sites Not Permitted From Intranet
947. Encrypt Credit Card Numbers & Other Payment Data When Not Used
948. Credit Card Numbers Must Be Used Only For Payment Processing
949. New Account Opening Requires Robust Identity Authentication
950. Any Demonstrated Fraud Forces Immediate Financial Account Closure
954. All New Workers Must Receive Information Security Policy Pamphlet
955. Information Security Training Only After Workers Pass Other Basic Training
957. Information Security Policy Change Notices Distributed To All Workers
962. Information Security Training Course Prior To Gaining System Access
967. Computer Crime Investigation Information Is Legally Privileged
979. Reporting Unauthorized Data Changes & Questionable System Use
992. Every Information System Privilege Not Specifically Allowed Is Forbidden
995. Dedicated Computers & Networks For High-Security/High-Reliability
999. Network Security Measures Must Not Be Backwards Compatible
1001. Systems Must Be Configured & Customized According To Templates
1006. Best-Of-Breed Solutions For Critical Information Security Functions
1010. Non-Enforcement Of Any Policy Does Not Constitute Consent
1013. Approval Before Disabling Critical Components Of Security Infrastructure
1020. Outsourced Hosting Arrangements Require Backup Plan And Testing
1021. External Firms Gathering Company X Information Must Make It Available
1025. Financial Condition Of Critical Vendors Reviewed Annually
1027. Researchers Must Disclose Sponsors And All Potential Conflicts

1034. Immediate Notification Of Employees Regarding Worker Terminations
1035. Informing Relevant Contractors And Vendors Of Worker Terminations
1037. Security Guard Escort For Workers Who Are Involuntarily Terminated
1054. Staff Qualifications For Working On Most Sensitive Company X Projects
1055. Workers In Positions Of Trust Must Not Also Be Company X Customers
1061. Staff Must Pass Background Check Before Accessing Private Information
1062. Sensitive Product Information Access Requires Background Check
1066. Significant Unexplained Increases In Wealth Must Be Investigated
1086. Risk Assessments Performed By Organizational Units Managing Systems
1094. Annual Review Of Trade Secrets, Copyrights, Etc. By Legal Department
1137. Escorts Required For All Visitors Outside Normal Business Hours
1140. Removal Of Badges After Leaving Company X Facilities
1141. Handling Badges When Workers Are Away From Company X Facilities
1143. No Visitors Allowed In Data Center Or Information Systems Department
1145. Computer & Communications Equipment Rack Doors Must Be Locked
1146. Internet Commerce & Financial Systems Must Be Physically Isolated
1151. Computer Center Authorized Staff Access List Reviewed Quarterly
1155. Locked Communications Equipment Areas And Escorted Access
1158. Printers, Copiers, And Fax Machines Banned From Secret Information Areas
1163. Computer Equipment Locations Must Have Water Damage Precautions
1169. Secondary Computer Center Doors Must Have Alarmed Crash Bars

Appendix 11.
Index To Policies By Policy Numbers

The numbers on the left side of the page are policy numbers, not page numbers. When doing key word searches in the files entitled POLICY1.DOC, POLICY2.DOC, and POLICY3.DOC, the policy writer should keep in mind that there are two spaces between each policy number and the related policy title. Separately, note that this file can also be searched by key word for a quick overview of policies related to a certain area. The policies described below begin in the chapter entitled "Specific Policies." Due to quirk in certain versions of MS Word, the numbers listed on the left side of this appendix may not be locatable through the key word search (find) command; policy writers having trouble with this bug in MS Word, who are wishing to search the numbers on the left side of this appendix, should use the text version of the same file, or else the MS Word version of Appendix 12 (which does not use MS Word's "AUTONUM" function).

1. Minimum Password Length
2. Minimum Password Length Constrained By System Limitations
3. Difficult-To-Guess Passwords Required
4. Cyclical Passwords Prohibited
5. User-Chosen Passwords Must Not Be Reused
6. Passwords Must Contain Both Alphabetic And Non-Alphabetic Characters
7. Passwords Must Contain Both Upper And Lower Case Characters
8. Seed For System-Generated Passwords
9. Pronounceable System-Generated Passwords
10. Storage Of System-Generated Passwords
11. Zeroization Of Password Generation Materials
12. Protection Of Password Generation Algorithms
13. Previous Password History File
14. Anonymous User-IDs
15. Display And Printing Of Passwords
16. User-Chosen Passwords Must Be Entered Twice If Masked When Entered
17. Periodic Forced Password Changes
18. Password Change Interval Synchronization Across Platforms
19. Assignment Of Expired Passwords
20. Initial Passwords Transmitted To Remote Users By Authorized Means
21. Limit On Consecutive Unsuccessful Attempts To Enter A Password
22. Single Sign-On Process
23. All Workstations Must Have Password-Based Boot Protection
24. Passwords Never In Readable Form When Outside Workstations
25. Customer Service Fixed Passwords Not Displayed By Company X Systems
26. Fixed Password Changes Confirmed By Regular Mail To Detect Abuse
27. Protection Of Passwords Sent Through The Mail
28. Re-registration Required For All Users Forgetting Fixed Passwords
29. Password Guessing Lockout Requires Help Desk Password Reset
30. Storage Of Passwords In Readable Form
31. Encryption Of Passwords
32. Incorporation Of Passwords Into Software
33. Prevention Of Password Retrieval
34. Reliance On Operating System User Authentication Process
35. Special Privileges Associated With Secret User-IDs Or Passwords Prohibited
36. System Access Control With Individualized Passwords (Not Lockwords)
37. Unique Passwords For Each Internal Network Device

38. Use Of Duress Passwords
39. Changing Vendor Default Passwords
40. Requirement For Different Passwords On Different Systems
41. Permission To Use Same Password On Different Systems
42. Suspected Disclosure Forces Password Changes
43. Password Changes After Compromise Of A Multi-User Computer System
44. Writing Passwords Down And Leaving Where Others Could Discover
45. Passwords Must Never Be Written Down Near Related Access Devices
46. No Fixed Passwords Stored In Dial-Up Programs Or Internet Browsers
47. User Controlled Machines Must Not Employ Cookies For Automatic Log-In
48. Dynamic Password Tokens Must Not Be Stored In Portable Cases
49. Personal Identification Numbers (PINs) Constructed Using Password Rules
50. Writing Passwords Down Using Secrecy Techniques
51. Password Sharing Prohibition
52. Users Responsible For All Activities Involving Personal User-IDs
53. Forced Change Of All Passwords After System Compromise
54. Forced Change Of All Passwords After Supervisor Account Compromise
55. In-Person Proof Of Identity To Obtain A Password
56. When And How Passwords May Be Disclosed By Security Administrators
57. Positive Identification Required For System Usage
58. Access Controls For Remote Systems Connecting To Production Systems
59. User-ID & Password Required For Computer-Connected Network Access
60. Unique User-ID And Password Required
61. Disclosure Of Incorrect Log-In Information
62. Prohibition Against Any Feedback In Response To Incorrect Log-In
63. Security Notice In System Log-in Banner
64. Disclosure Of Information In System Log-In Banner
65. Network Log-In Banner Wording Required
66. Notice Of Last Log-In Time And Date
67. Limitation On Number Of Daily Log-Ins Prevents Unauthorized Use
68. Prohibition Of Multiple Simultaneous On-Line Sessions
69. Automatic Log-Off Process
70. Leaving Sensitive Systems Without Logging-Off
71. Logging-Off Personal Computers Connected To Networks
72. Games May Not Be Stored Or Used On Company X Computer Systems
73. Personal Use Of Computer And Communications Systems
74. Incidental Personal Use Of Business Systems Permissible
75. Reasonable Personal Use Consistent With Conventional Ethical Standards
76. Prohibition Against Non-Approved System Uses
77. Internet Use For Personal Purposes Prohibited
78. Personal Use Of Company X Internet Facilities Only On Personal Time
79. Personal Use Time Limit And Prohibited Activities
80. Permissible Uses Of Company X Information
81. Granting User-IDs To Outsiders
82. Third Party Access To Company X Systems Requires Signed Contract
83. When Established, Outsider User-IDs Must Have Defined Expiration Date
84. Information Systems Access Privileges Terminate When Workers Leave
85. Time Limits For User-IDs And File Retention Period After Expiration
86. Disclaimer Of Responsibility For Damage To Data And Programs
87. Gaining Unauthorized Access Via Company X Information Systems
88. Where To Use Computer System Access Controls
89. Personal Digital Assistant Use For Corporate Business Information
90. No Sensitive Information On Personal Digital Assistants, Handhelds, Etc.
91. All Software Must Be Regulated By Access Control Systems Software

92. Systems Requiring Password-Based Access Control Package
93. Privilege Restriction Based On The Need-To-Know
94. Privilege Restriction Based On The Need-To-Withhold
95. Specific Information Access Policies Must Be Prepared
96. Information Ownership Must Be Assigned
97. No Read Up Permissions To Access Sensitive Information
98. No Write Down Permissions To Access Sensitive Information
99. Age Verification Required Prior To Adult Material Access
100. User-To-User Separation Of Activities And Data
101. Default File Permissions For Networked Systems
102. Existence Of User Access Capabilities Does Not Imply Usage Permission
103. User-IDs Must Each Uniquely Identify A Single User
104. Generic User-IDs Based On Job Function Prohibited
105. Re-Use Of Unique User-IDs Prohibited
106. Naming Standard For A Single User-ID Used On All Platforms
107. Separate User-IDs For Internet Connected & Internal Network Systems
108. Exclusive Personal Use Of Access Codes Such As User-IDs & Credit Cards
109. Positive Identification Required For Initiation of Computer Transactions
110. Support For Special Privileged Type Of Users
111. Restriction Of Special System Privileges
112. Restricted Remote Administration Of Internet-Connected Computers
113. Limited Number Of Privileged User-IDs
114. Two User-IDs Required For All Systems Administrators
115. Logging And Reporting On Privileged User-ID Activity
116. Default User Privileges And Need for Explicit Written Approvals
117. Approvals Required For User-ID Creation And Privilege Assignment
118. Restriction Of Third Party Dial-Up Privileges
119. Time Dependent Access Control
120. Dormant User-IDs And Automatic Privilege Revocations
121. Default To Denial Of Access Control Privileges
122. Trusted Host Relationships Must Not Be Established Without Permission
123. Unbecoming Conduct And The Revocation Of Access Privileges
124. End-User Access To Operating System Commands
125. Limiting End-User Knowledge Of System Capabilities And Commands
126. Termination Of User Processes Or Sessions And Removal Of User Files
127. Prohibition Against Testing Information System Controls
128. Prohibition Against Exploiting Systems Security Vulnerabilities
129. Recipient Screening For Distribution Of Powerful Security Tools
130. Removal Of Vulnerability Identification Software When Not In Use
131. Limitation Of Functionality For Powerful Information Systems Tools
132. Privileges For Modification Of Production Business Information
133. Controlled Process For Modification Of Production Business Information
134. Business Production Information Updates By Non-Production Staff
135. Database Updates Must Be Made Only Through Established Channels
136. Access Control Required For All Multi-User Production Applications
137. Technical Staff Privileges And Production System Change Control
138. Signed Forms Required For Issuance Of User-ID
139. Multi-Platform Systems Parameter Naming Conventions
140. Administrative Security Management For All Networked Computers
141. Tools For Determining Security Status of System
142. Periodic Review And Reauthorization Of User Access Privileges
143. Human Resources Sends Worker Status Changes To System Administrators
144. Reporting Changes In User Duties To Systems Security Administration
145. Users Must Inform Systems Administration About Status Changes

146. Maintenance Of Master User-ID And Privilege Database
147. Transfer Of Information Custodian Duties After Employee Terminations
148. Schedule For Deletion Of Files Following Worker Termination
149. Logs Required On Application Systems Handling Sensitive Information
150. Keystroke Logs Required For All Production System Privileged User-IDs
151. Inclusion Of Security Relevant Events In System Logs
152. Computer System Logs Must Support Audits
153. Accountability And Traceability For All Privileged System Commands
154. Contents Of Logs For Systems Running Production Applications
155. All Attempted System Log-Ins, Successful Or Not, Must Be Logged
156. Log-In Passwords Must Not Be Logged Unless In Encrypted Form
157. Required Retention Period Of Logs
158. Daily Removal Of Logs From Internet-Accessible Computers
159. Logs Of User-Initiated Security Relevant Activities
160. Retention Of Access Control Privilege Logs
161. Reconstructibility Of Changes To Production Information
162. Cryptographic Checksums To Detect Modifications Of System Logs
163. Information To Capture When Computer Crime Or Abuse Is Suspected
164. Logs Required For Rapid Resumption Of Production System Activities
165. Systems Architecture For Logging Activities
166. Clock Synchronization For Accurate Logging Of Events On Network
167. Logs Of All Inbound And Outbound Faxes
168. Resistance Of Logs Against Deactivation, Modification, Or Deletion
169. Writing Logs To WORM Storage Media Prevents Alteration
170. Externally Accessible Systems Must Employ Remotely Mirrored Logs
171. Digital Signatures & Sequence Numbers Required For System Logs
172. System Log Rotation & Archive Process For High Security Systems
173. Persons Authorized To View Logs
174. Regular And Prompt Review Of System Logs
175. Notification Of Users About Logging Of Security Violations
176. Users Must Not Attempt To Eradicate Computer Virus
177. Virus Eradication Requires Support Of Systems Administrator
178. Prohibition Against Down-Loading Software From Third Party Systems
179. Testing For Viruses Prior To Use On Company X Systems
180. Testing For Viruses On A Stand-Alone Non-Production Machine
181. All Outbound Software And Executable Files Must Be Virus Free
182. Virus Checking At Firewalls, Servers, And Desktop Machines
183. At Least Two Virus Screening Software Packages Must Be Employed
184. Virus Checking Decal Required For All Externally-Supplied Floppy Disks
185. Required Process For Checking Software Down-Loaded From Internet
186. System Integrity Checking Programs Required For Personal Computers
187. Approved Virus Checking Programs Required On PCs And LAN Servers
188. Current Virus Software Required For Certain Worker-Owned Computers
189. Material Must Be Decrypted Before Checking For Viruses
190. Write Protection For Software On Micros And Workstations
191. Initial Backup Copies Of Microcomputer Software
192. Testing Of Software And Information Prior To Third Party Distribution
193. Prohibition Against Programs Consuming Excessive System Resources
194. All User Involvement With Computer Viruses Prohibited
195. Security Requirements Identification Prior To Development/Acquisition
196. Developers Embed Security In Systems If Commercial Solution Exists
197. Compliance With Organizational Systems Development Conventions
198. Software Testing With Sanitized Rather Than Production Information
199. Software Developed In-House--Notice Of Failure To Properly Operate

200. Software Developed In-House--Notice When No Action Taken
201. Formal Specifications Required For Software Developed In-House
202. Removal Of All Unauthorized Access Paths In Production Software
203. Use Of Mature Development Tools And Techniques
204. Use Of Software Tools & Languages With Unproven Security Attributes
205. Use Of Higher Level Programming Languages
206. Re-Usability Of Software Developed In-House
207. Naming Convention For Production Files
208. Special Labeling For All Non-Production Business Transactions
209. Documentation Required For All Production Business Systems
210. Permissible Functionality Of Systems Developed In-House
211. Immediate System Interruption If Human Beings Are Jeopardized
212. Restricted Use Of Diagnostic Test Hardware And Software
213. Systems Utilities Resident On Production System Storage Media
214. Restricted And Monitored Use Of Systems Software Utilities
215. External Network Interfaces Must Be Approved By Information Security
216. Access To Production Business Information For System Testing
217. Separation Between Production And Development Environments
218. Separation Between Programming And Testing Environments
219. Development Staff Access To Production Application Information
220. System Developers Must Not Perform Formal Testing
221. Special Sign-Off Required For Projects Involving Human Safety Issues
222. Designers & Developers Must Notify Management Of Potential Problems
223. Complaints Regarding Errors & Security Problems Traced To Developers
224. Formal Change Control Procedure Required For All Production Systems
225. Production System Changes Must Be Consistent With Security Architecture
226. User Installation Of Software On Personal Computers Is Prohibited
227. Users Prohibited From Upgrading Software For Personal Computers
228. Access Controls Defined Prior To Cut-Over To Production Operation
229. Disabling Unnecessary Software Features At Installation Time
230. Disabling Privileged User-IDs Prior To Operating System Installation
231. Removal Of Unnecessary Systems Software At Installation Time
232. When To Prepare Production Systems Change Documentation
233. Training & Operating Documentation Required For Production Systems
234. Loading External Programs Onto Network-Connected Computers
235. Use Of Push Background Updates For Software Requires Approval
236. Testing Externally-Provided Software Prior To Use
237. Free Software May Not Be Used For Production Applications
238. Automatic Detection Of End-User Application Programs
239. Critical Business Logic Must Not Reside On Desktop Computers
240. Control Over Movement Of Software From Development To Production
241. Vendor Provided Systems Software Must Go Through Change Control
242. Review And Recompilation Required Before Movement To Production
243. Formal Change Control Process Required For Business Applications
244. Separate Approval Required For Production System Controls
245. Approvals Required For Production Multi-User Applications
246. Approval For End-User Production System Development Efforts
247. Approval Required For Changes To Production Operating Systems
248. Periodic Review Of Production Operating System Changes
249. Prohibition Against Trap Doors To Circumvent Access Controls
250. Prompt Implementation Of Security Problem Fix Software, Scripts, Etc.
251. Systems Software & Applications Software At Most Recent Stable Levels
252. Special Approval Required For Production Software Package Changes
253. Software Maintenance With Source Rather Than Object Code

254. Timing Of Changes To Company X Production Information Systems
255. Rapid Roll-Back To Prior Versions Of Production Software
256. Production Software Conversion Contingency Plans
257. When Information Security Impact Statements Are Required
258. Security Impact Statements For New Or Modified Business Applications
259. Vendor-Provided Written Integrity Statements
260. Packaged Software And Unilateral Deactivation By Third Party Vendor
261. Escrow For Software Used In Critical Business Activities
262. Software In Escrow Must Be Verified By Independent Third Party
263. Form Of Company X Software Distributed To Third Parties
264. Third Party Agreements On Usage Of Company X Software
265. Release Of Systems Documentation To Third Parties
266. Software Features & Functions Must Be Fully Revealed In Documentation
267. Access To Company X Letterhead, Check Stock, And Other Forms
268. Smoking, Eating And Drinking In The Computer Machine Room
269. Production Computer Systems Must Be Physically Located In Data Center
270. Computer Operator Logs Required For Multi-User Production Systems
271. Computer Operator Logs Must Be Periodically Reviewed
272. Information As An Important Company X Asset
273. Assignment Of Patent, Copyright, And Other Intellectual Property Rights
274. Property Rights To Computer Programs And Documentation
275. Legal Ownership Of Information Systems Files And Messages
276. Recovery Of Computer-Related Property Belonging To Company X
277. Attribution Of Sources For Information
278. Labelling For Paternity Rights To Intellectual Property
279. Copyright Notices On Computer Programs And Documentation
280. Workers May Make Multiple Copies Only If Reasonable And Customary
281. Periodic Review Of Software Licensing Agreements
282. Systems Acquisition And Evidence Of Software Licenses
283. Registration Of Information Systems Products With Vendors
284. Ordering Authorized Copies Of Software Needed For Business Activities
285. When Making Additional Copies Of Software Is Permissible
286. Removal Of Unauthorized Copyrighted Information And Software
287. Default Copyright Protection For Information Posted To Internet
288. Copying, Transferring, Or Disclosing Software Prohibited
289. Responsibility For Making Unauthorized Software And Data Copies
290. Tools Used To Break Systems Security Prohibited
291. Participation In Pirated Software Bulletin Boards & Related Internet Sites
292. Handling Of Third Party Confidential And Proprietary Information
293. Use Of Company X Information For Non-Business Purposes
294. Transfer Of Company X Information To Third Parties
295. Software Or Data Exchanges With Third Parties Require Agreements
296. Designation Of Software And Systems As Competitive Information
297. Monitoring Internet For Use Of Trademark And Copyrighted Materials
298. Internet Use Of Other Organization's Trademarks And Service Marks
299. Prohibition Against Any Third Party Use Of Company X's Name
300. Every Public Written Use Of Company X's Name Requires Approval
301. Loss Of Critical Knowledge And Employees Flying On Same Airplane
302. Right Of Management To Examine Data Stored On Company X Systems
303. Pretext Requests Used To Test Both Customer Service And Security Policies
304. Areas Where Electronic Monitoring Of Workers May Be Used
305. Disclosure Of Information On Company X Systems To Law Enforcement
306. Privacy Rights Waived When Collecting Bills Or Enforcing Contracts
307. Disclosures Of Private Information Without Data Subject Consent

308. Affected Individuals Notified About Material Changes In Privacy Policy
309. Privacy Policy Changes Require Posting Of Clear Differences Summary
310. Privacy Policy Pertains To All Types Of Interactions With Customers
311. Permissible Information To Collect From Prospective Employees
312. Collection Of Private Information Banned Except By Permission
313. Personal Information Necessary For Proper Functioning Of Business
314. Collecting Information About Expressions Of First Amendment Rights
315. Need To Collect Private Information Must First Be Justified
316. Private Data Collection Only If Lawful And Necessary
317. Surreptitious Collection Of Customer Private Data Prohibited
318. Personally-Identifiable Information Collection Requires Robust Notice
319. Childrens' Personal Information Gathering Needs Parental Consent
320. Personal Information Collection Permissible But Distribution Prohibited
321. Permissible Information To Collect From Customers
322. Least Intrusive Methods Available To Gather Private Information
323. Involuntary Capture Of Personal Biometric Information Prohibited
324. Prohibited Transfer Of Personal Biometric Data To Third Parties
325. Personal Data Gathering Points And Corporate Privacy Policy Posting
326. Name Of Organization Collecting Private Information Must Be Disclosed
327. Full Explanation Why Private Information Is Required
328. Performance Monitoring Information And Relevance To The Job
329. Privacy Expectations And Information Stored On Company X Systems
330. Employee Permission Required Before Monitoring Is Used
331. No Blanket Monitoring Of Employee Communications
332. Management Attention To Employee Off-the-Job Behavior
333. Notifying Subjects Of Existing Monitoring Systems
334. All User Monitoring Reported To User's Manager And Logged
335. Managers Receive Logs And Determine Appropriate Internet Usage
336. No Internet Customer Usage Profiles Will Be Compiled
337. Monitoring Or Recording Telephone Conversations
338. Group Monitoring Rather Than Individual Monitoring
339. Monitoring And Recording Activity In An Anonymous Fashion
340. Timing Of Notification About Electronic Performance Monitoring
341. Existence Of Secret Systems Containing Personnel Records
342. Guaranteed Access To Personal Information Held In Company X Records
343. Periodic Distribution Of Employee Personnel Records
344. Prospective Employees Given Opportunity To Decline Credit Checks
345. Disclosure Of Private Information To Third Parties
346. Transfer Of Private Data Only To Organizations With Sufficient Controls
347. Keeping Records Of All Third Parties Receiving Private Information
348. Transfer Of Private Information To Other Countries Requires Approval
349. Subjects Given Opportunity To Block Private Information Disclosures
350. Disclosure Of Worker Names, Titles, And Other Contact Particulars
351. Disclosure Of Reason For Termination Of An Employee
352. Disclosure Of Worker Change Of Status Information
353. Granting Workers Access To Disclosures Of Private Data Records
354. Privacy Of Individual Worker Performance Information
355. Confidentiality Of Internal Investigations Information
356. Mandatory Disclosure Of Worker Health And Safety Information
357. Use Of Tests To Determine Lifestyle, Political, & Religious Information
358. Privacy Of Personal Files Stored On Computers And In Desks
359. Keeping Records Of Private Information Disclosed To Third Parties
360. Protection Of The Privacy Of Customer Information
361. Disclosure Of Customer Information Including Customer Identity

362. Customer Right To Know Third Parties Receiving His Or Her Data
363. Customer Objection Opportunity For Subpoena Record Requests
364. Privacy Policy Considered Contract Made At Time Information Provided
365. Privacy Of Correspondent Email Addresses And Telephone Numbers
366. Telephone Disclosures Require Positive Caller Identification
367. No Discussions Of Private Information In Public Places
368. Customer Requests For Anonymity On Company X Systems
369. Public Acknowledgement Of Or Reference To Famous Customers
370. Distribution Of Statistical Information About Customer Records
371. Disclosure Of Computer Logs Reflecting Customer Activities
372. Deletion Of Log Information About Customer Activities
373. Monitoring Of Electronic Mail Messages
374. Worker Rights To Read Third Party Electronic Mail Messages
375. Employee Observance Of Company X's Right To Privacy
376. Informed Consent Required For Questionable System Actions
377. Record Creators Decide Whether Record Subjects May View Records
378. Disclosure Of Intended Uses Of Personal Information Prior To Collection
379. Customers Given Opportunity To Decide To Receive Direct Mail
380. Placement Of Internet Advertising Only With Firms Valuing Privacy
381. Making Copies Of Information Appearing In One's Personnel File
382. Conditions Under Which Employees May Examine Their Files
383. Employee Right To Add Explanatory Statement To Personnel File
384. Allegedly Incorrect Information To Be Corrected Or Labeled As Disputed
385. Required Efforts To Ensure Integrity Of All Personal Records
386. Documented Procedures Required For Personal Record Handling Activities
387. Required Efforts To Ensure Personal Records Are Used Only As Intended
388. Use Of Personal Information For New Purposes
389. Linking Anonymous Information With Personally-Identifiable Information
390. Use And Disclosure Of Personal Information About Customers
391. Customer's Right-To-Know Nature Of Personal Information
392. Resale Or Subsequent Dissemination Of Customer Contact Information
393. Distribution Of Unsolicited Company X Marketing Materials
394. Major Systems Changes And Privacy Impact Review Committee
395. Source And Purpose Of Cookies And Web Bugs Must Be Revealed
396. Compelling Need Required Prior To Usage Of Cookies Or Web Bugs
397. No Embedded Secret Personal Identifiers Or Serial Numbers
398. Personal Identifiers Must Not Appear On Publicly-Accessible Locations
399. Severing Link Between Identifying Information And Research Data
400. Retaining Personal Information Only As Long As Needed For Business
401. No Links Between Private Information And Other Information Types
402. Routine Destruction Of Transaction Logs Prevents Profile Compilation
403. Subjects Given Opportunity To Opt-Out Of Private Data Systems
404. All Marketing Communications Must Provide An Opt-Out Opportunity
405. Subjects Must Opt-In To Be Included In Systems Handling Private Data
406. Immediate Action For Individuals Requesting Database Removal
407. Subjects May Block Their Private Data From Being Used
408. Subjects Must Approve New Personal Data Uses After Merger/Acquisition
409. Business Structure Changes Do Not Permit Transfer Of Private Data
410. Maintenance Of Index To Databases Containing Private Information
411. Denial Of Benefits Due To Refusal To Provide Unnecessary Information
412. Confidentiality Agreements Required For All Company X Workers
413. Chain Of Trust Agreements Required For Private & Sensitive Information
414. Confidentiality Agreements Required For Office Machine Repair Staff
415. Changes In Employment Require Review Of Confidentiality Agreements

416. Default Restrictions On Dissemination Of Company X Information
417. Notification Of Suspected Loss Or Disclosure Of Sensitive Information
418. Revealing Information Systems Technical Details To Job Applicants
419. Disclosure Of Information System Control Specifics To Third Parties
420. Material Financial Information Disclosures To Selected Parties
421. Disclosure Of Information About Information System Vulnerabilities
422. Vulnerability Information Detail Level In Press Releases Must Be Low
423. Disclosure Of System Vulnerability Exploitation And Victim Data
424. Disclosure Of System Penetration Software Source Code And Analysis
425. Security Mechanisms Must Not Be Compromised for Customers
426. Presentation Of Low-Profile And Secure Image
427. Information Access Control Systems And The Mosaic Theory
428. Limitations On Third Party Collection Of Pricing Information
429. Identity Theft Prevention By Restricting Access To Personal Information
430. Data Warehouse Access Restricted To Top And Middle Management
431. Dithering To Conceal True Nature Of Signal
432. Right To Block, Conceal, Deny, Or Discontinue Service At Any Time
433. Information With Multiple Sensitivity Classifications On Single System
434. Choosing Computer Storage Media Data Classifications
435. Four Category Data Classification Scheme
436. Three Category Data Classification Scheme
437. Descriptive Prefixes For Data Classification Categories
438. Trade Secrets Specifically Identified Prior To Disclosure
439. Company X Trade Secrets Must Named & Described On Intranet Page
440. Chief Legal Counsel Is Sole Person To Declare Information A Trade Secret
441. Limited Data Classification System Labelling Requirements
442. Information Treated As Secret Whenever Sensitivity Label Unknown
443. Department Specific Data Classification Labels Permissible
444. Responsibility For Assigning Data Classification System Labels
445. Responsibility For Labelling Externally-Provided Information
446. Creator Must Select Data Classification Label For New Files & Messages
447. Comprehensive Data Classification System Labelling Requirements
448. Location On The Page Of Hardcopy Sensitivity Labels
449. Bound Hardcopy Material And Sensitivity Labels
450. Labelling & Presentation Of Sensitive Information To Computer Users
451. Use Of Labels Throughout Sensitive Information's Life Cycle
452. Maintaining, Propagating, And Reestablishing Data Classification Labels
453. Labels For Collections Of Information With Various Sensitivities
454. New Label After Storage Media Exposure To Secret Data Or Applications
455. User-Generated Classification Labels Do Not Bind Company X
456. Permission Required When Making Copies Of Sensitive Information
457. Tracking Copies Of Sensitive Information
458. Destruction Of Intermediate Products Containing Sensitive Information
459. Destruction Of Waste Copies Of Sensitive Information
460. Attended Operation Required When Printing Sensitive Information
461. Page Numbering and Accountability for Sensitive Information
462. Third Party Non-Disclosure Agreements And Sensitive Information
463. Disclosure Of Third Party Information In Possession Of Company X
464. Private And Confidential Information Sent By Internal Or External Mail
465. Secret Information Sent By Internal Or External Mail
466. Two Envelopes Required For Sensitive Information Sent By Mail
467. Permissible Methods For Transmitting Secret Hardcopy Information
468. Special Paper Preventing Copying Of Sensitive Documents
469. Secret Information May Only Be Printed On Paper Indicating Originals

470. Delivery Of Sensitive Computer Output To Intended Recipients
471. Delivery Via Courier Of Sensitive Hardcopy Information
472. Acknowledgement Required For Deliveries Of Secret Information
473. Immediate Written Acknowledgment Of Receipt For Secret Information
474. Log Book Reflecting Movement Of Secret Documents
475. Sequence Numbers For Secret Documents
476. Those With Custody Of Sensitive Information Must Restrict Access
477. Prior Notice And Attended Operation For Sensitive Information Faxing
478. Faxing Sensitive Information Requires Human Presence
479. Faxing Sensitive Information Via Untrusted Third Parties
480. Cover Sheet Receipt Confirmation Before Faxing Sensitive Information
481. When Faxing Sensitive Information Is Permissible
482. Destination Physical Security For Sensitive Information Faxing
483. Encryption Required For Sending Secret Information By Fax
484. Password Required For Sending Secret Information By Fax
485. Fax Cover Sheet Must Contain Restricted Dissemination Notice
486. Binding Signatures Must Be Sent By Traditional Paper Means
487. Discussion Of Secret Information And Use Of Speaker Phones
488. Guarded Terms For Telephone Discussions Of Sensitive Information
489. Use Of Cordless Or Cellular Telephones For Secret Discussions
490. Secret Discussions On Wireless Microphones And Radio Networks
491. Internet Telephone Facilities May Not Be Used For Secret Discussions
492. Secondary Dissemination Of Secret Information
493. Travelling On Public Transportation With Secret Information
494. Exposure Of Sensitive Information In Public Places
495. Secret Information Discussions In Company X Administrative Areas
496. Storing Secret Information On Transportable Computers
497. Controls For Transportable Computers With Sensitive Information
498. Transportable Computers Must Be Hand Luggage on Airplanes
499. Taking Secret Information Into A Foreign Country
500. Permission Required To Take Secret Information Into Foreign Country
501. Floppy Disk Input/Output Encryption Drivers Prevent Disclosure
502. Removal Of Sensitive Information From Company X Premises
503. Secret Information Must Not Leave Company X Offices In Any Form
504. Log for Sensitive Information Removed From Company X Premises
505. Handling Hardcopy Sensitive Information Off Company X Premises
506. Transfer Of Sensitive Information To Third Parties On Computer Media
507. Certificate Of Destruction Rather Than Return Of Storage Media
508. Confidentiality Of Company X Computer Related Documentation
509. Secret Information Sent By Electronic Mail
510. Diskless Workstations Must Be Used By R&D Department Workers
511. Information Systems Unsuitable For Time-Sensitive Information
512. Use Of Hard-Disk Drives For Storage Of Sensitive Information
513. Commingling Of Sensitive And Non-Sensitive Information
514. Clean Desks And Working Areas
515. Traditional Clean Desk Policy
516. Securing Sensitive Information In Unattended Rooms
517. Storage Of Sensitive Information On Personal Computers
518. Storage Of Sensitive Information When Not In Use
519. Retention Period Required For All Sensitive Information
520. Date For Declassification Must Be Specified If Known
521. Accelerated Declassification And Downgrading Of Sensitive Information
522. Extension Of Declassification Or Downgrading Date
523. Automatic Schedule For Downgrading Company X Information

524. Annual Declassification Review For Sensitive Information
525. Declassification Of Sensitive Information Required As Soon As Practical
526. Sensitive Information Destruction/Concealment Before Servicing Done
527. Release Of Computer Storage Media Prior To Degaussing/Zeroizing
528. Destruction Of Sensitive Information On Computer Storage Media
529. Zeroization Required For Erasure Of Sensitive Information
530. Approved Methods For Hardcopy Sensitive Information Disposal
531. Strip Shredders Must Not Be Used For Destruction Of Sensitive Information
532. Areas Containing Sensitive Information Must Have Shredders
533. Use Of Secure Containers For All But Secret Information Disposal
534. Security Staff Must Follow Information Destruction Instructions
535. Sensitive Information Destruction Must Follow Specified Procedures
536. Persons Authorized To Destroy Sensitive Company X Information
537. Use Of Metal Boxes To Hold Sensitive Information To Be Destroyed
538. Destruction Of Materials Used In Handling Sensitive Information
539. Approval Required Before Access To Sensitive Or Valuable Information
540. Access To Secret Information Granted On Individual (Not Group) Basis
541. Granting System Privileges By Chain Of Authority Delegation
542. Confidentiality Agreements And Disclosures Of Sensitive Information
543. Specific Handling Instructions For Recipients Of Sensitive Information
544. Requests For Company X Information Referred To Public Relations
545. Prohibition Against Disclosing Customer Projects, Strategies, Etc.
546. Marketing Information Must Never Be Shared With Competitors
547. Information Released To The Public Must Have Single Official Source
548. Approval Required Prior To Release Of Company X Information
549. Public Representations About Future Earnings Or New Product Prospects
550. Waiting Period Prior To External Disclosure Of Requested Information
551. Phased Public Release Of Controversial Sensitive Information
552. Approval For Help Wanted Ads And Disclosure Of Sensitive Material
553. Established Procedure For Review Of Information Released To Public
554. Prior Review For Speeches, Presentations, Technical Papers, Etc.
555. Conditions For Acceptance Of Third Party Sensitive Information
556. Signing Third Party Confidentiality Agreements Without Approval
557. Sensitive Information Access For Temporaries And Consultants
558. Workers Have Right To Know All Workplace Hazards
559. Nature Of Labels On Hazardous Products And Services
560. Refrain From Pressuring Employees Who Worked At Competitors
561. Disclosure Of Privacy Related Information Security Policies & Procedures
562. Uninvited Attendees At Meetings Covering Secret Information
563. Third Party Visitor Meetings In Enclosed Conference Rooms
564. Oral Disclosure Of Confidential Information In Meetings
565. Black Boards And White Boards Must Be Erased After Meetings
566. Erasure Of Sensitive Information On Black Boards And White Boards
567. Nature And Location Of Company X Information Is Confidential
568. Information Security Policies & Procedures Are For Internal Use Only
569. Location Of Data Processing Centers Considered Confidential
570. Browsing On Company X Systems And Networks Prohibited
571. Authorized Systems Administrator Examination Of Private User Files
572. Power Down Required For Systems Processing Sensitive Information
573. Covering Sensitive Information When Interrupted At Work
574. Never Lend Computers Containing Sensitive Information To Others
575. Locking File Cabinets Must Be Provided To And Used By All Workers
576. Prohibited Trading Dates For Employee Stock Transactions
577. Dictation Machines And Tape Recorders For Sensitive Information

578. Periodic Sweeps For Bugging, Interception, And Recording Equipment
579. Specific Quantitative Goal For System Availability
580. Limitation Of User Abilities To Delay Or Interrupt Service
581. Establishment And Use Of Control Override Facilities
582. Management Definition Of Circumstances For Use Of Control Overrides
583. Generation And Review Of Logs Showing Use Of Override Facilities
584. Computing Environment Supporting Equipment Required
585. Power Conditioning Equipment Required For All Microcomputers
586. Static Electricity Protection Equipment And Local Conditions
587. Dispersion Of Computer And Communication Systems
588. Web And Commerce Servers Must Not Store Critical Information
589. Avoidance Of Communication Network Central Point Of Failure
590. Diverse Long Distance Network Routing Required
591. Compliance With Standards Required For Emergency/Disaster Support
592. Framework For Segmenting Information Resources By Recovery Priority
593. Annual Criticality Rating For Multi-User Applications
594. Five Category Application Criticality Classification Scheme
595. Preparation And Maintenance Of Computer Emergency Response Plans
596. Continuous Computer Center Staffing For Prompt Problem Resolution
597. Organization/Maintenance Of Computer Emergency Response Team
598. Regular Simulated Incidents To Test Computer Emergency Response Team
599. Required Actions Following Suspected System Intrusion
600. Operations Staff Must Have Documented Intrusion Response Procedure
601. Regular Monitoring Of Information Security Vulnerability Advisories
602. Information Security Alert System
603. Users Must Not Distribute Information About System Vulnerabilities
604. Users Must Notify Help Desk About All Production System Problems
605. Notify Management Of Conditions That May Disrupt Work
606. Expected Employee Assistance During Business Restoration
607. Inventory Of Key Technical Jobs And Individuals Who Fill Them
608. Cross Training For Staff In Critical Technical Jobs
609. Preparation And Maintenance Of Computer Disaster Recovery Plans
610. Preparation And Maintenance Of Business Contingency Plans
611. Business And Computer Continuity Planning Process
612. Reversion To Manual Procedures Where Cost-Effectively Possible
613. Annual Inventory Of Information Systems Hardware, Software, Etc.
614. Equipment Custodians Must Control Inventory With Serial Numbers
615. Annual Determination Level Of Disaster/Emergency Support Levels
616. Computer And Communications System Contingency Plan Testing
617. Preventive Maintenance On Computer And Communication Systems
618. Information Systems Equipment Maintenance Requirements
619. Internet Domain Name Registration Payments Must Be Confirmed
620. Contact Numbers For Information Systems Department Staff
621. Access Control For End-User File Restoration Processes
622. What Data To Backup And Minimum Backup Frequency
623. Periodic And Supplementary Backups Required For Portable Computers
624. Do Not Use Hard Drives On Public Access Computers For Backup
625. Encrypting Backup Media Stored Off-Site
626. Two Copies Of Sensitive, Critical, Or Valuable Information
627. Two Copies Of Critical Company X Records Stored Off-Site
628. Management Review Of End-User Backup Process
629. Specification Of Backup Process And Frequency
630. Automatic Backup To Local Area Network Server
631. Users Notified That All Data Is Routinely Backed-Up

632. Make At Least One Copy of Critical Backed-Up Files Prior To Use
633. Production Batch Processing Only If Pre-Processing Backup Is Complete
634. Annual Audits To Determine Whether Production Backup Is Performed
635. Off-Site Storage Of Backup Media
636. Backup Media Stored In Separate Fire Zones From Originating Machine
637. Backup Media Storage Rooms, Vaults, & Cabinets Must Be Kept Locked
638. Archival Storage Of Every Version Of Internet Web & Commerce Sites
639. Quarterly Archival Backups Required For All Critical Information
640. Department Managers Must Identify Vital Records
641. Directory Of Information Held In Archival Storage
642. Acceptable Archival Storage Data Media
643. Regular Testing Of Archival Storage Data Media
644. Regular Testing Of Used Data Media Employed For Archival Storage
645. Preservation Of Data Held In Archival Storage
646. Minimum Information Retention Period
647. Definition Of Archival Storage Data Retention Schedule
648. Responsibility For Archival Storage Data Retention Schedule
649. Business Source Document Data Retention Requirements
650. Business Source Document Data Retention Period
651. Regular Purging Of Information Which Is No Longer Needed
652. Procedure For Release Of Used Equipment And Media To Third Parties
653. Information Destruction And Information Systems Equipment Disposal
654. Destruction Of Records Or Information Requires Management Approval
655. Record Destruction Prohibited Unless Authorized By List Or Schedule
656. Data Destruction Process Placed On Hold In Response To Discovery
657. Management Must Be Notified Of Information Integrity Attributes
658. Management Notification Of Information Integrity Controls Failure
659. Calculation Recipients Must Receive Information To Verify Correctness
660. Nature Of Information Modifications Must Be Disclosed
661. Source And Date Labels Required For Major Decision Input
662. Suppression Or Labelling Of Incomplete Or Obsolete Information
663. Production Input Transactions Must Have Sequence Numbers
664. Authorization Required For All Production System Input Transactions
665. Changes To Sensitive, Critical, Or Valuable Information
666. Input Data Validation And Rejected Item Handling
667. Email & Regular Mail Address Change Confirmed Via Previous Address
668. Double Keying Required For All Amounts Over $1,000
669. Line Numbering Required For Critical Free-Form Text Messages
670. Originator Of Transactions Must Be Clearly Identified
671. Data Warehouse Input Requires Source, Classification, And Other Labels
672. Official Documents Prepared By Hand Must Exclusively Use Ink
673. Review For Important Computer Analyses Done By Individuals
674. Controls For Data Used To Arrive At Decisions Involving $100,000
675. Acceptable Risk Of Undetected Information Alteration
676. Altered Photographs Must Be So Labeled
677. Handling Of Rejected Input Transactions Via Suspense Files
678. Time For Problem Resolution Of Items In Suspense Files
679. Input Validation Procedures For Rejected Or Suspended Input
680. Personal Information Changed Only After Correct Prior Values Provided
681. Authorization For Changes To Production Data And Programs
682. All Production Transactions Must Be Authorized By Management
683. Review Reasonableness And Accuracy Of Changes To Internal Records
684. Required Actions After Errors In Records Are Detected
685. Standard Control Procedures For Correcting Business Records

686. Cellular Phones Must Not Be Used Anywhere In Data Center
687. Truthful Representations By Company X Employees
688. Misrepresentation Of Identity On Electronic Communication Systems
689. Consistent Way Of Representing Employee Contact Information
690. Need For Cross-Validation Of Important Information
691. All Public Representations Must Be Cleared Through Public Relations
692. Right To Free Speech Does Not Apply To Company X Systems
693. Right To Censor Data On Organizational Systems
694. New Information Types Must Be Reflected In Corporate Data Dictionary
695. Right To Remove Offensive Material Without Warning
696. No Responsibility For Monitoring Content Of Information Systems
697. Prohibited Uses Of Company X Computer & Communication Facilities
698. Disclaimer Of Responsibility Or Liability For Message Contents
699. Comments On Systems Do Not Necessarily Reflect Company X Positions
700. Warnings Required If Recipients Might Be Offended Or Upset
701. All Information Posted To Internet Must Have Standard Content Labels
702. Network Message Protection Services Not Provided
703. Prohibition Against Sexual, Ethnic, And Racial Harassment
704. Restricted Behavior For Outbound Internet Communications
705. Internal Network Addresses Must Not Be Publicly Released
706. Access Control Packages Required For Computers On The Network
707. Access Control Packages For Network-Connected Computers
708. Large Networks Must Be Divided Into Separate Domains
709. Internet Connected Machines Must Have Intrusion Detection Systems
710. Permissible Internet Access Without Firewalls
711. All Internet Web Servers Must Be Firewall Protected
712. Internet Commerce Servers Must Be In Demilitarized Zone (DMZ)
713. Public Servers On Internet Must Be Placed On Separate Subnets
714. Internet Commerce Servers Must Use Digital Certificates & Encryption
715. Dial-Up Connections Must Always Utilize Firewalls
716. Real-Time External Network Connections Require Firewalls
717. Firewalls Must Be Configured So All Services Are Denied Unless Approved
718. Firewalls Must Run On Dedicated Computers
719. Firewall Configuration Change Requires Information Security Approval
720. Internet Connections Require Approved Firewalls
721. Trusted Host Relationships Prohibited For Internet Connected Machines
722. Direct Network Connections With Outside Organizations (Tunnels)
723. Inter-Processor Commands From Outside Locations Prohibited
724. Isolate Systems Containing Secret Information From Network
725. Customers Must Specifically Agree To Receive New/Enhanced Service
726. Prior Approval Required For All Communication Line Changes
727. Prior Approval Required For Set-Up Of Multi-User Systems
728. Prior Approval Required For In-House System Interconnection
729. Separate Subnet Required For Walk-Up Network Connections
730. Unattended Active Network Ports In Public Areas Prohibited
731. Network Ports In Vacant Offices Must Be Promptly Disabled
732. Configuration To Prevent/Detect Unauthorized Network Connections
733. Criteria For Connecting Company X Networks To Third Party Networks
734. Security Requirements For Network-Connected Third Party Systems
735. Approval Required For Internet Connection Establishment
736. Security Criteria A Prerequisite For Intranet Connection
737. Inventory Of Connections To External Networks
738. Standards Of Common Carriers Do Not Apply
739. Participation In Public Networks As Service Provider

740. Formation Of Binding Contracts Via Electronic Systems
741. Conducting Business Over The Internet With Foreign Companies
742. Trading Partner Agreement Required Prior To Use Of EDI
743. Only Designated Employees May Form Contracts Via Email
744. Criteria For Accepting And Acting On Computerized Transactions
745. Multiple Communication Channels For Electronic Offers & Acceptances
746. Internet Customers Must Specifically Agree To Terms & Conditions
747. Encryption Processes Must Not Be Used Unless Previously Approved
748. Use Of Any Encryption Process Requires Prior Written Approval
749. Encryption Utilities With User-Provided Passwords Or Keys Prohibited
750. Compliance With International Trade In Armaments Regulations
751. Secret Data Sent Over Networks Must Be Encrypted
752. Transportation Of Secret Data In Computer-Readable Storage Media
753. Secret Information Must Be Encrypted When Not In Active Use
754. Data Stored On Hard Disk Drives Must Be Encrypted
755. Government Standard Encryption Algorithm & Implementation
756. Deployed Encryption Algorithms Must Be Publicly Evaluated (Open)
757. Disclosure Of Encryption Keys Requires Special Approval
758. Encryption Key Management Systems And Separation Of Duties
759. Initialization Of Encryption Systems Requires Auditor Presence
760. Conditions For Delegation Of Key Management Responsibility
761. Protection Of Digital Certificate Root Keys At Certificate Authorities
762. Separate Communication Channel For Data And Encryption Keys
763. Automated Encryption Key Management Systems Preferred
764. Maximum Life Of Encryption Keys
765. Stated Life For All Encryption Keys
766. Process For Generating Encryption Keys
767. Minimum Length For User-Chosen Encryption Keys
768. Protection For Encryption Key Generation Materials
769. Protection For Plaintext Encryption Master Keys
770. Destruction Of Encryption Key Generation Materials
771. Time Frame For Destruction Of Key Exchange Material
772. Time Period For Protection Of Encryption Keys Used For Confidentiality
773. Time Period For Protection Of Private Digital Signature Keys
774. Never Automatically Backup Private Key Used For Digital Certificates
775. Duplication Of Encryption Keys For Data That Has Been Backed-Up
776. Prevention Of Unauthorized Disclosure Of Encryption Keys
777. Private Key For Digital Certificates Must Be Encrypted Or In Smart Card
778. Transmission Of Cleartext Private Encryption Keys Prohibited
779. Notifying Correspondents About Changes In Public Keys
780. Compromised Keys Revoked Back To Last Time Known To Be Safe
781. Storing Encryption Keys On Same Media As Protected Data Prohibited
782. Backup Encryption Keys Provided To Information Security Officer
783. General Purpose Encryption Systems Must Include Key Escrow
784. Digital Signature And User Authentication Keys Must Not Be Escrowed
785. Explicit Assignment Of Encryption Key Management Functions
786. Deletion Of Readable Data After Encrypted Version Has Been Made
787. Separate Keys For Encryption And Digital Signatures
788. Compression And Encryption Of Sensitive Data To Be Held In Storage
789. Tamper Resistant Hardware Modules For Encryption Processes
790. Insertion Of Computer-Related Contact Numbers In Directories
791. Periodic Changes In Computer Communications Line Numbers
792. Extended User Authentication Systems Required For Dial-Up Lines
793. Dial-Out User Identity Must Be Authenticated Before Session Established

794. Use Of Cable Modems For Business Communications
795. Modems On Workstations Connected To Internal Networks
796. Direct Dial Connections Prohibited Unless Modem Pool Is Used
797. Registry Of All Modem Lines And Related Advance Approval Process
798. Approval Required For Systems Accepting In-Coming Dial-Up Calls
799. Prohibition Against Personal Computer Modems In Autoanswer Mode
800. In-Coming Dial-Up Calls Must Not Be Answered Until Fourth Ring
801. Department Management Responsible For Dial-Up Compliance
802. Maximum Permissible Password Attempts For Dial-Up Users
803. Process For Down-Loading Software From An Internet Mirror Site
804. Controls Needed For Down-Loading Sensitive Company X Information
805. Down-Loading Sensitive Information Prohibited Without Permission
806. Automatic Device Synchronization Allowed Only With Permission
807. Collect And Third-Party Bill-To Calls Prohibited On Voicemail Lines
808. Disable Area Code 900 Calls On All Company X PBXs
809. PBX Defined Calling Areas Must Be Restricted
810. Workers Must Not Return Area Code 900 or Similar Calls
811. Unusual Phone Operation Requests Must Be Denied And Reported
812. Leaving Sensitive Information On Answering Machines
813. Voicemail Passwords Not Subject To Password Construction Standards
814. Heard Voicemail Messages Deleted After One Month In Storage
815. Placement Of Telephone Credit Card Calls Through PBX Systems
816. Use Of Credit Cards On Public Pay Phones
817. PBX - DISA Features Require Fraud Detection Facilities
818. Telephone Book Contains Restricted Information
819. Two-Party Consent For All Speaker Phone Use Or Tape Recording
820. Special Permission Required To Record Video-Conferencing Sessions
821. Use Of Telephones For Personal Purposes
822. Reimbursement For Personal Telephone Calls
823. Maintaining Accurate Records To Prevent Unwanted Telemarketing
824. Orders To Change Internal Records Placed Via Phone
825. Conference Bridge Activated Only When Needed
826. Computer Support Identification Codes
827. Using An Electronic Mail Account Assigned To Another Individual
828. Using Electronic Mail Addresses Other Than Official Company X Addresses
829. Sender Contact Information Must Be Included In Electronic Mail
830. Clearly Identified Source For Electronic Mail Marketing Material
831. Forwarding Electronic Mail To An External Network Address
832. Forwarding Externally Provided Electronic Mail Messages
833. Recording And Retention Of Electronic Mail
834. User Retention Of Electronic Mail Messages For Future Reference
835. Users Must Not Employ Electronic Mail Systems As A Database
836. Periodic Destruction Of Archived Electronic Mail Messages
837. Privacy Expectations And Electronic Mail
838. Treat Electronic Mail As Public Communications
839. Authorization To Read Electronic Mail Messages Of Other Workers
840. Modifying Electronic Mail Message Contents Or Header Prohibited
841. Profane, Obscene Or Derogatory Remarks In Electronic Mail Messages
842. Message Content Restrictions For Company X Information Systems
843. Notification Of Content Monitoring For Electronic Mail Transmissions
844. Reporting Offensive Electronic Mail Messages To Originator And HR
845. Sending Unsolicited Personal Email Messages After Request To Stop
846. Prohibition Against Unsolicited Bulk Email Advertisements (SPAM)
847. Forwarding Is Appropriate Response To Junk Email (SPAM)

848. Sending Large Quantities Of Unsolicited Email (Mail Bombing)
849. Electronic Mail Messages Are Company Records
850. All Electronic Mail Archived And Subject To Supervisory Review
851. Forwarding Copies Of Official Electronic Mail To Archival Records
852. Personal Use Of Electronic Mail Systems
853. Authorization To Issue Broadcasts On Electronic Mail And Voice Mail
854. Authorization To Issue Electronic Mail Or Voice Mail To Groups
855. Placement On Electronic Mail Distribution List Requires Opt-In
856. Prohibition Against Use Of Scanned Hand-Rendered Signatures
857. Prohibition Against Opening Attachments Unless They Were Expected
858. Inbound Attachments To Internet Electronic Mail Prohibited
859. Browser Electronic Mail Features Must Not Be Used For Business Activities
860. Telecommuting Data Entry Operators Must Employ Thin Clients
861. Permissible Equipment For Telecommuting
862. Alteration/Expansion Of Computers Provided By Company X
863. Reporting Of Damage To Company X Off-Site Systems
864. Protection Of Company X Property At Alternative Work Sites
865. Rights To Intellectual Property Developed Off-Site
866. Information Stored In Portable Computers Owned By Company X
867. Telecommuters And Structured Working Environments
868. Use Of Computer Systems Belonging To Workers On Company Property
869. Security Requirements For Work At Home Arrangements
870. Sensitive Information Retention For Destruction Via Approved Method
871. Telecommuter Remote System Information Security Procedures
872. Right To Conduct Inspections Of Telecommuter Environments
873. Training Course Required Prior To Use Of Remote Access Systems
874. Workers Must Keep Portable Computers In Their Possession Or Locked
875. Mobile Computer Alternatives For Protecting Company X Information
876. Access To Internet Requires Completion Of Training Course
877. Internet Privileges Reserved For Those With A Business Need
878. Workers Who Do Not Perform Research Denied Internet Web Access
879. Expiration Of User-IDs On Internet Accessible Computers
880. Company X Blocks Certain Non-Business Internet Web Sites
881. News Feeds From Internet For Company X Related Topics
882. Extended User Authentication Required For In-Bound Internet Users
883. Telnet Connections With Fixed Passwords Over Internet Prohibited
884. Updating Company X Information Through The Internet
885. Disabling Java Within Internet Web Browsers
886. Java Program Execution Prohibited Unless Digital Signature Validated
887. Firewalls Screen Out All Active Content (Java, Active X, Etc.)
888. Internet Access With Company X Computers Must Go Through Firewall
889. Disclaimer Must Accompany All Internet Personal Messages
890. Internet Representations Including Company X Affiliation
891. Internet Discussion Group And Chat Room Participation Forbidden
892. Internet Representations About Company X Products & Services
893. Disclosure Of Personal Contact Information In Public Internet Forums
894. Political Advocacy Statements And Product/Service Endorsements
895. Internet Discussion Group Participation And Release Of Trade Secrets
896. Validating The Identity Of External Parties On The Internet
897. Digital Certificate For All Company X Internet Web And Commerce Sites
898. Workers Must Not Conceal Their Identity When Using The Internet
899. Respecting The Intellectual Property Rights Of Others On The Internet
900. Sending Software And Other Sensitive Information Over The Internet
901. Removal Of Inappropriate Electronic Postings To Public Forums

902. Search Engines To Detect Misleading Web Sites With Similar Names
903. Posting Company X Material On The Internet
904. Establishing New Business Arrangements Via Internet
905. Production In-House Systems May Not Be Directly Internet Connected
906. Publicly-Writable Directories On Company X Computers Cleared Nightly
907. Encryption For Files Left On Anonymous FTP Servers
908. Encryption Of All Payment Information On Internet-Accessible Machines
909. Avoid Tipping-Off Competition Through Public Network Postings
910. Handling Software And Files Down-Loaded From Internet
911. Transferring Files Down-Loaded From Internet To Another Computer
912. Reliability Of Information Down-Loaded from Internet
913. Exchanges Of Information Over The Internet
914. Up-Loading Software To Other Machines Via The Internet
915. User Control Over Information Gathered Via Internet Web Site
916. Acceptance Of Unsolicited Ideas Through The Internet
917. Production Systems Must Not Rely On Free Internet Information
918. Unofficial Web Pages Permitted Only By Contract
919. Responsibility For Content Posted To Personal Web Pages
920. Company X Internet Web Page Management Committee
921. Internet Web Page Design Requirements
922. Management Approval Required For Internet Hot-Link Establishment
923. Internet Hot-Links Must Be Accompanied By Legal Disclaimer
924. Daily Review Of Contents And Hot-Links For Company X Web Page
925. Owner/Department Manager Permission Required For Intranet Postings
926. All Content Posted To Intranet Is Owned By Company X
927. User Checking Of Information Before Posting To The Intranet
928. Staging Area For New/Changed Intranet Content Review And Testing
929. Cleansing Process For Downloaded Internet Content Moved To Intranet
930. Intranet Sites Must Not Use Unapproved Active Content
931. Webmaster Review Of Intranet Web Pages Prior To Posting
932. All Information Posted On Intranet Pages Must Have Designated Owner
933. All Intranet Pages Must Include Information Owner Digital Signatures
934. Secret Information Must Not Be Placed On Internet Or Intranet Systems
935. Intranet Reviewed Quarterly To Confirm Sensitive Data Not Posted
936. Intranet Server Establishment Requires Information Systems Approval
937. Real-Time Connections To Company X Production Systems Via Intranet
938. Approval Required For Access To Internal Systems By Third Parties
939. Forwarding Information On Company X Intranet To Third Parties
940. Direct Transfer To Internet Sites Not Permitted From Intranet
941. Intranet Site Developers Must Use Company X Style Guide
942. Concealing Account Numbers On Customer Receipts
943. Receipt Must Be Provided For Every Purchase Or The Purchase Is Free
944. Payment Information Never Provided In Its Entirety To Customers
945. Disclosure Of Bank Account Numbers
946. Shredding Of Credit Card Receipts And Other Payment Information
947. Encrypt Credit Card Numbers & Other Payment Data When Not Used
948. Credit Card Numbers Must Be Used Only For Payment Processing
949. New Account Opening Requires Robust Identity Authentication
950. Any Demonstrated Fraud Forces Immediate Financial Account Closure
951. Alternative Communications Channel Confirmation For Transactions
952. Daily Balancing And Reconciliation Of Accounting Records
953. Receipt Must Be Confirmed Before Payment Token Will Be Activated
954. All New Workers Must Receive Information Security Policy Pamphlet
955. Information Security Training Required For All Information Workers

956. Information Security Training Only After Workers Pass Other Training
957. Information Security Policy Change Notices Distributed To All Workers
958. Information Security Department Responsible For Related Training
959. Information Security Training Time Required
960. Work According To Information Security Policies & Procedures
961. Attendance At Information Security Class Mandatory
962. Information Security Training Course Prior To Gaining System Access
963. Required Compliance With Corporate Code Of Conduct
964. Signed Acknowledgement For Understanding The Code Of Conduct
965. Required User Training For Production Systems
966. Required Reporting of Information Security Incidents
967. Computer Crime Investigation Information Is Legally Privileged
968. Issuance Of Cease And Desist Messages To Attackers
969. Inclusion Of Information Security Contact Information On Web Site
970. Internal Reporting Of Information Security Violations & Problems
971. Centralized Reporting Of Information Security Problems
972. Interference With Reporting Of Information Security Problems
973. Protection Of Workers Who Report Information Security Problems
974. External Reporting Of Information Security Violations
975. Reporting Problems To Investors & Government Regulatory Authorities
976. Public And Governmental Disclosure Of Computer System Attacks
977. Immediate Reporting Of Suspected Computer Virus Infestation
978. Required Reporting Of Software Malfunctions
979. Reporting Unauthorized Data Changes & Questionable System Use
980. Required Investigation Following Computer Crimes
981. When To Seek Assistance With Unauthorized Access Problems
982. Retention Of Information Security Violation & Problem Information
983. Annual Analysis Of Information Security Violations & Problems
984. Problem Reporting And Management Process
985. Systems Designers & Developers Must Inform Management Of Problems
986. Reliance On New Information Systems Security Products
987. Ease-Of-Use Required For Computer & Communications Security
988. Required User Acceptance Of Information Security Measures
989. Incorporation Of Security Into Systems Development Life Cycle
990. Hardware/Software Procurement Via Standard Purchasing Channels
991. Consistent Protection Of Information Regardless Of Manifestation
992. Every Information System Privilege Not Specifically Allowed Is Forbidden
993. Minimization Of Reliance On Common Mechanism For Controls
994. Independent Security Systems For Each Computer System
995. Dedicated Computers & Networks For High-Security/High-Reliability
996. Designing Controls With Large Margins Of Error
997. Use Of Most Current Computer Operating System Versions
998. Latest Software Release On Systems Interfacing External Networks
999. Network Security Measures Must Not Be Backwards Compatible
1000. Keeping Security Functionality Out Of Business Applications
1001. Systems Must Be Configured & Customized According To Templates
1002. Risk Assessments Required For Production Information Systems
1003. When To Perform An Information Systems Security Risk Assessment
1004. Vulnerability Identification Software For Internet-Connected Systems
1005. Purchase Rather Than Build Information Security Solutions
1006. Best-Of-Breed Solutions For Critical Information Security Functions
1007. Compliance With Industry Specific Information Security Standards
1008. Legal Framework For Information Security Policies
1009. Risk Acceptance Process And Permissible Exceptions To Policies

1010. Non-Enforcement Of Any Policy Does Not Constitute Consent
1011. Minimum Information System Controls Dictated By Standard Practice
1012. Response Required For Every Significant Information Security Risk
1013. Approval Before Disabling Critical Components Of Security Infrastructure
1014. Adequate Information Security Insurance Coverage Must Be Maintained
1015. Allocation Of Sufficient Resources To Address Information Security
1016. Information Security Is Overhead, Not A Charge-Back Item
1017. Security Measures Must Be Enforceable Prior To Installation
1018. Whenever They Are Available, Use Of Evaluated Products Required
1019. Agreements With Third Parties Which Handle Company X Information
1020. Outsourced Hosting Arrangements Require Backup Plan And Testing
1021. External Firms Gathering Company X Information Must Make It Available
1022. Security Responsibilities For Real-Time Connections With Third Parties
1023. Clear Definition Of Third Party Information Security Responsibilities
1024. Termination Of Outsourcing Contracts For Security Violations
1025. Financial Condition Of Critical Vendors Reviewed Annually
1026. Avoid Actual And Apparent Conflict of Interest
1027. Researchers Must Disclose Sponsors And All Potential Conflicts
1028. Workers May Not Have Romantic Relationships With Competitor Staff
1029. Disciplinary Measures For Information Security Non-Compliance
1030. Disciplinary Measures For Various Information Security Violations
1031. Unauthorized Information Disclosure and Loss of Stock Options
1032. Security Violations Requiring Instant Terminations
1033. Notification And Handling Of Employees Leaving For A Competitor
1034. Immediate Notification Of Employees Regarding Worker Terminations
1035. Informing Relevant Contractors And Vendors Of Worker Terminations
1036. Handling Involuntary Terminations Of Computer Workers
1037. Security Guard Escort For Workers Who Are Involuntarily Terminated
1038. Removal Of Information Upon Termination Of Employment
1039. Return Of Information By Contractors, Consultants, And Temporaries
1040. Return Of Company X Property At Time Of Separation From Company X
1041. Responsibility For Taking Action In Response To Worker Terminations
1042. Those Involuntarily Terminated Not To Be Re-Hired Or Retained
1043. Probationary Period For New, Re-Hired, Or Retained Again Workers
1044. Leave Without Pay Required During Extended Investigations
1045. Annual Signature On Agreement To Comply With Security Policies
1046. When To Prosecute Or Seek Restitution
1047. Human Intervention Required For Important Decisions
1048. Reliance On A Single Person For Important Systems Expertise
1049. Five Consecutive Days Of Vacation Required Each Year
1050. Second Job Impact On Objectivity And Competition With Employer
1051. Second Jobs Must Be Disclosed At Initial Interview Or When Taken
1052. Periodic Job Rotation For Computer-Related Workers
1053. Bonding Of Persons In Computer-Related Position Of Trust
1054. Staff Qualifications For Working On Most Sensitive Company X Projects
1055. Workers In Positions Of Trust Must Not Also Be Company X Customers
1056. Duty To Report Status Changes Affecting Eligibility For Certain Position
1057. Transfer Of Certain Workers To Positions With Less Exposure
1058. Use Of Convicted Felons And A Safe Work Place
1059. Use Of Convicted Felons In Computer-Related Positions Of Trust
1060. Background Checks For Computer-Related Positions Of Trust
1061. Staff Must Pass Background Check Before Accessing Private Information
1062. Sensitive Product Information Access Requires Background Check
1063. Fingerprinting For Employees With Access To Sensitive Information

1064. Honesty And Emotional Stability Tests For Computer-Related Workers
1065. Foreign Nationals Prohibited From Working On Information Systems
1066. Significant Unexplained Increases In Wealth Must Be Investigated
1067. Adequate Grievance Resolution Procedures
1068. Free Confidential Counselling Services For Workers
1069. Drug-Free And Alcohol-Free Work Place
1070. Agreements Not To Compete Required For Employees
1071. Technical Information Systems Staff Training & Continuing Education
1072. Information Security Management Committee
1073. Information Ownership And Management's Responsibilities
1074. Divisional Plans For Information Security Compliance
1075. Assignment Of Responsibility For Information Asset Controls
1076. Control Implementations Consistent With Standard Of Due Care
1077. Handling Variances From Generally Accepted Control Practices
1078. Information Security Is Every Worker's Duty
1079. Centralized Responsibility For Information Security
1080. Overview Of Tasks Performed By Information Security Department
1081. Specific Tasks Performed By The Information Security Department
1082. Information Security Department Mission Supports Company X Goals
1083. Authority To Create Information Security Standards And Procedures
1084. Annual Information Security Planning Process Required
1085. Annual Organization-Wide Information Security Risk Assessment
1086. Risk Assessments Performed By Organizational Units Managing Systems
1087. Current Information Security Manual Required
1088. Involvement Of In-House Information Security Department
1089. Prompt Review Of Invoices For Computer & Communications Services
1090. Who Must Comply With Information Security Requirements
1091. Designated Security Administrator For All Multi-User Systems
1092. Backup Security Administrator Must Be Designated And Trained
1093. Each Department Must Have An Information Security Liaison
1094. Annual Review Of Trade Secrets, Copyrights, Etc. By Legal Department
1095. Internal Audit Review Of Information System Controls
1096. Internal Audit Performs Information Security Compliance Checking
1097. Periodic Independent Review Of Information System Controls
1098. Information Security Responsibilities In Job Descriptions
1099. Information Security Considered In Employee Performance Evaluations
1100. Separation Of Duties And Control Over Company X Assets
1101. Building Systems So That Errors And Manipulations Come To Light
1102. Specific Instructions Regarding Separation Of Duties
1103. Incident Management Responsibilities
1104. High-Level Inventory Of Information Assets
1105. Criteria For Assigning Information Ownership
1106. Information Systems Department Must Not Be Owner Of Information
1107. Designated Custodian Required For All Major Information Types
1108. Security Responsibilities Of Information Custodians
1109. Security Responsibilities Of Information Users
1110. Process For Granting Access To Company X Information
1111. Restricted Delegation Of Information Owner Duties
1112. Physical Access Control For Areas Containing Sensitive Information
1113. When Personal Offices Are Not In Use, The Doors Must Be Locked
1114. Multi-User Computer Or Communications Systems In Locked Rooms
1115. Guards Or Receptionists For Areas Containing Sensitive Information
1116. Badges Must Be Worn In Visible Places When In Company X Premises
1117. Temporary Badges For Workers Who Have Forgotten Their Badges

1118. Reporting Lost/Stolen Identification Badges And System Access Tokens
1119. Each Individual Must Have Their Badge Read At Every Controlled Door
1120. No 'Piggybacking' Through Controlled Doors Permitted
1121. Propped-Open Doors To Computer Center Requires Presence Of A Guard
1122. Testing Physical Access Controls Forbidden
1123. Working Alone In Restricted Areas Forbidden
1124. Working In Restricted Areas Only During Official Business Hours
1125. Physical Security Or Encryption Required For All Sensitive Information
1126. Property Pass For Removal Of All Computer And Communications Gear
1127. Computer Storage Media Must Have A Pass When Leaving Premises
1128. Workers Must Show Contents Of Luggage When Leaving Premises
1129. Provision Of Lockable Metal Furniture To Staff Working At Home
1130. Maintaining Building Access Control System Records
1131. Changing Physical Access Control Codes On Worker Termination
1132. Access Rights To Restricted Areas Must Be Revoked On Termination
1133. Maintenance Of List Showing Those Permitted To Grant Physical Access
1134. Periodic Identification Badge Reports Issued To Department Heads
1135. Identification And Sign-In Process Required For All Visitors
1136. Escorts Required For All Visitors
1137. Escorts Required For All Visitors Outside Normal Business Hours
1138. Third Party Supervision In Areas Containing Sensitive Information
1139. Individuals Without Identification Badges Must Be Challenged
1140. Removal Of Badges After Leaving Company X Facilities
1141. Handling Badges When Workers Are Away From Company X Facilities
1142. Unescorted Visitors In Restricted Areas Must Be Challenged
1143. No Visitors Allowed In Data Center Or Information Systems Department
1144. All Workstations Must Use Metal Keys To Control Access
1145. Computer & Communications Equipment Rack Doors Must Be Locked
1146. Internet Commerce & Financial Systems Must Be Physically Isolated
1147. Equipment Isolation Between Company X And Third Party Systems
1148. Physical Security Measures For Computers & Communications Systems
1149. Critical Or Sensitive Activities Permitted Only In Physically Secure Areas
1150. Computer Center Is A Closed Shop
1151. Computer Center Authorized Staff Access List Reviewed Quarterly
1152. Centralization Of All Critical Voice And Data Networking Devices
1153. Restricted Access To Magnetic Tape, Disk, And Documentation Libraries
1154. Vacated Equipment Areas Must Be Locked And Periodically Checked
1155. Locked Communications Equipment Areas And Escorted Access
1156. Public Tours Of Computer Facilities Prohibited
1157. Cameras Plus Audio Or Video Recording Equipment Prohibited
1158. Printers, Copiers, & Fax Machines Banned From Secret Information Areas
1159. Location Of New Computer Or Communications Centers
1160. Redundant Supplies For Public Utility Resources
1161. Adequate Construction For Computer Or Communications Centers
1162. Computer And Communications Facility Location Within A Building
1163. Computer Equipment Locations Must Have Water Damage Precautions
1164. Intermediate Holding Area Required To Restrict Computer Room Access
1165. No Signs Indicating Location Of Computer Or Communications Center
1166. Computer Center Fire Resistance And Self-Closing Openings
1167. Computer Facilities And Doors Resistant To Forcible Entry
1168. Computer Facilities And Automatically Closing Doors
1169. Secondary Computer Center Doors Must Have Alarmed Crash Bars
1170. Computer-Assisted Equipment Tracking
1171. Marking Information Systems Equipment With Identification Codes

1172. Moving Microcomputer Equipment Without Approval Prohibited
1173. Fire, Water, And Physical Intrusion Alarms Trigger Immediate Action
1174. Positioning Of Computer Display Screens With Respect To Windows
1175. Electromagnetic Radiation (Emanation) Protection For Secret Systems

Appendix 12.
Index To Policies By Policy Names

The numbers on the right side of the page are policy numbers, not page numbers. When doing key word searches in the files entitled POLICY1, POLICY2, and POLICY3, the policy writer should keep in mind that there is a period and two spaces between each policy number and the related policy title. This file is most often used by policy writers who are using a hardcopy version of the book, who have found a reference to another policy at the bottom of a policy commentary that they have just read, and who wish to know the policy number of this additional reference.

Appendix 13.
Agreement To Comply With Information Security Policies

A signed paper copy of this form must be submitted with all requests for (1) authorization of a new user-ID, (2) authorization of a change in privileges associated with an existing user-ID, or (3) periodic reauthorization of an existing user-ID. Modifications to the terms and conditions of this agreement will not be accepted by Company X management.

User's Clearly Printed Name: ______________________________

User's Department: ______________________________________

User's Telephone Number: _________________________________

User's Office Physical Address & Mail Stop: ____________________

I, the user, agree to take all reasonable precautions to assure that Company X internal information, or information which has been entrusted to Company X by third parties (such as customers), will not be disclosed to unauthorized persons. At the end of my employment or contract with Company X, I agree to return to Company X all information to which I have had access as a result of my position with Company X. I understand that I am not authorized to use this information for my own purposes, nor am I at liberty to provide this information to third parties without the express written consent of the internal Company X manager who is the designated information owner.

I have access to a copy of the Company X Information Security Policies, I have read and understand these materials, and I understand how they impact my job. As a condition of continued employment at Company X, I agree to abide by these information security policies. I understand that non-compliance will be cause for disciplinary action up to and including system privilege revocation, dismissal from Company X, and perhaps criminal and/or civil penalties.

I agree to choose a difficult-to-guess password as described in the Company X Information Security Policies document, I agree not to share this password with any other person, and I agree not to write this password down unless it has been transformed in an unrecognizable way.

I also agree to promptly report all violations or suspected violations of information security policies to the Director of the Information Security Department (at XXX-XX-XXXX).

User Signature & Date: ______________________________

Appendix 14.
Identity Token Responsibility Statement

By signing this form, I acknowledge receipt of a dynamic password identity token (hereafter called a "token"). I understand that this token provides access to Company X information systems and restricted information stored thereon. I understand that the access privileges that go with this token may, at any time, be revoked by Company X management if they believe that I have not acted in a manner consistent with the Information Security Policy Statement, or if my employment with Company X for any reason is discontinued or suspended. I have read and understood the material contained in the Information Security Policy Statement and I agree to abide by these rules whenever using Company X information and information systems.

I understand that this token is exclusively for my personal use in the performance of Company X business, and I promise that I will not share it or the system privileges that it provides with any other person. Furthermore, I agree not to write or store the token's activating personal identification number (PIN) on anything that is stored anywhere near the token.

I agree that I will immediately report to the Information Security Department the fact that my token has been lost or stolen, or that I suspect that it has been lost or stolen. I furthermore agree to surrender the token at the time that I discontinue my work for Company X. At such a point in time, I additionally agree to surrender to Company X staff all other information as well as computer and communications equipment provided to me in order to perform my job (cellular phones, pagers, portable computers, copiers, etc.).

____

Employee Signature With Date

____

Printed Employee Name With Employee Number

Appendix 15.
Management Risk Acceptance Memo

When To Use This Form
This form must be employed when (1) an information system, a communications system, or an organizational unit is known to be out of compliance with Company X information security policies and/or standards, and (2) the responsible manager does not intend to come into full compliance within a three-month period.

RISK ACCEPTANCE MEMO

Regarding Company X policy or standard #_______, dealing with the topic of

____.

I understand that compliance with Company X information security policies and standards is expected for all organizational units, information systems, and communication systems. I have read the above-named policy or standard and I believe that the control(s) described therein should not be required for the following organizational unit, information system, or communication system (circle the relevant choice among these three options and describe briefly below):

____.

I furthermore understand that a control deficiency in one network-connected system can jeopardize other information systems because erroneous data may be inherited, or because a conduit for a intruder to enter Company X systems may be created. I also understand that non-compliance in this instance may adversely affect the morale or willingness of staff associated with other systems to comply with information security policies and standards.

I understand that an exception to information security policies and standards is appropriate only when it would: (a) adversely affect the accomplishment of Company X business, and/or (b) cause a major adverse financial impact that would not be offset by the reduced risk occasioned by compliance. I believe that an exception to this policy or standard is warranted because:

____

____

____.

I have prepared, or have had a staff member reporting to me prepare, a written assessment of the risks associated with being out-of-compliance with the above-mentioned policy or standard. This risk assessment has been reviewed and approved by the Manager of the Information Systems Security Department and the Manager of the Internal Audit Department.

I accept personal responsibility for this decision to be out of compliance with information security policies and/or standards. Personal responsibility does not mean that I am financially responsible for losses that may take place as a result of this out of compliance situation. Personal responsibility does mean that my job performance evaluation, my salary and bonus, and my continued employment status at Company X can be jeopardized or damaged if a major loss takes place because this out of compliance situation existed.

I also understand that this exception will expire one year from the date the above-mentioned approvals are obtained.

____
Signature of responsible manager

____
Printed name of responsible manager

____
Date signed

Procedural Note: If this out of compliance situation is to continue, the brief risk assessment regarding the out of compliance situation must be updated annually, the above-mentioned approvals must be obtained annually, and this form must be signed by the responsible manager annually. Each year the responsible manager must return a signed copy of this form to the Manager of the Information Security Department who will keep it on file.

Appendix 16.
Two Page Simple Non-Disclosure Agreement

This confidentiality agreement is entered into as of _______________ (date), by and between Company X, and ______________________________________ (recipient organization name), which together with its subsidiaries and affiliates, shall individually and collectively be referred to hereinafter as the "Recipient."

Company X and Recipient hereby agree as follows:

1. Company X created and is the owner and developer of an idea for a new product (hereinafter referred to as the "System"). By disclosing this information, Company X grants Recipient no license or right, by implication or otherwise, to use this information for any purpose other than the specific business purposes of Company X as found in written agreement(s) to be separately negotiated.

2. Recipient acknowledges that the System and all related documentation, including but not limited to descriptions of the System or its component parts, all product mock-ups, product prototypes, product samples, product technical specifications, product input data, product-related know-how, product-related new and different ideas, product technology, all or any of which may be derived from any of the foregoing (all of which, individually and collectively, shall hereinafter be referred to as the "Proprietary Information") are valuable, confidential, and proprietary to Company X.

3. Company X and Recipient wish to discuss mutually beneficial business arrangements and relationships which in some way concern, or are related to the System. Recipient acknowledges that disclosure of this information constitutes consideration for this agreement because it wishes to pursue the opportunity of business dealings with Company X. Recipient agrees not to use Proprietary Information for its own use or for any other purpose except to evaluate whether it desires to enter into a business relationship with Company X, or as necessary, to carry on such a relationship. Recipient furthermore agrees to manage all of its workers who come into contact with Proprietary Information such that the obligations and duties described in this agreement will be strictly enforced.

4. Recipient agrees to hold the Proprietary Information in strict confidence. Recipient furthermore agrees not to reproduce, transcribe, or disclose the Proprietary Information to third parties without prior written approval of Company X. Recipient also agrees not to make, have made, use, distribute or sell for its own purposes or for any purpose other than on behalf of Company X, any product incorporating Proprietary Information. Recipient furthermore agrees to promptly return all copies, renderings, transformations, and derivatives of such information to Company X at the termination of its discussions and/or work dealing with the System.

5. The obligations imposed by this Agreement shall not apply to any information that: (a) is rightfully received from a third party without accompanying use of disclosure restrictions, and can be documented as such, (b) is independently developed without access to Proprietary Information, (c) is or becomes publicly available through no wrongful act of the Recipient, (d) is already known to Recipient as evidenced by third-party documentation bearing a date prior to the date of Proprietary Information disclosure, or (e) is approved for release in writing by an authorized representative of Company X.

6. This agreement supercedes and replaces all existing agreements, written or otherwise, entered into between Recipient and Company X dealing with the subject matter discussed herein.

7. Recipient agrees that, in the event of a breach of this non-disclosure agreement, that Company X shall be entitled to an injunction to enforce the terms and conditions of this agreement, and to protect its Proprietary Information. Recipient additionally agrees that this shall not preclude Company X for pursuing further actions or remedies at law or in equity, for any breach or threatened breach of the terms of this agreement, including but not limited to the recovery of damages.

8. If any one or more of the terms of this agreement shall for any reason be held to be invalid, illegal, or unenforceable in any other respect, these problems shall not affect the overall intention of the agreement, nor shall it affect the degree to which the other terms remain binding, nor shall it interfere with the enforcement of or the duty to comply with the other terms found in this agreement. This agreement is governed by the laws of California [replace with relevant jurisdiction].

9. The terms of this agreement will be in effect for five (5) years from the time that the Recipient receives information from Company X. Each time that Company X provides new confidential information to Recipient, the period when this information must be held confidential will then continue for five years from that time. Termination of the proposed or actual working relationship between Recipient and Company X in no way invalidates the binding nature of this agreement or the period when it remains in effect.

10. The person signing below for Recipient represents that he or she is an authorized representative and/or corporate officer of the Recipient organization.

____

RECIPIENT SIGNING OFFICER (WITH DATE)

____

SIGNING OFFICER'S NAME TYPED OR PRINTED

____

COMPANY X OFFICER (WITH DATE)

Appendix 17.
About The Author

Charles Cresson Wood has worked full-time in the information security field for more than twenty-one years. In the late 1970s and early 1980s he worked as a computer security consultant at SRI International (formerly Stanford Research Institute, now known as Atomic Tangerine). In the mid-1980s he was lead data communications security officer at the Bank of America. For the last fifteen years he has been an independent information security consultant and researcher, and in this capacity he has done consulting work for over 125 different organizations in over twenty countries around the world.

Although Mr. Wood's consulting practice involves a variety of information security work, he most often provides Internet commerce security designs, new information system risk assessments, information systems security architectures, and security documentation compilations. He also prepares and reviews codes of conduct, standards, policies, procedures, budgets, action plans, mission statements, job descriptions, and other parts of an organizational infrastructure to support information security.

Mr. Wood has been quoted as an expert in news media such as Business Week, Cable News Network (CNN), CIO, Computerworld, Datamation, Government Technology, IEEE Spectrum, Information Week, Info World, LA Times, Network Computing, Network World, PC Week, The Wall Street Journal, and Time. Mr. Wood serves as the Senior North American Editor for both Computers & Security and Computer Fraud & Security Bulletin. He also sits on the editorial board of the white collar crime publication known as Inside Fraud. He has authored over 225 technical articles on information security, and for the last six years has written a monthly column on information security policies for Computer Security Alert. His other information security books are entitled Computer Security: A Comprehensive Controls Checklist (John Wiley & Sons, New York, New York, 1987), Effective Information Security Management (Elsevier Science Publishers, Oxford, England, 1991), How to Handle Internet Electronic Commerce Security: Risks, Controls & Product Guide (PentaSafe, Houston, Texas, 1996), Best Practices In Internet Commerce Security (PentaSafe, Houston, Texas, 1998), and Information Security Roles & Responsibilities Made Easy (InfoSecurity Infrastructure, Sausalito, California, 2001).

Mr. Wood holds an MBA in financial information systems and a BSE in accounting, both from the Wharton School at the University of Pennsylvania. He also holds an MSE degree in computer science from the Moore School of Engineering at the same University (birthplace of the ENIAC, the world's first general purpose electronic computer). In addition to passing the Certified Public Accountant (CPA) exam, he is both a Certified Information Systems Auditor (CISA) and a Certified Information Systems Security Professional (CISSP). In 1996, Mr. Wood received the Lifetime Achievement Award from the Computer Security Institute for his "sincere dedication to the computer security profession." He can be reached directly at ccwood@ix.netcom.com.